P9-CAH-853

Art &
Architecture
Thesaurus

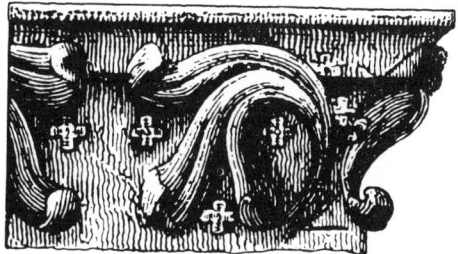

Toni Petersen
DIRECTOR

SECOND EDITION

Volume 3

Part III: Alphabetical Display

Published on behalf of
The Getty Art History Information Program

OXFORD UNIVERSITY PRESS

New York · 1994 · Oxford

Oxford University Press

Oxford   New York   Toronto
Delhi   Bombay   Calcutta   Madras   Karachi
Kuala Lumpur   Singapore   Hong Kong   Tokyo
Nairobi   Dar es Salaam   Cape Town
Melbourne   Auckland   Madrid

and associated companies in
Berlin   Ibadan

Copyright © 1990, 1992, 1994 by The J. Paul Getty Trust

Published by Oxford University Press, Inc.,
200 Madison Avenue, New York, New York 10016

Oxford is a registered trademark of Oxford University Press

All rights reserved. No part of this publication may be reproduced,
stored in a retrieval system, or transmitted, in any form or by any means,
electronic, mechanical, photocopying, recording, or otherwise, without
the prior written permission of Oxford University Press.

Library of Congress Cataloging-in-Publication Data

Art & architecture thesaurus / Toni Petersen, director. — 2nd ed.
        p. 21½ x 28 cm.
        "Published on behalf of the Getty Art History Information
Program."
        Includes bibliographical references.
        Contents: v. 1, pt. 1. Introduction. pt. 2. Hierarchical displays
— v. 2, pt. 2. Hierarchical displays (continued) — v. 3. pt.
3. Alphabetical display — v. 4, pt. 3. Alphabetical display
(continued) — v. 5, pt. 3. Alphabetical display (continued).
        ISBN 0-19-508756-9
        1. Subject headings—Art. 2. Subject headings—Architecture.
3. Art—Abstracting and indexing. 4. Architecture—Abstracting
and indexing. I. Petersen, Toni. II. Title: Art and architecture
thesaurus.
Z695.1.A7A76   1994   93-30628
025.4'97—dc20   CIP

Printing (last digit): 9 8 7 6 5 4 3 2 1

Printed in the United States of America
on acid-free paper

FINE ARTS DEPT
Reference

F-A
Z695
.1
.A7A76
1994
v.3

MAY 0 0 1995

LV

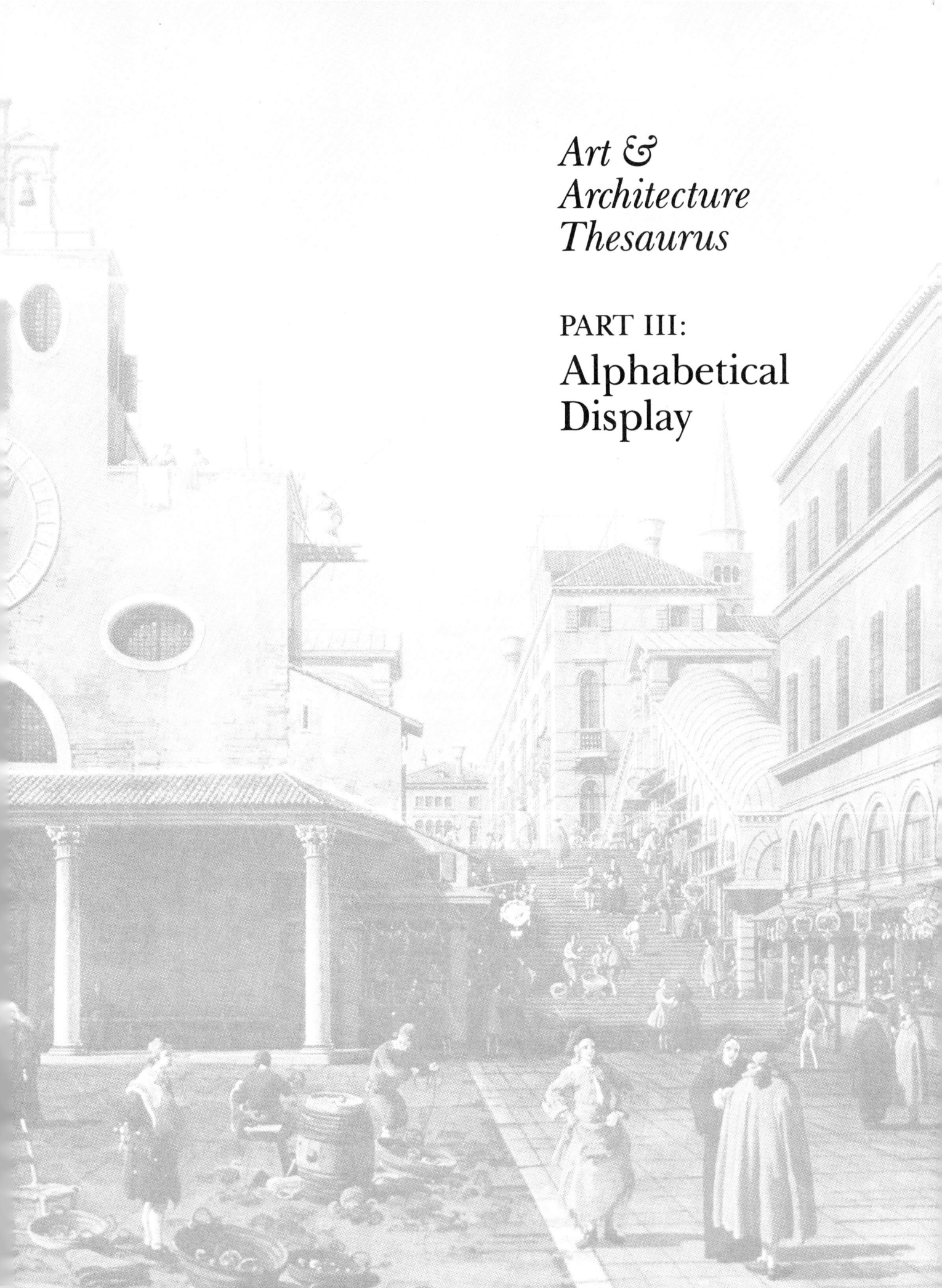

Art & Architecture Thesaurus

PART III:
Alphabetical Display

Overleaf: Canaletto, *The Vegetable Market and San Giacometto di Rialto* (detail), The National Gallery of Canada, Ottawa.

1-story
USE single-story

1st Dynasty
USE First Dynasty

2nd Dynasty
USE Second Dynasty

3-bay barns
USE English barns

3-story
USE three-story

3rd Dynasty
USE Third Dynasty

4th Dynasty
USE Fourth Dynasty

5th Dynasty
USE Fifth Dynasty

6th Dynasty
USE Sixth Dynasty

7th Dynasty
USE Seventh Dynasty

8th Dynasty
USE Eighth Dynasty

9th Dynasty
USE Ninth Dynasty

10-foot rods
USE ten-foot rods

10-pin bowling
USE tenpin bowling

10th Dynasty
USE Tenth Dynasty

11th Dynasty
USE Eleventh Dynasty

12th Dynasty
USE Twelfth Dynasty

13th Dynasty
USE Thirteenth Dynasty

14-carat gold
USE fourteen-carat gold

14th Dynasty
USE Fourteenth Dynasty

15th Dynasty
USE Fifteenth Dynasty

16th Dynasty
USE Sixteenth Dynasty

17th Dynasty
USE Seventeenth Dynasty

18-carat gold
USE eighteen-carat gold

18th Dynasty
USE Eighteenth Dynasty

19th Dynasty
USE Nineteenth Dynasty

20th Dynasty
USE Twentieth Dynasty

21st Dynasty
USE Twenty-first Dynasty

22nd Dynasty
USE Twenty-second Dynasty

23rd Dynasty
USE Twenty-third Dynasty

24-sheet posters
USE twenty-four-sheet posters

24-sheets
USE twenty-four-sheet posters

24th Dynasty
USE Twenty-fourth Dynasty

25th Dynasty
USE Twenty-fifth Dynasty

26th Dynasty
USE Twenty-sixth Dynasty

27th Dynasty
USE Twenty-seventh Dynasty

28th Dynasty
USE Twenty-eighth Dynasty

29th Dynasty
USE Twenty-ninth Dynasty

30th Dynasty
USE Thirtieth Dynasty

35mm cameras
TH.750   (L)
ALT 35mm camera
UF cameras, 35mm
cameras, thirty-five millimeter
thirty-five millimeter cameras

100% cotton rag board
USE museum board

136 armchairs
TC.509
HN January 1993 descriptor moved
ALT 136 armchair
UF armchairs, 136

1200 Style
USE Early Gothic

A and I services
USE abstracting and indexing services

à deux crayons
KT.390
HN May 1993 lead-in term added
SN A drawing technique, usually employing red chalk and black chalk or charcoal.
UF aux deux crayons
deux crayons

A-frame houses
RK.246   (B)
HN December 1991 scope note added
ALT A-frame house
SN Use for houses with steep gable roofs that extend to ground level on two sides; employed mostly for vacation and second homes.
UF houses, A-frame

à la poupée
KT.710
HN April 1990 descriptor added
SN Printing technique in which color is applied to specific areas of the plate with a pad or rolled piece of felt. (PRTT)
UF dolly method
method, dolly

A-shaped trestles
USE A trestles

A trestles
PJ.2736
HN March 1993 descriptor moved
ALT A trestle
UF A-shaped trestles
trestles, A
trestles, A-shaped

à trois crayons
KT.391
SN A drawing technique usually employing a combination of red, black, and white chalks on a yellowish or off-white paper; especially common in the 18th century. (LAD)
UF aux trois crayons
trois couleurs
trois crayons

à trois crayons (printmaking)
USE crayon manner

AA guns
USE antiaircraft guns

AA shells
USE antiaircraft shells

AAA
USE antiaircraft guns

AAS
USE atomic absorption spectroscopy

Ababua
USE Babwa

abaca
USE Manila hemp

abaci (capital components)
PJ.1504   (N)
HN March 1993 descriptor moved
May 1991 descriptor changed, was abaci
May 1991 alternate term changed, was abacus
ALT abacus (capital component)
SN Uppermost members of the capitals of columns; often plain square slabs, but sometimes molded or otherwise enriched. (HAS)

abaci (sideboards)
TC.1001
HN January 1993 descriptor moved
ALT abacus (sideboard)

SN Ancient Roman sideboards, generally having a tablelike lower member and an upper member with shelving; used to display highly prized ornaments. (RICHTE)

abacots
USE bycockets

abalone shell
MT.1331 (L)
HN March 1992 scope note added
March 1992 descriptor changed, was abalone
February 1992 descriptor moved
SN Bowl-like shells of the abalone mollusk, a source of mother of pearl.

abandoned buildings
USE derelict buildings

abandoned farms
RG.5 (L)
ALT abandoned farm
UF farms, abandoned

abas
TE.143 (N)
ALT aba
SN Loose, sleeveless mantles traditionally worn by Arabs.

Abash-adar
USE Bashadar

Abasian boxwood
USE boxwood

abat-jours
PJ.2152
HN March 1993 descriptor moved
November 1990 descriptor moved
November 1990 scope note changed
ALT abat-jour
SN Use for beveled openings in a wall or in a roof which admit light from above.

abat-voix
USE sounding boards

abatement, noise
USE noise control

abatement, smoke
USE smoke abatement

abattoirs
USE slaughterhouses

Abbasid
FL.3526 (A,L)
HN April 1990 descriptor changed, was Abbasid (dynasty)

<Abbasid pottery styles>
FL.3527

abbesses
HG.430 (L)
HN January 1993 descriptor added
ALT abbess
abbesses'
abbess's

SN Nuns who hold the office of superior of a convent.

Abbevillian
FL.2539
UF Chellean

abbey churches
RK.1049 (A,B)
ALT abbey church
UF churches, abbey
churches, conventual
conventual churches

abbeys
RG.208 (A,L,B,R)
ALT abbey
SN Designates independent and canonically erected monasteries, ruled by an abbot if occupied by monks and by an abbess if occupied by nuns.

abbots
HG.428 (L,R)
HN February 1993 descriptor moved
February 1993 scope note changed
December 1992 alternate terms added
ALT abbot
abbot's
abbots'
SN Monks who hold the office of superior of a monastery.

abbots' chairs
USE Glastonbury chairs

Abbotsford
FL.3373
UF Baronial

abbozzi
VC.586
ALT abbozzo
SN Use especially for sketches that are part of the underpainting and establish the tonal relationships of a painting; also, for a block of sculptural material at a stage where it has been worked to a rough form of the finished work.
UF abozzi

abbreviations
VW.225 (L)
HN June 1992 descriptor added
ALT abbreviation
SN Shortened forms of words or phrases that are not words themselves but stand for the original; often created by the omission of letters or the replacement of several letters by a symbol.

ABC
USE Minimal

ABC books
USE alphabet books

ABC quilts
USE alphabet quilts

'Abd-al-'Aziz
USE Abdülâziz

'Abd-al-Hamid I
USE Abdülhamid I

'Abd-al-Hamid II
USE Abdülhamid II

'Abd-al-Majid I
USE Abdülmecid I

Abdül Aziz
USE Abdülâziz

Abdül Hamid I
USE Abdülhamid I

Abdül-Hamid II
USE Abdülhamid II

Abdül Mecid I
USE Abdülmecid I

Abdülâziz
FL.3640
HN April 1993 descriptor moved
UF 'Abd-al-'Aziz
Abdül Aziz

Abdülhamid I
FL.3635
HN April 1993 descriptor moved
UF 'Abd-al-Hamid I
Abdül Hamid I

Abdülhamid II
FL.3642
HN April 1993 descriptor moved
April 1990 lead-in term deleted, was Abdül hamit II
UF 'Abd-al-Hamid II
Abdül-Hamid II
Abdülhamit II

Abdülhamit II
USE Abdülhamid II

Abdülmecid I
FL.3639
HN April 1993 descriptor moved
UF 'Abd-al-Majid I
Abdül Mecid I

abecedaria
USE alphabet books

Abelam
FL.3784 (L)

abherent
USE release agent

Abies
USE fir

Abies amabilis
USE silver fir

Abies balsamea
USE balsam fir

Abies fraseri
USE Fraser's balsam fir

Abies humilis
USE Fraser's balsam fir

Abigarrado
USE cursive

Abipón
    FL.1653   (L)

ablution fountains
    PJ.2511
HN March 1993 descriptor moved
        August 1990 scope note added
ALT ablution fountain
SN   Fountains for ritual cleansing, usually associated with religious buildings.
UF   fountains, ablution

Abnakee hooked rugs
USE Abnakee rugs

Abnakee rugs
    TC.119
ALT Abnakee rug
SN   Hooked rugs popular in the early 20th century with designs inspired by Native American rug motifs.
UF   Abnakee hooked rugs
        hooked rugs, Abnakee
        rugs, Abnakee
RT   hooking

Abnaki
    FL.1302   (L)
UF   Kennebec
        Wabanaki

abocockets
USE bycockets

abolitionists
    HG.983   (L)
HN February 1993 descriptor moved
        January 1993 alternate terms added
ALT abolitionist
        abolitionist's
        abolitionists'

Aboriginal
USE Australian Aboriginal

Aboriginal, Australian
USE Australian Aboriginal

abozzi
USE abbozzi

abrading
USE abrasion

Abraham of Kütahya
USE Kütahya

Abraham of Kütahya style Iznik pottery
USE Kütahya + ware

abrash
    DE.50
HN December 1992 descriptor moved
        June 1991 descriptor added
SN   Unintentional variations in the color of a rug caused by irregular dyeing of the yarn, or by using yarn from a different dye lot.

abrasion
    KT.906

HN April 1991 scope note changed
ALT abraded
SN   Material-removing process which results in the loss or disruption of a surface as a result of wearing, grinding, rubbing, or scraping.
UF   abrading

abrasion-resistant material
    MT.3067
HN April 1993 descriptor changed, was **abrasion-resistant materials**
UF   material, abrasion-resistant

abrasive
    MT.1674   (L)
HN April 1993 descriptor changed, was **abrasives**
SN   Any hard, sharp material that wears away a softer, less resistant surface when the two are rubbed together. (HORNB)

abrasive blasting
USE abrasive cleaning

abrasive cleaning
    KT.920
HN January 1993 descriptor moved
SN   Cleaning method that removes soil, discolorations, or coatings through the action of certain materials which impact and abrade the surface under pressure. (GRIMMR)
UF   abrasive blasting
        blast-cleaning
        blasting, abrasive
        cleaning, abrasive

abrasive paper
    TH.1061
UF   paper, abrasive

abrasive wheels
USE grinding wheels

abreuvoirs
    PJ.661
HN April 1993 descriptor moved
ALT abreuvoir
SN   Joints filled with mortar and located between masonry units. (MEANS)

abridged editions
USE abridgements

abridgements
    VW.226
HN June 1992 descriptor added
ALT abridgement
SN   Use for versions of written works produced by condensation and omission but with retention of the general meaning and manner of presentation of the original, often prepared by someone other than the author of the original. (ALAG)
UF   abridged editions
        abridgments
        condensations
        editions, abridged
        epitomes

abridgments
USE abridgements

Abron
USE Brong

ABS
USE acrylonitrile-butadiene-styrene copolymer

ABS plastic
USE acrylonitrile-butadiene-styrene copolymer

Absaroke
USE Crow

absolute alcohol
    MT.2446
UF   alcohol, absolute
        alcohol, anhydrous
        anhydrous alcohol

absolute dates
USE absolute dating

absolute dating
    KT.181
HN November 1992 descriptor added
SN   Techniques of dating which result in dates given in terms of calendar years. (CHAMP)
UF   absolute dates
        chronometric dating
        dates, absolute
        dating, absolute
        dating, chronometric

absolute humidity
    BM.328
HN November 1992 descriptor added
SN   The actual quantity of water vapor present in a given volume of air. (BATCOB)
UF   humidity, absolute

absolutism
USE despotism

absorbency
    DC.246   (L)
HN April 1993 scope note changed
        October 1992 descriptor moved
        May 1991 descriptor added
ALT absorbent
SN   The property by which a material is able to take up a liquid or a gas by capillary, osmotic, solvent, chemical, or other means.

absorbent materials
HN April 1993 descriptor split, use absorbent (ALT of absorbency) + material (ALT of materials)

absorbent paper
HN April 1993 descriptor split, use absorbent (ALT of absorbency) + paper

absorber
USE absorbent (ALT of absorbency) + material (ALT of materials)

absorptiometers
TN.328 (L)
ALT absorptiometer
SN Photoelectric instruments equipped to measure the absorption of nearly monochromatic light in the visible range by a gas or liquid and so determine the concentration of the absorbing constituents in the gas or liquid.

absorption
KT.817 (L)
HN January 1993 descriptor moved
March 1991 alternate term added
ALT absorbed
SN The process by which a liquid, or a mixture of gases and liquids, is drawn into and tends to fill permeable pores in a porous solid material; usually accompanied by a physical change, chemical change, or both. (DAC)

absorption fields
USE leaching fields

absorption, sound
USE sound absorption

Abstract
FL.3379 (L,R)
HN April 1993 related term added
SN Use with reference to 20th-century art; in other contexts use abstraction.
RT abstraction

Abstract Expressionist
FL.3849 (L,R)
HN April 1993 lead-in term added
ALT Abstract Expressionism
UF American-Type painting
Expressionist, Abstract
painting, American-Type

Abstract Imagist
FL.3850
SN Use for certain Abstract Expressionist paintings. Use Color-field to encompass Abstract Imagist painting and the works of the 1960s derived from it.
UF Imagist, Abstract

Abstract Impressionist
FL.3852 (L)
ALT Abstract Impressionism
UF Impressionist, Abstract

Abstract, Perceptual
USE Op art

abstracting
KG.107 (L)
SN Production of a document surrogate which summarizes the subject matter or describes other essential qualities of the document. For the process of making visual forms less representational, use abstraction.

abstracting and indexing services
HN.125 (L)
ALT abstracting and indexing service
SN Information services which provide access to documents in a specific subject field or fields by means of abstracts and indexes issued periodically on paper, in microform, or as machine-readable databases, available by subscription or fee. (ALAG)
UF A and I services
indexing and abstracting services
services, A and I
services, abstracting and indexing
services, indexing and abstracting

abstraction
BM.147
HN April 1993 related term added
SN Use for the general concept and approach. For the 20th-century movement and its products, use Abstract.
RT Abstract

abstraction, biomorphic
USE biomorphic abstraction

Abstraction, Chromatic
USE Color-field

abstraction, classical
USE geometric abstraction

abstraction, creative
USE biomorphic abstraction

Abstraction, Eccentric
USE Eccentric Abstraction

abstraction, geometric
USE geometric abstraction

Abstraction, Lyrical
USE Lyrical Abstraction

Abstraction Lyrique
USE Tachiste

Abstraction, Post-painterly
USE Color-field

abstracts
VW.231 (L)
HN November 1992 descriptor moved
ALT abstract
SN Brief summaries that provide the essential points of written works.
UF précis

Abua
FL.234 (L)

abuse, drug
USE drug abuse

abuse of substances
USE substance abuse

abuse, substance
USE substance abuse

abutments
PJ.1433 (L)
HN March 1993 descriptor moved
August 1990 scope note added

ALT abutment
SN Masses, usually of masonry, that support and receive the thrust of arches, vaults, or trusses.
UF butments

abutting joints
PJ.617
HN April 1993 descriptor moved
ALT abutting joint
SN Joints between two pieces of wood in which the direction of the grain of one piece is at an angle (usually 90 degrees) to the grain in the other. (DAC)
UF joints, abutting

Acacia
MT.2787 (L)
HN March 1992 descriptor moved
UF arabic tree, gum
gum arabic tree
tree, gum arabic

Acacia (black locust)
USE black locust

Acacia dealbata
USE silver wattle

Acacia, false
USE black locust

Acacia gum
USE gum arabic

Acacia koa
USE koa

Acacia melanoxylon
USE Australian locust

academic architecture
BM.166 (R)
SN Conforming to the architectural theories of the European and American academies of architecture.
UF architecture, academic

academic art
BM.174 (R)
SN Conforming to the official standards and principles of taste of European and American art academies.
UF art, academic

<academic ceremonies>
KM.20

academic libraries
RK.670
ALT academic library
UF libraries, academic

academicism
BM.133 (R)
HN February 1991 descriptor moved

academies
HN.2 (L)
HN May 1991 scope note added
ALT academy
SN Organizations of learned individuals united for the advancement of art, science, or literature. (W)

academies (schools)
USE schools

academies, military
USE military academies

academies, naval
USE naval schools

academies of art
USE art + schools

Academy blue
USE artificial ultramarine blue

academy board
　　MT.1454
HN February 1992 descriptor moved
SN Heavy, smooth cardboard coated with a ground that has sufficient roughness for the application of oil paint. (MAYER)
UF board, academy

Acadian houses
USE Creole cottages

acanthus
　　DG.66　　　　　　　　　　　　(R)
HN October 1990 lead-in terms added
SN Use for the conventionalized decorative motif based on the deeply serrated and scalloped leaves and curving stems of the acanthus plant. (IDO)
UF acanthus leaf
　　bear's breech
　　bear's foot
　　brank-ursine
　　breech, bear's
　　foot, bear's
　　leaf, acanthus

acanthus leaf
USE acanthus

acapau
USE partridgewood

acaroid resin
　　MT.1268
HN April 1992 descriptor moved
SN A gum resin from the base of the tufted trunk leaves of various species of Xanthorrhoea trees of Australia and Tasmania. (MH)
UF accroides
　　accroides, gum
　　Botany Bay gum
　　gum accroides
　　gum, Botany Bay
　　gum, yacca
　　resin, acaroid
　　xanthorrhoea
　　yacca gum

accelerated aging
　　KT.159　　　　　　　　　　　(L)
HN November 1992 descriptor added
SN Use for testing techniques that impose conditions on an object or material to cause it to age more rapidly than it would naturally.
UF aging, accelerated

aging, artificial
artificial aging

accelerated cement
　　MT.41　　　　　　　　　　　　(B)
HN April 1992 descriptor moved
SN Cement that will set hard in three days. (MH)
UF cement, accelerated
　　cement, rapid-hardening
　　rapid-hardening cement

accelerated weathering
　　KT.268
HN January 1993 descriptor added
SN Use for weathering that has been caused to proceed at an unusually fast pace, whether by special environmental conditions or by intentionally imposed testing conditions.
UF artificial weathering
　　weathering, accelerated
　　weathering, artificial

acceleration
　　BM.822　　　　　　　　　　　(L)
HN November 1992 descriptor moved
　　February 1992 scope note added
SN The rate at which the velocity of a body changes with time. (HEWPHY)

acceleration lanes
　　PJ.846
HN March 1993 descriptor moved
ALT acceleration lane
UF lanes, acceleration

accelerator
　　MT.1677
HN April 1993 descriptor changed, was **accelerators**
SN Any substance which hastens a reaction. (MAYER)

accelerators, circular
USE cyclotrons

accelerators, linear
USE linear accelerators

accelerators, magnetic resonance
USE cyclotrons

accelerators, particle
USE particle accelerators

accelerometers
　　TN.264　　　　　　　　　　　(L,N)
ALT accelerometer
SN Instruments for measuring, indicating, or recording accelerative forces, such as those imparted by gravity or aeronautical devices.

accent light
USE accent lighting

accent lighting
　　KT.761
HN May 1991 descriptor added
SN Localized lighting technique designed to emphasize a particular object or area.
UF accent light

light, accent
lighting, accent

acceptances
　　VK.172　　　　　　　　　　　(L)
ALT acceptance
SN Credit instruments specifying the drawer's intention to pay at the date of maturity; generally applied to drafts and bills of exchange.
RT commercial paper
　　credit instruments

access
　　BM.365　　　　　　　　　　　(A,L,B)
HN December 1992 descriptor moved
　　April 1990 lead-in term added
UF accessibility

access doors
　　PJ.2179
HN March 1993 descriptor moved
　　September 1991 scope note changed
ALT access door
SN Doors, usually small, opening through a finished construction, as into a duct or wall, and used to provide a means of inspection of equipment or services housed behind. (DAC)
UF doors, access

access floors
　　PJ.2064　　　　　　　　　　　(A)
HN March 1993 descriptor moved
　　November 1991 lead-in term deleted, was **raised flooring systems**
　　November 1991 lead-in term deleted, was **flooring systems, raised**
　　August 1990 lead-in terms added
ALT access floor
SN Flooring systems consisting of completely removable and interchangeable floor panels that are supported on adjustable pedestals or stringers to allow free access to the area underneath. (DAC)
UF floors, access
　　floors, raised
　　raised floors

access, handicapped
USE barrier-free design

access roads
　　RM.157　　　　　　　　　　　(L,B)
HN April 1993 descriptor moved
ALT access road
SN Use for public roads giving direct access to the land, premises, or highways on one or both sides.
UF access roads, highway
　　approach roads
　　highway access roads
　　roads, access
　　roads, approach
　　roads, highway access

access roads, highway
USE access roads

accessibility
USE access

accession catalogs
VW.24
HN November 1992 descriptor moved
ALT accession catalog
SN Records of the stock added to a collection; may be in book form, on cards, or online.
UF catalogs, accession

accession files
USE accession records

accession lists
USE accession registers

accession records
VW.515
HN November 1992 descriptor moved
ALT accession record
SN Records documenting additions to a collection, whether acquired by transfer under a legally based procedure, or by deposit, purchase, gift, or bequest. (ICA)
UF accession files
files, accession
records, accession

accession registers
VW.516
HN November 1992 descriptor moved
ALT accession register
SN Lists of additions to the holdings of a collection, usually in chronological order by date of receipt and giving the titles of the accessions. (ICA)
UF accession lists
lists, accession
registers, accession

accessioning
KG.112
ALT accessioned
SN Recording the entry of items into a collection in the order of acquisition. (W)

accessories, bathroom
USE bathroom hardware

accessories, washroom
USE bathroom hardware

<accessories worn above the waist>
TE.640

<accessories worn at the waist or below>
TE.673

<accessories worn on arms or hands>
TE.690

<accessories worn on the head>
TE.502

<accessories worn on the legs and feet>
TE.702

<accessory containers for food service>
TQ.540
RT spice boxes

<accessory door hardware>
PJ.284
HN April 1993 guide term moved

<accessory industrial buildings>
RK.575

<accessory table equipment>
TH.340
HN April 1993 guide term added
RT dish warmers

<accessory window and shutter hardware>
PJ.306
HN April 1993 guide term moved

accident reports
VW.915
HN November 1992 descriptor moved
ALT accident report
UF reports, accident

accidental color
USE reflected color

accidental colour
SEE reflected color

accolades
PJ.2125
HN April 1993 descriptor moved
ALT accolade
SN Ornamental treatments used over openings such as doors or windows, and composed of ogee arches the apex of which extends upward to form an ornamental finial.

accordion doors
USE folding doors

accordion fold books
USE folded books

accordion folds
USE accordion pleats

accordion pleats
PJ.3062
ALT accordion pleat
SN Use for wide, sharply pressed pleats, arranged in a row, evenly spaced and all turned in the same direction. For narrow pleats of a similar nature, use **knife pleats.**
UF accordion folds
folds, accordion
pleats, accordion
RT knife pleats

accordion shades
TC.334
ALT accordion shade
SN Shades with narrow, sharply pleated folds, resembling the musical instrument. For shades that pull up in wide horizontal pleats, use **Roman shades.**
UF shades, accordion
RT Roman shades

accordions
TT.129   (L,N)
ALT accordion

SN Portable reed organs consisting of an expandable bellows worked by the player's arm and a variable number of melody and bass keys.

account books
VW.581   (N,R)
HN November 1992 descriptor moved
ALT account book
SN Books in which financial accounts are kept. (GAHLM)
UF books, account

account books, household
USE housebooks

accountants
HG.610   (L)
HN December 1992 alternate terms added
ALT accountant
accountant's
accountants'

accounting
KG.242   (L,B)
SN Collecting data, usually in monetary terms, about economic activity, processing those data, and reporting them for the use of interested decision-makers. (PG)

accounting, cost
USE cost accounting

accounts
VW.582
HN November 1992 descriptor moved
ALT account
SN Documents in which monies or goods received and paid or given out are recorded in order to permit periodic totaling. (ICA)

accounts, churchwardens'
USE churchwardens' accounts

accreditation
USE accrediting

accrediting
KG.208   (L)
HN April 1993 lead-in term added
ALT accredited
SN Officially recognizing an institution as maintaining standards that render them eligible for membership in an association of similar institutions. (W)
UF accreditation

accretions
USE additions

accroides
USE acaroid resin

accroides, gum
USE acaroid resin

accruals
USE additions

Acer
USE maple

Acer macrophyllum
USE bigleaf maple

Acer mono
USE Japanese maple

Acer negundo
USE box elder

Acer nigrum
USE black maple

Acer rubrum
USE red maple

Acer saccharinum
USE silver maple

Acer saccharum
USE sugar maple

Aceraceae
USE maple

acetal
MT.1155 (L)
HN January 1993 descriptor moved
SN Highly crystalline resin that is among the strongest and stiffest types of thermoplastic. (MH12)
UF acetal resin
polyether
polyformaldehyde resin
polyformaldehydes
polyoxide
resin, acetal
resin, polyformaldehyde

acetal, polyvinyl
USE polyvinyl acetal

acetal resin
USE acetal

acetate, amyl
USE amyl acetate

acetate, butyl
USE butyl acetate

acetate butyrate, cellulose
USE butyrate

acetate, cellulose
USE cellulose acetate

acetate, ethyl
USE ethyl acetate

acetate, isopropyl
USE isopropyl acetate

acetate, N-butyl
USE butyl acetate

acetate, normal butyl
USE butyl acetate

acetate, polyvinyl
USE polyvinyl acetate

acetic acid
MT.3069 (L)
HN February 1992 descriptor moved
UF acid, acetic
acid, ethanoic
ethanoic acid

acetone
MT.2456 (L)
UF dimethyl ketone
ketone, dimethyl

acetone, methyl
USE methyl acetone

acetylene black
USE carbon black

acetylene burners
PJ.2909
ALT acetylene burner
SN Burners used for controlled burning of acetylene gas. (MYERS)
UF acetylene tips
burners, acetylene
tips, acetylene

acetylene lamps
TC.1374 (L)
ALT acetylene lamp
SN Lamps equipped with containers for calcium carbide, a reservoir of water with a controlled drip, and a nozzle or burner for the combustion of the acetylene gas produced by bringing the water into contact with the calcium carbide; also lamps with acetylene burners connected to a central source of acetylene.
UF cap lamps
lamps, acetylene
lamps, cap

acetylene tips
USE acetylene burners

acetylene torches
TH.511 (N)
ALT acetylene torch
SN Torches operated by compressed acetylene gas and oxygen; used in welding and metal-cutting. (DAC)
UF torches, acetylene

Achaemenid
FL.3103 (A,L,B)

Achagua
FL.1645 (L)

Acheulian
FL.2540 (L)

Achi
FL.260

achievements, funereal
USE hatchments

Acholi
FL.673

Achomawi
FL.1261 (L)

achromatic colors
USE neutrals

acid
MT.3068 (L)
HN February 1993 scope note added
February 1992 descriptor moved

SN A substance capable of forming hydrogen ions when dissolved in water. (BATCOB)

acid, acetic
USE acetic acid

acid-biting
USE biting

acid, carbolic
USE carbolic acid

acid copper chromate
MT.2394
UF chromate, acid copper
copper chromate, acid

acid etching
USE frosting

acid, ethanoic
USE acetic acid

acid, fatty
USE fatty acid

acid-free
DC.11
HN October 1992 descriptor added
SN Use to describe materials having a pH of 7 or higher when the concern is that there be little or no acid present to accelerate aging or deterioration.

acid, hydrochloric
USE hydrochloric acid

acid, hydrofluoric
USE hydrofluoric acid

acid igneous rock
MT.626
HN April 1992 descriptor moved
SN Igneous rock containing a high percentage of silica.
UF igneous rock, acid
rock, acid igneous

acid, muriatic
USE hydrochloric acid

acid, nitric
USE nitric acid

acid, orthophosphoric
USE phosphoric acid

acid, phosphoric
USE phosphoric acid

acid precipitation
USE acid rain

acid rain
BM.345 (A,L)
HN February 1991 lead-in terms added
SN Form of precipitation (rain, snow, sleet, or hail) containing high levels of sulfuric or nitric acids. (COLENC)
UF acid precipitation
precipitation, acid
rain, acid

acid resist
USE resist

acid resistance
DC.12 (B)
HN April 1993 alternate term added
October 1992 descriptor moved
ALT acid-resistant
UF resistance, acid

acid-resistant materials
HN April 1993 descriptor split, use acid-resistant (ALT of **acid resistance**) + material (ALT of **materials**)

acid, sulfuric
USE sulfuric acid

acid, sulphuric
SEE sulfuric acid

acid, tannic
USE tannin

acidimeters
TN.130 (N)
ALT acidimeter
SN Instruments for measuring the amount of acid in a solution. (RHDEL2)

acidity
DC.13
HN October 1992 descriptor moved
June 1992 alternate term added
ALT acidic
SN Use generally for the degree of acid content of a substance. Use particularly with reference to solutions having a pH value less than 7. (MH)

acknowledgements
USE acknowledgments

acknowledgments
VW.332 (L)
HN March 1993 lead-in term added
November 1992 descriptor moved
ALT acknowledgment
SN Written recognitions of acts or achievements. (WCOL9)
UF acknowledgements

Acolapissa
FL.1445
HN April 1991 descriptor added

Acoma
FL.1483 (L)

acorn clocks
TN.157
ALT acorn clock
SN American 19th-century clocks generally resembling an acorn in outline and available in shelf, wall, and mantel styles.
UF clocks, acorn

acorn cups
TQ.403
ALT acorn cup
SN Silver standing cups of which the bowl and cover together are in the form of an acorn and generally with a trunklike stem; of a type made in England from the late 16th century. (HNSIL)
UF cups, acorn

acoustic equipment
TH.1108 (N)
SN Encompasses objects used in the study of sound and for transmitting sound.
UF equipment, acoustic

acoustic insulating material
USE acoustical insulation

acoustic insulation
SEE acoustical insulation

acoustic interferometers
TN.359
ALT acoustic interferometer
SN Devices for measuring the velocity and attenuation of sound waves in a gas or liquid by studying the interference pattern set up by two waves generated from the same source.
UF interferometers, acoustic

acoustical ceilings
PJ.2048 (B)
HN March 1993 descriptor moved
ALT acoustical ceiling
SN Ceilings covered with a material designed to absorb sound.
UF ceilings, acoustical

acoustical engineering
HN April 1993 descriptor split, use **acoustical** (ALT of **acoustics**) + engineering

acoustical engineers
HN April 1993 descriptor split, use **acoustical** (ALT of **acoustics**) + engineers

acoustical insulation
MT.1805 (L)
HN April 1993 lead-in term changed, was **acoustic insulating materials**
August 1992 lead-in term added
June 1991 descriptor moved
UK acoustic insulation
SN Insulation used in a building to resist passage of sound waves. (STEIN)
UF acoustic insulating material
insulating material, acoustic
insulation, acoustic
insulation, acoustical
insulation, sound
material, acoustic insulating
sound insulation

acoustical plaster
MT.1869
SN Finishing plaster designed to correct sound reverberations or reduce noise intensity. (STEIN)
UF plaster, acoustical

acoustical properties
DC.6 (L)

HN October 1992 descriptor moved
UF properties, acoustical

acoustical tile
MT.1662
SN Any tile composed of materials having the property of absorbing sound waves. (PUTNAM)
UF tile, acoustical

acoustics
KD.191 (A,L,B,R)
HN December 1992 descriptor moved
January 1991 alternate term added
ALT acoustical

<acoustics concepts>
BM.765
HN April 1993 guide term moved
November 1992 guide term changed, was *<sound and related concepts>*

acquiring
USE procuring

acquisition
KG.113
SN Obtaining materials for a library, documentation center, archive, or other collection, including selection, ordering, and obtaining by exchange or gift. (LG)

Acra red (TM)
USE quinacridone red

acridone red
USE quinacridone red

acroliths
VC.537
ALT acrolith
SN Ancient Greek sculptures in which the extremities are made of stone and the torso is made of another material, usually wood.

acropolises
RG.301 (B)
ALT acropolis
SN The higher and usually fortified sections of ancient Greek cities, typically containing temples and some public buildings and used as places of refuge.

acroteria
PJ.2354 (A,L)
HN March 1993 descriptor moved
ALT acroterion
SN The figures or ornaments at the lower angles or apex of a pediment, generally supported on plinths. (DINSMR)

acrylate resin
USE acrylic

acrylic
MT.1156 (L,B,R)
HN January 1993 descriptor moved
December 1991 scope note changed
April 1990 lead-in term added

SN Colorless, transparent, thermoplastic synthetic resin made by the polymerization of acrylic acid derivatives; used for adhesives, consolidants, protective coatings, finishes, and as a paint medium.
UF acrylate resin
acrylic plastic
acrylic resin
Acryloid (TM)
plastic, acrylic
PMMA
resin, acrylate
resin, acrylic

acrylic color
USE acrylic paint

acrylic paint
MT.1942
HN January 1993 descriptor moved
July 1990 lead-in terms added
UF acrylic color
acrylic resin paint
Aqua-Tec (TM)
color, acrylic
Liquitex (TM)
magna
paint, acrylic
paint, acrylic resin
paint, plastic
plastic paint
resin paint, acrylic

acrylic painting
KT.439 (L)
HN April 1993 scope note added
June 1990 descriptor added
SN The art or practice of producing creative works with acrylic paint.
UF painting, acrylic
painting, polymer
polymer painting

acrylic paintings
VC.273
ALT acrylic painting
SN Creative works in the medium of acrylic paint.
UF paintings, acrylic

acrylic plastic
USE acrylic

acrylic resin
USE acrylic

acrylic resin paint
USE acrylic paint

Acryloid (TM)
USE acrylic

acrylonitrile-butadiene-styrene copolymer
MT.1162 (B)
HN January 1993 descriptor moved
UF ABS
ABS plastic
copolymer, acrylonitrile-butadiene-styrene
plastic, ABS

Act of Parliament clocks
TN.174
ALT Act of Parliament clock
SN British pendulum wall clocks of the mid- to late 18th century, with large dials and wooden cases, generally made for public gathering places, such as inns.
UF clocks, Act of Parliament
clocks, Parliament
Parliament clocks

actinographs
TN.241 (N)
ALT actinograph
SN Recording actinometers. (MHDSTT)

actinometers
TN.240 (L,N)
ALT actinometer
SN Any instrument used to measure the intensity of radiant energy, especially of the sun. (MHDSTT)

action, blow-forward
USE blow-forward action

action, blowback
USE blowback action

action, capillary
USE capillarity

<action components>
PJ.3217

action, double
USE double action

action figures
USE dolls

Action painting
FL.3851 (R)
UF Gestural painting
painting, Action
painting, Gestural

action playgrounds
USE adventure playgrounds

action, single
USE single action

action theater
USE happenings

actions (sound device components)
PJ.3216
ALT action (sound device component)
SN Mechanisms by means of which the strings or pipes of a keyboard instrument are sounded when a key is depressed, or, in harps, that alter the pitch of strings when a pedal is depressed. (NGDMI)
RT harps (chordophones)
keyboard instruments

actions (works of art)
VC.593
ALT action (work of art)
SN Direct, literal events carried out by artists, especially in Germany and Austria, attempting to destroy barri-

ers between art and life; often brutal and obscene.
UF Aktionen

<actions and action components>
PJ.3215

actions, bolt
USE bolt actions

actions, lever
USE lever actions

actions, pump
USE pump actions

actions, slide
USE pump actions

actions, trombone
USE pump actions

activation analysis
USE neutron activation analysis

activation analysis, neutron
USE neutron activation analysis

active solar heating
PC.154
HN March 1993 descriptor moved
February 1991 scope note added
SN Use for solar heating systems that include mechanical equipment and hardware to collect and transport heat; for solar heating systems without mechanical assistance, use passive solar heating.
UF solar heating, active

activists
HG.971
HN February 1993 descriptor moved
January 1993 alternate terms added
ALT activist
activist's
activists'

actons
USE aketons

actors
HG.246 (L,R)
HN February 1993 lead-in term added
November 1992 alternate terms added
ALT actor
actor's
actors'
SN Persons who portray roles in dramatic productions to interpret character or present characterization to an audience. (DOT)
UF actresses
players (actors)

actresses
USE actors

acts, legislative
USE legislative acts

actuaries
HG.611 (L)

HN December 1992 alternate terms added
ALT actuaries'
actuary
actuary's
SN Persons trained in mathematics and statistics whose business it is to calculate insurance and annuity premiums, reserves, and dividends. (W)

acute arches
USE lancet arches

Adam Style
FL.3401 (B,R)
UF Adamesque

<Adamawa-Eastern branch>
FL.201

Adamesque
USE Adam Style

Adampa
USE Adangme

Adangme
FL.299 (L)
UF Adampa

adaptability
DC.7 (B)
HN October 1992 descriptor moved

adaptable furniture
USE adjustable furniture

adaptations
PE.15 (H,L)
HN December 1992 descriptor added
ALT adaptation
SN Works that are modifications of other works done for a purpose, use, or medium other than that for which the original was intended. (ALAG)

adaptive reuse
BM.381 (A,B)
HN December 1992 descriptor moved
April 1992 lead-in terms added
UF adaptive use
conversion of buildings
reuse, adaptive
use, adaptive

adaptive use
USE adaptive reuse

Adarawa
FL.389

addenda
VW.239
HN April 1993 related term added
November 1992 descriptor moved
ALT addendum
SN Printed matter included with or added to a text after it has been set.
RT additions

addendum drawings
USE clarification drawings

addiction
BM.566
HN January 1991 descriptor added
SN The state of being physically or psychologically habituated to a substance or practice to such an extent that its cessation causes severe trauma. For the long term or excessive use or misuse of narcotics, alcohol, or other substances, use **substance abuse**. (RHDEL2)
RT addicts
substance abuse

addiction, drug
USE drug addiction

addiction, narcotic
USE drug addiction

addicts
HG.992
HN January 1993 alternate terms added
January 1991 descriptor added
ALT addict
addict's
addicts'
SN Those who are addicted to an activity, habit, or substance. (RHDEL2)
RT addiction
substance abuse

addicts, dope
USE drug addicts

addicts, drug
USE drug addicts

addicts, narcotic
USE drug addicts

additions
PJ.3 (A,B)
HN May 1993 related term added
March 1993 descriptor moved
February 1991 related term added
ALT addition
SN Use for parts added onto an object or structure. In architecture, if a modification does not substantially increase a structure's volume, use **alterations**. With regard to printed matter, use **addenda**.
UF accretions
accruals
extensions
RT addenda
alterations

additive
MT.1676 (A,L)
HN April 1993 descriptor changed, was **additives**
April 1993 lead-in term changed, was **admixtures**
UF admixture

<additive and joining processes and techniques>
KT.6
HN November 1992 guide term added

additive, antistatic
USE antistatic agent

additive color
USE additive mixture

additive color mixture
USE additive mixture

additive color processes
KT.504
UK additive colour processes
UKA additive colour process
SN Photographic processes that record a color image by making three records of the scene on a monochrome plate or film, each record filtered for one of the three primary colors (red, green, and blue). The image is viewed by reassembling in register each of the separate records, each record being shown by the light of its own record, that is, the red record is displayed with red light.
UF additive processes

additive colour processes
SEE additive color processes

additive mixture
DL.22
HN February 1992 descriptor moved
SN Mixture of colored light, so called because as the colors are combined the mixture becomes successively lighter. (PREBLE)
UF additive color
additive color mixture
color, additive
color mixture, additive
mixture, additive

additive processes
USE additive color processes

address books
VW.814 (N)
HN November 1992 descriptor moved
ALT address book
SN Books listing names with residences, usually in alphabetical order. (GAHLM)
UF books, address

addresses
USE speeches

Adena
FL.893 (L)

adenkums
TT.498
ALT adenkum
SN Stamping tubes made from gourds, played by the Ashanti women of Ghana.

adeudeus
TT.224
ALT adeudeu
SN Arched harps of the Teso of Uganda and Kenya, with a very slim

elongated body and five or six strings.
UF akidiaits
     amagaraits

adhering
USE adhesion

adhesion
     KT.7   (L)
HN January 1993 descriptor moved
     October 1991 scope note changed
SN The joining of two surfaces by means of a generally viscous, sticky composition such as an adhesive or through physical or chemical force. (DAC)
UF adhering

adhesive
     MT.1714   (A,L,B)
HN April 1993 descriptor changed, was **adhesives**
     April 1993 lead-in term changed, was **bonding agents**
     April 1993 lead-in term changed, was **bonding materials**
     July 1990 lead-in term added
UF agent, bonding
     bonding agent
     bonding material
     cement (adhesive)
     material, bonding

adhesive anchors
     PJ.20
HN April 1993 descriptor moved
ALT adhesive anchor
UF anchors, adhesive

adhesive binding
     KT.776
HN January 1993 descriptor added
SN Those methods for bookbinding that rely on adhesives to hold together the leaves of the volume.
UF binding, adhesive
RT adhesive bindings

adhesive bindings
     PJ.3341
ALT adhesive binding
SN Bindings that rely on adhesives to hold together the leaves of the volume.
UF bindings, adhesive
RT adhesive binding

<adhesive by composition or origin>
     MT.1715

<adhesive by form>
     MT.1740

<adhesive by function>
     MT.1747

adhesive, hot-melt
USE hot-melt adhesive

adhesive, organic
USE organic adhesive

adhesive tape
USE pressure-sensitive tape

adhesive, vegetable
USE vegetable adhesive

adhocism
     BM.150   (B)
SN Term coined by the architectural historian Charles Jencks to describe design which comes about, not by formulating new solutions to problems, but by combining pre-existing elements to achieve a new result. (THDAT)

adinkra
     MT.1631
HN March 1993 descriptor moved
SN Asante stamped cloth.
UF adinkra cloth
     cloth, adinkra

adinkra cloth
USE adinkra

adire
     MT.1625
HN March 1993 descriptor moved
SN Yoruba indigo dyed cloth.

Adirondack chairs
     TC.451
HN May 1993 related terms added
     January 1993 descriptor moved
ALT Adirondack chair
SN Angular chairs with slatted seats and backs; not known to have originated in the Adirondacks. (GILBOR)
UF chairs, Adirondack
RT outdoor furniture
     Westport chairs

Adirondack guideboats
     TX.355   (L,N)
ALT Adirondack guideboat
SN Use for light, bevel-lapped double-ended guideboats from New York State's Adirondack region, ranging from 13 to 18 feet long, fitted with a carrying yoke, having a flat bottom board, and planked over natural crook frames in the style of dories; planking is usually smooth or carvel.
UF boats, Adirondack guide
     guideboats, Adirondack

Adja
     FL.303   (L)
HN June 1990 lead-in term added
UF Aja

adjudicating
     KG.4   (L)
HN February 1991 alternate term added
ALT adjudicated
SN Settling disputes by legal process. (RLG7)

adjustable ball hinges
     PJ.372
HN April 1993 descriptor moved
ALT adjustable ball hinge

SN Hinges so designed that, when the door is closed, only a ball-type knuckle is exposed. Such hinges have an adjustment for vertical control within limited scope. (STEIN)
UF ball hinges, adjustable
     hinges, adjustable ball

adjustable candleholders
     TC.1227
ALT adjustable candleholder
SN Candleholders with a device for raising and lowering the height of the candle within its holder or of the holder itself.
UF candleholders, adjustable

adjustable furniture
     TC.1197   (B)
HN January 1993 descriptor moved
UF adaptable furniture
     furniture, adaptable
     furniture, adjustable

adjustable inserts
     PJ.137
HN April 1993 descriptor moved
ALT adjustable insert
UF inserts, adjustable

adjustable keys
     PJ.596
HN March 1993 descriptor moved
ALT adjustable key
SN Keys for sliding-door locks, having a stem or shank adjustable in length to adapt the key to doors of various thicknesses. (STEIN)
UF extension keys
     keys, adjustable
     keys, extension

adjustable lamps
     TC.1342
ALT adjustable lamp
SN Lamps equipped with a mechanism for regulating the position of the light source.
UF lamps, adjustable

adjustable pipe hangers
     PJ.88
HN April 1993 descriptor moved
ALT adjustable pipe hanger
UF hangers, adjustable pipe
     pipe hangers, adjustable

adjustable wrenches
     TH.1310   (N)
ALT adjustable wrench
SN Wrenches with one fixed jaw and one adjustable jaw; generally refers to wrenches with crescent-shaped jaws.
UF crescent wrenches
     wrenches, adjustable
     wrenches, crescent

adjusters, casement
USE casement stays

adjusting
     KT.154

HN January 1993 descriptor added
ALT adjusted
SN Arranging or regulating something to bring it into a proper state or position or to put it in good working order.

adjusting nuts
PJ.210
HN April 1993 descriptor moved
ALT adjusting nut
SN Threaded nuts, used for alignment of an object, that are often coupled with a locking nut to secure them in position. (MEANS)
UF nuts, adjusting

adjusting screws
PJ.238
HN April 1993 descriptor moved
ALT adjusting screw
SN Screws, used for alignment of an object, that are often coupled with a locking nut to secure them in position. (MEANS)
UF screws, adjusting

Adler-Kazaks
USE sunburst Kazaks

administering
KG.205   (L,B,R)
HN February 1991 scope note changed
February 1991 related term added
February 1991 alternate term added
ALT administered
SN Use for the activity of directing the business affairs and human and material resources of an organization, project, or enterprise, involving primarily the formulation of policy. When the application rather than the formulation of policy is the primary aspect, use **managing**. For directly overseeing the activities of an organization or enterprise, use **supervising**.
UF administrating
RT managing

administrating
USE administering

administration buildings
RK.875   (B)
ALT administration building
UF administrative buildings
administrative facilities
administrative office buildings
administrative services buildings
buildings, administration
buildings, administrative office
buildings, administrative services
facilities, administrative
office buildings, administrative

administration, letters of
USE letters of administration

administration, museum
USE museum administration

<*administrative bodies*>
HN.3
HN February 1993 scope note added
SN Collocates terms for organizations consisting of a governing authority together with a population and an area of land which are under its jurisdiction in some or all respects.

<*administrative bodies by degree of independence*>
HN.4
HN December 1992 guide term added

<*administrative bodies by governing person*>
HN.37
HN December 1992 guide term added

administrative buildings
USE administration buildings

administrative facilities
USE administration buildings

administrative office buildings
USE administration buildings

administrative papers
USE administrative records

administrative records
VW.517
HN November 1992 descriptor moved
ALT administrative record
SN Records that relate to budget, personnel, supply, and similar facilitative operations within an organization. (ICA)
UF administrative papers
housekeeping records
papers, administrative
records, administrative
records, housekeeping

administrative regulations
VW.741   (L)
HN November 1992 descriptor moved
ALT administrative regulation
SN Regulations issued by a governmental agency, having the force of law, to interpret or implement the provisions of a statute. For acts of a legislature declaring, commanding, or prohibiting something, and that constitute the law, use **statutes**. (BLACKS)
UF regulations, administrative

<*administrative reports*>
VW.913
HN November 1992 guide term moved

<*administrative reports by frequency*>
VW.918
HN November 1992 guide term moved

<*administrative reports by function*>
VW.914
HN November 1992 guide term moved

administrative services buildings
USE administration buildings

administrators
HG.137   (L)
HN January 1993 scope note added
December 1992 alternate terms added
ALT administrator
administrator's
administrators'
SN Those involved in planning, organizing, directing, and controlling human or material resources to accomplish specific goals.

administrators, public
USE public administrators

Admiral carpets
TC.99
ALT Admiral carpet
SN Early Spanish carpets with three major types of ornamentation derived from Persian or Anatolian rugs, an octagonal-hexagonal design, stepped lozenges design, and star and lozenge design; they are often embellished with coats of arms, and incorporate non-Islamic motifs such as animal or human figures.
UF Admiral rugs
admiral's carpets
armorial carpets, Spanish
carpets, Admiral
carpets, Spanish armorial
rugs, Admiral
Spanish armorial carpets

Admiral rugs
USE Admiral carpets

admirals
HG.124   (L)
HN January 1993 descriptor added
ALT admiral
admiral's
admirals'
SN Officers of the highest rank in a navy.

admiral's carpets
USE Admiral carpets

admiralty brass
USE admiralty metal

admiralty bronze
USE admiralty metal

admiralty charts
USE marine charts

Admiralty Islands
USE Manus

admiralty metal
MT.388
HN March 1993 lead-in terms added
March 1993 descriptor moved
SN Alloy consisting of about 70% copper, 1% tin, and the remainder zinc. (MH)
UF admiralty brass
admiralty bronze
brass, admiralty

bronze, admiralty
metal, admiralty

admission
USE admitting

admission tickets
    VK.187
HN March 1993 descriptor moved
ALT admission ticket
SN Paper slips or cards indicating that the holder has paid for or is entitled to entrance or admission. (AHD)
UF tickets, admission

admitting
    KG.206
HN February 1991 alternate term added
ALT admitted
SN Authorizing entrance as in admission to an institution or program. (RLG7)
UF admission

admixture
USE additive

admixture, air-entraining
USE air-entraining agent

admixture, water-reducing
USE water reducer

adobe
    MT.130   (A,B)
HN May 1993 scope note changed
    April 1992 descriptor moved
    January 1992 lead-in terms added
SN Unfired, sundried brick composed of soil or similar binder and sometimes sand or straw.
UF adobe brick
    brick, adobe
    brick, sun-baked
    brick, unburnt
    brick, unfired
    later crudus
    sun-baked brick
    sun-dried mud brick
    unburnt brick
    unfired brick

adobe brick
USE adobe

adolescence
    BM.577   (H,L)
HN February 1991 descriptor added
SN Transitional stage between childhood and adulthood in the development of a living being; in humans, it extends mainly over the teen years and terminates legally when the official age of majority is reached.
UF teen-age

adolescents
    HG.51   (L)
HN March 1992 alternate terms added
    February 1991 scope note added
    February 1991 descriptor changed, was **teenagers**

February 1991 alternate term changed, was **teenager**
February 1991 lead-in term changed, was **adolescents**
ALT adolescent
    adolescent's
    adolescents'
SN People in the transitional stage of development between childhood and adulthood, commonly considered as those of 13 to 17 years of age.
UF teenagers

Adoptionism
    BM.535   (L,R)
SN Doctrine that Jesus became son of God by exaltation that was not his at birth. (W)

ADs
USE assessment districts

ads
USE advertisements

adsorption
    KT.818   (L)
HN January 1993 descriptor moved
    March 1991 alternate term added
ALT adsorbed
SN The taking up of the molecules of gases, dissolved substances, or liquids by the surfaces of solids and liquids with which they are in contact. (W)

adult day care centers
    RK.1130   (A,L)
ALT adult day care center
SN Use for alternatives to nursing homes providing for aged and disabled members, if their needs are appropriate, a structured program of activities, meals, and medical and psychological services during daytime hours only; members spend evenings in their own homes.
UF adult day health centers
    centers, adult day care
    centers, adult day health
    day care centers, adult
    health centers, adult day

adult day health centers
USE adult day care centers

adult education centers
USE continuing education centers

adulthood
    BM.578   (L)
HN February 1991 descriptor added
SN Stage at which a living being is fully grown or developed.

adults
    HG.48   (L)
HN November 1992 alternate terms added
    February 1991 scope note changed
ALT adult

adult's
adults'
SN People who are fully grown and developed, commonly considered to be those aged 18 years or older.

Aduma
USE Duma

advancement
USE promoting

advantage, pieces of
USE double pieces

Advent
    KM.173   (L)
HN April 1991 descriptor added
SN Christian religious season lasting from the fourth Sunday before Christmas until Christmas, observed by some as a period of prayer and fasting. (WCOL9)

adventure playgrounds
    RM.104   (B)
HN April 1993 descriptor moved
ALT adventure playground
SN Use for supervised play areas featuring exercise-oriented equipment often built and freely arranged by children from readily available loose materials, such as crates, tires, and ropes.
UF action playgrounds
    junk playgrounds
    playgrounds, action
    playgrounds, adventure
    playgrounds, junk
    playgrounds, Robinson Crusoe
    Robinson Crusoe playgrounds
    workyards

adventurers
    HG.893   (L)
HN January 1993 descriptor added
ALT adventurer
    adventurer's
    adventurers'
SN Men who pursue hazardous, risky, unscrupulous, or questionable enterprises and activities, either to gain wealth, power, or social position, or for the sake of excitement.

adventurers, women
USE adventuresses

adventures, joint
USE joint ventures

adventuresses
    HG.894   (L)
HN February 1993 descriptor added
ALT adventuress
    adventuresses'
    adventuress's
SN Women who pursue hazardous, risky, unscrupulous, or questionable enterprises and activities, either to gain wealth, power, or social position, or for the sake of excitement.

UF adventurers, women
　　women adventurers

Adventus books
USE festival books

adversaria
USE marginalia

adverse weather lamps
USE fog lights

advertisements
　　VW.373　　　　　　　　　　(L,N)
HN June 1992 descriptor added
ALT advertisement
SN Public notices or paid announce-
　　ments, especially those in print. For
　　announcements paid for by an ad-
　　vertiser and broadcast on radio or
　　television, use **commercials**.
UF ads

advertisements, bid
USE bidding announcements

advertisements for bidders
USE bidding announcements

advertising
　　KD.238　　　　　　　　　(L,B,R)
HN June 1992 scope note added
SN The nonpersonal presentation of
　　goods, services, or ideas for action,
　　openly paid for by an identified en-
　　tity. (KAUFAD)

advertising, broadcast
USE broadcast advertising

advertising campaigns
　　KM.10　　　　　　　　　　　(L)
HN May 1991 alternate term added
ALT advertising campaign
UF campaigns, advertising

advertising cards
　　VW.1120　　　　　　　　(H,L,N)
HN June 1992 descriptor added
ALT advertising card
SN Use for cards distributed by mer-
　　chants or manufacturers to adver-
　　tise or promote their business or
　　product, sometimes as premiums.
　　For small printed sheets or cards
　　bearing tradesmen's advertisements
　　from the 17th through the 19th
　　century, use **trade cards**. For cards
　　made later, bearing the name and
　　address of a business concern and
　　the name of its representative, and
　　intended more for information than
　　for advertising, use **business cards**.
　　For cards made later and issued pri-
　　marily to be collected, with or with-
　　out advertisements on them, use
　　collecting cards. For cards intended
　　to be posted as public advertise-
　　ments, use **posters** or its narrower
　　terms.
UF cards, advertising
　　cards, show
　　show cards

　　showcards
RT business cards
　　collecting cards
　　posters
　　premiums
　　trade cards

advertising design
HN January 1993 descriptor split, use
　　advertising + design

advertising fliers
HN June 1992 descriptor split, use ad-
　　vertising + fliers (printed matter)

<advertising functions>
　　KG.40
HN February 1993 guide term added

advertising mail
USE direct mail

advertising, outdoor
USE outdoor advertising

advertising photography
HN April 1993 descriptor split, use ad-
　　vertising + photography

advertising, point-of-purchase
USE point-of-purchase displays

advertising, point-of-sale
USE point-of-purchase displays

advertising, print
USE print advertising

advertising trade cards
USE trade cards

advertising, transit
USE transit advertising

advice centers
USE information centers

advice, letters of
USE letters of advice

advisers
SEE advisors

advising
USE counseling

advisors
　　HG.895　　　　　　　　　　　(L)
HN April 1993 related term added
　　December 1992 alternate terms
　　　added
ALT advisor
　　advisor's
　　advisors'
UK advisers
UKA adviser
SN Use for persons who give advice ei-
　　ther nonprofessionally, or in an of-
　　ficial or professional context, usually
　　on an ongoing basis. For persons
　　called on for professional advice re-
　　garding matters in their field of spe-
　　cial knowledge or training, usually

　　for specific projects or problems,
　　use **consultants**.
RT consultants

advisors, investment
USE investment advisors

advocating
　　KG.45
HN April 1991 lead-in term added
SN Representing and supporting the
　　interests of a person, group, project,
　　or program. (RLG7)
UF promoting (advocating)

adyta
　　PJ.1282
HN March 1993 descriptor moved
ALT adytum
SN Use for small inner rooms adjacent
　　to or within the naos, found in some
　　ancient temples.

Adyukru
USE Ajukru

adze-hatchets
　　TH.1467
ALT adze-hatchet
SN Two-bladed tools with the larger
　　blade in the shape of a hatchet and
　　the smaller shaped like an adz, as
　　distinguished from **hatchet-adzes** in
　　which the adz-shaped blade is the
　　larger.

adzes
　　TH.523　　　　　　　　　　(L,N)
ALT adz
SN Long-handled tools with a curved
　　blade set perpendicular to the han-
　　dle; used for dressing lumber.
　　(MEANS)

adzes, bunging
USE bunging adzes

adzes, carpenters'
USE carpenters' adzes

adzes, cleaving
USE cleaving adzes

adzes, coopers'
USE coopers' adzes

adzes, dished
USE hollowing adzes

adzes, dubbing
USE lipped adzes

adzes, gouge
USE hollowing adzes

adzes, hatchet
USE hatchet-adzes

adzes, hollowing
USE hollowing adzes

adzes, lipped
USE lipped adzes

adzes, saucer
USE hollowing adzes

adzes, ship carpenters'
USE shipwrights' adzes

adzes, shipwrights'
USE shipwrights' adzes

adzes, stowing
USE trussing adzes

adzes, trussing
USE trussing adzes

adzes, wheelers'
USE wheelwrights' adzes

adzes, wheelwrights'
USE wheelwrights' adzes

<adzes: woodworking tools>
TH.1387

Adzhina-Tepe
FL.1869
HN April 1993 descriptor moved

aedes
RK.1077
SN Use only in ancient Roman contexts when distinguishing a sacred precinct (called a temple) from the building within the precinct housing a cult image or the treasure of a deity.
UF aedes sacrae

aedes sacrae
USE aedes

aedicula frames
USE tabernacle frames

aediculae
PJ.1420   (R)
HN March 1993 descriptor moved
ALT aedicula
SN Use for niches, often intended for sculpture, or for frameworks around doors or windows formed of columns, corbeling, or pilasters, supporting a pediment or canopy.
UF edicules
tabernacles (aediculae)

aedicular frames
USE tabernacle frames

Aegean
FL.2618   (L,B)

<Aegean architecture styles>
FL.2675

<Aegean Bronze Age periods>
FL.2624

<Aegean Neolithic periods>
FL.2620

<Aegean periods>
FL.2619

<Aegean pottery styles>
FL.2680

<Aegean sculpture styles>
FL.2764

<Aegean styles>
FL.2672

aegicranes
DG.32
HN March 1993 lead-in terms added
April 1991 lead-in terms added
ALT aegicrane
SN Motifs representing the head of a ram or goat; used originally in Greek and Roman temple decoration and later in classicizing styles. (LDDO)
UF goats' heads
ram's heads
rams' heads

Aeneolithic
USE Eneolithic

aeolian harps
TT.625   (L)
ALT aeolian harp
SN Ambient sound makers with strings, usually tuned in unison, which are sounded by the natural wind blowing across them.
UF harps, aeolian

aeolian landforms
RD.165
ALT aeolian landform
SN Landforms whose constituents have been carried and laid down by air currents. (WAYTA)
UF aeolian sediments
eolian landforms
landforms, aeolian
landforms, eolian
sediments, aeolian

aeolian sediments
USE aeolian landforms

Aeolic
FL.2676
UF Proto-Aeolic
Proto-Ionic
Pseudo-Ionic

Aeolic capitals
PJ.1491
HN March 1993 descriptor moved
August 1990 lead-in terms added
ALT Aeolic capital
SN Use for a broad range of capital designs found in the Mediterranean world prior to the Classical period and generally characterized by paired, vertically rising volutes.
UF capitals, Aeolic
capitals, proto-Ionic
capitals, pseudo-Ionic
proto-Ionic capitals
pseudo-Ionic capitals

aeoliphones
USE wind chimes

aeraria
RK.925
ALT aerarium

SN Use for ancient Roman public treasury buildings.

aerated concrete
USE air-entrained concrete

aëres
TC.181
ALT aër
SN Textile coverings for communion vessels, used in the Orthodox Eastern Church.

<aerial activities>
KQ.38

aerial bombs
TK.103   (L)
ALT aerial bomb
SN Bombs designed to be dropped from aircraft, first seriously developed during the First World War.
UF bombs, aerial

aerial charts
USE aeronautical charts

aerial ladders
TH.1040   (L)
ALT aerial ladder
SN Extension ladders capable of reaching very high places; often mounted on a vehicle such as a fire truck. (DAC)
UF ladders, aerial

aerial mosaics
USE photomosaic maps

aerial perspective
USE atmospheric perspective

aerial perspectives
USE bird's-eye perspectives

aerial photogrammetry
KT.199   (L)
HN January 1993 descriptor moved
UF aerial photographic surveying
photogrammetry, aerial
photographic surveying, aerial

aerial photographic surveying
USE aerial photogrammetry

aerial photographs
VC.366   (L)
HN April 1992 descriptor moved
ALT aerial photograph
SN Use for photographs of the earth taken from aircraft. For photographs taken from beyond the earth's atmosphere, use **space photographs**. For photographs of celestial bodies or astronomical phenomena, use **astrophotographs**.
UF air photographs
photographs, aerial
photographs, air

aerial photography
KT.582   (A,L,B,R)
SN Use for the activity of photographing from aircraft. When em-

phasis is on the view achieved by photographing from aircraft or other high locations, use **aerial views**. For photography beyond the earth's atmosphere, use **space photography**; for photography of celestial phenomena, use **astronomical photography**.

UF   air photography
      balloon photography
      photography, aerial
      photography, air
      photography, balloon

aerial prospecting
USE aerial surveying

aerial prospection
USE aerial surveying

aerial surveying
    KT.287
HN November 1992 descriptor added
SN The systematic examination of land or water areas from aircraft.
UF   aerial prospecting
      aerial prospection
      prospecting, aerial
      prospection, aerial
      surveying, aerial

aerial transport
USE air transport

aerial views
    VC.21   (L,B)
HN April 1991 descriptor moved
ALT aerial view
SN Use to designate views achieved by photographing from an aircraft or other high location. When emphasizing the photograph itself, use **aerial photographs**. For nonphotographic depictions having high viewpoints, use **bird's-eye views** or **bird's-eye perspectives**.
UF   air views
      views, aerial
      views, air

aerial views (perspective drawings)
USE bird's-eye perspectives

aerodrome beacons
USE airport beacons

aerodrome identification beacons
USE airport beacons

aerodrome obstruction lights
USE obstruction lights

aerodromes
USE airports

aerodynamical laboratories
    RK.1105   (A,L,B)
ALT aerodynamical laboratory
UF   laboratories, aerodynamical

aerodynamics
    BM.823   (A,L,R)
HN March 1993 scope note added
      November 1992 descriptor moved

SN Physical forces related to the motion of air and other gaseous fluids, including the forces acting on bodies when they move through such fluids, or when such fluids move against or around bodies.

aerodynes
USE heavier than air aircraft

aerogrammes
    VW.1110   (L)
HN June 1992 descriptor added
ALT aerogramme
SN Sheets of lightweight paper, bearing an official postal stamp imprint, that are folded to form their own envelopes and can be sent via airmail at a special, low rate. (RHDEL2)
UF   air letter sheets
      air letters
      letter sheets, air
      letters, air

aerographs
USE meteorographs

aerometers
    TN.295   (N)
ALT aerometer
SN Instruments for determining the weight or density of air or other gases.

aeronautical beacons
    TC.1433
ALT aeronautical beacon
SN Visual aids to navigation displaying flashes of white or colored light or both, used to indicate the location of airports, landmarks, and certain points of the federal airways in mountainous terrain and to mark hazards. (MHDSTT)
UF   beacons, aeronautical

aeronautical charts
    VW.126   (L)
HN November 1992 descriptor moved
ALT aeronautical chart
SN Maps designed primarily for use in air navigation, giving surface features of aeronautical importance. (GAHLM)
UF   aerial charts
      aeronautical maps
      charts, aerial
      charts, aeronautical
      maps, aeronautical

aeronautical engineering
    KD.111
HN April 1993 related term added
SN Branch of aerospace engineering dealing with the design, development, and production of aircraft that function within the atmosphere, and their related systems. (RHDEL2)
UF   engineering, aeronautical
RT   aeronautical engineers

aeronautical engineers
    HG.856   (L)
HN April 1993 related term added
      December 1992 alternate terms added
ALT aeronautical engineer
      aeronautical engineer's
      aeronautical engineers'
UF   engineers, aeronautical
RT   aeronautical engineering

aeronautical ground lights
    RM.218   (L,N)
HN April 1993 descriptor moved
      May 1990 descriptor added
ALT aeronautical ground light
SN Any light specially provided as an aid to air navigation, other than a light displayed on an aircraft. (IESREF)
UF   ground lights, aeronautical
      lights, aeronautical ground

aeronautical laboratories
HN April 1993 descriptor split, use **aeronautical (ALT of aeronautics) + laboratories**

aeronautical lights, aircraft
USE aircraft aeronautical lights

aeronautical maps
USE aeronautical charts

aeronautical museums
    RK.387   (A,L)
ALT aeronautical museum
UF   air and space museums
      aviation museums
      museums, aeronautical
      museums, air and space
      museums, aviation

aeronautical schools
HN May 1991 descriptor split, use **aeronautical engineering + schools**

<aeronautical site elements>
    RM.217
HN April 1993 guide term moved
      August 1990 guide term added

aeronautics
    KD.100   (L,R)
HN May 1991 alternate term added
ALT aeronautical
SN Science and practice of flight. (RHDEL2)

Aeropainting
USE Aeropittura

<aerophone components>
    PJ.3222

<aerophone components: pipes>
    PJ.3240

aerophones
    TT.2
ALT aerophone
SN Sound devices that produce their sound by using the air itself as the primary vibrating agent. (NGDMI)

UF aerophonic instruments
   instruments, aerophonic
RT <instrumentalists: wind instruments>
   wind instruments

aerophones, free reed
USE free reeds

aerophones, whirling
USE whirling aerophones

aerophonic instruments
USE aerophones

Aeropittura
   FL.3495
UF Aeropainting

aeroplanes
SEE airplanes

aerosol
   MT.1371   (L)
HN February 1992 scope note changed
SN A colloidal system such as a mist or
   fog, in which the dispersion me-
   dium is a gas.

aerospace engineering
   KD.110
HN April 1993 related term added
SN Branch of engineering that deals
   with the design, development, testing, and production of aircraft,
   spacecraft, missiles, rocket propulsion systems, and other equipment
   operating both within and beyond
   the earth's atmosphere. (RHDEL2)
UF engineering, aerospace
RT aerospace engineers

aerospace engineers
   HG.855   (L)
HN April 1993 related term added
   December 1992 alternate terms
   added
ALT aerospace engineer
   aerospace engineer's
   aerospace engineers'
UF engineers, aerospace
RT aerospace engineering

aerospace planes
USE aerospace vehicles

aerospace vehicles
   TX.4
ALT aerospace vehicle
SN Use for vehicles capable of flight
   both within and outside the sensible
   atmosphere. (NASATH)
UF aerospace planes
   planes, aerospace
   vehicles, aerospace

aerostats
USE lighter than air aircraft

aeruca
USE verdigris

aerugo
USE verdigris

aes grave
   VK.21
SN Designates cumbersome, heavy,
   bronze Roman cast coins, generally
   of the 3rd century BCE.

aes rude
   VK.3
SN Earliest type of Roman money, essentially rough, unmade, or unfin-
   ished lumps of bronze of irregular
   weights. (DOFARC)

aes signatum
   VK.53
SN Use for ancient Roman cast bronze
   coins, usually in the form of ingots,
   and in circulation before 300 BCE,
   preceding the aes grave.

Aesculus
USE buckeye

Aesculus californica
USE California buckeye

Aesculus flava
USE yellow buckeye

Aesculus hippocastanum
USE horse chestnut

Aesculus octandra
USE yellow buckeye

Aesculus pavia
USE dwarf buckeye

<aesthetic concepts>
   BM.396

aesthetic, machine
USE machine aesthetic

Aesthetic Movement
   FL.3402   (A,L,R)
UF Aestheticism (art movement)

aesthetic urge
USE Kunstwollen

aestheticians
   HG.387
HN April 1993 related term added
   December 1992 alternate terms
   added
ALT aesthetician
   aesthetician's
   aestheticians'
SN Specialists in aesthetics. (W)
RT aesthetics

aestheticism
   BM.418
SN A theory of art which maintains that
   the philosophy of art is separate
   from any other philosophy and that
   art can be judged only by its own
   standards. (THDAT)

Aestheticism (art movement)
USE Aesthetic Movement

aesthetics
   KD.73   (A,L,B,R)

HN April 1993 related term added
UF art, philosophy of
   esthetics
   philosophy of art
RT aestheticians

aetherophones
USE theremins

Afanasievo
   FL.2196
UF Afanasyevskaya

Afanasyevskaya
USE Afanasievo

Afar
   FL.615   (L)
UF Danakil

afara
USE limba

affection
USE love

affiches déchirées
USE affiches lacérées

affiches lacérées
   VC.76   (R)
SN An art form popular in the 1950s
   consisting of layers of posters with
   parts torn away; for the process or
   art of making them, use **décollage.**
UF affiches déchirées
   décollages

affidavits
   VW.616   (L)
HN November 1992 descriptor moved
ALT affidavit
SN Sworn statements in writing; espe-
   cially made upon oath before an au-
   thorized magistrate or officer.
   (GAHLM)

affordable housing
   RG.69   (A)
HN January 1993 related term added
   January 1991 related term added
SN Designates housing for people who
   are unable to purchase or rent
   homes through normal marketplace
   mechanisms; includes such options
   as low cost housing, low income
   housing, shelters for the homeless,
   or mobile homes.
UF housing, affordable
RT single room occupancy hotels
   Usonian houses

Afghan
   FL.1891   (L,B)
HN April 1993 descriptor moved
UF Bokhara

Afghan (Ersari)
USE Ersari

**<Afghan and Bactrian historic styles and
   periods>**
   FL.1790
HN April 1993 guide term added

Afghan carpets
USE Afghan + rugs

Afghan door rugs
USE Afghan + rugs

afghans
TC.164 (L,N)
ALT afghan
SN Knitted or crocheted throws composed of strips or squares sewn or crocheted together.

Afghans (rugs)
USE Afghan + rugs

Afikpo
FL.261

Afo
FL.206

afochês
USE cabacas

Afrasiab
FL.1884
HN April 1993 descriptor moved
UF Afrosiab
Samarkand (Sogdian)
Samarqand (Sogdian)

African
FL.34 (B,R)

African American
FL.1742 (H,L,R)
UF Afro-American
Black (style)
Negro

African Americans
HN June 1991 descriptor deleted

African blackwood
MT.2891
HN March 1992 descriptor moved
UF blackwood, African
congo-wood
Dalbergia melanoxylin
ebony, Senegal
Senegal ebony

African cedar
MT.2949
HN March 1992 descriptor moved
UF cedar, African
Juniperus procera

<African Epipaleolithic periods>
FL.40

African mahogany
MT.2797
HN March 1992 descriptor moved
UF khaya
mahogany, African

<African Paleolithic periods>
FL.37

<African sculpture styles>
FL.713

<African styles by region>
FL.174

Africano, marmor
USE marmor Africano

Afro-American
USE African American

Afro-Portuguese
FL.171 (H)
UF Sherbro (Afro-Portuguese)

Afrosiab
USE Afrasiab

Afsar carpets
USE Afshar + rugs

Afshar
FL.3727
HN April 1993 descriptor added

Afshars
USE Afshar + rugs

after-five dresses
USE cocktail dresses

afterimages
BM.111 (L)
HN January 1991 alternate term added
ALT afterimage
SN Visual sensation occurring after the external cause has disappeared.

afternoon costume
USE afternoon dress

afternoon dress
BM.268
HN August 1992 descriptor added
SN Dress for daytime social functions.
UF afternoon costume
costume, afternoon
dress, afternoon
RT tea gowns

Ag
USE silver

agal-agal
USE agar-agar

agalmatolite
USE pagoda stone

Agano
FL.2089 (L)

agar
USE agar-agar

agar-agar
MT.992 (L)
HN April 1992 descriptor moved
SN Gelatinous extract from seaweed. (MH)
UF agal-agal
agar

Agata glass
MT.268
HN March 1992 descriptor added
SN Term used in the glass trade for a type of art glass first produced by the New England Glass Co. in 1886, characterized by a glossy mottled surface created by first coating the

object with metallic stain and then spattering it with a volatile liquid; the finish is fixed by a light firing. (AAT)
UF glass, Agata

agate
MT.578 (L)
HN April 1992 descriptor moved
February 1992 related term added
February 1992 scope note changed
SN A cryptocrystalline variety of quartz being a banded chalcedony.
RT gemstone

Agate Basin
FL.763 (L)

agate glass
MT.266
HN April 1993 descriptor added
SN Decorative opaque glass made by mixing different colors in order to imitate natural semi-precious stones. Also a type of art glass developed by Tiffany that resembles agate stone.
UF glass, agate
RT holly amber glass

Age, Bronze
USE Bronze Age

age cracking
USE age cracks

age crackle
USE age cracks

age cracks
DE.9
SN A pattern of crackle in paintings occurring after all layers have dried, often penetrating the ground as well, resulting from subtle movements in the support, such as from changes of temperature or humidity.
UF age cracking
age crackle
convection crackle
cracking, age
crackle, age
crackle, convection
cracks, age
cracks, late
late cracks

age discrimination
BM.1071 (L)
HN February 1993 descriptor moved
February 1991 scope note added
January 1991 alternate term added
ALT ageist
SN Discriminatory attitudes or practices toward people on the basis of their age. (ERIC12)
UF ageism
discrimination, age

age, golden
USE golden age

Age, Iron
USE Iron Age

age, middle
USE middle age

age, old
USE old age

age, spirit of the
USE Zeitgeist

Age, Stone
USE Stone Age

aged
USE elderly

aged, housing for the
USE housing for the elderly

ageism
USE age discrimination

agencies
HN.58
HN February 1993 scope note changed
ALT agency
SN Organizations that provide a service; also certain administrative units of government. (RHDEL2)

agencies, employment
USE employment agencies

agencies, funding
USE funding agencies

agencies, granting
USE funding agencies

agencies, library service
USE library service agencies

agencies, state art
USE art commissions

agencies, travel
USE travel agencies

agendas
VW.518
HN November 1992 descriptor moved
ALT agenda
SN Documents, often in list form, stating things to be done, as items of business or discussions to be brought up at a meeting; includes programs consisting of such items. (GAHLM)

agent, air-entraining
USE air-entraining agent

agent, anti-foaming
SEE antifoaming agent

agent, antifoaming
USE antifoaming agent

agent, antifungal
USE fungicide

agent, antistatic
USE antistatic agent

agent, binding
USE binder

agent, bonding
USE adhesive

agent, buffing
USE buffing composition

agent, cleaning
USE cleaning compound

agent, curing
USE curing agent

agent, dispersing
USE dispersing agent

agent, emulsifying
USE emulsifier

agent, fire-proofing
SEE fireproofing agent

agent, fireproofing
USE fireproofing agent

agent, foaming
USE foaming agent

agent, mold release
USE mold release agent

agent, mould release
SEE mold release agent

agent, permeability
USE permeability agent

agent, release
USE release agent

agent, rust removing
USE rust removing agent

agent, stabilizing
USE stabilizer

agent, surface active
USE surface active agent

agent, suspending
USE suspending agent

agent, water-reducing
USE water reducer

agent, wetting
USE wetting agent

agents
USE commercial agents

agents, business
USE commercial agents

agents, commercial
USE commercial agents

agents, estate
USE real estate agents

agents, house
USE real estate agents

agents, insurance
USE insurance agents

agents, real estate
USE real estate agents

agents, travel
USE travel agents

Ages, Dark
USE Dark Ages
Migration period

Agfacolor (TM)
KT.557

agglomerations
RD.17   (L)
ALT agglomeration
SN Use.for large, unplanned clusterings of urban populations, that, as a result of urban sprawl, have outgrown local governmental boundaries.

agglutinant
SEE agglutinin

agglutinin
MT.1758   (L)
UK agglutinant
SN A substance that causes the union of separate materials or particles into a group or mass; includes glue or other adhesive that serves this function in making aqueous paint, pastels, and ink for drawing.

aggregate
MT.1678   (L,B)
HN April 1993 descriptor changed, was **aggregates**
SN Inert granular material such as natural sand, manufactured sand, or gravel that, when bound into a conglomerate mass, forms concrete or mortar. (DAC)

<aggregate by size>
MT.1679

<aggregate by weight>
MT.1683

aggregate, coarse
USE coarse aggregate

aggregate, fine
USE fine aggregate

Aghem
USE Wum

Aghlabid
FL.3534
HN April 1993 descriptor moved

agiasteria
USE sanctuaries

aging, accelerated
USE accelerated aging

aging, artificial
USE accelerated aging

aging persons
USE elderly

agitable lamps
TC.1305
ALT agitable lamp
SN Lamps with usually one or two vertical wick tubes projecting from a tightly closed reservoir. From the patent of John Miles of Birmingham, England, 1787; so called because the fuel is protected from spillage when agitated.
UF common lamps
lamps, agitable
lamps, common
lamps, Miles patent
Miles patent lamps

agitation propaganda
USE agitprop

agitprop
BM.164   (R)
SN Derived from agitation propaganda, meaning intended to inspire political action. With reference to visual art, use for the specific art movement arising in Soviet Russia following the Bolshevik revolution.
UF agitation propaganda

Agkhand
FL.3578
HN April 1993 descriptor added

Agkhand ware
HN April 1993 descriptor split, use Agkhand + ware

aglets
TE.482
ALT aglet
SN Any of various ornamental cords, studs, pins, or the like used for decoration on costume.

Agni
USE Anyi

agnosticism
BM.536   (L)
HN January 1991 alternate term added
ALT agnostic
SN Doctrine affirming that the existence of God is possible, but denying that there are any sufficient reasons for holding either that God does or does not exist. (W)

agoras
RM.191   (A,B)
HN April 1993 descriptor moved
ALT agora
SN In ancient Greek settlements, open spaces used as marketplaces or general public meeting places.

Agra
FL.2385
HN April 1993 descriptor added

agrafes (clasps)
PJ.75
ALT agrafe (clasp)
SN Clasps, often richly ornamented, in the form of a hook sewn to one side of a garment or armor, to be attached to a loop or ring sewn on the other side.

agrafes (sculpture)
VC.526
ALT agrafe (sculpture)
SN Reliefs found on the face of a voussoir or keystone.

Agras
USE Agra + rugs

agreements
VW.617   (L)
HN November 1992 descriptor moved
ALT agreement
SN Writing made to evidence the terms and conditions, or the fact, of an accord or arrangement. (GAHLM)
UF articles of agreement

agreements, apprenticeship
USE articles of apprenticeship

agreements, collective labor
USE collective labor agreements

agreements, cost plus fee
USE cost plus fee agreements

agreements, international
USE international agreements

agreements, master
USE collective labor agreements

agreements, owner-contractor
USE owner-contractor agreements

agreements, partnership
USE partnership agreements

agricultural aircraft
TX.43
SN Light aircraft specially equipped for agricultural applications, such as crop dusting. (NASATH)
UF agricultural airplanes
aircraft, agricultural
airplanes, agricultural

agricultural airplanes
USE agricultural aircraft

agricultural buildings
RK.42   (B)
ALT agricultural building
SN Use for buildings used for the science or art of cultivating the soil, harvesting crops, or raising livestock, not used for human habitation, employment, or processing, and not used by the public.
UF agricultural facilities
agricultural works
buildings, agricultural
facilities, agricultural
works, agricultural

<agricultural complexes>
RG.3

<agricultural equipment>
TH.417
HN December 1992 guide term added

agricultural facilities
USE agricultural buildings

<agricultural functions>
KG.238
HN May 1991 guide term added

agricultural laboratories
HN April 1993 descriptor split, use agricultural (ALT of agriculture) + laboratories

agricultural land
RD.250
UF agricultural landscape
land, agricultural
landscape, agricultural

agricultural landscape
USE agricultural land

agricultural museums
USE agriculture

agricultural settlements
RD.47
ALT agricultural settlement
UF agricultural villages
farming villages
settlements, agricultural
villages, agricultural
villages, farming

<agricultural structures>
RK.41

agricultural villages
USE agricultural settlements

agricultural works
USE agricultural buildings

agriculture
KD.102   (L,R)
HN February 1991 alternate term added
ALT agricultural
SN Science or art of cultivating the soil, harvesting crops, and raising livestock. (W)

agriculture museums
HN April 1993 descriptor split, use agriculture + museums

agricultural museums
USE agriculture + museums

agriculturists
HG.559   (L)
HN February 1993 descriptor moved December 1992 alternate terms added
ALT agriculturist
agriculturist's
agriculturists'
SN Persons trained in the theory or science of agriculture. (W)
UF agronomists

agronomists
USE agriculturists

AGT
USE   personal rapid transit

Aguada
FL.1205

Ägyptisch Blau
USE   Egyptian blue

Ägyptischblau
USE   Egyptian blue

Ahmad I
USE   Ahmed I

Ahmad II
USE   Ahmed II

Ahmad III
USE   Ahmed III

Ahmadnagar
FL.2301   (L)
HN   February 1991 descriptor moved

Ahmed I
FL.3623
HN   April 1993 descriptor moved
UF   Ahmad I
     Ahmet I

Ahmed II
FL.3629
HN   April 1993 descriptor moved
UF   Ahmad II
     Ahmet II

Ahmed III
FL.3631
HN   April 1993 descriptor moved
     November 1991 lead-in terms
     added
UF   Ahmad III
     Ahmet III

Ahmet I
USE   Ahmed I

Ahmet II
USE   Ahmed II

Ahmet III
USE   Ahmed III

Aht
USE   Nootka

Ahtena
FL.1239   (L)
UF   Atnah
     Atnatana

ai
USE   indigo

Ai-Hanum
FL.1791
HN   April 1993 descriptor moved
UF   Ai-Khanum

Ai-Khanum
USE   Ai-Hanum

aid, federal
USE   federal aid

aid, student
USE   student aid

aids, audiovisual
USE   audiovisual materials

aids, finding
USE   finding aids

aids, visual
USE   visual aids

aigrettes
TE.503
ALT   aigrette
SN   Upright plumes of feathers of an
     egret or heron arranged as a hair
     ornament. Also, similar jeweled or-
     naments in the shape of feathers,
     especially those worn on the head.
UF   egrets
RT   jewelry
     plumes

aiguilles
TH.1345
HN   December 1992 descriptor moved
ALT   aiguille
SN   Slender drills used for boring or
     drilling a blasthole in rock. (DAC)

Aija
USE   Recuay

ailerons
PJ.1942
HN   March 1993 descriptor moved
     November 1990 descriptor moved
     November 1990 scope note changed
ALT   aileron
SN   Half gables, such as those that close
     the end of a penthouse roof or the
     roof over a side aisle of a church;
     may be scrolled, curved, or other-
     wise ornamented.

Aimoré
USE   Botocudo

air
MT.1311   (H,L,B)
HN   April 1992 descriptor added

air and space museums
USE   aeronautical museums

<air and space transportation buildings>
RK.1174
HN   March 1993 guide term added

<air and space transportation equipment>
TH.405
HN   March 1993 guide term added

<air and space transportation vehicles>
TX.3

air art
VC.77   (L,R)
HN   April 1991 scope note changed
     April 1991 descriptor moved
SN   Use for works of art, first appearing
     in the late 1960s, that exploit the
     possibilities of compressed air, or
     the natural force of the wind, usu-

ally in association with plastic envelopes.
UF   art, air

air balloons, hot
USE   hot-air balloons

air barriers
USE   air infiltration barriers

air bases
RG.130   (A,L)
ALT   air base
UF   air bases, military
     Air Force bases
     bases, air
     bases, Air Force
     bases, military air
     military air bases

air bases, military
USE   air bases

air bases, naval
USE   naval air bases

air brick
MT.97   (B)
HN   April 1992 descriptor moved
SN   A perforated brick or perforated
     metal unit of brick size which is built
     into a wall for ventilation. (DAC)
UF   brick, air
     brick, ventilating
     ventilating brick

air bubbles
USE   air traps

air cleaners
USE   air filters
     air washers

air conditioners
TH.490   (N)
ALT   air conditioner
SN   Devices for controlling the tempera-
     ture, humidity, and sometimes the
     purity of the air in an interior
     space. (RHDEL2)
UF   conditioners, air

air conditioning
PC.141   (A,L,B)
HN   March 1993 descriptor moved
     August 1990 scope note changed
SN   Building systems in which air is
     treated to control its temperature,
     humidity, cleanliness, or distri-
     bution.
UF   air conditioning systems
     systems, air conditioning

air conditioning, central
USE   central air conditioning

air conditioning, incremental
USE   incremental air conditioning

air conditioning locks
PJ.547
HN   May 1993 descriptor moved
ALT   air conditioning lock
UF   locks, air conditioning

air conditioning systems
USE air conditioning

air cooling
PC.144
HN March 1993 descriptor moved
August 1990 scope note added
SN Building system for the lowering of air temperature, as for comfort, process control, or food preservation. (MHEST6)
UF cooling systems
systems, cooling

air-cooling coils
USE cooling coils

air curtains
PJ.2156   (A,L,B,R)
HN March 1993 descriptor moved
ALT air curtain
SN Streams of high-velocity, temperature-controlled air which are directed downward across an opening to prevent transfer of heat across it, thus making it possible to air condition a space having an open entrance.
UF air doors
doors, air

air diffusers
PJ.812
HN March 1993 descriptor moved
August 1990 scope note changed
ALT air diffuser
SN Outlets in an air supply duct for distributing and blending air in an enclosure, usually mounted in suspended ceilings. (MEANS)
UF diffusers, air

air distribution systems
PJ.813
HN March 1993 descriptor moved
ALT air distribution system
SN That part of a ventilation system which includes supply and return air ducts and plenum chambers. (STEIN)
UF systems, air distribution

air doors
USE air curtains

air-dried lumber
MT.3027
HN March 1992 descriptor moved
SN Any lumber from which sap has been removed by seasoning. (PUTNAM)
UF air-seasoned lumber
dry lumber
dry wood
lumber, air-dried
lumber, air-seasoned
lumber, dry
wood, dry

air drills
USE pneumatic drills

air ducts
PJ.814   (L)
HN March 1993 descriptor moved
August 1990 scope note changed
ALT air duct
SN Includes any tubes or conduits for conveying air to and from enclosed spaces or corridors within a wall or other structure used for conveying air. (STEIN)
UF ducts, air

air-entrained concrete
MT.211   (A,L,B)
HN April 1992 descriptor moved
SN Concrete containing minute air bubbles that improve its workability and frost resistance. (MEANS)
UF aerated concrete
cellular concrete
concrete, aerated
concrete, air-entrained
concrete, cellular

air-entraining admixture
USE air-entraining agent

air-entraining agent
MT.1685
HN April 1993 descriptor changed, was air-entraining agents
SN Additive to natural cement, concrete, or mortar that causes entrained air to be incorporated into it. (STEIN)
UF admixture, air-entraining
agent, air-entraining
air-entraining admixture

air filters
PJ.815   (L)
HN March 1993 descriptor moved
ALT air filter
SN Devices for removing undesirable gaseous or solid particles from ambient air. (MEANS)
UF air cleaners
cleaners, air
filters, air

Air Force bases
USE air bases

air forces
HN.61   (L)
ALT air force

air frames
USE airframes

air freighters
USE cargo aircraft

air guns
TK.214   (L)
ALT air gun
SN Guns that operate using the propulsive power of compressed air.
UF airguns
guns, air
guns, wind
wind guns

air guns, bellows
USE bellows guns

air guns, pump-up
USE pump-up air guns

air guns, spring
USE spring air guns

air hammers
USE jackhammers

air handlers
USE air-handling units

air-handling units
PJ.818
HN March 1993 descriptor moved
ALT air-handling unit
SN Devices, such as fans or blowers, that distribute a conditioned air supply to a room or space.
UF air handlers
handlers, air

air-heating coils
USE heating coils

air infiltration barriers
MT.1776   (A)
HN April 1993 alternate term added
ALT air infiltration barrier
SN Use for plastic sheeting, building paper, or similar materials that wrap the walls of a building beneath the outermost surface, serving to diminish the infiltration and exfiltration of air.
UF air barriers
barriers, air
barriers, air infiltration
infiltration barriers, air

air-inflated structures
PJ.1754
HN March 1993 descriptor moved
ALT air-inflated structure
SN Pneumatic structures in which closed membranes, used as building elements, are inflated; for pneumatic structures supported by pressurization of the habitable space, use **air-supported structures**.
UF inflatable structures
structures, air-inflated
structures, inflatable

air letter sheets
USE aerogrammes

air letters
USE aerogrammes

air locks
PJ.1150
HN March 1993 descriptor moved
July 1991 scope note changed
ALT air lock
SN Airtight spaces permitting passage between spaces of different air pressures or qualities, or between underwater and air-filled spaces.
UF locks, air

air locks (motifs)
USE   air traps

air meters
TN.249   (N)
ALT   air meter
SN   Devices used to measure the rate of flow of air or gas. (CHAMBD)
UF   airometers
meters, air

air photographs
USE   aerial photographs

air photography
USE   aerial photography

air pollution
BM.338   (A,L,B)
HN   September 1992 scope note added
SN   Pollution of the earth's atmosphere.
UF   atmospheric pollution
pollution, air
pollution, atmospheric

air pollution, indoor
USE   indoor air pollution

air pressure
BM.847
HN   November 1992 descriptor moved
February 1992 scope note added
SN   Pressure that the air exerts on any surface in contact with it. (MHDSTT)
UF   pressure, air

air purification
KG.166   (L)
HN   December 1992 descriptor moved
UF   purification, air
purification of air

air quality
BM.312   (L)
HN   November 1992 descriptor moved
February 1992 scope note added
SN   Degree to which air is polluted, such that air quality is deemed to be high when air pollution levels are low. (ALLAB3)
UF   quality, air

air quality, indoor
USE   indoor air quality

air raid shelters
PJ.1085   (A,L,N,B)
HN   March 1993 descriptor moved
ALT   air raid shelter
UF   bomb shelters
shelters, air raid
shelters, bomb

air rifles
TK.215   (L)
ALT   air rifle
SN   Air guns with rifled bore. (RHDEL2)
UF   rifles, air
RT   rifles (long guns)

air rights
BM.904   (A,L,B)
HN   March 1993 lead-in term deleted, was **airspace (law)**
February 1993 descriptor moved
SN   Development rights to the space above a piece of real estate; the owner of the land may sell or lease these rights to another party.
UF   airspace rights
rights, air
rights, airspace

air-seasoned lumber
USE   air-dried lumber

air shafts
PJ.1226   (B)
HN   March 1993 descriptor moved
ALT   air shaft
SN   Use for very small courts that are enclosed within the walls of a building and supply ventilation to windows. Prefer **light courts** for somewhat larger courts supplying significant light as well as ventilation, or courts supplying only light.
UF   air wells
shafts, air
wells, air

air superiority fighter aircraft
USE   air superiority fighters

air superiority fighters
TX.50   (L)
ALT   air superiority fighter
SN   Use for fighters designed and equipped to remove hostile aircraft from a given volume of airspace and so establish control of the air without prohibitive interference from enemy aircraft.
UF   air superiority fighter aircraft
aircraft, air superiority fighter
fighter aircraft, air superiority
fighters, air superiority

air-supported furniture
USE   inflatable furniture

air-supported structures
PJ.1755   (A,L,B,R)
HN   March 1993 descriptor moved
November 1990 lead-in term added
November 1990 scope note changed
ALT   air-supported structure
SN   Use for pneumatic structures supported by pressurization of the habitable space; for pneumatic structures in which closed membranes, used as building elements, are inflated, use **air-inflated structures.**
UF   expandable structures
inflatable structures
structures, air-supported
structures, expandable

air tankers
USE   water bombers

air terminals
USE   airport (ALT of airports) + terminals

air transport
BM.1111   (L,B)
UF   aerial transport
transport, air

<air transportation complexes>
RG.232

<air transportation spaces>
RM.112
HN   April 1993 guide term moved

air transports
USE   transport aircraft

air-traps
SEE   air traps

air traps
DG.12
HN   December 1992 descriptor added
UK   air-traps
SN   Decoration of glass in the form of embedded air pockets, larger than usual air bubbles or tears, arranged in a decorative pattern, often in criss-crossed diagonal rows. (ILDIGL)
UF   air bubbles
air locks (motifs)
air twists

air twists
USE   air traps

air views
USE   aerial views

air washers
PJ.790
HN   March 1993 descriptor moved
ALT   air washer
SN   Parts of air conditioning systems in which the air is freed from dust and given the desired humidity by means of a spray of water. (W)
UF   air cleaners
washers, air

air wells
USE   air shafts

airbrush technique
USE   airbrushing

airbrushes
TH.719   (N)
HN   February 1993 descriptor added
ALT   airbrush
SN   Implements resembling fountain pens with attached reservoirs using compressed air to deliver a fine spray of paint or other coating.
RT   airbrushing

airbrushing
KT.417   (L)
HN   January 1993 descriptor moved
December 1992 related term added
October 1990 descriptor moved
ALT   airbrushed
SN   A method of painting by means of a small, finely controllable mechanical paint sprayer; used also in the retouching of photographs. (THDAT)
UF   airbrush technique
RT   airbrushes

aircraft
TX.5 (N)
SN Use for vehicles that navigate through the air, either supported for flight by buoyancy or by the dynamic action of the air on their surfaces; usually designed to accommodate one or more persons.
UF craft

aircraft aeronautical lights
PJ.3298
ALT aircraft aeronautical light
SN Aeronautical lights specially provided on an aircraft. (IESREF)
UF aeronautical lights, aircraft
    lights, aircraft aeronautical

aircraft, agricultural
USE agricultural aircraft

aircraft, air superiority fighter
USE air superiority fighters

<aircraft and spacecraft components>
PJ.3297

aircraft, attack
USE attack aircraft

aircraft bodies
USE fuselages

aircraft, bomber
USE bombers

aircraft, business
USE business aircraft

<aircraft by construction>
TX.61

<aircraft by form>
TX.6

<aircraft by function>
TX.38

<aircraft by method of propulsion>
TX.64

aircraft, cargo
USE cargo aircraft

aircraft carriers
TX.428 (L,N)
ALT aircraft carrier
SN Use for the largest warships acting as floating mobile air stations with facilities for the takeoff, landing, and servicing of aircraft.
UF carriers, aircraft

aircraft, commuter
USE commuter aircraft

aircraft, company
USE business aircraft

aircraft, corporate
USE business aircraft

aircraft, experimental
USE research aircraft

aircraft, fighter
USE fighters

aircraft, fixed-wing
USE fixed-wing aircraft

aircraft, freight
USE cargo aircraft

aircraft, GA
USE general aviation aircraft

aircraft, general aviation
USE general aviation aircraft

aircraft hangars
USE hangars

aircraft, heavier than air
USE heavier than air aircraft

aircraft, interceptor
USE interceptors

aircraft, jet
USE jet aircraft

aircraft, light
USE light aircraft

aircraft, lighter than air
USE lighter than air aircraft

aircraft, military
USE military aircraft

aircraft, passenger
USE passenger aircraft

aircraft, personal
USE private aircraft

aircraft, private
USE private aircraft

aircraft, pursuit
USE pursuit planes

aircraft, reconnaissance
USE reconnaissance aircraft

aircraft, research
USE research aircraft

aircraft, rotary-wing
USE rotary-wing aircraft

aircraft, swing-wing
USE variable-sweep aircraft

aircraft, tail-first
USE canards

aircraft, tilt-rotor
USE tilt-rotor aircraft

aircraft, training
USE training aircraft

aircraft, transport
USE transport aircraft

aircraft, turbofan
USE turbofan aircraft

aircraft, turbojet
USE jet aircraft

aircraft, turboprop
USE turboprop aircraft

aircraft, ultralight
USE ultralight aircraft

aircraft, utility
USE utility aircraft

aircraft, variable geometry
USE variable-sweep aircraft

aircraft, variable-sweep
USE variable-sweep aircraft

aircraft, vertical take-off and landing
USE vertical take-off and landing aircraft

aircraft, vertical takeoff
USE vertical take-off and landing aircraft

aircraft, VTOL
USE vertical take-off and landing aircraft

airers, linen
USE clotheshorses
    towel racks

airfields
RM.113 (L,B)
HN April 1993 descriptor moved
ALT airfield
SN Use for areas prepared for the landing and takeoff of aircraft; may or may not be provided with associated buildings, equipment, or other installations. (DODDIC)
UF fields, landing
    landing fields

airframes
PJ.3301 (L,N)
ALT airframe
SN Use for the structural components and external coverings of aircraft and missiles.
UF air frames
    frames, air

airguns
USE air guns

airline maps
VW.127 (L)
HN November 1992 descriptor moved
ALT airline map
UF maps, airline

airliners
TX.59 (L)
ALT airliner
SN Passenger aircraft operated by commercial airline companies.

airmail postage stamps
USE airmail stamps

airmail stamps
VK.180 (L)
ALT air mail stamp
SN Postage stamps authorizing the delivery of mail by air.
UF airmail postage stamps
    airmails
    stamps, airmail

airmails
USE airmail stamps

airometers
USE air meters

airplanes
TX.9 (A,H,L,N,B,R)
ALT airplane
UK aeroplanes
UKA aeroplane
SN Nontechnical term for heavier than air fixed-wing aircraft designed to utilize the pressures created by their motion through the air to lift and transport people and cargo; if possible use a more precise term.
UF planes (airplanes)

airplanes, agricultural
USE agricultural aircraft

airplanes, business
USE business aircraft

airplanes, canard
USE canards

airplanes, commuter
USE commuter aircraft

airplanes, company
USE business aircraft

airplanes, corporate
USE business aircraft

airplanes, jet
USE jet aircraft

airplanes, jet propelled
USE jet aircraft

airplanes, light
USE light aircraft

airplanes, military
USE military aircraft

airplanes, personal
USE private aircraft

airplanes, private
USE private aircraft

airplanes, ultralight
USE ultralight aircraft

airport beacons
TC.1434
ALT airport beacon
SN Aeronautical beacons used to indicate the location of an airport. (IESREF)
UF aerodrome beacons
aerodrome identification beacons
airport light beacons
beacons, aerodrome
beacons, airport

airport buildings
HN March 1993 descriptor split, use airport (ALT of airports) + buildings

airport control towers
USE control towers

airport light beacons
USE airport beacons

airport runways
USE runways

airport terminals
HN March 1993 descriptor split, use airport (ALT of airports) + terminals

airports
RG.233 (A,L,N,B,R)
ALT airport
UF aerodromes

airships
TX.28 (A,L,N,B,R)
ALT airship
SN Use for self-propelled and steerable lighter than air vehicles dependent on the displacement of air by a lighter gas for lift; generally composed of a streamlined hull, usually prolate ellipsoids, with one or more cells, a cabin for crew and passengers, and a propulsion system.
UF balloons, dirigible
dirigible balloons
dirigibles

airspace rights
USE air rights

airstrips
RM.117 (L,B)
HN April 1993 descriptor moved
ALT airstrip
SN Use for runways without normal airport facilities.
UF landing strips
strips, landing

airtankers
USE water bombers

airtightness
DC.256 (A,L)
HN October 1992 descriptor moved
ALT airtight
SN Use for the condition of being impervious to air penetration, or nearly so.

airway beacons
TC.1435
ALT airway beacon
SN Revolving aeronautical beacons of high intensity used to indicate the course of a runway.
UF beacons, airway

aisles
PJ.1024 (A,B,R)
HN March 1993 descriptor moved
ALT aisle
SN Includes both passages between sections of seats and the side divisions of buildings where the interior is divided into parts by columns or piers.

aisles, apse
USE ambulatories

aiwans
USE iwans

Aizo
FL.304

Aja
USE Adja

Ajmer
FL.2367

Ajukru
FL.291 (L)
UF Adyukru

Ak-Beshim
FL.1870
HN April 1993 descriptor moved

Ak Koyunlu
USE Akkoyunlu

Ak-Kuyunli
USE Akkoyunlu

akadindas
TT.523
ALT akadinda
SN Xylophones of the Ganda of Uganda, consisting of 17 (formerly 22) wood slabs set on two banana trunks and held in position by two shoulders carved on the underside of the slabs. They require up to six players and are traditionally associated with royalty. (NGDMI)
UF akandindas

Akamba
USE Kamba

Akan
FL.280 (L)

Akan, Coastal
USE Coastal Akan

<Akan cultures>
FL.279

akandindas
USE akadindas

Akbar
FL.2315

Akem
USE Akyem

aketons
TE.304
ALT aketon
SN Plain quilted or padded coats of textile or leather, often sleeveless, worn either under metal armor or as the sole protective garment, in use from at least the 12th to the early 15th century.
UF actons
RT soft armor

akidiaits
USE adeudeus

Akikuyu
USE Kikuyu

Akita Ranga School
FL.2128 (L)

Akkadian
FL.3056 (L)

Akkoyunlu
FL.3678 (L)
HN April 1993 descriptor moved
UF Ak Koyunlu
Ak-Kuyunli
Aq Qoyunlu

Akmak
FL.819

Aksum
USE Axum

Aktionen
USE actions (works of art)

Akuapem
USE Akwapim

Akwamu
FL.282

Akwapim
FL.283
UF Akuapem

Akye
USE Attie

Akyem
FL.281 (L)
UF Akem

Al
USE aluminum

'Ala'-ad-Din 'Ali
FL.3594
HN April 1993 descriptor moved

'Ala'-ad-Din b. Khalil
FL.3592
HN April 1993 descriptor moved

'Ala'-ad-Din Khalil
FL.3591
HN April 1993 descriptor moved

Alabama cream marble
MT.761
HN April 1992 descriptor moved
UF cream marble, Alabama
marble, Alabama cream

Alabama limestone
MT.857
HN April 1992 descriptor moved
UF limestone, Alabama

alabaster
MT.558 (A,L,B)
HN December 1992 descriptor moved
December 1992 scope note changed
SN Fine-grained marblelike variety of
gypsum. Regarding ancient Egyptian artifacts, the term is sometimes
used for calcium carbonate. (MH)

alabaster (color)
USE pale yellowish pink
yellowish gray

alabastra
TQ.220
ALT alabastron
SN Small ancient Greek or Roman vessels for holding oils, ointments, or
perfumes; usually elongated in
form, almost cylindrical, and
rounded at the bottom. They either
have no handles or one small handle at the side.

Alacaluf
FL.1705 (L)
UF Alikaluf
Alikuluf
Alookooloop
Alukoelúf

Aladdin lamps
TC.1324
ALT Aladdin lamp
SN Kerosene lamps employing a central
draft burner and an incandescent
mantel. Based on a 1909 patent,
they are usually made of metal or
glass.
UF lamps, Aladdin
RT kerosene lamps

Aladian
USE Alagya

alae
PJ.968
HN March 1993 descriptor moved
ALT ala
SN Alcoves or small room openings off
the atrium of an ancient Roman
house. (HAS)

Alagya
FL.292 (L)
UF Aladian
Alangua
Alladians

Alamannic
FL.3194 (L,R)
UF Alemannic

alamedas
RM.188
HN April 1993 descriptor moved
ALT alameda
SN Use both for shaded promenades,
often with plantings and seating areas, in Spanish-speaking countries
and for public gardens or parks with
similar characteristics in the southwest United States.

Alamgir
USE Aurangzeb

alamorus
TT.14
ALT alamoru
SN End-blown flutes of the Teso and
Karamojong areas of Uganda, cut

off at a slanting angle at the bottom
end and blown obliquely; there are
two sizes, the longer having a hemispherical gourd bell attached at the
lower end.

Alangua
USE Alagya

Alani
FL.1842 (R)
HN April 1993 descriptor moved
UF Alans

Alans
USE Alani

alarm clocks
TN.180 (N)
ALT alarm clock
SN Clocks with a bell or buzzer that can
be set to sound at a particular time,
as to awaken someone. (RHDEL2)
UF clocks, alarm

alarm systems, fire
USE fire alarm systems

alarm systems, local fire
USE local fire alarm systems

alarm systems, proprietary fire
USE proprietary fire alarm systems

alarms, burglar
USE burglar alarms

alarms, intruder
USE burglar alarms

Alaskan Eskimo, North
USE Inupiaq

<Alaskan Native styles>
FL.1212

Alaskan pine
USE western hemlock

alba, terra
USE gypsum

albanene tracing paper
USE tracing vellum

Albanian
FL.3125 (L,B)

albany cutters
TX.290 (N)
ALT albany cutter
SN Use for sleighs originally designed
by James Gould of Albany, New
York, and generally characterized
by sweeping lines and rounded, or
swelled, bodies; often with colorfully
decorated panels.
UF cutters, albany
cutters, gould
cutters, swell-body
cutters, swell-side
gould cutters
swell-body cutters
swell-side cutters

Albany slip clay
MT.64
HN April 1992 descriptor moved
SN Clay used by potters to produce a natural black or brown glaze on stoneware. (W)
UF clay, Albany slip
slip clay, Albany

albarelli
TQ.125 (H)
ALT albarellos
SN Jars more or less cylindrical in form but with concave sides, used originally as containers for drugs, pigments, and the like. Often made of maiolica or faience.

albas
USE albs

Alberene stone
MT.819
HN April 1992 descriptor moved
SN A bluish gray stone quarried in Virginia; commonly used for building trim and for chemical laboratory tables and sinks; hard varieties employed for stair treads and flooring. (MH)
UF stone, Alberene

Albert key system
USE Albert system

Albert system
PJ.3229
SN Keywork for the clarinet developed by the Belgian instrument maker Eugène Albert around 1860.
UF Albert key system
key system, Albert
system, Albert

albite
MT.551 (L)
HN February 1992 descriptor added
SN A white or colorless triclinic mineral of the feldspar group. (AGI)

Albizia lebbeck
USE East India walnut

Albizia odoratissima
USE Ceylon rosewood

albs
TE.244 (H,N)
ALT alb
SN Long, close-sleeved vestments with a full skirt, usually of linen. White in the Western Church, of varying colors in the Eastern Church. Also, similar secular garments, especially those worn in Greco-Roman times.
UF albas
RT main garments

album quilts
TC.241
ALT album quilt
SN Quilts constructed of blocks, made and signed by a number of different people as a remembrance, as would be the pages of an autograph album. Often pieced or appliquéd with pictorial motifs. (QCRS)
UF quilts, album
RT pictorial quilts
presentation quilts
sampler quilts
signature quilts

album quilts, Baltimore
USE Baltimore album quilts

albumen
MT.2520
HN January 1993 lead-in term deleted, was **egg white**
March 1992 scope note added
February 1992 descriptor moved
SN Use for egg white in the context of photographic materials and processes.

albumen photoprints
USE albumen prints

albumen print process
USE albumen process

albumen prints
VC.319
HN April 1993 lead-in term added
April 1992 descriptor moved
ALT albumen print
SN Use for photographic prints having albumen as the binder; always black-and-white, though they may be toned to a monochrome hue.
UF albumen photoprints
albumen prints, silver
albumen silver prints
photoprints, albumen
prints, albumen
prints, albumen silver
prints, silver albumen
silver albumen prints
silver prints, albumen

albumen prints, silver
USE albumen prints

albumen process
KT.509
SN Use for photographic processes in which albumen is used as the binder. Common for photographic prints and occasionally for lantern slides, but rarely used for negatives on glass.
UF albumen print process
albumen silver process
silver albumen process

albumen silver prints
USE albumen prints

albumen silver process
USE albumen process

albumin
MT.1227 (L)
HN April 1992 descriptor moved
February 1992 scope note changed
SN Water-soluble and alcohol-soluble protein obtained from blood, egg, or milk; used in adhesive, finishes, coatings, varnish, and as a clarifying agent for tannin and in-oil emulsion. (MH)

albumin, animal blood
USE albumin glue

albumin glue
MT.1724
HN March 1992 descriptor moved
June 1991 scope note added
SN Glue obtained from rapidly drying the serum from blood. (PCC)
UF albumin, animal blood
animal blood albumin
glue, albumin

albums
VW.993 (L,N)
HN November 1992 descriptor moved
June 1992 scope note changed
ALT album
SN Use for unpublished sets of pages, bound or loose-leaf, either intended to have, or assembled after having, material affixed to them or writing or other images made on them. (GMGPC)

albums, autograph
USE autograph albums

albums, photograph
USE photograph albums

albums, postcard
USE postcard albums

albums, presentation
USE presentation albums

albums, scrap
USE scrapbooks

albums, souvenir
USE viewbooks

albums, stamp
USE stamp albums

albums, view
USE viewbooks

alcazars
RK.412
ALT alcazar
SN Use for Spanish or Moorish castles, fortresses, or fortified palaces.

alchemists
HG.604 (L)
HN January 1993 descriptor added
ALT alchemist
alchemist's
alchemists'
SN Those who study or practice alchemy.
RT alchemy

alchemy
KD.327 (L,R)
HN February 1993 related term added

February 1992 scope note changed
October 1991 scope note changed
SN A form of chemistry and speculative philosophy practiced in the Middle Ages and the Renaissance and concerned principally with discovering methods for transmuting base metal into gold and with finding a universal solvent and an elixir of life. (RHDEL2)
RT alchemists

alcohol
MT.2440 (L)
UF spirit

alcohol, absolute
USE absolute alcohol

alcohol, amyl
USE amyl alcohol

alcohol, anhydrous
USE absolute alcohol

alcohol, butyl
USE butyl alcohol

alcohol, denatured
USE denatured alcohol

alcohol dependency
USE alcoholism

alcohol, di-acetone
SEE diacetone alcohol

alcohol, diacetone
USE diacetone alcohol

alcohol, ethyl
USE ethyl alcohol

alcohol, grain
USE ethyl alcohol

alcohol, industrial
USE methyl alcohol

alcohol, isopropyl
USE isopropyl alcohol

alcohol, methyl
USE methyl alcohol

alcohol, normal butyl
USE butanol

alcohol, polyvinyl
USE polyvinyl alcohol

alcohol resin, furan-furfuryl
USE furan

alcohol-resin varnish
USE spirit varnish

alcohol, wood
USE methyl alcohol

alcoholics
HG.994 (L,B)
HN January 1993 alternate terms added
January 1991 descriptor added
ALT alcoholic
alcoholic's
alcoholics'

SN Those who are addicted to alcoholic beverages.
RT alcoholism

alcoholism
BM.567 (L)
HN January 1991 descriptor added
SN Addiction to alcoholic beverages.
UF alcohol dependency
dependency, alcohol
RT alcoholics

alcoholometers
TN.131 (L,N)
ALT alcoholometer
SN Devices that measure the quantity of alcohol in a liquid. (MHDSTT)

alcove beds
USE box beds

alcoves
PJ.967 (A,R)
HN March 1993 descriptor moved
ALT alcove
SN Use to designate small recessed spaces off of larger rooms.
UF nooks
recesses

alcoves, dining
USE dining alcoves

aldanite
HN February 1992 descriptor deleted

alder
MT.2679 (L)
HN March 1992 descriptor moved
UF Alnus

alder, American green
USE American green alder

alder, black
USE common alder

alder, common
USE common alder

alder, European green
USE European green alder

alder, Formosan
USE seaside alder

alder, red
USE red alder

alder, seaside
USE seaside alder

ale glasses
TQ.425 (N)
ALT ale glass
SN Glasses intended for drinking ale or beer. Early 17th- and 18th-century examples are often similar in form to elongated wine glasses with ogee or rounded funnel bowls, resting on stems of varying length; bowl capacity is usually between 3 and 5 ounces. Modern examples are often in the form of tall, thin glasses, generally of 12-ounce capacity, which

taper at the bottom and rest on solid bases.
UF ales
glasses, ale
glasses, malt-beverage
malt-beverage glasses

ale glasses, dwarf
USE dwarf ale glasses

alehouses
USE pubs

Alemannic
USE Alamannic

alembics
TQ.38 (N)
ALT alembic
SN Apparatus of glass or metal formerly used in distillation. They are in the shape of an inverted bowl with an internal gutter along the rim into which the condensed vapor descends and from which extends a long horizontally sloping tube to the receptacle for the distilled liquid. (ILDIGL)

aleppo oak
MT.2818 (L)
HN March 1992 descriptor moved
UF oak, aleppo
Quercus infectoria

ales
USE ale glasses

ales, dwarf
USE dwarf ale glasses

alettes
PJ.1562
HN March 1993 descriptor moved
July 1991 scope note changed
ALT alette
SN In Roman and later classicizing architecture, those parts of a pier that form arch abutments and flank a central engaged column or pilaster carrying an architrave.

Aleut
FL.799

Alexandria blue
USE Egyptian blue

alfa
USE esparto

algae
RD.227 (L,B)
ALT alga

algaitas
TT.171
ALT algaita
SN West African shawms having a bell, pirouette, and five or six fingerholes; the pipe and bell are made from a single piece of wood and covered with leather.
UF algaitu

gaitas
gaitu
ghaitas
ghaitu

algaitu
USE algaitas

algal limestone
MT.843
HN April 1992 descriptor moved
UF limestone, algal

algaroba
USE mesquite

algebra
KD.146 (L)

algicide
MT.1764 (L)
HN April 1993 descriptor changed, was
algicides

Algonkin
FL.1232 (L,R)

algorithms
BM.649
HN January 1991 alternate term added
ALT algorithm

Ali Kosh
FL.3095

aligning punches
USE drift punches

alignment
BM.47
ALT aligned
UF alinement

Alikaluf
USE Alacaluf

Alikuluf
USE Alacaluf

alinement
USE alignment

aliphatic hydrocarbon
MT.2425
HN April 1993 descriptor changed, was
aliphatic hydrocarbons
UF hydrocarbon, aliphatic

alizari
USE madder

alizarin
MT.2012 (L)
HN May 1992 lead-in term added
May 1992 related terms added
January 1992 descriptor moved
October 1991 scope note changed
SN An orange or red crystalline compound prepared from the madder plant, the chief coloring agent of madder; now made synthetically from anthraquinone. Used primarily in making red pigment and dye.
UF alizarina
dihydroxy anthraquinone

RT lake (pigment)
madder
synthetic dye

alizarin crimson
USE alizarin madder

alizarin madder
MT.2198
HN April 1992 descriptor moved
UF alizarin crimson
crimson, alizarin
lake, madder
madder, alizarin
madder lake
madder, rose
madder, synthetic
rose madder
synthetic madder

alizarin violet
MT.2219
HN April 1992 descriptor moved
SN A transparent violet pigment made from synthetic purpurin, not sufficiently permanent for artists' use, since it turns dark or blackish on long exposure to light. (MAYER)
UF madder lake, violet
violet, alizarin
violet madder lake

alizarin yellow
MT.2297
HN April 1992 descriptor moved
SN A dull, brownish, translucent yellow pigment. (MAYER)
UF yellow, alizarin

alizarina
USE alizarin

alizarine pink
USE deep pink
strong pink

alkali
MT.3082
HN February 1993 descriptor moved
SN Compounds having highly basic properties. (MHEST7)

alkali feldspar
MT.544
HN March 1992 descriptor added
UF feldspar, alkali

alkalimeters
TN.132 (N)
ALT alkalimeter
SN Apparatus for measuring either the quantity of alkali in a solid or liquid or the quantity of carbon dioxide formed in a reaction.

alkaline glaze
MT.1987
SN A ceramic glaze whose flux is an alkali. (MAYER)
UF glaze, alkaline

alkalinity
DC.14
HN October 1992 descriptor added

ALT alkaline
SN The quality of having a pH value greater than 7 or of having the properties of an alkali.

alkanet
MT.2028
HN April 1992 descriptor moved
SN A red natural dyestuff from the alkanet root. (MAYER)

alkyd, oil-modified
USE oil-modified alkyd

alkyd plastic
USE alkyd resin

alkyd resin
MT.1199 (L)
HN January 1993 descriptor moved
UF alkyd plastic
plastic, alkyd
resin, alkyd

all-over patterns
SEE allover patterns

alla prima
KT.418 (L)
SN A method of oil painting in which the final effects are achieved in the initial application of paint as opposed to covering the canvas layer by layer. (MAYER)
UF au premier coup
direct painting
painting, direct

alla Romana locks
USE Italian miquelets

Alladians
USE Alagya

allées
RM.178
HN April 1993 descriptor moved
January 1993 lead-in term added
April 1990 descriptor added
ALT allée
SN Use for walkways bordered by formally planted trees, clipped hedges, or shrubs; usually found in formal gardens or parks.
UF alleys (walkways)

allées couvertes
USE gallery graves

allegories
VW.260 (H,L)
HN June 1992 descriptor added
ALT allegory
SN Works that employ symbolic, fictional figures and actions to express truths or generalizations about human conduct or experience. (W)

allegory
BM.14 (L,R)
HN November 1992 alternate term added
ALT allegorical

Allen head screws
USE   Allen screws

Allen head wrenches
USE   Allen wrenches

Allen screws
PJ.232
HN   April 1993 descriptor moved
ALT   Allen screw
SN   Screws with a hexagonal recess to receive an Allen wrench. (MEANS)
UF   Allen head screws
     screws, Allen

Allen wrenches
TH.1313   (N)
ALT   Allen wrench
SN   Wrenches which consist of a steel bar, hexagonal in section, bent to form a right angle; used for Allen screws. (DAC)
UF   Allen head wrenches
     wrenches, Allen
     wrenches, Allen head

alleys
RM.137   (A,L,B,R)
HN   April 1993 descriptor moved
ALT   alley

alleys (walkways)
USE   allées

alleys, blind
USE   blind alleys

alleys, bowling
USE   bowling alleys

alleys, skittle
USE   skittle alleys

alliance rings
USE   eternity rings

alliances
HN.67   (L)
HN   December 1992 descriptor added
ALT   alliance
SN   Associations expressly formed for integrated joint action by two or more political powers, typically for a specific purpose such as mutual defense, trade, or the acquisition or sharing of power.

allies
HG.995
HN   January 1993 descriptor added
ALT   allies'
     ally
     ally's
SN   Those who have entered into an alliance with others, including both individuals and organizations such as sovereign states.

alligator crackle
USE   traction crackle

alligator cracks
USE   traction crackle

alligator shears
USE   lever shears

alligatoring
USE   traction crackle

allocating
USE   funding

allotment gardens
RM.46   (B)
HN   April 1993 descriptor moved
ALT   allotment garden
SN   Garden areas which have been divided into plots, or allotments, for assignment or rental to individuals for cultivation; may also be used for the resulting gardens on those plots.
UF   allotments
     gardens, allotment

allotments
USE   allotment gardens

allover backing
USE   lining (process)

allover mounting
USE   lining (process)

allover patterns
DG.114
HN   February 1993 related terms added
ALT   allover pattern
UK   all-over patterns
UKA   all-over pattern
SN   Use for patterns that extend broadly over a surface. For a continuous pattern that proceeds more directionally, use **running ornament**.
UF   over-all patterns
     overall patterns
     patterns, allover
     patterns, over-all
     patterns, overall
RT   arabesques
     millefleurs
     running ornament

alloy
MT.492   (L,B)
HN   April 1993 related term added
     March 1993 descriptor moved
     March 1993 descriptor changed, was **alloys**
     March 1993 lead-in term changed, was **metal alloys**
SN   Substance having metallic properties, consisting of two or more metallic elements or of metallic and nonmetallic elements, which are miscible with each other when molten, and do not separate into distinct layers when solid. (HORNB)
UF   alloy, metal
     metal alloy
RT   solder

alloy, aluminium-zinc
SEE   aluminum-zinc alloy

alloy, aluminum
USE   aluminum alloy

alloy, aluminum-silicon
USE   aluminum-silicon alloy

alloy, aluminum-zinc
USE   aluminum-zinc alloy

alloy, bearing
USE   Babbitt metal

alloy, brazing
USE   hard solder

alloy, chromium
USE   chromium alloy

alloy constructional steel
USE   high-strength low-alloy steel

alloy, copper
USE   copper alloy

alloy, copper-beryllium
USE   copper-beryllium alloy

alloy, copper-nickel
USE   copper-nickel alloy

alloy, copper-silicon
USE   copper-silicon alloy

alloy, copper-tin
USE   bronze

alloy, copper-zinc
USE   brass (alloy)

alloy, ferrous
USE   iron alloy

alloy, gold
USE   gold alloy

alloy, iron
USE   iron alloy

alloy, Koeller's
USE   Koeller's alloy

alloy, lead
USE   lead alloy

alloy, lead-antimony-tin
USE   white metal

alloy, mercury
USE   amalgam

alloy, metal
USE   alloy

alloy, Monel
USE   Monel (TM)

alloy, nickel
USE   nickel alloy

alloy, nickel-copper
USE   copper-nickel alloy

alloy, non-ferrous
SEE   nonferrous alloy

alloy, nonferrous
USE   nonferrous alloy

alloy, plastic
USE   plastic alloy

alloy, silver
USE silver alloy

alloy, soldering
USE solder

alloy steel
    MT.355 (L,B)
HN March 1993 descriptor moved
    March 1993 descriptor changed,
      was **steel alloys**
    March 1993 lead-in term changed,
      was **alloy steels**
UF alloy, steel
    steel alloy
    steel, alloy

alloy, steel
USE alloy steel

alloy, steel-aluminum
USE steel-aluminum alloy

alloy, tin
USE tin alloy

alloy, zinc
USE zinc alloy

allusion
    BM.4

alluvial fans
    RD.156 (L)
ALT alluvial fan
SN Designates sloping, fan-shaped
    masses of sediment deposited by a
    watercourse at the place where it
    leaves a constricted course or up-
    land and emerges into a broad val-
    ley or a plain.
UF fans, alluvial

allyl plastic
USE allyl resin

allyl resin
    MT.1201
HN January 1993 descriptor moved
UF allyl plastic
    plastic, allyl
    resin, allyl

Alma
    FL.959

Alma plain
    FL.960
UF plain, Alma

Alma rough
    FL.961
UF rough, Alma

almanacs
    VW.815 (L,R)
HN November 1992 descriptor moved
ALT alamanac
SN Publications, usually annuals, con-
    taining a variety of useful facts of
    miscellaneous nature, or statistical
    information; originally included
    projections of coming days, months,
    and holidays. (LG)

almemars
USE bemas

Almerian
    FL.2575

almeries
USE aumbries

almimbars
USE minbars

Almohad
    FL.3537 (H,L)
HN April 1993 descriptor moved

almond
    MT.2874 (L)
HN March 1992 descriptor moved

almond oil
    MT.1077
HN April 1992 descriptor moved
    October 1990 descriptor moved
SN A colorless or pale yellow bland and
    nearly odorless nondrying fatty oil
    used as an emollient. (W)
UF oil, almond

almond-shaped
    DC.57
HN October 1992 descriptor moved

almoners
USE aulmonieres

almoners cupboards
USE livery cupboards

Almoravid
    FL.3536 (L)
HN April 1993 descriptor moved

alms basins
USE alms dishes

alms dishes
    TQ.152
ALT alms dish
SN Large, circular, dishlike vessels
    upon which money, collected in
    church from the congregation in
    smaller containers, is assembled and
    presented at the altar.
UF alms basins
    altar dishes
    basins, alms
    dishes, alms
    dishes, altar

almshouses
    RK.750 (A,L,B,R)
ALT almshouse
UF farms, poor
    poor farms
    poorhouses
    workhouses (almshouses)

almuces
    TE.633
ALT almuce
SN Fur-lined hoods with two long ends
    meant to hang down in front; of a

type originating in the Medieval period and worn especially by clergy.
RT *<liturgical costume>*

almuces (amices)
USE amices

alners
USE aulmonieres

Alnus
USE alder

Alnus cremastogyne
    MT.2680
HN March 1992 descriptor moved

Alnus crispa
USE American green alder

Alnus glutinosa
USE common alder

Alnus maritima
USE seaside alder

Alnus oregona
USE red alder

Alnus pendula
    MT.2681
HN March 1992 descriptor moved

Alnus rubra
USE red alder

Alnus viridis
USE European green alder

Alookooloop
USE Alacaluf

alpaca
    MT.2570 (L)
HN February 1992 descriptor moved
SN Use for hair of the alpaca.

alpargatas
USE espadrilles

alpenhorns
USE alphorns

alphabet blocks
    TV.141 (N)
ALT alphabet block
SN Use for cubical objects of wood,
    plastic, or other material having let-
    ters of the alphabet on most or all
    sides and used as teaching toys.
UF blocks, alphabet
RT educational toys

alphabet books
    VW.4 (H)
HN June 1992 descriptor added
ALT alphabet book
SN Use for books designed to display
    the letters of the alphabet, often
    with accompanying illustrations,
    sometimes to teach the alphabet and
    sometimes as vehicles for an illustra-
    tor's art.
UF ABC books
    abecedaria
    alphabets (primers)

books, ABC
books, alphabet

alphabet quilts
TC.250
ALT   alphabet quilt
SN   Quilts decorated with the letters of the alphabet, sometimes illustrated with appropriate objects, such as an apple with the letter A.
UF   ABC quilts
      quilts, ABC
      quilts, alphabet

alphabets (primers)
USE   alphabet books

alphorns
TT.97   (L,N)
ALT   alphorn
SN   Wood trumpets of conical bore, made of a young tree curving upwards naturally from the roots to form the bell, found in pastoral communities in the Alps.
UF   alpenhorns

alpine architecture
USE   hillside architecture

alpine candleholders
TC.1228
ALT   alpine candleholder
SN   Devices with a wrought iron standard, often ornate, supporting a horizontal flat ring and spring for clamping whatever is placed within the ring. May have been intended for holding a torch or link rather than an ordinary candle.
UF   candleholders, alpine
      candleholders, spring
      spring candleholders (alpine candleholders)

alpine skiing
KQ.93   (L)
UF   skiing, alpine

Alpine zithers
USE   zithers

Alpujarra
FL.3541   (L)
HN   April 1993 descriptor added

Alpujarras
USE   Alpujarra + rugs

Alsea
FL.1348   (L)

Altai
FL.2215
UF   Altaitsy
      Altay

Altaitsy
USE   Altai

<altar and altar component coverings and hangings>
TC.345

altar canopies
USE   baldachins

altar cavities
USE   sepulchers

altar cloths
TC.346   (H,L,N,R)
ALT   altar cloth
SN   Cloth coverings for altars often with decorative edgings and individual embroidered motifs.
UF   cloths, altar

<altar components>
PJ.2515
HN   March 1993 guide term moved

altar cruets
TQ.153
ALT   altar cruet
SN   Small stoppered vessels for wine and water used in the celebration of the Eucharist. (CBHOS)
UF   burettes
      cruets, altar
RT   cruets

altar dishes
USE   alms dishes

altar facings
USE   altar frontals

altar frontals
VC.49   (H,N,B,R)
HN   April 1993 related term added
      April 1993 lead-in term deleted, was antependia
      February 1993 lead-in terms added
      February 1993 descriptor moved
      February 1993 scope note changed
ALT   altar frontal
SN   Carved, painted, embroidered, or otherwise decorated panels or hangings covering the front of a Christian altar. (STOK)
UF   altar facings
      altar fronts
      facings, altar
      frontals
      frontals, altar
      fronts, altar
RT   antependia

altar fronts
USE   altar frontals

altar lamps
USE   sanctuary lamps

altar rails
PJ.2519   (B)
HN   March 1993 descriptor moved
ALT   altar rail
SN   Low rails or barriers in front of the altar, separating the officiating clergy from the other worshippers. (HAS)
UF   rails, altar

altar screens
PJ.2537   (L,B,R)
HN   March 1993 descriptor moved

ALT   altar screen
SN   Use for screens that separate the altar area from the space behind it. Distinct from reredoses, which relate visually to the altar and may form part of the inner side of an altar screen.
UF   screens, altar

altar slabs
USE   mensas

altar stones
USE   mensas

altar tombs
RK.450
ALT   altar tomb
SN   Use for tombs or tomb monuments whose location or decoration resembles that of altars.
UF   high tombs
      tombs, altar
      tombs, high

<altarpiece components>
VC.54

altarpieces
VC.51   (A,N,R)
HN   March 1993 related terms added
      February 1993 descriptor moved
      February 1993 scope note changed
ALT   altarpiece
SN   Religious images on, above, or behind the altar of a Christian church. (THDAT)
RT   dossals
      superfrontals

<altarpieces and altarpiece components>
VC.50

altars
PJ.2513   (A,L,N,B,R)
HN   March 1993 descriptor moved
      October 1991 scope note changed
ALT   altar
SN   Use for constructions upon which religious sacrifice is offered. Includes both small, tablelike fixtures and larger, free-standing, outdoor structures. For the surface at which communion is celebrated in Protestant churches, use communion tables.

<altars and altar components>
PJ.2512
HN   May 1993 guide term moved
      April 1993 related term added
RT   tabernacles

altars, fire
USE   fire altars

altars, high
USE   high altars

altars, main
USE   high altars

Altay
USE   Altai

alteration
  KT.156
HN August 1992 scope note added
ALT altered
SN Use for the process of changing something in some particular characteristic such as measure, dimension, course, arrangement, or inclination, without changing into something else. For the modifications themselves, use **alterations**. (W)

alterations
  PJ.5   (A,L,B,R)
HN March 1993 descriptor moved
    February 1991 related terms added
ALT alteration
SN Use for modifications to an object or structure. Refers especially to the physical evidence of the change. In architecture, use **additions** if the change increases the structure's volume; **alterations** if it does not.
RT additions
    pentimenti

altered photographs
USE manipulated photographs

altered prints (photographs)
USE manipulated photographs

alternative press publications
USE alternative publications

alternative publications
  VW.966   (L)
HN May 1991 descriptor added
ALT alternative publication
UF alternative press publications
    publications, alternative
    publications, alternative press

alternative schools
USE free schools

alternative spaces
  PJ.1037   (H)
HN March 1993 descriptor moved
    May 1991 descriptor added
ALT alternative space
SN Use for display and study spaces providing artists, especially new, emerging artists, the opportunity to exhibit their works outside the traditional gallery and museum context.
UF spaces, alternative
RT exhibiting

alternative technology
USE appropriate technology

althorns
  TT.82   (L,N)
ALT althorn
SN Valved brass instruments of the cornet family, of alto range, having a conical bore and medium-sized bell; the tube can be coiled in tuba, orchestral trumpet, or helicon shape.
UF alto cornets
    alto horns

cornets, alto
horns, alto

alti fagotti
USE caledonicas

altimeters
  TN.106   (L,N)
ALT altimeter
SN Instruments that measure and indicate the altitude of an object above a fixed level, such as sea level or ground level.

alto
  DC.201
HN October 1992 descriptor added

alto cornets
USE althorns

alto horns
USE althorns

alto rilievo
USE high relief

alto rilievos
USE high reliefs

Altoperuvian
  FL.1726
HN June 1991 descriptor moved

Altstadts
USE old towns

Alukoelúf
USE Alacaluf

alum
  MT.512   (L)
HN January 1993 scope note changed
    February 1992 descriptor moved
    July 1990 descriptor added
SN Colorless-to-white crystalline potassium aluminum sulfate; has a wide range of uses, including in treatment of leather and textile, in sizing paper, as a mordant in dyeing, and as a water-purifying agent. (MH12)
UF alum, potash
    potash alum

alum dressing
USE tawing

alum, potash
USE alum

alum tanning
USE tawing

alum tawing
USE tawing

aluminate cement
USE aluminous cement

aluminium
SEE aluminum

aluminium alloy
SEE aluminum alloy

aluminium, structural
SEE structural aluminum

aluminium-zinc alloy
SEE aluminum-zinc alloy

aluminizing
  KT.1104
HN March 1991 alternate term added
ALT aluminized
SN The application of an aluminum coating such as to iron and steel sheet. (HORNB)

aluminous cement
  MT.11   (B)
HN April 1992 descriptor moved
SN Cement made with bauxite and containing a high percentage of alumina; valued for its fast setting and high strength properties. (MH12)
UF aluminate cement
    cement, aluminate
    cement, aluminous
    cement, high alumina
    cement, high speed
    HAC
    high alumina cement
    high-speed cement

aluminum
  MT.373   (A,L,R)
HN April 1993 related term added
    March 1993 scope note added
    March 1993 descriptor moved
    December 1992 lead-in term added
UK aluminium
SN Use for the pure metallic element having symbol Al and atomic number 13; a hard, strong, silver white metal. Use also for this metal as processed and formed, usually in combination with other substances, to make objects and materials.
UF Al
RT structural aluminum

aluminum (color)
USE light gray
    medium gray

aluminum alloy
  MT.374   (L,B)
HN March 1993 descriptor moved
    March 1993 descriptor changed, was **aluminum alloys**
UK aluminium alloy
UF alloy, aluminum

<aluminum and aluminum alloy>
  MT.372
HN March 1993 guide term added

aluminum bronze
  MT.406   (L)
HN March 1993 descriptor moved
SN A copper-aluminum alloy with aluminum as the chief alloying element. (MH)
UF bronze, aluminum

aluminum hydrate white
  MT.2239

HN April 1992 descriptor moved
UF white, aluminum hydrate

aluminum oxide
USE corundum

aluminum paint
MT.1933
SN Paint containing aluminum alloy, effective in preventing discoloration of painted surfaces from mildew. (PUTNAM)
UF paint, aluminum

aluminum paper
MT.1428
HN February 1992 descriptor moved
July 1990 descriptor added
SN Paper of silvery appearance coated with powdered aluminum. (W)
UF paper, aluminum

aluminum-silicon alloy
MT.375
HN March 1993 descriptor moved
SN Refers to alloys with from 5 to 22% silicon characterized by ease of casting, corrosion resistance, lightness, and ease of welding. (MH)
UF alloy, aluminum-silicon

aluminum stearate white
MT.2240
HN April 1992 descriptor moved
UF white, aluminum stearate

aluminum, structural
USE structural aluminum

aluminum-zinc alloy
MT.376   (L)
HN March 1993 descriptor moved
UK aluminium-zinc alloy
UF alloy, aluminium-zinc
alloy, aluminum-zinc

alumni centers
RK.1125
HN September 1990 descriptor added
ALT alumni center
SN Use for college buildings housing alumni associations and having entertainment and assembly facilities for graduates.
UF centers, alumni

alumni directories
VW.834   (L)
HN November 1992 descriptor moved
ALT alumni directory
SN Directories of names, addresses, and other data about former students of schools, colleges, or universities. (AHD)
UF directories, alumni

Alunda
USE Lunda

alveated domes
USE beehive domes

alveolar erosion
USE alveolar weathering

alveolar pattern
USE alveolar weathering

alveolar weathering
KT.269   (L)
HN January 1993 descriptor added
SN A distinctive effect of weathering, often affecting stone, characterized by a pattern of small cavities.
UF alveolar erosion
alveolar pattern
alveolation
erosion, alveolar
erosion, honeycomb
honeycomb erosion
pattern, alveolar
weathering, alveolar

alveolation
USE alveolar weathering

amadindas
TT.524
ALT amadinda
SN Xylophones of the Ganda of Uganda, consisting of twelve wood slabs placed across two banana trunks and separated by tall thin sticks driven into the stems; they are played by three players.
UF madindas

amagaraits
USE adeudeus

Amahuaca
FL.1585   (L)
UF Ipitinere
Sayaco

amalgam
MT.433   (L)
HN March 1993 descriptor moved
March 1993 descriptor changed, was **amalgams**
March 1993 lead-in term changed, was **mercury alloys**
February 1991 descriptor added
SN Alloy of mercury with another metal. (W)
UF alloy, mercury
mercury alloy

amalgam gilding
KT.140
HN April 1993 descriptor changed, was **amalgam-gilding**
January 1993 descriptor moved
March 1991 alternate term added
ALT amalgam-gilded
SN Technique of applying gold leaf in which gold is mixed with mercury and applied to the surface of the object; the object is then heated to dispel the mercury. (SCHNEI)
UF fire gilding
gilding, amalgam
gilding, fire

amalgam silvering
KT.148
HN April 1993 descriptor changed, was **amalgam-silvering**

January 1993 descriptor moved
March 1991 alternate term added
ALT amalgam-silvered
SN Technique of applying silver leaf in which silver is mixed with mercury and applied to the surface of the object; the object is then heated to dispel the mercury. (SCHNEI)

Aman-Kutan
FL.1847
HN April 1993 descriptor moved

amaranth
USE purpleheart

Amargosa
FL.915

amargosite
USE bentonite

amarillo de cadmio
USE cadmium yellow

amarillo de cromo
USE chrome yellow

amarillo de Nápoles
USE Naples yellow

amarillo de plomo-estano
USE lead-tin yellow

amarillo de zinc
USE zinc yellow

amarillo indio
USE Indian yellow

Amarna age
USE Amarna period

Amarna period
FL.2908
UF Amarna age

amateur art
BM.175   (L,R)
HN May 1993 related term added
SN Includes any art created by nonprofessional artists practicing for pleasure or self-expression. For nonprofessional art valued for the roughness or rawness of its artistic impulse, use art brut.
UF art, amateur
RT art brut

amateur voice horns
USE ballad horns

amateurism
BM.282   (L,R)

amateurs
HG.879
HN January 1993 alternate terms added
ALT amateur
amateur's
amateurs'
SN Persons who engage in a particular pursuit, study, or science as a pastime rather than as a profession. (W)

amatl
USE   bark cloth

Amatle
FL.1039

Amba
FL.506   (L)
UF   Baamba

Ambamba
USE   Mbamba

ambassadors
HG.175   (L)
HN   January 1993 descriptor moved
December 1992 alternate terms added
December 1990 descriptor added
ALT   ambassador
ambassador's
ambassadors'
SN   Diplomats of the highest rank, sent by one sovereign or state to another or to an international organization as its chief representative. (RHDEL2)

amber (color)
USE   dark orange yellow
deep orange yellow
light yellow
moderate orange yellow
moderate yellow

amber (fossil resin)
MT.1263   (L,R)
HN   April 1992 descriptor moved
May 1991 descriptor changed, was amber

Amber (Mughal style)
FL.2321
HN   April 1993 descriptor moved
April 1993 descriptor changed, was Amber (painting style)
UF   Jaipur

amber glass
USE   Amberina glass

amber glass, holly
USE   holly amber glass

amber gold
USE   grayish yellow
light yellowish brown

amber, light
USE   dark orange yellow
moderate orange yellow

amber, Prussian
USE   succinite

amber yellow
USE   brilliant yellow
light yellow

Amberina glass
MT.269
HN   December 1991 descriptor added
SN   Term used in the glass trade for un-cased art glass developed by the New England Glass Company in 1883, which varies in shading from light amber to deep ruby, the ruby areas result when part of the glass is reheated and the gold particles in the glass develop a ruby color.
UF   amber glass
glass, amber
glass, Amberina

Ambete
USE   Mbete

ambient energy
USE   solar power

ambient light photography
USE   available light photography

<ambient sound makers>
TT.624

ambiente
USE   environmental art

Ambo
FL.575   (L)
UF   Ovambo

ambones
USE   ambos

ambos
PJ.2533   (A,R)
HN   March 1993 descriptor moved
March 1991 descriptor moved
November 1990 alternate term changed, was ambon
ALT   ambo
SN   In Early Christian churches, pulpits in the nave for reading the Gospels or the Epistles. In present-day balkan and Greek churches, large pulpits or reading desks. (HAS)
UF   ambones

amboyna
USE   oil of cloves

ambries
USE   aumbries

ambrotype
KT.514   (L)
HN   February 1991 descriptor moved
SN   A variant of the wet collodion pro-cess to produce a direct-positive camera original. The collodion is coated on glass, the image underex-posed and then underdeveloped, the glass backed with black lacquer or black cloth, and the whole mounted in a case or frame. Occa-sionally, the image was made on ruby glass.

ambrotypes
VC.301   (H,L,N,R)
HN   April 1992 descriptor moved
ALT   ambrotype
SN   Photographs produced by mounting a negative (made by a variant of the wet collodion process) that is on glass with a dark backing, which makes the image appear as a pos-itive.

UF   collodion glass positives
glass-collodion positives
glass positives, collodion
positives, collodion glass
positives, glass-collodion

ambry veils
USE   aumbry veils

Ambrym
FL.3809   (L)

ambulance stations
RK.702   (A,B)
ALT   ambulance station
UF   stations, ambulance

ambulances
TX.213   (L,N)
ALT   ambulance
SN   Emergency land vehicles designed and equipped for conveying the sick or injured to medical facilities.

ambulantes
USE   tables ambulantes

ambulatories
PJ.1247
HN   March 1993 descriptor moved
ALT   ambulatory
SN   Semicircular or polygonal circula-tion spaces enclosing an apse or a straight-ended sanctuary. (PDARC)
UF   aisles, apse
apse aisles
deambulatories

Ambuun
USE   Mbun

Ameca
USE   Ameca-Zacoalco

Ameca-Zacoalco
FL.1084
UF   Ameca

amending
KG.108
HN   April 1993 lead-in term added
January 1991 descriptor added
ALT   amended
SN   Officially correcting written text or recorded data by addition, deletion, or modification.
UF   amendment

amendment
USE   amending

amendments
VW.519   (L)
HN   November 1992 descriptor moved
ALT   amendment
SN   Any writing made or proposed as an addition to or improvement of some principal writing; in legislation, re-fers to modifications or alterations in a bill or enacted law. (BLACKS)

amenta
TK.220
ALT   amentum

SN Leather thongs, Greco-Etruscan in origin and adopted by the Romans, attached to the shafts of javelins and used to throw them with more propulsion than was possible by hand alone.

UF ammae

Amer

    FL.696

UF Beni Amer

American

    FL.727   (L,B,R)

SN Use in the context of or associated specifically with the modern political entity of the United States of America.

UF U.S.

American arbor vitae

    MT.2924   (L)

HN March 1992 descriptor moved

UF arbor-vitae
    arbor vitae, American
    thuja accidentalis
    thuya occidentalis

American ash

USE white ash

American aspen

    MT.2863

HN March 1992 descriptor moved

SN A wood used chiefly for match stems and making excelsior; also for some inside construction work. (MH)

UF American poplar
    aspen (American aspen)
    aspen, American
    aspen, quaking
    poplar, American
    Populus tremuloides
    quaking aspen

American bass viols

USE church basses

American basswood

USE linden

American beech

    MT.2692

HN March 1992 descriptor moved

UF beech, American
    Fagus grandifolia

American black cherry

USE black cherry

American black walnut

USE black walnut

American blue

USE Prussian blue

American bond

USE common bond

American, Central

USE Central American

American cherry

USE black cherry

American chestnut

    MT.2719   (L)

HN March 1992 descriptor moved

UF American sweet chestnut
    Castanea dentata
    chestnut, American
    chestnut, American sweet
    sweet chestnut, American

American chrome yellow

USE chrome yellow

American Colonial

    FL.1720   (L)

SN Style of furniture, architecture, and domestic articles built or made in the United States in the Colonial period or somewhat later. Popular term; when possible prefer a more specific descriptor, such as Georgian.

UF American, Early
    Colonial, American
    Colonial North American
    Early American
    North American, Colonial

American Deco

USE Art Deco

American dulcimers

USE Appalachian dulcimers

American, Early

USE American Colonial

American elm

    MT.2732   (L)

HN March 1992 descriptor moved

SN Fine-grain, durable wood used chiefly for ax handles, and for parts requiring a combination of strength, bending qualities, and ability to withstand rough usage. (MH)

UF American white elm
    elm, American
    elm, American white
    elm, white
    Ulmus americana
    white elm
    white elm, American

American Federal

USE Federal

American film

    MT.2365

HN April 1992 descriptor moved

SN An invention of George Eastman, a photographic material consisting of a gelatino-bromide emulsion over plain gelatin; first appeared in 1888 on a paper support and later on nitrocellulose film. (HCOP)

UF film, American

American football

SEE football

American green alder

    MT.2682

HN March 1992 descriptor moved

UF alder, American green

Alnus crispa
    green alder, American

American hammer dulcimers

USE hammer dulcimers

American hop hornbeam

    MT.2771

HN March 1992 descriptor moved

UF hop hornbeam, American
    hornbeam, American hop
    ironwood (American hop hornbeam)
    Ostrya virginiana

American horse chestnut

USE buckeye

American Indian

USE Native American

American ivorytypes

USE ivorytypes

American, Latin

USE Latin American

American limewood

USE linden

American long rifles

    TK.191   (L,N)

ALT American long rifle

SN American-made muzzleloading flintlock rifles manufactured, mainly in Pennsylvania, from the Revolution to the late 19th century, characterized by a long octagonal barrel, maple stock, brass fittings, and ornamental openwork mounts.

UF American rifles
    guns, Kentucky long
    guns, Pennsylvania long
    Kentucky long guns
    Kentucky rifles
    long guns, Kentucky
    long guns, Pennsylvania
    long rifles
    long rifles, American
    Pennsylvania long guns
    Pennsylvania rifles
    rifles, American
    rifles, American long
    rifles, Kentucky
    rifles, long
    rifles, Pennsylvania

American, Mexican

USE Mexican American

American, Native

USE Native American

American, North

USE North American

American organs

USE melodeons (reed organs)

<American paper money>

    VK.148

American plane

USE sycamore

American poplar
USE American aspen

<American regions>
FL.717

American Renaissance
USE Renaissance Revival

American rifles
USE American long rifles

American sassafras
MT.2897
HN March 1992 descriptor moved
UF Sassafras albidum
sassafras, American

American Scene
FL.1774   (R)
SN Movement of American figurative
painting active from the 1920s to
the 1940s, committed to the establishment of a genuinely American
art by the realistic depiction of contemporary American life and the re-
pudiation of contemporary nonreal-
ist styles introduced by the Armory
Show.
UF painting, American Scene
Scene, American

American, South
USE South American

American sweet chestnut
USE American chestnut

American sycamore
USE sycamore

American-Type painting
USE Abstract Expressionist

American vermilion
USE chrome red

American walnut
USE black walnut

American white ash
USE white ash

American white elm
USE American elm

Amerindian
USE Native American

amethyst
MT.575   (L)
HN April 1992 descriptor moved
February 1992 scope note changed
February 1992 related term added
SN A purple or bluish-violet variety of
quartz. (AGI)
RT gemstone

amethyst (color)
USE dark purple
grayish purple
grayish reddish purple
moderate purple

amethyst, light
USE moderate purple

amethyst violet
USE vivid purple

Amhara
FL.637   (L)

Amherst sandstone
MT.901
HN April 1992 descriptor moved
SN A stone from Ohio, containing up
to 95% silica with 4% aluminum ox-
ide, and colored gray and buff with
iron oxides. (MH)
UF sandstone, Amherst

Ami School
FL.2129

amianto
MT.793
HN April 1992 descriptor moved
UF amiantus, lapis
lapis amiantus

amiantus, lapis
USE amianto

amices
TE.641   (N)
ALT amice
SN Rectangular pieces of white cloth,
usually linen, worn around the neck
and partly under the alb; designed
to protect other vestments from per-
spiration.
UF almuces (amices)
RT *<liturgical costume>*

amino acid dating
KT.182
HN November 1992 descriptor added
SN The technique for dating that exam-
ines the relation between elapsed
time and the degradation of amino
acids in proteins, specifically the
racemization of amino acids in collagen. (HOLHZR)
UF amino acid racemization dating
dating, amino acid
dating, epimerization
dating, racemization
epimerization dating
racemization dating

amino acid racemization dating
USE amino acid dating

amino resin
MT.1202   (L)
HN January 1993 descriptor moved
UF aminoplastics
resin, amino

aminoaldehyde resin
MT.1205
HN January 1993 descriptor moved
UF resin, aminoaldehyde

aminoplastics
USE amino resin

Amish
BM.470   (L,B,R)
UF Old Order Amish

ammae
USE amenta

ammeters
TN.219   (L,N)
ALT ammeter
SN Instruments for measuring the
strength of electric current flow,
amperage, in amperes.

ammonia
MT.4   (L)
HN April 1992 descriptor moved
February 1992 lead-in term added
UF ammonium hydroxide

ammonia, aqua
USE ammonia water

ammonia, aqueous
USE ammonia water

ammonia process
KT.371
HN March 1993 descriptor added
SN Two-component diazo process in
which both the diazonium salts and
the coupler are on the base, and development is achieved by neutralizing the acidic stabilizers with vapors
derived from evaporating ammonia
water.
UF diazo process, dry
diazo process, vapor
dry diazo process
vapor diazo process

ammonia water
MT.2471
UF ammonia, aqua
ammonia, aqueous
aqua ammonia
aqueous ammonia
hartshorn, spirit of
spirit of hartshorn
water, ammonia

ammoniac, sal
USE ammonium chloride

ammoniacal copper arsenate
MT.2395
UF copper arsenate, ammoniacal

ammonium chloride
MT.955
HN April 1992 descriptor moved
July 1990 descriptor added
SN White crystalline powder used in
electric batteries, in printing, as a
soldering flux, and in making other
compounds. (MH12)
UF ammoniac, sal
chloride, ammonium
sal ammoniac

ammonium hydroxide
USE ammonia

ammonium Prussian blue
USE Prussian blue

ammunition
TK.244   (L)

SN Use generally for the projectiles and propellants used to operate firearms.
RT gunpowder
  priming powder
  propellant

ammunition, ball
USE balls (bullets)

ammunition, drill
USE drill ammunition

ammunition, dummy
USE drill ammunition

ammunition, fixed
USE fixed ammunition

<ammunition for artillery>
  TK.247

<ammunition for small arms>
  TK.259

ammunition, semifixed
USE semifixed ammunition

Amol
  FL.3528
HN April 1993 descriptor added
UF Amul

Amol ware
HN April 1993 descriptor split, use Amol + ware

Amorgos group
  FL.2632

amorphous
  DC.45   (L)
HN October 1992 descriptor added
SN Use to describe materials having no stratification or crystalline structure, or, more generally, things having no pattern or structure.

amortization
  BM.863   (L)
HN February 1993 descriptor moved
SN Gradual reduction of a financial obligation by payment of a part of the principal, contribution to a sinking fund, or the gradual depreciation of an asset.

amortizements
  PJ.2046
HN March 1993 descriptor moved
ALT amortizement
SN Sloping tops of buttresses or projecting piers.

amphibians
USE amphibious vehicles

amphibious assault ships
  TX.417   (L)
ALT amphibious assault ship
SN Warships designed to transport and land troops, equipment, and supplies, often with the aid of helicopters. (QCKDWT)

UF assault ships, amphibious
  ships, amphibious assault

amphibious vehicles
  TX.78   (L,N)
ALT amphibious vehicle
SN Use for transportation vehicles capable of travel equally well in water and on land, or in water and in the air.
UF amphibians
  vehicles, amphibious
RT *<amphibious warships>*
  seaplanes

<amphibious warships>
  TX.416
RT amphibious vehicles

amphiprostyle
  DC.145
HN October 1992 descriptor moved

amphitheaters
  RK.892   (A,L,N,B,R)
HN September 1990 scope note added
ALT amphitheater
UK amphitheatres
UKA amphitheatre
SN Use for circular or elliptical structures in which a central performance area is surrounded by rising tiers of seats.
UF coliseums

amphitheatres
SEE amphitheaters

amphorae
  TQ.649   (H,L)
ALT amphora
SN Ancient Greek and Roman storage vessels of many variations usually having a large oval body with a narrow neck and two or more handles extending from the mouth or neck to the shoulders on the body.
UF amphorae, storage
  storage amphorae
RT loutrophoroi

amphorae (Panathenaic)
USE Panathenaic amphorae

amphorae, belly
USE continuous curve amphorae

amphorae, continuous curve
USE continuous curve amphorae

amphorae, neck
USE neck amphorae

amphorae, nikosthenic
USE nikosthenic amphorae

amphorae, Nolan
USE Nolan amphorae

amphorae, Panathenaic
USE Panathenaic amphorae

amphorae, pointed
USE diotae

amphorae, storage
USE amphorae

amphorae, type c neck
USE Panathenaic amphorae

amphorae, type I
USE continuous curve amphorae

amphorae type II
USE neck amphorae

amphorae, type II
USE neck amphorae

amphorae type IIa
USE Nolan amphorae

amphorae, type IIa
USE Nolan amphorae

amphorae type IIc
USE Panathenaic amphorae

amphorae type IIc
USE Panathenaic amphorae

ampullae
  TQ.132   (H,L,N)
ALT ampulla
SN Vessels, varying in shape and size, used in churches and at coronations for holding liquids. Also, Roman vessels with one or two handles, often globular in form, used for perfumes, ointments, or serving drinks.

Amratian
  FL.2872
UF Early Naqada
  Naqada I

Amritsar
  FL.2386
HN April 1993 descriptor added

Amstel
  FL.3444   (R)
HN May 1990 descriptor added
UF Amstel porcelain
  porcelain, Amstel

Amstel porcelain
USE Amstel

Amul
USE Amol

Amul ware
USE Amol + ware

amulets
  PE.60   (H,L,N)
HN December 1992 descriptor added
ALT amulet
SN Small objects worn as protecting charms, as to ward off evil, harm, or illness, or to bring good fortune. For objects specifically cut with astrological or magical symbols, intended to protect the bearer, but not necessarily worn, use **talismans**. (RHDEL2)
RT talismans

Amuq B
    FL.3022
  HN March 1993 descriptor added

Amuq B ware
  HN April 1993 descriptor split, use
      Amuq B + ware

amusement arcades
    RK.976   (B)
  HN September 1990 scope note added
  ALT amusement arcade
  SN Entertainment buildings containing
      a variety of games and other amuse-
      ments that can be played for a nom-
      inal fee.
  UF arcades, amusement

<amusement park structures>
  HN January 1992 guide term deleted

amusement parks
    RG.158   (A,L,B,R)
  ALT amusement park
  UF parks, amusement

amusement rides
    RK.959   (A,L,N)
  HN January 1992 descriptor moved
      September 1990 scope note added
  ALT amusement ride
  SN Recreation structures containing ve-
      hicles or other devices in or on
      which people may ride for amuse-
      ment for a nominal fee and for a
      limited time.
  UF rides
      rides, amusement

Amuzgo
    FL.1526   (L)

amyl acetate
    MT.2451
  HN June 1990 lead-in term added
  UF acetate, amyl
      banana oil

amyl alcohol
    MT.2441
  UF alcohol, amyl

amylin
  USE dextrine

amz'ads
  USE imzads

An-yang
  USE Anyang (Shang style)

ana
  USE epigrams

Anachronism (Pittura Colta)
  USE Pittura Colta

anaglyphs
    VC.376   (R)
  HN April 1992 descriptor moved
  ALT anaglyph
  SN Stereoscopic photographs in which
      the two images are in contrasting
      colors and produce a three-dimen-

sional effect when viewed through
colored filters. (W)

Anaglypta
    TC.373
  SN Embossed paper wall coverings
      which were painted after being
      hung; made by a process patented
      by T. J. Palmer in 1887.

anagrams
    VW.946   (L)
  HN June 1992 descriptor added
  ALT anagram
  SN Words or phrases made by transpos-
      ing the letters of other words or
      phrases. (W)

analogy
    BM.19   (L)

analysing
  SEE analyzing

analysis
  USE analyzing

<analysis and testing techniques>
    KT.158

analysis, chemical
  USE chemical analysis

analysis, content
  USE subject analysis

analysis, cost benefit
  USE cost benefit analysis

analysis, discourse
  USE pragmatics

analysis, gravimetric
  USE gravimetric analysis

analysis, literary
  USE literary criticism

analysis, mass spectrum
  USE mass spectrometry

analysis, needs
  USE needs assessment

analysis, neutron activation
  USE neutron activation analysis

analysis, nondestructive
  USE nondestructive testing

analysis, plastic
  USE plastic design

analysis, qualitative
  USE qualitative analysis

analysis, quantitative
  USE quantitative analysis

analysis, radioactivation
  USE neutron activation analysis

analysis, site
  USE site analysis

analysis, spatial
  USE spatial analysis

analysis, spectrum
  USE spectroscopy

analysis, stability
  USE structural stability

analysis, stress
  USE structural analysis

analysis, structural
  USE structural analysis

analysis, subject
  USE subject analysis

analysis, systems
  USE systems analysis

analysis, terrain
  USE terrain analysis

analysis, thermal
  USE thermal analysis

analysis, trace element
  USE trace element analysis

analysis, ultimate-strength
  USE plastic design

analysts, handwriting
  USE graphologists

analysts, systems
  USE systems analysts

Analytic Cubist
  USE Analytical Cubist

analytical balances
    TN.284   (N)
  ALT analytical balance
  SN Use for precision balances with a
      sensitivity of 0.1 to 0.01 mg.
  UF balances, analytical

analytical bibliography
    BM.244   (L)
  SN The study of the history of book
      production and the description of
      books as physical objects, including
      study of the relationships of varying
      texts or multiple editions of a work.
  UF bibliography, analytical
      bibliography, critical
      bibliography, descriptive
      bibliography, historical
      critical bibliography
      descriptive bibliography
      historical bibliography

Analytical Cubist
    FL.3383
  HN June 1990 lead-in term added
  ALT Analytical Cubism
  UF Analytic Cubist
      Cubist, Analytical
      Cubist, Facet
      Facet Cubist

<analytical functions>
    KG.3

analyzers, sound
  USE sound analyzers

analyzing
KG.5 (A,L)
HN February 1991 alternate term added
ALT analyzed
UK analysing
UKA analysed
SN Examining an object, action, material, or concept in detail by separating it into its fundamental elements or component parts.
UF analysis

anamometers
USE anemometers

anamorphic lenses
USE wide-angle lenses

anamorphoses
VC.10 (R)
HN April 1991 descriptor moved
July 1990 scope note changed
ALT anamorphosis
SN Images so executed as to give a distorted shape to the object represented but which, if viewed from a certain point or using a curved mirror or other instrument, show the object in true proportion. (OCA)

Anang
FL.240 (L)

Anangula
FL.800

Anan'ino
FL.1836
HN April 1993 descriptor moved

anarchism
BM.969 (L,R)
HN February 1993 descriptor moved
January 1991 alternate term added
ALT anarchist

anarchists
HG.972 (L)
HN February 1993 descriptor moved
January 1993 alternate terms added
ALT anarchist's
anarchists'
SN Persons who promote disorder or excite revolt against any established rule, law, or custom. (RHDEL2)

Anasazi
FL.971 (A,L)
UF Basketmaker-Pueblo

anastatic printing
KT.700
HN October 1991 descriptor moved
October 1990 scope note changed
SN A process of relief etching, usually on zinc plates, used in the 19th century to reproduce existing printed material, including drawings and pages of type. (LG)
UF etching, zinc
printing, anastatic
zinc etching

anastylosis
KT.876
SN The reconstruction of a monument or other structure from fallen parts. (W)

anatase
USE titanium dioxide white

Anatolian
FL.2936 (L)

<Anatolian Islamic pottery styles after Manzikert>
FL.3647
HN April 1993 guide term added

<Anatolian Islamic styles after Manzikert>
FL.3645
HN April 1993 guide term added

<Anatolian Islamic styles and periods after Manzikert>
FL.3587
HN April 1993 guide term added

<Anatolian Islamic textile styles after Manzikert>
FL.3653
HN April 1993 guide term added

<Anatolian Paleolithic periods>
FL.2938

<Anatolian periods>
FL.2937

<Anatolian pottery styles>
FL.2954

Anatolian Seljuq
USE Seljuk of Rum

<Anatolian styles>
FL.2951

anatomical illustration
HN May 1991 descriptor split, use anatomical (ALT of anatomy) + illustration

anatomical illustrations
HN May 1991 descriptor split, use anatomical (ALT of anatomy) + illustrations

anatomical models
HN March 1991 descriptor split, use anatomical (ALT of anatomy) + models (representations)

anatomical studies
HN May 1991 descriptor split, use anatomical (ALT of anatomy) + studies (visual works)

anatomists
HG.581 (L)
HN April 1993 related term added
December 1992 alternate terms added
ALT anatomist
anatomist's
anatomists'
SN People who study anatomy.
RT anatomy

anatomy
KD.155 (L,B,R)
HN April 1993 related term added
December 1992 descriptor moved
February 1991 alternate term added
ALT anatomical
SN Discipline concerned with the structure, function, and development of the cells, tissues, and organs constituting the animal body. (PG)
RT anatomists

Anau
FL.1852
HN April 1993 descriptor moved

anchor bolts
PJ.42
HN April 1993 descriptor moved
ALT anchor bolt
SN Threaded bolts, usually embedded in a foundation, for securing a sill, framework, or machinery. (MEANS)
UF bolts, anchor
bolts, foundation
bolts, hold-down
foundation bolts
hold-down bolts

anchor davits
USE davits

anchor escapements
PJ.2654
ALT anchor escapement
SN Escapements in which wedge-shaped pallets of an anchor-shaped component engage an escape wheel causing the wheel to recoil slightly at every release.
UF escapements, anchor
escapements, recoil
recoil escapements

anchor hinges
PJ.410
HN April 1993 descriptor moved
ALT anchor hinge
UF hinges, anchor

anchor lights
TC.1430 (N)
ALT anchor light
SN Lights shown at night by a vessel at anchor.
UF lights, anchor

anchor plates
PJ.21
HN April 1993 descriptor moved
ALT anchor plate
SN Plates attached to an object to which accessories or structural members may be attached by welding, screwing, nailing, or bolting. (MEANS)
UF plates, anchor

anchor ties
PJ.22

HN April 1993 descriptor moved
ALT anchor tie
SN Fasteners used to secure the parts of a wall to some stable object, such as another wall. (PUTNAM)
UF ties, anchor

anchors (fasteners)
PJ.19 (L)
HN April 1993 descriptor moved
ALT anchor (fastener)
SN Metal ties or plates used to fasten together timbers or masonry.

anchors (watercraft equipment)
TH.413 (H,L,N)
HN March 1993 descriptor added
ALT anchor (watercraft equipment)
SN Use for any of various devices dropped to the bottom of a body of water and designed to bury themselves there in order to restrict the movement of watercraft or other floating objects. (RHDEL2)

anchors, adhesive
USE adhesive anchors

anchors, beam
USE beam anchors

anchors, buck
USE buck anchors

anchors, dog
USE dogs

anchors, double end
USE double end anchors

anchors, dovetail wire
USE dovetail wire anchors

anchors, dowel
USE dowel anchors

anchors, drive
USE drive anchors

anchors, furring
USE slot anchors

anchors, joist
USE beam anchors
joist anchors

anchors, lewis bolt
USE lewis bolt anchors

anchors, plate
USE sill anchors

anchors, rawlplug
USE rawl plugs

anchors, rod
USE rod anchors

anchors, screw
USE screw anchors

anchors, sill
USE sill anchors

anchors, slot
USE slot anchors

anchors, stone
USE stone anchors

anchors, strap
USE strap anchors

anchors, wall
USE beam anchors

anchors, Z
USE Z anchors

ancient
FL.2 (A,L,B,R)

<ancient African styles and periods>
FL.74

<ancient Central African styles and periods>
FL.121

<ancient East African styles and periods>
FL.147

Ancient Elamite
USE Old Elamite

<ancient European styles and periods>
FL.2537

<ancient Inland Niger Delta styles>
FL.84

<ancient Italian architecture styles>
FL.2829

<ancient Italian periods>
FL.2787

<ancient Italian pottery styles>
FL.2832

<ancient Italian sculpture styles>
FL.2848

<ancient Italian styles>
FL.2817

<ancient Italian styles and periods>
FL.2786

<ancient Italian wall painting styles>
FL.2853

<ancient North African styles and periods>
FL.166

<ancient Southern African pottery styles>
FL.143

<ancient Southern African styles and periods>
FL.127

<ancient West African styles and periods>
FL.75

ancillaries
USE outbuildings

ancones
HN January 1992 descriptor deleted, made lead-in to consoles

ancones
USE consoles

Andachtsbilder
VC.58
ALT Andachtsbild
SN Devotional images, especially from the Late Gothic and Renaissance periods, intended to inspire meditation and usually emphasizing subjects of grief and suffering.

Andaman marblewood
USE marblewood

Andaqui
FL.1670 (L)

Ande
USE Campa

andesite
MT.655
HN April 1992 descriptor moved
December 1991 scope note changed
SN An extrusive, usually dark grayish igneous rock consisting essentially of oligoclase or andesine feldspar with augite, hornblende, hypersthene, or biotite. (W)

Andhra
FL.2271 (L)
HN June 1990 lead-in term changed, was Satvahana
UF Andhra-Satavahana
Satavahana

Andhra, Early
USE Early Andhra

Andhra, Later
USE Later Andhra

Andhra-Satavahana
USE Andhra

Andoke
FL.1671 (L)

Andorobo
USE Dorobo

andra
PJ.1334
HN March 1993 descriptor moved
ALT andron
SN Use for the parts of ancient Greek houses used only by men.

Andronovo
FL.2198

Andumbo
USE Ndumbo

anechoic chambers
USE anechoic rooms

anechoic rooms
PJ.1341
HN March 1993 descriptor moved
ALT anechoic room
SN Rooms with sound-absorbent walls, especially designed for acoustic experiments. (W)
UF anechoic chambers

chambers, anechoic
rooms, anechoic

anemoclinometers
TN.356   (L)
ALT anemoclinometer
SN   Instruments that measure the inclination of the wind from the horizontal plane. (MHDSTT)

anemometers
TN.357   (L,N)
ALT anemometer
SN   Instruments designed to measure the speed or force of the wind.
UF anamometers

aneroid barographs
TN.352   (N)
ALT aneroid barograph
SN   Aneroid barometers equipped with an automatic recording mechanism. (RHDEL2)
UF aneroidographs
barographs, aneroid
barometrographs

aneroid barometers
TN.350   (L,N)
ALT aneroid barometer
SN   Barometers that depend on neither hydrostatic equilibrium nor the laws of gases but instead on measurement of force exerted by the atmosphere on some component of the mechanical system; often calibrated for use as altimeters.
UF barometers, aneroid

aneroidographs
USE aneroid barographs

Angas
FL.224   (L)

angel beds
USE lits à la duchesse

angel canopies
USE canopies (bed components)

angel lights
PJ.2277
HN March 1993 descriptor moved
June 1991 scope note changed
ALT angel light
SN   Small triangular lights between subordinate arches of the tracery of a window.
UF lights, angel

anger
BM.997   (L,R)
HN February 1993 descriptor moved
UF rage
wrath

Angevin Gothic
FL.3228
UF Gothic, Angevin

angiospermae
USE flowers

angiportus
RM.138
HN April 1993 descriptor moved
SN   Designates narrow, ancient Roman lanes, often leading to a dead end.

Angkor Thom
FL.2436

Angkor Vat
FL.2439

Angkorean
FL.2413   (A,L,B)
UF Khmer (Angkorean)

<Angkorean periods by reign>
FL.2414

<Angkorean styles>
FL.2435

angle arches, obtuse
USE drop arches

angle bars
USE angles (rolled sections)

angle bonds
PJ.23
HN April 1993 descriptor moved
ALT angle bond
SN   In masonry work, brick or metal ties used to bind the angles or corners of the walls together. (PUTNAM)
UF bonds, angle

angle braces
HN November 1990 descriptor deleted, made lead-in to **knee braces**

angle braces
USE hand drills
knee braces

angle brackets
PJ.1666
HN March 1993 descriptor moved
October 1991 scope note changed
ALT angle bracket
SN   Use for brackets projecting from the intersection of two walls; when on the exterior, often to support a cornice; when on the interior, often to support a rafter.
UF brackets, angle

angle brick
MT.74
HN April 1992 descriptor moved
SN   Any brick having an oblique shape to fit an oblique salient corner. (DAC)
UF brick, angle

angle buttresses
PJ.1449
HN March 1993 descriptor moved
ALT angle buttress
SN   Use for paired buttresses set at right angles, forming the corner of a structure.
UF buttresses, angle

angle capitals
PJ.1492
HN March 1993 descriptor moved
November 1990 scope note changed
ALT angle capital
SN   Capitals of corner columns.
UF capitals, angle
capitals, corner
corner capitals

angle chairs
USE corner chairs

angle cleats
PJ.78
HN April 1993 descriptor moved
ALT angle cleat
SN   Short sections of angle iron used to attach structural members, such as precast panels, to structural steel. (MEANS)
UF angle clips
cleats, angle
clips, angle

angle clips
USE angle cleats

angle columns
HN February 1991 descriptor split, use **corner + columns (architectural elements)**

angle dozers
TH.441
ALT angle dozer
SN   Bulldozers whose blades are set on an angle. (DAC)
UF angling dozers
dozers, angle
dozers, angling

angle floats
TH.1150
HN December 1992 descriptor moved
ALT angle float
SN   Trowels with two surfaces meeting at a right angle; used to finish plaster or concrete in a corner. (MEANS)
UF floats, angle

angle irons
USE angles (rolled sections)

angle joints
PJ.618
HN April 1993 descriptor moved
ALT angle joint
SN   Joints formed where two construction members meet at an angle. (PUTNAM)
UF joints, angle

<angle measuring devices>
TN.4

angle paddles
TH.1141
HN December 1992 descriptor moved
ALT angle paddle
SN   Hand tools used to finish a plastered surface. (DAC)
UF paddles, angle

angle planes
 TH.1142
 HN December 1992 descriptor moved
 ALT angle plane
 SN Plastering tools used to prepare surfaces for a finish coat by knocking down high spots, cleaning angles, and scraping. (PUTNAM)
 UF planes, angle

angle plows
 TH.1143
 HN December 1992 descriptor moved
 ALT angle plow
 SN Plastering tools primarily used on inside corners to apply pressure to finish setting materials. (PUTNAM)
 UF plows, angle

angle rafters
 USE hip rafters

angle ridges
 USE hip rafters

angle saws
 USE dovetail saws

angle sections
 USE angles (rolled sections)

angle ties
 USE knee braces

angle trowels
 USE margin trowels

angle views
 USE oblique views

angled stairs
 USE quarter-turn stairs

angles (mathematics)
 BM.654   (L)
 HN May 1991 alternate term changed, was **angled**
 ALT angle (mathematics)

angles (rolled sections)
 PJ.2038
 HN March 1993 descriptor moved
   July 1991 scope note changed
   November 1990 lead-in terms added
 ALT angle (rolled section)
 SN Use for metal members having an L-shaped section.
 UF angle bars
   angle irons
   angle sections
   bars, angle
   irons, angle
   sections, angle

Anglican
 BM.471   (L,B)
 HN May 1993 related term added
 SN Use with regard to the Church of England; with regard to the Episcopal Church in America, use **Episcopal.**
 RT Episcopal

Anglican (Episcopal)
 USE Episcopal

angling dozers
 USE angle dozers

angling lodges
 USE fishing lodges

Anglo-Chinoise
 USE Chinoiserie

Anglo-Japanese
 USE Japonaiserie

Anglo-Norman
 FL.3207   (A)

Anglo-Saxon
 FL.3209   (A,L,B)

Angoni
 USE Ngoni

angons
 TK.50   (H,N)
 ALT angon
 SN Javelins of the ancient Franks, having a barbed iron head forged at the top of an iron haft with a socket for mounting it on a long wooden staff.

angora
 USE angora wool

angora wool
 MT.2571
 HN March 1992 scope note added
   March 1992 lead-in term added
   March 1992 descriptor changed, was **angora**
   February 1992 descriptor moved
 SN Hair of the Angora goat or the Angora rabbit.
 UF angora
   wool, angora

Angostura
 FL.764

angular
 DC.58
 HN October 1992 descriptor moved

angular harps
 TT.222
 ALT angular harp
 SN Open harps in which the neck makes a sharp angle with the resonator. (NGDMI)
 UF harps, angular

angular perspectives
 USE two-point perspectives

Anguru
 USE Lomwe

anhydrite white
 MT.2241
 HN April 1992 descriptor moved
 UF white, anhydrite

anhydrous alcohol
 USE absolute alcohol

anhydrous gypsum plaster
 MT.1858
 UF class C gypsum plaster
   gypsum plaster, anhydrous
   gypsum plaster, class C
   plaster, anhydrous gypsum
   plaster, class C gypsum

anhydrous lime
 USE quicklime

aniconism
 BM.284   (R)
 SN Use generally for opposition to the use of idols. For more vehement movements against religious images, use **iconoclasm.**

anil
 USE indigo

anil nilah
 USE indigo

anilin
 USE aniline dye

aniline
 USE aniline dye

aniline black
 MT.2081   (L)
 HN April 1992 descriptor moved
 UF black, aniline

aniline black (color)
 USE dark grayish purple
   dark purplish gray

aniline blue, dark
 USE dark grayish blue
   dark grayish purple

aniline dye
 MT.2043   (L)
 HN April 1993 lead-in term added
   April 1992 descriptor moved
 SN Dye produced from aniline, a poisonous, oily liquid. Used to make the earliest synthetic dyes.
 UF anilin
   aniline
   dye, aniline

aniline printing
 USE aniline process

aniline process
 KT.369   (L)
 HN March 1993 descriptor moved
 SN A photographic process usually used for reproducing technical drawings. The image is formed using aniline dyes and appears blue-black.
 UF aniline printing
   printing, aniline

aniline purple
 USE mauve

aniline violet
 USE light violet
   mauve

aniline yellow
USE deep yellow

<animal adhesive>
HN March 1992 guide term deleted

animal blood albumin
USE albumin glue

animal cemeteries
USE pet cemeteries

<animal equipment>
TH.14
HN February 1993 guide term added

<animal exhibition buildings>
RK.367

animal fiber
HN June 1991 descriptor deleted

animal glue
MT.1725
HN March 1992 descriptor added
SN An adhesive made from a solution of degraded or denatured collagen in water.
UF glue, animal
RT gelatin

animal homes
USE animal shelters

animal hospitals
USE veterinary hospitals

animal housing
RK.78   (A,L,B)
HN December 1991 scope note added
SN Use for the broad class of agricultural structures that provide shelter for animals.
UF animal shelters (farm structures)
buildings, livestock
housing, animal
livestock buildings
shelters, animal

<animal husbandry containers>
TQ.115

animal material
MT.2514   (L)
HN April 1993 descriptor changed, was animal materials
February 1992 descriptor moved
SN Use for material of animal origin.
UF material, animal

<animal material by form or function>
MT.2515
HN February 1992 guide term added

animal oil
MT.1065   (L)
HN April 1992 descriptor moved
July 1990 scope note added
SN Oil obtained from animal substances. (W)
UF oil, animal

animal painters
HG.290   (L)
HN February 1993 descriptor moved

November 1992 alternate terms added
ALT animal painter
animal painter's
animal painters'
UF painters, animal

animal parks
USE wild animal parks

animal pedigrees
USE studbooks

animal pigment
MT.2059   (L)
HN April 1992 descriptor moved
UF pigment, animal

animal pounds
USE animal shelters

animal-powered engines
TH.933   (L)
ALT animal-powered engine
UF engines, animal-powered

animal sculptors
HG.318   (L)
HN February 1993 descriptor moved
December 1992 alternate terms added
ALT animal sculptor
animal sculptor's
animal sculptors'
UF sculptors, animal

animal shelters
RK.752   (L,B)
ALT animal shelter
UF animal homes
animal pounds
estrays
homes, animal
pounds (animal shelters)
pounds, animal
shelters, animal

animal shelters (farm structures)
USE animal housing

animal size
MT.2493   (L)
HN December 1992 scope note changed
June 1991 lead-in term deleted, was animal glue
SN An animal glue or gelatin used for surface-sizing paper or textile. (W)
UF size, animal

Animal Style
FL.3108   (H)

<animal trappings>
TH.15
HN February 1993 guide term added

animal wax
MT.1289
HN April 1992 descriptor moved
December 1990 descriptor moved
UF wax, animal

Animalier
FL.3463   (L)

animated books
USE movable books

animation
KT.348   (L,R)
ALT animated

animation, computer
USE computer animation

animators
HG.334   (L)
HN February 1993 descriptor moved
November 1992 alternate terms added
ALT animator
animator's
animators'
SN Persons who contribute to the production of an animated cartoon or other animation, as by making drawings. (W)

animé
USE East African copal

animes
TE.313
ALT anime
SN Laminated cuirasses first appearing in Italy in the first quarter of the 16th century, built up of horizontal overlapping lames joined by leather straps and sliding rivets on the inner side. They went out of fashion in western Europe by the end of the 16th century, but continued to be popular throughout the 17th century in eastern Europe, particularly in Hungary and Poland where they were used by heavy cavalry.

animism
BM.537   (L,R)
HN July 1991 related term added
January 1991 alternate term added
ALT animist
RT spirit houses

anisometric projections
USE trimetric drawings

anisotropism
USE anisotropy

anisotropy
DC.351
HN October 1992 descriptor added
ALT anisotropic
SN The quality of having different characteristics, as properties or dimensions, along different axes.
UF anisotropism
nonisotropy
onisotropy

ankhs
DG.18
ALT ankh
SN Figures like a cross having a loop instead of an upper vertical, used especially in ancient Egypt as a symbol of life. (W)

UF ansate crosses
crosses, ansate
crosses, Egyptian
cruces ansatae
Egyptian crosses
keys of life
life, keys of

ankle bracelets
USE anklets

ankle ornaments
USE anklets

ankle rings
USE anklets

anklets
TE.480 (L,N)
ALT anklet
SN Ornamental bands, rings, or chains worn around the ankle.
UF ankle bracelets
ankle ornaments
ankle rings
bracelets, ankle
ornaments, ankle
rings, ankle

Ankole
USE Nkole

Ankwe
USE Goemai

annals
VW.276 (L)
HN June 1992 descriptor added
ALT annal
SN Use for records of events arranged in yearly sequence, usually without comment or interpretation by the compiler. For more connected and full descriptions of events in chronological order, use **chronicles**. (W)

annals (chronicles)
USE chronicles

Annamese
FL.2521

annatto
MT.2259 (L)
HN April 1992 descriptor moved
UF orlean
terra orellana

annealing
KT.998
HN January 1993 descriptor moved
May 1991 descriptor moved
May 1991 scope note changed
ALT annealed
SN Process by which materials, such as metal and glass, are softened and made workable by heating and controlled cooling. (THDAT)

annexation
USE annexing

annexes (building divisions)
PJ.945

HN March 1993 descriptor moved
March 1993 descriptor changed, was **annexes**
March 1993 alternate term changed, was **annex**
ALT annex (building division)
SN Use for subsidiary supplementary structures, whether additions to a main building or separate from it, but usually visibly distinct and often with a separate entrance.

annexes (districts)
RG.302
HN January 1993 descriptor added
ALT annex (district)
SN Districts, including those originally possessing a degree of political independence or self-government, which have been incorporated into the boundaries of another administrative body.
RT possessions

annexing
KG.263 (L)
HN April 1993 lead-in term added
February 1991 alternate term added
ALT annexed
SN Including or appropriating an area within the limits of a governmental unit. (W)
UF annexation

anniversaries
KM.13 (L)
HN April 1992 scope note added
May 1991 alternate term added
ALT anniversary
SN Annual or multiannual commemorations, often occurring on the specific calendar date of the event remembered.

annotated bibliographies
VW.173
HN November 1992 descriptor moved
ALT annotated bibliography
SN Bibliographies with notes added to the entries to elucidate, evaluate, or describe the subject and contents of the entries.
UF bibliographies, annotated

annotations
VW.240 (B)
HN November 1992 descriptor moved
April 1992 scope note changed
ALT annotation
SN Notes added as comment or explanation.
UF notations

announcements
VW.374 (N)
HN November 1992 descriptor moved
ALT announcement
SN Printed or published statements or notices that inform the reader of an event or other news.
UF notices

announcements, bidding
USE bidding announcements

announcements, business
USE business announcements

announcements of bidding
USE bidding announcements

announcers
HG.474
HN December 1992 alternate terms added
ALT announcer
announcer's
announcers'
SN Persons who introduce television or radio programs, often act as masters of ceremonies, make commercial announcements, and read brief items such as news summaries and sports reviews. (W)

annual gift books
USE gift books

annual indexes
VW.864
HN November 1992 descriptor moved
ALT annual index
UF indexes, annual

annual reports
VW.922 (L)
HN November 1992 descriptor moved
ALT annual report
SN Documentation summarizing the activities of an organization over the course of a year.
UF reports, annual

annual reports of corporations
USE corporation reports

annuals (gift books)
USE gift books

annuals (plants)
RD.233 (L)
ALT annual (plant)
SN Designates plants that complete their cycle from seed to seed in a single year. (ALLAB2)

annuals (publications)
VW.968 (L)
HN November 1992 descriptor moved
May 1991 descriptor changed, was **annuals**
May 1991 alternate term changed, was **annual**
ALT annual (publication)
SN Use generally for yearly publications.

annuals, keepsake
USE keepsakes (books)

annular
DC.59
HN October 1992 descriptor moved
SN Ringlike; composed of ringlike sections. (THDAT)
UF ring-shaped

annular bits
USE   tenon-cutting bits

annular French lamps
USE   astral lamps

annular lamps
　　　TC.1306
ALT   annular lamp
SN   Lamps with a ring-shaped reservoir with a burner or burners located in the center of the ring at the same level or below the level of the reservoir and connected to it by two tubes through which fuel is fed.
UF   lamps, annular

annular moldings
USE   roll moldings

annular nails
USE   ring-shank nails

annular ring nails
USE   ring-shank nails

annular vaults
　　　PJ.1876
HN   March 1993 descriptor moved
　　　November 1990 scope note changed
ALT   annular vault
SN   Use for barrel vaults covering a space the plan of which is formed by the area between two concentric circles, or any portion of such a space.
UF   vaults, annular

annulated columns
　　　PJ.1460
HN   March 1993 descriptor moved
　　　March 1991 scope note changed
　　　March 1991 lead-in terms added
ALT   annulated column
SN   Use for columns or clusters of shafts encircled by annulets or shaft rings, common in Medieval architecture.
UF   annulated shafts
　　　columns, annulated
　　　shafts, annulated

annulated shafts
USE   annulated columns

annulets
　　　PJ.2117
HN   April 1993 descriptor moved
　　　November 1990 descriptor moved
　　　November 1990 scope note changed
ALT   annulet
SN   Use generally for small decorative moldings, usually angular bands or fillets, encircling column shafts; specifically designates the fillets around the bottom of the echinus of a Doric capital. For the grooves encircling the bottom of a Doric capital and masking the joint between capital and shaft, use **hypotrachelia**. For molded bands around Gothic column shafts, often masking the joint

between two sections of shaft, prefer **shaft rings**.
UF   bandelets

anodic
　　　DC.22　　　　　　　　　　　(L)
HN   October 1992 descriptor added
SN   Use to describe things pertaining to anodes, especially phenomena taking place in the vicinity of anodes or materials formed by such phenomena.

anodizing
　　　KT.1132　　　　　　　　　(L,B)
ALT   anodized
SN   Process in which the surface of a metal is coated with a protective or decorative layer through electrolytic action.

anonymous architecture
USE   vernacular architecture

anorthoclase
　　　MT.545
HN   April 1992 descriptor moved

ansate crosses
USE   ankhs

antae
　　　PJ.1558
HN   March 1993 descriptor moved
ALT   anta
SN   Piers produced by the thickening of walls at their termination. (W)

Antandroy
　　　FL.554　　　　　　　　　　(L)

Antanosy
　　　FL.555

ante-rooms
SEE   anterooms

antebellum
　　　FL.1739
HN   June 1991 descriptor added

antecabinets
USE   anterooms

antechambers
USE   anterooms

antechoirs
　　　PJ.1248
HN   March 1993 descriptor moved
ALT   antechoir
SN   Spaces of a divided choir farthest from the sanctuary. (W)
UF   choirs, fore
　　　fore choirs

antecourts
USE   forecourts

antefixes
　　　PJ.2355　　　　　　　　　　(N)
HN   March 1993 descriptor moved
　　　November 1990 scope note changed
　　　November 1990 alternate term changed, was **antefixe**

ALT   antefix
SN   Use for ornaments at the ridge or eaves of a roof, in classical architecture and derivatives, that close or conceal the open end of a row of cover tiles.

antemurals
USE   outworks

antenna systems, television
USE   television antenna systems

antennas, dish
USE   satellite home antennas

antennas, satellite
USE   satellite home antennas

antennas, satellite home
USE   satellite home antennas

antependia
　　　TC.355　　　　　　　　　　(N,B)
ALT   antependium
SN   Hangings for the front of an altar, pulpit, or lectern. (W)
UF   frontals
RT   altar frontals

antependia, pulpit
USE   pulpit falls

anterooms
　　　PJ.1075
HN   March 1993 descriptor moved
ALT   anteroom
UK   ante-rooms
UKA   ante-room
SN   Rooms preceding or serving as a lobby or means of access to another and more important room. (RS)
UF   antecabinets
　　　antechambers

anthemions
　　　DG.67
ALT   anthemion
SN   Use for series of conventionalized flower and foliage motifs, usually palmettes alternating with lotus, or other similar forms having lobe or leaf shapes radiating from a base. Sometimes used for individual such motifs. Found in Greek and later classicizing styles.
UF   honeysuckle motifs
　　　motifs, honeysuckle

anthocyanin
　　　MT.2061　　　　　　　　　(L)
HN   April 1992 descriptor moved

anthologies
　　　VW.954　　　　　　　　　　(L)
HN   November 1992 descriptor moved
　　　June 1992 lead-in term added
　　　April 1991 lead-in term added
ALT   anthology
SN   Collections of choice extracts, from the writings of one author, or various authors, and usually having a common characteristic such as subject matter or literary form. (LG)

UF florilegia (anthologies)
   miscellanies

anthracene green
USE moderate bluish green

anthracene purple
USE dark grayish purple
   dark purplish red

anthracene violet
USE moderate violet

anthracene violet, dark
USE dark grayish purple
   dark purple

anthracite
   MT.1017   (L)
HN April 1992 descriptor moved
UF anthracite coal
   coal, anthracite

anthracite coal
USE anthracite

anthro-geography
USE human geography

anthropological archaeologists
HN April 1993 descriptor split, use anthropological (ALT of anthropology) + archaeologists

anthropological archaeology
HN April 1993 descriptor split, use anthropological (ALT of anthropology) + archaeology

anthropological linguistics
   KD.45   (L)
SN Study of speech communities, particularly those with no writing system, by the application of anthropological and linguistic techniques. (ERIC9)
UF anthropology, linguistic
   linguistic anthropology
   linguistics, anthropological

anthropological materials
USE ethnographic objects

anthropological museums
USE anthropology + museums

anthropologists
   HG.441   (L)
HN April 1993 related term added
   December 1992 alternate terms added
ALT anthropologist
   anthropologist's
   anthropologists'
RT anthropology

anthropologists, cultural
USE social anthropologists

anthropologists, physical
USE physical anthropologists

anthropologists, social
USE social anthropologists

anthropology
   KD.210   (L,B,R)
HN April 1993 related term added
   February 1992 scope note added
   September 1991 descriptor moved
   February 1991 alternate term added
ALT anthropological
SN The scientific study of human history in its biological, linguistic, and social aspects. (HOLHZR)
RT anthropologists

anthropology, cultural
USE social anthropology

anthropology, demographic
USE demographic anthropology

anthropology, linguistic
USE anthropological linguistics

anthropology museums
HN May 1993 descriptors moved
   March 1993 descriptor split, use anthropology + museums

anthropology of religion
   KD.85
UF religion, anthropology of

anthropology, philosophical
USE philosophical anthropology

anthropology, physical
USE physical anthropology

anthropology, psychological
USE ethnopsychology

anthropology, social
USE social anthropology

anthropology, structural
USE structural anthropology

anthropometrics
USE anthropometry

anthropometry
   KD.217   (L,B)
HN September 1991 descriptor moved
SN Study of human body measurements on a comparative basis. (W)
UF anthropometrics

anthropomorphic
   DC.46
HN October 1992 descriptor moved
SN Resembling a human form. (RHDEL2)

<anthropomorphic supporting elements>
   PJ.1434
HN March 1993 guide term moved

anthropomorphism
   BM.419   (A,L,R)
HN January 1991 alternate term added
ALT anthropomorphist
SN Interpretation of what is not human in terms of human characteristics. (W)

anthroposophy
   BM.551   (L,R)

HN January 1991 alternate term added
ALT anthroposophist
SN 20th-century spiritual and mystical doctrine centering on human development, deriving mainly from the religious ideology theosophy.

Anti
USE Campa

anti-art
   BM.151
SN Use to describe work which has the character of art, but which mocks or challenges preconceptions about the nature of art. (THDAT)

anti-foaming agent
SEE antifoaming agent

Anti-form
USE Post-Minimal

anti-fouling paint
SEE antifouling paint

anti-freeze
SEE antifreeze

anti-freeze solution
USE antifreeze

anti-oxidant
SEE antioxidant

anti semitism
USE antisemitism

anti-semitism
USE antisemitism

anti-submarine detection investigation committee
USE sonar

antiabrasion layer
USE supercoat

antiaircraft artillery
USE antiaircraft guns

antiaircraft guns
   TK.156   (L,N)
ALT antiaircraft gun
SN Artillery designed to fire at enemy aircraft in flight.
UF AA guns
   AAA
   antiaircraft artillery
   artillery, antiaircraft
   flak
   guns, AA
   guns, antiaircraft

antiaircraft shells
   TK.256
ALT antiaircraft shell
SN Artillery shells designed to be fired from the ground at flying aircraft.
UF AA shells
   shells, AA
   shells, antiaircraft

antibacterial paint
USE antifouling paint

antibiotic
MT.1765 (L)
HN April 1992 descriptor added
SN A chemical substance produced by microorganisms that has the capacity, in dilute solutions, to inhibit the growth of other microorganisms or destroy them. (CCDICT)

antifoamer
USE antifoaming agent

antifoaming agent
MT.1686 (L)
HN April 1993 lead-in term changed, was **antifoamers**
April 1993 descriptor changed, was **antifoaming agents**
UK anti-foaming agent
UF agent, anti-foaming
agent, antifoaming
antifoamer

antifouling paint
MT.1967 (L)
UK anti-fouling paint
UF antibacterial paint
mold-resistant paint
mould-resistant paint
paint, anti-fouling
paint, antibacterial
paint, antifouling
paint, mold-resistant
paint, mould-resistant

antifreeze
MT.1687 (L)
HN April 1993 lead-in term added
April 1993 lead-in term changed, was **antifreeze compounds**
April 1993 lead-in term changed, was **antifreeze solutions**
December 1991 lead-in term added
June 1990 lead-in term changed, was **anti-freeze solutions**
UK anti-freeze
UF anti-freeze solution
antifreeze compound
antifreeze solution
compound, antifreeze
solution, antifreeze

antifreeze compound
USE antifreeze

antifreeze solution
USE antifreeze

antifriction bolts
USE antifriction latch bolts

antifriction latch bolts
PJ.551
HN March 1993 descriptor moved
ALT antifriction latch bolt
UF antifriction bolts
bolts, antifriction latch
latch bolts, antifriction

antifungal agent
USE fungicide

antimacassars
TC.191 (N)
ALT antimacassar
SN Small washable mats, often crocheted, used in the 19th century to protect the backs and arms of upholstered seating and reclining furniture from the stains caused by Macassar oil or other hair preparations. In the late 19th century, these were replaced by **tidies.**
UF backs, chair
chair backs
RT mats (furniture coverings)
tidies

antimensia
TC.350 (H,L)
ALT antimension
SN Consecrated linen or silk altar coverings containing relics, used by the Orthodox Eastern Church.
UF eilitons

Antimongelb
USE Naples yellow

antimony
MT.378 (L)
HN March 1993 scope note changed
April 1992 descriptor moved
SN Use for the pure metallic element having symbol Sb and atomic number 51; a bright, hard, silvery to bluish white metal. Use also for this metal as processed and formed, usually in combination with other substances, to make various objects and materials, particularly alloys and pigments.
UF Sb
stibium

antimony orange
MT.2191 (L)
HN April 1992 descriptor moved
UF antimony red
orange, antimony
red, antimony

antimony oxide
MT.2224
HN April 1992 descriptor moved
UF oxide, antimony

antimony red
USE antimony orange

antimony vermilion
MT.2182
HN April 1992 descriptor moved
UF vermilion, antimony

antimony white
MT.2225
HN April 1992 descriptor moved
UF timonox
white, antimony

antimony yellow
USE moderate orange yellow
Naples yellow

antimycotic
USE fungicide

antioxidant
MT.1688 (L)
HN April 1993 descriptor changed, was **antioxidants**
UK anti-oxidant
SN Substance that opposes or inhibits oxidation. (W)

antiparabemata
PJ.1251
HN March 1993 descriptor moved
ALT antiparabema
SN Chapels at the west end of Byzantine churches, especially of the Armenian type.

antipersonnel grenades
TK.108 (N)
ALT antipersonnel grenade
SN Grenades specifically designed to explode into and scatter fragments, used against personnel rather than mechanized vehicles, installations, or structures.
UF defensive grenades
fragmentation grenades
grenades, antipersonnel
grenades, defensive
grenades, fragmentation
RT shrapnel

antiphonals
USE antiphonaries

antiphonaries
VW.887 (L,R)
HN November 1992 descriptor moved
December 1990 descriptor added
ALT antiphonary
SN Collections of psalms, anthems, or verses to be sung responsively.
UF antiphonals

Antiplano
USE Puná

antiqua
PJ.3454
SN A formal script developed in the 15th century in Italy based largely on Caroline minuscule.
UF humanistic round
humanistic textual

antiquarianism
BM.285 (R)
SN Interest in or devotion to things of the past, especially of ancient times. The term implies admiration of a style or object simply because it is old. (MAYER)

antiquaries
HG.896 (L,B)
HN December 1992 alternate terms added
ALT antiquaries'
antiquary
antiquary's

SN Experts on, or students or collectors of, antiquities. (RHDEL2)

antique green
USE verd antique

Antique, Late
USE Late Antique

antique porphyry, red
USE red antique porphyry

antique shops
USE antique (ALT of antiques) + stores

antique stores
HN March 1993 descriptor split, use antique (ALT of antiques) + stores

Antique, the
BM.220
SN Use generally to mean belonging to or after the manner of ancient Greece or Rome. Use specifically to refer to those aspects of classical art, particularly the representation of the human figure in ancient sculpture and also the use of ornament in ancient art, when they are used as models of perfection in other periods.
UF the Antique

antiques
PE.5 (A,L)
HN November 1990 descriptor moved
ALT antique

antiquing
KT.453
ALT antiqued
SN The process of finishing or refinishing so as to give the appearance of age to an object. (W)

antisemitism
BM.1072 (L,R)
HN February 1993 descriptor moved
February 1991 scope note added
February 1991 lead-in terms added
January 1991 alternate term added
ALT antisemitic
SN Economic, religious, or racial discrimination against Jews. (TSIT)
UF anti semitism
anti-semitism

antiseptic
MT.1767 (L)
HN April 1993 descriptor changed, was antiseptics

antistatic additive
USE antistatic agent

antistatic agent
MT.1750 (L)
HN April 1993 lead-in term added
April 1993 descriptor changed, was antistatic agents
July 1990 lead-in terms added
SN Material that prevents build-up or promotes discharge of static electricity, as in film or textile. (MH)

UF additive, antistatic
agent, antistatic
antistatic additive
antistatic treatment
treatment, antistatic

antistatic treatment
USE antistatic agent

antitank artillery
USE antitank guns

antitank grenades
TK.109 (L,N)
ALT antitank grenade
SN Grenades designed specifically for use against tanks or other armored vehicles.
UF grenades, antitank

antitank guns
TK.157 (L,N)
ALT antitank gun
SN Guns designed for use against tanks or other armored vehicles.
UF antitank artillery
artillery, antitank
guns, antitank

antler
MT.1315 (L,R)
HN March 1992 scope note added
March 1992 related term added
February 1992 descriptor moved
SN Paired deciduous outgrowths of bone, projecting from the frontal bones of ungulates of the deer family. Distinguished from **horn**, which is modified skin tissue or compacted hair.
RT horn

Antonine
FL.2803 (R)

antoniniani
VK.54 (L)
ALT antoninianus
SN Designates Roman coins of the 3rd century CE distinguished by a radiate crown on the depiction of the emperor; originally of silver and probably a double denarius, later debased.
UF radiates

Antwerp blue
MT.2110
HN April 1992 descriptor moved
SN Pale variety of Prussian blue. (MAYER)
UF blue, Antwerp
blue, Haarlem
blue, mineral
Haarlem blue
mineral blue

Antwerp blue (color)
USE dark blue
grayish blue

Anuradhapura
FL.2390

<anvil accessories>
TH.1191

<anvil components>
PJ.2571
HN March 1993 guide term moved

anvil cutters
USE hardies

anvil dies
TH.1009
HN March 1992 descriptor added
ALT anvil die
SN Use for the lower of two dies between which coins are struck. (PGNUM)
UF dies, anvil
dies, pile
pile dies

anvil tongs
USE pickup tongs

anvils (idiophones)
TT.504 (N)
ALT anvil (idiophone)
SN Orchestral percussion instruments, consisting of one or two metal bars mounted on a resonating frame; occasionally, they are actual blacksmiths' anvils. (NGDMI)

anvils (tools)
TH.1189 (N)
HN April 1993 descriptor changed, was anvils
April 1993 alternate term changed, was anvil
ALT anvil (tool)
SN Heavy, usually steel or iron blocks on which metal is shaped by hand hammering or forging. (W)

<anvils and anvil accessories>
TH.1188

anvils, bench
USE bench anvils

anvils, stake
USE stakes

anxiety
BM.998 (L,R)
HN February 1993 descriptor moved

Anyang (Nigerian)
FL.235 (L)
HN August 1990 lead-in term added
UF Banyangi
Nyangi

Anyang (Shang style)
FL.1929
UF An-yang
Yinxu

Anyi
FL.284 (L)
UF Agni

Ao Kutani
FL.2103
UF Green Kutani

Kutani, Ao
Kutani, Green

Aoba
USE   Oba

Aona
USE   Ona

Aowin
  FL.285   (L)
UF   Brisa

Apache
  FL.1464   (L)

Apache, Chiricahua
USE   Chiricahua Apache

Apache, Eastern
USE   Eastern Apache

Apache fiddles
USE   kízh kízh díhís

Apache, Jicarilla
USE   Jicarilla Apache

Apache, Kiowa
USE   Kiowa Apache

Apache, Lipan
USE   Lipan Apache

Apache, Mescalero
USE   Mescalero Apache

Apache, Mohave
USE   Yavapai

Apache, Western
USE   Western Apache

Apalai
  FL.1586   (L)

apartment buildings
USE   apartment houses

apartment hotels
  RK.354   (A,B)
HN   March 1993 scope note changed
   January 1993 related term added
ALT   apartment hotel
SN   Hotels providing apartments, usually furnished, to long-term tenants
  and including some services not
  available to the general public. For
  similar housing but providing
  smaller accommodations for short-
  or long-term rental at very low
  rates, often with shared facilities,
  and fewer services, use **single room
  occupancy hotels.**
UF   hotels, apartment
  hotels, residential
  residential hotels
RT   single room occupancy hotels

apartment houses
  RK.355   (A,L,B,R)
ALT   apartment house
UF   apartment buildings
  blocks of flats
  buildings, apartment

flats, blocks of
houses, apartment

apartment houses, cooperative
USE   cooperative apartment houses

apartments
  PJ.1208   (A,L,N,B)
HN   May 1993 descriptor moved
  May 1990 scope note changed
  May 1990 lead-in terms added
ALT   apartment
SN   Use for rooms or sets of rooms used
  as dwellings or private living quarters and located in houses, hotels, or
  within apartment houses.
UF   domestic wings
  dwelling units
  family quarters, private
  living quarters
  living units
  private family quarters
  private wings
  quarters, private family
  residential wings
  units, dwelling
  units, living
  wings, domestic
  wings, private
  wings, residential

apartments, bachelor
USE   studio apartments

apartments, cooperative
USE   cooperative apartment houses

apartments, duplex
USE   duplex apartments

apartments, efficiency
USE   studio apartments

apartments, garden
USE   garden apartments

apartments, model
USE   model apartments

apartments, railroad
USE   railroad flats

apartments, studio
USE   studio apartments

apatite
  MT.513   (L)
HN   April 1992 descriptor moved
  February 1992 related term added
  February 1992 scope note changed
SN   A calcium phosphate mineral com-
  monly used as a source of phospho-
  rus, containing up to 20% phospho-
  rus pentoxide. (MH)
RT   gemstone

APCs
USE   armored personnel carriers

Apennine
  FL.2789
UF   Extra Terramaricolan

apertometers
  TN.83   (L,N)

ALT   apertometer
SN   Instruments designed to measure
  the numerical aperture of microscope objectives. (MHDSTT)

aperture cards
  VW.1052
HN   November 1992 descriptor moved
ALT   aperture card
SN   Cards with one or more openings
  into each of which is mounted a
  frame cut from a strip of microfilm.
  (LG)
UF   cards, aperture
  cards, image
  cards, peephole
  image cards
  peephole cards

Aphrodisian
  FL.2850
UF   School of Aphrodisias

apiaries
  RK.79   (A,N,B)
HN   December 1991 scope note added
ALT   apiary
SN   Use for structures where bees are
  kept; especially collections of hives
  or colonies of bees kept for their
  honey. (W)
UF   bee houses
  houses, bee
  mellaria

apocalyptic art
  BM.176   (L,R)
SN   Use for any art which deals with the
  final doom or ultimate destiny of
  the world, including that in the Bib-
  lical story of Armageddon in the
  Book of Revelations.
UF   art, apocalyptic

apodyteria
  PJ.1011
HN   March 1993 descriptor moved
  June 1990 scope note changed
ALT   apodyterium
SN   Dressing rooms in ancient Greek
  and Roman baths and palaestrae.
  (W)
UF   gymnasteria

Apollo lyres
USE   lyre-guitars

Apono
USE   Punu

apophyges
  PJ.1516
HN   March 1993 descriptor moved
  November 1990 lead-in term
  changed, was **conges**
ALT   apophyge
SN   In columns, concave sweep where
  the shaft springs from the base or
  terminates in the capital; also, hol-
  lows or scotias beneath the echinus
  of some Archaic Doric capitals.
UF   apotheses

congés
scapes

apothecae
HN January 1992 descriptor deleted

apothecaries
USE drugstores
pharmacists

apothecary bottles
TQ.126   (H,L,N,R)
ALT apothecary bottle
SN Cylindrical bottles with short necks
and glass stoppers, of a type originally sold to an apothecary in sets of
four or more and labeled with the
name of a standard medicine. For
unmarked bottles of varying size
used by an apothecary use **medicine
bottles.** (JSSG)
UF apothecary jars
bottles, apothecary
jars, apothecary
RT bottles
medicine bottles

<apothecary containers>
TQ.124

apothecary jars
USE apothecary bottles

apothecary scales
USE prescription scales

apotheses
USE apophyges

Appalachee
FL.902

Appalachian dulcimers
TT.369   (L)
ALT Appalachian dulcimer
SN Use for folk instruments from the
Appalachian region of the United
States, usually consisting of a long
figure-eight shaped box, a fretted
fingerboard set centrally along its
entire length, and from three to five
metal strings tensioned by lateral
pegs. For the American chordophones of similar construction, but
struck with hammers instead of
plucked, use **hammer dulcimers.**
UF American dulcimers
dulcimers, American
dulcimers, Appalachian
dulcimers, Kentucky
dulcimers, mountain
Kentucky dulcimers
mountain dulcimers
mountain zithers
zithers, mountain
RT hammer dulcimers

apparatus, drying
USE dryers

apparatus, photographic
USE photographic equipment

appareilles
HN May 1991 descriptor deleted

apparels
PJ.3000
ALT apparel
SN Rectangular panels used to decorate
albs, amices, dalmatics, and tunicles;
made of precious materials, in brocade, appliqué, or a variety of needlework techniques.

appentices
PJ.946
HN April 1993 related term added
March 1993 descriptor moved
June 1990 scope note changed
ALT appentice
SN Use to designate minor structures
with roofs of single slope built
against the sides of buildings. For
freestanding structures of this type,
use **lean-tos.**
UF pentices
pents
RT lean-tos

apple, common
USE applewood

apple corers
USE corers

apple parers
TH.127
HN April 1993 descriptor added
ALT apple parer
SN Cranked, but not necessarily geared,
devices of wood or iron for mechan-
ically paring apples. (HEARTH)
UF apple peelers
parers, apple
peelers, apple

apple peelers
USE apple parers

apple presses
USE cider presses

apple, wild
USE applewood

applewood
MT.2850
HN March 1992 descriptor moved
UF apple, common
apple, wild
common apple
malus
Pyrus malus
wild apple

application forms
VW.40
HN November 1992 descriptor moved
ALT application form
SN Forms used by persons requesting
assistance, authorization, employ-
ment, admission, or other action.
UF forms, application

applications, job
USE job applications

applied arts
USE decorative arts

applied columns
USE engaged columns

applied decoration
DG.2
HN November 1992 descriptor added
SN Use for decorative forms that are
attached to the surface of an object
after the object has been formed.
UF applied ornament
applied relief
decoration, applied
ornament, applied
relief, applied

applied linguistics
KD.44   (L)
SN Application of the findings of linguistic science to practical language
problems, such as language teaching, lexicography, translation, and
speech therapy. (ERIC9)
UF linguistics, applied

applied mathematics
KD.147
UF mathematics, applied

applied moldings
PJ.744
HN April 1993 descriptor moved
January 1992 lead-in terms added
ALT applied molding
SN Moldings which are nailed, laid on,
or otherwise fastened to the work
rather than cut into the solid material. (HAS)
UF applied trim
moldings, applied
moldings, planted
planted moldings
trim, applied

applied ornament
USE applied decoration

applied physics
KD.192
HN April 1993 scope note added
April 1993 lead-in terms added
December 1992 descriptor moved
SN Field concerned with the application
of techniques developed in engineering to problems in physics, and
the application of new concepts developed in the basic sciences, particularly physics, to engineering
problems.
UF engineering physics
physics, applied
physics, engineering

applied relief
USE applied decoration

applied science
USE technology

applied trim
USE applied moldings

applied work
SEE appliqué

appliqué
    KT.1218 (L,R)
HN March 1993 lead-in terms added
    March 1993 descriptor moved
    August 1992 scope note added
    June 1991 descriptor moved
ALT appliquéd
UK applied work
SN Technique of forming a design by applying cut out pieces of a material to a ground material; generally associated with needleworking but also used in ceramics, leatherworking, woodworking, and metalworking.
UF appliquéing
    laid on work
    laid work
    onlay
    work, laid
    work, laid on

appliqué, chintz
USE broderie perse

appliqué, cretonne
USE broderie perse

appliqué, cut-out chintz
USE broderie perse

appliqué, inlaid
USE reverse appliqué

appliqué, inlay
USE reverse appliqué

appliqué perse
USE broderie perse

appliqué, reverse
USE reverse appliqué

appliquéing
USE appliqué

appointing
    KG.216 (L)
HN April 1993 lead-in term added
    February 1991 alternate term added
ALT appointed
SN Naming to or placing in an office or position. (RHDEL2)
UF appointment

appointment
USE appointing

appointment books
    VW.333
HN November 1992 descriptor moved
ALT appointment book
SN Books for recording engagements; usually containing calendars.
UF books, appointment
    books, date
    date books

apportioning
    KG.264 (L)
HN January 1991 scope note added
ALT apportioned
SN Dividing and assigning according to some rule of proportional distribution.

appraisal
USE appraising

appraisals
    VW.562 (L,B)
HN November 1992 descriptor moved
ALT appraisal
SN Printed or written statements of evaluation or estimate of the market or other value, cost, utility or other attribute of land, buildings, works of art, or other objects of property, by qualified persons.

appraisers
    HG.615 (L)
HN December 1992 alternate terms added
ALT appraiser
    appraiser's
    appraisers'
SN Persons who engage in appraising.
UF evaluators

appraising
    KG.82 (L,B)
HN April 1993 lead-in term added
    February 1991 alternate term added
ALT appraised
SN Determining an item's market value, as done by the estimate of an authorized person.
UF appraisal
    valuation

appreciation, art
USE art appreciation

apprehension
USE perception

apprentices
    HG.891 (L,B,R)
HN January 1993 alternate terms added
ALT apprentice
    apprentice's
    apprentices'
SN Persons who learn by practical experience under skilled workers a trade or art, usually for a prescribed period of time and for a prescribed compensation. (W)

apprenticeship agreements
USE articles of apprenticeship

apprenticeship, articles of
USE articles of apprenticeship

approach, global
USE globalism

approach-light beacons
USE approach lights

approach lights
    RM.219
HN April 1993 descriptor moved
    May 1990 descriptor added
ALT approach light
SN Aeronautical ground lights indicating a desirable line of approach to a landing area. (MHDSTT)
UF approach-light beacons
    beacons, approach-light
    lights, approach

approach roads
USE access roads

approach, worldwide
USE globalism

approaches, bridge
USE bridge approaches

appropriate technology
    BM.1102 (L,B)
UF alternative technology
    intermediate technology
    technology, alternative
    technology, appropriate
    technology, intermediate

appropriated imagery
USE appropriation

appropriated images
USE appropriation

appropriation
    BM.221
HN February 1992 lead-in terms added
    May 1990 descriptor added
SN In Postmodern art, the practice of borrowing pre-existing forms or images in order to bring into question issues of originality in art.
UF appropriated imagery
    appropriated images
    appropriationism
    imagery, appropriated
    images, appropriated

appropriationism
USE appropriation

approved schools
USE reformatories

approximate symmetry
    BM.91
SN The use of similar forms around a center of balance. The forms may give a feeling of equal relationships, but are varied to prevent visual monotony.
UF dynamic symmetry
    symmetry, approximate
    symmetry, dynamic

apricot
    MT.2875 (L)
HN March 1992 descriptor moved

apricot gum
    MT.1051
HN April 1992 descriptor moved

SN A clear, pale gum that exudes from apricot trees. (MAYER)
UF gum, apricot

apron pieces
PJ.2400
HN March 1993 descriptor moved
November 1990 scope note changed
ALT apron piece
SN Pieces of lumber protruding from a wall to support carriage pieces or strings of a wooden stair at their upper ends or at landings. (MEANS)
UF pieces, apron
pieces, pitching
pitching pieces

apron pieces (furniture components)
USE aprons (furniture components)

apron pieces (stage components)
USE forestages

apron stages
USE forestages

aprons (costume)
TE.272   (H,L,N,R)
ALT apron (costume)
SN Garments worn over main garments for protection and sometimes ornamentation. Usually cover the front of the body and tie at the waist with strings, but may have a bib or shoulder straps.
RT <costume accessories worn>

aprons (furniture components)
PJ.2704   (N)
HN March 1993 descriptor moved
ALT apron (furniture component)
SN Extensions below the bottom edge of the seat of a chair, or frame of a table or cabinet. (BEARD)
UF apron pieces (furniture components)
lambrequins (furniture components)
pieces, apron
skirts (furniture components)

aprons (stages)
USE forestages

apse aisles
USE ambulatories

apses
PJ.1198   (A,L,B,R)
HN March 1993 descriptor moved
ALT apse
SN Use for semicircular or polygonal extensions off of a larger space; common in Roman basilicas and Christian churches.
UF tribunes (apses)

apses, counter
USE counter apses

apsidal buildings
RK.16   (A,B)
HN December 1991 scope note added
ALT apsidal building
SN Use for buildings the plans of which

feature at least one apse, the most common arrangement being one apse at the end of the longitudinal axis.
UF buildings, apsidal

apsidioles
PJ.1199
HN March 1993 descriptor moved
ALT apsidiole
SN Small apses, especially those which project from a larger apse.

Apulian
FL.2721   (L)

apungas
USE ponges

Aq Qoyunlu
USE Akkoyunlu

aqua
USE light bluish green
light greenish blue

aqua ammonia
USE ammonia water

aqua blue
USE light greenish blue
very light greenish blue

aqua blue, light
USE pale blue
very light greenish blue

aqua blue, pale
USE very pale blue

aqua, bright
USE brilliant bluish green
light bluish green
light greenish blue
very light greenish blue

aqua fortis
MT.2480
SN Latin for nitric acid, a dilution of which is the principal mordant used in etching.

aqua gray
USE bluish gray
grayish blue
light bluish gray
pale green

aqua green
USE light bluish green
light greenish blue

aqua green, bright
USE brilliant bluish green
light bluish green
very light bluish green

aqua green, light
USE pale green
very light bluish green

aqua green, pale
USE very light bluish green
very pale green

aqua, light
USE pale blue
pale green
very light greenish blue

aqua, pale
USE very pale blue
very pale green

aqua regia
MT.3074
HN February 1992 descriptor moved
SN Acid used for dissolving or testing gold and platinum; consisting of three parts hydrochloric acid and one part nitric acid. (MH)

Aqua-Tec (TM)
USE acrylic paint

aquamaniles
TQ.74   (H)
ALT aquamanile
SN Ewers used for washing hands, especially those made of pottery and used in Roman times, and metal versions, often in animal forms, made in the Medieval period, used for hand washing at the table.

aquamarine
MT.518
HN April 1992 descriptor moved
February 1992 related term added
February 1992 scope note added
SN A transparent, light bluish green gem variety of beryl. (AGI)
RT gemstone

aquamarine (color)
USE light greenish blue
pale blue

aquamarine green
USE moderate bluish green

aquaplanes
TV.82   (N)
ALT aquaplane
SN Use for small platforms designed to skim over the water when towed at high speed by motorboats and upon which riders stand during certain aquatic sports.

aquarelle
KT.440
HN July 1990 lead-in terms added
SN Use for watercolor painting done in transparent washes of color as distinguished from the opaque method using gouache.
UF transparent watercolor
watercolor, transparent

aquariums (buildings)
RK.368   (A,L,N,B,R)
HN March 1993 descriptor changed, was **aquariums**
March 1993 alternate term changed, was **aquarium**
ALT aquarium (building)

UF aquariums, public
   public aquariums

aquariums (containers)
   TQ.116   (H,L,N)
ALT aquarium (container)
 SN Term applied to a wide variety of
    glass-sided tanks, bowls, or the like
    in which fish or other aquatic ani-
    mals or plants are kept.

aquariums, marine
USE marine aquariums

aquariums, public
USE aquariums (buildings)

aquariums, saltwater
USE marine aquariums

Aquarius symbols
   DG.91   (R)
ALT Aquarius symbol

aquatic environments
   BM.319   (L)
 HN November 1992 descriptor added
 SN Environments completely or mainly
    under water.
 UF environment, underwater
    environments, aquatic
    environments, underwater
    underwater environment
    underwater environments

aquatint
   KT.681   (L,R)
 HN October 1991 descriptor moved
    October 1991 scope note changed
 SN A printing process in which resin or
    other substance is applied to a plate
    to make a porous ground, and the
    plate is then heated and etched,
    producing a range of tonal value;
    often combined with line work.
    (PRTT)

aquatint (photomechanical process)
USE photoaquatint

aquatint bags
USE dust bags

aquatint boxes
USE dust boxes

aquatint chambers
USE dust boxes

aquatint dust boxes
USE dust boxes

aquatint etching, lift-ground
USE lift-ground

aquatint, lift-ground
USE lift-ground

aquatint photogravure
USE photoaquatint

aquatint, sugar
USE sugar-lift

aquatint, sugar-lift
USE sugar-lift

aquatints
   VC.471   (L,R)
ALT aquatint
 SN Prints produced by the aquatint
    process.

aquatints, sand-grain
USE sandpaper aquatints

aquatints, sandpaper
USE sandpaper aquatints

aqueduct bridges
USE aqueducts

aqueducts
   RK.539   (A,L,B,R)
ALT aqueduct
 SN Use for artificial water channels for
    carrying water over long distances,
    usually by means of gravity, and for
    bridgelike structures that carry the
    channel or canal across a valley,
    river, or other obstacle.
 UF aqueduct bridges
    aqueducts, canal
    bridges, aqueduct
    bridges, canal
    canal aqueducts
    canal bridges

aqueducts, canal
USE aqueducts

aqueous
   DC.271   (L)
 HN October 1992 descriptor added
 SN Use to describe materials, solutions,
    or treatments that involve water.
 UF water-based

aqueous ammonia
USE ammonia water

<aqueous paint>
 HN August 1992 guide term deleted

Aquia Creek sandstone
   MT.902
 HN April 1992 descriptor moved
 UF Aquia sandstone
    sandstone, Aquia
    sandstone, Aquia Creek

Aquia sandstone
USE Aquia Creek sandstone

aquifers
   RD.109   (L)
ALT aquifer

Ar
USE argon

arabesques
   DG.122   (A,L,R)
 HN April 1993 scope note changed
    April 1993 related terms added
 SN Decorative patterns of stylized fo-
    liage characterized by a continuous
    stem which splits regularly, produc-
    ing a series of counterpoised, leafy,
    secondary stems. Used also gener-

ally for allover patterns of fanciful
foliate scrollwork.
 UF rumi
    waqwaq
 RT allover patterns
    scrollwork

Arabian
   FL.2969   (L,B)

*<Arabian Peninsula Islamic styles and
   periods>*
   FL.3558
 HN April 1993 guide term added

<Arabian periods>
   FL.2970

Arabic arches
USE horseshoe arches

Arabic figures
USE Arabic numerals

arabic, gum
USE gum arabic

Arabic numbers
USE Arabic numerals

Arabic numerals
   PJ.3504   (L)
ALT Arabic numeral
 SN The symbols 0, 1, 2, and so forth,
    derived from Arabic numerical no-
    tation in the late Middle Ages in
    Europe.
 UF Arabic figures
    Arabic numbers
    figures, Arabic
    numbers, Arabic
    numerals, Arabic

<Arabic scripts>
   PJ.3436

arabic tree, gum
USE Acacia

arable land
   RD.251
 UF land, arable

arachis oil
USE peanut oil

arae
   RK.1027
ALT ara
 SN Ancient Roman altars.

araghil
USE arghuls

Arak
   FL.3732
 HN April 1993 descriptor added
 UF Sultanabad (textile style)

Araks
USE Arak + rugs

Aranda
USE Arunta

Arapaho
    FL.1384   (L)

arariba
USE balaustre

Araucanian
    FL.1634   (L)
UF Mapuche

Arawak
    FL.1579   (L)

arbitrating
    KG.8   (L,B)
HN April 1993 lead-in term added
SN Determining disputes, as done by
    one or more outside, disinterested
    parties. (BOCLD)
UF arbitration

arbitration
USE arbitrating

arbitrators
    HG.507   (L,B)
HN December 1992 alternate terms
    added
ALT arbitrator
    arbitrator's
    arbitrators'

arbitrators, industrial
USE industrial arbitrators

arbor-vitae
USE American arbor vitae

arbor vitae, American
USE American arbor vitae

arboretums
    RM.25   (A,L,B,R)
HN April 1993 descriptor moved
ALT arboretum

arboriculture
    KD.104   (L)
HN February 1992 related term added
    April 1990 descriptor added
SN Raising and care of trees and
    shrubs, usually in gardens or for or-
    namental purposes. For the cultiva-
    tion and study of forest trees, use
    silviculture.
RT arboriculturists
    silviculture

arboriculturists
    HG.561
HN February 1993 descriptor moved
    December 1992 alternate terms
    added
    April 1990 descriptor added
ALT arboriculturist
    arboriculturist's
    arboriculturists'
RT arboriculture

arbors
    RK.1271   (A,R)
ALT arbor
SN Designates light, open structures
    formed from trees, shrubs, or vines

closely planted and twined together
to be self-supporting or supported
on a latticework frame.

Arbutus menziesii
USE madrona

arc brazing
    KT.1077
HN March 1993 descriptor moved
    March 1991 alternate term added
ALT arc-brazed
SN Brazing with an electric arc, that is,
    the electrical discharge between two
    electrodes.
UF brazing, arc

arc lamps
    PJ.2951   (L,R)
ALT arc lamp
SN Electric lamps in which the current
    is made to traverse an air gap be-
    tween two electrodes, usually of car-
    bon. The air in the gap as well as
    the two electrodes become heated to
    a brilliant incandescence.
UF arc lamps, Holmes
    arc lights
    Holmes arc lamps
    lamps, arc
    lamps, Holmes arc
    lights, arc

arc lamps, Holmes
USE arc lamps

arc lights
USE arc lamps

arc welders
USE arc welding machines

arc welding
    KT.1089   (L,B)
HN March 1991 alternate term added
ALT arc-welded
SN The joining of metal parts by fusion
    in which the necessary heat is pro-
    duced by means of an electric arc,
    that is, the electrical discharge be-
    tween two electrodes. (DAC)
UF electric arc welding
    electrical arc welding
    welding, arc
    welding, electric arc

arc-welding equipment
USE arc welding machines

arc welding machines
    TH.1282   (L,N)
ALT arc welding machine
UF arc welders
    arc-welding equipment
    electric welders
    equipment, arc-welding
    machines, arc welding
    welders, arc
    welders, electric

arc welding, shielded metal
USE shielded metal arc welding

arcades
    PJ.1421   (A,H,L,N,B,R)
HN March 1993 descriptor moved
ALT arcade
SN Use both for lines of arches raised
    on columns or piers and for covered
    walks with such lines of arches along
    one or both sides.

arcades (shopping arcades)
USE shopping arcades

arcades, amusement
USE amusement arcades

arcades, blank
USE blind arcades

arcades, blind
USE blind arcades

arcades, interlacing
USE interlacing arcades

arcades, intersecting
USE interlacing arcades

arcades, penny
USE penny arcades

arcades, shopping
USE shopping arcades

arcades, surface
USE blind arcades

arcades, video
USE video arcades

arcades, wall
USE blind arcades

arcading
    DG.126
HN January 1993 descriptor added
ALT arcaded
SN Decorative pattern imitating an ar-
    cade, as on a piece of furniture.

arcae
    TC.864
HN January 1993 descriptor moved
ALT arca
SN Chests for the safe-keeping of valu-
    ables usually made of wood and
    sheathed in iron; of a type made in
    the ancient and Medieval periods.
    (RICHTE)
UF arcula
    capsa
    cista
    loculus
    scrinium

arcanists
    HG.798
HN December 1992 alternate terms
    added
    March 1991 descriptor added
ALT arcanist
    arcanist's
    arcanists'
SN Persons professing a special secret
    knowledge concerning ceramics, es-

pecially the making of porcelain. (RHDEL2)

arch bands
USE archivolts

arch blocks
USE voussoirs

arch braces
PJ.1439
HN March 1993 descriptor moved
ALT arch brace
SN Curved braces, usually in pairs, used to support a roof frame and give the effect of an arch. (DAC)
UF braces, arch

arch brick
USE compass brick

arch bridges
RK.1215   (L)
ALT arch bridge
SN Bridges in which the main supporting elements are arches. (W)
UF bridges, arch

arch buttresses
USE flying buttresses

<arch components>
PJ.1638
HN April 1993 related term added
March 1993 guide term moved
RT <structural element components>

arch dams
RK.490   (L)
ALT arch dam
SN Use for dams resisting water pressure by use of the arch principle and having, in plan, the form of a single arch abutted by natural rock formation.
UF dams, arch

<arch, dome or vault components>
PJ.2011
HN March 1993 guide term moved

arch ribs
USE transverse ribs

arch-trusses, bowstring
USE bowstring trusses

archaeological illustration
HN May 1991 descriptor split, use archaeological (ALT of archaeology) + illustration

archaeological materials
USE archaeological objects

archaeological museums
HN March 1993 descriptor split, use archaeological (ALT of archaeology) + museums

archaeological objects
PE.94   (H)
HN December 1992 descriptor added
ALT archaeological object
SN Use for articles found in contexts of archaeological research, more specifically, those unearthed from periods before usually the 19th century and from extinct cultures. For articles originating in any culture still living or known through relatively recent history when those articles are the concern of ethnographic or ethnological study, prefer **ethnographic objects**.
UF archaeological materials
materials, archaeological
objects, archaeological

archaeological sites
RG.217
ALT archaeological site
UF sites, archaeological

archaeological societies
HN.79   (L,B)
ALT archaeological society
UF societies, archaeological

archaeological surveying
HN April 1993 descriptor split, use archaeological (ALT of archaeology) + surveying

archaeological trails
USE heritage trails

archaeologists
HG.446   (A,L)
HN April 1993 related term added
December 1992 alternate terms added
ALT archaeologist
archaeologist's
archaeologists'
RT archaeology

archaeologists, industrial
USE industrial archaeologists

archaeology
KD.203   (A,L,B,R)
HN April 1993 related term added
February 1992 scope note added
February 1991 alternate term added
ALT archaeological
SN Study of human history through the remnants of material culture, environment, and animal remains.
RT archaeologists

archaeology, classical
USE classical archaeology

archaeology, industrial
USE industrial archaeology

archaeology, marine
USE underwater archaeology

archaeology museums
USE archaeological (ALT of archaeology) + museums

archaeology, submarine
USE underwater archaeology

archaeology, underwater
USE underwater archaeology

archaeomagnetic dating
KT.183
HN November 1992 descriptor added
SN Method of dating by measuring the direction and intensity of the archaeomagnetism in materials and comparing the results to known records of fluctuations in the earth's magnetic field.
UF archaeomagnetism dating
dating, archaeomagnetic
dating, archaeomagnetism

archaeomagnetism
BM.757
HN November 1992 descriptor added
ALT archaeomagnetic
SN Use for remanence that is being examined or analyzed with regard to archaeological remains. When examined with regard to geologic materials, especially those predating human civilization, prefer **paleomagnetism**.

archaeomagnetism dating
USE archaeomagnetic dating

archaeometry
KD.204   (L,R)
SN Branch of archaeology that deals with the dating of archaeological specimens through scientific techniques, such as radiocarbon dating and amino-acid dating. (RHDEL2)
UF archeometry

Archaic (Greek)
FL.2652
HN March 1993 lead-in term added
May 1991 descriptor changed, was **Archaic**
UF Archaic period

Archaic (North American)
FL.769

Archaic (Persian pottery style)
FL.3112
HN April 1993 descriptor added
UF Archaic painted
painted, Archaic

Archaic (Preclassic)
USE Preclassic

Archaic, Boreal
USE Boreal Archaic

Archaic, Desert
USE Desert Tradition

Archaic, Early
USE Early Archaic

Archaic, Eastern
USE Eastern Archaic

Archaic, Hassuna
USE Hassuna Archaic

Archaic, Late
USE Late Archaic

Archaic, Middle
USE Middle Archaic

Archaic, Northern
USE Northern Archaic

Archaic painted
USE Archaic (Persian pottery style)
Hassuna Archaic

Archaic painted ware
USE Archaic (Persian pottery style) +
ware
Hassuna Archaic + ware

Archaic period
USE Archaic (Greek)
Early Dynastic (Egyptian)

Archaic ware
HN April 1993 descriptor split, use Archaic (Persian pottery style) +
ware

Archaic, Western
USE Western Archaic

archaism
BM.286   (L,R)

Archaistic
FL.2771

archangel fir
USE Scotch pine

archbishop-electors
HN February 1993 descriptor deleted

archbishoprics
USE archdioceses

archbishops
HG.402   (L,R)
HN February 1993 descriptor moved
December 1992 alternate terms
added
ALT archbishop
archbishop's
archbishops'
SN Bishops of the highest rank, who
preside over archdioceses. (RHDEL2)

archcitterns
TT.303
ALT archcittern
SN Bass citterns in use chiefly in France
and Germany in the 17th and 18th
centuries, patterned on the theorbo,
with two peg boxes, one for the on-
board strings which were stopped by
the fingers, and one for the off-
board unstopped strings. (MARCUS)

archdioceses
HN.29   (L)
HN February 1993 descriptor moved
February 1993 scope note added
ALT archdiocese
SN Administrative divisions of a
church, under the authority of an
archbishop.
UF archbishoprics

archduchies
HN.38
HN January 1993 descriptor added
ALT archduchy
SN Administrative bodies subject to an
archduke or archduchess.

arched
DC.60
HN October 1992 descriptor moved

arched barrel roofs
USE barrel roofs

arched butments
USE flying buttresses

arched buttresses
USE flying buttresses

arched harps
TT.223
ALT arched harp
SN Open harps in which the strings are
at one end attached to a resonator
and at the other to an onbuilt
curved neck rising away from it.
UF bow harps
harps, arched
harps, bow

arched stretchers
USE saltire stretchers

archeometry
USE archaeometry

archery ranges
RG.154
ALT archery range
UF ranges, archery

arches
PJ.1579   (A,L,N,B,R)
HN March 1993 descriptor moved
ALT arch
SN Structural elements, typically
curved, spanning openings and
transmitting vertical loads to either
side of the opening; also, structural
elements or freestanding structures
that resemble arches or act structurally like arches.

Arches (TM) paper
MT.1429
HN January 1993 lead-in term added
January 1993 descriptor changed,
was Arches paper
February 1992 descriptor moved
July 1990 descriptor added
UF Arches paper
Arches watercolor paper
paper, Arches
watercolor paper, Arches

arches, acute
USE lancet arches

<arches and arch components>
PJ.1578
HN March 1993 guide term moved

arches, Arabic
USE horseshoe arches

arches, back
USE back arches

arches, barrel
USE semicircular arches

arches, basket
USE three-centered arches

arches, basket handle
USE three-centered arches

arches, bell
USE bell arches

arches, blind
USE blind arches

arches, blunt
USE drop arches

arches, broken
USE broken pediments

<arches by form>
PJ.1580
HN March 1993 guide term moved

<arches by form: construction>
PJ.1606
HN March 1993 guide term moved

<arches by form: hinging>
PJ.1616
HN March 1993 guide term moved

<arches by form: number of centers>
PJ.1619
HN March 1993 guide term moved

<arches by form: plan>
PJ.1624
HN March 1993 guide term moved

<arches by function>
PJ.1627
HN March 1993 guide term moved

<arches by location or context>
PJ.1631
HN March 1993 guide term moved

arches, Byzantine
USE horseshoe arches

arches, camber
USE camber arches

arches, catenary
USE catenary arches

arches, chancel
USE chancel arches

arches, circular
USE semicircular arches

arches, compass-headed
USE semicircular arches

arches, composite
USE four-centered arches

arches, contrasted
USE ogee arches

arches, corbel
USE corbel arches

arches, counter
USE counter arches

arches, crescent
USE horseshoe arches

arches, cusped
USE cusped arches

arches, depressed
USE drop arches

arches, diaphragm
USE diaphragm arches

arches, discharging
USE relieving arches

arches, drop
USE drop arches

arches, Dutch
USE French arches

arches, elliptical
USE elliptical arches

arches, equilateral
USE equilateral arches

arches, equilateral pointed
USE equilateral arches

arches, extradosed
USE extradosed arches

arches, false
SEE corbel arches

arches, flat
USE flat arches

arches, Florentine
USE Florentine arches

arches, fluing
USE splayed arches

arches, foiled
USE cusped arches

arches, four-centered
USE four-centered arches

arches, four-centered Tudor
USE Tudor arches

arches, four-centred
SEE four-centered arches

arches, French
USE French arches

arches, gauged
USE gauged arches

arches, Gothic
USE pointed arches

arches, honorific
USE memorial arches

arches, horseshoe
USE horseshoe arches

arches, inflected
USE inverted arches

arches, inverted
USE inverted arches

arches, Italian pointed
USE Italian pointed arches

arches, jack
USE flat arches

arches, keel
USE ogee arches

arches, lancet
USE lancet arches

arches, lobed
USE cusped arches

arches, memorial
USE memorial arches

arches, miter
USE triangular arches

arches, monumental
USE memorial arches

arches, Moorish
USE horseshoe arches

arches, oblique
USE skew arches

arches, obtuse angle
USE drop arches

arches, ogee
USE ogee arches

arches, ogival
USE ogee arches

arches, one-centered
USE one-centered arches

arches, Palladian
USE Palladian windows

Arches paper
USE Arches (TM) paper

arches, peak
USE pointed arches

arches, pier
USE pier arches

arches, pointed
USE pointed arches

arches, pointed segmental
USE pointed segmental arches

arches, proscenium
USE proscenium arches

arches, raking
USE rampant arches

arches, rampant
USE rampant arches

arches, rear
USE back arches

arches, recessed
USE back arches

arches, relieving
USE relieving arches

arches, rising
USE rampant arches

arches, rollock
USE rowlock arches

arches, Roman
USE semicircular arches

arches, rough
USE relieving arches

arches, round
USE semicircular arches

arches, rowlock
USE rowlock arches

arches, safety
USE relieving arches

arches, sconcheon
USE back arches

arches, segmental
USE segmental arches

arches, semi-circular stilted
USE surmounted arches

arches, semicircular
USE semicircular arches

arches, semielliptical
USE elliptical arches

arches, Serlian
USE Palladian windows

arches, shouldered
USE shouldered arches

arches, single-center
USE one-centered arches

arches, skew
USE skew arches

arches, sluing
USE splayed arches

arches, soldier
USE soldier arches

arches, splayed
USE splayed arches

arches, squinch
USE squinches

arches, stepped
USE stepped arches

arches, stilted
USE stilted arches

arches, straight
USE flat arches

arches, strainer
USE straining arches

arches, straining
USE straining arches

arches, surbased
USE surbased arches

arches, surmounted
USE surmounted arches

arches, three-centered
USE three-centered arches

arches, three-centred
SEE three-centered arches

arches, three-hinged
USE three-hinged arches

arches, three-pinned
USE three-hinged arches

arches, transverse
USE transverse arches

arches, triangular
USE triangular arches

arches, triumphal
USE chancel arches
      triumphal arches

arches, trumpet
USE squinches

arches, Tudor
USE Tudor arches

arches, two-centered
USE two-centered arches

arches, two-centered segmental
USE pointed segmental arches

arches, two-centred
SEE two-centered arches

arches, two-hinged
USE two-hinged arches

Arches watercolor paper
USE Arches (TM) paper

archil
USE orchil

architect-consultant contracts
      VW.633
HN November 1992 descriptor moved
ALT architect-consultant contract
UF contracts, architect-consultant

architect-designed
      DC.31   (A,L,B)
HN October 1992 descriptor added
SN Use to describe objects or structures
      when emphasizing that they have
      been designed by architects.

architect-designed houses
HN March 1993 descriptor split, use ar-
      chitect-designed + houses

architects
      HG.259   (A,L,B,R)
HN February 1993 descriptor moved
      November 1992 alternate terms
      added

ALT architect
      architect's
      architects'

architects, associated
USE associated architects

architects, garden
USE landscape architects

architects, government
USE government architects

architects' homes
USE architects' (ALT of architects) +
      houses

architects' houses
HN April 1993 descriptor split, use ar-
      chitects' (ALT of architects) +
      houses

architects' lamps
      TC.1325
ALT architect's lamp
UF drafting lamps
      lamps, architects'
      lamps, drafting
      lamps, Luxo
      Luxo lamps

architects, landscape
USE landscape architects

architects, marine
USE naval architects

architects' marks
HN March 1993 descriptor split, use ar-
      chitects' (ALT of architects) +
      marks (symbols)

architects, military
USE military engineers

architects, naval
USE naval architects

architects' office buildings
USE architects' (ALT of architects) + of-
      fices

architects' offices
HN March 1993 descriptor split, use ar-
      chitects' (ALT of architects) + of-
      fices

architects, official
USE government architects

architects, project
USE project architects

architects, public
USE government architects

architects' rules
USE architects' scales

architects' scales
      TN.63   (N,B)
ALT architect's scale
SN Flat beveled or triangular bars, usu-
      ally of wood or plastic, with a variety
      of graduations so that scale draw-
      ings can be drawn and measured.

UF architects' rules
      draftsmen's scales
      rules, architects'
      scales, architects'
      scales, draftsmen's

architects, supervising
USE supervising architects

architectural acoustics
HN April 1993 descriptor split, use ar-
      chitectural (ALT of architecture)
      + acoustics

architectural associations
USE architectural societies

architectural bronze
      MT.398
HN March 1993 scope note changed
      March 1993 descriptor moved
SN Bronze of very high copper content,
      formulated for color.
UF art bronze
      bronze, architectural
      bronze, art

architectural canopies
USE canopies (structural elements)

architectural centers
      RK.654   (A,B)
HN October 1990 descriptor moved
ALT architectural center
SN Use for buildings constructed as re-
      source and information centers for
      documents, exhibitions, and other
      events and data of relevance to ar-
      chitects.
UF centers, architectural

architectural clubs
USE architectural societies

architectural criticism
      KD.22   (A,L,B,R)
HN April 1993 related term added
UF criticism, architectural
RT architectural critics

architectural critics
      HG.340   (A,L,B)
HN April 1993 related term added
      December 1992 alternate terms
      added
ALT architectural critic
      architectural critic's
      architectural critics'
UF critics, architectural
RT architectural criticism

architectural design
HN January 1993 descriptor split, use
      architectural (ALT of architecture)
      + design

architectural detailing
USE architectural drawing

architectural draftsmen
HN January 1993 descriptor split, use
      architectural (ALT of architecture)
      + draftsmen (technical)

architectural drawing
KT.388　　　　　　　　(A,L,B,R)
UF　architectural detailing
　　detailing, architectural
　　drawing, architectural

architectural drawings
VC.225　　　　　　　　(A,L,N,B)
HN　April 1992 descriptor moved
ALT　architectural drawing
SN　Use for drawings of architecture and drawings for architectural projects, whether the project was executed or not.
UF　drawings, architectural

architectural education
KD.262　　　　　　　　(A,H,B,R)
HN　October 1990 descriptor moved
UF　architectural training
　　education, architectural
　　training, architectural

architectural elements
PJ.1373　　　　　　　　(A)
HN　April 1993 scope note added
　　March 1993 descriptor moved
ALT　architectural element
SN　Forms, structural or decorative, developed originally or primarily as components of architecture, often adapted to other habitable spaces, such as in large vehicles, and often borrowed or imitated for structural or decorative use on other objects.
UF　elements, architectural

<architectural elements by building type>
PJ.2464
HN　March 1993 guide term moved

architectural engineering
HN　April 1993 descriptor split, use **architectural** (ALT of **architecture**) + **engineering**

architectural fantasies
USE　fantastic architecture

architectural firms
HN.108　　　　　　　　(A,L,R)
HN　April 1993 descriptor reinstated
　　March 1991 descriptor split, use architecture + firms
ALT　architectural firm
UF　firms, architectural

architectural follies
USE　follies

architectural frames
TC.416
ALT　architectural frame
SN　Use for frames which incorporate architectural features.
UF　frames, architectural

architectural furniture
TC.1198
HN　April 1993 lead-in term deleted, was **architect-designed furniture**
　　January 1993 descriptor moved
SN　Use for furniture designed by archi-

tects or to match or accord with the architectural features of the rooms for which it is intended.
UF　furniture, architectural

architectural glass
MT.310
HN　March 1993 descriptor moved
UF　glass, architectural

architectural guidebooks
HN　April 1993 descriptor split, use architectural (ALT of **architecture**) + **guidebooks**

architectural hardware
USE　finish hardware

architectural historians
HG.341　　　　　　　　(A,L)
HN　April 1993 related terms added
　　December 1992 alternate terms added
ALT　architectural historian
　　architectural historian's
　　architectural historians'
UF　historians, architectural
RT　architectural history
　　historians

architectural history
KD.23　　　　　　　　(A,L,B,R)
HN　April 1993 related terms added
SN　Study of the development over time of the human built environment.
UF　architecture, history of
　　history, architectural
　　history of architecture
RT　architectural historians
　　history

architectural libraries
HN　March 1993 descriptor split, use architectural (ALT of **architecture**) + **libraries (buildings)**

architectural lighting
PC.206　　　　　　　　(A,L)
HN　March 1993 descriptor moved
　　April 1991 scope note added
　　April 1991 lead-in term deleted, was **outline lighting**
　　April 1991 lead-in term deleted, was **decorative lighting**
SN　Lighting systems for the illumination of building elements, spaces, or exteriors for visual effects.
UF　lighting, architectural

architectural materials
USE　building materials

architectural mirrors
TC.1471
ALT　architectural mirror
SN　Use for mirrors contained in frames that have strong architectural features, often including side columns and pediments.
UF　mirrors, architectural

architectural models
HN　March 1991 descriptor split, use ar-

chitectural (ALT of **architecture**) + **models (representations)**

<architectural moldings by form>
PJ.2074
HN　April 1993 guide term moved
　　April 1993 scope note added
　　April 1993 guide term changed, was *<moldings by form>*
SN　Collocates descriptors for molding types originally developed in architecture, though often adapted for use on other objects.

<architectural moldings by form: motif>
PJ.2077
HN　April 1993 guide term moved
　　April 1993 guide term changed, was *<moldings by form: motif>*

<architectural moldings by form: section>
PJ.2091
HN　April 1993 guide term moved
　　April 1993 guide term changed, was *<moldings by form: section>*

<architectural moldings by location or context>
PJ.2116
HN　April 1993 guide term moved
　　April 1993 guide term changed, was *<moldings by location or context>*

architectural museums
HN　April 1993 descriptor split, use architectural (ALT of **architecture**) + **museums**

architectural orders
PJ.1424　　　　　　　　(A,L,B,R)
HN　March 1993 descriptor moved
ALT　architectural order
SN　In classical architecture, a particular ensemble of column with its entablature, having standardized details. (HAS)
UF　classical orders
　　orders, architectural
　　orders, classical

architectural photographers
HN　February 1993 descriptor split, use **architectural** (ALT of **architecture**) + **photographers**

architectural photography
HN　April 1993 descriptor split, use architectural (ALT of **architecture**) + **photography**

architectural presentation drawings
USE　presentation drawings (proposals)

architectural psychology
USE　environmental psychology

architectural records
VW.537
HN　November 1992 descriptor moved
ALT　architectural record
SN　Records documenting the design and construction of buildings or other structures.
UF　records, architectural

architectural renderings
USE   renderings

architectural schools
HN   May 1991 descriptor split, use archi-
      tectural (ALT of architecture) +
      schools

architectural societies
      HN.80   (A,B)
ALT   architectural society
UF   architectural associations
      architectural clubs
      associations, architectural
      clubs, architectural
      societies, architectural

Architectural Style
USE   Second Style

architectural surveys
HN   October 1992 descriptor deleted

architectural terracotta
      MT.192
HN   April 1992 descriptor moved
      October 1990 descriptor added
SN   A hard-burnt, glazed or unglazed
      clay unit used in building construc-
      tion, machine extruded or hand-
      made. (HAS)
UF   terracotta, architectural

architectural theory
      BM.250   (A,B,R)
UF   architecture, philosophy of
      philosophy of architecture
      theory, architectural

architectural toys
      TV.145   (A)
ALT   architectural toy
SN   Use for construction toys that are
      architectural or architectonic in
      form or purpose.
UF   toys, architectural

architectural training
USE   architectural education

architecture
      KD.15   (A,L,B,R)
HN   October 1990 alternate term added
ALT   architectural
SN   Art or science of designing and
      building structures, especially habit-
      able structures, in accordance with
      principles determined by aesthetic
      and practical or material considera-
      tions. Refers also to the structures
      created.

architecture, academic
USE   academic architecture

architecture, alpine
USE   hillside architecture

architecture, anonymous
USE   vernacular architecture

architecture, bank
USE   banks (buildings)

architecture, bizarre
USE   fantastic architecture

architecture, cave
USE   cave architecture

architecture, church
USE   churches

architecture, community
USE   participatory design

architecture, domestic
USE   dwellings

architecture, ecclesiastical
USE   religious buildings

architecture, fantastic
USE   fantastic architecture

architecture feinte
USE   fictive architecture

architecture, fictive
USE   fictive architecture

architecture, folk
USE   vernacular architecture

architecture, futuristic
USE   visionary architecture

<architecture genres>
      BM.165

architecture, grotto
USE   cave architecture

architecture, grouped domestic
USE   cluster housing

architecture, hillside
USE   hillside architecture

architecture, history of
USE   architectural history

architecture, imaginary
USE   fantastic architecture

architecture, indigenous
USE   vernacular architecture

architecture, industrial
USE   industrial buildings

architecture, landscape
USE   landscape architecture

architecture, library
USE   libraries (buildings)

architecture, liturgical
USE   religious buildings

architecture, marine
USE   naval architecture

architecture, military
USE   military buildings
      military engineering

architecture, mountain
USE   hillside architecture

architecture, museum
USE   museums

architecture museums
USE   architectural (ALT of architecture)
      + museums

architecture, naval
USE   naval architecture

architecture, non-pedigreed
USE   vernacular architecture

architecture, organic
USE   organic architecture

architecture parlante
USE   mimetic buildings

architecture, philosophy of
USE   architectural theory

architecture, primitive
USE   primitive architecture

architecture, programmatic
USE   mimetic buildings

architecture, religious
USE   religious buildings

architecture, rock-cut
USE   rock-cut architecture

architecture schools
USE   architectural (ALT of architecture)
      + schools

architecture, spontaneous
USE   vernacular architecture

architecture, temporary
USE   temporary buildings

architecture, trompe-l'oeil
USE   fictive architecture

architecture, vernacular
USE   vernacular architecture

architecture, visionary
USE   visionary architecture

<architrave components>
      PJ.1677
HN   March 1993 guide term moved
      March 1991 guide term added

architrave cornices
      PJ.1673
HN   March 1993 descriptor moved
      November 1990 lead-in terms
      added
ALT   architrave cornice
SN   Entablatures in which the cornice
      rests directly on the architrave, the
      frieze being omitted. (DAC)
UF   cornices, architrave
      entablatures, friezeless
      friezeless entablatures

architraves
      PJ.1676   (A)
HN   March 1993 descriptor moved
      March 1991 descriptor moved
ALT   architrave
SN   Includes the lowermost element of a
      classical entablature, and similar fea-

tures when carried around doorways or other openings.
UF epistyles

<architraves and architrave components>
PJ.1675
HN March 1993 guide term moved
March 1991 guide term added

archival
USE archival quality

archival calendars
VW.455   (L)
HN November 1992 descriptor moved
ALT archival calendar
SN Lists of descriptions of individual documents in a collection or of a specified kind, usually arranged in chronological order.
UF calendars, archival

archival catalogs
VW.456   (L)
HN November 1992 descriptor moved
ALT archival catalog
UF catalogs, archival

archival finding aids
USE finding aids

archival guides
VW.457
HN November 1992 descriptor moved
ALT archival guide
SN Includes finding aids that give a general account of the holdings of one or more archives, including background history, usually arranged by record group, thereunder by series; also, finding aids that describe the holdings of one or more archives relating to particular subjects or to specified types of documents. (ICA)
UF guides, archival

archival inventories
VW.458   (L)
HN November 1992 descriptor moved
October 1992 related term added
ALT archival inventory
SN Finding aids, whose normal unit of entry is the series. Usually include a brief history and description of the organization that produced the records, descriptive lists of each record series, and sometimes supplementary information, such as selective indexes. (SAA)
UF inventories, archival
RT inventories

archival processing
KT.599
SN Photographic processing designed to preserve a print or negative for as long as possible by protecting it against deterioration due to chemical reactions. For activities involving the arrangement and description of archival materials use **processing**

plus terms for the form of material being processed.

archival quality
DC.272
HN October 1992 descriptor added
SN Use broadly to describe materials, such as paper or mat board, or processing methods that are expected to allow items to be stored for extended periods of time without loss of quality.
UF archival
conservation quality
quality, archival
quality, conservation

archival registers
VW.459
HN November 1992 descriptor moved
ALT archival register
SN Finding aids developed at the Library of Congress to describe groups of papers, collections, and records by giving their provenance and conditions of administration, their scope and general content, including span and bulk dates, biographical notes about the person, group, or organization whose material it is, its arrangement, a container or folder listing, and, on occasion, selective document indexes. (SAA)
UF registers, archival

archive buildings
USE archives (buildings)

archive repositories
USE repositories

archives (buildings)
RK.655   (A,L,B,R)
HN January 1992 descriptor changed, was **archives**
January 1992 alternate term changed, was **archive**
April 1991 related term added
September 1990 lead-in terms added
ALT archive (building)
UF archive buildings
buildings, archive
RT collections

archives (rooms)
PJ.1126
HN March 1993 descriptor moved
January 1992 lead-in term deleted, was **rooms, archives**
January 1992 scope note added
January 1992 descriptor changed, was **archives rooms**
January 1992 alternate term changed, was **archives room**
ALT archive (room)
SN Rooms or sets of rooms for the systematic maintenance and storage of records and documents.

archives, family
USE family papers

archiving
KG.114
ALT archived
SN Filing or collecting (as records or documents) in an archive or other repository. (W)

archivists
HG.460   (L)
HN December 1992 alternate terms added
ALT archivist
archivist's
archivists'
SN Persons concerned with collecting, evaluating, systemizing, preserving, and making available for reference public records and documents of historical significance. (DOT)

archivolts
PJ.1639   (R)
HN March 1993 descriptor moved
November 1991 lead-in terms added
November 1990 scope note changed
ALT archivolt
SN Molded or decorated bands around an arch, as, for example, in a series framing a tympanum.
UF arch bands
bands, arch

archways
PJ.2299   (N)
HN March 1993 descriptor moved
November 1990 scope note changed
ALT archway
SN Use for openings under arches.

arcichitarras
USE chitarrones

arciviolataliras
USE liras da gamba

arcs doubleaux
USE transverse ribs

arcs formerets
USE wall ribs

<Arctic and Subarctic Native American styles>
FL.1210

arctic climate
USE polar climate

Arctic Inuit, Western
USE Western Arctic Inuit

<Arctic Native American styles>
FL.1211

arcuballistae
USE ballistae

arcula
USE arcae

Ardabil carpets
TC.93
ALT Ardabil carpet
SN Refers to two carpets traditionally

thought to have been made for use at the Ardabil shrine. Also, term applied to any carpet made in India, Turkey, Iran, or elsewhere that copies the original carpets made for use at the Ardabil shrine; and any 20th century carpet made in the area of Ardabil.
  UF Ardebibs
       Ardebil rugs
       Ardebils
       carpets, Ardabil
       rugs, Ardebil

Ardebibs
  USE Ardabil carpets

Ardebil rugs
  USE Ardabil carpets

Ardebils
  USE Ardabil carpets

area
     DC.92
  HN October 1992 descriptor moved

area code maps, telephone
  USE telephone area code maps

area drains
     PJ.885
  HN March 1993 descriptor moved
  ALT area drain
  SN Receptacles designed to collect surface or rainwater from open areas. (STEIN)
  UF drains, area

<area plans>
     VC.119
  HN April 1992 guide term moved

area rugs
     TC.27
  ALT area rug
  SN Use for decorative rugs which define a living space in a room by providing an often colorful focus. (ARCCM)
  UF rugs, area

area, vanishing
  USE vanishing area

area-ways
  SEE areaways

areas, commercial
  USE business districts

areas, development
  USE development areas

areas, growth
  USE growth centers

areas, historic
  USE historic districts

areas, metropolitan
  USE metropolitan areas

areas, picnic
  USE picnic areas

areas, recreation
  USE recreation areas

areas, residential
  USE residential districts

areas, rural
  USE rural areas

areas, spoil
  USE spoil banks

Areas, Standard Metropolitan Statistical
  USE Standard Metropolitan Statistical Areas

areas, statistical
  USE statistical areas

areas, unincorporated
  USE unincorporated areas

areas, urban
  USE urban areas

areas, wilderness
  USE wilderness areas

areaways
     PJ.974   (L)
  HN March 1993 descriptor moved
  ALT areaway
  UK area-ways
  UKA area-way
  SN Open subsurface spaces around a basement window or doorway, adjacent to the foundation walls. (PUTNAM)

arena theaters
     RK.889   (L,B)
  HN September 1990 scope note added
  ALT arena theater
  UK arena theatres
  UKA arena theatre
  SN Theaters in which seating for the audience surrounds the stage in the middle. (EAA)
  UF arenas (theaters)
       theaters, arena
       theaters-in-the-round
       theatres, arena
       theatres-in-the-round

arena theatres
  SEE arena theaters

arenaceous limestone
  USE siliceous limestone

arenaceous rock
  USE sandstone

Arenal
     FL.1036

arenas
     RK.990   (A,B)
  ALT arena
  SN Use both for buildings housing central stages, rings, or areas used for sports or other entertainment events and for the central open spaces of ancient amphitheaters.
  UF arenas, sports

       coliseums
       sports arenas

arenas (theaters)
  USE arena theaters

arenas, sports
  USE arenas

Arequipa
     FL.1729
  HN June 1991 descriptor moved

Arévalo
     FL.1032

Argand burners
     PJ.2905   (L,N)
  ALT Argand burner
  SN Burners employing a circular wick mounted between two metal tubes through which a current of air rises to feed the inside of the wick; also used for gas burners with multiple holes arranged in a circle with a hollow center providing a central draft.
  UF burners, Argand

Argand lamps
     TC.1307   (N)
  ALT Argand lamp
  SN Lamps with a burner that has a cylindrical wick sandwiched between two metal tubes that admit a current of air to the inside of the flame and a chimney to enclose the flame and direct air to the outside of it; use especially for such lamps with a separate fuel reservoir from which fuel is fed to the font and burner on the bird-fountain principle.
  UF lamps, Argand

Argentine
     FL.731   (L,B)

argentotype
  USE kallitype

arghools
  USE arghuls

arghuls
     TT.154
  ALT arghul
  SN Near Eastern double clarinets with one melody pipe with six fingerholes and one drone pipe, very much longer and with several detachable extensions to vary the pitch.
  UF araghil
       arghools
       arguls
  RT drone pipes
       melody pipes

argillaceous limestone
     MT.839
  HN April 1992 descriptor moved
  SN Limestone containing 10 to 50% clay. (STEIN)
  UF limestone, argillaceous

argillaceous rock
    MT.824
  HN May 1993 lead-in term changed, was **pelites**
      April 1992 descriptor moved
  SN Rock, especially limestone and sandstone, containing clay.
  UF pelite
      rock, argillaceous

argillaceous sandstone
    MT.891
  HN April 1992 descriptor moved
  UF sandstone, argillaceous

argillite
    MT.825   (L)
  HN March 1992 scope note changed
      March 1992 descriptor moved
  SN Compact argillaceous sedimentary rock that is cemented by silica. (W)

Argive Minyan
    FL.2748
  HN April 1993 descriptor added
  UF Minyan, Argive

Argive Minyan ware
  HN April 1993 descriptor split, use Argive Minyan + ware

Argive School
    FL.2772

Argive shields
  USE hoplite shields

argon
    MT.5   (L)
  HN January 1993 lead-in term added
      April 1992 descriptor moved
      December 1991 scope note changed
  SN Inert noble gas used in metalworking and as a filler for electric incandescent and fluorescent light bulbs.
  UF Ar

argon-potassium dating
  USE potassium-argon dating

arguls
  USE arghuls

argyles
    TQ.324
  ALT argyle
  SN Serving vessels in which gravy, sauce, or the like, is kept warm by hot water, or sometimes embers, contained in an internal chamber.
  UF gravy warmers
      warmers, gravy

Ariabel dark blue 300308
  USE Prussian blue

Aries symbols
    DG.92
  ALT Aries symbol

Arikara
    FL.1385   (L)
  UF Ree

aristo paper
    MT.1486
  HN April 1993 lead-in term changed, was **aristotype papers**
      February 1992 descriptor moved
  UF aristotype paper
      aristotypie
      paper, aristo
      paper, aristotype

aristocracy
    HG.19   (L,R)
  HN February 1993 related term added
      November 1991 descriptor moved
  SN Class of persons holding exceptional rank, power, and privileges in a society. (RHDEL2)
  RT aristocrats

aristocrats
    HG.996
  HN January 1993 descriptor added
  ALT aristocrat
      aristocrat's
      aristocrats'
  SN Members of the aristocracy.
  RT aristocracy

Aristotelianism
    BM.420   (R)
  HN January 1991 alternate term added
  ALT Aristotelian
  SN Philosophy incorporating essential features of the thinking of Aristotle. (W)

aristotype
    KT.510   (L)
  SN Used loosely for various photographic processes employing silver chloride printing-out paper with either gelatin or collodion as the binder; popular from the late 1880s to the early 20th century. At one time a trade name, but the term fell into generic use.

aristotype paper
  USE aristo paper

aristotypes
    VC.320
  HN April 1992 descriptor moved
  ALT aristotype

aristotypie
  USE aristo paper

Arita
    FL.2090

arithmetic
    KD.148   (L,R)

arithmetic progressions
    BM.703   (L)
  SN Sequences or series of mathematical objects or quantities, in which each entry is determined from its predecessors by some algorithm. (MHDSTT)
  UF arithmetic series

progressions, arithmetic
series, arithmetic

arithmetic series
  USE arithmetic progressions

Arizona flagstone
    MT.885
  HN April 1992 descriptor moved
  UF flagstone, Arizona

ark chests
  USE arks

ark curtains
  USE parokhets

ark curtains, Torah
  USE parokhets

arkose
  USE feldspathic sandstone

arks
    TC.823   (L,R)
  HN May 1993 related terms added
      January 1993 descriptor moved
  ALT ark
  SN Various forms of chests, coffers, and other covered receptacles generally made of strong and durable construction and used to store articles of great value, such as the Torah scrolls in synagogues.
  UF ark chests
      arks, holy
      Arks of the Law
      chests, ark
      holy arks
      shrines, Torah
      Torah shrines
  RT chests
      coffers (furniture)

arks, holy
  USE arks

arks, Noah's
  USE Noah's arks

Arks of the Law
  USE arks

arm chairs, continuous
  USE continuous-bow Windsor armchairs

<arm components>
    PJ.2716
  HN March 1993 guide term moved

arm-guards
  USE vambraces

arm lamps, mantel
  USE mantel lamps

arm lamps, swing
  USE swing arm lamps

arm pads
    PJ.2717
  HN March 1993 descriptor moved
      February 1993 lead-in term added
  ALT arm pad
  UF armpads

elbow pads
manchettes
pads, arm
pads, elbow

arm palettes
TH.745
HN February 1993 descriptor added
ALT arm palette
SN Palettes designed to be supported by the painter's forearm and larger than palettes held in the hand.
UF palettes, arm
palettes, studio
studio palettes

arm posts
USE arm supports

arm rails
PJ.2718
HN March 1993 descriptor moved
ALT arm rail
UF rails, arm

arm stumps
USE arm supports

arm supports
PJ.2719
HN March 1993 descriptor moved
ALT arm support
SN Vertical or curved uprights supporting the front end of chair arms.
UF arm posts
arm stumps
posts, arm
stumps, arm
supports, arm

armada chests
TC.873
HN January 1993 descriptor moved
ALT armada chest
SN 19th-century term for heavy iron-bound coffers used for the storage of valuables; generally of German make and rarely dating from before the 17th century. (DDA)
UF chests, armada

armadios
TC.914
HN May 1993 related terms added
January 1993 descriptor moved
ALT armadio
SN Italian cupboards, originally, a cassone with doors instead of a lid, but later (16th century) developing into a two-tiered piece similar to the English press cupboard. Generally having massive architectural decoration, including pilasters supporting a monumental cornice; frequently made for sacristies.
RT cassoni
press cupboards

armament
USE armor

armaria
TC.915

HN January 1993 descriptor moved
ALT armarium
SN Ancient Roman cupboards, generally having a rectangular case, mounted on feet, with doors reaching more or less from top to bottom, a gabled or flat top, and interior shelving. (RICHTE)

armarios
HN May 1993 descriptor deleted

armatures
PJ.3332
ALT armature
SN Rigid frameworks or skeletons used by sculptors to support plastic material during modeling.

armchairs
TC.452 (N)
HN May 1993 related terms added
January 1993 descriptor moved
ALT armchair
SN Term applied to a wide variety of chairs with arms, to distinguish them from side chairs which have no arms.
UF chaises à bras
RT curricles (chairs)
dining tables
hunting chairs
lolling chairs
Morris chairs
porters' chairs
reading chairs
side chairs
sleeping chairs
Sleepy Hollow chairs
student chairs

armchairs, 136
USE 136 armchairs

armchairs, cabriole
USE cabriole chairs

armchairs, continuous-bow Windsor
USE continuous-bow Windsor armchairs

armchairs, great
USE great chairs

armchairs, Plona folding
USE Plona folding armchairs

armchairs, Windsor low-back
USE low-back Windsor chairs

armchairs, Winsor continuous-bow
USE continuous-bow Windsor armchairs

armed conflicts
KM.2
HN December 1992 related term added
December 1992 scope note added
November 1990 descriptor added
ALT armed conflict
SN Use generally for occurrences of physical combat between or among people furnished with weapons.
RT jousts
revolutions

armed forces
HN.60 (L)
HN February 1991 related term added
UF armed services
forces, armed
military, the
services, armed
RT military personnel

armed services
USE armed forces

Armenian bole
USE bole
red bole

armets
TE.282
ALT armet
SN Close-fitting helmets with a rounded skull, large hinged cheekpieces overlapping on the chin, and a pivoted visor, in use from the 15th to the 17th century.

armies
HN.62 (L)
HN March 1992 related term added
ALT army
RT soldiers

armillae (jewelry)
TE.467 (H,N)
ALT armill (jewelry)
SN Archaeological term for bracelets or armlets, especially those worn by royalty and sometimes as part of the coronation regalia.
RT armlets
bracelets (jewelry)

armillae (stoles)
TE.169 (H,N,R)
ALT armilla (stole)
SN Stoles worn by a British king at his coronation.

armillary spheres
VW.1035 (L,N)
HN October 1992 descriptor added
ALT armillary sphere
SN Skeleton models of the celestial sphere, generally having the earth at the center, consisting of a framework of rings depicting the relative position of such astronomical elements as the celestial equator, the ecliptic, the zodiac, and the planets; developed by the ancient Greeks and used especially during the 14th through 16th centuries as an aid to navigation.
UF spheres, armillary

arming-caps
SEE arming caps

arming caps
PJ.3009
ALT arming cap
UK arming-caps
UKA arming-cap
SN Close-fitting cloth skullcaps, typi-

cally quilted, having a padded circlet and ear flaps which end in laces to be tied under the chin. They were worn in Medieval times under helmets and either under or over mail coifs, to prevent chafing and act as a buffer against the impact of blows.
UF caps, arming

arming-doublets
SEE arming doublets

arming doublets
PJ.3002
ALT arming doublet
UK arming-doublets
UKA arming-doublet
SN Quilted textile garments for the upper body with sleeves and often a skirt, furnished with laces for the attachment of armor pieces of hard material, and often inset with mail gussets for the armpits. They were worn in the 14th and 15th centuries under other armor for added protection and to prevent chafing.
UF doublets, arming

arming swords
TK.90
ALT arming sword
SN General term for fighting swords carried by mounted knights attached to the belt, used for both cutting and thrusting.
UF swords, arming

armlets
TE.468   (H,N,R)
ALT armlet
SN Ornamental bands or circlets worn on the upper arm. Use **bracelets (jewelry)** for similar articles worn on the lower arm.
UF armrings
RT armillae (jewelry)
   bracelets (jewelry)
   bullae

armoires
TC.1011   (N,R)
HN January 1993 descriptor moved
ALT armoire
SN Use with reference to French-styled wardrobes for the storage of clothing or linens.
UF buffets (armoires)

armoires à deux corps
TC.1012
HN January 1993 descriptor moved
ALT armoire à deux corps
SN French case furniture consisting of two cupboards, set one above the other, each with two doors, the front and sides of the upper cupboard being recessed. They generally have an architectural framework with pilasters and a crowning pediment. (DDA)

armoires à encoignure
USE encoignures

armoires à livres
USE bibliothèques

armoires-bibliothèque
USE bibliothèques

armoires bonnetières
USE bonnetières

armoires d'encoignure
USE encoignures

armoires dressoirs
USE dressers (cupboards)

armoires en bibliothèque
USE bibliothèques

armoires, mural
USE hanging cupboards

armonicas
TT.442   (L)
ALT armonica
SN Musical glasses developed by Benjamin Franklin around 1761, in which glass bowls fitted concentrically on a horizontal rod, the largest on the left, were turned by a crank attached to a pedal as the player rubbed the rims. In a slightly later development, the rims of the glasses were moistened automatically by means of a shallow trough of water which they barely touched as they rotated.

armor
TE.273   (H,L,N,B,R)
UK armour
SN Use generally for that category of costume designed to be worn or carried to protect the body in combat. Armor pieces which are always physical parts of or are affixed to other pieces and cannot function alone are collocated under *<armor components>*. For specifically groups of armor pieces designed as a whole to possess particular physical characteristics in order to suit a particular purpose or occasion, use **armors.**
UF armament
   suits of armor
RT *<armor components>*
   armors
   doublets

armor, body
USE body armor

<armor by form>
TE.274

<armor by function>
TE.365

<armor components>
PJ.3001
SN Collocates armor pieces which are physical parts of or are affixed to other pieces and cannot function alone. For individual armor pieces

which can be worn and function individually or in sets, use **armor.**
RT armor
   double pieces

armor, garnitures of
USE garnitures

<armor groupings>
PC.30

armor, horse
USE horse armor

armor-piercing bullets
TK.262   (N)
ALT armor-piercing bullet
SN Bullets designed to penetrate hard targets such as armored vehicles, generally consisting of a hard core inside a casing of softer metal.
UF bullets, armor-piercing

armor-piercing shells
TK.257
ALT armor-piercing shell
SN Artillery shells designed to penetrate hard targets such as armored vehicles and warships.
UF shells, armor-piercing

armor plates
PJ.296
HN April 1993 descriptor moved
ALT armor plate
SN Metal plates which protect the lower part of a door from kicks and scratches; similar to kickplates but covering the door to a greater height, usually 39 inches (1 meter) or more from the bottom of the door. (DAC)
UF plates, armor

armor, soft
USE soft armor

armored cable
PJ.774
HN March 1993 descriptor moved
   November 1992 scope note added
   November 1992 lead-in terms added
UK armoured cable
SN Rubber-insulated electrical wires wrapped with a flexible steel covering. (PUTNAM)
UF BX cable
   cable, armored
   cable, armoured
   cable, BX
   cable, metal-clad
   metal-clad cable

armored cars
TX.226   (L,N)
ALT armored car
SN Land vehicles with armorplated bodies and extra strong doors, locks, and windows, such as trucks for carrying money and valuables or auto-

mobiles specially designed for dignitaries.

UF cars, armored

armored personnel carriers
TX.130 (L,N)
ALT armored personnel carrier
SN Use for lightly armored, highly mobile, fully tracked vehicles primarily for transporting personnel on and off the battlefield; usually fitted with light armament.
UF APCs
carriers, armored personnel
personnel carriers, armored
RT tracklaying vehicles

armorers
HG.730 (L)
HN December 1992 alternate terms added
ALT armorer
armorer's
armorers'
UK armourers
UKA armourer
SN Persons that make armor or arms, or that repair, assemble, and test firearms. (W)

armorers' marks
HN March 1993 descriptor split, use armorers' (ALT of armorers) + marks (symbols)

armorial (porcelain style)
FL.3377
HN April 1993 descriptor added

armorial bindings
PJ.3352 (L)
ALT armorial binding
SN Bindings decorated with arms or other devices of royalty or nobility. (LG)
UF bindings, armorial

armorial carpets, Spanish
USE Admiral carpets

armorial porcelain
HN April 1993 descriptor split, use armorial (porcelain style) + porcelain

armorial ware
USE armorial (porcelain style) + porcelain

armories
RK.835 (A,H,L,N,B,R)
HN March 1993 related term added
ALT armory
SN Distinguished from arsenals by being used both for military training and storage of arms and equipment.
RT arsenals

armors
PC.31
ALT armor
UK armours
UKA armour

SN Use specifically for sets of armor pieces designed as a whole to possess particular physical characteristics, usually to suit a particular purpose. For the general meaning of all costume designed to be worn or carried to protect the body in combat, either entire sets or individual pieces, use **armor**.
UF suits of armor
RT armor

armors, barrier
USE armors for the barriers

<armors by function>
PC.35

armors, ceremonial
USE parade armors

armors, coat
USE coat armors

armors, field
USE field armors

armors, foot-combat
USE foot-combat armors

armors for the barriers
PC.47
ALT armor for the barrier
UK armours for the barriers
UKA armour for the barrier
SN Armors used in the 16th century for tournament combat fought on foot over a wooden barrier, emphasizing protection for the head, arms, and upper body.
UF armors, barrier
barrier armors
barriers, armors for the
barriers, armours for the

armors for the foot tourney
USE foot-combat armors

armors, half
USE half armors

armors, hosting
USE field armors

armors, parade
USE parade armors

armors, three-quarter
USE three-quarter armors

armors, tilt
USE tilt armors

armors, tournament
USE tournament armors

armour
SEE armor

armour, body
SEE body armor

armour, horse
SEE horse armor

armour, soft
SEE soft armor

armoured cable
SEE armored cable

armourers
SEE armorers

armours
SEE armors

armours, coat
SEE coat armors

armours, field
SEE field armors

armours, foot-combat
SEE foot-combat armors

armours for the barriers
SEE armors for the barriers

armours for the foot tourney
SEE foot-combat armors

armours, half
SEE half armors

armours, hosting
SEE field armors

armours, parade
SEE parade armors

armours, three-quarter
SEE three-quarter armors

armours, tilt
SEE tilt armors

armours, tournament
SEE tournament armors

armpads
USE arm pads

armrests
USE arms

armrings
USE armlets

arms
PJ.2706
HN March 1993 descriptor moved
March 1993 descriptor changed, was arms (furniture components)
March 1993 alternate term changed, was arm (furniture component)
ALT arm
SN Supports for the elbow and forearm used in seating furniture. (W)
UF armrests
elbows

arms (weapons)
USE weapons

<arms and arm components>
PJ.2705
HN March 1993 guide term moved

arms, balance
USE beams (balance components)

<*arms by form*>
PJ.2707
HN March 1993 guide term moved

<*arms by function*>
PJ.2714
HN March 1993 guide term moved

arms, candle
USE candle brackets

arms, coats of
USE coats of arms

arms, combined
USE combination guns

arms, edged
USE edged weapons

arms, hollowed
USE hollowed arms

arms, knuckled
USE knuckled arms

arms, martial
USE martial arms

arms, mast
USE brackets (lighting device components)

arms, military
USE martial arms

arms of the hilt
PJ.3134
SN Curving metal bands located one on each side of a sword hilt, between the quillons and the lower guard.
UF pas d'ânes

arms, open
USE open arms

arms, pole
USE staff weapons

arms, roll-over
USE rolled arms

arms, rolled
USE rolled arms

arms, scroll-over
USE scrolled arms

arms, scrolled
USE scrolled arms

arms, shoulder
USE long guns

arms, small
USE small arms

arms, swan
USE swan arms

arms, swan-neck
USE swan arms

arms, tablet
USE tablet-arm chairs
writing arms

arms, voluted
USE scrolled arms

arms, writing
USE writing arms

army bases
RG.132   (L)
HN March 1993 lead-in term added
ALT army base
UF army posts
bases, army
posts, army

army camps
RG.138   (B)
ALT army camp
UF camps, army

army housing
USE military housing

army posts
USE army bases

Arnaudon's green
USE chromium oxide green

Arnhem Land
FL.3752   (L)

Arnoaldi
FL.2827

aromas
USE odors

aromatic hydrocarbon
MT.2429
HN April 1993 lead-in term changed, was **aromatic solvents**
April 1993 descriptor changed, was **aromatic hydrocarbons**
SN One of four main types of hydrocarbon found in crude oil belonging to the class of organic compounds that has an unsaturated ring of carbon atoms, considered generally more volatile and active than an oliphatic hydrocarbon. (GOTTS)
UF aromatic solvent
hydrocarbon, aromatic
solvent, aromatic

aromatic solvent
USE aromatic hydrocarbon

aromatic vinegar boxes
USE vinaigrettes

arpanettas
TT.390
ALT arpanetta
SN Upright double psalteries with a trapeziform box acting as a soundboard between two rows of strings.

arpeggiones
TT.234   (L)
ALT arpeggione
SN Fiddles combining qualities of the guitar and the violoncello, being smooth-waisted like a guitar, with a guitarlike tuning and fitted with 24 frets, but of the size of the violon-

cello and bowed in the same manner.
UF bowed guitars
guitar violoncellos
guitares d'amour
guitars, bowed
violoncellos, guitar

arquebuses
USE harquebuses

Arraiolos carpets
TC.120
ALT Arraiolos carpet
SN Embroidered rugs named after and made in Arraiolos, Portugal. The technique is herringbone or cross-stitch on a linen cloth foundation. (EB1584)
UF Arraiolos rugs
carpets, Arraiolos
rugs, Arraiolos

Arraiolos rugs
USE Arraiolos carpets

arrangers
HG.214
HN February 1993 descriptor moved
November 1992 alternate terms added
ALT arranger
arranger's
arrangers'
SN Persons who transcribe music for voices or instruments for which it was not originally written or adapt it to a style suitable to a particular group of performers. (W)

arrangers, flower
USE floral designers

arrangers, makeup
USE makeup arrangers

arras
USE tapestries

arrests
USE lance rests

arrests, lance
USE lance rests

Arretine
FL.2846   (L)
HN April 1993 descriptor added

Arretine pottery
USE Arretine + ware

Arretine ware
HN April 1993 descriptor split, use Arretine + ware

arricciato
USE arriccio

arriccio
MT.1873
HN November 1992 related term added
SN In the preparation of a wall for fresco, the second coat of plaster,

over the roughcast and under the intonaco. (PDAT)
UF arricciato
brown coat
RT frescoes

arrière-voussures
USE back arches

arris gutters
PJ.890
HN March 1993 descriptor moved
November 1990 scope note changed
ALT arris gutter
SN V-shaped gutters usually of wood.
UF gutters, arris

arris tile
HN November 1992 descriptor deleted

arrondissements
HN.15
HN February 1993 descriptor moved
February 1993 scope note changed
ALT arrondissement
SN Divisions of French departments and some French cities.

<arrow components>
PJ.3153
RT arrows
shafts (tool components)

arrow feet
USE therm feet

arrow loops
USE loopholes

arrow-root
SEE arrowroot

arrow spindles
PJ.2880
HN March 1993 descriptor moved
ALT arrow spindle
UF spindles, arrow

arrowheads
PJ.3154   (L,N)
ALT arrowhead
SN The pointed or edged heads of arrows.
RT projectile points

arrowroot
MT.1284   (L)
HN April 1992 descriptor moved
UK arrow-root
SN A nutritive starch obtained from the rootstock of the arrowroot plant. (W)
UF arrowroot starch
starch, arrowroot

arrowroot starch
USE arrowroot

arrows
TK.236   (H,L,N,R)
ALT arrow
SN Projectiles generally consisting of a straight, slender shaft with a sharp point or carrying a sharp edged or

pointed head of stone or metal, shot from a bow. More developed versions also had flights near the butt to stabilize their trajectory.
RT <arrow components>
bows (weapons)
edged weapons
nocks

arroyos
RD.158   (L)
ALT arroyo
SN Use for flat-bottomed and often steep-walled dry watercourses occupied by streams only after heavy rains; common in the southwest United States.

Arsacid
USE Parthian

Arsari
USE Ersari

arsenals
RK.816   (A,L,B,R)
HN March 1993 related term added
ALT arsenal
SN Distinguished from **armories** by being exclusively a repository or magazine for arms and military equipment.
RT armories

arsenate, chromated copper
USE chromated copper arsenate

arsenate, pale cobalt
USE pale cobalt arsenate

Arsenblende
USE orpiment

arsenic
MT.6   (L)
HN April 1992 descriptor added
SN A grayish-white element having a metallic luster, vaporizing when heated, and forming poisonous compounds. (RHDEL2)
UF As

arsenic orange
USE realgar

arsenic yellow
USE orpiment

arsenikon
USE orpiment

arsonists
HG.912
HN January 1993 descriptor added
ALT arsonist
arsonist's
arsonists'
SN Those who set fire to buildings, vehicles, or other property with criminal intent.
UF incendiaries

art
KD.18   (A,L,B,R)

HN March 1991 scope note changed
SN Use with reference to the study or practice of the fine arts or the fine and decorative arts together. With reference to the visual and performing arts together, use **arts**. For actual works or objects of the fine or decorative arts, use **works of art** or **art objects**.

art, academic
USE academic art

art academies
USE art + schools

art, air
USE air art

art, amateur
USE amateur art

art, apocalyptic
USE apocalyptic art

art appreciation
KD.263   (L,R)
HN October 1990 descriptor moved
UF appreciation, art

Art Autre
USE Art Informel

art, body
USE body art

art, book
USE artists' books

art bronze
USE architectural bronze

art brut
BM.177   (L,R)
HN May 1993 related term added
SN Use for art where the artistic impulse appears in a raw, uncivilized state, particularly work created by people isolated from society such as prisoners and the mentally ill. Use **amateur art** when referring to any art created by nonprofessionals.
UF art of the insane
art, outsider
art, psychiatric
art, psychotic
art, raw
brut, art
insane, art of the
l'art brut
outsider art
psychiatric art
psychotic art
raw art
RT amateur art

art, cave
USE cave art

art centers
RK.1135   (A,L,B)
ALT art center
UF art centers, community

centers, art
community art centers

art centers, community
USE art centers

art centres
SEE performing arts centers

art, children's
USE children's art

art, clip
USE clip art

art colleges
USE art + schools

art colonies
USE artists' colonies

art, commercial
USE commercial art

art commissions
HN.95 (L,R)
ALT art commission
SN Governmental agencies having administrative, legislative, or judicial powers concerning the arts.
UF agencies, state art
arts agencies, state
commissions, art
state arts agencies

art, community
USE community art

art, computer
USE computer art

Art Concret
USE Concrete art

art, Concrete
USE Concrete art

art, copy
USE copy art

art, corporal
USE body art

art, correspondence
USE mail art

art, court
USE court art

art criticism
KD.24 (L,R)
HN April 1993 related term added
UF criticism, art
RT art critics

art critics
HG.342 (A,L,R)
HN April 1993 related term added
December 1992 alternate terms added
ALT art critic
art critic's
art critics'
UF critics, art
RT art criticism

Art Deco
FL.3342 (A,L,B,R)
UF American Deco
Art Décoratif
Art Moderne
Jazz Modern
Modern, Jazz
Moderne
Style Moderne

Art Décoratif
USE Art Deco

art, devotional
USE devotional images

art, didactic
USE didactic art

art, Direct
USE Direct art

art directors
HG.266 (L)
HN February 1993 descriptor moved
November 1992 alternate terms added
ALT art director
art director's
art directors'
SN Persons who formulate concepts and supervise workers engaged in executing layout designs for art work and copy to be presented by visual communications media, such as magazines, books, newspapers, television, film, posters, and packaging. (DOT)
UF directors, art

art, dissident
USE dissident art

art, distributional
USE floor pieces

art, earth
USE earthworks (sculpture)

art, eco
USE earthworks (sculpture)

art, ecological
USE earthworks (sculpture)

art education
KD.264 (L,B,R)
HN October 1990 descriptor moved
UF education, art

art, environmental
USE environmental art

art, ethnic
USE ethnic art

art, event
USE happenings

art, fantastic
USE fantastic art

art, fiber
USE fiber art

art, fibre
SEE fiber art

art, figurative
USE figurative art

art, floor
USE floor pieces

art, folk
USE folk art

art for art's sake
BM.222 (L,R)
HN April 1990 descriptor added
UF l'art pour l'art

art, funerary
USE funerary art

art furniture
TC.1199
HN January 1993 descriptor moved
SN Term applied in the 1860s to furniture produced by firms which employed leading designers and architects. Designs tended toward simple forms with hand-carved and painted decoration.
UF furniture, art

art galleries
RK.140 (A,L,B,R)
ALT art gallery
SN Use only for stores in which works of art are displayed for sale.
UF art galleries, commercial
commercial art galleries
galleries (art galleries)
galleries, art

art galleries (museums)
USE art + museums

art galleries, commercial
USE art galleries

<art genres>
BM.173

<art genres by medium>
HN October 1991 guide term deleted

art glass
PE.131 (L,R)
HN January 1993 descriptor moved
January 1991 descriptor added
SN Glassware, of the mid- to late 19th century, that was made for ornamental more than for utilitarian purposes and that incorporated newly developed techniques for producing colors and surface textures.
UF glass, art

art, ground
USE floor pieces

art historians
HG.343 (A,L,R)
HN April 1993 related terms added
December 1992 alternate terms added
ALT art historian

art historian's
art historians'
UF historians, art
RT art history
historians

art history
KD.25 (L,B,R)
HN April 1993 related terms added
SN Study of man-made visual forms in periods from prehistory to the present, including their use in communication, decoration, and aesthetic and intellectual stimulation.
UF history, art
history of art
RT art historians
history

Art in motion
USE Kinetic

Art Informel
FL.3853 (R)
UF Art Autre
Informal art
L'Art informel

art, junk
USE junk sculpture

art, land
USE earthworks (sculpture)
environmental art

art, laser
USE laser art

art libraries
HN April 1993 descriptor split, use **art** + **libraries (buildings)**

art, light
USE light art

art, line
USE line copy

art, mail
USE mail art

art market
KG.253 (L,R)
HN January 1991 scope note changed
November 1990 descriptor moved
January 1990 lead-in terms added
SN Use for the buying, selling, and trading of works of art.
UF art trade
market, art
trade, art

art materials
USE artists' materials

art, Matter
USE Matter art

art metalworking
HN December 1992 descriptor deleted

Art Moderne
USE Art Deco

art, mourning
USE funerary art

art, multimedia
USE multimedia works

art, municipal
USE public art

art museums
HN April 1993 descriptor split, use **art** + **museums**

art, naive
USE naive art

art, nonconformist
USE dissident art

art, nonfigurative
USE nonrepresentational art

art, nonrepresentational
USE nonrepresentational art

Art Nouveau
FL.3343 (A,L,B,R)
UF Arte Joven
Modern Style (Art Nouveau)
Modernismo
Nieuwe Kunst
Palingstijl
Quaint Style
Style Guimard
Yachting Style

art, object
USE object sculpture

art, objective
USE figurative art

art objects
PE.6 (L,B,R)
HN December 1992 descriptor moved
March 1991 scope note changed
November 1990 descriptor moved
ALT art object
SN Use for works of the fine or decorative arts when their qualities as discrete and coherent individual objects are emphasized, e.g., in relation to conservation or inventorying. When the aesthetic nature of works is emphasized, use **works of art**. When referring to the study or practice of the fine arts or the fine and decorative arts together, use **art**.
UF objects, art
objets d'art
objets de vertu

art of the insane
USE art brut

art, Op
USE Op art

art, Optical
USE Op art

art, outsider
USE art brut

art, peasant
USE folk art

art, performance
USE performance art

art, philosophy of
USE aesthetics

art photography
FL.1776 (L)
HN April 1990 descriptor added
SN Use for the movement in England and the United States, from around 1890 into the early 20th century, which promoted various aesthetic approaches. Historically, has sometimes been applied to any photography whose intention is aesthetic, as distinguished from scientific, commercial, or journalistic; for this meaning, use **photography**. For discussion of photography as a fine art, use **photography** plus **art theory**. Regarding photography of art, use **photography** plus **art objects** or **works of art**.
UF artistic photography
fine art photography
photography, art
photography, artistic
photography, fine art

art, postal
USE mail art

art pottery
PE.104 (L)
HN January 1993 descriptor moved
October 1990 descriptor added
SN Ornamental pottery produced by artists and craftsmen who emphasized the artistic nature of their work; of a type closely associated with the Arts and Crafts movement.
UF pottery, art

Art Povera
USE Arte Povera

art, primitive
USE primitive art

art, Procedural
USE Process art

art, Process
USE Process art

art, psychiatric
USE art brut

art, psychotic
USE art brut

art, public
USE public art

art, raw
USE art brut

art, representational
USE figurative art

art, reprographic
USE copy art

art restoration laboratories
USE conservation + laboratories

art, rock
USE rock art

art schools
HN May 1991 descriptor split, use **art + schools**

art, scrap
USE junk sculpture

art, sequential
USE serial art

art, serial
USE serial art

art, series
USE serial art

art, sofa
USE sofa art

art, soft
USE soft sculpture

art squares
TC.126
ALT art square
SN Late-19th-century ingrain carpets which were woven in one piece, with border and fringe. They could be used as crumbcloths, and were easy to move and clean.
UF big floor rugs
rugs, big floor
squares, art
RT crumbcloths

art, street
USE street art

art supplies
USE artists' materials

art, Systems
USE Systems art

art theory
BM.253   (H,B,R)
UF theory, art

art therapy
KD.26   (H,L)
SN Study and practice of the therapeutic use of images and objects, to foster nonverbal communication, creativity, and physical interaction, and to uncover verbal associations and interpretations, helping to identify and understand patients' emotional, motor, and perceptual dysfunctions.
UF creative arts therapy
therapy, art
therapy, creative arts

art, total
USE happenings

art trade
HN January 1991 descriptor deleted, made lead-in to **art market**

art trade
USE art market

art unions
HN.68
HN July 1990 descriptor added
ALT art union
SN 19th-century associations for promoting the arts, especially through the distribution of paintings and prints by lottery. (W)
UF unions, art

art, unofficial
USE dissident art

art, video
USE video art

art, visionary
USE fantastic art

art, word
USE visual poetry

art, works of
USE works of art

art, xerographic
USE copy art

art, Xerox
USE copy art

Arte Joven
USE Art Nouveau

Arte Metafisica
USE Metaphysical

Arte Povera
FL.3855   (L,R)
UF Art Povera

artefacts
USE artifacts

arterial roads
USE arterial streets
arterials

arterial streets
RM.151   (B)
HN April 1993 descriptor moved
ALT arterial street
SN Urban thoroughfares handling major portions of traffic, often larger than most streets and having medians; use primarily when referring to the flow of traffic within a transportation system.
UF arterial roads
roads, arterial
streets, arterial

arterials
RM.158   (B)
HN April 1993 descriptor moved
ALT arterial
SN Intercity roads, usually with entrances at restricted locations and channelized intersections, designed to move large volumes of traffic; use only with reference to the flow of traffic within a transportation system.
UF arterial roads
roads, arterial

artesian wells
RK.564   (L)
ALT artesian well
SN Wells bored into a confined aquifer which overflow the wellhead, because the water level of the aquifer lies above the level of the wellhead; the water rises under its own pressure through the borehole. (W)
UF wells, artesian

articles
VW.950
HN November 1992 descriptor moved
ALT article
SN Literary compositions prepared for publication as an independent portion of a magazine, newspaper, encyclopedia, or other work. (GAHLM)

articles, desk
USE desk sets

articles, holy
USE sacred objects

articles of agreement
USE agreements

articles of apprenticeship
VW.655
HN November 1992 descriptor moved
ALT article of apprenticeship
SN Written agreements between masters and minors under which a minor agrees to work for a master for a stated period of time in return for instruction in a trade by a master. (BLACKS)
UF agreements, apprenticeship
apprenticeship agreements
apprenticeship, articles of

articles of association
USE articles of incorporation

articles of incorporation
VW.641   (L)
HN November 1992 descriptor moved
ALT article of incorporation
SN Written agreements embodying the purposes or other conditions of the association of a number of persons for the pursuit of a joint enterprise; especially those duly executed and filed with a state's administrative authorities so as to have the force of a charter under general incorporation law. (GAHLM)
UF articles of association
association, articles of
incorporation, articles of

articles, religious
USE religious objects

articles, sacred
USE sacred objects

articulation
BM.48
SN Use when referring to the manner in which contiguous shapes are joined or formed in architectural or decorative designs or in works of art; also, the clarification of an architectural design by emphasizing certain elements of the structure.
UF spatial articulation

artifacts
PE.2
HN January 1993 scope note changed November 1990 descriptor moved
ALT artifact
SN Objects made, modified, or used by humans. (HOLHZR)
UF artefacts
realia

artificial
DC.8   (A,L,B)
HN October 1992 descriptor added
SN Use to describe things produced by human action, as opposed to by natural causes, usually those things intended to substitute for their natural counterparts. For things produced by human action but not substituting for natural counterparts, use **man-made**. For things produced specifically by synthesis, use **synthetic**.
RT man-made
synthetic

artificial aging
USE accelerated aging

artificial asphalt
MT.1008
HN April 1992 descriptor moved
SN A term applied to the bituminous residue from coal distillation mechanically mixed with sand or limestone. (MH)
UF asphalt, artificial

artificial calcium carbonate
USE precipitated chalk

artificial candles
USE gas candles

artificial crinolines
USE cage crinolines

artificial illumination
USE artificial light

artificial inorganic black pigment
MT.2078
HN April 1992 descriptor moved
UF black pigment, artificial inorganic
black pigment, synthetic inorganic
inorganic black pigment, artificial
inorganic black pigment, synthetic
pigment, artificial inorganic black

pigment, synthetic inorganic black
synthetic inorganic black pigment

artificial inorganic blue pigment
MT.2094
HN April 1992 descriptor moved
UF blue pigment, artificial inorganic
blue pigment, synthetic inorganic
inorganic blue pigment, artificial
inorganic blue pigment, synthetic
pigment, artificial inorganic blue
pigment, synthetic inorganic blue
synthetic inorganic blue pigment

artificial inorganic brown pigment
MT.2124
HN April 1992 descriptor moved
UF brown pigment, artificial inorganic
brown pigment, synthetic inorganic
inorganic brown pigment, artificial
inorganic brown pigment, synthetic
pigment, artificial inorganic brown
pigment, synthetic inorganic brown
synthetic inorganic brown pigment

artificial inorganic green pigment
MT.2147
HN April 1992 descriptor moved
UF green pigment, artificial inorganic
green pigment, synthetic inorganic
inorganic green pigment, artificial
inorganic green pigment, synthetic
pigment, artificial inorganic green
pigment, synthetic inorganic green
synthetic inorganic green pigment

artificial inorganic pigment
MT.2053
HN April 1992 descriptor moved
UF artificial mineral pigment
inorganic pigment, artificial
mineral pigment, artificial
pigment, artificial inorganic
pigment, artificial mineral

artificial inorganic red pigment
MT.2190
HN April 1992 descriptor moved
UF inorganic red pigment, artificial
inorganic red pigment, synthetic
pigment, artificial inorganic red
pigment, synthetic inorganic red
red pigment, artificial inorganic
red pigment, synthetic inorganic
synthetic inorganic red pigment

artificial inorganic violet pigment
MT.2214
HN April 1992 descriptor moved
UF inorganic violet pigment, artificial
inorganic violet pigment, synthetic
pigment, artificial inorganic violet
pigment, synthetic inorganic violet
synthetic inorganic violet pigment
violet pigment, artificial inorganic
violet pigment, synthetic inorganic

artificial inorganic yellow pigment
MT.2268
HN April 1992 descriptor moved
UF inorganic yellow pigment, artificial
inorganic yellow pigment, synthetic

pigment, artificial inorganic yellow
pigment, synthetic inorganic yellow
synthetic inorganic yellow pigment
yellow pigment, artificial inorganic
yellow pigment, synthetic inorganic

artificial islands
HN March 1993 descriptor split, use **artificial + islands**

artificial ivory
MT.3091
SN Material made to imitate ivory; usually consisting of celluloid, a synthetic resin, or, before 1881, ceramic.
UF ivory, artificial

artificial ivorytypes
USE ivorytypes

artificial light
BM.779   (A,L,B)
HN April 1993 descriptor moved
September 1992 lead-in term added
UF artificial illumination
artificial lighting
light, artificial
lighting, artificial

artificial lighting
USE artificial light

artificial mineral pigment
USE artificial inorganic pigment

artificial mounds
USE mounds

artificial negatives
USE clichés-verre

artificial organic black pigment
USE synthetic organic black pigment

artificial organic blue pigment
USE synthetic organic blue pigment

artificial organic green pigment
USE synthetic organic green pigment

artificial organic pigment
USE synthetic organic pigment

artificial organic red pigment
USE synthetic organic red pigment

artificial organic violet pigment
USE synthetic organic violet pigment

artificial organic yellow pigment
USE synthetic organic yellow pigment

artificial perspective
USE linear perspective

artificial resin
USE plastic

artificial rubber
USE elastomer

artificial ruins
RK.1317
ALT artificial ruin
UF ruins, artificial

ruins, sham
sham ruins

artificial satellites
TX.74   (L,N,B)
ALT artificial satellite
SN Use for specially designed unmanned spacecraft intended to
maintain an orbit around a celestial
body. For unmanned spacecraft designed for nonorbital missions, use
space probes.
UF orbiting vehicles
satellites
satellites, artificial
vehicles, orbiting
RT space probes

artificial ski slopes
RK.1019   (B)
ALT artificial ski slope
SN Usually small structures with artifi-
cial surfaces, often plastic, upon
which to practice skiing. (HSRBD)
UF ski slopes, artificial

artificial stone
MT.3092   (A,L,B)
UF stone, artificial

artificial teeth
USE dentures

artificial ultramarine
USE artificial ultramarine blue
strong blue
strong purplish blue

artificial ultramarine blue
MT.2095
HN January 1992 lead-in terms added
January 1992 lead-in term deleted,
was **outremer**
January 1992 descriptor moved
UF Academy blue
artificial ultramarine
blue, artificial ultramarine
blue, French
blue, Gmelin's
blue, Guimet's
blue, lime
blue, new
blue, permanent
blue, royal
French blue
French ultramarine
Gmelin's blue
Guimet's blue
lime blue
new blue
permanent blue
royal blue
sky blue
synthetic ultramarine
Ultramarinblau
ultramarine blue, artificial
ultramarine, French
ultramarine, synthetic

artificial vermilion
USE grayish purplish red

<artificial water channels>
RK.482

artificial weathering
USE accelerated weathering

Artigue process
KT.541
SN A variant of the carbon process to
produce contact prints; the image is
formed from a pigment, usually carbon black, in a colloid suspension
that has been made light-sensitive
with bichromates. Marketed under
the name Charbon Velours.
UF Artigueotype
Charbon Velours

Artigueotype
USE Artigue process

artillery
TK.136   (L,N,R)
SN Firearms generally having a bore of
over 1 inch in diameter, designed to
be supported on a gun mount or
carriage when operated and requiring a crew of at least two people.
UF guns (artillery)
ordnance
RT gun carriages
gun mounts
machine guns

artillery, antiaircraft
USE antiaircraft guns

artillery, antitank
USE antitank guns

<artillery by form>
TK.137

<artillery by function>
TK.155

<artillery by location or context>
TK.161

artillery, coastal
USE coastal artillery

artillery, field
USE field artillery

artillery, fortress
USE garrison artillery

artillery, garrison
USE garrison artillery

artillery, naval
USE naval guns

artillery, railroad
USE railway artillery

artillery, railway
USE railway artillery

artillery, self-propelled
USE self-propelled artillery

artillery, siege
USE siege artillery

Artisan Mannerist
FL.3291   (B)
ALT Artisan Mannerism
UF Mannerist, Artisan

artisans
USE craftsmen

artisans' marks
HN March 1991 descriptor deleted

artist-designed frames
TC.429   (H)
ALT artist-designed frame
SN Use for frames designed by artists,
usually for specific works they have
done. (IJMMC)
UF artists' frames
frames, artist-designed
frames, artists'

artist supplies
USE artists' materials

<artistic concepts>
BM.2

<artistic devices>
BM.3

<artistic devices: literature>
BM.18

artistic dissenters
USE dissident artists

artistic masterpiece
USE masterpiece

artistic photography
USE art photography

artists
HG.267   (A,L,B,R)
HN February 1993 descriptor moved
November 1992 alternate terms
added
ALT artist
artist's
artists'
SN Use specifically for people who produce work in the visual arts. For
those in the performing arts, use
performing artists.

artists' books
VW.1017   (H,L,R)
HN June 1992 descriptor added
ALT artist's book
SN Use for books, whether unique or
multiple, made or conceived by artists. For texts written by artists for
the sake of their informational content, use **artists'** (ALT of **artists**) plus
writings. For artists' books that emphasize the physical book as a work
of art, use **bookworks.** For works
that look like or incorporate books
but do not communicate in the ways
characteristic of books, use **book objects.**
UF art, book

book art
books, artists'
RT book objects

artists' brushes
    TH.720   (L)
HN February 1993 descriptor added
ALT artist's brush
SN Brushes made for use by artists from animal hair or synthetic material in a variety of shapes and sizes, but generally small enough to be handled with precision. The term pencil was used until the 19th century to describe small pointed sable or camel hair brushes. For larger brushes made for applying paint over large areas, especially as a protective coating, use **paintbrushes.**
UF brushes, artists'
    pencils (brushes)
RT brushes
    paintbrushes

<artists' brushes by form>
    TH.721
HN February 1993 guide term added

<artists' brushes by function>
    TH.727
HN February 1993 guide term added

<artists' brushes by material>
    TH.736
HN February 1993 guide term added

artists' colonies
    RD.72   (A,L,R)
HN March 1993 alternate term changed, was **artist's colony**
ALT artists' colony
UF art colonies
    colonies, art
    colonies, artists'

artist's color
    MT.1961
HN April 1993 descriptor changed, was **artists' colors**
    August 1992 lead-in term added
    August 1990 descriptor added
UK artist's colour
SN A paint intended for use by artists, especially as opposed to wall or bulk paint. (MAYER)
UF color, artist's
    colour, artist's

artists' colormen
    HG.769
HN December 1992 alternate terms added
ALT artists' colorman
    artists' colorman's
    artists' colormen's
UK artists' colour-men
UKA artists' colour-man
SN Persons who develop and supply artists' colors.
UF artists' colourmen
    color makers
    colormen, artists'

colour makers
colour-men, artists'
colourmen, artists'
makers, color
makers, colour

artist's colour
SEE artist's color

artists' colour-men
SEE artists' colormen

artists' colourmen
SEE artists' colormen

artists, commercial
USE commercial artists

artists, conceptual
USE conceptual artists

artists' contracts
HN April 1993 descriptor split, use **artists'** (ALT of **artists**) + **contracts**

artists, display
USE display designers

artists, dissident
USE dissident artists

artists, doll
USE dollmakers

artists, environmental
USE environmental artists

artists, fashion
USE fashion illustrators

artists, fiber
USE fiber artists

artists, fibre
SEE fiber artists

artists, folk
USE folk artists

artists' frames
USE artist-designed frames

artists, graphic
USE draftsmen (artists)
    illustrators
    printmakers

artists' houses
HN March 1993 descriptor split, use **artists'** (ALT of **artists**) + **houses**

artists' illustrated books
USE livres d'artistes

artists-in-residence
    HG.268
HN February 1993 descriptor moved
    November 1992 alternate terms added
ALT artist-in-residence
    artist's-in-residence
    artists'-in-residence
SN Artists officially associated with an organization.

artists' marks
HN March 1993 descriptor split, use **art-**

ists' (ALT of **artists**) + **marks (symbols)**

artists' materials
    MT.1751   (L,R)
HN January 1993 scope note added
    July 1992 lead-in terms added
    July 1990 lead-in terms added
SN Use generally for materials used by artists. Most descriptors for the specific materials will be found in the *<materials by composition>* section.
UF art materials
    art supplies
    artist supplies
    artists' supplies
    materials, art
    materials, artists'
    supplies, artists'

artists, naive
USE naive artists

artists, performance
USE performance artists

artists, performing
USE performing artists

artists' prints
USE prints

artists' proofs
    VC.436
HN April 1993 descriptor changed, was **artist's proofs**
ALT artist's proof
SN Proofs numbered separately from the edition, but often made at the same time as the edition, for the use of the artist.
UF épreuves d'artiste
    proofs, artists'

artists' residences
USE artists' (ALT of **artists**) + **houses**

artists' rights
    BM.905
HN February 1993 descriptor moved
SN Use with regard to legal protection for the work of visual artists, including copyright, protection from mutilation, and royalty payments.
UF rights, artists'

artists' sketchbooks
HN April 1993 descriptor split, use **artists'** (ALT of **artists**) + **sketchbooks**

artists' statements
    VW.380   (H)
HN May 1993 descriptor moved
    May 1991 descriptor added
ALT artist's statement
SN Use for texts by artists, often brief, that state, for example, explanations of the artists' work or theoretical concepts on which their work is based.
UF statements, artists'

artists' supplies
USE artists' materials

artists' tables
USE   drawing tables

artists, tattoo
USE   tattoo artists

artists, woodblock
USE   wood engravers

arts
KD.4   (L,R)
SN   Use broadly for the areas of activity
     that encompass both performing
     and visual arts. With reference to
     the fine arts or the fine and decora-
     tive arts together, use **art**.

arts agencies, state
USE   art commissions

Arts and Crafts
FL.3403   (A,L,B,R)
HN   July 1991 related term added
ALT Arts and Crafts Movement
RT   Craftsman

<arts and related disciplines>
KD.3

arts, applied
USE   decorative arts

arts centers, performing
USE   performing arts centers

arts centres, performing
SEE   performing arts centers

arts, decorative
USE   decorative arts

arts, dramatic
USE   drama

arts, fine
USE   fine arts

arts, forbidden
USE   forbidden arts

arts, graphic
USE   drawing (image-making)
      illustration
      printmaking

arts, illiberal
USE   mechanical arts

arts, liberal
USE   liberal   arts   (cross-disciplinary
      studies)
      liberal arts (Medieval studies)

arts, mechanical
USE   mechanical arts

arts, minor
USE   decorative arts

arts, performing
USE   performing arts

arts, popular
USE   popular culture

<arts-related disciplines>
KD.21

arts, theater
USE   theater

arts, visual
USE   visual arts

artwork, line
USE   line copy

artworks
USE   works of art

Arua
FL.1587

Arunta
FL.3748   (L)
UF   Aranda

Arusha
FL.642   (L)

Arusi
FL.616
UF   Galla

Aryan
USE   Vedic

Aryavarta
USE   Nagara

aryballoi
TQ.221
ALT aryballos
SN   Relatively small ancient Greek ves-
     sels with a globular body, a short
     neck, a flat disk-shaped mouth with
     a small orifice, and a handle (or
     sometimes two) extending from the
     shoulder to the rim; used for hold-
     ing oils and ointments.

arzica
USE   weld

As
USE   arsenic

as-built drawings
VC.172
HN   April 1992 descriptor moved
     April 1990 scope note changed
ALT as-built drawing
SN   Use regarding the modern building
     trade for drawings that indicate
     changes made during construction
     from the work proposed in the
     working drawings. For these and
     other drawings or copies of draw-
     ings that are kept as file records of
     a completed project, use **record
     drawings**. For scale drawings of ex-
     isting structures, generally, use **mea-
     sured drawings**; for drawings that
     generally depict actual locations, use
     topographical views.
UF   drawings, as-built

<as coins>
VK.22

Asante
FL.286   (L)

HN   January 1992 descriptor changed,
     was **Ashanti**
     January 1992 lead-in term changed,
     was **Asante**
UF   Ashanti

asarota
HN   April 1991 descriptor deleted

asbestine
MT.593
HN   April 1992 descriptor moved
SN   Finely fibrous variety of talc used es-
     pecially as a filler for rubber and pa-
     per and as an extender and white
     pigment in paint. (W)

asbestos
MT.514   (A,L,B)
HN   April 1992 descriptor moved
     February 1992 scope note changed
SN   A commercial term for a type of sili-
     cate mineral readily separable into
     thin, strong fiber that is flexible,
     heat resistant, and chemically inert,
     used in a wide variety of industrial
     products. (AGI)

asbestos-cement
MT.12   (L,B)
HN   April 1992 descriptor moved
     June 1990 scope note added
SN   Fire-resistant, waterproofing mate-
     rial made by combining portland ce-
     ment with asbestos fiber. (PUTNAM)

asbestos curtains
TC.320
HN   May 1993 descriptor moved
     May 1993 related term added
ALT asbestos curtain
SN   Curtains which close the stage of a
     theater from the auditorium in case
     of fire, preventing the spread of
     flame and smoke; usually fabricated
     of woven asbestos and steel wire.
     (DAC)
UF   curtains, asbestos
     curtains, fire
     curtains, safety
     fire curtains
     safety curtains
RT   *<protective equipment>*

asbestos, serpentine
USE   chrysotile

Ascension Day
KM.102   (L,R)
SN   The day 40 days after Easter ob-
     served   in   commemoration   of
     Christ's   ascension   into   heaven.
     (WCOL9)

ascots
TE.656   (N)
ALT ascot
SN   Neckcloths with broad ends usually
     looped and tied under the chin and
     sometimes secured by a stickpin.

asdic
USE   sonar

aseismic design
USE   earthquake-resistant construction

ash (residue)
    MT.3061   (L,B)
HN   February 1992 descriptor moved
SN   Earthy or mineral residue that re-
    mains after combustible substances
    have been thoroughly burned. (W)
UF   ash, fly
    fly ash

ash (wood)
    MT.2687   (L)
HN   March 1992 descriptor moved

ash, American
USE   white ash

ash, American white
USE   white ash

ash, blue ultramarine
USE   moderate blue

ash, Canadian
USE   white ash

ash, common
USE   European ash

ash, European
USE   European ash

ash, fly
USE   ash (residue)

ash glaze
    MT.1988
SN   Ceramic glaze, utilizing wood or
    vegetable ash as the fluxing ingredi-
    ent. (MAYER)
UF   glaze, ash

ash-leafed maple
USE   box elder

ash, mountain
USE   mountain ash

ash, pearl
USE   potash

ash, soda
USE   sodium carbonate

ash, ultramarine
USE   ultramarine blue

ash, ultramarine gray
USE   light greenish gray

ash urns
USE   cremation urns

Ash Wednesday
    KM.103
SN   The first day of Lent. (WCOL9)

ash, white
USE   white ash

Ashanti
USE   Asante

Ashberry metal
    MT.455

HN   March 1993 descriptor moved
SN   Pewter for tableware, containing
    some nickel and aluminum. (MH)
UF   metal, Ashberry

Ashcan School
    FL.1777   (L,R)

ashes, blue
USE   azurite
    blue verditer

Ashikaga
USE   Muromachi

Ashira
USE   Shira

ashlar
    MT.940   (H,B)
HN   April 1992 descriptor moved
SN   Small dimension stone with a flat
    faced surface, usually square or
    rectangular.
UF   ashlar masonry
    masonry, ashlar

ashlar brick
    MT.105
HN   April 1992 descriptor moved
UF   brick, ashlar
    brick, rock-faced
    rock-faced brick

ashlar masonry
USE   ashlar

Ashluslay
    FL.1654   (L)

Ashogo
USE   Tsogo

Ashoka
USE   Asoka

ashpits
    PJ.2453
HN   March 1993 descriptor moved
    November 1990 lead-in term de-
    leted, was **ash dumps**
ALT   ashpit
SN   Chambers located below fireplaces
    or fireboxes for the collection and
    removal of ashes.
UF   cleanouts

ashtray stands
USE   smokers

ashtrays
    TQ.238   (N)
ALT   ashtray
SN   Receptacles for smokers' tobacco
    ashes, made in a great range of sizes
    and designs.

Asian
    FL.1788   (L,B,R)
UF   Oriental

Asian, Central
USE   Central Asian

<Asian coins>
    VK.124

<Asian coins by denomination name>
    VK.125

<Asian coins by descriptive name>
    VK.130

Asian, East
USE   East Asian

Asian, South
USE   South Asian

Asian, Southeast
USE   Southeast Asian

Asiatic bases
    PJ.1485
HN   March 1993 descriptor moved
    June 1991 descriptor moved
ALT   Asiatic base
SN   Use for bases of Ionic columns fol-
    lowing a pattern developed in Asia
    Minor, with an upper torus sur-
    mounting a disk generally com-
    posed of shallow scotias, both ele-
    ments being usually horizontally
    fluted.
UF   bases, Asiatic

Asiatic boxwood
USE   boxwood

askoi
    TQ.39   (L)
ALT   askos
SN   Small ancient Greek flasklike vessels
    with a circular body, wider than
    high, with a convex top and an
    arched handle extending from one
    side across the top to a spout on the
    other side; used for pouring oil.

asmalyks
    TH.16
HN   October 1992 descriptor added
ALT   asmalyk
SN   Pentagonal knotted-pile weavings
    made in pairs to decorate the flanks
    of a camel. (TURKMN)
UF   asmylaks
    azmalyks
    camel flank hangings
    hangings, camel flank
RT   rugs

Asmat
    FL.3766   (L)

asmylaks
USE   asmalyks

Asoka
    FL.2269
UF   Ashoka

asparagus forks
    TH.250
HN   April 1993 descriptor added
ALT   asparagus fork
SN   Broad, flat forks with four or five

tines used to serve hot or cold asparagus.
UF asparagus servers
 forks, asparagus
 servers, asparagus

asparagus servers
USE asparagus forks

asparagus tongs
 TH.294 (N)
HN April 1993 descriptor added
SN Tongs intended primarily for serving individual portions of asparagus; having either narrow or broad blades and made either as U-shaped sprung tongs or as scissorlike devices.
UF sandwich tongs
 steak tongs
 tongs, asparagus
 tongs, sandwich
 tongs, steak

aspect
USE orientation

aspen
 MT.2864 (L)
HN March 1992 descriptor moved
UF Populus tremula

aspen (American aspen)
USE American aspen

aspen, American
USE American aspen

aspen, big toothed
USE big toothed aspen

aspen, quaking
USE American aspen

aspersoriums
 TQ.154
ALT aspersorium
SN Basins for holy water, used both in religious and in secular contexts.
UF buckets, holy water
 holy water buckets
 stoups (aspersoriums)

aspes
 TE.354
ALT aspis
SN Round, oval, or bilobated shields of Classical Greece and later, Doric in origin, made of layers of cow hide and large enough to protect most of the body. Early models were held in the hand; later versions had an armlet set diagonally, with a handle near the edge, and were carried on the arm.

asphalt
 MT.1003 (A,L,B)
HN April 1992 descriptor moved
 March 1992 lead-in terms added
UF asphalt, native
 asphalt, natural
 native asphalt

natural asphalt
pitch (asphalt)

asphalt, artificial
USE artificial asphalt

<asphalt by composition or origin>
HN March 1992 guide term deleted

<asphalt by form>
HN March 1992 guide term deleted

<asphalt by function>
HN March 1992 guide term deleted

<asphalt by property>
HN March 1992 guide term deleted

asphalt cement
 MT.13 (L)
HN April 1992 descriptor moved
UF cement, asphalt

asphalt concrete
 MT.197 (A,L)
HN April 1992 descriptor moved
SN High-quality, thoroughly controlled hot mixture of asphalt cement and well-graded, high-quality aggregate, thoroughly compacted into a uniform dense mass. (STEIN)
UF asphaltic concrete
 concrete, asphalt

asphalt, emulsified
USE emulsified asphalt

asphalt emulsion mixtures
USE emulsified asphalt

asphalt, lake
USE lake asphalt

asphalt, native
USE asphalt

asphalt, natural
USE asphalt

asphalt oil
USE petroleum asphalt

asphalt, oil
USE petroleum asphalt

asphalt, paving
USE paving asphalt

asphalt, petroleum
USE petroleum asphalt

asphalt prepared roofing
USE tar paper

asphalt, rapid-curing
USE rapid-curing asphalt

asphalt, rock
USE rock asphalt

asphalt, slow-curing
USE slow-curing asphalt

asphalters
 HG.813
HN December 1992 alternate terms added

ALT asphalter
 asphalter's
 asphalters'
SN Persons who lay down asphalt. (OED)

asphaltic concrete
USE asphalt concrete

asphaltite
 MT.1014
HN March 1992 descriptor added
SN Any one of the naturally occurring black solid bitumens that are soluble in carbon disulphide and fuse above 230 degrees Fahrenheit. (AGI)

asphaltum
 MT.2115
HN April 1992 descriptor moved
UF bitumen (brown pigment)

asphaltum (color)
USE dark grayish yellowish brown

assassinations
 KM.162 (L)
HN May 1991 alternate term added
ALT assassination
SN Murders of high public officials or other prominent persons, whether by persons acting alone or in conspiracy with others. (DOAP)

assault rifles
 TK.193 (L)
ALT assault rifle
SN Automatic rifles developed from submachine guns during the Second World War for use with cartridges intermediate in size and power between pistol and rifle cartridges.
UF rifles, assault

assault ships, amphibious
USE amphibious assault ships

assay balances
USE assay scales

assay scales
 TN.296 (L,N)
ALT assay scale
SN Weighing devices for assaying.
UF assay balances
 balances, assay
 scales, assay
RT assayers
 assaying

assayers
 HG.532 (L)
HN December 1992 alternate terms added
 September 1992 related term added
 July 1991 related term added
ALT assayer
 assayer's
 assayers'
SN Chemists who analyze the value and quantity of metals in ores and alloys. (W)

RT assay scales
   assaying

assaying
   KT.160   (L)
HN March 1992 descriptor added
SN Testing to determine the percentage
   of pure metal in a specimen of ore,
   bullion, or alloy.
RT assay scales
   assayers
   metal
   ore

assemblage
   KT.803   (L)
HN April 1991 descriptor moved
   November 1990 lead-in term added
SN A 20th-century technique of creating a three-dimensional work of art
   by combining various elements, especially found objects; may include
   elements painted, carved, or modeled by the artist. (MAYER)
UF assembling (sculpture technique)

assemblages
   VC.556   (L,N,R)
ALT assemblage
SN Use for sculptural works created
   since about 1945 by the technique
   of assemblage. For such works created earlier in the 20th century, use
   object sculpture.
UF constructions (assemblages)

assemblers
   HG.659
HN December 1992 alternate terms
   added
ALT assembler
   assembler's
   assemblers'
SN Persons who assemble component
   parts of an item of manufacture.
   (W)

assemblies, column and beam
USE post-and-beam structures

assemblies, major
USE assembly drawings

assemblies, minor
USE minor assembly drawings

assembling
   KT.10
HN January 1993 descriptor moved
   August 1992 scope note added
ALT assembled
SN Fitting together various parts to
   make an operative whole. (W)

assembling (sculpture technique)
USE assemblage

*<assembling and disassembling
   construction equipment>*
   TH.423

assembling bolts
   PJ.43

HN April 1993 descriptor moved
ALT assembling bolt
SN Threaded bolts for holding together
   temporarily parts of a structure dur-
   ing riveting. (DAC)
UF bolts, assembling

assembly buildings
USE assembly halls

assembly drawings
   VC.192
HN April 1993 lead-in terms added
   April 1992 descriptor moved
ALT assembly drawing
UF assemblies, major
   assembly drawings, major
   drawings, assembly
   major assemblies
   major assembly drawings

assembly drawings, major
USE assembly drawings

assembly drawings, minor
USE minor assembly drawings

assembly facilities
USE assembly halls

assembly halls
   RK.1126   (A,L,B)
ALT assembly hall
UF assembly buildings
   assembly facilities
   buildings, assembly
   facilities, assembly
   halls (assembly halls)
   halls, assembly
   halls, public
   public halls

assembly plants
   RK.584   (B)
ALT assembly plant
SN Factories where parts for a complete
   unit are put together, as in automo-
   bile manufacturing. (RHDEL2)
UF plants, assembly

assembly rooms
   PJ.1063   (A,B)
HN March 1993 descriptor moved
ALT assembly room
SN Use for rooms, primarily of the 18th
   century, in which social gatherings
   and balls (commonly referred to as
   assemblies) were held.
UF rooms, assembly

<assembly spaces>
   PJ.997
HN March 1993 guide term moved

asses (coins)
   VK.23   (L)
ALT as (coin)
SN Use both for bronze coins of the Roman Republic and for copper coins
   used during the Roman Empire
   from the 1st century BCE through
   the 3rd century CE.

assessing
   KG.265   (L)
HN April 1993 lead-in term added
ALT assessed
SN Determining the value of property
   for taxation purposes.
UF assessment

assessment
USE assessing

assessment districts
   RG.257
ALT assessment district
UF ADs
   districts, assessment

assessment, needs
USE needs assessment

assignats
   VK.156   (L)
ALT assignat
SN Denotes paper money issued by the
   French revolutionary government
   between 1789 and 1796.

assimilation
   DL.20
HN March 1993 descriptor changed,
   was **assimilation (color)**
   February 1992 descriptor moved
SN Phenomenon of visual perception
   which occurs when interlocking areas of contrasting colors are combined on the retina and perceived as
   a mixed color.

Assiniboin
   FL.1386   (L)
UF Stoney

assistance
USE assisting

<assistance vessels>
   TX.444

assistants
   HG.880   (B)
HN January 1993 alternate terms added
ALT assistant
   assistant's
   assistants'
SN Persons who act as subordinates to
   another or as an official in a subordinate capacity. (W)
UF hands (assistants)
   helpers
   mates

assisting
   KG.84   (L)
HN June 1991 lead-in term added
SN Providing direct economic or finan-
   cial aid. (RLG7)
UF assistance

associated architects
   HG.260
HN February 1993 descriptor moved
   November 1992 alternate terms
   added
ALT associated architect

associated architect's
associated architects'
SN   Architects working with other architects in a temporary agreement or partnership of joint venture. (STEIN)
UF   architects, associated

association, articles of
USE   articles of incorporation

association buildings
USE   societies' buildings

association football
USE   soccer

association of ideas
USE   associationism

associationism
         BM.987   (R)
HN   February 1993 descriptor moved
        April 1990 descriptor added
ALT   associationist
SN   The doctrine that mental and moral phenomena may be accounted for by association of ideas. (OED)
UF   association of ideas

associations
         HN.66   (L,B,R)
ALT   association

associations, architectural
USE   architectural societies

associations, civic
USE   community organizations

associations, educational
USE   educational associations

associations, professional
USE   professional associations

associations, trade
USE   trade associations

associations, voluntary
USE   voluntary associations

assurance, quality
USE   quality control

Assyrian
         FL.3066   (A,L,B)

Assyrian Colony period
         FL.2942
UF   Old Assyrian Colony period

Assyrian, Late
USE   Late Assyrian

Assyrian, Middle
USE   Middle Assyrian

Assyrian, Old
USE   Old Assyrian

Assyro-Babylonian
         FL.3073   (A,L)
SN   Use for art or architecture that is not distinctly Assyrian or Babylonian but has characteristics of both.

astragal ends
         PJ.2787
HN   March 1993 descriptor moved
ALT   astragal end
UF   ends, astragal
        ends, ovolo
        ovolo ends

astragal planes
USE   bead planes

astragals
         PJ.2106   (B)
HN   April 1993 descriptor moved
ALT   astragal
SN   Small moldings having a rounded, convex section. (RS)
UF   bagnettes
        baguets
        chaplets (astragals)

astral lamps
         TC.1308   (N)
ALT   astral lamp
SN   Lamps with a ring-shaped reservoir and central Argand burner or burners; the name was originally used for hanging lamps, thus the name astral from star.
UF   annular French lamps
        lamps, annular French
        lamps, astral

astral lamps, solar
USE   solar astral lamps

Astrolabe Bay
         FL.3773

astrolabes
         TN.24   (L,N)
ALT   astrolabe
SN   Use for instruments designed to observe the positions and measure the altitude of celestial bodies; used from the 2nd century BCE, until superseded by sextants.
RT   astronomical instruments

astrologers
         HG.605   (L)
HN   January 1993 descriptor added
ALT   astrologer
        astrologer's
        astrologers'
SN   Those who study or practice astrology.
RT   astrology

astrological charts
         VW.142   (L)
HN   November 1992 descriptor moved
ALT   astrological chart
UF   charts, astrological

astrology
         KD.328   (L,R)
HN   February 1993 related term added
        February 1991 alternate term added
ALT   astrological
RT   astrologers

astronautical charts
         VW.96   (L)
HN   November 1992 descriptor moved
ALT   astronautical chart
SN   Charts used for navigation beyond the earth's atmosphere, including interplanetary or interstellar space.
UF   charts, astronautical

astronautical museums
         RK.388   (A,L)
ALT   astronautical museum
UF   museums, astronautical

astronomers
         HG.522   (L,R)
HN   April 1993 related terms added
        December 1992 alternate terms added
ALT   astronomer
        astronomer's
        astronomers'
RT   astronomical instruments
        astronomy

astronomical charts
         VW.97   (L,R)
HN   November 1992 descriptor moved
        April 1992 lead-in terms added
ALT   astronomical chart
UF   atlases, celestial
        celestial atlases
        celestial charts
        charts, astronomical
        charts, celestial
        charts, star
        maps, star
        star charts
        star maps

astronomical clocks
         TN.181   (L,N)
ALT   astronomical clock
SN   Clocks that display astronomical phenomena, such as the phases of the moon, or clocks that show sidereal time.
UF   clocks, astronomical

astronomical equipment
USE   astronomical instruments

astronomical instruments
         TH.1115   (L,N,R)
HN   December 1992 descriptor added
ALT   astronomical instrument
SN   Tools and equipment used in the observation, measurement, and recording of objects and events outside of the earth's atmosphere. (NOM)
UF   astronomical equipment
        astronomical tools
        equipment, astronomical
        instruments, astronomical
        tools, astronomical
RT   astrolabes
        astronomers
        astronomy
        cross-staffs
        octants
        sextants

astronomical museums
HN March 1993 descriptor split, use as-tronomical (ALT of **astronomy**) + museums

astronomical observatories
HN March 1993 descriptor split, use as-tronomical (ALT of **astronomy**) + observatories

astronomical photographs
USE astrophotographs

astronomical photography
KT.489 (L)
SN Use for techniques to record images of subjects located outside the atmo-sphere of the earth and certain phe-nomena associated with the iono-sphere, such as aurorae and meteor showers. For the taking of photo-graphs from beyond the earth's at-mosphere, use **space photography**. For photography of the earth from aircraft, use **aerial photography**.
UF astrophotography
celestial photography
photography, astronomical
photography, celestial

astronomical tools
USE astronomical instruments

astronomy
KD.165 (A,L,B,R)
HN April 1993 related terms added
December 1992 descriptor moved
February 1992 scope note added
February 1991 alternate term added
ALT astronomical
SN The science that deals with the ma-terial universe beyond the earth's at-mosphere. (RHDEL2)
RT astronomers
astronomical instruments

astronomy museums
USE astronomical (ALT of **astronomy**) + museums

astrophotographs
VC.400
HN April 1992 descriptor moved
ALT astrophotograph
SN Use for photographs taken of celes-tial bodies or astronomical phenom-ena. For photographs taken from beyond the earth's atmosphere, use **space photographs**. For photo-graphs of the earth taken from air-craft, use **aerial photographs**.
UF astronomical photographs
celestial photographs
photographs, astronomical
photographs, celestial

astrophotography
USE astronomical photography

astrophysics
KD.166 (L)
HN December 1992 descriptor moved
February 1991 alternate term added

ALT astrophysical
SN Study of astronomical phenomena in terms of the underlying physical processes. (PG)

Asturian
FL.2564 (L)

astylar
DC.134
HN March 1993 descriptor added
SN Without columns or pilasters or without the repetitive use of them in important locations or as influential elements of design; used especially with reference to facades.

Asuka
FL.2052
UF Suiko

asukusuks
TT.98
ALT asukusuk
SN Trumpets of the Teso of Uganda, consisting of a straight wood tube with a bottle-shaped calabash bell; they are played by men in sets of three as accompaniment for dancing.

asylum camps, first
USE refugee camps

asylum locks
PJ.521
HN April 1993 descriptor moved
ALT asylum lock
SN Locks used on doors of psychiatric institutions providing special protec-tion against tampering. (STEIN)
UF locks, asylum

asylums
RK.753 (A,L,B,R)
HN April 1990 scope note added
ALT asylum
SN Designates buildings used as refuges for the sick or destitute who need care rather than medical treatment; for institutional facilities treating the mentally ill, use **psychiatric hospi-tals** or **psychiatric clinics**, and for those treating the chronically ill, use **sanatoriums**.
UF homes

asylums (psychiatric hospitals)
USE psychiatric hospitals

asylums, insane
USE psychiatric hospitals

asylums, orphan
USE orphanages

<asymmetrical-ended watercraft>
TX.307

asymmetrical knots
PJ.2683
ALT asymmetrical knot
SN Knots of rugs tied on pairs of warp

strands, looping under one strand and then over and around the other, the ends of the knot coming up individually between each single warp strand to form a pile. They can be tied so that the knot ends come up either to the right or to the left of the encircled warp strands.
UF farsibaff
figure 8 knots
knots, asymmetric
knots, asymmetrical
knots, figure 8
knots, open
knots, Persian
knots, sehna
knots, senna
open knots
Persian knots
sehna knots
senna knots
senneh knots

asymmetry
BM.49 (B,R)
ALT asymmetrical

Atabeg
FL.3585
HN April 1993 descriptor moved

Atacama
USE Atacameño

Atacameño
FL.1197 (L)
HN June 1990 lead-in term deleted, was **Atacaman**
UF Atacama
Chincha-Atacaman

ataduras
PJ.2118
HN April 1993 descriptor moved
July 1991 scope note changed
November 1990 lead-in ..rms added
ALT atadura
SN In Mayan architecture, tripartite fa-cade moldings consisting of a cen-tral vertical band framed on top and bottom by flaring members; charac-teristic of Puuc architecture.
UF binder moldings
moldings, binder

Atakapa
FL.1446

Atarco
FL.1174

Atchana
FL.3023
HN April 1993 descriptor added
UF Billa
Hurrian
Mitannian (pottery style)

Atchana ware
HN April 1993 descriptor split, use **Atchana** + **ware**

atefs
USE pschents

ateliers
USE studios (organizations)
 studios (work spaces)
 workshops (organizations)
 workshops (work spaces)

Aterian
 FL.38

Athabaskan
 FL.1240

atheism
 BM.538 (L)
HN January 1991 alternate term added
ALT atheist
SN Doctrine that there is neither God nor any other deity. (W)

athenaeums
 RK.1142
ALT athenaeum

athéniennes
 TC.1040
HN January 1993 descriptor moved
ALT athénienne
SN Ornate, multifunctional tripods, especially those in the style of antique bronzes from Herculaneum; common in Neoclassical French furniture.

athletes
 HG.897 (H,L)
HN January 1993 descriptor added
ALT athlete
 athlete's
 athletes'
SN People trained or gifted in activities or contests involving physical skill, agility, stamina, or strength.

athletic clubs
 RK.973 (A,L)
HN April 1991 scope note added
 April 1991 lead-in term deleted, was health clubs
ALT athletic club
UK sports clubs
UKA sports club
SN Buildings with sports and recreation facilities offered only on a membership basis.
UF clubs, athletic
 clubs, sports

athletic facilities
USE sports complexes

athletic fields
 RM.86 (A,L,B)
HN April 1993 descriptor moved
 March 1993 related term added
ALT athletic field
UF fields, athletic
 fields, playing
 grounds, sports
 playfields

 playing fields
 sports grounds
RT <field sports>

athletic shoes
 TE.743 (L)
ALT athletic shoe
UK trainers
SN Shoes designed to be worn for sports.
UF shoes, athletic
 shoes, sport
 shoes, training
 sport shoes
 training shoes
RT sports clothing

athletics buildings
USE sports buildings

Atie
USE Attie

Atisha Style
USE Kadam School

atlantes
 PJ.1435 (A,R)
HN March 1993 descriptor moved
 November 1990 alternate term changed, was **atlante**
ALT atlas
SN Male figures used as supports or apparent supports.
UF telamones

Atlantic cedar
 MT.2925
HN March 1992 descriptor moved
UF atlas cedar
 cedar, Atlantic
 cedar, atlas
 Cedrus atlantica

Atlantic white cedar
USE white cypress

atlas cedar
USE Atlantic cedar

atlases
 VW.48 (L,R)
HN November 1992 descriptor moved
ALT atlas
SN Volumes of maps, with or without descriptive text, which may be issued to supplement or accompany texts or be published independently. (LG)

<atlases by subject>
HN March 1993 guide term deleted

<atlases by subject: location>
HN March 1993 guide term deleted

atlases, celestial
USE astronomical charts

atlases, fire insurance
USE fire insurance maps

atlases, historical
USE historical atlases

atlases, insurance
USE fire insurance maps

atlases, national
USE national atlases

atlases, regional
USE regional atlases

atlases, statistical
USE statistical atlases

atlases, world
USE world atlases

atlatls
 TK.233 (L)
ALT atlatl
SN Throwing-sticks of the Aztec culture of pre-Columbian Mexico, used to throw spears.

Atlatongo
USE Aztec II

atmidometers
USE atmometers

atmometers
 TN.341 (L,N)
ALT atmometer
SN Instruments for measuring the rate of evaporation of water into the atmosphere.
UF atmidometers
 evaporation gauges
 evaporimeters
 gauges, evaporation

atmospheric corrosion
 KT.253 (L)
HN January 1993 descriptor added
SN Corrosion caused by pollutants in the atmosphere.

atmospheric humidity
USE relative humidity

atmospheric perspective
 KT.467
HN February 1991 scope note changed
 February 1991 descriptor changed, was **aerial perspective**
 February 1991 lead-in term changed, was **atmospheric perspective**
SN Use for the means of suggesting pictorial depth by depicting more distant things with less clarity of outline and detail and, where color is involved, by alteration of hue toward blue, and decrease of color saturation and value contrast. (A-Z)
UF aerial perspective
 perspective, aerial
 perspective, atmospheric

atmospheric pollution
USE air pollution

atmospheric pressure
 BM.848 (L)
HN November 1992 descriptor moved
 February 1992 scope note added

SN Pressure exerted in every direction at any given point by the weight of the atmosphere. (W)
UF pressure, atmospheric

atmospheric sciences
USE meteorology

ATMs
USE automated teller machines

Atnah
USE Ahtena

Atnatana
USE Ahtena

atokes
TT.468
ALT atoke
SN Boat-shaped clapperless iron bells of the Ewe of Ghana; they are held in the palm of the hand and struck with a metal rod.

atolls
RD.189   (L)
ALT atoll
SN Designates circular, elliptical, or horseshoe-shaped islands or a ring of such islands, usually formed by coral reefs and enclosing a lagoon.

atom smashers
USE particle accelerators

atomic absorption spectrometry
USE atomic absorption spectroscopy

atomic absorption spectrophotometry
USE atomic absorption spectroscopy

atomic absorption spectroscopy
KT.214   (L)
HN November 1992 descriptor added
UF AAS
atomic absorption spectrometry
atomic absorption spectrophotometry
spectrometry, atomic absorption
spectrophotometry, atomic absorption
spectroscopy, atomic absorption

atomic bomb shelters
USE nuclear bomb shelters

atomic clocks
TN.192   (L)
ALT atomic clock
SN Extremely accurate electronic clocks regulated by the resonance frequency of atoms or molecules, such as cesium or ammonia. (RHDEL2)
UF clocks, atomic

atomic energy
USE nuclear power

atomic furnaces
USE nuclear reactors

atomic piles
USE nuclear reactors

atomic power plants
USE nuclear power plants

atomic power stations
USE nuclear power plants

atomic test sites
USE nuclear test sites

atomic warfare
USE nuclear wars

atomic wars
USE nuclear wars

atomizers
TQ.128   (L,N)
ALT atomizer
SN Containers with a spraying device used for atomizing liquids.

Atonement, Day of
USE Yom Kippur

atrament
SEE atramentum

atramentum
MT.1916
HN June 1991 descriptor moved
UK atrament
UF ink, Roman
Roman ink

atrium houses
RK.258   (A,L,B)
HN March 1993 related term added
ALT atrium house
SN Use for ancient Roman houses or similarly styled houses containing internal courtyards with impluvia but without colonnades; for houses with internal courtyards having colonnades, use peristyle houses.
UF houses, atrium
RT peristyle houses

atriums (church courtyards)
PJ.980   (A,L,B,R)
HN March 1993 descriptor moved
ALT atrium (church courtyard)
SN Use for the colonnaded forecourts of Early Christian churches.

atriums (interior spaces)
PJ.1201   (A,L,B,R)
HN March 1993 descriptor moved
ALT atrium (interior space)
SN Use for many-storied, skylit spaces in or between high-rise buildings, common since 1960.

atriums (Roman halls)
PJ.975   (A,L,B,R)
HN March 1993 descriptor moved
ALT atrium (Roman hall)
SN Use for the main inner halls of Roman houses having a compluvium (opening in the roof) for rainwater and an impluvium (rectangular basin) to collect the water.

Atsahuaca
FL.1621

Atsina
FL.1387   (L)
UF Gros Ventre

Atsugewi
FL.1262   (L)
HN June 1990 lead-in term changed, was Pit River Indians
UF Pit River

attaché cases
TQ.185   (L,N)
ALT attaché case
SN Flat, rigid, rectangular containers with a handle used for carrying business papers or other relatively flat documents. For flat, flexible rectangular containers use briefcases.
UF cases, attaché
RT briefcases
<costume accessories carried>
traveling bags

attached
DC.318
HN October 1992 descriptor moved

attached columns
USE engaged columns

attachments
PJ.6   (N)
ALT attachment

attachments, flash
USE flash attachments

attack aircraft
TX.47   (L)
SN Late 20th-century term for multiweapon bombers carrying non-nuclear payloads.
UF aircraft, attack
attack bombers
attack planes
bombers, attack
planes, attack

attack bombers
USE attack aircraft

attack planes
USE attack aircraft

attapulgite
MT.526   (L)
HN February 1992 descriptor added
SN A chain-lattice clay mineral, also a group name for lightweight fibrous clay minerals characterized by their bleaching and absorbent qualities.
UF palygorskite

attendance lists
VW.171
HN November 1992 descriptor moved
ALT attendance list
UF lists, attendance

attendance records
VW.527

HN November 1992 descriptor moved
ALT attendance record
UF records, attendance

Attic
FL.2703

Attic bases
PJ.1486
HN March 1993 descriptor moved
June 1991 descriptor moved
ALT Attic base
SN Use for column bases consisting of a scotia between an upper and lower torus, usually found on the Ionic order.
UF bases, Attic

Attic helmets
TE.283
ALT Attic helmet
SN Helmets used in Greece from about the mid-6th century BCE on, consisting of a skull with a short neck guard and two movable cheekpieces hinged to the skull. They were often highly decorated and surmounted by an elaborate crest.
UF helmets, Attic

attic stories
USE attics (exterior stories)

attics (exterior stories)
PJ.1355   (A)
HN April 1993 lead-in term added
March 1993 descriptor moved
ALT attic (exterior story)
SN Use to designate the exterior walled portions of buildings, above the uppermost cornice, whether fenestrated or not.
UF attic stories
stories, attic

attics (interior spaces)
PJ.1202   (A,L,B)
HN March 1993 descriptor moved
ALT attic (interior space)
SN Use for spaces under sloping roofs, between the roof and the ceiling of the uppermost story.
UF cocklofts
garrets

Attie
FL.293   (L)
UF Akye
Atie
Kuroba

attiring houses
USE tiring houses

attorney, letters of
USE powers of attorney

attorney, powers of
USE powers of attorney

attorneys
USE lawyers

attributes (characteristics)
DC.3
HN October 1992 descriptor added
ALT attribute (characteristic)
SN Refers most often to characteristics of individual objects, items, or entities, mostly expressions used to describe the thing. Often readily apparent though not quantifiable by an established standard.

attributes (symbols)
VC.67   (H)
ALT attribute (symbol)
SN Objects, and sometimes animals or plants, closely associated with a specific person or deity and used in an image to identify that figure.

<attributes and properties>
DC.1
HN October 1992 guide term changed, was *<design attributes>*

<attributes and properties by general type>
DC.2
HN October 1992 guide term added

<attributes and properties by specific type>
DC.5
HN October 1992 guide term added

attributing
USE attribution

attribution
KG.9   (L)
HN April 1993 lead-in terms added
January 1991 scope note added
January 1991 alternate term added
ALT attributed
SN Ascription of an action or manmade object to an agent or creator, place or date; used particularly with regard to ascribing a work of art to a particular artist or school of artists. (W)
UF attributing
reattributing
reattribution

atukpanis
USE atumpans

atumpans
TT.583
ALT atumpan
SN Large double-conical drums of West Africa with a tubular open foot at the base, played upright, usually in pairs, each being of a different pitch; one of the pair often has a jingle suspended across the drum head. They serve as talking drums on ceremonial occasions, and as accompaniment ritual to singing and dancing.
UF atukpanis
atungblans
ntumpani
RT talking drums

atungblans
USE atumpans

Au
USE gold

au premier coup
USE alla prima

Aua
FL.3814
UF Dourour
Durour

Aubusson
FL.3300   (R)

Aubusson carpets
TC.122   (R)
ALT Aubusson carpet
SN Use for tapestries or flat-woven rugs made in southern France, used as floor coverings or wall hangings.
UF Aubusson rugs
Aubussons
carpets, Aubusson
rugs, Aubusson

Aubusson rugs
USE Aubusson carpets

Aubussons
USE Aubusson carpets

auction catalogs
VW.28   (L)
HN April 1993 descriptor moved
ALT auction catalog
SN Catalogs of objects, manuscripts, books, or other items offered for sale at auction.
UF catalogs, auction

auction galleries
USE auction houses

auction houses
RK.141   (A)
ALT auction house
UF auction galleries
galleries, auction
houses, auction

auctioneers
HG.616   (L)
HN December 1992 alternate terms added
ALT auctioneer
auctioneer's
auctioneers'
SN Persons who conduct the sale of goods at public auction, usually as agents on commission. (W)

auctions
KM.180   (L,R)
HN May 1991 alternate term added
ALT auction
SN Public sales of property to the highest bidder, as by successive increased bids. (W)

audience halls
USE presence chambers

audience rugs
　　TC.28
ALT　audience rug
SN　Single rugs woven to represent the arrangement of four rugs often used in the main chambers of important Islamic houses, composed of the mian farsh, kelleyeh, and two kenares. (ORR)
UF　carpets, audience
　　rugs, audience
　　rugs, triclinium
　　triclinium rugs
RT　kelleyehs
　　kenares
　　mian farsh

<audience spaces>
　　PJ.1295
HN　March 1993 guide term moved

audiences
　　HG.25　　　　　　　　(L)
HN　May 1991 descriptor added
ALT　audience
SN　Use for groups of spectators or viewers.
RT　spectators
　　viewers

audio cartridges
USE　audio cassettes

audio cassettes
　　VW.1090
HN　November 1992 descriptor moved
ALT　audio cassette
UF　audio cartridges
　　cartridges, audio
　　cassettes, audio

audio recordings
USE　sound recordings

audio tapes
　　VW.1089　　　　　　(L,N,B)
HN　November 1992 descriptor moved
ALT　audio tape
SN　Sound recordings on magnetic tape. (ICA)
UF　phonotapes
　　recordings, tape
　　sound tapes
　　tape recordings
　　tapes, audio
　　tapes, sound

audio-visual centres
SEE　audiovisual centers

audio-visual librarians
SEE　audiovisual librarians

audio-visual materials centers
USE　audiovisual centers

audiometers
　　TN.360　　　　　　　(L,N)
ALT　audiometer
SN　Instruments for measuring and recording the acuity of hearing.

audiovisual aids
USE　audiovisual materials

audiovisual centers
　　PJ.1162　　　　　　　(L)
HN　April 1993 lead-in terms added
　　March 1993 descriptor moved
ALT　audiovisual center
UK　audio-visual centres
UKA　audio-visual centre
SN　Instructional areas with equipment for storage and use of audiovisual aids. (ERIC9)
UF　audio-visual materials centers
　　audiovisual materials centers
　　centers, audiovisual
　　centers, instructional materials
　　centres, audio-visual
　　educational media centers
　　instructional materials centers
　　materials centers, audiovisual
　　media centers, educational

audiovisual librarians
　　HG.501
HN　December 1992 alternate terms added
ALT　audiovisual librarian
　　audiovisual librarian's
　　audiovisual librarians'
UK　audio-visual librarians
UKA　audio-visual librarian
SN　Library personnel who plan audiovisual programs and administer libraries of film and audiovisual materials. (DOT)
UF　film librarians
　　librarians, audio-visual
　　librarians, audiovisual
　　librarians, film

audiovisual materials
　　VW.990　　　　　　(L,B,R)
HN　November 1992 alternate term deleted, was audiovisual material
　　November 1992 descriptor moved
　　November 1992 scope note changed
SN　Use broadly for nonprint materials, such as slides, transparencies, motion pictures, or filmstrips, that make use of sight and sound to convey information; refers especially to such materials when used for instruction.
UF　aids, audiovisual
　　audiovisual aids
　　audiovisual records
　　materials, audiovisual
　　materials, nonbook
　　materials, nonprint
　　nonbook materials
　　nonprint materials
　　records, audiovisual

audiovisual materials centers
USE　audiovisual centers

audiovisual records
USE　audiovisual materials

audit reports
USE　audits

auditing
　　KG.10　　　　　　　(L)

SN　Reviewing a practice or set of practices to certify that they are being conducted in accordance with established principles. (RLG7)

auditoriums
　　PJ.998　　　　　　(A,L,B)
HN　March 1993 descriptor moved
ALT　auditorium
SN　Use for either rooms or entire buildings designed for a variety of activities such as would occur on a stage before a seated audience; for rooms or buildings used only for theatrical performances, use theaters; for rooms with fixed seating designed for lectures, use lecture halls.

auditors
　　HG.612　　　　　　　(L)
HN　December 1992 alternate terms added
ALT　auditor
　　auditor's
　　auditors'
SN　Persons authorized to examine and verify accounts. (W)

audits
　　VW.563
HN　November 1992 descriptor moved
ALT　audit
SN　Final reports following formal examinations of accounts. (W)
UF　audit reports
　　reports, audit

auger bits
　　PJ.2575　　　　　　　(L)
HN　March 1993 descriptor moved
ALT　auger bit
SN　Bits having a square tapered shank fitted into and rotated by a brace; used for drilling holes in wood. (DAC)
UF　bits, auger

auger bits, ship
USE　ship auger bits

augers
　　TH.524　　　　　　　(L,N)
ALT　auger
SN　Hand tools with a long steel bit, usually not larger than 1 inch in diameter, with a wood handle that is usually set perpendicular to the bit; used for boring holes in wood.

augers, breast
USE　breast augers

augers, burn
USE　burn augers

augers, cylinder
USE　cylinder augers

augers, downcutting
USE　nose augers

augers, nose
USE　nose augers

augers, pipe
USE nose augers

augers, pod
USE shell augers

augers, pump
USE taper augers

augers, raft
USE raft augers

augers, screw
USE spiral augers

augers, shell
USE nose augers
        shell augers

augers, ship
USE ship auger bits

augers, snail
USE shell augers

augers, spiral
USE spiral augers

augers, tap
USE taper augers

augers, taper
USE taper augers

augers, taper shell
USE taper augers

augers, twist
USE spiral augers
        spiral bits

<augers: woodworking tools>
        TH.1398

augite
        MT.516
HN April 1992 descriptor moved
SN Mineral occurring in igneous rocks
        such as basalt. (W)

Augustan
        FL.2798

aulmonieres
        TE.674
ALT aulmoniere
SN Medieval pouches or bags sus-
        pended from the girdle and worn by
        nobles. (CDC)
UF almoners
        alners
        aumeres
        aumers
        aumoners
        aunonieres
        awmeners
        awners
RT girdles (belts)
        pouches

auloi
        TT.187   (L)
ALT aulos
SN Reedpipes of ancient Greece, con-
        sisting of two separate slender cylin-
        drical pipes of wood or metal each

with a reed, single or double; the
pipes were held at a divergent angle
and both reeds held in the mouth
together.

aumbries
        TC.916   (L,R)
HN May 1993 related terms added
        January 1993 descriptor moved
ALT aumbry
SN Medieval term for enclosed cup-
        boards or storage niches enclosed by
        doors; often a receptacle for provi-
        sions to be given away as alms. The
        term remained in use chiefly for the
        aumbries, enclosed in or hung on a
        wall, near the altar in churches in
        which sacramental vessels were
        kept. When referring to such forms
        enclosed by doors from the 17th
        century on, use **cupboards**.
UF almeries
        ambries
        close cupboards
        cupboards, close
RT cupboards
        livery cupboards

aumbry veils
        TC.275
ALT aumbry veil
SN Curtains, occasionally embroidered,
        which cover the aumbry. (PCTND)
UF ambry veils
        veils, ambry
        veils, aumbry

aumeres
USE aulmonieres

aumers
USE aulmonieres

aumoners
USE aulmonieres

aunonieres
USE aulmonieres

aural hospitals
        RK.728   (A,L,B)
ALT aural hospital
UF hospitals, aural

Aurangabad
        FL.2302
HN February 1991 descriptor moved

Aurangzeb
        FL.2318
UF Alamgir

aurei
        VK.28
ALT aureus
SN Gold coins in use in the Roman
        world from the time of Caesar to
        that of Constantine, but primarily
        from the later Roman Republic
        through the middle years of the Ro-
        man Empire.
UF denarius aureus

Aurene glass
        MT.270
HN December 1991 descriptor added
SN Term used in the glass trade for a
        type of art glass developed at the
        Steuben Glass Works with either a
        purplish, bluish, or golden metallic
        appearance created by spraying the
        glass at the fire with stannous chlo-
        ride or lead chloride under con-
        trolled atmospheric conditions.
UF glass, Aurene

aureolin
USE brilliant yellow
        cobalt yellow
        strong yellow
        vivid yellow

Auricular
        FL.3273   (H)
UF Knorpelwork
        Kwabornament
        Lobate

Aurignacian
        FL.2554   (L)

Auripigment
USE orpiment

auripigmento
USE orpiment

aurocoline
USE cobalt yellow

Aurora
        FL.1038

Aurora yellow
USE cadmium yellow

Ausonian
        FL.2790

austenitic stainless steel
        MT.359   (L)
HN April 1993 lead-in term added
        March 1993 descriptor moved
SN Stainless steel containing up to 30%
        chromium and 20% nickel; used
        chiefly in aircraft and other trans-
        port equipment because of its high
        strength and corrosion resistance.
        (MH)
UF austenitic steel
        stainless steel, austenitic
        steel, austenitic
        steel, austenitic stainless

austenitic steel
USE austenitic stainless steel

Austral Island
        FL.3825
UF Tubuai Island

Australian
        FL.3746   (L,B)

Australian Aboriginal
        FL.3747   (A,L,R)
UF Aboriginal
        Aboriginal, Australian

Australian blackwood
USE   Australian locust

Australian locust
        MT.2789
HN   March 1992 descriptor moved
SN   A wood employed for cabinetwork,
        reddish brown to black in color and
        beautifully grained; similar to rose-
        wood. (MH)
UF   Acacia melanoxylon
        Australian blackwood
        blackwood, Australian
        blackwood, Tasmanian
        locust, Australian
        Tasmanian blackwood

<*Australian regional styles*>
        FL.3751

Austrian
        FL.3126   (L,B)

Austrian black pine
USE   Austrian pine

Austrian blinds
SEE   Austrian shades

Austrian oak
        MT.2819
HN   March 1992 descriptor moved
UF   oak, Austrian

Austrian pine
        MT.2962   (L)
HN   March 1992 descriptor moved
UF   Austrian black pine
        black pine
        black pine, Austrian
        pine, Austrian
        pine, Austrian black
        pine, black

Austrian poufs
USE   Austrian shades

Austrian shades
        TC.304
ALT   Austrian shade
UK   Austrian blinds
UKA Austrian blind
SN   Shirred curtains which are perma-
        nently gathered both across the
        width and down the length and
        which are raised or lowered by cords
        and rings; generally made of light-
        weight and often sheer fabric that
        drapes well and gives the effect of
        many rows of horizontal swags.
UF   Austrian poufs
        blinds, Austrian
        poufs, Austrian
        shades, Austrian
RT   pull-up curtains
        shades (coverings)

authenticating
        KG.11   (L)
HN   April 1993 lead-in term added
        March 1991 alternate term added
ALT   authenticated
SN   Determining the legitimacy of a
        document or other artifact, or val-
        idating a document, as done by an
        authorized person.
UF   authentication

authentication
USE   authenticating

authenticity
        BM.385   (L)
HN   September 1992 alternate term
        added
        February 1992 scope note added
ALT   authentic
SN   The quality of being genuine or
        original. (AAT)
UF   genuineness

author catalogs
        VW.18
HN   November 1992 descriptor moved
ALT   author catalog
SN   Catalogs of works arranged alpha-
        betically by authors' names or by
        other persons responsible for the in-
        tellectual content of the works, such
        as editors or translators.
UF   catalogs, author

author indexes
        VW.870
HN   November 1992 descriptor moved
ALT   author index
SN   Indexes consisting of the names of
        authors.
UF   indexes, author

authority control
        KG.142
SN   Establishing,   maintaining,   and
        applying consistent spellings and
        forms of proper names and terms
        used as the descriptive and access
        language for collections of docu-
        ments and objects.
UF   authority work
        control, authority
        control, terminological
        control, vocabulary
        terminological control
        vocabulary control
        work, authority

authority files
        PC.90   (L)
HN   March 1993 descriptor moved
ALT   authority file
SN   Documentation of the form of
        names or subject headings used in a
        catalog, inventory, or information
        retrieval system.
UF   files, authority

authority files, name
USE   name authority files

authority files, subject
USE   subject authority files

authority work
USE   authority control

authorization
USE   authorizing

authorizing
        KG.207
HN   April 1993 lead-in term added
SN   Giving sanction to an action or ob-
        ject, as done by a valid authority.
UF   authorization

authors
        HG.356   (L,R)
HN   February 1993 related term added
        December 1992 alternate terms
        added
ALT   author
        author's
        authors'
SN   Persons who write or otherwise
        compose books, articles, poems,
        plays, or other works which involve
        literary composition and are in-
        tended for publication. (W)
UF   writers
RT   lyricists

authorship
        BM.26   (L)

auto courts
USE   motor courts

Auto-destructive
USE   Destructive Art

auto ferries
USE   car ferries

auto rack cars
USE   rack cars

auto washes
USE   car washes

autobiographies
        VW.263   (L)
HN   November 1992 descriptor moved
ALT   autobiography
SN   Biographies of individuals written
        by themselves.

autobiography
        BM.211

autobody shops
USE   body shops

autocars
USE   automobiles

autochrome
SEE   Autochrome process

Autochrome process
        KT.505   (L)
UK   autochrome
SN   An additive color process using a
        color screen with an irregular pat-
        tern formed from dyed starch
        grains. The screen was coated on a
        glass plate and a panchromatic
        black-and-white emulsion coated on
        top of the screen. The image is ex-

posed through the glass and viewed from the emulsion side.
UF Lumière process

Autochromes
VC.344
HN April 1992 descriptor moved
ALT Autochrome
SN Photographs made by the Autochrome process.

autocycles
USE mopeds

autodromes
USE automobile racetracks

autogiros
TX.25 (L,N)
ALT autogiro
SN Use for aircraft with unpowered horizontally placed rotors which provide lift, akin to those on helicopters, and conventional engine-driven propellers that pull the vehicles forward, as on airplanes.
UF gyroplanes

autograph albums
VW.994 (L,N,R)
HN November 1992 descriptor moved
ALT autograph album
SN Books, loose-leaf binders, or other volumes containing blank leaves, on which persons have written sentiments, quotations, or signatures. (GAHLM)
UF albums, autograph
autograph books
books, autograph

autograph books
USE autograph albums

autograph quilts
USE signature quilts

autographs
VW.959 (L)
HN November 1992 descriptor moved
November 1992 scope note changed
ALT autograph
SN Documents written in, and usually signed with, the writer's own hand.

autographs (signatures)
USE signatures (names)

autoharps
TT.370 (L,N)
ALT autoharp
SN Zitherlike chordophones with a shallow soundbox, furnished with a series of button-controlled chord bars lying across the strings which damp all strings not required for the chord being played at the moment.

automata
PE.32 (H,L,N)
HN December 1992 descriptor added
ALT automaton
SN Mechanical figures or contrivances constructed to move as if by their own power, generally by intricate hidden mechanisms; known since at least the Hellenistic period, as toys, amusements, and in clocks.
UF automatic toys
automatons
toys, automatic

automated guideway transit
USE personal rapid transit

automated guideway works
USE personal rapid transit

automated peoplemovers
USE personal rapid transit

automated teller machines
TH.1102 (L)
HN November 1992 descriptor added
ALT automated teller machine
SN Use for banking machines capable of automatic processing of various transactions between depository institutions and customers; may be on or off the premises of the depository institution.
UF ATMs
automated tellers
automatic teller machines
cash machines
machines, automated teller
machines, automatic teller
machines, cash
machines, money
money machines
teller machines, automated
teller machines, automatic
tellers, automated

automated tellers
USE automated teller machines

automated typesetting
USE computerized composition

automatic
DC.221 (L,N)
HN November 1992 descriptor added
SN Use to describe firearms in which, after initial manual or mechanical loading, the process of firing, extraction, ejection, and reloading continues without intermission as long as the trigger is pressed and the supply of ammunition lasts. To describe firearms which reload automatically after firing but require a squeeze of the trigger for each shot, use **semiautomatic**.
RT semiautomatic

automatic cameras
USE electric eye cameras

automatic data processing
USE data processing

automatic doors
PJ.2183 (L)
HN March 1993 descriptor moved
May 1991 scope note added
May 1991 lead-in term changed, was **automatic doors**
May 1991 descriptor changed, was **mechanically operated doors**
May 1991 alternate term changed, was **mechanically operated door**
ALT automatic door
SN Use for power-operated doors that open and close at the approach of a person or vehicle. (MEANS)
UF doors, automatic
doors, mechanically operated
mechanically operated doors

automatic drills
USE push drills

automatic elevators
PC.132 (L)
HN March 1993 descriptor moved
June 1991 scope note added
ALT automatic elevator
SN Use for elevators that can be operated by the passengers, having at least automatic doors and leveling at landings.
UF elevators, automatic

automatic teller machines
USE automated teller machines

automatic toys
USE automata

automatic watches
USE self-winding watches

automating
USE automation

automation
KG.236 (A,L)
HN April 1993 lead-in term added
November 1992 lead-in term deleted, was **computerization**
January 1991 scope note added
January 1991 lead-in term added
January 1991 alternate term added
ALT automated
SN Installing mechanical or electronic devices, processes, or systems which take the place of human effort, observation, or decision, and which require minimal human intervention in their operation.
UF automating

automatism
BM.988 (L,R)
HN February 1993 descriptor moved
June 1991 alternate term deleted, was **automatist**

automatons
USE automata

Automats (TM)
RK.113 (B)
ALT Automat (TM)
UF restaurants, self-service
self-service restaurants

automobile dealerships
USE automobile showrooms

automobile factories
HN March 1993 descriptor split, use automobile (ALT of automobiles) +
     factories

automobile graveyards
     RM.79   (L)
HN April 1993 descriptor moved
ALT automobile graveyard
UF automobile junkyards
     graveyards, automobile
     junkyards, automobile

automobile junkyards
USE automobile graveyards

automobile museums
HN March 1993 descriptor split, use automobile (ALT of automobiles) +
     museums

automobile race-courses
SEE automobile racetracks

automobile racetracks
     RG.191   (L,B,R)
ALT automobile racetrack
UK automobile race-courses
UKA automobile race-course
UF autodromes
     race-courses, automobile
     racetracks, automobile
     speedways

automobile rack cars
USE rack cars

automobile service stations
USE service stations

automobile showrooms
     PJ.1042   (A,L,B)
HN March 1993 descriptor moved
ALT automobile showroom
SN Includes both places where automobiles are displayed and entire dealership complexes including the
     sales-and-service building and surrounding lot.
UF automobile dealerships
     dealerships, automobile
     showrooms, automobile

automobiles
     TX.137   (A,L,N,B,R)
ALT automobile
SN Use for self-propelled vehicles designed primarily to transport passengers over ordinary roads.
UF autocars
     automobiles, gasoline
     carriages, horseless
     cars (automobiles)
     cars, passenger
     gasoline automobiles
     horseless carriages
     motorcars
     passenger cars (automobiles)

<automobiles by form>
     TX.138

<automobiles by function>
     TX.149

automobiles, convertible
USE convertibles

automobiles, gasoline
USE automobiles

automobiles, jeep
USE jeeps

automobiles, scout
USE scout cars

automobiles, three wheel
USE three-wheelers

automotive museums
USE automobile (ALT of automobiles) +
     museums

automotive vehicles
USE motor vehicles

Autoperipatetikos
USE walking dolls

autopositive printing
     KT.611
HN March 1993 descriptor added
SN Use for those processes of making
     photographic prints that employ
     materials which yield a positive image when exposed to a positive and
     then processed, or a negative image
     when exposed to a negative and
     processed. (CMM)
UF printing, autopositive
RT direct positive processes

autoradiography
     KT.593   (L,R)
HN January 1993 descriptor moved
     December 1992 scope note changed
SN Process that records the location
     and distribution in an object of radioactive substances, or those made
     radioactive in order to be detected,
     when radiation from these substances act on a photographic emulsion placed in close contact with the
     object. When used on a painting,
     identifies areas of pigments through
     elemental half lives.
UF radioautography

autotype
USE carbon process

autowalks
USE moving walkways

autoxidation
     KT.847   (L)
HN January 1993 descriptor added
ALT autoxidized
SN Oxidation caused by the atmosphere
     or self-catalyzed and spontaneous.
     (MHDSTT)

autumn
     BM.726   (L,R)
HN March 1993 scope note added
     November 1992 descriptor moved
SN The season of the year which is the
     transition period from summer to

winter, occurring as the sun approaches the winter solstice, its beginning marked by the autumnal
equinox.
UF fall

aux deux crayons
USE à deux crayons

aux trois crayons
USE à trois crayons

auxiliaries
USE auxiliary views

auxiliaries, naval
USE naval auxiliary ships

auxiliary cartoons
     VC.196
HN April 1992 descriptor moved
ALT auxiliary cartoon
UF cartoons, auxiliary

auxiliary dead latches
     PJ.467
HN April 1993 descriptor moved
ALT auxiliary dead latch
UF auxiliary latch bolts
     auxiliary latches
     bolts, auxiliary latch
     bolts, trigger
     dead latches, auxiliary
     deadlocking latch bolts
     deadlocking latches
     latches, auxiliary dead
     latches, deadlocking
     trigger bolts

auxiliary drawings
USE auxiliary views

auxiliary fire alarm systems
     PC.229
HN March 1993 descriptor moved
ALT auxiliary fire alarm system
SN Use for fire alarm systems that
     transmit an alarm over a municipal
     system to the fire station.
UF fire alarm systems, auxiliary
     systems, auxiliary fire alarm

<auxiliary health care facilities>
     RK.701

auxiliary latch bolts
USE auxiliary dead latches

auxiliary latches
USE auxiliary dead latches

<auxiliary powered watercraft>
     TX.529

auxiliary rim locks
     PJ.511
HN April 1993 descriptor moved
ALT auxiliary rim lock
SN Surface-mounted locks in addition
     to the main lock on a door. (MEANS)
UF locks, auxiliary rim
     rim locks, auxiliary

auxiliary sections
     VC.155

HN April 1992 descriptor moved
ALT auxiliary section
SN Use for oblique sections that are intended to show true shape of an oblique plane in the structure or object.
UF sections, auxiliary

auxiliary ships, naval
USE naval auxiliary ships

auxiliary vessels, naval
USE naval auxiliary ships

auxiliary views
VC.103
HN April 1992 descriptor moved
ALT auxiliary view
SN Use for orthographic drawings projected at an angle other than the usual plan, section, or elevation, in order to show true shape of an oblique plane.
UF auxiliaries
auxiliary drawings
drawings, auxiliary
views, auxiliary

available light photography
KT.589 (L)
UF ambient light photography
existing light photography
low-light photography
photography, ambient light
photography, available light
photography, existing light
photography, low-light

avalanche control
USE avalanche protection

avalanche protection
KG.175 (L)
HN December 1992 descriptor moved
UF avalanche control
control, avalanche
protection, avalanche

avalanches
KM.126 (L,B)
HN March 1993 scope note changed
May 1991 alternate term added
ALT avalanche
SN Occurrences of rapid descent of large masses of snow or ice down a mountainside.

avant-corps
USE pavilions (building divisions)

avant-garde
BM.287 (L,R)
SN Use to describe attitudes, ideas, or works of art or architecture, especially from the late 19th to the mid-20th century, that depart from the existing norm in an original and experimental way.

avant-lettre proofs
USE proofs before letters

Avar
FL.3192 (L,R)

aventails
PJ.3010
ALT aventail
SN Tippets of mail attached around the lower edge and face opening of helmets, commonly basnets, to protect the shoulders, neck, and part of the face; used in the 14th and 15th centuries.
UF camails
RT tippets (costume accessories)

aventurine
MT.576
HN April 1992 descriptor moved
March 1992 lead-in terms added
February 1992 related term added
SN Form of quartz crystal that comes from the Ural mountains and from India, made synthetically for costume jewelry under the name of goldstone. (MH)
UF aventurine quartz
quartz, aventurine
RT gemstone

aventurine glass
MT.278 (H,R)
HN December 1991 descriptor added
SN A translucent glass flecked with metallic particles to imitate the appearance of brownish aventurine quartz.
UF glass, aventurine
glass, goldstone
goldstone glass

aventurine quartz
USE aventurine

avenues
RM.140 (L,B)
HN April 1993 descriptor moved
ALT avenue
SN Use for wide, straight, usually tree-lined roads or approaches.

average
USE mean

aviaries
RK.81 (A,L,N,B,R)
HN March 1993 related term added
ALT aviary
SN Houses, enclosures, or large cages for confining live birds; distinguished from birdhouses which house birds but do not confine them.
RT birdhouses

aviation
KD.101 (L,B)
HN June 1991 descriptor added
SN Branch of aeronautics ·which includes the design, production, and operation of aircraft, particularly heavier-than-air aircraft. (RHDEL2)

aviation museums
USE aeronautical museums

aviation schools
USE aeronautical engineering + schools

aviator jackets
USE bomber jackets

Avignon berry
USE buckthorn berry

Avshars
USE Afshar + rugs

awards
BM.1092 (A,L,N,B,R)
HN February 1993 descriptor moved
September 1992 scope note changed
September 1992 lead-in term deleted, was prizes
September 1992 lead-in term deleted, was certificates of award
ALT award
SN Honors conferred or bestowed, usually including a document or token indicating or symbolizing the award, or remuneration.

awards, contract
USE contract awards

awe
BM.999 (L)
HN February 1993 descriptor moved

awl pikes
TK.54 (N)
ALT awl pike
SN Pikes with a long, spiked blade quadrangular in section and fitted with a disk at the base.
UF pikes, awl

awls
TH.927 (N)
ALT awl
SN Sharp metal points with wood handles; used to make small holes in wood or leather. (BLACKB)

awls, burning
USE burning awls

awls, chisel-end marking
USE scribe awls

awls, flooring
USE bradawls

awls, marking
USE scribe awls

awls, peg
USE peg awls

awls, scratch
USE scribe awls

awls, scribe
USE scribe awls

<awls: woodworking tools>
TH.1407

awmeners
USE aulmonieres

awners
USE aulmonieres

awning hardware
PJ.585
HN April 1993 descriptor moved
UF hardware, awning

awning windows
PJ.2248
HN March 1993 descriptor moved
ALT awning window
SN Windows that have one or more top-hinged, out-swinging sashes. (STEIN)
UF top hung windows
windows, awning
windows, top hung

ax chairs
TC.460
HN January 1993 descriptor moved
ALT ax chair
UF chairs, ax

axatses
TT.546
ALT axatse
SN Gourd rattles of the Ewe of Ghana, made of a calabash covered with a mesh of string, beads, shells, and pieces of bamboo.

axed brick
MT.134
HN April 1992 descriptor moved
SN A brick that has been shaped with an ax and not trimmed when laid. (DAC)
UF brick, axed
brick, rough-axed
rough-axed brick

axes (mathematics)
BM.655
HN January 1991 alternate term added
ALT axis (mathematics)

axes (tools)
TH.525   (L,N,R)
HN March 1993 scope note changed
March 1993 related term added
September 1991 descriptor changed, was **axes**
September 1991 alternate term changed, was **ax**
ALT ax (tool)
SN Use for cutting tools that consist of a relatively heavy edged head fixed to a handle, the edge or edges being parallel to the handle so as to be suited for striking. For axes used as weapons, typically having wider blades, use **axes (weapons)**.
RT axes (weapons)

axes (weapons)
TK.5   (H,N,R)
ALT ax (weapon)
SN Cutting weapons consisting basically of a relatively heavy, flat blade fixed to a handle, wielded by either striking or throwing. For axes used for other purposes, typically having narrower blades, use **axes (tools)**.

RT axes (tools)
gisarmes
halberds
pollaxes

axes, barking
USE barking axes

axes, beginning
USE beginning axes

axes, boatbuilders'
USE shipwrights' axes

axes, carpenters'
USE shipwrights' axes

axes, chip
USE chip axes

axes, cross
USE twivels

axes, dill
USE froes

axes, felling
USE felling axes

axes, fire
USE fire axes

axes, firemen's
USE fire axes

axes, fitting
USE beginning axes

axes, hewing
USE broadaxes

axes, jedding
USE cavils

axes, lath
USE froes

axes, lopping
USE lopping axes

axes, marking
USE marking axes

axes, masons'
USE axhammers

axes, mast
USE mast axes

axes, mast and spar
USE mast axes

axes, mastmakers'
USE mast axes

axes, meat
USE cleavers

axes, mortising
USE mortising axes

axes, pole
USE froes

axes, post
USE mortising axes

axes, rending
USE froes

axes, riving
USE froes

axes, shedding
USE lopping axes

axes, ship
USE shipwrights' axes

axes, ship carpenters'
USE shipwrights' axes

axes, shipbuilders'
USE shipwrights' axes

axes, shipwrights'
USE shipwrights' axes

axes, spar
USE mast axes

axes, split
USE froes

<axes: stone and masonry working equipment>
TH.1330
HN December 1992 guide term moved
December 1992 guide term changed, was *<axes: masonry and plastering tools>*

axes, throwing
USE throwing axes

axes, topping
USE lopping axes

axes, wheelwrights'
USE shipwrights' axes

<axes: woodworking tools>
TH.1411

axhammers
TH.1352   (N)
HN March 1993 lead-in term changed, was **mason's axes**
March 1993 lead-in term changed, was **axes, mason's**
January 1993 scope note changed
December 1992 descriptor moved
ALT axhammer
SN Striking tools having two cutting edges, or one cutting edge and one hammer face, used for dressing or spalling rough stone. (PUTNAM)
UF axes, masons'
masons' axes

axial balance
USE axial symmetry

axial loads
BM.600   (L)
HN March 1993 scope note added
November 1992 descriptor moved
January 1991 alternate term added
ALT axial load
SN Loads or forces acting through the center of gravity of the section of structural members, therefore per-

pendicular to the plane of the section.
UF loads, axial

axial perspective
KT.468
SN Use for a perspective system in which parallels converge to points on a vertical axis.
UF herringbone perspective
perspective, axial
perspective, herringbone

axial-plan
DC.139
HN October 1992 descriptor moved
UF longitudinal-plan

axial sections
USE longitudinal sections

axial stress
BM.640
HN November 1992 descriptor moved
SN Tension and compression forces that are collinear with the long axes of structural members. (DS)
UF normal forces
stress, axial

axial symmetry
BM.92
SN Balanced arrangement of compositional units on either side of a central axis.
UF axial balance
axiality
balance, axial
symmetry, axial

axiality
USE axial symmetry

axiology
KD.74   (L,R)
SN Study of values, primarily of intrinsic values (as those in ethics, aesthetics, and religion), but also of instrumental values (as those in economics), particularly with reference to the manner in which they can be known or experienced, their nature and kinds, and their ontological status. (W)
UF philosophy of value
theory of value
value, philosophy of
value theory
value, theory of

axis, vanishing
USE vanishing axis

Axminster carpets
TC.144   (R)
ALT Axminster carpet
SN Knotted pile carpets originally produced in Axminster, Devon, England. They are woven in one piece with weaving of high quality.
UF Axminsters
carpets, Axminster
RT moquettes

Axminsters
USE Axminster carpets

axonometric drawings
VC.92
HN April 1992 descriptor moved
June 1991 lead-in term added
ALT axonometric drawing
SN Use for drawings in which projectors are parallel, and at least one of the three spatial axes is inclined to the plane of projection. In modern architectural parlance, sometimes used only for strictly orthographic drawings with the object tilted to the plane.
UF axonometric projections
axonometrics
drawings, axonometric
drawings, paraline
paraline drawings
projections, axonometric

axonometric projection
KT.478   (L)
SN Historically, has meant projection in which projectors are parallel, and at least one of the three spatial axes is inclined to the plane of projection. In modern architectural parlance, sometimes used only for strictly orthographic project ion with the object tilted to the plane.
UF projection, axonometric

axonometric projections
USE axonometric drawings

axonometrics
USE axonometric drawings

Axum
FL.148
UF Aksum

ayatollahs
HG.410
HN February 1993 descriptor moved
December 1992 alternate terms added
ALT ayatollah
ayatollah's
ayatollahs'

Ayios Onouphrios
FL.2754
HN April 1993 descriptor added

Ayios Onouphrios ware
HN April 1993 descriptor split, use
Ayios Onouphrios + ware

Aymará
FL.1635   (L)

Ayudhya
FL.2505
UF Ayuthya School
Ayutthaya

Ayuthya School
USE Ayudhya

Ayutthaya
USE Ayudhya

Ayyubid
FL.3550   (L)
HN April 1993 descriptor moved

<Ayyubid painting styles>
FL.3551
HN April 1993 guide term moved

<Ayyubid pottery styles>
FL.3554
HN April 1993 guide term moved

Azande
USE Zande

Azanian
FL.149

Azilian
FL.2565

azimuth circles
PJ.2631   (N)
ALT azimuth circle
SN Graduated rings designed to fit over compasses, compass repeaters, or similar direction finders and often equipped with sighting vanes for measuring azimuths.
UF circles, azimuth

azmalyks
USE asmalyks

Aztalan
FL.829

Aztatlán
FL.1080

Aztec
FL.1014   (A,L,B,R)
UF Mexica

Aztec I
FL.1009
UF Culhucán
Mazapán
Tula-Mazapán

Aztec II
FL.1010
UF Atlatongo
Tenayuca

Aztec III
FL.1011
UF Tenochtitlán

Aztec IV
FL.1012
UF Teocalco
Tlatelolco

Aztec paper
USE bark cloth

azul-indigo
USE indigo

azulejo
MT.187   (B)
HN April 1992 descriptor moved

SN Earthenware tile of Spanish manu-facture, painted and enameled in rich colors. (HAS)

azur d'acre
USE ultramarine blue

azure
USE ultramarine blue

azure blue
USE smalt

azure cobalt
USE cobalt blue

azure d'Alemagna
USE azurite

azurite
MT.2084
HN May 1992 lead-in terms added
May 1992 related term added
May 1992 lead-in term deleted, was **chessylite**
May 1992 lead-in term deleted, was **Armenian stone**
May 1992 lead-in term deleted, was **blue malachite**
January 1992 descriptor moved
UF ashes, blue
azure d'Alemagna
azurro della magna
azzurrite
azzurro della magna
Bergblau
bergblau, Teutonic
bice, blue
bise
bise, Spanish
bleu d'Allemagne
bleu de montagne
bleu Paul Véronèse
blue ashes
blue bice
blue, Bremen
blue, cendre
blue, copper
blue mineral
blue, mountain
Bremen blue
cendre
cendre blue
cendres bleues
cenizas
copper blue
lapis Armenius
mineral blue
mountain blue
Spanish bise
Teutonic bergblau
RT blue verditer

azurite blue
USE grayish blue
moderate greenish blue
moderate purplish blue

azuro oltramarino
USE ultramarine blue

azurro della magna
USE azurite

azurro oltramarino
USE ultramarine blue

azurrum ultramarinum
USE ultramarine blue

azurum transmarinum
USE ultramarine blue

azurum ultramarine
USE ultramarine blue

azzurrite
USE azurite

azzurro della magna
USE azurite

azzurro di smalto
USE smalt

azzurro ultramarino
USE ultramarine blue

B & Bs
USE bed-and-breakfasts

B-and-Bs
USE bed-and-breakfasts

B-ES
USE environmental psychology

Baamba
USE Amba

Babanki
USE Banki

babbar garayas
USE komos

Babbit metal
SEE Babbitt metal

Babbitt
USE Babbitt metal

Babbitt metal
MT.453   (L)
HN April 1993 lead-in term changed, was **Babbits**
April 1993 lead-in term changed, was **bearing alloys**
March 1993 descriptor moved
UK Babbit metal
SN The original name for tin-antimony-copper alloy used for machinery bearings; now used for almost any bearing alloy with either a tin or lead base. (MH)
UF alloy, bearing
Babbitt
bearing alloy
metal, Babbit
metal, Babbitt

Babembe
USE Bembe (Lower Zaire)

Babeo
FL.519

babies
USE infants

Baboma
USE Boma

babool gum
USE gum arabic

babul gum
USE gum arabic

Babunda
USE Mbun

Babur
FL.2313

babushkas
TE.613
ALT babushka
SN Kerchiefs, triangular or folded tri-angularly, with two of the ends tied under the chin; often open at the back.

Babwa
FL.518   (L)
UF Ababua
Boa

Babwendi
USE Bwende

baby blue
USE bluish gray
light bluish gray
pale blue
very light blue
very light greenish blue
very pale blue

baby bonnets
TE.571
ALT baby bonnet
SN Infants' soft hats with hood-shaped crown fitted to the head with a frilled surround, tied under the chin. (FDOF)
UF bonnets, baby

baby books
VW.995   (L)
HN November 1992 descriptor moved
ALT baby book
UF books, baby

baby buggies
USE baby carriages

baby carriages
TX.152   (H,N)
ALT baby carriage
SN Any of various wheeled vehicles for carrying infants; may be pushed or pulled and are often wagonlike or carriagelike in appearance.
UF baby buggies
buggies, baby
carriages, baby
perambulators
prams (baby carriages)

baby doll pajamas
TE.269
UK baby doll pyjamas
SN A form of pajamas in which ex-

posed panties match the fabric of a hip-length top. (NMAHDC)
UF baby dolls (pajamas)
  pajamas, baby doll
  pyjamas, baby doll

baby doll pyjamas
SEE baby doll pajamas

baby dolls
  TV.156
ALT baby doll
SN Use for dolls whose expressions, proportions, and dress mimic those of infants.
UF dolls, baby

baby dolls (pajamas)
USE baby doll pajamas

baby grand pianos
  TT.412   (N)
ALT baby grand piano
SN Grand pianos of the smallest size. (MARCUS)
UF baby grands
  grand pianos, baby
  pianos, baby grand

baby grands
USE baby grand pianos

baby houses
USE dollhouses

baby napkins
SEE diapers

baby pink
USE light pink
  light yellowish pink
  moderate pink
  moderate yellowish pink
  pale purplish pink

baby spoons
  TH.336   (N)
HN April 1993 descriptor added
ALT baby spoon
SN Spoons scaled down in size for use by infants, or for serving small portions of food to an infant.
UF spoons, baby

babyhood
USE infancy

Babylonian
  FL.3074   (L,B,R)

Babylonian, Early
USE Old Babylonian

Babylonian, Old
USE Old Babylonian

baccarat
  KQ.23   (L)

Bacham
USE Cham (Bamileke)

Bachama
  FL.225   (L)

bachelor apartments
USE studio apartments

bachelors (academics)
  HG.881
HN January 1993 alternate terms added
  April 1991 descriptor added
ALT bachelor (academic)
  bachelor's (academic)
  bachelors' (academics)
SN Those who have been awarded a bachelor's degree. (RHDEL2)

bachelors' chests
  TC.891
HN March 1993 descriptor changed, was **bachelor's chests**
  March 1993 lead-in term changed, was **chests, bachelor's**
  January 1993 descriptor moved
ALT bachelor's chest
SN Chests of drawers having a folding top which, when open, serves as a writing board; of a type made in 18th-century England.
UF chests, bachelors'

bacini
  PJ.1959   (A)
HN March 1993 descriptor moved
ALT bacino
SN Ceramic basins pressed into walls as ornament.

back
USE rear

back arches
  PJ.1632
HN March 1993 descriptor moved
  November 1990 scope note changed
ALT back arch
SN Use for arches that carry the primary thickness of a wall over an opening, usually a door or window, when the rest of the wall is carried by other means, such as a lintel, an arch of different form or size, or a decorated frame.
UF arches, back
  arches, rear
  arches, recessed
  arches, sconcheon
  arrière-voussures
  rear arches
  rear vaults
  recessed arches
  sconcheon arches
  vaults, rear

back boards
USE backboards (furniture components)

back catches
  PJ.320
HN April 1993 descriptor moved
UF catches, back

back catches (dog catches)
USE dog catches

back checks
USE door checks

back clips
  PJ.79
HN April 1993 descriptor moved
ALT back clip
SN Special clips used on the back of gypsum board in certain applications, as in some demountable partitions, to hold the board in place by insertion into slots or other receptacles in the framing. (MEANS)
UF clips, back

<back components>
  PJ.2725
HN March 1993 guide term moved

back elevations
USE rear + elevations (building divisions)

back frames
  TC.424
ALT back frame
SN Use for frames to which decorative carved moldings may be attached, often made of wood inferior in quality to that of the carved moldings. (BRESTA)
UF blind frames
  frames, back
  frames, blind

back gutters
  PJ.891
HN March 1993 descriptor moved
ALT back gutter
SN Gutters installed on the uphill side of a chimney on a sloping roof; used to divert water around the chimney. (HAS)
UF gutters, back

back hearths
  PJ.2460
HN March 1993 descriptor moved
  November 1990 descriptor moved
  November 1990 scope note added
ALT back hearth
SN Use for that part of hearths on which the fire is built.
UF hearths, back
  hearths, inner
  inner hearths

back-lighting
SEE backlighting

back matter
  VW.244
HN June 1992 descriptor added
SN Use collectively for the parts of a book that follow the main text, including, for example, appendices, notes, or indexes.
UF backmatter
  end matter
  matter, back
  matter, end

back nuts
PJ.211
HN April 1993 descriptor moved
ALT back nut
SN Threaded nuts which help to create a watertight joint, as on the long thread of a pipe connector, and whose one dished side accepts a grommet. (MEANS)
UF nuts, back

back painting
USE reverse painting on glass
verre églomisé

back plates
USE backplates (finish hardware)

back posts
USE back rails

back rails
PJ.2726
HN March 1993 descriptor moved
ALT back rail
SN Extensions of back legs which support the chair back.
UF back posts
posts, back
rails, back
uprights

back-scatter
USE backscattering

back-scattering
USE backscattering

back splats
USE splats

back stamps
VW.433
HN January 1993 scope note added
November 1992 descriptor moved
ALT back stamp
SN 20th-century term sometimes applied to any marks placed on the underside of any ceramic object but strictly applicable to only such marks made with rubber stamps. (IDC89)
UF stamps, back

back-stool chairs
USE backstools

backboards (furniture components)
PJ.2721
HN April 1993 descriptor changed, was **backboards**
April 1993 alternate term changed, was **backboard**
March 1993 descriptor moved
ALT backboard (furniture component)
SN The board or boards that make up the back of a piece of case furniture and sometimes extend above the top. (KETCH)
UF back boards
boards, back

backboards (sports equipment)
TV.26   (N)

ALT backboard (sports equipment)
SN Use for the flat vertical surfaces at either end of basketball courts to which the baskets are attached.
UF backboards, basketball
basketball backboards
RT basketball

backboards, basketball
USE backboards (sports equipment)

backbones
USE spines

backchoirs
USE retrochoirs

backflap hinges
PJ.373
HN April 1993 descriptor moved
ALT backflap hinge
SN Hinges in two leaves, screwed to the face of a door which is not thick enough to permit the use of butt hinges. (PUTNAM)
UF flap hinges
hinges, backflap

backgammon
KQ.14   (L,N)
UF tric-trac
RT backgammon tables

backgammon tables
TC.1152
HN May 1993 related terms added
January 1993 descriptor moved
ALT backgammon table
SN Gaming tables with tops marked as boards for playing backgammon.
UF tables, backgammon
RT backgammon
tables de tric-trac

background
BM.56
SN In pictorial arts, that part of the composition that appears to be farthest from the viewer. (MAYER)

background brushes
TH.790
ALT background brush
SN Soft camel hair brushes used in lab work, photography, and photoengraving. (QCKAIE)
UF brushes, background

backhoes
TH.446   (L,N)
ALT backhoe
SN Excavating machines used for cutting trenches with a boom-mounted bucket which is drawn through the ground toward the machine.
UF drag shovels
pull shovels
shovels, drag
shovels, pull

backing
MT.1555   (L)
HN November 1992 descriptor added

SN Textile forming the back of something, or placed at or attached to the back of something to support, strengthen, stiffen, or protect it.

backing (process)
USE lining (process)

backing, allover
USE lining (process)

backing brick
MT.98
HN April 1992 descriptor moved
SN A relatively low-quality brick used behind face brick or other masonry. (DAC)
UF backup brick
brick, backing
brick, backup

backing drawknives
TH.1477   (N)
ALT backing drawknife
SN Drawknives with a slight downward thrust of the handles for cutting outside curves, such as on the outside of barrel staves. (SALAM)
UF drawknives, backing

backing-out punches
TH.1211   (N)
ALT backing-out punch
SN Punches mounted on a handle; often used in conjunction with square and round punches in farriers' work.
UF pin punches
punches, backing-out
punches, pin

backlight
USE backlighting

backlighting
KT.746
HN April 1991 descriptor added
UK back-lighting
SN Illumination from behind, and often above, a subject; a technique to produce highlights along edges as well as to separate an object from its background. (IESREF)
UF backlight
lighting, rim
rim lighting

backmatter
USE back matter

backpack baskets
USE pack baskets

backpacks
USE knapsacks

backplates (body armor)
TE.305   (N)
ALT backplate (body armor)
SN Pieces of armor protecting the back of the trunk, consisting either of several wide lames buckled together, or of a single plate, fastened to the

breastplate by straps, hinges, or other means. (TARA)

backplates (finish hardware)
PJ.436
HN April 1993 descriptor moved
April 1993 lead-in terms added
April 1993 descriptor changed, was **backplates**
April 1993 alternate term changed, was **backplate**
ALT backplate (finish hardware)
SN Plates that serve as mounts for knobs or pulls and intervene between them and the cabinetry to which they are attached. (DITTRI)
UF back plates
plates, back

backs (furniture components)
PJ.2724
HN March 1993 descriptor moved
December 1992 scope note added
December 1992 related term added
July 1991 alternate term changed, was **backs**
March 1991 descriptor changed, was **backs**
ALT back (furniture component)
SN Use for the parts of seating furniture that support sitters' backs. For the rearmost surfaces or portions of objects in general, use **backs (portions)**.
RT backs (portions)

backs (portions)
PJ.753
ALT back (portion)
SN Use for surfaces or portions of objects that are opposite to those regarded as fronts or to the most important or useful surfaces. For the adjective describing the location of something at or near the back of something, use **rear**. For the parts of seating furniture that supports sitters' backs, use **backs (furniture components)**.
RT backs (furniture components)
rear

<backs and back components>
PJ.2723
HN March 1993 guide term moved

backs, chair
USE antimacassars
tidies

backs, chimney
USE firebacks

backs, hollow
USE hollow back bindings

backs, tight
USE tight back bindings

backs, turtle
USE whaleback vessels

backsaws
TH.1561 (N)
ALT backsaw
SN Small handsaws whose back edge is stiffened with a steel or brass strip; used in finish carpentry for cutting mitered joints and other joinery work. (MEANS)
UF saws, back

backsaws, fancy
USE bead saws

backscatter
USE backscattering

backscattering
KT.819 (L)
HN November 1992 descriptor added
SN The scattering of radiation, such as x-rays, in a direction approximately opposite to that of the incident radiation and due to reflection from particles of the medium traversed; sometimes produced and examined as a technique for analyzing materials. (RHDEL2)
UF back-scatter
back-scattering
backscatter

Backstein Gothic
USE Backsteingotik

Backsteingotik
FL.3233
UF Backstein Gothic
Gothic, Backstein

backstools
TC.461
HN May 1993 related terms added
January 1993 descriptor moved
ALT backstool
SN Chairs in the form of a four-legged stool to which a back has been added. The term first appeared in the 16th century and was sometimes used in the 17th and 18th centuries for a chair without arms. (DDA)
UF back-stool chairs
chairs, back-stool
chairs, low back (backstools)
chaises à demoiselle
chaises à vertugadin
low back chairs (backstools)
RT caquetoires
stools

backstools, upholstered joined
USE farthingale chairs

backstrips
USE spines

backswords
TK.68 (N)
ALT backsword
SN Heavy military swords with broad blades having a single cutting edge, a flattened back edge, and a well de-

veloped defense for the hand, usually a basket hilt or a shell guard.
RT cutting swords

backup brick
USE backing brick

backwaters
RD.135 (L)
ALT backwater
SN Areas of virtually stagnant water that are joined to a stream but relatively unaffected by its current. (DNE)

Bactrian
FL.1792 (L)
HN April 1993 descriptor moved

Bad Painting
USE Neo-Expressionist

Badarian
FL.2871
UF Tasian

baddeleyite
USE zirconium oxide

badge of Tamarlane
USE chintamani

badge of Tamberlaine
USE chintamani

badge of Timur
USE chintamani

badge, Timur's
USE chintamani

badger blenders
USE blenders (artists' brushes)

badger-hair blenders
USE blenders (artists' brushes)

badger-hair brushes
USE blenders (artists' brushes)

badger planes
TH.1499 (N)
ALT badger plane
SN Large wood hand planes, the mouths of which are cut obliquely from side to side, so that they can work close to a corner. (DAC)
UF planes, badger
planes, rabbet
rabbet planes (badger planes)

badgers
TH.1144
HN December 1992 descriptor moved
ALT badger
SN Tools used inside a pipe or culvert to remove excess mortar or deposits. (DAC)

badges
VW.1158 (L,N,B)
HN June 1992 descriptor added
ALT badge
SN Use for special or distinctive marks, tokens, or devices worn on the per-

son as signs of allegiance, membership, authority, or achievement.
(RHDEL2)

badigeon
MT.2326
HN December 1991 scope note changed
SN Stiff paste often composed of plaster and powdered stone used to fill
holes or cover defects in stone or
wood.

Badin
FL.841

Badjok
USE Chokwe

badminton
KQ.58   (L,B)
RT shuttlecocks

badminton courts
HN March 1993 descriptor split, use
badminton + courts (built works)

badminton halls
USE badminton + courts (built works)

Badr-al-Din Mahmud
FL.3590
HN April 1993 descriptor moved

Baehr Hopewell
FL.848
UF Hopewell, Baehr

baeta
USE baize

baff
USE knots (rug components)

Baffin Island Inuit
FL.1221
UF Baffinland Eskimo
Eskimo, Baffinland
Inuit, Baffin Island
Nunatsiaqmiut

Baffinland Eskimo
USE Baffin Island Inuit

baffles
PJ.2897   (B)
ALT baffle
SN Single opaque or translucent elements which shield a source from
direct view at certain angles and absorb unwanted light. (STEIN)
UF baffles, light
light baffles

baffles, light
USE baffles

Bafia
USE Fia

Bafo
FL.185
UF Fo

Bafum
USE Fum

Bafumungu
USE Fumu

bag tables
USE work tables

Baga
FL.343

Bagam
FL.179
UF Gam

baganas
TT.339
ALT bagana
SN Large, usually rectangular but occasionally round, box lyres of Ethiopia
and the Sudan with ten strings
tuned in pairs in octaves, played
with a plectrum. (KAUF)
UF begannas
begennas
begs

Baganda
USE Ganda

bagasse
MT.1383   (L)
HN February 1992 descriptor moved
June 1990 lead-in term added
SN The residue left after grinding sug-
arcane and extracting the juice, employed in making paper and fiber
building board. (MH)
UF bagasse, sugar cane
megass
sugar cane bagasse

bagasse, sugar cane
USE bagasse

bagatelle
KQ.15   (L,N)

bagatelle boards
USE bagatelle tables

bagatelle tables
TC.1119
HN January 1993 descriptor moved
ALT bagatelle table
UF bagatelle boards
bagatelles
boards, bagatelle
tables, bagatelle

bagatelles
USE bagatelle tables

baggage
USE luggage

baggage cars
TX.270   (N)
ALT baggage car
SN Use for passenger train cars in
which travelers' luggage is carried.
UF cars, baggage

baggage rooms
PJ.1127
HN March 1993 descriptor moved
ALT baggage room

SN Rooms for receiving, checking, and
handling luggage. (RS)
UF rooms, baggage

Baggara
FL.692   (L)

bagh
RM.8
HN April 1993 descriptor moved
SN Use for Islamic formal gardens.

Baghdad portieres
USE cicims

Baghdad School
FL.3553
HN April 1993 descriptor moved

Baghdad strips
USE cicims

Bagirmi
FL.366   (L)

bagnettes
USE astragals

bagpipe players
USE bagpipers

bagpipers
HG.234   (L)
HN January 1993 descriptor added
ALT bagpiper
bagpiper's
bagpipers'
SN Those who play on bagpipes.
(OED2)
UF bagpipe players
players, bagpipe
RT bagpipes

bagpipes
TT.188   (H,L,N)
ALT bagpipe
SN Composite reedpipes consisting of
an air-tight skin, cloth, or (rarely)
rubber bag which serves as the air
reservoir, one or more chanters with
fingerholes on which the melody is
played, and often one or more
drone pipes which sound a continuous background to the melody. All
sounding pipes have reeds and are
attached to the bag by being inserted into tubular wooden stocks
which are tied into openings in the
bag.
RT bagpipers
chanters
drone pipes

bagpipes, Lowland
USE Lowland pipes

bagpipes, Northumbrian
USE Northumbrian pipes

bagpipes, Polish
USE dudas

bagpipes, Scotch
USE Highland pipes

bagpipes, Spanish
USE gajdes

bags (containers)
TQ.3 (L,N)
ALT bag (container)
SN Containers or receptacles of leather, cloth, paper, or other flexible material capable of being closed at the mouth. (RHDEL2)
RT mafrashes
okbashes

bags (costume accessories)
TE.409 (L,N)
ALT bag (costume accessory)
SN Soft or rigid accessories for carrying personal articles, often having a drawstring closure. For bags having a fixed frame and clasp use **purses**.
UF pocketbooks

bags, aquatint
USE dust bags

bags, book
USE schoolbags

bags, carriage
USE traveling bags

bags, chatelaine
USE chatelaine bags

bags, ditty
USE ditty bags

bags, duffel
USE duffel bags

bags, dust
USE dust bags

bags, evening
USE evening bags

bags, garment
USE garment bags

bags, Gladstone
USE Gladstone bags

bags, hot-water
USE hot-water bottles

bags, ice
USE ice bags

bags, kit
USE kit bags

bags, light
USE punching bags

bags, matzah
USE matzah covers

bags, money
USE moneybags

bags, pastry
USE pastry bags

bags, pouch
USE pouches

bags, pounce
USE pounce bags

bags, punching
USE punching bags

bags, resin
USE dust bags

bags, rosin
USE dust bags

bags, saddle
USE saddlebags

bags, salt
USE salt bags

bags, shoe
USE shoe bags

bags, shopping
USE shopping bags

bags, shoulder
USE shoulder bags

bags, spoon
USE salt bags

bags, striking
USE punching bags

bags, tote
USE tote bags

bags, traveling
USE traveling bags

bags, wall
USE wall bags

bags, woolwork
USE carpetbags

baguets
USE astragals

baguettes
USE bead moldings

bagwigs
TE.521
ALT bagwig
SN Wigs in which the backhair was enclosed in an ornamental bag. (EMAEA)

Baham
USE Cham (Bamileke)

Bahía
FL.1132

Baholoholo
USE Holoholo

Bahuana
USE Huana

bahuts
TC.874
HN January 1993 descriptor moved
ALT bahut
SN Medieval French term for portable coffers or chests used for personal luggage, covered in leather and studded with nails and usually having a rounded top. Eventually they took the form of a chest mounted on feet, used for storing goods. The current French form is a decorative high chest or cabinet with an arched or curved top.
UF coffres à bahut

Bahzad School
USE Bihzad School

Bai miao
FL.2013
UF Pai miao

bail bonds
VW.643
HN November 1992 descriptor moved
ALT bail bond
SN Bonds executed by defendants or those legally liable for debt, that state defendants will appear in court when required and that in the event defendants fail to appear, the signers of the bonds will pay to the court the amount of money specified. (BLACKS)
UF bonds, bail

bail handles
PJ.278
ALT bail handle
SN Arched overhead handles which are either fixed or swivelling.
UF bails
bale handles
falling handles
handles, bail
handles, bale
handles, falling

bail pulls
PJ.346
HN April 1993 descriptor moved
December 1992 lead-in term deleted, was **bail handles**
December 1992 lead-in term deleted, was **handles, bail**
August 1990 lead-in terms added
ALT bail pull
UF pulls, bail

bailey bridges
RK.1236 (L,B)
ALT bailey bridge
SN Use for temporary bridges designed for rapid construction of prefabricated, interchangeable, steel-truss panels bolted together.
UF bridges, bailey

baileys
PJ.2466
HN March 1993 descriptor moved
July 1991 scope note changed
November 1990 lead-in term added
ALT bailey
SN The enclosed open spaces within castles; especially applied to Medieval fortifications; sometimes also

used to refer to the outer walls of such spaces.
- UF ballia
  - bayles
  - wards

baileys, inner
- USE inner baileys

baileys, outer
- USE outer baileys

bails
- USE bail handles

bain-marie pans
- USE bains-marie

bain-marie saucepans
- USE bains-marie

Baining
- FL.3759 (L)

Bainov phase
- FL.2209

bains-marie
- TQ.300
- ALT bain-marie
- SN Open vessels meant to be filled with boiling water and into which other containers are placed to warm or cook food. (RHDEL2)
- UF bain-marie pans
  - bain-marie saucepans
  - pans, bain-marie
  - saucepans, bain-marie

baize
- MT.1614
- HN March 1993 scope note changed
  - March 1993 lead-in terms added
  - March 1993 descriptor moved
- SN Loosely woven wool or cotton tabby, finished with a long nap to imitate felt and dyed in solid colors. Used as a protective covering for furnishings, as well as for costume, especially the lining of outerwear.
- UF baeta
  - bay
  - bayes

<Baja Californian Native American>
- FL.1287

Bajokwe
- USE Chokwe

Bajun
- FL.609 (L)
- HN June 1990 lead-in term deleted, was Bajuni

bake boards
- USE bannock boards

bake kettles
- USE Dutch ovens

bake ovens
- TH.53 (H,B)
- HN May 1993 descriptor moved
  - May 1993 related term added

May 1992 lead-in terms added
July 1991 descriptor added
- ALT bake oven
- SN Chambers encased in thick, fire-proof vaults of clay, brick, or stone used for baking bread and other food stuffs.
- UF bakers' ovens
  - baking ovens
  - beehive ovens (bake ovens)
  - Dutch ovens (bake ovens)
  - ovens, bake
  - ovens, baking
  - ovens, beehive
  - ovens, Dutch
- RT ovens

bake ovens (Dutch ovens)
- USE Dutch ovens

bakeboards
- USE bannock boards

baked brick
- USE fired brick

baked enamel
- MT.1848
- HN July 1990 descriptor added
- UF enamel, baked

Bakedi
- USE Teso

Bakelite (TM)
- MT.1212 (L)
- HN January 1993 descriptor moved
- SN The original name for phenol plastic, but now usually covers a range of different types of plastic.

Bakerewe
- USE Kerewe

bakeries
- RK.155 (A,L,B,R)
- HN March 1993 lead-in term changed, was baker's shops
  - March 1993 lead-in term changed, was shops, baker's
- ALT bakery
- UF bakers' shops
  - shops, bakers'

bakers
- HG.770 (L,R)
- HN December 1992 alternate terms added
  - December 1992 descriptor moved
- ALT baker
  - baker's
  - bakers'
- SN Persons who specialize in the making of breads, cakes, cookies, and pastries. (W)

bakers' lamps
- TC.1316
- ALT baker's lamp
- SN Lamps used to inspect ovens, commonly either of tin with a long oval font and tubular handle at one end and a whale oil burner at the other,

or a cast iron cup-shaped font with a wick channel, attached saucer base and usually a hinged lid.
- UF bakers' oven lamps
  - lamps, bakers'
  - lamps, bakers' oven
  - lamps, oven
  - lamps, witch
  - oven lamps
  - oven lamps, bakers'
  - witch lamps

bakers' oven lamps
- USE bakers' lamps

bakers' ovens
- USE bake ovens

bakers' sheets
- USE baking pans

bakers' shops
- USE bakeries

bakers, tin
- USE tin kitchens

bakestones
- TH.87
- HN April 1993 descriptor added
- ALT bakestone
- SN Flat pieces of stone, ceramic materials, or iron used for baking.
- UF baking stones
  - bannock stones
  - stones, bake
  - stones, baking
  - stones, bannock

Bakete
- USE Kete

bakeware
- TQ.283
- SN Any of various heat-resistant containers intended primarily for baking.

Bakheng
- FL.2440
- UF Phnom Bakhen

Bakhtiari
- USE Bakhtiyari

Bakhtiari kilims
- USE Bakhtiyari + rugs

Bakhtiari rugs
- USE Bakhtiyari + rugs

Bakhtiari-Shustar kilims
- USE Bakhtiyari + rugs

Bakhtiaris
- USE Bakhtiyari + rugs

Bakhtiyari
- FL.3721
- HN April 1993 descriptor added
- UF Bakhtiari

baking dishes
- TQ.284 (N)
- ALT baking dish

SN Dishes intended primarily for baking.
UF dishes, baking
RT dishes

baking ovens
USE bake ovens

baking pans
TQ.290　(L,N)
ALT baking pan
SN Pans intended primarily for baking.
UF bakers' sheets
pans, baking
sheets, bakers'
RT pans (containers)

baking stones
USE bakestones

Bakongo
USE Kongo

Bakongo Kingdom
USE Kongo Kingdom

Bakosi
USE Kossi

Bakota
USE Kota

Baku
FL.1804
HN April 1993 descriptor added

Bakuba
USE Kuba (Zaire)

Bakuba Kingdom
USE Kuba Kingdom

Bakus
USE Baku + rugs

Bakusu
USE Kusu

Bakwele
USE Kwele

Bakwese
USE Kwese

Bakwiri
USE Kpe

Bal-bris
FL.2252
UF Bal'bris
Nepalese School

balabaykas
USE balalaikas

balaclava helmets
USE balaclavas

balaclavas
TE.634
ALT balaclava
SN Heavy knitted or crocheted hoods that cover the head, neck and tops of the shoulders; worn especially by soldiers or mountaineers.

UF balaclava helmets
helmets, balaclava

balafons
USE balos

balalaikas
TT.297　(L,N)
ALT balalaika
SN Russian plucked lutelike chordophones consisting of a triangular body with a flat back and slightly arched belly, a long neck with frets, and three strings; it is made in six different sizes.
UF balabaykas
balalaykas

balalaykas
USE balalaikas

Balali
USE Lali

Balalyk-Tepe
FL.1794
HN April 1993 descriptor moved

balance
BM.50　(L,R)
SN Use for the impression of visual equilibrium in a composition.
UF equilibrium (composition)

balance arms
USE beams (balance components)

balance, axial
USE axial symmetry

balance beams
TV.48　(L,N)
ALT balance beam
SN Narrow, and relatively long, wooden or steel beams set horizontally several feet above the floor and upon which performers demonstrate balancing acts and gymnastic moves.
UF balance boards
beams, balance
boards, balance

balance boards
USE balance beams

balance bridges
USE balance cocks

balance cocks
PJ.2643　(L)
ALT balance cock
SN Use for detachable brackets in clocks and watches that carry the upper pivot of the axis of the balance.
UF balance bridges
bridges, balance
cocks, balance

balance pans
USE pans (scale components)

balance, radial
USE radial symmetry

balance scales
USE balances

balance scales, even
USE balances

balance sheets
VW.583　(L)
HN November 1992 descriptor moved
ALT balance sheet
SN Statements of the financial condition, as of a corporation, at a given date showing the equality of total assets to total liabilities plus net worth, or of total liabilities to total assets plus deficit. (W)
UF sheets, balance

balance springs
PJ.2644　(L)
ALT balance spring
SN Coiled springs that determine the time of vibration of balance wheels, with which they work to regulate the progress of the hands on timepieces.
UF springs, balance

balance, symmetrical
USE bilateral symmetry

balance weights
USE weights

balance wheels
PJ.2646　(L)
ALT balance wheel
SN Wheels that oscillate against the tension of balance springs to regulate the beats of clocks or watches.
UF balances (timepiece components)
wheels, balance

balanced steps
PJ.2418
HN March 1993 descriptor moved
ALT balanced step
SN Series of winders arranged so that the small ends of the steps are not much narrower than the parallel steps of the same stair. (PUTNAM)
UF dancing steps
dancing winders
steps, balanced
steps, dancing
winders, dancing

balances
TN.283　(L,N)
ALT balance
SN Scales with a horizontal bar pivoting about a central fulcrum, creating equal-length arms; suspended from the ends of the arms are pans or baskets, in one of which is placed the item being weighed and in the other, a premeasured weight.
UF balance scales
balance scales, even
balances, equal-armed
equal-arm scales
equal-armed balances
even balance scales

scales, balance
scales, equal-arm
scales, even balance

balances (timepiece components)
USE   balance wheels

balances, analytical
USE   analytical balances

balances, assay
USE   assay scales

balances, coin
USE   coin scales

balances, equal-armed
USE   balances

balances, platform
USE   platform scales

balances, spring
USE   spring balances

balances, torsion
USE   torsion balances

balaphons
USE   balos

balasarasvatis
USE   mayuris

balaustre
MT.2690
HN   March 1992 descriptor moved
UF   arariba
canarywood
centrolobium

Balawaste
FL.1818
HN   April 1993 descriptor moved

Bal'bris
USE   Bal-bris

balconets
PJ.971
HN   March 1993 descriptor moved
ALT   balconet
UK   balconettes
UKA   balconette
SN   Use to designate very small balcon-
ies, usually not large enough to
stand on and consisting of little
more than a protective railing.

balconettes
SEE   balconets

balconies
PJ.970   (A,L,N,B,R)
HN   March 1993 descriptor moved
ALT   balcony
SN   Use for railed platforms projecting
from the exterior walls of buildings.
Use also for similar interior features, when small. For larger platforms which extend the length of
one side of a room or are recessed
behind an arcade, use **galleries
(rooms)**.

baldacchinos
USE   baldachins

baldachins
PJ.1750   (A,N,B,R)
HN   March 1993 descriptor moved
May 1991 descriptor moved
November 1990 scope note added
ALT   baldachin
SN   Use for canopies over such features
as thrones, altars, tombs, or doorways; may be suspended, projecting,
or free-standing. For roofed structures with columns built over altars,
use **ciboria (structures)**. (PDARC)
UF   altar canopies
baldacchinos
baldaquins
canopies, altar

baldachins (furniture components)
USE   canopies (bed components)

baldaquins
USE   baldachins

bale handles
USE   bail handles

balection moldings
USE   bolection moldings

baleen
MT.2578   (L)
HN   February 1992 descriptor added
SN   A horny keratinous substance that
grows in the mouth of whales. (W)
UF   whalebone
RT   scrimshaws

Balega
USE   Lega

Balekeshir
USE   Balikesir

Balekesir
USE   Balikesir

Balesa
USE   Lese

Bali
USE   Li

Balikeshir
USE   Balikesir

Balikesir
FL.3654
HN   April 1993 descriptor added
UF   Balekeshir
Balekesir
Balikeshir

Balinese
FL.2459   (L)
ALT   Bali

balisht
TC.46

balk
MT.3038
HN   April 1993 lead-in term added

April 1993 descriptor changed, was
balks
March 1992 descriptor moved
November 1990 descriptor moved
November 1990 scope note changed
SN   Use for large, squared timber.
UF   baulk

ball ammunition
USE   balls (bullets)

ball-and-claw feet
USE   claw-and-ball feet

ball and spear pulls
PJ.347
HN   April 1993 descriptor moved
ALT   ball and spear pull
SN   Hand-forged pulls mounted with
plates shaped like balls with single
spear points projecting from them;
similar to onion pulls. (DITTRI)
UF   pulls, ball and spear

ball-bearing hinges
PJ.375
HN   April 1993 descriptor moved
ALT   ball-bearing hinge
SN   Butt hinges having ball bearings po-
sitioned between the knuckles to re-
duce friction. (MEANS)
UF   hinges, ball-bearing

ball breakers
USE   wrecking balls

ball-burnishing
KT.298
HN   January 1993 descriptor moved
March 1991 alternate term added
ALT   ball-burnished
SN   Smoothing or brightening of sur-
faces by means of metal pellets,
balls, or other metal shapes in a ro-
tating container. (STEIN)

ball caps
USE   baseball caps

ball catches
PJ.321
HN   April 1993 descriptor moved
ALT   ball catch
SN   Catches whose strike holds a com-
municating projection or finger by
means of the pressure exerted by
one or two spring-loaded balls.
(DITTRI)
UF   catches, ball

ball clay
MT.55   (L)
HN   April 1992 descriptor moved
SN   A kind of ceramic clay of exception-
ally small particle size and, consequently, very good plasticity; used
to impart plasticity to other clay
bodies. (MAYER)
UF   clay, ball

ball cocks
PJ.577

HN April 1993 descriptor moved
ALT ball cock
SN Float valves incorporating a spherical float; used to control the height of water. (MEANS)
UF cocks, ball

ball courts
　　RK.964
ALT ball court
SN Use only to designate the generally I-shaped playing area and associated viewing platforms of the ancient Mesoamerican ritual ball game.
UF courts, ball
　　pok-ta-poks
　　tlachtlis

ball feet
　　PJ.2791
HN March 1993 descriptor moved
ALT ball foot
SN Spherical feet, used mainly on tables and case furniture in the second half of the 17th century. (TOMLIN)
UF feet, ball

ball-flowers
SEE ballflowers

<ball game equipment>
　　TV.25

<ball game sets>
　　PC.57

ball games
　　KQ.5　　　　　　　　　　　　(L)
UF games, ball

ball hinges, adjustable
USE adjustable ball hinges

ball joints
　　PJ.685
HN April 1993 descriptor moved
ALT ball joint
SN Flexible mechanical joints that allow the axis of one part to be set at an angle to the other by virtue of the design of the two components. One possesses a fixed spherical shell to accommodate the ball-shaped end of the other. (MEANS)
UF joints, ball

ball mills
　　TH.714　　　　　　　　　　　(L,N)
HN February 1993 descriptor added
ALT ball mill
SN Devices for dispersing pigment in a vehicle, consisting of a rotating cylinder containing pigment, vehicle, and ball bearings or pebbles. (GOTTS)
UF mills, ball
　　pebble mills

ball-peen hammers
　　TH.1022　　　　　　　　　　(N)
HN April 1993 lead-in terms added
ALT ball-peen hammer

SN Hammers having a hemispherical peen, the end opposite the hammering face.
UF ball peen hammers
　　hammers, ball-peen
　　peen hammers, ball

ball peen hammers
USE ball-peen hammers

ball-point pens
　　TH.690　　　　　　　　　　　(L,N)
ALT ball-point pen
SN Pens having as the writing point a small ball that rotates in its socket and inks itself by contact with an inner magazine of ink. (W)
UF pens, ball-point

<ball striking or snaring and throwing equipment>
　　TV.27

ball valves
　　PJ.575
HN April 1993 descriptor moved
ALT ball valve
SN Spherically shaped gate valves which provide a very tight shut-off for fluids in a high-pressure piping system. (MEANS)
UF valves, ball

ballad horns
　　TT.79
ALT ballad horn
SN Aerophones of conical bore, constructed in circular shape with three piston valves and the bell directed either upward or forward; invented around 1870 by one of the English Distin family.
UF amateur voice horns
　　horns, amateur voice
　　horns, ballad
　　horns, vocal
　　horns, voice
　　vocal horns
　　voice horns
　　voice horns, amateur

ballad horns (mellophones)
USE mellophones

ballast
　　MT.1680
SN Heavy material, such as water, sand, or iron, used to increase weight, as in a machine. (STEIN)

ballast resistors
USE ballasts

ballasts
　　PJ.2898　　　　　　　　　　(L)
ALT ballast
SN Devices used with an electric discharge lamp to obtain and maintain the necessary circuit conditions, such as voltage, current, and wave form, for starting and operating. (IESREF)

UF ballast resistors
　　resistors, ballast

ballasts, reference
USE reference ballasts

ball'd candlesticks
　　TC.1236
ALT ball'd candlestick
UF candlesticks, ball'd

ballerinas
　　HG.251　　　　　　　　　　　(L)
HN January 1993 descriptor added
ALT ballerina
　　ballerina's
　　ballerinas'
SN Use specifically for women who dance in classical ballet.

ballet
　　KD.7　　　　　　　　　　　(L,B,R)
HN February 1993 related term added
RT ballet dancers

ballet-dancers
SEE ballet dancers

ballet dancers
　　HG.250　　　　　　　　　　　(L)
HN January 1993 descriptor added
ALT ballet dancer
　　ballet dancer's
　　ballet dancers'
UK ballet-dancers
UKA ballet-dancer
　　ballet-dancer's
　　ballet-dancers'
SN Those who practice the art of ballet.
UF dancers, ballet
RT ballet

ballet shoes
USE ballet slippers

ballet slippers
　　TE.731　　　　　　　　　　(L,N)
ALT ballet slipper
UK dancing sandals
UKA dancing sandal
SN Soft shoes, often of leather or leatherlike fabric, with a rounded toe and little or no heel. Those worn for dance usually have a partial sole which extends from the heel to the ball of the foot.
UF ballet shoes
　　sandals, dancing
　　shoes, ballet
　　slippers, ballet

ballflowers
　　DG.69
ALT ballflower
UK ball-flowers
UKA ball-flower
SN Motifs consisting of three- or four-petal flowers, usually nearly closed over a ball, frequently occurring in hollow moldings in English Gothic architecture. (RS)

ballia
USE baileys

ballistae
    TK.221   (L,N)
ALT ballista
SN Ancient projectile launchers used by the Imperial Romans, built like large crossbows and used to hurl javelins, large rocks, and other large projectiles.
UF arcuballistae

ballistic missile submarines
    TX.440   (N)
ALT ballistic missile submarine
SN Naval submarines carrying ballistic missiles.
UF missile submarines, ballistic
    submarines, ballistic missile

ballistics
    BM.829   (H,L)
HN December 1992 descriptor added
ALT ballistic
SN The motion and behavior of projectiles in flight.

ballnut
USE mockernut hickory

ballock daggers
    TK.17
ALT ballock dagger
UK ballock-knives
UKA ballock-knife
SN Civilian daggers with a hilt resembling a phallic symbol, having a guard formed by two rounded lobes and reinforced on top with a shaped metal washer. Appearing first in the 13th century, they were in wide use until the 17th century, particularly in Flanders, England, and Scotland.
UF ballock knives
    daggers, ballock
    daggers, kidney
    dudgeon-daggers
    kidney daggers
    kidney-daggers
    knives, ballock

ballock-knives
SEE ballock daggers

ballock knives
USE ballock daggers

<balloon and platform frame components>
    PJ.2027
HN March 1993 guide term moved

balloon-back chairs
    TC.550
HN January 1993 descriptor moved
ALT balloon-back chair
SN Chairs with open backs and usually horizontal splats with the top rail and uprights rounded to give an overall balloon shape to the back. (FAIRB)
UF chairs, balloon-back

balloon-back Windsor chairs
    TC.526
HN January 1993 descriptor moved
ALT balloon-back Windsor chair
SN Windsor chairs with a bowlike back comprised of three sawn pieces of wood containing a central vertical back splat, sometimes spindles; common in the mid-19th century. (EVANS)
UF chairs, balloon-back Windsor
    Windsor chairs, balloon-back

balloon barrages
USE barrage balloons

balloon clocks
    TN.162
ALT balloon clock
SN Late-18th-century bracket clocks having a round upper portion, waisted central section, and a rectangular base, with or without small feet, vaguely resembling ascension balloons.
UF clocks, balloon

balloon frame construction
USE balloon frames

balloon frames
    PJ.1410   (B)
HN March 1993 descriptor moved
    August 1991 scope note changed
ALT balloon frame
SN Wooden frameworks in which all vertical structural elements, posts and studs, of the exterior bearing walls and partitions extend the full height of the frame from sill to roof plate.
UF balloon frame construction
    balloon framing
    construction, balloon frame
    frame construction, balloon
    frames, balloon

balloon framing
USE balloon frames

balloon glasses
USE snifters

balloon hats
    TE.567
ALT balloon hat
SN Women's hats with a wide brim, generally of light material over a framework to create an inflated crown; named in commemoration of the pioneering balloon ascent of 1783. (HFC)
UF balloons (hats)
    hats, balloon
    hats, Lunardi
    hats, parachute
    hats, Rubens
    Lunardi hats
    lunardis
    parachute hats
    parachutes (hats)
    Rubens hats

balloon pants
USE shalwar

balloon photography
USE aerial photography

balloon shades
    TC.305
ALT balloon shade
SN Popular term for curtains raised or lowered by cords and rings, made in several variations and distinguished mainly by their bottom hem which, when the curtain is raised, billows in a series of graceful puffs suggesting balloons.
UF shades, balloon
RT pull-up curtains
    shades (coverings)

balloon structures
USE pneumatic structures

balloon views
USE bird's-eye views

ballooning
    KQ.39   (L)
RT hot-air balloons

balloons
    TX.31   (H,L,N)
ALT balloon
SN Use for nonporous, flexible spherical bags made of a lightweight material inflated with heated air or a gas that is lighter than air and designed to rise and float in the atmosphere, usually while carrying aloft passengers or scientific instruments.

balloons (hats)
USE balloon hats

balloons, barrage
USE barrage balloons

<balloons by function>
    TX.32

<balloons by lifting method>
    TX.36

balloons, dirigible
USE airships

balloons, hot-air
USE hot-air balloons

balloons, meteorological
USE meteorological balloons

balloons, sounding
USE sounding balloons

balloons, weather
USE meteorological balloons

ballot boxes
    TQ.600   (L,N)
ALT ballot box
UF boxes, ballot
    boxes, voting
    voting boxes
RT boxes (containers)

ballots
VW.520 (L,N)
HN November 1992 descriptor moved
ALT ballot
SN Sheets of paper, cards, or other devices used to cast a vote or announce a slate of candidates. (GMGPC)
UF ballots, election
election ballots
election tickets
papers, voting
tickets, election
voting papers

ballots, election
USE ballots

ballrooms
PJ.1064 (A,B,R)
HN March 1993 descriptor moved
ALT ballroom

balls (bullets)
TK.263 (N)
ALT ball (bullet)
SN Use for solid bullets of spherical or conical shape, containing no propellant or explosive, fired from small arms. For the spherical projectiles made to be fired from cannons, use **cannonballs**.
UF ammunition, ball
ball ammunition
RT cannonballs

balls (foot components)
PJ.2826 (R)
HN March 1993 descriptor moved
ALT ball (foot component)

balls (parties)
KM.153 (L,R)
HN May 1991 alternate term added
ALT ball (party)

balls (recreational artifacts)
TV.2 (H,L,N)
ALT ball (recreational artifact)
SN Round or roundish objects of various materials and sizes, inflated, soft, or solid used in many sports and games.
RT cricket
lacrosse

balls, breaker
USE wrecking balls

balls, cannon
USE cannonballs

balls, chain
USE chain shot

balls, coffee
USE tea balls

balls, cup and
USE cup-and-ball toys

balls, fancy
USE fancy dress balls

balls, fancy dress
USE fancy dress balls

<balls for sports>
TV.34

balls, headache
USE wrecking balls

balls, ink
USE ink balls

balls, inking
USE ink balls

balls, medicine
USE medicine balls

balls, Minié
USE Minié balls

balls, tea
USE tea balls

balls, volley
USE volleyballs

balls, wrecking
USE wrecking balls

balm of Gilead
MT.2870
HN March 1992 descriptor moved
UF balsam, hybrid
Gilead, balm of
hybrid balsam
Populus candicans
Populus gileadensis

balmorals (boots)
TE.708
ALT balmoral (boot)
SN Closed-front, laced ankle boots characterized by the vamp wings being extended along either side to form a galosh. (NMST)
UF bals

Balmorals (caps)
TE.528 (N)
ALT Balmoral (cap)
SN Round, flat caps with the crown projecting on all sides. (W)

Balmorals (petticoats)
TE.233
ALT Balmoral (petticoat)
SN Very full, ankle-length petticoats of gray or white horsehair, worn to hold out the skirt before and in place of the cage crinoline.

balnea
RK.747
HN March 1993 related term added
ALT balneum
SN Use for public or private ancient Roman baths or bath buildings of ordinary size. For the great ancient Roman baths, use **thermae**.
RT thermae

Baloch
USE Baluch

Balochi rugs
USE Baluch + rugs

Balochis
USE Baluch + rugs

Balochs
USE Baluch + rugs

balofons
USE balos

Baloi
USE Loi

Balombo
USE Lumbu

Balooch
USE Baluch

Baloochs
USE Baluch + rugs

balos
TT.531 (L)
ALT balo
SN Xylophones of the Manding people of West Africa, having wood keys thinned on the ends and undersides for tuning and with a gourd resonator beneath each; they are played exclusively by male professional musicians, using a rubber-tipped hammer in each hand and often with bells strapped to their wrists.
UF balafons
balaphons
balofons

Balouch
USE Baluch

Balovale
USE Lwena

bals
USE balmorals (boots)

balsa wood
MT.2922 (L)
HN March 1992 descriptor moved
UF Ochroma lagopus
wood, balsa

balsam
MT.1235 (L)
HN April 1992 descriptor moved
UF oleoresin

balsam, Canada
USE Canada balsam

balsam, copaiba
USE copaiba balsam

balsam fir
MT.2940 (L)
HN March 1992 descriptor moved
UF Abies balsamea
fir, balsam

balsam, hybrid
USE balm of Gilead

balsam, Maracaibo
USE   Maracaibo balsam

balsam of Peru
USE   Peru balsam

balsam, para
USE   para balsam

balsam, Peru
USE   Peru balsam

balsam poplar
       MT.2871
HN   March 1992 descriptor moved
UF   poplar, balsam
       Populus balsamifera
       Populus tacamahaca
       tacamahac

balsam poplar, western
USE   black cottonwood

balsam, tolu
USE   tolu balsam

baltei
       PJ.1505
HN   March 1993 descriptor moved
       November 1990 scope note changed
ALT   balteus
SN   Decorative bands often encircling
       and seeming to constrain the middle
       of the bolsters on Ionic capitals.

Baltic chests
USE   Nonsuch chests

Baltic pine
USE   Scotch pine

Baltic redwood
USE   Scotch pine

Baltimore album quilts
       TC.242
ALT   Baltimore album quilt
SN   Particularly fine album quilts made
       by a group of women living in the
       Baltimore area in the mid-19th
       century.
UF   album quilts, Baltimore
       Baltimore brides' quilts
       Baltimore quilts
       brides' quilts, Baltimore
       quilts, Baltimore
       quilts, Baltimore album
       quilts, Baltimore brides'

Baltimore brides' quilts
USE   Baltimore album quilts

Baltimore clippers
       TX.301
ALT   Baltimore clipper
SN   Use for fast, powerful seagoing wa-
       tercraft, usually schooner- or brig-
       rigged, with fine entrance, long run,
       moderate to pronounced drag, and
       strong deadrise; built in the first
       half of the 19th century and often
       involved in illegal trades, either as

smugglers or slavers, or as revenue
vessels trying to catch smugglers.
UF   clippers, Baltimore

Baltimore quilts
USE   Baltimore album quilts

Balualua
USE   Lwalwa

Baluba
USE   Luba

Baluch
       FL.1892
HN   April 1993 descriptor added
UF   Baloch
       Balooch
       Balouch
       Baluchi
       Belouch
       Bolochi

Baluchi
USE   Baluch

Baluchi carpets
USE   Baluch + rugs

Baluchi rugs
USE   Baluch + rugs

Baluchis
USE   Baluch + rugs

Baluchs
USE   Baluch + rugs

Balumbu
USE   Lumbu

baluster columns
       PJ.1461   (A)
HN   March 1993 descriptor moved
       October 1991 scope note changed
ALT   baluster column
SN   Columns resembling balusters, com-
       posed of a base, a potlike element, a
       bulbous shaft, and a capital.
UF   baluster shafts
       columns, baluster
       shafts, baluster

baluster legs
       PJ.2838
HN   March 1993 descriptor moved
ALT   baluster leg
UF   baluster turned legs
       bulbous legs
       legs, baluster
       legs, baluster turned
       legs, bulbous
       turned legs, baluster

baluster shafts
USE   baluster columns

baluster turned legs
USE   baluster legs

balusters
       PJ.2345   (L,N,R)
HN   March 1993 descriptor moved
ALT   baluster
SN   Short vertical members used to sup-

port a stair handrail or coping,
often circular in section with a vase-
shaped outline. Used also in furniture, as on the backs of chairs.
UF   banisters

balusters (capital components)
USE   bolsters (capital components)

<balustrade and railing components>
       PJ.2344
HN   March 1993 guide term moved

balustrades
       PJ.2342   (A,B,R)
HN   March 1993 descriptor moved
ALT   balustrade
SN   Parapets or low screens composed
       of balusters and carrying a rail or
       other horizontal member that is
       usually heavy in proportion to the
       balusters themselves. (RS)

<balustrades, railings and their
*   components>*
       PJ.2341
HN   March 1993 guide term moved

Bamana
USE   Bambara

Bambala
USE   Mbala (Western Zaire)

Bambara
       FL.373   (L)
HN   June 1990 lead-in terms added
       June 1990 descriptor changed, was
       Bamana
UF   Bamana
       Banmana

Bambete
USE   Mbete

bambocciate
       VC.610   (R)
ALT   bambocciata
SN   Small paintings depicting low-life
       and peasant genre scenes, originally
       those created in the 17th century by
       Northern artists living in Italy.

Bambole
USE   Mbole

bamboo
       MT.2622   (A,L,B,R)
HN   March 1992 descriptor moved

bamboo, split
USE   split bamboo

Bamenjo
       FL.180   (L)
UF   Menjo

Bamileke
       FL.178   (L)
UF   Mileke

bamsuris
USE   bansuris

Bamum
FL.194   (L)
UF Mum
    Mun

Ban Chieng
FL.2489
UF Ban Jieyang

Ban Jieyang
USE Ban Chieng

bana
USE banjis

Banana
USE Masa (Sudanese)

banana boats
TQ.496
ALT banana boat
SN Term used by tableware designers
    and glass manufacturers at the end
    of the 19th century for U-shaped
    dishes set on a high stem and in-
    tended to hold bananas.
UF banana bowls
    banana dishes
    boats, banana
    bowls, banana
    dishes, banana
RT bowls (vessels)

banana bowls
USE banana boats

banana dishes
USE banana boats

banana oil
USE amyl acetate

banc lits
USE settle beds

bancelles
USE banquettes (benches)

banco
MT.56
HN April 1992 descriptor moved

bancos
USE benches

Band ceramics
USE Bandkeramik

band cups
TQ.467
ALT band cup
SN Black-figure kylikes characterized by
    decoration in a band, generally in
    the zone of the handles.
UF cups, band

band-masters
SEE bandmasters

band patterns
USE running ornament

band saws
TH.543   (L,N)
ALT band saw
SN Power saws with a continuous piece

of flexible steel running around two
pulleys and with teeth on one or
both sides; used primarily to cut
wood, but with the proper blade
may be used to cut metal.
UF endless saws
    ribbon saws
    saws, band
    saws, endless
    saws, ribbon

band shells
RK.878   (A,B)
ALT band shell
SN Concave,   acoustically   resonant
    structures at the back of outdoor
    bandstands. (RHDEL2)
UF orchestra shells
    shells, band
    shells, orchestra

bandannas
TE.424   (L,N)
ALT bandanna
SN Large silk or cotton handkerchiefs
    that usually have a solid ground of
    red or blue with simple figures or
    geometric forms in white or yellow
    and which are often printed by tie-
    dyeing. (W)

bandboxes
TQ.186   (H,L,N,R)
ALT bandbox
SN Boxes, usually cylindrical, of paste-
    board or thin wood for holding light
    articles of attire such as ruffs, col-
    lars, and hats. (W)
RT hatboxes

bandeaux
TE.605
ALT bandeau
SN Headbands, generally of soft mate-
    rial, tied horizontally around the top
    of the head, across the forehead.

bandeaux (brassieres)
USE brassieres

banded (pottery style)
USE Bandkeramik

banded columns
PJ.1462
HN March 1993 descriptor moved
    November   1991   lead-in   terms
    added
    September 1991 lead-in term de-
    leted, was **rusticated columns**
    September 1991 lead-in term de-
    leted, was **columns, rusticated**
ALT banded column
SN Use for columns with drums alter-
    nately larger and smaller, or plainer
    and richer.
UF blocked columns
    columns, banded
    columns, blocked
    columns, ringed
    ringed columns

Banded ware
USE Bandkeramik

Banded ware, Incised
USE Stichbandkeramik

bandelets
USE annulets

banderillas
TK.240   (N)
ALT banderilla
SN Ornamented barbed darts thrust
    into the neck and shoulders of the
    bull during a bullfight.

Bandi
USE Gbande

banding
DG.3
HN March 1993 descriptor moved
SN Decorative border of contrasting
    types of wood cut at varying angles
    to the grain, such as for finishing
    the edges and rims of furniture.

banding, cross
USE cross banding

banding, feather
USE feather banding

banding, herringbone
USE feather banding

banding planes
TH.1500   (N)
ALT banding plane
SN Wide planes with a rabbet taken out
    of one side and a blade that cuts
    flush with the rabbet; used for cut-
    ting wide bands of particular
    depths, the depth determined by
    the depth of the rabbet and the
    width determined by the width of
    the blade. (MERCER)
UF planes, banding

banding, straight
USE straight banding

Bandirma
FL.3655
HN April 1993 descriptor added
UF Panderma

bandits, one-armed
USE slot machines

Bandkeramik
FL.2591   (L)
UF Band ceramics
    banded (pottery style)
    Banded ware
    ceramics, Band
    ware, Banded

bandleaders
USE bandmasters

bandmasters
HG.216   (L)
HN February 1993 descriptor moved

November 1992 alternate terms added
June 1990 lead-in term added
ALT bandmaster
    bandmaster's
    bandmasters'
UK band-masters
UKA band-master
UF bandleaders

bands (collars)
    TE.651
ALT band (collar)
SN Flat, stand-up collars, starched, wired, or otherwise stiffened, especially those commonly worn by men and women in the 17th century.

bands (ensembles)
    HG.27   (L)
HN December 1991 descriptor added
ALT band (ensemble)
SN Use for groups of musicians which either play related groups of instruments, such as all brass, or which serve a particular function, such as for rehearsals, dances, or parades.

bands, arch
USE archivolts

bands, chevroned
USE zigzags

bands, cloud
USE cloud bands

bands, fret
USE frets (patterns)

bands, ophrey
USE orphreys

bands, steel
USE steel bands

bands, swaddling
USE swaddling bands

bands, undulate
USE undulate bands

bands, window
USE ribbon windows

bandsmen
    HG.215   (L)
HN February 1993 descriptor moved
    November 1992 alternate terms added
ALT bandsman
    bandsman's
    bandsmen's
SN Members of a band of musicians. (W)

bandstands
    RK.879   (H,L,B)
HN September 1990 scope note added
ALT bandstand
SN Use for structures with raised platforms on which a band or orchestra plays; often roofed when sited outdoors.

Bandwurmstil
USE Jugendstil

bandy legs
USE cabriole legs

Bangi
    FL.525

bangios
USE banjos

Bangkok
    FL.2508
UF Ratanakosin

bangle bracelets
USE bangles

bangles
    TE.470   (N)
ALT bangle
SN Nonflexible bracelets that slip over the hand or which are hinged and closed by a clasp. (HNDOJ)
UF bangle bracelets
    bracelets, bangle

Bangombe
USE Ngombe

Bangomo
USE Ngom

Bangongo
USE Ngongo

Bangor limestone
    MT.858
HN April 1992 descriptor moved
UF limestone, Bangor

Bangua
USE Ngwa

Bangwa
USE Ngwa

banians
USE banyans

banister-back chairs
    TC.551
HN January 1993 descriptor moved
ALT banister-back chair
UF banister chairs
    chairs, banister
    chairs, banister-back

banister-back chairs, harp
USE lyre-back chairs

banister chairs
USE banister-back chairs

banister planes
USE capping planes
    handrail planes

banisters
USE balusters
    handrails

Banjabi
USE Nzebi

banjars
USE banjos

banjis
    TC.86
ALT banji
SN Multicolored spotted rugs produced in ancient southwestern China. (ROSTOV)
UF bana

banjo clocks
    TN.175   (L)
ALT banjo clock
SN American pendulum wall clocks having a circular case for the dial, a narrow tapering body, and a boxlike base, resembling a banjo; design invented and patented by Simon Willard in 1802.
UF clocks, banjo
    improved patent timepieces
    patent timepieces, improved
    timepieces, improved patent

banjo players
USE banjoists

banjoists
    HG.225   (L)
HN January 1993 descriptor added
ALT banjoist
    banjoist's
    banjoists'
SN Those who play the banjo. (OED2)
UF banjo players
    players, banjo
RT banjos

banjors
USE banjos

banjos
    TT.298   (L,N)
ALT banjo
SN American plucked chordophones with a long, guitarlike fretted neck and a circular belly of tautly stretched skin, parchment, or plastic against which the bridge is pressed by the strings, varying in number from four to six in different models.
UF bangios
    banjars
    banjors
RT banjoists

banjos, finger-style
USE five-string banjos

banjos, five-string
USE five-string banjos

bank architecture
USE banks (buildings)

bank barns
    RK.55
HN February 1992 scope note added
ALT bank barn
SN Use for two-story barns, usually dug into a hillside thus providing

ground-level entrances to both stories.
UF barns, bank

bank barns, German
USE Pennsylvania bank barns

bank barns, Pennsylvania
USE Pennsylvania bank barns

bank buildings
USE banks (buildings)

bank checks
USE checks

bank drafts
HN July 1991 descriptor deleted, made lead-in to **drafts (negotiable instruments)**

bank drafts
USE drafts (negotiable instruments)

bank lobbies
USE banking rooms

bank notes
USE paper money

bank notes, national
USE national bank notes

bank statements
VW.571   (L,N)
HN November 1992 descriptor moved
ALT bank statement
SN The statements, usually monthly, rendered by a bank to a depositor. (GAHLM)
UF statements, bank

bankbooks
VW.564   (N)
HN November 1992 descriptor moved
ALT bankbook
SN Books held by depositors in which a bank enters a record of the depositor's transactions. (RHDEL2)
UF passbooks

banker-marks
USE masons' (ALT of masons) + marks (symbols)

banker masons
HG.828
HN December 1992 alternate terms added
ALT banker mason
banker mason's
banker masons'
SN Persons who perform the final preparation work on stone masonry blocks. (W)
UF masons, banker

bankers
HG.617   (L)
HN April 1993 related term added
December 1992 alternate terms added
ALT banker

banker's
bankers'
RT banking

Banki
FL.195
UF Babanki

banking
KG.244   (L)
HN April 1993 related term added
January 1991 scope note added
SN Business of receiving and safeguarding money on deposit, loaning money, eextending credit, and facilitating the transfer of funds by check, draft, or exchange.
RT bankers

banking halls
USE banking rooms

banking rooms
PJ.1163
HN March 1993 descriptor moved
ALT banking room
SN Use for rooms in banks open to the public for doing business and generally containing the tellers' stations, writing desks, and sometimes also officers' platforms.
UF bank lobbies
banking halls
halls, banking
lobbies, bank
rooms, banking

Banko
FL.2094

bankruptcy, petitions for
USE petitions for bankruptcy

bankruptcy proceedings
VW.607
HN November 1992 descriptor moved
UF proceedings, bankruptcy

banks (benches)
USE benches

banks (buildings)
RK.130   (A,L,B,R)
HN March 1993 descriptor changed, was **banks**
March 1993 alternate term changed, was **bank**
ALT bank (building)
UF architecture, bank
bank architecture
bank buildings
buildings, bank

banks (containers)
TQ.165   (L)
ALT bank (container)
SN Small containers often ornamental or mechanical for holding coins. (W)
UF banks, coin
banks, penny
coin banks
penny banks

banks (riverbanks)
USE riverbanks

banks, blood
USE blood banks

banks, branch
USE branch banks

banks, coin
USE banks (containers)

banks, drive-in
USE drive-in banks

banks, Federal Reserve
USE Federal Reserve banks

Banks Island
FL.3810   (L)

banks, loading
USE loading docks

banks, mechanical
USE mechanical banks

banks, mechanical coin
USE mechanical banks

banks, mechanical penny
USE mechanical banks

banks, mobile
USE mobile banks

banks, penny
USE banks (containers)

banks, piggy
USE piggy banks

banks, savings
USE savings banks

banks, spoil
USE spoil banks

Bankutshu
USE Nkutshu

Banmana
USE Bambara

banner screens
USE pole screens

banners
VW.1124   (H,L,N)
HN June 1992 descriptor added
ALT banner
SN Use for pieces of cloth or other flexible material painted with signs or decorative designs and intended to be displayed by hanging or suspending. In heraldry, use for square flags bearing heraldic devices. For other cloths intended to symbolize or to signal, prefer **flags**.

Bannock
FL.1322   (L)

bannock boards
TH.88
HN April 1993 descriptor added
ALT bannock board

SN Thick wooden planks, sometimes with a short one-legged support, on which cakes are baked before a fire. (HEARTH)
UF bake boards
    bakeboards
    boards, bake
    boards, bannock

bannock stones
USE bakestones

banquet cameras
    TH.767
ALT banquet camera
SN Cameras with wide-angle lenses capable of producing oversized, wide-angle images of great depth and clarity.
UF cameras, banquet

banquet halls
    PJ.1047   (H,B)
HN March 1993 descriptor moved
ALT banquet hall
SN Large rooms, halls, or apartments designed or used for festive or state functions.
UF banquet rooms
    halls, banquet
    rooms, banquet

banquet lamps
    TC.1266
ALT banquet lamp
SN Ornate kerosene table lamps with a high stem dating to the late 19th and early 20th centuries.
UF lamps, banquet
RT kerosene lamps

banquet rooms
USE banquet halls

banquet tables
USE dining tables

banquettes (benches)
    TC.706
HN May 1993 related term added
    January 1993 descriptor moved
    May 1991 descriptor changed, was
        banquettes
    May 1991 alternate term changed,
        was **banquette**
ALT banquette (bench)
SN Small benches usually with upholstered seats; in form they resemble a tabouret lengthened and supported on six or more legs. (DDA)
UF bancelles
RT tabourets

banquettes (defensive wall components)
    PJ.2483
HN March 1993 descriptor moved
ALT banquette (defensive wall component)
SN Steps made on the ramparts of works near the parapets, for the troops to stand upon, in order to fire over the parapet. (UMD)

banquettes (pouffes)
USE pouffes

banquettes (sidewalks)
USE sidewalks

banquettes de croisée
    TC.721
HN January 1993 descriptor moved
ALT banquette de croisée
SN Banquettes made to stand in the embrasure of a window. (DDA)
UF banquettes d'embrasure

banquettes d'embrasure
USE banquettes de croisée

bansuris
    TT.6   (L)
ALT bansuri
SN Large transverse flutes used in Hindustani or North Indian classical music. (NGDMI)
UF bamsuris
    basuris

Bantéai Chhmar
USE Banteay Chmar

Banteay Chmar
    FL.2441
UF Bantéai Chhmar

Banteay Srei
    FL.2442

Bantu Kavirondo
    FL.674   (L)
UF Kavirondo

Banyamituku
USE Metoko

Banyangi
USE Anyang (Nigerian)

Banyankole
USE Nkole

banyans
    TE.4
ALT banyan
SN Men's loose-skirted wraps worn informally from the 17th to early 19th century; so called from their resemblance to similar garments worn by Banyans, a caste of Hindu merchants.
UF banians
    indian nightgowns
    nightgowns, indian

Banyoro
USE Nyoro

Banyun
    FL.335

Banza
USE Mbanza

baolis
    RK.565   (A)
ALT baoli
SN Use for well constructions of India,

often architecturally embellished, with steps deeply cut down to a water-drawing area.
UF stepped wells
    wavs
    wells, stepped

Baotou
USE Pao-t'ou

Baotou-Suiyuan
USE Pao-t'ou

Baoulé
USE Baulé

Bapende
USE Pende

Baphuon
    FL.2437

baptismal basins
    TQ.155   (H,N,R)
ALT baptismal basin
SN Circular or oval vessels used for the sacrament of baptism by aspersion. Many are unornamented and bear no religious emblems.
UF baptismal bowls
    basins, baptismal
    bowls, baptismal
RT basins

baptismal bowls
USE baptismal basins

baptismal certificates
    VW.706   (L,N)
HN November 1992 descriptor moved
ALT baptismal certificate
SN Certificates which record the administration of the sacrament of baptism for an individual; often substituted for birth records that are unobtainable. (GAHLM)
UF certificates, baptismal

baptismal fonts
USE fonts (religious building fixtures)

baptismal registers
    VW.710
HN November 1992 descriptor moved
ALT baptismal register
SN Registers which record the administration of the sacrament of baptism; often substituted for birth records that are unobtainable. (GAHLM)
UF registers, baptismal

baptisms
    KM.37   (H,L,R)
HN February 1991 alternate term added
    February 1991 descriptor changed,
        was **baptism**
ALT baptism

Baptist
    BM.472   (L,B)

baptisteries
    RK.1037   (A,L,B,R)
ALT baptistery

SN Use for separate buildings or parts of buildings containing a font for the baptismal rite.

baptizing
KG.301
SN Ceremonially immersing in or applying water to someone as an initiation rite or sacrament of the Christian church. (RHDEL2)

bar (glass)
USE cane (glass)

bar-b-ques
USE barbecue grills

bar-back chairs
TC.579
HN January 1993 descriptor moved
ALT bar-back chair
UF chairs, bar-back

bar-back sofas
USE chair-back settees

bar brooches
SEE bar pins

bar clamps
TH.1623   (N)
HN April 1993 lead-in term changed, was **bar clamps**
April 1993 alternate term changed, was **joiner's clamp**
March 1993 descriptor changed, was **joiner's clamps**
March 1993 lead-in term changed, was **clamps, joiner's**
ALT bar clamp
SN Long bar-type clamps either of wood or metal with an adjustable stop at one end, and a screw-type stop at the other. (SALAM)
UF clamps, bar
clamps, joiners'
joiners' clamps

bar feet
USE runner feet

bar graphs
VW.152
HN November 1992 descriptor moved
ALT bar graph
UF graphs, bar

bar handles
PJ.334
HN April 1993 descriptor moved
ALT bar handle
UF handles, bar

bar joists
USE open web joists

bar mitzvahs
KM.38   (L)
HN May 1991 alternate term added
ALT bar mitzvah

bar pins
TE.486

ALT bar pin
UK bar brooches
UKA bar brooch
SN Long, narrow ornamental pins.
UF brooches, bar
pins, bar

bar shot
TK.248   (N)
SN Shot for cannons, consisting of two spheres, hemispheres, or cylinders connected by a bar of iron, used primarily to destroy masts or rigging in naval combat. (QCKDWT)
UF shot, bar

bar spoons
USE barspoons

bar stools
USE barstools

bar tracery
PJ.2326
HN March 1993 descriptor moved
SN Openwork of molded mullions that divide a window into lights in decorative patterns; common in the Gothic style.
UF tracery, bar

Bara
FL.556   (L)

Baradostian
FL.3089

Barat, Irian
USE Irian Jaya

baratine
USE barium sulfate

Barawa
FL.210

Barba
USE Bargu

Barbacoa
FL.1672

Barbarian
USE Migration period

barbecue grills
TH.59
HN April 1993 descriptor added
ALT barbecue grill
SN Portable grills with metal racks on which food is broiled directly over a charcoal fire or other heat source.
UF bar-b-ques
barbecues
charcoal grills
grills, barbecue
grills, charcoal

barbecues
USE barbecue grills

barbed dowel pins
PJ.218
HN April 1993 descriptor moved
ALT barbed dowel pin

SN Short, headless pins with a sharp point on one end and barbs between the two ends, used largely for fastening the mortise-and-tenon joints in a window sash and for door work. (PUTNAM)
UF dowel pins, barbed
pins, barbed dowel

barbed nails
PJ.179
HN April 1993 descriptor moved
ALT barbed nail
UF nails, barbed

barbed wire
MT.508   (L)
HN April 1992 descriptor moved
UF wire, barbed

barbells
TV.45   (L,N)
ALT barbell
SN Use for the apparatus used in weightlifting, consisting generally of a bar with replaceable, disk-shaped weights fastened to the ends. (RHDEL2)

barbers
HG.87   (L)
HN November 1992 alternate terms added
December 1990 descriptor added
ALT barber
barber's
barbers'
SN Those whose occupation is to shave or trim the beard and to cut and dress the hair of their primarily male clientele.

barbers' basins
USE shaving basins

barbers' bowls
USE shaving basins

barbers' chairs
TC.591   (L,N)
HN May 1993 related term added
March 1993 descriptor changed, was **barber's chairs**
January 1993 descriptor moved
ALT barber's chair
UF chairs, barbers'
RT mechanical furniture

barbers' chairs (corner chairs)
USE corner chairs

barbershops
RK.189   (A,L,B)
ALT barbershop

barbicans
PJ.2498   (A,B)
HN March 1993 descriptor moved
ALT barbican
SN Outworks in Medieval fortifications, such as gate towers, but more fre-

quently an advance work used to flank the approach to a gateway. (RS)

barbières
USE   shaving stands

barbuts
      TE.284
ALT   barbut
SN   Open helmets usually forged in one piece, having at first an ogival-shaped skull, later a rounded one, which extended down to protect the cheeks, leaving a small opening for the face. They were in use from the mid-14th to the late 15th century.
UF   burbuts

Barcelona chairs
      TC.463
HN   January 1993 descriptor moved
ALT   Barcelona chair
UF   chairs, Barcelona

bardiches
USE   berdyshes

bardiglio
      MT.722
HN   April 1992 descriptor moved
SN   An Italian marble commonly having a dark gray or bluish ground traversed by veins and occurring in its principal varieties in the neighborhood of Carrara and Corsica. (W)

bardiglio fiorito
      MT.724
HN   April 1992 descriptor moved

bardiglio 'scuro
      MT.723
HN   April 1992 descriptor moved

bardings
USE   bards

bards
      TH.21
HN   February 1993 descriptor added
ALT   bard
SN   Use for complete sets of horse armor.
UF   bardings
RT   field armors
      great garnitures

Bare Island
      FL.881

barens
      TH.812
HN   February 1993 descriptor added
ALT   baren
SN   Term of Japanese origin for smooth, flat, round, or oval pads with handles used to press a sheet of paper against the face of a relief printing block to form an impression. (MAYER)

barge rafters
USE   bargeboards

barge spikes
      PJ.251
HN   April 1993 descriptor moved
      April 1993 descriptor changed, was **boat spikes**
      April 1993 lead-in term changed, was **barge spikes**
      April 1993 alternate term changed, was **boat spike**
ALT   barge spike
SN   Long, square spikes used in heavy timber construction. (PUTNAM)
UF   boat spikes
      spikes, barge
      spikes, boat

barge stones
      PJ.1972
HN   March 1993 descriptor moved
      November 1990 scope note changed
ALT   barge stone
SN   Stones which form the sloping edge of a gable built of masonry.
UF   stones, barge

bargeboards
      PJ.1832   (N,B)
HN   March 1993 descriptor moved
      February 1992 lead-in terms added
      February 1992 lead-in term deleted, was **fascia rafters**
      February 1992 lead-in term deleted, was **rafters, fascia**
ALT   bargeboard
SN   Boards which hang from the projecting end of a roof, covering the gables; often elaborately carved and ornamented. (HAS)
UF   barge rafters
      fly rafters
      gableboards
      rafters, barge
      rafters, fly
      vergeboards

barges (ceremonial watercraft)
      TX.343   (N)
ALT   barge (ceremonial watercraft)
SN   Watercraft, usually highly decorated and propelled by oars or paddles, used for transporting important persons, either alive or dead, on state occasions or for ceremonial visits.
UF   barges, funerary
      funerary barges

barges (flat-bottomed watercraft)
      TX.327   (L,N)
ALT   barge (flat-bottomed watercraft)
SN   Capacious, flat-bottomed vessels, usually intended to be pushed or towed, primarily for transporting cargo.

barges (ships' boats)
      TX.462
ALT   barge (ship's boat)
SN   Use for ships' boats assigned to flag officers, especially since 1750; generally smaller and lighter than launches and longboats, usually hav-ing more than 10 oars, and often decorated and fitted out with accommodations for the assigned officer.

barges, funerary
USE   barges (ceremonial watercraft)

Bargu
      FL.349   (L)
HN   October 1991 lead-in terms added
UF   Barba
      Bariba
      Bongu

bargueños
USE   vargueños

Bari
      FL.617   (L)

Bariba
USE   Bargu

barite
USE   barium sulfate

baritone
      DC.203
HN   October 1992 descriptor added

baritones
      TT.80   (L,N)
ALT   baritone
SN   Three-valved aerophones pitched in B flat, popular as brass band instruments.

barium carbonate
      MT.2242   (L)
HN   April 1992 descriptor moved
UF   carbonate, barium

barium chromate
USE   barium yellow

barium chrome
USE   barium yellow

barium sulfate
      MT.2243
HN   May 1992 related term added
      March 1992 lead-in terms added
      January 1992 descriptor moved
      January 1992 descriptor changed, was **blanc fixe**
      January 1992 lead-in term changed, was **barium sulfate**
      October 1991 lead-in term added
      June 1990 lead-in terms added
UF   baratine
      barite
      baryta
      baryta white
      barytes
      Barytweiss
      blanc baryte
      blanc fixe
      blanco fijo
      Bologna stone
      constant white
      enamel white
      heavy spar
      permanent white

Permanentweiss
process white
spar, heavy
stone, Bologna
sulfate, barium
sulfate de barium
sulfato de bario
Tyrol white
white, baryta
white, constant
white, enamel
white, permenent
white, process
RT   mineral

barium yellow
    MT.2269
HN   May 1992 lead-in terms added
      January 1992 descriptor moved
UF   barium chromate
      barium chrome
      baryta yellow
      Barytgelb
      chromate, barium
      chrome, barium
      jaune de baryte
      lemon yellow
      permanent yellow
      Steinbühl yellow
      ultramarine yellow
      yellow, barium
      yellow, baryta
      yellow, lemon
      yellow, permanent
      yellow, Steinbühl
      yellow ultramarine

barium yellow (color)
USE   brilliant yellow
      light greenish yellow
      moderate greenish yellow

barjairs
USE   bergères

bark
    MT.2612   (L)
HN   March 1992 descriptor moved

bark cloth
    MT.1516   (L,R)
HN   March 1993 descriptor moved
      March 1993 lead-in term deleted,
        was **kapa**
      March 1993 lead-in term deleted,
        was **tapa**
UF   amatl
      Aztec paper
      bark cloth, beaten
      bark paper
      bark paper, cannabis
      bark paper, fig
      beaten bark cloth
      cannabis bark paper
      cloth, bark
      cloth, beaten bark
      cloth, tapa
      fiber paper, plant
      fig bark paper
      huun
      paper, Aztec
      paper, bark

paper, cannabis bark
paper, fig bark
paper, plant fiber
plant fiber paper

bark cloth, beaten
USE   bark cloth

bark mills
    TH.1377   (N)
ALT   bark mill
SN   Horse-powered mills used for grind-
      ing bark.
UF   mills, bark

bark paper
USE   bark cloth

bark paper, cannabis
USE   bark cloth

bark paper, fig
USE   bark cloth

bark strip
    MT.2613
HN   March 1992 descriptor moved
UF   strip, bark

barkentines
    TX.572
ALT   barkentine
UK   barquentines
UKA   barquentine
SN   Use for sailing vessels of three or
      more masts, square-rigged on the
      foremast only; the remaining masts
      are fore-and-aft-rigged.
UF   barquantines

barkers
    TH.1378   (L)
ALT   barker
SN   Machines used especially in pulp
      mills to remove bark from logs. (W)
UF   barking machines
      debarkers
      machines, barking

barking axes
    TH.1412   (N)
ALT   barking ax
SN   Axes used to split timber before re-
      moval of the bark. (SLOANE)
UF   axes, barking

barking chisels
    TH.1428   (N)
ALT   barking chisel
SN   Chisels used in the debarking of
      timber.
UF   chisels, barking
      chisels, peeling
      peeling chisels

barking drawknives
    TH.1478   (N)
ALT   barking drawknife
SN   Large drawknives of varying shapes
      with the blade's bevel facing down
      so that the knife will not dig into the
      timber as it is removing the bark.
      (SALAM)
UF   drawknives, barking

barking irons
    TH.1422   (N)
ALT   barking iron
SN   Tools with a round, semicircular, or
      spade-shaped blade often socketed
      and mounted on a wood handle;
      used for stripping bark from logs.
      (SALAM)
UF   irons, barking
      irons, peeling
      irons, rinding
      irons, wrong
      peeling irons
      rinding irons
      spuds
      wrong irons

barking machines
USE   barkers

barks
    TX.573   (L)
ALT   bark
SN   Use for sailing vessels of three or
      more masts, square-rigged on all but
      the aftermost mast, which is fore-
      and-aft-rigged.
UF   barques

barks, jackass
USE   jackass barks

barley straw
    MT.2665
HN   March 1992 descriptor moved
UF   straw, barley

barn-board
SEE   barnboard

barn-door hangers
    PJ.91
HN   April 1993 descriptor moved
ALT   barn-door hanger
SN   Hangers used for heavy exterior
      sliding or rolling doors, consisting
      of two pulleys secured to the top of
      the door in tandem, connected by a
      heavy metal strap. The door is
      moved by rolling along a horizontal
      track which either hangs from the
      lintel or is anchored to a parallel
      member projecting slightly from it.
      (MEANS)
UF   hangers, barn-door

barn-door latches
    PJ.474
HN   April 1993 descriptor moved
ALT   barn-door latch
UF   latches, barn-door

barn-door pulls
    PJ.362
HN   April 1993 descriptor moved
ALT   barn-door pull
SN   Large cupped pulls for heavy
      doors. (STEIN)
UF   pulls, barn-door

barn-door rollers
    PJ.285

HN   April 1993 descriptor moved
ALT barn-door roller
UF   rollers, barn-door

barn door shutters
USE barn doors

barn-door stays
PJ.286
HN   April 1993 descriptor moved
ALT barn-door stay
SN   Small pulleys or wheels which facilitate and direct the movement of a sliding barn (or other) door by rolling along a horizontal track or rail. (MEANS)
UF   stays, barn-door

barn doors
PJ.2900
ALT barn door
SN   Sets of adjustable flaps, usually two or four, that are attached to the front of a luminaire in order to partially control the shape and spread of the light beam. (IESREF)
UF   barn door shutters
     blinders
     doors, barn
     shutters, barn door

barn siding
USE barnboard

Barnack rag
USE Barnack stone

Barnack stone
MT.875
HN   April 1992 descriptor moved
UF   Barnack rag
     rag, Barnack
     stone, Barnack

barnboard
MT.3052
HN   March 1992 descriptor moved
UK   barn-board
UF   barn siding
     barnwood
     siding, barn

barns
RK.43   (A,L,N,B,R)
ALT barn
SN   Agricultural buildings with large, usually sliding doors, prominent roofs, and predominantly open spaces on the interior, primarily used as storage buildings for hay, grains, and farm equipment and shelters for livestock; does not include those structures, often termed barns, used for the processing of food and other agricultural produce, such as hop barns and tobacco barns.

barns, 3-bay
USE English barns

barns, bank
USE bank barns

<barns by form>
RK.44

<barns by function>
RK.48

<barns by location or context>
RK.54

barns, carriage
USE carriage houses

barns, cattle
USE cattle barns

barns, cider
USE cider mills

barns, coach
USE carriage houses

barns, connected
USE connected barns

barns, Connecticut
USE English barns

barns, continuous
USE connected barns

barns, cow
USE dairy barns

barns, crib
USE crib barns

barns, dairy
USE dairy barns

barns, Dutch
USE Dutch barns

barns, English
USE English barns

barns, German bank
USE Pennsylvania bank barns

barns, hop
USE hop barns

barns, horse
USE horse barns

barns, New England
USE English barns

barns, New England connected
USE connected barns

barns, New World Dutch
USE Dutch barns

barns, Pennsylvania bank
USE Pennsylvania bank barns

barns, Pennsylvania German
USE Pennsylvania bank barns

barns, Pennsylvania standard
USE Pennsylvania bank barns

barns, sheep
USE sheep barns

barns, sugar
USE sugar houses

barns, three-bay
USE English barns

barns, tithe
USE tithe barns

barns, tobacco
USE tobacco barns

barns, Yankee
USE English barns

barnwood
USE barnboard

barnyards
RM.213
HN   April 1993 descriptor moved
ALT barnyard
SN   Yards connected to and associated with a barn; usually fenced livestock yards separated from general work and activity areas. (BIGHSE)

Barocchetto
FL.3321

barographs
TN.351   (N)
ALT barograph
SN   Recording barometers.

barographs, aneroid
USE aneroid barographs

barometers
TN.349   (L,N)
ALT barometer
SN   Instruments for measuring atmospheric pressure.
UF   sympiesometers

barometers, aneroid
USE aneroid barometers

barometers, mercurial
USE mercury barometers

barometers, mercury
USE mercury barometers

barometrographs
USE aneroid barographs

Baronial
USE Abbotsford

Baronial, Scottish
USE Scottish Baronial

barons
HG.998
HN   January 1993 descriptor added
ALT baron
     baron's
     barons'
SN   Nobles bearing the title of baron. In Great Britain and Japan, a member of the lowest rank of nobility; on the continent of Europe, a noble whose rank and status relative to others varies from country to country.

Baroque
FL.3261   (A,L,B,R)

Baroque, Early
USE Early Baroque

Baroque, High
USE High Baroque

Baroque, High Edwardian
USE Baroque Revival

Baroque, Late
USE Late Baroque

Baroque Revival
FL.3354   (H,R)
UF Baroque, High Edwardian
High Edwardian Baroque
Neo-Baroque
Revival, Baroque

barothermographs
TN.343
ALT barothermograph
SN Meteorological instruments that automatically record temperature and pressure.

barothermohygrographs
TN.344
ALT barothermohygrograph
SN Instruments that automatically record graphically atmospheric pressure, temperature, and humidity.

Barotse
USE Lozi

barouches
TX.162   (N)
ALT barouche
SN Use for four-wheeled carriages generally characterized by high outside seats for the driver, passenger seats with either folding or fixed tops, and coachlike lower quarters and undercarriage.

Barozi
USE Lozi

Barozwi
USE Rozwi

barquantines
SEE barkentines

barquentines
SEE barkentines

barques
USE barks

barques, jackass
SEE jackass barks

barracks
RK.219   (A,L,B,R)
HN February 1992 scope note added
SN Use for buildings or sets of buildings erected as common living quarters for groups of soldiers or workers.

barracks, disciplinary
USE military prisons

barrage balloons
TX.33   (N)
ALT barrage balloon
SN Balloons anchored to the ground and grouped as protective screens to prevent or hinder operations by enemy aircraft.
UF balloon barrages
balloons, barrage
barrages, balloon

barrages
RK.494   (L,B)
ALT barrage
SN Artificial dams placed in a watercourse to increase the depth of water or to divert it into a channel for navigation or irrigation. (W)

barrages, balloon
USE barrage balloons

Barrancoid
USE Los Barrancos

Barre granite
MT.637
HN April 1992 descriptor moved
UF granite, Barre

Barreales
FL.1206

barred keys
USE pipe keys

barrel arches
USE semicircular arches

barrel bolts
PJ.552
HN March 1993 descriptor moved
ALT barrel bolt
SN Cylindrical bolts that are mounted on a plate having a raised case that contains the bolt and guides it into a recess in a jamb or some other suitable cylindrical socket. (DITTRI)
UF bolts, barrel

barrel-burnishing
USE barreling

barrel ceilings
PJ.2049
HN March 1993 descriptor moved
ALT barrel ceiling
SN Ceilings of semicylindrical shape. (DAC)
UF ceilings, barrel

barrel chairs
TC.464
HN January 1993 descriptor moved
ALT barrel chair
SN Chairs with a solid, rounded wood back, the cruder type being made by cutting away parts of a barrel. For easy chairs having a semicircular back use **circular easy chairs**.
UF chairs, barrel
chairs, tub
tub chairs

barrel chairs (circular easy chairs)
USE circular easy chairs

<barrel components>
PJ.3159

barrel drills
TH.593
ALT barrel drill
SN Tools consisting of a long drill bit which pierces a spool-shaped object; used in conjunction with a bow to drill holes in brass, iron, and steel. Most often used by clock- and watchmakers.
UF drills, barrel

barrel drums
TT.569
ALT barrel drum
SN Membranophones having a larger diameter at the middle than at the ends and a curvilinear body. (NGDMI)
UF barrel-shaped drums
drums, barrel
drums, barrel-shaped

barrel-finishing
USE barreling

barrel keys
USE pipe keys

barrel organs
TT.111   (L,N,B)
ALT barrel organ
SN Mechanical pipe organs operated by a rotary handle, which both works the bellows to supply air, and turns a pinned cylinder which, as it is turned, raises keys which cause the sounding of the appropriate pipes.
UF hand organs
handle organs
organs, barrel
organs, hand
organs, handle
RT mechanical instruments

barrel pianos
TT.418   (N)
ALT barrel piano
SN Mechanical upright pianos devoid of a keyboard, operated by pinned cylinders set in motion by a crank, often mounted on wheels for playing in the streets. (MARCUS)
UF cylinder pianos
pianos, barrel
pianos, cylinder
pianos, street
street pianos
RT mechanical instruments

barrel roofs
PJ.1782   (A)
HN March 1993 descriptor moved
ALT barrel roof
SN Roofs that are semicircular in section or, sometimes, roofs that incorporate a semicircular ceiling.
UF arched barrel roofs

barrel roofs, arched
barrel shell roofs
cradle roofs
roofs, arched barrel
roofs, barrel shell
roofs, cradle
roofs, wagon
wagon roofs

barrel roofs, arched
USE barrel roofs

barrel scales
USE cylinder scales

barrel-shaped drums
USE barrel drums

barrel shell roofs
USE barrel roofs

barrel vaults
    PJ.1875   (B)
HN March 1993 descriptor moved
    May 1991 scope note changed
    May 1991 lead-in term added
    May 1991 lead-in term deleted, was
    transverse barrel vaults
    May 1991 lead-in term deleted, was
    barrel vaults, transverse
    May 1991 lead-in term deleted, was
    vaults, transverse barrel
ALT barrel vault
SN Vaults of plain, semicircular cross
    section supported by parallel walls
    or arcades. (DAC)
UF cradle vaults
    tunnel vaults
    vaults, barrel
    vaults, cradle
    vaults, tunnel
    vaults, wagon
    vaults, wagonhead
    wagon vaults
    wagonhead vaults

barrel vaults, half
USE half barrel vaults

barrel vaults, rampant
USE rampant barrel vaults

barrel vaults, uncentered
USE pitched-brick vaults

barreling
    KT.294
HN January 1993 descriptor moved
ALT barreled
UK barrelling
UKA barrelled
SN Use both for application of paint to
    small articles by tumbling them in a
    barrel containing paint, and the
    process of improving the surface
    finish of objects by processing them
    in a barrel along with abrasive par-
    ticles.
UF barrel-burnishing
    barrel-finishing
    burnishing, barrel
    finishing, barrel
    tumbling

barrelling
SEE barreling

barrels (aerophone components)
    PJ.3223
ALT barrel (aerophone component)
SN Short cylindrical sections of aero-
    phones which couple the mouth-
    piece to the rest of the tube.

barrels (containers)
    TQ.5   (L,N)
ALT barrel (container)
SN Cylindrical, usually wooden, con-
    tainers with slightly bulging sides
    made of staves hooped together,
    and with flat, parallel ends.
    (RHDEL2)
RT casks
    kegs
    puncheons (casks)

barrels (firearm components)
    PJ.3158
ALT barrel (firearm component)
SN In firearms, metal tubes closed at
    one end that hold the projectile and
    the propellant charge and, utilizing
    the explosive force of the charge,
    act as the path for the projectile.
    They may be smoothbore or rifled.
    (TARA)

<barrels and barrel components>
    PJ.3157

barrettes
    TE.507   (N)
ALT barrette
UK hair-slides
UKA hair-slide
SN Decorative devices designed to hold
    the hair in place.
UF slides (barrettes)

barriadas
    RG.291
ALT barriada
SN Use for self-built shantytowns lo-
    cated on the outskirts of large cities
    in Latin America.

barrier armors
USE armors for the barriers

<barrier elements>
    PJ.2340   (B)
HN March 1993 guide term moved

barrier-free design
    BM.366   (A,L,B)
HN March 1993 scope note added
    December 1992 descriptor moved
    May 1990 lead-in term added
SN The creation of buildings which are
    intended to be universally accessible
    or usable, regardless of the individ-
    ual user's abilities or disabilities.
UF access, handicapped
    design, barrier-free
    handicapped access
    X factor

barriers
    PJ.2339   (B)
HN March 1993 descriptor moved
    November 1990 scope note added
ALT barrier
SN Objects or sets of objects that sepa-
    rate, keep apart, demarcate, or serve
    as barricades. (W)

barriers, air
USE air infiltration barriers

barriers, air infiltration
USE air infiltration barriers

<barriers and barrier elements>
    PJ.2338
HN March 1993 guide term moved

barriers, armors for the
USE armors for the barriers

barriers, armours for the
SEE armors for the barriers

barriers, fire
USE fire walls

barriers, radiant
USE radiant barriers

barriers, vapor
USE vapor barriers

barriers, vapour
SEE vapor barriers

barrios
    RG.285
ALT barrio
SN Use only to denote the Spanish-
    speaking quarters of cities or towns.

barristers
    HG.514   (L)
HN December 1992 alternate terms
    added
ALT barrister
    barrister's
    barristers'
SN Counsels admitted to plead at the
    bar and undertake the public trial of
    causes in the higher courts of law.
    (W)

Barrow culture
USE Kurgan

barrowcoats
USE buntings

barrows
USE burial mounds

barrows, long
USE burial mounds

barrs
USE stretchers (furniture components)

bars (building materials)
    MT.1777   (L)
HN April 1993 alternate term added
    December 1992 lead-in term added
ALT bar (building material)
UF rods (building materials)

bars (commercial buildings)
  RK.104   (A,L,B,R)
  HN May 1991 descriptor changed, was
        bars
        May 1991 alternate term changed,
        was **bar**
  ALT bar (commercial building)
  SN Places with counters where bever-
        ages, usually liquors, and light meals
        are served to customers. (RHDEL2)

bars (taverns)
  USE taverns

bars, angle
  USE angles (rolled sections)

bars, channel
  USE channels (rolled sections)

bars, chimney
  USE chimney bars

bars, chinning
  USE horizontal bars

bars, claw
  USE claw bars

bars, cocktail
  SEE cocktail lounges

bars, deformed
  USE deformed bars

bars, glazing
  USE muntins

bars, grab
  USE grab bars

bars, high
  USE horizontal bars

bars, horizontal
  USE horizontal bars

bars, meeting
  USE meeting rails

bars, milk
  USE milk bars

bars, monkey
  USE junglegyms

bars, parallel
  USE parallel bars

bars, pinch
  USE pinch bars

bars, pry
  USE crowbars

bars, pull
  USE pull bars

bars, push
  USE push bars

bars, reinforcing
  USE reinforcing bars

bars, ripping
  USE pinch bars

bars, sand
  USE sand bars

bars, sash
  USE muntins

bars, shutter
  USE shutter bars

bars, snack
  USE snack bars

bars, stall
  USE stall bars

bars, tie
  USE tie rods

bars, towel
  USE towel bars

bars, transom
  USE transoms

bars, turning
  USE chimney bars

bars, uneven
  USE uneven parallel bars

bars, uneven parallel
  USE uneven parallel bars

bars, water
  USE water bars

bars, wrecking
  USE pinch bars

barspoons
  TH.146   (N)
  HN April 1993 descriptor added
  ALT barspoon
  SN Long-handled spoons, usually with
        the capacity of a teaspoon, used for
        measuring ingredients or mixing
        drinks.
  UF bar spoons
        spoons, bar

barstools
  TC.690   (N)
  HN January 1993 descriptor moved
  ALT barstool
  SN High stools that are usually one of a
        row of such stools standing in front
        of a bar; often taking the form of a
        rounded seat fixed on a central
        post. (W)
  UF bar stools
        stools, bar

bartizans
  PJ.2484
  HN March 1993 descriptor moved
        November 1990 scope note added
        November 1990 lead-in term de-
        leted, was **echauguettes**
  ALT bartizan
  SN Small turrets projecting from angles
        on top of towers or parapets, usually
        as part of a fortification.
  UF turrets, watch
        watch turrets

bartons
  USE farmyards

Barwa chairs
  TC.465
  HN January 1993 descriptor moved
  ALT Barwa chair
  UF chairs, Barwa

barware
  PE.61
  HN January 1993 descriptor added
  SN Glassware or utensils used in serving
        alcoholic beverages. (W)

barwood
  MT.2188
  HN April 1992 descriptor moved

baryta
  USE barium sulfate

baryta paper
  MT.1482
  HN February 1992 descriptor moved
  SN Paper with a gelatin/barium sulfate
        surface preparation. (REILLY)
  UF paper, baryta

baryta white
  USE barium sulfate

baryta yellow
  USE barium yellow

barytes
  USE barium sulfate

Barytgelb
  USE barium yellow

barytons
  TT.262   (L,N)
  ALT baryton
  SN Viols of bass range, similar to the
        bass viol but with ten or more addi-
        tional wire strings that pass close to
        the belly and under the neck so that
        several of them can be plucked by
        the left thumb.
  UF paradons
        violas di bordone
  RT sympathetic strings

Barytweiss
  USE barium sulfate

bas-de-pages
  PJ.3415
  ALT bas-de-page
  SN The bottom margins of pages in
        Medieval manuscripts; also, illumi-
        nations appearing in that area.

bas-relief
  KT.808   (A,L)
  HN April 1991 descriptor moved
        November 1990 scope note changed
  SN Sculptural relief technique in which
        the projection of the forms is rela-
        tively shallow.
  UF basso rilievo
        low relief

bas-reliefs
VC.562   (A,L,B)
ALT bas-relief
SN Use for works executed in relatively shallow relief.
UF basso-relievos
low reliefs
reliefs, low

Basa
USE Bassa

Basal Neolithic
HN October 1990 descriptor deleted

basal rims
USE foot rings

basal rings
USE foot rings

Basalampasu
USE Salampasu

basalt
MT.650   (L)
HN April 1992 descriptor moved
December 1991 scope note changed
SN A dense, hard, dark brown-to-black volcanic igneous rock, consisting of feldspar and mafic minerals such as augite or olivine.
UF lapis basanites

basalt glass
USE tachylite

basanite
USE touchstone

Basari
FL.350   (L)
UF Bassari

bascinets
USE basnets

bascinets, great
USE great basnets

bascule bridges
RK.1219
ALT bascule bridge
SN Bridges in which sections of the span are pivoted upward by use of counterweights.
UF bridges, bascule

base
MT.3081   (L)
HN February 1993 descriptor added
SN Substance that yields hydroxyl ions when dissolved in water. (CTRRH)

base (inert pigment)
USE inert pigment

base bid specifications
VW.542
HN November 1992 descriptor moved
October 1990 lead-in term added
ALT base bid specification
SN Specifications listing or describing only the materials, equipment, and methods of construction upon

which a base bid must be predicated, exclusive of any alternate bids. (MEANS)
UF documents, base bid
specifications, base bid

base burlap
USE base cloths (upholstery foundation components)

base cloths (upholstery foundation components)
PJ.2693
ALT base cloth (upholstery foundation component)
SN Layer of coarsely woven, heavyweight textile used in upholstery, fixed over webbing to form a seat cavity and to keep the stuffing from falling through.
UF base burlap
bottom linen
burlap, base
cloths, base (upholstery foundation components)
linen, bottom

<base components: columns>
PJ.1487
HN March 1993 guide term moved
December 1992 guide term changed, was <base components>
June 1991 guide term moved

base-courts
PJ.977
HN March 1993 descriptor moved
ALT base-court
SN Use for the outer or lesser courts of mansions or castles.
UF basse-cours

base flashing
PJ.2132
HN March 1993 descriptor moved
July 1991 scope note changed
November 1990 lead-in term added
SN Watertight membranes, along roofs or other flat surfaces, that turn up against and cover the intersection with vertical surfaces, such as chimneys or parapets; the exposed upper edge is normally covered by counterflashing.
UF flashing, base
under-flashing

base light
USE base lighting

base lighting
KT.756
HN April 1991 descriptor added
SN General lighting providing uniform, diffuse illumination approaching a shadowless condition acceptable for the filming of motion pictures and television programs. (IESREF)
UF base light
light, base
lighting, base

base lights
TC.1431
ALT base light
SN Lighting devices which produce a uniform, diffuse illumination approaching a shadowless condition; may be supplemented by other lighting. (STEIN)
UF lights, base

base lights (fill lights)
USE fill lights

base maps
VW.67   (L)
HN November 1992 descriptor moved
ALT base map
SN Outline maps showing the important natural and man-made features of an area, to which specific information may be added for any of various purposes.
UF maps, base

base metal
MT.493
HN March 1993 descriptor added
SN Metal or alloy not considered to have high intrinsic value.
UF metal, base

base ring (pottery style)
FL.2989
HN April 1993 descriptor added
UF ring, base (pottery style)

base ring ware
HN April 1993 descriptor split, use **base ring (pottery style)** + **ware**

base-rings
SEE base rings

base rings
PJ.3087
ALT base ring
UK base-rings
UKA base-ring
SN Rings of glass added to the undersides of glass vessels after their bodies have been made. They are usually flattened so that their edges extend beyond the bottom of the vessels. (ILDIGL)

base, safety
USE safety film

base, transparent
USE transparent base

base valances
TC.266
ALT base valance
SN Valances hanging from the lower edge of a bed or bedcover; used decoratively to conceal the base of the bed.
UF bases (bed valances)
bedskirts
bottom valances
lower valances
pantes

pants
valances, base
valances, bottom
valances, lower

baseball
KQ.69 (A,L)
RT baseballs
bats

baseball caps
TE.552
ALT baseball cap
SN Close-fitting caps with a visor, gen-
erally having a gored crown with a
button on top.
UF ball caps
caps, ball
caps, baseball
RT sports clothing

baseball cards
VW.1026 (L,N)
HN January 1993 descriptor moved
ALT baseball card
UF cards, baseball

baseball fields
RM.87 (B)
HN April 1993 descriptor moved
ALT baseball field
UF fields, baseball

baseball stadiums
HN March 1993 descriptor split, use
baseball + stadiums

baseballs
TV.35 (N)
ALT baseball
SN Use for the ball thrown or batted in
the game of the same name; usually
9 to 9 1/4 inches in circumference,
weighing about 5 ounces, and consisting of a cork center wound
round with twine and covered with
white leather.
RT baseball

baseboard heaters
USE baseboard units

baseboard heating
USE baseboard units

baseboard radiator units
USE baseboard units

baseboard units
PJ.808 (B)
HN March 1993 descriptor moved
November 1990 scope note changed
ALT baseboard unit
SN Use for heating elements that are
housed in special panels placed horizontally along the baseboards of a
wall.
UF baseboard heaters
baseboard heating
baseboard radiator units
heaters, baseboard
heating, baseboard

radiator units, baseboard
units, baseboard

baseboards
PJ.1977 (A,B)
HN March 1993 descriptor moved
ALT baseboard
SN Flat or molded projections from interior walls or partitions at the floor,
covering the joint between the floor
and the wall.
UF boards, skirting
skirting boards
skirtings

baselards
TK.18 (N)
ALT baselard
SN Long civilian daggers with a hilt
shaped like a capital letter I, originating in southern Germany or
Switzerland in the late 13th century
and remaining in wide use throughout Europe until the late 15th century. Some models are as long as
short swords.
UF basilards

basement windows
PJ.2264
HN March 1993 descriptor moved
ALT basement window
SN Windows of a type commonly used
in residential basements, usually
having between one and three
lights only.
UF windows, basement

basements
PJ.1356 (A,L,B,R)
HN March 1993 descriptor moved
ALT basement
SN Use to designate stories wholly or
partly underground. For similar
spaces used solely for storage, par-
ticularly food, prefer cellars.

Basengele
USE Sengele

bases (artists' materials)
USE supports (artists' materials)

bases (bed valances)
USE base valances

bases (components)
PJ.7 (L)
HN April 1993 alternate term changed,
was base
March 1993 descriptor moved
December 1992 related terms added
March 1991 scope note changed
March 1991 descriptor · changed,
was bases
ALT base (component)
SN Use for relatively massive elements
at the bottoms of structures or objects upon which the upper parts
rest or are supported. For terminal
elements upon which objects rest
and that are small in relation to the
body of the object, use feet.

RT <bases: column components>
<bases: furniture components>

bases (furniture components)
HN September 1991 descriptor deleted

bases (military installations)
USE military bases

bases (skirts)
TE.337
ALT bases (skirt)
SN Flared and pleated skirts of cloth,
often velvet or brocade, or of mail
or plate metal, worn over or in place
of tassets in early 16th-century
Europe.

bases, air
USE air bases

bases, Air Force
USE air bases

<bases and base components: columns>
PJ.1483
HN March 1993 guide term moved
December 1992 guide term
changed, was <bases and base com-
ponents>
June 1991 guide term moved

bases, army
USE army bases

bases, Asiatic
USE Asiatic bases

bases, Attic
USE Attic bases

<bases: column components>
PJ.1484
RT bases (components)

bases, extraterrestrial
USE extraterrestrial bases

<bases: furniture components>
PJ.2734
HN March 1993 guide term moved
December 1992 related term added
March 1991 guide term added
RT bases (components)

bases, guided missile
USE guided missile bases

bases, lunar
USE lunar bases

bases, military
USE military bases

bases, military air
USE air bases

bases, missile
USE guided missile bases

bases, moon
USE lunar bases

bases, naval
USE naval bases

bases, naval air
USE naval air bases

bases, pad
USE pad bases

bases, space
USE extraterrestrial bases

bases, submarine
USE submarine bases

Bashadar
FL.2216
UF Abash-adar

Bashilele
USE Lele

basic igneous rock
MT.649
HN April 1992 descriptor moved
UF basic rock
igneous rock, basic
rock, basic
rock, basic igneous

basic liquid epoxy
MT.1208
HN January 1993 descriptor moved
UF DGEBA
epoxy, basic liquid
liquid epoxy, basic

basic rock
USE basic igneous rock

Basikasingo
USE Kasingo

basilards
USE baselards

Basilian
BM.490   (L)

basilicas
RK.19   (A,L,B,R)
ALT basilica
SN Use for religious or secular buildings characterized by an oblong
plan divided into a nave with two or
more side aisles, the former higher
and wider than the latter and lit by
clerestory windows; usually termi-
nated by an apse.

basin stands
TC.1070
HN May 1993 scope note changed
January 1993 descriptor moved
ALT basin stand
SN Small stands for washing, often having a molded ring to hold the basin,
small drawers below the frieze, and
a shelf for a pitcher beneath.
UF bowl stands
stands, basin
stands, bowl
stands, toilet
toilet stands

basin stands, corner
USE corner basin stands

basin stands, corner enclosed
USE corner enclosed basin stands

basin stands, enclosed
USE enclosed basin stands

basinets
USE basnets

basins
TQ.40   (H,N,R)
ALT basin
SN Open, rounded vessels formerly
used for holding either liquids or
solids, today largely for holding liquids. In 17th-century England the
term implied a shallow dish,
whereas there today it means a deep
bowl. In the United States the term
has always meant either a deep dish
or shallow bowl. (LBFT)
RT baptismal basins
bowls (vessels)
ewers
shaving basins

basins, alms
USE alms dishes

basins, baptismal
USE baptismal basins

basins, barbers'
USE shaving basins

basins, butter
USE butter dishes

basins, catch
USE catch basins

basins, sedimentation
USE settling basins

basins, settling
USE settling basins

basins, shaving
USE shaving basins

basins, slop
USE slop bowls

basins, stilling
USE stilling basins

basins, storm water retention
USE storm water retention basins

basins, wash
USE washbowls

basins, water retention
USE storm water retention basins

basket (pottery style)
FL.3024
HN April 1993 descriptor added

basket arches
USE three-centered arches

basket capitals
PJ.1493
HN March 1993 descriptor moved
November 1990 scope note changed

ALT basket capital
SN Use for capitals having interlaced
bands resembling the weave of a
basket; found in Medieval and Byzantine architecture.
UF capitals, basket

basket chairs
TC.466
HN January 1993 descriptor moved
ALT basket chair
SN Wicker chairs with arms that are a
forward continuation of the back,
usually with a cane-shaped base in
lieu of legs.
UF chairs, basket

basket-guards
SEE basket hilts

basket handle arches
USE three-centered arches

basket-handled jars
USE situlae

basket-hilts
SEE basket hilts

basket hilts
PJ.3140
ALT basket hilt
UK basket-hilts
UKA basket-hilt
SN Hilts with a guard wrought like bas-
ketwork, made of a number of con-
necting bars that completely cover
the hand.
UF basket-guards
hilts, basket

basket makers
HG.771   (L)
HN April 1993 related term added
December 1992 alternate terms
added
ALT basket maker
basket maker's
basket makers'
RT basketmaking

basket-making
SEE basketmaking

basket spits
TH.77
HN April 1993 descriptor added
ALT basket spit
SN Spits made with a central basket
formed of thin iron strips.
UF cradle spits
spits, basket
spits, cradle

basket torches
USE cressets

basket ware
HN April 1993 descriptor split, use basket (pottery style) + ware

basketball
KQ.54   (L)

RT   backboards (sports equipment)
        basketballs

basketball backboards
USE   backboards (sports equipment)

basketball courts
HN   March 1993 descriptor split, use
        basketball + courts

basketballs
        TV.36   (N)
ALT   basketball
SN   Use for the inflated spherical balls
        bounced or thrown in the game of
        the same name; generally about 30
        inches in circumference and
        weighing 20 to 22 ounces.
RT   basketball

Basketmaker
        FL.972   (L)

Basketmaker-Pueblo
USE   Anasazi

basketmaking
        KT.766   (L,R)
UK   basket-making
UF   basketry
RT   basket makers

basketry
USE   basketmaking

basketry-covered bottles
USE   carboys
        demijohns

baskets
        TQ.7   (H,L,N,R)
ALT   basket
SN   Containers made of twigs, rushes,
        thin strips of wood, or other flexible
        material woven together. (RHDEL2)
RT   bread baskets
        cake baskets
        cheese baskets
        cooking baskets
        creels
        dough baskets
        feather baskets
        flower baskets
        gathering baskets
        goose baskets
        hampers
        laundry baskets
        loom baskets
        market baskets
        picnic baskets
        pigeon baskets
        sewing baskets
        storage baskets
        wastebaskets
        wool-rinsing baskets

baskets, backpack
USE   pack baskets

baskets, berry
USE   berry baskets

baskets, berry-picking
USE   berry baskets

baskets, bobbin
USE   loom baskets

baskets, bread
USE   bread baskets

baskets, bread-raising
USE   dough baskets

baskets, cake
USE   cake baskets

baskets, cheese
USE   cheese baskets

baskets, cheese curd
USE   cheese baskets

baskets, clothes
USE   laundry baskets

baskets, comb
USE   loom baskets

baskets, cooking
USE   cooking baskets

baskets, curd
USE   cheese baskets

baskets, cutflower
USE   flower baskets

baskets, cutting
USE   flower baskets

baskets, darning
USE   sewing baskets

baskets, dough
USE   dough baskets

baskets, dough-rising
USE   dough baskets

baskets, feather
USE   feather baskets

baskets, fire
USE   cressets

baskets, flower
USE   flower baskets

baskets, food drying
USE   drying trays

baskets, fruit
USE   berry baskets

baskets, fruit-drying
USE   drying trays

baskets, gathering
USE   gathering baskets

baskets, goose
USE   goose baskets

baskets, hip
USE   egg baskets

baskets, jai alai
USE   cestas

baskets, jug
USE   egg baskets

baskets, knitting
USE   sewing baskets

baskets, laundry
USE   laundry baskets

baskets, loom
USE   loom baskets

baskets, market
USE   market baskets

baskets, mending
USE   sewing baskets

baskets, needlework
USE   sewing baskets

baskets, pack
USE   pack baskets

baskets, picnic
USE   picnic baskets

baskets, pigeon
USE   pigeon baskets

baskets, provender
USE   flower baskets

baskets, ring
USE   ring baskets

baskets, sandwich
USE   flower baskets

baskets, scrap
USE   wastebaskets

baskets, sewing
USE   sewing baskets

baskets, shopping
USE   market baskets

baskets, storage
USE   storage baskets

baskets, trappers'
USE   pack baskets

baskets, treasure
USE   storage baskets

baskets, trout
USE   creels

baskets, Victorian
USE   flower baskets

baskets, wash
USE   laundry baskets

baskets, waste
USE   wastebaskets

baskets, wastepaper
USE   wastebaskets

baskets, wool
USE   wool-rinsing baskets

baskets, wool-rinsing
USE   wool-rinsing baskets

basnets
        TE.285   (N)
ALT   basnet

SN Helmets, generally ogival or egg-shaped with a pointed apex, and often fitted with an aventail and a hinged or pivoted visor, usually a pig-faced visor; used from the 13th to the 15th century. In the 15th century they became more globular and the aventail was replaced by gorget plates.
UF bascinets
 basinets
 bassinets (helmets)
RT pig-faced visors

basnets, great
USE great basnets

Basoga
USE Soga (African)

Basohli
 FL.2352

Basonge
USE Songye

Basongo Meno
USE Nkutshu

basquines
 TE.217
ALT basquine
SN Tight-fitting corsetlike underbodices of heavy material worn especially in the 16th century. (W)
UF vasquines
RT corsets

Basra Gördes
USE Gördes + rugs

bass
 DC.204
HN October 1992 descriptor added

bass drums
 TT.616   (L,N)
ALT bass drum
SN Large cylindrical drums, usually double-headed, with a rather shallow body, the diameter always being greater than the length. When played, each head faces sideways and is struck close to the rim with a padded stick. (MARCUS)
UF drums, bass
 long drums

bass drums, gong
USE gong drums

bass horns
 TT.74   (L,N)
ALT bass horn
SN Early variety of serpent, consisting of a conical tube about 230 cm long, generally made of copper, with six fingerholes, three or four keys, a swan-neck crook, and terminating in a widely flared bell. (NGDMI)
UF basshorns
 horns, bass

bass players
USE bassists

bass players, double
USE bassists

bass viols
USE violas da gamba

bass viols, American
USE church basses

bass viols, church
USE church basses

bass viols, Yankee
USE church basses

Bassa
 FL.186   (L)
HN August 1990 lead-in terms added
UF Basa
 Betjek
 Koko

Bassari
USE Basari

bassboats
 TX.353
ALT bassboat
SN Use for open outboard-powered boats in the 15- to 18-foot range, configured especially for freshwater sport fishing.

basse-cours
USE base-courts

basse-taille
 KT.94
HN March 1993 descriptor moved
SN Use for the enameling process developed in Mughal, India, which uses both translucent and opaque enamel applied over gold and silver and carved into a bas-relief.

basses
USE double basses
 marbles

basses, church
USE church basses

basses, double
USE double basses

basses, helicon
USE helicons

basses, stand-up
USE double basses

basses, string
USE double basses

basset horns
 TT.150   (L,N)
ALT basset horn
SN Elongated clarinets pitched in F, their compass extended downward by means of a box device set in the tube through which the bore zigzags up and down before emerging into a large metal bell; the tube may be

straight, sharply angled, or steeply curved.
UF horns, basset

basset tables
 TC.1123
HN January 1993 descriptor moved
ALT basset table
SN Small card tables for playing bassette, a card game popular in Italy and France in the late 17th century and in England in the early 18th century.
UF tables, basset

basshorns
USE bass horns

bassinets
 TC.764   (N)
HN January 1993 descriptor moved
ALT bassinet
SN Use for infants' beds, especially those with a hood over one end.

bassinets (helmets)
USE basnets

bassists
 HG.226   (L)
HN January 1993 descriptor added
ALT bassist
 bassist's
 bassists'
SN Use specifically for those who play the double bass. May also be used generally for those who play bass instruments of any kind.
UF bass players
 bass players, double
 bassists, double
 contrabass players
 contrabassists
 double bass players
 double bassists
 players, bass
 players, contrabass
 players, double bass
RT double basses
 violas da gamba

bassists, double
USE bassists

basso-relievos
USE bas-reliefs

basso rilievo
USE bas-relief

bassons Forveilles
USE serpents Forveilles

bassoon serpents
USE Russian bassoons

bassoons
 TT.180   (L,N)
ALT bassoon
SN Wood reedpipes with a double reed and a conical bore which doubles back upon itself like a hairpin. (NGDMI)

RT caledonicas
tenoroons

bassoons, double
USE contrabassoons

bassoons, Russian
USE Russian bassoons

bassoons, tenor
USE tenoroons

basswood
USE linden

basswood, American
USE linden

bast
MT.1384   (L)
HN February 1992 descriptor moved
UF bast fiber
fiber, bast

bast fiber
USE bast

bastard (scripts)
USE bastarda

bastard cedar
USE incense cedar

bastard culverins
USE serpentines (cannons)

bastard swords
TK.69
ALT bastard sword
SN Long, straight-bladed swords with a
grip long enough to allow them to
be grasped by one hand plus two or
three fingers of the other, used in
the 15th and 16th centuries.
UF hand-and-a-half swords
swords, bastard
swords, hand-and-a-half

bastarda
PJ.3449
SN Use for Gothic scripts employed especially in the 14th and 15th centuries that combine characteristics of
the Gothic cursive and the more formal textura.
UF bastard (scripts)
bastardus
Gothic hybrid
hybrid
hybrid Gothic
hybrida

bastardus
USE bastarda

bastel houses
RK.228
HN October 1991 scope note changed
ALT bastel house
SN Use for partly fortified houses often
having a vaulted ground floor, usually for livestock, and housing domestic spaces on upper levels; generally found along the Scottish
border.

UF houses, bastel
peel towers
peels (bastel houses)
towers, peel

basters
TH.89
HN April 1993 descriptor added
ALT baster
SN Large glass, plastic, or metal tubes
having a rubber bulblike piece at
one end to produce vacuum suction
when squeezed and a small opening
at the other, used for basting food.
(RHDEL2)

bastides
RD.32
ALT bastide
SN Use for Medieval planned settle-
ments built for defense and often
laid out on an orthogonal grid.

basting
KT.1237
HN March 1993 related term added
March 1993 descriptor moved
March 1993 scope note changed
ALT basted
SN Temporarily joining two or more
pieces of material together by sew-
ing with long loose stitches in order
to hold them in place until final
sewing. For a slight or temporary
fastening done by other means, use
tacking.
RT tacking

basting spoons
TH.90   (N)
HN April 1993 descriptor added
ALT basting spoon
SN Spoons having a long handle and a
large deep bowl used for basting
food.
UF spoons, basting

<bastion components>
PJ.2471
HN March 1993 guide term moved

bastioned forts
RK.416
ALT bastioned fort
UF forts, bastioned

bastions
PJ.2470   (B)
HN March 1993 descriptor moved
ALT bastion
SN The projecting portions of the outer
wall of a fortification.

<bastions and bastion components>
PJ.2469
HN March 1993 guide term moved

bastwork
PE.128   (L)
HN October 1992 descriptor moved

Basuku
USE Suku

basuris
USE bansuris

Basuto
USE Sotho

bat
USE brickbat

bat printing
KT.1161
HN March 1991 alternate term changed,
was bat printed
ALT bat-printed
SN Technique of applying glaze to pottery in which oil is applied to a
printing plate, then transferred to
the pottery by means of a gelatin
plate. The pottery is then dusted
with color material which adheres to
the oiled areas. (SCHNEI)
UF printing, bat

Batavia dammar
MT.1256
HN April 1992 descriptor changed, was
Batavia damar
February 1992 descriptor moved
UF dammar, Batavia

batch
MT.332
HN December 1992 descriptor added
SN Mixture of the unmelted raw mate-
rials, such as sand and cullet, prop-
erly proportioned and ready for fu-
sion into glass.
UF mixture

bateaux
TX.498   (N)
ALT bateau
SN Use for large, dorylike vessels with
straight posts and flat sides; com-
monly found in upper New England
and Canada.
UF batteaux

bateaux, two-sail
USE skipjacks

bateaux, V-bottomed
USE skipjacks

Bateke
USE Teke

batement lights
PJ.2278
HN March 1993 descriptor moved
July 1991 scope note changed
ALT batement light
SN Windows or tracery lights having a
curved or inclined bottom caused
by, for example, the arched heads of
other lights below.
UF lights, batement

Bateso
USE Teso

Batesville marble
MT.859
HN April 1992 descriptor moved

SN Limestone from Arkansas, gray or cream colored. (MAYER)
UF marble, Batesville

Batetela
USE Tetela

bath chairs
TC.614
HN January 1993 descriptor moved
ALT bath chair
SN Type of elaborate wheelchairs, sometimes glassed, especially those made in England in the mid-19th century and used at spas and seaside resorts.
UF chairs, bath

<bath, dressing and sanitary spaces>
PJ.1003
HN March 1993 guide term moved

bath mitzvahs
KM.39   (L)
ALT bath mitzvah

Bath oolite
USE Bath stone

bath, Smillie's
USE Smillie's bath

Bath stone
MT.860
HN April 1992 descriptor moved
UF Bath oolite
    oolite, Bath
    stone, Bath

bath towels
TH.395
HN February 1993 descriptor added
ALT bath towel
UF towels, bath

bathers
HG.900   (R)
HN April 1993 related term added
    December 1992 alternate terms added
    December 1990 descriptor added
ALT bather
    bather's
    bathers'
SN Use for people washing themselves with water, or immersed in water. For people actively propelling themselves through the water by natural means, use **swimmers**.
RT swimmers

bathhouses
RK.1011   (A,B,R)
ALT bathhouse
SN Use only for structures containing dressing rooms or lockers for bathers, as at the seashore. For buildings housing public swimming and bathing facilities, use **public baths**.
UF bathing pavilions
    houses, pool
    pavilions, bathing
    pool houses

bathhouses (public baths)
USE public baths

bathing beaches
RG.161   (L,B,R)
ALT bathing beach
UF beaches, bathing

bathing caps
TE.553   (N)
ALT bathing cap
UK swimming caps
UKA swimming cap
SN Tight-fitting waterproof caps, made of rubber or rubberized fabric, worn to keep the hair dry while swimming or bathing.
UF caps, bathing
    caps, swimming
RT sports clothing

bathing pavilions
USE bathhouses

bathing suits
TE.387   (H,L,N)
ALT bathing suit
UK swimsuits
UKA swimsuit
SN Garments worn for bathing or swimming.
UF cossies
    suits, bathing
    suits, swim
    swim suits
    swimwear

bathing suits, two-piece
USE two-piece bathing suits

bathing trunks
SEE trunks (costume)

bathometers
TN.102   (L,N)
ALT bathometer
SN Oceanographic instruments for measuring the depth of water.

Bathonga
USE Thonga

bathrobes
TE.261   (H,N)
ALT bathrobe
SN Loose-fitting knee-length or ankle-length garments, often tied with a belt, usually of a warm absorbent material, worn before and after bathing or informally around the house.
UF robes (bathrobes)
RT robes

bathroom accessories
USE bathroom hardware

bathroom hardware
PJ.586
HN April 1993 descriptor moved
UF accessories, bathroom
    accessories, washroom
    bathroom accessories
    hardware, bathroom
    washroom accessories

bathroom hooks
PJ.127
HN April 1993 descriptor moved
ALT bathroom hook
UF hooks, bathroom

bathroom scales
TN.297   (N)
ALT bathroom scale
SN Household accessories, usually portable, meant for persons to stand on in order to ascertain their weight.
UF scales, bathroom

bathrooms
PJ.1004   (A,L,B)
HN March 1993 descriptor moved
ALT bathroom
SN Use for rooms containing a bathtub or shower, and usually a toilet and lavatory; for rooms containing only a toilet and lavatory, use **lavatories (rooms)**; for public facilities containing toilets and lavatories, use **rest rooms**.
UF baths

baths
USE bathrooms
    bathtubs
    public baths

baths, Finnish
USE saunas

baths, mineral
USE spas

baths, public
USE public baths

baths, shower
USE shower stalls

baths, steam
USE steam baths

baths, swimming
USE swimming pools

baths, thermal
USE steam baths

baths, Turkish
USE Turkish baths

baths, vapor
USE steam baths

bathtubs
PJ.909   (L,N,B)
HN March 1993 descriptor moved
    November 1990 scope note added
ALT bathtub
SN Plumbing fixtures, usually in the form of tubs or basins, in which baths can be taken.
UF baths
    tubs (bathtubs)

bathymetric charts
USE bathymetric maps

bathymetric maps
VW.131 (L)
HN November 1992 descriptor moved
ALT bathymetric map
UF bathymetric charts
charts, bathymetric
maps, bathymetric

bathyscaphes
TX.486 (L,N)
ALT bathyscaphe
SN Use for relatively small, navigable submersibles designed for exploring ocean depths.

bathythermographs
TN.305 (L)
ALT bathythermograph
SN Oceanographic instruments that measure and record temperature at various depths in the ocean; often used by ships underway.

Bati
USE Beti

Batie
FL.181

batik
KT.1210 (H,L)
HN March 1993 descriptor moved
SN Resist dyeing in which wax is used as the resist.

bating
KT.1050
HN January 1993 descriptor added
ALT bated
SN Treating unhaired hides or skins with a solution in order to remove undesirable constituents and impart a quality of softness and flexibility to the final leather.

batiste
MT.1565
HN March 1993 descriptor moved
July 1990 descriptor added
SN Fine, soft, sheer cloth of plain weave made of any of the principal types of fiber, such as cotton, linen, rayon, silk, or wool. (W)

Batonga
USE Tonga

batons (music equipment)
TH.1106 (H,N)
HN January 1993 descriptor added
ALT baton (music equipment)
SN Sticks with which the conductor of an orchestra or similar ensemble beats the time. (NGDMI)
UF batons, conductors'
conductors' batons

batons (symbols of office)
VW.1177
HN June 1992 descriptor added
ALT baton (symbol of office)
SN Staffs, clubs, or truncheons carried as marks of office or authority. (RHDEL2)
UF batons, military
military batons

batons, conductors'
USE batons (music equipment)

batons, military
USE batons (symbols of office)

bâtons rompus
PJ.2129
HN March 1993 descriptor moved
November 1991 scope note changed
August 1991 alternate term deleted, was bâton rompus
SN Short, straight billets or portions of molding usually of rounded section forming the zigzag molding in Romanesque architecture; for the complete molding, use zigzag (ALT of zigzags) + moldings.

batoon
USE batten

bats
TV.28 (L,N)
ALT bat
SN Long, elongated, and usually wooden clubs of various sizes and shapes used to strike balls in certain sports, such as baseball and cricket.
RT baseball
cricket

BATs
USE bon à tirer proofs

Batshioko
USE Chokwe

batswing burners
PJ.2912
ALT batswing burner
SN Gas burners having a domical top pierced by a narrow slit across it, producing a fanlike sheet of flame. (MYERS)
UF batswings
burners, batswing
burners, flat-flame
flat-flame burners

batswings
USE batswing burners

batt
USE batt insulation

batt insulation
MT.1801
HN April 1993 lead-in term changed, was batts
June 1991 descriptor moved
June 1991 scope note added
June 1991 lead-in term added
June 1991 lead-in term deleted, was blanket insulation
SN Use for thermal or acoustical insulation available in precut, standard lengths.

UF batt
insulation, batt

batteaux
USE bateaux

batten
MT.3007
HN April 1993 descriptor changed, was battens
April 1993 lead-in term changed, was batoons
March 1992 descriptor moved
SN Thin, narrow strip of wood covering the joint between two parallel boards.
UF batoon
battening

batten, board and
USE board and batten

batten joints
PJ.724
HN April 1993 descriptor moved
ALT batten joint
UF joints, batten

battened columns
HN May 1991 descriptor deleted

battened walls
PJ.1902
HN March 1993 descriptor moved
ALT battened wall
SN Walls to which battens have been affixed. (HAS)
UF strapped walls
walls, battened
walls, strapped

battening
USE batten

battered walls
PJ.1903 (B)
HN March 1993 descriptor moved
November 1990 scope note changed
ALT battered wall
SN Walls that incline as they rise.
UF talus walls
walls, battered
walls, talus

battered women's shelters
USE crisis shelters

batteries
PJ.2473 (A,L)
HN March 1993 descriptor moved
ALT battery
SN Use for fixed platforms on which artillery is mounted.

battering rams
TK.122 (L,N)
ALT battering ram
SN Devices, known since antiquity, used to batter through the walls or gates of a fortified place, basically consisting of a large beam with a heavy metal head, mounted on a wheeled carriage or a frame from which it

could be swung back and forth, or
carried by people.
UF   rams (battering rams)
     rams, battering

batters
USE   mauls

battery wagons
      TX.131   (N)
ALT   battery wagon
SN   Horse-drawn military vehicles used
      in the 19th century to transport
      tools and materials for repairing an
      artillery battery's equipment.
UF   wagons, battery
RT   wagons

batting
      MT.1536
HN   November 1992 descriptor added
UK   wadding
SN   Sheet or roll of soft slightly matted
      fiber, traditionally carded cotton or
      wool, used especially for stuffing,
      padding, and interlining in quilting.
UF   cotton, padding
      padding cotton
RT   quilts

Battle-ax (pottery style)
USE   Corded

battle-axes
      TK.6   (N)
ALT   battle-ax
UKA   battle-axe
SN   Axes used in combat and warfare
      since prehistoric times, made in var-
      ious forms and sizes from one geo-
      graphic region and culture to an-
      other, but typically having a broad
      blade with a convex cutting edge
      and a handle, and wielded with one
      or two hands to strike cutting blows
      or to throw.

battledore
USE   battledore and shuttlecock

battledore and shuttlecock
      KQ.59   (L)
UF   battledore
      shuttlecock, battledore and
RT   shuttlecocks

battledores
USE   hornbooks

battlefield maps
      VW.113   (L)
HN   November 1992 descriptor moved
ALT   battlefield map
UF   maps, battlefield

battlefields
      RG.225   (A,L)
ALT   battlefield
UF   battlegrounds

battlegrounds
USE   battlefields

<battlement components>
      PJ.2487
HN   March 1993 guide term moved

battlements
      PJ.2486   (A)
HN   March 1993 descriptor moved
ALT   battlement
SN   Fortified parapets with alternate
      solid parts and openings.
UF   castellations
      crenelated parapets
      crenellations
      embattlements
      parapets, crenelated

<battlements and battlement components>
      PJ.2485
HN   March 1993 guide term moved

battles
      KM.3   (L)
HN   December 1992 scope note added
      November 1990 descriptor added
ALT   battle
SN   Use for individual instances of
      armed conflict between two or
      more groups.

battleships
      TX.429   (L,N)
ALT   battleship
SN   Use for the most heavily armored
      warships carrying the most powerful
      armament and deployed directly in
      the line of battle.
UF   dreadnoughts

Batwa
USE   Twa

Batwana
USE   Tswana

Baudou
USE   Pao-t'ou

Bauhaus
      FL.3472   (B,R)

Baulé
      FL.287   (L)
UF   Baoulé

baulk
USE   balk

Baumer
      FL.860

bauxite, ferroginous
USE   laterite

baviers
USE   bevors

Bavili
USE   Vili

bawdyhouses
USE   brothels

bawns
      RK.403
ALT   bawn

SN   Use for enclosure walls, usually for-
      tified, around Irish castles and some
      Irish houses.

Bawongo
USE   Wongo

Bawoyo
USE   Woyo

Bawumbu
USE   Hum
      Wumu

bay
USE   baize

bay laurel
USE   laurel (wood)

bay windows
      PJ.2222   (A,B)
HN   March 1993 descriptor moved
ALT   bay window
SN   Windows, either single or in a series,
      forming a bay or recess in a room
      and projecting outward from the
      wall in a rectangular, curved, or
      polygonal form. (W)
UF   jut windows
      windows, bay
      windows, jut

Bayaka
USE   Yaka

Bayanzi
USE   Yanzi

Bayard's process
      KT.520
SN   A direct positive process to make
      photographic prints in which a
      physically developed, unfixed print
      containing exposed silver chloride is
      soaked in a solution of potassium io-
      dide and is bleached in relation to
      exposure in the camera.

Bayat
      FL.3098

Bayazid I
      FL.3612
HN   April 1993 descriptor moved
UF   Beyazit I
      Beyazit, Lightning
      Lightning Beyazit

Bayazid II
      FL.3617
HN   April 1993 descriptor moved
UF   Beyazit II

bayes
USE   baize

bayles
USE   baileys

Bayombe
USE   Yombe

Bayon
      FL.2438

bayonet saws
USE saber saws

bayonet sockets
　　PJ.2991
ALT bayonet socket
UF sockets, bayonet

bayonets
　　TK.10　　　　　　　　　　(H,L,N)
ALT bayonet
SN Edged steel weapons resembling daggers or short swords, designed to be attached to the muzzle end of a firearm barrel.

bayonets, integral
USE integral bayonets

bayonets, knife
USE knife bayonets

bayonets, plug
USE plug bayonets

bayonets, retractable
USE integral bayonets

bayonets, socket
USE socket bayonets

bayonets, sword
USE sword bayonets

bayous
　　RD.136　　　　　　　　　　(L)
ALT bayou
SN Denotes marshy creeks or other sluggish swampy watercourses, generally found along the lower Mississippi River and other alluvial lowlands.

bays (bodies of water)
　　RD.111　　　　　　　　　　(L)
HN September 1991 descriptor changed, was bays
　　September 1991 alternate term changed, was bay
ALT bay (body of water)
SN Denotes wide, open, curving indentations of a shoreline, larger than coves and smaller than gulfs.

bays (building divisions)
　　PJ.947　　　　　　　　　　(A)
HN March 1993 descriptor moved
ALT bay (building division)
SN Use for repeated, similar divisions or compartments of a building or part of a building, as defined by recurring architectural features, such as arches, vaults, openings, or pilasters.

bays (vault components)
USE vault bays

bays, loading
USE loading docks

bays, vault
USE vault bays

Baysonqur
　　FL.3681
HN April 1993 descriptor moved

Baysonqur Style
USE Baysunghur Style

Baysunghur Style
　　FL.3702
HN April 1993 descriptor moved
UF Baysonqur Style

Baytown
　　FL.861

baywood
USE South American mahogany

bazaars
　　RG.41　　　　　　　　　　(L,B)
ALT bazaar
UF bazaars, Oriental
　　Oriental bazaars
　　suqs

bazaars, Oriental
USE bazaars

Bäzäklik
　　FL.1819
HN April 1993 descriptor moved

bazookas
　　TK.159　　　　　　　　　　(N)
ALT bazooka
SN Official nickname for a type of tube-shaped smoothbore portable rocket launcher, held atop the shoulder when fired, introduced as antitank weapons during the Second World War.
RT small arms

bazookas (kazoos)
USE kazoos

bazoos
USE kazoos

BB guns
　　TK.219　　　　　　　　　　(N)
ALT BB gun
SN Smoothbore spring air guns designed to fire BB shot.
UF guns, BB

BB shot
　　TK.260
SN Small pellets 0.175 or 0.18 inch in diameter, used in shotgun cartridges or for use in BB guns.
UF beebees
　　shot, BB
RT shot

beach chairs
　　TC.634　　　　　　　　　　(N)
HN January 1993 descriptor moved
ALT beach chair
UF chairs, beach

beach clubs
　　RK.974　　　　　　　　　　(B)
HN September 1990 scope note added
ALT beach club

SN Use for clubhouses whose primary recreational focus is a bathing beach.
UF clubs, beach

beach cobble
　　MT.926
HN April 1992 descriptor moved
UF cobble, beach

beach houses
　　RK.308　　　　　　　　　　(A,B)
ALT beach house
UF houses, beach

beach pajamas
　　TE.391
UK beach pyjamas
SN Trousered garments worn casually on the beach; in use from about 1920 to 1950. (NMAHDC)
UF pajamas, beach
　　pyjamas, beach
RT trousers

beach pyjamas
SEE beach pajamas

beach ridges
　　RD.159　　　　　　　　　　(L)
ALT beach ridge
SN Low ridges of stratified, unconsolidated sand and gravel created by the wave action of lakes or oceans and representing previous coastlines. (WAYTA)
UF ridges, beach

beaches
　　RD.196　　　　　　　　　　(A,L,B,R)
ALT beach

beaches, bathing
USE bathing beaches

beachwear
　　TE.386
SN Clothing for wear at the beach. (W)

beacons
　　TC.1432
ALT beacon
SN Lights, electronic apparatus, or other devices that emit identifying signals related to their position to guide or warn navigators or pilots of aircraft or ships. (MHDSTT)

beacons, aerodrome
USE airport beacons

beacons, aeronautical
USE aeronautical beacons

beacons, airport
USE airport beacons

beacons, airway
USE airway beacons

beacons, approach-light
USE approach lights

beacons, cemetery
USE lanterns of the dead

beacons, hazard
USE obstruction beacons

beacons, landmark
USE landmark beacons

beacons, lighthouse
USE lighthouse lamps

beacons, obstruction
USE obstruction beacons

bead and reel moldings
PJ.2078
HN April 1993 descriptor moved
ALT bead and reel molding
SN Round convex moldings with disks alternating singly or in pairs with oblong beads. (W)
UF moldings, bead and reel
moldings, reel and bead
reel and bead moldings

bead molding planes
USE bead planes

bead moldings
PJ.2107
HN April 1993 descriptor moved
ALT bead molding
SN Small, convex moldings of semicircular or greater profile. (HAS)
UF baguettes
beads (moldings)
chaplets (bead moldings)
moldings, bead
roundels (moldings)

bead planes
TH.1539 (N)
ALT bead plane
SN Planes having a curved cutting edge which makes bead moldings along a wood surface.
UF astragal planes
bead molding planes
molding planes, bead
planes, astragal
planes, bead
planes, bead molding

bead saws
TH.1562 (N)
ALT bead saw
SN Small backsaws, 3 to 6 inches in length, with very fine teeth and very little set; used for fine work. (SALAM)
UF backsaws, fancy
fancy backsaws
saws, bead

bead screws, stop
USE stop bead screws

bead-work
SEE beadwork

beaded dovetail seams
PJ.693
HN April 1993 descriptor moved
March 1993 alternate term added
ALT beaded dovetail seam

UF dovetail seams, beaded
seams, beaded dovetail

beaded joints
PJ.619
HN April 1993 descriptor moved
ALT beaded joint
UF joints, beaded

beadhouses
RK.751
ALT beadhouse
SN Almshouses in which the residents were required to pray for the founder. (RHDEL2)
UF bedehouses

beading (beadwork)
USE beadwork

beading (edging pattern)
DG.127 (L)
ALT beaded (edging pattern)
SN Enrichment consisting of a line of tiny beads; common on silver and furniture. (LDDO)
UF pearling

beading (process)
KT.1221
HN January 1993 descriptor added
ALT beaded
SN Trimming, furnishing, adorning, or covering with beads. (W)
RT beadwork

beadmaking
KT.767
HN December 1992 related term added
RT beads (round objects)

beads (moldings)
USE bead moldings

beads (necklaces)
TE.457 (L)
SN Use for necklaces consisting of one or more strands of beads.
RT beads (round objects)

beads (round objects)
PE.33 (H,L,N)
HN December 1992 descriptor added
ALT bead (round object)
SN Small objects, often balls or cylinders, but can be any shape or material, pierced to be strung or to be attached, as by sewing.
RT beadmaking
beads (necklaces)
beadwork

beads and quirks
USE quirk beads

beads, quirk
USE quirk beads

beadwork
PE.98 (L,R)
HN December 1992 related terms added
December 1992 descriptor moved
December 1992 scope note changed

December 1992 alternate term deleted, was beaded
December 1992 lead-in term changed, was beading (textiles)
UK bead-work
SN Arrangements of beads, often attached to textiles.
UF beading (beadwork)
RT beading (process)
beads (round objects)

beak
MT.2556
HN March 1992 descriptor added
SN The bill of a bird or similar horny mouthpart in other animals. (RHDEL2)

beak irons
PJ.2572 (N)
HN March 1993 descriptor moved
ALT beak iron
SN The tapered ends of anvils. (W)
UF bick irons
bickerns
irons, beak
irons, bick

beak moldings
PJ.2099
HN April 1993 descriptor moved
ALT beak molding
SN Use for fillet moldings with the front portion pendant; for moldings with a beaked head ornamental motif, use beakhead moldings.
UF hawksbeak moldings
moldings, beak
moldings, hawksbeak

Beaker
USE Bell Beaker
Funnel Beaker

beakers (drinking vessels)
TQ.387 (H,N,R)
ALT beaker (drinking vessel)
SN Drinking vessels without handles, cylindrical or conical, generally with a flat base.
UF cups, mint julep
mint julep cups
RT beakers (vessels)
church plate
flip glasses

beakers (vessels)
TQ.42 (N,R)
ALT beaker (vessel)
SN Flat-bottomed, cylindrical vessels usually with a pouring lip, especially those used by chemists and pharmacists.
RT beakers (drinking vessels)

beakers, maiden
USE wager cups

beakhead moldings
PJ.2079
HN April 1993 descriptor moved
ALT beakhead molding
SN Use for moldings with bird, animal,

or human heads biting a roll molding as the ornamental motif; for fillet moldings with the front portion pendant, use **beak moldings.**
UF   bird's beak moldings
moldings, beakhead
moldings, bird's beak

beakhorn stakes
TH.1224
ALT beakhorn stake
SN   Stakes or small bench anvils having a slender horn on one side. (W)
UF   stakes, beakhorn

beaking joints
PJ.620
HN   April 1993 descriptor moved
ALT beaking joint
UF   joints, beaking

beaks
PJ.3112
ALT beak
SN   A type of lip on a container that extends to a point.

beam anchors
PJ.24
HN   April 1993 descriptor moved
ALT beam anchor
SN   Metal ties for securing a beam, joist, or floor firmly to a wall. (MEANS)
UF   anchors, beam
anchors, joist
anchors, wall
joist anchors (beam anchors)
wall anchors

beam-and-girder constructions
USE one-way beam and slab systems

beam-and-slab floor constructions
USE one-way beam and slab systems
two-way beam and slab systems

beam-and-slab floors
USE one-way beam and slab systems
two-way beam and slab systems

beam and slab systems, one-way
USE one-way beam and slab systems

beam and slab systems, two-way
USE two-way beam and slab systems

beam ceilings
PJ.2050
HN   March 1993 descriptor moved
ALT beam ceiling
SN   Ceilings having beams, either structural or decorative, that are visible. (DAC)
UF   ceilings, beam

beam compasses
TH.657   (N)
HN   February 1993 scope note changed
ALT beam compass
SN   Instruments consisting of a long horizontal bar on which two movable heads slide, one of which carries a pencil, and the other a pin or tracer; used to draw large circles or

arcs of circles as for full-scale working drawings, cask gauging, or carpentry work. (DAC)
UF   compasses, beam

beam hangers
PJ.100
HN   April 1993 descriptor moved
ALT beam hanger
SN   Wires, straps, or other hardware devices used to hang the formwork for concrete beams.
UF   beam saddles
hangers, beam
saddles, beam

beam hangers, steel-to-steel
USE steel-to-steel beam hangers

beam projector floodlights
USE beam projectors

beam projectors
TC.1447
ALT beam projector
SN   Projectors whose lamp may be moved toward or away from the reflector to vary the beam spread.
UF   beam projector floodlights
BPs
floodlights, beam projector
parabolic spotlights
projector floodlights, beam
projector spots
projectors, beam
spotlights, parabolic
spots, projector
spots, sun
sun spots
washtubs (beam projectors)

beam saddles
USE beam hangers

beams (balance components)
PJ.2635
ALT beam (balance component)
SN   Use for the crossbars of balances, from the ends of which the pans or baskets are suspended. (RHDEL2)
UF   arms, balance
balance arms

beams (structural elements)
PJ.1643   (A,H,L,B)
HN   March 1993 descriptor moved
March 1993 descriptor changed, was **beams**
March 1993 alternate term changed, was **beam**
ALT beam (structural element)
SN   Structural members whose primary function is to carry transverse loads.

beams, balance
USE balance beams

beams, box
USE box beams

beams, built-up
USE built-up beams

<beams by form>
PJ.1644
HN   March 1993 guide term moved

<beams by location or context>
PJ.1655
HN   March 1993 guide term moved

<beams by support condition>
PJ.1662
HN   March 1993 guide term moved

beams, candle
USE candle beams

beams, cased
USE cased beams

beams, channel
USE channels (rolled sections)

beams, collar
USE collar beams

beams, compound
USE built-up beams

beams, continuous
USE continuous beams

beams, dragging
USE dragon beams

beams, dragon
USE dragon beams

beams, end-supported
USE simple beams

beams, flitch
USE flitch beams

beams, flitch plate
USE flitch beams

beams, ground
USE sill plates

beams, hammer
USE hammer beams

beams, jesting
USE jesting beams

beams, percussion
USE percussion beams

beams, plate
USE plate girders

beams, ridge
USE ridgeboards

beams, sandwich
USE flitch beams

beams, simple
USE simple beams

beams, simply supported
USE simple beams

beams, straining
USE straining beams

beams, tie
USE tie beams

beams, WF
USE wide-flange beams

beams, wide-flange
USE wide-flange beams

beams, wind
USE collar beams

bean
    MT.2653   (L)
HN March 1992 descriptor moved

bean pod, locust
USE locust bean pod

bean pulls
    PJ.348
HN April 1993 descriptor moved
ALT bean pull
SN Hand-forged pulls mounted with lima bean-shaped plates. (DITTRI)
UF pulls, bean

bean roasters, coffee
USE coffee roasters

bean tree
USE catalpa

bean tree, Indian
USE catalpa

beanbag chairs
    TC.467
HN January 1993 descriptor moved
ALT beanbag chair
SN Large, soft frameless chairs resembling a beanbag; typically a clothlike plastic shell filled with plastic chips, that molds itself readily to the contour of the occupant. (RHDEL2)
UF chairs, beanbag

beanies
    TE.543   (N)
ALT beanie
SN Small, round skullcaps, often brightly colored, worn especially by children and collegians.

beano
USE bingo

bear-paw sabatons
    TE.350
ALT bear-paw sabaton
SN Sabatons with broad, blunt toe caps, popular in the mid-16th century.
UF bear's paw solerets
    broad sabatons
    duck-billed solerets
    sabatons, bear-paw
    sabatons, broad
    solerets, bear's paw
    solerets, duck-billed

bear spears
    TK.62
ALT bear spear
SN Long spears used in hunting bears.
UF spears, bear

bearing alloy
USE Babbitt metal

bearing cloths
    TE.238
ALT bearing cloth
SN Large squares of cloth, often edged with lace or embroidery, which were wrapped around a swaddled baby during a baptism.
UF christening palms
    cloths, bearing
    palms, christening

bearing stress
    BM.641
HN November 1992 descriptor moved
SN Stress developed at the point of contact between two loaded structural members. (DS)
UF stress, bearing

bearing swords
    TK.92
ALT bearing sword
SN Swords carried during public ceremonies and rituals to signify the authority of the owner or wearer. They were often carried point up by a body guard or other attendant following the owner, rather than worn by him.
UF swords, bearing

bearing walls
    PJ.1911   (A,B)
HN March 1993 descriptor moved
    March 1991 lead-in term changed, was **bearing walls**
    March 1991 descriptor changed, was **loadbearing walls**
    March 1991 alternate term changed, was **loadbearing wall**
ALT bearing wall
SN Walls that support a vertical load in addition to their own weight. (PUTNAM\
UF loadbearing walls
    walls, bearing
    walls, loadbearing

bear's breech
USE acanthus

bear's foot
USE acanthus

bear's paw solerets
USE bear-paw sabatons

bears, teddy
USE teddy bears

beatae
USE blessed

beaten bark cloth
USE bark cloth

beaters (culinary tools)
    TH.135   (N)
HN April 1993 descriptor added
ALT beater (culinary tool)
SN Tools used for beating, stirring, or whipping.
UF whippers

beaters (mauls)
USE mauls

beaters, egg
USE eggbeaters

beaters, rotary
USE eggbeaters

beaters, rotary egg
USE eggbeaters

beati
USE blessed

beatifications
    KM.169   (L)
HN May 1991 alternate term added
ALT beatification
SN Official acts of the pope whereby deceased persons are declared to be enjoying the happiness of heaven and therefore proper subjects of religious honor. (RHDEL2)

Beau-Brummel dressing tables
    TC.1143
HN January 1993 descriptor moved
ALT Beau-Brummel dressing table
SN Men's or ladies' dressing boxes on a tall stand with a lid that opens to reveal a fitted interior, usually with drawers beneath. Unlike other dressing tables, it has taller legs and lacks a full case of drawers beneath. (ANTIQS)
UF Beau-Brummel tables
    Beau-Brummels
    dressing tables, Beau-Brummel
    tables, Beau-Brummel dressing

Beau-Brummel tables
USE Beau-Brummel dressing tables

Beau-Brummels
USE Beau-Brummel dressing tables

beautification
    KG.60
HN April 1993 lead-in term added
    January 1991 scope note added
    January 1991 alternate term added
ALT beautified
SN Activity of making something beautiful or repairing or enhancing its appearance.
UF beautifying

beautification, highway
USE roadside improvement

beautification, urban
USE urban beautification

beautifying
USE beautification

beauty
    BM.397   (L,B,R)
UF the Beautiful

beauty, line of
USE Hogarth's line

beauty parlors
USE beauty shops

beauty patches
USE patches (costume accessories)

beauty salons
USE beauty shops

beauty shops
RK.190 (A,L,B)
ALT beauty shop
UF beauty parlors
    beauty salons
    hairdressers
    hairdressing salons
    parlors, beauty
    salons, beauty
    salons, hairdressing
    shops, beauty

beauty spots
USE patches (costume accessories)

Beaux-Arts
FL.3368 (A,L,B,R)

Beaver
FL.1241 (L)
UF Tsattine

Beaverboard (TM)
USE fiberboard

beavers
TE.601
ALT beaver
SN Top hats made of beaver fur or of a fabric simulating this fur. Prefer **castors (hats)** for other men's hats of beaver fur made in varying form.
RT castors (hats)

beavers (armor)
USE bevors

Becton white
USE lithopone

bed-and-breakfast inns
USE bed-and-breakfasts

bed-and-breakfasts
RK.901 (A,L)
ALT bed-and-breakfast
SN Inns, hotels, or private homes offering a room for the night and breakfast the next morning for one inclusive price. (RHDEL2)
UF B & Bs
    B-and-Bs
    bed-and-breakfast inns
    inns, bed-and-breakfast

bed bolt covers
PJ.62
HN March 1993 descriptor moved
ALT bed bolt cover
UF bedstead bolt covers
    bolt covers, bed
    covers, bed bolt

bed bolts
PJ.55
HN April 1993 descriptor moved
    April 1993 lead-in term deleted, was
    bedstead bolts
ALT bed bolt
UF bolts, bed

bed canopies
USE canopies (bed components)

bed chairs
TC.592 (N)
HN May 1993 related term added
    January 1993 descriptor moved
ALT bed chair
SN Chairs with backs which may be lowered and seats that are hinged to unfold or that can otherwise be extended to form beds.
UF chair-beds
RT beds (furniture)

bed-chests
USE press beds (deception beds)

<bed components>
PJ.2737
HN March 1993 guide term moved

bed coverings
TC.195
ALT bed covering
SN Term generally applied to any textile used to cover a bed.
UF coverings, bed
RT blankets (coverings)
    throws

bed covers
USE bedcovers

bed curtains
TC.261
ALT bed curtain
SN Curtains on or around a bed, that can be opened or closed for privacy, control of light and drafts, or protection against dust.
UF curtains, bed
RT curtains

bed flounces
USE dust ruffles

bed furniture
TC.259
SN Period term referring to both bedcovers and bed hangings.
UF furniture, bed
RT bed hangings
    bedcovers

bed hangings
TC.260
ALT bed hanging
SN Curtains and other cloth hangings on or around a bed; used for decoration, privacy, control of light and drafts, or as protective coverings.
UF hangings, bed
RT bed furniture

bed jackets
TE.262 (N)
ALT bed jacket

SN Waist-length jackets or capes worn in bed.
UF jackets, bed
RT jackets

bed joints
PJ.678
HN April 1993 descriptor moved
ALT bed joint
SN Joints between different courses or layers of bricks. (AGS6)
UF joints, bed

bed keys
USE bed wrenches

bed mantles
USE bedcovers

bed mold planes
USE cornice planes

bed moldings
PJ.2119
HN April 1993 descriptor moved
    November 1990 descriptor moved
    November 1990 scope note changed
ALT bed molding
SN Use both for small cornice moldings situated beneath the corona and above the frieze in Classical architecture and its derivatives, and for moldings located beneath an overhanging horizontal surface, as below the eaves.
UF bed molds
    moldings, bed
    molds, bed

bed molds
USE bed moldings

bed-outshots
SEE bed-outshuts

bed-outshuts
PJ.960 (A)
HN March 1993 descriptor moved
ALT bed-outshut
UK bed-outshots
UKA bed-outshot
SN Use for small additions to houses, accommodating a bed, common in South Wales.

bed pillars
USE bedposts

bed plates
USE press beds (printing press components)

bed quilts
USE quilts

bed rugs
TC.197 (L)
ALT bed rug
SN Heavy ruglike bedcovers, done in a variety of techniques such as flat or pile weaves or needlework.
UF rugs, bed
RT rugs

bed sheets
USE sheets (bed coverings)

bed slats
PJ.2738
HN March 1993 descriptor moved
ALT bed slat
SN Boards supporting the bedsprings, usually extending from side to side of a bedstead. (W)
UF bed staffs
bed sticks
slats, bed
staffs, bed
sticks, bed

bed springs
USE bedsprings

bed staffs
USE bed slats

bed steps
TC.1028   (N)
HN January 1993 descriptor moved
ALT bed step
SN Steps used to climb into a bed. (W)
UF steps, bed

bed sticks
USE bed slats

bed tables
TC.1117
HN January 1993 descriptor moved
ALT bed table
UF tables, bed

bed tents
USE sparvers

bed throws
USE bedspreads

bed trays
TQ.541   (N)
ALT bed tray
SN Meal trays with legs or supports at each end to fit across the lap of a person sitting in bed. (RHDEL2)
UF trays, bed
RT trays

bed valances
TC.265
ALT bed valance
SN Horizontal cloth hangings fixed to the tester or canopy of a bed; generally used as decorative headings to conceal the tops of bed curtains and their hardware. For valances around the base of a bed, use **base valances**.
UF bed valances, upper
top valances
upper bed valances
valances, bed
valances, top
valances, upper
valances, upper bed
RT valances

bed valances, upper
USE bed valances

bed wrenches
TH.1314
ALT bed wrench
SN Wrenches for adjusting the nuts and bolts of a bedstead. (W)
UF bed keys
keys, bed
wrenches, bed

bedboards
PJ.2739
HN March 1993 descriptor moved
ALT bedboard
SN Stiff, thin, wide boards inserted usually between bedspring and mattress. (W)

bedchamber candlesticks
USE chambersticks

bedchamber lamps
USE chamber lamps

bedchambers
USE bedrooms

bedcovers
TC.196   (R)
ALT bedcover
SN Bed coverings used as the topmost cover of a bed during the day.
UF bed covers
bed mantles
covers, bed
mantles, bed
RT bed furniture
catalognes
palampores
suzani

bedding, carpet
USE carpet beds

bedding, massed
USE carpet beds

beddles
USE beetles

bedehouses
USE beadhouses

Bedford stone
MT.863
HN April 1992 descriptor moved
UF stone, Bedford

bedframes
PJ.2740
HN March 1993 descriptor moved
ALT bedframe

Bedja
USE Beja

Bedouin
FL.693   (A,L)

Bedouin carpets
USE Berber + rugs

bedpans
TQ.173   (L,N)
ALT bedpan
SN Shallow containers designed to be

used for urination or defecation by persons confined to bed.

bedposts
PJ.2741
HN March 1993 descriptor moved
ALT bedpost
SN Upright supports on a bedstead, such as those which support the tester on a high-post bed.
UF bed pillars
pillars, bed

bedquilts
USE quilts

bedroom pianos, convertible
USE piano beds

bedroom slippers
TE.749   (N)
ALT bedroom slipper
SN Low-cut slippers, often with a flexible sole and either heelless or with a low heel, intended for indoor use.
UF house slippers
slippers, bedroom
slippers, house

bedrooms
PJ.1102   (A,L,B)
HN March 1993 descriptor moved
ALT bedroom
UF bedchambers
chambers (bedrooms)

beds (furniture)
TC.749   (L,N,R)
HN May 1993 related terms added
March 1993 descriptor changed, was **beds**
March 1993 alternate term changed, was **bed**
January 1993 descriptor moved
ALT bed (furniture)
SN A term signifying either the bedding (mattress and cover), or the bedsteads, or both. (DDA)
UF bedsteads
bedstocks
RT bed chairs
couch beds
sofa beds

beds (printing press components)
USE press beds (printing press components)

beds (site elements)
RM.247
HN March 1993 descriptor added
ALT bed (site element)
SN Use for areas of gardens or lawns demarcated from their surroundings and devoted to the cultivation of a particular group of plants.

beds (swaddling garments)
TE.400
ALT bed (swaddling garment)
SN Period term for rectangular pieces of cloth wrapped around an infant and pinned in place to keep the

arms fixed by the sides and the legs
straight.

beds à la duchesse
USE lits à la duchesse

beds, alcove
USE box beds

beds, angel
USE lits à la duchesse

beds, boat
USE sleigh beds

beds, bookcase
USE bookcase beds

beds, box
USE box beds

beds, bunk
USE bunk beds

beds, bureau
USE bureau beds

<beds by form or function>
TC.750
HN January 1993 guide term moved

<beds by form: size>
TC.751
HN January 1993 guide term moved
January 1993 guide term changed,
was *<beds by size>*

beds, cabinet
USE cabinet beds

beds, camp
USE field beds

beds, canopy
USE canopy beds
tester beds

beds, cant
USE field beds

beds, carpet
USE carpet beds

beds, chiffonier
USE chiffonier beds

beds, chiffonier folding
USE chiffonier beds

beds, closet
USE press beds (deception beds)

beds, concealed
USE deception beds

beds, convertible
USE sofa beds

beds, couch
USE couch beds

beds, crib
USE cribs

beds, cupboard
USE box beds
press beds (deception beds)

beds, davenport
USE davenports (sofas)

beds, deception
USE deception beds

beds, dome
USE dome beds

beds, double
USE double beds

beds, duchesse
USE lits à la duchesse

beds, field
USE field beds

beds, folding
USE folding beds

beds, four-posted
USE tester beds

beds, French
USE French beds
sleigh beds

beds, full
USE double beds

beds, gondola
USE sleigh beds

beds, gondola-shaped
USE sleigh beds

beds, Grecian
USE sleigh beds

beds, half-tester
USE half-tester beds

beds, hideaway
USE hideaway beds

beds, high-post
USE high-post beds

beds, hollywood
USE hollywood beds

beds, hospital
USE hospital beds

beds, Jenny Lind
USE spool beds

beds, king-size
USE king-size beds

beds, library press
USE library press beds

beds, livery
USE livery beds

beds, low-post
USE low-post beds

beds, Murphy
USE Murphy beds

beds, pencil-post
USE pencil-post beds

beds, piano
USE piano beds

beds, piano folding
USE piano beds

beds, plantation
USE tester beds

beds, platform
USE platform beds

beds, post
USE high-post beds
low-post beds

beds, press
USE press beds (deception beds)
press beds (printing press components)

beds, queen-size
USE queen-size beds

beds, rest
USE daybeds

beds, river
USE river beds

beds, settee
USE settle beds

beds, settle
USE settle beds

beds, single
USE twin beds

beds, sleigh
USE sleigh beds

beds, slope
USE field beds

beds, sofa
USE sofa beds

beds, sparver
USE sparver beds

beds, sperver
USE sparver beds

beds, spindle
USE spool beds

beds, spool
USE spool beds

beds, state
USE state beds

beds, stump
USE stump beds

beds, suitcase
USE suitcase beds

beds, summer
USE summer beds

beds, swinging crib
USE swinging cribs

beds, table
USE table beds

beds, tall-post
USE high-post beds

beds, tent
USE field beds

beds, tester
USE tester beds

beds, toilet table
USE toilet table beds

beds, truckle
USE trundle beds

beds, trundle
USE trundle beds

beds, trunk
USE trundle beds

beds, turn-up
USE folding beds
    press beds (deception beds)

beds, twin
USE twin beds

beds, water
USE water beds

bedsheets
USE sheets (bed coverings)

bedside cabinets
USE night tables

bedside cupboards
USE night tables

bedside tables
USE night tables

bedskirts
USE base valances

bedspreads
    TC.198   (L,N,R)
ALT bedspread
SN Term used from the mid-19th century onward for a variety of bedcovers, especially those which are large, lightweight cloths that cover the full bed and pillow and often extend to the floor.
UF bed throws
    spreads
    throws, bed
RT counterpanes

bedspreads, candlewick
USE candlewick spreads

bedsprings
    PJ.2744   (N)
HN March 1993 descriptor moved
ALT bedspring
SN Springs supporting a mattress. (W)
UF bed springs
    springs, bed

bedstands
USE night tables

bedstead bolt covers
USE bed bolt covers

bedsteads
USE beds (furniture)

bedsteads, box
USE box beds

bedsteads, buroe
USE bureau beds

bedsteads, cabinet
USE press beds (deception beds)

bedsteads, cot
USE cots

bedsteads, crib
USE cribs

bedsteads, field
USE field beds

bedsteads, high-post
USE high-post beds

bedsteads, library press
USE library press beds

bedsteads, low-post
USE low-post beds

bedsteads, sparver
USE sparver beds

bedsteads, table
USE table beds

bedsteads, tent
USE field beds

bedstocks
USE beds (furniture)

bee glue
USE propolis

bee houses
USE apiaries

beebees
USE BB shot

beech
    MT.2691   (L)
HN March 1992 descriptor moved
UF Fagus

beech, American
USE American beech

beech, black
USE New Zealand beech

beech, Chinese
USE Chinese beech

beech, common
USE European beech

beech, European
USE European beech

beech, Japanese
USE Japanese beech

beech, New Zealand
USE New Zealand beech

beech, Oriental
USE Oriental beech

beech, red
USE red beech

beech, Siebold's
USE Siebold's beech

beech, white
USE white beech

beehive coke ovens
USE beehive ovens

beehive domes
    PJ.1734   (B)
HN March 1993 descriptor moved
ALT beehive dome
SN Use for domes in the form of a cone with curved sides.
UF alveated domes
    domes, alveated
    domes, beehive

beehive dwellings
USE beehive houses

beehive houses
    RK.247   (B,R)
HN February 1992 scope note added
ALT beehive house
SN Designates a class of simple dwellings, circular in plan and with beehive domes.
UF beehive dwellings
    beehive huts
    dwellings, beehive
    houses, beehive
    huts, beehive

beehive huts
USE beehive houses

beehive kilns
USE beehive ovens

beehive ovens
    TH.497   (N)
ALT beehive oven
SN Kilns used to convert coal into coke, characterized by a dome-shaped roof. (RHDEL2)
UF beehive coke ovens
    beehive kilns
    beehives (ovens)
    coke ovens, beehive
    kilns, beehive
    ovens, beehive

beehive ovens (bake ovens)
USE bake ovens

beehive tombs
USE tholos tombs

beehives
    RK.80   (L,N,B,R)
ALT beehive
UF skeps

beehives (ovens)
USE beehive ovens

beepers
    TT.648
ALT beeper
SN Electric devices that, when activated,

produce short, relatively high-pitched tones, at regular intervals over a period of time, as in portable pagers or animal tracking collars.

beer cellars
    PJ.1129   (A)
HN March 1993 descriptor moved
ALT beer cellar
SN Use for cellars in which beer is stored.
UF cellars, beer

beer gardens
    RK.110
ALT beer garden
SN Distinguished from other drinking establishments (e.g., bars, saloons) by being family-oriented, by having chairs and tables rather than a bar, by emphasizing food as much as beer, by having music, and by being more impersonal than saloons.
UF gardens, beer

beer halls
    RK.108   (A)
ALT beer hall
SN Use for establishments chiefly serving beer and usually offering entertainment.
UF halls, beer

Beer limestone
USE Beer stone

Beer stone
    MT.848
HN April 1992 descriptor moved
UF Beer limestone
    limestone, Beer
    stone, Beer

beers, pillow
USE pillowcases

Beersheba-Ghassulian
USE Ghassulian

bees-wax
SEE beeswax

bees-wax, unbleached
SEE unbleached beeswax

beeswax
    MT.1291   (L)
HN April 1992 descriptor moved
    December 1991 scope note changed
    December 1990 descriptor moved
UK bees-wax
SN Natural wax produced by bees as a by-product of honey production; used chiefly in polish, candles, encaustic, leather dressing, adhesive, cosmetics, as a protective coating for etching, and occasionally to modify paint. (MH)

beeswax, bleached
USE bleached beeswax

beeswax, bleached white
USE bleached beeswax

beeswax, unbleached
USE unbleached beeswax

beetles
    TH.1661   (N)
HN May 1993 descriptor changed, was **beetles (mallets)**
    May 1993 alternate term changed, was **beetle (mallet)**
ALT beetle
SN Large sledgehammers made of wood, used for driving pegs or wedges, knocking heavy wood beams into place, or in other applications where material might sustain damage if struck with a conventional sledgehammer. (MEANS)
UF beddles
    bittels
    bittles, wedge
    commanders (mallets)
    wedge bittles

beetles, potato
USE potato mashers

before letters
USE proofs before letters

begannas
USE baganas

begennas
USE baganas

beggars
    HG.901   (L,R)
HN December 1992 alternate terms added
    December 1990 descriptor added
ALT beggar
    beggar's
    beggars'
SN Those who subsist by asking for alms. (WCOL9)
UF mendicants

beggars' quilts
USE charm quilts

beginning axes
    TH.1413
ALT beginning ax
SN Axes used to make rough cuts before an adz is used to produce a curved surface in wood. (HUMMEL)
UF axes, beginning
    axes, fitting
    fitting axes

begs
USE baganas

béguinages
    RG.202   (L)
ALT béguinage
SN Communal facilities established for the sisterhood of Béguines.

<behavior and mental disorders>
    BM.989
HN February 1993 guide term moved
    February 1991 guide term added

behavior, deviant
USE deviant behavior

behavior disorders
    BM.990   (L)
HN February 1993 descriptor moved
    January 1991 descriptor added
ALT behavior disorder
UF disorders, behavior

behavior, environment and
USE environmental psychology

behavior-environment studies
USE environmental psychology

behavior, human
USE human behavior

behavior, proxemic
USE spatial behavior

behavior, spatial
USE spatial behavior

behavioral sciences
    KD.209   (L)
HN August 1992 lead-in term added
    September 1991 descriptor added
ALT behavioral science
UK behavioural sciences
UKA behavioural science
SN Area of study typically including anthropology, psychology, and sociology. (IESS)
UF sciences, behavioral
    sciences, behavioural
RT ethics (philosophy)

behavioural sciences
SEE behavioral sciences

beholders
USE spectators
    viewers

Behzad School
USE Bihzad School

beige
USE grayish yellow
    light grayish brown
    light grayish yellowish brown
    light olive brown
    pale yellow

beige brown
USE grayish yellowish brown

beige gray
USE medium gray
    yellowish gray

beige, light
USE grayish yellow
    light grayish yellowish brown

beige, light rose
USE grayish yellowish pink

beige, yellow
USE light yellowish brown
    moderate yellowish brown

Beijing
USE Peking

Beinschwarz
USE   bone black

Beja
FL.695   (L)
UF   Bedja

Belbasi
FL.2939

Beldibi
FL.2940

Belén
FL.1200

Belfast trusses
USE   bowstring trusses

belfries
PJ.1082   (A,L,N,B,R)
HN   March 1993 descriptor moved
ALT   belfry
SN   Use for the rooms or spaces in which bells are hung in a tower; for the entire tower structure, use **bell towers.**

belfries (bell towers)
USE   bell towers

belfrys (sheds)
RK.1154
ALT   belfry (shed)
SN   Use only for vernacular British sheds for cattle, wagons, or farm equipment from the 16th to the 18th century.

Belgian
FL.3127   (L,B)

Belgian black marble
MT.714
HN   April 1992 descriptor moved
UF   black marble, Belgian
        marble, Belgian black
        noir belge

Belgian block
MT.948
HN   October 1992 related term added
        April 1992 descriptor moved
SN   A type of paving stone generally cut in a truncated, pyramidal shape; laid with the base of the pyramid down. (DAC)
UF   block, Belgian
RT   blocks (shaped masses)

Belgian Earth
USE   green earth

Belgian linen
MT.1524
HN   March 1993 descriptor moved
        July 1990 descriptor added
UF   linen, Belgian

Belgian marble
USE   rance

Belgian trusses
USE   Fink trusses

Belgischestil
USE   Jugendstil

bell-and-spigot joints
PJ.686
HN   April 1993 descriptor moved
ALT   bell-and-spigot joint
SN   Commonly used joints in cast iron pipe. Each piece is made with an enlarged diameter or bell at one end into which the plain or spigot end of another piece is inserted. The joint is sealed by cement, oakum, lead, or rubber caulked into the bell around the spigot. (MEANS)
UF   joints, bell-and-spigot
        joints, spigot-and-socket
        spigot-and-socket joints

bell arches
PJ.1581
HN   March 1993 descriptor moved
ALT   bell arch
SN   Use for round arches supported by large corbels with curved lower edges, giving the opening a bell-shaped outline.
UF   arches, bell

Bell Beaker
FL.2594   (L)
UF   Beaker

bell canopies
USE   bell cotes

bell capitals
PJ.1494
HN   March 1993 descriptor moved
        November 1990 scope note added
ALT   bell capital
SN   Capitals whose basic form is shaped like a bell or an inverted bell; may be enriched with carving.
UF   capitals, bell

bell corslets
TE.314
ALT   bell corslet
SN   Bronze cuirasses of ancient Greece, typically consisting of two pieces hinged on one side and joined by metal pins or loops on the other, and characterized by an inward curve near the waist below which the lower rim curves strongly out. They were common until the late 6th century BCE.
UF   bell-shaped corslets
        corslets, bell
        corslets, bell-shaped

bell cotes
PJ.1811
HN   April 1993 alternate term changed, was **bellcote**
        March 1993 descriptor moved
        November 1990 scope note changed
        November 1990 descriptor changed, was **bellcotes**
ALT   bell cote
SN   Use for small, open structures erected on a roof, wall, or gable of a church or other structure, carrying and sheltering bells.
UF   bell canopies
        bell gables
        canopies, bell
        cotes, bell
        gables, bell

bell flower motifs
USE   husks (motifs)

bell-founders
SEE   bell founders

bell founders
HG.731   (L)
HN   December 1992 alternate terms added
        July 1992 descriptor changed, was **bell-founders**
        July 1992 lead-in term changed, was **bell founders**
        July 1992 alternate term changed, was **bell-founder**
ALT   bell founder
        bell founder's
        bell founders'
UK   bell-founders
SN   Founders, casters, or makers of bells. (OED)

bell gables
USE   bell cotes

bell glasses
TQ.611
ALT   bell glass
SN   Bell-shaped glass domes placed over delicate plants to protect them from the weather and to force their growth.
UF   bell jars (bell glasses)
        bells, garden
        cloches (bell glasses)
        garden bells
        glasses, bell

bell glasses (bell jars)
USE   bell jars

bell harps
TT.391
ALT   bell harp
SN   Wire-strung psalteries which are swung while being played. (NGDMI)
UF   harps, bell

bell houses
USE   bell towers

bell jars
TQ.81   (N)
ALT   bell jar
SN   Bell-shaped glass jars or covers for protecting delicate instruments or natural or fabricated objects from dust or damage. Also, vessels for containing gases or a vacuum in chemical experiments. (RHDEL2)
UF   bell glasses (bell jars)
        display domes
        domes, display

glasses, bell
jars, bell

bell jars (bell glasses)
USE bell glasses

bell kraters
  TQ.91
ALT bell krater
SN Kraters in the form of an inverted bell with handles placed high on the body.
UF kraters, bell

bell metal
  MT.399
HN March 1993 descriptor moved
SN Bronze used chiefly for casting large bells. Its standard composition is 78% copper and 22% tin but is varied to give varying tones.
UF metal, bell

bell-ringing toys
USE bell toys

bell-shaped
  DC.61
HN October 1992 descriptor moved
SN The shape, in full or in outline, of a cross section of an inverted cup with flaring rim and convex crown, very like a bell. (W)

bell-shaped corslets
USE bell corslets

bell towers
  RK.33   (A,L,N,B,R)
HN February 1992 scope note added
ALT bell tower
SN Use for towers fitted and prepared for containing bells, can be either freestanding or attached to buildings or other structures.
UF belfries (bell towers)
    bell houses
    houses, bell
    kolokolnya
    towers, bell

bell toys
  TV.139   (N)
ALT bell toy
SN Use for wheeled toys, usually meant to be pulled, in which bells or chimes ring as the wheels turn; popular since the 1860s.
UF bell-ringing toys
    toys, bell
    toys, bell-ringing

Bella Bella
  FL.1349   (L)

Bella Coola
  FL.1350   (L)
UF Bellacoola

Bellacoola
USE Bella Coola

bellarmines
  TQ.46

ALT bellarmine
SN Narrow-necked stoneware bottles, globular or pear-shaped, ornamented with a bearded mask and often with a coat of arms; of a type made in the 16th and 17th centuries.
UF bottles, d'Alva
    d'Alva bottles
    graybeards
    greybeards
    longbeards

bellboys
USE bellpeople

bellexion moldings
USE bolection moldings

bellflowers
USE husks (motifs)

bellhops
USE bellpeople

bellies
  PJ.3278
ALT belly
SN Upper surfaces of the soundboxes of chordophones over which the strings pass and which play a major part in transmitting the vibration of the strings to the surrounding atmosphere.
UF soundtables
    tables (resonators)
RT <chordophone components>
    lutes

Bellini prayer rug
USE re-entrant rugs

Bellini rugs
USE re-entrant rugs

bellmen
USE bellpeople

bellows air guns
USE bellows guns

bellows guns
  TK.216
ALT bellows gun
SN Air guns having a pair of flat bellows in the butt which are squeezed together by a spring or springs when the trigger is pressed, producing a strong blast of air to propel the projectile. They were popular in southern Germany and Austria in the 18th and early 19th centuries.
UF air guns, bellows
    bellows air guns
    guns, bellows
    guns, bellows air

bellows visors
  PJ.3023
ALT bellows visor
SN Visors with deep horizontal ridges, used in the late 15th and early 16th centuries.
UF visors, bellows

bellpeople
  HG.88   (L)
HN February 1993 lead-in term added
    February 1993 descriptor changed, was **bellmen**
    February 1993 alternate term changed, was **bellman**
    November 1992 alternate terms added
ALT bellpeople's
    bellperson
    bellperson's
SN Hotel or club employees who escort guests to rooms, assist them with luggage, and run errands. (WCOL9)
UF bellboys
    bellhops
    bellmen

bells (aerophone components)
  PJ.3224
ALT bell (aerophone component)
SN Flared or bulbous terminals found on many open-ended aerophone tubes.

bells (idiophones)
  TT.466   (A,H,L,N,B)
ALT bell (idiophone)
SN Percussion vessels consisting of a hollow object, usually of metal but in some cultures of hard clay, wood, or glass, which when struck emits a sound by the vibration of most of its mass; they are held in position at their vertex, the point farthest from their rim, and their zone of maximum vibration is towards the rim. (NGDMI)
RT tubular bells

<*bells and sets of bells*>
  TT.465

bells, clapper
USE clapper bells

bells, cow
USE cowbells

bells, door
USE doorbells

bells, garden
USE bell glasses

bells, pellet
USE pellet bells

bells, resting
USE resting bells

bells, sacring
USE sanctus bells

bells, saints'
USE sanctus bells

bells, sanctus
USE sanctus bells

bells, sleigh
USE sleigh bells

bells, smoke
USE   smoke bells

bells, tubular
USE   tubular bells

belly amphorae
USE   continuous curve amphorae

Belouch
USE   Baluch

belows
USE   furbelows

belt conveyors
TH.910   (L,N,B)
ALT   belt conveyor
SN   Continuous belts passing over pul-
      leys, providing a track on which
      loose materials or small articles are
      carried from one point to another.
      (PUTNAM)
UF   conveyors, belt

belt courses
USE   stringcourses

belt highways
USE   beltways

belt pistols
TK.176
ALT   belt pistol
SN   Large pocket pistols.
UF   overcoat pistols
      overcoat pocket pistols
      pistols, belt
      pistols, overcoat
      pistols, overcoat pocket
      pocket pistols, overcoat

belt-pistols
USE   holster pistols

belt racks
PJ.446
HN   April 1993 descriptor moved
ALT   belt rack
UF   racks, belt

belt sanders
TH.1083   (N)
HN   January 1991 lead-in terms added
ALT   belt sander
SN   Portable tools with power-driven,
      abrasive-coated continuous belts,
      used to smooth surfaces. (DAC)
UF   electric files
      files, electric
      sanders, belt

belts (costume accessories)
TE.675   (H,L,N)
ALT   belt (costume accessory)
SN   Flexible straps or bands encircling
      the waist or hips and usually having
      some type of fastener, such as a
      buckle; worn for decoration, sup-
      port, or the containment of money,
      documents or the like.
RT   ties (fasteners)

belts (tool components)
PJ.2573   (L)
HN   March 1993 descriptor moved
ALT   belt (tool component)
SN   Continuous bands of tough, flexible
      material such as leather, fabric, rub-
      ber, or wire; used for transmitting
      motion and power from one pulley
      to another or for conveying materi-
      als. (W)

belts, chastity
USE   chastity belts

belts, garter
USE   garter belts

belts, money
USE   money belts

belts, safety
USE   safety belts

belts, Sam Browne
USE   Sam Browne belts

belts, suspender
SEE   garter belts

belts, sword
USE   sword belts

belts, weight
USE   weight belts

beltways
RM.125   (L,B)
HN   April 1993 descriptor moved
ALT   beltway
UF   belt highways
      circumferential highways
      highways, belt
      highways, circumferential
      ring roads
      roads, ring

Beluchis
USE   Baluch + rugs

Beluchs
USE   Baluch + rugs

Beludjs
USE   Baluch + rugs

belvederes
PJ.1812   (N,B,R)
HN   March 1993 descriptor moved
      November 1990 scope note changed
ALT   belvedere
SN   Use for rooftop pavilions intended
      as lookouts or for the enjoyment of
      a view. For unroofed platforms, use
      widows' walks; for rooftop struc-
      tures that are primarily ornamental,
      use **cupolas**, for small pavilions, in a
      garden setting, intended for enjoy-
      ment of a view, use **gazebos**.

belvederes (gazebos)
USE   gazebos

bemas
PJ.2067

HN   March 1993 descriptor moved
      October 1991 scope note changed
ALT   bema
SN   Refers to raised speaking platforms
      in pre-Christian and Early Christian
      basilicas and meeting places, in syn-
      agogues, and in Orthodox Eastern
      churches.
UF   almemars
      bimahs
      tevahs

Bemba
FL.542   (L)

Bembe (Lower Zaire)
FL.475   (L)
UF   Babembe

Bembe (Northeastern Zaire)
FL.507   (L)
UF   Wabembe

bembes
TT.617
ALT   bembe
SN   Snared double-headed cylindrical
      drums of the Yoruba people of Ni-
      geria, used with clapperless bells to
      accompany song and dance at har-
      vest   thanksgiving   ceremonies.
      (NGDMI)

bembés
TT.610
ALT   bembé
SN   Afro-Cuban drums, generally sin-
      gle-headed and with nail tension,
      approximately cylindrical or barrel-
      shaped and open at the bottom;
      they are played with two drumsticks.

Bena
FL.582   (L)
UF   Wabena

Bena Kanioka
USE   Kanioka

Bena Lulua
USE   Lulua

Bena Luluwa
USE   Lulua

Benacci
FL.2828

bench anvils
TH.1190
ALT   bench anvil
SN   Anvils with two shaped ends.
      (HAND)
UF   anvils, bench

bench chisels
TH.1429
ALT   bench chisel
SN   A class of woodworking chisels.
      (BLACKB)
UF   chisels, bench

bench clamps
TH.1625

ALT bench clamp
SN Simple tools used in conjunction with a workbench which hold a piece of wood firmly in place in a V-shaped mouth.
UF clamps, bench

bench dogs
TH.1636
ALT bench dog
SN Pegs or pins partially inserted into a hole at an edge or end of a workbench to help secure a piece of work or prevent it from sliding off the bench. (MEANS)
UF bench stops (bench dogs)
   dogs, bench
   stops, bench

bench hooks
TH.1618 (N)
ALT bench hook
SN Devices, usually made of hardwood, used in carpentry to secure the work at the back of the workbench, in order to protect the surface of the workbench from being scarred or damaged by movement of the work. (MEANS)
UF hooks, bench
   hooks, side
   side hooks

bench knives
TH.1474 (N)
ALT bench knife
SN Adjustable stops with a projecting knife or hook that holds a piece of work on a workbench. (W)
UF knives, bench

bench marks
VW.395 (L,N)
HN November 1992 descriptor moved
ALT bench mark
SN Marks on a fixed and enduring object, indicating a particular elevation and used as a reference, such as in topographic surveys and tidal observations. (BLACKS)
UF marks, bench

bench planes
TH.1518
ALT bench plane
SN A class of planes used for reducing, leveling, and smoothing wood. (BLACKB)
UF planes, bench

bench plates
TH.1193 (N)
ALT bench plate
UF plates, bench

bench rules
TN.45
ALT bench rule
SN Woodworking rules graduated into eighths of an inch along one edge and sixteenths of an inch along the other edge and usually made of ma-

ple or hickory with brass tips; may also be metrically divided.
UF rules, bench

bench saws
TH.1570 (N)
HN January 1991 lead-in terms added
ALT bench saw
SN Name given to the ensemble of a circular saw mounted on a bench.
UF benches, saw
   joiner saws
   saw benches
   saws, bench
   saws, joiner

bench shears
TH.1262 (N)
SN Large shears used in sheet metal work typically having one handle bent to go into a hole in the top of the workbench so that they rest on the surface when in use. (RUSERW)
UF shears, bench

bench stops
TH.1619 (N)
ALT bench stop
SN Adjustable apparatus, often made of metal, used to secure wood near the end of the workbench; usually used during planing.
UF stops, bench

bench stops (bench dogs)
USE bench dogs

bench tables
PJ.1945
HN March 1993 descriptor moved
ALT bench table
SN Projecting courses of masonry at the foot of an interior wall, or around a column; generally wide enough to form a seat. (HAS)
UF tables, bench

bench vises
TH.644 (N)
ALT bench vise
SN Vises attached to a workbench to hold material while it is being worked. (PUTNAM)
UF vises, bench

Bencharong
FL.2510

benches
TC.704 (L,N,B,R)
HN May 1993 related term added
   January 1993 descriptor moved
ALT bench
SN Seats for two or more persons, generally without a back.
UF bancos
   banks (benches)
RT stools

benches, bucket
USE water benches

<benches by form or function>
TC.705
HN January 1993 guide term moved

<benches by location or context>
TC.715
HN January 1993 guide term moved

benches, carpenters'
USE workbenches

benches, cradle
USE cradle benches

benches, deacons'
USE deacons' benches

benches, garden
USE garden seats

benches, mammas'
USE cradle benches

benches, mammies'
USE cradle benches

benches, meeting house
USE deacons' benches

benches, milk
USE water benches

benches, monks'
USE box settles
   chair-tables

benches, piano
USE piano benches

benches, picnic
USE picnic benches

benches, rocking
USE cradle benches

benches, saw
USE bench saws

benches, settle
USE settles

benches, wagon
USE wagon seats

benches, water
USE water benches

benches, window
USE window seats

bend hangers, bottom
USE bottom bend hangers

bend hangers, bottom and flange
USE bottom and flange bend hangers

benday artists
HN February 1993 descriptor deleted

Bende (Igbo)
FL.262

Bende (Kenya)
FL.643
HN June 1990 lead-in terms added
UF Kawende
   Wabende

bended-back chairs
TC.553
HN January 1993 descriptor moved
ALT bended-back chair
SN Early 18th-century chairs with or without arms, having a vase-shaped splat in the back which was curved to give comfortable support to the back. (GLOAG)
UF chairs, bended-back
chairs, Hogarth
Hogarth chairs

bending
KT.303 (L)
HN August 1992 scope note added
ALT bent
SN Turning, pressing, or forcing with stress concentrated at specific points in order to form angular or curved forms. (W)

bending stress
BM.642
HN November 1992 descriptor moved
SN Stress induced by loads perpendicular to the member. (STEIN)
UF stress, bending

bends
PJ.2756
HN March 1993 descriptor moved
ALT bend
SN Curving members which connect the front and back legs on an object, such as on a chair, cradle, or bench, allowing it to rock.
UF rockers (furniture components)
runners (furniture components)

Benedictine
BM.491 (A,L)

benedictionals
VW.882 (H,L)
HN June 1992 descriptor added
ALT benedictional
SN Books containing benedictions; often for liturgical use, especially by bishops.

benefactors
USE patrons

Beneventan
USE Beneventan minuscule

Beneventan minuscule
PJ.3445
SN A script developed in South Italy in the 8th century and in use until the 13th century.
UF Beneventan
Beneventan scripts
Lombardic (scripts)
minuscule, Beneventan
scripts, Beneventan

Beneventan scripts
USE Beneventan minuscule

Bengal cutch
USE cutch

Beni Amer
USE Amer

beni-e
VC.492
SN Japanese prints on which the principal hand coloring was executed with beni, a red pigment. (SMPJ)

Benin
FL.92 (L,B)

Benin, Early
USE Early Benin

Benin, Late
USE Late Benin

Benin, Middle
USE Middle Benin

benizuri-e
VC.495
SN Japanese prints in which colors, red (beni) and usually green, were printed rather than hand-colored.

bent gouges
TH.1458
ALT bent gouge
SN Gouges whose shank is either curved for its entire length or straight for most of its length with a sharp bend near the tip. (MAYER)
UF gouges, bent
gouges, spade
gouges, spoon
spade gouges
spoon gouges

bent-wire chairs
USE ice-cream parlor chairs

bentonite
MT.65 (L)
HN March 1992 lead-in terms added
February 1992 descriptor moved
SN A soft plastic light-colored clay formed by the chemical alteration of volcanic ash; it can swell to several times its original volume when placed in water.
UF amargosite
clay, soap
clay, volcanic
gumbrin
mineral soap
soap clay
soap, mineral
volcanic clay

bents
PJ.1411
HN March 1993 descriptor moved
November 1990 descriptor moved
ALT bent
SN Frameworks usually designed to carry both lateral and vertical loads and that are transverse to the length of a framed structure.

bentwood
MT.3000 (L,R)
HN March 1992 descriptor moved

SN Use to describe wood that is bent rather than cut into shape.

<Benue-Congo branch>
FL.205

benzene
MT.2430 (L)
UF benzol

benzene, methyl
USE toluene

benzine
USE naphtha

benzoin
MT.1247 (L)
HN April 1992 descriptor moved
SN A balsamic resin, used chiefly in treating irritations of the skin, as a fixative in perfume, and as incense. (W)

benzol
USE benzene

benzol black
USE carbon black

Beothuk
FL.1233 (L)

bequests
BM.924 (L)
HN February 1993 descriptor moved
January 1991 alternate term added
ALT bequest
SN Gifts of personal property by will. (BOCLD)
UF legacies

Berber
FL.698 (L)
HN April 1993 descriptor moved

Berber carpets
USE Berber + rugs

Berber knots
PJ.2684
ALT Berber knot
UF knots, Berber

Berbers, Moroccan
USE Berber + rugs

berdyshes
TK.46 (N)
ALT berdyshe
SN Pollaxes with a very long, narrow, curved blade, elongated at the upper end for thrusting, used primarily in northeastern Europe, particularly Russia.
UF bardiches

beres, pillow
USE pillowcases

berets
TE.529 (L,N)
ALT beret
SN Soft, flat-topped, visorless caps with

a tight-fitting headband; of a type originally worn by Basque peasants.

Berëzovsk phase
FL.2204
HN June 1990 lead-in term deleted, was **Berezovo phase**

Bergama
FL.3656
HN April 1993 descriptor added
UF Yüncü

Bergamas
USE Bergama + rugs

Bergamees
USE Bergama + rugs

Bergamos
USE Bergama + rugs

Bergamots
USE Bergama + rugs

Bergblau
USE azurite

bergblau, Teutonic
USE azurite

Bergdama
FL.550

bergère chairs
USE bergères

bergère hats
TE.568
ALT bergère hat
SN Straw hats with a low crown and a wide brim. (HFC)
UF bergères (hats)
hats, bergère
hats, shepherdess
shepherdess hats

bergères
TC.453
HN January 1993 descriptor moved
ALT bergère
SN Upholstered armchairs, differing from other armchairs in being upholstered between the arms and seats.
UF barjairs
bergère chairs
cabriole bergères
chairs, bergère
fauteuils à panneaux
fauteuils en bergère

bergères (hats)
USE bergère hats

bergères à joue
USE bergères en confessional

bergères à la reine
TC.561
HN January 1993 descriptor moved
ALT bergère à la reine
SN Bergères with flat backs; distinct from bergères with concave backs called **bergères en cabriolet**.

bergères à oreilles
USE bergères en confessional

bergères en cabriolet
TC.555
HN January 1993 descriptor moved
ALT bergère en cabriolet
SN Bergères with concave backs; distinct from bergeres with flat backs called **bergères à la reine**.

bergères en confessional
TC.490
HN January 1993 descriptor moved
ALT bergère en confessional
SN Large and deep armchairs with sides and wings.
UF bergères à joue
bergères à oreilles
confessionals (chairs)

bergères en gondole
TC.499
HN January 1993 descriptor moved
ALT bergère en gondole
SN U-shaped armchairs, the upper rail of the back gently sloping down to the arms. Most popular during the Louis XV period.

Berggrün
USE malachite (pigment)

berimbaus
TT.347   (L)
ALT berimbau
SN Brazilian musical bows of African origin, with a single wire string and sometimes a gourd resonator, held against the chest during play. One hand holds the bow and occasionally applies a metal coin to the string to alter its pitch, while the other strikes it with a stick. (NGDMI)
UF urucungus

Bering Sea, Old
USE Old Bering Sea

Berlin blue
USE dark blue
Prussian blue

berlin coaches
TX.167   (H,N)
ALT berlin coach
SN Use for coaches hung on berlin undercarriages, employing two light perches instead of a single heavy one to connect the front transom with the rear axle.
UF berlins
coaches, berlin

Berlin woolwork
KT.1223
HN November 1992 descriptor added
SN Type of 19th- and 20th-century embroidery, usually worked in worsted yarns following a colored pattern drawn on a graphed chart; named as such because early major supplies

of these patterns, yarns, and canvas came from Berlin.
UF Berlin work
woolwork, Berlin
work, Berlin

Berlin work
USE Berlin woolwork

berlins
USE berlin coaches

berms
RM.249   (A)
HN April 1993 descriptor moved
ALT berm
SN Use for banks of earth piled against exterior walls.

Bermuda shorts
TE.89
SN Knee-length walking shorts worn by men and women. (W)
UF shorts, Bermuda

berry
MT.2618   (L)
HN March 1992 descriptor moved

berry, Avignon
USE buckthorn berry

berry baskets
TQ.579   (N)
ALT berry basket
SN Tightly woven and relatively deep baskets seldom made larger than 2-quart size; most are a quart or less in capacity.
UF baskets, berry
baskets, berry-picking
baskets, fruit
berry-picking baskets
fruit baskets

berry, buckthorn
USE buckthorn berry

berry forks
USE strawberry forks

berry, French
USE buckthorn berry

berry, Persian
USE buckthorn berry

berry-picking baskets
USE berry baskets

berry spoons
TH.284
HN April 1993 descriptor added
ALT berry spoon
SN Popular name for spoons with a broad deep bowl, sometimes silver gilt and may be pierced or embossed with fruit motifs; used to serve berries and other juicy foods. Often made by altering plain tablespoons.
UF spoons, berry
RT tablespoons

berry, yellow
USE buckthorn berry

bertha collars
SEE berthas

berthas
TE.652 (N)
ALT bertha
SN Deep, capelike collars, often of lace or silk, worn about the shoulders by women.
UF bertha collars
collars, bertha

berths (sleeping spaces)
PJ.3282
ALT berth (sleeping space)
SN Use for shelflike platforms or other similar sleeping spaces on board transportation vehicles, such as boats, trains, or travel trailers.

berths (waterfront spaces)
RM.209
HN April 1993 descriptor moved
March 1993 related terms added
April 1990 descriptor changed, was **berths**
April 1990 alternate term changed, was **berth**
ALT berth (waterfront space)
SN Use for unoccupied, open water spaces allotted to vessels when alongside a landing place; when such spaces are set between adjacent piers or perpendicular to landing places, use **slips (waterfront spaces)**. Use **docks** for open water spaces when occupied by vessels made fast to landing places.
RT docks
slips (waterfront spaces)

berths, building
USE slipways

Bertoia chairs
USE diamond chairs

beryl
MT.517 (L)
HN April 1992 descriptor moved
February 1992 related term added
February 1992 scope note added
SN A hexagonal mineral, which includes several varieties of gemstone such as emerald and aquamarine.
RT gemstone

beryl, golden
USE golden beryl

beryllium bronze
USE copper-beryllium alloy

beryllium copper
USE copper-beryllium alloy

besagews
PJ.3003
ALT besagew
SN Small pieces of plate armor, usually round or oval, attached by straps, rivets, or laces to upper body armor such as pauldrons, spaudlers, and vambraces, to protect the open joints at the armpits and elbows.
UF besagnes
rondels (besagews)

besagnes
USE besagews

besems
USE desemers

Beshir
USE Ersari

Beshire
USE Ersari

Besiri rugs
USE Ersari + rugs

besoms
USE curling brooms

bestiaries
VW.261 (H,L)
HN June 1992 descriptor added
ALT bestiary
SN Collections of moralized fables, especially as written in the Middle Ages, about actual or mythical animals. (RHDEL2)

beta particles
USE beta rays

beta radiation
USE beta rays

beta rays
BM.792 (L)
HN November 1992 descriptor added
SN Streams of electrons or positrons emitted from an atomic nucleus in a certain type of radioactive decay. (RHDEL2)
UF beta particles
beta radiation

Bété
FL.311 (L)

Beti
FL.408 (L)
UF Bati

Betjek
USE Bassa

béton
MT.198 (A,L)
HN April 1992 descriptor moved
SN Concrete consisting of lime, sand, and gravel. (DAC)

bettering houses
USE workhouses

betties, Ipswich
USE Ipswich betty lamps

betties, Portsmouth
USE Portsmouth betties

betting-houses
USE betting parlors

betting parlors
RK.191 (A)
ALT betting parlor
SN Designates licensed bookmaking establishments that take off-track bets, especially with relation to horse racing.
UF betting-houses
betting shops
parlors, betting
shops, betting

betting shops
USE betting parlors

betty lamps
TC.1320 (N)
ALT betty lamp
SN Lamps having a shallow font of oval or pear shape with a wick support attached to the bottom of the font at the narrow end, usually partly or fully covered by a hinged or sliding lid and often a half-bail support at the end opposite the wick support with an attached halbred hook and wire wick pick.
UF bettys
judies
kays
lamps, betty

betty lamps, Ipswich
USE Ipswich betty lamps

betty saws
USE felloe saws

bettys
USE betty lamps

Betula
USE birch

Betula alleghaniensis
USE yellow birch

Betula lenta
USE sweet birch

Betula lutea
USE yellow birch

Betula nana
USE dwarf birch

Betula nigra
USE river birch

Betula papyrifera
USE paper birch

Betula pendula
USE silver birch

Betula populifolia
USE gray birch

Betula pubescens
USE downy birch
European birch

Betula utilis
USE Himalayan birch

bevel locks, reverse
USE   reverse bevel locks

bevel siding
USE   clapboard siding

bevel squares
   TH.1001   (N)
HN   May 1993 lead-in term changed,
        was **T bevels**
        May 1993 lead-in term deleted, was
        bevels, T
ALT   bevel square
SN   Tools similar to the try square ex-
        cept that they have an adjustable
        blade which can be set at any angle.
        (MEANS)
UF   bevels
        bevels, sliding
        bevels, tee
        sliding bevels
        squares, bevel
        T-bevels
        tee bevels

beveled butt joints
USE   oblique joints

beveled closer
USE   king closer

beveling
   KT.304
ALT   beveled
UK   bevelling
UKA   bevelled
SN   Cutting or shaping the edge or end
        of a material to form an angle that
        is not a right angle. In the context
        of furniture, prefer **chamfering**.

bevelling
SEE   beveling

bevels
USE   bevel squares

bevels, sliding
USE   bevel squares

bevels, tee
USE   bevel squares

beverage processing plants
   RK.588   (L)
ALT   beverage processing plant
UF   plants, beverage processing
        processing plants, beverage

beverage shakers
USE   cocktail shakers

beverage spoons, iced
USE   iced-tea spoons

<bevor components>
   PJ.3011

bevors
   TE.277
ALT   bevor
SN   Armor pieces protecting the throat
        and lower part of the face, worn ei-
        ther independently or attached to
        the helmet skull by pivoting rivets.

UF   baviers
        beavers (armor)
RT   falling buffes
        wrappers (armor)

bevors, falling
USE   falling buffes

bevors, lower
USE   lower bevors

bevors, reinforcing
USE   wrappers (armor)

bevors, upper
USE   upper bevors

Beyazit I
USE   Bayazid I

Beyazit II
USE   Bayazid II

Beyazit, Lightning
USE   Bayazid I

Beyshire
USE   Konya

bezels
   PJ.8
ALT   bezel
SN   Rims or bands that surround and
        hold a stone or other ornament,
        such as on a ring or snuff box, or a
        crystal, such as on a watch case or
        clock, or a glass or plastic covering,
        such as on a headlight.

Bhaca
   FL.567   (L)

Bhaktapur
USE   Bhatgaon

Bharatpur
USE   Bhatgaon

Bhatgaon
   FL.2242
UF   Bhaktapur
        Bharatpur

Bhoti
   FL.2353

Bhutanese
   FL.2228   (L)

Bi
USE   billon

bi-gum
USE   gum bichromate process

bi-level cars
   TX.267
ALT   bi-level car
SN   Use for railroad passenger cars with
        seating areas on two levels, the up-
        per of which may or may not extend
        the full length of the car.
UF   bilevel cars
        cars, bi-level

bi-pack
SEE   bipack

bi-pack, integral
SEE   integral bipack

biacca di piombo
USE   lead white

bianco de zinco
USE   zinc white

bianco di piombo
USE   lead white

bianco di titanio
USE   titanium dioxide white

bianco e giallo
USE   bianco e giallo antico

bianco e giallo antico
   MT.744
HN   April 1992 descriptor moved
UF   bianco e giallo
        marble, phengites
        marmor phengite
        phengites marble

bianco sangiovanni
USE   lime white

bib taps
USE   faucets

bibcocks
USE   faucets

biberons
   TQ.389   (H)
ALT   biberon
SN   Drinking vessels with usually one
        elongated spout, but sometimes
        more, used for feeding children or
        invalids.
RT   spout cups

Bible boxes
   TQ.601   (N)
ALT   Bible box
SN   Boxes, usually of oak and with a
        slanting top, used to hold a Bible,
        books, or writing materials.
UF   boxes, Bible
        boxes, desk
        desk boxes
        desks, table
        table desks
RT   boxes (containers)

Bible paper
USE   India paper

Bible quilts
   TC.244
ALT   Bible quilt
SN   Quilts illustrating Bible stories or in-
        cluding   scriptural   quotations,
        adages, maxims, or proverbs con-
        veying religious or moral precepts.
        (QIA)
UF   quilts, Bible
        quilts, Scripture
        Scripture quilts

Bible records
VW.799
HN November 1992 descriptor moved
ALT Bible record
SN Family records of births, baptisms, marriages, and deaths written on blank or printed formlike pages of Bibles. (GAHLM)
UF records, Bible

Bibles
HN January 1992 descriptor deleted

Bibles moralisées
VW.883
HN June 1992 descriptor added
ALT Bible moralisée
SN Illustrated Biblical commentaries first produced in France in the 13th century, characterized by pairs of medallions containing depictions of the Biblical story and its moralization.
UF Bibles, moralized
moralized Bibles

Bibles, moralized
USE Bibles moralisées

Biblia pauperum
VW.884 (L)
HN November 1992 descriptor moved
June 1992 alternate term deleted, was **Biblium pauperum**
SN Medieval picture books of scriptural subjects, with descriptive vernacular text. (LG)

Biblical studies
KD.91 (L)
UF studies, Biblical

bibliographers
HG.371 (L)
HN December 1992 alternate terms added
ALT bibliographer
bibliographer's
bibliographers'
SN Persons who compile lists of books, periodical articles, and audiovisual materials on specialized subjects, annotate bibliographies with physical descriptors, and analyze subject content of materials; also those who advise on the acquisition of materials in special subjects. (DOT)

bibliographic databases
VW.36 (L)
HN November 1992 descriptor moved
ALT bibliographic database
UF databases, bibliographic

bibliographic utilities
HN.126 (L)
ALT bibliographic utility
SN Organizations that maintain large online bibliographic databases and offer cataloging support and related products to libraries and other customers who access those databases on an online, time-sharing basis. (SAF6BU)
UF bibliographical services
services, bibliographical
utilities, bibliographic

bibliographical services
USE bibliographic utilities

bibliographies
VW.172 (A,L,B,R)
HN November 1992 descriptor moved
ALT bibliography
SN Lists of books or other textual materials arranged in some logical order giving brief information about the works, such as author, date, publisher, and place of publication; may be works by a particular author, or on a particular topic.
UF book lists
lists, book

bibliographies, annotated
USE annotated bibliographies

bibliographies, bibliographies of
USE bibliographies of bibliographies

bibliographies, enumerative
USE systematic enumerative bibliographies

bibliographies, local
USE local bibliographies

bibliographies, national
USE national bibliographies

bibliographies of bibliographies
VW.177 (L)
HN November 1992 descriptor moved
ALT bibliography of bibliographies
UF bibliographies, bibliographies of

bibliographies, partial
USE selective bibliographies

bibliographies, selective
USE selective bibliographies

bibliographies, subject
USE subject bibliographies

bibliographies, systematic
USE systematic enumerative bibliographies

bibliographies, systematic enumerative
USE systematic enumerative bibliographies

bibliographies, trade
USE trade bibliographies

bibliography, analytical
USE analytical bibliography

bibliography, critical
USE analytical bibliography

bibliography, descriptive
USE analytical bibliography

bibliography, historical
USE analytical bibliography

bibliothecae
USE libraries (buildings)

bibliothèques
TC.825
HN January 1993 descriptor moved
ALT bibliothèque
SN Cupboards containing bookshelves and closed with doors usually of glass or sometimes fitted with grilles.
UF armoires à livres
armoires-bibliothèque
armoires en bibliothèque
bibliothèques basses

bibliothèques basses
USE bibliothèques

bibs
TE.373 (N)
ALT bib
SN Small panels, usually attached at the neck, which cover the chest and are worn to protect a main garment when eating. Also, any similar part of a garment.
RT <costume components>

bibs (faucets)
USE faucets

bibs, breast
USE breastplates (tools)

bice
USE smalt

bice, blue
USE azurite
blue verditer

bice, green
USE green earth

bicentennial quilts
TC.227
ALT bicentennial quilt
SN Quilts made to commemorate a two-hundredth anniversary.
UF quilts, bicentennial

bichromate, gum
USE gum bichromate process

bichromate prints, gum
USE gum bichromate prints

bichromate processes
KT.539
SN Processes for making photographic prints using a bichromate compound which, when exposed to light, causes its colloid binder to harden; unhardened areas are washed or abraded away. Pigments may be incorporated before exposure or during development. Though the expression dichromate is now preferred in chemistry, bi-

chromate remains common usage in photography.
UF   bichromated pigment processes
     dichromate processes

bichromated pigment processes
USE   bichromate processes

bick irons
USE   beak irons

bickerns
USE   beak irons

biclinia
     TC.812
HN   January 1993 descriptor moved
ALT   biclinium

biconical drums
USE   double-conical drums

bicorne hats
USE   bicornes

bicornes
     TE.582
ALT   bicorne
SN   19th-century name for cocked hats with the brim turned up flat against the front and back to form two corners.
UF   bicorne hats
     hats, bicorne
RT   chapeaux bras

bicycle paths
USE   cycling paths

bicycle sheds
     RK.1155   (A,B)
ALT   bicycle shed
UF   bicycle shelters
     cycle sheds
     sheds, bicycle
     sheds, cycle
     shelters, bicycle

bicycle shelters
USE   bicycle sheds

bicycle tracks
USE   cycling paths
     velodromes

bicycle trails
USE   cycling paths

bicycle-wheel roofs
USE   double-cable structures

bicycles
     TX.153   (H,L,N)
ALT   bicycle
SN   Vehicles with two wheels in tandem propelled by the rider straddling a frame which holds the wheels and handlebars for steering.
UF   bikes
RT   motorbikes

bicycles, motorized
USE   mopeds

bid advertisements
USE   bidding announcements

bid bonds
     VW.644
HN   November 1992 descriptor moved
ALT   bid bond
SN   Surety bonds executed by the bidder on a construction project that serve as a guarantee that the bidder will enter into a contract within a specified time and furnish any required bonds ensuring completion of the work.
UF   bonds, bid
     bonds, proposal
     proposal bonds

bid calls
USE   bidding announcements

bid forms
     VW.555
HN   November 1992 descriptor moved
ALT   bid form
SN   Forms, furnished to bidders, on which to submit their bids. (MEANS)
UF   forms, bid

bid instructions
USE   instructions to bidders

bid, invitation to
USE   bidding announcements

bid invitations
USE   bidding announcements

bidders
     HG.618
HN   December 1992 alternate terms added
ALT   bidder
     bidder's
     bidders'

bidders, advertisements for
USE   bidding announcements

bidders, instructions to
USE   instructions to bidders

biddery
USE   bidri

bidding
     KG.87   (L,B)
HN   January 1991 scope note added
     January 1991 alternate term added
ALT   bid
SN   Offering a specific sum as the price one will pay or charge. (RHDEL2)
UF   competitive bidding
     competitive tendering
     tendering

bidding announcements
     VW.556
HN   November 1992 descriptor moved
ALT   bidding announcement
SN   Documents advertising for bids to be submitted for a particular job.
UF   advertisements, bid
     advertisements for bidders

announcements, bidding
announcements of bidding
bid advertisements
bid calls
bid, invitation to
bid invitations
bidders, advertisements for
calls, bid
invitations, bid
invitations to bid

bidding documents
     VW.554
HN   November 1992 descriptor moved
ALT   bidding document
UF   bidding requirements documents
     documents, bidding

bidding requirements documents
USE   bidding documents

bidery metal
USE   bidri

bidet stands
USE   bidets (box stools)

bidets (box stools)
     TC.664
HN   May 1993 related term added
     January 1993 descriptor moved
ALT   bidet (box stool)
SN   Box stools with a china bowl and cover. Use **commode chairs** for chairs having a chamber pot.
UF   bidet stands
     stands, bidet
RT   commode chairs

bidets (plumbing fixtures)
     PJ.910   (N,B)
HN   March 1993 descriptor moved
     May 1991 descriptor changed, was **bidets**
     May 1991 alternate term changed, was **bidet**
     November 1990 scope note added
ALT   bidet (plumbing fixture)
SN   Bathroom fixtures used for hygienic washing of the genitals and posterior parts. (MEANS)

bidets, portable
USE   portable bidets

bidets, traveling
USE   traveling bidets

bidonvilles
     RG.292
ALT   bidonville
SN   Use for impoverished shantytowns, jerry-built of cut and flattened metal drums, located in France or North Africa.

bidri
     MT.474
HN   March 1993 scope note changed
     March 1993 lead-in term deleted, was **tutenag**
     March 1993 descriptor moved
     December 1992 related term added

SN Copper-zinc alloy of India, finished with a velvety-black color by a solution of copper sulfate.
UF biddery
biddery metal
metal, bidery
RT bidriware

Bidri-ware
SEE bidriware

bidriware
PE.99   (L)
HN December 1992 related term added
December 1992 descriptor moved
UK Bidri-ware
SN Articles made from bidri, a metal alloy, that has been inlaid with gold or silver.
RT bidri

bids
VW.557   (B)
HN November 1992 descriptor moved
ALT bid
SN Offers to perform a contract for work and labor or to supply materials or goods at a specified price. (BLACKS)
UF tenders (bids)

Bidyogo
USE Bijogo

Biedermeier
FL.3344   (A,L,R)

biege, light rose
USE brownish pink

biennials
RD.234   (L)
ALT biennial

bifolia
PJ.3371
ALT bifolium
SN The individual sheets folded into two leaves that together form a gathering.
UF bifolios

bifolios
USE bifolia

big floor rugs
USE art squares

Big Game Hunting
USE Paleo-Indian (Pre-Columbian North American)

big houses
USE plantation houses

big-leaf maple
SEE bigleaf maple

big shellbark hickory
MT.2760
HN March 1992 descriptor moved
UF Carya lactiniosa
hickory, big shellbark

hickory, king nut
king nut hickory
shellbark hickory, big

big toothed aspen
MT.2865   (L)
HN March 1992 descriptor moved
UF aspen, big toothed
Populus grandidentata

bigas
TX.118
ALT biga
SN Ancient war or racing chariots drawn by two horses abreast.
UF birigas

biggins (caps)
TE.530   (N)
ALT biggin (cap)
SN Close-fitting caps, often of mesh, worn by young children in the 16th and 17th centuries; also, soft caps worn by children and adults while sleeping.
RT nightcaps

biggins (vessels)
TQ.521
ALT biggin (vessel)
SN Coffeepots having separate containers, often in the form of a muslin bag, in which the coffee is immersed while being boiled and usually a stand with a heating device for keeping the coffee warm.
UF biggins, coffee
coffee biggins

biggins, coffee
USE biggins (vessels)

bigio antico
MT.725
HN April 1992 descriptor moved
UF marmor batthium

bigio e nero antico
MT.726
HN April 1992 descriptor moved
UF marmor proconnesium

bigio e nero di francia
MT.727
HN April 1992 descriptor moved
UF marmor celticum

bigio morato
MT.728
HN April 1992 descriptor moved
UF mormor luculleum

bigleaf maple
MT.2806
HN August 1992 lead-in term added
March 1992 descriptor moved
UK big-leaf maple
UF Acer macrophyllum
broadleaved maple
maple, big-leaf
maple, bigleaf
maple, broadleaved

maple, Oregon
Oregon maple

bigotry
USE discrimination

Bihara
USE New Britain

Bihzad School
FL.3708
HN April 1993 descriptor moved
UF Bahzad School
Behzad School

Biisk phase
USE Biysk phase

Bijapur
FL.2303
HN February 1991 descriptor moved

Bijar
FL.3733
HN April 1993 descriptor added

Bijars
USE Bijar + carpets

Bijogo
FL.336
UF Bidyogo
Bissago

Bikaner
FL.2368

bike paths
USE cycling paths

bikes
USE bicycles

bikeways
USE cycling paths

bikinis
TE.390
ALT bikini
SN Very abbreviated two-piece bathing suits with the bottom half cut below the waist.

Bikom
USE Kom

bilanders
TX.556
ALT bilander
SN Use for sailing vessels lateen-rigged on the mainmast and square-rigged on a smaller mizzenmast.
UF billanders

Bilaspur
FL.2354
UF Kahlur

bilateral symmetry
BM.93
SN Extreme regularity of balance achieved by the correspondence of identical compositional units on either side of a central axis.
UF balance, symmetrical

symmetrical balance
symmetry, bilateral

bilbao looking glasses
USE bilbao mirrors

bilbao mirrors
TC.1472
ALT bilbao mirror
SN Mirrors having frames partly or fully of marble and often ornamented with filigree or openwork cresting; popular in the late 18th and early 19th centuries and thought to have originated in Bilbao, Spain.
UF bilbao looking glasses
bilbaos
bilboa looking glasses
bilboa mirrors
bilboas
looking glasses, bilbao
looking glasses, bilboa
mirrors, bilbao
mirrors, bilboa

bilbaos
USE bilbao mirrors

bilboa looking glasses
USE bilbao mirrors

bilboa mirrors
USE bilbao mirrors

bilboas
USE bilbao mirrors

bilboquets
USE cup-and-ball toys

bilection moldings
USE bolection moldings

bilevel cars
USE bi-level cars

bilinear scripts
USE majuscule

bilingual dictionaries
USE foreign-language dictionaries

Billa
USE Atchana

Billa ware
USE Atchana + ware

billanders
USE bilanders

billboard posters
USE twenty-four-sheet posters

billboards
RM.228   (A,H,L,N,B)
HN August 1992 descriptor added
ALT billboard
SN Use for flat surfaces or boards, sometimes substantial structures, constructed for or used for posting announcements or advertisements.

billboards (posters)
USE twenty-four-sheet posters

billet moldings
PJ.2080
HN April 1993 descriptor moved
July 1991 scope note changed
ALT billet molding
SN Used to designate moldings formed by a series of regularly spaced cubical or short cylindrical projections; found in Romanesque architecture and usually appearing in multiple rows.
UF moldings, billet

billet moldings, roll
USE roll billet moldings

billet moldings, round
USE roll billet moldings

billets
USE thumbpieces

billheads
VW.41
HN November 1992 descriptor moved
ALT billhead
SN Printed forms, characterized by a heading containing the name of a company or name and address, on which a statement of money due is recorded.

billiard-halls
SEE billiard rooms

billiard halls
USE pool halls

billiard lamps
USE billiard lights

billiard lights
TC.1361
ALT billiard light
SN Lighting devices designed for use over a billiard table.
UF billiard lamps
lamps, billiard
lights, billiard

billiard parlors
USE pool halls

billiard rooms
PJ.1070   (A,B)
HN March 1993 descriptor moved
March 1993 related term added
ALT billiard room
UK billiard-halls
UKA billiard-hall
UF rooms, billiard
RT billiards

billiard tables
TC.1118   (N)
HN May 1993 related terms added
January 1993 descriptor moved
ALT billiard table
SN Tables with a slate surface covered with cloth and surrounded by cushioned rails, on which the game of billiards is played. Distinct from **pool tables** which are similar in form but have six pockets.

UF tables, billiard
RT billiards
pool tables

billiards
KQ.98   (H,L)
RT billiard rooms
billiard tables
cues
pool halls

billing
KG.88   (L)
SN Issuing a list of charges payable. (RLG7)

billon
MT.447
HN March 1992 descriptor added
SN An alloy of silver mixed with an equal or greater amount of a base metal, usually copper.
UF Bi

bills (handbills)
USE handbills

bills (invoices)
USE invoices

bills (legislative records)
VW.766   (L)
HN November 1992 descriptor moved
ALT bill (legislative record)
SN Drafts of proposed laws introduced in a legislative body. (LG)
UF bills, legislative
legislative bills

bills (paper money)
USE paper money

bills (posters)
USE posters

bills (staff weapons)
TK.36   (N)
ALT bill (staff weapon)
SN European staff weapons having a long blade with one cutting edge, convex or of flattened S-shape, divided at the top into a vertical spike and a forward curving hook, and with a horizontal fluke in the center of the back. They were used from at least the middle of the 13th until the 17th century, and were one of the most widely used foot soldiers' weapons. (BLEAA)

bills, House of Commons
USE House of Commons bills

bills, House of Lords
USE House of Lords bills

bills, legislative
USE bills (legislative records)

bills of exchange
VK.164   (L)
ALT bill of exchange
SN Historically a form of paper currency used in Europe from the late

Medieval to the early Modern period often used as credit among merchants. Now refers to written orders to pay a specific sum of money on demand or at a specified future time; used with reference to foreign transactions; for similar orders to pay usually restricted to domestic transactions, use **drafts (negotiable instruments)**.

UF exchange, bills of
RT commercial paper
    drafts (negotiable instruments)

bills of fare
USE menus

bills of lading
    VW.674   (L)
HN November 1992 descriptor moved
ALT bill of lading
SN Written receipts given by a carrier for goods accepted for transportation. (RHDEL2)
UF lading, bills of

bills of material
USE quantity surveys

bills of quantity
USE quantity surveys

bills of sale
    VW.601   (L,N)
HN November 1992 descriptor moved
ALT bill of sale
SN Formal instruments attesting to the transfer of ownership of personal property. (W)

bills, tax
USE tax bills

billy-cocks
SEE derbies

billycock hats
USE derbies

billycocks
USE derbies

billys
USE jumpers (tools)

bimahs
USE bemas

Bimal
    FL.618

bin labels
    VW.1168
HN June 1992 descriptor added
ALT bin label
SN Ceramic plaques pierced with holes to hang from wine barrels and inscribed with the names of the contents.
UF labels, bin

bin pulls
    PJ.363

HN April 1993 descriptor moved
ALT bin pull
UF pulls, bin

Binburra
USE white beech

binder
    MT.1757   (B,R)
HN April 1993 descriptor changed, was binders
    April 1993 lead-in term changed, was **binding agents**
    April 1993 lead-in term changed, was **image-bearing colloids**
    April 1993 lead-in term changed, was **mediums (photographic binders)**
    March 1992 lead-in term added
    March 1992 scope note changed
SN Use for a substance that produces or promotes cohesion among loosely assembled materials; also includes the substance in a photograph or photographic film that holds the final image material. For the combined material of photographic binder and image material, use **emulsion**.
UF agent, binding
    binding agent
    binding medium
    colloid, image-bearing
    image-bearing colloid
    medium (photographic binder)
    medium, binding

binder moldings
USE ataduras

binders
    TE.239   (N)
ALT binder
SN Broad bands of cloth, such as those wound around a baby's waist to support the back and stomach.

binders (bookbinders)
USE bookbinders

binders' tickets
    VW.1169
HN October 1992 descriptor added
ALT binder's ticket
SN Small engraved or printed labels, usually found on the upper outside corner of one of the front flyleaves, giving the name and usually the address of the bookbinder; common in the 18th and early 19th centuries. (BATCOB)
UF tickets, binders'

binders, Torah
USE Torah binders

binding (bookbinding)
USE bookbinding

binding, adhesive
USE adhesive binding

binding agent
USE binder

binding, caoutchouc
USE caoutchouc binding

binding, case
USE case binding

binding, Chinese
USE Japanese binding

<binding components>
    PJ.3363

binding, edition
USE edition binding

binding, hand
USE hand binding

binding, Japanese
USE Japanese binding

binding joists
HN April 1991 descriptor deleted

binding, library
USE library binding

binding, mechanical
USE mechanical binding

binding medium
USE binder

binding of books
USE bookbinding

binding, perfect
USE perfect binding

binding, saw-kerf
USE saw-kerf binding

binding, thermoplastic
USE perfect binding

binding warp
    PJ.3072
SN A secondary warp that binds weft floats. In weft-faced compound woven textiles, the binding warp binds the weft. In woven textiles with more than one weft, the binding warp's primary function is to bind specifically the brocading weft or pattern weft, thus making a supplementary binding.
UF binding yarn
    crimp warp
    warp, binding
    warp, crimp
    yarn, binding

binding yarn
USE binding warp

bindings
    PJ.3339
ALT binding
SN Collectively the parts of books applied in the process of attaching the leaves and covering them.
UF bookbindings
RT bookbinding

bindings, adhesive
USE adhesive bindings

\<bindings and binding components\>
PJ.3338

bindings, armorial
USE armorial bindings

bindings, blocked
USE panel stamp bindings

\<bindings by structure\>
PJ.3340

\<bindings by style or decoration\>
PJ.3351

bindings, cameo
USE cameo bindings

bindings, cameo-stamped
USE cameo bindings

bindings, caoutchouc
USE caoutchouc bindings

bindings, case
USE case bindings

bindings, chained
USE chained bindings

bindings, fanfare
USE fanfare bindings

bindings, fanfare style
USE fanfare bindings

bindings, fast back
USE tight back bindings

bindings, Greek fashion
USE Greek style bindings

bindings, Greek style
USE Greek style bindings

bindings, Grolier
USE Grolieresque bindings

bindings, Grolieresque
USE Grolieresque bindings

bindings, gutta-percha
USE caoutchouc bindings

bindings, half
USE half bindings

bindings, hollow back
USE hollow back bindings

bindings, Jansenist
USE Jansenist style bindings

bindings, Jansenist style
USE Jansenist style bindings

bindings, Jansenite style
USE Jansenist style bindings

bindings, library
USE library bindings

bindings, limp
USE limp bindings

bindings, loose back
USE hollow back bindings

bindings, mechanical
USE mechanical bindings

bindings, open back
USE hollow back bindings

bindings, panel-stamped
USE panel stamp bindings

bindings, perfect
USE perfect bindings

bindings, plaquette
USE cameo bindings

bindings, quarter
USE quarter bindings

bindings, royal
USE royal bindings

bindings, thermoplastic
USE perfect bindings

bindings, tight back
USE tight back bindings

bindings, tightbacked
USE tight back bindings

bingo
KQ.16   (L,N)
UF beano
RT bingo halls

bingo halls
RK.979   (B)
HN March 1993 related term added
September 1990 scope note added
ALT bingo hall
SN Use for buildings, generally having large open interior spaces, that accommodate a series of tables on which bingo, and derivative games, can be played.
UF bingo parlors
halls, bingo
parlors, bingo
RT bingo

bingo parlors
USE bingo halls

Binh Dinh
FL.2524
UF Thap-mam

Bini
FL.247   (L)

Bini-Portuguese
FL.172

binious
TT.189   (L)
ALT biniou
SN Small mouth-blown bagpipes of Brittany, with a sheepskin bag, drone pipe, and conical wide-bore chanter with seven fingerholes and double reed. (MARCUS)

bins
USE vinas

bins, grain
USE grain bins

biocatalyst
USE enzyme

biochemistry
KD.168   (L)
HN February 1993 related term added
December 1992 descriptor moved
January 1991 alternate term added
ALT biochemical
UF biological chemistry
chemistry, biological
RT biochemists

biochemists
HG.533   (L)
HN January 1993 descriptor added
ALT biochemist
biochemist's
biochemists'
SN Scientists trained or working in the field of biochemistry.
RT biochemistry
biologists

biocorrosion
USE biodeterioration

biodegradable
DC.273   (L)
HN October 1992 descriptor added
SN Use to describe materials capable of decaying through the action of living organisms.

biodegradation
USE biodeterioration

biodeterioration
KT.232   (L)
HN January 1993 descriptor added
SN Deterioration caused by bacteria or other microorganisms.
UF biocorrosion
biodegradation
biological corrosion
biological degradation
corrosion, biological
degradation, biological

biographers
HG.357   (L)
HN December 1992 alternate terms added
ALT biographer
biographer's
biographers'

biographical dictionaries
VW.824   (L)
HN November 1992 descriptor moved
ALT biographical dictionary
UF dictionaries, biographical

biographical notes
USE biographies

biographical sketches
USE biographies

biographies
VW.262 (L)
HN November 1992 descriptor moved
ALT biography
SN Written accounts of the lives of individuals. (GAHLM)
UF biographical notes
biographical sketches
notes, biographical
sketches, biographical

biographies, collective
USE collective biographies

biography
BM.210 (L,B,R)
HN September 1992 scope note added
SN The genre of nonfiction that concerns written accounts of the lives of individuals.

biography files
PC.95
HN March 1993 descriptor moved
ALT biography file
SN Files of records, giving information about individuals. (LG)
UF files, biographical

biological chemistry
USE biochemistry

<biological concepts>
BM.556

<biological control agents>
MT.1763

biological corrosion
USE biodeterioration

biological degradation
USE biodeterioration

biological illustration
HN May 1991 descriptor split, use biological (ALT of biology) + illustration

biological illustrations
HN May 1991 descriptor split, use biological (ALT of biology) + illustrations

biological laboratories
HN March 1993 descriptor split, use biological (ALT of biology) + laboratories

biological sciences
KD.154
HN December 1992 descriptor moved
UF sciences, biological

biologists
HG.523 (L)
HN April 1993 related terms added
December 1992 alternate terms added
ALT biologist
biologist's
biologists'
RT biochemists
biology

biologists, marine
USE marine biologists

biology
KD.156 (A,L,B,R)
HN February 1993 related term added
December 1992 descriptor moved
February 1991 alternate term added
ALT biological
RT biologists

biology, molecular
USE molecular biology

Biombo
FL.429

biomedical engineers
HG.857 (L)
HN December 1992 alternate terms added
ALT biomedical engineer
biomedical engineer's
biomedical engineers'
UF engineers, biomedical

biometrics
KD.149 (L)
SN Statistical study of biological observations and phenomena. (W)
UF biometry

biometry
USE biometrics

biomorphic abstraction
BM.148
UF abstraction, biomorphic
abstraction, creative
concretions, humor
creative abstraction
humor concretions

biotechnology
BM.1103 (L,B,R)
SN Aspect of technology concerned with the application of biological and engineering data to problems relating to the mutual adjustment of man and machine. (W)

biotite
MT.567 (L)
HN February 1992 descriptor added
SN Common rock-forming mineral of the mica group. (AGI)

bipack
MT.2371
HN April 1993 descriptor changed, was bipacks
April 1992 descriptor moved
UK bi-pack
SN Color film formed of two separate emulsions bound in register. For film with an integral, two-layer emulsion, use **integral bipack**.

bipack, integral
USE integral bipack

biplanes
TX.18 (L)
ALT biplane

SN Airplanes with two sets of wings, one above and usually slightly forward of the other. (RHDEL2)

birch
MT.2701 (L)
HN March 1992 descriptor moved
UF Betula

birch, black
USE river birch
sweet birch

birch, canoe
USE paper birch

birch, cherry
USE sweet birch

birch, common
USE silver birch

birch, downy
USE downy birch

birch, dwarf
USE dwarf birch

birch, European
USE European birch

birch, gray
USE gray birch

birch, grey
SEE gray birch

birch, Himalayan
USE Himalayan birch

birch, mahogany
USE sweet birch

birch, paper
USE paper birch

birch, river
USE river birch

birch, silver
USE silver birch

birch, sweet
USE sweet birch

birch, white
USE silver birch

birch, yellow
USE yellow birch

bird carpets
USE bird Ushaks

bird ovens
USE bird roasters

bird pattern rugs
USE bird Ushaks

bird refuges
USE bird sanctuaries

bird roasters
TH.73
HN April 1993 descriptor added
ALT bird roaster
SN Reflector ovens specifically designed

for roasting fowl, with hooks to hold the bird and a drip pan.
UF   bird ovens
     bird roasting ovens
     ovens, bird
     ovens, bird roasting
     roasters, bird
     roasting ovens, bird

bird roasting ovens
USE   bird roasters

bird rugs
USE   bird Ushaks

bird sanctuaries
     RM.62   (A,L)
HN   April 1993 descriptor moved
ALT   bird sanctuary
UF   bird refuges
     refuges, bird
     sanctuaries, bird

bird Ushaks
     TC.110
ALT   bird Ushak
SN   White-ground Anatolian rugs with an endless repeat of stylized angular leaves.
UF   bird carpets
     bird pattern rugs
     bird rugs
     carpets, bird
     carpets, white ground
     rugs, bird
     Ushaks, bird
     white ground carpets

birdbaths
     RM.229   (L,N,B)
HN   April 1993 descriptor moved
ALT   birdbath

birdcage candlesticks
USE   wire candlesticks

birdcage supports
USE   birdcages (furniture components)

birdcage Windsor chairs
USE   square-back Windsor chairs

birdcages (containers)
     TQ.118   (L,N)
ALT   birdcage (container)
SN   Cages for confining birds. (RHDEL2)

birdcages (furniture components)
     PJ.2757
HN   March 1993 descriptor moved
ALT   birdcage (furniture component)
SN   Double-block devices with columns fitted between the top and the shaft of a tilt-top table that allows the top to tilt and rotate. (FAIRB)
UF   birdcage supports
     boxes (furniture components)
     cages, squirrel (furniture components)
     squirrel cages (furniture components)
     supports, birdcage

birdhouses
     RK.82   (A,L,N)
HN   March 1993 related term added
ALT   birdhouse
SN   Enclosures, often resembling houses, built as resting, nesting, or feeding places for birds; distinguished from **aviaries** by the lack of emphasis on confinement.
RT   aviaries

birding pieces
USE   fowling pieces

birds
USE   shuttlecocks

bird's beak moldings
USE   beakhead moldings

bird's-eye maple
     MT.2807
HN   March 1992 descriptor moved
UF   maple, bird's-eye

bird's eye marble
USE   coral limestone

bird's-eye perspectives
     VC.166
HN   April 1992 descriptor moved
ALT   bird's-eye perspective
SN   Use for perspective drawings having a viewpoint well above normal eye level; for other nonphotographic depictions from a high viewpoint, where perspective is not used or is not emphasized, use **bird's-eye views**. For photographs taken from high locations, use **aerial views** or **aerial photographs**.
UF   aerial perspectives
     aerial views (perspective drawings)
     bird's-eye views (perspective drawings)
     perspectives, aerial
     perspectives, bird's-eye
     views, aerial
     views, bird's-eye

bird's-eye views
     VC.22
HN   April 1991 descriptor moved
ALT   bird's-eye view
SN   Use with reference to nonphotographic depictions having a viewpoint well above normal eye level; if these are architectural drawings in precise perspective, use **bird's-eye perspectives**. For photographs, use **aerial views** or **aerial photographs**.
UF   balloon views
     views, balloon
     views, bird's-eye

bird's-eye views (perspective drawings)
USE   bird's-eye perspectives

birefraction
USE   birefringence

birefringence
     DC.231   (L)
HN   October 1992 descriptor added
SN   The tendency of a material to cause a ray of light to separate, or the degree to which the ray separates, into two unequally refracted, plane-polarized rays of orthogonal polarizations.
UF   birefraction
     double refraction
     extraordinary ray
     ordinary ray
     pockels effect
     refraction, double

biremes
     TX.524
ALT   bireme
SN   Use for ancient Mediterranean warships propelled by oarsmen arranged in two levels.
UF   diereis
RT   warships

birettas
     TE.554   (N)
ALT   biretta
SN   Ecclesiastical caps, generally square in form and having three or four upright projections extending from the center of the top to the edge. Either red, purple, or black, corresponding to the rank of cardinal, bishop, or priest.
RT   *<liturgical costume>*

birigas
USE   bigas

Birnick
     FL.820

Birnin Gazargamo
     FL.107

birth certificates
     VW.690   (L,N)
HN   November 1992 descriptor moved
ALT   birth certificate
SN   Formal documents certifying the date and place of persons' births and their parentage, as issued by an official in charge of such records. (BLACKS)
UF   certificates, birth

birth control clinics
     RK.706   (L)
ALT   birth control clinic
UF   clinics, birth control
     clinics, family planning
     family planning clinics

birth records
     VW.689
HN   November 1992 descriptor moved
ALT   birth record
SN   Official documentation concerning dates and places of persons' births, as well as parentage. (BLACKS)
UF   records, birth

birth registers
     VW.691   (L)

HN November 1992 descriptor moved
ALT birth register
UF registers, birth

birth-stone
USE birthstone

birthday cards
　　VW.345
HN November 1992 descriptor moved
ALT birthday card
UF cards, birthday

birthdays
　　KM.14
HN April 1992 scope note added
　　May 1991 alternate term added
ALT birthday
SN Observances, usually celebratory in nature, marking the anniversary of someone's birth.

births
　　KM.158　　　　　　　　　　(L,R)
HN March 1993 lead-in term changed, was **childbirth**
　　May 1991 alternate term added
　　February 1991 descriptor changed, was **birth**
　　February 1990 lead-in term added
ALT birth
UF childbirths

birthstone
　　MT.950　　　　　　　　　　(L)
HN April 1993 lead-in term added
　　April 1993 descriptor changed, was **birthstones**
　　April 1992 descriptor moved
UF birth-stone

bisc
USE biscuit

biscuit
　　MT.149　　　　　　　　　　(H,L)
HN March 1993 descriptor added
SN Unglazed porcelain or earthenware that has been fired only once; generally producing a grainy texture; frequently used for modeling ornament or making small statues, dolls, or vessels. Distinct from **parian (porcelain)** which is silky in texture and marblelike in appearance.
UF bisc
　　biscuit porcelain
　　bisk
　　bisque
　　porcelain, biscuit
RT parian (porcelain)

biscuit boxes
　　TQ.589
ALT biscuit box
SN Covered containers of varying form intended primarily for storing biscuits.
UF boxes, biscuit
RT boxes (containers)

biscuit cutters
　　TH.98　　　　　　　　　　(N)

HN April 1993 descriptor added
ALT biscuit cutter
SN Shaped devices, generally of sheet metal, used for cutting biscuits from rolled dough.
UF cutters, biscuit

biscuit porcelain
USE biscuit

biscuit quilts
USE puff quilts

bise
USE azurite

bise, Spanish
USE azurite

bisellia
　　TC.722
HN January 1993 descriptor moved
ALT bisellium

bisexuality
　　BM.1031　　　　　　　　　　(L)
HN February 1993 descriptor moved
SN Sexuality characterized by romantic love or sexual desire toward members of either sex.

bishoprics
USE dioceses

bishops (chessmen)
　　TV.8
ALT bishop (chessman)
SN Use for those chess pieces that move as bishops are designated to move.

bishops (prelates)
　　HG.403　　　　　　　　　(H,L,B,R)
HN February 1993 descriptor moved
　　December 1992 descriptor changed, was **bishops**
　　December 1992 alternate term changed, was **bishop**
　　December 1992 alternate terms added
ALT bishop (prelate)
　　bishop's
　　bishops'
SN Clergymen of the highest order in Christian churches, usually charged with an administrative function such as the supervision of a diocese. (W)

bishops' palaces
HN March 1993 descriptor split, use **bishops'** (ALT of **bishops (prelates)**) + **palaces**

bisk
USE biscuit

bismars
USE desemers

bismuth white
　　MT.2226
HN May 1992 lead-in terms added
　　January 1992 descriptor moved
UF Bougival white
　　pearl white

　　Spanish white
　　white, bismuth
　　white, Bougival
　　white, pearl
　　white, Spanish

bisque
USE biscuit
　　brownish pink
　　grayish yellow
　　grayish yellowish pink
　　light grayish brown
　　light grayish yellowish brown
　　moderate yellowish pink
　　pale orange yellow
　　yellowish gray

bisque dolls
　　TV.157　　　　　　　　　　(L)
ALT bisque doll
SN Use for dolls made primarily of unglazed porcelain; produced since the mid-19th century.
UF dolls, bisque

Bissago
USE Bijogo

bister
　　MT.2117
HN April 1992 descriptor moved
UK bistre
UF brown lampblack
　　brown, soot
　　lampblack, brown
　　soot brown

bistre
SEE bister

bistre
USE dark orange yellow
　　dark yellow
　　deep yellow
　　grayish brown
　　grayish yellow
　　grayish yellowish brown
　　light brown
　　light brownish gray
　　light grayish olive
　　light grayish yellowish brown
　　light olive brown
　　light yellowish brown
　　moderate greenish yellow
　　moderate olive brown
　　moderate orange yellow
　　moderate yellow
　　moderate yellowish brown
　　pale yellow
　　strong yellowish brown

bistre brown
USE light brown
　　light brownish gray
　　light olive
　　light olive brown
　　light yellowish brown
　　moderate yellowish brown
　　moderate yellowish pink

bistre, brown
USE light grayish yellowish brown

bistre, deep
USE   light olive brown

bistre, gray
USE   light grayish yellowish brown
light olive brown
light yellowish brown

bistre, olive
USE   light olive
light olive brown
light olive gray

bistre, purplish
USE   brownish pink

bistros
USE   cafés

bit
USE   bitstone

bit braces
USE   braces (woodworking tools)

bit-hilani
RK.342
SN   Designates ancient Near Eastern and Anatolian palaces having two long rooms fronted by a portico, often flanked by projecting ells; may also refer to some ancient entrance buildings or gatehouses.

bit key locks
PJ.488
HN   April 1993 descriptor moved
ALT   bit key lock
UF   key locks, bit
locks, bit key

bit pads
USE   graphics tablets

bit stocks
USE   braces (woodworking tools)

bit-stone
SEE   bitstone

bit tongs, right-angle
USE   side tongs

bite, creeping
USE   creeping bite

bite, deep
USE   deep etching

biting
KT.953
HN   March 1991 alternate term added
October 1990 descriptor moved
July 1990 scope note changed
July 1990 lead-in terms added
July 1990 descriptor changed, was acid-biting
ALT   bitten
SN   Use for the specific step of corroding a material by the action of acid.
UF   acid-biting
biting in
etching (biting)

biting, brush
USE   spit biting

biting, false
USE   foul biting

biting, foul
USE   foul biting

biting in
USE   biting

biting, open
USE   open biting

biting, spit
USE   spit biting

<biting techniques>
KT.711
HN   October 1990 guide term added

bits (coins)
USE   reales

bits (key components)
PJ.613
HN   March 1993 descriptor moved
ALT   bit (key component)
SN   Parts of keys which are inserted into a lock and engage the tumblers or bolt. (MEANS)
UF   key bits

bits (tool components)
PJ.2574   (L,N)
HN   March 1993 descriptor moved
May 1991 descriptor changed, was bits
May 1991 alternate term changed, was bit
ALT   bit (tool component)
SN   Tool components of varying sizes that fit into a brace or drill and are rotated to bore a hole. (MEANS)
UF   bits, drill
cherries
drill bits
reamers (bits)

bits, annular
USE   tenon-cutting bits

bits, auger
USE   auger bits

bits, brush
USE   brush bits

bits, button
USE   button bits

bits, center
USE   center bits

bits, chair
USE   spoon bits

bits, cock plug
USE   tenon-cutting bits

bits, countersink
USE   countersink bits

bits, crook
USE   crook-bit tongs

bits, deck dowelling
USE   tenon-cutting bits

bits, dowel
USE   spoon bits

bits, drill
USE   bits (tool components)

bits, expansion
USE   expansion bits

bits, flat
USE   flat tongs

bits, Foerstner
USE   Forstner bits

bits, Forstner
USE   Forstner bits

bits, gimlet
USE   gimlet bits

bits, gouge
USE   gouge bits

bits, modesty
USE   modesties

bits, nose
USE   nose bits

bits, pin
USE   spoon bits

bits, pivot
USE   tenon-cutting bits

bits, plug
USE   tenon-cutting bits

bits, plug center
USE   tenon-cutting bits

bits, quill
USE   spoon bits

bits, reamer
USE   reamer bits

bits, shell
USE   shell bits

bits, ship auger
USE   ship auger bits

bits, spiral
USE   spiral bits

bits, spoon
USE   spoon bits

bits, sprig
USE   bradawls

bits, tenon-cutting
USE   tenon-cutting bits

bits, twist
USE   spiral bits

bits, wimble
USE   nose bits

bitstone
MT.1772

HN April 1993 descriptor moved
April 1993 scope note changed
UK bit-stone
SN Coarse particles of hard material, such as crushed quartz or flint, used in making ceramics, spread beneath delicate articles to prevent their sticking or being blemished by contact during firing.
UF bit

bittels
USE beetles

bitternut hickory
MT.2761
HN March 1992 descriptor moved
UF Carya cordiformis
hickory, bitternut

bitters bottles
TQ.60   (L)
ALT bitters bottle
SN Small bottles used for holding bitters and having a metal dropper. Also, bottles of varying form used for holding patent medicine or other medical products.
UF bottles, bitters

bittles, wedge
USE beetles

bitudobe
MT.131
HN April 1992 descriptor moved

bitumen
MT.1002   (L,B)
HN April 1992 descriptor moved
March 1992 lead-in terms added
March 1992 scope note changed
SN Use generally for a number of types of natural combustible material rich in carbon and hydrogen.
UF bitumen, natural
natural bitumen

bitumen (brown pigment)
USE asphaltum

bitumen (color)
USE dark grayish yellowish brown

bitumen, natural
USE bitumen

bitumen process
USE heliography

bituminised paper
USE tar paper

bituminous coal
MT.1018   (L)
HN April 1992 descriptor moved
UF coal, bituminous
coal, soft
soft coal

bituminous coating
MT.1846

HN April 1993 descriptor changed, was bituminous coatings
UF coating, bituminous

bituminous earth
USE Vandyke brown

bituminous felt
USE tar paper

bituminous limestone
USE carbonaceous limestone

bituminous material
MT.993   (L)
HN April 1993 descriptor changed, was bituminous materials
April 1993 lead-in term deleted, was bituminous products
April 1992 descriptor moved
UF material, bituminous

bituminous rock
USE rock asphalt

biwa
TT.283
SN Pear-shaped, short-necked Japanese lutelike chordophones made of wood, commonly with four strings and a pegbox sharply angled back from the neck.

Biysk phase
FL.2203
UF Biisk phase

bizarre architecture
USE fantastic architecture

Bizen
FL.2095   (L)

Bka'gdams
USE Kadam School

black
DL.336   (L,R)
UF black, dull violet
black, grayish
black, greenish slate
black, jet
black, lamp
black, slate
blackish green gray
blue, midnight
brown, iron
centroid color 267
charcoal (color)
dark navy
dull violet black
graphite (color)
grayish black
green gray, blackish
greenish slate black
iron (color)
iron brown
jet black
lamp black
midnight blue
navy, dark
slate black
slate black, greenish
violet black, dull

Black (style)
USE African American

black, acetylene
USE carbon black

black alder
USE common alder

black-and-gold marble
USE portor marble

black-and-white film
MT.2368
HN April 1992 descriptor moved
UF film, black-and-white

black-and-white negatives
VC.290
HN April 1992 descriptor moved
ALT black-and-white negative
SN Use for negatives whose images are composed of gray tones, black, and white or clear areas; may include one hue as a result of process, toning, or discoloration.
UF negatives, black-and-white

black-and-white photographs
VC.347
HN April 1992 descriptor moved
ALT black-and-white photograph
SN Use for the broad class of photographs whose images are composed of gray tones, black, and white, and sometimes one hue (which can result from chemical processes used, including toning, or from aging).
UF photographs, black-and-white

black-and-white photography
KT.568
HN June 1991 scope note added
SN The art or practice of taking and/or processing photographs whose images are composed of gray tones, black, and white, and sometimes one hue, which may result from toning or aging.
UF photography, black-and-white

black-and-white photoprints
USE black-and-white prints (photographs)

black-and-white prints
VC.447
ALT black-and-white print
SN Prints composed using only black and white, usually black ink on white paper. For black-and-white photographs, use **black-and-white prints (photographs)**.
UF black-on-white prints
prints, black-and-white

black-and-white prints (photographs)
VC.316
HN April 1992 descriptor moved
ALT black-and-white print (photograph)
SN Use for photographic prints whose images are composed of gray tones, black, and white; may include one

hue as a result of process, toning, discoloration, or the use of a colored support.
UF black-and-white photoprints
photoprints, black-and-white
prints, black-and-white

black-and-white slides
VC.358
HN April 1992 descriptor moved
ALT black-and-white slide
SN Use for slides whose images are composed of gray tones, black, and clear areas; may include one hue as a result of process, toning, or discoloration.
UF slides, black-and-white

Black and White Style (architecture)
FL.3292

Black and White Style (pottery)
FL.2731

black-and-white transparencies
VC.341
HN April 1992 descriptor moved
ALT black-and-white transparency
SN Use for transparencies whose images are composed of gray tones, black, and clear areas; may include one hue as a result of process, toning, or discoloration.
UF transparencies, black-and-white

black, aniline
USE aniline black
dark grayish purple
dark purplish gray

black beech
USE New Zealand beech

black, benzol
USE carbon black

black birch
USE river birch
sweet birch

black, blue
USE bluish gray
dark bluish gray
vine black

black, blue violet
USE dark gray
dark purplish gray

black, bluish
USE bluish black

Black Bobo
USE Bobo-Fing

black, bone
USE bone black

black brown
USE brownish gray
dark grayish brown
grayish brown
grayish olive
light brownish gray
olive gray

black, brownish
USE brownish black

black burnished (Helladic pottery style)
FL.2741
HN April 1993 descriptor added
UF burnished, black

black-burnished (Mesopotamian pottery style)
FL.3079
HN April 1993 descriptor added

black-burnished ware
HN April 1993 descriptor split, use black-burnished (Mesopotamian pottery style) + ware

black burnished ware (Helladic pottery)
HN April 1993 descriptor split, use black burnished (Helladic pottery style) + ware

black, carbon
USE carbon black

black carbon ink
MT.1917
HN June 1991 descriptor moved
June 1990 lead-in term added
UF carbon ink
carbon ink, black
ink, black carbon

black chalk
MT.48
HN December 1992 descriptor moved
SN Natural chalk containing carbon or shale and used for drawing especially since the Renaissance.
UF chalk, black
chalk, Italian
Italian chalk

black, charcoal
USE charcoal black

black cherry
MT.2877
HN March 1992 descriptor moved
UF American black cherry
American cherry
black cherry, American
cherry, American
cherry, American black
cherry, black
cherry, rum
Prunus serotina
rum cherry

black cherry, American
USE black cherry

black, cork
USE vine black

black cornetts
USE curved cornetts

black cottonwood
MT.2872
HN March 1992 descriptor moved
UF balsam poplar, western
cottonwood, black
poplar, western balsam
Populus trichocarpa
western balsam poplar

black, deep purplish
USE dark purplish gray

black, diamond
USE carbon black

black, drop
USE bone black
vine black

black, dull blue green
USE blackish blue
bluish black
dark grayish blue

black, dull greenish
USE dark gray
dark greenish gray

black, dull violet
USE black

black ebony
MT.2726
HN March 1992 descriptor moved
UF Diospyros dendo
ebony, black

Black-figure
FL.2732

black, flame
USE carbon black

black, Frankfort
USE bone black

black, fruit stone
USE fruit stone black

black, gas
USE carbon black

black, German
USE vine black

black granite
USE diabase
diorite

black, gray
USE greenish gray
light brownish gray
light olive gray
medium gray
olive gray

black, grayish
USE black

black, green
USE dark grayish green
dark greenish gray

black, greenish
USE greenish black

black, greenish slate
USE black

black gum
MT.2746

HN March 1992 descriptor moved
UF black tupelo
    gum, black
    Nyssa sylvatica
    tupelo, black

black hemlock
USE mountain hemlock

black hickory
    MT.2762
HN March 1992 descriptor moved
UF Carya texana
    hickory, black

black, ink
USE dark bluish gray

black iron oxide
USE Mars black

black, ivory
USE ivory black

black jacks
USE blackjacks (drinking vessels)

black, jet
USE black

black, kernel
USE peach black

black, lamp
USE black

black lead
USE graphite

black letter
    PJ.3479
SN Group of typefaces characterized by
    heavy faces and angular outlines,
    based on Gothic hand-written
    scripts.
UF black letter typefaces
    blackletter
    gothic typefaces
    letter, black
    text letter typefaces
    text typefaces (black letter)
    texts, wedding
    typefaces, black letter
    typefaces, gothic
    typefaces, text (black letter)
    typefaces, text letter
    typefaces, wedding
    types, wedding
    wedding texts
    wedding typefaces
    wedding types

black letter (script)
USE textura

black letter typefaces
USE black letter

black locust
    MT.2790   (L)
HN March 1992 descriptor moved
UF Acacia (black locust)
    Acacia, false
    false Acacia
    locust, black

locust, red
red locust
Robinia pseudoacacia

black lustrous (pottery style)
    FL.2990
HN April 1993 descriptor added
UF lustrous, black

black lustrous ware
HN April 1993 descriptor split, use
    black lustrous (pottery style) +
    ware

black manner
USE mezzotint

black maple
    MT.2808
HN March 1992 descriptor moved
UF Acer nigrum
    maple, black

black marble
    MT.713
HN April 1992 descriptor moved
UF marble, black

black marble, Belgian
USE Belgian black marble

black marble, Irish
USE Irish black marble

black marble, Rockingham royal
USE Rockingham royal black marble

black, Mars
USE Mars black

black metal
USE pewter

black-mouthed
    FL.2926
HN April 1993 descriptor added

black-mouthed ware
HN April 1993 descriptor split, use
    black-mouthed + ware

black oak
    MT.2820   (L)
HN March 1992 descriptor moved
UF oak, black
    Quercus velutina

black oak, California
USE California black oak

black oil
    MT.1112
HN April 1992 descriptor moved
    October 1990 descriptor moved
SN Linseed oil cooked at a high tem-
    perature with as much white lead or
    litharge as will combine with it.
    (MAYER)
UF oil, black

black, oil
USE carbon black

black olive
USE dark olive

black, olive
USE olive black

black-on-buff
    FL.3080
HN April 1993 descriptor added

black-on-buff ware
HN April 1993 descriptor split, use
    black-on-buff + ware

black-on-red
    FL.2955
HN April 1993 descriptor added

black-on-red ware
HN April 1993 descriptor split, use
    black-on-red + ware

black-on-white, Mimbres
USE Mimbres black-on-white

black-on-white prints
USE black-and-white prints

black, Paris
USE Paris black

black, peach
USE peach black

black persimmon
USE persimmon

black pigment
    MT.2067
HN April 1993 descriptor moved
UF pigment, black

black pigment, artificial inorganic
USE artificial inorganic black pigment

black pigment, artificial organic
USE synthetic organic black pigment

black pigment, organic
USE organic black pigment

black pigment, synthetic inorganic
USE artificial inorganic black pigment

black pigment, synthetic organic
USE synthetic organic black pigment

black pine
USE Austrian pine

black pine, Austrian
USE Austrian pine

black plum
USE dark grayish purple
    dark purplish gray
    purplish black

black poplar
    MT.2860
HN March 1992 descriptor moved
UF black poplar, European
    English poplar
    European black poplar
    Lombardy poplar
    poplar, black
    poplar, English
    poplar, European black

poplar, Lombardy
Populus nigra

black poplar, European
USE black poplar

Black pottery (period)
USE Longshan

black powder
USE gunpowder

black, purplish
USE purplish black

black, reddish
USE reddish black

black slate
MT.807
HN April 1992 descriptor moved
UF slate, black

black, slate
USE black

black-slip-and-combed
FL.2991
HN April 1993 descriptor added

black-slip-and-combed ware
HN April 1993 descriptor split, use
black-slip-and-combed + ware

black, Spanish
USE vine black

black spruce
MT.2988   (L)
HN March 1992 descriptor moved
UF Picea nigra
pine, spruce
spruce, black
spruce pine

black-topped
FL.2927
HN April 1993 descriptor added

black-topped pottery
HN April 1993 descriptor split, use
black-topped + pottery

black-topped red
FL.2928
HN April 1993 descriptor added
UF red, black-topped

black-topped red ware
HN April 1993 descriptor split, use
black-topped red + ware

black tupelo
USE black gum

black, vegetable
USE carbon black
charcoal black

black, vine
USE vine black

black violet
USE blackish purple
dark grayish purple

dark purplish red
very dark purplish red

black, violet
USE dark grayish red
dark purplish gray

black walnut
MT.2912   (L)
HN March 1992 descriptor moved
UF American black walnut
American walnut
black walnut, American
Juglans nigra
walnut, American
walnut, American black
walnut, black

black walnut, American
USE black walnut

black watercolor
USE Japanese ink

black-white-red
FL.1189

black willow
MT.2917   (L)
HN March 1992 descriptor moved
UF Salix nigra
willow, black

black willow, western
USE western black willow

black, yeast
USE vine black

blackamoors
USE guéridons

blackboard slate
MT.814
HN April 1992 descriptor moved
SN Select, unfading, black slate of uniform color and thickness with all
edges   ground   and   accurately
squared so that joints can be made
tight, smooth, and on the same
plane. (HORNB)
UF slate, blackboard

blackbutt
MT.2739
HN March 1992 descriptor moved
UF Eucalyptus pilulares

Blackfoot
FL.1388

blackhouses
RK.266
HN January 1992 descriptor added
ALT blackhouse
SN Use for low, single-story, stone, of-
ten windowless, housebarns of
Scotland.

blackish blue
DL.256
UF black, dull blue green
blue, blackish
blue, dull
blue, dull greenish

blue, dull reddish
blue, graphite
blue green black, dull
blue, midnight
centroid color 188
dark navy
dull blue
dull blue green black
dull greenish blue
dull reddish blue
graphite blue
green black, dull blue
greenish blue, dull
greenish navy
indigo (color)
midnight blue
navy
navy, dark
navy, greenish
reddish blue, dull
slate (color)

blackish brown
USE brownish gray
dark grayish brown
dark reddish gray

blackish green
DL.208
UF blue green, dark
bluish green, dull
centroid color 152
dark blue green
dark slate green
dull bluish green
dull green
green, blackish
green, dark blue
green, dark slate
green, dull
green, dull bluish
hemlock (color)
slate green, dark

blackish green blue
USE dark greenish blue

blackish green, dull
USE dark grayish green

blackish green gray
USE black

blackish purple
DL.312
UF black violet
blue, midnight
bluish violet, dull
brown, dark violet
centroid color 230
dark eggplant
dark navy
dark plum
dark violet brown
dull bluish violet
dull reddish violet
dull violet
eggplant, dark
logwood (color)
midnight blue
navy
navy, dark

plum, dark
purple, blackish
reddish violet, dull
violet, black
violet brown, dark
violet, dull
violet, dull bluish
violet, dull reddish

blackish red
DL.76
HN November 1991 lead-in term changed, was **lilac, grayish**
May 1990 lead-in term changed, was **grayish lilac**
UF brown, dull reddish
brown, lilac
brown, red
centroid color 21
dull reddish brown
gray lilac
lilac brown
lilac, gray
red, blackish
red brown
reddish brown, dull

blackish red purple
USE dark purplish red

blackish slate
USE dark gray

blackish violet
USE dark violet
grayish violet
moderate violet

blackish violet gray
USE dark gray
dark purplish gray

blackjacks (drinking vessels)
TQ.390
ALT blackjack (drinking vessel)
SN Capacious vessels for beer or ale usually of tar-coated leather. (W)
UF black jacks
jacks, leather
leather jacks
RT tankards

blackjacks (weapons)
TK.123 (N)
ALT blackjack (weapon)
SN Small percussive weapons typically consisting of a leather-covered piece of lead or other heavy material with a short flexible handle such as a strap or springy shaft.

blackletter
USE black letter

blackline prints
VW.1080 (L)
HN March 1993 descriptor moved
ALT blackline print
SN Use for prints made on light-sensitized surfaces that produce black lines on neutral backgrounds.
UF blacklines
prints, blackline

blackline process
USE ferrogallic process

blacklines
USE blackline prints

blacksmith shops
USE smithies

blacksmithing
KT.1070 (L,R)
HN August 1992 scope note added
SN The craft or job of a blacksmith.

blacksmiths
HG.715 (H,L)
HN December 1992 alternate terms added
ALT blacksmith
blacksmith's
blacksmiths'
SN Persons who make iron into tools, horseshoes, machine parts, and other objects by heating it in a forge and hammering it into shape on an anvil. (W)

blackwood, African
USE African blackwood

blackwood, Australian
USE Australian locust

blackwood, Tasmanian
USE Australian locust

bladder
MT.2536
HN February 1992 descriptor added
SN The membraneous sac of an animal that serves as a receptacle for fluid or gas; historically sometimes removed and used by people to store liquid materials. (W)

bladder green
USE sap green

blades
PJ.2593 (L)
HN March 1993 descriptor moved
November 1992 related term added
ALT blade
RT <edged weapon components>

blades (graders)
USE graders

blades (rafters)
USE principal rafters

blades, cleaving
USE cleaving blades

blades, razor
USE razor blades

blades, saw
USE saw blades

blanc baryte
USE barium sulfate

blanc d'argent
USE lead white

blanc de lait
USE opaque white glass

blanc de plomb
USE lead white

blanc de zinc
USE zinc white

blanc fixe
USE barium sulfate

blanc titane
USE titanium dioxide white

blanco de cinc
USE zinc white

blanco fijo
USE barium sulfate

blank arcades
USE blind arcades

blank-books
USE blankbooks

blank cartridges
TK.270 (N)
ALT blank cartridge
SN Cartridges containing an explosive propellant but no projectile, designed to produce a loud noise on firing and used for signalling, training, firing salutes, or to mimic the effect of real gunfire in theatrical performances.
UF blanks (cartridges)
cartridges, blank
RT <sound devices by function>

blank doors
USE false doors

blank forms
VW.42
HN June 1992 descriptor added
ALT blank form
SN Forms whose spaces provided for information have not been filled.
UF forms, blank

blank leaves
PJ.3384
ALT blank leaf
SN Unprinted leaves in books, often placed at each end of a book by the printer or the binder.
UF leaves, blank

blank tracery
USE blind tracery

blank walls
PJ.1904
HN March 1993 descriptor moved
ALT blank wall
SN Walls whose whole surfaces are unbroken by windows, doors, or other openings.
UF blind walls
dead walls
walls, blank
walls, blind
walls, dead

blank windows
USE   blind windows

blankbooks
    VW.1004   (L)
HN   June 1992 descriptor added
ALT   blankbook
SN   Books of blank, mostly blank, or
      ruled pages, or of printed forms.
UF   blank-books

blanket chests
    TC.865   (N)
HN   January 1993 descriptor moved
ALT   blanket chest
UF   chests, blanket

blanket-coats
USE   mackinaws

blanket insulation
    MT.1802
HN   April 1993 descriptor moved
      June 1991 descriptor added
SN   Denotes flexible, lightweight, faced
      or unfaced thermal or acoustical in-
      sulation formed in long continuous
      rolls.
UF   blankets (insulation)
      insulation, blanket
      insulation, roll
      roll insulation

blanket rails
    PJ.2746
HN   March 1993 descriptor moved
ALT   blanket rail
UF   rails, blanket

blanket sheets
USE   winter sheets

blanketing
    MT.1558
HN   November 1992 descriptor added
SN   Textile made for blankets and simi-
      lar items, woven by the yard.

blankets (coverings)
    TC.9   (L,N)
ALT   blanket (covering)
SN   Large rectangular coverings of thick
      but soft material, used especially
      for warmth.
RT   bed coverings
      lap robes
      plaids
      throws
      wearing blankets
      winter sheets

blankets (insulation)
USE   blanket insulation

blankets (printing press components)
    PJ.2622
ALT   blanket (printing press component)
SN   Rectangles of piano felt or foam
      rubber used between the paper and
      the roller on a rolling press. (PRTT)
UF   blankets, etching
      blankets, press
      etching blankets

      felts
      press blankets

blankets, button
USE   button blankets

<blankets by form or function>
    TC.10

<blankets by pattern or motif>
    TC.17

blankets, camp
USE   utility blankets

blankets, chief
USE   chief blankets

blankets, chief pattern
USE   chief blankets

blankets, chiefs'
USE   chief blankets

blankets, electric
USE   electric blankets

blankets, etching
USE   blankets (printing press compo-
      nents)

blankets, Hudson's Bay
USE   Hudson's Bay blankets

blankets, Moki
USE   Moki blankets

blankets, Moki pattern
USE   Moki blankets

blankets, nobility
USE   nobility blankets

blankets, Pendleton
USE   Pendleton blankets

blankets, Pendleton Indian
USE   Pendleton blankets

blankets, pictorial
USE   pictorial blankets

blankets, point
USE   point blankets

blankets, pound
USE   pound blankets

blankets, press
USE   blankets (printing press compo-
      nents)

blankets, rose
USE   rose blankets

blankets, rose wheel
USE   rose blankets

blankets, Saltillo
USE   Saltillo sarapes

blankets, sandpainting
USE   sandpainting rugs

blankets, shadda
USE   shadda

blankets, sheet
USE   winter sheets

blankets, shoulder
USE   shoulder blankets

blankets, trade
USE   trade blankets

blankets, utility
USE   utility blankets

blankets, wearing
USE   wearing blankets

blankets, yei
USE   yei rugs

blankets, yeibichai
USE   yeibichai rugs

blanking
    KT.1117   (L)
SN   Cutting desired shapes out of a ma-
      terial such as metal to be used for
      forming or other manufacturing op-
      erations. (STEIN)

blanks
    PE.34
HN   March 1992 descriptor added
ALT   blank
SN   Semifinished items prepared to be
      made into something else by further
      operations. (W)
UF   flans

blanks (cartridges)
USE   blank cartridges

blast-cleaning
USE   abrasive cleaning

blast-furnace slag
USE   slag

blast furnaces
    RK.645   (H,L,N,B)
ALT   blast furnace
SN   Large, vertical structures for
      smelting iron from ore, using a solid
      fuel, designed so as to direct a con-
      tinuous blast of air through the fuel
      to assure a high rate of combustion.
UF   furnaces, blast

blasters
    HG.814
HN   December 1992 alternate terms
      added
ALT   blaster
      blaster's
      blasters'
SN   Construction workers whose work is
      blasting with an explosive. (W)
UF   shot-firers

blasting
    KT.273   (L,B)
ALT   blasted
SN   The process of loosening rock, or
      other hard-packed materials, with
      explosives. (MEANS)

blasting, abrasive
USE abrasive cleaning

<blasting equipment>
TH.419
HN January 1993 guide term added

Blaugrünoxid
USE blue-green oxide

blazers
TE.55
ALT blazer
SN Lightweight semi-tailored jackets usually made with a notched collar, patch pockets, and sometimes an insignia on the breast pocket. So called because originally made in brilliant colors or striped to distinguish schools, colleges, teams, or the like.

blazoners
HG.269
HN January 1993 descriptor added
ALT blazoner
blazoner's
blazoners'
SN Those who depict coats of arms in proper form and color.
RT heralds

bleach
MT.1773
HN March 1992 related term added
RT bleaching

bleach-out process
USE silver-dye bleach process

bleach process, dye
USE silver-dye bleach process

bleached beeswax
MT.1292
HN April 1992 descriptor moved
December 1990 descriptor moved
UF beeswax, bleached
beeswax, bleached white
bleached white beeswax
cera alba
wax, white
white beeswax, bleached
white wax

bleached white beeswax
USE bleached beeswax

bleacheries
RK.651
ALT bleachery
UF bleachworks

bleaching
KT.908 (L)
HN January 1993 descriptor moved
February 1992 related terms added
February 1992 scope note changed
ALT bleached
SN The process of whitening or lightening the color of a material by means of oxidation through the use of chemicals or exposure to sunlight.

RT bleach
fuller's earth

bleachworks
USE bleacheries

bled-to-the edge
USE bleeding (printing technique)

bleed prints
USE bled (ALT of bleeding (printing technique)) + prints

bleeding (printing technique)
KT.705
HN March 1991 descriptor added
ALT bled
SN Printing an image so that it extends to the edge of the paper or other printing surface.
UF bled-to-the-edge

bleeding (seeping)
KT.225
HN January 1993 descriptor moved
March 1992 scope note changed
SN The loss or migration of colorant due to contact with liquids, especially water; also in painting the diffusion or migration of coatings or the pigments in them into surrounding layers or surfaces.
UF bleeding through

bleeding bowls
TQ.174 (N)
ALT bleeding bowl
SN Shallow bowls from 4 to 6 inches in diameter, with one flat handle usually flush with the rim, employed by barber-surgeons of the 17th and 18th centuries in bleeding a patient. In England the term is also sometimes applied to what in America is known as porringers.
UF bowls, bleeding
bowls, cupping
cupping bowls
RT bowls (vessels)
porringers

bleeding through
USE bleeding (seeping)

bleeds
USE bled (ALT of bleeding (printing technique)) + prints

Blei-Zinn Gelb
USE lead-tin yellow

Bleiglätte
USE litharge

Bleimennige
USE red lead

Bleintimoniat
USE Naples yellow

Bleiweiss
USE lead white

blenders (artists' brushes)
TH.730

HN February 1993 descriptor added
ALT blender (artist's brush)
SN Large round brushes that fan out to a flat end, used particularly in oil painting to soften or blend edges or textures; usually made of badger hair.
UF badger blenders
badger-hair blenders
badger-hair brushes
blenders, badger
blenders, badger-hair
blenders, oil
brushes, badger-hair
oil blenders
softeners
sweeteners

blenders (culinary equipment)
TH.137 (L,N)
HN April 1993 descriptor added
ALT blender (culinary equipment)
SN Tools used for blending food, especially culinary appliances consisting of a container with a fixed propellerlike blade at the bottom which rotates at different speeds to chop, mix, purée, or whip foods.
UF blendors
RT food processors
mixers (culinary equipment)

blenders, badger
USE blenders (artists' brushes)

blenders, badger-hair
USE blenders (artists' brushes)

blenders, bread
USE bread makers

blenders, dough
USE pastry blenders

blenders, fan
USE fan brushes

blenders, oil
USE blenders (artists' brushes)

blenders, pastry
USE pastry blenders

blending
KT.71
HN January 1993 descriptor moved
ALT blended
SN Mingling or combining so that the separate constituents or the line of demarcation cannot be distinguished. In painting, includes the gradation of color so that two hues or values merge imperceptibly.

blendors
USE blenders (culinary equipment)

blessed
HG.33 (L)
HN February 1993 descriptor moved
January 1993 alternate term added
ALT blessed's
UF beatae
beati

blessing
 KG.302 (L)
 SN Consecrating or sanctifying by a holy rite; also, invoking God's favor upon a person. (RHDEL2)

bleu céleste
 USE cerulean blue

bleu d'alexandrie
 USE Egyptian blue

bleu d'Allemagne
 USE azurite

bleu d'azur
 USE ultramarine blue

bleu de cobalt
 USE cobalt blue

bleu de mangane
 USE manganese blue

bleu de montagne
 USE azurite

bleu de Pouzzoles
 USE Egyptian blue

bleu de Prusse
 USE Prussian blue

bleu d'Egypte
 USE Egyptian blue

bleu d'émail
 USE smalt

bleu egiziano
 USE Egyptian blue

bleu Egyptian
 USE Egyptian blue

bleu fritté
 USE Egyptian blue

bleu héliogène
 USE phthalocyanine blue

bleu Paul Véronèse
 USE azurite

blight
 USE urban blight

blimps
 TX.29 (A,L,N,R)
 ALT blimp
 SN Use for nonrigid airships having several balloonlike compartments.

blind
 HG.41 (A,L,B,R)
 HN February 1993 descriptor moved
 SN People having no sight or such limited vision that hearing and touch are the chief means of perception. (ERIC9)

blind alleys
 RM.139
 HN April 1993 descriptor moved
 ALT blind alley
 SN Restricted to alleyways open only at one end; for larger thoroughfares

having access at only one end, use **dead-end streets** or **culs-de-sac.**
 UF alleys, blind

blind arcades
 PJ.1422
 HN April 1993 lead-in term added
 March 1993 descriptor moved
 ALT blind arcade
 SN Arcades closed at the back and serving only as decorative features.
 UF arcades, blank
 arcades, blind
 arcades, surface
 arcades, wall
 blank arcades
 surface arcades
 wall arcades

blind arches
 PJ.1582
 HN March 1993 descriptor moved
 ALT blind arch
 SN Arches in which the opening is permanently closed by the wall construction. (DAC)
 UF arches, blind

blind catches
 PJ.322
 HN April 1993 descriptor moved
 ALT blind catch
 UF catches, blind

blind contour drawing
 KT.394
 SN The technique of drawing the contours of an object while looking at the object and not at the drawing.
 UF contour drawing, blind
 drawing, blind contour

blind contour drawings
 VC.211
 HN April 1992 descriptor moved
 ALT blind contour drawing
 UF contour drawings, blind
 drawings, blind contour

blind doors
 USE false doors

blind dovetail joints
 PJ.716
 HN April 1993 descriptor moved
 ALT blind dovetail joint
 UF dovetail joints, blind
 joints, blind dovetail

blind drawers
 PJ.2770
 HN March 1993 descriptor moved
 ALT blind drawer
 UF drawers, blind

blind embossed prints
 USE embossed prints

blind embossing
 KT.980
 HN January 1993 descriptor moved
 April 1990 descriptor added

 ALT blind-embossed
 SN Creating raised letters or designs without ink, foil, or other color.
 UF blind intaglio
 embossing, blind
 embossing, uninked
 inkless intaglio
 intaglio, blind
 intaglio, inkless
 uninked embossing

blind frames
 USE back frames

blind hinges
 USE concealed hinges

blind intaglio
 USE blind embossing

blind joints
 PJ.679
 HN April 1993 descriptor moved
 ALT blind joint
 SN Use for concealed joints in masonry.
 UF joints, blind

blind stamping
 KT.992
 HN February 1993 descriptor moved
 June 1991 descriptor added
 ALT blind-stamped
 SN Impressing an image into a surface using a tool that is cut intaglio with a complete design, resulting in a relief image; used especially in bookbinding.
 UF blind-stamping
 stamping, blind

blind-stamping
 USE blind stamping

blind tracery
 PJ.2330
 HN March 1993 descriptor moved
 SN Tracery applied to a surface without being pierced through.
 UF blank tracery
 tracery, blank
 tracery, blind

blind trumpets
 USE trumpet spirals

blind walls
 USE blank walls

blind windows
 PJ.1943 (B)
 HN March 1993 descriptor moved
 October 1991 alternate term changed, was **false window**
 March 1991 descriptor moved
 March 1991 scope note changed
 March 1991 descriptor changed, was **false windows**
 March 1991 lead-in term changed, was **blind windows**
 ALT blind window
 SN Representations of windows inserted to complete a series of win-

dows, or to give the appearance of symmetry to a facade.
UF blank windows
false windows
windows, blank
windows, blind
windows, false

blinders
USE barn doors

blindman's rules
TN.46
ALT blindman's rule
SN Wooden rules having extra large and bold numbers; produced during the first half of the 20th century.
UF rules, blindman's

blindness
BM.586   (L,R)

blinds (coverings)
TC.298   (L,B)
ALT blind (covering)
SN Flexible or removable devices used to obstruct or regulate vision or light consisting of horizontal or vertical slats that can be opened or closed, often with the angle of the slats adjustable to admit varying amounts of light. For blinds permanently affixed to buildings, use **shutters**. For assemblies of adjustable blades, slats, or baffles, use **louvers**. Prefer **shades (coverings)** for flexible screens, usually of paper, cloth, bamboo, or similar materials and sometimes mounted on a roller, used to obstruct or regulate vision or light.
UF blinds, window
window blinds
RT shutters

blinds (shelters)
RK.1121   (A)
ALT blind (shelter)

blinds (shutters)
USE shutters

blinds, Austrian
SEE Austrian shades

blinds, mini
USE miniblinds

blinds, roller
SEE roller shades

blinds, Roman
SEE Roman shades

blinds, venetian
USE venetian blinds

blinds, venetian window
USE venetian blinds

blinds, vertical
USE vertical blinds

blinds, window
USE blinds (coverings)

blister glaze
MT.1997
SN Ceramic glaze that produces a broken blister effect. Made by combining an ordinary glaze with grains of a material that will become gaseous under firing. (MAYER)
UF glaze, blister

blistering
KT.245
HN January 1993 descriptor moved
ALT blistered
SN Bulging out from the main mass or surface, such as paint. (W)

blisters
DE.2

blitz-back saws
TH.1563
ALT blitz-back saw
SN Back saws with removable interchangeable blades and a thumb hook at the toe. (SALAM)
UF blitz saws
saws, blitz
saws, blitz-back

blitz saws
USE blitz-back saws

blizzards
KM.146   (L,R)
HN May 1991 alternate term added
February 1991 descriptor moved
February 1991 scope note added
ALT blizzard
SN Long, severe snowstorms, often accompanied by strong winds. (WCOL9)

Blochflöten
USE recorders

block and spindle stretchers
PJ.2890
HN March 1993 descriptor moved
ALT block and spindle stretcher
UF block and turned stretchers
stretchers, block and spindle
stretchers, block and turned

block and tackle
TH.484   (N,B)
SN Mechanisms or apparatus as ropes and pulley blocks; used for hoisting, lowering, and shifting objects or materials. (RHDEL2)
UF tackles

block and turned stretchers
USE block and spindle stretchers

block, Belgian
USE Belgian block

block bond
USE stack bond

block books
VW.1019   (H,L)
HN June 1992 descriptor added
ALT block book
SN Books in which the entire text and illustrations for each individual page is printed from a single carved wood block.
UF block-books
blockbooks
books, block
xylographica

block-books
USE block books

block capitals
USE cushion capitals

block carriages
USE block mountings

block, cinder
USE cinder block

block, clinker
USE cinder block

block cornices
PJ.1681
HN March 1993 descriptor moved
ALT block cornice
SN Use for cornices of slight projection, with plain blocklike modillions and simple bed moldings.
UF cornices, block

block cutters
USE wood engravers

block diagrams
VW.149
HN November 1992 descriptor moved
ALT block diagram
SN Diagrams using labeled blocks connected by straight lines to represent the relationship of parts or phases. (W)
UF diagrams, block

block engravers
USE wood engravers

block feet
PJ.2793
HN March 1993 descriptor moved
ALT block foot
SN Feet on furniture in the shape of a cube, generally used with square untapered legs. (W)
UF feet, block

block-front
SEE blockfront

block, hollow
USE hollow masonry units

block knives
TH.1475   (N)
ALT block knife
UF knives, block
knives, stock
stock knives

block letter
USE sans serif

block mountings
PJ.3173
ALT block mounting
SN Gun mounts featuring a block made of two rigidly joined triangular or trapezoidal side panels, supporting the trunnions on which the gun barrel rests.
UF block carriages
carriages, block
mountings, block

block planes
TH.1519   (N)
ALT block plane
SN Small hand-held planes, either of wood or metal, with low-angled cutting blades; used for small work, to clean up rough spots, and especially to clean up end grain and miters.
UF planes, block

block planes, straight
USE strike blocks

block plans
VC.121
HN April 1992 descriptor moved
ALT block plan
SN Use for plans of building sites with structures indicated by simple outlines or shapes.
UF plans, block

block printing
KT.694   (L,R)
HN January 1993 related term added
November 1991 lead-in term deleted, was block printing, relief
October 1991 descriptor moved
April 1991 scope note changed
March 1991 alternate term added
October 1990 lead-in terms added
October 1990 lead-in term deleted, was relief block printing
ALT block-printed
SN Use for printing from wooden blocks, as in block books before movable type, or from wood or occasionally metal blocks on textile. Sometimes used loosely with reference to relief printmaking processes; there prefer relief printing.
UF printing, block
printing, wood block
wood block printing
RT wood blocks

block prints
USE relief prints

<block quilts>
TC.214
RT blocks (quilt components)

block scrapers
TH.1145
HN December 1992 descriptor moved
ALT block scraper
SN Flat, rigid pieces of steel having ei-

ther plain or toothed edges; used for applications such as smoothing plaster and clay. (QCKAIE)
UF scrapers, block

blockboard
MT.3053   (B)
HN March 1992 descriptor moved
SN A plywood board in which veneer layers used in the core are replaced by blocks of wood, the direction of grain of the blocks running at right angles to that of the adjacent veneer. (W)

blockbooks
USE block books

blocked bindings
USE panel stamp bindings

blocked columns
HN September 1991 descriptor deleted, made lead-in to banded columns

blocked columns
USE banded columns

blockfront
DC.79
HN October 1992 descriptor moved
UK block-front
SN Use with reference to furniture pieces having a front the center of which recedes in a flattened curve between convex sections of similar flattened curves. (DDA)
UF swell'd front

blockhouses
RK.823   (A,N)
ALT blockhouse
SN Fortified log structures with loopholes or ports in their sides which permit gunfire in all directions. (HAS)

blocking chisels
TH.1334
HN December 1992 descriptor moved
ALT blocking chisel
SN Any rugged, broad-edged stone masons' chisels. (MEANS)
UF bolsters (blocking chisels)
chisels, blocking

blocking in
USE laying in

blocking out
USE stopping out

blocks (city blocks)
USE city blocks

blocks (printing)
USE printing blocks

blocks (pulley blocks)
USE pulley blocks

blocks (quilt components)
PJ.2674

ALT block (quilt component)
SN The basic unit of many quilt tops which, sewn together or to setting blocks or sashes, create the design. Blocks are composed of one or many patches, either pieced or appliquéd. Blocks are commonly square, but can also be in other geometric shapes such as hexagons or circles.
UF blocks, pattern
blocks, quilt
pattern blocks
quilt blocks
quilt squares
squares (quilt components)
squares, quilt
RT <block quilts>
contained crazy quilts
four-patch quilts
nine-patch quilts
patches (quilt components)

blocks (shaped masses)
PE.35   (A,L,B)
HN October 1992 descriptor moved
October 1992 scope note added
October 1992 related terms added
October 1992 alternate term added
October 1992 descriptor changed, was block
ALT block (shaped mass)
SN Solid masses or hollow units having approximately flat faces.
RT Belgian block
blocks (toys)
masonry units
miter blocks
shaving blocks

blocks (toys)
TV.140   (L,N)
ALT block (toy)
SN Lightweight solids, usually cubical and often of wood, plastic, or similar material, occurring in sets and designed as children's toys.
UF blocks, toy
toy blocks
RT blocks (shaped masses)

blocks, alphabet
USE alphabet blocks

blocks, arch
USE voussoirs

blocks, building
USE building blocks

blocks, Chinese
USE woodblocks

blocks, chopping
USE chopping blocks

blocks, city
USE city blocks

blocks, color
USE color blocks

blocks, colour
SEE color blocks

blocks, corner
USE corner blocks

blocks, dapping
USE dapping blocks

blocks, end-grain
USE end-grain blocks

blocks, filing
USE filing blocks

blocks, fixing
USE nailing blocks

blocks, gage
USE gage blocks

blocks, gauge
USE gage blocks

blocks, holding
USE holding blocks

blocks, impost
USE impost blocks

blocks, key
USE key blocks

blocks, lino
USE linoleum blocks

blocks, linoleum
USE linoleum blocks

<blocks: metalworking tools>
TH.1194

blocks, miter
USE miter blocks

blocks, mitre
SEE miter blocks

blocks, nailing
USE nailing blocks

blocks of flats
USE apartment houses

blocks, pattern
USE blocks (quilt components)

blocks, picture
USE picture blocks

blocks, plank
USE plank-grain blocks

blocks, plank-grain
USE plank-grain blocks

blocks, plate
USE plate number blocks

blocks, plate number
USE plate number blocks

blocks, point
USE point blocks

blocks, precision
USE gage blocks

blocks, printing
USE printing blocks

blocks, pulley
USE pulley blocks

blocks, punch
USE punch blocks

blocks, quilt
USE blocks (quilt components)

blocks, sanding
USE sanding blocks

blocks, setting
USE setting blocks

blocks, shaving
USE shaving blocks

blocks, side-grain
USE plank-grain blocks

blocks, size
USE gage blocks

blocks, skew
USE kneelers (gable components)

blocks, slab
USE slab blocks

blocks, strike
USE strike blocks

blocks, striking
USE striking blocks

blocks, temple
USE temple blocks

blocks, text
USE text blocks

blocks, tower
USE skyscrapers

blocks, toy
USE blocks (toys)

blocks, whetting
USE saw clamps

blocks, wood
USE wood blocks
woodblocks

blockwork breakwaters
RK.525
ALT blockwork breakwater
UF breakwaters, blockwork

blood (animal material)
MT.2537 (L,R)
HN March 1992 scope note added
March 1992 descriptor changed, was **blood**
February 1992 descriptor moved
SN Fluid that circulates in the principal vascular system of vertebrate animals. (W)

Blood (Native American)
FL.1389 (L)
UF Kainah

blood banks
PJ.1234 (L)
HN March 1993 descriptor moved
ALT blood bank
SN Includes spaces in rooms as well as rooms and buildings where blood or blood plasma is collected, processed, stored, and distributed.
UF banks, blood

blood, dragon's
USE dragon's blood

blood red
USE moderate red
strong red
vivid red

blood-stone
SEE bloodstone

blood-wood
SEE bloodwood

bloodstone
MT.579
HN April 1992 descriptor moved
March 1992 related term added
February 1992 scope note added
UK blood-stone
SN A green chalcedony sprinkled with red dots.
UF heliotrope
RT gemstone

bloodwood
MT.2740
HN March 1992 descriptor moved
UK blood-wood

bloom
DE.3
HN November 1992 descriptor moved
November 1990 descriptor added
SN Whitish or foggy effect on various types of surfaces, such as may appear on the varnish of a painting.
UF chill

bloom, peach
USE peach bloom

bloomers
TE.227 (N)
UK knickers
SN Drawers with full, loose legs gathered above or below the knee; worn by women and children.
RT camiknickers
drawers (underpants)

blot drawing
KT.392
SN A technique, usually in watercolor, in which the design is derived from an accidental mark or blot. (THDAT)
UF drawing, blot

blot drawings
VC.201
HN April 1992 descriptor moved
ALT blot drawing
UF drawings, blot

blotters
VW.584 (N)
HN November 1992 descriptor moved
ALT blotter
SN Books in which entries of transactions or occurrences are made as they take place, usually pending their transfer to permanent record books; such as a police blotter or general merchandise store blotter. (GAHLM)

blotting paper
MT.1464
HN April 1993 descriptor moved
UF paper, blotting

blouses
TE.44 (L,N)
ALT blouse
SN Women's or children's main garments for the upper body, usually lightweight and loose-fitting, made with or without sleeves and worn over or tucked in the waistband of a skirt or trousers. Also, women's garments cut in the style of a man's classic, tailored-cut shirt, having a notch collar, collar band, front placket opening, and usually long sleeves with cuffs.

blouses, middy
USE middy blouses

blouses, peek-a-boo
USE peek-a-boo blouses

blouses, tailored
USE shirtwaists

blow dryers
TH.386
HN January 1993 descriptor added
ALT blow dryer
SN Small, usually hand-held electrical appliances that dry hair by emitting a stream of warm air. (RHDEL2)
UF dryers, blow

blow-forward action
DC.222
HN November 1992 descriptor added
SN Use to describe automatic and semi-automatic firearms in which the pressure of the propellant gas is used to force the barrel forward from a standing breech to open the action and eject the fired case. A spring brings the barrel back to firing position and also reloads and cocks the firearm. (QCKDWT)
UF action, blow-forward
blow-forward system
system, blow-forward

blow-forward system
USE blow-forward action

blow-irons
SEE blowpipes

blow joints
USE blown joints

blow lamps
USE blowtorches

blow molding
KT.328
HN March 1993 alternate term changed, was blow molded
August 1992 lead-in term added
ALT blow-molded
UK blow moulding
UKA blow-moulded
SN Forming process whereby a hollow unit is formed and then forced, by internal pneumatic pressure, against a surrounding mold shaped to form a bottle or other container. Usually used with reference to glass and plastics.
UF mold-blowing
molding, blow
moulding, blow

blow moulding
SEE blow molding

blow-pipes (glassmaking tools)
SEE blowpipes

blow-pipes (weapons)
SEE blowguns

blow-tubes
SEE blowpipes

blow-up furniture
USE inflatable furniture

blowback action
DC.223
HN November 1992 descriptor added
SN Use to describe automatic and semi-automatic firearms in which the pressure of the propellant gas is used to force the bolt to the rear, independently of the barrel, which does not move relative to the receiver. (QCKDWT)
UF action, blowback
blowback operation
blowback system
operation, blowback
system, blowback

blowback operation
USE blowback action

blowback system
USE blowback action

blowers
PJ.819 (L)
HN March 1993 descriptor moved
November 1990 scope note added
ALT blower
SN Use for heavy-duty fans, such as those for ventilating building shafts or forcing air through large ducted systems.

blowers, hair
USE hair dryers

blowguns
TK.222 (L,N)
ALT blowgun
UK blow-pipes (weapons)
UKA blow-pipe (weapon)
SN Projectile weapons consisting basically of a long narrow tube of wood, cane, reed, or metal, through which small darts or pellets are propelled by means of the user's breath.
UF blowpipes (weapons)

blowhorn stakes
TH.1225 (N)
ALT blowhorn stake
SN Long, tapered stakes used for a variety of shaping tasks with sheet metal. (RUSERW)
UF stakes, blowhorn

blowing irons
USE blowpipes

blowing pipes
USE blowpipes

blowirons
USE blowpipes

blowlamps
USE blowtorches

blown glass
MT.279
HN March 1993 descriptor moved
February 1993 scope note added
SN Glassware shaped by blowing air through a blowpipe into a glob of molten glass.
UF glass, blown

blown joints
PJ.687
HN April 1993 descriptor moved
ALT blown joint
SN Plumbing joints sealed with the use of a blowtorch. (MEANS)
UF blow joints
joints, blown

blown molded glass
USE blown three-mold glass

blown oil
MT.1109
HN April 1992 descriptor moved
SN A thickened oil obtained by blowing a fatty acid, such as linseed oil or fish oil; used in paint and varnish as a drying oil and in lubricant. (W)
UF oil, blown

blown papers
USE flock papers

blown three-mold glass
MT.282
HN December 1992 descriptor added
SN Term of convenience used to describe a type of mold-blown glassware blown in full-size molds that usually consist of three parts, but occasionally the term is used to de-

scribe glassware made in two-, four-, or five-part molds.
UF blown molded glass
glass, blown molded
glass, blown three-mold
glass, three mold
three mold glass

blowpipes
TH.1135   (L,N)
HN December 1992 descriptor added
ALT blowpipe
UK blow-pipes (glassmaking tools)
SN Long metal tubes on the end of which a quantity of molten glass is gathered and through which air is blown to expand and shape it. (W)
UF blow-irons
blow-tubes
blowing irons
blowing pipes
blowirons
blowtubes

blowpipes (weapons)
USE blowguns

blowtorches
TH.512   (L,N)
ALT blowtorch
UF blow lamps
blowlamps

blowtubes
USE blowpipes

blowups
USE enlargements

bludgeons
USE clubs (weapons)

blue
DL.243   (L,R)

blue, Alexandria
USE Egyptian blue

blue-and-green
FL.2014

blue-and-white, Transitional
USE Kraak

blue, Antwerp
USE Antwerp blue
dark blue
grayish blue

blue, aqua
USE light greenish blue
very light greenish blue

blue, artificial ultramarine
USE artificial ultramarine blue

blue ashes
USE azurite
blue verditer

blue, azure
USE smalt

blue, azurite
USE grayish blue

moderate greenish blue
moderate purplish blue

blue, baby
USE bluish gray
light bluish gray
pale blue
very light blue
very light greenish blue
very pale blue

blue, Berlin
USE dark blue
Prussian blue

blue bice
USE azurite
blue verditer

blue black
USE bluish gray
dark bluish gray
vine black

blue, blackish
USE blackish blue

blue, Bremen
USE azurite
blue verditer
light greenish blue
moderate bluish green

blue brick
MT.103
HN April 1992 descriptor moved
SN A brick of high strength whose blue color results from firing in a kiln with a flame of low oxygen content. (DAC)
UF blue brick, Staffordshire
brick, blue
brick, sewer
brick, Staffordshire blue
sewer brick
Staffordshire blue brick

blue brick, Staffordshire
USE blue brick

blue, bright
USE brilliant blue
brilliant greenish blue
light greenish blue
moderate greenish blue
strong blue
strong bluish green
strong greenish blue
vivid blue

blue, bright cerulean
USE moderate blue
strong greenish blue

blue, bright copen
USE strong blue

blue, bright greenish
USE vivid greenish blue

blue, bright open
USE brilliant blue

blue, bright peacock
USE brilliant greenish blue
strong greenish blue

blue, bright periwinkle
USE light violet

blue, bright reddish
USE vivid purplish blue

blue, bright teal
USE dark greenish blue
moderate greenish blue

blue, bright turquoise
USE brilliant greenish blue
strong bluish green
strong greenish blue

blue, brilliant greenish
USE brilliant greenish blue

blue, brilliant peacock
USE strong greenish blue

blue, brilliant purplish
USE brilliant purplish blue

blue, bronze
USE Prussian blue

blue, Brunswick
USE Prussian blue

blue carmine
MT.2089
HN April 1992 descriptor moved
UF carmine, blue

blue, cendre
USE azurite
blue verditer

blue, cerulean
USE cerulean blue
light blue
moderate blue
strong blue
strong greenish blue
vivid blue
vivid greenish blue

blue, Chinese
USE Prussian blue

blue, cobalt
USE cobalt blue
strong greenish blue
vivid blue

blue collar workers
HG.73   (L)
HN March 1992 alternate terms added
ALT blue collar worker
blue collar worker's
blue collar workers'
SN Wage earners performing manual work which usually calls for the wearing of work clothes or protective clothing on the job.
UF manual workers
workers, blue collar
workers, manual

blue, copen
USE light blue
moderate blue
strong blue

blue, copper
USE azurite
blue verditer

blue, cornflower
USE cornflower blue
moderate purplish blue

blue, cyan
USE moderate bluish green
moderate greenish blue

blue, cyanine
USE dark purplish blue
moderate purplish blue

blue, dark
USE dark blue

blue, dark aniline
USE dark grayish blue
dark grayish purple

blue, dark cerulean
USE dark greenish blue
grayish blue

blue, dark delft
USE dark grayish blue

blue, dark grayish
USE dark grayish blue

blue, dark greenish
USE dark greenish blue

blue, dark peacock
USE dark greenish blue

blue, dark purplish
USE dark purplish blue

blue, dark steel
USE grayish blue

blue, dark teal
USE dark grayish blue
dark greenish blue

blue de tungstène
USE tungsten blue

blue, deep
USE deep blue

blue, deep cerulean
USE dark greenish blue
deep greenish blue
moderate blue
moderate greenish blue

blue, deep delft
USE grayish blue

blue, deep greenish
USE deep greenish blue

blue, deep peacock
USE dark greenish blue
moderate greenish blue

blue, deep purplish
USE deep purplish blue

blue, deep royal
USE dark blue
deep blue
deep purplish blue
moderate purplish blue

blue, deep sapphire
USE dark blue
deep blue
moderate purplish blue

blue, deep teal
USE dark bluish green
dark greenish blue
moderate greenish blue

blue, delft
USE dark blue
grayish blue
grayish purplish blue
moderate blue
pale purplish blue

blue, della robbia
USE light blue
moderate blue

blue denim jackets
USE jean jackets

blue, diamin azo
USE dark grayish purple
grayish violet

blue, dull
USE blackish blue
dark bluish gray
dark grayish blue
deep blue
grayish blue
grayish purplish blue
light blue
moderate blue
pale blue
pale purplish blue
strong blue
very pale blue
very pale purplish blue

blue, dull greenish
USE blackish blue
dark grayish blue
grayish blue
pale blue
very pale blue

blue, dull reddish
USE blackish blue
dark grayish blue
grayish blue
grayish purplish blue
pale blue
pale purplish blue
very pale blue
very pale purplish blue

blue, dumont
USE smalt

blue, Egyptian
USE Egyptian blue

blue, French
USE artificial ultramarine blue
light purplish blue
strong purplish blue
vivid purplish blue

blue frit
USE Egyptian blue

blue, gentian
USE moderate purplish blue

blue, genuine ultramarine
USE strong blue
vivid blue

blue, Gmelin's
USE artificial ultramarine blue

blue, granite
USE light gray

blue, graphite
USE blackish blue
dark grayish blue
dark purplish blue
grayish purplish blue

blue gray
USE bluish gray
light greenish gray
medium gray

blue, gray
USE light bluish gray
light purplish gray
moderate blue
pale blue
pale purplish blue

blue, grayish
USE grayish blue

blue, grayish purplish
USE grayish purplish blue

blue green
USE brilliant bluish green
brilliant green
light bluish green
light green
light yellowish green
moderate bluish green
moderate green
strong bluish green
strong green
very light green
vivid bluish green

blue-green
USE moderate greenish blue

blue green black, dull
USE blackish blue
dark grayish blue

blue green, bright
USE brilliant green
strong green
vivid green

blue green, dark
USE blackish green
dark grayish green
dark green

light bluish green
moderate bluish green
moderate greenish blue
strong bluish green
strong green
very dark green

blue green, dark grayish
USE dark gray
dark greenish gray

blue green, deep grayish
USE grayish green

blue green, grayish
USE grayish green
moderate bluish green

blue green, light
USE brilliant green
light bluish green
light green

blue green, moderate
USE moderate bluish green

blue-green oxide
MT.2148
HN April 1992 descriptor moved
UF Blaugrünoxid
Grünblauoxid
oxide, blue-green

blue green, pale
USE pale green
very pale green

blue, greenish
USE greenish blue

blue, Guimet's
USE artificial ultramarine blue

blue gum
MT.2743   (L)
HN March 1992 descriptor moved
UF Eucalyptus globulus
gum, blue

blue, Haarlem
USE Antwerp blue

blue, Hungary
USE cobalt blue
smalt

blue, indanthrone
USE indanthrone blue

blue, Indian
USE indigo

blue, indigo
USE dark grayish blue
grayish blue
grayish purplish blue

blue, ink
USE dark grayish blue

blue, intense
USE indigo
phthalocyanine blue

blue, irgazin
USE irgazin blue

blue, iron
USE dark gray
Prussian blue

blue, Italian
USE Egyptian blue

blue jean jackets
USE jean jackets

blue jeans
USE jeans

blue, kingfisher
USE strong greenish blue

blue, king's
USE cobalt blue

blue lake
MT.2090
HN April 1992 descriptor moved
UF lacree
lake, blue

blue, lapis lazuli
USE deep blue
moderate blue

blue lavender
USE pale purplish blue

blue, lazuline
USE ultramarine blue

blue, Leithner's
USE Leithner's blue

blue, light
USE light blue

blue, light aqua
USE pale blue
very light greenish blue

blue, light cerulean
USE brilliant greenish blue
light blue
strong greenish blue

blue, light copen
USE light blue

blue, light cornflower
USE light purplish blue
light violet
moderate purplish blue
moderate violet

blue, light gray
USE grayish blue
pale blue

blue, light greenish
USE light greenish blue

blue, light methyl
USE brilliant blue

blue, light periwinkle
USE light purplish blue
light violet
very pale violet

blue, light purplish
USE light purplish blue

blue, light turquoise
USE light greenish blue
very light greenish blue

blue, lime
USE artificial ultramarine blue
blue verditer

blue lines
USE bluelines

blue, logwood
USE dark bluish gray

blue mahoe
USE mahoe

blue, manganese
USE manganese blue

blue, Maya
USE Maya blue

blue, Mayan
USE Maya blue

blue, medium
USE dark blue
dark greenish blue
grayish purplish blue
moderate blue
moderate greenish blue

blue, medium teal
USE moderate greenish blue

blue, medium turquoise
USE moderate greenish blue

blue, methyl
USE vivid blue

blue, midnight
USE black
blackish blue
blackish purple
bluish black
dark bluish gray
dark purplish blue

blue, Milori
USE Prussian blue

blue mineral
USE azurite

blue, mineral
USE Antwerp blue

blue, moderate
USE moderate blue

blue, moderate greenish
USE moderate greenish blue

blue, moderate purplish
USE moderate purplish blue

blue, Monastral
USE dark blue
moderate purplish blue
phthalocyanine blue

blue, Monastral fast
USE phthalocyanine blue

blue, mountain
USE   azurite
   blue verditer

blue, navy
USE   dark purplish blue
   grayish purplish blue
   moderate purplish blue

blue, Neuwieder
USE   blue verditer

blue, new
USE   artificial ultramarine blue
   cobalt blue

blue ocher
   MT.2085
HN   August 1992 lead-in term added
   April 1992 descriptor moved
UK   blue ochre
UF   ocher, blue
   ochre, blue
   vivianite

blue ochre
SEE   blue ocher

blue, olympia
USE   cobalt blue

blue, pale
USE   pale blue

blue, pale aqua
USE   very pale blue

blue, pale cerulean
USE   light blue
   very light blue

blue, pale grayish
USE   very pale blue

blue, pale periwinkle
USE   very pale purple
   very pale purplish blue

blue, pale purplish
USE   pale purplish blue

blue, pale Windsor
USE   light blue

blue, Paris
USE   Prussian blue
   strong blue

blue, paste
USE   Prussian blue

blue, pastel
USE   grayish blue
   pale blue
   very pale blue

blue, peacock
USE   dark greenish blue
   moderate greenish blue
   strong greenish blue

blue, pearl
USE   light gray

blue, periwinkle
USE   light purplish blue
   light violet

blue, permanent
USE   artificial ultramarine blue
   strong purplish blue

blue, phenyl
USE   vivid purplish blue

blue, phthalocyanine
USE   phthalocyanine blue

blue pigment
   MT.2082
HN   April 1993 descriptor moved
UF   pigment, blue

blue pigment, artificial inorganic
USE   artificial inorganic blue pigment

blue pigment, artificial organic
USE   synthetic organic blue pigment

blue pigment, inorganic
USE   inorganic blue pigment

blue pigment, organic
USE   organic blue pigment

blue pigment, synthetic inorganic
USE   artificial inorganic blue pigment

blue pigment, synthetic organic
USE   synthetic organic blue pigment

blue plum
USE   dark grayish purple
   dark violet
   grayish violet

blue, Pompeian
USE   Egyptian blue

blue, powder
USE   bluish gray
   deep blue
   moderate blue
   pale blue
   pale purplish blue

blue, Pozzuoli
USE   Egyptian blue

blue-printing
SEE   blueprint process

blue process prints
USE   blueprints

blue, Prussian
USE   dark greenish blue
   deep greenish blue
   moderate blue
   Prussian blue
   strong blue

blue, purplish
USE   purplish blue

blue, reddish
USE   brilliant purplish blue
   dark purplish blue
   deep purplish blue
   light purplish blue

   moderate purplish blue
   strong purplish blue
   very light purplish blue

blue, royal
USE   artificial ultramarine blue
   dark blue
   deep blue
   deep purplish blue
   moderate blue
   moderate purplish blue
   strong blue
   strong purplish blue
   vivid blue
   vivid purplish blue

blue, Sanders
USE   blue verditer

blue, sapphire
USE   dark blue
   deep purplish blue
   strong blue
   strong purplish blue
   vivid blue
   vivid purplish blue

blue, Saxon
USE   smalt

blue shale
USE   bluestone

blue slate
   MT.808
HN   April 1992 descriptor moved
UF   slate, blue

blue, slate
USE   dark bluish gray
   grayish blue
   moderate bluish green

blue, smalt
USE   vivid purplish blue

blue spruce
   MT.2989
HN   March 1992 descriptor moved
UF   blue spruce, Colorado
   Colorado blue spruce
   Colorado spruce
   Picea pangens
   pine, spruce
   spruce, blue
   spruce, Colorado
   spruce, Colorado blue
   spruce pine

blue spruce, Colorado
USE   blue spruce

blue, steel
USE   grayish blue
   Prussian blue

blue-stone
SEE   bluestone

blue-stone, Hudson
SEE   Hudson bluestone

blue-stone, North River
SEE   North River bluestone

blue, strong
USE strong blue

blue, strong greenish
USE strong greenish blue

blue, strong purplish
USE strong purplish blue

blue, teal
USE dark grayish blue
 dark greenish blue
 moderate greenish blu

blue, Thalo (color)
USE very dark greenish blue
 dark greenish blue

blue, Thalo (TM)
USE phthalocyanine blue

blue, Thénard's
USE cobalt blue

blue, tungsten
USE tungsten blue

blue, Turnbull's
USE Prussian blue

blue turquoise
USE brilliant greenish blue
 light greenish blue

blue, turquoise
USE light bluish green
 light greenish blue
 moderate greenish blue
 strong greenish blue

blue, ultramarine
USE ultramarine blue
 vivid blue
 vivid purplish blue

blue ultramarine ash
USE moderate blue

blue, Venetian
USE Egyptian blue

blue verditer
 MT.2096
 HN May 1992 lead-in terms added
 May 1992 related term added
 January 1992 descriptor moved
 UF ashes, blue
 bice, blue
 blue ashes
 blue bice
 blue, Bremen
 blue, cendre
 blue, copper
 blue, lime
 blue, mountain
 blue, Neuwieder
 blue, Sanders
 Bremen blue
 copper blue
 Kalkblau
 lime blue
 mountain blue
 Neuwied blue

 Neuwieder blue
 Sanders blue
 verditer
 verditer, blue
 RT azurite

blue verditer (color)
USE moderate blue

blue, very dark greenish
USE very dark greenish blue

blue, very light
USE very light blue

blue, very light greenish
USE very light greenish blue

blue, very light purplish
USE very light purplish blue

blue, very pale
USE very pale blue

blue, very pale purplish
USE very pale purplish blue

blue, Vestorian
USE Egyptian blue

blue, Vienna
USE cobalt blue

blue violet
USE light purplish blue
 vivid purplish blue
 vivid violet

blue, violet
USE strong purplish blue

blue violet black
USE dark gray
 dark purplish gray

blue violet, dark grayish
USE grayish violet

blue violet, deep
USE vivid purplish blue
 vivid violet

blue violet, dull
USE brilliant violet
 moderate violet
 strong purplish blue
 strong violet

blue violet, grayish
USE light purplish blue
 moderate purplish blue
 moderate violet
 strong purplish blue
 strong violet

blue violet, light
USE vivid purplish blue

blue violet, light grayish
USE light purplish blue

blue violet, pale
USE brilliant purplish blue

blue violet, pale grayish
USE very pale purplish blue

blue violet, soft
USE brilliant violet

blue, vivid
USE vivid blue

blue, vivid cerulean
USE strong greenish blue

blue, vivid greenish
USE vivid greenish blue

blue, vivid peacock
USE strong greenish blue

blue, vivid purplish
USE vivid purplish blue

blue, vivid turquoise
USE moderate greenish blue
 strong bluish green
 strong greenish blue

blue, white
USE light bluish gray

blue, Williamson's
USE Prussian blue

bluebooks
USE social registers

blueline prints
 VW.1081 (N)
 HN March 1993 descriptor moved
 ALT blueline print
 SN Use for prints made on light-sensitized surfaces that produce blue images on neutral backgrounds. For white images on blue backgrounds, use blueprints.
 UF bluelines (whiteprints)
 prints, blueline

bluelines
 VW.1194
 HN March 1993 descriptor added
 ALT blueline
 SN Proofs of copy prepared for printing, made on light-sensitive paper from negatives stripped and ready for platemaking.
 UF blue lines
 blueprints (proofs)
 blues

bluelines (whiteprints)
USE blueline prints

blueprint process
 KT.532 (L,B)
 UK blue-printing
 SN A photographic process using iron salts and producing an image in Prussian blue. For the resulting prints, use blueprints if they are reproductions of technical drawings, or cyanotypes if they are camera images or photograms.
 UF cyanotype
 ferroprussiate process

blueprints
 VW.1067 (A,L,N)

HN March 1993 lead-in term changed,
     was **cyanotypes (reproductions)**
     March 1993 descriptor moved
ALT blueprint
SN Use for reproductive prints of archi-
     tectural and other technical draw-
     ings having white images on blue
     backgrounds, produced by the blue-
     print process. For blue images on
     white backgrounds, use **blueline
     prints.** For blue-toned photographs
     produced by the blueprint process,
     use **cyanotypes.**
UF blue process prints
     cyanotypes (photocopies)
     iron process prints
     prints, blue process
     prints, iron process
     prints, white line
     white line prints

blueprints (photographs)
USE cyanotypes

blueprints (proofs)
USE bluelines

blues
USE bluelines

bluestone
     MT.892
HN March 1992 descriptor moved
UK blue-stone
UF blue shale
     shale, blue

bluestone, Hudson
USE Hudson bluestone

bluestone, North River
USE North River bluestone

Bluff-dweller
     FL.899

bluffs
USE cliffs

bluish black
     DL.261
UF black, bluish
     black, dull blue green
     blue, midnight
     centroid color 193
     dark navy
     dull blue green black
     midnight blue
     navy, dark

bluish gray
     DL.258
UF aqua gray
     baby blue
     black, blue
     blue, baby
     blue black
     blue gray
     blue, powder
     centroid color 191
     gray, aqua
     gray, blue
     gray, bluish

     gray, light Payne's
     light Payne's gray
     Payne's gray, light
     pewter (color)
     powder blue
     slate (color)

bluish gray, dark
USE dark bluish gray

bluish gray green
USE grayish green
     pale green

bluish gray green, dark
USE dark bluish green
     dark grayish green
     grayish green
     moderate bluish green

bluish gray green, deep
USE grayish green

bluish gray, light
USE light bluish gray

bluish green
     DL.226
UF green, bluish

bluish green, bright
USE vivid bluish green

bluish green, brilliant
USE brilliant bluish green

bluish green, dark
USE dark bluish green

bluish green, deep
USE deep bluish green

bluish green, dull
USE blackish green
     dark grayish green
     grayish green
     pale green
     very pale green

bluish green, light
USE light bluish green

bluish green, moderate
USE moderate bluish green

bluish green, strong
USE strong bluish green

bluish green, very dark
USE very dark bluish green

bluish green, very light
USE very light bluish green

bluish green, vivid
USE vivid bluish green

bluish lavender
USE light violet

bluish lavender, pale
USE very pale purple

bluish lavender, pale bluish
USE very pale violet

bluish olive
USE dark grayish olive green
     dark olive green
     deep olive green
     grayish olive green
     moderate olive green
     strong olive green

bluish pink
USE brilliant purplish pink
     dark purplish pink
     deep purplish pink
     grayish purplish pink
     light grayish purplish red
     light purplish pink
     moderate purplish pink
     pale purplish pink
     strong purplish pink

bluish red
USE deep purplish red
     moderate purplish red
     strong purplish red
     very deep purplish red

bluish red, dull
USE dark purplish red
     moderate purplish red
     very dark purplish red

bluish slate black
USE dark blue

bluish violet
USE brilliant violet
     dark violet
     deep violet
     light violet
     moderate violet
     strong violet
     very light violet
     vivid purplish blue
     vivid violet

bluish violet, bright
USE vivid violet

bluish violet, dark
USE dark violet
     grayish purple
     grayish violet

bluish violet, dark dull
USE dark purple
     grayish violet
     moderate violet

bluish violet, deep dull
USE grayish purplish blue
     moderate violet
     pale purplish blue
     pale violet
     strong violet

bluish violet, dull
USE blackish purple
     brilliant violet
     dark grayish purple
     grayish violet
     light violet
     moderate violet
     pale purple
     strong violet

very pale purple
very pale violet

bluish violet, light
USE brilliant purplish blue
     brilliant violet
     strong purplish blue

bluish violet, light dull
USE light violet

bluish violet, pale
USE brilliant purplish blue

bluish white
     DL.257
UF centroid color 189
     white, bluish

blunderbuss pistols
     TK.173
ALT blunderbuss pistol
SN Pistols with a flaring muzzle like a
     blunderbuss, intended to be loaded
     with shot for use at close range.
     They were extremely popular from
     the mid-18th to the early 19th cen-
     tury. (BPOW)
UF boarding pistols
     musketoon pistols
     pistols, blunderbuss
     pistols, boarding
     pistols, musketoon

blunderbusses
     TK.196   (N)
ALT blunderbuss
SN Short-barrelled shotguns with a
     wide bore expanding gradually
     throughout its length, typically ter-
     minating in a flared or thickened
     muzzle, and often carrying a spring-
     activated bayonet that folded back
     along the barrel when not in use.
     They were designed to fire a quan-
     tity of shot at once against a mass of
     opponents, and were popular weap-
     ons for defending stage coaches,
     ships, and prisons from the 17th to
     the 19th century.

blunt arches
HN March 1991 descriptor deleted,
     made lead-in to **drop arches**

blunt arches
USE drop arches

blunt nails
     PJ.180
HN April 1993 descriptor moved
ALT blunt nail
UF nails, blunt

Boa
USE Babwa

boar-spear swords
     TK.99
ALT boar-spear sword
SN Hunting swords having a long,
     straight, slender blade widening to a
     heavy point like a spearhead, often
     with a cross bar at the base to pre-

vent the impaled prey from running
up the blade. (BLEAA)
UF boar swords
     swords, boar
     swords, boar-spear

boar-spears
SEE boar spears

boar spears
     TK.63
ALT boar spear
UK boar-spears
UKA boar-spear
SN Spears designed for hunting wild
     boars and other large game, having
     a transverse bar fitted below the
     broad blade.
UF boar-staffs
     spears, boar

boar-staffs
SEE boar spears

boar swords
USE boar-spear swords

board, 100% cotton rag
USE museum board

board, academy
USE academy board

board and batten
     MT.1796
SN Siding in which joints between verti-
     cally placed boards are covered by
     narrow strips of wood. (MEANS)
UF batten, board and

board, bristol
USE bristol board

board, building
USE building board

board, canvas
USE canvas board

board chairs
     TC.468
HN January 1993 descriptor moved
ALT board chair
SN Simple chairs consisting of a slab
     seat, four stick legs, and a plank
     back inserted into a slot in the seat.
     (BOYCE)
UF chairs, board
     chairs, plank
     plank chairs

board, chemical wood pulp
USE conservation board

board chests
     TC.866
HN January 1993 descriptor moved
ALT board chest
SN Simple chests constructed of six
     boards butted, lapped, nailed, and
     hinged together; an economical al-
     ternative to joined chests. (FAIRB)
UF boarded chests
     chests, board

chests, six-board
six-board chests

board, conservation
USE conservation board

board, coquille
USE coquille board

board, corrugated
USE corrugated board

board, fiber
USE fiberboard

board, fiber building
USE fiberboard

board figures, dummy
USE dummy board figures

board, flake
USE particle board

board, foamcore
USE Fome-Cor (TM)

board, form
USE form lumber

<board games>
     KQ.13
RT games

board games
     PC.60   (L,N)
ALT board game
SN Use for games in which a primary
     activity involves the moving of game
     pieces across a gameboard.
UF games, board

board, gypsum
USE gypsum board

board hammers
USE drop hammers

board, illustration
USE illustration board

board insulation
USE rigid (ALT of rigidity) + insulation

board, ivory
USE ivory board

board, jute
USE jute board

board knives
USE utility knives

board, mat
USE mat board

board, matched
USE matched lumber

board measure rules
USE board rules

board, mounting
USE mounting board

board, museum
USE museum board

board nails, gypsum
USE   gypsum board nails

board, particle
USE   particle board

board, poster
USE   poster board

board, pressing
SEE   pressboard

board, rag
USE   museum board

board-rooms
SEE   boardrooms

board, Ross (TM)
USE   Ross board (TM)

board rules
TN.55
ALT   board rule
SN   Measuring devices, usually in the form of flat sticks, bearing various scales for computing board feet.
UF   board measure rules
board sticks
rules, board
rules, board measure
sticks, board
sticks, tally
tally sticks

board saws
USE   pit saws

board sticks
USE   board rules

board, wall
USE   wallboard

board, wood-pulp
USE   pulpboard

boarded chests
USE   board chests

boarding homes
USE   rest homes

boarding houses
USE   lodging houses

boarding pikes
TK.55   (N)
ALT   boarding pike
SN   Pikes with comparatively short, stout staffs, used as weapons aboard warships from the 16th into the 20th century either when boarding a ship or to repel boarders.
UF   pikes, boarding

boarding pistols
USE   blunderbuss pistols

boarding schools
RK.763   (L,B)
ALT   boarding school
SN   Educational institutions at the elementary-secondary level in which

students are in residence while enrolled in an instructional program. (ERIC9)
UF   residential schools
schools, boarding
schools, residential

boardrooms
PJ.1000   (B)
HN   March 1993 descriptor moved
ALT   boardroom
UK   board-rooms
UKA   board-room
SN   Rooms that are designated for meetings of a board and usually contain a large conference table. (W)

boards (binding components)
PJ.3364
ALT   board (binding component)
SN   Stiff upper and lower covers of books, of various materials, often covered with leather, cloth or other material.

boards (flat objects)
PE.36   (N,B)
HN   November 1992 descriptor moved
November 1992 scope note added
November 1992 alternate term added
November 1992 descriptor changed, was **board**
ALT   board (flat object)
SN   Thin, flat, rigid objects, of considerable length or breadth compared to thickness, most often of wood, paperboard, or composite fiber materials.

boards (gameboards)
USE   gameboards

boards (organizations)
HN.94
ALT   board (organization)
SN   Groups of persons appointed to or elected to sit in council for the management or investigation of a public or private business, trust, or other organization or institution. (W)
UF   commissions (boards)

boards (stage floors)
USE   stage floors

boards (tables)
USE   tables (support furniture)

boards, back
USE   backboards (furniture components)

boards, bagatelle
USE   bagatelle tables

boards, bake
USE   bannock boards

boards, balance
USE   balance beams

boards, bannock
USE   bannock boards

boards, bread
USE   breadboards

boards, cake
USE   springerle boards

boards, candle
USE   candle slides

boards, cheese
USE   cheeseboards

boards, chopping
USE   cutting boards

boards, comb
USE   saddle boards

boards, corner
USE   corner boards

boards, counter
USE   counters

boards, cribbage
USE   cribbage boards

boards, cutting
USE   cutting boards

boards, dart
USE   dart boards

boards, dough
USE   breadboards

boards, dummy
USE   dummy board figures

boards, eaves
USE   eaves boards

boards, end
USE   end boards

boards, fascia
USE   fascia boards

boards, fat
USE   hawks

boards, governing
USE   boards of trustees

boards, health
USE   health boards

boards, hunting
USE   huntboards

boards, hymn
USE   hymn boards

boards, ironing
USE   ironing boards

boards, kneading
USE   breadboards

boards, ledger
USE   ledger boards

boards, lever
USE   louver boards

boards, louver
USE   louver boards

boards, luffer
USE   louver boards

boards, miter
USE   miter boards

boards, molding
USE   pastry boards

boards, mortar
USE   hawks

boards of directors
    HN.96   (L)
ALT   board of directors
UF   corporations, directors of
      directors, boards of
      directors of corporations

boards of health
USE   health boards

boards of trade
    HN.97   (L,B)
ALT   board of trade
SN   Organizations that regulate, pro-
      mote, supervise, or protect commer-
      cial or business enterprises. (W)
UF   chambers of commerce
      commerce, chambers of
      trade, boards of

boards of trustees
    HN.98
ALT   board of trustees
UF   boards, governing
      governing boards
      trustees, boards of

boards of zoning adjustment
USE   zoning boards

boards, park
USE   park commissions

boards, paste
USE   pastry boards

boards, pastry
USE   pastry boards

boards, public health
USE   health boards

boards, ribbon
USE   ledger boards

boards, saddle
USE   saddle boards

boards, sandwich
USE   sandwich boards

boards, serving
USE   sideboards

boards, skirting
USE   baseboards

boards, snow
USE   snow guards

boards, sounding
USE   sounding boards

boards, spot
USE   hawks

boards, springerle
USE   springerle boards

boards, surf
USE   surfboards

boards, table
USE   tables (support furniture)

boards, tea
USE   tea tables
      tea trays

boards, tilt
USE   table easels

boards, window
USE   window sills

boards, writing
USE   writing arms

boards, zoning
USE   zoning boards

boardwalks
    RM.179
HN   April 1993 descriptor moved
      January 1991 descriptor added
ALT   boardwalk
SN   Use for walkways of boards or
      planks, usually located along shores,
      especially beaches.

boas
    TE.661   (N)
ALT   boa
SN   Very long, elliptical neckpieces
      made of feathers, fur, or similar
      fluffy materials, especially popular
      in the 1890s.

boasted work
    KT.914
HN   January 1993 descriptor moved
      November 1990 descriptor added
UF   work, boasted

boasters
    TH.1335
HN   January 1993 scope note changed
      December 1992 descriptor moved
ALT   boaster
SN   Flat, broad chisels used in carving or
      dressing stone. (MEANS)

boat beds
USE   sleigh beds

boat clubs
    RG.172   (B)
HN   January 1992 scope note added
      November 1991 descriptor moved
ALT   boat club
SN   Water recreation complexes includ-
      ing clubhouse, marina, and associ-
      ated boating facilities.
UF   clubs, boat

boat davits
USE   davits

boat foundations
USE   raft foundations

boat lumber
    MT.3032
HN   March 1992 descriptor moved
SN   A term commonly applied to wide
      boards (12 inches to 16 inches in
      width) of lightweight clear wood,
      such as cedar, redwood, or white
      pine. (PUTNAM)
UF   lumber, boat

boat ramps
USE   launching ramps

boat spikes
USE   barge spikes

boatbuilders' axes
USE   shipwrights' axes

boater hats
USE   boaters

boaters
    TE.569   (N)
ALT   boater
SN   Straw hats with a straight brim, flat
      crown and a ribbon band.
UF   boater hats
      hats, boater

boathouses
    RK.1209   (A,L)
ALT   boathouse
SN   A building usually built partly in the
      water for the housing or storing of
      boats. (W)

boating
    KQ.101   (H)
RT   boats

boatneck sweaters
    TE.75
ALT   boatneck sweater
SN   Pullover sweaters having a neckline
      following the curve of the collar
      bone; high in the front and back,
      wide at the sides, and ending in
      shoulder seams.
UF   sweaters, boatneck

boats
    TX.297   (A,L,B,R)
ALT   boat
SN   Use for watercraft generally smaller
      and less seaworthy than ships and
      generally not designed to cross large
      open waters.
UF   craft, small
      small craft
RT   boating

boats, Adirondack guide
USE   Adirondack guideboats

boats, banana
USE   banana boats

boats, bum
USE   bumboats

boats, bushwack
USE   bushwack boats

boats, canal
USE   canal boats

boats, cargo
USE   cargo vessels

boats, class
USE   class boats

boats, deadrise
USE   deadrise boats

boats, development class
USE   development class boats

boats, duck
USE   gunning boats

boats, excursion
USE   excursion boats

boats, fishing
USE   fishing vessels

boats, flying
USE   flying boats

boats, gravy
USE   sauceboats

boats, guide
USE   guideboats

boats, gunning
USE   gunning boats

boats, hydrofoil
USE   hydrofoils

boats, incense
USE   incense boats

boats, jackass
USE   jackass barks

boats, jolly
USE   jolly boats

boats, lobster
USE   lobsterboats

boats, long
USE   longboats

boats, measurement-class
USE   development class boats

boats, motor torpedo
USE   motor torpedo boats

boats, packet
USE   packets

boats, picket
USE   picket boats

boats, pilot
USE   pilot boats

boats, pleasure
USE   yachts

boats, PT
USE   motor torpedo boats

boats, pulling
USE   pulling boats

boats, push
USE   yawl boats

boats, race
USE   raceboats

boats, rail-bird
USE   rail skiffs

boats, raised deck
USE   raised deck boats

boats, Rangeley
USE   Rangeley boats

boats, Rangeley Lake
USE   Rangeley boats

boats, restricted class
USE   development class boats

boats, seine
USE   seiners

boats, shanty
USE   houseboats

boats, ships'
USE   ships' boats

boats, skin
USE   skin boats

boats, sportfishing
USE   sportfishermen

boats, submarine
USE   submarines

boats, una
USE   catboats

boats, water
USE   water boats

boats, waterfowl
USE   gunning boats

boats, yawl
USE   yawl boats

boatswains' calls
USE   boatswains' whistles

boatswains' pipes
USE   boatswains' whistles

boatswains' whistles
      TT.37
ALT   boatswain's whistle
SN   Metal whistles traditionally used on
      ships by boatswain's mates to relay
      orders or to pipe senior naval offi-
      cers aboard; they were grasped in
      the hand when blown, the pitch ris-
      ing or falling as the hand was
      opened or closed.
UF   boatswains' calls
      boatswains' pipes
      bosuns' whistles
      calls, boatswains'
      pipes, boatswains'
      whistles, boatswains'
      whistles, bosuns'

boatyards
USE   shipyards

bob punches
USE   countersinks

bob-sleighs
USE   bobsleds

bob wigs
      TE.522
ALT   bob wig
SN   Wigs with the bottom locks turned
      up into bobs or short curls; always
      intended to be worn for undress.
      (EMAEA)
UF   bobs
      wigs, bob

bobaches
USE   bobeches

bobbin baskets
USE   loom baskets

bobbin lace
      MT.1577   (L)
HN   March 1993 lead-in terms added
      March 1993 descriptor moved
SN   Handmade lace made by inter-
      twisting threads wound on bobbins
      and worked over a pillow on which
      the pattern is marked out by pins.
      (W)
UF   bone lace
      cushion lace
      lace, bobbin
      lace, bone
      lace, cushion
      lace, pillow
      pillow lace

bobbin lace, Brussels
USE   Brussels lace (bobbin lace)

bobby pins
      TE.518   (N)
ALT   bobby pin
UK   hair-grips
UKA   hair-grip
SN   Flat, springlike metal hairpins used
      for both styling and holding the
      hair, having the prongs held close
      together by tension.
UF   grips
      kirby-grips
      pins, bobby

bobeches
      PJ.2901   (N)
ALT   bobeche
SN   Drip catchers fitted to the sockets of
      candleholders, may be fixed or re-
      movable and are usually made of
      metal or glass.
UF   bobaches
      catchers, drip
      drip catchers
      drip pans
      pans (lighting device components)
      pans, drip

Bobo
      FL.379   (L)

Bobo, Black
USE Bobo-Fing

Bobo-Fing
FL.380 (L)
UF Black Bobo
Bobo, Black

Bobo-Ule
USE Bwa

bobruns
USE bobsled runs

bobs
USE bob wigs
shillings

bobs, plumb
USE plumb bobs

bobsled runs
RK.1020 (B)
HN September 1990 scope note added
ALT bobsled run
SN Use for ice-covered courses for bob-sledding consisting of chutes with high walls, banked turns, and straightaways. (RHDEL2)
UF bobruns
runs, bobsled

bobsleds
TV.86 (L,N)
ALT bobsled
SN Use for heavy, sturdy sleds having two pairs of runners, a brake, and steering mechanism that enables the front rider to direct the sled down steeply banked chutes; found in two- and four-rider versions.
UF bob-sleighs
RT sleds

bocals
PJ.3226
ALT bocal
SN S-shaped crooks on bassoons and English horns that carry the mouth-piece.

bocks
TT.190
ALT bock
SN German mouth-blown bagpipes with a single horn-belled chanter and a bass drone. (NGDMI)

bodegónes
VC.602 (R)
ALT bodegón
SN Images, especially Spanish, in which still life predominates, though it may be part of a kitchen or eating scene.

bodhráns
TT.586 (L)
ALT bodhrán
SN Single-headed frame drums of Ireland, with a membrane of animal skin and a criss-cross arrangement of cord, sticks, or wire over the open end by which they are held with one

hand; they are struck by the free hand or alternately by the knobs at each end of the stick.

bodices
TE.50 (H,L,N,R)
ALT bodice
SN Close-fitting garments worn on the upper body, often laced and worn over a dress or blouse. Also, the upper part of a dress.
RT <costume components>
dresses

bodices, bust
USE brassieres

bodied oil
MT.1110
HN April 1992 descriptor moved
October 1990 descriptor moved
SN A drying oil whose drying properties have been increased.
UF oil, bodied

bodies (container components)
PJ.3088
ALT body (container component)
SN Those parts of containers that enclose the contents, as distinguished from accessory components such as covers, handles, and applied decoration.

bodies (land vehicle components)
PJ.3304 (L)
ALT body (land vehicle component)
SN Use for the main portions of land vehicles on or in which the passengers or loads are contained; excludes those components necessary to make the vehicles move. For similar main portions of watercraft, use **hulls**, and of aircraft, use **fuselages**.
UF bodywork

bodies (stays)
USE stays (corsets)

bodies (underbodices)
USE underbodices

bodies, aircraft
USE fuselages

bodies of water
RD.91
ALT body of water
UF water, bodies of

<bodies of water and components of bodies of water>
RD.90

<bodies of water by location>
RD.108

<bodies of water by size>
RD.92

<bodies of water by state>
RD.119

bodkins
TE.519 (N)

ALT bodkin
SN Ornamental hairpins; used especially with reference to Renaissance examples.

body armor
TE.275
UK body armour
SN Pieces of armor worn on the human body.
UF armor, body
armour, body
body-armour

<body armor: hand and forearm>
TE.324
RT gauntlets
vamplates

<body armor: helmets>
TE.280
RT helmets

<body armor: lower extremities>
TE.336
RT codpieces

<body armor: neck and head>
TE.276

<body armor: torso>
TE.303

<body armor: upper extremities>
TE.323

body armour
SEE body armor

body-armour
SEE body armor

body art
VC.78 (L,R)
SN Use for works produced since the 1960s that employ human bodies as the medium of expression; may be in the form of performance art, or the artist using his own body as a focus or theme.
UF art, body
art, corporal
body sculpture
body works
corporal art
sculpture, body
works, body

body Brussels
TC.146
SN Heavy resilient multi-framed Brussels carpets in which all the colored worsted pattern yarns are carried along with the body or structure of the carpet and pick up into the pattern as the design requires. (ARCCM)

body color
HN June 1991 descriptor deleted, made lead-in to **gouache**

body color
USE gouache
mass color

body plans
VC.112
HN April 1992 descriptor moved
ALT body plan
SN Drawings that are end elevations of ships, indicating curvature at certain points along the ship's length. When appearing with a half-breadth plan and a sheer plan, use **lines drawings** for the set.
UF plans, body

body rub parlors
USE massage parlors

body sculpture
USE body art

body-shells
USE shells (drum components)

body shops
RK.581
ALT body shop
SN Factories or machine shops in which bodies of vehicles are manufactured or repaired. (RHDEL2)
UF autobody shops
shops, autobody
shops, body

body type
USE text type

body works
USE body art

bodygros
SEE creepers

bodysuits
SEE creepers

bodywork
USE bodies (land vehicle components)

Boehm clarinets
USE Boehm system + clarinets

Boehm flutes
USE Boehm system + flutes (aerophones)

Boehm keywork
USE Boehm system

Boehm system
PJ.3230
SN Keywork for the flute developed by Theobald Boehm in the 1830s, involving an improved placement of fingerholes and a key mechanism to provide full venting and bring all fingerholes within easy control of the fingers. Other instrument makers later adapted the system for the clarinet, oboe, bassoon, and other aerophones.
UF Boehm keywork
keywork, Boehm
system, Boehm

RT clarinets
flutes (aerophones)

Boeotian
FL.2707

bog spruce
MT.2990
HN March 1992 descriptor moved
UF Picea mariana
spruce, bog

bogs
RD.137 (L)
HN March 1993 related term added
ALT bog
SN Designates waterlogged spongy ground with a characteristic plant-life, such as sphagnum mosses, and in which vegetation is decaying, ultimately producing highly acidic peat. Distinct from **fens**, in which the water remains alkaline.
RT fens

bogs, peat
USE peat bogs

bohça
USE bokches

Bohemian earth
MT.2138
HN April 1992 descriptor moved
UF earth, Bohemian

Bohemianism
BM.288 (L,R)

boiled linseed oil
USE boiled oil

boiled oil
MT.1111
HN April 1992 descriptor moved
October 1990 descriptor moved
UF boiled linseed oil
linseed oil, boiled
oil, boiled
oil, boiled linseed

boiler houses
RK.576 (B)
ALT boiler house
UF houses, boiler

boiler-makers
SEE boilermakers

boiler rooms
PJ.1160
HN March 1993 descriptor moved
ALT boiler room
SN Spaces provided for the boilers used for heating, ventilation, or power generation. (RS)
UF rooms, boiler

boiler suits
SEE coveralls

boilermakers
HG.732
HN December 1992 alternate terms added

ALT boilermaker
boilermaker's
boilermakers'
UK boiler-makers
UKA boiler-maker

boilers (HVAC components)
PJ.791 (A,L,B)
HN March 1993 descriptor moved
March 1993 descriptor changed, was **boilers**
March 1993 alternate term changed, was **boiler**
November 1990 scope note added
ALT boiler (HVAC component)
SN Use for a wide range of pressure vessels in which water or other fluid is heated and then discharged to supply hot water for heating or steam for heating or power generation.

boilers (vessels)
TQ.43 (L)
ALT boiler (vessel)
SN Lidded vessels used for boiling or heating, usually oval or rectangular and often made of tin-lined copper.

boilers, coffee
USE coffeepots

boilers, double
USE double boilers

boilers, egg
USE egg coddlers

boilers, fish
USE fish kettles

boilers, hot water
USE hot water boilers

boilers, laundry
USE washboilers

boilers, steam
USE steam boilers

boilers, steam wash
USE washboilers

boilers, wash
USE washboilers

boiling point
DC.367 (L)
HN October 1992 descriptor moved

bois d'arc
USE Osage orange

boiserie
TC.377 (R)
HN May 1993 descriptor moved
SN Wood paneling on interior walls, usually floor to ceiling; as a rule enriched by carving, gilding, painting, or sometimes inlaying. (DAC)

bokches
TQ.664
ALT bokche
SN Turkish woven squares used for

wrapping or sewn into baglike containers with one side left unsewn, to be folded like an envelope.
UF bohça
   boktche
   buqchah
   hogca
RT rugs

Bokhara
USE Afghan
    Bukhara

Bokhara rugs
USE Bukhara + rugs

Bokhara School
USE Bukhara School

Bokharas
USE Afghan + rugs
    Bukhara + rugs

Boki
   FL.236

boktche
USE bokches

bolas
   TK.238   (L,N)
ALT bola
SN Projectile weapons consisting of two or more stone or iron balls attached to the ends of a cord, whirled and thrown to entangle an animal or human being.

bold typefaces
USE boldface

boldface
   PJ.3493
SN Typefaces that are a thicker version of the same typeface style.
UF bold typefaces
   typefaces, bold

bole
   MT.67
HN November 1992 descriptor added
SN Soft, unctuous clays of various colors, used as pigments.
UF Armenian bole
   bolus
   burnish clay
   clay, gilder's
   clay, gilder's burnishing
   gilder's burnishing clay
   gilder's clay
   poliment

bole, Armenian
USE red bole

bole, red
USE red bole

bolection moldings
   PJ.746
HN April 1993 descriptor moved
   November 1991 lead-in term deleted, was **moldings, belection**

November 1990 lead-in term deleted, was **belection moldings**
   November 1990 scope note changed
ALT bolection molding
SN Moldings or groups of moldings used to cover the joint between two surfaces on different levels and projecting beyond the surface of both.
UF balection moldings
   bellexion moldings
   bilection moldings
   moldings, balection
   moldings, bellexion
   moldings, bolection
   moldings, raised
   moldings, risen
   raised moldings
   risen moldings

boleros
   TE.56   (N)
ALT bolero
SN Jackets of waist length or shorter, with or without sleeves and worn open in the front; especially those of Spanish origin.

Bolia
   FL.526   (L)
UF Lia

Bolidist
HN May 1990 descriptor deleted

Bolivian
   FL.732   (L,B)

bollards
   RM.230   (A,N,B)
HN April 1993 descriptor moved
ALT bollard
SN Use for low stone piers that hold the line of a moored boat or prevent passage by automobiles.

bolo ties
   TE.663   (L)
ALT bolo tie
SN Neckties of thin cord fastened in front with an ornamental clasp or other device. (RHDEL2)
UF bolos
   rope ties
   ties, bolo
   ties, rope

Bolochi
USE Baluch

Bologna stone
USE barium sulfate

bolombatas
USE bolons

bolometers
   TN.244   (L,N)
ALT bolometer
SN Instruments that measure minute amounts of electromagnetic radiation by determining the changes in resistance of a conductor caused by

the heating effect of the radiation; used in meteorology.

bolons
   TT.225
ALT bolon
SN Large harps of the Fula and the Malinke people of Africa, with an arched neck, three strings, and a gourd resonator. (KAUF)
UF bolombatas
   bulumbatas

bolos
   TK.31   (N)
ALT bolo
SN Long, heavy single-edged Philippine knives similar to machetes, used as weapons.

bolos
USE bolo ties

Bol'shaia Rechka
   FL.2202

bolster cases
   TC.291
ALT bolster case
SN Sacklike removable and washable coverings for a bolster. If used on sleeping furniture, they often match pillowcases and sheets; if used on seating furniture, they often match other slipcovers.
UF bolster casings
   cases, bolster
   casings, bolster
RT pillowcases
   slipcovers

bolster casings
USE bolster cases

bolsters (blocking chisels)
USE blocking chisels

bolsters (capital components)
   PJ.1506
HN March 1993 descriptor moved
   March 1993 descriptor changed, was **bolsters**
   March 1993 alternate term changed, was **bolster**
ALT bolster (capital component)
SN Use for the rolls, faced at either end with volutes, forming the sides of an Ionic capital.
UF balusters (capital components)

bolsters (soft furnishings)
   TC.1485   (N)
ALT bolster (soft furnishing)
SN Long, often cylindrical, pillows or cushions that are used to support the head of a person lying on a bed, couch, or similar form of furniture.

bolt actions
   PJ.3164   (L)
ALT bolt action
SN Mechanisms on breechloading firearms featuring a manually operated

cylindrical bolt with an external lever which the shooter pulls back to open the breech and extract the empty case of a fired cartridge and pushes forward to push a fresh cartridge into firing position and close the breech.
UF actions, bolt
RT bolts (breechblocks)

bolt anchors, lewis
USE lewis bolt anchors

bolt clippers
TH.1263 (N)
HN April 1993 alternate term added
ALT bolt clipper
SN Heavy hand shears used for cutting bolts in two. (SMITH)
UF clippers, bolt

bolt clippers (bolt cutters)
USE bolt cutters

<bolt components>
PJ.61
HN March 1993 guide term moved

bolt covers, bed
USE bed bolt covers

bolt cutters
TH.1270 (N)
ALT bolt cutter
SN Tools which take a variety of forms; used for cutting threads in metal pegs to make bolts.
UF bolt clippers (bolt cutters)
clippers, bolt
cutters, bolt

bolt tongs
TH.1290 (N)
UF tongs, bolt

bolted joints
PJ.621
HN April 1993 descriptor moved
ALT bolted joint
UF joints, bolted

boltels
USE roll moldings

bolting
KT.35
HN March 1993 descriptor moved
ALT bolted

bolting cloth
MT.1566
HN January 1993 descriptor added
SN A firm cloth usually of silk woven in various mesh sizes for various uses such as bolting flour or for use in screen printing or needleworking. (W)
UF bolting cloth, silk
cloth, bolting
cloth, silk bolting
silk bolting cloth

bolting cloth, silk
USE bolting cloth

Bolton coverlets
TC.207
ALT Bolton coverlet
SN All-white cotton coverlets with distinctive geometric designs in weft loop weave. Originally made in Bolton, England, and copied in North America.
UF caddows
coverlets, Bolton
RT boutonné coverlets
candlewick spreads

bolts (arrows)
TK.237
ALT bolt (arrow)
SN Short, thick arrows fitted with flights and a head of any of various shapes, often square or blunt, designed to be shot by crossbows.
UF carreaux
quarrels (arrows)
RT crossbows

bolts (breechblocks)
PJ.3169
ALT bolt (breechblock)
SN Sliding breechblocks incorporating a firing pin, cartridge case extractor, and one or more lugs to lock them into firing position, found in bolt action, automatic, and semiautomatic breechloading rifles, machine guns, and submachine guns with blowback action. They guide ammunition into the chamber and rotate to lock the breech mechanism.
RT bolt actions
machine guns

bolts (fasteners)
PJ.40 (L,N)
HN April 1993 descriptor moved
September 1991 descriptor changed, was bolts
September 1991 alternate term changed, was bolt
ALT bolt (fastener)
SN Small metal rods used as fasteners having a head and often helical threading and being usually secured by a nut or by riveting. (W)

bolts (latch and lock components)
PJ.550
HN March 1993 descriptor moved
ALT bolt (latch and lock component)
SN The protruding parts of latches or locks that prevent a door from opening. (MEANS)

bolts, anchor
USE anchor bolts

<bolts and bolt components>
PJ.39

bolts, antifriction latch
USE antifriction latch bolts

bolts, assembling
USE assembling bolts

bolts, auxiliary latch
USE auxiliary dead latches

bolts, barrel
USE barrel bolts

bolts, bed
USE bed bolts

bolts, bookcase
USE bookcase bolts

bolts, bottom
USE bottom bolts

bolts, box
USE box bolts

bolts, button-headed
USE carriage bolts

<bolts by form>
PJ.41
HN April 1993 guide term moved

<bolts by location or context>
PJ.54
HN April 1993 guide term moved

bolts, Canada
USE box bolts

bolts, cane
USE cane bolts

bolts, carriage
USE carriage bolts

bolts, chain
USE chain bolts

bolts, cremorne
USE cremorne bolts

bolts, dead
USE dead bolts

bolts, door
USE door bolts

bolts, double-door
USE double-door bolts

bolts, double throw
USE double throw bolts

bolts, Dutch-door
USE Dutch-door bolts

bolts, espagnolette
USE espagnolette bolts

bolts, expansion
USE expansion bolts

bolts, extension
USE extension flush bolts

bolts, extension flush
USE extension flush bolts

bolts, eye
USE eyebolts

bolts, fire exit
USE panic bolts

bolts, flush
USE flush bolts

bolts, foot
USE foot bolts

bolts, foundation
USE anchor bolts

bolts, gutter
USE gutter bolts

bolts, handrail
USE handrail bolts

bolts, hanger
USE hanger bolts

bolts, hinged latch
USE swinging latch bolts

bolts, hold-down
USE anchor bolts

bolts, joint
USE handrail bolts

bolts, knob
USE knob latches

bolts, lag
USE lag bolts

bolts, latch
USE latch bolts

bolts, lewis
USE lewis bolt anchors

bolts, live
USE latch bolts

bolts, machine
USE machine bolts

bolts, mortise
USE mortise bolts

bolts, necked
USE necked bolts

bolts, night
USE night latches

bolts, panic
USE panic bolts
panicproof locks

bolts, rail
USE handrail bolts

bolts, self-latching
USE self-latching bolts

bolts, split dead
USE split dead bolts

bolts, square
USE square bolts

bolts, star expansion
USE star expansion bolts

bolts, stove
USE stove bolts

bolts, swinging latch
USE swinging latch bolts

bolts, thumb
USE thumb bolts

bolts, tie
USE tie rods

bolts, toggle
USE toggle bolts

bolts, tower
USE tower bolts

bolts, trigger
USE auxiliary dead latches

bolts, window spring
USE window spring bolts

bolus
USE bole

Boma
FL.460   (L)
UF Baboma

bomb ketches
USE bomb vessels

bomb shelters
USE air raid shelters

bomb vessels
TX.430
ALT bomb vessel
SN Use for sailing warships carrying one or more heavy mortars or how-itzers mounted on specially con-structed platforms or in heavily re-inforced pits; often ketch-rigged to give mortars a clearer field of fire forward and used in bombarding coastal towns or fortresses.
UF bomb ketches
bombs (warships)
bombships
ketches, bomb
vessels, bomb
RT sailing vessels

bombards (cannons)
TK.139
ALT bombard (cannon)
SN Early cannons in use from the 14th to the 16th century, typically of large bore, made of wrought iron or cast bronze and firing stone cannon-balls.

bombards (shawms)
TT.172
ALT bombard (shawm)
SN The lower-pitched shawms devel-oped between the 14th and 16th centuries, being long and slender with a narrow, slightly conical bore ending in a flare, six fingerholes in two groups of three, and at least one key. (MARCUS)

Bombay mastic
USE mastic

bombé
DC.80
HN October 1992 descriptor moved

SN Having rounded, outward bulging, or swelling sides and front, used with reference to furniture. (FAIRB)
UF kettle (bombé)

bomber aircraft
USE bombers

bomber jackets
TE.127   (L)
ALT bomber jacket
SN Jackets, often made of leather with ribbed trim, resembling those worn by Second World War bomber crews. (RHDEL2)
UF aviator jackets
flight jackets
jackets, aviator
jackets, bomber
jackets, flight
RT jackets

bombers
TX.46   (L)
ALT bomber
SN Use for military aircraft designed to be used primarily against surface targets and equipped to carry and drop bombs, generally characterized by long range, low maneuverability, and large weapon-carrying capacity.
UF aircraft, bomber
bomber aircraft

bombers, attack
USE attack aircraft

bombers, strategic
USE strategic bombers

bombers, water
USE water bombers

bombillas
TH.300
HN April 1993 descriptor added
ALT bombilla
SN Small tubes with a strainer at one end used in drinking maté. (W)
UF maté sippers
sippers, maté

bombing and gunnery ranges
USE firing ranges

bombproof building
USE bombproof construction

bombproof construction
KT.29   (A,L)
HN January 1993 descriptor moved
UF bombproof building
building, bombproof
construction, bombproof

bombs
TK.102   (L)
ALT bomb
SN Use for projectiles or stationary de-vices containing both a detonating mechanism and a harmful agent such as an explosive, poison gas, bi-ological poison, or incendiary sub-stance, set off by a time fuse or by

impact. For the hollow projectiles containing shrapnel, explosives, incendiary or poisonous chemicals, or other harmful agents, designed to be fired from artillery, use **shells (ammunition)**.

RT shells (ammunition)

bombs (warships)
USE bomb vessels

bombs, aerial
USE aerial bombs

bombs, depth
USE depth charges

bombs, fire
USE incendiary bombs

bombs, incendiary
USE incendiary bombs

bombs, nuclear
USE nuclear bombs

bombships
USE bomb vessels

bomoi
RK.1028
ALT bomos
SN Ancient Greek altars to supreme gods. (OCD)

bon à tirer
USE bon à tirer proofs

bon à tirer proofs
VC.441
ALT bon à tirer proof
SN Proofs designated by the artist to serve as the standard, both aesthetically and technically, for the printing of the edition. Sometimes identical with the printers' proofs of the edition.
UF BATs
bon à tirer
OK to print
proofs, bon à tirer

bon-bon quilts
USE yo-yo spreads

bon-bon spreads
USE yo-yo spreads

bonang
TT.488
SN Gong chimes of Southeast Asia, in which the gongs are arranged in single rows or in L- or U-shaped frames. They constitute an important element of the gamelan.
RT gamelan

bonbon dishes
TQ.348   (H,N)
ALT bonbon dish
SN Shallow dishes for candies or other sweets; may have a lid or stem.
UF bonbonnières

bonbonnieres
dishes, bonbon
RT comfit boxes

bonbonnieres
USE bonbon dishes

bonbonnières
USE bonbon dishes

bonces
USE marbles

bond, American
USE common bond

bond, block
USE stack bond

bond breaker
MT.2404
HN April 1993 descriptor changed, was **bond breakers**
SN A material, such as form oil, used to prevent adhesion of newly placed concrete to the forms, wall, or other support. (PUTNAM)
UF breaker, bond

bond, common
USE common bond

bond courses
PJ.1946
HN March 1993 descriptor moved
ALT bond course
SN Courses of bondstones that affix the facing masonry to the backing masonry. (DAC)
UF courses, bond
lockbands

bond, English
USE English bond

bond, Flemish
USE Flemish bond

bond paper
MT.1502
HN February 1992 descriptor moved
UF paper, bond

bond, running
USE running bond

bond, stack
USE stack bond

bond-stone
SEE bondstone

bond stone
USE bondstone

bond, stretcher
USE running bond

bonded warehouses
RK.1170   (L)
ALT bonded warehouse
UF warehouses, bonded

Bondei
FL.594   (L)

bonder
USE bondstone

bonding (financial)
KG.89   (L)
HN January 1991 scope note added
SN Placing under the conditions of a bond. (W)

bonding (joining)
KT.49   (L,B)
HN January 1993 descriptor moved
July 1991 related term added
ALT bonded
SN Includes the process of binding or tying, usually by lapping one unit over another, as various masonry units, and holding or adhering together firmly by means of a binder or bond, as the fibers in paper. (W)
RT cladding

bonding agent
USE adhesive

bonding, hydrogen
USE hydrogen bonding

bonding material
USE adhesive

bonds (legal records)
VW.642   (N)
HN November 1992 descriptor moved
July 1991 scope note changed
ALT bond (legal record)
SN Use for agreements pledging liability for financial or personal loss caused to another party.

bonds (masonry)
MT.1814   (B)
HN October 1992 descriptor moved
ALT bond (masonry)
SN Arrangements of, or patterns formed by, the exposed faces of laid masonry units. (MEANS)

bonds (negotiable instruments)
VK.173   (L,N)
HN March 1993 scope note changed
March 1993 related term added
March 1993 descriptor changed, was **bonds (financial records)**
March 1993 alternate term changed, was **bond (financial record)**
July 1991 descriptor moved
ALT bond (negotiable instrument)
SN Use for interest-bearing certificates of public or private debt, usually offered in series, constituting promises to pay the lender a certain amount of money at a fixed future date.
RT credit instruments

bonds, angle
USE angle bonds

bonds, bail
USE bail bonds

bonds, bid
USE bid bonds

bonds, labor and material
USE   labor and material bonds

bonds, payment
USE   payment bonds

bonds, performance
USE   performance bonds

bonds, proposal
USE   bid bonds

bonds, subcontractor
USE   subcontractor bonds

bonds, surety
USE   surety bonds

bondstone
　　MT.1824
HN   April 1993 lead-in term added
　　April 1993 lead-in term changed,
　　　was **bonders**
　　April 1993 descriptor changed, was
　　　bondstones
　　October 1992 descriptor moved
UK   bond-stone
SN   In stone masonry, stone usually set
　　with its longest dimension perpen-
　　dicular to the wall.
UF   bond stone
　　bonder
　　stone, bond

bone
　　MT.1313   (A,L)
HN   March 1992 scope note added
　　March 1992 related term added
　　February 1992 descriptor moved
SN   Organic and/or inorganic material
　　combination composed primarily of
　　collagen and calcium phosphate
　　composing the skeleton of most ver-
　　tebrates.
RT   collagen

bone black
　　MT.2070   (L)
HN   April 1992 descriptor moved
UF   Beinschwarz
　　black, bone
　　black, drop
　　black, Frankfort
　　drop black
　　Frankfort black
　　noire d'os

bone brown
　　MT.2118
HN   April 1992 descriptor moved
UF   brown, bone

<bone by form>
　　MT.1314
HN   February 1992 guide term moved

bone china
　　MT.151   (H)
HN   December 1992 descriptor added
SN   Porcelain made with the addition of
　　bone ash making it pure white in
　　color.
UF   bone porcelain
　　china, bone

china, English
English china
English soft paste porcelain
porcelain, English soft paste

<bone components>
　　MT.1323
HN   January 1992 guide term added

<bone dating techniques>
　　KT.184
HN   January 1993 guide term moved

bone dishes
　　TQ.542   (N)
ALT   bone dish
SN   Shallow dishes placed alongside a
　　dinner plate for the bones and other
　　remains of an elaborate meal; often
　　included as part of a standard place
　　setting in the 19th century. (WKPP)
UF   dishes, bone
RT   dishes

bone glue
　　MT.1726
HN   March 1992 descriptor moved
　　February 1992 scope note changed
　　June 1991 descriptor moved
　　June 1991 scope note added
SN   Glue made from degraded or dena-
　　tured collagen obtained from bones.
UF   glue, bone

bone houses
USE   ossuaries (buildings)

bone lace
USE   bobbin lace

bone porcelain
USE   bone china

bone white
　　MT.2244
HN   May 1992 lead-in term deleted, was
　　　bone ash
　　January 1992 descriptor moved
UF   white, bone

bones
　　TT.453   (L)
SN   Thin flat clappers of bone, ivory, or
　　hardwood played in pairs, usually a
　　pair in each hand.

bones (dominoes)
USE   dominoes (game pieces)

bonfire firing
　　KT.1000
HN   January 1993 descriptor moved
UF   firing, bonfire

Bongo
　　FL.619   (L)

bongo drums
USE   bongos

bongos
　　TT.611   (L,N)
ALT   bongo
SN   Small single-headed drums, Afro-
　　Cuban in origin, with conical or cy-

lindrical hardwood shells; they generally occur in pairs joined together
horizontally, one being larger in diameter than the other. Existing in
tunable and nontunable versions,
they are played with the bare hands.
UF   bongo drums
　　drums, bongo

Bongu
USE   Bargu

bonheurs-du-jour
　　TC.990
HN   January 1993 descriptor moved
ALT   bonheur-du-jour
SN   Women's small writing tables with a
　　gradin (cabinet) at the back; often
　　elaborately decorated and occasion-
　　ally fitted for toilet purposes as well
　　as writing.
UF   tables à gradin

boning knives
　　TH.99   (N)
HN   April 1993 descriptor added
ALT   boning knife
SN   Small knives with a narrow blade
　　used to remove bones from meat,
　　fish, or similar foods.
UF   knives, boning

bonnet boxes
USE   hatboxes

bonnet glasses
　　TQ.325
ALT   bonnet glass
SN   Small glass vessels intended for salt
　　or sweetmeats, usually with double
　　ogee or cup-shaped bowls.
UF   glasses, bonnet
　　monteiths (bonnet glasses)

bonnet hip tile
　　MT.183
HN   April 1992 descriptor moved
SN   A tile that resembles a bonnet; used
　　to cover the hip on a hip roof. (HAS)
UF   cone hip tile
　　cone tile
　　hip tile, bonnet
　　hip tile, cone
　　tile, bonnet hip
　　tile, cone
　　tile, cone hip

bonnet tops
　　PJ.2833
HN   March 1993 descriptor moved
ALT   bonnet top
SN   Triangular closed backs forming the
　　hood or top to a tall piece of case
　　furniture. (FAIRB)
UF   bonnet tops, closed
　　closed bonnet tops
　　hooded tops
　　tops, bonnet
　　tops, closed bonnet
　　tops, hooded

bonnet tops, closed
USE   bonnet tops

bonnetières
TC.844
HN   January 1993 descriptor moved
ALT   bonnetière
SN   Tall, narrow, and deep cabinets to accommodate the elaborate bonnets peculiar to Normandy and Brittany in the 18th century. (ARONS)
UF   armoires bonnetières
chapelières
coiffières

bonnets
TE.570   (H,N)
ALT   bonnet
SN   Soft hats with a front brim which usually tie under the chin; formerly worn by women, but now mostly children.

bonnets (chimney caps)
USE   chimney caps

bonnets, baby
USE   baby bonnets

bonnets, fanchon
USE   fanchons

bonnets, glengarry
USE   glengarries

bonnets, poke
USE   poke bonnets

boob-tubes
SEE   tube tops

boobams
TT.612
ALT   boobam
SN   Percussion instruments originating in the United States in the 1950s, consisting of a set of small tunable drums, in which the drum heads are stretched across the top of an open bamboo stem or deep wooden shell. (NGDMI)

boobies
USE   booby huts

booby hacks
USE   booby huts

booby hutches
USE   booby huts

booby huts
TX.288   (N)
ALT   booby hut
SN   Elegant sleighs with enclosed bodies; term used in New England from the mid-18th century until the end of the carriage era. (BERKCT)
UF   boobies
booby hacks
booby hutches
hacks, booby
hutches, booby
huts, booby

book art
USE   artists' books

book bags
USE   schoolbags

book cabinets
USE   bookcases

book catalogs
VW.14   (L)
HN   November 1992 descriptor moved
ALT   book catalog
SN   Catalogs containing the surrogate descriptions of books or other bibliographic material in a collection.

book cupboards
TC.826
HN   January 1993 descriptor moved
ALT   book cupboard
SN   Bookcases having solid, as opposed to glazed, doors.
UF   cupboards, book

book hand, Gothic
USE   textura

book hands
PJ.3475
ALT   book hand
SN   Those styles of handwriting designed for legibility and used in transcribing manuscript books.
UF   book-hands
book scripts
bookhands
bookscripts
hands, book
literary scripts
scripts, book
scripts, literary

book-hands
USE   book hands

book harmoniums
TT.133
ALT   book harmonium
SN   Very small harmoniums in the shape of a large book. (MARCUS)
UF   harmoniums, book

book illustration
HN   May 1991 descriptor split, use book (ALT of **books**) + illustration

book illustrations
HN   May 1991 descriptor split, use book (ALT of **books**) + illustrations

book illustrators
HN   January 1993 descriptor split, use book (ALT of **books**) + illustrators

book jackets
PJ.3373   (H,L,N)
ALT   book jacket
SN   Use for the detachable, flexible coverings for books, usually of paper and made flush with the edges of the covers at top and bottom and folded around the fore edges of the covers. For attached outer sheets or boards, use **covers (gathered matter components)**.
UF   covers, dust

dust covers (book jackets)
dust jackets
dust wrappers
jackets (book jackets)
jackets, book
jackets, dust
wrappers (book jackets)
wrappers, dust

book-keepers
SEE   bookkeepers

book labels
USE   bookplates

book lists
USE   bibliographies

book-marks
USE   bookmarks

book match covers
USE   matchbooks

book objects
VC.504
ALT   book object
SN   Use for works of sculpture, usually one-of-a-kind, that look like books or incorporate books but that do not communicate in the ways characteristic of books, such as containing print or images, being experienced sequentially or in fragments, as page by page. For books made or conceived by visual artists, use **artists' books** or **bookworks**.
UF   objects, book
RT   artists' books
bookworks

book paper
MT.1494
HN   February 1992 descriptor moved
SN   A paper suitable for printing books, magazines, and advertising matter including many grades of plain and coated papers but excluding newsprint. (W)
UF   paper, book

book presses (bookcases)
USE   bookcases

book reviews
HN   April 1993 descriptor split, use book (ALT of **books**) + reviews

book scripts
USE   book hands

book shelves
USE   bookshelves

book slipcases
USE   slipcases

book spines
USE   spines

book stands
USE   bookstands

book tea chests
USE   tea chests

book tile
MT.158
HN April 1992 descriptor moved
SN Flat, cellular roofing tile having two parallel edges, one of which is convex and the other concave, so that a number may be fit together edge-to-edge between rafters, joists, or the like. (RHDEL2)
UF tile, book

bookbinders
HG.670   (L,R)
HN April 1993 related term added
December 1992 alternate terms added
ALT bookbinder
bookbinder's
bookbinders'
UF binders (bookbinders)
bookmakers
RT bookbinding

bookbinding
KT.769   (L,B,R)
HN January 1993 descriptor moved
January 1993 scope note added
January 1993 lead-in term added
January 1993 related terms added
SN The process, involving various procedures done by hand or machine, of securing leaves or gatherings, usually within covers, to form a book.
UF binding (bookbinding)
binding of books
books, binding of
RT bindings
bookbinders

<bookbinding and bookbinding processes and techniques>
KT.768
HN January 1993 guide term added

bookbinding marks
HN April 1993 descriptor split, use bookbinding + marks (symbols)

<bookbinding processes and techniques>
KT.775
HN January 1993 guide term added

bookbindings
USE bindings

bookblocks
USE text blocks

bookcase and secretaries
USE secretary-bookcases

bookcase beds
TC.773
HN May 1993 related term added
January 1993 descriptor moved
ALT bookcase bed
SN Deception beds which fold into a dummy bookcase. (GILBR2)
UF beds, bookcase
RT bookcases

bookcase bolts
PJ.56
HN April 1993 descriptor moved
ALT bookcase bolt
UF bolts, bookcase

bookcases
TC.824   (A,L,N,B,R)
HN May 1993 related terms added
January 1993 descriptor moved
ALT bookcase
SN Cases for holding books generally having several shelves enclosed by doors; distinct from **bookshelves** which are open shelves for holding books.
UF book cabinets
book presses (bookcases)
cabinets, book
presses, book (bookcases)
RT bookcase beds
bookshelves

bookcases, counting-house
USE counting-house bookcases

bookcases, desks and
USE desks and bookcases

bookcases, dwarf
USE dwarf bookcases

bookcases, library
USE library bookcases

bookcases, movable
USE moving libraries

bookcases, portable library
USE moving libraries

bookcases, secretary
USE desks and bookcases

bookcases, secretary and
USE secretary-bookcases

bookcases, sectional
USE sectional bookcases

bookcases, sisters' cylinder
USE cylinder desks and bookcases

bookhands
USE book hands

bookkeepers
HG.613   (L)
HN December 1992 alternate terms added
ALT bookkeeper
bookkeeper's
bookkeepers'
UK book-keepers
UKA book-keeper
SN Those who keep accounts but are not formally trained in accounting.

bookkeeping records
VW.580   (L)
HN November 1992 descriptor moved
ALT bookkeeping record
UF records, bookkeeping

bookkeeping registers
VW.585
HN November 1992 descriptor moved
ALT bookkeeping register
UF registers, bookkeeping

booklets
USE pamphlets

bookmakers
USE bookbinders

bookmarks
TH.972   (L,N,R)
HN January 1993 descriptor added
ALT bookmark
SN Devices of any sort intended for marking a particular opening between the leaves of a book.
UF book-marks
signets

bookplates
VW.1170   (L,N,R)
HN November 1992 descriptor moved
ALT bookplate
SN Labels pasted in books to mark their ownership, and sometimes to indicate their location in a library. (LG)
UF book labels
ex libris
labels, book

books
VW.991   (L,N,R)
HN November 1992 descriptor moved
June 1992 lead-in term added
ALT book
SN Collections of wood or ivory tablets, or sheets of paper, parchment, or similar material, that are blank, written on, or printed, and are strung or bound together; commonly many folded and bound sheets containing continuous printing or writing; especially, when printed, a bound volume, or a volume of some size.
UF codices (gathered leaves)

books, ABC
USE alphabet books

books, accordion fold
USE folded books

books, account
USE account books

books, address
USE address books

books, Adventus
USE festival books

books, alphabet
USE alphabet books

books, animated
USE movable books

books, appointment
USE appointment books

books, artists'
USE artists' books

books, artists' illustrated
USE   livres d'artistes

books, autograph
USE   autograph albums

books, baby
USE   baby books

books, binding of
USE   bookbinding

books, block
USE   block books

books, bridal
USE   bridal books

<books by conditions of production>
VW.1016
HN   June 1992 guide term added

<books by external form>
VW.1010
HN   June 1992 guide term added
SN   Collocates descriptors for books having distinctive physical characteristics in their binding or overall form. For books having distinctive physical characteristics within the page and text block areas, use descriptors under *<books by internal form>*.

<books by form or function>
HN   June 1992 guide term deleted

<books by internal form>
VW.992
HN   June 1992 guide term added

<books by subject>
HN   June 1992 guide term deleted

books, carol
USE   carol books

books, chained
USE   chained bindings

books, christening
USE   christening books

books, Christmas
USE   gift books

books, clothbound
USE   hardcover books

books, coloring
USE   coloring books

books, comic
USE   comic books

books, commonplace
USE   commonplace books

books, concertina fold
USE   folded books

books, courtesy
USE   courtesy books

books, cradle
USE   incunabula

books, date
USE   appointment books

books, deed
USE   deed books

books, double leaf
USE   folded books

books, emblem
USE   emblem books

books, festival
USE   festival books

books, field
USE   field notes

books, flip
USE   flip books

books, folded
USE   folded books

books, folding
USE   folded books

books, gift
USE   gift books

books, girdle
USE   girdle books

books, grade
USE   grade books

books, guest
USE   guest registers

books, hardbound
USE   hardcover books

books, hardcover
USE   hardcover books

books, household account
USE   housebooks

books, irregularly shaped
USE   shaped books

books, large print
USE   large print books

books, large type
USE   large print books

books, letter
USE   letter books

books, manipulative
USE   movable books

books, mass
USE   missals

books, minute
USE   minute books

books, model
USE   pattern books

books, movable
USE   movable books

books, movable picture
USE   movable books

books of courtesy
USE   courtesy books

books of hours
VW.885   (L,R)
HN   November 1992 descriptor moved
ALT   book of hours
SN   Books containing the prescribed order of prayers, readings from the Scripture, and rites for the canonical hours. (RHDEL2)
UF   hours, books of

books, paperback
USE   paperbacks

books, parade
USE   festival books

books, participation
USE   movable books

books, pattern
USE   pattern books

books, penitential
USE   penitentials

books, penmanship
USE   copybooks

books, phone
USE   telephone directories

books, picture
USE   picture books

books, plan
USE   pattern books

books, plat
USE   plat books

books, pop-up
USE   pop-up books

books, prayer
USE   prayer books

books, price
USE   price books

books, prompt
USE   prompt books

books, psalm
USE   psalters

books, receipt (cookbooks)
USE   cookbooks

books, recipe
USE   cookbooks

books, reference
USE   reference books

books, sample
USE   sample books

books, service
USE   choirbooks
         service books

books, shaped
USE   shaped books

books, sight-saving
USE large print books

books, softbound
USE paperbacks

books, song
USE songbooks

books, specially shaped
USE shaped books

books, specimen
USE sample books

books, stand-up
USE pop-up books

books, tax warrant
USE warrant books

books, telephone
USE telephone directories

books, time
USE time books

books, toy
USE toy books

books, trade
USE trade books

books, turn-up
USE harlequinades

books, visitors'
USE visitors' books

books, warrant
USE warrant books

books, zig-zag fold
USE folded books

bookscripts
USE book hands

booksellers
HG.646   (A,L)
HN April 1993 related term added
        December 1992 alternate terms
        added
        October 1992 scope note added
ALT bookseller
        bookseller's
        booksellers'
SN People or firms that buy and sell
        books. In contexts before about
        1800, use also for those responsible
        for issuing books, later called **pub-
        lishers**.
RT publishers

booksellers' catalogs
HN October 1992 descriptor split, use
        booksellers' (ALT of **booksellers**)
        + **catalogs**

bookshelves
TC.820   (B)
HN May 1993 related term added
        January 1993 descriptor moved
ALT bookshelf
SN Open shelves for holding books; dis-
        tinct from **bookcases** which gener-

ally have several shelves enclosed
by doors.
UF book shelves
        shelves, book
        shelves, standing (bookshelves)
        standing shelves (bookshelves)
RT bookcases

bookshops
USE bookstores

bookstalls
RK.149   (B)
ALT bookstall

bookstands
TC.1042   (N,B)
HN January 1993 descriptor moved
ALT bookstand
UF book stands
        dictionary stands
        stands, book
        stands, dictionary

bookstores
RK.156   (A,B)
ALT bookstore
UF bookshops

bookworks
VW.1018   (L)
HN June 1992 descriptor added
ALT bookwork
SN Use for artists' books that exploit
        the book form or alter its physical
        structure as part of the content of
        the work. Also includes works where
        emphasis is on the fine crafting of
        the book. For sculptures that look
        like or incorporate books but do not
        communicate in the ways character-
        istic of books, use **book objects**.
RT book objects

boom towns
SEE boomtowns

boomerangs
TK.243   (L,N)
ALT boomerang
SN Highly developed throwing-sticks of
        the Australian aborigines, known
        also in India, Africa, the Americas,
        and ancient Egypt, being basically
        curved or angular flat sticks de-
        signed so that they can be thrown so
        as to return to their starting point.
        They have been used in warfare, for
        hunting, and as recreational objects.
RT *<noncompetitive play equipment>*

boomtowns
RD.48   (A)
ALT boomtown
UK boom towns
UKA boom town
SN Towns that have grown very rapidly
        as a result of sudden prosperity.
        (RHDEL2)

booster rockets
USE boosters

boosters
TH.406
HN March 1993 descriptor added
ALT booster
SN Auxiliary or initial propulsion sys-
        tems for aircraft, missles, or space-
        craft which may or may not separate
        from the parent craft when their
        fuel has been consumed.
UF booster rockets
        rockets, booster

boot camps
RG.143
ALT boot camp
UF camps, boot

boot cuffs
TE.431
ALT boot cuff
SN Very deep, turned-back cuffs on a
        man's coat; they frequently reached
        the bend of the elbow. Fashionable
        from 1727 to the 1740s. (EMAEA)
UF cuffs, boot

boot-hooks
SEE boot hooks

boot hooks
TH.347   (N)
HN January 1993 descriptor added
ALT boot hook
UK boot-hooks
UKA boot-hook
SN Long, usually metal hooks for pull-
        ing on riding boots by the straps.
        (W)
UF hooks, boot

boot-jacks
SEE bootjacks

boot-trees
SEE boot trees

boot trees
TH.348
HN January 1993 descriptor added
ALT boot tree
UK boot-trees
UKA boot-tree
SN Devices of wood, metal, or plastic
        inserted in boots to maintain their
        shape when they are not being
        worn.
UF trees, boot

bootees
TE.705   (N)
ALT bootee
SN Soft, socklike footwear, usually knit-
        ted or crocheted. (NMAHDC)
RT socks

booths
PJ.1203
HN March 1993 descriptor moved
ALT booth
SN Use generally for small enclosures
        or stands, permanent or temporary,
        and freestanding or not, used for

selling goods or to afford privacy to their occupants.

booths, exhibition
USE   exhibition booths

booths, phone
USE   telephone booths

booths, telephone
USE   telephone booths

bootjack feet
PJ.2794
HN   March 1993 descriptor moved
ALT bootjack foot
UF   feet, bootjack

bootjacks
TH.349   (N)
HN   January 1993 descriptor added
ALT bootjack
UK   boot-jacks
UKA boot-jack
SN   V-shaped devices for catching the heel of a boot to aid in removing it. Also, notches or moldings cut into a piece of furniture intended for the same purpose. (RHDEL2)

boots
TE.706   (H,L,N,R)
ALT boot
SN   Footwear, the leg of which extends above the ankle joints. (NMST)
RT   crakows

<boots by form>
TE.707

<boots by function>
TE.715

boots, carriage
USE   carriage boots

boots, cowboy
USE   cowboy boots

boots, hip
USE   hip boots

boots, riding
USE   riding boots

boots, ski
USE   ski boots

Borana
FL.620   (L)

borax
MT.522   (L)
HN   April 1992 descriptor moved
       February 1992 lead-in term added
SN   A white or colorless crystalline mineral used in glass and ceramic enamel mixes, as a scouring and cleansing agent, as a flux in melting materials and in soldering, and as a source of boron. (MH)
UF   tincal

bordellos
USE   brothels

border inspection stations
RK.949   (B)
HN   June 1991 descriptor added
ALT border inspection station
SN   Built works erected at or near border crossings where persons or vehicles are halted for examination and clearance by government officials.
UF   border posts
       border stations
       checkpoints
       customs posts
       inspection stations, border
       posts, border
       posts, customs
       stations, border
       stations, border inspection
RT   inspecting

border posts
USE   border inspection stations

border stations
USE   border inspection stations

bordering wax
MT.1309
HN   April 1992 descriptor moved
       December 1990 descriptor added
SN   Wax formed into an edge around a printing plate so that the plate may be bitten before immersion; used especially for extra-large plates. (PRTT)
UF   walling wax
       wax, bordering
       wax, walling

borderlights
TC.1458
ALT borderlight
UF   borders (lighting devices)
       lights, border
       lights, toning
       toning lights

borders
DG.104   (L)
ALT border

borders (lighting devices)
USE   borderlights

Boreal Archaic
FL.882
UF   Archaic, Boreal

boreal forests
USE   taigas

bored locks
PJ.489
HN   April 1993 descriptor moved
ALT bored lock
SN   Locks manufactured to fit into a circular hole in a door. (MEANS)
UF   locks, bored

borers
HG.815
HN   December 1992 alternate terms added
ALT borer

borer's
borers'
SN   Workers who bore holes. (W)

borers, cylindrical bung
USE   cylinder augers

bores
PJ.3160
ALT bore
SN   The tubular hollow interiors of the barrels of firearms.

boring
USE   drilling

boring machinery
TH.588   (L,N)
UF   machinery, boring

Borjeño
FL.1299

borjs
RK.303
ALT borj
SN   Use for multistory, Islamic towerlike dwellings often seasonally occupied and located on the fringes of urban areas, especially in North Africa.

Bornean
FL.2461   (L)
UF   Kalimantan

Borneo cedar
USE   Borneo mahogany

Borneo mahogany
MT.2798
HN   March 1992 descriptor moved
UF   Borneo cedar
       cedar, Borneo
       mahogany, Borneo
       seraya

Borneo rosewood
MT.2887
HN   March 1992 descriptor moved
UF   ringas
       rosewood, Borneo

bornes
TC.736
HN   January 1993 descriptor moved
ALT borne
SN   French type of sofa, oval or round, with an upholstered pillar-like back in the center of the seat. Intended to stand in the center of the room.
UF   canapés confidents à quatre places
       canapés ronds
       milieu de salon

Bororo (African)
FL.391   (L)

Bororo (South American)
FL.1690   (L)

borosilicate glass
MT.236
HN   March 1993 descriptor moved
UF   glass, borosilicate

boroughs
HN.16 (L)
HN February 1993 descriptor moved
February 1993 scope note changed
ALT borough
SN Incorporated, primarily urban divisions whose population and, usually, territorial area are smaller than those of cities.

borrow soil
MT.1345
HN April 1992 descriptor moved
SN Soil borrowed from another location to be used in construction. (PUTNAM)
UF soil, borrow

borstals
USE reformatories

boskets
RM.5
HN April 1993 descriptor moved
ALT bosket
SN Use for garden areas composed of ornamental groupings of trees pierced by walkways.
UF bosquets

bosom friends
TE.642
ALT bosom friend
SN Chest protectors of wool, flannel, or fur, which also served as bust-improvers. In use in the late 18th and early 19th centuries. (EMAEA)
UF friends, bosom
RT *<supporting and shaping garments and accessories>*

bosoms, shirt
USE dickeys

bosquets
USE boskets

Boss Style
FL.2605

bosses
PJ.11 (A,L,B,R)
HN March 1993 descriptor moved
October 1990 descriptor added
ALT boss

bostan
USE bustanim

Boston chairs
TC.471
HN January 1993 descriptor moved
ALT Boston chair
SN High-back chairs with broad central splats, generally having leather-upholstered backs and seats; popular in 18th-century America.
UF Boston leather chairs
chairs, Boston
chairs, crook'd-back leather
chairs, crooked-back
chairs, leather (Boston chairs)
chairs, leather-upholstered (Boston chairs)
crook'd-back leather chairs
crooked-back chairs
leather chairs (Boston chairs)
leather chairs, Boston
leather chairs, crook'd-back
leather-upholstered chairs (Boston chairs)

Boston leather chairs
USE Boston chairs

Boston rockers
TC.655
HN May 1993 related term added
January 1993 descriptor moved
ALT Boston rocker
SN 19th-century American rocking chairs derived from Windsor chairs and having wooden seats which curve upwards to meet the spindles of the noticeably high, curved back with a scrolled top rail; usually grained or painted with fine ornamental detail.
UF Boston rocking chairs
chairs, Boston rocking
rockers, Boston
rocking chairs, Boston
RT Windsor chairs

Boston rocking chairs
USE Boston rockers

bosuns' whistles
USE boatswains' whistles

botanical gardens
RM.26 (A,L,B,R)
HN April 1993 descriptor moved
ALT botanical garden
SN Primarily outdoor areas where a variety of plants are grown and displayed for scientific, educational, or artistic purposes.
UF gardens, botanical

botanical illustration
HN May 1991 descriptor split, use botanical (ALT of botany) + illustration

botanical illustrations
HN May 1991 descriptor split, use botanical (ALT of botany) + illustrations

botanical museums
HN March 1993 descriptor split, use botanical (ALT of botany) + museums

botanical societies
USE garden clubs
horticultural societies

botanists
HG.524 (L)
HN April 1993 related term added
December 1992 alternate terms added
ALT botanist

botanist's
botanists'
RT botany

botany
KD.157 (L,R)
HN April 1993 related term added
December 1992 descriptor moved
February 1991 alternate term added
ALT botanical
RT botanists

Botany Bay gum
USE acaroid resin

botany museums
USE botanical (ALT of botany) + museums

Botecudos
USE Botocudo

bothies
RK.237
ALT bothy
SN Denotes certain Scottish huts.

Botocudo
FL.1691 (L)
UF Aimoré
Botecudos

bottegas
USE studios (organizations)
workshops (organizations)

Böttger
FL.3316 (L)
HN April 1993 descriptor added

Böttger porcelain
USE Böttger + ware

Böttger stoneware
USE Böttger + ware

Böttger ware
HN April 1993 descriptor split, use Böttger + ware

Botticino marble
MT.688
HN April 1992 descriptor moved
April 1990 descriptor added
UF marble, Botticino

bottle cases
TQ.573
ALT bottle case
UF cases, bottle
RT case bottles
cases (containers)

bottle decanters
USE decanter bottles

bottle-decanters
USE decanter bottles

bottle drawers
USE celleret drawers

bottle glass
USE green glass

bottle labels (bottle tickets)
USE   bottle tickets

bottle makers' marks
VW.442   (L)
HN   November 1992 descriptor moved
ALT   bottle maker's mark
UF   marks, bottle makers'

bottle openers
TH.174   (N)
HN   April 1993 descriptor added
ALT   bottle opener
SN   Tools used for removing caps on
      bottles.
UF   openers, bottle

bottle plates
USE   wine coasters

bottle slides
USE   wine coasters

bottle stands
USE   wine coasters

bottle tickets
VW.1171   (H,L)
HN   November 1992 descriptor moved
      June 1992 scope note added
      June 1992 lead-in terms added
      June 1992 descriptor changed, was
         wine labels
      June 1992 alternate term changed,
         was **wine label**
      June 1992 lead-in term changed,
         was **bottle tickets**
ALT   bottle ticket
SN   Use for plaques, often of silver, with
      a chain for suspending around the
      neck of a bottle and lettered with
      the name of the contents; usually
      for wine or liquor, sometimes for
      other substances.
UF   bottle labels (bottle tickets)
      decanter labels
      labels, bottle (bottle tickets)
      labels, decanter
      labels, wine
      liquor labels
      tickets, bottle
      tickets, wine
      wine labels
      wine-tickets

bottled gas
USE   liquefied petroleum gas

bottles
TQ.44   (H,L,N,R)
ALT   bottle
SN   Vessels having a neck and mouth
      considerably narrower than the
      body, used for packaging and con-
      taining liquid and dry preparations.
      (MCKWBF)
RT   apothecary bottles
      carafes
      casting bottles
      cruets
      decanter bottles
      decanters
      hot-water bottles

ink bottles
jars
jugs
perfume bottles
smelling bottles
snuff bottles
whiskey jugs

bottles, apothecary
USE   apothecary bottles

bottles, basketry-covered
USE   carboys
      demijohns

bottles, bitters
USE   bitters bottles

<*bottles by form*>
TQ.45

<*bottles by function*>
TQ.59

bottles, case
USE   case bottles

bottles, casting
USE   casting bottles

bottles, chestnut
USE   chestnut bottles

bottles, cruet
USE   cruets

bottles, d'Alva
USE   bellarmines

bottles, decanter
USE   decanter bottles

bottles, gemel
USE   gemel bottles

bottles, hairpin
USE   hairpin boxes

bottles, hot-water
USE   hot-water bottles

bottles, ink
USE   ink bottles

bottles, junk
USE   junk bottles

bottles, Ludlow
USE   chestnut bottles

bottles, medicine
USE   medicine bottles

bottles, perfume
USE   perfume bottles

bottles, pilgrim
USE   pilgrim bottles

bottles, poison
USE   poison bottles

bottles, scent
USE   scent bottles

bottles, serving
USE   decanter bottles

bottles, smelling
USE   smelling bottles

bottles, snuff
USE   snuff bottles

bottles, soda
USE   soda bottles

bottles, soda syphon
USE   syphons

bottles, soda water
USE   soda bottles

bottles, soft drink
USE   soda bottles

bottles, syphon
USE   syphons

bottles, wine
USE   wine bottles

bottling plants
RK.589   (A,B)
ALT   bottling plant
UF   plants, bottling

bottom
DC.310
HN   April 1993 related term added
      October 1992 descriptor moved
      October 1992 scope note added
SN   Use to describe something situated
      at or near the lowest or deepest part
      of an object. For the noun denoting
      these parts of objects, use **bottoms**
      from the Components hierarchy.
RT   bottoms

bottom and flange bend hangers
PJ.101
HN   April 1993 descriptor moved
ALT   bottom and flange bend hanger
UF   bend hangers, bottom and flange
      hangers, bottom and flange bend

<*bottom-based watercraft*>
TX.494

bottom bend hangers
PJ.102
HN   April 1993 descriptor moved
ALT   bottom bend hanger
UF   bend hangers, bottom
      hangers, bottom bend

bottom bolts
PJ.457
HN   April 1993 descriptor moved
ALT   bottom bolt
SN   Vertically mounted bolts on the bot-
      tom of a door which slide into a
      socket in the floor. (MEANS)
UF   bolts, bottom

bottom double seams
PJ.694
HN   April 1993 descriptor moved
ALT   bottom double seam
UF   double seams, bottom
      seams, bottom double

bottom linen
USE base cloths (upholstery foundation components)

bottom plates
USE sill plates

bottom rails
HN June 1991 descriptor split, use bottom + rails

bottom seams, insert
USE insert bottom seams

bottom seams, lap
USE lap bottom seams

bottom seams, single
USE single bottom seams

bottom sheets
USE fitted sheets

bottom valances
USE base valances

bottoms
PJ.756
ALT bottom
SN Use for the lowest or deepest parts of objects. For the adjective describing the location of something at or near the bottom of something, use **bottom** from the Attributes and Properties hierarchy.
RT bottom

bottoms, false
USE bustles

Bou Sbaa
USE Chichaoua + carpets

bouchardes
USE bushhammers

bouclé
USE weft loop weave

bouclé weave
USE weft loop weave

boudeusses
TC.737
HN January 1993 descriptor moved
ALT boudeusse
SN 19th-century sofas with a central backrest on either side of which people can sit. (DDA)
UF dos-à-dos

boudoir
DC.121
HN April 1993 descriptor added
SN A size of card photograph on a mount measuring 8 1/2 by 5 1/2 or 8 1/4 by 5 inches; popular from the 1870s to 1890s. (SAPSP)
RT boudoir midget mounts

boudoir caps
TE.555   (N)
ALT boudoir cap
SN Soft caps worn for lounging or as nightwear.

UF boudoirs (headgear)
    caps, boudoir
RT nightcaps

boudoir midget mount card photoprints
USE boudoir midget mounts

boudoir midget mounts
VC.351
HN April 1993 descriptor moved
    April 1993 related term added
    April 1993 lead-in term deleted, was **mounts, boudoir midget**
ALT boudoir midget mount
SN Commercial card photographs whose mounts measure about 3 3/8 by 2 inches; primarily used for portraits. (SAPSP)
UF boudoir midget mount card photoprints
    card photoprints, boudoir midget mount
    midget mounts, boudoir
RT boudoir

boudoir prints
HN April 1993 descriptor deleted

boudoirs
PJ.1107
HN March 1993 descriptor moved
ALT boudoir
SN Use for rooms adjacent to a lady's bedroom, serving as private sitting rooms and dressing rooms.

boudoirs (headgear)
USE boudoir caps

Bougainville
FL.3800   (L)

bougard marble
MT.729
HN April 1992 descriptor moved
UF marble, bougard

bouges
USE marlis

boughpots
TQ.612
ALT boughpot
SN Containers, usually of pottery or porcelain, with a perforated cover in which cut flowers, boughs, or branches are held or displayed.
UF bowpots
RT vases

bougie boxes
USE candle boxes
    taper jacks

bougies
TC.1221
ALT bougie

Bougival white
USE bismuth white

bouillon cups
TQ.326   (N)
ALT bouillon cup

SN Shallow cuplike vessels with two side handles intended primarily for serving bouillon; often accompanied by a matching saucer.
UF bowls, broth
    broth bowls
    cups, bouillon
    cups, soup
    soup cups
RT bouillon spoons
    cups

bouillon spoons
TH.322   (N)
HN April 1993 descriptor added
ALT bouillon spoon
SN Small spoons with a circular bowl used to consume bouillon and other clear soups. For larger spoons with a circular or oval bowl and used to consume soup use **soup spoons.**
UF spoons, bouillon
RT bouillon cups
    soup spoons

bouillotte lamps
TC.1229
ALT bouillotte lamp
SN Devices holding two to four candles and made of gilt brass with an adjustable painted metal shade.
UF lamps, bouillotte

boulder
MT.920   (L)
HN April 1992 descriptor moved

bouleuteria
RK.938
ALT bouleuterion
SN Use for the council chambers of ancient Greek cities, the place where the Boulé, a senate, met.

boulevards
RM.141   (L,B)
HN April 1993 descriptor moved
ALT boulevard
SN Wide city streets characterized by rows of trees or other plantings decoratively laid out along the sides or in a median strip.

boulle
USE boulle work

boulle marquetry
USE boulle work

boulle work
KT.134   (H,R)
HN January 1993 descriptor moved
    June 1991 lead-in term added
SN Marquetry comprised of brass and tortoise shell, applied to furniture especially in the late 17th and early 18th centuries.
UF boulle
    boulle marquetry
    buhl
    buhl work
    marquetry, boulle

boultels
TH.179
HN April 1993 descriptor added
ALT boultel
SN Cloth bags in which flour or meal is shaken as a means of sifting.
UF boulters

boulters
USE boultels

boultines
USE roll moldings

bouncers, recreation
USE trampolines

bound, half
USE half bindings

bound, quarter
USE quarter bindings

boundaries
BM.931   (L,B)
HN February 1993 descriptor moved
      January 1991 alternate term added
ALT boundary

boundary lights
RM.220
HN April 1993 descriptor moved
      May 1990 descriptor added
ALT boundary light
SN Aeronautical ground lights used to indicate the limits of the landing area of an airport. (W)
UF lights, boundary

boundary maps
USE cadastral maps

boundary stones
RM.231   (L)
HN April 1993 descriptor moved
ALT boundary stone
UF stones, boundary

boundary walls
RM.242
HN April 1993 lead-in term added
      April 1993 descriptor moved
ALT boundary wall
SN Use for walls enclosing an area or defining a boundary.
UF bounding walls
      walls, boundary
      walls, bounding

bounders, yellow
USE post chaises

bounding tables
USE trampolines

bounding walls
USE boundary walls

Bouneparte chairs
USE Trafalgar chairs

bouquet holders
TE.417
ALT bouquet holder
SN Decorative accessories for holding flowers in the hand, consisting of a tube or funnel of metal, open at one end; may convert to allow holder to stand and serve as miniature vase. (NMAHDC)
UF holders, bouquet
      holders, posie
      posie holders

bouquet stands
USE plant stands

bourdalous
TQ.182
ALT bourdalou
SN Small urinary containers for female use, of compressed elliptical shape with an incurved rim on the front end. Generally made of ceramic or occasionally silver.
UF chamber-pots, oval
      coach-pots
      oval chamber-pots
      slippers (containers)

Bourdon gages
TN.267   (L)
ALT Bourdon gage
SN Mechanical pressure-measuring instruments employing as sensing elements a curved or twisted metal tube, flattened in cross-section and closed. (MHDSTT)
UF Bourdon pressure gages
      Bourdon tubes
      gages, Bourdon
      gages, Bourdon pressure
      pressure gages, Bourdon
      tubes, Bourdon

Bourdon pressure gages
USE Bourdon gages

Bourdon tubes
USE Bourdon gages

bourgeoisie
HG.16   (L,R)
HN November 1991 descriptor moved
SN One of the social classes whose income derives from the profits of commercial and industrial enterprise, especially as distinguished from the landed gentry, wage earners, farmers, and the professions. (W)

bourkhas
USE burkas

bourses
USE exchanges

bousillage
MT.1781
HN April 1990 descriptor added
SN Mixture of mud, moss, and lime (often in the form of ground shells) used as infill between wall timbers, characteristic of French-influenced architecture of the southern United States, especially Louisiana.

bousines
USE buisines

bouteilleries
USE pantries

boutiques
RK.182   (A,B)
ALT boutique
SN Use for small, upscale specialty shops generally specializing in fashionable clothing or accessories or a special collection of other merchandise; may also be used for individual departments within larger stores if featuring a similar line of goods. (RHDEL2)

boutonné coverlets
TC.208
ALT boutonné coverlet
SN Handloomed coverlets with weft loop weave patterning, often in colored wools, in the French-Canadian tradition.
UF coverlets, boutonné
RT Bolton coverlets
      candlewick spreads

boutonnieres
TE.643   (N)
ALT boutonniere
SN Flowers or small bouquets worn, usually by a man, in the buttonhole of the lapel. (RHDEL2)

bovedas
USE pitched-brick vaults

Bovidean Pastoral phase
FL.69

bow-back Windsor chairs
TC.527
HN January 1993 descriptor moved
ALT bow-back Windsor chair
SN Windsor chairs having a back of medium height consisting of spindles contained within a bent bow that is anchored in the seat; may or may not have arms. (EVANS)
UF chairs, bow-back Windsor
      chairs, dining Windsor
      chairs, oval-back Windsor
      dining Windsor chairs
      oval-back Windsor chairs
      Windsor chairs, bow-back
      Windsor chairs, dining
      Windsor chairs, oval-back

bow compasses
TH.658   (N)
HN October 1992 descriptor added
ALT bow compass
SN Any of several types of compasses having the legs joined by a bow-shaped piece. (RHDEL2)
UF bows (bow compasses)
      compasses, bow
      compasses, spring bow
      spring bow compasses
      spring bows

bow drills
TH.594 (N)
ALT bow drill
SN Drills rotated by a cord or string wrapped tightly around it and strung to a bow. (RHDEL2)
UF drills, bow
drills, fiddle
drills, thong
fiddle drills
thong drills

bow harps
USE arched harps

bow lutes
USE pluriarcs

bow saws
TH.1579 (N)
ALT bow saw
SN Hand saws with a thin blade held in place between the two ends of a frame. (MEANS)
UF saws, bow
saws, sweep
saws, turning
sweep saws
turning saws

bow ties
TE.664 (N)
ALT bow tie
SN Small neckties tied in a bow knot.
UF ties, bow

bow tongs
USE sugar tongs

bow windows
PJ.2223 (H)
HN March 1993 descriptor moved
ALT bow window
SN Bay windows that are curved in plan.
UF compass windows
curved windows
windows, bow
windows, compass
windows, curved

bowed guitars
USE arpeggiones

bowed legs
USE cabriole legs

bowfront
DC.81
HN October 1992 descriptor moved

bowie-knives
SEE bowie knives

bowie knives
TK.32 (L,N)
ALT bowie knife
UK bowie-knives
UKA bowie-knife
SN Large hunting and fighting knives with a heavy blade, typically from 10 to 15 inches long, that is straight and single-edged for most of their length until it curves concavely and

acquires a double edge at the end. They were first produced for the American Colonel James Bowie in 1830.
UF knives, bowie

bowl capitals
HN May 1991 descriptor deleted

bowl gouges
TH.1459
ALT bowl gouge
SN Short bowl-shaped gouges. (BLACKB)
UF gouges, bowl

bowl lyres
TT.330
ALT bowl lyre
SN Lyres having a natural or man-made bowl for a resonator and a membrane belly. (MARCUS)
UF lyres, bowl

<bowl-shaped drums>
TT.574

bowl stands
USE basin stands

bowler hats
SEE derbies

bowlers
SEE derbies

bowling
KQ.40 (L)
UF bowling games
games, bowling
RT sports

bowling, 10-pin
USE tenpin bowling

<bowling alley sports>
KQ.41
RT bowling alleys
bowling pins

bowling alleys
RK.999 (A,L,B)
HN March 1993 related term added
September 1990 scope note added
ALT bowling alley
SN Designates buildings housing wooden lanes, equipped with facilities for setting bowling pins and returning balls to the user, for the indoor sport of bowling.
UF alleys, bowling
bowling lanes
lanes, bowling
RT <bowling alley sports>

bowling, candlepin
USE candlepin bowling

bowling, duckpin
USE duckpin bowling

bowling games
USE bowling

<bowling green sports>
KQ.45
RT bowling greens

bowling greens
RM.96 (H,L,B)
HN April 1993 descriptor moved
March 1993 scope note changed
March 1993 related term added
ALT bowling green
SN Designates closely mown, level pieces of ground reserved for the playing of lawn bowls.
UF greens, bowling
RT <bowling green sports>

bowling lanes
USE bowling alleys

bowling, lawn
USE lawn bowls

bowling pins
TV.41 (N)
ALT bowling pin
SN Use for the club-shaped or candle-shaped wooden or plastic targets set up for the various games of bowling.
UF pins (bowling equipment)
pins, bowling
RT <bowling alley sports>
targets (sports equipment)

bowling, tenpin
USE tenpin bowling

bowls (container components)
PJ.3089 (N,R)
ALT bowl (container component)
SN Rounded, cuplike, hollow parts of containers; especially the body of a stemmed vessel.

bowls (vessels)
TQ.66 (H,L,N,R)
ALT bowl (vessel)
SN Rounded vessels which are generally wider than they are high and which often have a spreading base or foot ring and sometimes two handles or a cover.
RT banana boats
basins
bleeding bowls
brandy bowls
chopping bowls
compotes
dinner services
dishes
finger bowls
fishbowls
fruit bowls
mixing bowls
punch bowls
rose bowls
salad bowls
saucers
slop bowls
soup bowls
standing bowls
sugar bowls

tea bowls
washbowls

bowls, banana
USE   banana boats

bowls, baptismal
USE   baptismal basins

bowls, barbers'
USE   shaving basins

bowls, bleeding
USE   bleeding bowls

bowls, brandy
USE   brandy bowls

bowls, broth
USE   bouillon cups

bowls, chopping
USE   chopping bowls

bowls, covered
USE   covered bowls

bowls, cricket
USE   cricket fields

bowls, cupping
USE   bleeding bowls

bowls, finger
USE   finger bowls

bowls, fish
USE   fishbowls

bowls, flower
USE   rose bowls

bowls, fraternity
USE   bratinas

bowls, fruit
USE   fruit bowls

bowls, indoor
USE   indoor bowls

bowls, lawn
USE   lawn bowls

bowls, mixing
USE   mixing bowls

bowls, monteith
USE   monteiths

bowls, punch
USE   punch bowls

bowls, rose
USE   rose bowls

bowls, salad
USE   salad bowls

bowls, shaving
USE   shaving basins

bowls, slop
USE   slop bowls

bowls, soup
USE   soup bowls

bowls, spitting
USE   spittoons

bowls, standing
USE   standing bowls

bowls, sugar
USE   sugar bowls

bowls, tea
USE   tea bowls

bowls, voiding
USE   slop bowls

bowls, wash
USE   washbowls

bowls, waste
USE   slop bowls

bowpots
USE   boughpots

bows (bow compasses)
USE   bow compasses

bows (chordophone components)
PJ.3248   (L)
ALT   bow (chordophone component)
SN   Flexible sticks of wood, very rarely of metal or plastic, carrying stretched between the two ends a length of horsehair or other stringlike material which is used to brush against the strings of a chordophone, causing them to sound. Historically bows have been evenly curved, curved only at one end, or straight in the middle with both ends curved; modern Western bows typically have a concave curve.
RT   <*lutelike chordophones: bowed*>
       Stroh violins
       <*zitherlike chordophones: bowed*>

bows (tools)
PJ.2595
HN   March 1993 descriptor moved
ALT   bow (tool)
SN   Tools that consist of a bent elastic rod with ends connected by a string; used for various purposes, as for giving reciprocating motion to a drill. (W)

bows (weapons)
TK.223   (H,L,N)
ALT   bow (weapon)
SN   Stringed projectile weapons designed to propel arrows, generally consisting of a long stave of wood, metal, fiberglass, or other flexible material, with a length of strong string fastened to the tips of the stave which is bent in a curve, either permanently or from the tension of the string. The string is drawn back, holding the arrow by means of a notch in its rear tip, and propels the arrow upon release.
RT   arrows
       nocks

bows, composite
USE   composite bows

bows, diddley
USE   diddley bows

bows, earth
USE   ground bows

bows, English
USE   longbows

bows, European
USE   self bows

bows, ground
USE   ground bows

bows, harp
USE   harp zithers

bows, knuckle
USE   knuckle guards

bows, mouth
USE   mouth bows

bows, musical
USE   musical bows

bows, self
USE   self bows

bows, simple
USE   self bows

bowstring arch-trusses
USE   bowstring trusses

bowstring trusses
PJ.1703   (B)
HN   March 1993 descriptor moved
       August 1991 scope note changed
       March 1991 descriptor moved
ALT   bowstring truss
SN   Trusses having a bow-shaped top chord, often semicircular or parabolic, and a straight or cambered member that ties together the two ends of the bow.
UF   arch-trusses, bowstring
       Belfast trusses
       bowstring arch-trusses
       trusses, Belfast
       trusses, bowstring

bowtells
USE   roll moldings

box beams
PJ.1645   (A,L,B)
HN   March 1993 descriptor moved
       July 1991 scope note changed
ALT   box beam
SN   Use for built-up hollow beams of rectangular section, whether metal or wood.
UF   beams, box
       box girders
       girders, box

box beds
TC.757   (H)
HN   January 1993 descriptor moved
ALT   box bed

SN Beds enclosed with paneling on all sides but one, where there was a curtain over the opening; usually stood against the wall and, in some cases, were built into the wall or incorporated into the scheme of paneling. (THORN2)
UF alcove beds
   beds, alcove
   beds, box
   beds, cupboard
   bedsteads, box
   box bedsteads
   close-beds
   cupboard beds
   lits alcoves
   lits carrosses
   lits chapelles
   lits clos
   lits en forme d'armoire
   lits fermés
   wall-beds

box bedsteads
USE box beds

box bolts
   PJ.554
HN March 1993 descriptor moved
ALT box bolt
UF bolts, box
   bolts, Canada
   Canada bolts

box cameras
   TH.751   (N)
ALT box camera
SN Early type of camera consisting of a lightproof box, with lens, shutter, and viewfinder, and employing film rather than a plate. (HCOP)
UF cameras, box

box chivs
USE howell planes

box coats
USE surtouts

box, common
USE boxwood

box elder
   MT.2809
HN March 1992 descriptor moved
UF Acer negundo
   ash-leafed maple
   elder, box
   maple, ash-leafed

box, European
USE boxwood

box frames
   PJ.1417   (B)
HN March 1993 descriptor moved
   November 1990 lead-in terms added
   November 1990 descriptor moved
   November 1990 scope note changed
ALT box frame
SN Structural frames of monolithic reinforced concrete with walls and floors in the form of slabs creating a cellular appearance.
UF cellular frames
   construction, cross-wall
   cross-wall construction
   frames, box
   frames, cellular

box girders
USE box beams

box hammer tongs
   TH.1296
SN Tongs to hold hammers being reforged. The prong fits into one eye of the hammer, while the bottom piece keeps the head from twisting sideways. (SMITH)
UF tongs, box hammer

box locks
   PJ.3177
ALT box lock
SN Firearm locks in which the entire mechanism is either set into the stock or contained within a metal boxlike frame, rather than mounted on external side plates.
UF locks, box

box locks (door locks)
USE rim locks

box lyres
   TT.338
ALT box lyre
SN Lyres having a built-up wooden box serving as a resonator and a wooden soundboard, existing today primarily in Ethiopia. (MARCUS)
UF lyres, box

box nails
   PJ.147
HN April 1993 descriptor moved
ALT box nail
SN Nails similar to common nails with the same penny designation of length but having a shank smaller in diameter. (MEANS)
UF nails, box

box pews
   PJ.2528
HN March 1993 descriptor moved
   July 1991 scope note changed
ALT box pew
SN Pews screened and enclosed by high backs and sides. (HAS)
UF pews, box

box pleats
   PJ.3063
ALT box pleat
SN Wide double pleats, with the material folded under at each side. For wide double pleats having the flat fold turned in rather than out, use **inverted pleats.**
UF pleats, box

box scrapers
   TH.1610
ALT box scraper
SN Scraping tools whose blade is perpendicular to the handle and set at the end of two parallel arms.
UF scrapers, box

box settles
   TC.712
HN May 1993 related term added
   March 1993 lead-in term changed, was monk's benches (box settles)
   March 1993 lead-in term changed, was **benches, monk's (box benches)**
   January 1993 descriptor moved
ALT box settle
SN Settles with a box seat with a hinged lid which allows access to a storage space beneath.
UF benches, monks'
   chest-benches
   monks' benches
   settles, box
   settles, storage
   storage settles
RT settles

box springs
   PJ.2745   (N)
HN March 1993 descriptor moved
   March 1993 scope note added
ALT box spring
SN Bedsprings that consist of spiral springs attached to a foundation and enclosed in a cloth-covered frame. (W)
UF springs, box

box stalls
   PJ.1292
HN March 1993 descriptor moved
ALT box stall
SN In barns or stables, individual compartments in which an animal may move about freely. (DAC)
UF boxes, loose
   loose boxes
   stalls, box

box stools
   TC.663
HN January 1993 descriptor moved
ALT box stool
SN Stools with the seat board hinged to the seat-rail in the form of a small lidded chest. (CHINNE)
UF stools, box

box stoops
   PJ.990
HN March 1993 descriptor moved
ALT box stoop
SN High stoops making a quarter turn, reached by a flight of stairs along a building front. (DAC)
UF stoops, box

box stretcher desks-on-frames
USE desks-on-frames

box stretchers
   PJ.2891

HN March 1993 descriptor moved
ALT box stretcher
UF stretchers, box

box strikes
    PJ.64
HN March 1993 descriptor moved
ALT box strike
SN Strikes with enclosed recesses to receive lock bolts. (MEANS)
UF strikes, box

box tongs
    TH.1291   (N)
UF tongs, box

box vises
    TH.1649
ALT box vise
UF vises, box

boxcars
    TX.246   (N)
ALT boxcar
SN Totally enclosed boxlike freight cars, with floor, roof, sides, and ends, usually with large doors on the sides or sides and ends.

boxer shorts
    TE.223   (L,N)
SN Loose-fitting underpants for men, having short, trouserlike legs rather then leg openings.
UF boxers
    shorts, boxer

boxers
USE boxer shorts

boxes (audience spaces)
    PJ.1296   (A)
HN March 1993 descriptor moved
ALT box (audience space)
UF boxes, theater
    theater boxes

boxes (containers)
    TQ.11   (H,L,N,R)
ALT box (container)
SN Rigid, often rectangular containers usually with a lid or cover in which something nonliquid is kept or carried. (W)
RT ballot boxes
    Bible boxes
    biscuit boxes
    bread boxes
    brideboxes
    caskets
    cheese boxes
    cigar boxes
    cigarette boxes
    collar and cuff boxes
    comfit boxes
    ditty boxes
    dressing cases
    file boxes
    freedom boxes
    glove boxes
    hairpin boxes
    handkerchief boxes
    hatboxes

    patch boxes
    pillboxes (containers)
    pounce boxes
    salt boxes
    sardine boxes
    sewing boxes
    soap boxes
    spice boxes
    stamp boxes
    <storage boxes>
    sugar boxes
    tobacco boxes
    workboxes

boxes (furniture components)
USE birdcages (furniture components)

boxes (soundboxes)
USE soundboxes

boxes, aquatint
USE dust boxes

boxes, aquatint dust
USE dust boxes

boxes, aromatic vinegar
USE vinaigrettes

boxes, ballot
USE ballot boxes

boxes, Bible
USE Bible boxes

boxes, biscuit
USE biscuit boxes

boxes, bonnet
USE hatboxes

boxes, bougie
USE candle boxes
    taper jacks

boxes, bread
USE bread boxes

boxes, brides'
USE brideboxes

boxes, call
USE telephone booths

boxes, candle
USE candle boxes

boxes, cases of
USE cabinets (case furniture)

boxes, cheese
USE cheese boxes

boxes, cigar
USE cigar boxes

boxes, cigarette
USE cigarette boxes

boxes, collar and cuff
USE collar and cuff boxes

boxes, comfit
USE comfit boxes

boxes, desk
USE Bible boxes

boxes, ditty
USE ditty boxes

boxes, dough
USE dough troughs

boxes, dredging
USE dredgers (containers)

boxes, dressing
USE dressing cases

boxes, drudging
USE dredgers (containers)

boxes, dust
USE dust boxes

boxes, file
USE file boxes

boxes, fire alarm
USE manual stations

boxes, flower
USE window boxes

boxes, folding
USE cartons

boxes, freedom
USE freedom boxes

boxes, glove
USE glove boxes

boxes, hairpin
USE hairpin boxes

boxes, handkerchief
USE handkerchief boxes

boxes, ice
USE iceboxes

boxes, kneading
USE dough troughs

boxes, letter
USE mailboxes

boxes, loose
USE box stalls

boxes, mail
USE mailboxes

boxes, miter
USE miter boxes

boxes, music
USE music boxes

boxes, needlework
USE sewing boxes

boxes, outlet
USE power outlets

boxes, packing
USE packing boxes

boxes, paint
USE paint boxes

boxes, paper
USE cartons

boxes, patch
USE   patch boxes

boxes, pill
USE   pillboxes (containers)

boxes, pin
USE   hairpin boxes

boxes, pounce
USE   pounce boxes

boxes, powder
USE   spice boxes

boxes, press
USE   press boxes

boxes, punch
USE   jack-in-the-boxes

boxes, quill
USE   slip cups

boxes, rosin
USE   dust boxes

boxes, rosin dust
USE   dust boxes

boxes, salt
USE   salt boxes

boxes, sardine
USE   sardine boxes

boxes, screw
USE   screw boxes

boxes, seal
USE   freedom boxes

boxes, sentry
USE   sentry boxes

boxes, sewing
USE   sewing boxes

boxes, signal
USE   signal towers

boxes, sneak
USE   sneak boxes

boxes, soap
USE   soap boxes

boxes, solander
USE   solander boxes

boxes, sound
USE   soundboxes

boxes, spice
USE   spice boxes

boxes, spill
USE   spill holders

boxes, stamp
USE   stamp boxes

boxes, stilling
USE   stilling basins

boxes, sugar
USE   sugar boxes

boxes, sweetmeat
USE   sugar boxes

boxes, taper
USE   candle boxes

boxes, theater
USE   boxes (audience spaces)

boxes, tobacco
USE   tobacco boxes

boxes, tool
USE   toolboxes

boxes, vesta
USE   matchboxes

boxes, voting
USE   ballot boxes

boxes, window
USE   window boxes

boxes, wood
USE   woodbins

boxes, work
USE   workboxes

boxing planes
USE   rabbet planes

boxing shutters
USE   folding + shutters

boxwood
MT.2712   (L)
HN   March 1992 descriptor moved
UF   Abasian boxwood
      Asiatic boxwood
      box, common
      box, European
      boxwood, Abasian
      boxwood, Asiatic
      boxwood, common
      boxwood, European
      boxwood, Indian
      Buxus sempervirens
      common box
      common boxwood
      European box
      European boxwood
      Indian boxwood

boxwood, Abasian
USE   boxwood

boxwood, Asiatic
USE   boxwood

boxwood, common
USE   boxwood

boxwood, European
USE   boxwood

boxwood, Indian
USE   boxwood

boxwood, Maracaibo
USE   Maracaibo boxwood

boxwood, West Indian
USE   Maracaibo boxwood

Boyela
USE   Yela

Boylston
FL.883

Boyo
FL.508

Bozo
FL.374   (L)

bozzetti
VC.588   (R)
HN   May 1991 scope note changed
      April 1991 descriptor moved
ALT   bozzetto
SN   Use for fairly developed sketches,
      most often three-dimensional ones
      for sculpture, but may be painted or
      drawn. With regard to sketches
      for architecture, use **preliminary
      sketches**. For rougher sculptural
      sketches, use **maquettes**.

BPs
USE   beam projectors

bra slips
TE.193
ALT   bra slip
SN   Slips with a foundation included in
      the bodice portion.
UF   slips, bra
RT   brassieres

braced frames
PJ.1412
HN   March 1993 descriptor moved
      November 1990 descriptor moved
      November 1990 scope note changed
ALT   braced frame
SN   Use for wooden building frames
      that use diagonal bracing between
      full-height corner posts and the
      plates; generally found in construc-
      tion with timbers heavy enough to
      be mortised.
UF   frames, braced

braced tables
USE   sawbuck tables

bracelets (foot components)
PJ.2827
HN   March 1993 descriptor moved
ALT   bracelet (foot component)
SN   Modern American term for a band
      separating the leg and foot of a ta-
      ble or stand.

bracelets (jewelry)
TE.469   (H,L,N,R)
ALT   bracelet (jewelry)
SN   Ornamental bands or circlets worn
      on the lower arm. Use **armlets** for
      similar articles worn on the upper
      arm.
RT   armillae (jewelry)
      armlets

bracelets, ankle
USE   anklets

bracelets, bangle
USE bangles

bracelets, charm
USE charm bracelets

bracelets, ID
USE identification bracelets

bracelets, identification
USE identification bracelets

bracelets, identity
SEE identification bracelets

braces
SEE suspenders (garment supports)

braces (shield handles)
USE enarmes

braces (supporting elements)
PJ.1438   (N)
HN March 1993 descriptor moved
     May 1991 descriptor changed, was
       braces
     May 1991 alternate term changed,
       was **brace**
ALT brace (supporting element)
SN Use for rigid stays, usually of wood
     or metal, and commonly in com-
     pression.
UF struts

braces (woodworking tools)
TH.1423   (H,N)
ALT brace (woodworking tool)
SN Hand tools with a handle, crank,
     and chuck; used for turning a bit or
     auger to drill a hole by hand. (DAC)
UF bit braces
     bit stocks
     braces, bit
     braces, hand
     breast stocks
     breast wimbles
     hand braces
     stocks (woodworking tools)
     stocks, bit
     stocks, breast
     sways
     sweeps
     whimbles
     wimbles, breast

braces, angle
USE hand drills
     knee braces

braces, arch
USE arch braces

braces, bit
USE braces (woodworking tools)

braces, bracket
USE bracket feet

braces, drill
USE hand drills

braces, gearing
USE hand drills

braces, hand
USE braces (woodworking tools)

braces, knee
USE knee braces

braces, medial
USE medial braces

braces, ratchet
USE ratchet braces

braces, smiths'
USE smiths' braces

braces, spur
USE spurs (architectural elements)

braces, sweep
USE medial braces

braces, wind
USE wind braces

bracket braces
USE bracket feet

bracket capitals
PJ.1495
HN March 1993 descriptor moved
     November 1990 scope note changed
ALT bracket capital
SN Use for capitals whose upper bear-
     ing surface has been greatly ex-
     tended by projecting elements
     placed along the planes loaded by
     beams or roof members, generally
     used to lessen the span between
     supports.
UF capitals, bracket

bracket clocks
TN.161
ALT bracket clock
SN Small, spring-driven or pendulum,
     wood-cased clocks intended to be
     placed on a bracket on the wall, set
     on a mantel, or carried from room
     to room; the brackets were often de-
     signed to match the style of clocks;
     generally from the 17th and 18th
     centuries.
UF clocks, bracket

bracket feet
PJ.2795
HN March 1993 descriptor moved
ALT bracket foot
SN Feet shaped like a bracket, in com-
     mon use on case furniture in the
     first half of the 18th century.
     (TOMLIN)
UF braces, bracket
     bracket braces
     brackets (feet)
     Chinese feet
     feet, bracket
     feet, Chinese
     feet, Goddard
     Goddard feet

bracket feet, common
USE French feet

bracket feet, flaring
USE French feet

bracket feet, ogee
USE ogee bracket feet

bracket lamps
USE brackets (lighting devices)

bracket saws
USE fretsaws

bracket scaffolding
TH.1050
SN Scaffolding supported by metal
     brackets which are temporarily
     attached to a building or column.
     (DAC)
UF bracket staging
     scaffolding, bracket
     staging, bracket

bracket staging
USE bracket scaffolding

bracket tables
USE console tables

bracket tables, console
USE eagle console tables

Bracketed mode
USE Italian Villa Style

brackets (consoles)
USE consoles

brackets (feet)
USE bracket feet

brackets (finish hardware)
PJ.314   (L,N,B)
HN April 1993 descriptor moved
     May 1990 descriptor added
ALT bracket (finish hardware)

brackets (lighting device components)
PJ.2902   (N,B)
ALT bracket (lighting device component)
SN Attachments to a lamp post or pole
     from which a lamp or lighting fix-
     ture is suspended. (STEIN)
UF arms, mast
     brackets, lamps
     lamp brackets
     mast arms

brackets (lighting devices)
TC.1215
ALT bracket (lighting device)
SN Lamps or candleholders that are
     attached to, or suspended from,
     some form of bracket by which they
     can be hung on a wall or that is af-
     fixed to the wall.
UF bracket lamps
     brackets, wall
     lamps, bracket
     wall brackets
RT wall lamps

brackets (structural elements)
PJ.1665   (L,N,B)
HN March 1993 descriptor moved

November 1991 alternate term changed, was **bracket**

May 1990 descriptor changed, was **brackets**

ALT bracket (structural element)

SN Use for elements, usually of generally triangular shape, that project from a wall, pier, or other structure and which serve to support vertical loads or strengthen an angle by transferring the load against the face of the structure from which they project; sometimes more decorative than functional.

brackets, angle
USE angle brackets

brackets, candle
USE candle brackets

brackets, handrail
USE handrail brackets

brackets, knee
USE knee brackets

brackets, lamps
USE brackets (lighting device components)

brackets, shelf
USE shelf brackets

brackets, stifted
USE stifted brackets

brackets, swing
USE swing brackets

brackets, wall
USE brackets (lighting devices)

bracteates (coins)
VK.6 (H,L,R)
ALT bracteate (coin)
SN Use for very thin, usually silver, coins struck with an obverse die only so that the design shows through on the reverse; used in Germany and neighboring territories between the 12th and 18th centuries.

bracteates (pendants)
TE.437 (L)
ALT bracteate (pendant)
SN Pendants in the form of discs of thin, beaten gold or silver with stamped decoration based on Roman coin or medallion prototypes or with runic inscriptions. Suspended by means of a circular attachment and intended to be worn on a thong or other support around the neck.

brad nails
USE brads

brad nails, flooring
USE flooring nails

brad pushers
TH.1620
ALT brad pusher
SN Special tools used to grip and insert brads in an inaccessible location. (MEANS)
UF brad squeezers
pushers, brad
squeezers, brad

brad squeezers
USE brad pushers

bradawls
TH.1408 (N)
ALT bradawl
SN Tools resembling ice picks, used to make holes for brads and wood screws. (MEANS)
UF awls, flooring
bits, sprig
flooring awls
sprig bits

brads
PJ.161 (N)
HN April 1993 descriptor moved
ALT brad
SN Slender, smooth nails each having a small deep head used for finish carpentry work. (MEANS)
UF brad nails
nails, brad

brads, flat-head wire
USE flat-head wire brads

Brah Pahdona
USE Pra Patom

Brahmanism
BM.500 (L)
ALT Brahmanic

braid
MT.2498
HN December 1992 descriptor added
SN A narrow trimming made by a variety of techniques such as tablet weaving or braiding. It comes in a variety of fibers and weights, but is heavier than ribbon and flatter than cord.

braiding
KT.1173 (L)
HN March 1993 lead-in term deleted, was **braid**
March 1993 descriptor moved
March 1993 scope note changed
ALT braided
SN Flat over-and-under oblique interlacing using the undifferentiated elements of a single set of strands, characterized by the oblique crossings of the elements and their common directional trend.
UF plaiting

braille
PJ.3433 (L)
SN System of writing or printing for the use of the visually impaired in which combinations of dots or points are used to represent characters and are read by touch.

braille maps
VW.57
HN November 1992 descriptor moved
January 1991 lead-in term added
ALT braille map
SN Maps for the blind utilizing symbols and the braille system of writing. (CM)
UF maps, braille
tactile orientation models

brain
MT.2538 (L)
HN February 1992 descriptor added
SN The part of the central nervous system enclosed in the cranium of humans and other vertebrates. (RHDEL2)

braising pans
USE braziers (culinary equipment)

brake-vans
SEE cabooses

brakes (carriages)
USE breaks

brakes, dough
USE bread makers

branch banks
RK.131 (L)
ALT branch bank
UF banks, branch

branch libraries
RK.666 (L,B)
ALT branch library
SN Libraries in a system other than the main or central library. (ERIC9)
UF libraries, branch

branch mahogany
USE crotch mahogany

branch sewers
RK.517
ALT branch sewer
SN Sewers that receive sewage from a relatively small area and are connected to main sewers or manholes. (MEANS)
UF sewers, branch

branches, candle
USE candle branches

branching crackle
USE traction crackle

Brancovan
FL.3295 (H,R)

branding irons
USE brands

brands
TH.900 (L,N)
HN January 1991 lead-in terms added
ALT brand
SN Iron rods which terminate in a flat surface on which is a device or letter set in relief; used after heating to mark livestock, tools, or manufac-

tured goods with indelible evidence of ownership.
UF branding irons
    brands, burn
    brands, marking
    burn brands
    irons, branding
    irons, marking
    marking brands
    marking irons

brands, burn
USE brands

brands, marking
USE brands

brandy bowls
     TQ.391
ALT brandy bowl
SN   Drinking vessels similar to but usually larger than a dram cup.
UF   bowls, brandy
RT   bowls (vessels)
     dram cups
     écuelles
     porringers

brandy glasses
USE snifters

brandy inhalers
USE snifters

brandy-saucepans
USE pipkins

brandy snifters
USE snifters

brank-ursine
USE acanthus

bras
USE brassieres

bras, chapeaux
USE chapeaux bras

brasers
USE braziers (culinary equipment)

brasil
USE logwood

brass (alloy)
     MT.387   (A,L,B,R)
HN   April 1993 related term added
     March 1993 scope note added
     March 1993 lead-in terms added
     March 1993 descriptor moved
     May 1991 descriptor changed, was **brass**
SN   Alloy of copper and zinc, usually with copper as the major alloying element and zinc up to 40% by weight. (MMAHM)
UF   alloy, copper-zinc
     copper-zinc alloy
RT   hard solder

brass (color)
USE dark yellow
     moderate yellow

Brass (Ijo)
     FL.266

brass, admiralty
USE admiralty metal

brass, cartridge
USE cartridge brass

brass instruments
     TT.643   (L)
ALT brass instrument
SN   Lip-vibrated aerophones made of brass or other metals.
UF   instruments, brass
RT   bugles
     crooks
     sarrusophones

brass knuckles
     TK.28   (N)
ALT brass knuckle
SN   American weapons consisting of a band of metal, either with holes for four fingers or a single large opening to slip the main part of the hand into, leaving the thumb outside, used to increase the effect of a blow with the fist.
UF   knuckle-dusters
     knuckles, brass

brass, naval
USE naval brass

brass, red
USE red brass

brass rubbing
HN   July 1990 descriptor split, use **brass (memorial)** (ALT of **brasses (memorials)**) + **rubbing**

brass-smithing
     KT.1066   (L)
UF   brasswork (brass-smithing)
     smithing, brass

brass, tin
USE naval brass

brass-work
SEE brasswork

brass, yellow
USE cartridge brass

brasseries
     RK.114   (A,B)
ALT brasserie
SN   Use for unpretentious restaurants serving fresh, simply prepared foods, beers, and ales in an informal, casual atmosphere.

brasses (furniture hardware)
USE furniture hardware

brasses (memorials)
     VC.516   (A,L,B,R)
ALT brass (memorial)
SN   Incised brass plates serving as memorials to the dead, often showing a portrait or coat of arms.
UF   brasses, church

     brasses, memorial
     brasses, monumental
     brasses, sepulchral
     brasses, tomb
     church brasses
     memorial brasses
     monumental brasses
     sepulchral brasses
     tomb brasses

brasses, church
USE brasses (memorials)

brasses, memorial
USE brasses (memorials)

brasses, monumental
USE brasses (memorials)

brasses, sepulchral
USE brasses (memorials)

brasses, tomb
USE brasses (memorials)

brassieres
     TE.196   (L,N)
ALT brassiere
SN   Close-fitting underwear worn for bust support, varying in width from a band to a waist-length bodice, made with or without cups or straps and often boned or wired for additional support or separation.
UF   bandeaux (brassieres)
     bodices, bust
     bras
     bust bodices
     uplifts
RT   bra slips
     bust forms
     corselets

brassieres, bust-confining
USE bust reducers

brasswork
     PE.133   (L)
HN   October 1992 descriptor moved
UK   brass-work

brasswork (brass-smithing)
USE brass-smithing

bratinas
     TQ.392
ALT bratina
SN   Russian ceremonial drinking vessels, globular in form and sometimes having a cover and a low foot ring; usually of silver and sometimes richly enamelled or ornamented with gems.
UF   bowls, fraternity
     fraternity bowls
RT   <ceremonial vessels>

brattishing
     PJ.2356
HN   March 1993 descriptor moved
     March 1993 related term added
SN   Ornamental cresting on the top of a screen or cornice, usually formed of leaves, Tudor flowers, or miniature

battlements; found especially in English Late Gothic architecture. (PDARC)
RT cresting

brayers
TH.839   (N)
HN February 1993 descriptor added
ALT brayer
SN Soft rubber rollers attached to wooden or metal handles; used to ink wood blocks, linoleum blocks, lithographic stones, or printing plates. (QCKAIE)

brayers, gelatin
USE gelatin brayers

brayers, gelatine
USE gelatin brayers

braze welding
KT.1087   (L)
HN March 1993 related term added
    March 1993 lead-in term deleted, was **brazing**
    March 1991 alternate term added
    November 1990 lead-in term added
ALT braze-welded
SN Method of welding whereby a groove, fillet, plug, or seat weld is made using a nonferrous filler metal having a melting point below that of base metals. (STEIN)
UF welding, braze
RT brazing

brazeros
USE braziers (culinary equipment)

braziers (culinary equipment)
TH.54   (H,L,N)
HN April 1993 descriptor added
ALT brazier (culinary equipment)
SN Metal receptacles with a base designed to hold live coals, and generally with a pierced cover or lid, used for cooking and warming food and in some cases for heating a room.
UF braising pans
    brasers
    brazeros
    pans, braising
RT chafing dishes

braziers (metalworkers)
HG.710
HN January 1993 descriptor changed, was **braziers**
    January 1993 alternate term changed, was **brazier**
    December 1992 alternate terms added
ALT brazier (metalworker)
    brazier's
    braziers'
SN Persons who work in brass. (W)

Brazilian
FL.733   (L,B)

Brazilian rosewood
MT.2888

HN March 1992 descriptor moved
UF Dalbergia nigra
    jacaranda
    jacaranda wood
    pao rosa
    rosewood, Brazilian
    wood, jacaranda

Brazilian Style
FL.270   (A)

Brazilian walnut
USE imbuia

brazilwood
MT.2714
HN March 1992 descriptor moved
UF Caesalpinia brasiliensis
    Caesalpinia echinata
    ébano

brazing
KT.1076   (L)
HN March 1993 lead-in terms added
    March 1993 descriptor moved
    March 1993 related terms added
    March 1993 scope note changed
ALT brazed
SN Use for the process of joining two pieces of metal by inserting filler metal of very high melting point, such as hard solder, between them and applying heat, at temperatures ranging between 750 and 900 degrees Celsius; sometimes but not necessarily involves softening or melting the surfaces to be joined. For the similar process carried out at temperatures below 750 degrees Celsius, use **soldering**. For the process of joining two pieces of metal that necessarily involves softening or melting the surfaces to be joined but not necessarily the insertion of filler metal, use **welding**.
UF hard soldering
    soldering, hard
RT braze welding
    hard solder
    soldering
    welding

brazing alloy
USE hard solder

brazing, arc
USE arc brazing

brazing, dip
USE dip brazing

brazing, furnace
USE furnace brazing

brazing, induction
USE induction brazing

brazing, resistance
USE resistance brazing

brazing solder
USE hard solder

brazing, torch
USE torch brazing

brazing, vacuum
USE vacuum brazing

bread-and-butter plates
TQ.362   (N)
ALT bread-and-butter plate
SN Plates for holding an individual serving of bread, similar to but smaller than dessert plates.
UF bread plates
    butter plates
    plates, bread
    plates, bread-and-butter
    plates, butter
RT dessert plates
    place settings

bread and cheese cupboards
USE livery cupboards

bread baskets
TQ.321   (N)
ALT bread basket
SN Baskets or basketlike containers for bread or rolls. (RHDEL2)
UF baskets, bread
RT baskets
    cake baskets

bread baskets (dough baskets)
USE dough baskets

bread blenders
USE bread makers

bread boxes
TQ.574   (N)
ALT bread box
SN Airtight or nearly airtight, boxlike containers, of metal or plastic, for storing bread and other baked goods to keep them fresh. (RHDEL2)
UF boxes, bread
RT boxes (containers)

bread-brakes
USE dough troughs

bread coolers
USE cooling racks

bread graters
TH.119
HN April 1993 descriptor added
ALT bread grater
SN Metal graters for making bread crumbs.
UF bread rasps
    graters, bread
    rasps, bread

bread knives
TH.260   (N)
HN April 1993 descriptor added
ALT bread knife
SN Knives with a long blade and a serrated or scalloped cutting edge. Similar in form to **cake knives,** but having larger teeth set further apart.

UF knives, bread
RT cake knives

bread makers
TH.141 (L,N)
HN April 1993 descriptor added
ALT bread maker
SN Devices intended primarily for mixing and kneading bread dough;
used especially with reference to
pail-like containers with large, hand-
cranked kneading paddles or
blades; also, for electrical devices
that mix, knead, and bake bread
dough.
UF blenders, bread
brakes, dough
bread blenders
bread-makers
bread mixers
bread-mixers
dough brakes
dough-brakes
dough kneaders
dough-kneaders
dough makers
dough-makers
dough mixers
kneaders, dough
makers, bread
makers, dough
mixers, bread
mixers, dough

bread-makers
USE bread makers

bread mixers
USE bread makers

bread-mixers
USE bread makers

bread pans
TQ.291 (N)
ALT bread pan
SN Pans, often metal, intended primar-
ily for baking bread; made in vary-
ing size and form.
UF pans, bread

bread peels
USE peels

bread plates
USE bread-and-butter plates

bread raisers
TQ.277
ALT bread raiser
SN Large, tin, bowl-shaped vessels with
a perforated lid; used to protect and
cover bread dough while it rises.
UF raisers, bread

bread-raising baskets
USE dough baskets

bread rasps
USE bread graters

bread trays
TQ.322 (N)
ALT bread tray

SN Shallow receptacles used to serve
bread at the table; often rectangular
with upcurving sides. (HNSIL)
UF trays, bread
RT trays

bread troughs
USE dough troughs

breadboards
TH.49 (N)
HN April 1993 descriptor added
ALT breadboard
SN Boards on which dough is kneaded
or rolled and bread is cooled and
cut.
UF boards, bread
boards, dough
boards, kneading
dough boards
kneading boards
RT cutting boards

break-front
SEE breakfront

break joints
PJ.622
HN April 1993 descriptor moved
ALT break joint
SN Arrangements of modular structural
units, such as masonry or plywood
sheathing, so that the vertical joints
of adjacent units do not line up.
(MEANS)
UF broken joints
joints, break
joints, broken
joints, shift
joints, staggered
shift joints
staggered joints

break-open
DC.215
HN November 1992 descriptor added
SN Use to describe firearms that hinge
open at the barrel breech to allow
ammunition to be loaded.

breaker balls
USE wrecking balls

breaker, bond
USE bond breaker

breakers, ball
USE wrecking balls

breakers, circuit
USE circuit breakers

breakers, sun
USE brise-soleils

breakers, sword
USE sword breakers

breakfast nooks
PJ.1048 (A)
HN March 1993 descriptor moved
ALT breakfast nook
SN Alcoves where light meals are taken;

usually containing a built-in table
and seating.
UF nooks, breakfast

breakfast rooms
PJ.1049
HN March 1993 descriptor moved
ALT breakfast room
SN Small rooms for the morning meal;
usually, but not always, adjoining
the chief dining room; in northern
climates often specially arranged
with an eastern exposure to catch
the morning sun. (RS)
UF rooms, breakfast

breakfast services
PC.19 (H)
ALT breakfast service
SN Services intended for use at breakfast generally including a teapot,
coffeepot or chocolate pot; creamer
and sugar bowl; cups and saucers;
bowls and plates; toast rack or other
accessories for service and sometimes flatware and cutlery.
UF services, breakfast
RT chocolate pots
coffee cups
coffeepots
creamers
cutlery
egg stands
eggcups
flatware
jam pots
saucers
sugar bowls
teacups
teapots
toast racks

breakfast tables
TC.1120 (N)
HN January 1993 descriptor moved
ALT breakfast table
SN Moderate-sized tables lacking the
raised edge of a tea table or the
scale of a dining table and having
drop leaves and sometimes a small
drawer or two in the apron.
(DOWNS)
UF tables, breakfast

breakfront
DC.82
HN October 1992 descriptor moved
UK break-front
SN Having a slightly projecting central
section, used with reference to case
furniture. (THDAT)
UF broken front

breaking
KT.275
HN August 1992 scope note added
ALT broken
SN Splitting into pieces or smashing
into parts or fragments, typically by
a blow or stress and with sudden-
ness or violence. (W)

breaking strength
DC.185
SN The greatest stress, especially in tension, that a material, such as a fiber, can withstand without rupture.
UF strength, breaking

breaks
TX.197
ALT break
SN Heavy driving vehicles with a high driving seat and no body designed for training horses for carriage driving or for exercising or breaking horses; not used for pleasure driving.
UF brakes (carriages)

breaks, thermal
USE thermal breaks

breakwaters
RK.524 (A,L,R)
ALT breakwater
SN Use for structures, usually located offshore, built to protect an area from waves.
UF moles

breakwaters, blockwork
USE blockwork breakwaters

breakwaters, mound
USE mound breakwaters

breast augers
TH.1399
ALT breast auger
SN Augers having a wood stock with a shell or nose bit; turned by a wood bar passing through a hole in the top of the stock. (SALAM)
UF augers, breast

breast bibs
USE breastplates (tools)

breast drills
TH.595
ALT breast drill
SN Manual rotary drills which have an attachment for applying pressure with the chest; used by carpenters for drilling horizontal holes. (MEANS)
UF drills, breast

breast stocks
USE braces (woodworking tools)

breast wimbles
USE braces (woodworking tools)

breastpins
USE brooches

<breastplate components>
PJ.3004

breastplates (body armor)
TE.306 (N)
ALT breastplate (body armor)
SN Pieces of armor protecting the front of the torso, consisting either of a

single contoured plate, or of two or more plates or lames overlapping.

breastplates (tools)
TH.1426 (N)
ALT breastplate (tool)
SN Pieces of hardwood against which a workman presses his breast in operating a breast drill or similar tool. (W)
UF bibs, breast
breast bibs

breastplates, reinforcing
USE plackarts

breasts, chimney
USE chimney breasts

breastworks
PJ.2478
HN March 1993 descriptor moved
June 1991 scope note changed
ALT breastwork
SN Defensive walls about breast high.

breccia
MT.915 (L)
HN March 1992 scope note added
March 1992 descriptor moved
SN A coarse-grained clastic rock, composed of angular broken rock fragments held together by a mineral cement or a fine-grained matrix. (AGI)

breccia a semesanto
MT.692
HN April 1992 descriptor moved

breccia corallina
MT.693
HN April 1992 descriptor moved

breccia di Settebasi
MT.694
HN April 1992 descriptor moved

breccia marble
MT.691
HN April 1992 descriptor moved
UF marble, breccia

breccia marble, Egyptian
USE Egyptian breccia marble

breccia, Potomac
USE Potomac breccia

breccia traccagnina
MT.695
HN April 1992 descriptor moved

breche violette marble
MT.696
HN April 1992 descriptor moved
UF marble, breche violette

breech, bear's
USE acanthus

breech-loaders
USE breechloading + firearms

<breech mechanism components>
PJ.3167

<breech mechanisms>
PJ.3163

<breech mechanisms and breech mechanism components>
PJ.3162

breechblocks
PJ.3168
ALT breechblock
SN Movable metal blocks fitting into the breeches of firearms, serving to close and seal the breech opening of the barrel during firing.

breechcloths
USE loincloths

breeches (barrel components)
PJ.3161
ALT breech (barrel component)
SN Rear sections of the barrels of firearms, containing the chamber in which the charge is ignited.

breeches (trousers)
TE.101 (N,R)
SN Knee-length trousers commonly worn by men and boys in the 17th, 18th, and early 19h centuries.
UF breeches, knee
knee breeches

breeches, jodhpurs
USE jodhpurs

breeches, knee
USE breeches (trousers)

breeches of mail
USE brekes of mail

breechloaders
USE breechloading + firearms

breechloading
DC.214 (N)
HN November 1992 descriptor added
SN Use to describe firearms that are loaded at the rear end of the barrel. (TARA)

breeders, horse
USE horse breeders

breeders, livestock
USE livestock breeders

breeders, stock
USE livestock breeders

breeding stations, fish
USE fish hatcheries

breeze
MT.1684 (B)
HN April 1993 descriptor moved
April 1993 scope note changed
SN Lightweight aggregate made from the residue from the making of coke or charcoal.

UF breeze, pan
    pan breeze

breeze, pan
USE breeze

breeze-ways
SEE breezeways

breezeways
    PJ.1187
HN March 1993 descriptor moved
ALT breezeway
UK breeze-ways
UKA breeze-way
SN Use for roofed passages connecting two parts of a house or a house and garage; common after 1930. Distinct from **dogtrots**, which occur in folk architecture and log houses.

brekes of mail
    TE.338
ALT breke of mail
SN Pieces of mail to protect the genitals, worn attached to the center of the lower edge of a shirt of mail or appended to the fork of a plate armor skirt. They took various forms, including short skirts or breeches, and could incorporate a codpiece.
UF breeches of mail
    mail, breeches of
    mail, brekes of

breloques
    TE.440   (N)
ALT breloque
SN Small seals or charms, intended to be worn from a watch chain. (W)

Bremen blue
HN January 1992 descriptor deleted, made lead-in to **azurite**

Bremen blue
USE azurite
    blue verditer
    light greenish blue
    moderate bluish green

Bremen green
USE malachite (pigment)

bretelles
    TE.644
ALT bretelle
SN Decorative attachments resembling suspenders, with shaped straps which pass over each shoulder, and sometimes connect to a matching waistband. The straps are sometimes connected by horizontal bands across the chest or back. (NMAHDC)
RT suspenders (garment supports)

Brettstuhls
    TC.469
HN January 1993 descriptor moved
ALT Brettstuhl
SN German variety of the board chair. (BOYCE)

Breuer chairs
USE Cesca chairs
    Wassily chairs

breviaries
    VW.888   (L,R)
HN November 1992 descriptor moved
ALT breviary
SN Books containing all daily psalms, hymns, prayers, lessons, and other religious recitations necessary to enable a cleric to recite the daily Divine Office. (RHDEL2)

breweries
    RK.590   (A,L,B,R)
ALT brewery

brewers
    HG.772   (L)
HN January 1993 descriptor added
ALT brewer
    brewer's
    brewers'
SN Those whose occupation is brewing beer and other malt liquors.

Brewster chairs
    TC.458
HN May 1993 related term added
    January 1993 descriptor moved
ALT Brewster chair
SN Collector's term for 17th-century American turned great chairs styled after one that belonged to Elder William Brewster of Plymouth Colony. Such chairs have boldly turned posts and decorative spindles, but unlike Carver chairs they have spindles below the seat as well as in the back and below the arms.
UF chairs, Brewster
RT Carver chairs

brick
    MT.71   (A,L,B,R)
HN April 1992 descriptor moved

brick, adobe
USE adobe

brick, air
USE air brick

brick, angle
USE angle brick

brick, arch
USE compass brick

brick, ashlar
USE ashlar brick

brick, axed
USE axed brick

brick, backing
USE backing brick

brick, backup
USE backing brick

brick, baked
USE fired brick

brick, blue
USE blue brick

brick, building
USE building brick

brick, bull-nose
SEE bullnose brick

brick, bullnose
USE bullnose brick

brick, burned
USE fired brick

brick, burnt
USE fired brick

<brick by form>
    MT.72
HN April 1992 guide term moved

<brick by form: shape or size>
    MT.73
HN April 1992 guide term moved

<brick by form: solidity>
    MT.92
HN April 1992 guide term moved

<brick by function>
    MT.96
HN April 1992 guide term moved

<brick by location or context>
    MT.115
HN April 1992 guide term moved

<brick by technique>
    MT.120
HN April 1992 guide term moved

<brick by technique: drying process>
    MT.121
HN April 1992 guide term moved

<brick by technique: shaping process>
    MT.132
HN April 1992 guide term moved

brick, calcium silicate
USE calcium silicate brick

brick, cant
USE splay brick

brick, capping
USE capping brick

brick cement
    MT.42
HN April 1992 descriptor moved
SN Waterproof cement used in masonry work. (DAC)
UF cement, brick

brick chisels
USE brick sets

brick, clinker
USE clinker brick

brick, common
USE building brick

brick, compass
USE compass brick

brick, coping
USE capping brick

brick, copper
USE copper brick

brick, dog-leg
SEE dogleg brick

brick, dogleg
USE dogleg brick

brick, Dutch
USE clinker brick

brick, economy
USE jumbo brick

brick, end-cut
USE end-cut brick

brick, engineering
USE engineering brick

brick, face
USE face brick

brick, facing
USE face brick

brick, featheredge
USE compass brick

brick, fire
USE fire brick

brick, fired
USE fired brick

brick, Flemish
USE Flemish brick

brick, floor
USE floor brick

brick, furring
USE furring brick

brick, gauged
USE gauged brick

brick, great
USE great brick

brick, hand-made
SEE handmade brick

brick, handmade
USE handmade brick

brick, hard
USE hard-burned brick

brick, hard-burned
USE hard-burned brick

brick, hard-burnt
SEE hard-burned brick

brick, hollow
USE hollow brick

brick, jumbo
USE jumbo brick

brick, key
USE compass brick

brick, kiln-burned
USE fired brick

brick kilns
TH.502 (N,B)
ALT brick kiln
UF kilns, brick

brick, modular
USE modular building brick

brick, modular building
USE modular building brick

brick, molded
USE molded brick

brick, Norman
USE Norman brick

brick, paving
USE paving brick

brick, paviour
USE paving brick

brick, perforated
USE perforated brick

brick, pilaster
USE pilaster brick

brick, place
USE place brick

brick, plinth
USE plinth brick

brick, pressed
USE pressed brick

brick, radial
USE compass brick

brick, radiating
USE compass brick

brick, radius
USE compass brick

brick red
USE dark red
grayish red
moderate red
strong reddish orange

brick, refractory
USE fire brick

brick, rock-faced
USE ashlar brick

brick, Roman
USE Roman brick

brick, rough-axed
USE axed brick

brick, rustic
USE rustic brick

brick, saddle-back coping
USE saddle-back coping brick

brick, salmon
USE place brick

brick, sammel
USE sammel brick

brick, sand-faced
USE sand-struck brick

brick, sand-lime
USE sand-lime brick

brick, sand-struck
USE sand-struck brick

brick, SCR
USE SCR brick

brick sets
TH.1336 (N)
HN December 1992 descriptor moved
ALT brick set
SN Chisels or bolsters for cutting brick. (DAC)
UF brick chisels
chisels, brick
sets, brick

brick, sewer
USE blue brick

brick, side-cut
USE side-cut brick

brick slip
MT.75
HN April 1992 descriptor moved
SN A solid tile used to simulate brick-work. (DAC)
UF slip, brick

brick, slop
USE water-struck brick

brick, soft
USE soft brick

brick, soft-burned
USE soft brick

brick, soft-mud
USE soft-mud brick

brick, solid
USE solid brick

brick, splay
USE splay brick

brick, squint
USE squint brick

brick, Staffordshire blue
USE blue brick

brick stamps
VW.434 (L,R)
HN November 1992 descriptor moved
ALT brick stamp
UF stamps, brick

brick, stiff-mud
USE stiff-mud brick

brick, stock
USE stock brick

brick, stone
USE hard-burned brick

brick, sun-baked
USE adobe
    sun-dried brick

brick, sun-dried
USE sun-dried brick

brick, sun-dried mud
USE sun-dried brick

brick, tax
USE tax brick

brick trowels
    TH.1174
HN December 1992 descriptor moved
ALT brick trowel
SN Trowels having a flat, triangular steel blade in an offset handle, used to pick up and spread mortar. (DAC)
UF trowels, brick

brick, unburnt
USE adobe
    sun-dried brick

brick, underburned
USE soft brick

brick, unfired
USE adobe
    soft brick
    sun-dried brick

brick, ventilating
USE air brick

brick, voussoir
USE compass brick

brick, water-struck
USE water-struck brick

brick, well-burned
USE hard-burned brick

brick, wire-cut
USE wire-cut brick

brick, wood
USE nailing blocks

brick-work, moulded
SEE molded brick

brickbat
    MT.76
HN November 1992 descriptor moved
    November 1992 scope note changed
    November 1992 lead-in term added
    November 1992 related term added
SN Pieces of broken brick, especially those with one end of the brick left whole.
UF bat
    half bat
    header, snap
    snap header
RT fragments

bricklayers
    HG.829   (A,L,R)
HN December 1992 alternate terms added

ALT bricklayer
    bricklayer's
    bricklayers'

bricklayers' scaffolding
    TH.1051
HN March 1993 descriptor changed, was **bricklayer's scaffolding**
    March 1993 lead-in term changed, was **scaffolding, bricklayer's**
SN Scaffolding composed of framed wood squares which support a platform; limited to light and medium duty. (DAC)
UF scaffolding, bricklayers'

bricklaying
    KT.73   (A,L,B)
HN January 1993 descriptor moved

bricklaying profiles
    TH.1332   (B)
HN December 1992 descriptor moved
ALT bricklaying profile
SN Guides used to set out brick work or block work accurately. (DAC)
UF profiles, bricklaying

brickmakers
    HG.773   (L)
HN April 1993 related term added
    December 1992 alternate terms added
ALT brickmaker
    brickmaker's
    brickmakers'
RT brickmaking

brickmaking
    KT.787   (A,L,B)
HN November 1992 descriptor added
SN The act or process of making bricks. (W)
RT brickmakers

bricks, building
USE building blocks

brickwork
    MT.1820   (A,L,B)
HN October 1992 descriptor moved

brickworks
    RK.594   (A,H,L,B)
ALT brickwork

bridal books
    VW.996   (L)
HN November 1992 descriptor moved
ALT bridal book
UF books, bridal
    brides' books

bridal chests
USE dower chests

bridal cups
USE wager cups

brideboxes
    TQ.187   (N)
ALT bridebox
SN Oval boxes of light wooden-splint construction used to hold delicate finery or trinkets.
UF boxes, brides'
    brides' boxes
RT boxes (containers)

brides' books
USE bridal books

brides' boxes
USE brideboxes

brides' quilts, Baltimore
USE Baltimore album quilts

bridewell houses
USE workhouses

bridewells
USE workhouses

bridge approaches
    PJ.833   (L)
HN March 1993 descriptor moved
ALT bridge approach
SN Embankments, trestles, or other structures that provide access at either end of a bridge. (W)
UF approaches, bridge

bridge cloths
    TC.288
ALT bridge cloth
SN Small tablecloths for use on card tables.
UF cloths, bridge

bridge cranes
    TH.467   (L)
ALT bridge crane
SN Cranes used in manufacturing or assembling heavy objects, composed of a bridge spanning two overhead rails and a hoisting device which moves laterally along the bridge. The bridge can move longitudinally along the rails. (MEANS)
UF cranes, bridge

bridge cranes (gantry cranes)
USE gantry cranes

<bridge elements>
    PJ.832
HN March 1993 guide term moved

bridge failures
    BM.625   (A,L)
HN November 1992 descriptor moved
    January 1991 alternate term added
ALT bridge failure
UF failures, bridge

bridge harps
USE harp lutes

bridge lutes
USE harp lutes

bridge spouts
    PJ.3124
ALT bridge spout
SN Type of spout that is attached to a

pouring vessel by a horizontal bar or
decorative ornament.
UF   spouts, bridge

bridge trusses
HN   March 1991 descriptor split, use
bridge (built work) (ALT of bridges (built works)) + trusses

bridgeboards
USE   open strings

bridges (built works)
RK.1213   (A,L,N,B,R)
HN   March 1993 descriptor changed,
was **bridges**
March 1993 alternate term changed,
was **bridge**
ALT   bridge (built work)

bridges (chordophone components)
PJ.3249
ALT   bridge (chordophone component)
SN   Wedge- or barlike devices, usually
of hardwood, inserted between the
strings and soundboard of chordophones for the purpose of raising
the strings to a required distance
and of transmitting the vibrations of
the strings to the soundboard.

bridges (hand rests)
TH.832
HN   February 1993 descriptor added
ALT   bridge (hand rest)
SN   Devices used to protect image areas
of a printing plate or stone from
contact with the hand during draw-
ing. (SAFF)
UF   hand rests
rests, hand

bridges, aqueduct
USE   aqueducts

bridges, arch
USE   arch bridges

bridges, bailey
USE   bailey bridges

bridges, balance
USE   balance cocks

bridges, bascule
USE   bascule bridges

<bridges by construction>
RK.1235

<bridges by form>
RK.1214

<bridges by function>
RK.1227

bridges, cable braced
USE   cable-stayed bridges

bridges, cable-stayed
USE   cable-stayed bridges

bridges, canal
USE   aqueducts

bridges, cantilever
USE   cantilever bridges

bridges, cold
USE   thermal bridges

bridges, continuous
USE   continuous bridges

bridges, covered
USE   covered bridges

bridges, deck
USE   deck truss bridges

bridges, deck truss
USE   deck truss bridges

bridges, floating
USE   pontoon bridges

bridges, flying
USE   skybridges

bridges, girder
USE   girder bridges

bridges, heat
USE   thermal bridges

bridges, lift
USE   lift bridges

bridges, military
USE   military bridges

bridges, movable
USE   movable bridges

bridges, multispan
USE   multispan bridges

bridges, pedestrian
USE   footbridges

bridges, pile
USE   pile bridges

bridges, pontoon
USE   pontoon bridges

bridges, railroad
USE   railroad bridges

bridges, railway
USE   railroad bridges

bridges, road
USE   road bridges

bridges, single span
USE   single span bridges

bridges, skew
USE   skew bridges

bridges, skywalk
USE   skybridges

bridges, stayed
USE   cable-stayed bridges

bridges, stayed girder
USE   cable-stayed bridges

bridges, suspension
USE   suspension bridges

bridges, swing
USE   swing bridges

bridges, thermal
USE   thermal bridges

bridges, toll
USE   toll bridges

bridges, truss
USE   truss bridges

bridges, vertical lift
USE   lift bridges

bridging
PJ.1440
HN   March 1993 descriptor moved
November 1990 scope note changed
SN   Braces or systems of braces, placed
between horizontal or vertical structural members, to stiffen them, hold
them in place, and to help distribute
the load. (DAC)

bridging, cross
USE   cross bridging

bridging, diagonal
USE   cross bridging

bridging joists
USE   joists

bridle gauntlets
USE   elbow gauntlets

bridle joints
PJ.721
HN   April 1993 descriptor moved
ALT   bridle joint
SN   Mortise-and-tenon joints used when
two timbers are joined at an angle
of less than 90 degrees. (MEANS)
UF   joints, bridle

bridle paths
RM.183   (A,L)
HN   April 1993 descriptor moved
ALT   bridle path
SN   Paths cleared and compacted, reserved for riding horses and barred
to vehicles. (DAC)
UF   bridle roads
bridle trails
bridle ways
paths, bridle
riding trails
roads, bridle
trails, bridle
trails, riding
ways, bridle

bridle roads
USE   bridle paths

bridle trails
USE   bridle paths

bridle ways
USE   bridle paths

briefcases
TQ.188   (L,N)
ALT   briefcase

SN Flat, flexible rectangular containers with a handle used for carrying books, papers, or the like, and often made of leather. For flat, rigid, rectangular containers use **attaché cases.**
RT attaché cases
    <costume accessories carried>
    traveling bags

briefs (legal documents)
    VW.609   (L)
HN November 1992 descriptor moved
    May 1991 descriptor changed, was
        briefs
    May 1991 alternate term changed,
        was **brief**
ALT brief (legal document)
SN Concise statements of the arguments of a party to a case in dispute, submitted to the court or other body hearing the case. (GAHLM)

briefs (papal)
USE papal briefs

briefs (programs)
USE programs

briefs (underpants)
    TE.224   (N)
SN Snug-fitting underpants with leg openings, made in a variety of styles for men, women, and children.

briefs, papal
USE papal briefs

brig-schooners
USE brigantines

brig-sloops
USE sloops (warships)

brigandines
    TE.307
ALT brigandine
SN Armored sleeveless jackets used by infantry from the mid-14th century to the beginning of the 17th century, consisting of small rectangular metal plates, overlapping in vertical strips, mounted on a fabric or hide support in parallel rows, the whole being sewn to a quilted jacket which gave the garments their final shape. (TARA)
RT jackets

brigantines
    TX.567
ALT brigantine
SN Use for two-masted vessels square-rigged on the foremast, but primarily fore-and-aft-rigged on the mainmast, although some vessels carried square topsails on the mainmast.
UF brig-schooners
    brigs, hermaphrodite
    hermaphrodite brigs
    hermaphrodites (watercraft)

brigantins
USE field beds

bright aqua
USE brilliant bluish green
     light bluish green
     light greenish blue
     very light greenish blue

bright aqua blue
USE light greenish blue

bright aqua green
USE brilliant bluish green
     light bluish green
     very light bluish green

bright blue
USE brilliant blue
     brilliant greenish blue
     light greenish blue
     moderate greenish blue
     strong blue
     strong bluish green
     strong greenish blue
     vivid blue

bright blue green
USE brilliant green
     strong green
     vivid green

bright bluish green
USE vivid bluish green

bright bluish red
USE vivid purplish red

bright bluish violet
USE vivid violet

bright cerulean blue
USE moderate blue
     strong greenish blue

bright chartreuse
USE brilliant yellow green
     strong yellow green
     vivid yellow green

bright chartreuse yellow
USE strong greenish yellow
     vivid greenish yellow

bright copen blue
USE strong blue

bright-cut engraving
USE bright cutting

bright cutting
    KT.948
HN December 1992 descriptor added
ALT bright-cut
SN Engraving produced by short repetitive strokes of a cutting tool, especially on metal.
UF bright-cut engraving
    cutting, bright

bright emerald green
USE brilliant bluish green
     brilliant green
     strong bluish green
     strong green

bright fuchsia purple
USE deep purplish red

deep reddish purple
strong reddish purple

bright fuchsia rose
USE moderate purplish red

bright gold
USE deep yellow
     vivid yellow

bright green
USE brilliant bluish green
     brilliant green
     deep green
     deep yellowish green
     moderate green
     strong bluish green
     strong green
     strong yellowish green
     vivid green
     vivid yellowish green

bright green yellow
USE vivid yellow green

bright greenish blue
USE vivid greenish blue

bright greenish yellow
USE vivid greenish yellow

bright jade green
USE brilliant bluish green
     strong bluish green
     strong green

bright kelly green
USE brilliant green
     strong green
     strong yellowish green
     vivid yellowish green

bright lavender
USE light purple
     light violet
     moderate purple
     moderate violet

bright lemon yellow
USE vivid greenish yellow

bright lime green
USE brilliant yellow green
     brilliant yellowish green
     strong yellow green
     vivid yellow green

bright navy
USE dark blue
     deep blue
     moderate blue
     moderate purplish blue

bright olive green
USE light olive
     moderate olive
     moderate olive green
     moderate yellow green

bright open blue
USE brilliant blue

bright orange
USE strong orange
     vivid orange

bright peach
USE strong yellowish pink

bright peacock blue
USE brilliant greenish blue
strong greenish blue

bright periwinkle blue
USE light violet

bright red
USE strong red
vivid red

bright red violet
USE strong purple
strong reddish purple
vivid purple
vivid reddish purple

bright reddish blue
USE vivid purplish blue

bright reddish orange
USE vivid reddish orange

bright reddish violet
USE vivid reddish purple

bright reddish yellow
USE vivid orange yellow
vivid yellow

bright rose
USE deep pink
deep purplish pink
grayish purplish red
moderate purplish red
strong purplish red
strong red
vivid purplish red

bright rose violet
USE deep purplish pink

bright teal blue
USE dark greenish blue
moderate greenish blue

bright turquoise
USE brilliant bluish green
strong bluish green

bright turquoise blue
USE brilliant greenish blue
strong bluish green
strong greenish blue

bright turquoise green
USE brilliant bluish green
light bluish green
moderate bluish green
strong bluish green

bright ultramarine
USE strong blue
strong purplish blue
vivid blue
vivid purplish blue

bright violet
USE light violet
moderate purple
moderate violet

strong purple
vivid purple
vivid violet

bright yellow
USE brilliant orange yellow
light orange yellow
moderate orange yellow
strong orange yellow
vivid yellow

bright yellowish green
USE vivid yellow green
vivid yellowish green

bright yellowish orange
USE vivid orange yellow

bright yellowish red
USE vivid red
vivid reddish orange

brightness
DC.232
HN March 1993 related term added
October 1992 descriptor moved
October 1992 alternate term added
ALT bright
SN Use when referring generally to the
relative degree of lightness or dark-
ness given to a surface by the
amount of light reflected from it.
When referring to the degree of
lightness or darkness of a color, use
value (color).
UF lightness
RT value (color)

brightness (color)
USE value (color)

brights
TH.722
HN February 1993 descriptor added
ALT bright
SN Square-ended artists' brushes with
shorter bristles than flats.

brigs
TX.568
ALT brig
SN Use for two-masted vessels carrying
a full set of square sails on each
mast, although the mainmast also
carries a gaff-rigged spanker or
driver sail; the mainmast is taller
than the foremast.

brigs, four-masted
USE jackass barks

brigs, hermaphrodite
USE brigantines

brilliant blue
DL.245
UF blue, bright
blue, bright open
blue, light methyl
bright blue
bright open blue
centroid color 177

light methyl blue
methyl blue, light
ultramarine

brilliant bluish green
DL.228
UF aqua, bright
aqua green, bright
blue green
bluish green, brilliant
bright aqua
bright aqua green
bright emerald green
bright green
bright jade green
bright turquoise
bright turquoise green
centroid color 159
emerald green, bright
emerald green, light
green, bright
green, bright aqua
green, bright emerald
green, bright jade
green, bright turquoise
green, brilliant bluish
green, light emerald
green, turquoise
jade green, bright
light emerald green
turquoise (color)
turquoise, bright
turquoise green
turquoise green, bright

brilliant-cut glass
MT.291
HN January 1992 descriptor added
SN Use to describe glassware with very
deep, complex, and polished
cutting.
UF glass, brilliant-cut

brilliant green
DL.196
UF blue green
blue green, bright
blue green, light
bright blue green
bright emerald green
bright green
bright kelly green
centroid color 140
chrysocolla green
emerald (color)
emerald green (color)
emerald green, bright
emerald green, light
green, bright
green, bright emerald
green, bright kelly
green, brilliant
green, chrysocolla
green, emerald
green, light emerald
green, Paris
green, viridian
kelly green, bright
light blue green
light emerald green

Paris green
viridian green

brilliant greenish blue
DL.265
UF blue, bright
blue, bright peacock
blue, bright turquoise
blue, brilliant greenish
blue, light cerulean
blue turquoise
bright blue
bright peacock blue
bright turquoise blue
centroid color 168
cerulean blue, light
greenish blue, brilliant
light cerulean blue
peacock blue, bright
turquoise, blue
turquoise blue, bright

brilliant greenish yellow
DL.167
UF centroid color 98
chartreuse
chartreuse yellow
chartreuse yellow, light
citron
green yellow
greenish yellow, brilliant
lemon yellow
lemon yellow, light
light chartreuse yellow
light lemon yellow
lime yellow
strontium yellow
sulphur yellow
yellow, brilliant greenish
yellow, chartreuse
yellow, lemon
yellow, light chartreuse
yellow, light lemon
yellow, strontium
yellow, sulphur

brilliant orange
DL.93
UF cadmium orange (color)
centroid color 49
orange, brilliant
orange, cadmium
orange pink
pink, orange

brilliant orange yellow
DL.158
UF bright yellow
centroid color 67
Indian yellow (color)
ocher (color)
orange yellow, brilliant
orange, yellowish
reddish yellow
yellow, bright
yellow, brilliant orange
yellow, Indian
yellow, reddish
yellowish orange

brilliant peacock blue
USE strong greenish blue

brilliant purple
DL.299
UF centroid color 217
mauve (color)
purple, brilliant
rose purple

brilliant purplish blue
DL.275
UF blue, brilliant purplish
blue, reddish
blue violet, pale
bluish violet, light
bluish violet, pale
centroid color 195
deep lavender blue
grayish violet blue, light
lavender blue
lavender blue, deep
light bluish violet
light grayish violet blue
light violet
pale blue violet
pale bluish violet
purplish blue, brilliant
reddish blue
ultramarine
violet blue, light grayish
violet, light
violet, light bluish
violet, pale bluish

brilliant purplish pink
DL.47
UF bluish pink
centroid color 246
pink, bluish
pink, brilliant purplish
purplish pink, brilliant

brilliant scarlet
USE iodine scarlet

brilliant violet
DL.287
UF blue violet, dull
blue violet, soft
bluish violet
bluish violet, dull
bluish violet, light
centroid color 206
dull blue violet
dull bluish violet
lavender violet
light bluish violet
mauve (color)
soft blue violet
violet, bluish
violet, brilliant
violet, dull bluish
violet, light bluish

brilliant yellow
DL.144
UF amber yellow
aureolin
barium yellow (color)
buff, orange
canary yellow
centroid color 83
cobalt yellow (color)
gold, light

lemon yellow
light gold
Naples yellow (color)
ocher (color)
orange buff
orpiment (color)
reddish yellow
Turner's yellow (color)
yellow, amber
yellow, barium
yellow, brilliant
yellow, canary
yellow, cobalt
yellow, lemon
yellow, Naples
yellow, reddish
yellow, Turner's

brilliant yellow (pigment)
USE cadmium yellow
Naples yellow

brilliant yellow green
DL.187
HN April 1990 lead-in terms added
UF bright chartreuse
bright lime green
centroid color 116
chartreuse, bright
chartreuse green
chartreuse, light
green, bright lime
green, brilliant yellow
green, chartreuse
green, light lime
light chartreuse
light lime green
lime green, bright
lime green, light
lime yellow
yellow green, brilliant
yellow, lime

brilliant yellowish green
DL.217
UF bright lime green
centroid color 130
emerald (color)
emerald green (color)
green, bright lime
green, brilliant yellowish
green, emerald
green, light lime
green, Paris
light lime green
lime green, bright
lime green, light
Paris green
yellowish green, brilliant

brims
USE marlis

brimstone
USE sulfur

Brisa
USE Aowin

brisé fans
TE.420
ALT brisé fan
SN Fans without a leaf, comprised of

flat, overlapping sticks which broaden towards the outer edge where they are secured, one to another, by a ribbon or cord. (CASF)
UF fans, brisé

brise-soleils
PJ.2273 (B)
HN March 1993 descriptor moved
ALT brise-soleil
SN Fixed or movable devices, such as louvers, designed to block the direct entrance of sun rays into buildings. (HAS)
UF breakers, sun
louvers, sun
shades, sun
sun breakers
sun louvers
sun shades

briskers
USE britzkas

bristle
MT.2565 (L)
HN April 1992 descriptor changed, was bristles
March 1992 scope note added
February 1992 descriptor moved
SN Short, stiff, coarse hair. (W)

bristle brushes
TH.738
HN February 1993 descriptor added
ALT bristle brush
SN Artists' brushes made of hog, pig, or boar bristle. (SAITZY)
UF brushes, bristle
brushes, hog-hair
hog-hair brushes

bristol board
MT.1445
HN February 1992 descriptor moved
SN A high-grade white cardboard, supercalendered with China clay; also made by pasting together sheets of heavy ledger paper. (MH)
UF board, bristol

Bristol glaze
MT.1990
SN A low-fire glaze usually containing zinc oxide. (W)
UF glaze, Bristol

britannia metal
MT.456 (R)
HN March 1993 descriptor moved
SN A type of pewter that usually contains copper. Its color is silvery white with a bluish tinge, or with a yellowish tinge if the copper content is high.
UF metal, britannia

britannia metal, English
USE English britannia metal

British
FL.3128 (L,B)

British Colonial
FL.3280 (A)
HN May 1991 descriptor added
UF Colonial, British

<British Colonial Indian styles>
FL.2329

British gum
MT.1734
HN March 1992 descriptor moved
SN Grade of dextrin used as a paper adhesive and in the manufacture of gouache, watercolor, and other aqueous paint. (MAYER)
UF gum, British

<British Isles Medieval architecture styles>
FL.3212

<British Isles Medieval pottery styles>
FL.3218

<British Isles Medieval styles>
FL.3208

British oak
USE English oak

<British Renaissance-Baroque architecture styles>
FL.3290

<British Renaissance-Baroque styles>
FL.3279

<British Renaissance-Baroque styles by reign>
FL.3281

British Solomon Island
USE Solomon Island

British warms
TE.151
ALT British warm
SN Double-breasted overcoats of a type originally worn by British army officers.
UF warms, British

brittle (pottery style)
FL.2838
HN April 1993 descriptor added

brittle-painted (pottery style)
FL.3025
HN April 1993 descriptor added

brittle-painted ware
HN April 1993 descriptor split, use brittle-painted (pottery style) + ware

brittle ware
HN April 1993 descriptor split, use brittle (pottery style) + ware

brittleness
DC.174 (L)
HN October 1992 descriptor moved
February 1992 scope note added
ALT brittle
SN The property of being hard and rigid with little tensile strength,

tending to break readily with a comparatively smooth fracture. (RHDEL2)

britzkas
TX.163
ALT britzka
SN Carriages developed in Poland and Austria in the early 19th century and eventually popular in England for long-distance travel since the interior seating compartment could be converted into sleeping quarters; often featuring a large rear-facing seat to accommodate servants.
UF briskers

Brno chairs
TC.472
HN January 1993 descriptor moved
ALT Brno chair
UF chairs, Brno

broach spires
PJ.1348
HN March 1993 descriptor moved
ALT broach spire
SN Octagonal spires rising from a square tower without an intervening parapet, the four angles of the tower being covered by corner segments of a pyramid seeming to penetrate the tower. (W)
UF spires, broach

broaching
KT.909 (L)
HN March 1991 alternate term added
ALT broached
SN Drilling or cutting out material left between adjacent holes in a row of closely spaced drill holes; process used especially in mining and quarrying. (W)

broad glass
USE cylinder glass

broad hatchets
USE hewing hatchets

Broad Manner
FL.3322
HN July 1990 descriptor added
UF Manner, Broad

broad sabatons
USE bear-paw sabatons

broadaxes
TH.1414 (N)
ALT broadax
SN Axes having a large, broad blade bevelled on one side, used for the rough dressing of timber. (DAC)
UF axes, hewing
hewing axes

broadcast advertising
KG.41 (L)
HN February 1993 descriptor added

SN Use for advertising via the broadcast media of radio or television.
UF advertising, broadcast

broadcasters
HG.475   (L)
HN April 1993 related term added
      December 1992 alternate terms added
ALT broadcaster
      broadcaster's
      broadcasters'
RT broadcasting

broadcasters, radio
USE radio broadcasters

broadcasting
KD.239   (L,B)
HN April 1993 related term added
RT broadcasters

broadcasting houses
SEE broadcasting stations

broadcasting, radio
USE radio broadcasting

broadcasting stations
RK.203   (H,L,B)
HN March 1993 related term added
      April 1990 scope note changed
ALT broadcasting station
UK broadcasting houses
UKA broadcasting house
SN Telecommunications buildings containing studios, production and technical offices, equipment spaces, and control facilities for sending and receiving microwave transmissions; for rooms and spaces designed for the origination or recording of radio or television programs, use **broadcasting studios**.
UF houses, broadcasting
      stations, broadcasting
RT broadcasting studios

broadcasting studios
PJ.1164   (A,B)
HN March 1993 related term added
      March 1993 descriptor moved
      April 1990 scope note added
ALT broadcasting studio
SN Use for rooms and spaces designed for the origination or recording of radio or television programs; for telecommunications buildings containing facilities for sending and receiving microwave transmissions, use **broadcasting stations**.
UF studios, broadcasting
RT broadcasting stations

broadcasting, television
USE television broadcasting

broadleaved maple
USE bigleaf maple

broadloom carpets
USE broadlooms

broadlooms
TC.29
ALT broadloom
SN Use for machine-made carpets woven on a wide loom, usually measuring 54 inches or wider.
UF broadloom carpets
      carpets, broadloom

broadsheets
USE broadsides

broadsides
VW.1125   (H,L,N)
HN November 1992 descriptor moved
      June 1992 scope note changed
ALT broadside
SN Sizeable single-sheet notices or advertisements printed on one or both sides, often chiefly textual rather than pictorial, and printed to be read unfolded. For folded sheets having printed matter that generally does not cross the folds, use **folders (printed matter)**.
UF broadsheets

broadswords
TK.70   (N)
ALT broadsword
SN Term applied from at least the 17th century to heavy military swords with a large, straight, double-edged blade and a basket hilt or shell guard, designed primarily for cutting.
RT cutting swords

brocade
MT.1589   (H,L)
HN November 1992 descriptor added
SN Textile produced by brocading, typically richly figured and incorporating metal thread.

brocade (weaving)
USE brocading

brocade pictures
USE nishiki-e

brocade prints
USE nishiki-e

Brocade Style
FL.3077

brocading
KT.1201   (L)
HN March 1993 descriptor moved
      March 1993 scope note changed
      March 1993 lead-in term added
      February 1993 descriptor changed, was **brocade**
ALT brocaded
SN Weft patterning technique of weaving raised patterns on a woven textile. For the process of stitching decorative designs into cloth, leather, or paper by hand or machine, use **embroidering**.
UF brocade (weaving)

brocading filling
USE brocading weft

brocading weft
PJ.3079
SN A discontinuous supplementary weft which does not travel from selvage to selvage, but rather is limited to the area where it is required by the pattern.
UF brocading filling
      filling, brocading
      weft, brocading

brocatelle
MT.1590
HN March 1993 descriptor moved
SN Use for brocade done in high relief.

brocatelle marble
MT.745
HN August 1992 lead-in term added
      April 1992 descriptor moved
UK Brocatello marble
UF marble, brocatelle
      marble, Brocatello

brocatello
MT.706
HN April 1992 descriptor moved
UF marmor schiston

Brocatello marble
SEE brocatelle marble

broccatellone
MT.697
HN April 1992 descriptor moved

brochs
RK.828   (A,L)
ALT broch
SN Use for circular stone towers having a double wall, found in Scotland and neighboring islands.

brochures
USE pamphlets

broderie perse
KT.1219
HN November 1992 descriptor added
SN 18th-century form of appliqué in which motifs such as flowers and animals are cut from cotton textiles, especially chintz, and stitched to a plain ground.
UF appliqué, chintz
      appliqué, cretonne
      appliqué, cut-out chintz
      appliqué perse
      chintz appliqué
      chintz appliqué, cut-out
      cretonne appliqué
      cretonne work
      cut-out chintz appliqué
      embroidery, Persian
      Persian embroidery
      work, cretonne

brogan shoes
USE brogans

brogans
　　TE.747
ALT　brogan
SN　Heavy shoes, especially coarse leather work shoes reaching to the ankles. (W)
UF　brogan shoes
　　shoes, brogan

brogue shoes
USE　brogues

brogues
　　TE.738
ALT　brogue
SN　Oxfords trimmed with perforations, stitchings, pinkings, or the like.
UF　brogue shoes
　　shoes, brogue
　　tips, wing
　　wing tips

broilers
　　TH.56　　　　　　　　　　　　(N)
HN　April 1993 descriptor added
ALT　broiler
SN　Devices used to broil meat, fish, poultry, or other foods.
RT　toasters

brokages
　　VK.9
ALT　brokage
SN　Use for coins generated through a minting error which produced the same design on the obverse and reverse, one in relief and the other incuse; the coins are created when a preceding coin remained in the die and consequently left its impression on the next coin.

broken
　　DC.47
HN　October 1992 scope note changed
　　October 1992 descriptor moved
SN　Use in the sense of interrupted. For the sense of damaged, use **broken** (ALT of **breaking**).
UF　discontinuous

broken arches
HN　June 1991 descriptor deleted, made lead-in to **broken pediments**

broken arches
USE　broken pediments

broken front
USE　breakfront

broken joints
USE　break joints

broken-out sections
　　VC.149
HN　April 1992 descriptor moved
ALT　broken-out section
SN　Use for orthographic drawings of the exterior of a structure or object with a small portion removed to show an interior detail. When a more substantial portion is re-

moved, use **half sections** or **sectional elevations**.
UF　sections, broken-out

broken pediments
　　PJ.2004
HN　March 1993 descriptor moved
　　July 1991 scope note changed
　　June 1991 lead-in terms added
ALT　broken pediment
SN　Use for pediments whose lines are interrupted either at the apex or the base, or in both locations; found especially on Late Antique, Baroque, and Mannerist architecture, and on Chippendale furniture.
UF　arches, broken
　　broken arches
　　open pediments
　　pediments, broken
　　pediments, open

broken stone
USE　crushed stone

broken twill
　　MT.1620
HN　November 1992 descriptor added
SN　Any form of twill in which the diagonal lines have been deliberately broken. The binding points are not regularly set over by one end on each successive pick, but breaks occur at regular intervals. (WRPWFT)
UF　twill, broken

brokers
　　HG.626　　　　　　　　　　　(L)
HN　December 1992 alternate terms added
ALT　broker
　　broker's
　　brokers'
SN　Middlemen who for a fee or commission negotiate contracts of purchase and sale between buyers and sellers. (W)

brokers, real estate
USE　real estate agents

brokers, stock
USE　stockbrokers

broletti
　　RK.957
ALT　broletto
SN　Use for town hall buildings in smaller Italian communities, especially in Lombardy.

bromide
USE　silver bromide

bromoil photoprints
USE　bromoil prints

bromoil prints
　　VC.331
HN　April 1992 descriptor moved
ALT　bromoil print
UF　bromoil photoprints

photoprints, bromoil
prints, bromoil

bromoil process
　　KT.547
SN　Use for the photographic process that is a variant of the oil process in which the developed silver in a gelatin print is used as a catalyst to tan the gelatin. The untanned highlights become saturated when the print is soaked in water and will resist a greasy ink, while the tanned shadows accept the ink. The original print may be the end product or may be used as a master for transferring the image to another support.

Brong
　　FL.297　　　　　　　　　　　(L)
UF　Abron

bronze
　　MT.397　　　　　　　　(A,L,B,R)
HN　March 1993 related term added
　　March 1993 lead-in terms added
　　March 1993 descriptor moved
SN　Copper alloy that has as the principle alloying element a metal other than nickel or zinc. (MMAHM)
UF　alloy, copper-tin
　　copper-tin alloy
RT　manganese bronze

bronze (color)
USE　moderate olive brown
　　moderate yellowish brown

bronze, admiralty
USE　admiralty metal

Bronze Age
　　FL.25　　　　　　　　　　(A,L,R)
UF　Age, Bronze

Bronze Age, Early
USE　Early Bronze Age

Bronze Age, Late
USE　Late Bronze Age

Bronze Age, Middle
USE　Middle Bronze Age

bronze, aluminum
USE　aluminum bronze

bronze, architectural
USE　architectural bronze

bronze, art
USE　architectural bronze

bronze, beryllium
USE　copper-beryllium alloy

bronze blue
USE　Prussian blue

bronze brown
USE　brownish gray

bronze disease
　　DE.33

SN The destructive formation of a soft powdery mineral on copper or any of its alloys caused by the presence of chlorides and moisture.
UF disease, bronze

bronze gold
USE strong yellow

bronze green
USE chrome green

bronze, lead
USE lead bronze

bronze, manganese
USE manganese bronze

bronze, naval
USE naval brass

bronze, nickel
USE nickel bronze

bronze, ordnance
USE lead bronze

bronze paint
MT.1937
HN July 1990 descriptor added
UF paint, bronze

bronze, phosphor
USE phosphor bronze

bronze powder
MT.476
HN April 1992 descriptor moved
     July 1990 descriptor added
SN Any metal, as a copper alloy or aluminum, in fine flake form used as a pigment to give the appearance of a metallic surface. (W)
UF powder, bronze

bronze sculpture
USE bronzes

bronze, silicon
USE silicon bronze

bronze-smiths
SEE bronzeworkers

bronze, statuary
USE statuary bronze

bronze, steel
USE phosphor bronze

bronzers
HG.672
HN December 1992 alternate terms added
ALT bronzer
     bronzer's
     bronzers'

bronzes
VC.538   (H,L,B,R)
SN Use collectively for the class of sculptures executed in bronze, especially figures or figure groups. When possible, use the material term plus a more specific object name, such as **bronze + figurines.**

UF bronze sculpture
     sculpture, bronze

bronzeworkers
HG.711
HN December 1992 alternate terms added
ALT bronzeworker
     bronzeworker's
     bronzeworkers'
UK bronze-smiths
UKA bronze-smith

bronzing
KT.138   (L)
HN January 1993 descriptor moved
ALT bronzed
SN The painting of a surface to give the appearance of bronze. In printmaking, refers to printing with metallic inks. (TBL)
UF hand-bronzing

brooches
TE.487   (H,L,N,R)
ALT brooch
SN Ornamental pins made in a variety of forms.
UF breastpins
RT clips (jewelry)

brooches
SEE pins (jewelry)

brooches, bar
SEE bar pins

brooches, disc
USE disc brooches

brooches, penannular
USE penannular brooches

brooches, plaque
USE plaques (brooches)

brooks
RD.106   (L,R)
HN April 1993 lead-in term changed, was **rivurets**
ALT brook
SN Use for small streams, generally smaller than creeks.
UF riverets
     rivulets

Brook's curves
TH.994   (N)
HN November 1992 descriptor moved
ALT Brook's curve
UF curves, Brook's

broom closets
PJ.1136
HN March 1993 descriptor moved
     August 1992 lead-in term added
ALT broom closet
UK broom cupboards
UKA broom cupboard
UF closets, broom
     cupboards, broom

broom cupboards
SEE broom closets

broom-makers
SEE broommakers

broommakers
HG.774
HN December 1992 alternate terms added
ALT broommaker
     broommaker's
     broommakers'
UK broom-makers
UKA broom-maker

brooms
TH.890   (H,L,N)
ALT broom

brooms (curling equipment)
USE curling brooms

brooms, curling
USE curling brooms

brooms, whisk
USE whisk brooms

Brosium aubletti
USE snakewood

broth bowls
USE bouillon cups

brothels
RK.192   (A,L,R)
HN July 1991 related terms added
ALT brothel
UF bawdyhouses
     bordellos
     cat houses
     houses, cat
     houses of ill repute
     houses of prostitution
     houses, panel
     houses, sporting
     panel houses
     sporting houses
     whorehouses
RT prostitutes
     prostitution

brotherhoods
HN.81   (L)
HN February 1993 descriptor moved
ALT brotherhood

brothers
HG.62   (L)
HN March 1992 alternate terms added
     December 1990 descriptor added
ALT brother
     brother's
     brothers'
SN Male siblings.

broughams
TX.168   (N)
ALT brougham
SN Compact, low-hung coaches with the driver's perch outside, space for two or more passengers, and generally with a straight front; may also be used for early automobiles whose form borrowed the characteristic

closed carriage-style body and open driver's area.
RT coupés (carriages)

brougnes
USE hauberks

brow reinforces
PJ.3014
ALT brow reinforce
SN Metal plates on some sallets and armets, curving down over the skull to the line of the eyebrows and serving as extra protection for the forehead. Early forms first appearing before the middle of the 15th century consisted of a single heavy contoured plate, cusped and pointed, riveted to the skull; in the late 15th century a detachable form made of two plates was introduced and remained in use on German jousting helmets until the mid-16th century.
UF brows, helmet
helmet brows
reinforces, brow

brown
DL.107   (L)

brown, beige
USE grayish yellowish brown

brown bistre
USE light grayish yellowish brown
light olive brown

brown, bistre
USE light brown
light brownish gray
light olive
light olive brown
light yellowish brown
moderate yellowish brown
moderate yellowish pink

brown black
USE brownish gray

brown, black
USE brownish gray
dark grayish brown
grayish brown
grayish olive
light brownish gray
olive gray

brown, blackish
USE brownish gray
dark grayish brown
dark reddish gray

brown, bone
USE bone brown

brown, bronze
USE brownish gray

brown, Caledonian
USE burnt sienna

brown, Cappagh
USE umber

brown carmine
USE dark red
very deep red

brown, Cassel
USE moderate brown

brown, chestnut
USE burnt umber

brown coal
USE lignite

brown coat
USE arriccio

brown, dark
USE dark brown

brown, dark grayish
USE dark grayish brown

brown, dark grayish reddish
USE dark grayish reddish brown

brown, dark grayish yellowish
USE dark grayish yellowish brown

brown, dark olive
USE dark olive brown

brown, dark reddish
USE dark reddish brown

brown, dark rose
USE dark grayish red
dark reddish gray

brown, dark violet
USE blackish purple
dark grayish purple
dark purplish red
very dark purplish red

brown, dark yellowish
USE dark yellowish brown

brown, deep
USE deep brown

brown, deep red
USE grayish reddish brown

brown, deep reddish
USE deep reddish brown

brown, deep yellowish
USE deep yellowish brown

brown, dull
USE brownish pink
dark grayish brown
grayish brown
light grayish brown

brown, dull reddish
USE blackish red
dark grayish red
dark grayish reddish brown
dark red
dark reddish brown
grayish red
grayish reddish brown
light grayish reddish brown
light reddish brown
very dark red

brown, dull yellowish
USE dark grayish yellowish brown
dark yellowish brown
grayish yellowish brown
light grayish yellowish brown
light yellowish brown
moderate yellowish brown

brown, ebony
USE dark gray
dark reddish gray
reddish black

brown, Egyptian
USE mummy

brown, garnet
USE dark red
deep red

brown, gold
USE brownish orange
strong brown

brown, golden
USE deep yellowish brown
moderate yellowish brown

brown, gray
USE light brownish gray
light grayish reddish brown
light olive brown
light olive gray

brown, grayish
USE grayish brown

brown, grayish reddish
USE grayish reddish brown

brown, grayish yellowish
USE grayish yellowish brown

brown, iron
USE black

brown iron oxide
MT.2126
HN April 1992 descriptor moved
UF brown, Mars
iron oxide, brown
Mars brown

brown, jacaranda
USE burnt umber

brown lake
USE moderate red

brown lampblack
USE bister

brown, light
USE light brown

brown, light copper
USE strong brown

brown, light grayish
USE light grayish brown

brown, light grayish reddish
USE light grayish reddish brown

brown, light grayish yellowish
USE light grayish yellowish brown

brown, light olive
USE light olive brown

brown, light reddish
USE light reddish brown

brown, light rose
USE dark grayish red
grayish red

brown, light yellowish
USE light yellowish brown

brown, lilac
USE blackish red
light brownish gray
reddish gray

brown, Mars
USE brown iron oxide
moderate brown

brown, metallic
USE deep brown
deep reddish brown

brown, moderate
USE moderate brown

brown, moderate olive
USE moderate olive brown

brown, moderate reddish
USE moderate reddish brown

brown, moderate yellowish
USE moderate yellowish brown

brown, mummy
USE dark yellowish brown
grayish brown
grayish yellowish brown
moderate brown

brown, mustard
USE moderate olive

brown ocher
MT.2125
HN April 1992 descriptor moved
UK brown ochre
UF ocher, brown
ochre, brown

brown, ocher
USE golden ocher

brown ochre
SEE brown ocher

brown olive
USE light olive brown

brown, olive
USE olive brown

brown-on-cream
FL.2956
HN April 1993 descriptor added

brown-on-cream ware
HN April 1993 descriptor split, use
brown-on-cream + ware

brown orange
USE brownish orange
deep orange

grayish reddish orange
light brown
light yellowish brown
moderate orange
moderate orange yellow
moderate yellow
moderate yellowish pink
strong orange
strong orange yellow

brown, orange
USE brownish orange
dark red
deep orange
grayish reddish orange
light brown
light grayish brown
light grayish yellowish brown
moderate brown
moderate reddish orange
strong brown
strong reddish brown

brown, pale
USE light brown
light grayish reddish brown
light grayish yellowish brown
light yellowish brown
moderate orange

brown, pale reddish
USE light reddish brown

brown, pale yellowish
USE light grayish yellowish brown

brown pigment
MT.2111
HN April 1993 descriptor moved
UF pigment, brown

brown pigment, artificial inorganic
USE artificial inorganic brown pigment

brown pigment, inorganic
USE inorganic brown pigment

brown pigment, organic
USE organic brown pigment

brown pigment, synthetic inorganic
USE artificial inorganic brown pigment

brown pink
USE Dutch pink

brown purple
USE grayish purple

brown red
USE grayish red
grayish reddish brown
light grayish red
vivid red

brown, red
USE blackish red
brownish orange
dark red
dark reddish orange
deep orange
grayish red
grayish yellowish pink
light brown

light grayish red
light reddish brown
moderate brown
moderate olive brown
moderate orange
moderate reddish brown
moderate reddish orange
moderate yellowish brown
pale yellowish pink
reddish gray
strong yellowish brown

brown, reddish
USE reddish brown

brown, rose
USE dark grayish red
deep purplish red
deep red
grayish red
grayish reddish brown
very deep purplish red
very deep red
vivid red

brown rot
DE.53   (L)
SN A decay of wood caused by fungus
that decomposes cellulose and the
associated pentosans, leaving the lignin more or less unaltered; the resultant mass is powdery and occurs
in various shades of brown. (TOWT)
UF rot, brown

brown, Rubens'
USE Vandyke brown

brown, sepia
USE dark grayish yellowish brown
dark olive brown
dark yellowish brown

brown, Sicilian
USE raw umber

brown, sienna
USE moderate brown

brown-slipped (pottery style)
FL.2957
HN April 1993 descriptor added

brown-slipped ware
HN April 1993 descriptor split, use
brown-slipped (pottery style) +
ware

brown, soot
USE bister

brown, Spanish
USE strong reddish brown

brown-stone
SEE brownstone

brown, strong
USE strong brown

brown, strong reddish
USE strong reddish brown

brown, strong yellowish
USE strong yellowish brown

brown, taupe
USE brownish gray
dark grayish purple
grayish brown
grayish reddish brown

brown, transparent
USE transparent brown

brown, umber
USE grayish brown

brown, Van Dyck
USE Vandyke brown

brown, Van Dyke
USE Vandyke brown

brown, Vandyke
USE grayish brown
moderate brown

brown, Verona
USE transparent brown

brown, Veronese
USE transparent brown

brown, very dark
USE dark brown
dark yellowish brown

brown, very dark grayish
USE dark grayish yellowish brown
moderate olive brown

brown, very pale
USE brownish pink
light grayish yellowish brown
light yellowish brown
pale orange yellow

brown violet
USE dark purplish red
grayish purplish red

brown, violet
USE dark purplish red
grayish purple
grayish red

brown, yellow
USE brownish orange
brownish pink
dark orange yellow
dark reddish orange
light brown
light olive
light reddish brown
moderate orange
strong brown
strong yellowish brown

brown, yellowish
USE yellowish brown

browning brushes
TH.1147
HN December 1992 descriptor moved
ALT browning brush
SN Tools used to throw water on the surface of applied mortar to provide lubrication to the tools used to straighten the surface. (PUTNAM)
UF brushes, browning

brownish black
DL.118
UF black, brownish
centroid color 65

brownish gray
DL.116
UF black brown
blackish brown
bronze brown
brown black
brown, black
brown, blackish
brown, bronze
brown, taupe
centroid color 64
dark rose taupe
gray, brownish
gray, rose
gray, very dark
rose gray
rose taupe, dark
taupe
taupe brown
taupe, dark rose
very dark gray

brownish gray, light
USE light brownish gray

brownish olive
USE light olive brown
moderate olive brown

brownish olive, dull
USE dark olive brown

brownish olive, light
USE light olive brown

brownish orange
DL.106
UF brown, gold
brown orange
brown, orange
brown, red
brown, yellow
centroid color 54
gold brown
gold ocher, transparent
ocher, transparent gold
orange brown
orange, brown
orange, brownish
raw sienna (color)
red brown
red, yellow
sienna, raw
terra cotta
terra sienna
transparent gold ocher (color)
yellow brown
yellow red

brownish pink
DL.64
UF biege, light rose
bisque
bistre, purplish
brown, dull
brown, very pale
brown, yellow

buff
centroid color 33
dull brown
gray, lilac
light rose beige
lilac gray
pink, brownish
purplish bistre
rose beige, light
very pale brown
yellow brown

brownish white
USE yellowish white

brownish yellow
USE dark orange yellow

brownline prints
VW.1082
HN March 1993 descriptor moved
ALT brownline print
SN Use for prints made on light-sensitized surfaces that produce brown lines on neutral backgrounds. For white images on brown backgrounds, use **brownprints**. For brownline prints on translucent paper, use **sepia prints**.
UF brownlines
prints, brownline

brownlines
USE brownline prints

brownprints
VW.1068
HN March 1993 descriptor moved
ALT brownprint
SN Use for prints made on light-sensitized surfaces that produce white images on brown backgrounds. For brown images on neutral backgrounds use **brownline prints** or **sepia prints**.
UF photoprints, Van Dyke
photoprints, Van Dyke brown
prints, Van Dyke
Van Dyke brown photoprints
Van Dyke photoprints
Van Dyke prints

brownstone
MT.886
HN March 1992 scope note added
March 1992 descriptor moved
UK brown-stone
SN A brown or reddish-brown sandstone whose grains are generally coated with iron oxide. (AGI)

brownstones
RK.269   (B)
ALT brownstone
SN Dwellings, often row houses, faced with brownstone. (HAS)

brows, helmet
USE brow reinforces

brun Vandyck
USE Vandyke brown

Brunings
USE diazotypes

Brunswick blue
USE Prussian blue

Brunswick green
    MT.2164
HN April 1992 descriptor moved
UF green, Brunswick
    green, Prussian
    Prussian green

brush biting
USE spit biting

brush bits
    PJ.2577
HN March 1993 descriptor moved
ALT brush bit
UF bits, brush

brush cleaners
USE brush washers

brush graining
USE graining

brush-makers
SEE brushmakers

brush marks
USE brush strokes

brush strokes
    PJ.3322   (L)
ALT brush stroke
SN Use for the marks made in paint by
    the action of the painter's brush.
UF brush marks
    marks, brush
    strokes, brush

brush technique
USE brushwork

brush washers
    TH.740
HN February 1993 descriptor added
ALT brush washer
SN Devices used for cleaning artists'
    brushes, or to prevent them from
    drying out. (GETTEN)
UF brush cleaners
    cleaners, brush
    studio brush cleaners
    washers, brush

brush-work
SEE brushwork

brushes
    TH.1064   (L,N)
HN May 1993 related terms added
    March 1993 scope note changed
ALT brush
SN Implements consisting of bristles,
    hair, or the like, set in or attached
    to a handle; used for painting,
    cleaning, polishing, or grooming.
    (RHDEL2)
RT artists' brushes
    <brushes: maintenance tools>
    <brushes: personal use>
    <brushes: photographic equipment>
    <brushes: plaster, concrete and mortar
    working equipment>

brushes, artists'
USE artists' brushes

brushes, background
USE background brushes

brushes, badger-hair
USE blenders (artists' brushes)

brushes, bristle
USE bristle brushes

brushes, browning
USE browning brushes

brushes, camel hair
USE camel hair brushes

brushes, cloth
USE clothes brushes

brushes, clothes
USE clothes brushes

brushes, dusting
USE dusting brushes
    fan brushes

brushes, fan
USE fan brushes

brushes, filbert
USE filberts

brushes, file
USE file brushes

brushes, flat
USE flats (brushes)

brushes, food
USE pastry brushes

brushes, fountain
USE fountain brushes

brushes, glazing
USE pastry brushes

brushes, hair
USE hair brushes
    hairbrushes

brushes, hog-hair
USE bristle brushes

brushes, lather
USE shaving brushes

brushes, lettering
USE lettering brushes

<brushes: maintenance tools>
    TH.892
HN May 1993 related term added
RT brushes

brushes, oval
USE filberts

brushes, paint
USE paintbrushes

brushes, paperhanging
USE wallpaper brushes

brushes, pastry
USE pastry brushes

<brushes: personal use>
    TH.372
HN February 1993 guide term added
RT brushes

<brushes: photographic equipment>
    TH.789
HN May 1993 related term added
RT brushes

<brushes: plaster, concrete and mortar
   working equipment>
    TH.1146
HN May 1993 related term added
    December 1992 guide term moved
    December 1992 guide term
    changed, was *<brushes: masonry*
    and plastering tools>
RT brushes

brushes, rasp
USE file brushes

brushes, rigger
USE riggers

brushes, round
USE rounds

brushes, scrub
USE scrub brushes

brushes, shaving
USE shaving brushes

brushes, sky
USE wash brushes

brushes, stencil
USE stencil brushes

brushes, tooth
USE toothbrushes

brushes, wallpaper
USE wallpaper brushes

brushes, wash
USE wash brushes

brushes, watercolor
USE watercolor brushes

brushes, watercolour
SEE watercolor brushes

brushes, wire
USE wire brushes

brushing
USE napping

brushmakers
    HG.775
HN December 1992 alternate terms
    added
ALT brushmaker
    brushmaker's
    brushmakers'

UK brush-makers
UKA brush-maker

brushwork
KT.120 (L)
HN January 1993 descriptor moved
UK brush-work
UF brush technique

Brussels bobbin lace
USE Brussels lace (bobbin lace)

Brussels carpeting
USE Brussels carpets

Brussels carpets
TC.145 (R)
ALT Brussels carpet
SN Carpets that were made with variously colored worsted yarn first fixed in a foundation web of strong linen thread and then drawn up in loops to form the pattern. (W)
UF Brussels carpeting
carpeting, Brussels
carpets, Brussels

Brussels lace (bobbin lace)
MT.1578
HN December 1992 descriptor added
SN Bobbin lace made in and around Brussels, especially a fine 18th-century lace in which individual motifs or small sections of the pattern are made separately and joined on a net ground.
UF bobbin lace, Brussels
Brussels bobbin lace
lace, Brussels

Brussels lace (needlepoint)
MT.1583
HN December 1992 descriptor added
SN Needle lace made in and around Brussels, especially a flat lace made with very fine thread and decorated with elaborated fillings.
UF Brussels needle lace
Brussels needlepoint
lace, Brussels
needle lace, Brussels
needlepoint, Brussels

Brussels needle lace
USE Brussels lace (needlepoint)

Brussels needlepoint
USE Brussels lace (needlepoint)

Brussels, tapestry
USE tapestry Brussels

brut, art
USE art brut

Brutalist
FL.3843 (A,L,B,R)
ALT Brutalism
SN Includes late works of Le Corbusier and other architecture influenced by it, characterized by raw concrete and undisguised functional features.
UF Neo-Brutalist
New Brutalist

bruzz chisels
USE corner chisels

Brya ebenus
USE granadilla

bryozoa limestone
MT.844
HN April 1992 descriptor moved
UF limestone, bryozoa

Bubalus phase
FL.67
UF Hunter period
Large wild fauna phase

bubble lamps
TC.1267
ALT bubble lamp
UF lamps, bubble

Bubi
USE Bulu

Bucchero
FL.2834 (L)
HN April 1993 descriptor added

Bucchero ware
HN April 1993 descriptor split, use Bucchero + ware

buccinae
TT.46
ALT buccina
SN Curved Roman brass aerophones of conical bore, their range limted to a few notes of the natural scale and filling primarily a signalling function. (NGDMI)
UF buccinas
RT *<sound signaling devices>*

buccinas
USE buccinae

buccins
TT.99 (N)
ALT buccin
SN Signal instruments of Europe, made of horn or wood, later imitated in metal, having a straight conical tube with a slight flare at the end. (MARCUS)

bûches
USE épinettes des Vosges

buck anchors
PJ.25
HN April 1993 descriptor moved
ALT buck anchor
UF anchors, buck

buck-eye
SEE buckeye

buck-eye, California
SEE California buckeye

buck-eye, dwarf
SEE dwarf buckeye

buck-eye, Ohio
SEE Ohio buckeye

buck-eye, yellow
SEE yellow buckeye

buck wagons
USE buckboards

buckboards
TX.164 (N)
ALT buckboard
SN Use for light four-wheeled carriages with simple bodies set on long elastic planks, instead of springs, attached to the axles and with seats mounted directly on the floorboards near their center; developed in the United States in the early 19th century; later modified versions may have springs.
UF buck wagons
wagons, buck

Bückelkeramik
USE knobbed (pottery style)

bucket benches
USE water benches

bucket lamps
TC.1230
ALT bucket lamp
SN Small, glass, cup-shaped containers that hold oil and a float wick or candles, used especially for outdoor decoration and illumination.
UF lamps, bucket

bucket loaders
TH.459
ALT bucket loader
UF loaders, bucket

bucket loaders, chain
USE chain bucket loaders

buckets (construction equipment)
TH.461 (L)
ALT bucket (construction equipment)
SN Attachments for a materials-handling or excavating machine. (DAC)

buckets (vessels)
TQ.68 (H,L,N)
ALT bucket (vessel)
SN Typically, round wooden vessels for drawing water from a well; also, any comparable vessel for catching, holding, or carrying liquids or solids. (W)
RT ice buckets
pails

buckets, clamshell
USE clamshell buckets

buckets, dinner
USE lunchboxes

buckets, dipper
USE dippers (construction equipment)

buckets, dragline
USE dragline buckets

buckets, grab
USE clamshell buckets

buckets, holy water
USE aspersoriums

buckets, ice
USE ice buckets
wine coolers

buckeye
MT.2674
HN March 1992 descriptor moved
UK buck-eye
UF Aesculus
American horse chestnut
chestnut, American horse
horse chestnut, American

buckeye, California
USE California buckeye

buckeye, dwarf
USE dwarf buckeye

buckeye, Ohio
USE Ohio buckeye

buckeye, sweet
USE yellow buckeye

buckeye, yellow
USE yellow buckeye

buckle tongs
USE sliding tongs

bucklers
TE.355 (N)
ALT buckler
SN Small shields with an internal grip,
held in the left hand during foot
combat; they were used from the
13th to the 17th century.

buckles
PJ.69 (H,L,N,R)
ALT buckle
SN Devices used for fastening and
sometimes decoration consisting of
a frame, usually metal, covered or
uncovered, and one or more teeth,
chapes, or catches.
RT <costume components>

buckling
KT.246 (L)
HN January 1993 descriptor moved
November 1992 scope note changed
ALT buckled
SN Severe bending, warping, or bulg-
ing; in the case of a structural mem-
ber, failure caused by lateral or tor-
sional instability.

buckling, elastic
USE elastic buckling

buckling, inelastic
USE inelastic buckling

buckling, lateral
USE lateral buckling

bucks, door
USE door bucks

bucks, rough
USE door bucks

bucks, vaulting
USE vaulting horses

bucksaws
TH.1581 (N)
HN March 1993 lead-in term changed,
was **woodcutter's saws**
March 1993 lead-in term changed,
was **saws, woodcutter's**
ALT bucksaw
SN Saws with a fixed blade set in an H-
shaped frame, used mainly for cutting across the grain of lumber and
firewood.
UF saws, buck
saws, woodcutters'
woodcutters' saws

buckskin
MT.2588 (L)
HN March 1992 scope note added
March 1992 lead-in term added
February 1992 descriptor moved
SN Skin from deer or deer family ani-
mals from which the grain has been
removed. Generally treated with an-
imal oils, formaldehyde, or a combi-
nation of both.
UF buckskin leather
leather, buckskin

buckskin leather
USE buckskin

buckthorn berry
MT.2029
HN April 1992 descriptor moved
UF Avignon berry
berry, Avignon
berry, buckthorn
berry, French
berry, Persian
berry, yellow
French berry
Persian berry
yellow berry

buckthorn lake
USE Persian berries lake

bucranes
USE bucrania

bucrania
DG.33
ALT bucranium
SN Motifs representing the head or
skull of an ox, often garlanded,
common in classical style friezes.
(HAS)
UF bucranes

bud vases
TQ.613 (N)
ALT bud vase
SN Relatively tall containers with a narrow mouth intended primarily for
holding one or a few buds or
flowers.

UF vases, bud
RT vases

Buddhism
BM.448 (A,L,B,R)
ALT Buddhist

Buddhism, Ch'an
USE Ch'an

Buddhism, Hinayana
USE Hinayana

Buddhism, Mahayana
USE Mahayana

Buddhism, Pali
USE Theravada

Buddhism, Southern
USE Theravada

Buddhism, Theravada
USE Theravada

Buddhism, Vajrayana
USE Vajrayana

Buddhism, Zen
USE Zen

budgeting
KG.90
SN Planning, coordinating, and allocating financial resources and expenditures.

budgets
VW.565 (L)
HN November 1992 descriptor moved
ALT budget

Budu
FL.520
UF Mabudu

bufetes
TC.1145
HN January 1993 descriptor moved
ALT bufete
SN Small Spanish tables, usually in a
woman's room. (BURR2)

bufetillos
TC.981
HN January 1993 descriptor moved
ALT bufetillo
SN Castilian name for small writing ta-
bles with hidden places for jewels
and other valuables. (BUENO)

buff
USE brownish pink
dark orange yellow
grayish yellow
light grayish yellowish brown
light orange
light yellowish brown
moderate orange
moderate orange yellow
moderate yellow
moderate yellowish pink
pale orange yellow
pale yellow

pale yellowish pink
yellowish gray
yellowish white

buff (pottery style)
FL.3113
HN April 1993 descriptor added

buff coats
TE.308
ALT buff coat
SN Sleeveless jackets made of leather, worn in 16th- and 17th-century Europe either under a cuirass or as an independent protection against edged weapons. (TARA)
UF coats, buff
RT jackets
soft armor

buff, cream
USE pale yellow

buff, dull
USE grayish yellowish pink
moderate orange yellow
pale orange yellow
pale yellowish pink

buff, gritty
USE gritty buff

buff, light
USE pale orange yellow
pale yellow

buff, orange
USE brilliant yellow
light orange yellow
light yellow
moderate orange yellow
moderate yellow
moderate yellowish pink
strong yellow

buff, pale pinkish
USE pale orange yellow

buff, red-washed
USE red-washed buff

buff ware
HN April 1993 descriptor split, use **buff (pottery style)** + **ware**

buff yellow
USE moderate yellow

buff, yellow
USE grayish yellow
light yellowish brown
moderate orange yellow
pale orange yellow
pale yellow

buffer
MT.3083   (L)
HN May 1993 descriptor added
SN Any substance capable in solution of neutralizing both acids and bases and thereby maintaining the original acidity or basicity of the solution. (WCOL9)

UF buffer solution
solution, buffer

buffer solution
USE buffer

buffer zones
RG.297   (L)
ALT buffer zone
SN Strips established to separate and protect one type of land use from another (e.g., industry versus housing). (LOC)
UF zones, buffer

buffering, humidity
USE humidity control

buffers (cutters)
TH.1248   (N)
HN May 1992 descriptor changed, was **buffers**
May 1992 alternate term changed, was **buffer**
ALT buffer (cutter)
SN Tools used for cutting horseshoe nails. (KNIGHT)
UF clinch cutters
cutters, clinch

buffers (surface working tools)
TH.1068   (N)
HN January 1993 descriptor added
ALT buffer (surface working tool)
SN Any of various devices used for polishing or buffing.

buffes, falling
USE falling buffes

buffet forks
USE cold-meat forks

buffet spoons
USE sugar spoons

buffet stools
TC.668
HN January 1993 descriptor moved
ALT buffet stool
SN 16th-century English and early 17th-century American stools, usually upholstered and covered with sumptuous fabric and fringe. Term also applied to a variety of small, low stools generally with socketed legs.
UF cricket stools (buffet stools)
stools, buffet
stools, cricket (buffet stools)

buffets
TC.1002
HN May 1993 related term added
March 1993 descriptor changed, was **buffets (sideboards)**
March 1993 alternate term changed, was **buffet (sideboard)**
January 1993 descriptor moved
ALT buffet
SN Term used loosely for a variety of serving cupboards or tables since

the 16th century, now generally called **sideboards**. (FAIRB)
RT cupboards

buffets (armoires)
USE armoires

buffets (sideboard tables)
USE sideboard tables

buffets (sideboards)
USE sideboards

buffing
USE polishing

buffing agent
USE buffing composition

buffing composition
MT.2007
HN April 1993 lead-in term added
April 1993 descriptor changed, was **buffing compositions**
SN Material used for buffing or polishing metal, originally of dolomitic lime with from 18 to 25% saponifiable grease as a bond. (MH)
UF agent, buffing
buffing agent
composition, buffing

buffs
TH.1069
ALT buff
SN Devices, such as sticks or blocks, having a soft absorbent surface; used to apply polishing material. (W)

bugel horns
USE bugles

bugelhorns
USE bugles

bugeyes
TX.495   (L,N)
ALT bugeye
SN Use for double-ended, log-bottom boats or later flat-bottom, shallow-draft boats of similar shape, but built plank-on-frame, with two masts raking aft carrying a jib and triangular sails; used for offshore fishing and general cargo transport in the Chesapeake Bay area.

buggies (carriages)
TX.177
ALT buggy (carriage)
SN Use for light, simply constructed, four-wheeled carriages with or without collapsible tops and usually accommodating only one or two passengers; developed in England in the late 18th century; may also be used for early automobile designs with similar body styles.

buggies (equipment)
TH.1123
ALT buggy (equipment)

SN Devices for transporting concrete. (DAC)
UF carts, concrete
concrete carts

buggies, baby
USE baby carriages

buggies, doll
USE doll carriages

bugle players
USE buglers

buglers
    HG.235
HN January 1993 descriptor added
ALT bugler
bugler's
buglers'
SN Those who play the bugle, including those who use it to sound signals, as in an army.
UF bugle players
players, bugle
RT bugles
keyed bugles

bugles
    TT.47   (L,N)
ALT bugle
SN Keyless valveless aerophones with a coiled wide conical bore and a cup mouthpiece, now used chiefly for military and parade use. (MARCUS)
UF bugel horns
bugelhorns
clairons
horns, bugle
RT brass instruments
buglers
keyed bugles

bugles, Kent
USE keyed bugles

bugles, keyed
USE keyed bugles

bugles, Royal Kent
USE keyed bugles

Buhágana
USE Macuna

buhl
USE boulle work

buhl saws
    TH.1585   (N)
ALT buhl saw
SN Fretsaws having a very deep frame and a short blade; used for inlay work. (DISSTO)
UF inlaying saws
saws, buhl
saws, inlaying

buhl work
USE boulle work

builder-designed houses
    RK.286   (B)

ALT builder-designed house
UF houses, builder-designed

builders
    HG.816   (A,H,B)
HN December 1992 alternate terms added
ALT builder
builder's
builders'

builders' finish hardware
USE finish hardware

builders' guides
    VW.470
HN November 1992 descriptor moved
    June 1991 descriptor moved
ALT builder's guide
UF carpenters' handbooks
guides, builders'
handbooks, carpenters'

builders' hardware
USE finish hardware

builders, organ
USE organ builders

building
USE construction

building berths
USE slipways

building blocks
    TV.142   (L)
ALT building block
SN Use for toy blocks capable of being stacked to make simple constructions.
UF blocks, building
bricks, building
building bricks
RT construction toys

building board
    MT.1782   (L,B)
HN October 1992 descriptor moved
SN Multipurpose structural insulating board. (STEIN)
UF board, building

building board, fiber
USE fiberboard

building, bombproof
USE bombproof construction

building brick
    MT.99
HN April 1992 descriptor moved
SN Brick made from natural clay and having no special surface treatment. (W)
UF brick, building
brick, common
common brick

building brick, modular
USE modular building brick

building bricks
USE building blocks

building caretakers
USE caretakers

⟨building ceremonies⟩
    KM.23

building codes
    VW.743   (A,L,B)
HN November 1992 descriptor moved
ALT building code
SN Laws, ordinances, or government regulations concerning fitness for habitation setting forth standards and requirements for the construction, maintenance, operation, occupancy, use, or appearance of buildings, premises, and dwelling units. (BLACKS)
UF building laws
building regulations
codes, building
laws, building
regulations, building

building design, green
USE green design

building diagnostics
    KG.19   (A)
SN Judging how well a building performs its functions, through an understanding of the building's purpose, present use, environment, and history.
UF diagnostics, building

building directories
    VW.842
HN November 1992 descriptor moved
    February 1991 descriptor added
ALT building directory
SN Devices informing users of a building or complex about the location of or directions to individuals, organizations, or services within that building or complex.
UF directories, building

⟨building divisions⟩
    PJ.944
HN March 1993 guide term moved

⟨building elevation attributes⟩
    DC.133
HN October 1992 guide term moved
    March 1991 guide term moved
    November 1990 guide term changed, was ⟨building plan attributes: number of stories⟩

building envelopes
    BM.943   (A)
HN February 1993 descriptor moved
    January 1991 alternate term added
ALT building envelope
SN Use for the three-dimensional space within which a structure is permitted to be built on a zoning lot; used especially in relation to zoning regulations concerned with land use and access to light and air.
UF bulk envelopes

envelopes, building
envelopes, bulk

building equipment
USE construction equipment

building evaluation
USE post-occupancy evaluation

building failures
BM.626 (A)
HN November 1992 descriptor moved
January 1991 alternate term added
ALT building failure
UF failures, building

building, fast
USE fast-track method

building heating systems
USE heating systems

building land
USE building sites

building laws
USE building codes

building lines
BM.944 (L,B)
HN February 1993 descriptor moved
January 1991 alternate term added
ALT building line
SN Lines on a land plot beyond which
the law forbids the erection of a
building. (PUTNAM)
UF lines, building

building lots
USE lots

building machinery
USE construction equipment

building materials
MT.1775 (A,L,B,R)
UF architectural materials
construction materials
materials, architectural
materials, building
materials, construction

building paper
MT.1465 (L)
HN February 1992 descriptor moved
SN Paper used for insulation, as in
walls, roofs, and between floors. (W)
UF paper, building
paper, sheathing
sheathing paper

building pathology
KG.20
SN Use for the evaluation of building
performance in terms of technical
and physical aspects of structures
after construction, such as structural
integrity, mechanical system performance, and properties of materials.
UF pathology, building

building permits
VW.503 (L)
HN November 1992 descriptor moved
ALT building permit

SN Permits required by local governmental bodies for new building, or
for major alteration or expansion of
existing structures. Applications,
building plans, estimated costs, and
a fee are usually required before a
permit is issued. (BLACKS)
UF lining petitions
permits, building
petitions, lining

<building plan attributes>
DC.138
HN October 1992 guide term moved

<building plan attributes: column layouts>
DC.144
HN October 1992 guide term moved

<building plans>
VC.126
HN April 1992 guide term moved

building plots
USE building sites

building programs
VW.214 (A)
HN November 1992 descriptor moved
ALT building program
SN Written statements setting forth
design objectives, constraints, and
criteria for a building project, including space requirements and relationships, site requirements, and
other considerations. (MEANS)
UF programs, building

building regulations
USE building codes

building sand
MT.1360
HN April 1992 descriptor moved
SN Selected sand used for concrete, for
mortar, for laying bricks, and for
plastering. (MH)
UF sand, building

building sections
USE longitudinal sections

building security
USE burglary protection

building services
USE building systems

building sites
RG.220 (A,L,B)
ALT building site
UF building land
building plots
construction sites
land, building
plots, building
sites, building
sites, construction

building, slab (pottery technique)
USE slab method

building slips
USE slipways

building stone
MT.938 (L)
HN April 1992 descriptor moved
SN Any stone used for building.
UF stone, building

building, stormproof
USE stormproof construction

building surveys
HN October 1992 descriptor deleted

building systems
PC.239 (B)
HN March 1993 descriptor moved
November 1990 scope note added
November 1990 lead-in terms
added
ALT building system
SN Use for networks of equipment that
provide nonstructural services, such
as HVAC or electricity throughout a
building or complex.
UF building services
service, building
systems, building

buildings
RK.4 (A,L,B,R)
ALT building
SN Use for structures, generally enclosed, that are used or intended to
be used for sheltering an activity or
occupancy.

buildings, abandoned
USE derelict buildings

buildings, administration
USE administration buildings

buildings, administrative office
USE administration buildings

buildings, administrative services
USE administration buildings

buildings, agricultural
USE agricultural buildings

buildings, apartment
USE apartment houses

buildings, apsidal
USE apsidal buildings

buildings, archive
USE archives (buildings)

buildings, assembly
USE assembly halls

buildings, association
USE societies' buildings

buildings, athletics
USE sports buildings

buildings, bank
USE banks (buildings)

buildings, business
USE commercial buildings

buildings, capitol
USE capitols

buildings, church
USE churches

buildings, civic
USE public buildings

buildings, commercial
USE commercial buildings

buildings, communications
USE communications buildings

buildings, community
USE community centers

buildings, computer
USE computer centers

buildings, containment
USE reactor containment buildings

buildings, conventual
USE convents

buildings, cultural
USE cultural centers

buildings, demountable
USE demountable buildings

buildings, derelict
USE derelict buildings

buildings, earth sheltered
USE earth sheltered buildings

buildings, educational
USE schools

buildings, embassy
USE embassy buildings

buildings, employees'
USE employees' buildings

buildings, energy efficient
USE energy efficient buildings

buildings, entertainment
USE entertainment buildings

buildings, exhibition
USE exhibition buildings

buildings, experimental
USE experimental buildings

buildings, exposition
USE exhibition buildings

buildings, factory
USE factories

buildings, fair
USE exhibition buildings

buildings, farm
USE farm buildings

buildings, floating
USE floating buildings

buildings, foundation
USE societies' buildings

buildings, fraternal
USE fraternal lodges

buildings, funerary
USE funerary buildings

buildings, government
USE public buildings

buildings, government office
USE government office buildings

buildings, health care
USE health facilities

buildings, heritage
USE historic buildings

buildings, high
USE skyscrapers

buildings, high-rise
USE high-rise buildings

buildings, historic
USE historic buildings

buildings, illegal
USE illegal buildings

buildings, industrial
USE industrial buildings

buildings, intelligent
USE intelligent buildings

buildings, landmark
USE landmark buildings

buildings, legislative
USE legislative buildings

buildings, library
USE libraries (buildings)

buildings, listed
USE landmark buildings

buildings, livestock
USE animal housing

buildings, local authority
USE municipal buildings

buildings, local government
USE municipal buildings

buildings, loft
USE loft buildings

buildings, low-energy
USE energy efficient buildings

buildings, low-rise
USE low-rise buildings

buildings, masonic
USE masonic buildings

buildings, medium-rise
USE mid-rise buildings

buildings, mercantile
USE mercantile buildings

buildings, mid-rise
USE mid-rise buildings

buildings, military
USE military buildings

buildings, mimetic
USE mimetic buildings

buildings, mine
USE mine buildings

buildings, mobile
USE portable buildings

buildings, movable
USE portable buildings

buildings, multi-storey
SEE multistory buildings

buildings, multi-storied
SEE multistory buildings

buildings, multipurpose
USE multipurpose buildings

buildings, multistoreyed
SEE multistory buildings

buildings, multistory
USE multistory buildings

buildings, municipal
USE municipal buildings

buildings, office
USE office buildings

buildings, organizations'
USE societies' buildings

buildings, out-patient
USE clinics

buildings, parliament
USE parliament buildings

buildings, personnel
USE employees' buildings

buildings, phys-ed
USE physical education buildings

buildings, physical education
USE physical education buildings

buildings, portable
USE portable buildings

buildings, public
USE public buildings

buildings, public safety
USE public safety buildings

buildings, railway
USE railway buildings

buildings, reactor containment
USE reactor containment buildings

buildings, recreation
USE recreation buildings

buildings, religious
USE religious buildings

buildings, research
USE research buildings

buildings, residential
USE dwellings

buildings, revolving
USE revolving + buildings

buildings, school
USE schools

buildings, service station
USE service stations

buildings, slab
USE slab blocks

buildings, smart
USE intelligent buildings

buildings, societies'
USE societies' buildings

buildings, society and association
USE societies' buildings

buildings, solar
USE solar buildings

buildings, spa
USE spas

buildings, sports
USE sports buildings

buildings, store
USE stores

buildings, subterranean
USE underground buildings

buildings, sun-heated
USE solar buildings

buildings, tall
USE skyscrapers

buildings, temporary
USE temporary buildings

buildings, terminal
USE terminals

buildings, textile mill
USE textile mills

buildings, tower
USE tower buildings

buildings, transportable
USE portable buildings

buildings, transportation
USE transportation buildings

buildings, underground
USE underground buildings

buildings, underwater
USE underwater buildings

buildings, welfare
USE welfare buildings

buildings, windowless
USE windowless buildings

built-in furniture
TC.1200   (A,L,B)
HN May 1993 related terms added
    January 1993 descriptor moved
UF fitted furniture

furniture, built-in
furniture, fitted
RT cabinets (case furniture)
    corner cupboards
    counters
    cupboards
    window seats

built-up beams
PJ.1646
HN March 1993 descriptor moved
    November 1990 scope note changed
ALT built-up beam
SN Beams, whether of metal, wood, or
    concrete, which are made up of sep-
    arate parts fastened together.
UF beams, built-up
    beams, compound
    compound beams

built-up roofing
MT.1792
SN Continuous roof covering of lami-
    nations or piles of saturated or
    coated felt, alternated with layers of
    bitumen and surfaced with mineral
    aggregate or asphaltic material.
    (STEIN)
UF composition roofing
    roofing, built-up
    roofing, composition

buisines
TT.48
ALT buisine
SN Long straight trumpetlike aero-
    phones of slightly conical bore,
    made of brass or silver with several
    joints, their junctions concealed by
    ornamental bosses, and a flared bell.
    They were used as heralds' trum-
    pets in Medieval Europe and often
    bore the standard of a noble person.
UF bousines
    buysines
    buzines

Bujinga
USE Nanga

Buka
FL.3801

Bukhara
FL.1902
HN April 1993 descriptor added
UF Bokhara

Bukhara (Ersari)
USE Ersari

Bukhara School
FL.1889
HN April 1993 descriptor moved
UF Bokhara School

Bukharas
USE Bukhara + rugs

bukkehorns
TT.65
ALT bukkehorn
SN Simple end-blown aerophones of

Norway made of goat's horn, having
three to five fingerholes but no
mouthpiece. (MARCUS)
UF goat horns
    horns, goat
    prillar horns

bulb plants
USE bulbs

bulbous domes
USE onion domes

bulbous feet
USE bun feet

bulbous legs
USE baluster legs

bulbs
RD.235   (L)
ALT bulb
SN Plants with swollen, underground
    food-storage organs ringed with
    fleshy scale-like leaves enclosing
    next year's buds.
UF bulb plants
    plants, bulb

bulbs (lighting device components)
USE lamps (lighting device components)

bulbs, light
USE lamps (lighting device components)

bulbs, neon
USE neon lamps

bulbs, photoflood
USE photoflood lamps

Bulgarian
FL.3132   (L,B)

Buli
FL.495   (L)
UF Long-faced Style
    Luba, Northern
    Northern Luba

bulk cargo ships
USE bulk carriers

bulk carriers
TX.391
ALT bulk carrier
SN Use for vessels designed to carry dry
    bulk cargoes, such as grain, coal, or
    ore, loose in large compartments.
UF bulk cargo ships
    bulkers
    cargo ships, bulk
    carriers, bulk
    ships, bulk cargo

bulk envelopes
USE building envelopes

bulkers
USE bulk carriers

bulkheads
PJ.1918   (A,N)
HN March 1993 descriptor moved
ALT bulkhead

SN Walls used to resist pressure caused by rock or water, such as to separate land and water areas. (BROOKS)

bulky color
USE volume color

bulky colour
SEE volume color

bull floats
TH.1151
HN December 1992 descriptor moved
ALT bull float
SN Wood, aluminum, or magnesium boards mounted on poles; used to spread and smooth freshly placed, horizontal concrete surfaces. (MEANS)
UF floats, bull

bull header
MT.1827
HN October 1992 descriptor moved
SN In masonry, a brick having one rounded corner, usually laid with the short face exposed to form the brick sill under and beyond a window frame; also used as a quoin or around doorways. (PUTNAM)
UF header, bull

bull laurel
USE magnolia graniflora

bull-nose brick
SEE bullnose brick

bull-roarers
TT.203   (N)
ALT bull-roarer
SN Aerophones consisting of a spatulate piece of wood, bone, stone, or similar material, tied to a string and sounded by being whirled through the air by the player holding the free end of the string. (NGDMI)
UF bullroarers

bullae
TE.438
ALT bulla
SN Small pendants, usually of gold but sometimes of leather, designed as containers for amulets; use especially for those of Etruscan origin.
RT armlets

bulldozers
TH.440   (L,N,B)
HN November 1992 related term added
ALT bulldozer
SN Tractors with caterpillar treads, used to push away debris for clearing an area. (PUTNAM)
UF dozers
RT tracklaying vehicles

bullet catches
PJ.323
HN April 1993 descriptor moved
ALT bullet catch
SN Door latches employing a spring-loaded steel ball. The loaded ball holds the door closed but rolls free when the door is pulled. (MEANS)
UF catches, bullet

bullet-resistant glass
MT.328
HN March 1993 descriptor moved
UF bulletproof glass
glass, bullet-resistant
glass, bulletproof

bullet trains
PC.72   (L)
ALT bullet train
SN High-speed passenger trains used on some routes in Japan. (RHDEL2)
UF trains, bullet

bulletins
USE newsletters

bulletins, church
USE church bulletins

bulletins, news
USE news bulletins

bulletproof glass
USE bullet-resistant glass

bulletproof vests
TE.309   (N)
ALT bulletproof vest
SN Garments worn on the torso as protection against bullets. In the 20th century, they commonly incorporate plates of steel, aluminum, fiberglass, or ceramic, or numerous layers of heavy-weave polymer fiber cloth.
UF vests, bulletproof
RT vests (main garments)

bullets
TK.261   (L,N)
ALT bullet
SN Use for small metal projectiles, round, cylindro-conical, or pointed and streamlined in shape, usually consisting of a lead core in an envelope of some lighter metal and often but not always housed in cartridges, designed to be fired from small arms singly with each firing. For the small solid lead or steel pellets fired from shotguns in multiples with each firing, use **shot**.
RT shot

bullets, armor-piercing
USE armor-piercing bullets

bullets, dumdum
USE dumdums

bullets, expanding
USE expanding bullets

bullets, incendiary
USE incendiary bullets

bullets, Minié
USE Minié balls

bullets, tracer
USE tracer bullets

bullion
MT.477   (L)
HN March 1992 descriptor added
SN Gold or silver considered in mass rather than in value, often in ingot or bar form. (RHDEL2)

bullnose brick
MT.77
HN April 1992 descriptor moved
UK bull-nose brick
UF brick, bull-nose
brick, bullnose

bullnose planes
TH.1509   (N)
ALT bullnose plane
SN Small planes whose mouths can be adjusted for coarse or fine work; used in corners and other difficult to reach places. (PUTNAM)
UF bullnose rabbet planes
planes, bullnose
planes, bullnose rabbet
rabbet planes, bullnose

bullnose rabbet planes
USE bullnose planes

bullnose steps
PJ.2413
HN March 1993 descriptor moved
ALT bullnose step
SN Steps, usually the lowest in a flight, having one or both ends rounded to a semicircle and projecting beyond the face of the stair string and the newel. (HAS)
UF steps, bullnose

bullrings
RK.1001   (B)
HN September 1990 scope note added
ALT bullring
SN Arenas for bullfights. (W)

bullroarers
USE bull-roarers

bulls
VW.707   (L)
HN March 1993 lead-in term added
November 1992 descriptor moved
ALT bull
SN Formal documents issued by the pope that are sealed with a bulla (a round, usually lead, seal) or sealed with a red-ink imprint of the device on the bulla.
UF bulls, papal
papal bulls

bull's eye lamps
TC.1268
ALT bull's eye lamp
SN Lamps fitted with from one to four lenses to concentrate and intensify light, most commonly made of pewter or of tinned sheet iron with a separate glass font.

UF lamps, bull's eye
   lamps, lens
   lens lamps
   lenses (lamps)

bull's eye lanterns
   TC.1396
ALT bull's eye lantern
SN Lanterns fitted with a lens or lenses, sometimes of knobbed or faceted glass to concentrate and intensify light. May be four-sided with lenses on three sides and a handle on the fourth, or have a lens on one side and a handle on the opposite side, or be cylindrical with a hinged door on which the lens or lenses are mounted.
UF dark lanterns (bull's eye lanterns)
   hand lanterns, bull's-eye
   lanterns, bull's eye
   lanterns, dark
   lanterns, policemen's
   policemen's lanterns

bull's eye mirrors
USE convex mirrors

bull's eye windows
USE oculi

bulls, papal
USE bulls

Bulom
USE Sapi-Portuguese
   Sherbro

bulrush
   MT.2627
HN March 1992 descriptor moved

Bulu
   FL.409   (L)
UF Bubi

bulumbatas
USE bolons

bulwarks
USE ramparts

bum rolls
USE bustles

bumbasses
   TT.364
ALT bumbass
SN European zitherlike chordophones consisting of a heavy gut string attached at each end to a long wooden pole and passing over an inflated pig's bladder which serves as a resonator. They are sounded with a notched stick or horsehair bow, to provide a droning accompaniment to folksong or dance.

bumboats
   TX.460
ALT bumboat
SN Use for small open boats used for carrying supplies and provisions to

sell to ships lying in harbor; also employed to take garbage ashore.
UF boats, bum

bumper stickers
   VW.1096   (L,N)
HN June 1992 descriptor added
ALT bumper sticker
SN Stickers intended to be placed on the bumpers of motor vehicles, usually bearing messages such as slogans, witticisms, or advertisements.
UF bumper strips
   stickers, bumper
   strips, bumper

bumper strips
USE bumper stickers

bumpers
USE door bumpers

bumpers, door
USE door bumpers

bumping glasses
USE firing glasses

bums
USE bustles

bums, false
USE bustles

bun feet
   PJ.2798
HN March 1993 descriptor moved
ALT bun foot
SN Flattened ball feet, used on furniture from the mid-17th century. (BEARD)
UF bulbous feet
   feet, bulbous
   feet, bun
   feet, onion
   onion feet
   pieds d'oignon

buna N
USE nitrile elastomer

buna S
USE styrene-butadiene rubber

Bunda
USE Mbun

Bundelkhand
   FL.2348   (L)

Bundi
   FL.2369

bundle piers
HN May 1991 descriptor deleted

bung borers, cylindrical
USE cylinder augers

bung floggers
USE bungstarts

bungalows
   RK.229   (A,L,B,R)
ALT bungalow

bungholes
   PJ.3090
ALT bunghole
SN Small holes, usually near the base of a container, through which liquid can be poured; usually found in rundlets and water coolers. (WKPP)

bunging adzes
   TH.1388   (N)
ALT bunging adz
SN Tools similar to rounding adzes, but used for rougher work, including, but not limited to, cross-cutting bungs and stock for bungs. (SALAM)
UF adzes, bunging

bungs
   PJ.3101   (N)
ALT bung
SN Stoppers for the openings of casks. (RHDEL2)
RT casks

bungstarters
USE bungstarts

bungstarts
   TH.1662   (N)
ALT bungstart
UF bung floggers
   bungstarters
   floggers, bung

Bunjin-ga
USE Nanga

Bunjinga
USE Nanga

bunk beds
   TC.758   (L,N)
HN January 1993 descriptor moved
ALT bunk bed
SN Beds for two people with one sleeping place above the other in the manner of tiered bunks. (W)
UF beds, bunk
   lits superposés

bunkers
   RK.824   (A)
ALT bunker
SN Fortification chambers mostly below ground level built of reinforced concrete or similar material and usually provided with embrasures; also, dugouts that are reinforced (as with logs or bags of sand) and usually have firing slits. (W)

bunkhouses
   RK.220
ALT bunkhouse
SN Rough buildings often with bunk beds, used for sleeping quarters, as for ranch hands, migratory workers, and campers. (RHDEL2)

buntings
   TE.128   (L,N)
ALT bunting

SN Baglike wraps for infants which may be made with or without hood and structured sleeves but which always encase the lower body in one closed bag. May be made in one piece, or with closures at the waist. (NMAHDC)
UF barrowcoats
sleepers (buntings)

Bünyan
USE Kayseri + carpets

Bunyoro
USE Nyoro

Bunzlau
FL.3478 (R)
HN April 1993 descriptor added

Bunzlau pottery
HN April 1993 descriptor split, use **Bunzlau + pottery**

buon fresco
USE fresco painting

buqchah
USE bokches

bur oak
MT.2822 (L)
HN March 1992 descriptor moved
UF mossy-cup oak
oak, bur
oak, mossy-cup
Quercus macrocarpa

bur reed
MT.2628
HN March 1992 descriptor moved
UF reed, bur

Bura
FL.226

burbuts
USE barbuts

bureau beds
TC.774
HN May 1993 related term added
January 1993 descriptor moved
ALT bureau bed
SN Deception beds concealed in a carcase that outwardly resembles a bureau. (GILBR2)
UF beds, bureau
bedsteads, buroe
buroe bedsteads
RT bureaus

bureau-bookcases
TC.944
HN May 1993 related term added
January 1993 descriptor moved
ALT bureau-bookcase
SN Use for English desks with a steeply sloping lid (usually a 45-degree angle) surmounted by a bookcase. For similar American examples use **desks and bookcases.**
UF desks, secretary

scrutoires
secretary desks
RT desks and bookcases

bureau-cabinets
USE fall-front desks

bureau dressing tables
USE bureau tables

bureau tables
TC.937
HN May 1993 related terms added
January 1993 descriptor moved
ALT bureau table
SN Kneehole writing or dressing tables. (GILBR2)
UF bureau dressing tables
buroe dressing tables
combined dressing tables and desks
combined writing and dressing tables
desks, kneehole
dressing tables and desks, combined
dressing tables, bureau
kneehole desks (bureau tables)
kneehole tables
tables and desks, combined dressing
tables, bureau
tables, bureau dressing
tables, combined writing and dressing
tables, kneehole
writing and dressing tables, combined
RT dressing tables
writing tables

bureaucrats
HG.171
HN December 1992 alternate terms added
ALT bureaucrat
bureaucrat's
bureaucrats'

bureaus
TC.951
HN May 1993 related term added
January 1993 descriptor moved
ALT bureau
SN English desks having a lid sloping at an acute angle (usually 45 degrees) that folds out as a writing surface, above drawers. (BEARD)
RT bureau beds

bureaus (chests of drawers)
USE chests of drawers

bureaus, cheval
USE cheval dressers

bureaus, cylinder
USE bureaux à cylindre

bureaus, information
USE information centers

bureaus, travel
USE travel agencies

bureaux (kneehole desks)
USE kneehole desks

bureaux (writing tables)
USE writing tables

bureaux à cylindre
TC.941
HN January 1993 descriptor moved
ALT bureau à cylindre
SN Large French desks popular in the late Louis XV and the Louis XVI periods with a roll top in the shape of a quarter cylinder. This type was occasionally imitated in other countries, besides France, particularly in Germany and Scandinavia in the last decade of the 18th century and virtually every western country during the 19th and 20th centuries.
UF bureaus, cylinder
bureaux à la Kaunitz
bureaux à panse
bureaux à rouleau
cylinder bureaus
secrétaires à cylindre
secrétaires à panse
secrétaires à rouleau

bureaux à dos d'âne
USE bureaux en pente

bureaux à gradin
TC.984
HN January 1993 descriptor moved
ALT bureau à gradin
SN Bureaux plats with a set of drawers or pigeonholes along one side of the top. (DDA)

bureaux à la Bourgogne
USE secrétaires à la Bourgogne

bureaux à la Kaunitz
USE bureaux à cylindre

bureaux à panse
USE bureaux à cylindre

bureaux à rouleau
USE bureaux à cylindre

bureaux de dame
TC.991
HN January 1993 descriptor moved
ALT bureau de dame

bureaux debout
TC.970
HN May 1993 related term added
January 1993 descriptor moved
ALT bureau debout
SN French form of standing desk, sometimes having a pupitre.
RT pupitres

bureaux, dressing
USE dressing tables

bureaux en pente
TC.952
HN January 1993 descriptor moved
ALT bureau en pente
SN Slant-front desks generally intended for a woman's use.
UF bureaux à dos d'âne
bureaux en tombeau

secrétaires à dessus brisé
secrétaires à pupitre
secrétaires en pente
secrétaires en tombeau

bureaux en pupitre
TC.982
HN May 1993 related term added
January 1993 descriptor moved
ALT bureau en pupitre
SN Writing tables with a pop-up reading stand.
RT pupitres

bureaux en tombeau
USE bureaux en pente

bureaux Mazarins
TC.956
HN May 1993 related terms added
January 1993 descriptor moved
ALT bureau Mazarin
SN Bureaux with two tiers of drawers flanking a kneehole recess, some forms intended to be used as writing desks, others as dressing tables; of a type popular in France during the second half of the 17th century.
RT dressing tables
writing desks

bureaux plats
TC.983
HN May 1993 related terms added
January 1993 descriptor moved
ALT bureau plat
SN Large flat-top writing tables, usually with drawers in the frieze.
RT cartonniers
serre papiers
tables à écrire

burettes
USE altar cruets

burgas
USE burkas

burginots
USE burgonets

burglar alarms
PJ.943   (A,L,N)
HN March 1993 descriptor moved
November 1992 lead-in terms added
November 1992 lead-in term deleted, was **burglar alarm systems**
November 1992 lead-in term deleted, was **systems, burglar alarm**
October 1990 descriptor added
ALT burglar alarm
SN Use for automatic devices that give an alarm when such items as doors, windows, or safes are tampered with or opened without authorization, as by burglars. (RHDEL2)
UF alarms, burglar
alarms, intruder
intruder alarms

burglar-proofing
USE burglary protection

burglary
BM.1063   (L)
HN February 1993 descriptor moved
January 1991 descriptor added
ALT burglarized
SN Breaking into and entering any building belonging to another with the intent to commit theft. (RHDEL2)

burglary protection
KG.170   (A,L,B)
HN December 1992 descriptor moved
UF building security
burglar-proofing
housing security
protection, burglary
security, building
security, housing

burgomaster chairs
USE corner chairs

burgomeister chairs
USE corner chairs

burgonets
TE.287   (N)
ALT burgonet
SN Light open helmets of ogival or hemispherical form, commonly furnished with a comb, a pointed peak projecting over the eyes, and hinged cheekpieces or earflaps. They were worn by infantry and light cavalry during the 16th and 17th centuries.
UF burginots
RT gorget plates

burgonets, closed
USE closed burgonets

burgonets, lobster-tailed
USE Zischäggen

Burgundian
FL.3195   (A,L,R)

Burgundy pitch
MT.1237
HN April 1992 descriptor moved
UF pitch, Burgundy

Burgundy turpentine
MT.1236
HN April 1992 descriptor moved
UF turpentine, Burgundy

Burgundy violet
USE manganese violet

burial chambers
PJ.1330   (A)
HN March 1993 descriptor moved
ALT burial chamber
UF chambers, burial

burial cloths
USE shrouds

burial-cloths
USE shrouds

burial gifts
USE grave goods

burial grounds
USE cemeteries

Burial Mound I
FL.779

Burial Mound II
FL.780

Burial Mound period
FL.778

burial mounds
RK.425   (A,L)
HN March 1993 related terms added
ALT burial mound
SN Use for piles of earth erected over grave sites; for piles of stones built over grave sites, use **cairns**; for piles of earth used generally and not over burials, use **mounds**.
UF barrows
barrows, long
conical mounds
kurgans
long barrows
mounds, burial
mounds, conical
tumuli
RT cairns
mounds

burial records
VW.693
HN November 1992 descriptor moved
ALT burial record
UF records, burial

burial registers
VW.711
HN November 1992 descriptor moved
ALT burial register
UF registers, burial

burial shrouds
USE shrouds

buried
DC.300   (L)
HN October 1992 descriptor added
SN Use to describe objects that are or have been in the ground and covered with, often in direct contact with, earth. For structures intentionally built below the earth's surface, use **underground structures**. With regard to the effects of being buried, use **underground environments**.

buried cable maps
VW.118   (L)
HN November 1992 descriptor moved
ALT buried cable map
UF maps, buried cable

buried cities
RD.40   (A,L)
ALT buried city
UF cities, buried

burins
TH.846   (N)

HN February 1993 descriptor added
ALT burin
SN Tools used in printmaking for engraving metal plates or end-grain wood blocks, consisting of a small steel rod, of square or lozenge section, with a sharpened point, and having a half-round wood handle that fits in the palm of the hand. For various tools for chasing or engraving metal or wood, use **gravers**.
RT gravers

burkas
TE.5 (N)
ALT burka
SN Loose garments covering the entire body and having a veiled opening for the eyes, worn by Muslim women. (RHDEL2)
UF bourkhas
burgas
burkhas

burkhas
USE burkas

burl veneer
MT.1666
UF veneer, burl

burlap
MT.1568 (L,B)
HN March 1993 descriptor moved
SN Coarse canvas made of jute, used mainly for sacks and wrapping.
UF gunny
hessian

burlap, base
USE base cloths (upholstery foundation components)

burled walnut
MT.2909
HN March 1992 descriptor moved
UF walnut, burled

Burmese
FL.2393 (L,B)

Burmese glass
MT.271 (R)
HN May 1993 descriptor added
SN Term used in the glass trade for a type of art glass developed by the Mt. Washington Glass Company, shaded from pink to yellow with pink at the top caused by the presence of gold and uranium.
UF glass, Burmese

burn augers
TH.1400 (N)
ALT burn auger
SN Augers whose points are heated to burn holes in wood and then twisted to enlarge the holes.
UF augers, burn

burn brands
USE brands

burn care units
PJ.1238 (L)
HN March 1993 descriptor moved
ALT burn care unit

burned
USE burning

burned brick
USE fired brick

burners
PJ.2903
ALT burner
SN That part of a lamp that supports and permits adjustment of the wick and is the seat of combustion that provides the light. (RUSHL)

burners, acetylene
USE acetylene burners

burners, Argand
USE Argand burners

burners, batswing
USE batswing burners

burners, burning fluid
USE burning fluid burners

<burners by form>
PJ.2904

<burners by fuel type>
PJ.2908

burners, cockscomb
USE cockscomb burners

burners, cockspur
USE cockspur burners

burners, cork disc
USE cork disc burners

burners, drop
USE drop burners

burners, duplex
USE duplex burners

burners, Empire
USE governor burners

burners, fishtail jet
USE fishtail burners

burners, flat-flame
USE batswing burners
fishtail burners

burners, flat wick
USE flat wick burners

burners, fluid
USE burning fluid burners

burners, gas
USE gas burners

burners, governor
USE governor burners

burners, incense
USE incense burners

burners, Jones
USE Jones burners

burners, rat-tail
USE rat-tail burners

burners, union jet
USE fishtail burners

burners, Vienna
USE Vienna burners

burners, whale oil
USE whale oil burners

burning
KT.820
HN January 1993 scope note changed
January 1993 related term added
November 1992 descriptor moved
ALT burnt
SN Use for the process of altering, injuring, or consuming something by fire or heat. For events where something is totally or partially consumed by fire, whether intentionally or by accident, use **fires**.
UF burned
RT fires

burning awls
TH.1409
ALT burning awl
SN Awls used for burning holes in wood, often to remove sap from trees. (SLOANE)
UF awls, burning

burning fluid burners
PJ.2910
ALT burning fluid burner
SN Burners with one or more thin, tapering wick tubes extending above the burner plate but cut off immediately below it to prevent conducting heat into the font containing highly volatile fuel (a mixture of alcohol and redistilled turpentine). When there is more than one tube, they diverge from base to top. Usually small caps are attached by chains to each tube for use in extinguishing the flame and to prevent evaporation of the fuel.
UF burners, burning fluid
burners, fluid
fluid burners

burning fluid lamps
TC.1375 (N)
ALT burning fluid lamp
SN Lamps with fonts, either of metal or glass, which are high and narrow, generally tapering from top to bottom, and which have one to six diverging wick tubes that extend well beyond the height of the burner. Small metal caps attached by chains are furnished to extinguish the flame and retard evaporation of the volatile fuel (alcohol and redistilled turpentine or camphene).
UF fluid lamps

lamps, burning fluid
lamps, fluid

burning in (painting)
KT.446
HN October 1990 descriptor moved
ALT burned-in (painting)
SN The stage of encaustic painting in which the surface of a painting is heated so that the colors may be manipulated and blended.
UF inustion

burning in (photography)
KT.612
HN March 1993 descriptor moved
ALT burned-in (photography)
SN Use for the mechanical process employed in the darkroom to darken a portion of a print, by means of additional exposure. (HCOP)

burning mirrors
TC.1464   (L)
ALT burning mirror
SN Use for concave or convex mirrors designed to start fires by focusing rays of sunlight.
UF mirrors, burning

burnish clay
USE bole

burnished, black
USE black burnished (Helladic pottery style)

burnished, dark-faced
USE dark-faced burnished

burnished, gray
USE gray burnished (Mesopotamian pottery style)
Syrian gray-black

burnished, red
USE red burnished (pottery style)

burnished, red-black
USE Khirbet Kerak

burnished, red-pattern
USE red-pattern burnished

burnishers (metalworkers)
HG.721
HN January 1993 descriptor added
ALT burnisher (metalworker)
burnisher's
burnishers'

burnishers (tools)
TH.1070   (N)
HN April 1993 descriptor changed, was burnishers
April 1993 alternate term changed, was burnisher
January 1993 scope note changed
ALT burnisher (tool)
SN Implements with a hard smooth rounded end or surface; used for smoothing and polishing. In printmaking, used to smooth rough areas of an intaglio plate. (MAYER)

burnishing (photography)
KT.600
ALT burnished (photography)
SN Method of obtaining a glossy surface on collodion prints by pressing them between rollers.

burnishing (polishing)
KT.297   (L)
HN April 1993 alternate term changed, was burnished (polishing)
January 1993 descriptor moved
September 1991 alternate term changed, was burnished
May 1991 descriptor changed, was burnishing
ALT burnished (polished)
SN Making shiny or lustrous by rubbing with a tool that compacts or smooths. (W)

burnishing, barrel
USE barreling

burnouses
TE.134   (N)
ALT burnous
SN Long, hooded cloaks woven in one piece worn by Arabs and monks. Also, similar cloaks worn by women at various periods in Europe and the United States.

burnt brick
USE fired brick

burnt carmine
MT.2119
HN April 1992 descriptor moved
SN A deep brownish purple pigment made by carefully roasting or charring carmine. (MAYER)
UF carmine, burnt

burnt daga
MT.1347
HN April 1992 descriptor moved
UF daga, burnt

burnt green earth
USE transparent brown

burnt Italian earth
USE dark reddish orange

burnt Italian ocher
USE dark reddish orange

burnt lime
USE quicklime

burnt ocher
MT.2127
HN April 1992 descriptor moved
UK burnt ochre
UF gebrannter Ocker
ocher, burnt
ochre, burnt
ocre brûlée

burnt ocher (color)
USE moderate reddish orange

burnt ochre
SEE burnt ocher

burnt-oil varnish
USE litho varnish

burnt sienna
MT.2129
HN April 1992 descriptor moved
UF brown, Caledonian
Caledonian brown
gebrannte Siena
Italian earth
sienna, burnt
terre de Sienne brûlée

burnt sienna (color)
USE dark reddish orange
strong reddish brown

burnt terre verte
USE transparent brown

burnt umber
MT.2132
HN April 1992 descriptor moved
UF brown, chestnut
brown, jacaranda
chestnut brown
euchrome
jacaranda brown
terre d'ombre brûlée
umber, burnt
Umbra gebrannt

burnt umber (color)
USE grayish reddish brown
moderate brown

buroe bedsteads
USE bureau beds

buroe dressing tables
USE bureau tables

Burr arch trusses
PJ.1704
HN March 1993 descriptor moved
March 1991 descriptor moved
ALT Burr arch truss
SN Trusses, patented in the early 19th century by Theodore Burr, combining a wood arch with a series of metal king-post trusses.
UF trusses, Burr arch

burr puzzles
TV.130   (N)
ALT burr puzzle
SN Use for usually solid, geometric puzzles composed of interlocking notched rods of wood or plastic whose final assembled form is highly symmetrical. (PUZZLS)
UF Chinese puzzles
puzzles, burr
puzzles, Chinese

burses
TQ.149   (H,N,R)
ALT burse
SN Cases formed from two squares of stiffened material, usually varying in color according to the season, in

which cloths used in the Christian liturgy are kept. (LITG)

bursting strength
DC.186
HN   October 1992 descriptor moved
SN   Ability of a material, usually in sheet form, to withstand hydrostatic pressure without rupture. (MH)
UF   strength, bursting

burying-grounds
USE   cemeteries

bus ducts
USE   busways

bus lanes
PJ.847   (L)
HN   March 1993 descriptor moved
       June 1990 scope note added
ALT   bus lane
SN   Street or highway lanes intended for use primarily by buses but also used by other traffic for such purposes as right turns. (DDT)
UF   lanes, bus

Bus Mordeh
FL.3094

bus rapid transit
USE   bus transit systems

bus route maps
VW.124
HN   November 1992 descriptor moved
ALT   bus route map
UF   maps, bus route

bus shelters
RK.1188   (A,B)
HN   March 1993 related term added
ALT   bus shelter
SN   Use for minimal structures providing weather protection for patrons at bus stops; for more substantial buildings along bus routes, usually with sales and service facilities, use **bus stations.**
UF   shelters, bus
RT   bus stations

bus stations
RK.1189   (A,L,B)
HN   March 1993 related terms added
ALT   bus station
SN   Use only for intermediate stops along bus routes, usually containing sales and service facilities; use **bus shelters** for structures at bus stops affording weather protection but having no sales or service facilities; use **bus terminals** only to refer to buildings or other structures located at bus route endpoints.
UF   stations, bus
RT   bus shelters
       bus terminals

bus stops
PJ.854

HN   March 1993 descriptor moved
       December 1990 descriptor moved
ALT   bus stop

bus systems
USE   bus transit systems

bus terminals
RK.1190   (A,L)
HN   March 1993 related term added
ALT   bus terminal
SN   Use only to refer to buildings or other structures placed at the endpoints of bus routes; use **bus stations** only for intermediate stops along bus routes; use **bus shelters** for structures at bus stops affording weather protection but having no sales or service facilities.
UF   motor bus terminals
       terminals, bus
       terminals, motor bus
RT   bus stations

bus transit
USE   bus transit systems

bus transit systems
PC.177
HN   March 1993 descriptor moved
ALT   bus transit system
UF   bus rapid transit
       bus systems
       bus transit
       motor bus systems
       rapid transit, bus
       systems, bus
       systems, bus transit
       systems, motor bus
       transit, bus
       transit systems, bus

busbies
TE.576   (N)
ALT   busby
SN   Tall, cylindrical, brimless hats of black fur or feathers, with or without a plume or cockade and usually a bag draped from the crown to the right.
RT   plumes

buscs
USE   busks

buses
TX.154   (H,L,N)
ALT   bus
SN   Use for large, motorized, public street vehicles for large numbers of persons, generally having long bodies and equipped with benches or seats for passengers.
UF   coaches (buses)

buses, double-deck
USE   double-deck buses

buses, school
USE   school buses

buses, trolley
USE   trolleybuses

bush
RD.266
UF   bushland

bush coats
USE   bush jackets

bush jackets
TE.57   (N)
ALT   bush jacket
UK   safari jackets
UKA   safari jacket
SN   Hip-length, belted jackets with two sets of patch pockets and a notched collar.
UF   bush coats
       bush shirts
       coats, bush
       jackets, bush
       jackets, safari
       shirts, bush

bush shirts
USE   bush jackets

bushhammers
TH.1353   (N)
HN   December 1992 descriptor moved
       December 1992 lead-in term added
ALT   bushhammer
SN   Chunky hammers with two striking surfaces covered with rows of pyramidal metal teeth or points; used in stone carving. (MAYER)
UF   bouchardes
       hammers, bush

bushland
USE   bush

Bushmen
USE   San

Bushong
USE   Kuba Kingdom

Bushongo
USE   Kuba Kingdom
       Mbala (Kuba Folk style)

bushwack boats
TX.378
ALT   bushwack boat
SN   Use for dory-type waterfowling boats with wide stern found on the Susquehanna Flats of the upper Chesapeake Bay during the late 19th and early 20th centuries; generally having a hole in the transom for a sculling oar.
UF   boats, bushwack

business
KG.241   (L,R)
HN   February 1993 related term added
       February 1991 descriptor moved
       January 1991 scope note changed
SN   Use for the broad area of commercial or mercantile activity involving the exchange of commodities, services, or financial resources. (W)
UF   commerce
RT   *<people in commerce and business>*

business agents
USE commercial agents

business aircraft
TX.40   (L)
SN Light aircraft used for business, usually seating fewer than ten passengers.
UF aircraft, business
       aircraft, company
       aircraft, corporate
       airplanes, business
       airplanes, company
       airplanes, corporate
       business airplanes
       company aircraft
       company airplanes
       corporate aircraft
       corporate airplanes

business airplanes
USE business aircraft

<business and related functions>
KG.240
HN February 1991 guide term added

business announcements
VW.375   (L)
HN November 1992 descriptor moved
ALT business announcement
UF announcements, business

business buildings
USE commercial buildings

business cards
VW.1162   (L,N,R)
HN April 1993 lead-in term added
       January 1993 related term added
       January 1993 lead-in term deleted, was **trade cards**
       January 1993 lead-in term deleted, was **advertising cards**
       January 1993 lead-in term deleted, was **tradesmen's cards**
       November 1992 descriptor moved
       June 1992 scope note changed
ALT business card
SN Small cards produced since the 19th century bearing the name and address of a business concern and one of its representatives, and intended more for information than advertisement. For small printed sheets or cards bearing tradesmen's advertisements from the 17th through the 19th century, use **trade cards**. For cards made later and distributed for advertisement, use **advertising cards.**
UF cards, business
       cards, show
       show cards
       showcards
RT advertising cards

business centers
USE central business districts

business colleges
RK.773   (B)

HN March 1993 related term added
       July 1991 scope note changed
ALT business college
SN Schools for training students in the clerical aspects of business and commerce, such as typing and bookkeeping; for schools devoted to the professional study of the aspects of commercial enterprise, use **business schools.**
UF colleges, business
       colleges, commercial
       commercial colleges
RT business schools

business directories
USE commercial directories

business districts
RG.276   (B)
ALT business district
UF areas, commercial
       commercial areas
       commercial districts
       commercial zones
       districts, business
       districts, commercial
       zones, commercial

business districts, central
USE central business districts

business enterprises
HN.103   (L)
ALT business enterprise
UF business organizations
       businesses
       commercial enterprises
       enterprises
       enterprises, business
       enterprises, commercial
       organizations, business

business facilities
USE commercial buildings

business letters
VW.352   (L)
HN November 1992 descriptor moved
ALT business letter
UF letters, business

business organizations
USE business enterprises

business parks
USE office parks

business records
VW.702   (L,R)
HN November 1992 descriptor moved
ALT business record
SN Records generated by a commercial or industrial enterprise. (GAHLM)
UF company records
       records, business
       records, company

<business-related functions>
KG.254
HN February 1991 guide term added

business schools
RK.772

HN March 1993 related term added
       September 1990 scope note added
ALT business school
SN Use for schools devoted to the professional study of the organization and management of commercial enterprises, usually at the baccalaureate level and above. For schools devoted to training students in the clerical aspects of business and commerce, use **business colleges.**
UF commercial schools
       schools, business
       schools, commercial
RT business colleges

businesses
USE business enterprises

businessmen
HG.621   (L)
HN February 1993 descriptor moved
       February 1993 scope note changed
       December 1992 alternate terms added
ALT businessman
       businessman's
       businessmen's
SN Men who engage in business as their primary occupation or function.

businesspeople
HG.620
HN February 1993 descriptor added
ALT businesspeople's
       businessperson
       businessperson's
SN Those who engage in business as their primary occupation or function.

businesswomen
HG.622   (L)
HN February 1993 descriptor added
ALT businesswoman
       businesswoman's
       businesswomen's
SN Women who engage in business as their primary occupation or function.

buskins
TE.760
ALT buskin
SN Silk stockings decorated with gold thread worn by Roman Catholic clergy.
RT *<liturgical costume>*

buskins (boots)
USE cothurni

busks
PJ.3033
ALT busk
SN Thin strips, as of whalebone, steel, or wood, worn in front of a corset or stays for stiffening. (NMAHDC)
UF buscs
       busks, spoon
       spoon busks

busks, spoon
USE busks

bust bodices
USE brassieres

bust-confining brassieres
USE bust reducers

bust forms
TE.197 (N)
ALT bust form
SN Pads, ruffles, or shaped inserts placed inside a corset or brassiere to fill out the bust. (NMAHDC)
UF forms, bust
RT brassieres
corsets

bust reducers
TE.199
ALT bust reducer
SN Bands of tape, webbing, or elasticized fabric arranged in an oblong panel which may be slightly curved over the bustline. Worn to compress the breasts. (NMAHDC)
UF brassieres, bust-confining
bust-confining brassieres
reducers, bust

busta
RK.430
ALT bustum
SN Ancient Roman enclosures for cremation and for deposition of cremation urns.

bustan
USE bustanim

bustanim
RM.48 (A)
HN April 1993 descriptor moved
UF bostan
bustan

buster suits
TE.115
ALT buster suit
SN Suits for small boys consisting of a shirt and shorts made of matching or coordinating fabric and held together by buttons at the waist.
UF suits, buster

bustiers
TE.51
ALT bustier
SN Women's or girls' close-fitting, sleeveless tops, often elasticized and usually having boning or facing to give shape and bust support.

bustle pads
TE.200
ALT bustle pad
SN Rectangular pads, generally filled with horsehair, stitched into the top back of the skirt to act as a bustle.
UF pads, bustle

bustles
TE.201 (L,N)

ALT bustle
SN Pads or frames worn at or below the waist in the back to distend the garment backward at the hips. (NMAHDC)
UF bottoms, false
bum rolls
bums
bums, false
cork rumps
culs postiches
false bottoms
false bums
rolls, bum
rumps
rumps, cork

busts
VC.606 (L,N,B,R)
ALT bust
SN Use for representations of only the head and shoulders of a human figure. (THDAT)

busut
USE rugs

busways
PJ.782 (L)
HN March 1993 descriptor moved
November 1990 lead-in term changed, was **busducts**
ALT busway
SN Electric conduits prefabricated in sections and containing heavy conductors for transmission of large currents at relatively low voltage. (W)
UF bus ducts

butane
MT.1129 (L)
HN April 1992 descriptor moved

butanol
MT.2443 (L)
UF alcohol, normal butyl
butyl alcohol, normal
normal butyl alcohol

butcher knives
TH.100 (N)
HN April 1993 descriptor added
ALT butcher knife
SN Large knives with a broad blade, sometimes curved at the tip, used to cut and trim uncooked meat.
UF knives, butcher

butcher paper
MT.1500
HN February 1992 descriptor moved
UF paper, butcher

butchers' cleavers
USE cleavers

butchers' scales
USE platform scales

butlers (chests)
USE cellerets

butlers' desks
TC.892
HN March 1993 descriptor changed, was **butler's desks**
March 1993 lead-in term changed, was **desks, butler's**
January 1993 descriptor moved
ALT butler's desk
SN Chests of drawers with a secretary drawer at the top. (MONTGO)
UF desks, butlers'

butlers' enemies
USE tantaluses

butlers' pantries
PJ.1143
HN March 1993 descriptor moved
March 1993 descriptor changed, was **butler's pantries**
March 1993 lead-in term changed, was **pantries, butler's**
ALT butler's pantry
SN Service rooms between kitchens and dining rooms, typically equipped with counters, a sink, and storage space for china and silver. (RHDEL2)
UF pantries, butlers'

butlers' trays
TQ.543
ALT butler's tray
SN Rectangular trays with hinged sides of curved profile that may be folded down to form a flat oval; may also have attached folding legs or an accompanying stand.
UF trays, butlers'
RT trays

butments
USE abutments

butments, arched
USE flying buttresses

butt chisels
TH.1430
ALT butt chisel
SN Chisels with a short blade; used especially for setting hinges on doors and door frames. (MEANS)
UF chisels, butt

butt hinges
PJ.374
HN April 1993 descriptor moved
ALT butt hinge
SN Hinges mortised into the edge of a door and the edge of the jamb against which the edge of the door will butt when closed. (DITTRI)
UF butts (hinges)
hinges, butt

butt hinges, capped
USE capped butt hinges

butt hinges, loose-joint
USE loose-joint hinges

butt hinges, pocket
USE pocket butt hinges

butt hinges, rising
USE rising hinges

butt joints
PJ.623
HN April 1993 descriptor moved
ALT butt joint
SN Square joints between two members at right angles to each other. The contact surface of the outstanding member is cut square and fits flush to the surface of the other member. (MEANS)
UF end joints
joints, butt
joints, end

butt joints, beveled
USE oblique joints

butt joints, oblique
USE oblique joints

butt stiles
USE hanging stiles

butter basins
USE butter dishes

butter chips
TQ.349
ALT butter chip
SN Small dishes used by an individual diner to hold a pat or small serving of butter. For dishes intended to hold and serve butter at the table use **butter dishes.**
UF butter dishes (butter chips)
RT butter dishes

butter churns
USE churns

butter-coolers
SEE butter coolers

butter coolers
TQ.375
ALT butter cooler
UK butter-coolers
UKA butter-cooler
SN Cylindrical or oval covered vessels designed to serve chilled butter at the table; often with a drainer intended to contain the butter as it is cooled in iced water. Also includes similar vessels made without a drainer but with perforations on the sides and bottom for ventilation. Use **butter dishes** for other dishes intended to hold and serve butter at the table.
UF coolers, butter
RT butter dishes

butter cupboards
USE livery cupboards

butter curlers
TH.198 (N)
HN April 1993 descriptor added
ALT butter curler

SN Culinary tools used to shape butter into fluted scrolls.
UF curlers, butter

butter cutters
TH.101 (N)
HN April 1993 descriptor added
ALT butter cutter
SN Devices used to slice butter.
UF butter slicers
cutters, butter
slicers, butter

butter dishes
TQ.376 (N)
ALT butter dish
SN Dishes for holding and serving butter at the table. Use **butter chips** for small dishes used by an individual diner to hold a pat or small serving of butter. Use **butter coolers** for vessels designed to serve chilled butter at the table.
UF basins, butter
butter basins
dishes, butter
RT butter chips
butter coolers
butter knives
butter tubs

butter dishes (butter chips)
USE butter chips

butter forks
USE pickle forks

butter hands
USE Scotch hands

butter knives
TH.261 (N)
HN April 1993 descriptor added
ALT butter knife
SN Small knives with a wide but dull blade and often with a rounded tip used to cut or serve butter from a butter dish. For similar knives used as a place piece by an individual diner use **butter spreaders.**
UF butter serving knives
knives, butter
knives, butter serving
serving knives, butter
RT butter dishes
butter spreaders

butter molds
TH.202 (L,N)
HN April 1993 descriptor added
ALT butter mold
SN Culinary tools used to form butter into decorative shapes.
UF molds, butter

butter packing tamps
USE butter tamps

butter picks
USE pickle forks

butter plates
USE bread-and-butter plates

butter presses
USE butter prints

butter printers
USE butter prints

butter prints
TH.199 (L,N)
HN April 1993 descriptor added
ALT butter print
SN Culinary tools used to impress designs on butter.
UF butter presses
butter printers
butter stamps
presses, butter
printers, butter
prints, butter
stamps, butter

butter rollers
USE Scotch hands

butter scoops
TH.167 (N)
HN April 1993 descriptor added
ALT butter scoop
SN Long-handled wood scoops used to remove butter from a churn. (WKABW)
UF scoops, butter
RT scoops (serving utensils)

butter serving knives
USE butter knives

butter slicers
USE butter cutters

butter spreaders
TH.315
HN April 1993 descriptor added
ALT butter spreader
SN Small knives with a wide but dull blade used as a place piece by an individual diner to spead butter on bread, rolls, or similar foods. For similar knives used as a serving piece to cut or serve butter from a butter dish use **butter knives.**
UF spreaders
spreaders, butter
RT butter knives

butter stamps
USE butter prints

butter tamps
TH.50 (N)
HN April 1993 descriptor added
ALT butter tamp
SN Flat-headed wooden devices used to pack butter into storage containers.
UF butter packing tamps
tampers
tamps, butter
RT mashers

butter tubs
TQ.575 (N)
ALT butter tub
SN Wooden staved tubs with close-fit-

ting tops used for butter storage or sale.
- UF tubs, butter
- RT butter dishes

butter workers
TH.180 (N)
- HN April 1993 descriptor added
- ALT butter worker
- SN Triangular wooden trays with either a corrugated pin or wooden arm with a metal blade used to work butter.
- UF workers, butter

butterfly chairs
- USE Hardoy chairs

butterfly hinges
PJ.381
- HN April 1993 descriptor moved
- ALT butterfly hinge
- SN Surface-mounted cabinet hinges that have the appearance of a butterfly when opened out flat. (DITTRI)
- UF hinges, butterfly

butterfly joints
PJ.735
- HN April 1993 descriptor moved
- ALT butterfly joint
- UF joints, butterfly

butterfly roofs
PJ.1761 (L,B)
- HN March 1993 descriptor moved
- ALT butterfly roof
- SN Use for roofs sloping downward from eaves on either side to a central valley.
- UF butterfly-shell roofs
  roofs, butterfly
  roofs, butterfly-shell

butterfly-shell roofs
- USE butterfly roofs

butterfly tables
TC.1080
- HN January 1993 descriptor moved
- ALT butterfly table
- UF tables, butterfly

butteries
- USE pantries

buttering trowels
TH.1175
- HN December 1992 descriptor moved
- ALT buttering trowel
- SN Small trowels used to spread mortar on brick before it is laid. (DAC)
- UF trowels, buttering

butternut
MT.2913 (L)
- HN March 1992 descriptor moved
  January 1992 scope note added
  January 1992 lead-in term added
- SN Lightweight, soft walnut, ranging in color from light chestnut brown with darker zones in the heartwood

to pale yellow or white in the sapwood. It has been used for furniture, interior trim, and general carpentry.
- UF juglans cinerea
  walnut, white
  white walnut

buttery hatches
PJ.2216
- HN March 1993 descriptor moved
  November 1990 scope note changed
- ALT buttery hatch
- SN Half-doors giving entrance to a pantry and over which are served out the contents of the pantry. (RS)
- UF hatches, buttery

buttes
RD.175
- ALT butte
- SN Use for erosional landforms that are carved from flat-lying sediment or rocks having resistant top layers and characterized as conspicuous, isolated flat-topped hills with relatively steep sides; smaller in extent than mesas.

button bits
PJ.2578
- HN March 1993 descriptor moved
- ALT button bit
- SN Bits used to inscribe, smooth, and cut out circles from thin bone plates in the production of buttons. (MERCER)
- UF bits, button

button blankets
TE.175
- ALT button blanket
- SN Northwest Coast Native American blankets with totemic designs outlined in buttons, often of abalone shell or pearl, used ceremonially to indicate status and power.
- UF blankets, button
  button robes
  robes, button
- RT hangings
  shoulder blankets

button-headed bolts
- USE carriage bolts

button-hooks
- SEE buttonhooks

button pulls
PJ.349
- HN April 1993 descriptor moved
- ALT button pull
- UF pulls, button

button robes
- USE button blankets

button rugs
TC.149
- ALT button rug
- SN Rugs composed of small fabric circles which have been folded into

quarters and sewn in rows onto a foundation cloth.
- UF dollar mats
  dollar rugs
  mats, dollar
  pile surface button rugs
  rugs, button
  rugs, dollar
  rugs, pile surface button

buttonball
- USE sycamore

buttonholes
PJ.70 (L)
- ALT buttonhole
- SN Holes, slits, or loops through which a button is passed and by which it is secured. (RHDEL2)

buttonhooks
TH.350 (L,N)
- HN January 1993 descriptor added
- ALT buttonhook
- UK button-hooks
- UKA button-hook
- SN Hooks for drawing small buttons through buttonholes, especially on shoes and gloves.

buttoning
KT.1244
- HN December 1992 descriptor added
- ALT buttoned
- SN Fastening an upholstery covering and padding in place by the use of buttons, usually in a pattern such as a diamond or square for a decorative effect.

buttoning, deep
- USE deep buttoning

buttons (fasteners)
PJ.71 (H,L,N,R)
- ALT button (fastener)
- SN Disks, balls, or devices of other shape having holes or a shank by which they are sewn or secured to an article and that are used as fasteners by passing through a buttonhole or loop or a trimming.
- RT <costume components>
  cuff links

buttons (information artifacts)
VW.1022 (N)
- HN June 1992 descriptor added
- ALT button (information artifact)
- SN Ornaments or badges for wearing, as on a lapel, stamped or printed with designs or slogans.

buttons, collar
- USE collar buttons

buttons, stud
- USE studs (buttons)

buttonwood
- USE sycamore

buttress dams
RK.491 (L)

ALT buttress dam
UF dams, buttress

buttress piers
PJ.1559
HN March 1993 descriptor moved
ALT buttress pier
SN Use for piers serving both as buttresses and as regular supporting and dividing elements.
UF piers, buttress

buttresses
PJ.1447   (A,L,N,B,R)
HN March 1993 descriptor moved
November 1990 scope note added
November 1990 lead-in term deleted, was **abamuri**
ALT buttress
SN Pierlike masonry elements built to strengthen or support walls or resist the lateral thrust of vaults.

buttresses, angle
USE angle buttresses

buttresses, arch
USE flying buttresses

buttresses, arched
USE flying buttresses

buttresses, clasping
USE clasping buttresses

buttresses, diagonal
USE diagonal buttresses

buttresses, flying
USE flying buttresses

buttresses, hanging
USE hanging buttresses

buttresses, setback
USE setback buttresses

butts
TQ.22
ALT butt
SN Large casks of varying capacity, especially those used for wine, beer, or water, and formerly for salmon and shrimps. (W)

butts (hinges)
USE butt hinges

butts, skew
USE kneelers (gable components)

butyl acetate
MT.2452
SN A colorless liquid ester of acetic acid that has a fruity odor and is used as a solvent, especially in cellulose nitrate lacquer. (W)
UF acetate, butyl
acetate, N-butyl
acetate, normal butyl
butyl acetate, normal
N-butyl acetate
normal butyl acetate

butyl acetate, normal
USE butyl acetate

butyl alcohol
MT.2442   (L)
HN December 1991 scope note changed
SN Any of four types of flammable liquid alcohol containing four carbons and used chiefly in organic synthesis and as a solvent.
UF alcohol, butyl

butyl alcohol, normal
USE butanol

butyl lactate
MT.2419
SN Volatile solvent used in lacquer and other industrial coating materials as a retardant, to delay setting or drying.
UF lactate, butyl

butyl rubber
MT.1030   (L)
HN January 1993 descriptor moved
UF elastomer, isobutylene-isoprene
isobutylene-isoprene elastomer
rubber, butyl

butyral, polyvinyl
USE polyvinyl butyral

butyrate
MT.1163
HN January 1993 descriptor moved
SN Thermoplastic made by the esterification of cellulose with acetic acid and butyric acid in the presence of a catalyst; particularly valued for coatings, insulation, varnish, and lacquer. (MH)
UF acetate butyrate, cellulose
butyrate, cellulose acetate
CAB
cellulose acetate butyrate

butyrate, cellulose acetate
USE butyrate

Buvayhid
USE Buyid

Buwaihid
USE Buyid

Buwayhid
USE Buyid

Buxus sempervirens
USE boxwood

Buye
USE Hemba

buyers
HG.623   (L)
HN December 1992 alternate terms added
ALT buyer
buyer's
buyers'
SN Persons who have charge of the se-

lection, purchasing, pricing, and display of goods. (W)
UF purchasers

buyers' guides
VW.471
HN November 1992 descriptor moved
ALT buyer's guide
UF guides, buyers'

Buyid
FL.3563   (L)
HN April 1993 descriptor moved
UF Buvayhid
Buwaihid
Buwayhid

buying
USE purchasing

buysines
USE buisines

Buzi
USE Loma

buzines
USE buisines

buzz saws
USE circular saws

buzzers
TT.649   (N)
ALT buzzer
SN Electric signaling devices that produce a buzzing sound. (W)

Bwa
FL.381   (L)
UF Bobo-Ule

Bwaka
USE Ngbaka

Bwende
FL.476   (L)
HN July 1990 lead-in term added
UF Babwendi

BX cable
USE armored cable

bycocket hats
USE bycockets

bycockets
TE.577
ALT bycocket
SN Hats with a high crown and a brim turned up behind and rising to a peak at front; worn from the 14th to 17th century.
UF abacots
abocockets
bycocket hats
hats, bycocket

bylaws
VW.521   (L,B)
HN November 1992 descriptor moved
ALT bylaw
SN Laws, ordinances, or regulations made by a public or private corporation, association, or unincorporated

society for the regulation of its own local or internal affairs, for its dealings with others, or for the government of its members. (GAHLM)

bylaws (municipal)
USE ordinances

bypass roads
USE bypasses

bypasses
    RM.159   (L,B)
HN April 1993 descriptor moved
ALT bypass
UF bypass roads
     roads, bypass

byre-houses
USE housebarns

byres
USE dairy barns

byrnies
USE hauberks

Byzantine
    FL.3157   (A,L,B,R)

Byzantine arches
USE horseshoe arches

Byzantine, Early
USE Early Byzantine

Byzantine, Late
USE Late Byzantine

Byzantine, Middle
USE Middle Byzantine

<Byzantine regional styles>
    FL.3169

Byzantine Renaissance
USE Palaeologan

Byzantine Revival
    FL.3355   (R)
UF Neo-Byzantine
     Revival, Byzantine

C-14 dating
USE radiocarbon dating

C-clamps
    TH.1626   (N)
ALT C-clamp
SN Clamps in the shape of the letter C in which force is applied by rotating a threaded shaft through one jaw of the C to force the work against the other jaw; frequently used in carpentry and joinery. (MEANS)
UF circle clamps
     circle-end clamps
     clamps, C
     clamps, circle
     clamps, circle-end
     clamps, G
     clamps, gee
     G-clamps
     gee clamps

C-scrolls
    DG.81
ALT C-scroll
SN Ornamental scrolls that coil in only one direction, i.e., not reversing direction, as do S-scrolls.

CA
USE cellulose acetate

CAB
USE butyrate

cabacas
    TT.547
ALT cabaca
SN Latin American rattles consisting of a natural or synthetic round or pear-shaped gourd covered with a network of beads and finishing in a short handle, sometimes also containing rattling pieces. (NGDMI)
UF afochês

Cabahiba
USE Parintintin

Caballine phase
USE Horse phase

cabañas
    RK.1012   (A)
HN September 1990 scope note added
ALT cabaña
SN Use for small cabins, simple enclosures, or tentlike structures erected at beaches or swimming pools as bathhouses.

cabarets
    RK.881   (A,L,B,R)
ALT cabaret
SN Use for cafélike facilities often with a dance floor or small stage and featuring entertainment generally of an improvisational, satirical, or topical nature.

cabassets
    TE.289
ALT cabasset
SN Open helmets characterized by an almond- or pear-shaped skull, usually topped by a short spike, and a narrow, flat brim.
UF morions, Spanish
     Spanish morions

cabbage cutters
    TH.102   (N)
HN April 1993 descriptor added
ALT cabbage cutter
SN Rectangular pieces of wood with one or several diagonal blades used to cut or shred cabbage.
UF cabbage graters
     cabbage planes
     cabbage slicers
     cutters, cabbage
     cutters, slaw
     graters, cabbage
     machines, sauerkraut
     planes, cabbage

     sauerkraut machines
     slaw cutters
     slicers, cabbage

cabbage graters
USE cabbage cutters

cabbage knot
USE chou

cabbage-knot
USE chou

cabbage planes
USE cabbage cutters

cabbage slicers
USE cabbage cutters

cabin camps
USE motor courts

cabin cars
USE cabooses

cabin door hooks
    PJ.128
HN April 1993 descriptor moved
ALT cabin door hook
SN Use for heavy hooks and eyes, generally used on marine installations. Distinguished from **cabin hooks**, which are generally used on cabinets.
UF door hooks, cabin
     hooks, cabin door

cabin hooks
    PJ.129
HN April 1993 descriptor moved
ALT cabin hook
SN Use for small hooks and eyes, generally used on cabinets. Distinguished from **cabin door hooks**, which are generally used on marine installations.
UF hooks, cabin

cabin houses
USE cabin launches

cabin launches
    TX.336
ALT cabin launch
SN Use for engine-powered launches with high glass-sided cabins, which provide easy standing headroom and may be three feet or more higher than the basic hull.
UF cabin houses
     glass-cabin launches
     houses, cabin
     launches, cabin
     launches, glass-cabin

cabin, rustic
USE primitive hut

cabinet beds
    TC.775
HN January 1993 descriptor moved
ALT cabinet bed
UF beds, cabinet

cabinet bedsteads
USE press beds (deception beds)

cabinet card photographs
USE cabinet photographs

cabinet card photoprints
USE cabinet photographs

cabinet cards
USE cabinet photographs

cabinet chairs
TC.603
HN January 1993 descriptor moved
ALT cabinet chair
SN Form of late 19th-century commode chair, often associated with invalids, having a chamber pot concealed within a small cabinet under the seat; such cabinets usually have a door in the back so the chamber pot can be removed without disturbing the patient.
UF cabinet commode chairs
chairs, cabinet commode
commode chairs, cabinet

cabinet commode chairs
USE cabinet chairs

cabinet dressing tables, ladies'
USE ladies' cabinet dressing tables

cabinet files
TH.1450
ALT cabinet file
SN Single-cut files which are half-round on one side and flat on the other. (DAC)
UF files, cabinet

cabinet knobs
PJ.338
HN April 1993 descriptor moved
ALT cabinet knob
UF cupboard knobs
drawer knobs
knobs, cabinet
knobs, cupboard
knobs, drawer

cabinet latches
PJ.476
HN April 1993 descriptor moved
ALT cabinet latch
UF latches, cabinet

cabinet locks
PJ.540
HN April 1993 descriptor moved
ALT cabinet lock
SN Spring bolts or magnetic latches, usually found on cabinets. (MEANS)
UF locks, cabinet

cabinet locks, push-pull
USE push-pull cabinet locks

cabinet-makers
SEE cabinetmakers

cabinet makers
USE cabinetmakers

cabinet-making
SEE cabinetmaking

cabinet nests of drawers
USE cabinets of drawers

cabinet oblique drawings
VC.97
HN April 1992 descriptor moved
ALT cabinet oblique drawing
SN Use for drawings in oblique projection in which a vertical plane is parallel to the plane of projection (drawing surface), and receding planes are drawn at half the scale of that vertical plane.
UF cabinet projections
drawings, cabinet oblique
oblique drawings, cabinet
projections, cabinet

cabinet office secretaries
USE Wooton cabinet office secretaries

cabinet officers
HG.153   (L)
HN January 1993 descriptor moved
December 1992 alternate terms added
ALT cabinet officer
cabinet officer's
cabinet officers'
UF officers, cabinet

cabinet organs
USE chamber organs

cabinet photographs
VC.352   (L,N,R)
HN April 1992 descriptor moved
January 1991 lead-in terms added
ALT cabinet photograph
SN Use for card photographs on mounts measuring 4 1/4 by 6 1/2 inches.
UF cabinet card photographs
cabinet card photoprints
cabinet cards
cabinet prints
cabinet-sized photographs
cabinets (photographs)
card photographs, cabinet
card photoprints, cabinet
cards, cabinet
photographs, cabinet
photoprints, cabinet card
prints, cabinet

cabinet pianofortes
USE cabinet pianos

cabinet pianos
TT.419
ALT cabinet piano
SN Type of large upright piano invented by William Southwell of Dublin in 1807, remaining popular until the mid-19th century. It was from 6 to 6 1/2 feet in height with a large, open front panel covered with cloth. (MARCUS)
UF cabinet pianofortes

pianofortes, cabinet
pianos, cabinet

cabinet pictures
VC.254
ALT cabinet picture
SN Small easel paintings of the late 17th to 19th century, intended for hanging in small rooms and viewing at close range. (MAYER)
UF pictures, cabinet

cabinet prints
USE cabinet photographs

cabinet projections
USE cabinet oblique drawings

cabinet rasps
TH.1492
ALT cabinet rasp
SN Rasps which are half-round on one side and flat on the other.
UF cabinet rasps, half-round
half-round cabinet rasps
rasps, cabinet
rasps, half-round cabinet

cabinet rasps, half-round
USE cabinet rasps

cabinet saws
TH.1592
ALT cabinet saw
SN Saws with a reversible handle and a blade which has teeth on either side; one set is fine and the other coarse.
UF saws, cabinet

cabinet scrapers
TH.1611
ALT cabinet scraper
SN Flat steel blades used to smooth wood surfaces after planing, or for scraping paint. (DAC)
UF planes, scraper
scraper planes
scrapers, cabinet

cabinet-sized photographs
USE cabinet photographs

cabinet stands
TC.1032
HN May 1993 related term added
January 1993 descriptor moved
ALT cabinet stand
SN Low tables, often with a raised rim around the edge, intended to support a cabinet, chest, or other piece of case furniture. Intended to stand against a wall, and thus usually undecorated on one side. (BOYCE)
UF cabinet tables
casket stands
stands, cabinet
stands, casket
tables, cabinet
RT taquillónes

cabinet tables
USE cabinet stands

cabinet windows
    PJ.2261
  HN March 1993 descriptor moved
       April 1991 scope note added
  ALT cabinet window
  SN Use for show-windows that project
       outward from the principal plane of
       a building.
  UF windows, cabinet

cabinet-workers
  USE cabinetmakers

cabinetmakers
    HG.781   (A,L,B,R)
  HN April 1993 related term added
       March 1993 scope note added
       February 1993 lead-in term added
       December 1992 alternate terms
       added
  ALT cabinetmaker
       cabinetmaker's
       cabinetmakers'
  UK cabinet-makers
  UKA cabinet-maker
  SN Those whose occupation is cabinet-
       making.
  UF cabinet makers
       cabinet-workers
  RT cabinetmaking

cabinetmakers' marks
  HN March 1993 descriptor split, use
       cabinetmakers' (ALT of cabinet-
       makers) + marks (symbols)

cabinetmaking
    KT.794   (L,R)
  UK cabinet-making
  SN The making of fine furniture and
       intricate woodwork. Use **carpentry**
       for constructing buildings and other
       structures with wood, including in-
       stallation of floors, windows, and
       other trim work. Use **woodworking**
       broadly for the activity of fashioning
       in wood.
  RT cabinetmakers

cabinets (case furniture)
    TC.834   (N,R)
  HN May 1993 scope note changed
       May 1993 related terms added
       January 1993 descriptor moved
       May 1991 descriptor changed, was
         cabinets
       May 1991 alternate term changed,
         was **cabinet**
  ALT cabinet (case furniture)
  SN Case furniture consisting of a set of
       shelves, small drawers, or pigeon-
       holes, fronted by one or more
       doors, and intended for the storage
       and sometimes the display of small
       objects. Also, similar built-in or fit-
       ted cases often designed for specific
       purposes, as in a kitchen or
       bathroom.
  UF boxes, cases of
       cases of boxes
  RT built-in furniture
       commodes (chests of drawers)

cabinets (photographs)
  USE cabinet photographs

cabinets (rooms)
    PJ.1106   (A)
  HN March 1993 descriptor moved
  ALT cabinet (room)
  SN Use for small, private rooms, usually
       adjacent to bedrooms in great
       houses, serving as sitting and dress-
       ing rooms and often containing col-
       lections of art objects.
  UF closets (rooms)

cabinets and stands
  USE cabinets on stands

cabinets and writing tables, ladies'
  USE ladies' cabinet dressing tables

cabinets, bedside
  USE night tables

cabinets, book
  USE bookcases

<cabinets by form>
    TC.835
  HN January 1993 guide term moved

<cabinets by function>
    TC.843
  HN January 1993 guide term moved

cabinets, china
  USE china cabinets

cabinets, corner
  USE corner cabinets

cabinets, dental
  USE dental cabinets

cabinets, drop-front
  USE fall-front desks

cabinets, drying
  USE print dryers

cabinets, filing
  USE filing cabinets

cabinets, gun
  USE gun cabinets

cabinets, hanging
  USE hanging cabinets

cabinets, Hoosier
  USE Hoosier cabinets

cabinets, jewel
  USE jewel cabinets

cabinets, ladies'
  USE cheverets
       ladies' writing tables

cabinets, music
  USE music cabinets

cabinets of drawers
    TC.836
  HN January 1993 descriptor moved
  ALT cabinet of drawers
  UF cabinet nests of drawers
       drawers, cabinets of

       drawers, pedestals with
       nests of drawers, cabinet
       pedestals with drawers

cabinets on stands
    TC.837
  HN May 1993 related term added
       January 1993 descriptor moved
  ALT cabinet on stand
  UF cabinets and stands
       stands, cabinets and
       stands, cabinets on
  RT jewel cabinets

cabinets, piano roll
  USE pianola roll cabinets

cabinets, pianola
  USE pianola roll cabinets

cabinets, pianola roll
  USE pianola roll cabinets

cabinets, record
  USE record cabinets

cabinets, smokers'
  USE smoking stands

cabinets, spice
  USE spice cabinets

cabinets, thread
  USE thread cabinets

cabinets, utility
  USE utility cabinets

cabinets, wax work
  USE wax museums

cabinets, Welsh
  USE tridarns

cabinetwork
  USE joinery

cabins
    RK.230   (A,L,N,B,R)
  ALT cabin

cabins, log
  USE log cabins

cabins, slave
  USE slave quarters

cabins, tourist
  USE tourist cabins

Cabistan
  USE Kuba (Caucasus)

Cabistans
  USE Kuba (Caucasus) + carpets

cable, armored
  USE armored cable

cable, armoured
  SEE armored cable

cable-beam structures
  USE double-cable structures

cable braced bridges
  USE cable-stayed bridges

cable, BX
USE   armored cable

cable car railways
USE   cable railroads

cable laying
KT.75
HN   January 1993 descriptor moved
November 1992 related term added
RT   electric cables

cable-laying ships
USE   cable ships

cable, metal-clad
USE   armored cable

cable moldings
PJ.2082
HN   April 1993 descriptor moved
December 1990 scope note changed
December 1990 lead-in term added
ALT   cable molding
UK   cable mouldings
UKA   cable moulding
SN   Convex moldings resembling a rope
or cable.
UF   moldings, cable
moldings, rope
mouldings, cable
rope moldings
ropework (cable moldings)

cable mouldings
SEE   cable moldings

cable net structures
PJ.1389   (L,B)
HN   March 1993 descriptor moved
July 1991 scope note changed
July 1991 lead-in terms added
ALT   cable net structure
SN   Use for cable structures in which a
field of crossed cables, of different
and often reverse curvatures, make
up the primary roof surface.
UF   cable nets
cable-supported tents
cable tent structures
double curvature net structures
net structures
net structures, cable
net structures, double curvature
nets (net structures)
nets, cable
structures, cable net
structures, cable tent
structures, net
tent structures, cable
tents, cable-supported

cable nets
USE   cable net structures

cable railroads
PC.182   (A,L)
HN   March 1993 descriptor moved
ALT   cable railroad
UK   cable railways
UKA   cable railway
SN   Use for light rail transit in which
railroad-type vehicles are pulled by

a moving continuous cable or belt,
usually located beneath the railway.
UF   cable car railways
cable railway works
cable transportation
cableways
railroads, cable
railways, cable
railways, cable car
transportation, cable

cable railway works
USE   cable railroads

cable railways
SEE   cable railroads

cable releases
TH.769   (N)
ALT   cable release
SN   Long, flexible, cablelike plungers
that permit the photographer to re-
lease the shutter without touching
the camera. (SWED)
UF   releases, cable

cable roofs
USE   cable structures

cable ships
TX.447   (L)
ALT   cable ship
SN   Use for vessels fitted for laying and
repairing underwater communications cables.
UF   cable-laying ships
ships, cable
ships, cable-laying

cable-stayed bridges
RK.1237   (L)
HN   March 1993 alternate term added
November 1992 related term added
ALT   cable-stayed bridge
UF   bridges, cable braced
bridges, cable-stayed
bridges, stayed
bridges, stayed girder
cable braced bridges
stayed bridges
stayed girder bridges
RT   cable-stayed structures

cable-stayed structures
PJ.1390
HN   March 1993 descriptor moved
November 1992 related term added
August 1991 scope note changed
August 1991 lead-in terms added
ALT   cable-stayed structure
SN   Cable structures that use vertical or
sloping compression masts from
which straight cables run to critical
points or to horizontally spanning
or cantilevered members.
UF   cable-supported cantilever roofs
cable-supported structures
cantilever roofs, cable-supported
guyed structures
roofs, cable-supported cantilever
stayed cable structures
structures, cable-stayed

structures, cable supported
structures, guyed
structures, stayed cable
RT   cable-stayed bridges

cable structures
PJ.1388   (L)
HN   March 1993 descriptor moved
November 1992 related term added
July 1991 lead-in terms added
ALT   cable structure
SN   Use for structures in which cables
are essential to the system of sup-
port, as for example by suspension
or staying.
UF   cable roofs
roofs, cable
structures, cable
RT   cables

cable structures, suspension
USE   suspension structures

cable-supported cantilever roofs
USE   cable-stayed structures

cable-supported roofs, double-layer
USE   double-cable structures

cable-supported structures
USE   cable-stayed structures

cable-supported tents
USE   cable net structures

cable tent structures
USE   cable net structures

cable thread
USE   cabled yarn

cable transportation
USE   cable railroads

cabled fluting
DG.129
SN   Fluting in which the lower part of
each groove is filled with a solid
convex form. (PDARC)
UF   fluting, cabled
fluting, ribbed
ribbed fluting

cabled fluting
USE   cabling

cabled yarn
MT.1545
HN   November 1992 descriptor added
SN   Yarn produced by twisting together
two or more strands of plied yarn;
the final twist is opposite to that of
the plied ends.
UF   cable thread
thread, cable
yarn, cabled

cablegrams
USE   telegrams

cables
PE.38   (L)
HN   November 1992 descriptor moved
November 1992 related term added

November 1992 alternate term
added

November 1992 descriptor changed,
was **cable**

ALT cable

UF rope, wire
wire rope

RT cable structures

cables (column components)

USE cabling

cables, electric

USE electric cables

cableways

USE cable railroads

cabling

PJ.1517

HN March 1993 descriptor moved
November 1992 lead-in terms
added

SN The convex fillings of the lower part
of the flutes of classical columns or
pilasters.

UF cabled fluting
cables (column components)
fluting, cabled
rudenture

cabochons

DG.13

ALT cabochon

SN Motifs consisting of a smooth, convex circular or oval ornament; much
used during the 16th and 17th centuries and revived in kidney shape
on the cabriole knees of chairs and
tables in the mid-18th century.
(EDWARD)

caboose cars

USE cabooses

cabooses

TX.256   (L,N)

ALT caboose

UK brake-vans

UKA brake-van

SN Railroad cars providing offices and
quarters for conductors and train-
men while in transit and attached to
the end of freight trains.

UF cabin cars
caboose cars
cars, cabin
cars, caboose
cars, way
vans (railroad cars)
way cars

cabriole armchairs

USE cabriole chairs

cabriole bergères

USE bergères

cabriole chairs

TC.473   (N)

HN January 1993 descriptor moved

ALT cabriole chair

SN Chairs with a stuffed oval or car-

touche-shaped back; of a type popular in the late 18th century.

UF armchairs, cabriole
cabriole armchairs
cabrioles
cabriolets
chairs, cabriole
chairs, French
French chairs

cabriole legs

PJ.2839

HN March 1993 descriptor moved

ALT cabriole leg

SN Legs with a double curve, convex
above concave, introduced about
1700. (TOMLIN)

UF bandy legs
bowed legs
cabrioles
legs, bandy
legs, bowed
legs, cabriole

cabriole seats

USE cabriole sofas

cabriole sofas

TC.738

HN January 1993 descriptor moved

ALT cabriole sofa

SN Period term for late 18th- and early
19th-century sofas having a high-
pitch back.

UF cabriole seats
seats, cabriole
sofas, cabriole

cabrioles

USE cabriole chairs
cabriole legs

cabriolet hammers

TH.1096

HN March 1993 lead-in term changed,
was **French upholsterer's hammers**

March 1993 lead-in term changed,
was **hammers, French upholsterer's**

March 1993 lead-in term changed,
was **coach trimmer's cabriolet
hammers**

March 1993 lead-in term changed,
was **cabriolet hammers, coach
trimmer's**

March 1993 lead-in term changed,
was **hammers, coach trimmer's
cabriolet**

ALT cabriolet hammer

SN Hammers with very small narrow
faces used in upholstery for show-
wood or neat work. (SALAM)

UF cabriolet hammers, coach trimmers'
coach trimmers' cabriolet hammers
French upholsterers' hammers
hammers, cabriolet
hammers, coach trimmers' cabriolet
hammers, French upholsterers'

cabriolet hammers, coach trimmers'

USE cabriolet hammers

cabriolets

TX.187   (N)

ALT cabriolet

SN Use for European two-wheeled carriages pulled by a single horse and
having bodies resembling nautilus
shells.

cabriolets

USE cabriole chairs

Cabristans

USE Kuba (Caucasus) + carpets

cabs

USE hackney coaches
hansom cabs
taxicabs

cabs, hansom

USE hansom cabs

cabs, hansom safety

USE hansom cabs

cabstands

USE taxi stands

cachemere

USE cashmere

cachemire

USE cashmere

cachepots

TQ.614   (N)

ALT cachepot

SN Ornamental containers for holding
and concealing a flowerpot.

RT flowerpots
jardinières (containers)

cachou

USE cutch

cacqueteuses

USE caquetoires

cacquetoires

USE caquetoires

CAD

USE computer-aided design

cadastral maps

VW.70   (A,H,L)

HN November 1992 descriptor moved
May 1991 scope note changed

ALT cadastral map

SN Maps showing boundaries of subdi-
visions of land, buildings, or other
details for purposes of describing
and recording ownership. (DOD)

UF boundary maps
cadastral plans
cadastral surveys
land ownership maps
maps, boundary
maps, cadastral
maps, land ownership
maps, property
maps, real estate
maps, real property
maps, tax
plans, cadastral

plans, property
property maps
property plans
real estate maps
real property maps
surveys, cadastral
tax maps

cadastral plans
USE cadastral maps

cadastral surveys
USE cadastral maps

cadavres exquis
VC.202
HN March 1993 alternate term added
April 1992 descriptor moved
June 1990 descriptor added
ALT cadavre exquis
SN Images composed by several persons where each participant is not allowed to see the previous contributions. Popular among the Surrealists.
UF corpses, exquisite
exquisite corpses

caddies
TQ.12   (N)
ALT caddy
SN Containers, racks, or other devices for holding, organizing, or storing items. (RHDEL2)
RT tea caddies

caddies, tea
USE tea caddies
tea tables

caddinets
TQ.544
ALT caddinet
SN Receptacles consisting of a tray upon which to rest a napkin and having along the rear end a box divided into two or more compartments for eating utensils and spices.
UF cadenas
nef-à-cadenas
RT nefs

Caddo
FL.867   (L)

Caddo, Fulton
USE Fulton Caddo

Caddo, Gibson
USE Gibson Caddo

caddows
USE Bolton coverlets

caddy ladles
USE caddy spoons

caddy scoops
USE caddy spoons

caddy shells
USE caddy spoons

caddy spoons
TH.285   (L)

HN April 1993 descriptor added
ALT caddy spoon
SN Small spoons, often decorative, intended primarily for removing and measuring dry tea from a tea caddy.
UF caddy ladles
caddy scoops
caddy shells
ladles, caddy
scoops, caddy
shells, caddy
spoons, caddy
RT tea caddies

cadenas
USE caddinets

cadet jackets
USE Nehru jackets

Cadie gum
USE gamboge (pigment)

Cadioéo
USE Caduveo

cadmia
USE cadmium yellow

cadmium
MT.379   (L)
HN March 1993 scope note changed
December 1992 lead-in term added
February 1992 descriptor moved
SN Use for the pure metallic element having symbol Cd and atomic number 48; a silver white crystalline metal, very ductile, and which can be rolled or beaten into thin sheets; resembles tin but is harder. Use also for this metal as processed and formed, usually in combination with other substances, to make objects and materials.
UF Cd

cadmium carmine
USE strong red

cadmium green
MT.2149
HN April 1992 descriptor moved
UF green, cadmium

cadmium, light
USE vivid yellow

cadmium orange
MT.2271
HN April 1992 descriptor moved
UF cadmium yellow, orange
Kadmiumgelb orange
orange, cadmium
orange cadmium yellow
yellow, orange cadmium

cadmium orange (color)
USE brilliant orange
strong orange
vivid orange

cadmium purple
USE deep red
moderate red

cadmium red
MT.2192
HN April 1992 descriptor moved
UF Kadmiumrot
red, cadmium
red, selenium
rouge de cadmium
selenium red

cadmium red (color)
USE moderate red
strong red
vivid red
vivid reddish orange

cadmium red lithopone
MT.2193
HN April 1992 descriptor moved
UF lithopone, cadmium red
red lithopone, cadmium

cadmium sulfide
USE cadmium yellow

cadmium vermilion
USE moderate red
strong red

cadmium yellow
MT.2270
HN April 1992 descriptor moved
January 1992 lead-in terms added
UF amarillo de cadmio
Aurora yellow
brilliant yellow (pigment)
cadmia
cadmium sulfide
daffodil
giallo di cadmio
jaune brillant
jaune de cadmium
Kadmiumgelb
neutral orange
orient yellow
radiant yellow
yellow, Aurora
yellow, brilliant
yellow, cadmium

cadmium yellow (color)
USE moderate orange
moderate orange yellow
strong orange
strong orange yellow

cadmium yellow, deep
USE deep cadmium yellow

cadmium yellow, lemon
USE lemon cadmium yellow

cadmium yellow lithopone
MT.2272
HN April 1992 descriptor moved
UF cadmopone
lithopone, cadmium yellow
yellow lithopone, cadmium

cadmium yellow, middle
USE middle cadmium yellow

cadmium yellow, orange
USE cadmium orange

cadmium yellow, pale
USE   pale cadmium yellow

cadmopone
USE   cadmium yellow lithopone

Caduveo
FL.1655   (L)
HN   June 1990 lead-in term added
UF   Cadioéo

Caen limestone
USE   Caen stone

Caen stone
MT.861
HN   April 1992 descriptor moved
UF   Caen limestone
       kane stone
       limestone, Caen
       stone, Caen
       stone, kane

Caeretan
FL.2689

caeruleum
USE   cerulean blue

Caesalpinia brasiliensis
USE   brazilwood

Caesalpinia echinata
USE   brazilwood

Caesalpinia sappan
USE   sappanwood

Caesarian
FL.2807

café chairs
USE   ice-cream parlor chairs

café curtains
TC.306
ALT   café curtain
SN   Short straight-hanging curtains, of-
       ten in tiers, used to cover the lower
       and sometimes upper portions of a
       window or door.
UF   curtains, café
       curtains, half
       half curtains
RT   cottage curtains

café tables
USE   ice-cream tables

cafés
RK.115   (A,L,B,R)
HN   February 1991 lead-in term added
ALT   café
SN   Designates informal eating facilities
       with plated table service, a limited
       food-oriented menu generally of
       simply prepared items and coffee,
       and a social atmosphere emphasiz-
       ing bustle and noise.
UF   bistros

cafés (coffeehouses)
USE   coffeehouses

cafés, outdoor
USE   outdoor cafés

cafeterias
PJ.1050   (A,L,B)
HN   March 1993 descriptor moved
       June 1990 scope note added
ALT   cafeteria
SN   Self-service establishments provid-
       ing prepared food and drinks from
       long counters for on-premise or im-
       mediate consumption.
UF   restaurants, self-service
       self-service restaurants

caftans
TE.6   (N)
ALT   caftan
SN   Long, coatlike garments, fastened at
       the waist with a sash, having extra
       long sleeves. Usually of brightly col-
       ored cotton or silk, often striped.

Caga
USE   Chagga

cage crinolines
TE.206
ALT   cage crinoline
SN   Use for bell-shaped crinolines of
       whalebone or steel worn in the mid-
       19th century. Use **hoops (shaping
       garments)** for 18th-century shaping
       garments consisting of a series of
       concentric hoops of whalebone or
       bamboo.
UF   artificial crinolines
       cage petticoats
       cages (crinolines)
       crinolines, artificial
       crinolines, cage
       petticoats, cage
RT   hoops (shaping garments)

cage-cups
TQ.69   (R)
ALT   cage-cup
SN   Vessels decorated by undercutting
       so that the surface decoration stands
       free of the body of the glass, sup-
       ported by struts. The vessels appear,
       therefore, to be enclosed in an
       openwork cage. (DHGOC)
UF   diatretae vasae
       diatretons
       vasae diatretae

cage petticoats
USE   cage crinolines

cages
PJ.972
HN   March 1993 descriptor moved
ALT   cage
SN   Use for any boxlike enclosures hav-
       ing openwork of bars, wires, or the
       like used to confine or protect its oc-
       cupant, or to admit light or venti-
       lation.

cages (crinolines)
USE   cage crinolines

cages, squirrel (furniture components)
USE   birdcages (furniture components)

Cahokia
FL.862

Cahuilla
FL.1263   (L)
UF   Coahuila
       Kawia

Caingang
FL.1692   (L)
UF   Caiuá
       Cayuá
       Kaingua

cairns
RK.1296   (L)
HN   March 1993 related terms added
ALT   cairn
SN   Designates piles of stones heaped
       up for landmarks, monuments, me-
       morials, or as coverings over tombs.
       For piles of earth, generally, use
       mounds; for piles of earth used spe-
       cifically over tombs, use **burial
       mounds.**
RT   burial mounds
       mounds

caisson foundations
USE   pier foundations

caisson piles
PJ.1532
HN   March 1993 descriptor moved
       December 1990 scope note changed
ALT   caisson pile
SN   Piles formed by driving a hollow
       tube into the ground, excavating
       within the tube, and filling it with
       concrete.
UF   piles, caisson

caissons
PJ.1455   (L)
HN   March 1993 descriptor moved
       April 1991 descriptor moved
       April 1991 scope note changed
ALT   caisson
SN   Use for watertight boxes or cylin-
       ders serving to hold out water dur-
       ing excavation below the water ta-
       ble, often used for foundations.

caissons (coffers)
USE   coffers (ceiling components)

Caiuá
USE   Caingang

Cakchiquel
FL.1548   (L)

cake baskets
TQ.327   (N)
ALT   cake basket
SN   Shallow vessels made in the form of
       an open basket with a high, bail
       handle; presumably for serving
       cakes and cookies.
UF   baskets, cake
RT   baskets

bread baskets
tea services

cake boards
USE springerle boards

cake cutters
USE cookie cutters

cake forms
USE cake molds

cake knives
TH.262 (N)
HN April 1993 descriptor added
ALT cake knife
SN Large knives with a long blade and a serrated or scalloped cutting edge. May be accompanied by a cake server. For knives similar in form but having smaller teeth set closer together, use **bread knives.**
UF knives, cake
RT bread knives
cake servers

cake makers
USE cake mixers

cake mixers
TH.142 (N)
HN April 1993 descriptor added
ALT cake mixer
SN Devices intended primarily for mixing cake batter; used especially with reference to manually operated mixers with hand-cranked gears attached across the top of a straight-sided container.
UF cake makers
dough mixers
makers, cake
mixers, cake
mixers, dough

cake molds
TH.203 (L,N)
HN April 1993 descriptor added
ALT cake mold
SN Molds, often metal or earthenware, for baking cakes in distinctive shapes, such as in the form of animals.
UF cake forms
forms, cake
molds, cake

cake pans
TQ.292 (N)
ALT cake pan
SN Pans, often metal, intended primarily for baking cake; made in varying size and form.
UF pans, cake

cake plates
TQ.328 (N)
ALT cake plate
SN Platelike vessels from which cake and similar food is served.
UF cake trays

plates, cake
trays, cake
RT plates (dishes)

cake plates (dessert plates)
USE dessert plates

cake servers
TH.276 (N)
HN April 1993 descriptor added
ALT cake server
SN Term applied to a wide variety of special-purpose utensils designed to serve cake and similar foods, especially those with a flat wedge-shaped surface. May be accompanied by a cake knife.
UF cake slicers
cake-slicers
cake slices
cake-slices
servers, cake
slicers, cake
slices, cake
RT cake knives

cake slicers
USE cake servers

cake-slicers
USE cake servers

cake slices
USE cake servers

cake-slices
USE cake servers

cake stands
USE muffin stands

cake trays
USE cake plates

cake turners
USE turners (culinary tools)

cakes
USE upholstery foundations

Calamari
FL.1673

calamities
USE disasters

calamities, natural
USE natural disasters

Calapooya
USE Kalapuya

calasciones
USE colasciones

calashes
TE.635
ALT calash
SN Large hoods supported by an arrangement of hoops and designed to be collapsible; worn by women in the 18th century.

calc sinter
USE travertine

calcareous clay
USE marl

calcareous rock
USE carbonate rock

calcareous sandstone
MT.908
HN April 1992 descriptor moved
UF firestone
malmstone
sandstone, calcareous

calcareous tufa
USE travertine

Calchaqui
USE Diaguita

calcimeters
TN.133 (N)
ALT calcimeter
SN Devices for measuring the amount of lime in soils. (STEIN)

calcimine
MT.1947
HN August 1992 descriptor moved
August 1991 descriptor moved
UF kalsomine

calcined gypsum
HN March 1992 descriptor deleted

calcite
MT.523 (L)
HN May 1992 related terms added
February 1992 scope note added
February 1992 descriptor moved
SN A common rock-forming mineral, usually white or gray, it is the chief constituent of limestone and most marble. (AGI)
RT *<calcium carbonate white pigment>*
lapis lazuli

calcite marble
HN March 1992 descriptor deleted

calcium carbonate
MT.7 (L)
HN March 1992 descriptor added
SN A white crystalline powder occurring naturally chiefly as the minerals calcite and aragonite.
UF carbonate, calcium

calcium carbonate, artificial
USE precipitated chalk

<calcium carbonate white pigment>
MT.2245
HN May 1992 guide term added
RT calcite
chalk
coral
precipitated chalk
whiting

calcium chromate
MT.2277

245

HN   May 1992 descriptor added
UF   Gelbin
      Steinbühler Gelb

calcium silicate brick
      MT.45
HN   April 1992 descriptor moved
UF   brick, calcium silicate
      silicate brick, calcium

calcium sulfate dihydrate
USE gypsum

calculations
      VW.5   (B)
HN   December 1992 descriptor added
SN   Documents containing numerical
      determinations, such as of quanti-
      ties, distances, or amounts of time.
UF   computations
      reckoning

calculators
      TH.549   (L,N,R)
ALT calculator
SN   Small electronic or mechanical de-
      vices that perform calculations, re-
      quiring manual action for each indi-
      vidual operation. (RHDEL2)
UF   calculators, desk
      calculators, office
      desk calculators
      office calculators

calculators, desk
USE calculators

calculators, office
USE calculators

calculators, pocket
USE pocket calculators

calculus
      KD.150   (L)
HN   February 1992 scope note added
SN   A method of calculation and espe-
      cially one of several highly system-
      atic methods of treating problems
      by a special system of algebraic no-
      tations, as differential or integral
      calculus. (RHDEL2)

caldaria
      PJ.1012
HN   March 1993 descriptor moved
ALT caldarium
SN   The vapor baths or hot plunges in
      Roman baths. (HAS)

caldrons
USE cauldrons

Caledonian brown
USE burnt sienna

Caledonian white
      MT.2227
HN   April 1992 descriptor moved
UF   white, Caledonian

caledonicas
      TT.143
ALT caledonica

SN   Single reedpipes of conical bore,
      with the shape of a bassoon.
UF   alti fagotti
RT   bassoons

calefactories
      PJ.1108
HN   March 1993 descriptor moved
      June 1990 scope note added
ALT calefactory
SN   Use for the heated parlors or sitting
      rooms in monasteries. (RHDEL2)

calendar clocks
      TN.183
ALT calendar clock
SN   Use for clocks that show the day,
      date, month, and usually also the
      phases of the moon, as well as time
      of day. (MHDSTT)
UF   clocks, calendar

calendar watches
      TN.203   (L)
ALT calendar watch
SN   Use for watches that display, for ex-
      ample, the date of the month and
      day of the week, in addition to the
      time. (RHDEL2)
UF   watches, calendar

calendars
      VW.6   (L,N,R)
HN   November 1992 descriptor moved
      May 1991 scope note changed
ALT calendar
SN   Use for registers of days. (WCOL9)

calendars, archival
USE archival calendars

calendars, court
USE dockets

calendars, devotional
USE devotional calendars

calendars, perpetual
USE perpetual calendars

calendars, project
USE project calendars

calendars, religious
USE religious calendars

calendars, trial
USE dockets

calendering
      KT.337   (L)
HN   October 1992 scope note changed
ALT calendered
SN   The process of giving paper or cloth
      a flat, smooth, glossy, or embossed
      surface by running it between roll-
      ers under strong pressure.

Calene
      FL.2723
HN   April 1993 descriptor added

Calene ware
HN   April 1993 descriptor split, use
      Calene + ware

calf
      MT.2594
HN   October 1992 descriptor added
SN   Leather made of the skin of a calf,
      used especially for bookbinding.
UF   calfskin

calfskin
USE calf

caliche
      MT.835
HN   April 1992 descriptor moved
SN   Cemented deposits of calcium car-
      bonate materials. (MH)

calico
      MT.1632   (R)
HN   March 1993 descriptor moved
SN   Cotton textile, heavier than muslin,
      often dyed or with patterns printed
      in one or more colors. In the 18th
      and 19th centuries referred to
      printed cloth from India; now refers
      generally to cotton prints with small,
      stylized patterns. (NYLAN)

calico marble
USE Potomac breccia

calico rock
USE Potomac breccia

California black oak
      MT.2821   (L)
HN   March 1992 descriptor moved
      June 1990 lead-in term added
UF   black oak, California
      Kellogg's oak
      oak, California black
      Quercus kelloggii

California buck-eye
SEE California buckeye

California buckeye
      MT.2675   (L)
HN   March 1992 descriptor moved
UK   California buck-eye
UF   Aesculus californica
      buck-eye, California
      buckeye, California

California live oak
USE coast live oak

California redwood
USE redwood

California white oak
      MT.2823
HN   March 1992 descriptor moved
UF   oak, California white
      oak, valley
      Quercus lobata
      valley oak
      white oak, California

California Yuman
      FL.1288
UF   Yuman, California

Californian, Early period
USE Early period Californian

Californian Late period
USE   Late period Californian

Californian Middle period
USE   Middle period Californian

<Californian Native American styles>
FL.1260

Calima
FL.1124   (L)

caliper rules
TN.47   (N)
ALT caliper rule
SN   Use for measuring devices combining rulers with calipers having one jaw fixed to or integral with a graduated straight bar on which the other jaw slides.
UF   rules, caliper

calipers
TN.73   (L,N)
ALT caliper
UK   callipers
UKA calliper
SN   Instruments consisting usually of a pair of adjustable pivoted legs and used for measuring, for example, thickness or diameters.

calipers, double
USE   double calipers

calipers, inside
USE   inside calipers

calipers, micrometer
USE   micrometers

calipers, outside
USE   outside calipers

calipers, vernier
USE   vernier calipers

Caliphate, Orthodox
USE   Orthodox Caliphate

calite
USE   perlite

calk joints
PJ.688
HN   April 1993 descriptor moved
ALT calk joint
UF   joints, calk

calking
USE   caulking compound

calking compound
USE   caulking compound

call boxes
USE   telephone booths

calligraphers
HG.335   (L,B)
HN   April 1993 related term added
     February 1993 descriptor moved
     December 1992 alternate terms added
ALT calligrapher

calligrapher's
calligraphers'
UF   penmen
RT   calligraphy

calligraphers' marks
HN   March 1993 descriptor split, use calligraphers' (ALT of calligraphers) + marks (symbols)

calligraphic lettering pens
USE   lettering pens

calligraphy
KT.733   (A,L,B,R)
HN   April 1993 related term added
     January 1993 scope note added
SN   Elegant or brilliant writing or penmanship. (W)
RT   calligraphers

calling card cases
USE   card cases

calling card tables
USE   card stands

calling cards
USE   visiting cards

calliopes
TT.114   (L,N,R)
ALT calliope
SN   Organs involving a set of graded whistles operated by steam or compressed air, played by means of a keyboard, pinned cylinder, or paper roll. Producing a great volume of sound, their typical use has been outdoors, such as at circuses, fairgrounds, and on steamboats.
RT   mechanical instruments

callipers
SEE   calipers

callitype
USE   kallitype

calls, bid
USE   bidding announcements

calls, boatswains'
USE   boatswains' whistles

calorimeters
TN.306   (L,N)
ALT calorimeter
SN   Instruments for measuring heat quantities, such as the heat of combustion, specific heat, or vital heat in such processes as chemical reactions or changes of state.

calorimetry
KT.178   (L)
HN   November 1992 descriptor added
SN   Measurement of quantities of heat. (W)
UF   heat measurement

calottes
PJ.1735
HN   March 1993 descriptor moved
     December 1990 scope note added

ALT calotte
SN   Denotes hemispherical, caplike domes; the term applies to small semidomes lacking a drum or lantern, small shallow domes used in the ceilings of rooms to increase headroom, small domes not pierced by oculi, and domelike plaster surfaces suspended within double-shell domes and often decorated.

calottes (headgear)
USE   skullcaps

calotype
KT.551   (L)
SN   Use for Talbot's patented process to make negatives on paper; the image is formed from silver iodide coated on the base without a binder and is developed. In the mid-20th century, sometimes used incorrectly for any salted paper or paper negative process. Distinguished from **photogenic drawing**, in which the image was printed out.
UF   Talbotype

calotype negatives
USE   calotypes

calotype photonegatives
USE   calotypes

calotype photoprints
USE   salted paper prints

calotype positives
USE   salted paper prints

calotype prints
USE   salted paper prints

calotypes
VC.293   (R)
HN   April 1992 descriptor moved
ALT calotype
SN   Use for negatives on paper made by Talbot's patented calotype process, a developing-out process. Distinguished from Talbot's **photogenic drawings**, in which the image was printed out. For most prints made from these negatives, use **salted paper prints**. In the mid-20th century, sometimes used incorrectly for any other paper negatives or salted paper prints.
UF   calotype negatives
     calotype photonegatives
     negatives, calotype
     Talbotypes

Calukya
USE   Chalukyan

Calvary crosses
DG.23
ALT Calvary cross
SN   Latin crosses set upon three steps or upon a mount. (W)
UF   crosses, Calvary

crosses, passion
passion crosses

calves, downy
USE downy calves

calves, false
USE downy calves

calyx kraters
TQ.92
ALT calyx krater
SN Kraters so named for their resemblance to a calyx flower.
UF kraters, calyx

Camacan
FL.1693

camaieu
HN July 1990 descriptor deleted, made lead-in to **monochrome**

camaieu
USE monochrome

camails
USE aventails

camas de bilros
TC.790
HN January 1993 descriptor moved
ALT cama de bilros
SN Portuguese tester beds with turned elements and carvings on the headboard; generally having turned posts and either a plain or pagoda-shaped tester. Of a type made in the 16th century. (HAYWAR)

camber arches
PJ.1607
HN March 1993 descriptor moved
December 1990 descriptor moved
December 1990 scope note changed
ALT camber arch
SN Use for arches whose intrados, and possibly the extrados, has a very slight rise; for arches with no curvature, use **flat arches.**
UF arches, camber

camber windows
HN April 1991 descriptor split, use **camber arch** (ALT of **camber arches**) + **windows**

cambodiam
USE gamboge (pigment)

Cambodian
FL.2401   (L,B)

Cambridge lamps
USE student lamps

camel
USE light grayish yellowish brown
light olive brown
light yellowish brown
moderate yellowish brown

camel flank hangings
USE asmalyks

camel hair
MT.2560
HN February 1992 descriptor moved
February 1992 scope note changed
SN Fine body hair, or camel wool, used as a textile fiber. For artists' brushes usually made from the hair of squirrels, use **camel hair brushes.**
UF hair, camel

camel hair brushes
TH.739
HN February 1993 descriptor added
ALT camel hair brush
SN Artists' brushes made of squirrel hair or any other fine hair.
UF brushes, camel hair
camel hairs

camel hairs
USE camel hair brushes

camelback trusses
USE crescent trusses

cameo bindings
PJ.3354
ALT cameo binding
SN Bindings having the centers of the boards stamped in relief, in imitation of antique gems or medals. (ALAG)
UF bindings, cameo
bindings, cameo-stamped
bindings, plaquette
cameo-stamped bindings
plaquette bindings

cameo glass
MT.285   (L,R)
HN March 1993 descriptor moved
December 1991 scope note added
June 1990 descriptor added
SN Cased glass of two or more layers in contrasting colors. The outer layers are carved, cut, or engraved to produce a design which stands out from the background.
UF glass, cameo

cameo prints
VC.354
HN April 1992 descriptor moved
ALT cameo print
SN Cartes-de-visite which are raised, like medallions, by pressure to the back. (HCOP)
UF prints, cameo

cameo-stamped bindings
USE cameo bindings

cameos
VC.552   (H,L,N,R)
ALT cameo
SN Small reliefs made from gems, glass, ceramics, or shell having layers of different colors and carved so that the design stands out in one color against a background in another. (THDAT)

cameotypes
VC.382
HN April 1992 descriptor moved
ALT cameotype
SN Small vignette daguerreotypes, sometimes mounted like jewels. (WOODB)
UF crayon daguerreotypes
daguerreotypes, crayon
daguerreotypes, vignette
vignette daguerreotypes

<camera accessories>
TH.768
HN September 1992 related term added
RT exposure meters

camera copy
USE camera ready copy

camera lenses
USE photographic lenses

camera lucidas
TH.709   (R)
HN February 1993 descriptor added
ALT camera lucida
SN Instruments utilizing a prism to project an accurate image of an object onto a flat surface for the purpose of tracing.

camera obscuras
TH.710   (L,N,R)
HN February 1993 descriptor added
ALT camera obscura
SN Rooms or boxes with a single small opening, with or without a lens, through which an inverted image is projected from outside the box onto the opposite interior wall.

camera operators
USE cameramen

camera originals
USE direct positives

camera ready copy
VW.1186
HN March 1993 descriptor added
SN Originals of text or art copy ready to be photographed for reproduction.
UF camera copy
copy (camera ready)
copy, camera
CRC

cameraless photographs
USE photograms

cameramen
HG.207   (L)
HN April 1993 related term added
November 1992 alternate terms added
ALT cameramen's
cameraman
cameraman's
SN Operators of motion picture or television cameras. For persons who oversee all the aspects of photogra-

phy in a filmmaking or television project, use **cinematographers.**
UF camera operators
operators, camera
RT cinematographers

cameramen, lighting
USE cinematographers

cameras
TH.748 (L,N,R)
ALT camera
SN Lightproof boxes fitted with a lens through the aperture of which the image of an object is recorded on light-sensitive material. (W)

cameras, 35mm
USE 35mm cameras

<cameras and camera accessories>
TH.747

cameras, automatic
USE electric eye cameras

cameras, banquet
USE banquet cameras

cameras, box
USE box cameras

<cameras by form or function>
TH.749

cameras, circuit
USE panoramic cameras

cameras, cirkut
USE panoramic cameras

cameras, copy
USE process cameras

cameras, detective
USE detective cameras

cameras, double-lens
USE stereoscopic cameras

cameras, double-lens reflex
USE twin-lens reflex cameras

cameras, electric eye
USE electric eye cameras.

cameras, field
USE view cameras

cameras, flatbed
USE view cameras

cameras, graphic arts
USE process cameras

cameras, miniature
USE miniature cameras

cameras, motion-picture
USE motion-picture cameras

cameras, movie
USE motion-picture cameras

cameras, moving-picture
USE motion-picture cameras

cameras, panoramic
USE panoramic cameras

cameras, pinhole
USE pinhole cameras

cameras, process
USE process cameras

cameras, reflex
USE reflex cameras

cameras, single lens reflex
USE single lens reflex cameras

cameras, stereo
USE stereoscopic cameras

cameras, stereoscopic
USE stereoscopic cameras

cameras, subminiature
USE subminiature cameras

cameras, television
USE television cameras

cameras, thirty-five millimeter
USE 35mm cameras

cameras, twin-lens
USE stereoscopic cameras
twin-lens reflex cameras

cameras, twin-lens reflex
USE twin-lens reflex cameras

cameras, view
USE view cameras

<Cameroon grasslands>
FL.177

<Cameroonian groups below the escarpment>
FL.184

cames
PJ.2274 (H,R)
HN March 1993 descriptor moved
December 1990 scope note changed
ALT came
SN Slender bars of cast lead, with or without grooves, used in casement and stained glass windows to hold the pieces of glass in place.

cami-knickers
SEE camiknickers

camiknickers
TE.189
UK cami-knickers
SN Women's one-piece garments consisting of a camisole and bloomers.
RT bloomers
camisoles

Camirian
USE Rhodian (Island Greek pottery style)

camis
USE jamis

camisoles
TE.218 (N)
ALT camisole
SN Women's underbodices usually worn over corsets or brassieres, reaching to or just below the waist. Usually cut straight across the bustline, with straps structurally separate from the garment body.
RT camiknickers

camouflage
KT.863 (L,B,R)
HN January 1991 scope note added
January 1991 alternate term added
October 1990 descriptor moved
ALT camouflaged
SN The technique of disguising the appearance of beings or things so as to make them blend into their surroundings.

camp beds
USE field beds

camp blankets
USE utility blankets

camp ceilings
PJ.2051
HN March 1993 descriptor moved
ALT camp ceiling
SN Use for ceilings, usually within the roof of a building, characterized by sloping sides and a flat center.
UF ceilings, camp
ceilings, cum
ceilings, tent
ceilings, tray
cum ceilings
tent ceilings
tray ceilings

camp chairs
TC.648
HN May 1993 related term added
April 1993 descriptor moved
ALT camp chair
SN Light folding chairs, usually with canvas seats and backs. (RHDEL2)
UF chairs, camp
RT camp furniture

camp furniture
TC.1206
HN May 1993 related terms added
January 1993 descriptor moved
SN Portable furniture intended for use outdoors. (INNO)
UF furniture, camp
RT camp chairs
campstools
cots

camp sites
RM.97 (L,B)
HN April 1993 descriptor moved
ALT camp site
SN Use for individual locations, within organized campgrounds or as iso-

lated sites, set aside or otherwise marked for camping.
UF sites, camp

camp stools
USE campstools

Campa
FL.1622   (L)
UF Ande
    Anti

campaign chests
TC.867   (N)
HN January 1993 descriptor moved
ALT campaign chest
SN Popular name for low chests of drawers having handles on each end for lifting.
UF chests, campaign

campaign furniture
TC.1207
HN January 1993 descriptor moved
UF furniture, campaign

campaign posters
USE political posters

campaign torches
TC.1425
ALT campaign torch
SN Lamps with single or multiple wick tubes mounted at the end of a pole for carrying in political parades and torchlight processions. The lamp fonts are often shaped like stars, eagles, top hats, or other political symbols.
UF torches, campaign

campaign trim
PJ.317
HN April 1993 descriptor moved
SN Use for the decorative hardware used on chests and trunks.
UF trim, campaign

campaigning
KG.210
SN Engaging in or conducting a systematic course of aggressive activities for some special purpose. (RHDEL2)

campaigns
KM.9
HN May 1991 alternate term added
    January 1991 scope note added
ALT campaign
SN Systematic courses of aggressive activities designed to persuade or establish power over others.

campaigns, advertising
USE advertising campaigns

campaigns, political
USE political campaigns

campan marble
MT.746
HN April 1992 descriptor moved
UF marble, campan

Campanian
FL.2724

campaniles
RK.34   (A,L,B)
HN March 1993 alternate term added
ALT campanile
SN Use for Italian bell towers, usually of a church and usually free-standing.

campeachy lake
MT.2091
HN April 1992 descriptor moved
UF lake, campeachy

campeachy wood
USE logwood

camper trailers
USE camping trailers
     travel trailers

campers
USE camping trailers
     motor homes
     travel trailers

campgrounds
RG.162   (L)
ALT campground
UK camping-grounds
UKA camping-ground
SN Use for areas comprised of individual camp sites and providing facilities and conveniences for camping.

camphene lamps
TC.1376   (N)
ALT camphene lamp
SN Lamps designed to burn rectified turpentine, having an Argand burner without a separate reservoir, and a button-shaped deflector to spread the flame. (RUSHL)
UF lamps, camphene
    lamps, rectified turpentine
    rectified turpentine lamps
    turpentine lamps, rectified

camphor
MT.1248   (L)
HN April 1992 descriptor moved
SN The white resin of the Cinnamomum camphora, used for hardening nitrocellulose plastic, also in pharmaceuticals, disinfectants, and explosives.

camphor laurel
USE camphorwood

camphor tree
USE camphorwood

camphor-wood
SEE camphorwood

camphorwood
MT.2716   (L)
HN March 1992 descriptor moved
UK camphor-wood
UF camphor laurel
    camphor tree

laurel, camphor
tree, camphor

Campignian
FL.2566

camping-grounds
SEE campgrounds

camping trailers
TX.124   (L,N)
HN March 1993 descriptor moved
    March 1993 scope note changed
    March 1993 lead-in terms added
ALT camping trailer
SN Use for automobile-drawn, wheeled recreational vehicles with a folding shelter of canvas or other fabric, creating temporary accommodations as while camping.
UF camper trailers
    campers
    tent trailers
    trailers, camper
    trailers, camping
    trailers, tent

camps
RG.163   (A,L,B,R)
ALT camp

camps (military)
USE military camps

camps, army
USE army camps

camps, boot
USE boot camps

camps, cabin
USE motor courts

camps, church
USE church camps

camps, concentration
USE concentration camps

camps, day
USE day camps

camps, detention
USE concentration camps

camps, fishing
USE fishing lodges

camps, hunting
USE hunting lodges

camps, internment
USE concentration camps

camps, labor
USE labor camps

camps, labour
SEE labor camps

camps, logging
USE lumber camps

camps, lumber
USE lumber camps

camps, military
USE military camps

camps, military training
USE military training camps

camps, nudist
USE nudist camps

camps, prison
USE prison camps

camps, refugee
USE refugee camps

camps, religious
USE religious camps

camps, school
USE school camps

camps, summer
USE summer camps

camps, trailer
USE trailer camps

camps, work
USE prison camps

campstools
TC.695 (N)
HN May 1993 related term added
May 1993 lead-in terms added
April 1993 descriptor moved
ALT campstool
SN Small, folding stools with a detachable seat of canvas or leather. (GLOAG)
UF camp stools
stools, camp
RT camp furniture

campus planning
HN April 1993 descriptor split, use **campus** (ALT of **campuses**) + **planning**

campuses
RG.53 (A)
ALT campus

can openers
TH.175 (N)
HN April 1993 descriptor added
ALT can opener
SN Tools having various types of puncturing points and a cutting blade used for opening cans.
UF openers, can

Canaanean
USE Canaanite

Canaanite
FL.3015 (L)
UF Canaanean

Cañabal
USE Tojolabal

Canada balsam
MT.1238
HN April 1992 descriptor moved
UF balsam, Canada

Canada bolts
USE box bolts

Canada hemlock
USE eastern hemlock

Canadian
FL.728 (L,B)

<Canadian Arctic Native styles>
FL.1219
HN April 1991 related term added
RT *<Pre-Columbian Arctic and Subarctic styles>*

Canadian ash
USE white ash

Canadian Eskimo
USE Inuit

Canadian spruce
USE red spruce
white spruce

Çanakkale
FL.3646
HN April 1993 descriptor changed, was **Chanak Kalé**
April 1993 lead-in term changed, was **Çanakkale**
April 1993 descriptor moved
UF Chanak Kalé
Chanak Kalessi
Chanakkale

Çanakkale carpets
USE Çanakkale + rugs

canal aqueducts
USE aqueducts

canal boats
TX.490 (L,N)
ALT canal boat
SN Watercraft designed for use on canals generally long and narrow with bow and stern often nearly vertical for increased cargo capacity.
UF boats, canal

canal bridges
USE aqueducts

Canaletto frames
TC.403
ALT Canaletto frame
SN Use for frames with carved moldings and decorations of small mirrors and flowers interrupted by plain areas, named after the 18th-century Venetian painter Giovanni Antonio Canaletto.
UF frames, Canaletto

Canaliño
FL.916

canals
RK.486 (A,L,B,R)
ALT canal
SN Use for artificial navigable waterways.

canals, interoceanic
USE interoceanic canals

canals, sea level
USE interoceanic canals

canapés
TC.739
HN January 1993 descriptor moved
ALT canapé

canapés à confident
TC.740
HN May 1993 related term added
March 1993 scope note added
March 1993 lead-in terms added
March 1993 lead-in term deleted, was **canapés en confident**
March 1993 lead-in term deleted, was **canapés à la maintenon**
March 1993 lead-in term deleted, was **duchesses avec encoignures**
January 1993 descriptor moved
ALT canapé à confident
SN Use for S-shaped sofas with ends curving inward so two people could sit face to face. For straight-fronted sofas with small triangular seats (sometimes detachable) set outside the arms at either end use **confidantes.**
UF causeuses
confidents
confidents à deux place
têtes-à-têtes
vis-à-vis
RT confidantes

canapés à confident (confidantes)
USE confidantes

canapés à corbeille
TC.741
HN January 1993 descriptor moved
ALT canapé à corbeille
SN Canapés whose backs gently curve forward and downward to form the arms.

canapés à la maintenon
USE confidantes

canapés à marquise
USE marquises

canapés confidents à quatre places
USE bornes

canapés de l'amitié
USE marquises

canapés en confident
USE confidantes

canapés en lit
USE sofa beds

canapés-lits
USE sofa beds

canapés ronds
USE bornes

Cañar
FL.1656 (L)

canard airplanes
USE canards

canards
TX.10
ALT canard
SN Use for aircraft in which the horizontal stabilizers used for trim and control are positioned forward of the main wings.
UF aircraft, tail-first
airplanes, canard
canard airplanes
tail-first aircraft

Cañari
FL.1623   (L)

canary
USE moderate yellow

canary whitewood
USE tulipwood

canary yellow
USE brilliant yellow
light greenish yellow
light yellow
vivid yellow

canarywood
USE balaustre

cancellation impressions
USE cancellation proofs

cancellation marks
VW.413
HN February 1993 scope note added
February 1993 lead-in term deleted, was **deletion marks**
February 1993 lead-in term deleted, was **marks, deletion**
November 1992 descriptor moved
ALT cancellation mark
SN One or more marks made to deface something in order to indicate a change in its status, such as through a pottery factory mark, indicating the piece is defective or outmoded, or as across a printing plate, assuring that no prints are produced beyond a limited edition.
UF marks, cancellation

cancellation proofs
VC.438   (L)
ALT cancellation proof
SN Impressions made from a printing element that has been defaced after completion of an edition.
UF cancellation impressions
cancelled plate prints
proofs, cancellation

cancellations
VW.414   (L)
HN June 1992 descriptor added
ALT cancellation
SN Use only for defacements made by authorities for the primary purpose of preventing reuse of postage stamps; for official marks bearing

information about the time and place that a postal system accepted custody of a piece of mail, use postmarks.
RT postmarks
precancels

cancelled plate prints
USE cancellation proofs

Cancer symbols
DG.93
ALT Cancer symbol

canchas
RK.965   (B,R)
HN March 1993 related term added
September 1990 scope note added
ALT cancha
SN Denotes three-walled courts marked for playing jai alai.
UF courts, jai alai
courts, pelota
frontons
jai alai courts
pelota courts
RT jai alai

candelabras
TC.1231   (L,N,B,R)
HN May 1993 related term added
ALT candelabrum
SN Candleholders with two or more arms.
UF candelabrums
RT torchères (stands)

candelabrums
USE candelabras

Candelaria
FL.1207

candelilla wax
MT.1305
HN April 1992 descriptor moved
December 1990 descriptor moved
SN A brown vegetable wax obtained from a weed native to Texas and Mexico used to impart hardness to mixtures of wax and other compounds. (MAYER)
UF wax, candelilla

Candella
FL.2290   (L)
UF Chandella

candle arms
USE candle brackets

candle beams
TC.1254
HN April 1993 descriptor moved
April 1993 scope note changed
April 1993 lead-in term added
ALT candle beam
SN T-shaped or horizontal beamlike or rail-like candle supports, generally of wood although sometimes of wrought iron, found in liturgical contexts.

UF beams, candle
candlebeams

candle boards
USE candle slides

candle boxes
TQ.641   (N)
ALT candle box
SN Containers of varying form intended primarily for storing candles.
UF bougie boxes
boxes, bougie
boxes, candle
boxes, taper
chandleries (containers)
taper boxes
RT candles

candle brackets
TC.1216
ALT candle bracket
SN Supports for candles which attach to a wall; the supporting arm may be jointed or rigid. (DARBEE)
UF arms, candle
brackets, candle
candle arms

candle branches
TC.1255
ALT candle branch
UF branches, candle
candle chandeliers
chandeliers, candle

candle chandeliers
USE candle branches

candle ejectors
USE pushups

candle extinguishers
USE extinguishers

candle-fir
USE splints

candle glasses
TC.1232
ALT candle glass
UF glasses, candle

candle glasses
USE hurricane glasses

candle guards
USE candle screens

candle holders
USE candleholders

candle lamps
TC.1377   (N)
ALT candle lamp
SN Lamps using candles as the source of illumination and containing the candle within a vessel. For devices that hold a candle or candles from their bases use **candleholders**.
UF lamps, candle
RT candleholders

candle lamps, student
USE   student candle lamps

candle lifts
USE   pushups

candle-making
SEE   candlemaking

candle-nut oil
SEE   candlenut oil

candle screens
TC.433   (R)
HN   January 1993 descriptor moved
       August 1991 descriptor added
ALT   candle screen
SN   Small screens used to protect lighted
       candles; of a type made in the 18th
       century.
UF   candle guards
       candles, gauze
       gauze candles
       guards, candle
       lantern screens
       screens, candle
       screens, lantern
       table fire screens

candle slides
PJ.2878
HN   March 1993 descriptor moved
ALT   candle slide
SN   Small slides above the slant top in
       desks to support candlesticks.
UF   boards, candle
       candle boards
       slides, candle

candle snuffers
PJ.2926   (N,R)
ALT   candle snuffer
SN   Devices for trimming the wicks of
       candles and lamps to keep the end
       of the wick even and clean; usually
       in the form of scissors with one
       blade bearing a boxlike receptacle
       to catch the cut-off ends of the
       charred wick. For scissorlike devices
       with flat disc-shaped ends used for
       pinching out a candle flame, use
       douters. For cone-shaped devices
       used to extinguish flames, use **extin-
       guishers**.
UF   snuffers
       snuffers, candle

candle sockets
PJ.2927
ALT   candle socket
SN   Cylinders into which the base of the
       candle can be inserted to keep it up-
       right, either short to hold only the
       end of the candle or elongated, in
       the form of a tube, to hold the ma-
       jor part of a candle, with a lifting
       device to elevate the candle as it
       burns. Found on candleholders such
       as chambersticks and candlesticks,
       and on sconces and chandeliers.
UF   sockets, candle

candle stands
USE   candlestands (furniture)
       candlestands (lighting devices)

candle student lamps
USE   student candle lamps

candlebeams
USE   candle beams

candleholders
TC.1226   (L,N,R)
ALT   candleholder
SN   Term generally applied to a variety
       of devices having either a single
       spike or one or more candle sockets
       to hold candles; sometimes having
       drips to catch wax, push-ups and
       other devices for removing the stub,
       or adjustable features for control-
       ling the position of the flame.
UF   candle holders
       holders, candle
RT   candle lamps

candleholders, adjustable
USE   adjustable candleholders

candleholders, alpine
USE   alpine candleholders

candleholders, clip
USE   clip candleholders

candleholders, miners'
USE   miners' candlesticks

candleholders, socket
USE   candlesticks
       chambersticks

candleholders, spring
USE   alpine candleholders
       spring candleholders

candleholders, wire
USE   wire candlesticks

candlemaking
KT.788   (L)
UK   candle-making

candlenut oil
MT.1070
HN   April 1992 descriptor moved
       October 1990 descriptor moved
UK   candle-nut oil
UF   lumbang oil
       oil, candle-nut
       oil, candlenut
       oil, lumbang

candlepin bowling
KQ.42   (L)
UF   bowling, candlepin
       candlepins

candlepins
USE   candlepin bowling

candles
TC.1220   (L,N,R)
ALT   candle
SN   Long cylindrical masses typically of
       tallow or wax containing a wick or
       loosely twisted linen or cotton
       threads burned to give light; made
       by dipping or casting in a metal
       mold. (W)
RT   candle boxes

<candles and candleholders>
TC.1219

candles, artificial
USE   gas candles

candles, Easter
USE   paschal candles

candles, gas
USE   gas candles

candles, gauze
USE   candle screens

candles, King Alfred's
USE   time candles

candles, paschal
USE   paschal candles

candles, time
USE   time candles

candles, votive
USE   votive candles

candleshearers
USE   wick trimmers

candlestands (furniture)
TC.1044   (N,R)
HN   May 1993 lead-in terms added
       April 1993 descriptor changed, was
       candlestands
       April 1993 alternate term changed,
       was **candlestand**
       January 1993 descriptor moved
ALT   candlestand (furniture)
SN   Portable stands with a very small top
       intended to hold a candle or lamp;
       usually having a round or shaped
       top supported on a central pillar
       and with a tripod base. (MONTGO)
UF   candle stands
       stands, candle

candlestands (lighting devices)
TC.1233   (N,R)
ALT   candlestand (lighting device)
SN   Tall standards usually meant to rest
       on the floor supporting arms or
       branches fitted with candle sockets;
       also shorter versions for use on ta-
       bles or other raised surfaces.
UF   candle stands
       lamp stands
       lampstands
       stands, candle
       stands, lamp

candlestands, ratchet
USE   ratchet candlestands

candlestands, ratchet-base
USE   ratchet candlestands

candlestick lamps
USE   peg lamps

candlesticks
TC.1234 (L,N,R)
ALT candlestick
SN Candleholders with a single candle socket mounted on a support with a widened base or foot for balance; often the support is columnar in form. For candleholders with a single candle socket set on a flat saucer or traylike base, use **chambersticks.**
UF candleholders, socket
candlesticks, socket
socket candleholders
socket candlesticks
RT chambersticks

candlesticks, ball'd
USE ball'd candlesticks

candlesticks, bedchamber
USE chambersticks

candlesticks, birdcage
USE wire candlesticks

candlesticks, chamber
USE chambersticks

candlesticks, coil
USE spiral candlesticks

candlesticks, golden
USE Hanukkah lamps

candlesticks, hand
USE chambersticks

candlesticks, hogscraper
USE hogscraper candlesticks

candlesticks, miners'
USE miners' candlesticks

candlesticks, pricket
USE prickets

candlesticks, screw
USE screw candlesticks

candlesticks, screw-up
USE screw candlesticks

candlesticks, seven-branched
USE Hanukkah lamps

candlesticks, sheet hand
USE chambersticks

candlesticks, socket
USE candlesticks

candlesticks, spiral
USE spiral candlesticks

candlesticks, spring
USE spring candleholders

candlesticks, spring-action
USE spring candleholders

candlesticks, spring loaded
USE spring candleholders

candlesticks, stable
USE wire candlesticks

candlesticks, tea
USE tea candlesticks

candlesticks, telescopic
USE telescopic candlesticks

candlesticks, wire
USE wire candlesticks

candlesticks, worm
USE spiral candlesticks

candlewick
MT.1546
HN November 1992 descriptor added
SN Thick, loosely twisted, plied yarn, usually of cotton, used especially for embroidered bedspreads.
UF candlewick yarn
candlewicking (yarn)
yarn, candlewick
RT candlewicking

candlewick bedspreads
USE candlewick spreads

candlewick spreads
TC.199 (L)
ALT candlewick spread
SN Bedspreads, usually white and generally of cotton, with raised designs done either in weft loop weave or needlework, using a heavy thread resembling the wicks used by candlemakers.
UF bedspreads, candlewick
candlewick bedspreads
spreads, candlewick
RT Bolton coverlets
boutonné coverlets

candlewick yarn
USE candlewick

candlewicking
KT.1224
HN November 1992 descriptor added
ALT candlewick
SN Embroidering technique in which designs are stitched on a woven unbleached cotton or linen cloth using heavily plied yarn which is looped on the surface then cut, creating a tufted effect; used especially for bedspreads.
RT candlewick

candlewicking (yarn)
USE candlewick

candlewood
USE splints

Candy Creek
FL.903

candy molds
TH.204 (L,N)
HN April 1993 descriptor added
ALT candy mold
SN Molds, usually of tin or pewter, for forming chocolates and other candies.
UF molds, candy

cane (glass)
MT.257
HN March 1992 descriptor added
SN A slender rod of glass.
UF bar (glass)
rod

cane (plant material)
MT.2615
HN March 1993 descriptor changed, was **cane**
February 1992 descriptor moved

cane bolts
PJ.555
HN March 1993 descriptor moved
ALT cane bolt
UF bolts, cane

cane-work
SEE canework

canella
USE imbuia

canephorae
PJ.1437 (L)
HN March 1993 descriptor moved
December 1990 scope note added
December 1990 descriptor changed, was **canephores**
December 1990 alternate term changed, was **canephore**
ALT canephora
SN Caryatids with baskets on their heads.

canes
TH.399 (H,L,N,R)
HN February 1993 descriptor added
ALT cane
SN Walking sticks, especially those with a curved handle and made of cane or bamboo.

canes, log
USE log rules

canes, sword
USE sword sticks

canettes
USE canns

canework
PE.100
HN October 1992 descriptor moved
UK cane-work

caning
KT.1026
ALT caned
SN Process of weaving with split rattan such as for seats or backs of chairs. (W)

canions
PJ.3034 (N)
ALT canion
SN Close-fitting extensions of the hose which cover the leg below the knee-cap; worn by men during the Elizabethan and Jacobean periods.
UF cannons (canions)

canister shot
TK.249 (N)
UK case-shot
SN Inert artillery ammunition consisting of a metal cylindrical case containing shot or splinters of iron or lead, which splits open inside the bore when fired, so that the contents and case fragments are propelled from the barrel. They were developed in the early 18th century for use against personnel.
UF case shot
shot, canister
shot, case
RT shrapnel

canisters
TQ.13 (N)
ALT canister
SN Cylindrical or rectangular containers usually of lightweight metal, plastic, or laminated pasteboard used for holding dry products. (W)
RT tea caddies

cannabis bark paper
USE bark cloth

cannel coal
MT.1019 (L)
HN April 1992 descriptor moved
UF coal, cannel

canneries
RK.598 (A,L,B)
ALT cannery

cannikins
USE pannikins

cannon balls
USE cannonballs

cannon periers
USE pedreros

cannonballs
TK.250 (N)
ALT cannonball
SN Use for the spherical projectiles of stone or iron, usually solid, made to be fired from cannons. For the solid bullets of spherical or conical shape fired from small arms, use **balls (bullets)**.
UF balls, cannon
cannon balls
RT balls (bullets)

cannons (artillery)
TK.138 (H,L,N)
ALT cannon (artillery)
SN General term for large artillery pieces, developed in Europe since the 14th century, consisting basically of a long smoothbore iron, bronze, or steel barrel, cast in one piece or built up by a series of forgings, supported on a carriage or stationary mount, capable of firing very heavy projectiles.

cannons (body armor)
TE.332
ALT cannon (body armor)
SN Long cylindrical armor plates to protect the forearms and upper arms, either partially or completely encircling them; they were generally worn in pairs, linked at the elbows by cowters.
RT lower cannons
upper cannons

cannons (canions)
USE canions

cannons, hand
USE hand cannons

cannons, lower
USE lower cannons

cannons, serpentine
USE serpentines (cannons)

cannons, short
USE howitzers

cannons, upper
USE upper cannons

canns
TQ.393
ALT cann
SN Drinking vessels, usually in the form of a cylindrical cup but sometimes slightly tapering, having a flat base with a low foot ring and one vertical handle; especially those made of silver or pewter in the 18th and 19th centuries.
UF canettes
cans (drinking vessels)
RT cups

canoe birch
USE paper birch

canoes
TX.313 (L,N)
ALT canoe
SN Use for lightly built, slender, open craft of shallow draft that are paddled and not rowed and normally double-ended; may have sails.

canoes, dugout
USE dugouts

canoes, log
USE log canoes

canon law
VW.491 (H,L)
HN January 1993 descriptor added
SN The body of ecclesiastical law, especially of the Roman Catholic Church as promulgated in ecclesiastical councils and by the pope. (RHDEL2)
UF law, canon

canon tables
VW.156 (H,L)
HN June 1992 descriptor added
ALT canon table
SN Concordance tables showing parallel passages from the four Gospels.
UF tables, canon

canonical capitalis
USE rustic capitals

canonizations
KM.170 (L,R)
HN May 1991 alternate term added
ALT canonization
SN Official placements of deceased persons within the canon of saints. (RHDEL2)

canons
HG.396 (L)
HN February 1993 descriptor moved December 1992 alternate terms added
ALT canon
canon's
canons'
SN Clergy of a large church living as a community under a rule; also Medieval clergymen belonging to the chapter or the staff of a cathedral or collegiate church. (W)

cañons (canyons)
USE canyons

canons (psalteries)
USE qanuns

canopic jars
TQ.144 (L,N)
ALT canopic jar
SN Stone or ceramic jars in which the ancient Egyptians preserved the viscera of a deceased person usually for burial with the mummy. (W)
UF canopic vases
jars, canopic
vases, canopic

canopic vases
USE canopic jars

canopies (bed components)
PJ.2747 (A,N,R)
HN March 1993 descriptor moved
ALT canopy (bed component)
SN Use for rooflike components suspended over the head of a bed by means of a cord attached to the ceiling; usually a cone-shaped or domed bowl with a valance all around, and with two or three curtains long enough to reach and encompass the foot of the bed. Use **testers** for rooflike components supported above the bed by posts.
UF angel canopies
baldachins (furniture components)
bed canopies
canopies, angel
canopies, bed
impériales
pavillons

canopies (structural elements)
PJ.1749 (A,L,N,B,R)

HN March 1993 descriptor moved
March 1993 descriptor changed, was **canopies**
March 1993 alternate term changed, was **canopy**
May 1991 descriptor moved
May 1991 scope note changed
ALT canopy (structural element)
SN Use for small, rooflike structures, often suspended and often ornamental, that provide or suggest shelter; found, for example, at entrances or over thrones or sacred objects.
UF architectural canopies
canopies, architectural

canopies (testers)
USE testers

canopies, altar
USE baldachins

canopies, angel
USE canopies (bed components)

canopies, architectural
USE canopies (structural elements)

canopies, bed
USE canopies (bed components)

canopies, bell
USE bell cotes

canopies, half
USE half-testers

canopy beds
TC.759   (H,N)
HN May 1993 related term added
January 1993 descriptor moved
ALT canopy bed
SN Use for beds with suspended canopies, cone-shaped or domed and with curtains that reach and encompass the foot of the bed. Use **tester beds** for beds having a rooflike component supported on posts.
UF beds, canopy
RT tester beds

canopy beds (tester beds)
USE tester beds

canopy trees
RD.246
ALT canopy tree
UF trees, canopy

Canosa
FL.2725

cans
TQ.14   (L,N)
ALT can
SN Sealed metal containers for food or beverages. Also, other containers for holding or carrying liquids, such as oilcans, and metal or plastic containers for holding film on cores or reels.
UF cans, tin

tin cans
tins (cans)

cans (drinking vessels)
USE canns

cans, chimney
USE chimney pots

cans, garbage
USE trash cans

cans, sprinkling
USE watering cans

cans, tin
USE cans

cans, trash
USE trash cans

cans, watering
USE watering cans

cant beds
USE field beds

cant brick
USE splay brick

cant chisels
USE forming chisels

cant hooks
TH.1641   (N)
ALT cant hook
SN Wooden levers with metal hooks on their shafts, used to roll logs; later combined with the jam pike to become peavies.
UF hooks, cant

cant moldings
PJ.2092
HN April 1993 descriptor moved
ALT cant molding
SN Beveled moldings, either having a beveled back for nailing into a corner or angle, or one whose face or profile is a cant or oblique surface. (RS)
UF moldings, cant

canted corners
PJ.2762
HN March 1993 descriptor moved
ALT canted corner
SN Corners on furniture that have wide chamfers at the junctions of front and sides. (COLLEC)
UF corners, canted

canted moldings
USE raking moldings

canted vaults
USE pitched-brick vaults

canted walls
HN April 1991 descriptor deleted

canteens (containers)
TQ.576
ALT canteen (container)
SN Partitioned boxlike containers intended for use by travelers and mili-

tary personnel to carry flatware, cutlery, and other articles for eating and drinking.
RT canteens (vessels)

canteens (lunchrooms)
USE lunchrooms

canteens (post exchanges)
USE post exchanges

canteens (recreation centers)
USE recreation centers

canteens (vessels)
TQ.590   (N)
ALT canteen (vessel)
SN Flasklike vessels used to carry water or other liquids as by hikers or soldiers; typically made of metal and carried in a cloth jacket.
RT canteens (containers)
flasks (bottles)

canterburies (stands)
TC.1033
HN May 1993 related term added
January 1993 descriptor moved
ALT canterbury (stand)
SN 18th-century term for English stands in the form of a deep partitioned tray on legs intended to be placed near a table to hold plates and cutlery.
UF canterburies, supper
supper canterburies
supper trays
trays, supper
RT trays

canterburies (storage furniture)
TC.821   (N)
HN January 1993 descriptor moved
May 1991 descriptor changed, was **canterburies**
May 1991 alternate term changed, was **canterbury**
ALT canterbury (storage furniture)
SN Use for small racks with partitions intended to hold sheet music, books, or loose papers.
UF canterbury music cases
cases, canterbury music
music cases, canterbury

canterburies, supper
USE canterburies (stands)

canterbury music cases
USE canterburies (storage furniture)

cantilever bridges
RK.1238   (A,L)
ALT cantilever bridge
UF bridges, cantilever

cantilever construction
KT.13   (B)
HN January 1993 descriptor moved
ALT cantilevered
SN Construction employing a horizon-

tally projecting member unsupported at one end.
UF   construction, cantilever

cantilever footings
    PJ.1543
HN   March 1993 descriptor moved
      January 1991 descriptor moved
      January 1991 scope note added
      January 1991 descriptor changed,
        was **cantilevered footings**
      January 1991 alternate term
        changed, was **cantilevered footing**
ALT   cantilever footing
SN   Use for combined footings in which
    two independent footings are connected to each other to counterbalance an asymmetrical load on one of
    them, usually one supporting an
    off-center exterior wall or column.
UF   footings, cantilever

cantilever lamps
    TC.1343
ALT   cantilever lamp
UF   lamps, cantilever

cantilever roofs, cable-supported
USE   cable-stayed structures

cantilevered chairs
USE   Cesca chairs

cantilevered side chairs
USE   Cesca chairs

cantilevered stairs
USE   flying stairs

cantilevers
    PJ.1668
HN   March 1993 descriptor moved
    December 1990 scope note changed
ALT   cantilever
SN   Any projecting elements fixed at
    one end and free at the other.

canting lamps
    TC.1269
ALT   canting lamp
SN   Lamps with fonts that are pivoted so
    that, as fuel is consumed, the lamp
    will tilt, automatically or manually,
    feeding more fuel to the wick.
UF   lamps, canting

cantirs
    TQ.394   (N)
ALT   cantir
SN   Spanish drinking vessels with two
    spouts, one short and wide for filling, or sometimes pouring, and the
    other slender and tall for drinking
    (usually water); of a type made in
    the 17th and 18th centuries.
RT   jugs
    porrones

Canton
    FL.2015

cantonment towns
USE   cantonments

cantonments
    RG.139   (B)
ALT   cantonment
SN   Use for encampments formed by
    troops for long stays while on a
    campaign, especially during winter.
UF   cantonment towns
    towns, cantonment

cantons (administrative bodies)
    HN.17
HN   February 1993 scope note added
    May 1991 descriptor changed, was
      cantons
    May 1991 alternate term changed,
      was **canton**
ALT   canton (administrative body)
SN   Constituent political and administrative divisions within some European nations under a federal system, such as Switzerland.

cantons (wall components)
    PJ.1997   (R)
HN   March 1993 descriptor moved
ALT   canton (wall component)
SN   Corners of a building decorated
    with a projecting masonry course, a
    pilaster, or similar feature. (HAS)

cantorias
USE   choir lofts

cantors
    HG.414   (L)
HN   February 1993 descriptor moved
    December 1992 alternate terms
      added
    September 1990 lead-in terms
      added
ALT   cantor
    cantor's
    cantors'
SN   Synagogue officials who sing or
    chant liturgical music and lead the
    congregation in prayer. (W)
UF   cantors, Jewish
    Jewish cantors

cantors, Jewish
USE   cantors

canuns
USE   qanuns

canvas
    MT.1567   (L,B,R)
HN   March 1993 descriptor moved
    July 1991 scope note changed
SN   Use for closely woven textile made
    in various weights, usually of flax,
    hemp, jute, or cotton, used especially for sails, tarpaulins, awnings,
    upholstery, and as a support for oil
    painting. Also used for a latticelike
    mesh made of similar material, used
    as a needlepoint foundation.

canvas board
    MT.1455
HN   February 1992 descriptor moved
SN   Common gray cardboard or pasteboard to which a white cotton tex-

tile, prepared for oil painting, has
been glued or pasted. (MAYER)
UF   board, canvas

canvas, covering
USE   undercovers

canvas covers
USE   undercovers

canvas, foundation
USE   undercovers

canvas, glass
USE   fiberglass

canvas pliers
USE   stretching pliers

canvas, raw
USE   unprimed canvas

canvas, top
USE   undercovers

canvas, Tynecastle
USE   Tynecastle canvas

canvas, unprimed
USE   unprimed canvas

canvas, unsized
USE   unprimed canvas

canvases, shaped
USE   shaped canvases

canyons
    RD.160   (L,R)
HN   March 1993 related terms added
ALT   canyon
SN   Deep, steep-sided land depressions,
    often having a river at the bottom;
    common to arid and semi-arid areas; distinct from **valleys (landforms)**, which tend to have a flattish
    landscape rather than high, precipitous slopes; distinct from **gorges
    (landforms)**, which tend to be
    smaller, narrower, and more rocky.
UF   cañons (canyons)
RT   gorges (landforms)
    valleys (landforms)

caoutchouc binding
    KT.777
HN   January 1993 descriptor added
SN   Method of adhesive binding used in
    the mid-19th century employing a
    rubber solution.
UF   binding, caoutchouc
RT   caoutchouc bindings

caoutchouc bindings
    PJ.3342
ALT   caoutchouc binding
SN   Adhesive bindings produced in the
    mid-19th century using a rubber solution.
UF   bindings, caoutchouc
    bindings, gutta-percha
    gutta-percha bindings
RT   caoutchouc binding

cap covers
PJ.3094
ALT cap cover
SN Closures which are secured by friction and are usually low and flat-topped.
UF covers, cap
covers, pull-off
pull-off covers
slip-on covers

cap flashing
USE counterflashing

cap guns
USE cap pistols

cap lamps
USE acetylene lamps

cap locks
USE percussion locks

cap locks, percussion
USE percussion locks

cap moldings
PJ.2120
HN April 1993 descriptor moved
December 1990 lead-in terms added
ALT cap molding
SN Moldings which embellish the top of a piece of simple trim or casing, such as the top of a dado, base-board, or window casing.
UF cap trim
moldings, cap
trim, cap

cap pistols
TV.182   (N)
ALT cap pistol
SN Use for a variety of toy guns that utilize caps to imitate the sound of real pistols. (RHDEL2)
UF cap guns
guns, cap
pistols, cap
RT mechanical toys

cap screws
PJ.245
HN April 1993 descriptor moved
ALT cap screw
SN Threaded fasteners that screw into a threaded hole rather than into a nut. Cap screws are specified by diameter, length, and thread pitch. (MEANS)
UF screws, cap

cap strip seams
PJ.695
HN April 1993 descriptor moved
ALT cap strip seam
UF seams, cap strip
strip seams, cap

cap trim
USE cap moldings

capacity
DC.9   (L)
HN October 1992 descriptor added

SN The maximum amount or number that can be received or contained, or the ability to receive or contain.

cape chisels
TH.1245   (N)
ALT cape chisel
SN Long, cold chisels having long tapers and narrow cutting edges; used for cutting keyways and the like. (DAC)
UF chisels, cape
chisels, cope
cope chisels

Cape Cod lamps
USE kyals

Cape Indians
USE Makah

capes (landforms)
RD.187   (L)
ALT cape (landform)

capes (outerwear)
TE.129   (H,L,N,R)
ALT cape (outerwear)
SN Outer garments cut without sleeves and of varying length which fasten at the neck and fall loosely from the shoulders.

capillarity
BM.717   (L)
HN November 1992 descriptor added
SN A manifestation of surface tension by which the portion of the surface of a liquid coming in contact with a solid is elevated or depressed, depending on the adhesive or cohesive properties of the liquid. (RHDEL2)
UF action, capillary
capillary action
capillary attraction

capillary action
USE capillarity

capillary attraction
USE capillarity

capital
BM.864   (L)
HN February 1993 descriptor moved
SN Accumulated goods and financial resources devoted to the production of other goods or to generating income. (WCOL9)
UF capital goods
goods, capital

capital cities
RD.22   (A,L,B,R)
ALT capital city
UF capitals (cities)
cities, capital

<capital components>
PJ.1503
HN March 1993 guide term moved

capital goods
USE capital

capital letters
PJ.3508   (L)
ALT capital letter
SN In type, the largest letters in a given type size. In handwritten scripts, letters modeled on ancient Roman capital letters. For handwritten scripts without ascenders or descenders more generally, prefer **majuscule.**
UF capitals (letters)
capitals, full
caps (letters)
full capitals
letters, capital
letters, uppercase
uppercase
uppercase letters

capital plant
USE infrastructure

capitalis (rustic)
USE rustic capitals

capitalis cursive
USE older Roman cursive

capitalis elegans
USE square capitals

capitalis quadrata
USE square capitals

capitalis rustica
USE rustic capitals

capitalism
BM.874   (L,R)
HN February 1993 descriptor moved
January 1991 alternate term added
ALT capitalist
SN Economic system characterized by private or corporate ownership of capital goods, by investments that are determined by private decision rather than state control, and by prices, production, and the distribution of goods that are determined mainly by competition in a free market. (WCOL9)

capitals
PJ.1490   (A,L,B,R)
HN March 1993 descriptor moved
December 1990 scope note added
ALT capital
SN The uppermost members of columns, piers, or pilasters.
UF chapiters

capitals (cities)
USE capital cities

capitals (letters)
USE capital letters

capitals, Aeolic
USE Aeolic capitals

<capitals and capital components>
PJ.1489
HN March 1993 guide term moved

capitals, angle
USE angle capitals

capitals, basket
USE basket capitals

capitals, bell
USE bell capitals

capitals, block
USE cushion capitals

capitals, bracket
USE bracket capitals

capitals, corner
USE angle capitals

capitals, crocket
USE crocket capitals

capitals, cube
USE cushion capitals

capitals, cushion
USE cushion capitals

capitals, full
USE capital letters

capitals, lotus
USE lotus capitals

capitals, palm
USE palm capitals

capitals, papyriform
USE papyrus capitals

capitals, papyrus
USE papyrus capitals

capitals, pillow
USE cushion capitals

capitals, proto-Ionic
USE Aeolic capitals

capitals, protomai
USE protomai capitals

capitals, pseudo-Ionic
USE Aeolic capitals

capitals, rustic
USE rustic capitals

capitals, scalloped
USE scalloped capitals

capitals, small
USE small capitals

capitals, square
USE square capitals

capitals, vaulting
USE vaulting capitals

capitasti
USE capotastos

capitol buildings
USE capitols

capitols
　　RK.939　　　　　　　　(A,L,B,R)
ALT capitol

SN Use only for buildings in the United States occupied by a legislature; may also house one or more of the other branches of government.
UF buildings, capitol
　　capitol buildings
　　capitols, state
　　state capitols
　　statehouses

capitols, state
USE capitols

capitular records
USE church records

caplocks
USE percussion locks

capo dastos
USE capotastos

capotastos
　　PJ.3250
ALT capotasto
SN Movable nuts or pressure bars used in fretted chordophones and pianos to exert downward pressure on some or all of the strings, thereby shortening their speaking length.
UF capitasti
　　capo dastos

capotes (bonnets)
　　TE.572　　　　　　　　(N)
ALT capote (bonnet)
SN 19th-century women's bonnets, often with a soft gathered crown and a stiff brim with ribbons tied at the side or under the chin.

capotes (outerwear)
　　TE.132　　　　　　　　(N)
ALT capote (outerwear)
SN Long, full, and usually hooded cloaks or overcoats made of a rough cloth or skins; use especially for those worn during the Middle Ages or later by soldiers and travelers.
RT cloaks
　　overcoats

Cappadocian
　　FL.2958　　　　　　　　(L)
HN April 1993 descriptor added

Cappadocian ware
HN April 1993 descriptor split, use Cappadocian + ware

Cappagh brown
USE umber

capped butt hinges
　　PJ.382
HN April 1993 descriptor moved
ALT capped butt hinge
UF butt hinges, capped
　　hinges, capped butt

capping brick
　　MT.100
HN April 1992 descriptor moved
UF brick, capping

　　brick, coping
　　coping brick

capping planes
　　TH.1540　　　　　　　　(N)
HN March 1993 lead-in term changed, was **stairbuilder's planes**
　　March 1993 lead-in term changed, was **planes, stairbuilder's**
ALT capping plane
SN Planes used in conjunction with a set of handrail planes; the former cuts the top of the handrail and the latter cuts the sides. (SALAM)
UF banister planes
　　planes, banister
　　planes, capping
　　planes, stair
　　planes, starbuilders'
　　stair planes
　　starbuilders' planes

capping planes (handrail planes)
USE handrail planes

Capri pants
　　TE.105
SN Women's casual trousers with a tapered leg that ends above the ankle which often have a vertical slit at the outside bottom edge. (RHDEL2)
UF Capris
　　pants, Capri

capricci
　　VC.603　　　　　　　　(H,R)
HN April 1991 descriptor moved
ALT capriccio
SN Scenes of accurately rendered buildings grouped in an arbitrary, imaginary arrangement. Distinct from **vedute ideate**, in which scenes are realistically conceived but the elements are completely imaginary. Use especially with reference to 18th-century Italian paintings and prints.

Capricious Style
USE Third Style

Capricorn symbols
　　DG.94
ALT Capricorn symbol

Capris
USE Capri pants

caps (closures)
　　PJ.3093　　　　　　　　(N)
ALT cap (closure)
SN Items that cover, protect, or close a container or other object, usually by fitting around a cylindrical rim or collar.

caps (headgear)
　　TE.526　　　　　　　　(H,N)
ALT cap (headgear)
SN Brimless head coverings, often close-fitting and usually of a soft material; sometimes made with a visor.

caps (letters)
USE capital letters

caps (lock components)
PJ.563
HN March 1993 descriptor moved
ALT cap (lock component)
UF covers (lock components)

caps (pedestal components)
PJ.1550
HN March 1993 descriptor moved
ALT cap (pedestal component)
SN Use for the topmost projecting element of a pedestal classically divided by tripartation.
UF surbases

caps, arming
USE arming caps

caps, ball
USE baseball caps

caps, baseball
USE baseball caps

caps, bathing
USE bathing caps

caps, boudoir
USE boudoir caps

<caps by form>
TE.527

<caps by function>
TE.551

caps, chimney
USE chimney caps

caps, crown
USE crowns (closures)

caps, deerstalker
USE deerstalker caps

caps, flat
USE flatcaps

caps, forage
USE forage caps

caps, garrison
USE garrison caps

caps, glengarry
USE glengarries

caps, jockey
USE jockey caps

caps, lens
USE lens caps

caps, mob
USE mobcaps

caps, newel
USE newel caps

caps, overseas
USE garrison caps

caps, percussion
USE percussion caps

caps, Phrygian
USE Phrygian caps

caps, reed
USE wind caps

caps, round-eared
USE round-eared caps

caps, screw
USE screw caps

caps, skull
USE skullcaps

caps, small
USE small capitals

caps, stocking
USE stocking caps

caps, swimming
SEE bathing caps

caps, watch
USE watch caps

caps, wind
USE wind caps

capsa
USE arcae

Capsian
FL.41

capstan expanding tables
USE capstan tables

capstan tables
TC.1076
HN January 1993 descriptor moved
ALT capstan table
SN Tables with a circular top which expands on an iron frame to allow eight extra leaves to be inserted. Patented by Robert Jupe in 1835. (COLLAR)
UF capstan expanding tables
drum tables
expanding tables, capstan
tables, capstan
tables, capstan expanding
tables, drum

captains (military officers)
HG.125   (L)
HN January 1993 descriptor added
ALT captain (military officer)
captain's (military officer)
captains' (military officer)
SN Use for officers in the military, whose specific rank and extent of authority varies from one institution to another but who generally are in charge of a company of men or area of action, such as a ship, aircraft, or station. For officers of public services and institutions holding the same title, use **captains (public officers)**.
RT captains (public officers)

captains (public officers)
HG.154   (L)
HN January 1993 descriptor added
ALT captain (public officer)
captain's (public officer)
captains' (public officer)
SN Use for officers of this title in public services and institutions, their rank and extent of authority varying with the specific context, but generally holding authority over a group or area of activity. For military officers holding the same title, use **captains (military officers)**.
RT captains (military officers)
shipmasters

captains' chairs
USE low-back Windsor chairs

captains, ship
USE shipmasters

captains' walks
USE widows' walks

captions
VW.245   (L)
HN November 1992 descriptor moved
March 1991 descriptor added
ALT caption
SN Texts identifying or explaining, and printed in close proximity to, illustrations or other images.
UF legends (captions)

capuchins
TE.135   (H)
ALT capuchin
SN Women's hooded cloaks that resemble the habit of a Capuchin friar.
UF capuchons

capuchons
USE capuchins

caput mortuum
USE Indian red

caqueteuses
USE caquetoires

Caquetío
FL.1588

caquetoires
TC.474
HN May 1993 related term added
January 1993 descriptor moved
ALT caquetoire
SN Small, low armchairs, or backstools, often upholstered, which have a wide front, a very narrow back, and a trapezoidal seat.
UF cacqueteuses
caquetoires
caqueteuses
RT backstools

caquetoires (chauffeuses)
USE chauffeuses

car cards
VW.1133
HN June 1992 descriptor added
ALT car card

SN Use for posters intended to be placed in subway cars and buses.
UF cards, car
cards, poster
poster cards

car-ferries
SEE car ferries

car ferries
TX.404
ALT car ferry
UK car-ferries
UKA car-ferry
SN Ferries of various designs used to transport automobiles or railroad cars and accompanying passengers, if any.
UF auto ferries
car lighters (ferries)
ferries, auto
ferries, car
lighters, car (ferries)

car lighters (ferries)
USE car ferries

car lots, used
USE used car lots

car museums
USE automobile (ALT of automobiles) + museums

car parks
USE parking garages

car parks, multi-storey
USE parking garages

car-ports
SEE carports

car washes
RK.193 (A,L)
HN April 1990 descriptor added
ALT car wash
SN Structures with equipment and facilities for the washing, waxing, and polishing of motor vehicles.
UF auto washes
washes, car

Cara
FL.1674 (L)

Carabagh
USE Karabagh

Carabagh rugs
USE Karabagh + rugs

caraboard
MT.1835
SN A building material consisting of an overlap siding split from several species of deciduous trees and nailed directly to the roof-bearing walls' studs; perhaps uniquely Cameroonian. (OLIVER)

caracoles
USE spiral stairs

caracos
TE.58
ALT caraco
SN Women's short jackets extending to cover the spread of the panniers.

carafes
TQ.515 (N)
ALT carafe
SN Bottles for serving wine or water at the table.
RT bottles
decanters

Carajá
FL.1646 (L)
UF Karajá

Carancahua
USE Karankawa

caravan sites
USE trailer camps

caravans
TX.158 (L,N,B)
HN March 1993 descriptor moved
March 1993 scope note changed
March 1993 lead-in terms added
March 1993 related terms added
ALT caravan
SN Use for covered, nonmotorized animal-drawn vehicles equipped as traveling living quarters as used, for example, by gypsies, tinkers, or traveling salespeople; for motorized counterparts use **motor homes.**
UF gypsy vans
gypsy wagons
vans, gypsy
vardos
wagons, gypsy
wardos
RT houses
motor homes

caravans, motor
SEE motor homes

caravanserais
RK.902 (A,L,B)
ALT caravanserai
SN Use for stations along caravan routes providing overnight accommodations and facilities for caravans and individuals and their animals; generally characterized by large central courtyards, a single entrance and, often, shops.
UF choultries
dharmsalas

caravels
TX.310
ALT caravel
SN Small to medium-sized vessels, with plain head and square stern, originally developed as lateen-rigged coastal fishing vessels in Medieval Portugal, but eventually used as exploratory vessels in Iberian voyages to the New World in the late 15th and early 16th centuries; vessels of

exploration were often square-rigged for more efficient ocean-going travel.

Caraway
FL.842

carbines
TK.184 (L,N)
ALT carbine
SN Light, relatively short-barreled rifles and smoothbore long guns used by cavalry and lightly armed special troops, originating in Europe in the late 16th century and made in various sizes and with different firing mechanisms throughout their development down to the present day.

carbitol
MT.2420
SN A commercially prepared high-boiling ether alcohol used especially as an organic solvent. (W)

carbolic acid
MT.3071 (L)
HN February 1992 descriptor moved
UF acid, carbolic
phenol

carbolic oil
USE middle oil

carbolineum
MT.2388
SN A heavy, oily substance distilled from an anthracene-oil or creosote-oil fraction of coal tar, sometimes chlorinated or otherwise treated, and used as a wood preservative, disinfectant, or insecticide. (W)

carbometers
TN.134 (N)
ALT carbometer
SN Instruments for measuring the carbon content of steel. (STEIN)

carbon-14 dating
USE radiocarbon dating

carbon bisulfide
USE carbon disulfide

carbon black
MT.2069 (L)
HN April 1992 descriptor moved
UF acetylene black
benzol black
black, acetylene
black, benzol
black, carbon
black, diamond
black, flame
black, gas
black, oil
black, vegetable
diamond black
flame black
gas black
noir de bougie

oil black
vegetable black

carbon copies
VW.1069 (L)
HN November 1992 descriptor moved
ALT carbon copy
SN Copies of documents created simultaneously with the original manuscript or typescript by the use of an intermediate sheet of paper coated with carbon. (ICA)
UF copies, carbon

carbon dating
USE radiocarbon dating

carbon dioxide
MT.1023 (L)
HN February 1992 descriptor moved

carbon disulfide
MT.2421 (L)
UK carbon disulphide
SN Compound made by heating together carbon and sulfur; used as a solvent for rubber and other products. (MH)
UF carbon bisulfide

carbon disulphide
SEE carbon disulfide

carbon ink
USE black carbon ink

carbon ink, black
USE black carbon ink

carbon monoxide
MT.1024 (L)
HN February 1992 descriptor moved

carbon paper
MT.1468 (L)
HN February 1992 descriptor moved
UF paper, carbon

carbon photoprints
USE carbon prints

carbon print process
USE carbon process

carbon prints
VC.328
HN April 1992 descriptor moved
ALT carbon print
SN Use for photographic prints made by the carbon process.
UF carbon photoprints
photoprints, carbon
prints, carbon

carbon process
KT.540 (L)
SN A bichromate process to produce photographic prints using a carbon pigment to form the image. The most widely used carbon process was J.W. Swan's, introduced in 1864, which used sheets of pigmented gelatin that were trans-

ferred in processing to a paper support.
UF autotype
carbon print process
print process, carbon

carbon steel
MT.366 (L)
HN March 1993 descriptor moved
UF carbon steel, plain
carbon steel, straight
ordinary steel
plain carbon steel
steel, carbon
steel, ordinary
steel, plain carbon
steel, straight carbon
straight carbon steel

carbon steel, plain
USE carbon steel

carbon steel, straight
USE carbon steel

carbon tetrachloride
MT.2434 (L)

carbonaceous limestone
MT.834
HN April 1992 descriptor moved
UF bituminous limestone
limestone, bituminous
limestone, carbonaceous

carbonate, barium
USE barium carbonate

carbonate, calcium
USE calcium carbonate

carbonate ore
USE siderite

carbonate rock
MT.831 (L)
HN March 1992 scope note added
March 1992 descriptor moved
SN Any rock consisting chiefly of carbonate minerals such as calcite, dolomite, or siderite.
UF calcareous rock
rock, calcareous
rock, carbonate

carbonate, sodium
USE sodium carbonate

Carborundum (TM)
MT.1675 (L)
HN July 1990 descriptor added
SN Sharp, hard, artificial abrasive in solid or powdered form composed of silicon carbide.

carborundum paper
HN July 1990 descriptor split, use Carborundum (TM) + paper

carborundum stones
HN July 1990 descriptor split, use Carborundum (TM) + stone

carboys
TQ.47 (N)

ALT carboy
SN Bottles covered with wicker, wood, or other protective material, of a 1- to 20-gallon capacity; intended to contain corrosive liquids, acids, or distilled water. For similar large bottles covered with wicker and intended for noncorrosive liquids, use **demijohns.**
UF basketry-covered bottles
bottles, basketry-covered
RT demijohns

carbro process
KT.548 (L)
SN A carbon process to produce photographic prints in which the carbon transfer tissue is made sensitive when placed in contact with a developed silver bromide print. Distinguished from the **carbon process** by the chemical method for hardening the carbon transfer tissue and by the use of a silver bromide print, which allows carbro prints to be made from smaller negatives.
UF ozobrome
ozobrome process
ozotype

carbro tri-color
USE three-color carbro process

carbro trichrome
USE three-color carbro process

carcase furniture
USE case furniture

carcase grooving planes
USE dado planes

carcases
PJ.2758
HN March 1993 descriptor moved
ALT carcase
SN The body or main structure of furniture to which veneers are applied. (BEARD)

carcases (ammunition)
USE carcasses

carcass saws
TH.1569 (N)
ALT carcass saw
SN Thin saws with approximately 11 teeth per inch, stiffened with a metal rib along the top to prevent buckling; used to smooth cut the edges of tenons, dovetails, or miter fittings; a modern variety of the tenon saw.
UF saws, carcass

carcasses
TK.258 (N)
ALT carcass
SN Shells, oval or round in shape, filled with combustible materials and fired from mortars, howitzers, or artillery guns, used in the late 17th and 18th

centuries to set fire to buildings, ships, and fortifications.
UF carcases (ammunition)

Carcel lamps
TC.1284 (N)
ALT Carcel lamp
SN Mechanical lamps which have a spring-driven pump to maintain a uniform flow of oil to the top of the wick. Developed in France by Carcel in 1798.
UF lamps, Carcel

card cases
TQ.189 (L,N)
ALT card case
SN Small flat boxlike containers used to carry personal cards; used especially with reference to those used in the Victorian era to carry visiting cards.
UF calling card cases
cases, calling card
cases, card
cases, visiting card
visiting card cases
RT cases (containers)
visiting cards

card catalogs
VW.15 (L)
HN November 1992 descriptor moved
ALT card catalog
UF catalogs, card

card files
PC.86
HN November 1992 descriptor moved
ALT card file
SN Any files employing the use of cards. (GAHLM)
UF files, card

card frames
PJ.297
HN April 1993 descriptor moved
ALT card frame
SN Small frames that attach to a door surface for insertion of a name card or plate. (MEANS)
UF card holders
card plates
frames, card
holders, card
plates, card

<card games>
KQ.22
RT games

card games
PC.62 (H,L,N)
HN March 1993 descriptor moved
March 1993 scope note changed
April 1991 descriptor added
ALT card game
SN Sets composed of playing cards plus other items designed to be used together in games in which the primary activity during a round of play

involves the use of the playing cards.
UF games, card

card holders
USE card frames

card indexes
VW.856 (L)
HN November 1992 descriptor moved
ALT card index
SN Indexes recorded on cards of uniform size, arranged alphabetically, numerically, or by some other order. (ICA)
UF indexes, card

card keys
PJ.597
HN March 1993 descriptor moved
ALT card key
UF keys, card

card photographs
VC.350
HN April 1993 related term added
April 1992 descriptor moved
ALT card photograph
SN Photographic prints made by a variety of processes on commercially produced cardboard mounts of standard sizes. (GMGPC)
UF photographs, card
RT *<size: card photographs>*

card photographs (cartes-de-visite)
USE cartes-de-visite

card photographs, cabinet
USE cabinet photographs

card photoprints, boudoir midget mount
USE boudoir midget mounts

card photoprints, cabinet
USE cabinet photographs

card plates
USE card frames

card receivers
USE card stands

card-rooms
SEE cardrooms

card stands
TC.1047 (N)
HN January 1993 descriptor moved
ALT card stand
SN Small stands with a dished top intended to hold calling cards; of a type made in the late 19th century.
UF calling card tables
card receivers
card tables, calling
receivers, card
stands, card
tables, calling card

card stereographs
USE stereographs

<card, table and board game elements>
TV.4

<card, table and board game sets>
PC.59

card tables
TC.1122 (L,N)
HN May 1993 related term added
January 1993 descriptor moved
ALT card table
SN Tables with a smooth undecorated top, generally intended to be used for playing cards; often having a folding top and may have inset pockets to hold coins or counters. Distinguished from **gaming tables** which have tops marked as boards for playing chess, backgammon, or other games.
UF tables, card
RT gaming tables

card tables, calling
USE card stands

card tables, tripod
USE tripod card tables

card weaving
USE tablet weaving

Cardan lamps
TC.1270
ALT Cardan lamp
SN Lamps which utilize Cardan's (1550) adaptation of the barometric feed principle which permits a large reservoir to feed the fuel as needed without recourse to canting or pumping. (RUSL1)
UF lamps, Cardan
RT fountain lamps

cardboard
MT.1444 (L,N,B)
HN February 1992 descriptor moved
UF paperboard

cardboard, corrugated
USE corrugated board

cardboard cuts
USE cardboard relief prints

cardboard prints
USE cardboard relief prints

cardboard relief prints
VC.483
HN April 1993 related term added
ALT cardboard relief print
SN Relief prints made by inking pieces of cardboard that have been attached to a base.
UF cardboard cuts
cardboard prints
cuts, cardboard
prints, cardboard
prints, cardboard relief
relief prints, cardboard
RT collagraphs

cardenillo
USE verdigris

cardigan sweaters
USE cardigans

cardigans
　　TE.73　　　　　　　　　　(L)
ALT cardigan
SN Sweaters that open the full length of the center front and which have a round or V-shaped, usually collarless, neck.
UF cardigan sweaters
　　sweaters (cardigans)
　　sweaters, cardigan

cardinals (cloaks)
　　TE.136
ALT cardinal (cloak)
SN Women's hooded cloaks, usually three-quarters to full length, originally made in scarlet wool.

cardinals (prelates)
　　HG.404　　　　　　　　(L,R)
HN March 1993 descriptor changed, was **cardinals**
　　March 1993 alternate term changed, was **cardinal**
　　February 1993 descriptor moved
　　December 1992 alternate terms added
ALT cardinal (prelate)
　　cardinal's
　　cardinals'

cardines
　　RM.153
HN April 1993 descriptor moved
ALT cardo
SN Designates the north-south streets used in laying out ancient Roman countryside tracts and associated towns and thus, by extension, the main north-south streets, distinguished by greater width and scale of appointments, of planned Roman towns.

carding
　　KT.1185　　　　　　　　(L)
HN March 1993 descriptor moved
　　March 1991 alternate term added
ALT carded
SN Preparing relatively short fibers for spinning by cleansing, disentangling, and collecting them together using a card.

cardrooms
　　PJ.1071
HN March 1993 descriptor moved
ALT cardroom
UK card-rooms
UKA card-room
SN Use for rooms equipped for card playing.

cards
　　VW.1023　　　　　　　(L,R)
HN November 1992 descriptor moved
ALT card

cards (recreational artifacts)
USE playing cards

cards, advertising
USE advertising cards

cards, aperture
USE aperture cards

cards, baseball
USE baseball cards

cards, birthday
USE birthday cards

cards, business
USE business cards

cards, cabinet
USE cabinet photographs

cards, calling
USE visiting cards

cards, car
USE car cards

cards, catalog
USE catalog cards

cards, Chanukah
USE Hanukkah cards

cards, Christmas
USE Christmas cards

cards, cigarette
USE cigarette cards

cards, clipper
USE sailing cards

cards, clipper ship
USE sailing cards

cards, collecting
USE collecting cards

cards, collector
USE collecting cards

cards, collectors'
USE collecting cards

cards, compass
USE compass cards

cards, credit
USE credit cards

cards, dance
USE dance cards

cards, display
USE lobby cards

cards, Easter
USE Easter cards

cards, greeting
USE greeting cards

cards, Hanukkah
USE Hanukkah cards

cards, IBM (TM)
USE punched cards

cards, ID
USE identity cards

cards, identification
USE identity cards

cards, identity
USE identity cards

cards, image
USE aperture cards

cards, library
USE library cards

cards, lobby
USE lobby cards

cards, mass
USE mass cards

cards, memorial
USE memorial cards

cards, packs of
USE packs of cards

cards, peephole
USE aperture cards

cards, place
USE place cards

cards, playing
USE playing cards

cards, postal
USE postal cards

cards, poster
USE car cards

cards, punched
USE punched cards

cards, readers'
USE library cards

cards, report
USE report cards

cards, sailing
USE sailing cards

cards, ship
USE sailing cards

cards, show
USE advertising cards
　　business cards
　　trade cards
　　window cards

cards, store
USE store cards

cards, sure
USE cartes-de-visite

cards, time
USE time cards

cards, trade
USE trade cards

cards, trade advertising
USE trade cards

cards, tradesmen's
USE trade cards

cards, trading
USE collecting cards

cards, valentine's day
USE valentines

cards, visiting
USE visiting cards

cards, window
USE window cards

cardwork
USE cut-card work

care, day
USE day care

care facilities, extended
USE extended care facilities

care facilities, long-term
USE extended care facilities

care nurseries, intensive
USE neonatal intensive care units

care-takers
SEE caretakers

care units, neonatal intensive
USE neonatal intensive care units

career guidance
USE vocational guidance

caretakers
HG.91
HN November 1992 alternate terms added
ALT caretaker
caretaker's
caretakers'
UK care-takers
UKA care-taker
SN Persons placed usually as occupants in charge of the upkeep, repair, and protection of the house, estate, or farm of owners who may be absent. (W)
UF building caretakers
caretakers, building

caretakers, building
USE caretakers

cargo aircraft
TX.57   (L)
SN Aircraft designed or equipped primarily to transport cargo.
UF air freighters
aircraft, cargo
aircraft, freight
cargo liners
cargo planes
cargo transports
freight aircraft
freight planes
freighters
freighters, air
liners, cargo
planes, cargo
planes, freight
transports, cargo

cargo boats
USE cargo vessels

cargo liners
USE cargo aircraft

cargo planes
USE cargo aircraft

cargo ships
USE cargo vessels

cargo ships, bulk
USE bulk carriers

cargo transports
USE cargo aircraft

<cargo vehicles>
TX.94

<cargo vehicles by form>
TX.95

<cargo vehicles by function>
TX.115

cargo vessels
TX.390   (L,N)
ALT cargo vessel
SN Use for watercraft designed primarily to transport cargo.
UF boats, cargo
cargo boats
cargo ships
freighters
ships, cargo
vessels, cargo
RT tramps

Carib
FL.1580   (L)
UF Karinye

Caribbean
FL.721   (B)

Caribbean pine
USE Cuban pine

Caribou Eskimo
USE Caribou Inuit

Caribou Inuit
FL.1222
UF Caribou Eskimo
Eskimo, Caribou
Inuit, Caribou

caricatures
VC.11   (A,L,B,R)
HN April 1991 descriptor moved
ALT caricature
SN Use for representations, often portraits, that exaggerate certain features or characteristics to humorous or ludicrous effect.

caricaturists
HG.270   (L)
HN February 1993 descriptor moved
November 1992 alternate terms added
ALT caricaturist

caricaturist's
caricaturists'

Caríjona
FL.1589   (L)
UF Omagua
Umaua

carillons
TT.477   (H,L,B)
ALT carillon
SN Sets of stationary hanging bells, normally for outdoor use in an open tower chamber or on a high frame, played manually from a keyboard, automatically by clockwork, or electronically by pneumatic mechanism. More extensive than chimes, their range covers two octaves or more, with all but the lowest notes forming a fully chromatic scale. (NGDMI)
RT mechanical instruments

Caripuna
FL.1590

Carlo Maratta frames
USE Maratta frames

Carlovingian
USE Carolingian

Carlton House desks
USE Carlton House tables

Carlton House tables
TC.985
HN March 1993 lead-in term changed, was **lady's drawing and writing tables**
March 1993 lead-in term changed, was **drawing and writing tables, lady's**
March 1993 lead-in term changed, was **tables, lady's drawing and writing**
January 1993 descriptor moved
ALT Carlton House table
SN Writing tables with a low superstructure consisting of two or three tiers of small drawers rising from the back and curving around the sides. Presumably named in the late 18th century after the Prince Regent's Carlton House. (DDA)
UF Carlton House desks
Carlton tables
desks, Carlton House
drawing and writing tables, ladies'
ladies' drawing and writing tables
tables, Carlton
tables, Carlton House
tables, ladies' drawing and writing

Carlton tables
USE Carlton House tables

carmelita Van Dyck
USE Vandyke brown

carmine
MT.2013
HN March 1993 descriptor moved

March 1993 scope note added
May 1992 lead-in terms added
May 1992 related terms added
SN A red natural organic dye, also used as a lake pigment, prepared principally from two species of scale insect, cochineal and kermes.
UF carmine, cochineal
carmine, kermes
carmine lake
cochineal carmine
crimson
Florentine lake
globe lake
Karmesin lake
Karmin
Karminlack
kermes carmine
Kugel lake
lacque carminée
lake, carmine
lake, Florentine
lake, Munich
lake, Vienna
Munich lake
new red lake
Parisian lake
Venetian lake
Vienna lake
Viennese lake
RT cochineal
kermes
lake (pigment)

carmine (cochineal)
USE cochineal

carmine (color)
USE dark pink
deep purplish red
deep red
grayish red
moderate purplish red
moderate red
strong purplish red
strong red
vivid pink
vivid purplish red
vivid red

carmine, blue
USE blue carmine

carmine, brown
USE dark red
very deep red

carmine, burnt
USE burnt carmine

carmine, cadmium
USE strong red

carmine, cochineal
USE carmine

carmine, dark
USE moderate red
vivid red

carmine, kermes
USE carmine

carmine lake
USE carmine
moderate purplish red
moderate red
strong purplish red
strong red
vivid red

carmine, madder
USE moderate purplish red
moderate red

carmine rose
USE deep purplish pink
grayish red
moderate purplish red
moderate red
strong purplish red
strong red
vivid red

carmine, rose
USE moderate purplish red
strong purplish red
vivid purplish red

carmine, violet
USE dark purplish red
dark reddish purple
violet carmine

carmine, yellow
USE yellow carmine

carnauba wax
MT.1306 (L)
HN April 1992 descriptor moved
December 1990 descriptor moved
SN The hardest type of vegetable wax, obtained from the leaves of the Brazilian palm; used in compounds of wax and other material to impart hardness and durability. (MAYER)
UF wax, carnauba

Carnegie libraries
RK.667 (B)
ALT Carnegie library
SN Use for libraries, found in the United States and Great Britain, originally funded by Andrew Carnegie.
UF libraries, Carnegie

carnelian
MT.580
HN April 1992 descriptor moved
February 1992 scope note added
February 1992 related term added
SN A translucent red or orange variety of chalcedony, containing iron impurities. It is used for seals and signet rings. (AGI)
UF cornelian
RT gemstone

Carnival
KM.18 (L)
SN Use specifically for the festivals, merry-making, and revelry held a few days before Lent. For traveling amusement enterprises consisting of sideshows, games of chance, rides,

and such entertainments, use carnivals.
UF Fastnacht
Mardi Gras

carnival glass
MT.283 (L)
HN March 1992 descriptor added
SN Use to describe pressed glassware with an orange gold iridescence made with a colored spray rather than by the presence of metallic oxides.
UF glass, carnival
glassware, carnival

carnivals
KM.76 (H,L)
HN May 1991 alternate term added
ALT carnival
SN Use for traveling amusement enterprises, consisting of sideshows, games of chance, rides, and such entertainments. For the festivals, merry-making, and revelry held a few days before Lent, use Carnival.

carol books
VW.312
HN November 1992 descriptor moved
ALT carol book
UF books, carol

Carolean
USE Restoration (period)

Caroline Island
FL.3815 (L)

Caroline minuscule
PJ.3446
SN A script of great clarity, used in both books and documents, that combined characteristics of cursive and half-uncial; developed in Carolingian centers in the late 8th century and then predominant throughout Europe until the 13th century.
UF Caroline minuscule script
Carolingian (script)
Carolingian minuscule
minuscule, Carolingian
script, Caroline minuscule

Caroline minuscule script
USE Caroline minuscule

Carolingian
FL.3179 (A,L,B,R)
HN April 1993 lead-in term added
UF Carlovingian
Carolingian Renaissance
Renaissance, Carolingian

Carolingian (script)
USE Caroline minuscule

Carolingian minuscule
USE Caroline minuscule

Carolingian Renaissance
USE Carolingian

<Carolingian styles>
FL.3220

carols
USE   carrels

carotene
MT.2062   (L)
HN   April 1992 descriptor moved

Carpenter Gothic
FL.1744   (A,B)
HN   April 1991 lead-in terms added
      April 1991 descriptor changed, was
      Carpenter's Gothic
UF   Carpenteresque
      Gothic, Carpenter

Carpenteresque
USE   Carpenter Gothic

carpenters
HG.817   (A,L,B,R)
HN   January 1993 scope note added
      December 1992 alternate terms
      added
      September 1992 related terms
      added
ALT   carpenter
      carpenter's
      carpenters'
SN   Those who do carpentry, especially
      as an occupation.
RT   carpenters' rules
      carpentry

carpenters' adzes
TH.1389   (N)
HN   March 1993 descriptor changed,
      was **carpenter's adzes**
      March 1993 lead-in term changed,
      was **adzes, carpenter's**
ALT   carpenter's adz
SN   Long handled adzes whose blade is
      beveled on the inside; later adzes
      have polls on the head which are
      used as a maul.
UF   adzes, carpenters'

carpenters' axes
USE   shipwrights' axes

carpenters' benches
USE   workbenches

carpenters' dividers
USE   wing dividers

carpenters' handbooks
USE   builders' guides

carpenters' levels
TN.8
ALT   carpenter's level
SN   Hand tools which consist of a wood
      or metal bar about 2 feet long with
      four spirit levels set into it; used by
      carpenters to determine a horizontal
      or vertical plane or line. (MEANS)
UF   levels, carpenters'

carpenters' mallets
TH.1663   (N)

HN   March 1993 descriptor changed,
      was **carpenter's mallets**
      March 1993 lead-in term changed,
      was **mallets, carpenter's**
ALT   carpenter's mallet
UF   mallets, carpenters'

carpenters' pincers
USE   farriers' pincers

carpenters' rules
TN.56
ALT   carpenter's rule
SN   Rules containing graduations and
      various data conversion tables for
      making measurements and calcula-
      tions of use to carpenters; since
      about 1800 most commonly 2-foot,
      two-fold or four-fold rules.
UF   rules, carpenters'
RT   carpenters

carpenters' squares
TH.1002   (L,N)
HN   March 1993 descriptor changed,
      was **carpenter's squares**
      March 1993 lead-in term changed,
      was **squares, carpenter's**
      March 1993 lead-in term changed,
      was **squares (carpenter's squares)**
ALT   carpenter's square
SN   Flat, metal, L-shaped tools that con-
      stitute an accurate right angle and
      are engraved with divisions and
      markings useful to a carpenter in
      laying out and erecting framing.
      (MEANS)
UF   framing squares
      squares (carpenters' squares)
      squares, carpenters'
      squares, framing
      squares, steel
      steel squares

carpentry
KT.1254   (L,B,R)
HN   September 1992 related term added
SN   The art of building with wood, espe-
      cially in the construction of build-
      ings and other structures, including
      the installation of floors, windows,
      and other trim work. For the mak-
      ing of fine furniture and intricate
      woodwork, use **cabinetmaking**. For
      the activity of working in wood
      more generally, use **woodworking**.
RT   carpenters

carpet bedding
USE   carpet beds

carpet beds
RM.248
HN   March 1993 descriptor added
ALT   carpet bed
SN   Beds of foliage plants arranged in
      patterns similar to those on carpets;
      popular during the mid- to late 19th
      century, especially in England and
      the United States.
UF   bedding, carpet
      bedding, massed

beds, carpet
carpet bedding
massed bedding

carpet holders, stair
USE   stair carpet holders

carpet pages
PJ.3387
ALT   carpet page
SN   Use for pages covered with intricate
      ornament, sometimes with a central
      cross motif, as in certain Insular
      manuscripts, sometimes composed
      of minute script, as in certain He-
      brew manuscripts.
UF   pages, carpet

carpet tacks
PJ.258
HN   April 1993 descriptor moved
      March 1993 scope note added
ALT   carpet tack
SN   Flat-headed tacks used especially to
      fasten down carpets. (RHDEL2)
UF   tacks, carpet

carpet tiles
TC.31   (L)
ALT   carpet tile
SN   Small pieces of carpeting with adhe-
      sive backing. (STEIN)
UF   tiles, carpet
RT   tile

carpet, velvet
USE   velvet carpets

carpetbags
TQ.208   (N)
ALT   carpetbag
SN   Traveling bags, especially ones
      made of or simulating carpeting; of
      a type and style popular in the 19th
      century.
UF   bags, woolwork
      woolwork bags

carpeting
MT.1559
HN   November 1992 descriptor added
SN   Material woven by the yard to be
      made up into carpets.

carpeting, Brussels
USE   Brussels carpets

carpeting, Venetian
USE   Venetian carpets

carpets
TC.32   (A,L,N,B,R)
ALT   carpet
SN   Rugs of some size whose primary
      use is to cover a flat surface; carpets
      constitute the largest and most fa-
      miliar group of rugs. (DENNY2)
RT   güls
      millefleurs
      saddlebags

carpets, Admiral
USE   Admiral carpets

carpets, Afghan
USE Afghan + rugs

carpets, Afsar
USE Afshar + rugs

carpets, Ardabil
USE Ardabil carpets

carpets, Arraiolos
USE Arraiolos carpets

carpets, Aubusson
USE Aubusson carpets

carpets, audience
USE audience rugs

carpets, Axminster
USE Axminster carpets

carpets, Baluchi
USE Baluch + rugs

carpets, Bedouin
USE Berber + rugs

carpets, Bellini
USE re-entrant rugs

carpets, Berber
USE Berber + rugs

carpets, bird
USE bird Ushaks

carpets, broadloom
USE broadlooms

carpets, Brussels
USE Brussels carpets

carpets, Çanakkale
USE Çanakkale + rugs

carpets, cemetery
USE cemetery carpets

carpets, chessboard
USE chessboard rugs

carpets, Chodor
USE Chodor + rugs

carpets, column
USE pillar rugs

carpets, common Scotch
USE ingrain carpets

carpets, Coronation
USE Coronation carpets

carpets, cotton
USE dhurries

carpets, court
USE court carpets

carpets, Crivelli
USE Crivelli carpets

carpets, Dagestan
USE Dagestan + rugs

carpets, dragon
USE dragon rugs

carpets, eight lobed star Usak
USE star Ushaks

carpets, Ersari
USE Ersari + rugs

carpets, Ezine
USE Çanakkale + rugs

carpets, Feraghan
USE Feraghan + rugs

carpets, figure
USE pictorial rugs

carpets, flag
USE mats (floor coverings)

carpets, garden
USE garden carpets

carpets, Gördes
USE Gördes + rugs

carpets, Heris
USE Heriz + rugs

carpets, Heriz
USE Heriz + rugs

carpets, Holbein
USE Holbein carpets

carpets, Holbein type III
USE large pattern Holbeins

carpets, Indo-Herat
USE Indo-Herat carpets

carpets, Indo-Isfahan
USE Indo-Herat carpets

carpets, indoor-outdoor
USE indoor-outdoor carpets

carpets, ingrain
USE ingrain carpets

carpets, Joshaghan
USE Joshaghan + rugs

carpets, Kerman
USE Kirman + carpets

carpets, keyhole
USE re-entrant rugs

carpets, Khotanese
USE Khotan + carpets

carpets, Kidderminster
USE ingrain carpets

carpets, knotted-pile
USE pile-woven carpets

carpets, large-pattern Holbein
USE large pattern Holbeins

carpets, list
USE rag rugs

carpets, looped-pile
USE looped-pile carpets

carpets, Lotto
USE Lotto carpets

carpets, main
USE mian farsh

carpets, medallion Ushak
USE medallion Ushaks

carpets, meditation
USE khagangmas

carpets, Melas
USE Milas + rugs

carpets, Moroccan
USE Moroccan + rugs

carpets, Mudjur
USE Mucur + carpets

carpets, Mujur
USE Mucur + carpets

carpets, nomadic
USE tribal rugs

carpets, Oriental
USE Oriental rugs

carpets, Para-Mamluk
USE Para-Mamluk carpets

carpets, picture
USE pictorial rugs

carpets, pile
USE pile-woven carpets

carpets, pile-knotted
USE pile-woven carpets

carpets, pillar
USE pillar rugs

carpets, Polonaise
USE Polonaise carpets

carpets, Portuguese
USE Portuguese carpets

carpets, prayer
USE prayer rugs

carpets, rag
USE rag rugs

carpets, re-entrant
USE re-entrant rugs

carpets, Sanguszko
USE Sanguszko carpets

carpets, Savonnerie
USE Savonnerie carpets

carpets, Saxony
USE Saxony carpets

carpets, Scotch
USE ingrain carpets

carpets, Scots
USE ingrain carpets

carpets, shag
USE shag carpets

carpets, shaped
USE shaped carpets

carpets, Siebenbürgen
USE Transylvanian carpets

carpets, Spanish armorial
USE Admiral carpets

carpets, stair
USE stair carpets

carpets, star Ushak
USE star Ushaks

carpets, strip
USE striped rugs

carpets, striped
USE striped rugs

carpets, sunburst
USE sunburst Kazaks

carpets, table
USE table carpets

carpets, tapestry
USE tapestry Brussels

carpets, temple
USE temple rugs

carpets, Tibetan sitting
USE khagangmas

carpets, town
USE city rugs

carpets, Transylvanian
USE Transylvanian carpets

carpets, Transylvanian church
USE Transylvanian carpets

carpets, tribal
USE tribal rugs

carpets, Turcoman
USE Turkoman + rugs

carpets, turkey
USE turkey carpets

carpets, Turkman
USE Turkoman + rugs

carpets, Turkoman
USE Turkoman + rugs

carpets, vase
USE vase carpets

carpets, vase-technique
USE vase carpets

carpets, velvet pile
USE pile-woven carpets

carpets, Venetian
USE Venetian carpets

carpets, wall-to-wall
USE wall-to-wall carpets

carpets, white ground
USE bird Ushaks

carpets, Wilton
USE Wilton carpets

carpets, Wilton stair
USE stair carpets

carpets, workshop
USE city rugs

Carpinus betulus
USE European hornbeam

carports
PJ.1188 (L)
HN March 1993 descriptor moved
June 1990 scope note added
ALT carport
UK car-ports
UKA car-port
SN Roofed shelters for automobiles, often without walls; usually associated with or projecting from a separate building.

Carrack
USE Kraak

Carrack porcelain
USE Kraak + porcelain

carracks
TX.302
ALT carrack
SN Use for large, seagoing ships of the 15th through 17th century, distinguished by high sterncastle, high, overhanging forecastle, and a low waist; could be used either as a merchant vessel or warship; usually square-rigged on the fore- and mainmast and lateen-rigged on the remaining one to three masts.

Carrara marble
MT.764
HN April 1992 descriptor moved
UF marble, Carrara

Carrara structural glass
MT.311
HN March 1993 descriptor moved
UF glass, Carrara structural
structural glass, Carrara

carreau
MT.159
HN April 1992 descriptor moved

carreaux
USE bolts (arrows)

carrefours
USE intersections

carrels
PJ.1091 (B)
HN March 1993 descriptor moved
ALT carrel
SN Small individual compartments, alcoves, or furniture, such as in libraries, used for semiprivate study. (DAC)
UF carols
stalls (carrels)

carrene
USE methylene chloride

carriage bags
USE traveling bags

carriage barns
USE carriage houses

carriage bolts
PJ.44
HN April 1993 descriptor moved
ALT carriage bolt
SN Threaded bolts having a round smooth head; prevented from rotating in their holes by a square neck directly under the head. (MEANS)
UF bolts, button-headed
bolts, carriage
button-headed bolts

carriage boots
TE.709
ALT carriage boot
SN Fur-trimmed boots made for winter wear, usually lined with fur or felt. Of a type originally worn by women over shoes or slippers to keep their feet warm as they rode in carriages.
UF boots, carriage

carriage chairs
TC.601
HN January 1993 descriptor moved
ALT carriage chair
SN Adjustable highchairs which may be converted into a carriage or walker.
UF chairs, carriage
combination highchair and carriages
highchair and carriages, combination

carriage clocks
TN.184 (N)
ALT carriage clock
SN Small, portable clocks introduced in the 16th century for use when traveling; usually set in a brass, rectangular case with glass-paneled sides and having a hinged handle on top.
UF clocks, carriage

carriage cradles
TC.766
HN January 1993 descriptor moved
ALT carriage cradle
SN Cradles with two front wheels for transport.
UF carriages, cradles and
cradles and carriages
cradles, carriage

carriage houses
RK.1165 (A,B)
ALT carriage house
UF barns, carriage
barns, coach
carriage barns
carriage sheds
chaise houses
coach barns
coach houses
houses, carriage
houses, chaise
houses, coach

sheds, carriage
stables (carriage houses)

carriage lamps
TC.1397 (N)
ALT carriage lamp
SN Protected lamps or lanterns, fixed or removable, used on coaches or carriages. Commonly made of brass, they often were fitted with reflectors as well as red lenses to serve as tail lights.
UF carriage lanterns
coach lamps
lamps, carriage
lamps, coach
lanterns, carriage

carriage lanterns
USE carriage lamps

carriage pieces
PJ.2401
HN March 1993 descriptor moved
December 1990 lead-in term added
December 1990 lead-in term changed, was **rough strings**
December 1990 lead-in term deleted, was **strings, rough**
December 1990 lead-in term deleted, was **horses (stair components)**
ALT carriage piece
SN Inclined beams which support the steps or add support between the strings of a wooden staircase, usually between the wall and outer string. (DAC)
UF carriages (stair components)
pieces, carriage
roughstrings

carriage porches
USE porte-cochères

carriage sheds
USE carriage houses

carriages
TX.159 (A,H,L,N,R)
ALT carriage
SN Use for horse-drawn wheeled vehicles designed primarily to convey people in some comfort.
RT horse-drawn vehicles

carriages (gun carriages)
USE gun carriages

carriages (stair components)
USE carriage pieces
strings (stair components)

carriages, baby
USE baby carriages

carriages, block
USE block mountings

<carriages by form>
TX.160

<carriages by function>
TX.196

carriages, cradles and
USE carriage cradles

carriages, doll
USE doll carriages

carriages, gun
USE gun carriages

carriages, hackney
USE hackney coaches

carriages, horseless
USE automobiles

carriages, hose
USE hose carriages

carriages, wheel
USE wheel carriages

Carrier
FL.1242 (L)
UF Takulli

carrier rockets
USE launch vehicles

carriers, aircraft
USE aircraft carriers

carriers, armored personnel
USE armored personnel carriers

carriers, bulk
USE bulk carriers

carriers, roll-on/roll-off
USE Ro/Ros

carronades
TK.140 (N)
ALT carronade
SN Cannons first manufactured at the Carron Iron Company at Falkirk, Scotland, around 1778 and continuing in use until the late 19th century. They were short and light in relation to their bore, had no trunnions, and were used mainly on ships for firing broadsides at short range.

carrousels
USE merry-go-rounds

cars (automobiles)
USE automobiles

cars (railroad cars)
USE railroad cars

cars, armored
USE armored cars

cars, auto rack
USE rack cars

cars, automobile rack
USE rack cars

cars, baggage
USE baggage cars

cars, bi-level
USE bi-level cars

cars, cabin
USE cabooses

cars, caboose
USE cabooses

cars, club
USE lounge cars

cars, coach
USE coaches (railroad cars)

cars, container
USE container cars

cars, covered hopper
USE covered hopper cars

cars, depressed center
USE depressed center flatcars

cars, dining
USE dining cars

cars, dome
USE dome cars

cars, dump
USE dump cars

cars, estate
SEE station wagons

cars, express
USE express cars

cars, freight
USE freight cars

cars, freight train
USE freight cars

cars, funeral
USE hearses

cars, gondola
USE gondola cars

cars, governess
USE governess carts

cars, hand
USE handcars

cars, hopper
USE hopper cars

cars, horse
USE horsecars

cars, inspection
USE inspection cars

cars, light rail
USE light rail vehicles

cars, lounge
USE lounge cars

cars, parlor
USE lounge cars

cars, passenger
USE automobiles
passenger cars

cars, passenger train
USE passenger cars

cars, patrol
USE police cars

cars, pedal
USE pedal cars

cars, piggyback
USE piggyback cars

cars, piggyback rail
USE piggyback cars

cars, platform
USE flatcars

cars, police
USE police cars

cars, racing
USE racing cars

cars, rack
USE rack cars

cars, railroad
USE railroad cars

cars, railway
USE railroad cars

cars, railway freight
USE freight cars

cars, refrigerator
USE refrigerator cars

cars, restaurant
SEE dining cars

cars, saloon
USE sedans

cars, scout
USE scout cars

cars, sleeping
USE sleeping cars

cars, squad
USE police cars

cars, stock
USE stock cars

cars, subway
USE subway cars

cars, tank
USE tank cars

cars, trolley
USE trolley cars

cars, way
USE cabooses

cars, well
USE well cars

cars, well-hole
USE well cars

carstone
    MT.889   (L)
HN April 1992 descriptor moved
UF gingerbread stone
    stone, gingerbread

carte-de-visite photographs
USE cartes-de-visite

cartel clocks
    TN.176
ALT cartel clock
SN Decorative wall clocks originating in France in the early 18th century; usually spring-driven and set in gilt-bronze or carved wooden frames coming to a point at the bottom.
UF clocks, cartel

cartes-de-visite
    VC.353   (L,N,R)
HN April 1992 descriptor moved
ALT carte-de-visite
SN Use for card photographs on mounts measuring about 4 by 2 1/2 inches. Primarily used for portraits and functioning as calling cards; flourished from the 1860s to the 1880s.
UF card photographs (cartes-de-visite)
    cards, sure
    carte-de-visite photographs
    photographs, carte-de-visite
    sure cards

cartes de visite (visiting cards)
USE visiting cards

carthame
USE safflower

carthamin
USE safflower

Carthusian
    BM.493   (A,L)

cartoccios
USE cartouches

cartograms
    VW.58
HN November 1992 descriptor moved
ALT cartogram
SN Highly abstracted, simplified maps, which demonstrate a single idea or a specific type of data, often statistical, in a diagrammatic way. (LG)

cartographers
    HG.451   (L,R)
HN April 1993 related term added
    December 1992 alternate terms added
ALT cartographer
    cartographer's
    cartographers'
UF mapmakers
RT cartography

cartographic materials
    VW.47
HN March 1993 related term added
    November 1992 descriptor moved
SN Any materials representing, in whole or part, the earth or any celestial body at any scale. (AACR2)
UF cartographic records

    materials, cartographic
    records, cartographic
RT globes (cartographic spheres)

cartographic records
USE cartographic materials

cartography
    KT.350   (A,L,B,R)
HN April 1993 related term added
    July 1992 scope note added
    July 1992 lead-in term added
SN The science or art of making maps. (W)
UF chartography
    mapmaking
    mapping
RT cartographers

cartonniers
    TC.845
HN May 1993 related term added
    January 1993 descriptor moved
ALT cartonnier
SN Pieces of furniture fitted with pigeonholes or compartments to hold boxes made either as independent pieces of furniture or as pieces to be placed on top of a bureau plat.
RT bureaux plats

cartons
    TQ.16   (L,N)
ALT carton
SN Cardboard or plastic boxes used typically for storage or shipping, especially those which are relatively small and that when filled with merchandise are enclosed in a larger or stronger container for transport.
UF boxes, folding
    boxes, paper
    folding boxes
    paper boxes

cartoon strips
USE comic strips

cartooning
    KT.351   (L)
SN The activity of creating cartoons (humorous images).

cartoonists
    HG.271   (L)
HN February 1993 descriptor moved
    November 1992 alternate terms added
ALT cartoonist
    cartoonist's
    cartoonists'
SN Persons who draw cartoons (humorous images).

cartoons (humorous images)
    VC.35   (L,R)
HN April 1991 descriptor moved
ALT cartoon (humorous image)
SN Pictorial parodies using caricature, analogy, and ludicrous juxtaposition to comment on such things as contemporary events, social habits, or political trends. (ENCYB)

cartoons (working drawings)
VC.195   (R)
HN April 1992 descriptor moved
ALT cartoon (working drawing)
SN Use for full-size preparatory drawings made for the purpose of transferring a design to the working surface of a painting, tapestry, or other large work.

cartoons, auxiliary
USE auxiliary cartoons

cartoons, editorial
USE editorial cartoons

cartoons, political
USE political cartoons

cartouches
DG.105
ALT cartouche
SN Ornamental enframements, such as for an inscription, monogram, or coat of arms, or ornately framed tablets, often bearing inscriptions.
UF cartoccios

cartouches (cartridges)
USE cartridges

cartridge brass
MT.389
HN March 1993 descriptor moved
UF brass, cartridge
      brass, yellow
      yellow brass

cartridge paper
MT.1425
HN February 1992 descriptor moved
SN Fifty- to eighty-pound Manila paper, waxed on one side, originally used for muzzle-loading cartridges, but now employed where a stiff, waterproof material is needed. (MH)
UF paper, cartridge

cartridge pleats
PJ.3064
ALT cartridge pleat
SN Small cylindrical pleats arranged in a row, thus resembling a military cartridge belt, used decoratively to give a military effect to costume and hangings.
UF cartridge tucks
      pleats, cartridge
      tucks, cartridge

cartridge revolvers
TK.204
ALT cartridge revolver
SN Revolvers, generally breechloading, designed to fire cartridges.
UF revolvers, cartridge

cartridge tucks
USE cartridge pleats

cartridges
TK.269   (L)
ALT cartridge
SN Cylindrical cases containing a charge of powder and a bullet or quantity of shot for a single shot from a firearm, first appearing in the late 16th century. Early types had cases of paper, pasteboard, or linen which were ignited externally, while more recent ones have metal or plastic cases holding their own means of ignition, such as a percussion cap, at one end.
UF cartouches (cartridges)

cartridges, audio
USE audio cassettes

cartridges, blank
USE blank cartridges

cartridges, caseless
USE caseless cartridges

cartridges, center-fire
USE center-fire cartridges

cartridges, central-fire
USE center-fire cartridges

cartridges, centre-fire
SEE center-fire cartridges

cartridges, drill
USE drill ammunition

cartridges, dummy
USE dummy cartridges

cartridges, pin-fire
USE pinfire cartridges

cartridges, pinfire
USE pinfire cartridges

cartridges, rim-fire
SEE rimfire cartridges

cartridges, rimfire
USE rimfire cartridges

cartridges, video
USE videocassettes

cartridges, video tape
USE videocassettes

carts
TX.211   (A,H,L,N)
ALT cart
SN Use for two-wheeled, animal-drawn vehicles, primarily built for utility purposes, although some varieties were designed as sporting vehicles or for personal transportation.

carts, concrete
USE buggies (equipment)

carts, golf
USE golf carts

carts, governess
USE governess carts

carts, road
USE road carts

carts, tea
USE tea wagons

carts, tub
USE governess carts

cartularies
VW.188   (L)
HN November 1992 descriptor moved
ALT cartulary
SN Registers, usually in volume form, of copies of charters, title deeds, and other documents of significance belonging to a person, family, or institution. (ICA)
UF chartularies

cartunnel kilns
USE tunnel kilns

carvel-built
DC.34
HN February 1993 descriptor added
SN Use to describe wooden watercraft hulls in which the edges of planks are set flush resulting in a smooth exterior surface.
UF carvel construction
      construction, carvel

carvel construction
USE carvel-built

Carver chairs
TC.459
HN May 1993 related term added
      January 1993 descriptor moved
ALT Carver chair
SN Collector's term for 17th-century American turned great chairs styled after one that belonged to John Carver, Governor of Massachusetts Bay Colony. Such chairs have boldly turned posts and decorative spindles, but unlike Brewster chairs they have spindles only in the back and below the arms, and not below the seat.
UF chairs, Carver
RT Brewster chairs

carvers
HG.660
HN December 1992 alternate terms added
ALT carver
      carver's
      carvers'
SN Persons who engage in carving.

carvers' mallets
TH.1664   (N)
HN March 1993 descriptor changed, was carver's mallets
      March 1993 lead-in term changed, was mallets, carver's
ALT carver's mallet
SN Mallets whose head is a well-rounded truncated cone mounted upside down on a short handle. The shape enables the carver to strike the chisel from any angle without altering the hand's position on the tool. (SALAM)
UF mallets, carvers'

carvers' punches
TH.1485 (N)
HN March 1993 descriptor changed,
was **carver's punches**
March 1993 lead-in term changed,
was **punches, carver's**
ALT carver's punch
SN Steel punches with a decorative
face, used for marking wood to give
texture. (SALAM)
UF punches, carvers'

carving
KT.911 (L,R)
HN April 1993 related term added
January 1993 descriptor moved
November 1990 descriptor moved
ALT carved
SN The act of shaping wood, stone, or
another material by cutting or in-
cising.
RT sculpture techniques

<carving and carving techniques>
KT.910
HN January 1993 guide term moved
November 1990 guide term added

carving, chip
USE chip carving

carving, direct
USE direct carving

carving forks
TH.103 (N)
HN April 1993 descriptor added
ALT carving fork
SN Forks used to hold meat and similar
food as it is carved, generally having
two long tines which may be slightly
curved and which sometimes have
at the base of the handle a projection on which to rest one's forefin-
ger and thumb. May be accompanied by a carving knife.
UF forks, carving
RT carving knives
forks

carving, gem
USE lapidary

carving gouges
TH.1460 (N)
ALT carving gouge
SN Gouges sharpened both outside and
inside; the larger outside bevel is
used for hardwoods, and the smaller
inside bevel for softwoods. (SALAM)
UF gouges, carving

carving knives
TH.104 (N)
HN April 1993 descriptor added
ALT carving knife
SN Large knives with a sharp, curved,
and often pointed blade used to
carve or slice meat and similar food.
May be accompanied by a carving
fork.
UF knives, carving
RT carving forks

<carving techniques>
KT.913
HN January 1993 guide term moved
November 1990 guide term added

carvings
VC.553 (N,R)
ALT carving
SN Works executed by cutting a figure
or design out of a solid material
such as stone or wood.

carvings, ivory
USE ivories

carvings, jade
USE jades

carvings, rock
USE rock carvings

Carya
USE hickory

Carya amara
USE pignut hickory

Carya cordiformis
USE bitternut hickory

Carya glabra
USE pignut hickory

Carya illinoensis
USE pecan

Carya illoinesis
USE pecan

Carya lactiniosa
USE big shellbark hickory

Carya ovata
USE shagbark hickory

Carya texana
USE black hickory

Carya tomentosa
USE mockernut hickory

caryatids
PJ.1436 (A,L,B,R)
HN March 1993 descriptor moved
ALT caryatid
SN Supporting members serving the
function of a pier, column, or pilaster and carved or molded into the
form of a draped female human
figure.

caryophil oil
USE oil of cloves

Carystian marble
USE cipollino

casacas
USE reco-recos

Casali's green
USE viridian

Casas Grandes
FL.943

cascade of tails
USE tails (hangings)

cascades
RM.258 (A,R)
HN April 1993 descriptor moved
December 1990 descriptor moved
ALT cascade
SN Use for man-made stepped water-
falls, whether naturalistic or archi-
tectural in form.
UF waterfalls (man-made)

cascades (hangings)
USE tails (hangings)

cascades, central
USE pipes (hangings)

cascades, chain
USE water chains

cascades, cordonata
USE water chains

cascades, step
USE water stairs (landscaped-site elements)

cascading tails
USE tails (hangings)

cascadis fir
USE silver fir

case binding
KT.770
HN January 1993 descriptor added
ALT casebound
SN Method of bookbinding in which a
hard cover is made wholly separate
from the book and later is attached
to it by gluing the endpapers to the
inside of the boards of the case. Introduced in Great Britain in the
1820s.
UF binding, case
RT case bindings
casing-in
hardcover books

case bindings
PJ.3344
ALT case binding
SN Bindings in which the cover of the
book is made completely before it is
attached to the text block by means
of the endpapers.
UF bindings, case
cases (bindings)
RT case binding

case bottles
TQ.48
ALT case bottle
SN Four-sided bottles made to fit with
others in compartments in a bottle
case or box. (ILDIGL)
UF bottles, case
RT bottle cases

case clocks, dwarf tall
USE dwarf tall clocks

case clocks, long
USE   tall case clocks

case clocks, miniature tall
USE   dwarf tall clocks

case clocks, tall
USE   tall case clocks

case covers
SEE   slipcovers

case curtains
TC.262
ALT   case curtain
SN   Protective bed curtains, running on a separate outer rod, enclosing beds and their hangings when not in use.
UF   curtains, case

case files
PC.96
HN   March 1993 descriptor moved
ALT   case file
SN   Files relating to a specific action, event, person, place, project, or other subject. (ICA)
UF   dossiers
       files, case

case furniture
TC.822
HN   May 1993 related term added
       January 1993 descriptor moved
SN   Furniture that encloses a space and is generally boxlike in structure; intended for storage or display.
UF   carcase furniture
       case pieces
       cases (furniture)
       furniture, carcase
       furniture, case
       pieces, case
RT   containers

case-hardening
KT.1137   (L)
ALT   case-hardened
SN   Producing a hard surface layer on steel, as by carbonizing, cyaniding, and flame hardening. (DAC)

case histories
VW.277
HN   November 1992 descriptor moved
ALT   case history
UF   histories, case

case method
BM.388   (L)
UF   case teaching
       method, case
       teaching, case

case pieces
USE   case furniture

case-shot
SEE   canister shot

case shot
USE   canister shot

case teaching
USE   case method

Casearia praecox
USE   Maracaibo boxwood

casebooks
VW.816
HN   November 1992 descriptor moved
ALT   casebook
SN   Books containing records of cases illustrative of general principles or typifying significant situations; used for reference or instruction. (GAHLM)

cased beams
PJ.1648
HN   March 1993 descriptor moved
ALT   cased beam
SN   Use for beams enclosed in finished millwork.
UF   beams, cased
       cased-in timbers
       timbers, cased-in

cased concrete piles
USE   cased piles

cased glass
MT.284   (R)
HN   March 1993 descriptor moved
SN   Glass formed of two or more fused layers of different colored glass.
UF   glass, cased

cased-in timbers
USE   cased beams

cased photographs
VC.383
HN   April 1992 descriptor moved
ALT   cased photograph
SN   Use to describe photographs, usually daguerreotypes, ambrotypes, or tintypes, mounted in sturdy, boxlike cases.
UF   photographs, cased

cased piles
PJ.1533
HN   March 1993 descriptor moved
ALT   cased pile
SN   Use for concrete piles that are driven together with their steel casing, which is later removed and replaced by a permanent casing. (STEIN)
UF   cased concrete piles
       piles, cased

cased posts
PJ.1567
HN   March 1993 descriptor moved
ALT   cased post
SN   Use for interior posts or columns encased in finished millwork.
UF   posts, cased

casein
MT.1228   (L)
HN   April 1992 descriptor moved

March 1992 scope note changed
March 1992 related term added
SN   The primary protein of milk, used principally as a glue or pigment binder, precipitated from skim milk by acidification.
RT   tempera

casein color
USE   casein paint

casein colour
SEE   casein paint

casein glue
MT.1730
HN   March 1992 descriptor moved
SN   A cold-work, water-resistant paste made from casein by dispersion with a mild base such as ammonia. (MH)
UF   glue, casein

casein paint
MT.1953
HN   August 1992 descriptor moved
UK   casein colour
UF   casein color
       casein tempera
       color, casein
       colour, casein
       paint, casein
       tempera, casein

casein plastic
MT.1206
HN   January 1993 descriptor moved
UF   plastic, casein

casein tempera
USE   casein paint

caseless cartridges
TK.271   (N)
ALT   caseless cartridge
SN   Cartridges lacking the conventional metal case; instead the propellant is mixed with a binder, thus becoming a hard block which is shaped as required, with the bullet recessed into the forward end and a combustible cap fitted into the base.
UF   cartridges, caseless

casemates
PJ.2474
HN   March 1993 descriptor moved
       November 1990 descriptor moved
       November 1990 scope note added
ALT   casemate
SN   Use for chambers, often vaulted, in ramparts, bastions, or other outer fortification elements with openings for the firing of artillery.

casement adjusters
USE   casement stays

casement doors
USE   French doors

casement fasteners
USE   casement-window fasteners

casement hinges
PJ.411
HN April 1993 descriptor moved
ALT casement hinge
UF hinges, casement

casement stays
PJ.335
HN April 1993 descriptor moved
ALT casement stay
SN Braces or bars used to hold a casement window open in any of several positions. (MEANS)
UF adjusters, casement
casement adjusters
stays, casement

casement-window fasteners
PJ.324
HN April 1993 descriptor moved
ALT casement-window fastener
UF casement fasteners
fasteners, casement-window

casement windows
PJ.2246 (A,B)
HN March 1993 descriptor moved
November 1990 lead-in term added
ALT casement window
SN Windows having a sash that opens on hinges attached to the upright side of the frame.
UF casements
side hung windows
windows, casement
windows, side hung

casements
USE casement windows

casements, hopper
USE hopper windows

cases (bindings)
USE case bindings

cases (containers)
TQ.17 (H,N)
ALT case (container)
SN Protective containers, often small and portable, especially those shaped or with interiors fitted to encase or secure the object(s) they are meant to hold.
RT bottle cases
card cases
cigar cases
cigarette cases
etuis
eyeglass cases
key cases

cases (furniture)
USE case furniture

cases (kassen)
USE kassen

cases (lock components)
PJ.564
HN March 1993 descriptor moved
ALT case (lock component)
SN Lock housings. (MEANS)

cases (slipcovers)
USE slipcovers

cases, attaché
USE attaché cases

cases, bolster
USE bolster cases

cases, bottle
USE bottle cases

cases, calling card
USE card cases

cases, canterbury music
USE canterburies (storage furniture)

cases, card
USE card cases

cases, china
USE china cabinets

cases, cigar
USE cigar cases

cases, cigarette
USE cigarette cases

cases, clock
USE clock cases

cases, display
USE showcases

cases, dressing
USE dressing cases

cases, exhibit
USE exhibit cases

cases, eyeglass
USE eyeglass cases

cases, glove
USE glove boxes

cases, hairpin
USE hairpin boxes

cases, handkerchief
USE handkerchief boxes

cases, high
USE high chests of drawers

cases, key
USE key cases

cases, library
USE library bookcases

cases, low
USE low chests

cases, mummy
USE mummy cases

cases of boxes
USE cabinets (case furniture)

cases, packing
USE packing boxes

cases, pocket
USE etuis

cases, snap
USE snap cases

cases, solander
USE solander boxes

cases, spill
USE spill holders

cases, stamp
USE stamp boxes

cases, toilet
USE dressing cases

cases, vesta
USE matchboxes

cases, visiting card
USE card cases

cases, watch
USE watchcases

cash (Chinese money)
VK.126
SN Denotes Chinese base-metal cast coins with a square hole in the center issued from the 7th to the 19th centuries. (DOTY)
UF ch'ien
qian

cash journals
USE cashbooks

cash machines
USE automated teller machines

cashbooks
VW.586
HN November 1992 descriptor moved
ALT cashbook
SN Books of original entry in which a record is kept of all cash receipts, disbursements, or both. (GAHLM)
UF cash journals
journals, cash

cashmeer
USE cashmere

cashmere
MT.2572 (L)
HN February 1992 descriptor added
SN Fine, soft, light wool from the undercoat of the Kashmir goat; also yarn or fabric made from the wool.
UF cachemere
cachemire
cashmeer
cashmere wool
kashmir
Pashm
wool, cashmere

Cashmere (Kashmiri)
USE Kashmiri

cashmere wool
USE cashmere

casing
USE flashing (glassworking)

casing-in
KT.779
HN January 1993 descriptor added
SN The process of securing the text block and attached endpapers into a case that was produced as a separate operation. (BATCOB)
RT case binding

casing nails
PJ.163
HN April 1993 descriptor moved
ALT casing nail
SN Wire nails with a flaring head, used for outside finish and also for nailing floors. (PUTNAM)
UF nails, casing

casings, bolster
USE bolster cases

casings, door
USE doorframes

casings, pillow
USE pillowcases

casinos
RK.980   (A,L,B)
HN March 1993 related term added
ALT casino
SN Use for public entertainment buildings for meeting, dancing, and general recreation, often with eating and drinking facilities, music, and game rooms; for similar buildings equipped with gambling devices, use **gambling casinos.**
RT gambling casinos

casinos, gambling
USE gambling casinos

casket stands
USE cabinet stands

caskets
TQ.190   (H,L)
HN April 1993 descriptor moved
April 1993 related terms added
April 1993 descriptor changed, was **caskets (chests)**
April 1993 alternate term changed, was **casket (chest)**
ALT casket
SN Small boxes or chests for holding jewels, valuables, or small items; usually of wood or metal and often ornamented.
RT boxes (containers)
chests
reliquaries
toilet sets (dresser sets)

caskets (coffins)
USE coffins

casks
TQ.21   (N)
ALT cask
SN Barrel-shaped containers, especially those stronger and larger than barrels, made of staves, headings, and hoops usually closely fitted together so as to hold liquids.
RT barrels (containers)
bungs
hogsheads
kegs

cassapanche
TC.707
HN May 1993 related term added
January 1993 descriptor moved
ALT cassapanca
SN Italian wood benches with a chest under the seat, often in the form of a cassone with an upright back. (DDA)
RT cassoni

cassava
MT.1285   (L)
HN April 1992 descriptor moved
UF mandioca
manihot esculenta
manihot utilissima
manioc
tapioca
tapioca plant
yuca

Cassel brown
USE moderate brown

cassel cups
TQ.468
ALT cassel cup
SN Black-figure kylikes characterized by having a lip and body usually covered with simple patterned bands and often with rays above the foot; generally of the 6th century BCE.
UF cups, cassel

Cassel earth
USE moderate brown
Vandyke brown

Cassel yellow
USE Turner's yellow

casserole dishes
USE casseroles

casseroles
TQ.285   (L,N)
ALT casserole
SN Baking dishes, sometimes having a cover, in which food may be baked and served.
UF casserole dishes
dishes, casserole

cassetta frames
TC.404
ALT cassetta frame
SN Use for frames with simple lap-jointed back frames and entablature-derived moldings. (IRF)
UF entablature frames
frames, cassetta
frames, entablature
frames, panel
frames, plate
panel frames
plate frames

cassettes, audio
USE audio cassettes

cassettes, video tape
USE videocassettes

Cassite
USE Kassite

Cassler Umbra
USE Vandyke brown

cassocks
TE.7   (N)
ALT cassock
SN Ankle-length garments of various types, but usually having long, narrow sleeves; worn by men and women, especially members of the clergy and others participating in church services.
RT <liturgical costume>

cassolettes
TQ.129
ALT cassolette
SN Containers in which aromatic pastilles may be burned or liquid perfumes evaporated. Often in the form of a covered vase with holes on the shoulder or cover, or with pierced or openwork decoration. Sometimes made in the form of a tripod, especially an athenienne. For other containers of varying form used to hold burning incense for the purpose of scenting a room use **incense burners.** For covered vaselike containers intended primarily for liquid pot-pourri use **pot-pourri vases.**
UF cassoulettes
essence pots
essence vases
perfume-burners
pots, essence
vases, essence
RT incense burners
pot-pourri vases

cassoni
TC.868   (R)
HN May 1993 related terms added
January 1993 descriptor moved
ALT cassone
SN Italian 15th- and 16th-century chests, sometimes richly decorated; frequently intended as dower chests. (DDA)
RT armadios
cassapanche
dower chests

cassoons
USE coffers (ceiling components)

cassoulettes
USE cassolettes

cast concrete
USE cast-in-place concrete

cast-in-place concrete
MT.212   (B)
HN March 1993 descriptor added
SN Use for concrete that is deposited in liquid form in the place where it is required to harden as part of a structure; for concrete that is cast and cured in other than its final location, use **precast concrete**.
UF cast concrete
concrete, cast
concrete, cast-in-place
concrete, poured
concrete, poured-in-place
poured concrete
poured-in-place concrete
RT placing (concrete process)
precast concrete

cast-in-place piles
PJ.1531
HN March 1993 descriptor moved
ALT cast-in-place pile
SN Concrete piles that are poured at their permanent location.
UF formed piles, in situ
in situ formed piles
piles, cast-in-place

cast iron
MT.349   (A,L,B,R)
HN March 1993 descriptor moved

cast plate glass
USE rolled glass

cast products
USE castings

cast shadows
BM.819
HN April 1993 descriptor moved
January 1991 alternate term added
ALT cast shadow
UF shadows, cast

Castanea
USE chestnut

Castanea crenata
USE Japanese chestnut

Castanea dentata
USE American chestnut

Castanea mollissima
USE Chinese chestnut

Castanea sativa
USE European chestnut

Castanea vesca
USE European chestnut

castanets
TT.459   (N)
ALT castanet
SN Concussion instruments consisting of a pair of small shallow cup-shaped pieces of hardwood, strung together, hollow sides facing each

other, on a cord which loops around the player's thumb. The two pieces are clicked together by the fingers. Usually two pairs are played together, one higher-pitched than the other.

castellations
USE battlements

castelli (fortified towns)
RD.33
HN March 1993 descriptor changed, was **castelli**
ALT castellum
SN Small, ancient Roman fortified towns or outposts.

Castelli (maiolica style)
FL.3325
HN April 1993 descriptor added

castelli aquae
RK.546
ALT castellum aquae
SN Use for Roman water distribution structures, usually reservoirs, constructed at locations where water delivered by an aqueduct is diverted to various points in town.

Castelli maiolica
HN April 1993 descriptor split, use **Castelli (maiolica style)** + **maiolica**

Castelli majolica
USE Castelli (maiolica style) + maiolica

casters (finish hardware)
USE castors (finish hardware)

casters (people)
HG.661
HN January 1993 alternate terms added
ALT caster (person)
caster's
casters'
SN Persons who engage in casting.

casters (vessels)
TQ.333   (H,N)
ALT caster (vessel)
SN Small perforated containers of varying shape and material either made as one piece, with holes in the top and filled through a corked or otherwise plugged hole in the bottom, or made as two pieces, with a threaded stopper or screw cap; used for sprinkling sugar, salt, mustard, or other spices especially at the table.
RT dinner services
dredgers (containers)

casters, mustard
USE mustard casters

casters, sugar
USE sugar casters

castes
HG.13   (L)

HN January 1992 descriptor moved
January 1992 scope note added
January 1992 alternate term added
January 1992 descriptor changed, was **caste**
ALT caste
SN Closed social classes rigidly sanctioned by custom, law, or religion and based on heredity, that determine their members' prestige, occupation, and social relationships, especially marriage.

casting
KT.305   (L,R)
HN April 1993 scope note changed
ALT cast
SN The act or process of making casts or of shaping in a mold; usually refers to pouring liquid material into a mold, as distinguished from pressing a material into a mold, for which prefer **molding**.

casting bottles
TQ.545
ALT casting bottle
SN Bottles used for sprinkling scented water, spice, or pounce; often provided with devices which enable them to be suspended from chains. (MCDICT)
UF bottles, casting
RT bottles

casting, centrifugal
USE centrifugal casting

casting, continuous
USE continuous casting

casting, die
USE die casting

casting, investment
USE investment casting

casting, leaf
USE leafcasting

casting plaster
MT.1861
SN Type of plaster of Paris especially prepared to have the properties most desirable for casting and carving; it is very fine-grained, absorbent, brilliantly white, slow setting, and capable of taking fine detail. (MAYER)
UF plaster, casting

casting, sand
USE sand casting

casting, slip
USE slip casting

casting, slush
USE slush casting

casting, wax
USE lost-wax process

castings
PE.159 (B)
HN October 1992 alternate term added
January 1991 scope note added
November 1990 descriptor moved
August 1990 lead-in terms added
ALT casting
SN Use in industrial and building trade contexts for objects made by casting. For sculptural works made by casting, use **casts**.
UF cast products
products, cast

castles
RK.404 (A,L,N,B,R)
ALT castle
SN Use for buildings or groups of buildings intended primarily to serve as a fortified residence of a prince or nobleman. (AVERY)

castles (chessmen)
USE rooks

castles, moated
USE moated castles

castor oil
MT.1071 (L)
HN April 1992 descriptor moved
October 1990 descriptor moved
UF oil, castor

castor sets
PC.51
ALT castor set
SN Sets containing three or more castors generally accompanied by a metal frame or stand.
UF sets, castor

castors (finish hardware)
PJ.318 (N)
HN April 1993 descriptor moved
April 1993 lead-in term added
April 1993 descriptor changed, was **castors**
April 1993 alternate term changed, was **castor**
ALT castor (finish hardware)
SN Use for wheels set in a swivel and added to the feet on furniture to allow easy movement. Distinguished from **foot sockets** which serve to protect the feet on furniture as well as to allow easy movement.
UF casters (finish hardware)

castors (hats)
TE.578
ALT castor (hat)
SN Men's hats of varying form made of beaver fur; especially used for those worn from the 17th to 19th century. Prefer **beavers** for men's top hats made of beaver fur.
RT beavers

castra
RG.140
ALT castrum
SN Use for permanent ancient Roman military encampments laid out on a grid; may also designate later castles, forts, or fortified towers.

casts
VC.554 (H,L,N)
ALT cast
SN Use for sculptural works or reproductions made by casting. In industrial and building trade contexts, prefer **castings**.

casts (molds)
USE molds

casts, life
USE life masks

cat-boats
SEE catboats

cat houses
USE brothels

catacás
USE reco-recos

cataclysms
USE disasters

catacombs
RG.28 (A,L,B,R)
ALT catacomb
SN Underground systems of passages used as cemeteries, generally unsystematic and irregular in plan with networks of galleries and multiple levels over extensive areas. (TOYNBE)
UF coemeteria

catafalques
RK.426 (A,N,R)
ALT catafalque
SN Use for raised structures, often canopied, on which the coffin or effigy of a deceased person lies or is carried in state.

Çatal West
FL.2959
HN May 1993 descriptor added

Çatal West ware
HN May 1993 descriptor split, use Çatal West + ware

Catalan vaults
USE pitched-brick vaults
timbrel vaults

catalin
MT.1213
HN January 1993 descriptor moved
SN A thermosetting plastic made of a cast phenol-formaldehyde resin and having high compressive strength and ready machinability. (MH)

catalog cards
VW.1024 (L)
HN November 1992 descriptor moved
ALT catalog card
UF cards, catalog

catalogers
HG.498 (L)
HN April 1993 descriptor moved
April 1993 related term added
December 1992 alternate terms added
ALT cataloger
cataloger's
catalogers'
UK cataloguers
UKA cataloguer
RT cataloging

cataloging
KG.115 (L,B)
HN April 1993 related term added
January 1991 scope note added
ALT cataloged
UK cataloguing
UKA catalogued
SN Systematically analyzing and describing items in a collection and arranging the information into a catalog.
RT catalogers

cataloging, descriptive
USE descriptive cataloging

cataloging, subject
USE subject cataloging

catalognes
TC.21
ALT catalogne
UF laize du pays
RT bedcovers
floor coverings

catalogs
VW.12 (A,L,N,R)
HN November 1992 descriptor moved
November 1992 scope note changed
ALT catalog
UK catalogues
UKA catalogue
SN Enumerations of items, usually arranged systematically, with descriptive details; may be in book or pamphlet form, on cards, or online.

catalogs, accession
USE accession catalogs

catalogs, archival
USE archival catalogs

catalogs, auction
USE auction catalogs

catalogs, author
USE author catalogs

<catalogs by form>
VW.13
HN November 1992 guide term moved

<catalogs by function>
VW.23
HN January 1993 guide term changed, was *<catalogs by function or subject>*
November 1992 guide term moved

catalogs, card
USE card catalogs

catalogs, classed
USE classified catalogs

catalogs, classified
USE classified catalogs

catalogs, commercial
USE trade catalogs

catalogs, dictionary
USE dictionary catalogs

catalogs, exhibition
USE exhibition catalogs

catalogs, loose-leaf
USE loose-leaf catalogs

catalogs, mail order
USE mail order catalogs

catalogs, online
USE online catalogs

catalogs, sales
USE sales catalogs

catalogs, sheaf
USE loose-leaf catalogs

catalogs, subject
USE subject catalogs

catalogs, systematic
USE classified catalogs

catalogs, trade
USE trade catalogs

catalogs, union
USE union catalogs

cataloguers
SEE catalogers

catalogues
SEE catalogs

catalogues raisonnés
VW.25   (R)
HN November 1992 descriptor moved
ALT catalogue raisonné
UF oeuvre catalogues

cataloguing
SEE cataloging

cataloguing, descriptive
SEE descriptive cataloging

cataloguing, subject
SEE subject cataloging

catalpa
MT.2717   (L)
HN March 1992 descriptor moved
UF bean tree
    bean tree, Indian
    Indian bean tree
    tree, bean
    tree, Indian bean

catalyst
MT.1839   (L)

HN April 1993 descriptor changed, was
    catalysts

catamarans
TX.333   (L,N)
ALT catamaran
SN Use for watercraft, usually sailing
    vessels, with two hulls of equal size
    held apart above the water deck by
    rigid structural members.

catane d'acqua
USE water chains

catapults
TK.228   (L,N,R)
ALT catapult
SN Ancient military devices used to
    hurl heavy projectiles such as large
    stones, consisting essentially of a
    long upright arm with a spoon-
    shaped or slinglike holder to carry
    the projectile at the upper end, the
    lower end fastened to posts or a
    movable frame. The upper end is
    winched down by cords until paral-
    lel to the ground; when released,
    the torsion-generated force propels
    the projectile.
UF mangonels
    onagers

catapults (slingshots)
SEE slingshots

cataracts
RD.131   (L,R)
ALT cataract
SN Large, often high, thundering wa-
    terfalls; may also be used to desig-
    nate a series of rapids.

catastrophes
USE disasters

catathermometers
USE katathermometers

catboats
TX.552   (L)
ALT catboat
UK cat-boats
UKA cat-boat
SN Use for fore-and-aft-rigged vessels
    having a large boom and a single
    mast stepped well forward close to
    the stern and carrying no headsail.
UF boats, una
    una boats

catch basins
PJ.881
HN March 1993 descriptor moved
ALT catch basin
SN Receptacles that separate and retain
    greases, oil, dirt, gravel, and all
    other substances lighter or heavier
    than the liquid waste that bears
    them, such as to prevent their en-
    trance into the house sewer. (STEIN)
UF basins, catch

catch letters
USE catchwords

catchers, drip
USE bobeches

catchers, whale
USE whale catchers

catches
PJ.319
HN April 1993 descriptor moved
ALT catch
SN Use for holding devices that rely on
    a roller, magnet, or friction as the
    means of closure. Distinguished
    from **latches** which rely on some
    form of horizontal bar, such as a
    bolt, rod, or hook.

catches, back
USE back catches
    dog catches

catches, ball
USE ball catches

catches, blind
USE blind catches

catches, bullet
USE bullet catches

catches, cupboard
USE cupboard catches

catches, dog
USE dog catches

catches, eaves
USE eaves boards

catches, friction
USE friction catches

catches, magnetic
USE magnetic catches

catches, magnetic push
USE magnetic push catches

catches, roller
USE roller latches

catches, safety
USE safety catches

catches, screen-door
USE screen-door latches

catches, transom
USE transom catches

catchwords
PJ.3393
ALT catchword
SN Words placed at the bottom of a
    page repeating the first word on the
    following page; used especially at
    the very end of a gathering to guide
    the binder in assembling the gath-
    erings.
UF catch letters
    direction words
    guide words
    letters, catch

words, direction
words, guide

catechisms
VW.449 (L,R)
HN November 1992 descriptor moved
June 1992 scope note added
ALT catechism
SN Manuals or guides for instructing through a series of questions and answers, especially for religious instruction.

catechu
USE cutch

catenary arches
PJ.1583
HN March 1993 descriptor moved
ALT catenary arch
SN Arches constructed on the principle of the catenary, the shape assumed by a cord suspended at its ends from two supports in equilibrium under given forces.
UF arches, catenary

catercaps
USE mortarboards

catgut
USE gut

cathedrae
TC.594 (A,L,B,R)
HN January 1993 descriptor moved
ALT cathedra
SN Ancient Roman chairs with a rounded backboard resting on vertical stiles and curved legs. (RICHTE)

cathedral ceilings
PJ.2052
HN March 1993 descriptor moved
April 1991 scope note added
ALT cathedral ceiling
SN Use for ceilings formed by or suggesting open-timbered roofs, often higher than the ceilings of the other rooms in the building. (RHDEL2)
UF ceilings, cathedral

cathedral cities
RD.23
ALT cathedral city
UF cathedral towns
cities, cathedral
towns, cathedral

cathedral closes
USE closes

cathedral records
USE church records

Cathedral Style
USE Troubadour

cathedral towns
USE cathedral cities

cathedral windows (bedspreads)
TC.200
ALT cathedral window (bedspread)

SN Bedspreads made of plain textile squares folded to frame smaller squares of colored or printed textile, the total effect being somewhat like stained glass windows. (CHQEI)
RT quilts

cathedrals
RK.1050 (A,L,B,R)
ALT cathedral

cathedrals, double
USE double churches

cathedrals, twin
USE double churches

Catherine-wheel windows
USE rose windows

cathetometers
TN.107 (L,N)
ALT cathetometer
SN Instruments for measuring small differences in height, as for example between two columns of mercury. (MHDSTT)

cathodic
DC.23 (L)
HN October 1992 descriptor added
SN Use to describe things pertaining to cathodes, especially phenomena taking place in the vicinity of cathodes or materials formed by such phenomena.

cathodoluminescence
BM.806 (L)
HN November 1992 descriptor added
ALT cathodoluminescent
SN Luminescence produced when a substance is bombarded with cathode rays. (W)

Catholic Reformation
USE Counter-Reformation

Catholicism
BM.466 (L,B)
ALT Catholic
UF Roman Catholicism

catlinite
MT.57
HN April 1992 descriptor moved
UF pipestone

Catloltx
USE Comox

Catlow
FL.921

Catoquina
USE Catukina

cat's eye damar
USE Mata Kuching dammar

cat's eye resin
USE Mata Kuching dammar

cats' paws
USE tack pulls

cats, snow
USE snowmobiles

catslide houses
USE saltbox houses

catsteps
USE corbiesteps

cattle barns
RK.49 (L,B)
HN March 1993 related terms added
ALT cattle barn
SN Barns for beef cattle; for dairy cow housing, use **dairy barns**; for primarily open shelters for bovines, use **cow sheds**.
UF barns, cattle
cattle housing
housing, cattle
RT cow sheds
dairy barns

cattle housing
USE cattle barns

cattle ranches
RG.25 (A,L)
ALT cattle ranch
UF ranches, cattle

cattle sheds
USE cow sheds

Catukina
FL.1591 (L)
HN June 1990 lead-in term changed, was **Catoquina Indians**
UF Catoquina

catwalks
PJ.2365
HN March 1993 descriptor moved
November 1990 scope note changed
November 1990 lead-in term deleted, was **catladders**
November 1990 lead-in term deleted, was **duckboards**
ALT catwalk
SN Narrow fixed walkways providing access to an otherwise inaccessible area or to lighting units, such as used above an auditorium or stage.

Caucasian
FL.1798 (L)
HN April 1993 descriptor added

<Caucasian rugs by pattern>
TC.77

<Caucasian textile styles>
FL.1799
HN April 1993 guide term added

caudle cups
TQ.415 (H,N,R)
ALT caudle cup
SN Small unspouted cups with two vertical handles and usually a cover with a finial used to drink caudle; especially popular in the late 17th and the 18th centuries and typically made of silver. Formerly known as

posset pots or in England as porringers. For similar forms having a spout, use **spout cups**.
- UF caudle-urns
  cups, caudle
  porringers (caudle cups)
  small two-handled cups
- RT porringers
  posset pots
  spout cups
  two-handled cups

caudle-urns
USE caudle cups

cauldrons
    TQ.70   (H,N)
- ALT cauldron
- SN Large, open vessels, especially those used over an open fire.
- UF caldrons

cauliculi
    PJ.1507
- HN March 1993 descriptor moved
  November 1990 scope note changed
  November 1990 descriptor changed, was **caulicoles**
  November 1990 alternate term changed, was **caulicole**
- ALT cauliculus
- SN Ornamental stalks rising between the leaves of a Corinthian capital, from which the volutes spring and upon which the fleurons are sometimes supported.

caulk, latex
USE latex caulk

caulking
USE caulking compound

caulking chisels
USE caulking irons

caulking compound
    MT.2408   (A,L,B)
- HN April 1993 lead-in term added
  April 1993 descriptor changed, was **caulking compounds**
  April 1993 lead-in term changed, was **calking compounds**
  April 1993 lead-in term changed, was **caulking materials**
- UF calking
  calking compound
  caulking
  caulking material
  compound, calking
  compound, caulking
  material, caulking

caulking irons
    TH.1071   (N)
- ALT caulking iron
- SN Steel tools resembling chisels, most often characterized by a large, thick, flat blade cast as a single piece with a narrower handle and striking surface; used in conjunction with a caulking mallet to drive various ma-

terials into seams and crevices to make joints water- and airtight.
- UF caulking chisels
  caulking tools
  chisels, caulking
  irons, caulking
  tools, caulking

caulking mallets
    TH.1031   (N)
- HN March 1993 lead-in term changed, was **ship-carpenter's mallets**
  March 1993 lead-in term changed, was **mallets, ship-carpenter's**
- ALT caulking mallet
- SN Long-headed wooden mallets used for driving caulking irons. (SALAM)
- UF mallets, caulking
  mallets, ship-carpenters'
  ship-carpenters' mallets

caulking material
USE caulking compound

caulking tools
USE caulking irons

cauls (costume components)
    PJ.3035   (N)
- ALT caul (costume component)
- SN Soft crowns found on a bonnet or cap.

cauls (tools)
    TH.1621
- HN April 1993 descriptor changed, was **cauls**
  April 1993 alternate term changed, was **caul**
- ALT caul (tool)
- SN Tools used in forming veneer to the shape of a curved surface. (PUTNAM)

cauponae
    RK.913
- ALT caupona

causeuses
USE canapés à confident
    marquises

causeways
    RM.173   (L)
- HN April 1993 descriptor moved
- ALT causeway
- SN Use for roads or pathways raised above surrounding low, wet, or uneven ground.

caustic lime
USE quicklime

caustic potash
USE potassium hydroxide

caustic soda
USE sodium hydroxide

caution signs
USE warning signs

cavalier oblique drawings
    VC.98

- HN April 1992 descriptor moved
- ALT cavalier oblique drawing
- SN Use for drawings in oblique projection in which the vertical plane is parallel to the plane of projection (drawing surface), and all three spatial axes are drawn to the same scale.
- UF cavalier perspectives
  cavalier projections
  drawings, cavalier oblique
  military perspectives
  oblique drawings, cavalier
  perspectives, cavalier
  perspectives, military
  projections, cavalier

cavalier perspectives
USE cavalier oblique drawings

cavalier projections
USE cavalier oblique drawings

cavaliers (fortification elements)
    PJ.2475
- HN March 1993 descriptor moved
  March 1993 descriptor changed, was **cavaliers**
  March 1993 alternate term changed, was **cavalier**
  November 1990 scope note changed
- ALT cavalier (fortification element)
- SN Use for raised, defensible works erected within a fortified place or by besiegers to command enemy positions within firing range.

cavaliers (soldiers)
    HG.133
- HN January 1993 descriptor added
- ALT cavalier (soldier)
  cavalier's
  cavaliers'
- SN Fighting men on horseback, typically of upper class background, especially those who fought on the side of the Royalist party in 17th-century Great Britain.

cavalries
    HN.63   (H,L)
- HN March 1992 descriptor added
- ALT cavalry
- SN Groups of armed fighting men who fight or maneuver on horseback.

cavals
USE kavals

cave architecture
    RK.1287   (A,L)
- UF architecture, cave
  architecture, grotto
  grotto architecture

cave art
    BM.197
- HN May 1991 scope note added
  December 1990 descriptor moved
- SN Use for prehistoric art, especially Paleolithic, found in caves, includ-

ing paintings, carvings, and certain artifacts.
UF art, cave

cave churches
RK.1051   (A,L,B)
ALT cave church
UF churches, cave
churches, monolithic
churches, rock
monolithic churches
rock churches

cave drawings
HN October 1990 descriptor deleted, made lead-in to **cave paintings**

cave drawings
USE cave paintings

cave dwellings
RK.309   (L,B)
ALT cave dwelling
UF cave houses
dwellings, cave
houses, cave

cave houses
USE cave dwellings

cave paintings
VC.270   (L,B)
ALT cave painting
SN Paintings and other markings executed on the surface of the living rock in natural caves, especially during the Paleolithic period. For markings cut into the living rock, use **rock engravings.**
UF cave drawings
drawings, cave
paintings, cave

cave temples
RK.1082   (A,L,B)
ALT cave temple
UF temples, cave

caveae
PJ.1297
HN March 1993 descriptor moved June 1990 scope note added
ALT cavea
SN Use for the tiered, semicircular seating areas in ancient, especially Roman, theaters and amphitheaters.

Cavernas
USE Paracas Cavernas

caverns
RD.201   (A,L,R)
ALT cavern
SN Use for large, subterranean, naturally formed chambers, with entrances from the surface.

caves
RD.202   (A,L,B,R)
ALT cave

caves, chaitya
USE chaityas

caves, storm
USE storm cellars

cavetto cornices
PJ.1682
HN March 1993 descriptor moved
ALT cavetto cornice
SN Cornices consisting of a large cavetto molding, sometimes decorated.
UF cornices, cavetto
cornices, gorge
Egyptian gorges
gorge cornices
gorges, Egyptian

cavetto moldings
PJ.2093
HN April 1993 descriptor moved
November 1990 scope note changed
ALT cavetto molding
SN Moldings with a rounded concave surface, usually a quarter circle.
UF cove moldings
gorge moldings
hollow moldings
moldings, cavetto
moldings, cove
moldings, gorge
moldings, hollow
moldings, throat
throat moldings
trochili

cavils
TH.1331   (N)
HN December 1992 descriptor moved
ALT cavil
SN Axes having a flat face for knocking off projecting angular points and a pointed peen for reducing a surface to a desired form. (DAC)
UF axes, jedding
jedding axes
kevils

cavities, altar
USE sepulchers

cavity floors
USE suspended floors

cavity walls
PJ.1905   (B)
HN March 1993 descriptor moved
November 1990 scope note added
ALT cavity wall
SN Walls, usually of masonry, and usually exterior, consisting of two wythes separated by a continuous air space, the wythes held together by metal stays or wires.
UF hollow masonry walls
hollow walls
masonry walls, hollow
walls, cavity
walls, hollow
walls, hollow masonry

cavo relievo
USE intaglio

Cawahib
USE Parintintin

Cayapó
FL.1592   (L)
UF Kayapo

Cayuá
USE Caingang

Cayuga
FL.1307   (L)

Cayuse
FL.1420   (L)

CBDs
USE central business districts

CCUs
USE coronary care units

Cd
USE cadmium

CD-ROMs
VW.1044   (L)
HN November 1992 descriptor moved
September 1991 descriptor added
ALT CD-ROM
SN Compact disks on which a large amount of digitized read-only data can be stored. (RHDEL2)
UF compact disks read-only memory

CDCs
USE community design centers

CDs
USE certificates of deposit
compact disks

cedar
MT.2923   (L,R)
HN March 1992 descriptor moved
UF Cedrus

cedar, African
USE African cedar

cedar, Atlantic
USE Atlantic cedar

cedar, Atlantic white
USE white cypress

cedar, atlas
USE Atlantic cedar

cedar, bastard
USE incense cedar

cedar, Borneo
USE Borneo mahogany

cedar, Central American
USE Spanish cedar

cedar, Chinese
USE toon

cedar, cigar-box
USE Spanish cedar

cedar green
USE chrysocolla

cedar, Himalayan
USE deodar

cedar, incense
USE incense cedar

cedar, Lebanon
USE Lebanon cedar

cedar, oil of
USE oil of cedar

cedar, Oregon
USE Port Orford cedar

cedar, Paraguayan
USE Paraguayan cedar

cedar, pencil
USE red cedar

cedar, Port Orford
USE Port Orford cedar

cedar, red
USE red cedar

cedar, southern white
USE white cypress

cedar, Spanish
USE Spanish cedar

cedar, white
USE Port Orford cedar

cedar, yellow
USE yellow cypress

cedarwood oil
USE oil of cedar

Cedrela braziliensis
USE Paraguayan cedar

Cedrela odorata
USE Spanish cedar

Cedrela sinensis
USE toon

Cedrela toona
USE toon

Cedrus
USE cedar

Cedrus atlantica
USE Atlantic cedar

Cedrus deodara
USE deodar

Cedrus libani
USE Lebanon cedar

ceika
USE kapok

ceiling fixtures
TC.1403   (N)
ALT ceiling fixture
SN Lighting fixtures attached to or suspended from the ceiling.
UF ceiling lights
fixtures, ceiling

<ceiling hangers>
PJ.92
HN April 1993 guide term moved

ceiling hooks
PJ.130   (N)
HN April 1993 descriptor moved
ALT ceiling hook
SN Hooks that fasten to the ceiling or to the underside of shelves. (BROWNL)
UF hooks, ceiling

ceiling joists
PJ.1653
HN March 1993 descriptor moved
March 1991 descriptor moved
ALT ceiling joist
SN Joists which carry a ceiling; also small beams to which the ceiling of a room is attached.
UF joists, ceiling

ceiling lights
USE ceiling fixtures

ceiling papers
TC.394
ALT ceiling paper
SN Wallpapers designed for use on ceilings, often with tiny repeating patterns or astronomical motifs.
UF ceiling wallpapers
papers, ceiling
wallpapers, ceiling

ceiling plans, reflected
USE reflected ceiling plans

ceiling protectors
USE smoke bells

ceiling wallpapers
USE ceiling papers

ceilings
PJ.2047   (A,L,B,R)
HN March 1993 descriptor moved
November 1990 scope note changed
ALT ceiling
SN The overhead surfaces of interior spaces, sometimes constructed to mask building systems or structural elements.
UF plafonds

ceilings, acoustical
USE acoustical ceilings

ceilings, barrel
USE barrel ceilings

ceilings, beam
USE beam ceilings

ceilings, camp
USE camp ceilings

ceilings, cathedral
USE cathedral ceilings

ceilings, coffered
USE coffered ceilings

ceilings, compartment
USE compartment ceilings

ceilings, cove
USE cove ceilings

ceilings, cum
USE camp ceilings

ceilings, drop
USE suspended ceilings

ceilings, false
USE suspended ceilings

ceilings, luminous
USE luminous ceilings

ceilings, suspended
USE suspended ceilings

ceilings, tent
USE camp ceilings

ceilings, tray
USE camp ceilings

ceilometers
TN.108   (L,N)
ALT ceilometer
SN Automatic devices for measuring and recording cloud heights.

ceirnins
USE Irish harps

celadon
MT.1991

celadon (color)
USE very pale green

celadon gray
USE grayish yellow green
pale green

celadon green
USE grayish yellow green
green earth
moderate yellowish green
pale green

Celebes
USE Sulawesi

celebrating
KG.306
SN Observing, honoring, or commemorating with ceremonies, festivities, or wide public praise. (RHDEL2)

celebrations
KM.12   (R)
HN March 1993 related term added
April 1992 scope note added
May 1991 alternate term added
ALT celebration
SN Events demonstrating grateful or happy satisfaction or honor, marked by festivities, refraining from ordinary business, or other deviations from accustomed routine. For events serving specifically to call someone or something to remembrance, use **commemorations**.
RT commemorations

celebrations, centennial
USE centennials

celeries
USE celery glasses

celery dishes
TQ.377 (N)
ALT celery dish
SN Relatively long and narrow dishes with low vertical sides intended for serving stalks of celery. For vessels used to serve celery upright, use **celery glasses.**
UF celery trays
dishes, celery
trays, celery
RT celery glasses

celery glasses
TQ.329 (N)
ALT celery glass
SN Vaselike containers, typically made of glass, intended to be used on the dining table for serving stalks of celery. For relatively low and narrow dishes intended for serving celery, use **celery dishes.** For similar vaselike forms also used on the dining table but which often have a scalloped rim and are intended to hold spoons, use **spoon holders.** For vaselike forms which are often made of glass but sometimes made of wood or bone and which are usually kept near a fireplace or oil lamp, use **spill holders.**
UF celeries
celery stands
celery vases
glasses, celery
stands, celery
vases, celery
RT celery dishes
spill holders
spoon holders

celery stands
USE celery glasses

celery trays
USE celery dishes

celery vases
USE celery glasses

celestas
TT.510 (L,N)
ALT celesta
SN Keyboard instruments having the form of a small upright piano in which metal plates (usually steel) suspended over resonating boxes are struck by hammers and sustained in a manner similar to piano action.
RT keyboard instruments

celestial atlases
USE astronomical charts

celestial charts
USE astronomical charts

celestial globes
VW.1034 (L,R)
HN November 1992 descriptor moved
ALT celestial globe
UF globes, celestial

celestial photographs
USE astrophotographs

celestial photography
USE astronomical photography

celite
USE diatomaceous earth

cellae
PJ.1283
HN March 1993 descriptor moved
October 1990 descriptor added
ALT cella
SN Use for the sanctuaries of temples.

cellar lamps
USE miners' lamps

cellarets, wine
USE wine coolers

cellarette drawers
USE celleret drawers

cellarettes
USE cellerets

cellarettes, wine
USE cellerets

cellars
PJ.1128 (A,L,B)
HN March 1993 descriptor moved
ALT cellar
SN Use for rooms, wholly or mostly below ground level, used for storage, particularly of food; for similar areas serving utility purposes or as living spaces, use **basements.**

cellars, beer
USE beer cellars

cellars, cyclone
USE storm cellars

cellars, root
USE root cellars

cellars, storm
USE storm cellars

cellars, tornado
USE storm cellars

cellars, wine
USE wine cellars

celleret drawers
PJ.2774
HN March 1993 descriptor moved
ALT celleret drawer
UF bottle drawers
cellarette drawers
drawers, bottle
drawers, cellarette
drawers, celleret

celleret sideboards
TC.1003
HN May 1993 related term added
January 1993 descriptor moved
ALT celleret sideboard
SN Sideboards with a place at one end to hold bottles of wine and at the other end either a plain drawer or a drawer lined with lead, in which glasses could be washed.
UF sideboards, celleret
RT cellerets

cellerets
TC.869 (N)
HN May 1993 related terms added
January 1993 descriptor moved
ALT celleret
SN Use for small chests or cabinets, usually with locks and often fitted with side handles, designed to store bottles of wine or liquor. For metal-lined tubs or stands for cooling wine bottles, use **wine coolers.**
UF butlers (chests)
cellarettes
cellarettes, wine
cellerettes
chests, wine
gardes du vin
guardivines
sarcophagi (chests)
wine cellarettes
wine chests
RT celleret sideboards
wine coolers

cellerettes
USE cellerets

cellists
USE violoncellists

cello players
USE violoncellists

cellocuts
VC.448
ALT cellocut
SN Prints made from surfaces built up with liquid plastics on wood, metal, cardboard, or plastic support. May be printed intaglio or relief. (PETERD)

celloists
USE violoncellists

cellos
USE violoncellos

Cellosolve (TM)
USE ethylene glycol monoethyl ether

cells
PJ.1205
HN March 1993 descriptor moved
ALT cell
SN Single rooms usually housing only one person within a building having numerous similar rooms, as in a convent or in a prison. (W)

cells (vault components)
USE vaulting cells

cells, vault
USE vaulting cells

cells, vaulting
USE vaulting cells

cellular
    DC.48   (A,L,B)
HN October 1992 descriptor added
SN Use to describe a material having a structure composed of cells, whether biological cells, as in wood, or open cavities otherwise generated, as in some bricks.

cellular brick
HN April 1993 descriptor split, use cellular + brick

cellular concrete
USE air-entrained concrete

cellular frames
USE box frames

cellular glass
HN April 1993 descriptor split, use cellular + glass

cellular materials
HN April 1993 descriptor split, use cellular + material (ALT of materials)

cellular plastic
USE plastic foam

cellulated glass
USE cellular + glass

celluloid
    MT.1171   (L)
HN January 1993 descriptor moved
SN A tough, highly flammable but not usually explosive synthetic thermoplastic composed essentially of cellulose nitrate and camphor or other plasticizer. (W)

cellulose
    MT.1025   (L)
HN April 1992 descriptor moved

cellulose acetate
    MT.1165
HN January 1993 descriptor moved
UF acetate, cellulose
CA

cellulose acetate butyrate
USE butyrate

cellulose cement
    MT.1732
HN March 1992 descriptor moved
UF cement, cellulose

cellulose diacetate
    MT.1166
HN January 1993 descriptor moved
UF diacetate, cellulose

cellulose ether
    MT.1168
HN January 1993 descriptor moved
UF ether, cellulose

cellulose, ethyl
USE ethyl cellulose

cellulose fiber
USE excelsior

cellulose fiber, wood
USE excelsior

cellulose nitrate
USE nitrocellulose

cellulose triacetate
    MT.1167
HN January 1993 descriptor moved
SN Fully esterified cellulose acetate containing three acetyl groups per glucose unit. (NEBLET)
UF triacetate
triacetate, cellulose

cellulosic
    MT.1164
HN January 1993 descriptor moved
UF cellulosic plastic
plastic, cellulosic

cellulosic plastic
USE cellulosic

Celotex (TM)
USE fiberboard

celters
USE testers

Celtic
    FL.2611   (A,L,B,R)
UF Keltic

Celtic crosses
    DG.19
ALT Celtic cross
SN Crosses having a ring or halo about the intersection. (IDO)
UF crosses, Celtic
crosses, Iona
crosses, Irish
crosses of Iona
crosses, ring
crosses, wheel
crosses, wheel-head
Iona crosses
Irish crosses
ring crosses
wheel crosses (Celtic crosses)
wheel-head crosses

Celtic harps
USE Irish harps

Celtic trumpet motifs
USE trumpet spirals

celtis
USE hackberry

Celtis australis
USE European hackberry

Celtis mississippiensis
USE Mississippi hackberry

Celtis sinensis
USE Chinese hackberry

celures
USE testers

cembalons
USE cimbaloms

cembalos
USE harpsichords

cement
    MT.9   (L,B,R)
HN April 1992 descriptor moved
SN A material, usually in powder form that can be made into a paste when mixed with water, that is used as a construction material as an ingredient of mortar and concrete. (W)

cement (adhesive)
USE adhesive

cement, accelerated
USE accelerated cement

cement, aluminate
USE aluminous cement

cement, aluminous
USE aluminous cement

<cement and cement products>
    MT.8
HN April 1992 guide term moved

cement, asphalt
USE asphalt cement

cement, brick
USE brick cement

<cement by composition or origin>
    MT.10
HN April 1992 guide term moved

<cement by property>
    MT.40
HN April 1992 guide term moved

cement, cellulose
USE cellulose cement

cement clinker
USE clinker

cement-coated nails
    PJ.148
HN April 1993 descriptor moved
ALT cement-coated nail
SN Nails which are coated with cement in order to increase friction and holding power. (MEANS)
UF nails, cement-coated

cement color
HN March 1992 descriptor deleted

cement, expanding
USE expanding cement

cement, expansive
USE expanding cement

cement, extra-rapid-hardening
USE high-early-strength cement

cement, flooring
USE gypsum cement

cement, glass reinforced
USE glass reinforced cement

cement, granite-powder
USE granite-powder cement

cement, gypsum
USE gypsum cement

cement, high alumina
USE aluminous cement

cement, high-early
USE high-early-strength cement

cement, high-early-strength
USE high-early-strength cement

cement, high speed
USE aluminous cement

cement, hydraulic
USE natural cement

cement, hydraulic lime
USE natural cement

cement, joint
USE Spackle (TM)

cement, Keene's
USE Keene's cement

cement kilns
TH.503   (L)
ALT cement kiln
SN Kilns used to fire cement to less
than complete melting. (MHDSTT)
UF kilns, cement

cement, low-heat
USE low-heat cement

cement, Mack's
USE Mack's cement

cement, magnesia
USE magnesia cement

cement, Martin's
USE Martin's cement

cement, masonry
USE masonry cement

cement mixers
USE concrete mixers

cement, moderate portland
USE modified portland cement

cement, modified portland
USE modified portland cement

cement mortar
MT.2331
UF mortar, cement

cement, natural
USE natural cement

cement, neat
USE neat cement

cement, normal portland
USE standard portland cement

cement, oxychloric
USE oxychloric cement

cement, Parian
USE Parian cement

cement plants
RK.595   (H,L)
ALT cement plant
UF plants, cement

cement, plastic
USE plastic cement

cement, polymer-impregnated
USE polymer-impregnated cement

cement, portland
USE portland cement

cement, portland blast-furnace
USE portland slag cement

cement, portland blast-furnace-slag
USE portland slag cement

cement, portland-pozzolan
USE portland-pozzolan cement

cement, portland slag
USE portland slag cement

cement, pozzolan
USE pozzolan cement

cement, pozzuolana
USE pozzolan cement

<cement products>
MT.44
HN April 1992 guide term moved

cement, rapid-hardening
USE accelerated cement

cement, Roman
USE natural cement
pozzolan cement

cement, slag
USE slag cement

cement, soil
USE soil cement

cement, sorel
USE oxychloric cement

cement, standard portland
USE standard portland cement

cement stone
USE hydraulic limestone

cement, sulfate-resistant
USE sulfate-resistant cement

cement, sulfoaluminate
USE expanding cement

cement, sulfur
USE sulfur cement

cement, sulphate-resisting
SEE sulfate-resistant cement

cement, sulphur
SEE sulfur cement

cement, supersulphate
USE sulfur cement

cement, type I portland
USE standard portland cement

cement, type II portland
USE modified portland cement

cement, type III
USE high-early-strength cement

cement, type III portland
USE high-early-strength cement

cement, type IV
USE low-heat cement

cement, type V portland
USE sulfate-resistant cement

cement, waterproof
USE natural cement

cemeteries
RG.26   (A,L,B,R)
ALT cemetery
UF burial grounds
burying-grounds
graveyards
grounds, burial

cemeteries, animal
USE pet cemeteries

<cemeteries by form>
RG.27

<cemeteries by function>
RG.31

cemeteries, military
USE national cemeteries
war cemeteries

cemeteries, national
USE national cemeteries

cemeteries, pet
USE pet cemeteries

cemeteries, war
USE war cemeteries

cemetery beacons
USE lanterns of the dead

cemetery carpets
TC.101
ALT cemetery carpet
SN Turkish rugs with a design element
consisting of a tomb and trees.
UF carpets, cemetery
cemetery rugs
Mazarlek
Mazarlik
mezarliks
Mezars
rugs, cemetery

cemetery rugs
USE cemetery carpets

cendre
USE azurite

cendre blue
HN January 1992 descriptor deleted, made lead-in to azurite

cendre blue
USE azurite

cendres bleues
USE azurite

cenizas
USE azurite

cenobrium
USE vermilion

cenotaphs
   RK.445   (A,B,R)
ALT cenotaph
SN Sepulchral monuments erected to a person or persons buried elsewhere. (PDARC)

censers
   TQ.150   (H,L,N,R)
ALT censer
SN Containers in which incense is burned for ecclesiastical use. Use **incense burners** for containers for burning incense for the purpose of scenting a room.
UF thuribles
    thuribula
    thymiaterions
RT incense boats
    incense burners

censoring
   KG.109
ALT censored
SN Altering, deleting, or banning completely a report, document, art work, or any item bearing a message, information, or image which the censoring body wants to suppress.

censors
   HG.165
HN May 1993 alternate terms added
    February 1993 descriptor moved
    May 1991 descriptor added
ALT censor
    censor's
    censors'
SN Officials who examine publications, motion pictures, correspondence, or other forms of public or private communication for the purpose of suppressing any material in them deemed objectionable on moral, political, military, or other grounds.

censorship
   BM.1061   (L,R)
HN February 1993 descriptor moved

census districts
USE census tracts

census maps
   VW.116   (L)
HN November 1992 descriptor moved
ALT census map
UF maps, census

census records
   VW.560
HN November 1992 descriptor moved
ALT census record
SN Official, usually periodic, lists of persons or property with varying degrees of descriptive detail. (ICA)
UF census returns
    census schedules
    censuses
    records, census
    returns, census
    schedules, census

census returns
USE census records

census schedules
USE census records

census tracts
   RG.272   (L)
ALT census tract
UF census districts
    districts, census
    tracts, census

censuses
USE census records

<*cent pieces*>
   VK.58

cent pieces, fifty
USE half dollars

centavos
   VK.67
ALT centavo
SN Any of various coins valued at one-hundredth part of the monetary unit of several Spanish-American and Portuguese-speaking territories.

centenaries
USE centennials

centenionales
   VK.29
ALT centenionalis
SN Use for billon or copper coins of the Roman Empire issued from the mid-4th century.

centennial celebrations
USE centennials

centennial quilts
   TC.228
ALT centennial quilt
SN Quilts made to commemorate a hundredth anniversary.
UF quilts, centennial

centennials
   KM.15   (H,L)

HN April 1992 scope note changed
    March 1991 descriptor added
ALT centennial
SN One-hundredth anniversaries or their observances.
UF celebrations, centennial
    centenaries
    centennial celebrations

center and corner frames
   TC.405
ALT center and corner frame
UK centre and corner frames
UKA centre and corner frame
SN Use for frames in which the decoration of corners and centers is emphasized, usually by placement of cartouches. (WADSWO)
UF center-corner pattern leaf frames
    frames, center and corner
    frames, centre and corner
    leaf frames, center-corner pattern

center bits
   PJ.2579   (N)
HN March 1993 descriptor moved
ALT center bit
SN Tools used to start holes or make shallow borings in wood. They are held by braces and consist of a sharp point (or threaded center spur), a projecting scoring edge, and a sharp lip for cutting away the wood inside the circumference. (DAC)
UF bits, center

center bits, plug
USE tenon-cutting bits

center cars, depressed
USE depressed center flatcars

center cities
USE inner cities

center-corner pattern leaf frames
USE center and corner frames

center-fire cartridges
   TK.272   (N)
ALT center-fire cartridge
UK centre-fire cartridges
UKA centre-fire cartridge
SN Cartridges fired by the striking of a hammer or firing pin upon a primer located in the center of the base.
UF cartridges, center-fire
    cartridges, central-fire
    cartridges, centre-fire
    central-fire cartridges

center flatcars, depressed
USE depressed center flatcars

center-light chandeliers
   TC.1256
ALT center-light chandelier
SN Chandeliers having a burner located centrally, directly below the stem. (MYERS)
UF chandeliers, center-light

center of projection
BM.115
SN Use for the implied location of the viewer's eye in a perspective construction.
UF projection, center of

center-slide chandeliers
TC.1257
ALT center-slide chandelier
SN Chandeliers having a height-adjustable central burner which can be lowered to increase illumination when necessary, as at dinner or for reading. (MYERS)
UF center-slide fixtures
center slides
chandeliers, center-slide
chandeliers, slide
fixtures, center-slide
slide chandeliers

center-slide fixtures
USE center-slide chandeliers

center slides
USE center-slide chandeliers

center tables
TC.1181   (N)
HN January 1993 descriptor moved
ALT center table
SN Tables of any shape, finished on all sides and used in the center of a room for any purpose. (ARON)
UF tables, center

center tails
USE pipes (hangings)

centerbead molding planes
USE centerboard planes

centerboard planes
TH.1541   (N)
ALT centerboard plane
SN Planes that cut a bead or some other simple shape, and that are provided with a fence so that the molding can be cut in the middle of a piece of work. (SALAM)
UF centerbead molding planes
molding planes, centerbead
planes, centerbead molding
planes, centerboard

centered
DC.319
HN October 1992 descriptor moved
UK centred

centering
TH.425   (L,B)
HN April 1990 descriptor added
SN Temporary construction, usually of wood, over which arches and vaults are formed and held until they become self-supporting.

centerpieces
TC.1489   (R)
ALT centerpiece
SN Term generally applied to orna-

mental and often functional objects or ensemblages of objects placed in the center of a table.
UF pieces, center
RT dinner services
fruit bowls
plateaus (containers)
pyramids (containers)
sweetmeat stands

centers
BM.656
HN January 1991 alternate term added
ALT center

centers, adult day care
USE adult day care centers

centers, adult day health
USE adult day care centers

centers, adult education
USE continuing education centers

centers, advice
USE information centers

centers, alumni
USE alumni centers

centers, architectural
USE architectural centers

centers, art
USE art centers

centers, audiovisual
USE audiovisual centers

centers, business
USE central business districts

centers, child care
USE day care centers

centers, civic
USE civic centers

centers, college community
USE student unions

centers, commercial
USE central business districts

centers, community
USE community centers

centers, community design
USE community design centers

centers, community recreation
USE community centers

centers, computer
USE computer centers

centers, conference
USE convention centers

centers, continuing education
USE continuing education centers

centers, convention
USE convention centers

centers, crisis
USE crisis shelters

centers, cultural
USE cultural centers

centers, data processing
USE computer centers

centers, data processing service
USE computer centers

centers, day care
USE day care centers

centers, design
USE design centers

centers, detention
USE detention centers

centers, distribution
USE distribution centers

centers, documentation
USE documentation centers

centers, emergency medical
USE emergency medical centers

centers, fitness
USE health clubs

centers for the performing arts
USE performing arts centers

centers, growth
USE growth centers

centers, health
USE health facilities
medical centers

centers, immunization
USE vaccination centers

centers, information
USE information centers
information services

centers, instructional materials
USE audiovisual centers
learning resource centers

centers, job training
USE training centers

centers, juvenile detention
USE detention centers

centers, learning resource
USE learning resource centers

centers, medical
USE medical centers

centers, municipal
USE civic centers

centers, nature
USE nature centers

centers, parish
USE parish houses

centers, performing arts
USE performing arts centers

centers, physical fitness
USE health clubs

centers, physical training
USE physical education buildings

centers, pilgrimage
USE pilgrimage centers

centers, play
USE playgrounds

centers, poison control
USE poison control centers

centers, recreation
USE recreation centers

centers, rehabilitation
USE rehabilitation centers

centers, research
USE research centers

centers, school media
USE learning resource centers

centers, science
USE science + museums

centers, senior
USE senior centers

centers, shopping
USE shopping centers

centers, skill training
USE training centers

centers, social
USE community centers

centers, sports
USE sports complexes

centers, student
USE student unions

centers, tourist information
USE information centers

centers, training
USE training centers

centers, transport
USE terminals

centers, urban
USE central cities

centers, vaccination
USE vaccination centers

centers, village community
USE community centers

centers, visitors'
USE visitors' centers

centers, welfare
USE welfare buildings

centers, world trade
USE world trade centers

centers, youth
USE youth centers

centimes
VK.68
ALT centime

SN Any of various, usually copper or aluminum, coins issued since the late 18th century by several French-speaking countries and valued at one-hundredth part of their monetary unit.

central
DC.320
HN October 1992 descriptor moved

central air conditioning
PC.142
HN March 1993 descriptor moved
November 1990 scope note added
SN Air conditioning systems run from one or more centralized units that provide controlled air to an entire building or complex.
UF air conditioning, central
central systems

Central American
FL.718   (L,B,R)
UF American, Central

Central American cedar
USE Spanish cedar

<Central and Equatorial African styles>
FL.395

Central Asian
FL.1789   (L)
HN June 1990 lead-in term changed, was Transoxiana
UF Asian, Central
Transoxianan

<Central Asian Bronze Age styles and periods>
HN April 1993 guide term deleted

<Central Asian early historic painting styles>
HN April 1993 guide term deleted

<Central Asian early historic styles and periods>
HN April 1993 guide term deleted

<Central Asian Neolithic styles and periods>
HN April 1993 guide term deleted

<Central Asian Paleolithic styles and periods>
HN April 1993 guide term deleted

central business districts
RG.303   (A,L,B)
ALT central business district
SN Designates the high-density cores of cities, where activities are principally retail, commercial, service, and often governmental.
UF business centers
business districts, central
CBDs
centers, business
centers, commercial
commercial centers
districts, central business
downtowns

central cascades
USE pipes (hangings)

<Central Caucasian textile styles>
FL.1800
HN April 1993 guide term added

central cities
RG.304
ALT central city
SN Largest core areas within the incorporated limits of metropolitan areas; often used to distinguish the center from the suburban or newer outlying sections of metropolitan areas; generally excludes the central business district and inner city sections.
UF centers, urban
urban centers

central-fire cartridges
USE center-fire cartridges

Central Ge
FL.1694
UF Ge, Central

Central Indian
FL.2347
UF Indian, Central

<Central Italian Greek pottery styles>
FL.2688

Central Javanese
FL.2464
UF Javanese, Central

<Central Persian textile styles after the Mongols>
FL.3720
HN April 1993 guide term added

central perspective
USE one-point perspective

central perspectives
USE one-point perspectives

central-plan
DC.140
HN October 1992 descriptor moved
UF centralized-plan
centrally planned

<Central Plateau Mesoamerican periods>
FL.991

<Central Plateau Mesoamerican styles>
FL.1013

<Central Plateau Mesoamerican styles and periods>
FL.990

central projection
KT.476
SN Technique for representing three-dimensional objects in two dimensions using projecting lines that converge toward one or more points rather than running parallel, as in one-point, two-point, and three-point perspective.

UF perspective projection
    projection, central
    projection, perspective

central systems
USE central air conditioning

central tails
USE pipes (hangings)

<Central Tanzanian styles>
    FL.581

central towers
USE crossing towers

<Central Zaire>
    FL.427

centralized-plan
USE central-plan

centrally planned
USE central-plan

centre and corner frames
SEE center and corner frames

centre-fire cartridges
SEE center-fire cartridges

centred
SEE centered

centres, audio-visual
SEE audiovisual centers

centres, civic
SEE civic centers

centres, community-design
SEE community design centers

centres, conference
SEE convention centers

centres, detention
SEE detention centers

centres, growth
SEE growth centers

centres, nature
SEE nature centers

centres, performing arts
SEE performing arts centers

centres, pilgrimage
SEE pilgrimage centers

centres, remand
SEE detention centers

centres, shopping
SEE shopping centers

centres, sports
SEE sports complexes

centrifugal casting
    KT.310   (L)
HN March 1991 alternate term added
ALT centrifugal-cast
SN A method of casting by the lost-wax
    process using a machine in which
    the mold revolves so that its cavity is

filled with molten metal by centrifugal action and pressure. (MAYER)
UF casting, centrifugal

centrifugal force
    BM.824   (L)
HN November 1992 descriptor moved
SN Force that tends to impel matter
    outward from a center of rotation.
    (WCOL9)
UF force, centrifugal

centripetal force
    BM.825   (L)
HN November 1992 descriptor moved
SN Force that keeps an object moving
    in a circular path and that is di-
    rected inward toward the center of
    rotation. (WCOL9)
UF force, centripetal

centripetal spring chairs
    TC.653
HN May 1993 related term added
    January 1993 descriptor moved
ALT centripetal spring chair
SN Reclining chairs with a spring con-
    cealed under the seat which allows
    the chairs to recline and then snap
    into place; attributed to the Ameri-
    can Chair Company, Troy, NY,
    about 1850. (HAYWAR)
UF chairs, centripetal spring
    spring chairs, centripetal
RT patent furniture

centroid color 1
USE vivid pink

centroid color 10
USE pinkish gray

centroid color 100
USE deep greenish yellow

centroid color 101
USE light greenish yellow

centroid color 102
USE moderate greenish yellow

centroid color 103
USE dark greenish yellow

centroid color 104
USE pale greenish yellow

centroid color 105
USE grayish greenish yellow

centroid color 106
USE light olive

centroid color 107
USE moderate olive

centroid color 108
USE dark olive

centroid color 109
USE light grayish olive

centroid color 11
USE vivid red

centroid color 110
USE grayish olive

centroid color 111
USE dark grayish olive

centroid color 112
USE light olive gray

centroid color 113
USE olive gray

centroid color 114
USE olive black

centroid color 115
USE vivid yellow green

centroid color 116
USE brilliant yellow green

centroid color 117
USE strong yellow green

centroid color 118
USE deep yellow green

centroid color 119
USE light yellow green

centroid color 12
USE strong red

centroid color 120
USE moderate yellow green

centroid color 121
USE pale yellow green

centroid color 122
USE grayish yellow green

centroid color 123
USE strong olive green

centroid color 124
USE deep olive green

centroid color 125
USE moderate olive green

centroid color 126
USE dark olive green

centroid color 127
USE grayish olive green

centroid color 128
USE dark grayish olive green

centroid color 129
USE vivid yellowish green

centroid color 13
USE deep red

centroid color 130
USE brilliant yellowish green

centroid color 131
USE strong yellowish green

centroid color 132
USE deep yellowish green

centroid color 133
USE very deep yellowish green

centroid color 134
USE very light yellowish green

centroid color 135
USE light yellowish green

centroid color 136
USE moderate yellowish green

centroid color 137
USE dark yellowish green

centroid color 138
USE very dark yellowish green

centroid color 139
USE vivid green

centroid color 14
USE very deep red

centroid color 140
USE brilliant green

centroid color 141
USE strong green

centroid color 142
USE deep green

centroid color 143
USE very light green

centroid color 144
USE light green

centroid color 145
USE moderate green

centroid color 146
USE dark green

centroid color 147
USE very dark green

centroid color 148
USE very pale green

centroid color 149
USE pale green

centroid color 15
USE moderate red

centroid color 150
USE grayish green

centroid color 151
USE dark grayish green

centroid color 152
USE blackish green

centroid color 153
USE greenish white

centroid color 154
USE light greenish gray

centroid color 155
USE greenish gray

centroid color 156
USE dark greenish gray

centroid color 157
USE greenish black

centroid color 158
USE vivid bluish green

centroid color 159
USE brilliant bluish green

centroid color 16
USE dark red

centroid color 160
USE strong bluish green

centroid color 161
USE deep bluish green

centroid color 162
USE very light bluish green

centroid color 163
USE light bluish green

centroid color 164
USE moderate bluish green

centroid color 165
USE dark bluish green

centroid color 166
USE very dark bluish green

centroid color 167
USE vivid greenish blue

centroid color 168
USE brilliant greenish blue

centroid color 169
USE strong greenish blue

centroid color 17
USE very dark red

centroid color 170
USE deep greenish blue

centroid color 171
USE very light greenish blue

centroid color 172
USE light greenish blue

centroid color 173
USE moderate greenish blue

centroid color 174
USE dark greenish blue

centroid color 175
USE very dark greenish blue

centroid color 176
USE vivid blue

centroid color 177
USE brilliant blue

centroid color 178
USE strong blue

centroid color 179
USE deep blue

centroid color 18
USE light grayish red

centroid color 180
USE very light blue

centroid color 181
USE light blue

centroid color 182
USE moderate blue

centroid color 183
USE dark blue

centroid color 184
USE very pale blue

centroid color 185
USE pale blue

centroid color 186
USE grayish blue

centroid color 187
USE dark grayish blue

centroid color 188
USE blackish blue

centroid color 189
USE bluish white

centroid color 19
USE grayish red

centroid color 190
USE light bluish gray

centroid color 191
USE bluish gray

centroid color 192
USE dark bluish gray

centroid color 193
USE bluish black

centroid color 194
USE vivid purplish blue

centroid color 195
USE brilliant purplish blue

centroid color 196
USE strong purplish blue

centroid color 197
USE deep purplish blue

centroid color 198
USE very light purplish blue

centroid color 199
USE light purplish blue

centroid color 2
USE strong pink

centroid color 20
USE dark grayish red

centroid color 200
USE moderate purplish blue

centroid color 201
USE dark purplish blue

centroid color 202
USE very pale purplish blue

centroid color 203
USE pale purplish blue

centroid color 204
USE   grayish purplish blue

centroid color 205
USE   vivid violet

centroid color 206
USE   brilliant violet

centroid color 207
USE   strong violet

centroid color 208
USE   deep violet

centroid color 209
USE   very light violet

centroid color 21
USE   blackish red

centroid color 210
USE   light violet

centroid color 211
USE   moderate violet

centroid color 212
USE   dark violet

centroid color 213
USE   very pale violet

centroid color 214
USE   pale violet

centroid color 215
USE   grayish violet

centroid color 216
USE   vivid purple

centroid color 217
USE   brilliant purple

centroid color 218
USE   strong purple

centroid color 219
USE   deep purple

centroid color 22
USE   reddish gray

centroid color 220
USE   very deep purple

centroid color 221
USE   very light purple

centroid color 222
USE   light purple

centroid color 223
USE   moderate purple

centroid color 224
USE   dark purple

centroid color 225
USE   very dark purple

centroid color 226
USE   very pale purple

centroid color 227
USE   pale purple

centroid color 228
USE   grayish purple

centroid color 229
USE   dark grayish purple

centroid color 23
USE   dark reddish gray

centroid color 230
USE   blackish purple

centroid color 231
USE   purplish white

centroid color 232
USE   light purplish gray

centroid color 233
USE   purplish gray

centroid color 234
USE   dark purplish gray

centroid color 235
USE   purplish black

centroid color 236
USE   vivid reddish purple

centroid color 237
USE   strong reddish purple

centroid color 238
USE   deep reddish purple

centroid color 239
USE   very deep reddish purple

centroid color 24
USE   reddish black

centroid color 240
USE   light reddish purple

centroid color 241
USE   moderate reddish purple

centroid color 242
USE   dark reddish purple

centroid color 243
USE   very dark reddish purple

centroid color 244
USE   pale reddish purple

centroid color 245
USE   grayish reddish purple

centroid color 246
USE   brilliant purplish pink

centroid color 247
USE   strong purplish pink

centroid color 248
USE   deep purplish pink

centroid color 249
USE   light purplish pink

centroid color 25
USE   vivid yellowish pink

centroid color 250
USE   moderate purplish pink

centroid color 251
USE   dark purplish pink

centroid color 252
USE   pale purplish pink

centroid color 253
USE   grayish purplish pink

centroid color 254
USE   vivid purplish red

centroid color 255
USE   strong purplish red

centroid color 256
USE   deep purplish red

centroid color 257
USE   very deep purplish red

centroid color 258
USE   moderate purplish red

centroid color 259
USE   dark purplish red

centroid color 26
USE   strong yellowish pink

centroid color 260
USE   very dark purplish red

centroid color 261
USE   light grayish purplish red

centroid color 262
USE   grayish purplish red

centroid color 263
USE   white (neutral)

centroid color 264
USE   light gray

centroid color 265
USE   medium gray

centroid color 266
USE   dark gray

centroid color 267
USE   black

centroid color 27
USE   deep yellowish pink

centroid color 28
USE   light yellowish pink

centroid color 29
USE   moderate yellowish pink

centroid color 3
USE   deep pink

centroid color 30
USE   dark yellowish pink

centroid color 31
USE   pale yellowish pink

centroid color 32
USE   grayish yellowish pink

centroid color 33
USE   brownish pink

centroid color 34
USE vivid reddish orange

centroid color 35
USE strong reddish orange

centroid color 36
USE deep reddish orange

centroid color 37
USE moderate reddish orange

centroid color 38
USE dark reddish orange

centroid color 39
USE grayish reddish orange

centroid color 4
USE light pink

centroid color 40
USE strong reddish brown

centroid color 41
USE deep reddish brown

centroid color 42
USE light reddish brown

centroid color 43
USE moderate reddish brown

centroid color 44
USE dark reddish brown

centroid color 45
USE light grayish reddish brown

centroid color 46
USE grayish reddish brown

centroid color 47
USE dark grayish reddish brown

centroid color 48
USE vivid orange

centroid color 49
USE brilliant orange

centroid color 5
USE moderate pink

centroid color 50
USE strong orange

centroid color 51
USE deep orange

centroid color 52
USE light orange

centroid color 53
USE moderate orange

centroid color 54
USE brownish orange

centroid color 55
USE strong brown

centroid color 56
USE deep brown

centroid color 57
USE light brown

centroid color 58
USE moderate brown

centroid color 59
USE dark brown

centroid color 6
USE dark pink

centroid color 60
USE light grayish brown

centroid color 61
USE grayish brown

centroid color 62
USE dark grayish brown

centroid color 63
USE light brownish gray

centroid color 64
USE brownish gray

centroid color 65
USE brownish black

centroid color 66
USE vivid orange yellow

centroid color 67
USE brilliant orange yellow

centroid color 68
USE strong orange yellow

centroid color 69
USE deep orange yellow

centroid color 7
USE pale pink

centroid color 70
USE light orange yellow

centroid color 71
USE moderate orange yellow

centroid color 72
USE dark orange yellow

centroid color 73
USE pale orange yellow

centroid color 74
USE strong yellowish brown

centroid color 75
USE deep yellowish brown

centroid color 76
USE light yellowish brown

centroid color 77
USE moderate yellowish brown

centroid color 78
USE dark yellowish brown

centroid color 79
USE light grayish yellowish brown

centroid color 8
USE grayish pink

centroid color 80
USE grayish yellowish brown

centroid color 81
USE dark grayish yellowish brown

centroid color 82
USE vivid yellow

centroid color 83
USE brilliant yellow

centroid color 84
USE strong yellow

centroid color 85
USE deep yellow

centroid color 86
USE light yellow

centroid color 87
USE moderate yellow

centroid color 88
USE dark yellow

centroid color 89
USE pale yellow

centroid color 9
USE pinkish white

centroid color 90
USE grayish yellow

centroid color 91
USE dark grayish yellow

centroid color 92
USE yellowish white

centroid color 93
USE yellowish gray

centroid color 94
USE light olive brown

centroid color 95
USE moderate olive brown

centroid color 96
USE dark olive brown

centroid color 97
USE vivid greenish yellow

centroid color 98
USE brilliant greenish yellow

centroid color 99
USE strong greenish yellow

centrolobium
USE balaustre

cents
    VK.60   (L)
ALT cent
SN Designates various copper, copper alloy, steel, and copper-plated zinc coins valued at one-hundredth part of a dollar.
UF cents, large
    large cents
    one-cent pieces
    pennies (United States coins)
    pieces, one-cent

cents, half
USE half cents

cents, large
USE cents

Centuripe
FL.2726

cephalometers
TN.78 (N)
ALT cephalometer
SN Instruments for measuring the size of the skulls of living beings; for instruments that measure the skulls of deceased beings, use **craniometers.**
RT craniometers

cera alba
USE bleached beeswax

cera colla
MT.1759
SN A Medieval term for an emulsion of glue solution and molten beeswax; called for in old recipes as an ingredient of aqueous paint binder. (MAYER)

cera flava
USE unbleached beeswax

ceramic
MT.148
HN January 1993 descriptor added
UF ceramic material
material, ceramic

<ceramic and ceramic products>
MT.147
HN April 1992 guide term moved

ceramic color
HN March 1992 descriptor deleted

ceramic engineering
KD.141
HN April 1993 descriptor changed, was **ceramic science**
April 1993 lead-in term changed, was **ceramic engineering**
UF ceramic science
engineering, ceramic
science, ceramic

ceramic glaze
MT.1985
UF glaze, ceramic

<ceramic glaze by composition or origin>
MT.1986

<ceramic glaze by form>
MT.1994

<ceramic glaze by technique>
MT.1996

ceramic material
USE ceramic

ceramic metal
USE cermet

ceramic process
KT.543 (L)

SN Use for a variant of the dusting-on process in which the pigment is a vitrifiable powder, available in a wide range of colors, that is fired onto porcelain, earthenware, china, or the like; more broadly, use for any process to form an image on porcelain, china, earthenware, or similar material.
UF china process
enamel process
porcelain process

<ceramic products>
MT.155
HN April 1992 guide term moved

ceramic science
USE ceramic engineering

ceramic tile
MT.156 (A)
HN March 1993 scope note changed
November 1992 related term added
April 1992 descriptor moved
SN Fired clay in various shapes and thicknesses and with a variety of uses, as for surface covering, drainage, or construction. For flat, solid, and relatively thin durable material used primarily for surface covering, use **tile.**
UF tile, ceramic
RT tile

<ceramic tile by form>
MT.157
HN April 1992 guide term moved

<ceramic tile by function>
MT.162
HN April 1992 guide term moved

<ceramic tile by technique>
MT.186
HN April 1992 guide term moved

ceramic ware
USE ceramics

ceramicists
HG.689 (L,R)
HN February 1993 lead-in term added
February 1993 descriptor changed, was **ceramists**
February 1993 alternate term changed, was **ceramist**
December 1992 alternate terms added
ALT ceramicist
ceramicist's
ceramicists'
SN Persons who engage in ceramic arts, manufacturing, or technology. (W)
UF ceramists

ceramics
PE.102 (L,R)
HN January 1993 descriptor moved
January 1993 scope note added
January 1993 alternate term deleted, was **ceramic**

SN Use collectively for articles made of ceramic.
UF ceramic ware
keramics
ware, ceramic

ceramics, Band
USE Bandkeramik

ceramics, studio
USE studio ceramics

ceramists
USE ceramicists

Cerbat
FL.967

ceremonial armors
USE parade armors

<ceremonial chairs>
TC.593
HN January 1993 guide term moved
December 1992 related term added
RT ceremonial objects

<ceremonial containers>
TQ.130
RT ceremonial objects

<ceremonial costume>
TE.240
RT ceremonial objects
copes
crowns (headdresses)
headdresses
robes
tiaras
wreaths (costume accessories)

ceremonial objects
PE.62 (H,L)
HN December 1992 descriptor added
ALT ceremonial object
SN Use broadly for articles associated with or used in any context that may be considered a ceremony.
UF objects, ceremonial
objects, ritual
ritual objects
RT <ceremonial chairs>
<ceremonial containers>
<ceremonial costume>
ceremonial swords
<ceremonial watercraft>
ceremonies
flagons
hallah covers
loving cups
pokals
standing cups

ceremonial swords
TK.91
ALT ceremonial sword
SN Swords that play a part in public state or civic ceremonies or rituals, being variously worn, carried, or presented, as symbols of honor or power.
UF ritual swords

swords, ceremonial
swords, ritual
RT ceremonial objects

<ceremonial vessels>
TQ.131
RT bratinas
charkas
great salts
phialae
rhyta

<ceremonial watercraft>
TX.342
RT ceremonial objects

ceremonies
KM.19   (L,R)
HN March 1993 related terms added
April 1992 scope note changed
May 1991 alternate term added
January 1991 lead-in term added
ALT ceremony
SN Formal acts or series of acts, especially those conducted elaborately, solemnly, and as prescribed by the ritual or protocol of religious, state, court, social, or tribal procedure. For events serving to call someone or something to remembrance, use **commemorations.**
UF rites
RT ceremonial objects
commemorations

ceresin
MT.1301   (L)
HN April 1992 descriptor moved
December 1990 descriptor moved
SN Pure white or slightly yellowish mineral wax; suitable substitute for beeswax as an ingredient of polishes and protective coatings of sculptures. (MAYER)

cerise
USE deep purplish red
vivid purplish red

cerise pink
USE strong purplish red

cermet
MT.499   (L)
HN April 1993 descriptor changed, was **cermets**
April 1993 lead-in term changed, was **ceramic metals**
April 1992 descriptor moved
UF ceramic metal
metal, ceramic

cerography
KT.352   (L)
HN April 1993 lead-in term added
July 1990 lead-in term added
SN The art of making characters or designs in or with wax. (W)
UF engraving, wax
printing, wax
wax engraving
wax printing

cerography (wax painting)
USE encaustic painting

Cerro Mangote
FL.1101

Cerro Sechín
FL.1155
UF Sechín

cerrussa
USE lead white

certificates
VW.334
HN November 1992 descriptor moved
ALT certificate
SN Documents giving authoritative recognition of a fact, qualification, or promise.

certificates, baptismal
USE baptismal certificates

certificates, birth
USE birth certificates

certificates, copyright
USE copyright certificates

certificates, death
USE death certificates

certificates, gift
USE gift certificates

certificates, gold
USE gold certificates

certificates, hypothecation
USE hypothecation certificates

certificates, marriage
USE marriage certificates

certificates of compliance
USE certificates of occupancy

certificates of deposit
VW.566   (L)
HN June 1992 descriptor added
ALT certificate of deposit
SN Use for receipts from a bank certifying that a specified sum of money has been received for deposit, often for a specified length of time and at specified rates of interest.
UF CDs
deposit, certificates of
RT commercial paper

certificates of incorporation
VW.650   (L)
HN November 1992 descriptor moved
ALT certificate of incorporation
SN Documents issued by the Secretary of State or other state official, establishing a corporation. (GAHLM)
UF incorporation, certificates of

certificates of occupancy
VW.335
HN November 1992 descriptor moved
ALT certificate of occupancy
SN Documents officially certifying that

premises conform to provisions of the zoning ordinance and building code and may be used or occupied; granted for new construction or for alteration or additions to existing structures. (LOFZ)
UF certificates of compliance
compliance, certificates of
occupancy, certificates of
occupancy permits
permits, occupancy

certificates of origin
VW.336   (L)
HN November 1992 descriptor moved
ALT certificate of origin
SN Certificates attesting to the country of manufacture of a commodity, often required by the customs office before importation. (RHDEL2)
UF origin, certificates of

certificates of stock
USE stock certificates

certificates, share
USE stock certificates

certificates, silver
USE silver certificates

certificates, stock
USE stock certificates

certification
USE certifying

certified checks
VK.166
HN March 1993 scope note changed
July 1991 descriptor moved
ALT certified check
SN Checks that certify that the signature of the drawer is genuine and that the depositor has sufficient funds on deposit for payment. (ENCYBF)
UF checks, certified

certifying
KG.209   (L,B)
HN April 1993 lead-in term added
March 1991 alternate term added
ALT certified
SN Officially attesting that something is valid or meets a standard, or, with regard to people, that a standard degree of qualification has been met.
UF certification

certose
USE charterhouses

cerulean
USE light blue
light purplish blue

cerulean blue
MT.2097
HN April 1992 descriptor moved
UF bleu céleste
blue, cerulean
caeruleum

ceruleum
coelin
Coelinblau
coeruleum

cerulean blue (color)
USE light blue
     moderate blue
     strong blue
     strong greenish blue
     vivid blue
     vivid greenish blue

cerulean blue, bright
USE moderate blue
     strong greenish blue

cerulean blue, dark
USE dark greenish blue
     grayish blue

cerulean blue, deep
USE dark greenish blue
     deep greenish blue
     moderate blue
     moderate greenish blue

cerulean blue, light
USE brilliant greenish blue
     light blue
     strong greenish blue

cerulean blue, pale
USE light blue
     very light blue

cerulean blue, vivid
USE strong greenish blue

ceruleum
USE cerulean blue

cerusa
USE lead white

ceruse of tin
USE tin white

Cesca chairs
     TC.475
HN   January 1993 descriptor moved
ALT Cesca chair
UF   Breuer chairs
     cantilevered chairs
     cantilevered side chairs
     chairs, Breuer
     chairs, cantilevered
     chairs, Cesca
     side chairs, cantilevered

cesspools
     PJ.882   (L,B)
HN   March 1993 descriptor moved
ALT cesspool
SN   Covered pits into which raw sewage
     is discharged, the liquid portion
     seeping or leaching into the sur-
     rounding porous soil, and the solids
     being retained in the pit to undergo
     partial decomposition before re-
     moval. (STEIN)

cestas
     TV.29   (N)

ALT cesta
SN   Long, narrow, curved wicker baskets
     fitted to the end of a wooden handle
     with a glovelike compartment at the
     base used by players of jai alai to
     catch and throw the ball.
UF   baskets, jai alai
     jai alai baskets
RT   jai alai

ceteras
USE citterns

cetras
USE English guitars

Ceylon rosewood
     MT.2889
HN   March 1992 descriptor moved
UF   Albizia odoratissima
     rosewood, Ceylon

Ceylonese
USE Sri Lankan

CFC
USE chlorofluorocarbon

Chad Civilization
USE Sao Empire

*<Chad subfamily Afroasiatic language
groups>*
     FL.223

chafferns
USE chafing dishes

chafing dishes
     TH.60   (H,L,N)
HN   April 1993 descriptor added
ALT chafing dish
SN   Dishes supplied with a heat source
     (such as a fuel lamp or candle) used
     for cooking or keeping food warm.
     The term is sometimes applied to
     vessels containing charcoal or other
     fuel and upon which another con-
     tainer with food may be placed.
UF   chafferns
     dishes, chafing
RT   braziers (culinary equipment)
     dishes

Chagga
     FL.644   (L)
UF   Caga
     Wachaga

chahar bagh
     RM.9
HN   April 1993 descriptor moved
SN   Use   for   quadripartite   Islamic
     gardens.

chahar taqs
     RK.1079
ALT chahar taq
SN   Use for Zoroastrian· fire temples of
     the Sassanian period.
UF   char taqs
     tchahar taqs

chaifs
USE howell planes

Chaima
     FL.1647

chain
USE warp

chain balls
USE chain shot

chain bolts
     PJ.454
HN   April 1993 descriptor moved
ALT chain bolt
SN   Locks with a spring bolt at the top
     of the door that can be operated by
     pulling an attached chain. (MEANS)
UF   bolts, chain

chain bucket loaders
     TH.460
ALT chain bucket loader
SN   Mobile loaders that use a series of
     small buckets on a roller chain to el-
     evate excavated dirt or rock to the
     dumping point. (STEIN)
UF   bucket loaders, chain
     loaders, chain bucket

chain cascades
USE water chains

chain conveyors
     TH.911   (L)
ALT chain conveyor
UF   conveyors, chain

chain courses
     PJ.1947
HN   March 1993 descriptor moved
     April 1991 scope note changed
ALT chain course
SN   Masonry courses of headers fas-
     tened   together   continuously   by
     metal clamps. (RS)
UF   courses, chain

chain door fasteners
     PJ.455
HN   April 1993 descriptor moved
ALT chain door fastener
SN   Chains that can be secured by a
     slide bolt between a door stile and a
     door jamb to allow the door to be
     opened slightly while remaining se-
     curely fastened. (MEANS)
UF   door fasteners, chain
     fasteners, chain door

chain link fences
     RM.234
HN   April 1993 descriptor moved
ALT chain link fence
SN   Fences made of heavy steel wire fab-
     ric which is interwoven in such a
     way as to provide a continuous
     mesh without ties or knots, except at
     the ends. (DAC)
UF   fences, chain link

chain mail
USE mail

chain moldings
PJ.2083
HN April 1993 descriptor moved
ALT chain molding
SN Moldings carved with a motif resembling a chain. (DAC)
UF moldings, chain

chain-pipe vises
TH.1307
ALT chain-pipe vise
SN Portable vises used to hold pipes in the jaw by means of a chain. (DAC)
UF vises, chain-pipe

chain pipe wrenches
USE chain tongs

chain saws
TH.1571   (L,N)
ALT chain saw
SN Power-driven saws, usually hand-held, with a protruding arm that carries an endless chain into which the cutting teeth are set. (DAC)
UF saws, chain

chain shot
TK.251   (N)
SN Cannon shot consisting usually of two balls linked by a length of chain or wire, or sometimes of a single ball with a length of chain attached on opposite sides, used from the 17th to the 19th century to inflict damage on fortifications and most especially on the sails and rigging of ships.
UF balls, chain
chain balls
shot, chain

chain stores
RK.169   (L)
ALT chain store
UF stores, chain

chain tongs
TH.1315   (N)
SN Plumbers' tongs used for turning pipes, consisting of a lever arm which has sharp teeth that engage the pipe and a short adjustable chain which is wrapped around the pipe to hold it securely. (DAC)
UF chain pipe wrenches
pipe wrenches, chain
tongs, chain
wrenches, chain pipe

chain-track vehicles
USE tracklaying vehicles

chained bindings
PJ.3345   (L)
ALT chained binding
SN Bindings designed so that the book could be chained to a fixed feature such as a shelf or desk.
UF bindings, chained
books, chained
chained books

chained books
USE chained bindings

chaînes
PJ.1960
HN March 1993 descriptor moved
ALT chaîne
SN Type of wall decorations consisting of vertical bands of rusticated masonry which divide the surface into panels or bays; common in 17th-century French domestic architecture. (HAS)

chains
PE.39   (H,L,N)
HN November 1992 descriptor moved
November 1992 scope note added
November 1992 related term added
November 1992 alternate term added
November 1992 descriptor changed, was **chain**
ALT chain
SN Series of objects connected one after the other, usually rings passing through one another. (RHDEL2)
RT measuring chains

chains (measuring devices)
USE measuring chains

chains, engineers'
USE engineers' chains

chains, Gunter's
USE surveyors' chains

chains, measuring
USE measuring chains

chains, sash
USE sash chains

chains, surveyors'
USE surveyors' chains

chains, water
USE water chains

chair-back settees
TC.729
HN January 1993 descriptor moved
ALT chair-back settee
SN Small sofas formed of two or three combined chair backs, with arms, backs, and legs similar to those of the open-back chairs of the particular period. (FAIRB)
UF bar-back sofas
chairs, double
Darby and Joan settees
double chairs
settees, chair-back
settees, Darby and Joan
sofas, bar-back

chair backs
USE antimacassars
tidies

chair-beds
USE bed chairs

chair bits
USE spoon bits

chair-lift stations
USE ski-lift stations

chair lifts
RK.1023
HN July 1991 scope note changed
November 1990 descriptor moved
ALT chair lift
SN Use for a series of chairlike elements suspended from an endless cable designed for carrying skiers up a slope. (RHDEL2)
UF lifts, chair

chair lifts (ski lifts)
USE ski lifts

chair-makers
SEE chairmakers

chair rails
PJ.1978
HN March 1993 descriptor moved
ALT chair rail
SN Horizontal strips, usually of wood, affixed to walls at a height which prevents the backs of chairs from damaging the wall surface.
UF rails, chair

chair-tables
TC.476   (N)
HN May 1993 related term added
March 1993 lead-in term changed, was **monk's seats**
March 1993 lead-in term changed, was **seats, monk's**
March 1993 lead-in term changed, was **monk's chairs (chair-tables)**
March 1993 lead-in term changed, was **chairs, monk's (chair-tables)**
March 1993 lead-in term changed, was **monk's benches (chair-tables)**
March 1993 lead-in term changed, was **benches, monk's (chair-tables)**
January 1993 descriptor moved
ALT chair-table
SN Armchairs with large backs which are hinged so that they can be swung forward to rest on the arms, converting the piece into a table. Chairs of this type were made from the Middle Ages to the late 17th century in Europe and until the late 19th century in America. (DDA)
UF benches, monks'
chairs, monks'
monks' benches
monks' chairs
monks' seats
seats, monks'
table-chairs
RT tables (support furniture)

chair tidies
USE tidies

chair vises
TH.1650

ALT chair vise
UF   vises, chair

chair web saws
USE web saws

chairmakers
      HG.783   (A)
HN December 1992 alternate terms
      added
ALT chairmaker
      chairmaker's
      chairmakers'
UK   chair-makers
UKA chair-maker

chairs
      TC.449   (A,L,N,B,R)
HN May 1993 related terms added
      January 1993 descriptor moved
ALT chair
SN   Seats for one person with a back or
      a back and arms. Distinct from
      stools which have no back. (DDA)
RT   daybeds
      stools

chairs, abbots'
USE Glastonbury chairs

chairs, Adirondack
USE Adirondack chairs

chairs, angle
USE corner chairs

chairs, ax
USE ax chairs

chairs, back-stool
USE backstools

chairs, balloon-back
USE balloon-back chairs

chairs, balloon-back Windsor
USE balloon-back Windsor chairs

chairs, banister
USE banister-back chairs

chairs, banister-back
USE banister-back chairs

chairs, bar-back
USE bar-back chairs

chairs, barbers'
USE barbers' chairs
      corner chairs

chairs, Barcelona
USE Barcelona chairs

chairs, barrel
USE barrel chairs
      circular easy chairs

chairs, Barwa
USE Barwa chairs

chairs, basket
USE basket chairs

chairs, bath
USE bath chairs

chairs, beach
USE beach chairs

chairs, beanbag
USE beanbag chairs

chairs, bended-back
USE bended-back chairs

chairs, bent-wire
USE ice-cream parlor chairs

chairs, bergère
USE bergères

chairs, Bertoia
USE diamond chairs

chairs, birdcage Windsor
USE square-back Windsor chairs

chairs, board
USE board chairs

chairs, Boston
USE Boston chairs

chairs, Boston rocking
USE Boston rockers

chairs, Bouneparte
USE Trafalgar chairs

chairs, bow-back Windsor
USE bow-back Windsor chairs

chairs, Breuer
USE Cesca chairs
      Wassily chairs

chairs, Brewster
USE Brewster chairs

chairs, Brno
USE Brno chairs

chairs, burgomeister
USE corner chairs

chairs, butterfly
USE Hardoy chairs

<chairs by design>
      TC.646
HN January 1993 guide term moved

<chairs by form>
      TC.450
HN January 1993 guide term moved

<chairs by form: back form>
      TC.549
HN January 1993 guide term moved

<chairs by function>
      TC.590
HN January 1993 guide term moved

<chairs by location or context>
      TC.633
HN January 1993 guide term moved

<chairs by location or context: position>
      TC.636
HN January 1993 guide term moved

<chairs by location or context: rooms or
  spaces>
      TC.639
HN January 1993 guide term moved

chairs, cabinet commode
USE cabinet chairs

chairs, cabriole
USE cabriole chairs

chairs, café
USE ice-cream parlor chairs

chairs, camp
USE camp chairs

chairs, cantilevered
USE Cesca chairs

chairs, captains'
USE low-back Windsor chairs

chairs, carriage
USE carriage chairs

chairs, Carver
USE Carver chairs

chairs, centripetal spring
USE centripetal spring chairs

chairs, Cesca
USE Cesca chairs

chairs, chamber
USE commode chairs

chairs, Chiavari
USE Chiavari chairs

chairs, chicken-coop Windsor
USE square-back Windsor chairs

chairs, children's table
USE highchairs

chairs, Chinese
USE Chinese chairs

chairs, Chinese Chippendale
USE Chinese chairs

chairs, circular easy
USE circular easy chairs

chairs, cirricule
USE curricles (chairs)

chairs, cloath
USE cloath chairs

chairs, close-stool
USE commode chairs

chairs, club
USE club chairs

chairs, cockfight
USE reading chairs

chairs, comb-back Windsor
USE high-back Windsor chairs

chairs, commode
USE commode chairs

chairs, continuous arm
USE continuous-bow Windsor armchairs

chairs, continuous arm Windsor
USE continuous-bow Windsor armchairs

chairs, conversation
USE voyeuses

chairs, corner
USE corner chairs

chairs, coronation
USE thrones

chairs, counting-house
USE tall chairs

chairs, courting
USE love seats

chairs, Cromwellian
USE Cromwellian chairs

chairs, crook'd-back leather
USE Boston chairs

chairs, crooked-back
USE Boston chairs

chairs, curule
USE sellae curulis

chairs, cypher-back
USE cypher-back chairs

chairs, Dan Day
USE Mendlesham chairs

chairs, Dante
USE Dante chairs

chairs, Dantesca
USE Dante chairs

chairs, deck
USE deck chairs

chairs, dentists'
USE dentists' chairs

chairs, desk
USE desk chairs

chairs, devotional
USE prie-dieus

chairs, diamond
USE diamond chairs

chairs, dining
USE dining chairs

chairs, dining Windsor
USE bow-back Windsor chairs

chairs, directors'
USE directors' chairs

chairs, double
USE chair-back settees

chairs, double bow-back Windsor
USE double rod-back Windsor chairs

chairs, double rod-back Windsor
USE double rod-back Windsor chairs

chairs, draught
USE easy chairs

chairs, dressing
USE dressing chairs

chairs, easy
USE easy chairs

chairs, egg
USE egg chairs

chairs, egg easy
USE egg chairs

chairs, elastic
USE elastic chairs

chairs, elbow
USE elbow chairs

chairs, Elda 1005 upholstered
USE Elda 1005 upholstered chairs

chairs, exercising
USE chamber horses

chairs, fan-back
USE fan-back chairs

chairs, fan-back Windsor
USE fan-back Windsor chairs

chairs, farthingale
USE farthingale chairs

chairs, fiddle-back
USE fiddle-back chairs

chairs, fly
USE rout chairs

chairs, French
USE cabriole chairs
French elbow chairs

chairs, French elbow
USE French elbow chairs

chairs, fret-back
USE fret-back chairs

chairs, friars'
USE fraileros

chairs, garden
USE garden machines

chairs, Glastonbury
USE Glastonbury chairs

chairs, gondola
USE gondola chairs

chairs, gossiping
USE voyeuses

chairs, gouty
USE gouty chairs

chairs, grandfathers'
USE easy chairs

chairs, great
USE great chairs

chairs, Grecian rocking
USE Lincoln rockers

chairs, grotto
USE grotto chairs

chairs, gunstock Windsor
USE gunstock Windsor chairs

chairs, half-round
USE corner chairs

chairs, hall
USE hall chairs

chairs, hammock
USE hammock chairs

chairs, Hardoy
USE Hardoy chairs

chairs, harp-back
USE lyre-back chairs

chairs, harp banister-back
USE lyre-back chairs

chairs, harpsicord
USE music chairs

chairs, Harvard
USE great chairs

chairs, heart and shield back
USE heart-back chairs

chairs, heart-back
USE heart-back chairs

chairs, hearts and crown
USE hearts and crown chairs

chairs, high (tall chairs)
USE tall chairs

chairs, high-back Windsor
USE high-back Windsor chairs

chairs, hip-joint
USE X-chairs

chairs, Hitchcock
USE Hitchcock chairs

chairs, Hogarth
USE bended-back chairs

chairs, hoop-back Windsor
USE sack-back Windsor chairs

chairs, hunting
USE hunting chairs

chairs, ice-cream parlor
USE ice-cream parlor chairs

chairs, India
USE India chairs

chairs, invalids'
USE invalids' chairs

chairs, iron-wire
USE ice-cream parlor chairs

chairs, kitchen
USE kitchen chairs

chairs, klismos
USE klismoi

chairs, ladder-back
USE slat-back chairs

chairs, ladies'
USE ladies' chairs

chairs, lath-back Windsor
USE lath-back Windsor chairs

chairs, lattice-back
USE lattice-back chairs

chairs, leather (Boston chairs)
USE Boston chairs

chairs, leather-upholstered (Boston chairs)
USE Boston chairs

chairs, leather-upholstered (Cromwellian chairs)
USE Cromwellian chairs

chairs, library (reading chairs)
USE reading chairs

chairs, Lincoln rocking
USE Lincoln rockers

chairs, lolling
USE lolling chairs

chairs, loop-back Windsor
USE sack-back Windsor chairs

chairs, lounge
USE chaises longues

chairs, low back (backstools)
USE backstools

chairs, low-back Windsor
USE low-back Windsor chairs

chairs, lug
USE easy chairs

chairs, lunette-back
USE lunette-back chairs

chairs, lyre-back
USE lyre-back chairs

chairs, marquise
USE marquises

chairs, Martha Washington
USE lolling chairs

chairs, Mendlesham
USE Mendlesham chairs

chairs, Mendlesham Windsor
USE Mendlesham chairs

chairs, monks'
USE chair-tables
     fraileros

chairs, Morris
USE Morris chairs

chairs, MR
USE MR chairs

chairs, music
USE music chairs

chairs, necessary
USE commode chairs

chairs, necessity
USE commode chairs

chairs, Nelson's
USE Trafalgar chairs

chairs, nursing
USE nursing chairs

chairs, occasional
USE side chairs

chairs, office
USE office chairs

chairs, open-arm
USE elbow chairs

chairs, oval-back
USE oval-back chairs

chairs, oval-back Windsor
USE bow-back Windsor chairs

chairs, pages'
USE porters' chairs

chairs, panel-back
USE wainscot chairs

chairs, parlor
USE parlor chairs

chairs, pattern
USE pattern chairs

chairs, pedestal
USE pedestal chairs

chairs, pew
USE pew chairs

chairs, piano
USE music chairs

chairs, pillow back Windsor
USE high-back Windsor chairs

chairs, plank
USE board chairs

chairs, platform rocking
USE platform rockers

chairs, Plia folding
USE Plia folding chairs

chairs, pompador
USE ladies' chairs

chairs, porters'
USE porters' chairs

chairs, preaching
USE preaching chairs

chairs, press-back
USE press-back chairs

chairs, pretzel-back
USE pretzel-back chairs

chairs, pulpit
USE preaching chairs

chairs, reading
USE reading chairs

chairs, reception
USE reception chairs

chairs, reclining
USE reclining chairs

chairs, revolving
USE swivel chairs

chairs, ribbon-back
USE ribbon-back chairs

chairs, riding
USE chamber horses

chairs, rocking
USE rocking chairs

chairs, rod-back Windsor
USE square-back Windsor chairs

chairs, roll-top Windsor
USE roll-top Windsor chairs

chairs, round
USE corner chairs

chairs, round-top Windsor
USE sack-back Windsor chairs

chairs, roundabout
USE corner chairs

chairs, rout
USE rout chairs

chairs, S
USE S chairs

chairs, sack-back Windsor
USE sack-back Windsor chairs

chairs, saddle cheek
USE easy chairs

chairs, safari
USE directors' chairs

chairs, Savonarola
USE Savonarola chairs

chairs, Savonarola cross
USE Savonarola chairs

chairs, scissors
USE X-chairs

chairs, secretaries'
USE typewriter chairs

chairs, sedan
USE sedan chairs

chairs, shaving
USE corner chairs

chairs, sheaf-back
USE sheaf-back chairs

chairs, shell
USE diamond chairs

chairs, shield-back
USE shield-back chairs

chairs, shop
USE tall chairs

chairs, side
USE side chairs

chairs, single
USE side chairs

chairs, single bow Windsor
USE single rod-back Windsor chairs

chairs, single rod-back Windsor
USE single rod-back Windsor chairs

chairs, six-back
USE slat-back chairs

chairs, slat-back
USE slat-back chairs

chairs, slat-back Windsor
USE slat-back Windsor chairs

chairs, sleeping
USE sleeping chairs

chairs, Sleepy Hollow
USE Sleepy Hollow chairs

chairs, sling
USE sling chairs

chairs, slipper
USE slipper chairs

chairs, smoking
USE smoking chairs

chairs, soda
USE ice-cream parlor chairs

chairs, soda fountain
USE ice-cream parlor chairs

chairs, Spanish back
USE square-back chairs

chairs, spindle-back
USE spindle-back chairs

chairs, splat-back Windsor
USE splat-back Windsor chairs

chairs, spoon-back
USE spoon-back chairs

chairs, square-back
USE square-back chairs

chairs, square-back Windsor
USE square-back Windsor chairs

chairs, square easy
USE square easy chairs

chairs, stackable
USE stacking chairs

chairs, stacking
USE stacking chairs

chairs, state
USE state chairs

chairs, steamer
USE deck chairs

chairs, stenographers'
USE typewriter chairs

chairs, step
USE step chairs

chairs, step-ladder
USE step chairs

chairs, stick
USE sedan chairs

chairs, stick-back
USE spindle-back chairs

chairs, straight-back easy
USE square easy chairs

chairs, strapple
USE smoking chairs

chairs, student
USE student chairs

chairs, swan
USE swan chairs

chairs, swan easy
USE swan chairs

chairs, swept-leg
USE Trafalgar chairs

chairs, swing rocking
USE platform rockers

chairs, swivel
USE swivel chairs

chairs, tablet
USE tablet-arm chairs

chairs, tablet-arm
USE tablet-arm chairs

chairs, tablet top
USE Trafalgar chairs

chairs, tablet-top Windsor
USE tablet-top Windsor chairs

chairs, tall
USE tall chairs

chairs, three-seated
USE indiscrets

chairs, touring
USE touring chairs

chairs, Trafalgar
USE Trafalgar chairs

chairs, trellis-back
USE lattice-back chairs

chairs, tub
USE barrel chairs
circular easy chairs

chairs, tub-back easy
USE circular easy chairs

chairs, turkey work (Cromwellian chairs)
USE Cromwellian chairs

chairs, Turkish
USE Turkish chairs

chairs, Turkish frame
USE Turkish chairs

chairs, turned three-square great
USE great chairs

chairs, typewriter
USE typewriter chairs

chairs, urn back
USE shield-back chairs

chairs, vase back
USE shield-back chairs

chairs, vesper
USE prie-dieus

chairs, wainscot
USE wainscot chairs

chairs, Wassily
USE Wassily chairs

chairs, Waterloo
USE Trafalgar chairs

chairs, Wellington
USE Trafalgar chairs

chairs, Westport
USE Westport chairs

chairs, wheatsheaf-back
USE sheaf-back chairs

chairs, wheel-back
USE wheel-back chairs

chairs, window
USE window chairs

chairs, Windsor
USE Windsor chairs

chairs, Windsor rocking
USE Windsor rocking chairs

chairs, Windsor rod-back
USE square-back Windsor chairs

chairs, wing
USE easy chairs

chairs, wing-back
USE easy chairs

chairs, womb
USE womb chairs

chairs, writing
USE corner chairs

chairs, writing-arm Windsor
USE writing-arm Windsor chairs

chairs, X-shaped
USE X-chairs

chaise houses
USE carriage houses

chaises
TX.188 (N)
ALT chaise
SN Use for light, open, two-wheeled carriages drawn by a single horse, for one or two passengers, and with

or without foldable hoods; popular in England and the United States during the 18th and early 19th centuries.
UF shays

chaises à bras
USE armchairs

chaises à dame
USE chauffeuses

chaises à demoiselle
USE backstools
chauffeuses

chaises à femme
USE chauffeuses

chaises à la d'artois
TC.570
HN January 1993 descriptor moved
ALT chaise à la d'artois
SN French chairs with oval or medallion-shaped backs, the frames being carved in the center of the top with a ribbon bow. (WATSON)

chaises à la dauphine
USE perroquets

chaises à la reine
TC.562
HN May 1993 related term added
January 1993 descriptor moved
ALT chaise à la reine
SN Upholstered chairs with flat backs; distinct from those with concave backs called **chaises en cabriolet.**
UF sièges à la reine
RT chaises en cabriolet

chaises à médaillon
TC.571
HN January 1993 descriptor moved
ALT chaise à médaillon

chaises à porteur
USE sedan chairs

chaises à vertugadin
USE backstools
chauffeuses

chaises caquetoires
USE voyeuses

chaises chauffeuses
USE chauffeuses

chaises curules
USE sellae curulis

chaises de table
USE fauteuils de bureau

chaises du four
USE chauffeuses

chaises en cabriolet
TC.556
HN May 1993 related term added
January 1993 descriptor moved
ALT chaise en cabriolet
SN Upholstered chairs with slightly

concave backs to fit the contours of the human body; distinct from those with flat backs called **chaises à la reine.**
RT chaises à la reine

chaises en voyeuse
USE voyeuses

chaises longues
TC.477   (N)
HN May 1993 related term added
January 1993 descriptor moved
ALT chaise longue
SN Chairs, often upholstered, having a full-length leg rest and usually arms, designed for lounging. For similar chairs used outdoors, use **deck chairs.**
UF chairs, lounge
dormeuses (chaises longues)
lounge chairs
loungers
RT deck chairs

chaises percées
USE commode chairs

chaises, post
USE post chaises

chaitya caves
USE chaityas

chaitya halls
USE chaityas

chaityas
RK.1084
ALT chaitya
SN Use for Buddhist rock-cut shrines or sanctuaries.
UF caves, chaitya
chaitya caves
chaitya halls

Chaka
USE Saka

chalcedony
MT.577   (R)
HN April 1992 descriptor moved
February 1992 scope note changed
February 1992 related terms added
SN A cryptocrystalline variety of quartz, it is usually pale blue or gray. (AGI)
RT chert
gemstone

Chalcidian
FL.2708

chalcography
USE copper engraving
engraving (printing process)

Chalcolithic
FL.19   (L)
UF Copper Age
Cuprolithic

Chalcolithic, Early
USE Early Chalcolithic

Chalcolithic, Late
USE Late Chalcolithic

Chalcolithic, Middle
USE Middle Chalcolithic

chalcopyrite
MT.524   (L)
HN February 1992 descriptor added
SN A bright brass-yellow mineral, it constitutes the most important ore of copper. (AGI)
UF copper pyrite
pyrite, copper

Chaldean
FL.3071

chalets
RK.231   (A,N)
ALT chalet
SN Use both for Swiss herdsmen's houses, usually of wood with exposed structural members and overhanging upper floors, and for any house built in the Swiss style.

chalice capitals
HN November 1990 descriptor deleted

chalice covers
USE palls (chalice covers)

Chalice Style
FL.2696

chalice veils
TC.184   (N)
ALT chalice veil
SN Square textile coverings used to cover both chalice and paten before and after communion. For stiff squares covering just the top of the chalice, use **palls (chalice covers).**
UF veils, chalice
RT palls (chalice covers)

chalices
TQ.156   (H,L,N,R)
ALT chalice
SN Ecclesiastical drinking vessels for eucharistic wine having a stem, often with a central knop, and a foot; often made of precious metals and usually accompanied by a paten. Prefer **communion cups** when referring to similar but generally less ornate ecclesiastical drinking vessels used in the Protestant Church during or after the Reformation.
RT communion cups
drinking vessels
patens

chalk
MT.47   (L,N,B)
HN December 1992 descriptor moved
May 1992 related term added
November 1990 lead-in term deleted, was **lime white**
November 1990 lead-in term deleted, was **English white**
SN A fine-grained limestone, or soft,

earthy form of calcium carbonate; used chiefly in putty, crayons, paint, rubber products, linoleum, and as a pigment and abrasive. (MH12)
UF chalk, natural
natural chalk
RT <calcium carbonate white pigment>

chalk, black
USE black chalk

chalk engraving
USE crayon manner

chalk, fabricated
USE fabricated chalk

chalk, French
USE French chalk

chalk holders
USE portcrayons

chalk, Italian
USE black chalk

chalk manner
USE crayon manner

chalk method
USE crayon manner

chalk, natural
USE chalk

chalk, natural red
USE red chalk

chalk, precipitated
USE precipitated chalk

chalk, red
USE red chalk

chalk sticks
TH.654
ALT chalk stick
UF sticks, chalk

chalkware
PE.123 (L,R)
HN January 1992 descriptor added
SN Figures and ornaments made in plaster of Paris to imitate pottery and porcelain, popular in the United States in the 18th and 19th centuries.

challah cloths
USE hallah covers

chalmeyes
USE shawms

Chalukyan
FL.2283 (L)
UF Calukya

chalumeaux
TT.151 (L,N)
ALT chalumeau
SN Wood clarinets having a foot-joint like that of a recorder, seven fingerholes, one thumbhole, and two diametrically opposed keys.

chalwar
USE shalwar

Cham (Bamileke)
FL.182
UF Bacham
Baham

Cham (Vietnamese)
FL.2522 (L)
UF Champa

<Cham periods>
FL.2523

Chamacoco
FL.1657 (L)

Chamaecyparis nootkatensis
USE yellow cypress

Chamaecyparis thyoides
USE white cypress

Chamba (Nigerian)
FL.202

Chamba (Pahari)
FL.2355

Chamber
USE Fancy

chamber candlesticks
USE chambersticks

chamber chairs
USE commode chairs

chamber horses
TC.598
HN January 1993 descriptor moved
ALT chamber horse
SN Devices which allow the motions of horse exercise to be simulated indoors, consisting of springs encased in a concertinalike leather envelope, framed in mahogany. (GLOAG)
UF chairs, exercising
chairs, riding
exercising chairs
exercising machines, horse
horse exercising machines
horses, chamber
machines, horse exercising
riding chairs

chamber kilns
TH.498 (L)
ALT chamber kiln
SN Kilns consisting of a series of adjacent chambers in a ring or oval through which fire moves, taking several days to make a circuit. (MHDSTT)
UF kilns, chamber

chamber lamps
TC.1362
ALT chamber lamp
SN Small metal or glass lamps frequently with a saucer base meant for use in the bedchamber.
UF bedchamber lamps

lamps, bedchamber
lamps, chamber

chamber lye
USE urine

chamber organs
TT.115
ALT chamber organ
SN Small organs housed in a compact, furniture-quality wood cabinet, usually with one manual and no pedal keys, the wind being pumped into the pipes by the player's foot. Popular for domestic use in Europe and North America from the 17th to the 19th century, they were often made to resemble other pieces of furniture, such as tables, bureaus, and desks.
UF cabinet organs
organs, cabinet
organs, chamber

chamber pails
USE chamber pots

chamber pots
TQ.175 (H,L,N,R)
ALT chamber pot
SN Portable containers for elimination used in bedrooms. Usually in cylindrical form with shaped convex sides, a flat bottom, and a single loop or scroll handle; some have covers.
UF chamber pails
jordans
pails, chamber
pots, chamber
RT commode chairs
night tables
pots
urinals (containers)

chamber-pots, oval
USE bourdalous

chamber tables
TC.1140
HN May 1993 related term added
January 1993 descriptor moved
ALT chamber table
SN Contemporary name for plain dressing or writing tables in the 18th century. (GILBR2)
UF tables, chamber
RT writing tables

chamber tombs
RK.451 (H)
ALT chamber tomb
SN Use for communal burial places, cut into rock or hillslopes or constructed of masonry, whose chamber may or may not have an entry passage, usually covered by a mound.
UF tombs, chamber

chamber tombs, megalithic
USE megalithic chamber tombs

chamberlains
HG.109
HN January 1993 descriptor added
ALT chamberlain
    chamberlain's
    chamberlains'
SN Originally, high stewards of a sovereign or member of the nobility, having particular charge of the sovereign's or noble's private living quarters. Now used also as the title of officials serving as treasurers for public corporations or offices.

chambers
PJ.1326
HN March 1993 descriptor moved
ALT chamber
SN Use for the recessed part of an upper stage in an Elizabethan theater.
UF inner stages
    stages, inner

chambers (bedrooms)
USE bedrooms

chambers (rooms)
USE rooms

chambers, anechoic
USE anechoic rooms

chambers, aquatint
USE dust boxes

chambers, burial
USE burial chambers

chambers, drawing
USE drawing rooms

chambers of commerce
USE boards of trade

chambers, plenum
USE plenum chambers

chambers, presence
USE presence chambers

chambers sets
USE toilet sets (washing sets)

chambers, withdrawing
USE drawing rooms

chambersticks
TC.1242
ALT chamberstick
SN Candleholders with a single candle socket set on a flat saucer or traylike base. For candleholders with a single candle socket mounted on a support with a widened base or foot use **candlesticks.** (LDPC)
UF bedchamber candlesticks
    candleholders, socket
    candlesticks, bedchamber
    candlesticks, chamber
    candlesticks, hand
    candlesticks, sheet hand
    chamber candlesticks
    hand candlesticks
    hand candlesticks, sheet

    sheet hand candlesticks
    socket candleholders
RT candlesticks

Chambri
FL.3785 (L)
UF Tchambuli

chamfer knives
TH.1479 (N)
ALT chamfer knife
SN Drawknives used to cut an oblique surface.
UF guides, chamfer
    knives, chamfer

chamfer spokeshaves
TH.1614
ALT chamfer spokeshave
SN Spokeshaves which cut a chamfer on the edge of a piece of wood.
UF spokeshaves, chamfer

chamfering
KT.313
ALT chamfered
SN In the context of furniture, refers to cutting or shaping the edge or end of a material to form an angle that is not a right angle. In other contexts, prefer **beveling.**

chamfers, swelled
USE wave moldings

chammy
USE chamois

chamois
MT.2589 (L)
HN March 1992 scope note added
    March 1992 lead-in terms added
    February 1992 descriptor moved
SN Soft, pliable tawed or treated skin originally made from the skins of the chamois, Antilopa rupicapra, a small deer; now made from the skins of lamb, sheep, goat, or from the thin portion of split hides.
UF chammy
    chamoised leather
    leather, chamoised
    leather, wash
    shammy
    shamoy
    wash leather

chamois (color)
USE grayish yellow
    moderate yellow

chamois (yellow ocher)
USE yellow ocher

chamoised leather
USE chamois

chamoising
USE oil tanning

Champa
USE Cham (Vietnamese)

champagne glasses
TQ.449 (N)
ALT champagne glass
SN Glasses intended for drinking champagne, often having a shallow saucer-shaped bowl of 4- to 6-ounce capacity, which rests on a stemmed foot. For tall and narrow glasses used for drinking champagne, use **flute glasses.**
UF champagnes
    coupes (champagne glasses)
    glasses, champagne
RT flute glasses

champagne glasses, hollow stem
USE hollow stem champagnes

champagnes
USE champagne glasses

champlevé
KT.95 (L,R)
HN March 1993 descriptor moved
SN Enameling that is accomplished by carving away troughs or cells in metal, leaving a raised line that forms the outline of the design. The enamel is laid in the cells, fired, and then filed and polished. (QCKAIE)

Chamula
FL.1559 (L)

Ch'an
BM.455 (L)
UF Buddhism, Ch'an
    Chan
    Ch'an Buddhism
    Meditation, School of
    School of Meditation

Chan
USE Ch'an

Ch'an Buddhism
USE Ch'an

Chan-Kuo
USE Warring States

Chaná
FL.1706 (L)

Chanak Kalé
USE Çanakkale

Chanak kale rugs
USE Çanakkale + rugs

Chanak Kalessi
USE Çanakkale

Chanakkale
USE Çanakkale

chanakkale rugs
USE Çanakkale + rugs

chanakkales
USE Çanakkale + rugs

Chanapata
FL.1160

Chancay
　　FL.1181　　　　　　　　　　　(L)

chance, games of
USE　games of chance

chancel arches
　　PJ.1633
HN　March 1993 descriptor moved
ALT　chancel arch
SN　Use for the arch marking the separation of chancel from nave.
UF　arches, chancel
　　arches, triumphal
　　triumphal arches (church components)

chancel screens
　　PJ.2538　　　　　　　　　　　(R)
HN　March 1993 descriptor moved
　　September 1991 scope note changed
　　November 1990 lead-in term deleted, was **chancel enclosures**
ALT　chancel screen
SN　Use for partitions in Christian churches separating the chancel from the body of the church, particularly when the chancel does not also include a choir. Use **choir screens** for the screens around the choir when the choristers are seated in the chancel area. For screens separating the sanctuary from the nave in Orthodox Eastern churches, use **iconostases.**
UF　screens, chancel

chancelleries
USE　embassy buildings

chancellors
　　HG.138
HN　January 1993 descriptor added
ALT　chancellor
　　chancellor's
　　chancellors'
SN　Use for officials carrying this title serving in various administrative, judical, or secretarial capacities in various contexts, such as noble and royal houses, governments, the judiciary, churches, and universities.

chancels
　　PJ.1249　　　　　　　　　　　(A,R)
HN　March 1993 descriptor moved
　　August 1991 scope note changed
ALT　chancel
SN　Use for spaces in Christian churches containing the high altar and reserved for the use of the clergy. Includes the choir when present. Use **choirs** for the spaces in Christian churches, generally between the altar area and the nave, reserved for choristers.

chanceries
USE　embassy buildings

chancery documents
　　VW.745

HN　November 1992 descriptor moved
ALT　chancery document
UF　documents, chancery

chancery hand, Merovingian
USE　Merovingian chancery script

chancery script, Merovingian
USE　Merovingian chancery script

chandeliers
　　TC.1253　　　　　　　　　　　(L,N,B,R)
ALT　chandelier
SN　Lighting devices designed to hang from the roof or ceiling having two or more branches, usually upcurving, holding candles, burners, or lamps; often ornamental.
RT　hanging lamps

chandeliers, candle
USE　candle branches

chandeliers, center-light
USE　center-light chandeliers

chandeliers, center-slide
USE　center-slide chandeliers

chandeliers, rod-hung
USE　rod-hung chandeliers

chandeliers, rod-supported
USE　rod-hung chandeliers

chandeliers, rod-suspended
USE　rod-hung chandeliers

chandeliers, slide
USE　center-slide chandeliers

Chandella
USE　Candella

chandleries
　　PJ.1132
HN　March 1993 descriptor moved
ALT　chandlery
SN　Storage places for candles and other lighting devices.
UF　chandries

chandleries (containers)
USE　candle boxes

chandries
USE　chandleries

Chané
　　FL.1658　　　　　　　　　　　(L)

chanfrons
USE　shaffrons

chanfrons, half
USE　half shaffrons

change keys
USE　master keys

change order drawings
HN　April 1993 descriptor split, use
　　change order (ALT of **change orders**) + **drawings**

change orders
　　VW.539

HN　November 1992 descriptor moved
ALT　change order
SN　Written and signed legal documents authorizing a change from the original plans, specifications, or other contract documents, or authorizing a change in the cost of the project. (MEANS)
UF　orders, change
　　orders, variation
　　variation orders

change, population
USE　population change

change purses
USE　coin purses

changes (key components)
　　PJ.614
HN　March 1993 descriptor moved
ALT　change (key component)

changing rooms
USE　dressing rooms

channel bars
USE　channels (rolled sections)

channel beams
USE　channels (rolled sections)

channel inserts
　　PJ.138
HN　April 1993 descriptor moved
ALT　channel insert
UF　continuous inserts
　　inserts, channel
　　inserts, continuous

channel irons
USE　channels (rolled sections)

channel lamps, wick
USE　wick channel lamps

channel lights
　　RM.221
HN　April 1993 descriptor moved
　　May 1990 descriptor added
ALT　channel light
SN　Aeronautical ground lights along the sides of a channel of a water airport. (IESREF)
UF　lights, channel

channel moldings
　　PJ.2094
ALT　channel molding
SN　Concave moldings that are similar to scotias but less deep; used especially with reference to frames.
UF　moldings, channel

channel saddle hangers
　　PJ.107
HN　April 1993 descriptor moved
ALT　channel saddle hanger
UF　hangers, channel saddle
　　saddle hangers, channel

Channel School
USE　Channel Style

channel sections
 USE   channels (rolled sections)

Channel Style
  FL.3223
 UF   Channel School

channeled (pottery style)
  FL.144
 HN   April 1993 descriptor added
 UK   channelled (pottery style)

channeled ware
 HN   April 1993 descriptor split, use channeled (pottery style) + ware

channelled (pottery style)
 SEE   channeled (pottery style)

channels (rolled sections)
  PJ.2039
 HN   March 1993 descriptor moved
  November 1990 scope note changed
  November 1990 lead-in term added
  November 1990 descriptor changed, was **channel beams**
  November 1990 alternate term changed, was **channel beam**
 ALT   channel (rolled section)
 SN   Use for metal members having a C- or U-shaped section.
 UF   bars, channel
  beams, channel
  channel bars
  channel beams
  channel irons
  channel sections
  irons, channel
  sections, channel

channels (water body components)
  RD.124   (L)
 HN   September 1991 descriptor changed, was **channels**
  September 1991 alternate term changed, was **channel**
 ALT   channel (water body component)
 SN   Components of bodies of water characterized as being relatively long and narrow and axially located in relation to the waterway, such as used to designate the deepest part of streambeds where the main current runs, or stretches of sea between two land areas and linking two seas.

Channnukas
 USE   Hanukkah lamps

chanters
  PJ.3243
 ALT   chanter
 SN   Melody pipes on bigpipes; they may be of conical or cylindrical bore and be fitted with either a single or a double reed.
 RT   bagpipes

chantries
  PJ.1252   (A,L)
 HN   March 1993 descriptor moved
 ALT   chantry

 SN   Use for chapels, altars, or other parts of a church endowed for chanting of masses.
 UF   chantry chapels
  chapels, chantry

chantry chapels
 USE   chantries

chants
  VW.306   (L)
 HN   June 1992 descriptor added
 ALT   chant
 SN   Musical compositions characterized by single notes to which an indefinite number of syllables are intoned.

Chanukah
 USE   Hanukkah

Chanukah cards
 USE   Hanukkah cards

Chanukah lamps
 USE   Hanukkah lamps

chaparajos
 USE   chaps

chaparejos
 USE   chaps

chapbooks
  VW.952   (L,R)
 HN   November 1992 descriptor moved
  June 1992 scope note added
 ALT   chapbook
 SN   Small books or pamphlets, usually cheaply printed and containing such texts as popular tales, treatises, ballads, or nursery rhymes, formerly peddled by chapmen.

chapeaux bras
  TE.418
 ALT   chapeau bras
 SN   Flattened versions of the bicorne or tricorne adopted for court wear; intended to be carried under the arm and not worn on the head.
 UF   bras, chapeaux
 RT   bicornes
  hats
  tricornes

chapelières
 USE   bonnetières

chapels
  PJ.1250   (A,L,B,R)
 HN   March 1993 descriptor moved
 ALT   chapel
 SN   Includes both freestanding chapels and rooms or recesses serving as chapels in churches or other buildings.

chapels (kettle hats)
 USE   kettle hats

chapels, chantry
 USE   chantries

chapels, court
 USE   royal chapels

chapels de fer
 USE   kettle hats

chapels, domestic
 USE   private chapels

chapels, funeral
 USE   funeral chapels

chapels, lady
 USE   lady chapels

chapels, monumental
 USE   sepulchral chapels

chapels, mortuary
 USE   sepulchral chapels

chapels of ease
  RK.1045   (B)
 ALT   chapel of ease
 SN   Churches built within the bounds of a parish for the attendance of those who cannot reach the parish church conveniently. (DAC)

chapels, palace
 USE   royal chapels

chapels, private
 USE   private chapels

chapels royal
 USE   royal chapels

chapels, royal
 USE   royal chapels

chapels, sepulchral
 USE   sepulchral chapels

chaperons
  TE.563   (N)
 ALT   chaperon
 SN   Round, stuffed coverings for the head with wide streamers falling from the crown; worn in the 14th and 15th centuries.

chapiters
 USE   capitals

chaplains
  HG.397   (L)
 HN   February 1993 descriptor moved
  December 1992 alternate terms added
 ALT   chaplain
  chaplain's
  chaplains'
 SN   Christian clergy officially attached to the army or navy, to some public institution, or to a family or court. (W)

chaplets
  TE.564   (H)
 ALT   chaplet
 SN   Wreaths or garlands worn on the head, especially those of metal, often embellished with gems or pearls, common from the 14th to the 16th century.
 RT   wreaths (costume accessories)

chaplets (astragals)
USE astragals

chaplets (bead moldings)
USE bead moldings

chaps
TE.374 (N)
SN Leather leg coverings held together at the top by a belt or lacings, worn over trousers when horseback riding. (W)
UF chaparajos
chaparejos

chapter houses
RK.1127 (A,R)
HN April 1991 lead-in terms added
ALT chapter house
SN Designates assembly halls for the business meetings of religious or fraternal organizations.
UF chapter rooms
halls, synodal
houses, chapter
rooms, chapter
synodal halls

chapter rooms
USE chapter houses

chaptrels
HN April 1991 descriptor deleted

char taqs
USE chahar taqs

character dolls
TV.158
ALT character doll
SN Use for dolls made in the likeness of specific real people or human or humanoid fictional characters; use **character toys** for the broader category that includes these plus animal figures.
UF character-faced dolls
dolls, character
dolls, character-faced
RT character toys

character-faced dolls
USE character dolls

character toys
TV.151 (L)
ALT character toy
SN Figural toys made in the likeness of specific real persons or animals or human, humanoid, or animal fictional characters; use **character dolls** for the narrower category of figurines representing only specific real people or human or humanoid fictional characters.
UF toys, character
RT character dolls

charangos
TT.300
ALT charango
SN Small, fretted, plucked lutelike instruments of the Andes region of

South America, existing in many shapes and with differing numbers of strings; of the two main types, one is of wood and flat-backed, the other has a round back of armadillo shell.

Charbon Velours
USE Artigue process

charcoal
MT.2637 (L,R)
HN March 1992 descriptor moved

charcoal (color)
USE black
dark grayish blue
dark grayish brown
dark grayish purple
dark purplish gray

charcoal black
MT.2073
HN April 1992 descriptor moved
UF black, charcoal
black, vegetable
vegetable black

charcoal, compressed
USE charcoal sticks

charcoal gray
USE dark gray

charcoal grills
USE barbecue grills

charcoal paper
MT.1471
HN February 1992 descriptor moved
UF paper, charcoal

charcoal pencils
TH.683
ALT charcoal pencil
SN Pencils with lead of finely ground, highly compacted charcoal. Less messy, but not as versatile as charcoal sticks. (HAND)
UF pencils, charcoal

charcoal sticks
TH.655
HN December 1992 scope note changed
December 1992 lead-in terms added
ALT charcoal stick
SN Black crayons made of charred twigs of wood, usually willow or pieces of vine, or sticks of compressed charcoal.
UF charcoal, compressed
charcoal, vine
compressed charcoal
crayons, charcoal
sticks, charcoal
vine charcoal

charcoal, vine
USE charcoal sticks

charcoal, wood
USE wood charcoal

charets
SEE charettes

charettes
KM.70 (A)
HN March 1993 scope note changed
May 1991 alternate term added
ALT charette
UK charets
UKA charet
SN Periods of intense final effort made by architectural students to complete their solutions to a given architectural problem within an allotted time. (W)

charge plates
USE credit cards

charge, priming
USE priming powder

chargehands
USE foremen

chargers
TQ.380 (N)
ALT charger
SN Large platters, usually circular or oval, often earthenware or metal, used for serving meat. For other, circular or rectangular dishes, sometimes of wood, on which meat or other food is carved or served, use **trenchers**.
UF dishes, sideboard
shields (platters)
sideboard dishes
trays (platters)
RT trenchers

charges
USE fees
heraldic motifs

charges, depth
USE depth charges

charging
USE rolling up

Chariot sub-period
FL.71

chariots (ancient vehicles)
TX.117 (L,N)
ALT chariot (ancient vehicle)
SN Use for ancient Mesopotamian, Egyptian, Greek, and Roman animal-drawn, wheeled vehicles with a wide range of uses and forms, usually driven from the standing position and most often with two wheels; probably developed in Mesopotamia around the early 3rd millenium and could be pulled by up to ten animals.

chariots (carriages)
TX.165 (H,L,N,R)
ALT chariot (carriage)
SN Use for four-wheeled half-coaches lighter and less expensive than full coaches; popular luxury vehicles

from the mid-17th century until the development of broughams in the mid-19th century.

charitable institutions
USE   charities
       welfare buildings

charitable societies
      HN.82   (L)
HN   February 1993 descriptor moved
ALT charitable society
UF   societies, charitable

charities
      HN.118   (A,L,R)
ALT charity
SN   Organizations or institutions engaged in the free assistance of the poor, the suffering, or the distressed. (W)
UF   charitable institutions
       institutions, charitable

charkas
      TQ.397
ALT charka
SN   Russian cups for vodka, often with a horizontal handle flush with the rim.
UF   cups, vodka
       vodka cups
RT   <ceremonial vessels>

Charles X
USE   Restauration

Charlton white
USE   lithopone

charm bracelets
      TE.471   (L,N)
ALT charm bracelet
SN   Bracelets of metal links, to which are attached charms or trinkets, often acquired as souvenirs or mementos. (OED)
UF   bracelets, charm
RT   charms

charm quilts
      TC.222
ALT charm quilt
SN   Scrap quilts theoretically composed of 999 different printed cottons, no two of which could be alike. Always done in one-patch designs.
UF   beggars' quilts
       odd feller quilts
       odd fellows quilts
       quilts, beggars'
       quilts, charm
       quilts, odd feller
       quilts, odd fellows
RT   one-patch quilts

charms
      TE.439   (L,N)
ALT charm
SN   Small pendants worn for luck or decoration.
RT   charm bracelets
       lockets

charnel houses
USE   ossuaries (buildings)

Charrúa
      FL.1707   (L)

charter hands
USE   documentary scripts

charter rolls
      VW.746
HN   November 1992 descriptor moved
ALT charter roll
UF   rolls, charter

charter script, Merovingian
USE   Merovingian chancery script

charter scripts
USE   documentary scripts

charterhouses
      RG.209   (H,R)
ALT charterhouse
UF   certose
       chartreuses

charters
      VW.651   (H)
HN   November 1992 descriptor moved
ALT charter
SN   Documents, usually sealed, granting specific rights, setting forth aims and principles of a newly established entity, and often embodying formal agreements and authorizing special privileges or exemptions. (ICA)

chartography
USE   cartography

chartophylacia
      RK.656
ALT chartophylacium
SN   In Medieval ecclesiastical contexts, places for the safekeeping of records and other valuable documents.

chartreuse
USE   brilliant greenish yellow
       light greenish yellow
       moderate greenish yellow
       moderate yellow green
       strong greenish yellow
       strong yellow green

chartreuse, bright
USE   brilliant yellow green
       strong yellow green
       vivid yellow green

chartreuse green
USE   brilliant yellow green
       dark greenish yellow
       vivid yellow green

chartreuse, light
USE   brilliant yellow green
       light yellow green

chartreuse, pale
USE   light yellow green
       pale yellow green

chartreuse, vivid
USE   vivid yellow green

chartreuse yellow
USE   brilliant greenish yellow
       light greenish yellow
       moderate greenish yellow
       strong greenish yellow

chartreuse yellow, bright
USE   strong greenish yellow
       vivid greenish yellow

chartreuse yellow, light
USE   brilliant greenish yellow
       light greenish yellow
       moderate greenish yellow
       strong greenish yellow

chartreuses
USE   charterhouses

charts
      VW.141
HN   November 1992 descriptor moved
       July 1991 scope note added
ALT chart
SN   Arrangements of information in tabular form or in a graphic representation, as by curves, of a fluctuating variable.

charts (maps)
USE   maps

charts, admiralty
USE   marine charts

charts, aerial
USE   aeronautical charts

charts, aeronautical
USE   aeronautical charts

charts, astrological
USE   astrological charts

charts, astronautical
USE   astronautical charts

charts, astronomical
USE   astronomical charts

charts, bathymetric
USE   bathymetric maps

charts, celestial
USE   astronomical charts

charts, coastal
USE   coastal charts

charts, color
USE   color charts

charts, hydrographic
USE   nautical charts

charts, isogonic
USE   isogonic charts

charts, marine
USE   marine charts

charts, nautical
USE   nautical charts

charts, navigation
USE navigation charts

charts, organizational
USE organizational charts

charts, pilot
USE navigation charts

charts, plotting
USE plotting charts

charts, polar
USE polar charts

charts, portolan
USE portolanos

charts, portulan
USE portolanos

charts, progress
USE progress schedules

charts, river
USE river charts

charts, sea
USE marine charts

charts, solar
USE solar charts

charts, star
USE astronomical charts

charts, time zone
USE time zone maps

chartularies
USE cartularies

chasers
TH.1271
ALT chaser
SN Threading tools, many-toothed or with a single cut edge, shaped especially for cutting or finishing external or internal threads; usually used in conjunction with a lathe. (PUTNAM)

chases (type composition equipment)
TH.869 (N)
HN February 1993 descriptor added
ALT chase (type composition equipment)
SN Metal frame used to hold and secure matter for printing. (GDPTRM)

chases (wall spaces)
PJ.1151
HN March 1993 descriptor moved
March 1993 descriptor changed, was **chases**
March 1993 alternate term changed, was **chase**
ALT chase (wall space)
SN Use for continuous recesses or grooves built into walls to receive pipes, ducts, and other elements.
UF chases, pipe
chases, wall
pipe chases
wall chases

chases, pipe
USE chases (wall spaces)

chases, wall
USE chases (wall spaces)

chashitsu
USE teahouses

Chasidism
USE Hasidism

chasing
KT.1124 (L,R)
ALT chased
SN The process of adding detail or ornament on metal by indenting with a hammer and tools without a cutting edge. (W)
UF chasing, metal
metal chasing

chasing, flat
USE flat chasing

chasing, metal
USE chasing

Chasseen
FL.2576
UF Chassey

Chassey
USE Chasseen

chassis
PJ.3305
SN Use for the structural lower parts of motor vehicles that include the drive trains, exhaust systems, and steering, those components that make the vehicles move and that support the vehicle bodies.

chastity belts
TE.676 (L,N)
ALT chastity belt
SN Beltlike devices, worn by women especially in the Middle Ages, designed to prevent sexual intercourse. (RHDEL2)
UF belts, chastity

chasubles
TE.245 (H,N,R)
ALT chasuble
SN Sleeveless outer vestments in the form of a wide cloak or mantle that slips over the wearer's head and remains open at the sides; worn over the alb and stole by the celebrant at Mass.
UF planeta
RT cloaks
mantles

Château Style
FL.1753
UF Châteauesque

Châteauesque
USE Château Style

châteaus
USE châteaux

châteaux
RK.292 (A,L,B,R)
ALT château
SN Use for large country houses in France, which prior to the 16th century were usually fortified.
UF châteaus

chatelaine bags
TE.410
ALT chatelaine bag
SN Small bags suspended from a belt or waistband; popular from the mid- to the late 19th century.
UF bags, chatelaine

chatelaines
TE.684 (H,N)
ALT chatelaine
SN Ornamental chains, pins, or clasps usually worn at a woman's waist, to which trinkets, keys, purses, or other articles are attached.

châtelets
RK.405
ALT châtelet
SN Use for small French castles.

Châtelperronian
FL.2555

Chatino
FL.1527 (L)

chatônes
PJ.164
HN April 1993 descriptor moved
ALT chatône

Chaudor
USE Chodor

Chaudors
USE Chodor + rugs

chauffeuses
TC.480
HN January 1993 descriptor moved
ALT chauffeuse
SN Upholstered chairs with low seats and very high backs placed either beside or in front of the fire.
UF caquetoires (chauffeuses)
chaises à dame
chaises à demoiselle
chaises à femme
chaises à vertugadin
chaises chauffeuses
chaises du four
coins de feu
remailloteuses
sièges à langer
sièges de nourrice

chaufrons
USE shaffrons

chaufrons, half
USE half shaffrons

chausses
TE.339
ALT chausse

SN   Leg armor made of mail, worn from the 11th to the 14th century, consisting either of a strip of mail over the front of the leg laced at the back and under the sole, or a full stocking of mail laced around the leg and secured under the knee. (TARA)

UF   chausses of mail
hose of mail
mail, chausses of
mail, hose of

chausses of mail
USE   chausses

chauve-souris
USE   corsescas

Chavín horizon
FL.1156   (L)
HN   September 1991 descriptor moved

Chavín, Kotosh
USE   Kotosh Chavín

chawls
RK.359
HN   November 1992 descriptor added
ALT   chawl
SN   Use for tenement houses characteristic of Bombay and other industrial Indian cities; originally developed in the late 19th century to house migrant industrial workers.

chay
MT.2030
HN   April 1992 descriptor moved
SN   The root of an East Indian herb that yields a red dye. (W)

Che
USE   Zhe

check, damp
USE   damp course

check dams
RK.495
ALT   check dam
UF   dams, check

check pattern
USE   checker pattern

check planes
USE   rabbet planes

check-rooms
SEE   checkrooms

check stamping
KT.993
HN   February 1993 descriptor moved
March 1991 alternate term changed, was **check stamped**
ALT   check-stamped
UK   cheque-stamping
UKA   cheque-stamped
SN   The decorating of pottery with small, impressed squares, produced by a paddle or stamp. (JANA)
UF   cheque stamping

stamping, check
stamping, cheque

check stubs
VW.567
HN   November 1992 descriptor moved
ALT   check stub
UF   counterfoils
stubs, check

checkbooks
VW.568
HN   November 1992 descriptor moved
ALT   checkbook
SN   Books containing blank checks on a bank. (GAHLM)

checker (pattern)
USE   checker pattern

checker pattern
DG.143
HN   April 1993 lead-in terms added
ALT   checkered
UK   chequer-work
SN   A pattern of alternating squares or lozenges of contrasting color or texture. (THDAT)
UF   check pattern
checker (pattern)
checkered pattern
checkering
checkers (pattern)
checkerwork
checks (pattern)
chequer
chequer pattern
chequered pattern
chequering
chequerwork
pattern, check
pattern, checker
pattern, checkered
pattern, chequer

checker pieces
USE   checkers (game pieces)

checker tables
USE   chess tables

checkerboards
TV.20   (N)
ALT   checkerboard
SN   Gameboards marked off into 64 squares of alternating dark and light colors arranged eight vertically by eight horizontally; identical to chessboards.

checkered pattern
USE   checker pattern

checkering
USE   checker pattern

checkermen
USE   checkers (game pieces)

checkers (game pieces)
TV.6   (L,N)
ALT   checker (game piece)
UK   draughts
SN   Uniformly shaped wood, plastic, or

composition disks at least 1 inch in diameter and 1/2 inch thick, usually available in two colors and used as game pieces for such games as checkers and backgammon.
UF   checker pieces
checkermen
men, checker
pieces, checker

checkers (pattern)
USE   checker pattern

checkers (people)
HG.902
HN   January 1993 alternate terms added
ALT   checker (person)
checker's
checkers'
SN   Persons responsible for checking that a product or service meets required standards.

checkers, chinese
USE   chinese checkers

checkerwork
USE   checker pattern

checking floor hinges
PJ.413
HN   April 1993 descriptor moved
ALT   checking floor hinge
SN   Hinges containing a spring for closing a compression chamber in which the liquid escapes slowly, thus retarding the closing action to prevent slamming of the door. (STEIN)
UF   floor hinges, checking
hinges, checking floor

checklists
VW.181   (B)
HN   November 1992 descriptor moved
ALT   checklist
SN   Lists in which items can be compared, scheduled, verified, or identified. (AHD)

checkpoints
USE   border inspection stations

checkrooms
PJ.1133   (A)
HN   March 1993 descriptor moved
ALT   checkroom
UK   check-rooms
UKA   check-room
SN   Rooms at which baggage, parcels, clothing, or other personal articles are deposited with a clerk for temporary storage.

checks
VK.165   (L,N)
HN   March 1993 scope note changed
March 1993 lead-in term added
March 1993 related term added
July 1991 descriptor moved
ALT   check
SN   Written orders drawn on a bank or the Treasury of the United States to pay on demand a specified sum of

money to a named person, to his order, or to bearer, out of money on
deposit to the credit of the writer;
must be endorsed to be transferred.
(GAHLM)
UF bank checks
    checks, bank
RT commercial paper

checks (furniture backs)
USE wings (furniture components)

checks (pattern)
USE checker pattern

checks, back
USE door checks

checks, bank
USE checks

checks, certified
USE certified checks

checks, door
USE door checks

checks, travelers'
USE travelers' checks

chedi
USE stupas

cheekpieces
    PJ.3015
ALT cheekpiece
SN Side plates on many types of hel-
    mets that protect the cheeks and
    sometimes the ears or the chin.
    (TARA)
UF cheeks

cheeks
USE cheekpieces

cheeks, chimney
USE chimney cheeks

cheeks, door
USE doorjambs

cheeks, fireplace
USE fireplace cheeks

cheese baskets
    TQ.270   (N)
ALT cheese basket
SN Openwork, splint baskets used for
    making cheese.
UF baskets, cheese
    baskets, cheese curd
    baskets, curd
    cheese curd baskets
    cheese drainers
    cheese sieves
    curd baskets
    drainers, cheese
    sieves, cheese
    strainers, whey
    whey strainers
RT baskets

cheese boards
USE cheeseboards

cheese boxes
    TQ.577   (N)
ALT cheese box
SN Boxes or cases for holding cheese.
    (W)
UF boxes, cheese
RT boxes (containers)

cheese curd baskets
USE cheese baskets

cheese cutters
USE cheese slicer

cheese cutters, cider
USE cider cheese cutters

cheese dishes
    TQ.378   (N)
ALT cheese dish
SN Containers for storing and serving
    cheese, generally consisting of a flat
    dish with a dome cover. Use **cheese-
    boards** for boardlike trays use for
    serving cheese.
UF dishes, cheese
RT cheeseboards

cheese drainers
USE cheese baskets

cheese graters
    TH.120
HN April 1993 descriptor added
ALT cheese grater
SN Tools with numerous small teeth
    used for grating cheese.
UF graters, cheese

cheese knives (curd knives)
USE curd knives

cheese knives (food preparation tools)
    TH.105   (N)
HN April 1993 descriptor added
ALT cheese knife (food preparation tool)
SN Large spatulas used to break up the
    curd for cheesemaking. For knives
    with a curved blade used to cut
    cheese use **cheese knives (serving
    tools)**.
UF knives, cheese
RT cheese knives (serving utensils)
    curd knives

cheese knives (serving utensils)
    TH.263
HN April 1993 descriptor added
ALT cheese knive (serving utensil)
SN Knives with a curved blade used for
    cutting cheese. For large spatulas
    used to break up the curd for
    cheesemaking use **cheese knives
    (food preparation tools)**.
UF knives, cheese
RT cheese knives (food preparation
    tools)

cheese molds
    TH.205   (N)
HN April 1993 descriptor added
ALT cheese mold
SN Wood or metal containers in which

cheese curd is pressed to extract
moisture and to create distinctive
shapes.
UF molds, cheese

cheese planes
USE cheese slicers

cheese presses
    TH.225   (N,R)
HN April 1993 descriptor added
ALT cheese press
SN Devices for pressing cheese curds in
    a mold or hoop. (W)
UF presses, cheese

cheese scoops
    TH.168   (N)
HN April 1993 descriptor added
ALT cheese scoop
SN Pointed spoon-, spatula-, or shovel-
    like implements for scooping
    cheese.
UF scoops, cheese

cheese servers
    TH.277   (N)
HN April 1993 descriptor added
ALT cheese server
SN Term applied to a wide variety of
    special-purpose utensils designed to
    serve cheese.
UF servers, cheese

cheese sieves
USE cheese baskets

cheese slicers
    TH.106   (N)
HN April 1993 descriptor added
ALT cheese slicer
SN Tools having a stretched wire used
    as a cutting edge, or trowel-like tools
    with a central slitlike blade, used to
    slice cheese.
UF cheese cutters
    cheese planes
    cutters, cheese
    planes, cheese
    slicers, cheese

cheese toasters
    TH.79
HN April 1993 descriptor added
ALT cheese toaster
SN Utensils for toasting cheese on
    bread before an open fire. (HNSIL)
UF dishes, toasted-cheese
    toasted-cheese dishes
    toasters, cheese

cheese trays
USE cheeseboards

cheeseboards
    TH.246
HN April 1993 descriptor added
ALT cheeseboard
SN Boardlike trays for serving a variety
    of cheeses. Use **cheese dishes** for
    containers for storing or serving
    cheese, generally consisting of a flat
    dish with a dome cover.

UF boards, cheese
   cheese boards
   cheese trays
   trays, cheese
RT cheese dishes
   trays

chefs' knives
USE cooks' knives

Chehalis
   FL.1351 (L)

Chelaberds
USE sunburst Kazaks

Chelaberds, eagle
USE sunburst Kazaks

Chelaberds, Karabagh
USE sunburst Kazaks

Chellean
USE Abbevillian

Chelles-Acheul
   FL.50

Chemehuevi
   FL.1323 (L)

chemical analysis
   KT.161 (L)
HN August 1992 scope note added
SN Analysis of the chemical composition of a material.
UF analysis, chemical

chemical cleaning
HN October 1992 descriptor split, use chemical (ALT of chemistry) + cleaning

chemical closets
USE chemical toilets

chemical engineering
   KD.112 (L)
HN April 1993 related term added
SN Discipline in which chemistry, physics, and mathematics are combined with basic engineering principles to solve environmental, biomedical, societal, or technological problems arising in the application of chemistry. (PG)
UF engineering, chemical
RT chemical engineers

chemical engineers
   HG.858 (L)
HN April 1993 related term added
   December 1992 alternate terms added
ALT chemical engineer
   chemical engineer's
   chemical engineers'
UF engineers, chemical
RT chemical engineering

chemical inhibitor
USE inhibitor

chemical laboratories
HN April 1993 descriptor split, use

chemical (ALT of chemistry) + laboratories

chemical, petroleum
USE petrochemical

chemical pollution
   BM.346 (L)
UF pollution, chemical

chemical properties
   DC.10
HN October 1992 descriptor moved
   January 1991 alternate term added
ALT chemical property
UF properties, chemical

chemical pulp
   MT.2644
HN March 1992 descriptor moved
   July 1990 descriptor added
UF chemical wood pulp
   pulp, chemical
   wood pulp, chemical

chemical-resistant material
   MT.3084
HN April 1993 descriptor changed, was chemical-resistant materials
UF material, chemical-resistant

chemical-resistant paint
   MT.1968
UF paint, chemical-resistant

chemical toilets
   PJ.919
HN March 1993 descriptor moved
   June 1991 lead-in terms added
   June 1991 descriptor changed, was waterless toilets
   June 1991 alternate term changed, was waterless toilet
ALT chemical toilet
UF chemical closets
   closets, chemical
   toilets, chemical
   toilets, waterless
   waterless toilets

chemical wood pulp
USE chemical pulp

chemical wood pulp board
USE conservation board

chemiluminescence
   BM.807 (L)
HN November 1992 descriptor added
SN The emission of light by an atom or molecule that is in an excited state; also, the light so emitted. (W)

chemin de fer
   KQ.24

chemise dresses
   TE.18 (N)
ALT chemise dress
SN Dresses which hang straight from the shoulders, sometimes tapering slightly at hips.

UF chemise frocks
   chemise gowns
   chemises (dresses)
   dresses, chemise
   frocks
   frocks, chemise
   gowns, chemise

chemise frocks
USE chemise dresses

chemise gowns
USE chemise dresses

chemises (book coverings)
   PJ.3374
ALT chemise (book covering)
SN Use for loose covers for books, often of soft leather, having pockets into which the boards are inserted, used sometimes in the Middle Ages instead of binding. (LG)

chemises (dresses)
USE chemise dresses

chemises (underwear)
   TE.187 (N)
ALT chemise (underwear)
SN Loose-fitting, straight-hanging shirtlike underwear with or without sleeves usually extending to the hip or knee.
UF shifts
   smocks (chemises)

chemises, envelope
USE teddies

chemistry
   KD.167 (L,R)
HN February 1993 related term added
   December 1992 descriptor moved
   January 1991 alternate term added
ALT chemical
RT chemists

chemistry, biological
USE biochemistry

chemistry, inorganic
USE inorganic chemistry

chemistry, organic
USE organic chemistry

chemistry, physical
USE physical chemistry

chemists
   HG.531 (L)
HN February 1993 related term added
   December 1992 alternate terms added
ALT chemist
   chemist's
   chemists'
RT chemistry

chemists' shops
USE drugstores

Chen
   FL.1950 (L)
UF Ch'en

Ch'en
USE Chen

Chen-la
FL.2405

Chen-Yen
BM.456
UF Mi Tsung
True Word sect

cheneaux
PJ.2357
HN March 1993 descriptor moved
March 1993 related term added
ALT cheneau
SN Use for cresting occurring above the eaves or cornices of buildings, or for ornamental gutters.
RT cresting

Chenes
FL.1054
UF Los Chenes

cheng
USE zheng

Chêng chou
USE Zhengzhou

Chêng-chou
USE Zhengzhou

Ch'êng-hua
USE Chenghua

Chêng-tê
USE Zhengde

Chengchou
USE Zhengzhou

Chengchow
USE Zhengzhou

Chenghua
FL.1973
HN June 1990 lead-in term added
UF Ch'êng-hua

chenille
MT.1547
HN November 1992 descriptor added
SN Tufted yarn made by cross weaving a textile with warp ends in groups, then cutting it into narrow strips along the length between the groups.
UF chenille thread
chenille yarn
thread, chenille
yarn, chenille

chenille thread
USE chenille

chenille yarn
USE chenille

cheque-stamping
SEE check stamping

cheque stamping
SEE check stamping

chequer
USE checker pattern

chequer pattern
USE checker pattern

chequer-work
SEE checker pattern

chequerboard carpets
USE chessboard rugs

chequered pattern
SEE checker pattern

chequering
SEE checker pattern

chequerwork
SEE checker pattern

chermes
USE kermes

Cherokee
FL.1447   (L)

cherries
USE bits (tool components)

cherry
MT.2876   (L)
HN March 1992 descriptor moved

cherry, American
USE black cherry

cherry, American black
USE black cherry

cherry birch
USE sweet birch

cherry, black
USE black cherry

cherry, English
USE English cherry

cherry gum
MT.1052
HN April 1992 descriptor moved
UF cherry-tree gum
gum, cherry
gum, cherry-tree
gum, plum
plum gum

cherry pickers
TH.465
ALT cherry picker
SN Machines for lifting men or materials on a platform at the end of an extendable boom, usually mounted on a carrier with wheels to provide mobility. (DAC)

cherry pitters
USE cherry stoners

cherry, rum
USE black cherry

cherry, sour
USE sour cherry

cherry stoners
TH.164   (N)
HN April 1993 descriptor added
ALT cherry stoner
SN Mechanical pitters designed specifically to remove stones from cherries.
UF cherry pitters
pitters, cherry
stoners, cherry

cherry, sweet
USE sweet cherry

cherry-tree gum
USE cherry gum

cherry, wild
USE sweet cherry

chert
MT.878   (L,B)
HN April 1992 descriptor moved
March 1992 scope note changed
March 1992 lead-in term deleted, was **flint**
March 1992 related terms added
SN Fine-grained, dense sedimentary rock consisting of interlocking crystals of quartz approximately 30 microns in diameter. (DAC)
RT chalcedony
jasper

cherty limestone
USE siliceous limestone

Chesapeake Bay skiffs
USE crabbing skiffs

chess
KQ.17   (H,N)
RT chess sets

chess-board rugs
USE chessboard rugs

chess pieces
USE chessmen

chess sets
PC.61   (L)
ALT chess set
SN Use for the ensembles of chessboard and chessmen needed to play the game of chess.
UF sets, chess
RT chess

chess tables
TC.1153
HN January 1993 descriptor moved
ALT chess table
SN Tables with tops marked as a board for playing chess or checkers.
UF checker tables
tables, checker
tables, chess

chessboard carpets
USE chessboard rugs

chessboard plan
USE grid plan

chessboard rugs
TC.68
ALT chessboard rug
SN A name of convenience for a group of rugs that are similar in technique to Para-Mamluk carpets but that are not as finely woven and differ in color ranges. They have a characteristic field design of repeating rows of hexagonal or octagonal forms, often with a cartouche-rosette border.
UF carpets, chessboard
chequerboard carpets
chess-board rugs
chessboard carpets

chessboards
TV.21
ALT chessboard
SN Gameboards marked off into 64 squares of alternating dark and light colors arranged eight vertically by eight horizontally; identical to checkerboards.

chessmen
TV.7   (L)
ALT chessman
SN The pieces used in the game of chess. (RHDEL2)
UF chess pieces
pieces, chess

chest-benches
USE box settles

chest lifts
USE drawer pulls

chest pulls
USE drawer pulls

chesterfields (overcoats)
TE.152
ALT chesterfield (overcoat)
SN Single- or double-breasted fly-front coats usually of dark plain woolen fabric and often having a velvet collar. Of a type first worn by men in the 18th century and adapted for women in the 20th century.

chesterfields (sofas)
TC.742
HN March 1993 descriptor changed, was **chesterfields**
March 1993 alternate term changed, was **chesterfield**
January 1993 descriptor moved
ALT chesterfield (sofa)
SN Well-stuffed upholstered sofas with no wood showing. (DDA)

chestnut
MT.2718   (L)
HN March 1992 descriptor moved
UF Castanea

chestnut, American
USE American chestnut

chestnut, American horse
USE buckeye

chestnut, American sweet
USE American chestnut

chestnut bottles
TQ.49
ALT chestnut bottle
SN Free-blown bottles so named for their form which ranges from an often flattened globular shape to a completely round globelike vessel; a type known in both German and American glass.
UF bottles, chestnut
bottles, Ludlow
Ludlow bottles

chestnut brown
USE burnt umber

chestnut, Chinese
USE Chinese chestnut

chestnut, common horse
USE horse chestnut

chestnut, European
USE European chestnut

chestnut, horse
USE horse chestnut

chestnut, Indian rose
USE gangaw

chestnut, Italian
USE European chestnut

chestnut, Japanese
USE Japanese chestnut

chestnut oak
MT.2824   (L)
HN March 1992 descriptor moved
UF oak, chestnut

chestnut, Spanish
USE European chestnut

chestnut, sweet
USE European chestnut

chests
TC.863   (L,N,B,R)
HN February 1993 related terms added
January 1993 descriptor moved
ALT chest
SN Large boxes with hinged lids intended for the storage of textiles, clothing, and other articles. (GEWARD)
RT arks
caskets
press beds (deception beds)

chests, ark
USE arks

chests, armada
USE armada chests

chests, bachelors'
USE bachelors' chests

chests, Baltic
USE Nonsuch chests

chests, blanket
USE blanket chests

chests, board
USE board chests

chests, book tea
USE tea chests

chests, bridal
USE dower chests

chests, campaign
USE campaign chests

chests, chests upon
USE chests-on-chests

chests, clothes
USE clothes chests

chests, commode
USE commodes (chests of drawers)

chests, double
USE chests-on-chests

chests, dower
USE dower chests

chests, dressing
USE chests of drawers

chests, dug-out
USE dug-out chests

chests, French commode dressing
USE commode dressing tables

chests, half
USE low chests

chests, high
USE high chests of drawers

chests, hope
USE dower chests

chests, kneehole
USE kneehole desks

chests, lobby
USE lobby chests

chests, low
USE low chests

chests, marriage
USE dower chests

chests, medicine
USE medicine chests

chests, mule
USE mule chests

chests, Nonsuch
USE Nonsuch chests

chests of drawers
TC.890   (L,N)
HN May 1993 related terms added
January 1993 descriptor moved
ALT chest of drawers
SN Type of case furniture usually having four drawers but sometimes made with three, five, or more; generally supported on feet and some-

times resting directly on the floor. Use **commodes (chests of drawers)** for similar case pieces generally supported on short legs. Use **chests with drawers** for chests with one or more tiers of drawers below a deep storage space.
- UF bureaus (chests of drawers)
  chests, dressing
  drawers, chests of
  dressers (chests of drawers)
  dressing chests
- RT chests with drawers
  commodes (chests of drawers)

chests of drawers, double
USE chests-on-chests

chests of drawers, high
USE high chests of drawers

chests of drawers, kneehole
USE kneehole desks

chests of drawers, low
USE low chests

chests of drawers on frames
USE chests on frames

chests of drawers, tall
USE chiffoniers (chests of drawers)

chests-on-chests
TC.893 (L,N)
- HN January 1993 descriptor moved
- ALT chest-on-chest
- SN Two-part chests of drawers, one stacked on top of the other. (NEF)
- UF chests, chests upon
  chests, double
  chests of drawers, double
  chests upon chests
  double chests
  double chests of drawers
  drawers, double chests of

chests on frames
TC.894 (H,N)
- HN January 1993 descriptor moved
- ALT chest on frame
- SN Chests of drawers which sit on a framed stand. (NEF)
- UF chests of drawers on frames
  frames, chests of drawers on
  frames, chests on

chests over drawers
USE chests with drawers

chests, Rudd dressing
USE Rudd dressing chests

chests, sea
USE sea chests

chests, ship
USE sea chests

chests, six-board
USE board chests

chests, spice
USE spice chests

chests, sugar
USE sugar chests

chests, tea
USE tea chests

chests, tilting
USE tilting chests

chests upon chests
USE chests-on-chests

chests, wedding
USE dower chests

chests, wine
USE cellerets

chests with drawers
TC.870
- HN May 1993 related term added
  January 1993 descriptor moved
- ALT chest with drawers
- SN Chests with one or two tiers of drawers below a deep storage space; precursor to chests of drawers. Use **chests of drawers** for case furniture having two or more drawers but lacking a deep storage space. (NEF)
- UF chests over drawers
  drawers, chests with
- RT chests of drawers

cheval bureaus
USE cheval dressers

cheval dressers
TC.895
- HN January 1993 descriptor moved
- ALT cheval dresser
- SN Chests of drawers having a full-length mirror on one side and drawers on the other.
- UF bureaus, cheval
  cheval bureaus
  dressers, cheval

cheval dressing mirrors
USE cheval glasses

cheval fire screens
TC.435
- HN May 1993 related term added
  January 1993 descriptor moved
- ALT cheval fire screen
- SN Fire screens with a sliding panel set between two standards on four legs; distinguished from **pole screens** which have a tripod base and shaft which supports the fire screen.
- UF cheval screens
  fire screens, cheval
  fire screens, horse
  horse fire screens
  screens, cheval
  screens, cheval fire
  screens, horse fire
- RT pole screens

cheval glasses
TC.1473 (N)
- ALT cheval glass
- SN Use for full-length adjustable mir-

rors suspended on four-legged frames.
- UF cheval dressing mirrors
  cheval mirrors
  dressing glasses, horse
  dressing glasses, screen
  dressing mirrors, cheval
  glasses, cheval
  glasses, horse
  glasses, horse dressing
  glasses, screen dressing
  glasses, swing
  horse dressing glasses
  horse glasses
  large swingers (cheval glasses)
  mirrors, cheval
  mirrors, cheval dressing
  psychés
  screen dressing glasses
  swing glasses
  swingers (cheval glasses)
  swingers, large

cheval mirrors
USE cheval glasses

cheval screens
USE cheval fire screens

cheverets
TC.986
- HN January 1993 descriptor moved
  July 1992 lead-in term changed, was **lady's cabinets**
  July 1992 lead-in term changed, was **cabinets, lady's**
- ALT cheveret
- SN 18th-century English writing tables with oblong tops, shallow drawers below, and four slender tapering legs joined with a shelf; often made in satinwood. (DDA)
- UF cabinets, ladies'
  ladies' cabinets
  sheverets

cheves
USE howell planes

chevets
PJ.1260 (A)
- HN March 1993 descriptor moved
- ALT chevet
- SN Use for the combination of apse, ambulatory, and usually radial chapels of a church, especially French Gothic.

chevets (headboards)
USE headboards

chevets (night tables)
USE night tables

chevron twill
MT.1621
- HN November 1992 descriptor added
- SN Any form of twill in which the direction of the diagonal lines is reversed over groups of picks, or over groups of ends. (WRPWFT)
- UF chevron weave
  twill, chevron

twill, waved
waved twill
weave, chevron

chevron weave
USE chevron twill

chevroned bands
USE zigzags

chevrons
DG.36
ALT chevron
SN Simple geometric forms composed of Vs used singly, in a vertical series, or in a string to form a zigzag. (LDDO)
UF dancettes

Chewa
FL.543 (L)

Cheyenne
FL.1391 (L,R)

Cheyenne, Northern
USE Northern Cheyenne

Cheyenne, Southern
USE Southern Cheyenne

Ch'i, Northern
USE Northern Qi

Ch'i, Southern
USE Southern Qi

Chia-ch'ing
USE Jiaqing

Chia-ching
USE Jiajing

Chiadma
FL.706
HN April 1993 descriptor added

Chiadma rugs
USE Chiadma + carpets

Chian
FL.2695
UF Chiot
Naukratite

chian turpentine
USE turpentine

Chiang Mai
FL.2506
UF Chieng Mai
Jiang Hmai

chiaroscuro
KT.460 (H,L,R)
SN The technique of contrasting light and dark within a picture, especially one in which the forms are largely determined, not by sharp outlines, but by the meeting of lighter and darker areas.
UF clairobscur

chiaroscuro drawings
USE three-tone drawings

chiaroscuro woodcuts
VC.493
ALT chiaroscuro woodcut
SN Type of woodcut developed in the 16th century printed from two or more blocks to obtain differences in tone. (SAFF)
UF woodcuts, chiaroscuro

Chiavari chairs
TC.581
HN January 1993 descriptor moved
ALT Chiavari chair
UF chairs, Chiavari

Chibcha
FL.1675 (L)
UF Mosca
Muisca

Chicago Imagist
FL.3856 (R)
ALT Chicago Imagism
UF Imagist (Chicago Imagist)
Imagist, Chicago

Chicago School
FL.1754 (L,R)
HN June 1990 descriptor added

Chicago windows
PJ.2225
HN March 1993 descriptor moved
ALT Chicago window
SN Windows occupying the full width of a bay and divided into a large fixed sash flanked by a narrow movable sash on each side. (PDARC)
UF windows, Chicago

Chicanel
FL.1027

Chicano
USE Mexican American

Chichaoua
FL.707
HN April 1993 descriptor added

Chichaoua rugs
USE Chichaoua + carpets

Chichaouas
USE Chichaoua + carpets

Chichimec
FL.1515 (L)

Chickasaw
FL.1448 (L)

chicken-coop Windsor chairs
USE square-back Windsor chairs

chicken coops
USE chicken houses

chicken hatcheries
RK.92 (L)
ALT chicken hatchery
UF hatcheries, chicken

chicken houses
RK.91 (A,L,B)
ALT chicken house
UF chicken coops
chicken sheds
coops, chicken
hen houses
houses, chicken
houses, hen
sheds, chicken

chicken sheds
USE chicken houses

chicken-wire
SEE chicken wire

chicken wire
MT.509
HN April 1992 descriptor moved
UK chicken-wire
UF wire, chicken

chief blankets
TE.179
ALT chief blanket
SN Navajo shoulder blankets, woven wider than long and worn horizontally, characterized by a simple weft-banded design in weft-faced tabby weave, perhaps with tapestry-woven rectangles or diamonds. Not associated with rank.
UF blankets, chief
blankets, chief pattern
blankets, chiefs'
chief pattern blankets
chiefs' blankets
hanolchade
honal-chodi
honal-kladi
pattern blankets, chief
RT shoulder blankets

chief pattern blankets
USE chief blankets

chiefs' blankets
USE chief blankets

chieftains
HG.186
HN December 1992 alternate terms added
ALT chieftain
chieftain's
chieftains'

ch'ien
USE cash (Chinese money)

Ch'ien-lung
USE Qianlong

Chieng Mai
USE Chiang Mai

Chiengsen
USE Northern Thai

chiens-assis
PJ.1815
HN March 1993 descriptor moved
ALT chien-assis
SN Small, unglazed dormer windows used to provide light and ventilation

in an attic or space below a sloping roof; especially used in Medieval buildings. (HAS)

chiffonier beds
TC.776
HN May 1993 related term added
January 1993 descriptor moved
ALT chiffonier bed
SN Deception beds which fold into a dummy chiffonier.
UF beds, chiffonier
beds, chiffonier folding
chiffonier folding beds
folding beds, chiffonier
RT chiffoniers (chests of drawers)

chiffonier folding beds
USE chiffonier beds

chiffoniers (chests of drawers)
TC.896 (N)
HN May 1993 related term added
January 1993 descriptor moved
May 1991 descriptor changed, was **chiffoniers**
May 1991 alternate term changed, was **chiffonier**
ALT chiffonier (chest of drawers)
SN Tall chests of drawers with a mirror on top; common in late 19th and early 20th century.
UF chests of drawers, tall
drawers, tall chests of
tall chests of drawers
RT chiffonier beds

chiffonièrs (chiffonnières)
USE chiffonnières

chiffoniers (sideboards)
TC.1004
HN May 1993 related term added
January 1993 descriptor moved
ALT chiffonier (sideboard)
SN Anglicized name from French for a small cupboard with a top forming a sideboard. For small, low chests of drawers use **chiffonnières**.
RT chiffonnières

chiffonnières
TC.897 (N)
HN May 1993 related term added
January 1993 descriptor moved
ALT chiffonnière
SN 18th-century French term for a piece of furniture for the storage of stuffs (chiffons) and small articles of clothing. It is usually, but not necessarily, a small, low chest of drawers, narrower than the normal commode. For small cupboards with a top forming a sideboard, use **chiffoniers (sideboards)**.
UF chiffonièrs (chiffonnières)
RT chiffoniers (sideboards)

chiffonnières (tables)
USE tables en chiffonnière

chifforobes
TC.898

HN January 1993 descriptor moved
ALT chifforobe
SN Use for chests of drawers having a wardrobe cabinet built alongside.

chifforobes (wardrobes)
USE wardrobes (case furniture)

chika
MT.1354
HN April 1992 descriptor moved
SN Any kind of earth, especially clay, that is mixed with water to make mortar in Ethiopia. (OLIVER)

Chilcotin
FL.1243 (L)
UF Tsilkotin

child care centers
USE day care centers

childbirths
USE births

childhood
BM.575 (L)
HN February 1991 descriptor added
SN The earliest developmental stage of a living being.

childhood, early
USE infancy

children
HG.52 (L,R)
HN November 1992 alternate terms added
February 1991 scope note added
ALT child
children's
child's
SN People in the earliest developmental stage of life.

children (offspring)
USE offspring

children's art
BM.178 (L,R)
SN Art produced by children.
UF art, children's

<children's beds>
TC.763
HN January 1993 guide term moved

children's blankets
USE children's (ALT of children) + blankets (coverings)

children's chairs
HN April 1993 descriptor split, use children's (ALT of children) + chairs

<children's chairs>
TC.599

children's films
VW.1058 (L)
HN November 1992 descriptor moved
ALT children's film
SN Motion pictures produced primarily for children.
UF films, children's

children's gardens
RM.27 (A,L,B)
HN April 1993 descriptor moved
ALT children's garden
UF gardens, children's

children's homes
USE orphanages

children's hospitals
RK.729 (A,L,B)
ALT children's hospital
UF hospitals, children's
hospitals, pediatric
pediatric hospitals

children's hostels
USE orphanages
youth hostels

children's libraries
RK.676 (A,L,B)
ALT children's library
UF libraries, children's

children's museums
RK.374 (A,L)
ALT children's museum
UF junior museums
museums, children's
museums, junior

children's nurseries
USE nurseries (rooms)

children's parks
USE playgrounds

children's playgrounds
USE playgrounds

children's playhouses
RK.971 (A,L)
HN September 1990 scope note added
ALT children's playhouse
SN Use for small houselike structures designed for children to play in. (RHDEL2)
UF playhouses
playhouses, children's

children's table chairs
USE highchairs

children's villages
RG.38 (L,B)
ALT children's village
SN Use for residential treatment centers, often in a rural setting, which provide medical and counseling services for children with emotional problems.
UF villages, children's

children's zoological gardens
USE children's zoos

children's zoos
RG.245 (A,L)
ALT children's zoo
UF children's zoological gardens
gardens, children's zoological
zoos, children's

Chilean
FL.734 (L,B)

Chilean Diaguite
FL.1201
UF Diaguite, Chilean

chilia
USE Baku + rugs

Chilkat
FL.1379 (L)
HN June 1991 descriptor added

chill
USE bloom

chilled water systems
PC.145
HN March 1993 descriptor moved
November 1990 scope note added
ALT chilled water system
SN Air cooling systems in which cold water is circulated between mechanical refrigeration water chilling units and remote cooling equipment.
UF systems, chilled water
water systems, chilled

chills
USE crusies

Chimalhuacán
FL.1001

chimeres
TE.246
ALT chimere
SN Outer, sleeveless, floor-length garments, cut simply in the front and full from a shoulder blade yoke in back; generally made of scarlet or black silk; always worn over a rochet. (CMTWV)
RT rochets

chimes
TT.478 (H,L,N)
SN Sets of tuned stationary bells, hung indoors or out, and struck to sound. They are less extensive than carillons, having a range limited to within two octaves. (NGDMI)

chimes (container components)
USE foot rings

chimes, door
USE doorbells

chimes, gong
USE gong chimes

chimes, orchestral
USE tubular bells

chimes, wind
USE wind chimes

chiming clocks
TN.187 (L)
ALT chiming clock
SN Use for clocks that strike tunes or play musical notes periodically, as at the quarter hours.
UF clocks, chiming

chimney backs
USE firebacks

chimney bars
PJ.2437
HN March 1993 descriptor moved
November 1990 scope note changed
ALT chimney bar
SN Metal lintels that support the masonry above fireplace openings.
UF bars, chimney
bars, turning
turning bars

chimney breasts
PJ.2438
HN March 1993 descriptor moved
July 1991 scope note changed
November 1990 lead-in term deleted, was **chimney pieces**
ALT chimney breast
SN Use for portions of chimneys that project from the general wall plane into the room, often decorated with mantels and overmantels.
UF breasts, chimney
pieces, chimney

chimney cans
USE chimney pots

chimney caps
PJ.2439
HN March 1993 descriptor moved
July 1991 scope note changed
ALT chimney cap
SN Uppermost cornices, of masonry or other noncombustible material, atop chimneys; for extra components placed above and covering flue openings, use **chimney hoods**.
UF bonnets (chimney caps)
caps, chimney

chimney cheeks
PJ.2440
HN March 1993 descriptor moved
November 1990 scope note changed
ALT chimney cheek
SN Use for masonry on either side of a fireplace opening that supports the mantel and upper chimney construction. (MEANS)
UF cheeks, chimney

<chimney components>
PJ.2436
HN March 1993 guide term moved

chimney corners
USE inglenooks

chimney crickets
PJ.2441 (A)
HN March 1993 descriptor moved
ALT chimney cricket
SN Small false roofs built over the main roof behind a chimney; used to provide protection against water leakage where the chimney penetrates the roof. (HAS)
UF crickets
crickets, chimney

chimney flues
USE flues

chimney glasses
USE overmantel mirrors

chimney heads
USE chimney pots

chimney hoods
PJ.2442
HN March 1993 descriptor moved
July 1991 scope note changed
ALT chimney hood
SN Coverings that protect chimney openings; for cornicelike terminations to chimneys, use **chimney caps**, for extensions placed on top of chimneys to improve draft or appearance, and which generally extend the flue, use **chimney pots**.
UF hoods, chimney

chimney hooks
PJ.131
HN April 1993 descriptor moved
ALT chimney hook
UF hooks, chimney

chimney linings
USE flue linings

chimney looking glasses
USE overmantel mirrors

chimney pieces
USE mantels

chimney pots
PJ.2443 (A,N,B)
HN March 1993 descriptor moved
November 1990 scope note added
ALT chimney pot
SN Use for metal, masonry, or ceramic extensions which continue the flue on top of chimneys to improve draft or appearance; for extensions that protect chimney openings and may serve to block rain, use **chimney hoods**.
UF cans, chimney
chimney cans
chimney heads
heads, chimney
pots, chimney

chimney stacks
PJ.2434 (B)
HN March 1993 descriptor moved
November 1990 scope note changed
November 1990 lead-in terms added
ALT chimney stack
SN Use for chimneys containing a number of flues, especially when rising as shafts above a roof.
UF chimney stalks
chimney tuns

stacks, chimney
stalks, chimney
tuns, chimney

chimney stalks
USE chimney stacks

chimney throats
PJ.2445
HN March 1993 descriptor moved
ALT chimney throat
SN The narrowest portions of a chimney flue, between the gathering, or upward contraction above the fireplace, and the flue proper; often where the damper is located. (HAS)
UF chimney waists
fireplace throats
throats
throats, chimney
throats, fireplace
waists, chimney

chimney tuns
USE chimney stacks

chimney waists
USE chimney throats

chimney wings
PJ.2446
HN March 1993 descriptor moved
ALT chimney wing
SN The sides of chimneys above the fireplace opening that close in toward the chimney throat or damper opening. (MEANS)
UF wings, chimney

chimneys (architectural elements)
PJ.2433   (A,L,N,B,R)
HN March 1993 descriptor moved
March 1993 descriptor changed, was **chimneys**
March 1993 alternate term changed, was **chimney**
November 1990 scope note added
ALT chimney (architectural element)
SN Use for vertical noncombustible structures containing flues for drawing off into the outside air products of combustion from, for example, stoves, fireplaces, and furnaces.

chimneys (lighting device components)
PJ.2928
ALT chimney (lighting device component)
SN Tubular devices of glass, metal, or mica which extend upward from the rim of the burner and concentrate the hot air rising from the flame, thus producing a draft. (RUSHL)
UF glasses, lamp
lamp glasses

<chimneys and chimney components>
PJ.2432
HN March 1993 guide term moved

Chimú
FL.1182   (L)

Ch'in
USE Qin (style and period)

ch'in
USE qin (long zithers)

Chin
USE Jin (Golden Tartars)
Jin (Six Dynasties)

Chin, Eastern
USE Eastern Jin

Chin, Later
USE Later Jin

Chin, Western
USE Western Jin

china, bone
USE bone china

china cabinets
TC.846   (N)
HN January 1993 descriptor moved
ALT china cabinet
SN Use for glass-fronted cabinets used to hold and display china.
UF cabinets, china
cases, china
china cases
china closets
china presses
closets, china
presses, china

china cases
USE china cabinets

China clay
USE kaolin

china closets
USE china cabinets

china, English
USE bone china

china, flint
USE ironstone

China grass
USE ramie

china, hotel
USE ironstone

china, ironstone
USE ironstone

china, new
USE stone china

China paper
MT.1430
HN February 1992 descriptor moved
July 1990 descriptor added
UF Chinese paper
India paper (China paper)
India proof paper
paper, China
paper, India

china presses
USE china cabinets

china process
USE ceramic process

china shelves
TC.1015
HN January 1993 descriptor moved
ALT china shelf
SN Open hanging shelves for displaying china, often with lattice work on the sides. (GILBR2)
UF shelves, china

China silk
USE Chinese silk

China stone
MT.631
HN April 1992 descriptor moved
March 1992 descriptor changed, was **petuntze**
March 1992 lead-in term changed, was **China stone**
SN A partially decomposed feldspathic granite found in China and used with clay to make oriental porcelain. (MAYER)
UF petuntze
stone, China

china, stone
USE stone china

china tables
TC.1169
HN January 1993 descriptor moved
ALT china table
SN Use for those tea tables with a raised edge or gallery to protect china against damage.
UF dished-top tables
dished tops
fret tables
galleried tables
tables, china
tables, dished-top
tables, fret
tables, galleried
tops, dished

China trade
USE Chinese export

China trade porcelain
USE Chinese export + porcelain

China wood oil
USE tung oil

chinaberry
MT.2932
HN March 1992 descriptor moved

chinampas
RD.252   (L)
SN Mexican artificial fields made arable by piling onto the planting areas silt dredged from a criss-crossing series of irrigation canals plus organic wastes.

Chinantec
FL.1528   (L)

Chinatowns
RG.286 (L)
ALT Chinatown

Chinautla
FL.1041

Chincha
FL.1183

Chincha-Atacaman
USE Atacameño

chincing irons
TH.961 (N)
ALT chincing iron
SN Tools used by coopers to insert a cooper's flag between the head and staves of a barrel after the head is in place. (W)
UF irons, chincing

Chine sur commande
USE Compagnie des Indes

chiné technique
KT.52
HN January 1993 descriptor moved
SN Technique of dyeing threads of a fabric in different colors so as to produce an image. (SCHNEI)

Chinese
FL.1904 (A,L,B,R)

<Chinese architecture styles>
FL.1996

Chinese beech
MT.2693
HN March 1992 descriptor moved
UF beech, Chinese
Fagus englerana

Chinese binding
USE Japanese binding

Chinese blocks
USE woodblocks

Chinese blue
USE Prussian blue

<Chinese Buddhism>
BM.454

Chinese cedar
USE toon

<Chinese ceramics styles>
FL.1998
HN March 1993 guide term changed, was *<Chinese pottery styles>*

Chinese chairs
TC.565
HN January 1993 descriptor moved
ALT Chinese chair
SN Term used by Chippendale and others for fret-back chairs incorporating Chinese frets.
UF chairs, Chinese
chairs, Chinese Chippendale
Chinese Chippendale chairs
Chippendale chairs, Chinese

chinese checkers
KQ.18 (N)
UF checkers, chinese

Chinese chestnut
MT.2720 (L)
HN March 1992 descriptor moved
UF Castanea mollissima
chestnut, Chinese

Chinese Chippendale
FL.3427
UF Chippendale, Chinese

Chinese Chippendale chairs
USE Chinese chairs

Chinese, Cochin
USE Cochin Chinese

<Chinese dynastic styles and periods>
FL.1919

Chinese elm
MT.2733
HN March 1992 descriptor moved
UF elm, Chinese
Ulmus parrifolia

Chinese export
FL.1999 (H,R)
HN April 1993 descriptor added
SN Porcelain made and decorated in China to European order, as distinct from porcelain in native taste. (IDC74)
UF China trade
Chinese Lowestoft
export, Chinese
Lowestoft, Chinese
Lowestoft, Oriental
Oriental Lowestoft
trade, China

Chinese export porcelain
HN April 1993 descriptor split, use Chinese export + porcelain

Chinese feet
USE bracket feet

Chinese frets
DG.145
ALT Chinese fret
SN Frets characterized by elongated, right-angled meanderlike elements, originating in Chinese art and adapted to Chinoiserie in Europe in the 18th century.
UF frets, Chinese

Chinese fretwork
DG.148
SN A type of openwork pattern originating in Chinese art and adapted to Chinoiserie in Europe in the 18th century.
UF Chinese lattice
Chinese paling
Chinese railing
fretwork, Chinese
lattice, Chinese
paling, Chinese
railing, Chinese

Chinese gardens
RM.6 (L)
HN April 1993 descriptor moved
ALT Chinese garden
UF gardens, Chinese

Chinese green
USE lokao

Chinese hackberry
MT.2755
HN March 1992 descriptor moved
UF Celtis sinensis
hackberry, Chinese

Chinese ink
MT.1918
HN June 1991 descriptor moved
UF ink, Chinese

Chinese insect wax
MT.1295
HN April 1992 descriptor moved
December 1990 descriptor moved
SN Fairly hard, yellowish-white wax produced by insects that are cultivated by humans; used for general purposes and as a substitute for beeswax. (AHMT)
UF insect wax, Chinese
wax, Chinese insect

Chinese lattice
USE Chinese fretwork

Chinese Lowestoft
USE Chinese export

<Chinese Mesolithic periods>
FL.1909

Chinese nails
PJ.149
HN April 1993 descriptor moved
ALT Chinese nail
UF nails, Chinese

<Chinese Neolithic periods>
FL.1913

<Chinese painting styles>
FL.2012

<Chinese Paleolithic periods>
FL.1907

Chinese paling
USE Chinese fretwork

Chinese paper
USE China paper

Chinese papers
USE India papers

Chinese pavilions
USE jingling Johnnies

<Chinese prehistoric periods>
FL.1906

Chinese puzzles
USE burr puzzles

Chinese railing
USE Chinese fretwork

Chinese red
USE chrome red

<Chinese rugs by function>
TC.56

<Chinese rugs by pattern>
TC.85

Chinese silk
MT.1531 (L)
HN March 1993 descriptor moved
    March 1993 lead-in term added
    June 1991 descriptor moved
SN Lightweight silk of plain weave.
UF China silk
    petkin
    silk, China
    silk, Chinese

<Chinese styles>
FL.1994

<Chinese styles and periods>
FL.1905

<Chinese textile styles>
FL.2028
HN April 1993 guide term added

Chinese toon
USE toon

Chinese vermilion
MT.2183
HN April 1992 descriptor moved
UF vermilion, Chinese

Chinese vermilion (color)
USE vivid red

Chinese wallpapers
USE India papers

Chinese white
USE kaolinite (pigment)
    zinc white

Chinese woodblocks
USE temple blocks

Chinese yellow
USE orpiment

Ch'ing
USE Qing

Ch'ing-lien-kang
USE Qingliangang

Ch'ing-pai
USE Qingbai

Ch'ing-pai ware
USE Qingbai + ware

Ching-T'u
BM.457 (L)
UF Pure Land sect

chinkapin oak
USE chinquapin oak

chinning bars
USE horizontal bars

Chinoiserie
FL.3274 (A,B,R)
UF Anglo-Chinoise

Chinook
FL.1352 (L)

chinquapin oak
MT.2827
HN March 1992 descriptor moved
UF chinkapin oak
    oak, chinkapin
    oak, chinquapin

chintamani
DG.14
HN February 1993 descriptor added
SN Use for motifs consisting of two
    wavy lines set beneath three balls ar-
    ranged in a triangular shape.
UF badge of Tamarlane
    badge of Tamberlaine
    badge of Timur
    badge, Timur's
    chintamani design
    chintamani pattern
    design, chintamani
    pattern, chintamani
    Tamberlaine, badge of
    Timur's badge
RT rugs

chintamani design
USE chintamani

chintamani pattern
USE chintamani

chintz
MT.1626 (L,R)
HN April 1993 related term added
    March 1993 descriptor moved
SN Textile, usually cotton or linen,
    dyed in a number of colors and usu-
    ally glazed.
RT palampores

chintz appliqué
USE broderie perse

chintz appliqué, cut-out
USE broderie perse

Chios mastic
USE mastic

Chiot
USE Chian

chip axes
TH.526
ALT chip ax
SN Small axes for chipping wood or
    stone into shape. (DAC)
UF axes, chip

chip carving
KT.1256
HN March 1993 alternate term changed,
    was **chip carved**
ALT chip-carved
SN Hand carving of wood by cutting
    chips with a knife or other instru-

ment usually in simple geometric
designs. (W)
UF carving, chip

chip planes
USE splint planes

chipboard
MT.3058 (L,B)
HN March 1992 descriptor moved

chipendanis
TT.354
ALT chipendani
SN Braced mouth bows of the Shona of
    Zimbabwe, made from a single stick
    of wood and with the string looped
    to the bow at its center.
UF tshipendanis

Chipewyan
FL.1244 (L)
UF Yellowknife

Chippendale
FL.3426 (H,L,R)
UF Director Style

Chippendale chairs, Chinese
USE Chinese chairs

Chippendale, Chinese
USE Chinese Chippendale

chippers
TH.1379 (L,N)
ALT chipper
SN Machines for reducing something,
    such as pulpwood, to chips. (W)

Chippewa
USE Ojibwa

chipping
KT.250
HN January 1993 descriptor moved
ALT chipped
SN The separation of small pieces or
    fragments from an object or surface,
    such as masonry.

chips
USE gaming counters

chips, gambling
USE gaming counters

chips, poker
USE poker chips

Chiricahua Apache
FL.1465 (L)
UF Apache, Chiricahua

Chiricahua Cochise
FL.945
UF Cochise, Chiricahua

Chiricahua stage Mogollon
FL.951
UF Mogollon, Chiricahua stage

Chiriguano
FL.1593 (L)

chirimías
TT.173
ALT   chirimía
SN   Spanish and Latin American folk shawms made in treble and tenor sizes, having a pirouette and short, triangular reeds with a wide opening.
UF   chirimillas
       xirimías

chirimillas
USE   chirimías

Chiripa, Early
USE   Early Chiripa

Chiripa, Late
USE   Late Chiripa

Chiriqui
FL.1108
UF   Chiriqui, Classic
       Classic Chiriqui

Chiriqui, Classic
USE   Chiriqui

chiropractic
KD.132   (L)
HN   April 1993 related term added
SN   Study of the processes of human health and disease, giving special attention to spinal mechanics, musculoskeletal, neurological, vascular, nutritional, and environmental relationships. (PG)
RT   chiropractors

chiropractors
HG.582   (L)
HN   April 1993 related term added
       December 1992 alternate terms added
ALT   chiropractor
       chiropractor's
       chiropractors'
RT   chiropractic

chirulas
USE   chûrulas

chisel-end marking awls
USE   scribe awls

chisel nails
PJ.181
HN   April 1993 descriptor moved
ALT   chisel nail
UF   nails, chisel

chisel planes
USE   edge planes

chisels
TH.527   (L,N)
HN   May 1993 related terms added
ALT   chisel
SN   Metal hand tools with a cutting edge at one end, usually driven by a hammer or mallet; used in dressing, shaping, or working wood, stone, or metal. (MEANS)
RT   <chisels: metalworking tools>

<chisels: stone and masonry working equipment>
<chisels: woodworking tools>

chisels, barking
USE   barking chisels

chisels, bench
USE   bench chisels

chisels, blocking
USE   blocking chisels

chisels, brick
USE   brick sets

chisels, bruzz
USE   corner chisels

chisels, butt
USE   butt chisels

chisels, cant
USE   forming chisels

chisels, cape
USE   cape chisels

chisels, caulking
USE   caulking irons

chisels, claw
USE   tooth chisels

chisels, cold
USE   cold chisels

chisels, cope
USE   cape chisels

chisels, corner
USE   corner chisels

chisels, dogleg
USE   corner chisels

chisels, fishtail
USE   fishtail tools

chisels, flat
USE   flat chisels

chisels, floor
USE   floor chisels

chisels, forming
USE   forming chisels

chisels, framing
USE   framing chisels

chisels, heading
USE   mortise chisels

chisels, hinge
USE   hinge chisels

chisels, hot
USE   hot chisels

chisels, joiners'
USE   paring chisels

<chisels: metalworking tools>
TH.1243
HN   May 1993 related term added
RT   chisels

chisels, mortise
USE   mortise chisels

chisels, paring
USE   paring chisels

chisels, peeling
USE   barking chisels

chisels, pitching
USE   pitching chisels

chisels, plugging
USE   plugging chisels

chisels, pocket
USE   sash chisels

chisels, ripping
USE   ripping chisels

chisels, sash
USE   sash chisels

chisels, skew
USE   skew chisels

chisels, socket
USE   socket chisels

chisels, spline
USE   spline chisels

chisels, splitting
USE   splitting chisels

<chisels: stone and masonry working equipment>
TH.1333
HN   May 1993 related term added
       December 1992 guide term moved
       December 1992 guide term changed, was <chisels: masonry and plastering tools>
RT   chisels

chisels, stonecutters'
USE   tooth chisels

chisels, tooth
USE   tooth chisels

chisels, turners'
USE   turning chisels

chisels, turning
USE   turning chisels

<chisels: woodworking tools>
TH.1427
HN   May 1993 related term added
RT   chisels

chitarras
USE   guitars

chitarras battente
TT.309
ALT   chitarra battente
SN   Guitars of southern Italy, known from the 17th and 18th centuries, having a deep body, highly arched back, rounded edges, slender waist, and central soundhole covered with an ornamental rose. The metal strings, usually arranged in five

double or triple courses, are played with a plectrum.
UF guitarras battente

chitarrones
TT.301
ALT chitarrone
SN Large lutelike instruments, popular in Europe from about 1590 to 1655, with six double courses of stopped strings over the fingerboard and eight unstopped bass strings, about twice the length of the stopped strings, to accomodate which the neck is greatly extended beyond the pegbox of the stopped strings. Its primary use was to accompany the solo singing voice.
UF arichitarras

Chitimacha
FL.1449   (L)
UF Shetinasha

chitin
MT.1026   (L)
HN February 1992 descriptor added
SN Colorless substance that forms part of the outer integument and wings of insects, arthropods, and some other invertebrates.

chitons
TE.123
ALT chiton
SN Tunics, short or long, and generally of linen, worn by men and women in ancient Greece. (RICHTR)

chitons, Doric
USE peploses

Chitrasena
USE Mahendravarman

chits
USE froes

Ch'iu-tzu
USE Kuça

chiulas
USE chûrulas

chiv planes
USE howell planes

chives
USE howell planes

chivs, box
USE howell planes

chlamyses
TE.144
ALT chlamys
SN Short woolen mantles fastened on the right shoulder, worn by men of ancient Greece. (RICHTR)

chloride, ammonium
USE ammonium chloride

chloride, chromated zinc
USE chromated zinc chloride

chloride, ferric
USE ferric chloride

chloride, iron
USE ferric chloride

chloride, methylene
USE methylene chloride

chloride, polyvinyl
USE polyvinyl chloride

chloride, polyvinylidene
USE polyvinylidene chloride

chloride, potassium
USE potassium chloride

chloride, silver
USE silver chloride

chloride, sodium
USE sodium chloride

chlorinated hydrocarbon
MT.2433
HN April 1993 descriptor changed, was **chlorinated hydrocarbons**
SN Highly toxic material used as a solvent for fat, wax, oil, and plastic.
UF hydrocarbon, chlorinated

chlorite
MT.527   (L)
HN April 1993 scope note changed
    April 1992 descriptor moved
SN Widely occurring monoclinic mineral, usually green in color, associated with and resembling mica but chemically consisting of hydrous silicate of aluminum, ferrous iron, or magnesium.

chloro-copper phthalocyanine
USE phthalocyanine green

chlorofluorocarbon
MT.1027   (A)
HN April 1993 lead-in term changed, was CFCs
    April 1993 lead-in term changed, was Freons (TM)
    April 1993 descriptor changed, was **chlorofluorocarbons**
    April 1992 descriptor moved
    February 1991 alternate term added
    May 1990 lead-in term added
UF CFC
    Freon (TM)

Chlorophora excelsa
USE iroko

chlorophyll
MT.2063   (L)
HN April 1992 descriptor moved

chloroprene rubber
USE neoprene

chocalhos
TT.549
ALT chocalho

SN Generic term for Brazilian shaken and struck rattles. (NGDMI)
UF chocolos

Chocho
FL.1529   (L)

Chocó
FL.1676   (L)
UF Cholo
    Noaname

chocolate cups
TQ.416   (N)
ALT chocolate cup
SN Large cups for drinking hot chocolate, usually with two side handles, a cover, and a saucer. (IDC74)
UF cups, chocolate

chocolate mills
USE molinets

chocolate muddlers
USE muddlers

chocolate pots
TQ.516   (H,N)
ALT chocolate pot
SN Covered, spouted vessels for preparing and serving hot chocolate, often similar in form to coffeepots but invariably having a provision for inserting a molinet and often having a handle placed at a right angle to the spout.
UF pots, chocolate
RT breakfast services
    coffeepots
    molinets
    pots

chocolate spoons
TH.323
HN April 1993 descriptor added
ALT chocolate spoon
SN Small spoons, similar in size to coffee spoons, having a rounded bowl; introduced in the late 19th century as an individual place piece. Sometimes made in sets and accompanied by a muddler.
UF spoons, chocolate
RT coffee spoons
    muddlers

chocolos
USE chocalhos

Choctaw
FL.1450   (L)

Chodor
FL.1895
HN April 1993 descriptor moved
    April 1993 lead-in terms added
UF Chaudor
    Chudur
    Davolder
    Juvaldar
    Juvalder

Chodor carpets
USE Chodor + rugs

Chodors
USE   Chodor + rugs

Choga Mami Transitional
FL.3114
UF   Transitional, Choga Mami

choir enclosures
USE   choir screens

choir lofts
PJ.992
HN   March 1993 descriptor moved
February   1992   lead-in   term
changed, was *cantoriae*
ALT   choir loft
SN   Galleries appropriated to a choir.
(W)
UF   cantorias
lofts, choir

choir screens
PJ.2540   (A,L,R)
HN   March 1993 descriptor moved
August 1991 scope note changed
ALT   choir screen
SN   Use   for   screens   in   Christian
churches that separate the choir
from the nave and aisles of a
church. For partitions that separate
the chancel from the nave of the
church, use **chancel screens**.
UF   choir enclosures
enclosures, choir
screens, choir

choir stalls
PJ.2546   (A,L,B,R)
HN   March 1993 descriptor moved
August 1991 scope note changed
ALT   choir stall
SN   Stalls in the choir area of a church.
UF   stalls (choir stalls)
stalls, choir

choirbooks
VW.889   (H,L)
HN   November 1992 descriptor moved
June 1992 scope note added
ALT   choirbook
SN   General term for books used in
church   services   containing   the
chants of the Latin liturgy. (PACHT)
UF   books, service
service books (music)

choirs
PJ.1261   (A,R)
HN   March 1993 descriptor moved
September   1991   scope   note
changed
ALT   choir
SN   Use   for   spaces   in   Christian
churches, generally between the
altar area or sanctuary and the nave,
reserved for choristers. For spaces
containing the altar area and the
choir, when present, use **chancels**.
For elevated platforms from which a
choir, often composed of laity, sings,
use **choir lofts**.

choirs, fore
USE   antechoirs

Choiseul
FL.3802   (L)

chokers
TE.458   (N)
ALT   choker
SN   Short, narrow necklaces worn close
to the throat. For wide ornamental
bands worn tightly around the neck,
use **dog collars**.
RT   dog collars

Chokwe
FL.451   (L)
UF   Badjok
Bajokwe
Batshioko
Cokwe
Jokwe
Kioko
Kiokwe
Quioco
Tuchokwe

<Chokwe-Lunda>
FL.450

Chola
FL.2292   (A,L)
UF   Cola

cholees
USE   cholis

cholis
TE.45   (N)
ALT   choli
SN   Short-sleeved blouses with a low
neckline, and often cut to expose
part of the midriff, especially those
worn by Hindu women in India.
UF   cholees

Cholo
USE   Chocó

Chona I
USE   Monomotapa

Chona II
USE   Mambo

Chondzoresk rugs
USE   cloudband Kazaks

chondzoresks
USE   cloudband Kazaks

Chongzhen
FL.1980
UF   Ch'ung-chêng

Chono
FL.1708   (L)

Chontal
FL.1530   (L)

Chontal de Oaxaca
USE   Tequislatec

Chontales
FL.1090

Chontaquiro
USE   Piro

Chonyi
FL.601

choosing
USE   selecting

chop marks
VW.415   (L)
HN   June 1992 descriptor added
ALT   chop mark
SN   Use for small punched indentations,
usually Chinese characters, on coins
applied by Far Eastern bankers to
guarantee the coin's weight and purity; widely used between 1750 and
1920. (DOTY)
UF   marks, chop (coin marks)

chop marks (printers' marks)
USE   chops

chopblocks
USE   chopping blocks

Chopi
FL.578   (L)
HN   June 1990 lead-in term added
UF   Valenge

chopines
TE.733   (L,N)
ALT   chopine
SN   Women's overshoes with a mulelike
upper and a high stiltlike sole, usually of wood or cork; worn from the
16th to 18th century to increase
stature and protect the feet from
mud and dirt.
RT   mules

choppers
USE   chopping knives
food choppers

choppers, food
USE   food choppers

choppers, meat
USE   meat grinders

chopping blocks
TH.107   (N)
HN   April 1993 descriptor added
ALT   chopping block
SN   Thick, often large blocks of wood
on which food is placed for cutting,
trimming, chopping, and the like.
(RHDEL2)
UF   blocks, chopping
chopblocks

chopping boards
USE   cutting boards

chopping bowls
TQ.278   (N)
ALT   chopping bowl
SN   Wooden bowls in which food is
chopped.
UF   bowls, chopping

RT bowls (vessels)
chopping knives

chopping knives
TH.108 (N)
HN April 1993 descriptor added
ALT chopping knife
SN Tools with one to four blades connected to a handle used to mince and chop meat, vegetables, or other foods. Blades may be straight or curved, the latter for use in a chopping bowl or tray.
UF choppers
food-chopping knives
knives, chopping
knives, food-chopping
knives, mincing
mincers
mincing knives
RT chopping bowls
chopping trays

chopping trays
TQ.271 (N)
ALT chopping tray
SN Wooden trays in which food is chopped.
UF trays, chopping
RT chopping knives
trays

chops
VW.435
HN November 1992 descriptor moved
April 1990 descriptor added
ALT chop
SN Identifying marks stamped on prints by printers, artists, print workshops, or publishers; often embossed. (TYLER)
UF chop marks (printers' marks)
marks, chop (printers' marks)

chopsticks
TH.301 (L,N)
HN April 1993 descriptor added
ALT chopstick
SN Thin, tapered sticks, often of wood or ivory, held in one hand between the thumb and fingers and used chiefly in China, Japan, and other Asian countries for food preparation or lifting food to the mouth.

Chopunnish
USE Nez Percé

choragic monuments
RK.865
ALT choragic monument
SN In ancient Greece, monuments erected by leaders or winners of certain choral competitions; often quite elaborate.
UF monuments, choragic

Chorasmia
USE Khorezm

<chordophone components>
PJ.3247

RT bellies
soundboards

chordophones
TT.204 (H,L)
ALT chordophone
SN Sound devices that produce their sound by means of vibrating strings stretched between fixed points. (NGDMI)
UF chordophonic instruments
instruments, chordophonic
instruments, stringed
stringed instruments (chordophones)
RT *<instrumentalists: stringed instruments>*
stringed instruments
strings (chordophone components)

chordophonic instruments
USE chordophones

chords
PJ.1728
HN March 1993 descriptor moved
November 1990 scope note changed
ALT chord
SN Principal members of trusses that extend the length of the truss. (DAC)

choreographers
HG.208 (L,R)
HN November 1992 alternate terms added
ALT choreographer
choreographer's
choreographers'

Choris
FL.813

chorochromatic maps
VW.59
HN November 1992 descriptor moved
November 1992 scope note changed
ALT chorochromatic map
SN Maps in which aerial distribution is shown by distinctive colors or tints; most geological, soil, and political maps are of this type. (LG)
UF maps, chorochromatic

chorographic maps
VW.60
HN November 1992 descriptor moved
ALT chorographic map
SN Any maps representing large regions, such as countries or continents, on a small scale.
UF maps, chorographic

choroschematic maps
VW.61
HN November 1992 descriptor moved
November 1992 scope note changed
ALT choroschematic map
SN Maps in which small, semipictorial symbols such as dots or lines are used over the area of the map to represent distribution of land utili-

zation or vegetation, without indication of quantity. (LG)
UF maps, choroschematic

Chorotega
USE Mangue

Chorotegan
FL.1091 (L)
UF Manguean

<Chorotegan pottery styles>
FL.1092

Chorotí
FL.1659 (L)
UF Yofuaha

Chorrera
FL.1130

chortens
RK.1094
ALT chorten
SN Use for Tibetan stupas, generally characterized by bulbous domes set on square bases and surmounted by a spire of tiered disklike shapes.

chorus
USE crwths

choruses
USE crwths

Chosen
FL.2190

chou
MT.2500
HN December 1992 descriptor added
SN A cabbage-shaped ornament similar to a fabric rosette, but usually larger, softer, and three-dimensional rather than flat; used to trim costume, coverings, and hangings.
UF cabbage knot
cabbage-knot
knot, cabbage

Chou (Xia)
USE Xia

Chou (Zhou)
USE Zhou

Chou, Eastern
USE Eastern Zhou

Chou, Late
USE Late Zhou

Chou, Later
USE Later Zhou

Chou, Northern
USE Northern Zhou

Chou, Western
USE Western Zhou

Choukoutien
FL.1908

choultries
USE caravanserais

chovals
USE cuvals

CHP generating plants
USE cogeneration plants

chrismatories
HN November 1990 descriptor deleted

christening books
VW.339
HN November 1992 descriptor moved
ALT christening book
UF books, christening

christening palms
USE bearing cloths

christenings
KM.26 (L)
HN May 1991 alternate term added
ALT christening
SN Ceremonial namings of people, animals, or things, such as ships.

<Christian clergy>
HG.395
HN February 1993 guide term added
RT Christianity

Christian, Early
USE Early Christian

<Christian orders>
BM.489

<Christian religious building fixtures>
PJ.2518
HN March 1993 guide term moved

<Christian religious building spaces>
PJ.1246
HN March 1993 guide term moved

<Christian sects>
BM.481

Christianity
BM.465 (L,R)
HN February 1993 related term added
ALT Christian
RT *<Christian clergy>*

Christmas
KM.104 (L,R)

Christmas books
USE gift books

Christmas cards
VW.346 (L)
HN November 1992 descriptor moved
ALT Christmas card
UF cards, Christmas

chroma
USE intensity (color property)

chromascopes
TN.324 (N)
ALT chromascope
SN Instruments for measuring the optical effects of color. (MHDSTT)

chromate, acid copper
USE acid copper chromate

chromate, barium
USE barium yellow

chromated copper arsenate
MT.2396
UF arsenate, chromated copper
copper arsenate, chromated

chromated zinc chloride
MT.2397
UF chloride, chromated zinc
zinc chloride, chromated

Chromatic Abstraction
USE Color-field

<chromatic colors>
DL.33

chromatic frame harps
USE chromatic harps

chromatic harps
TT.211
ALT chromatic harp
SN Harps having a string for each semitone, and thus able to play a full chromatic range without the need for tuning devices such as pedals or hooks.
UF chromatic frame harps
frame harps, chromatic
harps, chromatic

chromatics
USE color

chromato de plomo
USE chrome yellow

chromatographic analysis
USE chromatography

chromatographic processes
USE chromatography

chromatography
KT.168 (L)
HN November 1992 descriptor added
SN The separation of chemical substances by making use of differences in the rates at which the substances travel through or along a stationary medium. (NASATH)
UF chromatographic analysis
chromatographic processes

chromatography, ion-exchange
USE ion-exchange chromatography

chromatography, liquid
USE liquid chromatography

chromatography, paper
USE paper chromatography

chromatography, thin layer
USE thin layer chromatography

chromatometers
TN.325 (N)
ALT chromatometer
SN Instruments for measuring color perception. (W)

chrome
USE chromium

chrome, barium
USE barium yellow

chrome, deep
USE strong orange yellow

chrome green
MT.2163
HN April 1992 descriptor moved
UF bronze green
cinnabar green
green, bronze
green, chrome
green, cinnabar
green, nitrate
green, oil
green, royal
green, Victoria
green, zinnober
nitrate green
oil green
royal green
verde chrome
vert de chrome
vert de cinabre
Victoria green
zinnober green
Zinnobergrün

chrome green (chromium oxide green)
USE chromium oxide green

chrome green (color)
USE moderate green
strong green
very dark yellowish green

chrome green, deep
USE dark yellowish green

chrome green, light
USE dark yellowish green

chrome green, medium
USE dark green
dark yellowish green

chrome green, zinc
USE zinc chrome green

chrome ocher
USE golden ocher

chrome orange
USE chrome red
vivid orange
vivid reddish orange

chrome oxide
USE chromium oxide green

chrome red
MT.2169
HN April 1992 descriptor moved
UF American vermilion
Chinese red
chrome orange
Chromrot
Derby red
orange, chrome
Persian red

red, Chinese
red, chrome
red, Derby
red, Persian
red, Victoria
red, Vienna
rouge de chrome
vermilion, American
Victoria red
Vienna red

chrome steel
    MT.356   (L)
  HN March 1993 lead-in terms added
       March 1993 descriptor moved
  UF chromium steel
       steel, chrome
       steel, chromium

chrome, strontium
  USE strontium chromate

chrome tannage
  USE chrome tanning

chrome tanning
    KT.1058
  HN February 1993 descriptor added
  ALT chrome-tanned
  SN Tanning hides or skins with chro-
      mium salts or chromic acid, used
      chiefly to produce light leathers.
  UF chrome tannage

chrome-vanadium steel
    MT.357   (L)
  HN March 1993 descriptor moved
  UF steel, chrome-vanadium

chrome yellow
    MT.2278   (L)
  HN May 1992 lead-in terms added
       May 1992 lead-in term deleted, was
         Baltimore yellow
       May 1992 lead-in term changed,
         was **Spooners chrome yellow**
       April 1992 descriptor moved
  UF amarillo de cromo
       American chrome yellow
       chromato de plomo
       chrome yellow, American
       chrome yellow, French
       chrome yellow, golden
       chrome yellow, jonquil
       chrome yellow, new
       chrome yellow, Spooner's
       Chromgelb
       Cologne yellow
       French chrome yellow
       giallo de cromo
       golden chrome yellow
       jaune de chrôme
       jaune de chrome
       Jonquil chrome yellow
       king's yellow (chrome yellow)
       Leipzig yellow
       lemon yellow
       new chrome yellow
       new yellow
       Paris yellow
       Spooner's chrome yellow

Vienna yellow
yellow, American chrome
yellow, chrome
yellow, Cologne
yellow, French chrome
yellow, golden chrome
yellow, Jonquil chrome
yellow, king's
yellow, Leipzig
yellow, lemon
yellow, new
yellow, new chrome
yellow, Paris
yellow, Spooner's chrome
yellow, Vienna

chrome yellow (color)
  USE strong orange yellow
       vivid orange yellow
       vivid yellow

chrome yellow, American
  USE chrome yellow

chrome yellow, deep
  USE moderate orange yellow

chrome yellow, French
  USE chrome yellow

chrome yellow, golden
  USE chrome yellow

chrome yellow, jonquil
  USE chrome yellow

chrome yellow, light
  USE strong yellow

chrome yellow, new
  USE chrome yellow

chrome yellow, Spooner's
  USE chrome yellow

chrome, zinc
  USE zinc yellow

Chromgelb
  USE chrome yellow

chromium
    MT.381   (L)
  HN March 1993 scope note changed
       March 1993 descriptor moved
       December 1992 lead-in term added
  SN Use for the pure metallic element
      having symbol Cr and atomic num-
      ber 24; an extremely hard, silvery
      white metal with a bluish tinge. Use
      also for the metal as processed and
      formed, usually in combination with
      other substances, to make various
      objects and materials, notably stain-
      less steel, heat-resistant alloy, high-
      strength alloy steel, and for wear-re-
      sistant electroplating.
  UF chrome
       Cr

chromium alloy
    MT.382   (L)

  HN March 1993 descriptor changed,
       was **chromium alloys**
      March 1993 descriptor moved
  UF alloy, chromium

<chromium and chromium alloy>
    MT.380
  HN March 1993 guide term added

chromium, emerald oxide of
  USE viridian

chromium, hydrated oxide of
  USE viridian

chromium oxide
  USE moderate yellowish green

chromium oxide green
    MT.2150
  HN May 1992 lead-in terms added
       April 1992 descriptor moved
  UF Arnaudon's green
       chrome green (chromium oxide
         green)
       chrome oxide
       chromium oxide green, opaque
       chromium, oxide of
       Chromoxidgrün
       Dingler's green
       green, Arnaudon's
       green, chrome
       green, chromium oxide
       green, Dingler's
       green, Plessy's
       green, Reading
       green, Schnitzer's
       oxide of chromium
       oxide verte de chrome opaque
       Plessy's green
       Reading green
       Schnitzer's green

chromium oxide green, opaque
  USE chromium oxide green

chromium oxide green, transparent
  USE viridian

chromium oxide, hydrated
  USE viridian

chromium, oxide of
  USE chromium oxide green

chromium oxide, transparent
  USE viridian

chromium steel
  USE chrome steel

chromo process
  USE chromolithography

chromogenic color prints
    VC.321
  ALT chromogenic color print
  UK chromogenic colour prints
  UKA chromogenic colour print
  SN Use for photographic prints made
      by chromogenic color processes.
  UF chromogenic development prints
       chromogenic prints
       color coupler prints

color prints, chromogenic
colour prints, chromogenic
coupler prints, color
coupler prints, dye
dye coupler photoprints
dye coupler prints
photoprints, dye coupler
prints, chromogenic
prints, chromogenic color
prints, chromogenic colour
prints, chromogenic development
prints, color coupler
prints, dye coupler

chromogenic colour prints
SEE chromogenic color prints

chromogenic development prints
USE chromogenic color prints

chromogenic development processes
USE chromogenic processes

chromogenic prints
USE chromogenic color prints

chromogenic processes
KT.556
SN Photographic processes in which subtractive dyes form from the reaction of the oxidation product of the developing agent (resulting from the development of the latent image) with a coupler, contained either in the film or in the developing solution. (HAIST)
UF chromogenic development processes
color coupler processes
color dye coupler processes
dye coupler processes
dye coupling processes

chromolithographs
VC.477   (L)
ALT chromolithograph
SN Use for color lithographs produced commercially in the latter half of the 19th century.
UF chromos

chromolithography
KT.688   (H,L)
HN March 1992 lead-in term added
October 1991 descriptor moved
October 1991 scope note changed
SN A type of color lithography used commercially in the latter half of the 19th century.
UF chromo process

chromophotography
USE color photography

chromos
USE chromolithographs

chromotypography
USE color printing

Chromoxidgrün
USE chromium oxide green

Chromoxidhydratgrün
USE viridian

chromoxylographs
USE color wood engravings

Chromrot
USE chrome red

chroniclers
HG.359
HN December 1992 alternate terms added
ALT chronicler
chronicler's
chroniclers'

chronicles
VW.278   (L,R)
HN November 1992 descriptor moved
June 1992 scope note changed
ALT chronicle
SN Use for histories in which events are described in chronological order. For records of events in yearly sequence but less connected or filled out by commentary or interpretation, use **annals**. (RBGENR)
UF annals (chronicles)

chronographs
TN.211   (L,N)
ALT chronograph
SN Timepieces used to register the time of an event or graphically register specific time intervals, such as for the duration of events. (MHDSTT)
RT stopwatches

chronology
BM.386   (L,R)
SN Use generally for a sequence or list of events in the order of time of their occurrence or appearance. In art or literary history, use specifically for the sequence of major events in the life of a painter, architect, writer, or other artist, including dates of the production of major works; use also for tables or lists detailing the sequence of development of major artistic works.

chronometer locks
USE time locks

chronometers
TN.212   (L,N)
ALT chronometer
SN Use either for strongly built precision timekeeping devices especially designed for use on ships or for extremely accurate wrist or pocket watches.

chronometric dating
USE absolute dating

chronophotographs
VC.367
HN April 1992 descriptor moved
May 1991 scope note changed
May 1991 related term added

ALT chronophotograph
SN Use for photographs that record movement or change in a series of images, regardless of the amount of time intervening. For a series of images capturing an action, as of a human figure or animal, use **motion photographs**. If photographs are arranged to be seen in a specified order, use **sequences**.
RT sequences

chronophotography
KT.571   (L,R)
HN May 1991 lead-in term deleted, was **serial photography**
May 1991 lead-in term deleted, was **sequential photography**
SN Use for the making of chronophotographs, recording motion or change with a series of photographic images, either discrete photographs taken sequentially or a single exposure capturing movement. (W)
UF motion photography
motion study photography
photochronography
photography, motion
photography, motion study

chronoscopes
TN.213   (N)
ALT chronoscope
SN Use for electronic devices for measuring extremely short intervals of time with great accuracy, such as for determining the velocity of projectiles.

chronothermometers
TN.318   (N)
ALT chronothermometer
SN Thermometers used to indicate mean temperature, consisting partly of a clock mechanism whose speed is a function of temperature. (MHDSTT)

chryselephantine sculpture
VC.539   (L,R)
SN Sculpture made of or covered with gold and ivory; used especially for ancient Greek figures.
UF sculpture, chryselephantine

chrysocalla
USE malachite (pigment)

chrysocolla
MT.2136
HN April 1992 descriptor moved
UF cedar green
gold solder
green, cedar
solder, gold

chrysocolla (color)
USE moderate yellowish green

chrysocolla green
USE brilliant green
strong green

chrysolite
USE olivine

chrysolith
USE olivine

chrysoprase
MT.581
HN April 1992 descriptor moved
February 1992 related term added
SN An apple-green variety of chalcedony valued as a gem. (W)
RT gemstone

chrysotile
MT.515 (L)
HN February 1992 descriptor added
SN A white, gray, or greenish mineral of the serpentine group; it constitutes the most important type of asbestos. (AGI)
UF asbestos, serpentine
serpentine asbestos
RT serpentine (mineral)

chuban
VC.424
SN Japanese prints of a standard size, about 11 by 8 inches. (HILLNA)

chucks
PJ.2596 (L,N)
HN March 1993 descriptor moved
ALT chuck
SN Devices with adjustable jaws used for centering and holding a cutting bit or a drill bit. (DAC)

Chudur
USE Chodor

chufti
USE jufti knots

Chugach
FL.1213 (L)

Chuguji
FL.2174

Chukchi
FL.2224 (L)
UF Chukotan

Chukotan
USE Chukchi

chullpas
RK.456
ALT chullpa
SN Use for tombs built as round or rectangular towerlike structures of stone or adobe found predominantly in pre-Inca Peru and Bolivia.
UF tomb towers
towers, tomb

Chumash
FL.1264 (L)
UF Chumashan

Chumashan
USE Chumash

Chün
USE Jun

Ch'un-ch'iu
USE Spring and Autumn Annals

Chün ware
USE Jun + ware

Ch'ung-chêng
USE Chongzhen

Chung-yuan
USE Chungwan

Chungwan
FL.1916
UF Chung-yuan

Chunqiu
USE Spring and Autumn Annals

Chuntaquiro
USE Piro

church and state
BM.950 (L,R)
HN February 1993 descriptor moved

church architecture
USE churches

church bass viols
USE church basses

church basses
TT.253
ALT church bass
SN Large bass-range chordophones of the violin family, made in 19th-century New England primarily for accompanying church choirs.
UF American bass viols
bass viols, American
bass viols, church
bass viols, Yankee
basses, church
church bass viols
Yankee bass viols

church brasses
USE brasses (memorials)

church buildings
USE churches

church bulletins
VW.708 (L)
HN November 1992 descriptor moved
ALT church bulletin
UF bulletins, church

church camps
RG.167 (L)
ALT church camp
UF camps, church

church costume
USE vestments

church halls
USE parish houses

church historians
HG.434 (L)
HN April 1993 related terms added

December 1992 alternate terms added
ALT church historian
church historian's
church historians'
UF historians, church
RT church history
historians

church history
KD.92 (L)
HN April 1993 related terms added
UF history, church
RT church historians
history

church houses
USE parish houses

Church, Mormon
USE Mormonism

church plate
PE.69 (L,R)
HN November 1992 descriptor added
SN Term generally applied to various articles such as alms dishes, chalices and censers, usually of silver or gold, intended for ecclesiastical use.
UF church silver
communion plate
ecclesiastical plate
plate, church
plate, communion
plate, ecclesiastical
silver, church
RT beakers (drinking vessels)
flagons
incense boats
<liturgical containers>

church records
VW.704 (L)
HN November 1992 descriptor moved
ALT church record
UF capitular records
cathedral records
records, capitular
records, cathedral
records, church

<church records by form or function>
VW.705
HN November 1992 guide term moved

<church records by provenance>
VW.714
HN November 1992 guide term moved

church registers
VW.709 (L)
HN November 1992 descriptor moved
ALT church register
UF records, vestry
registers, church
vestry records

church rugs
USE Transylvanian carpets

church schools
USE parochial schools

church silver
USE church plate

church symbolism
USE religious symbolism

church towers
 PJ.1363 (L,B,R)
HN March 1993 descriptor moved
ALT church tower
UF towers, church

church vestments
USE vestments

churches
 RK.1038 (A,L,B,R)
ALT church
UF architecture, church
 buildings, church
 church architecture
 church buildings
 kirks
 tabernacles (churches)

churches, abbey
USE abbey churches

<churches by form>
 RK.1039

<churches by function>
 RK.1044

<churches by location or context>
 RK.1048

churches, cave
USE cave churches

churches, collegiate
USE collegiate churches

churches, conventual
USE abbey churches

churches, double
USE double churches

churches, hall
USE hall churches

churches, mast
USE stave churches

churches, mission
USE mission churches

churches, monastic
USE monastic churches

churches, monolithic
USE cave churches

churches, parish
USE parish churches

churches, pilgrimage
USE pilgrimage churches

churches, rock
USE cave churches

churches, rock-cut
USE rock-cut churches

churches, stave
USE stave churches

churches, twin
USE double churches

churchwardens' accounts
 VW.715 (L)
HN November 1992 descriptor moved
ALT churchwarden's account
UF accounts, churchwardens'
 records, vestry
 vestry records

churchyards
 RG.32 (A,L,B,R)
ALT churchyard
SN Yards which belong to churches and
 are used as burial grounds. (W)

churns
 TH.139 (N)
HN April 1993 descriptor added
ALT churn
SN Containers in which milk or cream
 is stirred, beaten, or agitated by a
 plunging or revolving dasher, or by
 shaking, in order to separate the
 oily globules from the liquid and
 thus obtain butter.
UF butter churns
 churns, butter

churns, butter
USE churns

Churrigueresque
 FL.3335 (A)

chûrulas
 TT.25
ALT chûrula
SN Basque pipes of slightly conical
 bore, with two front fingerholes and
 one rear thumbhole, played with
 the left hand, the right usually being engaged in striking a Basque
 drum.
UF chirulas
 chiulas
 xiulas

Chust
 FL.1863
HN April 1993 descriptor moved

chutes
 PJ.1152 (B)
HN March 1993 descriptor moved
ALT chute
SN Inclined or vertical troughs or
 shafts, for conveying materials of
 any kind to a lower level. (RS)

chutes, clothes
USE laundry chutes

chutes, coal
USE coal chutes

chutes, drop
USE drop chutes

chutes, garbage
USE refuse chutes

chutes, laundry
USE laundry chutes

chutes, letter
USE mail chutes

chutes, mail
USE mail chutes

chutes, playground
USE slides (recreation equipment)

chutes, refuse
USE refuse chutes

chutes, rubbish
USE refuse chutes

chutes, trash
USE refuse chutes

chuvals
USE cuvals

Cibachrome (TM)
 KT.562
HN May 1991 scope note changed
SN A subtractive color process for making photographic prints and transparencies using a silver-dye bleach
 process. Also marketed under the
 name Cilchrome.
UF Cilchrome

Ciboney
 FL.1581 (L)
HN June 1990 lead-in term added
UF Siboney

ciboria (structures)
 PJ.2521 (A,L,N,B,R)
HN March 1993 descriptor moved
 March 1993 descriptor changed,
 was **ciboria**
 March 1993 alternate term changed,
 was **ciborium**
 July 1991 scope note changed
ALT ciborium (structure)
SN Roofed structures with four or more
 columns built over an altar; for suspended, projecting, or freestanding
 canopies over such features as
 altars, thrones, or doorways, use
 baldachins. (NCE)

ciboria (vessels)
 TQ.157 (H,N,R)
ALT ciborium (vessel)
UF footed pyxes
 pyxes, footed
RT pyxes

Ciceronian notes
USE tironian notes

cicims
 TC.123
ALT cicim
SN Turkish term for flat-woven rugs
 with a particular supplementary
 weft structure.
UF Baghdad portieres

Baghdad strips
djidjims
jijims
portieres, Baghdad
strips, Baghdad

cider barns
USE cider mills

cider cheese cutters
TH.109 (N)
HN April 1993 descriptor added
ALT cider cheese cutter
SN Shovel-like tools used to cut up and remove compacted mash and straw following cider pressing. (WKABW)
UF cheese cutters, cider
cutters, cider cheese

cider glasses
TQ.428
ALT cider glass
SN Drinking glasses intended for cider sometimes having engraved motifs of apple branches or apple blossoms.
UF glasses, cider

cider houses
USE cider mills

cider mills
RK.591 (A)
HN April 1990 descriptor added
ALT cider mill
SN Use for buildings in which apples are put through a press in order to produce cider.
UF barns, cider
cider barns
cider houses
houses, cider
mills, cider

cider presses
TH.226
HN April 1993 descriptor added
ALT cider press
SN Presses for `expressing juice from apples; used to make cider.
UF apple presses
presses, apple
presses, cider

cigar-box cedar
USE Spanish cedar

cigar boxes
TQ.240 (L)
ALT cigar box
SN Use for containers intended primarily for holding cigars, especially covered boxes of varying shape, similar to but larger than cigarette boxes, meant to be placed on a table, desk, or the like. For flat containers used to carry cigars, use **cigar cases**. For airtight containers for cigars, use **humidors**.
UF boxes, cigar
RT boxes (containers)
cigar cases

cigarette boxes
humidors

cigar cases
TQ.241 (N)
ALT cigar case
SN Flat, often rectangular cases, similar to but larger than cigarette cases, used to carry cigars. For covered boxes placed on a table, desk, or the like and used to hold cigars, use **cigar boxes**.
UF cases, cigar
RT cases (containers)
cigar boxes
cigarette cases

cigarette boxes
TQ.242 (N)
ALT cigarette box
SN Covered boxes of varying shape, similar to but smaller than cigar boxes, meant to be placed on a table, desk, or the like to hold cigarettes. For flat containers used to carry cigarettes, use **cigarette cases**. For open cylindrical containers used to hold cigarettes, use **cigarette holders (containers)**.
UF boxes, cigarette
cigarette jars
jars, cigarette
RT boxes (containers)
cigar boxes
cigarette cases
cigarette holders (containers)

cigarette cards
VW.1121 (L,N,R)
HN January 1993 related term added
November 1992 descriptor moved
March 1992 lead-in term added
ALT cigarette card
SN Cards containing pictures of birds, baseball players, celebrities, or other popular culture subjects packaged by manufacturers of cigarettes with their product during the 19th and early 20th centuries.
UF cards, cigarette
tobacco cards
RT premiums

cigarette cases
TQ.243 (H,N,R)
ALT cigarette case
SN Flat, usually rectangular containers similar to but smaller than cigar cases, used to carry cigarettes. For covered boxes used as containers for cigarettes and meant to be placed on a table, desk, or the like, use **cigarette boxes**.
UF cases, cigarette
RT cases (containers)
cigar cases
cigarette boxes

cigarette holders (containers)
TQ.244
ALT cigarette holder (container)
SN Open, usually cylindrical containers

used to hold cigarettes on a table, desk, or the like. For covered boxes used to hold cigarettes, use **cigarette boxes**.
UF holders, cigarette
RT cigarette boxes

cigarette holders (personal equipment)
TH.403 (N)
HN January 1993 descriptor added
ALT cigarette holder (personal equipment)
SN Hollow cylindrical devices used to hold a cigarette while it is being smoked.
UF holders, cigarette

cigarette jars
USE cigarette boxes

cigarette tables
USE smokers

Cilchrome
USE Cibachrome (TM)

cills
USE sills

cimas
USE cymas

cimbaloms
TT.406 (L,N)
ALT cimbalom
SN Hungarian gypsy dulcimers consisting of a shallow trapezoid box with from 20 to 35 courses of metal strings crossing two bridges, played while suspended from the player's neck by a strap or resting on four legs.
UF cembalons
cymbaloms
kimbaloms
kymbalons

cimbiae
USE shaft rings

cimeliarchs
PJ.1147
HN March 1993 descriptor moved
ALT cimeliarch
SN Rooms for keeping the valuables of a church. (RHDEL2)

cinabre
USE vermilion

cinabrio
USE vermilion

cinabro
USE vermilion

cinchers, waist
USE waist cinchers

cinctures (column components)
PJ.1518
HN March 1993 descriptor moved
March 1993 descriptor changed, was **cinctures**
March 1993 alternate term changed, was **cincture**

December 1990 descriptor moved
December 1990 scope note changed
ALT cincture (column component)
SN Use for moldings located at the top or bottom of column shafts, especially of Classical design; for molded bands on shafts in Gothic architecture, not located at the ends, use **shaft rings**. For angular bands around the base of the Doric echinus, use **annulets**.

cinctures (girdles)
TE.678
ALT cincture (girdle)
SN Cords, narrow bands, or the like worn at the waist, especially those worn as an ecclesiastical vestment.
RT <liturgical costume>

cinder
MT.3062
HN February 1992 descriptor moved
SN The incombustible residue of something burnt. (W)

cinder block
MT.231 (A,L)
HN April 1992 descriptor moved
UF block, cinder
block, clinker
clinker block

cinder concrete
MT.199
HN April 1992 descriptor moved
SN A lightweight concrete made with cinder as the coarse aggregate. (DAC)
UF concrete, cinder

cinema
USE film (performing arts)

cinemas
USE movie theaters

cinemas, drive-in
USE drive-in theaters

cinematographers
HG.300 (L)
HN April 1993 related terms added
February 1993 descriptor moved
November 1992 alternate terms added
ALT cinematographer
cinematographer's
cinematographers'
SN Persons who oversee all the aspects of photography in a television or filmmaking project, especially the lighting; they are particularly charged with achieving the photographic images and effects desired by the director. For operators of motion picture or television cameras, use **cameramen**.
UF cameramen, lighting
lighting cameramen
RT cameramen
cinematography

cinematography
KT.490 (L)
SN Science of motion picture photography. (W)
RT cinematographers

cinematography, stop-motion
USE stop-motion photography

cineraria
RG.33
ALT cinerarium
SN Use for places reserved for depositing ashes or ash urns of the dead.

cinerary urns
USE cremation urns

cingula
TE.679
ALT cingulum
SN Cinctures or belts for the alb.

cinnabar
USE vermilion

cinnabar green
USE chrome green

cinnaharis
USE dragon's blood

Cinquecentismo
USE Stile Umberto

cinquedeas
TK.19
ALT cinquedea
SN Heavy civilian daggers or short swords of 15th- and 16th-century Italy, characterized by a broad, flat double-edged triangular blade measuring five fingers in width at the hilt, a pair of short, arched quillons, a grip formed of two flat pieces riveted one on each side of the tang, and a pommel that is simply an arched cap fitted over the base of the grip. The blades are fluted and often elaborately decorated on the wider parts.
RT <swords by form>

cinquefoils
DG.37
ALT cinquefoil
SN Figures of five equal arcs or lobes, separated by cusps. (IDO)
UF quintfoils

ciphers
USE monograms

cipolin
SEE cipollino

cipollino
MT.747
HN April 1992 descriptor moved
UK cipolin
UF Carystian marble
marble, Carystian
marmor Carystium

cippi
RK.841
ALT cippus
SN Use for small Roman, Etruscan, or Greek stelae or stone pillars, usually inscribed, marking, for example, events, boundaries, or gravesites.

cirage
HN July 1990 descriptor deleted

circle clamps
USE C-clamps

circle-end clamps
USE C-clamps

circle shears
TH.1264 (N)
SN Term used for regular hand shears with a slight curve to their blade or mechanical shears, both of which are used to cut a circle out of sheet metal.
UF shears, circle

circles (plane figures)
BM.661 (H,B,R)
HN March 1993 descriptor changed, was **circles**
March 1993 alternate term changed, was **circle**
July 1991 alternate term added
ALT circle (plane figure)
circular

circles (road junctions)
USE traffic circles

circles (social groups)
HG.6
HN October 1992 descriptor added
ALT circle (social group)
SN Social groups sharing a common tie or interest such as a mode of life, activity, or social context.

circles, azimuth
USE azimuth circles

circles, color
USE color wheels

circles, interlocking
USE interlocking circles

circles, stone
USE cromlechs

circles, traffic
USE traffic circles

circuit breakers
PJ.771 (L,N)
HN March 1993 descriptor moved
ALT circuit breaker
SN Reusable electrical devices for discontinuing current flow during abnormal conditions.
UF breakers, circuit
circuit-breakers, electric
electric circuit-breakers

circuit-breakers, electric
USE circuit breakers

circuit cameras
USE   panoramic cameras

circuit interruptors, ground-fault
USE   ground-fault circuit interruptors

circuits
PJ.772   (L)
HN   March 1993 descriptor moved
       December 1990 scope note added
ALT   circuit
SN   Use for the complete paths taken by
       electric currents flowing through
       conductors, usually wires, from one
       terminal of a generating source
       through energy-consuming units
       and returning through different
       conductors, usually wires, back to
       another terminal on the power
       source. (STEIN)
UF   circuits, electric
       electric circuits

circuits, electric
USE   circuits

circular accelerators
USE   cyclotrons

circular arches
USE   semicircular arches

circular bookcases
USE   revolving + bookcases

circular easy chairs
TC.492
HN   May 1993 related term added
       January 1993 descriptor moved
ALT   circular easy chair
SN   18th-century term for easy chairs
       having a semicircular back forming
       a single upholstered piece with the
       wings and arms. For chairs with a
       solid, rounded wooden back or
       those made from cutting away parts
       of a barrel, use **barrel chairs.**
UF   barrel chairs (circular easy chairs)
       chairs, barrel
       chairs, circular easy
       chairs, tub
       chairs, tub-back easy
       easy chairs, circular
       easy chairs, tub-back
       tub-back easy chairs
       tub chairs
RT   square easy chairs

circular engine houses
USE   roundhouses

circular frames
USE   tondo frames

circular-front
DC.83
HN   October 1992 descriptor moved

circular graphs
VW.153
HN   November 1992 descriptor moved
ALT   circular graph
UF   graphs, circular

graphs, pie
pie graphs

circular letters
VW.353   (L)
HN   November 1992 descriptor moved
ALT   circular letter
SN   Letters intended for circulation, ei-
       ther widely or throughout a particu-
       lar group. (GAHLM)
UF   letters, circular

circular letters of credit
USE   letters of credit

circular notes
USE   letters of credit

circular saws
TH.1572   (L,N)
ALT   circular saw
SN   Thin steel disks, with teeth on their
       periphery, that rotate on a power-
       driven spindle; used either as hand
       tools   or   are   table-mounted.
       (MEANS)
UF   buzz saws
       saws, buzz
       saws, circular

circular saws, portable
USE   electric-portable saws

circular stairs
USE   spiral stairs

circulars
VW.1126   (L,N)
HN   June 1992 descriptor added
ALT   circular
SN   Use for printed pieces such as no-
       tices or advertisements, usually in
       the form of single sheets or leaflets,
       intended for wide distribution to the
       general public. For similar pieces in-
       tended for distribution by hand and
       often doubling as posters, use **hand-
       bills.**

circulars (memorandums)
USE   memorandums

circulating
USE   circulation   (collections
       management)

circulation (architecture)
BM.367   (B)
HN   December 1992 descriptor moved
SN   Use with reference to traffic pat-
       terns through areas or buildings, in-
       cluding the means of travel through
       a building, such as doors, corridors,
       stairs, or elevators. (DAC)

circulation (collections management)
KG.118   (L)
HN   April 1993 lead-in term added
       April 1993 alternate term deleted,
       was **circulating**
       July 1991 descriptor changed, was
       circulation
SN   Lending items from a collection to

outside users and keeping records
of such loans.
UF   circulating

<circulation elements>
PJ.2364
HN   March 1993 guide term moved

circulation librarians
HG.502
HN   December 1992 alternate terms
       added
ALT   circulation librarian
       circulation librarian's
       circulation librarians'
UF   librarians, circulation

<circulation spaces>
PJ.1023
HN   March 1993 guide term moved

circumcisions
KM.40   (H,L,R)
HN   February 1991 alternate term added
       February 1991 descriptor changed,
       was **circumcision**
ALT   circumcision

circumference
DC.93
HN   October 1992 descriptor moved
SN   Line that bounds a circular plane
       surface; the length of this line,
       equal to pi times the diameter. (W)

circumferential highways
USE   beltways

circus wagons
TX.109   (L,N)
ALT   circus wagon
SN   Various types of wagons, often
       horse-drawn, used by circuses to
       transport props, equipment, or ani-
       mals; often richly decorated.
UF   wagons, circus

circuses (performances)
KM.80   (L,R)
HN   May 1991 alternate term added
       May 1991 descriptor changed, was
       circuses
ALT   circus (performance)

circuses (Roman arenas)
RK.991   (A,L,B,R)
ALT   circus (Roman arena)
SN   Use for oblong ancient Roman en-
       closures which are curved at one
       end, with tiered seating on three
       sides, and built for chariot and
       horse racing.

cire perdue
USE   lost-wax process

cire-perdue process
USE   lost-wax process

cirkut cameras
USE   panoramic cameras

cirricule chairs
USE   curricles (chairs)

ciselé
USE ciselé velvet

ciselé velvet
MT.1603
HN November 1992 descriptor added
SN Velvet whose pattern is formed by cut and uncut pile. (WRPWFT)
UF ciselé
velvet, ciselé

ciseleur-doreurs
HG.692
HN December 1992 alternate terms added
December 1992 descriptor changed, was **ciseleurs-doreurs**
ALT ciseleur-doreur
ciseleur-doreur's
ciseleur-doreurs'
SN Craftsmen who gild the metal mounts on furniture. (HAYWAR)

ciselure
KT.1125
SN The final chasing or smoothing of a metal object. (THDAT)

cist graves
RK.457
ALT cist grave
SN Use to designate boxlike graves, normally rectangular and meant for single burial, dug into the ground and often lined with stone slabs and covered.
UF cist tombs
cists
cistvaens
graves, cist
tombs, cist

cist tombs
USE cist graves

cista
USE arcae

Cistercian
BM.494   (A,L)

cisterns
PJ.883   (A,L,N,B,R)
HN March 1993 descriptor moved
ALT cistern
SN May range in size from covered tanks to artificial reservoirs in which rainwater is stored for use when required.
UF cisterns, water storage
water storage cisterns

cisterns (wine coolers)
USE wine coolers

cisterns, water storage
USE cisterns

cisterns, wine
USE wine coolers

cisters
USE citterns

cistophori
VK.55   (L)
ALT cistophorus
SN Use for certain Hellenistic silver coins, chiefly of Pergamon, minted in the 2nd and 1st centuries BCE.

cistres
USE citterns

cists
USE cist graves

cistvaens
USE cist graves

citadels
RK.413   (B)
ALT citadel

citation indexes
VW.865   (L)
HN November 1992 descriptor moved
ALT citation index
SN Indexes to published materials that have cited a particular work; often includes subject and author indexes as well.
UF indexes, citation

citharas
USE kitharas

cither viols
USE sultanas

citherns
USE citterns

cithrens
USE citterns

cities
RD.11   (A,L,R)
HN January 1993 related term added
ALT city
SN Distinctions among villages, towns, and cities are relative and vary according to their individual regional contexts. Generally, cities designate large or important communities with population, status, and internal complexity greater than most towns in the region.
UF communities, urban
urban communities
RT city-states

cities, buried
USE buried cities

cities, capital
USE capital cities

cities, cathedral
USE cathedral cities

cities, center
USE inner cities

cities, colonial
USE colonial cities

cities, fortified
USE fortified towns

cities, future
USE future cities

cities, garden
USE garden cities

cities, history of
USE urban history

cities, ideal
USE ideal cities

cities, inner
USE inner cities

cities, linear
USE linear cities

cities, lost
USE lost cities

cities, mining
USE mining towns

cities, model
USE model cities

cities of the future
USE future cities

cities, pilgrimage
USE pilgrimage centers

cities, port
USE ports

cities, ruined
USE ruined cities

cities, satellite
USE new towns
satellite cities

cities, university
USE university towns

citizen participation
BM.951   (L,B)
HN February 1993 descriptor moved
February 1991 related term added
April 1990 lead-in terms added
UF community participation
participation, citizen
participation, community
participation, public
public participation
RT voting

citizens, senior
USE elderly

citizenship papers
VW.371
HN March 1993 alternate term deleted, was **citizenship paper**
November 1992 descriptor moved
SN Documents which evidence the status of being a citizen, such as passports and birth certificates. (GAHLM)
UF papers, citizenship

citoles
TT.284
ALT citole
SN European Medieval plucked lutelike

chordophones having a flat body, short neck and pegbox carved from a single piece of wood, with a bridge, one central or two lateral soundholes, frets, and usually four but sometimes three or five strings.

citras
USE English guitars

citrate, potassium
USE potassium citrate

citrine
MT.586
HN February 1992 descriptor added
SN The yellow variety of crystalline quartz, closely resembling topaz in color. (AGI)
UF quartz, topaz
topaz quartz

citron
USE brilliant greenish yellow
grayish greenish yellow

citron green
USE grayish greenish yellow
moderate greenish yellow

citron yellow
USE light greenish yellow
moderate greenish yellow
strong greenish yellow
strontium chromate
zinc yellow

citron yellow, light
USE light greenish yellow

citrus peelers
USE orange peelers

citrus spoons
USE grapefruit spoons

citterns
TT.302   (H,L,N)
ALT cittern
SN European wire-strung plucked lute-like chordophones played with a plectrum, very popular in the 16th and 17th centuries, having a wedge-shaped body with a curved bottom and straight shoulders narrowing towards the neck, and a low flat bridge held in position only by the strings it supports. Their most characteristic feature is a long, fretted neck which is half cut away from behind the fingerboard on the bass side, making a channel along which the player's left thumb can slide to facilitate very rapid shifts to and from high positions.
UF ceteras
cisters
cistres
citherns
cithrens

citterns, keyed
USE keyed guitars

city atlases
HN April 1993 descriptor split, use city (ALT of cities) + atlases

city beautification
USE urban beautification

City Beautiful Movement
FL.1755   (R)

city blocks
RM.192   (A,L)
HN April 1993 descriptor moved
ALT city block
SN Use for pieces of land within urban areas usually bounded on all sides by streets or other transportation routes, natural physical barriers, or public open space and not traversed by through streets. (LOFZ)
UF blocks (city blocks)
blocks, city

city crosses
USE market crosses

city directories
VW.844   (A,L)
HN November 1992 descriptor moved
ALT city directory
UF directories, city
directories, local
local directories

city forestry
USE urban forestry

city gates
RK.467   (A,R)
ALT city gate
UF gates, city

city guidebooks
HN January 1993 descriptor split, use city (ALT of cities) + guidebooks

city halls
RK.951   (A,L,B,R)
ALT city hall
SN Use for the chief public administration buildings of a city, generally housing the mayor's office and legislative chambers.
UF halls, city

city lighting
USE municipal lighting

city maps
HN April 1991 descriptor split, use city (ALT of cities) + maps

city noise
BM.332   (L)
HN November 1992 descriptor moved
UF noise, city
noise, urban
urban noise

city ordinances
USE ordinances

city parks
USE urban parks

city planners
HG.875   (A,L,B)
HN May 1993 alternate terms added
ALT city planner
city planner's
city planners'
UF planners, city
planners, town
planners, urban
town planners
urban planners
urbanists

city planning
KD.304   (A,L,B,R)
HN November 1991 lead-in term deleted, was **design, urban**
February 1991 lead-in term deleted, was **urban design**
UF civic design
civic planning
design, civic
planning, city
planning, civic
planning, town
planning, urban
town planning
urban planning

city plans
HN April 1991 descriptor split, use city (ALT of cities) + plans (drawings)

city rugs
TC.158
ALT city rug
UF carpets, town
carpets, workshop
rugs, city
rugs, town
rugs, workshop
town carpets
town rugs
workshop carpets
workshop rugs

city squares
USE squares (open spaces)

city-states
HN.33   (L)
HN January 1993 descriptor added
ALT city-state
SN Sovereign states consisting of a city and its contiguous dependent territories.
RT cities

city transit
USE local transit

city transportation
USE urban transportation

city views (creative works)
USE cityscapes

city walls
RK.408   (A,L,B,R)
ALT city wall
UF walls, city

city-wide parks
USE urban parks

cityscapes
VC.604
HN April 1993 lead-in term added
January 1993 scope note changed
January 1993 related terms added
January 1993 descriptor changed,
was **city views**
January 1993 alternate term
changed, was **city view**
January 1993 lead-in term deleted,
was **cityscapes (views)**
January 1993 lead-in term deleted,
was **townscapes (views)**
May 1991 descriptor moved
ALT cityscape
SN Use for creative works that depict
settlements that may be considered
cities. For creative works depicting
settlements that may be considered
towns, use **townscapes (representations)**. For images that are more
documentary than creative, prefer
views or **topographical views**.
UF city views (creative works)
urban views (creative works)
views, city (creative works)
views, urban (creative works)
RT topographical views
townscapes (representations)
views

cityscapes (built environment)
USE townscapes (built environment)

civic associations
USE community organizations

civic buildings
USE public buildings

civic centers
RG.279 (A,L)
ALT civic center
UK civic centres
UKA civic centre
SN Use for areas within a city where the
principal governmental and cultural
buildings are grouped; may also denote building complexes or individual buildings housing such a range
of functions, especially when the
construction was financed by municipal funds.
UF centers, civic
centers, municipal
centres, civic
municipal centers

civic centres
SEE civic centers

civic design
USE city planning

civic groups
USE community organizations

civic improvement
KG.62 (L)
HN January 1991 scope note added

SN Beautifying or improving the working condition of small-scale public
amenities in a municipality, such as
sidewalks, road signs, and green
areas.
UF improvement, civic
improvement, municipal
municipal improvement

civic organizations
USE community organizations

civic planning
USE city planning

civil court records
VW.756
HN November 1992 descriptor moved
ALT civil court record
UF records, civil court

<civil districts>
RG.258

civil engineering
KD.113 (L,B,R)
HN April 1993 related term added
SN Branch of engineering concerned
primarily with public works such as
highways, bridges, waterways, harbors, and water supply systems, but
also private enterprises such as land
drainage and railroad building. (W)
UF engineering, civil
RT civil engineers

civil engineers
HG.859 (A,L,B)
HN April 1993 related term added
December 1992 alternate terms
added
ALT civil engineer
civil engineer's
civil engineers'
UF engineers, civil
RT civil engineering

civil law
KD.296 (L)
SN Body of private law that has developed from the Roman law in states
where the legal system is substantially Roman but has been influenced by Germanic, ecclesiastical,
and purely modern institutions. (W)
UF law, civil

civil liberties
USE civil rights

civil rights
BM.952 (L)
HN February 1993 descriptor moved
September 1991 scope note added
September 1991 lead-in terms
added
September 1991 alternate term
added
ALT civil right
SN Personal liberties that belong to
each individual due to his or her sta-
tus as a citizen of a particular coun-
try or community. (GALAW)

UF civil liberties
liberties, civil
rights, civil

civil servants
USE government employees

civil wars
KM.6 (L)
HN January 1991 scope note added
January 1991 alternate term added
November 1990 descriptor moved
January 1990 descriptor changed,
was **civil war**
ALT civil war
SN Wars between different sections or
parties of the same nation. (W)
UF wars, civil

civilité
PJ.3491
SN Group of script typefaces based on
Gothic cursive hand-written scripts.

civilization
BM.264 (L)

Civitavecchia
FL.2835

clack idiophones
TT.447
ALT clack idiophone
SN Idiophones consisting of a lamella
carved in the surface of a nut, fruit
shell, or other spherical object
which serves as a resonator; the lamella is plucked by the player's
thumb. (MARCUS)
UF cricris
idiophones, clack

Clactonian
FL.2541

cladding
KT.1105 (L,R)
HN March 1993 scope note changed
January 1993 descriptor moved
July 1991 descriptor moved
July 1991 scope note changed
July 1991 related term added
July 1991 alternate term added
ALT clad
SN Coating one metal with another by
means of bonding, as to protect the
inner metal from corrosion or for
minting coins.
UF cladding, metal
metal cladding
RT bonding (joining)

cladding (siding)
USE siding

cladding, metal
USE cladding

claims
VW.610 (L)
HN November 1992 descriptor moved
November 1992 scope note changed
ALT claim
SN Documents asserting a right, includ-

ing titles to debts, privileges, or other things in possession of another; also includes titles to anything which another should give, concede, or confer on the claimant. (GAHLM)

claims, insurance
USE insurance claims

clairobscur
USE chiaroscuro

clairons
USE bugles

Clallam
USE Klallam

clam dredgers
TX.363
ALT clam dredger
SN Use for boats from the Chesapeake Bay rigged with hydraulic clam dredges; generally square-sterned deadrise motorboats, somewhat beamier than similar boats such as used in other Chesapeake fisheries.
UF dredgers, clam

clamp drills
USE drill clamps

clamp nails
PJ.188
HN April 1993 descriptor moved
ALT clamp nail
SN Mechanical fasteners designed to bridge a joint and pull the two pieces tightly together as they are driven in place. (MEANS)
UF nails, clamp

clamping-pliers
USE sliding tongs

clamping screws
PJ.233
HN April 1993 descriptor moved
ALT clamping screw
SN Screws that in connection with wood or metal jaws may be used to provide a clamping force. (MEANS)
UF screws, clamping

clamps
TH.634 (L,N)
HN May 1993 related term added
ALT clamp
SN Mechanical devices commonly used to hold items together or firmly in place while other operations are being performed. (MEANS)
UF cramps
glauns
RT <clamps: woodworking tools>

clamps, bar
USE bar clamps

clamps, bench
USE bench clamps

clamps, C
USE C-clamps

clamps, circle
USE C-clamps

clamps, circle-end
USE C-clamps

clamps, combination
USE universal clamps

clamps, corner
USE corner clamps

clamps, dovetail
USE dovetail clamps

clamps, drill
USE drill clamps

clamps, G
USE C-clamps

clamps, gee
USE C-clamps

clamps, hand
USE screw clamps

clamps, handscrew
USE screw clamps

clamps, hexagon
USE universal clamps

clamps, joiners'
USE bar clamps

clamps, panel
USE panel clamps

clamps, picture-framing
USE corner clamps

clamps, sash
USE sash clamps

clamps, saw
USE saw clamps

clamps, screw
USE screw clamps

clamps, slat-bending
USE slat-bending clamps

clamps, spring
USE spring clamps

clamps, universal
USE universal clamps

clamps, web
USE web clamps

<clamps: woodworking tools>
TH.1622
HN May 1993 related term added
RT clamps

clamshell buckets
TH.462 (N)
HN April 1993 lead-in terms added
January 1991 lead-in term added
ALT clamshell bucket
SN Buckets used on cranes or derricks for handling granular materials.

Their jaw-like halves close and open by cable or hydraulic action. (DAC)
UF buckets, clamshell
buckets, grab
clamshell grabs
clamshells
grab buckets

clamshell grabs
USE clamshell buckets

clamshells
USE clamshell buckets

clans
HG.9 (L)
HN May 1991 descriptor moved
ALT clan
SN Groups of families and households, the heads of which claim descent from a common ancestor. (W)

clap tables
USE console tables

clapboard siding
MT.1797 (A,B)
UF bevel siding
siding, bevel
siding, clapboard
siding, weatherboard
weatherboard siding

clapper bells
TT.470
ALT clapper bell
SN Suspended bells sounded by a swinging clapper attached inside.
UF bells, clapper

clappers (idiophones)
TT.452 (L)
ALT clapper (idiophone)
SN Concussion idiophones consisting of two or more objects in the form of sticks, plaques, troughs, or vessels of wood, bone, ivory, shell or other hard sonorous material, sounded by striking together; the component pieces may be hinged together at one end, hinged to a separate central piece, or be held one in each of the player's hands.
UF concussion idiophones
idiophones, concussion

clappers (percussion beaters)
PJ.3273
ALT clapper (percussion beater)
SN Tongues of metal or wood in various types of open bells which produce the sound by striking the side of the instrument; generally they take the form of a rod, or of a ball or pellet attached to a cord. (NGDMI)

clappers, stick
USE concussion sticks

clappers, vessel
USE concussion vessels

claret glasses
TQ.451
ALT claret glass
SN A 19th-century term for a type of stemmed wine glass intended for drinking red wine from Bordeaux.
UF clarets
glasses, claret

claret jugs
TQ.517
ALT claret jug
SN Decanters with a pouring lip and handle used for wine.
UF jugs, claret
RT decanters
jugs

clarets
USE claret glasses

clarification drawings
VC.175
HN April 1992 descriptor moved
ALT clarification drawing
SN Graphic interpretations of the drawings or other contractual documents issued by the architect. (DAC)
UF addendum drawings
drawings, addendum
drawings, clarification

clarinet players
USE clarinetists

clarinetists
HG.236 (L)
HN January 1993 descriptor added
ALT clarinetist
clarinetist's
clarinetists'
UK clarinettists
UKA clarinettist
clarinettist's
clarinettists'
SN Those who play the clarinet.
UF clarinet players
players, clarinet
RT clarinets

clarinets
TT.149 (L,N)
ALT clarinet
SN Use generally for all reedpipes with single reed and essentially cylindrical bore. May also be used specifically for those reedpipes with single reed used as solo and orchestral instruments in Western jazz, classical, folk, and band music; commonly, all have the Boehm system of keywork and fingering.
UF clarionets
RT Boehm system
clarinetists

clarinets, double
USE double clarinets

clarinettes d'amour
TT.152
ALT clarinette d'amour
SN Late 18th-century European clari-
nets, straight-bodied with a globular or pear-shaped bell with a narrow opening, and sometimes a curved metal crook to carry the mouthpiece.

clarinettists
SEE clarinetists

clarionets
USE clarinets

clarsaich
USE Irish harps

clasp knives
TH.534
ALT clasp knife
SN Large pocket knives whose blade or blades fold or shut into the handle. (W)
UF knives, clasp

clasp nails
USE cut nails

clasping buttresses
PJ.1450
HN March 1993 descriptor moved
ALT clasping buttress
SN Use for buttresses which in plan are squares or rectangles penetrated by the corner of a building.
UF buttresses, clasping

clasps (fasteners)
PJ.74 (H,L,N,R)
ALT clasp (fastener)
SN Two-part fasteners, usually metal, consisting of a hook and slot.
RT <costume components>

clasps (motifs)
DG.15
HN May 1992 descriptor added
ALT clasp (motif)
SN Straplike elements that encircle moldings, such as those applied to the center or corner of 17th-century frames.

clasps, tie
USE tie clasps

class B gypsum plaster
USE retarded hemihydrate plaster

class boats
TX.346
ALT class boat
SN Sailboats sufficiently alike or having differences under sufficient restrictions to enable them to race against each other as a class without the necessity of handicap allowances. (SCLASS)
UF boats, class

class boats, development
USE development class boats

class boats, restricted
USE development class boats

class C gypsum plaster
USE anhydrous gypsum plaster

class D gypsum plaster
USE Keene's cement

class differences
USE social stratification

class, laboring
USE working class

class, middle
USE middle class

class status
USE social status

class, upper
USE upper class

class, working
USE working class

classed catalogs
USE classified catalogs

classes, social
USE social classes

Classic
FL.982

Classic Chiriqui
USE Chiriqui

classic cypress
MT.2934
HN March 1992 descriptor moved
UF Cupressus sempervirens
cypress, classic
cypress, Mediterranean
Mediterranean cypress

Classic, Early
USE Early Classic

Classic Kerma
FL.159
UF Kerma, Classic

Classic, Late
USE Late Classic

Classic Maori
FL.3835
UF Maori, Classic

Classic, Middle
USE Middle Classic

Classic Revival
USE Classical Revival

Classic Veracruz
FL.1019
UF Veracruz, Classic

Classic Veraguas
USE Veraguas

Classical
FL.2666 (A)

classical abstraction
USE geometric abstraction

classical archaeology
  KD.205 (L)
  UF archaeology, classical

Classical, Early
  USE Early Classical

Classical, High
  USE High Classical

Classical Ife
  FL.100
  UF Ife, Classical

Classical, Late
  USE Late Classical

classical orders
  USE architectural orders

Classical Revival
  FL.3356 (A,B)
  HN May 1993 related terms added
  SN Use for late 18th- to early 20th-century architecture and ornament based relatively closely on ancient classical forms. For other architecture and art of the late 18th and the 19th centuries that follow principles of classicism, use **Neoclassical.**
  UF Classic Revival
      Neoclassical Revival
      Revival, Classic
      Revival, Classical
      Revival, Neoclassical
  RT classicism
      Neoclassical

Classical Revival (North American)
  USE Federal

classicism
  BM.134 (A,L,R)
  HN May 1993 related terms added
  ALT classicizing
  SN Includes any manifestation of the material culture of classical Greece and Rome. With reference to the period of late 18th- and 19th-century art and architecture which featured a return to classical principles, use **Neoclassical.** With reference to the period of architecture and ornament of the late 18th- to early 20th-century based relatively closely on ancient classical forms, use **Classical Revival.**
  RT Classical Revival
      Neoclassical

classicists
  HG.461 (L)
  HN April 1993 related term added
      February 1993 descriptor moved
      January 1993 alternate terms added
  ALT classicist
      classicist's
      classicists'
  SN Scholars of the ancient classical period or adherents of classicism in art or literature.
  RT classics

classics
  KD.40 (L)
  HN April 1993 related term added
  SN Area of study covering the civilizations of ancient Greece and Rome, including history, philosophy, language, literature, and to some extent art and archaeology. (PG)
  RT classicists
      papyrology

classification
  USE classifying

classification yards
  USE marshalling yards

classified catalogs
  VW.16 (L)
  HN November 1992 descriptor moved
  ALT classified catalog
  SN Subject catalogs in which entries are arranged by the class numbers of a classification schedule. (ALAG)
  UF catalogs, classed
      catalogs, classified
      catalogs, systematic
      classed catalogs
      systematic catalogs

classifying
  KG.110 (L,B,R)
  HN March 1991 alternate term added
  ALT classified
  SN Arranging systematically in groups or categories according to established criteria. (WCOL9)
  UF classification

classroom windows
  PJ.2226
  HN March 1993 descriptor moved
      December 1990 scope note changed
  ALT classroom window
  SN Windows designed to meet the requirements of school buildings, usually featuring large multipaned glass areas.
  UF windows, classroom

classrooms
  PJ.1167 (A,B)
  HN March 1993 descriptor moved
  ALT classroom
  SN Use for rooms devoted to formal instruction in schools.
  UF schoolrooms

Claudian stone
  USE Porta Santa marble

clavecins
  USE harpsichords

claves
  TT.457 (L,N)
  ALT clave
  SN Cuban concussion idiophones consisting of two cylindrical hardwood sticks; one stick rests lightly on the fingertips of one hand with the cupped palm acting as a resonator, while the other stick, held between the thumb and first two fingers, is used to strike the first. (NGDMI)

clavi
  PJ.3036
  ALT clavus
  SN Purple bands which ornamented Roman tunics, running up and over each shoulder from hem to hem, and indicated the rank of the wearer. Also, bands of this type and color used on vestments.
  RT tunics
      vestments

clavicembalos
  USE harpsichords

clavichords
  TT.402 (L,N,R)
  ALT clavichord
  SN Zitherlike instruments in the form of a rectangular box with a keyboard set in the long side. Strings, usually two per note, run diagonally from hitch pins on the left over a bridge to turning pins at the right. Brass tangents on the rear portion of each key strike the strings from below to produce sound.
  RT keyboard instruments
      tangents

clavichords, fretless
  USE unfretted clavichords

clavichords, fretted
  USE fretted clavichords

clavichords, unfretted
  USE unfretted clavichords

clavicorno
  USE clavicors

clavicors
  TT.100 (N)
  ALT clavicor
  SN European brass valve trumpets of tenor pitch, invented in 1837, having a narrow bore and three valves; their primary use was in French and Italian military bands in the 19th century.
  UF clavicorno

clavicytheria
  TT.374
  ALT clavicytherium
  SN Upright harpsichords having a vertical soundboard and a complicated action, often involving springs, in which the jacks move horizontally rather than vertically to pluck the strings. (NGDMI)

claviorgana
  USE claviorgans

claviorgans
  TT.631 (L)
  ALT claviorgan
  SN Keyboard instruments combining a harpsichord with an organ.

UF   claviorgana
claviorganums
harpsichords, organ
harpsichords, organized
organ harpsichords
organized harpsichords
RT   keyboard instruments

claviorganums
USE   claviorgans

claw-and-ball feet
    PJ.2805
HN   March 1993 descriptor moved
March 1993 lead-in term changed,
    was **eagle's feet**
March 1993 lead-in term changed,
    was **feet, eagle's**
ALT   claw-and-ball foot
SN   A termination mainly used on cabriole legs in the first half of the 18th century (though earlier examples occur), representing a bird's or dragon's claw clutching a ball. Of Oriental derivation. (TOMLIN)
UF   ball-and-claw feet
eagles' feet
feet, ball-and-claw
feet, claw-and-ball
feet, eagles'
feet, talon and ball
talon and ball feet

claw bars
    TH.963
ALT   claw bar
SN   Steel bars that have a straight chisel point at one end, and are bent at the other end, which has a notch for pulling nails; used for general demolition work. (MEANS)
UF   bars, claw

claw chisels
USE   tooth chisels

claw feet
    PJ.2804
HN   March 1993 descriptor moved
ALT   claw foot
SN   Feet, in the shape of claws, on a piece of furniture. (W)
UF   feet, claw

claw feet, rat
USE   rat claw feet

claw feet, retracted
USE   retracted claw feet

claw feet, winged
USE   winged claw feet

claw-hammer coats
USE   tail coats

claw hammers
    TH.1653   (N)
HN   January 1991 lead-in term added
ALT   claw hammer
SN   Hammers with a hardened face on one end of the head for driving nails, and curved forked tines on the

other end for pulling out nails. (MEANS)
UF   hammers, claw
khivi

claw hatchets
    TH.1471   (N)
ALT   claw hatchet
SN   Medium-sized hatchets with a nail-pulling claw at the side of a nail-driving poll. (BLACKB)
UF   hatchets, claw

claw tables
USE   pillar and claw tables

claw tools
USE   tooth chisels

claws
USE   talons

claws, nail
USE   tack pulls

claws, tack
USE   tack pulls

clay
    MT.53   (A,L,B,R)
HN   April 1992 descriptor moved
UF   clay, native
native clay

clay, Albany slip
USE   Albany slip clay

<clay and clay products>
    MT.52
HN   April 1992 guide term moved

clay-and-hair mortar
    MT.2333
UF   mortar, clay-and-hair

clay, ball
USE   ball clay

<clay by composition or origin>
    MT.54
HN   April 1992 guide term moved

<clay by function>
    MT.66
HN   April 1992 guide term moved

clay, calcareous
USE   marl

clay, Devonshire
USE   kaolin

clay, gilder's
USE   bole

clay, gilder's burnishing
USE   bole

clay, gilders red
USE   red bole

<clay minerals>
    MT.525
HN   February 1992 guide term added

clay mortar
    MT.2332
UF   mortar, clay

clay, native
USE   clay

clay pigeons
    TV.71
ALT   clay pigeon
SN   Use for disklike, saucer-shaped targets, about 4 1/2 inches in diameter and 1/2 inch thick hurled through the air from a trap in the sports of skeet and trapshooting; first developed in the 1860s and made of baked clay, now usually a mixture of river silt and pitch.
UF   pigeons, clay

clay, pipe
USE   pipe clay

clay, potter's
USE   potter's clay

clay products
HN   April 1993 descriptor deleted

<clay products>
    MT.70
HN   April 1993 guide term added

clay, refractory
USE   fireclay

clay shale
    MT.830
HN   April 1992 descriptor moved
UF   shale, clay

clay, slip
USE   slip

clay, soap
USE   bentonite

clay-stone
SEE   claystone

clay tile, structural
USE   structural clay tile

clay, volcanic
USE   bentonite

claymores
    TK.71   (N)
ALT   claymore
SN   Use for two-handed Scottish broadswords with a long, heavy double-edged blade, long diamond-section quillons angling toward the blade, and a tubular leather-covered hilt with a round pommel; they were used by Scottish Highlanders and mercenaries from the 15th to the 17th century. Use also for the one-handed Scottish broadswords with basket hilts in use in the British Army since the early 18th century.

claystone
    MT.826

HN April 1992 descriptor moved
March 1992 descriptor changed, was **clay stone**
UK clay-stone
SN Fine-grain rock largely composed of or derived by erosion of sedimentary silt and clay or any type of rock that contained clay. (STEIN)
UF siltstone (claystone)

<clayworking tools and equipment>
TH.1117

Clazomenian
FL.2691 (L)

clean rooms
PJ.1342 (A,L)
HN March 1993 descriptor moved
ALT clean room
SN Rooms in which efforts are made to keep contamination out, including atmospheric pollutants, by the use of air filters, mats, or other devices, as in assembly rooms for precision products or computer rooms.
UF rooms, clean

clean timber
USE clear lumber

cleaners
HG.89 (L)
HN March 1993 descriptor changed, was **cleaners (people)**
March 1993 alternate term changed, was **cleaner (person)**
November 1992 alternate terms added
ALT cleaner
cleaner's
cleaners'

cleaners, air
USE air filters

cleaners, brush
USE brush washers

cleaners, vacuum
USE vacuum cleaners

cleaning
KT.919 (A,L,B)
HN February 1993 related term added
November 1992 descriptor moved
August 1992 scope note added
ALT cleaned
SN Removing dirt, surface coatings, accretions, discolorations, or other matter from a substrate.
RT cleaning compound

cleaning, abrasive
USE abrasive cleaning

cleaning agent
USE cleaning compound

cleaning compound
MT.1841 (L)
HN April 1993 lead-in term changed, was **cleaning agents**

April 1993 descriptor changed, was **cleaning compounds**
February 1993 related term added
UF agent, cleaning
cleaning agent
compound, cleaning
RT cleaning

cleaning, dry
USE dry cleaning

cleaning-out planes
USE coopers' stoup planes

cleanouts
USE ashpits

clear glaze
MT.1995
UF glaze, clear

clear lumber
MT.3031
HN March 1992 descriptor moved
UF clean timber
lumber, clear
timber, clean

clearance lamps
PJ.3288
ALT clearance lamp
SN Lighting devices mounted on a vehicle for the purpose of indicating the overall width and height of the vehicle. (IESREF)
UF lamps, clearance

clearance, slum
USE slum clearance

clearing houses
SEE clearinghouses

clearinghouses
HN.127 (L)
HN February 1991 descriptor moved
February 1991 related term added
ALT clearinghouse
UK clearing houses
UKA clearing house
SN Organizations that serve as central agencies for the collection, organization, storage, and dissemination of documents and that perform referral services for researchers. (ALAG)
UF clearinghouses, information
information clearinghouses
RT collections

clearinghouses, information
USE clearinghouses

clearstories
USE clerestories

cleats
PJ.2759
HN March 1993 descriptor moved
ALT cleat

cleats, angle
USE angle cleats

cleavage
DE.4 (L)

SN Separation between layers, as between a paint or varnish film and other film layers, or between a film layer and its support, or separation along planes of weakness in crystalline materials.

cleavers
TH.110 (N)
HN April 1993 descriptor added
ALT cleaver
SN Sharp, broad-bladed and often short-handled knives used for cutting large pieces of meat into joints or roasts.
UF axes, meat
butchers' cleavers
cleavers, butchers'
cleavers, meat
meat-axes
meat cleavers

cleavers, butchers'
USE cleavers

cleavers, meat
USE cleavers

cleaving adzes
TH.1390 (N)
ALT cleaving adz
SN Short-handled adzes used for splitting wood. (HAND)
UF adzes, cleaving

cleaving blades
TH.1343
HN December 1992 descriptor moved
ALT cleaving blade
SN Sharp steel bars used to split stone so that the facet angles can be measured. (HAND)
UF blades, cleaving

cleaving irons
USE froes

cleaving wedges
USE splitting wedges

clench hammers
TH.1654 (N)
ALT clench hammer
SN Hammers with an octagonal or round face, chamfered neck, and a cross peen with thick rounded edges; used as an anvil when held behind the head of a rivet or nail to hold it in position while its point is hammered over. (SALAM)
UF flooring hammers
hammers, clench
hammers, flooring
hammers, roofing
roofing hammers

clench nails, rose
USE rose clench nails

clepsydras
USE water clocks

clerestories
PJ.1357 (A)

HN March 1993 descriptor moved
ALT clerestory
SN Upper zones of walls rising above adjacent roofs and pierced by windows so as to admit light to a high central room or space flanked by lower rooms or spaces.
UF clearstories

clergy
HG.393 (L,R)
HN February 1993 lead-in term deleted, was **ecclesiastics**
December 1992 alternate terms added
April 1991 alternate term added
ALT clergyman
clergyman's
clergy's
SN Religious officials or functionaries prepared and authorized to conduct religious services or attend to other official religious duties.
UF clerics

<clergy houses>
RK.329

clerical workers
HG.83 (L)
HN November 1992 alternate terms added
September 1990 lead-in term added
ALT clerical worker
clerical worker's
clerical workers'
SN Workers occupied in preparing, transcribing, systematizing, and preserving written communications and records, distributing information, or collecting accounts, usually in an office environment. (ERIC9)
UF clerks
office workers
workers, clerical
workers, office

clerics
USE clergy

clerks
USE clerical workers

clerks of the works
HG.818 (B)
HN December 1992 alternate terms added
ALT clerk of the works
clerk's of the works
clerks' of the works
SN On-site clerical workers who keep records of the workers on a building project, deliveries made, and progress of the job; they make reports, receive and catalog samples, and keep a log of job activities. (STEIN)

clichés-glace
USE clichés-verre

clichés-verre
VC.384 (L,R)
HN April 1993 lead-in terms added

April 1992 descriptor moved
May 1991 lead-in term added
ALT cliché-verre
SN Photographic prints produced from a glass plate that has been drawn on or painted and is then used like a negative.
UF artificial negatives
clichés-glace
factitious negatives
glass photoprints
glass prints
negatives, artificial
negatives, factitious
photoprints, glass
prints, glass

clients
HG.624
HN December 1992 alternate terms added
ALT client
client's
clients'
SN Persons who engage the professional advice or services of another. (W)

cliff dwellings
RK.310 (A,L,B)
ALT cliff dwelling
SN Houses built on ledges in the vertical sides of mesas, as in the American Southwest or similarly inaccessible locations.
UF dwellings, cliff

cliffs
RD.203 (L)
ALT cliff
UF bluffs

climate
BM.734 (L,B,R)
HN May 1993 related term added
March 1993 scope note added
January 1993 lead-in term deleted, was **microclimate**
November 1992 descriptor moved
SN The long-term total of atmospheric variations at a specific geographical location. Regarding shorter-term atmospheric conditions, use **weather**.
RT weather

climate, arctic
USE polar climate

climate control, indoor
USE HVAC

climate, desert
USE desert climate

climate, polar
USE polar climate

climate, temperate
USE temperate climate

climate, tropical
USE tropical climate

climatic charts
HN March 1991 descriptor split, use **climate + charts**

climatic maps
VW.98 (L)
HN November 1992 descriptor moved
ALT climatic map
UF maps, climatic

climbers
USE junglegyms

climbing cranes
TH.468
ALT climbing crane
SN Hoisting devices consisting of a horizontal boom, equipped with a winch and hoist line, and swung from the top of the vertical mast; used in the erection of high-rise buildings. (DAC)
UF cranes, climbing

climbing frames
USE junglegyms

climbing gyms
USE junglegyms

climbing plants
USE vines

climbing ropes
TV.49 (N)
ALT climbing rope
SN Use for special ropes, usually of four strands of selected manilla long fiber and about 1 1/2 inches in diameter, designed for gymnastic climbing or as practice for mountain climbing.
UF ropes, climbing

clinch-built
USE clinker-built

clinch cutters
USE buffers (cutters)

clinical laboratories
USE medical (ALT of medicine) + laboratories

clinical thermometers
TN.319 (L)
ALT clinical thermometer
SN Small thermometers used to measure accurately the temperature of the human body.
UF medical thermometers
thermometers, clinical
thermometers, medical

clinics
RK.705 (A,L,B,R)
ALT clinic
UF buildings, out-patient
clinics, medical
clinics, out-patient
departments, out-patient
medical clinics
out-patient buildings
out-patient clinics

out-patient departments
policlinics

clinics, birth control
USE   birth control clinics

clinics, dental
USE   dental clinics

clinics, family planning
USE   birth control clinics

clinics, medical
USE   clinics

clinics, mental health
USE   psychiatric clinics

clinics, mobile
USE   mobile hospitals

clinics, out-patient
USE   clinics

clinics, psychiatric
USE   psychiatric clinics

clinics, surgical
USE   surgical clinics

clinker
MT.3063
HN   February 1992 descriptor moved
UF   cement clinker
clinker, cement

clinker block
USE   cinder block

clinker brick
MT.124   (L)
HN   April 1992 descriptor moved
SN   Very hard-burnt brick whose shape
is distorted, owing to nearly com-
plete vitrification; used for paving.
(DAC)
UF   brick, clinker
brick, Dutch
clinker, Dutch
Dutch brick
Dutch clinker
klinkart

clinker-built
DC.35
HN   February 1993 descriptor added
SN   Use to describe wooden watercraft
hulls in which the lower ends of
each plank overlaps the top end of
the plank below it; the point of
overlap is usually pinned, nailed, or
riveted.
UF   clinch-built
lapstrake

clinker, cement
USE   clinker

clinker, Dutch
USE   clinker brick

clinographs
TN.25   (N)
ALT   clinograph
SN   Survey instruments used in mining

and construction that measure and
record the deviation from the vertical of, for example, boreholes or
well shafts.

clinometers
TN.26   (L,N)
ALT   clinometer
SN   Any of various instruments for mea-
suring vertical angles, as for inclina-
tion, slope, or elevation.

clip art
VC.38   (L)
SN   Stock images used by graphic artists
for decoration or illustration; traditionally on paper and clipped out
with scissors to be pasted into layouts, more recently, electronic images that can be transferred into a
computer application as needed.
UF   art, clip

clip candleholders
TC.1243
ALT   clip candleholder
UF   candleholders, clip

clip hangers
PJ.93
HN   April 1993 descriptor moved
ALT   clip hanger
UF   hangers, clip

clip-on earrings
USE   ear clips

clip pullers
USE   clip tongs

clip tongs
TH.1292   (N)
SN   Flat tongs whose faces are shaped to
pull or grip wire; used in welding
clips and in horseshoeing.
UF   clip pullers
draw tongs
pullers, clip
tongs, clip
tongs, draw

clipei (portraits)
VC.615
ALT   clipeus (portrait)
SN   Hellenistic and Roman portrait
heads or busts in round frames,
connoting honor or heroization.
(AGEOFS)
UF   imagines clipeatae

clipei (shields)
TE.356
ALT   clipeus (shield)
SN   Circular or oval shields of leather or
bronze covered with metal plates or
a sheet of bronze, used by Roman
heavy cavalry from the late 8th to
the 4th century BCE.
UF   clupei
clypei

clipped gable roofs
USE   jerkinhead roofs

clipper cards
USE   sailing cards

clipper ship cards
USE   sailing cards

clipper ships
TX.303   (L,N)
ALT   clipper ship
SN   Use for fast ocean-going sailing
ships generally characterized by
sharply raked stern, a long and low
hull with the draft deeper aft than
forward, an inclined, overhanging
counter stern, and a large spread of
canvas; developed in the mid-19th
century as cargo vessels, but their
speed lent the vessels to other uses;
typically having three masts and
square rigs.
UF   clippers (ships)
ships, clippers
RT   sailing ships

clippers
TH.528
HN   January 1993 descriptor added
ALT   clipper
SN   Term generally applied to a variety
of mechanical devices for clipping
or cutting.

clippers (ships)
USE   clipper ships

clippers, Baltimore
USE   Baltimore clippers

clippers, bolt
USE   bolt clippers
bolt cutters

clippers, nail
USE   nail clippers

clipping
KT.942
HN   March 1992 descriptor added
ALT   clipped
SN   Trimming or cutting away the edges
of gold or silver coins in order to
pilfer some of the precious metal.
(DOTY)

clippings
VW.1031   (L)
HN   November 1992 descriptor moved
ALT   clipping
SN   Illustrations, pages, articles, or columns of text removed from books,
newspapers, journals, or other
printed sources.
UF   clippings, newspaper
clippings, press
cuttings
cuttings, press
newspaper clippings
press clippings
press cuttings

clippings files
PC.87
HN   March 1993 descriptor moved

March 1990 alternate term changed,
was **clipping file**
ALT clippings file
SN Collections of cuttings from newspapers and periodicals, usually kept in folders in vertical files and arranged systematically. (LG)
UF cuttings files
files, clippings
files, cuttings
files, media
media files

clippings, newspaper
USE clippings

clippings, press
USE clippings

clips (fasteners)
PJ.77
HN April 1993 descriptor moved
March 1993 descriptor changed,
was **clips**
March 1993 alternate term changed,
was **clip**
February 1993 scope note changed
ALT clip (fastener)
SN Devices of varying form that grip and hold tightly.

clips (jewelry)
TE.483
ALT clip (jewelry)
SN Decorative items, similar in appearance to a brooch, but attached to a garment with a spring fastening.
RT brooches

clips, angle
USE angle cleats

clips, back
USE back clips

clips, corner
USE corner clips

clips, ear
USE ear clips

clips, nailing
USE nailing clips

clips, paper
USE paper clips

clips, tie
USE tie clasps

clips, truss
USE truss clips

clipsham stone
MT.849
HN April 1992 descriptor moved
UF stone, clipsham

cloacae
RK.518
ALT cloaca
SN Use for ancient Roman sewers. (BOETH)

cloak-rooms
SEE cloakrooms

cloakrooms
PJ.1134 (A,B)
HN March 1993 descriptor moved
ALT cloakroom
UK cloak-rooms
UKA cloak-room
SN Rooms in which coats or other garments may be placed during one's stay. (W)
UF coatrooms

cloaks
TE.133 (H,L,N,R)
ALT cloak
SN Sleeveless outer garments which fasten at the neck and fall loosely from the shoulders to cover the entire body; may have a yoke or some shaping from the neck to the shoulders.
RT capotes (outerwear)
chasubles
paletots
phelonions

cloaks, dust
USE dusters

cloath chairs
TC.493
HN January 1993 descriptor moved
ALT cloath chair
SN Chippendale's term for high-backed easy chairs stuffed all over and upholstered in wool fabric. (GILBR2)
UF chairs, cloath

clochans
RK.248
ALT clochan
SN Use for masonry, corbel-domed huts found from the Medieval period in Ireland and possibly built to house hermit monks.

cloches
TE.580 (N)
ALT cloche
SN Hats with a bell-shaped crown.

cloches (bell glasses)
USE bell glasses

clock and program systems
PC.106
HN March 1993 descriptor moved
ALT clock and program system
SN Use for systems that bring several clocks into conformity, and may ring bells or alarms at scheduled intervals.
UF school clock and program systems
systems, clock and program
systems, school clock and program

<clock and watch components>
PJ.2642

<clock and watch trains>
PJ.2647

clock cases
PJ.2650
ALT clock case
SN The protective and ornamental coverings that support and enclose a clock movement and dial. (IDOFC)
UF cases, clock

clock lamps
USE time lamps

clock-makers
SEE clockmakers

clock making
KT.789 (L)
RT clockmakers

clock towers
RK.36 (A,L,B,R)
ALT clock tower
UF towers, clock

clock watches
TN.204
ALT clock watch
SN Use for watches that strike the hours in passing; for timepieces that strike the hours at any time upon request, use **repeaters**.
UF watches, clock
RT repeaters

clockmakers
HG.776 (H,L,R)
HN April 1993 related term added
December 1992 alternate terms added
ALT clockmaker
clockmaker's
clockmakers'
UK clock-makers
UKA clock-maker
SN Persons who make or repair clocks. (W)
RT clock making

clockmakers' files
TH.1255
HN March 1993 descriptor changed,
was **clockmaker's files**
March 1993 lead-in term changed,
was **watchmaker's files**
March 1993 lead-in term changed,
was **files, clockmaker's**
March 1993 lead-in term changed,
was **files, watchmakers'**
ALT clockmaker's file
UF files, clockmakers'
files, watchmakers'
watchmakers' files

clocks
TN.155 (A,H,L,N,B,R)
ALT clock
SN Use for instruments that measure and indicate the passage of time, especially by mechanical means producing a regularly recurring action and indicating, usually by hands or changing numbers, the hours and minutes; not designed to be worn or otherwise carried about on a person.

For wearable timepieces, use
watches.
RT watches

clocks, acorn
USE acorn clocks

clocks, Act of Parliament
USE Act of Parliament clocks

clocks, alarm
USE alarm clocks

clocks, astronomical
USE astronomical clocks

clocks, atomic
USE atomic clocks

clocks, balloon
USE balloon clocks

clocks, banjo
USE banjo clocks

clocks, bracket
USE bracket clocks

<clocks by form>
TN.156

<clocks by function>
TN.179

<clocks by movement>
TN.190

clocks, calendar
USE calendar clocks

clocks, carriage
USE carriage clocks

clocks, cartel
USE cartel clocks

clocks, chiming
USE chiming clocks

clocks, cuckoo
USE cuckoo clocks

clocks, digital
USE digital clocks

clocks, digital electronic
USE digital clocks

clocks, dwarf tall
USE dwarf tall clocks

clocks, dwarf tall case
USE dwarf tall clocks

clocks, electronic
USE electronic clocks

clocks, equation
USE equation clocks

clocks, girandole
USE girandole clocks

clocks, Gothic
USE Gothic clocks

clocks, grandfathers'
USE tall case clocks

clocks, grandmother
USE dwarf tall clocks

clocks, lantern
USE lantern clocks

clocks, long case
USE tall case clocks

clocks, mantel
USE mantel clocks

clocks, mechanical
USE mechanical clocks

clocks, miniature tall case
USE dwarf tall clocks

clocks, musical
USE musical clocks

clocks, Parliament
USE Act of Parliament clocks

clocks, pedestal
USE pedestal clocks

clocks, pillar and scroll
USE pillar and scroll clocks

clocks, quartz
USE quartz clocks

clocks, quartz-crystal
USE quartz clocks

clocks, régulateur
USE regulators

clocks, self-winding
USE self-winding clocks

clocks, shelf
USE shelf clocks

clocks, ships'
USE ships' clocks

clocks, sidereal
USE sidereal clocks

clocks, skeleton
USE skeleton clocks

clocks, tabernacle
USE tabernacle clocks

clocks, table
USE table clocks

clocks, tall
USE tall case clocks

clocks, tall case
USE tall case clocks

clocks, tower
USE tower clocks

clocks, traveling
USE traveling clocks

clocks, turret
USE tower clocks

clocks, wall
USE wall clocks

clocks, water
USE water clocks

clocks, weight-driven
USE weight-driven clocks

clockwork toys
TV.198
ALT clockwork toy
SN Windup toys using the mechanisms and workings of clocks to move all or parts of the toy; popular since the mid-19th century, especially in the United States.
UF toys, clockwork

clogs
TE.718 (H,L,N)
ALT clog
SN Footwear with a thick sole typically of wood, but sometimes of rubber, cork, or the like.
UF shoes, wooden
wooden shoes

cloisonné
KT.96 (L,R)
HN March 1993 descriptor moved
SN A technique of enameling in which the design is laid down in thin metal strips on a metal or porcelain ground, forming chambers (cloisons) to receive the vitreous enamel pastes. (PDAT)
UF shippo

Cloisonnist
FL.3464 (R)
ALT Cloisonnism

cloister gardens
RM.36
HN April 1993 descriptor moved
ALT cloister garden
SN Use chiefly for Medieval gardens, generally found in monasteries, often formally arranged with planters and boxed sections.
UF gardens, cloister

cloister garths
PJ.978
HN March 1993 descriptor moved
June 1990 scope note changed
ALT cloister garth
SN Open courtyards surrounded by walkways, especially in a group of buildings of a monastery or college. (W)
UF garths
garths, cloister

cloister vaults
PJ.1868
HN March 1993 descriptor moved
October 1991 scope note changed
August 1991 lead-in term deleted, was **cloistered arches**
August 1991 lead-in term deleted, was **cloistered vaults**
August 1991 lead-in term deleted, was **arches, cloistered**

August 1991 lead-in term deleted,
was **vaults, cloistered**
ALT cloister vault
SN Use for vaults shaped like a pyramid
with sides that bow outward.
UF coved vaults
vaults, cloister
vaults, coved

cloisters
PJ.1262 (A,L,B,R)
HN March 1993 descriptor moved
June 1990 scope note changed
ALT cloister
SN Enclosed spaces composed of a
garth and surrounding walkways,
which are generally arcaded on the
courtyard side and walled on the
other; usually found in Christian religious building complexes. Use for
such features in secular buildings
only when closely resembling the
prototype.

close-beds
USE box beds

close cupboards
USE aumbries

close gauntlets
TE.331
ALT close gauntlet
SN Specialized type of mitten gauntlet,
in which the end finger lame was
extended so that, when the hand
was closed, it could be fastened to
the cuff, thus locking the hand in its
grip on a weapon; they were popular in the 16th century as double
pieces for foot-combat armor.
UF gauntlets, close
gauntlets, locking
locking gauntlets
RT double pieces

close helmets
TE.290
ALT close helmet
SN Closely fitting helmets with visor
and bevor, enclosing the head and
face; all main elements work on a
common set of pivots at the temples.
They were widely used from the
16th to the mid-17th century.
UF helmets, close
RT gorget plates

close nailing
KT.1246
HN December 1992 descriptor added
ALT close-nailed
SN Upholstering technique in which
nails are set close together to secure
the edges of the top cover, also cre-
ating a decorative feature.
UF nailing, close

close plating
KT.1110
HN December 1992 descriptor added
ALT close-plated

SN Process of plating with silver leaf on
steel, used especially on knives and
scissors; patented in 1779 by Rich-
ard Ellis as a technique less expensive than French plating. (HNSIL)
UF plating, close

close range photography
USE close-up photography

close-stool chairs
USE commode chairs

close stools
TC.667
HN January 1993 descriptor moved
ALT close stool
UF necessary stools
stools, close
stools, necessary

close-stools
USE commode chairs

Close Style
FL.2742

close-up photography
KT.583 (L)
UF close range photography
photography, close range
photography, close-up

close-up views
VC.23
HN April 1991 descriptor moved
ALT close-up view
SN Use when emphasis is on the close-
ness of the camera to the subject, as
distinct from **details**, where emphasis is on the partial nature of the
view.
UF close-ups
views, close-up

close-ups
USE close-up views

<closed automobiles>
TX.139

closed bonnet tops
USE bonnet tops

closed burgonets
TE.288
ALT closed burgonet
SN Helmets which are a cross between
burgonets and close helmets; they
are constructed like close helmets
but, like burgonets, have a peak,
cheekpieces, and a falling buffe instead of a visor and upper bevor.
UF burgonets, closed

closed composition
BM.53
UF composition, closed

closed eaves
PJ.1801
HN March 1993 descriptor moved
SN Use for eaves in which the support-

ing members are enclosed and
therefore not visible.
UF eaves, closed

closed greaves
TE.345
ALT closed greave
SN Greaves consisting of front and back
pieces, hinged together to enclose
the lower leg.
UF greaves, closed

closed knots
USE symmetrical knots

closed scorpers
TH.1607 (N)
ALT closed scorper
SN Two-handed scorpers having a
semicircular blade about 4 inches
wide and bent to bring the wood
handles in line with the blade.
(SALAM)
UF one-hand round shaves
round shaves, one-hand
scorpers, closed
shaves, one-hand round

closed specifications
VW.543
HN November 1992 descriptor moved
ALT closed specification
UF specifications, closed

closed system
PJ.3231
SN Keywork in which each fingerhole is
opened only for its own note, used
in Europe for a limited number of
instruments, such as ophicleides and
certain bagpipes.
UF system, closed

closer
MT.116
HN April 1992 descriptor moved
UF closure

closer, beveled
USE king closer

closer, king
USE king closer

closer, quarter
USE quarter closer

closer, queen
USE queen closer

closer, three-quarter
USE king closer

closers, door
USE door checks

closes
RG.267 (B)
HN March 1993 lead-in term added
ALT close
SN Use for the precincts, usually
walled, around cathedrals and their
dependent buildings.

UF cathedral closes
closes, cathedral

closes, cathedral
USE closes

closet beds
USE press beds (deception beds)

closet hardware
PJ.587
HN April 1993 descriptor moved
UF hardware, closet

closet knobs
PJ.339
HN April 1993 descriptor moved
ALT closet knob
SN A form of door hardware that consists of a single knob fastened to one end of a spindle, on the other end of which is a rose or plate used to secure the knob and spindle to the closet door. Distinguished from **doorknobs**, in which a pair of knobs on opposite ends of a spindle is used to release the door latch.
UF knobs, closet

closets
PJ.1135   (L,B)
HN March 1993 descriptor moved
ALT closet

closets (rooms)
USE cabinets (rooms)

closets, broom
USE broom closets

closets, chemical
USE chemical toilets

closets, china
USE china cabinets

closets, clothes
USE clothes closets

closets, linen
USE linen closets

closure
USE closer

closure, king
USE king closer

closure, quarter
USE quarter closer

closure, queen
USE queen closer

closures
PJ.3091
ALT closure
SN Object components which are used to cover or close a mouth or other openings on containers.

cloth
MT.1537   (A,L)
HN April 1993 related term added
March 1993 scope note changed
March 1993 descriptor moved

SN Use generally for textile that is woven, felted, knit, pounded, or otherwise made into a flat piece. For textile in the form of continuous strands made from filaments of fiber by reeling, spinning, twisting, or throwing, use **yarn**.
UF fabric
RT yarn

cloth, adinkra
USE adinkra

cloth, bark
USE bark cloth

cloth, beaten bark
USE bark cloth

cloth, bolting
USE bolting cloth

cloth brushes
USE clothes brushes

<cloth by composition or origin>
HN March 1993 guide term deleted

<cloth by form>
HN March 1993 guide term deleted

<cloth by surface treatment>
HN March 1993 guide term deleted

cloth, crocus
USE crocus cloth

cloth dolls
TV.161   (L)
ALT cloth doll
SN Use for dolls with bodies of cloth or cloth stuffed with various materials, as rags, sawdust, or papyrus leaves.
UF dolls, cloth
dolls, rag
rag dolls
RT soft toys

cloth, double
USE double weave

cloth, drafting
USE drafting cloth

cloth, emery
USE emery cloth

cloth, filling pile
USE weft pile weave

cloth, kente
USE kente

cloth, korhogo
USE korhogo cloth

cloth, luster
USE luster (textile)

cloth, mud
USE mud cloth

cloth, mud dyed
USE mud cloth

cloth, mud-resist
USE mud cloth

cloth, plain
USE tabby (textile)

cloth presses
USE clothes presses

cloth, rubberized
USE rubberized cloth

cloth, silk bolting
USE bolting cloth

cloth, tapa
USE bark cloth
tapa

cloth, terry
USE terry

cloth, tobacco
USE tobacco cloth

cloth, tracing
USE tracing cloth

cloth weave
USE tabby (textile)

cloth weave, plain
USE tabby (textile)

clothbound books
USE hardcover books

clothes
USE costume

clothes baskets
USE laundry baskets

clothes-brushes
SEE clothes brushes

clothes brushes
TH.351   (N)
HN January 1993 descriptor added
ALT clothes brush
UK clothes-brushes
UKA clothes-brush
SN Brushes used to remove loose hair, dirt, or dust off the surface of costume.
UF brushes, cloth
brushes, clothes
cloth brushes

clothes chests
TC.871
HN January 1993 descriptor moved
ALT clothes chest
UF chests, clothes

clothes chutes
USE laundry chutes

clothes closets
PJ.1137   (L)
HN March 1993 descriptor moved
ALT clothes closet
UK clothes cupboards
UKA clothes cupboard
UF closets, clothes
cupboards, clothes

clothes cupboards
SEE clothes closets

clothes cupboards
USE wardrobes (case furniture)

clothes designers
USE fashion designers

clothes, evening
USE evening dress

clothes hangers
USE coat hangers

clothes presses
TC.928   (R)
HN May 1993 related terms added
January 1993 descriptor moved
ALT clothes press
SN 18th-century term for large cupboards used to store clothes, having
sliding shelves behind closed doors.
For large case pieces fitted with
hooks, pegs, or rods to hang clothes,
use **wardrobes (case furniture)**.
UF cloth presses
presses à vêtements
presses, cloth
presses, clothes
RT presses (cupboards)
wardrobes (case furniture)

clothes presses, wing
USE wing clothes presses

clothes, sports
USE sports clothing

clothes, swaddling
USE swaddling clothes

clotheshorses
TC.1023
HN January 1993 descriptor moved
ALT clotheshorse
SN Racks on which to hang wet laundry
for drying.
UF airers, linen
drying racks
linen airers
racks, drying

clothing
USE costume

clothing, sports
USE sports clothing

clothing stores
RK.157   (A,B)
ALT clothing store
UF stores, clothing

cloths, altar
USE altar cloths

**cloths, base (upholstery foundation
components)**
USE base cloths (upholstery foundation
components)

cloths, bearing
USE bearing cloths

cloths, bridge
USE bridge cloths

cloths, burial
USE shrouds

cloths, challah
USE hallah covers

cloths, communion
USE corporals

cloths, credence
USE credence cloths

cloths, cupboard
USE cupboard cloths

cloths, dish
USE dishcloths

cloths, fair linen
USE fair linen cloths

cloths, floor
USE floor cloths

cloths, forehead
USE forehead cloths

cloths, hearse
USE funeral palls

cloths, houseling
USE houseling cloths

cloths, Kaaba
USE kiswas

cloths, Lenten
USE Lenten veils

cloths, matzah
USE matzah covers

cloths, pulpit
USE pulpit falls

cloths, saddle
USE saddlecloths

cloths, silence
USE silence cloths

cloths, tea
USE tea cloths

cloths, tea-table
USE tea cloths

cloths, tester
USE tester cloths

cloths, tray
USE tray cloths

cloths, wrapping
USE wrappers (containers)

cloud bands
DG.124
HN June 1990 lead-in terms added
ALT cloud band
SN A running ornament consisting of a
sinuous stylization of a cloud, common in Chinese art and in Oriental
rugs. (W)
UF bands, cloud
cloud pattern
pattern, cloud

cloud globe rugs
USE chintamani + rugs

cloud pattern
USE cloud bands

cloud point
DC.368
HN October 1992 descriptor added
SN The temperature at which a liquid
begins to cloud. (W)

cloud scrolls
DG.163
ALT cloud scroll
SN Characteristic Chinese motifs of the
Han Dynasty consisting of long,
convoluted, ribbonlike forms with
deep curls and curves constantly
changing direction, and at such
points widening into grotesque
shapes. (IDO)
UF scrolls, cloud

cloudband Kazaks
TC.80
ALT cloudband Kazak
SN Karabagh rugs with a pattern which
consists of one or more medallions
containing motifs which resemble
the cloud whisp motifs of Chinese
art.
UF Chondzoresk rugs
chondzoresks
Kazaks, cloudband
rugs, Chondzoresk

clout nails
PJ.165
HN April 1993 descriptor moved
ALT clout nail
SN Nails each having a large flat head,
round shank, and long flattened
point; used on sheet metal and dry
wallboard. (MEANS)
UF nails, clout

clouties
TC.211
ALT cloutie
SN Rag coverlets in the Scottish tra-
dition.

clove oil
USE oil of cloves

cloven feet
USE hoof feet

cloven-hoof feet
USE hoof feet

clover crossings
USE cloverleafs

clover-leaves
SEE cloverleafs

cloverleaf interchanges
USE cloverleafs

cloverleafs
PJ.843   (L,B)
HN March 1993 descriptor moved

June 1990 lead-in terms added
June 1990 scope note added
ALT cloverleaf
UK clover-leaves
UKA clover-leaf
SN Road arrangements, resembling four-leaf clovers in plan, for permitting easy traffic movement between intersecting highways. (RHDEL2)
UF clover crossings
  cloverleaf interchanges
  interchanges, cloverleaf

cloves, oil of
USE oil of cloves

Clovis
  FL.754

clowns
  HG.247   (L,R)
HN November 1992 alternate terms added
ALT clown
  clown's
  clowns'

club cars
USE lounge cars

club chairs
  TC.481
HN January 1993 descriptor moved
ALT club chair
SN Heavily upholstered chairs having solid sides and low backs. (RHDEL2)
UF chairs, club
  club divans
  divans, club

<club complexes>
  RG.171
HN November 1991 guide term added

club divans
USE club chairs

club feet
  PJ.2800
HN March 1993 descriptor moved
ALT club foot
SN Plain, circular feet used to terminate the cabriole leg, particularly in the early 18th century. When such feet are set on a disk, use **pad feet**.
UF feet, club

clubhouses
  RK.972   (A,L,R)
ALT clubhouse
SN Buildings occupied by a club or commonly used for club activities. (W)
UF lesches

clubhouses, faculty
USE faculty clubs

clubs (associations)
  HN.69   (A,L,B)
HN December 1991 descriptor changed, was **clubs**
  December 1991 alternate term changed, was **club**

ALT club (association)
SN Associations of persons for social and recreational purposes or for the promotion of some common object. (W)

clubs (golf equipment)
USE golf clubs

clubs (weapons)
  TK.124   (H,N)
ALT club (weapon)
SN Use generally for percussive weapons typically consisting of a staff of wood, metal, or other hard, heavy material, often carrying a head of stone or metal, wielded by hand as striking weapons.
UF bludgeons
  clubs, war
  war clubs

clubs, architectural
USE architectural societies

clubs, athletic
USE athletic clubs

clubs, beach
USE beach clubs

clubs, boat
USE boat clubs

clubs, country
USE country clubs

clubs, equestrian
USE riding clubs

clubs, faculty
USE faculty clubs

clubs, froe
USE froe clubs

clubs, frow
USE froe clubs

clubs, garden
USE garden clubs

clubs, gardening
USE garden clubs

clubs, golf
USE golf clubs

clubs, health
USE health clubs

clubs, horseback riding
USE riding clubs

clubs, Indian
USE Indian clubs

clubs, morning star
USE morning stars

clubs, officers'
USE officers' clubs

clubs, polo
USE polo clubs

clubs, riding
USE riding clubs

clubs, sports
SEE athletic clubs

clubs, tennis
USE tennis clubs

clubs, war
USE clubs (weapons)

clubs, yacht
USE yacht clubs

clubs, youth
USE youth centers

Cluniac
  BM.492   (A,L)

clupei
USE clipei (shields)

cluster housing
  RG.57   (A,L,B)
SN Dwellings grouped closely together to form relatively compact units, with the space between clusters usually allocated to pedestrian circulation and cooperative recreational use. (DAC)
UF architecture, grouped domestic
  domestic architecture, grouped
  grouped domestic architecture
  housing, cluster

cluster legs
  PJ.2840
HN March 1993 descriptor moved
ALT cluster leg
SN Legs having the form of a cluster of columns or shafts. (RHDEL2)
UF legs, cluster

clustered piers
USE compound piers

clutch pencils
USE mechanical pencils

Clutha glass
  MT.286   (R)
HN January 1992 descriptor added
SN A type of glass characterized by its mainly greenish, turquoise, yellow, brown-green, or smoky black color accented by air bubbles, streaks of pink and white, and speckles of aventurine; made by James Couper & Sons, Glasgow.
UF glass, Clutha

Cluthra glass
  MT.272
HN March 1992 descriptor added
SN Term used in the glass trade for a type of art glass characterized by large air bubbles of various sizes combined with larger unsifted glass particles, and cased with heavier clear glass; developed at Steuben Glass Works before 1930. (ILDIGL)
UF glass, Cluthra

clypei
USE clipei (shields)

CN
USE nitrocellulose

Co
USE cobalt

co-generation plants
SEE cogeneration plants

co-operative housing
SEE cooperative housing

co-ops
USE cooperative apartment houses
cooperative housing
cooperative stores

coach barns
USE carriage houses

coach cars
USE coaches (railroad cars)

coach framing hammers
USE framing hammers

coach horns
TT.60 (N)
ALT coach horn
SN English variety of post horn, having a straight conical tube of copper with silver mountings, wide bore, and a funnel-shaped unflared bell, and played with a cup mouthpiece.
UF horns, coach

coach houses
USE carriage houses

coach lamps
USE carriage lamps

coach-pots
USE bourdalous

coach screws
USE lag bolts

coach trimmers' cabriolet hammers
USE cabriolet hammers

coach varnish
MT.1891
UF coachbuilder's varnish
varnish, coach
varnish, coachbuilder's

coachbuilders' framing hammers
USE framing hammers

coachbuilder's varnish
USE coach varnish

coaches (buses)
USE buses

coaches (carriages)
TX.166 (H,L)
ALT coach (carriage)
SN Use for four-wheeled enclosed carriages characterized by roofs with fixed pillars, suspended bodies, and facing transverse seats accommodat-

ing four or six passengers; designed in the mid-15th century in Hungary.

coaches (people)
HG.903 (L)
HN March 1993 descriptor changed, was **coaches**
March 1993 alternate term changed, was **coach**
December 1992 alternate terms added
ALT coach (person)
coaches'
coach's

coaches (railroad cars)
TX.271 (N)
ALT coach (railroad car)
SN Use for ordinary passenger-carrying railroad cars for daytime travel.
UF cars, coach
coach cars
coaches, day
coaches, railway
day coaches
railway coaches

coaches, berlin
USE berlin coaches

coaches, concord
USE concord coaches

coaches, day
USE coaches (railroad cars)

coaches, funeral
USE hearses

coaches, hackney
USE hackney coaches

coaches, railway
USE coaches (railroad cars)

coaches, stage
USE stagecoaches

coaches, state
USE state coaches

coaches, trolley
USE trolleybuses

coaching-glasses
USE stirrup cups

coade stone
MT.189 (A,H,B,R)
HN April 1992 descriptor moved
February 1992 scope note added
SN Building material, composed of ceramic similar to stoneware, developed in England around 1769, used primarily for architectural decoration.
UF stone, coade

Coahuila
USE Cahuilla

coakels
USE spiral stairs

coal
MT.1016 (H,L,B,R)
HN April 1992 descriptor moved

coal, anthracite
USE anthracite

coal, bituminous
USE bituminous coal

coal, brown
USE lignite

coal-burning power plants
USE coal-fired power plants

coal, cannel
USE cannel coal

coal chutes
PJ.1153
HN March 1993 descriptor moved
ALT coal chute
UF chutes, coal

coal-fired power plants
RG.122 (L)
ALT coal-fired power plant
SN Steam-producing, electric power generating plants, using coal as the primary fuel.
UF coal-burning power plants
coal-fired steam electric power plants
plants, coal-fired power
power plants, coal-fired
steam electric power plants, coal-fired

coal-fired steam electric power plants
USE coal-fired power plants

coal hods
TQ.637 (N)
ALT coal hod
SN Small pails, generally made of metal, for holding or carrying coal, typically having a bail handle and one scooplike lip.
UF coal scuttles
coal vases
hods, coal
scuttles
scuttles, coal
vases, coal
RT pails

coal mines
RG.102 (L,B,R)
ALT coal mine
UF collieries
mines, coal

coal oil
USE kerosene

coal scuttles
USE coal hods

coal, soft
USE bituminous coal

coal tar
MT.996 (L)

HN April 1992 descriptor moved
March 1992 scope note added
SN Product of the destructive distillation of coal. (ABMVAA)
UF tar, coal

coal-tar color
USE synthetic organic pigment

coal tar creosote
MT.2390
UF creosote, coal tar

coal-tar dye
USE synthetic organic pigment

coal tar solvent
MT.2422
HN April 1993 lead-in term added
April 1993 descriptor changed, was coal tar solvents
SN Volatile solvent obtained by the distillation of coal tar; industrial grades are widely used as solvent for rubber and many resinous materials. (MAYER)
UF coal-tar solvent
solvent, coal tar

coal-tar solvent
USE coal tar solvent

coal tips
USE spoil banks

coal vases
USE coal hods

coal, wood
USE lignite

coaming
PJ.2307
HN March 1993 descriptor moved
SN Frames or curbs, around an opening in a roof or floor, raised above the surrounding level to prevent the flow of water into the opening. (DAC)

coarse aggregate
MT.1681
UF aggregate, coarse

coarse-grain material
MT.1642
HN April 1993 descriptor moved
April 1993 descriptor changed, was coarse-grain materials
UF material, coarse-grain

coarse stuff
MT.1854
UF stuff, coarse

Coast Chavin
USE Cupisnique

coast defense guns
USE coastal artillery

coast-lines
SEE coastlines

coast live oak
MT.2833   (L)
HN March 1992 descriptor moved
UF California live oak
live oak, California
live oak, coast
oak, California live
oak, coast live
Quercus agrifolia

coast redwood
USE Humboldt redwood

Coast Salish
FL.927   (L)
UF Salish, Coast

Coastal Akan
FL.290
UF Akan, Coastal

coastal artillery
TK.162   (N)
SN Artillery specially designed for defending coastal areas.
UF artillery, coastal
coast defense guns
defense guns, coast
guns, coast defense
guns, sea-coast
guns, seacoast
sea-coast guns
seacoast guns

coastal charts
VW.129
HN November 1992 descriptor moved
ALT coastal chart
SN Nautical charts used for navigation close to shore, such as for entering or leaving bays and harbors or for navigating inland waterways.
UF charts, coastal

coastal defenses
USE coastal fortifications

<Coastal East African styles>
FL.593

coastal environments
BM.321   (L)
HN November 1992 descriptor added
SN Use for environments along shores of bodies of water, affected by factors of both the land and the water. Regarding the geology or geography of coastal areas, prefer shores (landforms) or coastlines.
UF environments, coastal

coastal fortifications
RK.409   (L)
ALT coastal fortification
UF coastal defenses
fortifications, coastal

Coastal Tiahuanaco
USE Pacheco

coastal towns
RD.68   (A,B)
ALT coastal town
UF seaside towns

towns, coastal
towns, seaside

coastal zone maps
VW.101
HN November 1992 descriptor moved
ALT coastal zone map
UF maps, coastal zone

coasters (containers)
TQ.546   (L,N)
ALT coaster (container)
SN Small, shallow platelike containers or mats, usually circular, used to protect a surface from being scratched or damaged by heat or moisture.
RT <coverings and hangings for storage and support furniture>

coasters (watercraft)
TX.488   (L)
ALT coaster (watercraft)
SN Use for usually small or medium-sized vessels engaged in coastwise navigation; generally merchant vessels maintaining trade and communication among smaller ports and between major entrepôts and the hinterland.
UF coasting schooners
coasting vessels
schooners, coasting
vessels, coasting

coasters, roller
USE roller coasters

coasters, wine
USE wine coasters

coasters, wine-bottle
USE wine coasters

coastguard stations
RK.1210   (H,B)
ALT coastguard station
UF stations, coastguard

coasting schooners
USE coasters (watercraft)

coasting vessels
USE coasters (watercraft)

<coastline bodies of water>
RD.110

coastlines
RD.197   (L,B)
HN March 1993 related term added
ALT coastline
UK coast-lines
UKA coast-line
SN Use either generally for the lines forming boundaries between land and sea or specifically for the lines reached by the highest storm waves or the high-water marks of median tides; for strips of land bordering any large bodies of water, use shores (landforms).

UF   coasts
      shorelines
RT   shores (landforms)

coasts
USE   coastlines
       shores (landforms)

coat
USE   coating (material)

coat armors
      TE.310
ALT   coat armor
UK   coat-armours
UKA   coat-armour
SN   Textile garments worn over metal armor or on their own, from the mid-12th century to the first quarter of the 15th century. Their form varied greatly within this period, being variously long and loose-fitting, short and close-fitting, with or without sleeves, padded or quilted, or furnished on the inside with metal plates. Typically they were embellished with heraldic devices and other ornaments to distinguish the wearer.
UF   armors, coat
       armours, coat
       coat armours
       jupons
       surcoats
RT   soft armor

coat-armours
SEE   coat armors

coat armours
SEE   coat armors

coat-dresses
SEE   coatdresses

coat dresses
USE   coatdresses

coat-hangers
SEE   coat hangers

coat hangers
      TH.354   (L,N)
HN   January 1993 descriptor added
ALT   coat hanger
UK   coat-hangers
UKA   coat-hanger
SN   Hangers curved so as to fit the shoulders of a garment and having a hook by which they may be suspended.
UF   clothes hangers
       coathangers
       hangers, coat

<coat of arms elements>
      VW.398
HN   May 1993 guide term changed, was
       <coat of arms components>
       November 1992 guide term moved

coat, top
USE   supercoat

coatdresses
      TE.19
ALT   coatdress
UK   coat-dresses
UKA   coat-dress
SN   Tailored dresses styled like a coat and generally worn without an outer garment.
UF   coat dresses
       dresses, coat

coated paper
USE   prepared paper

coatees
      TE.9   (N)
ALT   coatee
SN   Close-fitting short coats having a short skirt, flaps, or tails. (PFASHN)

coathangers
USE   coat hangers

coating (material)
      MT.1844   (A,L)
HN   April 1993 lead-in terms added
       April 1993 descriptor changed, was **coatings**
       April 1993 lead-in term changed, was **surface-coatings**
SN   Use generally for any substance spread over a surface, usually for protection or decoration. (W)
UF   coat
       coating, surface
       surface coating

coating (process)
      KT.91   (L)
HN   April 1993 descriptor changed, was **coating**
       March 1993 descriptor moved
       November 1992 scope note added
ALT   coated
SN   Covering a surface with a layer of substance, especially a substance that is spread on.

coating, bituminous
USE   bituminous coating

<coating by composition or origin>
      MT.1845

<coating by form>
      MT.1913

<coating by function>
      MT.1978
HN   August 1992 guide term added

<coating by location or context>
      MT.1980

coating, concrete
USE   concrete coating

coating, paper
USE   paper coating

coating, powder
USE   powder coating

coating, protective
USE   protective coating

coating, roller
USE   roller painting

coating, substratum
USE   subbing layer

coating, surface
USE   coating (material)

coating, zinc
USE   electrogalvanizing

coatrooms
USE   cloakrooms

coats
      TE.8   (H,L,N)
ALT   coat
SN   Main garments usually fitted to the upper body, extending below the hip line, open at the front or side and generally having sleeves. Also, similar outer garments worn for warmth or protection from the weather.
RT   dusters
       jackets
       mackinaws
       outerwear
       overcoats
       paletots

coats, box
USE   surtouts

coats, buff
USE   buff coats

coats, bush
USE   bush jackets

coats, claw-hammer
USE   tail coats

coats, cutaway
USE   cutaways

coats, dinner
USE   dinner jackets

coats, dress
USE   tail coats

coats, dust
USE   dusters

coats, frock
USE   frock coats

coats, mackinaw
USE   mackinaws

coats, morning
SEE   cutaways

coats, Norfolk
USE   Norfolk jackets

coats of arms
      VW.400   (L,N,R)
HN   November 1992 descriptor moved
ALT   coat of arms
SN   Use for devices that include the full display of armorial bearings: the escutcheon plus its adjuncts (helm, crest, mantling, motto, supporters).

UF arms, coats of
 heraldic achievements

<coats of arms and coat of arms elements>
 VW.397
 HN May 1993 guide term changed, was
 *<coats of arms and coat of arms
 components>*
 November 1992 guide term moved

coats of plates
 TE.311
 ALT coat of plates
 SN Coat armors of cloth or leather hav-
 ing metal plates riveted on the in-
 side, widely used in 14th-century
 Europe.
 UF pairs of plates
 plates, coats of
 plates, pairs of

coats, pea
 USE pea jackets

coats, sack
 USE sack coats

coats, surtout
 USE surtouts

coats, swallow-tailed
 USE tail coats

coats, tail
 USE tail coats

coats, trench
 USE trench coats

coats, warning
 USE warning coats

coattails
 PJ.3037
 ALT coattail
 SN Rear flaps of a man's coat, such as
 on a tail coat, cutaway, or the like.

cob
 MT.190 (L,B)
 HN April 1992 descriptor moved

cobalt
 MT.383 (H,L)
 HN June 1992 descriptor added
 SN Use for the metallic element having
 the symbol Co and atomic number
 27; a white metal, resembling nickel
 but with a bluish instead of a yellow
 tinge. Use also for the metal as processed and formed, usually in combination with other substances, to
 make various objects and materials.
 UF Co

cobalt (blue pigment)
 USE cobalt blue

cobalt arsenate, pale
 USE pale cobalt arsenate

cobalt, azure
 USE cobalt blue

cobalt blue
 MT.2098
 HN April 1992 descriptor moved
 UF azure cobalt
 bleu de cobalt
 blue, cobalt
 blue, Hungary
 blue, king's
 blue, new
 blue, olympia
 blue, Thénard's
 blue, Vienna
 cobalt (blue pigment)
 cobalt, azure
 Hungary blue
 king's blue
 Kobaltblau
 new blue
 olympia blue
 Thénard's blue
 ultramarine, Vienna
 Vienna blue
 Vienna ultramarine

cobalt blue (color)
 USE strong greenish blue
 vivid blue

cobalt glass
 MT.238
 HN March 1992 descriptor added
 UF glass, cobalt
 smalt (cobalt glass)

cobalt green
 MT.2151
 HN April 1992 descriptor moved
 UF Gellert green
 green, cobalt
 green, Gellert
 green, Rinman's
 green, Saxony
 green smalt
 green, zinc
 Kobaltgrün
 Rinman's green
 Saxony green
 smalt, green
 vert de cobalt
 zinc green

cobalt green (color)
 USE moderate yellowish green

cobalt oxide
 MT.2099
 HN December 1992 descriptor added
 SN An oxide of cobalt used chiefly in
 coloring glass and ceramics.
 UF oxide, cobalt

cobalt phosphate, deep
 USE deep cobalt phosphate

cobalt ultramarine
 USE strong greenish blue

cobalt violet
 MT.2215
 HN April 1992 descriptor moved
 UF Kobaltviolet
 violet, cobalt
 violet de cobalt

cobalt violet (color)
 USE moderate purple
 strong purple

cobalt yellow
 MT.2279
 HN April 1992 descriptor moved
 January 1992 lead-in terms added
 UF aureolin
 aurocoline
 giallo di cobalto
 Indian yellow (cobalt yellow)
 jaune de cobalt
 jaune indien
 Kobaltgelb
 yellow, cobalt

cobalt yellow (color)
 USE brilliant yellow

cobangs
 USE kobans

Cobbeos
 USE Cubeo

cobble
 USE cobblestone

cobble, beach
 USE beach cobble

cobblers
 USE shoemakers

cobblestone
 MT.925 (A,L,B)
 HN April 1992 descriptor moved
 UF cobble

cobs
 VK.121 (L)
 ALT cob
 SN Irregularly shaped and uneven gold
 or silver coins struck in various parts
 of the Spanish Empire between the
 16th and 18th centuries. (DOTY)
 UF macuquinas

cocciniglia
 USE cochineal

Cochenille
 USE cochineal

cochenille
 USE cochineal

Cochin Chinese
 FL.2531
 UF Chinese, Cochin

cochineal
 MT.2014 (L)
 HN May 1992 descriptor moved
 May 1992 scope note added
 May 1992 lead-in terms added
 May 1992 related terms added
 SN A red natural organic dye, also used
 as a lake pigment, prepared from
 the bodies of the female scale insect,
 Dactylopius coccus Costa (formerly
 Coccus cacti). Its chief coloring com-
 ponent is carmine.
 UF carmine (cochineal)

cocciniglia
Cochenille
cochenille
cochinilla
grana cochinilla
Koschenille
Nopalschildlaus
zacatillo
RT carmine
    lake (pigment)

cochineal (color)
USE vivid red

cochineal carmine
USE carmine

cochinilla
USE cochineal

Cochise
    FL.944   (L)

Cochise, Chiricahua
USE Chiricahua Cochise

Cochise, San Pedro
USE San Pedro Cochise

Cochise, Sulphur Spring
USE Sulphur Spring Cochise

Cochiti
    FL.1484   (L)

cock plug bits
USE tenon-cutting bits

cockade fans
    TE.421
ALT cockade fan
SN Fans which open to a circle or semi-circle around a pivot set in the center rather than in the base. (CASF)
UF fans, cockade

cocked-hat lamps
    TC.1271
ALT cocked-hat lamp
SN Use in reference to ancient pottery lamps formed by folding or pinching in the edges of a shallow bowl or plate as soon as it was thrown. (DBGRPL)
UF lamps, cocked-hat
    lamps, shell-type
    shell-type lamps

cocked hats
    TE.581   (N)
ALT cocked hat
SN Men's stiff, round-crowned hats, usually of felt, the large brim cocked or rolled up against the crown; worn from the 17th to the 19th century.
UF hats, cocked

Cockeysville marble
    MT.765
HN April 1992 descriptor moved
UF marble, Cockeysville

cockfight chairs
USE reading chairs

cockfighting chairs
USE reading chairs

cocking pieces
USE sprockets

cockle
    DE.5
SN A condition of paper, paperboard, vellum, or cloth in which the material is wrinkled, puckered, warped, or rippled.

cockle stairs
USE spiral stairs

cockling
    KT.251
HN January 1993 descriptor added
ALT cockled
SN A process occurring in such materials as paper, paperboard, vellum, or cloth in which the material becomes wrinkled, puckered, warped, or rippled.

cocklofts
USE attics (interior spaces)

cocks (lighting device components)
    PJ.2929
ALT cock (lighting device component)
SN Devices used to control the flow of gas to a burner or lamp. (MYERS)
UF cocks, gas
    cocks, stop
    gas cocks
    petcocks
    stop cocks

cocks (lock components)
    PJ.3192
ALT cock (lock component)
SN The striking arms holding the gunflint in flintlocks, snaphances, and miquelet locks.

cocks, balance
USE balance cocks

cocks, ball
USE ball cocks

cocks' combs
    TH.1169
HN March 1993 descriptor changed, was **cock's combs**
    March 1993 lead-in term changed, was **combs, cock's**
    December 1992 descriptor moved
ALT cock's comb
SN Pieces of metal with a serrated edge; used to scratch plaster and create a rough gripping surface for the next coat. (MEANS)
UF combs, cocks'

cocks, gas
USE cocks (lighting device components)

cocks, stop
USE cocks (lighting device components)

cockscomb burners
    PJ.2913
ALT cockscomb burner
UF burners, cockscomb
    cockscombs

cockscombs
USE cockscomb burners

cockspur burners
    PJ.2914
ALT cockspur burner
UF burners, cockspur
    cockspurs

cockspurs
USE cockspur burners

cocktail bars
SEE cocktail lounges

cocktail dresses
    TE.28
ALT cocktail dress
SN Informal but rather elegant dresses suitable for late afternoon and evening events.
UF after-five dresses
    dresses, after-five
    dresses, cocktail

cocktail glasses
    TQ.429   (N)
ALT cocktail glass
SN Small drinking glasses for cocktails, with a foot, stem, and bowl, which varies in shape and size but is often funnel-shaped. (ILDIGL)
UF cocktails
    glasses, cocktail

cocktail lounges
    PJ.1051   (B)
HN March 1993 descriptor moved
ALT cocktail lounge
UK cocktail bars
UKA cocktail bar
SN Public rooms, as in hotels, clubs, or restaurants, where cocktails and other drinks are served. (W)
UF bars, cocktail
    lounges, cocktail

cocktail shakers
    TQ.518   (N)
ALT cocktail shaker
SN Any of various containers for shaking beverages to mix ingredients. (RHDEL2)
UF beverage shakers
    shakers
    shakers, beverage
    shakers, cocktail

cocktail tables
    TC.1128
HN January 1993 descriptor moved
ALT cocktail table
UF tables, cocktail

cocktails
USE cocktail glasses

Coclé
FL.1111

Cocle, Early
USE Conte Polychrome

cocoawood
USE granadilla

cocobolo
MT.2892 (L)
HN March 1992 descriptor moved
UF Dalbergia retusa
Honduran rosewood
rosewood, Honduran

Cocomaricopa
USE Maricopa

coconut cups
TQ.408 (R)
ALT coconut cup
SN Standing cups, generally made in silver or gold, with a bowl made of a coconut shell. Of a type which dates from the 15th century. (CHAES)
UF cups, coconut

Cocopa
FL.1471 (L)

cocos wood
USE granadilla

cocuswood
USE granadilla

coddlers
USE egg coddlers

coddlers, egg
USE egg coddlers

code maps, zip
USE zip code maps

codes
VW.742
HN November 1992 descriptor moved
ALT code
SN Systematically arranged and comprehensive collections of laws, or, more generally, systematic collections of regulations and rules of procedure or conduct. (AHD)

codes, building
USE building codes

codices
HN June 1992 descriptor deleted, made lead-in to **books**

codices (gathered leaves)
USE books

codices (Mesoamerican)
VW.961 (L)
HN August 1992 descriptor added
ALT codex (Mesoamerican)
SN Use for manuscripts from Mesoamerica, preconquest and into the early colonial period, taking various forms including folded and rolled. (MUSER)

codpieces
TE.685 (N)
ALT codpiece
SN Bagged appendages to the front of the close-fitting hose or breeches worn by men from the 15th to the 17th century, often conspicuous and ornamented. Also, similar appendages of female attire, worn on the breast. (OED)
RT <body armor: lower extremities>

Cody
FL.765

coefficient elasticity
USE modulus of elasticity

coefficient of reflection
USE reflectance

coefficient, reflection
USE reflectance

coelanaglyphic relief
KT.809
HN November 1990 descriptor added
SN Relief technique in which the surface of the block is allowed to remain as background and the figures are carved with positive projections within the surface. (OCA)
UF relief, coelanaglyphic
relief, sunk
sunk relief

coelin
USE cerulean blue

Coelinblau
USE cerulean blue

coemeteria
USE catacombs

coeruleum
USE cerulean blue
Egyptian blue

Coeur d'Alène
FL.1421

coffee balls
USE tea balls

coffee bean roasters
USE coffee roasters

coffee biggins
USE biggins (vessels)

coffee boilers
USE coffeepots

coffee cups
TQ.417 (N)
ALT coffee cup
SN Cups, with one or two handles, or sometimes with none, intended primarily for drinking coffee; often accompanied by a saucer.
UF cups, coffee
RT breakfast services
coffee services
place settings

coffee grinders
USE coffee mills

coffee houses
USE coffeehouses

coffee makers
TH.61 (L,N)
HN April 1993 descriptor added
ALT coffee maker
SN Any of various utensils in which coffee is infused, brewed, percolated, or boiled.
UF makers, coffee
RT coffeepots

coffee mills
TH.219 (L,N)
HN April 1993 descriptor added
ALT coffee mill
SN Small mechanical devices for grinding coffee beans.
UF coffee grinders
grinders, coffee
mills, coffee

coffee percolators
USE percolators

coffee pots
USE coffeepots

coffee-pots with spigot
USE coffee urns

coffee public houses
USE coffeehouses

coffee roasters
TH.63 (N)
HN April 1993 descriptor added
ALT coffee roaster
SN Devices for roasting coffee beans. (W)
UF bean roasters, coffee
coffee bean roasters
roasters (coffee roasters)
roasters, coffee
roasters, coffee bean

coffee services
PC.20 (H,R)
ALT coffee service
SN Services intended for use in serving coffee generally consisting of a coffeepot, creamer, sugar bowl, and often a matching tray. May also include matching cups and urn, saucers, or dessert plates.
UF coffee sets
services, coffee
sets, coffee
RT coffee cups
coffee urns
coffeepots
creamers
dessert plates
hot water urns
saucers
slop bowls
sugar bowls

coffee sets
USE coffee services

coffee shops
    RK.116   (A)
ALT coffee shop
SN Use for small, usually inexpensive, restaurants with a limited menu of light meals served at counters or tables.
UF shops, coffee

coffee spoons
    TH.324   (N)
HN April 1993 descriptor added
ALT coffee spoon
SN Small spoons, similar in size to chocolate spoons, used to stir coffee served in demitasses; often ornamental and sold in sets.
UF demitasse spoons
    spoons, coffee
    spoons, demitasse
RT chocolate spoons
    demitasses

coffee strainers
USE tea strainers

coffee tables
    TC.1129   (N)
HN January 1993 descriptor moved
ALT coffee table
UF tables, coffee

coffee urns
    TQ.519   (L,N)
ALT coffee urn
SN Vessels intended to hold or dispense coffee, either urnlike or in the form of a coffeepot and having, instead of a spout, one or more taps and a spigot; usually supported on legs or a stand and may have a heating device. May be part of a coffee service. Prefer **hot water urns** for urnlike vessels intended to hold or dispense hot water in connection with the serving of coffee and which may also be part of a coffee service.
UF coffee-pots with spigot
    urns, coffee
RT coffee services
    coffeepots
    hot water urns
    tea urns
    urns

coffeehouses
    RK.111   (A,L,B,R)
HN May 1993 lead-in terms added
ALT coffeehouse
SN Use for public places serving coffee and other refreshments and inexpensive foods; often meeting places for lively political discussions, especially popular in Europe from the 17th to the 19th century.
UF cafés (coffeehouses)
    coffee houses
    coffee public houses

houses, coffee
public houses, coffee

coffeepots
    TQ.520   (H,L,N,R)
ALT coffeepot
SN Covered spouted vessels for preparing and serving coffee, having a handle and sometimes small feet.
UF boilers, coffee
    coffee boilers
    coffee pots
    pots, coffee
RT breakfast services
    chocolate pots
    coffee makers
    coffee services
    coffee urns
    percolators
    pots
    tea services
    teapots

cofferdams
    RK.496   (L)
ALT cofferdam
SN Use for watertight enclosures from which water is pumped to expose an area in order to permit construction or repairs. (MEANS)

<coffered ceiling components>
    PJ.2055
HN April 1993 related term added
    March 1993 guide term moved
RT *<surface element components>*

coffered ceilings
    PJ.2054   (A)
HN March 1993 descriptor moved
ALT coffered ceiling
SN Ceilings treated with coffers.
UF ceilings, coffered

<coffered ceilings and coffered ceiling components>
    PJ.2053
HN March 1993 guide term moved

coffering
USE coffers (ceiling components)

coffers (ceiling components)
    PJ.2056
HN March 1993 descriptor moved
ALT coffer (ceiling component)
SN Recessed panels, usually square or octagonal, set into. ceilings, vaults, or soffits.
UF caissons (coffers)
    cassoons
    coffering
    lacunars

coffers (furniture)
    TC.872   (L,B)
HN May 1993 related term added
    January 1993 descriptor moved
ALT coffer (furniture)
SN Small chests for the storage of valuables which may also serve as seats or tables.

UF coffres
    coffrets
RT arks

coffers, traveling
USE trussing coffers

coffers, trussing
USE trussing coffers

coffin-cloths
USE funeral palls

coffin covers
USE funeral palls

coffin planes
USE smoothing planes

coffin stools
USE joint stools

coffins
    TQ.140   (H,L,N,R)
ALT coffin
SN Boxes or chests for a corpse to be buried in. (W)
UF caskets (coffins)

coffre à bijoux
USE jewel cabinets

coffres
USE coffers (furniture)

coffres à bahut
USE bahuts

coffrets
USE coffers (furniture)

cog railroads
USE rack railroads

cog rattles
    TT.555   (N)
ALT cog rattle
SN Scraped idiophones consisting of a cog wheel which is either revolved by means of a handle against one or more wood or metal tongues, or twirled so that the tongues strike the cogs of the wheel. (NGDMI)
UF ratchets
    rattles, cog
    scraped wheels
    wheels, scraped

cogboats
USE cogs (watercraft)

cogeneration facilities
USE cogeneration plants

cogeneration plants
    RG.114   (L)
HN December 1990 descriptor added
ALT cogeneration plant
UK co-generation plants
UKA co-generation plant
SN Use for power plants that simultaneously generate from the same source electrical energy and useful heat energy.
UF CHP generating plants

cogeneration facilities
cogeneration systems
combined cycle power plants
combined heat and power generating plants
facilities, cogeneration
generating plants, CHP
plants, CHP generating
plants, co-generation
plants, cogeneration
plants, combined cycle power
plants, combined heat and power generating
power generating plants, combined heat and
power plants, combined cycle
systems, cogeneration

cogeneration systems
USE cogeneration plants

cogged joints
PJ.626
HN April 1993 descriptor moved
ALT cogged joint
SN Joints consisting of two crossing pieces of wood, each piece notched to fit into the other. (MEANS)
UF joints, cogged

coggle wheels
USE coggles

coggles
TH.1118
HN December 1992 descriptor added
ALT coggle
SN Clayworking tools that consist mainly of a wheel or disk and are used to make indentations or grooves in the outer edges of plates.
UF coggle wheels
wheels, coggle

coggling wheels
USE jagging wheels

cognition
BM.995 (L,R)
HN February 1993 descriptor moved

cogs (machinery components)
PJ.2597
HN April 1993 descriptor changed, was cogs
April 1993 alternate term changed, was cog
March 1993 descriptor moved
ALT cog (machinery component)
SN Teeth on the rim of a wheel or gear. (W)

cogs (watercraft)
TX.496 (L)
ALT cog (watercraft)
SN Bottom-based merchant ships of the 13th to the 15th century, clinker-built with rounded bow and stern, fore and after castles, and very broad in the beam; occasionaly used as warships. (OCSS)
UF cogboats

RT merchant vessels
sailing ships

cogwheels
USE gears

Cohonina
FL.968 (L)

cohousing (TM)
RG.93 (A)
HN April 1990 descriptor added
SN A type of small communal housing development, designed and managed by the occupants, in which each resident family owns a home and shares with the group common facilities, such as kitchens, child care centers, and laundry rooms, and their associated tasks.

coiffeuses (chairs)
TC.482
HN January 1993 descriptor moved
ALT coiffeuse (chair)
SN French armchairs with the crest rail curving downward in the center to enable the hair to be dressed. (HAYWAR)

coiffeuses (tables)
TC.1148
HN May 1993 scope note changed
January 1993 descriptor moved
September 1991 descriptor changed, was coiffeuses
September 1991 alternate term changed, was coiffeuse
ALT coiffeuse (table)
SN Fitted dressing tables. The most typical 18th-century form has three rising flaps, the center one being fitted with a mirror. (WATSON)
UF poudreuses

coiffières
USE bonnetières

coifs
TE.531 (H)
ALT coif
SN Close-fitting caps made in a variety of shapes and sizes and worn at various periods of history by men and women, sometimes surmounted by a hat or headdress.

coigns
USE quoins

coil-bases
SEE coil bases

coil bases
PJ.3103
ALT coil base
UK coil-bases
UKA coil-base
SN A type of base on a glass vessel made by forming a ring on which the vessel stands by trailing molten glass around the bottom. (ILDIGL)

coil building
USE coiling

coil candlesticks
USE spiral candlesticks

coil construction
USE coiling

coil method
USE coiling

coil-spring seats
PJ.2868
HN March 1993 descriptor moved
ALT coil-spring seat
SN Upholstered seats with interior springs of coiled wire.
UF coiled inner-spring seats
inner-spring seats, coiled
seats, coil-spring

coiled inner-spring seats
USE coil-spring seats

coiling
KT.1155
HN November 1990 lead-in term added
ALT coiled
SN Pottery technique in which the piece is built up from ropelike coils of clay, without the use of a potter's wheel.
UF coil building
coil construction
coil method

coillons
USE quoins

coils (geometric figures)
USE spirals

coils (heat exchangers)
PJ.800
HN March 1993 descriptor moved
November 1992 related term added
November 1992 descriptor changed, was coils
November 1992 alternate term changed, was coil
December 1990 scope note added
ALT coil (heat exchanger)
SN Piping or tubing in various configurations employed in cooling or heating systems to serve as heat exchangers.
RT coils (spiral objects)

coils (spiral objects)
PE.40
HN November 1992 descriptor moved
November 1992 scope note added
November 1992 related term added
November 1992 alternate term added
November 1992 descriptor changed, was coil
ALT coil (spiral object)
SN Objects in the form of a long, thin material wound into a series of spirals or rings.
RT coils (heat exchangers)

coils, air cooling
USE   cooling coils

coils, air-heating
USE   heating coils

coils, cooling
USE   cooling coils

coils, dehumidifying
USE   dehumidifying coils

coils, heating
USE   heating coils

coin balances
USE   coin scales

coin banks
USE   banks (containers)

coin banks, mechanical
USE   mechanical banks

coin holders
TQ.168   (N)
ALT   coin holder
SN   Containers with one or more cylindrical channels for holding stacks of coins of identical size.
UF   holders, coin

coin moldings
USE   money pattern

coin operated laundries
USE   laundries

coin purses
TQ.218   (N)
ALT   coin purse
SN   Small bags with secure closings intended primarily for holding coins.
UF   change purses
purses, change
purses, coin

coin scales
TN.298
ALT   coin scale
SN   Scales, in use predominantly from the 13th to the 18th century, for weighing coins to prevent the circulation of pieces that were light or clipped.
UF   balances, coin
coin balances
scales, coin
tumbrels

coin silver
MT.448
HN   March 1993 descriptor added
SN   Silver of the fineness legalized for coins; 90% fine in the United States, 50% fine in Great Britain since 1920. (W)
UF   silver, coin

coinage
USE   coins
minting

coinage, emergency
USE   emergency currency

coinage, scyphate
USE   scyphate coins

coining
USE   minting

coins
VK.4   (H,L,N,B,R)
ALT   coin
SN   Pieces of metal stamped by government authority for use as money.
UF   coinage
specie
RT   minting
stamping (forming)

coins (cupboards)
USE   encoignures

coins (wall components)
USE   quoins

<coins by form or technique>
VK.5

<coins by function>
VK.15

<coins by origin>
VK.18

coins, counting
USE   jettons

coins de feu
USE   chauffeuses

coins, double-struck
USE   double-struck coins

coins, hoe
USE   spade money

coins, Maundy
USE   Maundy money

coins, nickel
USE   five-cent pieces

coins, obsidional
USE   siege pieces

coins, one-pound
USE   pounds

coins, pattern
USE   pattern coins

coins, proof
USE   proof coins

coins, punch-marked
USE   punch-marked coins

coins, scyphate
USE   scyphate coins

coins, siege
USE   siege pieces

coins, spade
USE   spade money

coins, token
USE   tokens

cointises
TE.504
ALT   cointise

coir
MT.1385   (L)
HN   February 1992 descriptor moved
SN   Stiff, coarse fiber from the outer bark of the coconut, used in making brushes, mats, cord, and coarse cloth.

coke ovens
TH.504   (A,H,L,N)
ALT   coke oven
SN   Closed refractory chambers in which coal is converted to coke by carbonization. (MHDSTT)
UF   ovens, coke

coke ovens, beehive
USE   beehive ovens

cokels
USE   spiral stairs

Cokwe
USE   Chokwe

Cola
USE   Chola

colanders
TH.181   (N)
HN   April 1993 descriptor added
ALT   colander
SN   Bowl-shaped or conical devices with perforated or pierced walls, used for draining and straining foods; usually set on a base or on legs. For other culinary tools used to filter foods, use **strainers (culinary tools)**.
UF   cullenders
RT   strainers (culinary tools)

colasciones
TT.307
ALT   colascione
SN   European lutelike chordophones, popular in 17th-century Italy, having a very long, narrow neck with up to 24 movable frets, a small bowl-shaped body, and two or three strings played with a plectrum.
UF   calasciones

Colastiné
FL.1709

colcothar
USE   Indian red

cold
DC.365   (H,L)
HN   October 1992 descriptor moved
October 1992 scope note added
SN   Use for the state of low temperature or to describe processes or situations that take place under conditions of low temperatures.

cold bridges
USE   thermal bridges

cold chisels
TH.1244 (N)
ALT cold chisel
SN Common form of chisel with a cutting edge of 60 degrees formed of tempered steel; used for cutting metal which has not been softened by heating. (DAC)
UF chisels, cold

cold composition
KT.634
HN February 1993 descriptor added
SN A term originating in the mid-20th century, originally to distinguish strike-on composition of type from hot-metal methods; later extended to include photographic methods. Use another term when possible.
UF cold-metal setting
cold type
composition, cold
setting, cold-metal
type, cold
RT cold-metal machines

cold-cut varnish
USE simple solution varnish

cold cutting
KT.1033
HN March 1993 descriptor added
ALT cold-cut
SN Cutting a raw block of glass that has not been previously cut to shape, using a rotating wheel fed with water. (COG)
UF cutting, cold

cold joints
PJ.655
HN April 1993 descriptor moved
ALT cold joint
SN Joints between two consecutive pours of concrete if the time elapsed between the first and second pours is such that the first pour has started to harden. (MEANS)
UF joints, cold

cold-meat forks
TH.251 (N)
HN April 1993 descriptor added
ALT cold-meat fork
SN Large and often ornamented forks used for serving meats and cold cuts.
UF buffet forks
forks, buffet
forks, cold-meat
meat forks, cold

cold-metal composing machines
USE cold-metal machines

cold-metal machines
TH.875
HN February 1993 descriptor added
ALT cold-metal machine
SN Machines for composing type that do not employ hot-metal casting at the time of composition. Includes those that assemble foundry type mechanically and those that do strike-on composition.
UF cold-metal composing machines
cold-metal typesetting machines
cold-type machines
composing machines, cold-metal
machines, cold-metal
machines, cold-metal composing
machines, cold-metal typesetting
machines, cold-type
typesetting machines, cold-metal
RT cold composition

cold-metal setting
USE cold composition

cold-metal typesetting machines
USE cold-metal machines

cold-pressed oil
MT.1113
HN April 1992 descriptor moved
SN Any vegetable oil that has been extracted from seeds or nuts by pressing them without the aid of heat. (MAYER)
UF oil, cold-pressed

cold-pressed paper
MT.1504
HN February 1992 descriptor moved
July 1990 descriptor added
SN Paper having a medium to rough finish created by running the sheets through a series of coated metal cylinders.
UF paper, cold-pressed

cold pressure welding
USE cold-welding

cold rooms
USE cold storage rooms

Cold Springs
FL.928

cold storage coolers
USE cold storage rooms

cold storage rooms
PJ.1139
HN March 1993 descriptor moved
ALT cold storage room
SN Rooms kept at low temperatures for the storage of perishable items.
UF cold rooms
cold storage coolers
coolers, cold storage
rooms, cold storage

cold type
USE cold composition

cold-type machines
USE cold-metal machines

cold-water flats
SEE coldwater flats

cold-welding
KT.1101 (L)

HN May 1993 descriptor changed, was cold welding
March 1991 alternate term changed, was cold welded
ALT cold-welded
SN The joining of metals at room temperature by subjecting to pressure. (DAC)
UF cold pressure welding
welding, cold

cold-working
KT.1139 (L)
HN April 1993 descriptor moved
ALT cold-worked
SN The process of hammering metal into shape without the use of heat.
UF working, cold

coldwater flats
PJ.1211
HN March 1993 descriptor moved
ALT coldwater flat
UK cold-water flats
UKA cold-water flat
SN Apartments provided with only cold running water, often in a building with no central heating. (RHDEL2)
UF flats, cold-water
flats, coldwater

Coles Creek
FL.870

Colima
FL.1081

coliseums
USE amphitheaters
arenas
stadiums

collage
KT.353 (A,L,R)
HN July 1990 scope note added
SN Use for the technique of making compositions in two dimensions or very low relief by gluing paper, fabrics, photographs, or other materials onto a flat surface. If heavy three-dimensional objects dominate, use assemblage. If the constituent fragments form a somewhat unified image, use montage.
UF collage technique
RT collagists

Collage Cubist
USE Synthetic Cubist

collage intaglio prints
USE collagraphs

collage prints
USE collagraphs

collage relief prints
USE collagraphs

collage technique
USE collage

collagen
MT.1229 (L)

HN February 1992 descriptor added
SN The structural protein of connective tissue. (TOCOMO)
RT bone
gelatin
glue
leather

\<collagenous material\>
MT.2547
HN February 1992 guide term added

collages
VC.79 (N)
ALT collage
SN Use for works produced by the technique of collage. If photographs dominate the composition, use **photocollages**.

collages (photocollages)
USE photocollages

collagists
HG.272
HN April 1993 related term added
February 1993 descriptor moved
November 1992 alternate terms added
ALT collagist
collagist's
collagists'
SN Artists who work in collage. (W)
RT collage

collagraph printing
KT.646 (L)
HN October 1991 descriptor moved
October 1991 scope note changed
October 1990 lead-in term added
UK collograph printing
SN Printing process in which the printing surface is created by gluing objects to a support; can be printed in intaglio or relief or can be blind printed. (PETERD)
UF collagraphy
printing, collagraph
printing, collograph

collagraphs
VC.449
ALT collagraph
SN Prints made by collagraph printing.
UF collage intaglio prints
collage prints
collage relief prints
collagraphs, relief
collographs
intaglio prints, collage
prints, collage
relief collagraphs
relief prints, collage
RT cardboard relief prints

collagraphs, relief
USE collagraphs

collagraphy
USE collagraph printing

collapse design
USE plastic design

collapsible top hats
USE opera hats

collar and cuff boxes
TQ.191 (N)
ALT collar and cuff box
SN Boxes, usually with round interior fittings, for the storage of collars and cuffs in a curved position. (NMAHDC)
UF boxes, collar and cuff
RT boxes (containers)

collar beam roofs
HN November 1990 descriptor split, use collar beam (ALT of **collar beams**) + roofs

collar beams
PJ.1843
HN March 1993 descriptor moved
December 1990 descriptor moved
ALT collar beam
SN Horizontal members which tie together and stiffen two opposite rafters, usually at a point about halfway up the rafters. (HAS)
UF beams, collar
beams, wind
collar ties
collars (beams)
strutbeams
ties, collar
wind beams

collar buttons
PJ.72
ALT collar button
SN Two buttons, one larger than the other, connected by a shank, inserted into shirt neck buttonholes. (NMAHDC)
UF buttons, collar
collar studs
studs, collar

collar joints
PJ.680
HN April 1993 descriptor moved
ALT collar joint
UF joints, collar

collar roofs
USE collar beam (ALT of **collar beams**) + roofs

collar studs
USE collar buttons

collar ties
USE collar beams

collars (beams)
USE collar beams

collars (container components)
PJ.3104
ALT collar (container component)
SN Encircling bands on containers and other objects. For flat, sharp-edged collars or knops on stemware, use **mereses**.
RT mereses

collars (armor)
USE gorgets

collars (lighting device components)
PJ.2930
ALT collar (lighting device component)
SN Ring-shaped attachments to lamps, usually of brass, which surround the opening of the font, and are threaded inside to receive the screw of the burner. (RUSHL)

collars (neckwear)
TE.650 (H,L,N)
ALT collar (neckwear)
SN Shaped articles worn at the neckline of a garment, either separate or attached.
RT *\<costume components\>*

collars, bertha
SEE berthas

collars, dog
USE dog collars

collars, newel
USE newel collars

collected works
VW.953
HN November 1992 descriptor moved
June 1992 alternate term deleted, was **collected work**
SN All the writings of an author, including those which have not been printed previously, published in one volume or a number of volumes in a uniform style of binding, usually with an inclusive title.
UF collections (collected works)
works, collected

collectibles
PE.7 (L,R)
HN November 1990 descriptor moved
ALT collectible
SN Objects collected by fanciers, especially items other than such traditionally collectible items as art, stamps, coins, and antiques. (W)

collecting
KG.119 (L,R)
SN Gathering things in order to retain them. (RLG7)

collecting cards
VW.1025 (L)
HN January 1993 scope note changed
January 1993 lead-in terms added
January 1993 related terms added
January 1993 descriptor changed, was **trading cards**
January 1993 alternate term changed, was **trading card**
January 1993 lead-in term changed, was **collecting cards**
November 1992 descriptor moved
May 1991 descriptor added
ALT collecting card
SN Use for cards issued singly or in sets since the 19th century, primarily to

be collected, bearing a wide variety of types of images, such as sports figures, movie stars, or flowers. Some may include advertising and thus also be a type of **advertising cards**; some may be included with a product and thus also be a type of **premiums**. For cards bearing tradesmen's advertisements, and sometimes a variety of images, produced from the 17th through the 19th century, use **trade cards**.

UF cards, collecting
   cards, collector
   cards, collectors'
   cards, trading
   collector cards
   collectors' cards
   trading cards
RT advertising cards
   premiums

collection developing
USE collection development

collection development
   KG.120   (L)
SN Building a coherent and reliable collection over a number of years. (LG)
UF collection developing
   developing, collection
   development, collection

collections
   PC.3   (A,L,R)
HN March 1993 descriptor moved
   April 1991 related terms added
   March 1991 scope note added
ALT collection
SN Use for groups of objects that have been brought together by an individual or organization.
RT archives (buildings)
   clearinghouses
   libraries (buildings)
   museums

collections (collected works)
USE collected works

collections, corporate
USE corporate collections

collections management
   KG.111
UF management, collections

collections, private
USE private collections

collective biographies
   VW.264
HN November 1992 descriptor moved
ALT collective biography
SN Works consisting of separate accounts of lives of people. (LG)
UF biographies, collective

collective farms
   RG.17   (L,B)
ALT collective farm
SN Farms consisting of many small holdings collected into a single unit

for joint operation by a community under public or state supervision.
UF farms, collective

collective labor agreements
   VW.618   (L)
HN November 1992 descriptor moved
ALT collective labor agreement
SN Bargaining agreements as to wages and conditions of work entered into by groups of employees, usually organized into a union on one side and one or more employers or corporations on the other side. (BLACKS)
UF agreements, collective labor
   agreements, master
   labor agreements, collective
   master agreements

collective settlements
   RD.78   (A,L,R)
ALT collective settlement
UF collectives
   communal settlements
   settlements, collective
   settlements, communal

collectives
USE collective settlements

collector cards
USE collecting cards

collectors
   HG.904   (L,R)
HN December 1992 alternate terms added
ALT collector
   collector's
   collectors'

<*collector's cabinets*>
HN April 1993 guide term deleted

collectors' cards
USE collecting cards

collectors' guides
   VW.340
HN November 1992 descriptor moved
   June 1992 scope note added
ALT collector's guide
SN Specialized books containing information pertinent to the collecting of particular types of artifacts.
UF guides, collectors'

collectors' marks
   VW.416   (L,R)
HN November 1992 descriptor moved
ALT collector's mark
UF marks, collectors'

collectors, solar
USE solar collectors

collectors, tax
USE tax collectors

college community centers
USE student unions

college housing
USE student housing

college towns
   RD.49   (L)
ALT college town
UF towns, college

college unions
USE student unions

colleges
   RK.802   (A,L,B)
HN September 1990 scope note added
ALT college
SN Use for buildings or groups of buildings that house institutions of higher learning that provide general or liberal arts education leading to bachelor's degrees; may be independent or parts of universities.

colleges, business
USE business colleges

colleges, commercial
USE business colleges

colleges, community
USE community colleges

colleges, dental
USE dental schools

colleges, junior
USE junior colleges

colleges, medical
USE medical (ALT of medicine) + schools

colleges, military
USE military academies

colleges, sixth-form
USE high schools

colleges, state
USE state colleges

colleges, teachers
USE teachers colleges

colleges, technical
USE polytechnics

colleges, veterinary
USE veterinary colleges

collegiate churches
   RK.1052   (B)
ALT collegiate church
UF churches, collegiate

Collens earth
USE Vandyke brown

collets
   PJ.2598   (L)
HN March 1993 descriptor moved
ALT collet
SN Casings or sockets which hold a drill or other tool. (W)

collieries
USE coal mines

colliers
TX.392
ALT collier
SN Use for vessels either designed for or engaged in the trade of carrying coal in bulk.

colliers de chien
USE dog collars

collies
USE crusies

collodion
MT.1172 (L)
HN January 1993 descriptor moved
SN Cellulose nitrate in a mixture of 60% ether and 40% alcohol for making fiber and film. (MH)

collodion dry plate photonegatives
USE dry collodion negatives

collodion dry-plate process
USE dry collodion process

collodion dry plates
USE dry collodion negatives

collodion glass positives
USE ambrotypes

collodion negatives
USE dry collodion negatives
wet collodion negatives

collodion negatives, dry
USE dry collodion negatives

collodion negatives, wet
USE wet collodion negatives

collodion pellicle
MT.2369
HN April 1992 descriptor moved
UF pellicle, collodion

collodion photonegatives
USE dry collodion negatives
wet collodion negatives

collodion photoprints
USE collodion prints

collodion prints
VC.322
HN April 1992 descriptor moved
ALT collodion print
SN Use for photographic prints having collodion as the binder.
UF collodion photoprints
photoprints, collodion
prints, collodion

collodion processes
KT.511 (L,R)
SN Use for photographic processes in which collodion is the binder. A silver halide is the light-sensitive agent, and the process may be used to produce positives (ambrotypes, tintypes) or negatives.

collodion transfers
VC.323

HN April 1992 descriptor moved
ALT collodion transfer
SN Collodion positives transferred from the glass plate to another support, usually paper. (HCOP)
UF transfers, collodion

collodion wet plate photonegatives
USE wet collodion negatives

collodion wet process
USE wet collodion process

collograph printing
SEE collagraph printing

collographs
USE collagraphs

colloid
MT.1372 (L)
HN February 1993 descriptor added
SN A material made up of finely divided particles dispersed in a continuous liquid, gaseous, or solid medium.

colloid, image-bearing
USE binder
emulsion

colloidal concrete
MT.200 (L)
HN April 1992 descriptor moved
SN Concrete in which the aggregate is bound by a grout that has the ability to retain dispersed solid particles in suspension.
UF concrete, colloidal

colloquiums
USE symposia

collotype
KT.664 (A,L,R)
HN April 1993 descriptor moved
SN A type of photolithography in which the printing plate is prepared using a bichromate process. Unhardened gelatin areas hold water and thus resist greasy ink; hardened areas accept ink and hold it in the characteristic wormlike pattern of cracks.
UF phototype

collotype prints
USE collotypes

collotypes
VC.416
HN April 1992 descriptor moved
ALT collotype
SN Photomechanical prints produced by the process called collotype.
UF collotype prints
prints, collotype

colobia
TE.124
ALT colobium
SN Half-sleeved or sleeveless tunics worn as ecclesiastical vestments before the 4th century. Also, similar

garments worn by monks and by kings as coronation robes.
RT *<liturgical costume>*
robes

Cologne earth
USE Vandyke brown

Cologne spirit
USE ethyl alcohol

Cologne yellow
USE chrome yellow

cololches
PJ.1456
HN March 1993 descriptor moved
December 1990 scope note changed
ALT cololche
SN Thin wood poles used in modern Mayan building construction. (DWELL)

Colombian
FL.735 (L,B)

colonels
HG.126
HN January 1993 descriptor added
ALT colonel
colonel's
colonels'
SN Commissioned officers in the armed forces; generally they rank as the superior officers of regiments.

<Colonial African styles>
FL.170

Colonial, American
USE American Colonial

<Colonial American styles>
FL.1718

Colonial, British
USE British Colonial

colonial cities
RD.24 (A)
ALT colonial city
SN Designates cities built in territories where no urban settlements existed before, generally created following an overall plan, and often established by an urban culture for purposes of local administration. (JOHNUG)
UF cities, colonial

Colonial, Dutch
USE Dutch Colonial

Colonial, French
USE French Colonial

<Colonial Indian styles>
FL.2328

<Colonial Latin American architecture styles>
FL.1728
HN June 1991 guide term moved

‹Colonial Latin American fine arts styles›
FL.1734
HN June 1991 guide term moved

‹Colonial Latin American styles›
FL.1725
HN June 1991 guide term moved

Colonial North American
USE American Colonial

‹Colonial North American styles›
FL.1719

Colonial, Portuguese
USE Portuguese Colonial

Colonial Revival
FL.1745   (A,L,B,R)
UF Revival, Colonial

Colonial Revival, Spanish
USE Spanish Colonial Revival

Colonial, Spanish
USE Spanish Colonial

colonials
HG.1001
HN January 1993 descriptor added
ALT colonial
       colonial's
       colonials'
SN Use for the inhabitants of a colony,
     either those who moved there or
     were born there. For those who take
     part in the initial founding of a col-
     ony, use **colonists.**
RT colonists

colonies
HN.9   (L)
HN January 1993 descriptor added
ALT colony
SN Areas outside the boundaries of sov-
     ereign states in which they have set-
     tled communities of their own peo-
     ple and which remain subject to or
     closely connected with the parent
     state.
RT colonization

colonies, art
USE artists' colonies

colonies, artists'
USE artists' colonies

colonies, penal
USE penal colonies

colonies, space
USE space colonies

colonists
HG.905
HN January 1993 descriptor added
ALT colonist
       colonist's
       colonists'
SN Use for those who take part in the
     initial founding of a colony. For
     those who inhabit a colony, either

those who moved there or were
born there, use **colonials.**
RT colonials

colonization
KG.266   (L,R)
HN January 1993 related term added
     June 1991 lead-in term added
     January 1991 alternate term added
     November 1990 descriptor moved
ALT colonized
SN Extension of political and economic
     control over an area by a foreign oc-
     cupying state that usually has orga-
     nizational and military superiority.
     (CCE)
UF colonizing
RT colonies

colonizing
USE colonization

colonnades
PJ.1430   (A,B,R)
HN March 1993 descriptor moved
     December 1990 scope note changed
ALT colonnade
SN Use for rows of columns supporting
     an entablature and often one side of
     a roof. Includes spaces behind such
     a feature when they are long and
     used for circulation.
UF orthostyles

colonnettes
PJ.1463
HN March 1993 descriptor moved
     November 1990 scope note changed
ALT colonnette
SN Use for small or slender columns;
     for small Medieval columns, usually
     attached to architectural features,
     use **shafts (Medieval columns).**

colophons
VW.246   (L)
HN November 1992 descriptor moved
     November 1992 scope note changed
ALT colophon
SN Use for closing statements placed at
     the ends of printed books giving de-
     tails of the book's production, such
     as the printer, place and date of
     printing, and author's name. For
     closing phrases of manuscripts and
     some early printed books, or of sec-
     tions of same, sometimes giving de-
     tails of the work's production, use
     explicits.

colophony
USE rosin

color
DL.2   (A,L,B,R)
HN February 1992 descriptor moved
UK colour
SN Use to refer to perceived qualities
     that result from the response of vi-
     sion to the wavelength of reflected
     or transmitted light. For individual

chromatic colors and achromatic
colors or neutrals, use **colors.**
UF chromatics

color, accidental
USE reflected color

color, acrylic
USE acrylic paint

color, additive
USE additive mixture

‹color and color-related phenomena›
DL.1
HN February 1992 guide term added

‹color and related concepts›
HN February 1992 guide term deleted

color, artist's
USE artist's color

color blocks
TH.858
HN February 1993 descriptor added
ALT color block
UK colour blocks
UKA colour block
SN Blocks for printing the individual
     colors in color woodcuts, registered
     onto the key block image.
UF blocks, color
       blocks, colour
RT color printing

color, body
USE gouache
       mass color

color, bulky
USE volume color

color, casein
USE casein paint

‹color changes›
KT.226
HN November 1992 guide term added

color charts
VW.143
HN November 1992 descriptor moved
ALT color chart
UF charts, color
       color diagrams
       diagrams, color

color circles
USE color wheels

color, coal-tar
USE synthetic organic pigment

color constancy
USE constancy

color coupler prints
USE chromogenic color prints

color coupler processes
USE chromogenic processes

color, dead
USE lay-in

color diagrams
USE color charts

color, dry
USE dry color

color dye coupler processes
USE chromogenic processes

color, earth
USE natural inorganic pigment

<color effects>
HN February 1992 guide term deleted

color, encaustic
USE encaustic paint

Color-field
FL.3857   (L,R)
SN Encompasses both Abstract Imagist painting and works of the 1960s derived from it.
UF Abstraction, Chromatic
     Abstraction, Post-painterly
     Chromatic Abstraction
     Post-painterly Abstraction

color film
MT.2370   (L)
HN April 1992 descriptor moved
UK colour film
UF film, color
     film, colour

color, film
USE film color

color filters
USE light filters

color, full
USE full-color printing

color lightfastness
USE lightfastness

color lithographs
VC.476
ALT color lithograph
UK colour lithographs
UKA colour lithograph
SN Lithographs printed in several colors.
UF lithographs, color
     lithographs, colour
     lithographs, multicolor
     lithographs, multicolour
     multicolor lithographs
     multicolour lithographs
RT color prints

color lithography
KT.687   (R)
HN March 1991 descriptor added
UK colour lithography
SN Printing by lithography using a separate stone or plate for each color. (LG)
UF lithography, color
     lithography, colour

color, local
USE local color

color, lost
USE lost color

color, luminous
USE luminous color

color makers
USE artists' colormen

color, mass
USE mass color

color measurement
USE colorimetry

<color measuring devices>
TN.323

color media
USE filters

color mediums
USE filters

color, metallic
USE metallic pigment

color mixture
DL.21
HN February 1992 descriptor moved
UK colour mixture
UF colorant mixture
     mixture, color
     mixture, colour
     mixture, optical
     optical mixture

color mixture, additive
USE additive mixture

color mixture, subtractive
USE subtractive mixture

color negatives
VC.291
HN April 1992 descriptor moved
ALT color negative
UK colour negatives
UKA colour negative
SN Use for photographic negatives that record on a single base the hue and lightness of a scene in complementary relation to the scene's perceived values; e.g., light blue is recorded as dark yellow. Use **color separation negatives** for images in which each color is recorded on a physically separate negative.
UF negatives, color
     negatives, colour

color, oil
USE oil paint

Color, Party of
USE Rubenism

color photographs
VC.348
HN April 1992 descriptor moved
ALT color photograph
UK colour photographs
UKA colour photograph
SN Use for the broad class of photographs whose images are composed of more than one hue, plus the neutral tones. For photographs having a range of tones within one hue, use **black-and-white photographs.**
UF photographs, color
     photographs, colour

color photography
KT.569   (L,R)
UK colour photography
UF chromophotography
     heliochromy (color photography)
     photography, color
     photography, colour

color photoprints
USE color prints (photographs)

color, polymer
USE polymer paint

color, poster
USE poster color

color printing
KT.647   (L,R)
HN January 1993 related terms added
     October 1991 descriptor moved
     May 1991 related term added
UK colour printing
UF chromotypography
     printing, color
     printing, colour
RT color blocks
     color prints
     key blocks
     key plates

color printing, process
USE full-color printing

color prints
VC.450   (L)
ALT color print
UK colour prints
UKA colour print
SN Images printed in two or more colors; if color is applied after printing, use **colored** (ALT of **coloring**) + **prints.** For color photographs, use **color prints (photographs).**
UF prints, color
     prints, colour
RT color lithographs
     color printing
     color prints (photographs)
     color proofs
     color wood engravings
     color woodcuts

color prints (photographs)
VC.317
HN April 1993 scope note changed
     April 1992 descriptor moved
     May 1991 related term added
ALT color print (photograph)
UK colour prints (photographs)
UKA colour print (photograph)
SN Use for photographic prints whose images are composed of more than one hue, plus the neutral tones. For photographic prints having a range

of tones within one hue, use **black-and-white prints (photographs).**
- UF color photoprints
  colour photoprints
  photoprints, color
  photoprints, colour
  prints, color
  prints, colour
- RT color prints

color prints, chromogenic
- USE chromogenic color prints

color, process
- USE full-color printing

color proofs
- VC.442
- ALT color proof
- UK colour proofs
- UKA colour proof
- SN Set of proofs showing each color from a color printing process on an individual impression. For a set of proofs showing the sequential and cumulative steps in a color printing process as each color is added, use **progressive proofs.**
- UF color separations (prints)
  colour separations (prints)
  flat proofs
  proofs, color
  proofs, colour
  proofs, flat
  proofs, successive
  separations, color (prints)
  separations, colour (prints)
  successive proofs
- RT color prints

<color properties>
- DL.10
- HN February 1992 guide term moved

color, reflected
- USE reflected color

<color-related attributes>
- DL.16
- HN February 1992 guide term moved

<color-related concepts>
- HN February 1992 guide term deleted

<color-related effects>
- DL.19
- HN February 1992 guide term added

color, scenic
- USE distemper

color screen processes
- USE screen processes

color screens
- USE filters

color separation
- KT.706   (L)
- HN October 1990 descriptor moved
- UK colour separation
- SN The technique of isolating individual colors on separate printing plates or photographic negatives, so

that a picture or design may be printed in multiple colors.
- UF separation, color
  separation, colour

color separation negatives
- VC.286
- HN April 1993 scope note changed
  April 1993 lead-in term added
  April 1992 descriptor moved
- ALT color separation negative
- UK colour separation negatives
- UKA colour separation negative
- SN Use for negatives that record in monochrome the ranges of lightness of one hue per negative, usually in sets of three negatives. Each is used to make a plate or matrix for printing one color, in register with the others, to form a full-color photomechanical print.
- UF color separation photonegatives
  colour separation photonegatives
  negatives, color separation
  negatives, colour separation
  negatives, separation
  photonegatives, color separation
  photonegatives, colour separation
  separation negatives
  separation negatives, color
  separation negatives, colour

color separation photonegatives
- USE color separation negatives

color separation phototransparencies
- USE color separation positives

color separation positives
- VC.337
- HN April 1993 scope note changed
  April 1993 lead-in term added
  April 1992 descriptor moved
- ALT color separation positive
- UK colour separation positives
- UKA colour separation positive
- SN Use for positive transparencies that record in monochrome the ranges of lightness of one hue per film, usually in sets of three films. Each is used to make a plate or matrix for printing one color, in register with the others, to form a full-color photomechanical print.
- UF color separation phototransparencies
  color separation transparencies
  colour separation phototransparencies
  colour separation transparencies
  phototransparencies, color separation
  phototransparencies, colour separation
  positives, color separation
  positives, colour separation
  positives, separation
  separation positives
  transparencies, color separation
  transparencies, colour separation

color separation transparencies
- USE color separation positives

color separations (prints)
- USE color proofs

color shift
- DE.6
- HN November 1992 descriptor moved
- UK colour shift
- SN Change in color brought about either by differential fade rates of dyes or by an imbalance of dyes in an image area. (CPEK)
- UF shift, color
  shift, colour

color, show-card
- USE poster color

color, size
- USE distemper

color slides
- VC.359   (L,R)
- HN April 1992 descriptor moved
- ALT color slide
- UK colour slides
- UKA colour slide
- SN Use for photographic slides whose images are composed of more than one hue, plus the neutral tones. For slides having a range of tones within one hue, use **black-and-white slides.**
- UF slides, color
  slides, colour

color spectrum
- USE visible spectrum

color, surface
- USE local color

color, symbolic
- USE symbolic color

color transparencies
- VC.342
- HN April 1992 descriptor moved
- ALT color transparency
- UK colour transparencies
- UKA colour transparency
- SN Use for transparencies whose images are composed of more than one hue, plus the neutral tones. For transparencies having a range of tones within one hue, use **black-and-white transparencies.**
- UF positive color transparencies
  positive colour transparencies
  transparencies, color
  transparencies, colour
  transparencies, positive color
  transparencies, positive colour

<color types>
- DL.337
- HN February 1992 guide term added

color, volume
- USE volume color

color wheels
- VW.144

HN November 1992 descriptor moved
ALT color wheel
UF circles, color
color circles
wheels, color

color wood engravings
VC.490
ALT color wood engraving
UK colour wood engravings
UKA colour wood engraving
UF chromoxylographs
engravings, color wood
wood engravings, color
RT color prints

color woodcuts
VC.494
ALT color woodcut
UK colour woodcuts
UKA colour woodcut
UF woodcuts, color
woodcuts, colour
RT color prints

Colorado blue spruce
USE blue spruce

Colorado spruce
USE blue spruce

Colorado yule statuary marble
MT.766
HN April 1992 descriptor moved
UF marble, Colorado yule statuary
statuary marble, Colorado yule

colorant
MT.2010 (L)
HN January 1992 descriptor moved
UK colourant
UF coloring matter
colouring matter
matter, coloring
matter, colouring

<colorant by form>
HN April 1992 guide term deleted

<colorant by function>
HN March 1992 guide term deleted

<colorant for dye and pigment>
MT.2011
HN May 1992 guide term added

colorant mixture
USE color mixture

colored ink
MT.1929
HN June 1991 descriptor moved
UK coloured ink
UF ink, colored
ink, coloured

colored pencils
TH.684 (N)
ALT colored pencil
UF pencils, colored

colorers
HG.671

HN December 1992 alternate terms
added
ALT colorer
colorer's
colorers'
UK colourers
UKA colourer
SN Persons who color by hand or spray
designs on cards, calendars, maps,
and related articles, using colored
inks and pens or airbrush, following
instructions or working drawings.
(DOT)

colorfastness
DC.274 (L)
HN October 1992 descriptor added
ALT colorfast
UK colour fastness
UKA colour fast
SN The property of a coloring matter
or material containing a coloring
matter to retain its original hue or
intensity. Refers especially to the
ability to resist running or fading
which most frequently results from
cleaning or exposure to light.

colorimeters
TN.326 (N)
ALT colorimeter
SN Instruments that measure color by
comparing a given color to a standard color, a scale of colors, or certain combinations of primary colors.
RT colorimetry
photometers

colorimetry
KT.174 (L)
HN December 1991 related term added
UK colour measurement
SN Use for the process of determining
and specifying colors.
UF color measurement
measurement, color
measurement, colour
RT colorimeters

coloring
KT.50
HN January 1993 descriptor moved
November 1992 scope note added
ALT colored
UK colouring
UKA coloured
SN Changing or altering the color of
something, whether by penetrating
or coating it.

coloring books
VW.31 (L)
HN November 1992 descriptor moved
ALT coloring book
UF books, coloring

coloring, hand
USE hand coloring

coloring matter
USE colorant

colorism
USE Rubenism

colormen, artists'
USE artists' colormen

colors
DL.32 (A,L,B,R)
UK colours
SN Use to refer to individual chromatic
colors in the spectrum and the achromatic colors or neutrals. With reference to theory and perception,
use color.

colors, achromatic
USE neutrals

colors, complementary
USE complementary colors

colors, cool
USE cool colors

colors, primary
USE primary colors

colors, secondary
USE secondary colors

colors, spectral
USE spectral colors

colors, tertiary
USE tertiary colors

colors, warm
USE warm colors

colorwashing
KT.92
HN March 1993 descriptor moved
March 1991 alternate term added
ALT colorwashed
UK colour-washing
UKA colour-washed
SN Applying a whitewash or a cold-
water paint tinted with colored pig-
ments. (W)

colossi
VC.571 (R)
ALT colossus
SN Sculptured figures of extraordi-
narily large size.

colour
SEE color

colour, accidental
SEE reflected color

colour, artist's
SEE artist's color

colour blocks
SEE color blocks

colour, bulky
SEE volume color

colour, casein
SEE casein paint

colour, dry
SEE dry color

colour, encaustic
SEE encaustic paint

colour fastness
SEE colorfastness

colour film
SEE color film

colour, film
SEE film color

colour, full
SEE full-color printing

colour lithographs
SEE color lithographs

colour lithography
SEE color lithography

colour, local
SEE local color

colour, lost
SEE lost color

colour, luminous
SEE luminous color

colour makers
SEE artists' colormen

colour, mass
SEE mass color

colour measurement
SEE colorimetry

colour-men, artists'
SEE artists' colormen

colour, metallic
SEE metallic pigment

colour mixture
SEE color mixture

colour negatives
SEE color negatives

colour, oil
SEE oil paint

colour photographs
SEE color photographs

colour photography
SEE color photography

colour photoprints
SEE color prints (photographs)

colour, polymer
SEE polymer paint

colour, poster
SEE poster color

colour printing
SEE color printing

colour printing, process
SEE full-color printing

colour prints
SEE color prints

colour prints (photographs)
SEE color prints (photographs)

colour prints, chromogenic
SEE chromogenic color prints

colour, process
SEE full-color printing

colour proofs
SEE color proofs

colour, reflected
SEE reflected color

colour separation
SEE color separation

colour separation negatives
SEE color separation negatives

colour separation photonegatives
SEE color separation negatives

colour separation phototransparencies
SEE color separation positives

colour separation positives
SEE color separation positives

colour separation transparencies
SEE color separation positives

colour separations (prints)
SEE color proofs

colour shift
SEE color shift

colour, show-card
USE poster color

colour slides
SEE color slides

colour transparencies
SEE color transparencies

colour, volume
SEE volume color

colour-washing
SEE colorwashing

colour wood engravings
SEE color wood engravings

colour woodcuts
SEE color woodcuts

colourant
SEE colorant

coloured ink
SEE colored ink

colourers
SEE colorers

colouring
SEE coloring

colouring, hand
SEE hand coloring

colouring matter
SEE colorant

colourmen, artists'
SEE artists' colormen

colours
SEE colors

colours, complementary
SEE complementary colors

colours, cool
SEE cool colors

colours, primary
SEE primary colors

colours, secondary
SEE secondary colors

colours, spectral
SEE spectral colors

colours, tertiary
SEE tertiary colors

colours, warm
SEE warm colors

colt feet
PJ.2809
HN March 1993 descriptor moved
March 1993 lead-in term added
March 1993 lead-in term changed, was colt's feet
ALT colt foot
SN Feet on baluster legs which end in a ball flanked by rings, over the beginning of another baluster facing downwards; resembling the foot of a colt. (KIRK)
UF colts' feet
feet, colt
feet, colts'

colts' feet
USE colt feet

columbaria
RG.29 (A,B)
ALT columbarium
SN Sepulchral chambers lined with rows of niches for cinerary urns.

columbaria (dovecotes)
USE dovecotes

columbariums
USE dovecotes

Columbia
USE Sinkiuse

Columbian spirit
USE methyl alcohol

columbine cups
TQ.404
ALT columbine cup
SN Standing cups often having a trefoil foot, baluster-shaped stem, and an embossed cup; so named from their resemblance to the columbine flower.
UF cups, columbine

column and beam assemblies
USE post-and-beam structures

column carpets
USE pillar rugs

<column components>
    PJ.1482
    HN April 1993 related term added
        March 1993 guide term moved
    RT *<structural element components>*

column figures
    VC.527
    ALT column figure
    SN Use for figures carved as part of, and projecting from, columns. For supporting members fully in human form, use such terms as **atlantes** or **caryatids**. (STOK)
    UF column statues
        columns, statue
        figures, column
        statue columns
        statues, column

column kraters
    TQ.93
    ALT column krater
    SN Kraters with columnlike handles extending from the shoulders to the rim.
    UF Corinthian kraters
        kraters, column
        kraters, Corinthian

column rugs
USE pillar rugs

column screens
USE columnar screens

column statues
USE column figures

columnae caelatae
    HN November 1990 descriptor deleted

columnae rostratae
USE rostral columns

columnar
    DC.62
    HN October 1992 descriptor moved
    SN Formed in columns; having the form of a column or shaft of a column. (W)

columnar prayer rugs
USE coupled-column rugs

columnar screens
    PJ.1731
    HN March 1993 descriptor moved
        April 1990 descriptor added
    ALT columnar screen
    SN Use for rows of columns that serve primarily to separate interior spaces.
    UF column screens
        columned screens
        screens, columnar

columned screens
USE columnar screens

columnists
    HG.479   (L)

    HN December 1992 alternate terms added
    ALT columnist
        columnist's
        columnists'
    SN Journalists who analyze news and write columns or commentary based on personal knowledge and experience for publication or broadcast. (DOT)

columns (architectural elements)
    PJ.1458   (A,L,N,B,R)
    HN March 1993 descriptor moved
        March 1993 descriptor changed, was **columns**
        March 1993 alternate term changed, was **column**
        July 1991 scope note changed
    ALT column (architectural element)
    SN Use for cylindrical, upright masonry members, usually either giving support or appearing to give support and usually comprised of three sections: a base, capital, and shaft; common also on furniture, especially as decorative elements. Use also for all uprights in steel frame or concrete frame structures. For square or rectangular members, either in masonry construction or classically treated, and for massive uprights in Medieval architecture, use **piers (supporting elements)**; for wooden square uprights, use **posts**.
    UF pillars

columns (layout features)
    PJ.3394
    ALT column (layout feature)
    SN Vertical lists of items or vertical sections of a printed page separated by rules or blank spaces.

columns (TM), Lally
USE Lally columns (TM)

<columns and column components>
    PJ.1457
    HN March 1993 guide term moved

columns, annulated
USE annulated columns

columns, applied
USE engaged columns

columns, attached
USE engaged columns

columns, baluster
USE baluster columns

columns, banded
USE banded columns

columns, blocked
USE banded columns

<columns by form>
    PJ.1459
    HN March 1993 guide term moved

<columns by location or context>
    PJ.1472
    HN March 1993 guide term moved

columns, coupled
USE coupled columns

columns, diminishing
USE diminishing columns

columns, doubled
USE doubled columns

columns, engaged
USE engaged columns

columns, flanked
USE flanked columns

columns, grouped
USE grouped columns

columns, half
USE half columns

columns, knotted
USE knotted columns

columns, median
USE median columns

columns, memorial
USE memorial columns

columns, mid-wall
USE mid-wall columns

columns, monolithic
USE monolithic columns

columns, monumental
USE memorial columns

columns, newspaper
USE newspaper columns

columns, paired
USE coupled columns

columns, ringed
USE banded columns

columns, rostral
USE rostral columns

columns, serpent
USE serpent columns

columns, Solomonic
USE spiral columns

columns, spiral
USE spiral columns

columns, statue
USE column figures

columns, trinity
USE trinity columns

columns, twisted
USE spiral columns

columns, wreathed
USE spiral columns

columns, zoophoric
USE zoophoric columns

colza oil
USE   rape oil

colza oil lamps
   TC.1388
ALT   colza oil lamp
SN   Lamps which burn colza oil.
UF   lamps, colza oil
   oil lamps, colza

COM
USE   computer-output microfiche
   computer-output microfilms
   computer-output microforms

comals
   TH.69
HN   April 1993 descriptor added
ALT   comal
SN   Ceramic griddles used to bake tortillas. (MUSER)

Comanche
   FL.1395   (L)

comb-back Windsor chairs
USE   high-back Windsor chairs

comb baskets
USE   loom baskets

comb boards
USE   saddle boards

combination clamps
USE   universal clamps

combination fixtures
   TC.1410
ALT   combination fixture
SN   Any lighting fixture using more than one method of illumination, usually with gas as one of the methods.
UF   combination gas and candle fixtures
   combination gas and electric fixtures
   combination gas and oil fixtures
   fixtures, combination
   fixtures, combination gas and candle
   fixtures, combination gas and electric
   fixtures, combination gas and oil
   fixtures, gas and electric
   gas and electric fixtures

combination gas and candle fixtures
USE   combination fixtures

combination gas and electric fixtures
USE   combination fixtures

combination gas and oil fixtures
USE   combination fixtures

combination guns
   TK.3   (N)
ALT   combination gun
SN   Combination weapons consisting of a small arm combined with either a different weapon or with some tool or article of everyday use, such as a walking stick.
UF   arms, combined
   combined arms

   combined firearms
   firearms, combined
   guns, combination
RT   *<small arms by form>*

combination highchair and carriages
USE   carriage chairs

<combination inorganic/organic animal material>
   MT.1312
HN   January 1992 guide term added

<combination inorganic/organic material>
   MT.1310
HN   January 1992 guide term added

<combination instruments>
   TT.630
SN   Collocates descriptors for devices consisting of two or more musical instruments or of a musical instrument with another type of device.

combination locks
   PJ.490
HN   April 1993 descriptor moved
ALT   combination lock
UF   dial locks
   locks, combination
   locks, dial

combination photoprints
USE   composite photographs

combination planes
   TH.1497   (N)
ALT   combination plane
SN   Planes with a moveable fence and interchangeable blades; used for a variety of grooving and molding purposes. (KEBABI)
UF   planes, combination

combination pliers
   TH.1286   (N)
SN   Any of several styles of pliers that can be used for cutting, swaging, or hammering, as well as for gripping. (MEANS)
UF   half-round pliers
   pliers, combination
   pliers, half-round

combination printing
   KT.613
HN   March 1993 descriptor moved
SN   Use for the technique of printing one photograph using images from more than one negative. For the technique of recording more than one image on a single sheet or frame of film, use **multiple exposure.**

combination prints
USE   composite photographs

combination tannage
USE   combination tanning

combination tanning
   KT.1056

HN   November 1992 descriptor added
ALT   combination tanned
SN   The use of two or more tanning processes, such as vegetable tanning and mineral tanning, to produce leather which possesses important characteristics of both methods.
UF   combination tannage
   tannage, combination
   tanning, combination

combination weapons
   TK.2
ALT   combination weapon
SN   Use for weapons which are combinations of two or more different kinds of weapon. May also be used for weapons that are hidden in or appear to be innocent articles of everyday use.
UF   weapons, combination
RT   sword sticks

combination windows
   PJ.2227
HN   March 1993 descriptor moved
ALT   combination window
SN   Windows equipped with removable or interchangeable screen and glass sections that make them suitable for either summer or winter use. (DAC)
UF   windows, combination

combination writing table and dressing stands
USE   ladies' cabinet dressing tables

combinations
   TE.188   (N)
ALT   combination
SN   One-piece garments combining an upper body covering, with or without sleeves, with a bifurcated lower body covering. (NMAHDC)
RT   creepers
   union suits

<combinations of rooms>
   PJ.1207
HN   March 1993 guide term moved

combined arms
USE   combination guns

combined cycle power plants
USE   cogeneration plants

combined dressing tables and desks
USE   bureau tables

combined escutcheon plates
   PJ.439
HN   April 1993 descriptor moved
ALT   combined escutcheon plate
SN   Escutcheons cut for both knob and keyhole or cylinder. (BROWNL)
UF   escutcheon plates, combined
   plates, combined escutcheon

combined firearms
USE   combination guns

combined footings
   PJ.1542

HN March 1993 descriptor moved
    January 1991 scope note changed
ALT combined footing
SN Use for footings that are slabs under two or more columns or columns and a wall, one of which is internal rather than on the perimeter so that the footing cannot take a beamlike form.
UF footings, combined

combined heat and power generating plants
USE cogeneration plants

combined loads
    BM.601
HN November 1992 descriptor moved
    January 1991 alternate term added
ALT combined load
SN Two or more different types of loads (such as dead load, live load, or wind load) occurring simultaneously on a structure. (DAC)
UF loads, combined

combined sewerage system
USE combined sewers

combined sewers
    RK.513   (L)
ALT combined sewer
SN Sewers that receive both storm water and sewage. (MEANS)
UF combined sewerage system
    sewerage system, combined
    sewers, combined

combined store-door locks
    PJ.523
HN April 1993 descriptor moved
ALT combined store-door lock
UF locks, combined store-door
    store-door locks, combined

combined stress
    BM.643
HN November 1992 descriptor moved
SN Bending or twisting stress in a structural member combined with direct tension or compression. (MHDSTT)
UF stress, combined

combined twill
USE composite twill

combined writing and dressing tables
USE bureau tables

combing
    KT.1186
HN March 1993 related term added
    March 1993 descriptor moved
ALT combed
SN Preparing fiber for spinning by cleansing, disentangling, and collecting together by the use of a comb; used to prepare relatively long fibers. (W)
RT combs (textile working equipment)

combing jackets
USE dressing jackets

combs (armor components)
    PJ.3016
ALT comb (armor component)
SN Raised ridges running from front to back over the top of the skulls of helmets, contributing to their strength and rigidity and providing a better glancing surface.

combs (grooming tools)
    TH.377   (H,L,N,R)
HN January 1993 descriptor added
ALT comb (grooming tool)
SN Tools with a row of teeth on one or both edges or sides that are used for adjusting, distangling, or cleaning the hair.
RT toilet sets (dresser sets)

combs (hair ornaments)
    TE.508   (H,L,N)
ALT comb (hair ornament)
SN Combs having three or more teeth and an ornamental upper portion intended to be seen when the teeth are inserted in the hair. (NMAHDC)
UF combs, ornamental
    haircombs
    ornamental combs

combs (textile working equipment)
    TH.1366   (H,N)
HN March 1993 descriptor added
ALT comb (textile working equipment)
SN Any of various toothed devices used in handling or ordering textile fibers. (W)
RT combing

combs, cocks'
USE cocks' combs

combs, ornamental
USE combs (hair ornaments)

combs, side
USE side combs

combustion
    KT.821   (L)
HN January 1993 descriptor moved
SN Use for the initial act or instance of burning and for the chemical processes in which light or heat are produced by the vigorous union of various substances with oxygen.

come-alongs
    TH.485   (N)
ALT come-along
SN Portable ratcheting winches consisting of a fastening device on one end and a hook attached to a cable at the other end. Operating a lever turns a drum which takes up the cable and exerts a pulling force on the hook. (MEANS)
UF hoists, ratchet
    pullers, ratchet
    ratchet hoists
    ratchet pullers

Comechingón
    FL.1636   (L)

comedians
    HG.248   (L,R)
HN November 1992 alternate terms added
ALT comedian
    comedian's
    comedians'

comedies
    VW.266   (L)
HN June 1992 descriptor added
ALT comedy
SN Light and amusing stories.

comedy
    BM.202   (L,R)

Comeya
USE Kamia

comfit boxes
    TQ.330
ALT comfit box
SN Boxes to hold comfits, a type of sweetmeat like crystallized fruit or a confection for sweetening the breath. (IDC89)
UF boxes, comfit
RT bonbon dishes
    boxes (containers)

comfit glasses
    TQ.359
ALT comfit glass
SN Small sweetmeat glasses, usually about 4 inches high, used for serving dry sweetmeats or confections.
UF glasses, comfit

comfort
    BM.1024   (L,B)
HN February 1993 descriptor moved
SN Sense of ease and satisfaction of bodily wants, with freedom from pain and anxiety. (RHDEL2)

comfort stations
    RK.711   (L,R)
ALT comfort station
SN Buildings with toilets and lavatory facilities for public use. (RHDEL2)
UF comfort stations, public
    pissoirs
    public comfort stations
    public toilets
    stations, comfort
    stations, public comfort
    toilets, public

comfort stations, public
USE comfort stations

comfortables
USE comforters

comforters
    TC.202   (N)
ALT comforter
SN Warm, heavily wadded bedcovers usually consisting of three layers (top, backing, and filling) which are

often tufted or tied rather than quilted.
UF comfortables
   comforts
RT quilts

comforts
USE comforters

comic books
   VW.33   (H,L)
HN June 1992 descriptor added
ALT comic book
SN Comics, often serialized, published in pamphlet form.
UF books, comic
   serial picture books

comic strips
   VW.34   (H,L)
HN June 1992 descriptor added
ALT comic strip
SN Comics, usually serialized and composed of a few frames, and often syndicated for publication in newspapers.
UF cartoon strips
   strips, cartoon
   strips, comic

comics
   VW.32   (H,L)
HN November 1992 descriptor moved
   September 1992 scope note changed
   June 1992 lead-in term added
   June 1992 lead-in term deleted, was comic strips
   June 1992 lead-in term deleted, was strips, comic
   June 1992 lead-in term deleted, was cartoon strips
   June 1992 lead-in term deleted, was strips, cartoon
   April 1991 descriptor moved
ALT comic
SN Use broadly for sequential graphic narratives, often serialized, and typically having dialogue written in balloons.
UF funnies

comitia
   RK.1128   (L)
ALT comitium
SN Use for ancient Roman places of political assembly for a variety of legal and administrative functions.

commandants
USE commanding officers

commanderies
   HN.39   (H)
HN January 1993 descriptor added
ALT commandery
SN Landed estates or groups of estates belonging to a military religious order of knights and placed under the charge of a member of the order, titled a commander.

commanders
   HG.127
HN January 1993 descriptor added
ALT commander
   commander's
   commanders'
SN Use for commissioned officers in the American and British navies, ranking immediately below captains. For chief officers in command of a military force, place, or station, use **commanding officers.**
RT commanding officers

commanders (commanding officers)
USE commanding officers

commanders (mallets)
USE beetles

commanding officers
   HG.128
HN January 1993 descriptor added
ALT commanding officer
   commanding officer's
   commanding officers'
SN Use for chief officers in command of a military force, place, or station. For commissioned officers in the American and British navies ranking immediately below captains, use **commanders.**
UF commandants
   commanders (commanding officers)
   officers, commanding
RT commanders
   condottieri

commedia dell'arte
   BM.203   (L,R)
SN Italian 16th- to 18th-century comedy performed by companies of actors trained to improvise dialogue, gesture, and movement from a written plot built around standardized situations and stock characters. (W)

commemorations
   KM.49   (H,L)
HN April 1992 descriptor added
ALT commemoration
SN Events, often but not always ceremonious or celebratory in nature, serving to call someone or something to remembrance or to honor people or past events. For events demonstrating grateful or happy satisfaction or honor, use **celebrations.** For formal events conducted elaborately, solemnly, and as prescribed by ritual or protocol, use **ceremonies.**
RT celebrations
   ceremonies

commemorations (memorials)
USE memorials

<commemorative containers>
   TQ.136
RT commemoratives

commemorative jewellery
SEE commemorative jewelry

commemorative jewelry
   TE.442
UK commemorative jewellery
SN Articles of jewelry worn to commemorate some occasion, such as a political event, royal marriage, coronation, or death. (HNDOJ)
UF jewellery, commemorative
   jewelry, commemorative
RT commemoratives

commemorative quilts
   TC.226
ALT commemorative quilt
SN Quilts made to commemorate events ranging from international to local significance, for example wars, political campaigns, or centennials.
UF quilts, commemorative
RT commemoratives
   patriotic quilts

commemoratives
   PE.70   (L,N)
HN January 1993 descriptor added
ALT commemorative
SN Use for items produced, issued, or worn to commemorate an event or occasion.
RT <commemorative containers>
   commemorative jewelry
   commemorative quilts
   dower chests

commencements
   KM.21
HN May 1991 alternate term added
ALT commencement
SN Ceremonies at which degrees or diplomas are conferred by an educational institution. (W)
UF graduations

commentaries
   VW.267   (H,L)
HN November 1992 descriptor moved
   June 1992 scope note changed
ALT commentary
SN Treatises or series of comments that systematically explain or annotate another work.

commerce
USE business

commerce, chambers of
USE boards of trade

commercial agents
   HG.625   (L)
HN December 1992 alternate terms added
   April 1991 lead-in terms added
ALT commercial agent
   commercial agent's
   commercial agents'
UF agents
   agents, business
   agents, commercial
   business agents

commercial areas
USE business districts

commercial art
BM.179 (L,R)
UF art, commercial

commercial art galleries
USE art galleries

commercial artists
HG.273 (L)
HN February 1993 descriptor moved December 1992 alternate terms added
ALT commercial artist
commercial artist's
commercial artists'
SN Designers whose work is commissioned for such uses as advertising, illustration, and the design, embellishment, or decoration of products. (MAYER)
UF artists, commercial

commercial buildings
RK.102 (A,L,N,B,R)
ALT commercial building
SN Use broadly to refer to buildings associated with any aspect of the various activities and business relationships of industry and trade; when referring to structures associated with the purchase, sale, or exchange of goods in business, use **mercantile buildings.** (RHDEL2)
UF buildings, business
buildings, commercial
business buildings
business facilities
commercial facilities
facilities, business
facilities, commercial

commercial catalogs
USE trade catalogs

commercial centers
USE central business districts

commercial colleges
USE business colleges

<commercial complexes>
RG.39

commercial correspondence
VW.364 (L)
HN November 1992 descriptor moved
UF correspondence, commercial

commercial directories
VW.835
HN November 1992 descriptor moved
ALT commercial directory
UF business directories
directories, business
directories, commercial
directories, trade
trade directories

commercial districts
USE business districts

commercial enterprises
USE business enterprises

commercial facilities
USE commercial buildings

commercial laundries
USE laundries

commercial letters of credit
USE letters of credit

commercial museums
USE company museums

commercial paper
VK.161 (L)
SN Use for short-term, usually three-to-six-month, negotiable instruments that arise from commercial, as opposed to speculative, investment, or real estate, and public or private transactions. (ENCYBF)
UF paper, commercial
RT acceptances
bills of exchange
certificates of deposit
checks
drafts (negotiable instruments)

commercial photography
USE advertising + photography

commercial portraiture
KT.491
SN Use for the activity of taking portrait photographs as a livelihood.
UF photography, professional portrait
portrait photography, professional
portraiture, commercial
portraiture, studio
professional portrait photography
studio portraiture

commercial schools
USE business schools

commercial specifications
VW.544
HN November 1992 descriptor moved
ALT commercial specification
UF specifications, commercial

commercial strips
RG.251 (A,L,B)
ALT commercial strip
UF strips, commercial

commercial vehicles
TX.116 (L)
ALT commercial vehicle
SN Use for road vehicles licensed or registered to transport goods or materials, other than passengers, for gain or reward. (DOFAE)
UF goods vehicles
vehicles, commercial
vehicles, goods

commercial zones
USE business districts

commercials
VW.303 (L)

HN June 1992 descriptor added
ALT commercial
SN Announcements paid for by an advertiser and broadcast on radio or television. For other public notices or paid announcements, especially those in print, use **advertisements.**

commissaries
USE lunchrooms
mess halls
post exchanges

commission merchants
HG.631 (L)
HN December 1992 alternate terms added
ALT commission merchant
commission merchant's
commission merchants'
UF merchants, commission

commissioners
HG.172
HN December 1992 alternate terms added
ALT commissioner
commissioner's
commissioners'

commissions
VW.498 (N)
HN November 1992 descriptor moved
ALT commission
SN Includes authorizations granting the power to perform a task or duty and documents appointing or hiring someone to perform a task.

commissions (boards)
USE boards (organizations)

commissions, art
USE art commissions

commissions, military
USE military commissions

commissions, park
USE park commissions

commissions, planning
USE planning commissions

committee rooms
USE conference rooms

committees
HN.111 (L,B)
ALT committee
SN Groups of persons delegated to consider, investigate, or take action upon and usually to report concerning some matter or business. (W)

commode chairs
TC.602
HN May 1993 related terms added
January 1993 descriptor moved
July 1992 lead-in terms added
ALT commode chair
SN Term generally applied to a variety of chairs fitted with a chamber pot.

Use **bidets (box stools)** for box stools with a chamber pot.
UF chairs, chamber
 chairs, close-stool
 chairs, commode
 chairs, necessary
 chairs, necessity
 chaises percées
 chamber chairs
 close-stool chairs
 close-stools
 fauteuils de bidet
 necessary chairs
 necessary stools
 necessity chairs
 stools, necessary
RT bidets (box stools)
 chamber pots

commode chairs, cabinet
USE cabinet chairs

commode chests
USE commodes (chests of drawers)

commode dressing chests, French
USE commode dressing tables

commode dressing tables
 TC.1141
HN January 1993 descriptor moved
ALT commode dressing table
UF chests, French commode dressing
 commode dressing chests, French
 commode tables
 dressing chests, French commode
 dressing tables, commode
 French commode dressing chests
 tables, commode

commode headdresses
USE commodes (headdresses)

commode steps
 PJ.2412
HN March 1993 descriptor moved
ALT commode step
SN Steps at the foot of a flight of stairs which have curved ends projecting beyond the string and surrounding the newel. (DAC)
UF steps, commode

commode tables
USE commode dressing tables

commode tables, French
USE commodes (chests of drawers)

commodes (chests of drawers)
 TC.899   (N)
HN May 1993 related terms added
 March 1993 descriptor changed, was **commode**
 March 1993 alternate term changed, was **commode**
 January 1993 descriptor moved
ALT commode (chest of drawers)
SN Chests of drawers or cabinets of chair-rail height, made for display as well as storage and often quite elaborately decorated. Term is applied especially to French forms,

and to English, American, and other styles to indicate a form inspired by French taste.
UF chests, commode
 commode chests
 commode tables, French
 French commode tables
 tables, French commode
RT cabinets (case furniture)
 chests of drawers
 encoignures

commodes (headdresses)
 TE.620
ALT commode (headdress)
SN Term applied to the tall lace headdresses worn by women in the 18th century. (HAH)
UF commode headdresses
 fontanges
 headdresses, commode
 tours (headdresses)
 towers (headdresses)

commodes (washstands)
USE washstands

commodes à battants anterieurs
USE commodes à vantaux

commodes à encoignures
 TC.900
HN January 1993 descriptor moved
ALT commode à encoignures
SN Commodes incorporating a tier of drawers flanked by open shelves or cupboards.

commodes à la régence
 TC.901
HN January 1993 descriptor moved
ALT commode à la régence
SN Term used in the 18th century for commodes with two tiers of drawers set on high legs; term later used for commodes with three or four tiers of drawers.
UF commodes en tombeau

commodes à vantaux
 TC.902
HN January 1993 descriptor moved
ALT commode à vantaux
SN Commodes with two cupboard doors instead of the more usual drawer front. Inside there may be drawers or open shelves.
UF commodes à battants anterieurs

commodes, corner
USE corner commodes

commodes en console
 TC.903
HN January 1993 descriptor moved
ALT commode en console
SN Commodes which consist of a single drawer set on tall legs presumably intended to stand beneath a mirror. (WATSON)
UF commodes en table d'applique

commodes en table d'applique
USE commodes en console

commodes en tombeau
USE commodes à la régence

commodes, petites
USE petites commodes

commodity exchanges
 RK.137   (A,H,L)
ALT commodity exchange
SN Organized markets where future delivery contracts for graded commodities (as grains, cotton, sugar, coffee, wool) are bought and sold. (W)
UF exchanges, commodity
 exchanges, produce
 produce exchanges

common alder
 MT.2683
HN March 1992 descriptor moved
UF alder, black
 alder, common
 Alnus glutinosa
 black alder

common apple
USE applewood

common ash
USE European ash

common beech
USE European beech

common birch
USE silver birch

common bond
 MT.1815
HN October 1992 descriptor moved
SN Pattern bond in which a course of full-length headers occurs at regular intervals, usually every five or six courses; other courses are composed only of stretchers.
UF American bond
 bond, American
 bond, common

common box
USE boxwood

common boxwood
USE boxwood

common bracket feet
USE French feet

common brick
USE building brick

common dimension lumber
USE dimension lumber

common fig
USE fig

common flutes
USE recorders

common hawthorn
USE hawthorn

common hemlock
USE eastern hemlock

common hornbeam
USE European hornbeam

common horse chestnut
USE horse chestnut

common joists
HN March 1991 descriptor deleted, made lead-in to **joists**

common joists
USE joists

common lamps
USE agitable lamps

common land
RD.278
HN March 1993 lead-in term added
UF communal land
land, common
land, communal

common lands
USE commons

common laurel
USE laurel (wood)

common lime
MT.2903 (L)
HN March 1992 descriptor moved
UF common linden
lime, common
linden, common
Tilia europea
Tilia vulgaris

common lime (quicklime)
USE quicklime

common linden
USE common lime

common nails
PJ.150
HN April 1993 descriptor moved
ALT common nail
SN General-use nails each having a head and a diamond-shaped point that are used where appearance is not important, as in framing. (MEANS)
UF nails, common

common papers
TC.381
ALT common paper
SN Wallpapers decorated with simple patterns or stripes, usually printed with only one or two colors and often lacking a ground color.
UF common wallpapers
papers, common
wallpapers, common

common pear
MT.2851
HN March 1992 descriptor moved
UF pear, common
Pyrus communis

common Persian walnut
USE English walnut

common persimmon
MT.2854 (L)
HN March 1992 descriptor moved
UF Diospyros virginiana
persimmon, common

common rafters
PJ.1835
HN March 1993 descriptor moved
ALT common rafter
SN Rafters which are at right angles to the eaves of a roof and extend from the plate to the ridgeboard.
UF intermediate rafters
rafters, common
rafters, intermediate
spars (rafters)

common rooms
PJ.1109
HN March 1993 descriptor moved
ALT common room
SN Use for public lounges or similar rooms in such places as hotels and colleges.
UF rooms, common

common salt
USE sodium chloride

common Scotch carpets
USE ingrain carpets

common spruce
MT.2991 (L)
HN March 1992 descriptor moved
UF deal, white
European spruce
fir, spruce
fir, white
Picea excelsa
pine, white
spruce, common
spruce, European
spruce fir
violin wood
white deal
white fir
white pine
wood, violin

common wallpapers
USE common papers

commonplace books
VW.165 (L)
HN November 1992 descriptor moved
ALT commonplace book
SN Books in which noteworthy literary passages, cogent quotations, poems, comments, recipes, prescriptions, and other miscellaneous document types are written. (GAHLM)
UF books, commonplace

commons
RM.194 (A,L,B,R)
HN April 1993 descriptor moved
ALT common
SN Use for expanses of land, paved or green, owned by the community as a whole. (DLA)
UF common lands

commons, student
USE student unions

commonwealths
HN.71
ALT commonwealth
SN Groups of sovereign states and their dependencies associated by their own choice and linked with common objectives and interests. For the concept of nations or states, use **nations.**

communal gardens
USE community gardens

communal housing
RG.92 (A,H,B)
HN March 1993 lead-in term added
UF communal residences
housing, communal
residences, communal

communal land
USE common land

communal living
BM.1096 (L)
HN February 1993 descriptor moved
SN Use for informal or formally organized cooperative living arrangements based on ideological, religious, or political affiliation. (LCSH)
UF communalism
living, communal

communal residences
USE communal housing

communal restaurants
USE soup kitchens

communal settlements
USE collective settlements

communalism
USE communal living

communes
RD.79 (L,B)
ALT commune
SN Use for self-supporting and self-governing communities comprised of small groups of people living together with minimal interference from outsiders.

communicating
KG.46 (L)
HN June 1991 lead-in term added
January 1991 scope note added
January 1991 alternate term added
ALT communicated
SN Conveying awareness, knowledge, or information to others.
UF communication

374

communicating-door locks
PJ.524
HN April 1993 descriptor moved
ALT communicating-door lock
UF connecting-door locks
  locks, communicating-door
  locks, connecting-door

communication
USE communicating

<communication functions>
KG.39

<communication system components>
PJ.768
HN March 1993 guide term moved

communication systems
PC.105
HN March 1993 descriptor moved
ALT communication system
SN Use for mechanical and electrical systems that relay information within buildings.
UF signal systems
  systems, communication
  systems, signal

communication systems (infrastructural systems)
USE telecommunication systems

<communication systems and communication system components>
HN March 1993 guide term deleted

communication systems, police
USE police communication systems

communications
KD.237   (L,B,R)

communications buildings
RK.200
ALT communications building
UF buildings, communications
  communications facilities
  facilities, communications

<communications concepts>
BM.860
HN February 1993 guide term added

communications facilities
USE communications buildings

communications museums
HN March 1993 descriptor split, use communications + museums

communications satellites
TX.75   (L,N)
ALT communications satellite
SN Use for artificial orbiting vehicles designed to reflect or relay electromagnetic signals among communications stations.
UF satellites, communications

<communications structures>
RK.199

<communications vessels>
TX.446

communion cloths
USE corporals

communion cups
TQ.158   (L,N)
ALT communion cup
SN Ecclesiastical drinking vessels used in the Protestant Church since the Reformation, sometimes in the form of a goblet wine cup or beaker. For other generally more ornate ecclesiastical drinking vessels, use **chalices.**
UF cups, communion
RT chalices
  drinking vessels

communion plate
USE church plate

communion plates
USE patens

communion rails
PJ.2520   (B)
HN March 1993 descriptor moved
ALT communion rail
SN Altar rails at which communicants receive communion. (W)
UF rails, communion

communion records
HN March 1991 descriptor split, use communion + records

communion sets
PC.52   (N)
ALT communion set
SN Sets of articles used for the Eucharist, including a chalice (or communion cup), paten, and flagon. (HNSIL)
UF sets, communion

communion tables
TC.1130   (L,R)
HN May 1993 related term added
  January 1993 descriptor moved
ALT communion table
UF tables, communion
RT *<religious building fixtures>*

communion tokens
VK.195   (L)
ALT communion token
SN Designates small tokens, of various metals and in various shapes, originally issued by the Calvinist Church as vouchers to members who qualified for communion, and later used in the United States by other Christian denominations.
UF tokens, communion

communions
KM.41   (L)
HN February 1991 alternate term added
  February 1991 descriptor changed, was communion
ALT communion

communiques
VW.924

HN November 1992 descriptor moved
ALT communique
SN Official announcements. (AHD)

communism
BM.875   (L,R)
HN February 1993 descriptor moved
  January 1991 alternate term added
ALT communist
SN Economic and political system in which land and capital goods are publicly owned, and the governing authorities control the means of production, prices, and distribution.

communities, golf course
USE golf course communities

communities, life care
USE life care communities

communities, new
USE new towns

communities, plant
USE plant communities

communities, religious
USE religious communities

communities, retirement
USE retirement communities

communities, satellite
USE satellite cities

communities, urban
USE cities

community architecture
USE participatory design

community art
BM.180   (R)
HN May 1993 related term added
SN Includes art undertaken in conjunction with particular communities, often socially deprived, usually with the idea of producing an effect or inspiring response specifically within those communities, with no reference to widely established standards. For art intended to beautify and enrich public places, use **public art.**
UF art, community
RT public art

community art centers
USE art centers

community based residences
USE group homes

community buildings
USE community centers

community centers
RK.1129   (A,H,L,B)
ALT community center
UF buildings, community
  centers, community
  centers, community recreation
  centers, social
  centers, village community

community buildings
community centers, village
community recreation centers
recreation centers, community
social centers
village community centers

community centers, college
USE student unions

community centers, village
USE community centers

community colleges
    RK.803 (L)
HN September 1990 scope note added
ALT community college
SN Colleges, typically without residential facilities, serving the educational needs of a specific community.
UF colleges, community

community design centers
    HN.136 (A)
HN July 1990 descriptor added
ALT community design center
UK community-design centres
UKA community-design centre
SN Use for multidisciplinary, nonprofit organizations comprised of professionals, generally architects and planners, and volunteers working to improve social and economic conditions in a neighborhood or community.
UF CDCs
centers, community design
centres, community-design
design centers, community
design centres, community

community-design centres
SEE community design centers

community development
    KG.64 (A,L)
HN January 1991 scope note added
SN Activity of solving or ameliorating a community's social and economic problems, organized and controlled mainly by the community itself. (TSIT)
UF development, community
development, regional
regional development

community development, rural
USE rural development

community gardens
    RM.45 (A,L,B)
HN April 1993 descriptor moved
ALT community garden
UF communal gardens
gardens, community
gardens, neighborhood
gardens, working-men's
neighborhood gardens
working-men's gardens

community organizations
    HN.141

ALT community organization
UF associations, civic
civic associations
civic groups
civic organizations
groups, civic
organizations, civic
organizations, community

community parks
    RM.66
HN April 1993 descriptor moved
ALT community park
UF parks, community

community participation
USE citizen participation

community recreation centers
USE community centers

community schools
    RK.764 (A,B)
HN April 1990 descriptor added
ALT community school
SN Designates schools whose facilities and programs are closely connected with the life and needs of, and may be shared by, the whole community.
UF schools, community

community transit
USE local transit

commuter aircraft
    TX.60 (L)
SN Small passenger aircraft operating either on a scheduled or nonscheduled basis, along short routes normally not serviced by airliners. (RHDEL2)
UF aircraft, commuter
airplanes, commuter
commuter airplanes

commuter airplanes
USE commuter aircraft

commuter rail
USE commuter railroads

commuter rail service
USE commuter railroads

commuter rail transit
USE commuter railroads

commuter railroads
    PC.192
HN March 1993 descriptor moved
ALT commuter railroad
UK commuter railways
UKA commuter railway
SN Rapid rail transit systems linking suburban districts with central city terminals; generally not operating on exclusive rights of way.
UF commuter rail
commuter rail service
commuter rail transit
commuter service, railroad
rail service, commuter
rail, suburban
railroad commuter service

railroads, commuter
railways, commuter
suburban rail

commuter railways
SEE commuter railroads

commuter service, railroad
USE commuter railroads

Comnene
USE Comnenian

Comnenian
    FL.3162 (R)
UF Comnene

Comox
    FL.1371 (L)
UF Catloltx
Sliammon

compact discs
USE compact disks

compact disks
    VW.1043 (L)
HN March 1993 lead-in terms added
November 1992 descriptor moved
September 1991 scope note added
July 1991 descriptor moved
ALT compact disk
SN Optical disks on which programs, data, or music are digitally encoded for a laser beam to scan, decode, and transmit to a playback system, computer monitor, or television set. (RHDEL2)
UF CDs
compact discs
discs, compact
disks, compact

compact disks read-only memory
USE CD-ROMs

compacting equipment
    TH.431
UF equipment, compacting

compaction
    KT.314 (L)
HN March 1991 alternate term added
ALT compacted
SN The process of consolidating or compressing substances to form a more dense unit, such as packing of the solid particles in freshly mixed concrete, mortar, or other mixture.
UF tamping

compactors
    TH.432 (N)
ALT compactor
SN Machines that use weight, vibration, or a combination of both, to achieve compaction. (DAC)

compacts
    TQ.222 (L,N)
ALT compact
SN Accessories for carrying cosmetics on the person. Usually made of metal or plastic and can be quite

decorative. Interior most often contains a mirror in the lid of one half and face powder in the other half, but may also have compartments for rouge or lipstick or a fitting for the attachment of a lipstick case. (NMAHDC)
RT cosmetics

Compagnie des Indes
FL.2000 (R)
HN April 1993 descriptor added
UF Chine sur commande
East India

Compagnie-des-Indes porcelain
USE Compagnie des Indes + ware

Compagnie des Indes ware
HN April 1993 descriptor split, use **Compagnie des Indes + ware**

companies
HN.104 (L)
ALT company
SN Use generally for associations of persons for carrying on commercial or industrial enterprises. (W)

companies, incorporated
USE corporations

companion pieces
USE companion portraits
pendants (companion pieces)

companion portraits
VC.616
ALT companion portrait
SN Use for pairs of portraits designed to be displayed together.
UF companion pieces
pieces, companion
portraits, companion

companions, ladies'
USE ladies' writing tables

companions, silent
USE dummy board figures

Company
FL.2330
UF Company School

company aircraft
USE business aircraft

company airplanes
USE business aircraft

company halls
USE guildhalls

company housing
USE industrial housing

company image
USE corporate image

company museums
RK.397 (L)
ALT company museum
UF commercial museums

museums, commercial
museums, company

company records
USE business records

Company School
USE Company

company stores
RK.170 (L)
ALT company store
UF industrial stores
stores, company
stores, industrial

company towns
RD.50 (A,L,B)
HN April 1993 lead-in terms added
ALT company town
SN Use for settlements whose inhabitants depend solely or chiefly on a single employer who also owns a substantial portion of the settlement's real estate and housing.
UF company towns, single
company villages
single company towns
towns, company
towns, single company
villages, company

company towns, single
USE company towns

company villages
USE company towns

comparative government
KD.309 (L)
UF comparative politics
government, comparative
politics, comparative

comparative literature
KD.65
UF literature, comparative

comparative politics
USE comparative government

comparative religion
KD.86 (L)
UF religion, comparative

comparing
KG.12 (L)
HN April 1993 lead-in term added
January 1991 scope note added
January 1991 alternate term added
ALT compared
SN Examining two or more entities in order to note relative similarities and differences.
UF comparison

comparison
USE comparing

comparison lamps
PJ.2967
ALT comparison lamp
SN Incandescent lamps having a constant but not necessarily known lu-

minous intensity against which other lamps are successively compared in a photometer. (W)
UF lamps, comparison

compartment ceilings
PJ.2057
HN March 1993 descriptor moved
ALT compartment ceiling
SN Ceilings divided into compartments or panels separated by moldings or ribs, particularly those in which the compartments or panels are not all uniform rectangles. (RS)
UF ceilings, compartment

compartments, toilet
USE toilet compartments

compartments, vaulting
USE vaulting cells

compartments, WC
USE toilet compartments

compass brick
MT.78
HN April 1992 descriptor moved
UF arch brick
brick, arch
brick, compass
brick, featheredge
brick, key
brick, radial
brick, radiating
brick, radius
brick, voussoir
featheredge brick
key brick
radial brick
radiating brick
radius brick
voussoir brick

compass cards
PJ.2632 (L,N)
ALT compass card
SN Use for that part of compasses on which the direction markings are placed, usually in the form of thin disks graduated in degrees clockwise from 0 to 360 and sometimes also indicating compass points. (MHDSTT)
UF cards, compass

compass-headed arches
USE semicircular arches

compass-headed roofs
USE compass roofs

compass maps
USE portolanos

compass planes
TH.1528 (N)
ALT compass plane
SN Planes having a curved baseplate, either concave or convex, used for smoothing curved woodwork. (DAC)
UF compass smoothing planes
heel planes

planes, compass
planes, compass smoothing
planes, heel
roundsils
smoothing planes, compass

<compass points>
DC.337
HN October 1992 guide term moved

compass roofs
PJ.1783
HN March 1993 descriptor moved
ALT compass roof
SN Use for timber roofs in which rafters, collar beams, and braces combine to suggest an arch; most common in Medieval architecture.
UF compass-headed roofs
cradle roofs
roofs, compass
roofs, compass-headed
roofs, cradle

compass saws
TH.1593   (N)
ALT compass saw
SN Hand saws having a narrow blade;
used to cut small intricate shapes or
circles of small radii. (DAC)
UF port saws
saws, compass
saws, port

compass seats
PJ.2864
HN March 1993 descriptor moved
ALT compass seat
SN Period term used to describe chair
seats which are rounded in the front
and which sometimes have in-
curving sides, forming an outline
like a horseshoe; most popular in
America between the 1730s and
1760s, although in many areas per-
sisting into the Federal period.
(FAIRB)
UF compass-shaped seats
horseshoe seats
seats, compass
seats, horseshoe

compass-shaped seats
USE compass seats

compass smoothing planes
USE compass planes

compass windows
USE bow windows

compasses (direction indicators)
TN.17   (L,N,R)
ALT compass (direction indicator)
SN Instruments for measuring and in-
dicating a horizontal reference di-
rection relative to magnetic north.

compasses (drawing instruments)
TH.656   (L)
HN September 1992 scope note
changed
September 1992 related term added

December 1991 descriptor changed,
was **compasses**
December 1991 alternate term
changed, was **compass**
ALT compass (drawing instrument)
SN Instruments for drawing circles and
measuring the distance between two
points; consisting of two pointed
legs, movable on a joint or pivot,
usually made so that one of the
points can be detached for the insertion of a pen or an extension. (DAC)
RT dividers

compasses (measuring devices)
USE dividers

compasses, beam
USE beam compasses

compasses, bow
USE bow compasses

compasses, dividing
USE dividers

compasses, gyroscopic
USE gyrocompasses

compasses, gyrostatic
USE gyrocompasses

compasses, mariners'
USE mariners' compasses

compasses, proportional
USE proportional compasses

compasses, solar
USE sun compasses

compasses, spring bow
USE bow compasses

compasses, sun
USE sun compasses

compasses, surveying
USE surveyors' compasses

compasses, surveyors'
USE surveyors' compasses

compendiums
VW.955
HN November 1992 descriptor moved
ALT compendium
SN Works containing in a smaller docu-
ment the substance or general prin-
ciples of larger works, often serving
as a supplement to the larger work.
UF digests (compendiums)

compensating hubs
PJ.569
HN March 1993 descriptor moved
ALT compensating hub
UF hubs, compensating

compensating planimeters
USE planimeters

compensation (economic concept)
BM.865   (L,B)
HN February 1993 descriptor moved
April 1991 scope note added

April 1991 lead-in term added
February 1991 descriptor changed,
was **compensation**
SN Something given or received in return for goods or services, or as settlement of a debt or injury. (TSIT)
UF remuneration

compensation (restoring)
KT.870
SN Use broadly for painting conservation treatments, such as oiling and
inpainting, intended to recreate the
original appearance of the design in
a defect that cannot be corrected.
Use a more specific term if possible.

<competition and recreation craft>
TX.344

<competition craft>
TX.345

competition designs
USE competition drawings

competition drawings
VC.173
HN April 1992 descriptor moved
ALT competition drawing
UF competition designs
designs, competition
drawings, competition

competitions
KM.51   (A,L,B,R)
HN May 1991 alternate term added
ALT competition

competitions, invited
USE invited competitions

competitions, limited
USE limited competitions

competitions, open
USE open competitions

competitions, student
USE student competitions

competitive bidding
USE bidding

competitive tendering
USE bidding

compilers
HG.372
HN December 1992 alternate terms
added
ALT compiler
compiler's
compilers'
SN Persons who assemble items of information. (W)

complementary colors
DL.338
HN February 1992 descriptor moved
February 1992 scope note changed
January 1991 alternate term added
ALT complementary color
UK complementary colours
UKA complementary colour

SN Two colors having maximum contrast with each other and which, when mixed additively produce white, and mixed subtractively produce black, at least in theory.
UF colors, complementary
colours, complementary

complementary colours
SEE complementary colors

<complex molding planes>
TH.1548

complexes
RG.1   (B)
ALT complex
SN Aggregations of buildings, other structures, and open spaces, often multifunctional, and more extensive, and usually shaped over a longer period of time by more participants, than single built works.

<complexes by development practice>
RG.250

<complexes by function>
RG.2

complexes, educational
USE educational complexes

complexes, farm
USE farms

complexes, housing
USE housing

complexes, industrial
USE industrial complexes

complexes, launch
USE launch complexes

complexes, office
USE office complexes

complexes, school
USE educational complexes

complexes, sports
USE sports complexes

complexity
BM.96   (L)
SN The state or quality of having many intricate or interrelated parts.

compliance, certificates of
USE certificates of occupancy

compluvia
PJ.2300
HN March 1993 descriptor moved
ALT compluvium
SN Apertures in the center of roofs of atriums in Roman houses, sloping inward to discharge rainwater into a cistern or tank, called an impluvium. (HAS)

compo
USE composition (material)

component drawings
USE minor assembly drawings

components
PJ.1
ALT component
SN Use for constituent parts of objects or structures. (W)

<components by general context>
PJ.2

<components by specific context>
PJ.766

<components of bodies of water>
RD.123

comports
USE compotes

composers
HG.217   (L,R)
HN February 1993 descriptor moved November 1992 alternate terms added
ALT composer
composer's
composers'

composing (printing preparation)
USE composition (printing preparation)

composing machines
TH.874   (L,N)
HN February 1993 descriptor added
ALT composing machine
SN Use for any of numerous machines used to set type, beginning with those of the early and mid-19th century, and including those for strike-on composition as well as electronic and photographic devices and systems.
UF keyboard typesetters
machines, composing
machines, type-composing
machines, typesetting
type-composing machines
typesetters (machines)
typesetters, keyboard
typesetting machines
RT machine composition

composing machines, cold-metal
USE cold-metal machines

composing machines, hot-metal
USE hot-metal machines

composing machines, typewriter
USE typewriter composing machines

composing sticks
TH.870   (N)
HN February 1993 descriptor added
ALT composing stick
SN Hand-held trays in which type is assembled before transfer to the larger galley.
UF sticks, composing

composing typewriters
USE typewriter composing machines

Composite
FL.2830

composite arches
USE four-centered arches

composite bows
TK.224
ALT composite bow
SN Bows, the shaft of which is composed of two or more organic materials, combined so as to enhance the elastic efficiency of each.
UF bows, composite

composite construction
KT.14   (A,L)
HN January 1993 descriptor moved
SN Use both for construction utilizing various different building materials and for the use of more than one type of construction method in a structure, such as a masonry building with a laminated wood beam roof.
UF construction, composite

composite drawings
VC.85
HN April 1992 descriptor moved
ALT composite drawing
SN Use for drawings in which two or more related images (e.g., different views of the same structure, or a figure in various poses) are displayed together or fused into one.
UF drawings, composite

composite, fibrous
USE fibrous composite

composite, filament reinforced
USE fibrous composite

composite green pigment
MT.2162
HN April 1992 descriptor moved
UF green pigment, composite
pigment, composite green

composite material
MT.1337   (L,B)
HN April 1993 descriptor changed, was composite materials
April 1993 lead-in term changed, was sandwich materials
April 1992 descriptor moved
UF material, composite
material, sandwich
sandwich material

Composite order
PJ.1425   (A,B,R)
HN March 1993 descriptor moved
December 1990 scope note added
SN Designates an architectural order characterized by capitals composed of foliate echini derived from the Corinthian order superposed by volutes derived from the Ionic order.
UF order, Composite

composite photographs
VC.391 (L)
HN April 1992 descriptor moved
ALT composite photograph
SN Use for photographic prints in which two or more negatives are printed as one unified image. For combinations of images, such as photographs with architectural drawings, use **photomontages**. When pieces of photographs or other relatively flat materials are pasted together into less unified images, use **collages**.
UF combination photoprints
combination prints
composite photoprints
composites
composites, photo
photo composites
photographs, composite
photoprints, composite
prints, combination

composite photoprints
USE composite photographs

<composite pieces>
TQ.548

composite pigment
MT.2302
HN April 1992 descriptor moved
SN Any pigment that contains more than one basic ingredient, as cadmium-barium yellow, which contains both cadmium sulfide and barium sulfate coprecipitated. (MAYER)
UF pigment, composite

composite, reinforced fibrous
USE fibrous composite

Composite Style
USE Fourth Style

composite twill
MT.1616
HN November 1992 descriptor added
SN Any form of twill woven using more than one binding system.
UF combined twill
composite weave
fancy twill
twill, combined
twill, composite
twill, fancy
weave, composite

composite weave
USE composite twill

composite white
MT.2228
HN April 1992 descriptor moved
UF mixed white
permalba
superba
superba white
ultra white
white, composite
white, mixed

white, superba
white, ultra

composites
USE composite photographs

composites, photo
USE composite photographs

composition (artistic arrangement)
BM.52 (A,H,L,B,R)
HN March 1993 descriptor changed, was **composition**
SN Structure or arrangement of the internal elements of a work of art, such as a drawing, sculpture, or written or musical work.

composition (material)
MT.1338
HN February 1993 descriptor added
SN Use for various aggregate materials formed artificially from two or more substances, such as whiting, resin, and size used for modeling ornament in the late 18th century, or plaster of Paris, sawdust, bran, and glue used for dollmaking, or plastic cement-based mortars used in construction.
UF compo
RT papier-mâché

composition (physicochemical makeup)
DC.276
HN October 1992 descriptor added
SN The makeup or constitution of a material or compound.

composition (printing preparation)
KT.630 (L)
HN February 1993 descriptor added
SN Preparation of copy in a form suitable for printing or for making printing plates, whether by hand, by mechanical devices, or by computer, including casting off and the arranging of type, spacing, and other material. For the specific process of arranging type, use **typesetting**.
UF composing (printing preparation)
RT compositors
<rules for type composition>
<type composition equipment>
typesetting

<composition and compositional elements>
BM.51

composition, buffing
USE buffing composition

composition, closed
USE closed composition

composition, cold
USE cold composition

composition, computerized
USE computerized composition

composition, direct impression
USE strike-on composition

composition drawings
VC.229
HN April 1992 descriptor moved
ALT composition drawing
SN Use for fairly finished drawings of whole compositions, whether as pattern drawings, working drawings, or done after a finished work.
UF drawings, composition

composition, hand
USE hand composition

composition, hot-metal
USE hot-metal composition

composition, hot-metal machine
USE hot-metal composition

composition leaf
USE Dutch metal

composition, machine
USE machine composition

composition machines, typewriter
USE typewriter composing machines

composition, mechanical
USE machine composition

composition, open
USE open composition

composition, photographic
USE photocomposition

composition roofing
USE built-up roofing

composition sketches
HN April 1991 descriptor split, use **composition (artistic arrangement)** + **sketches**

composition, slug
USE linecasting

composition, strike-on
USE strike-on composition

composition studies
HN April 1991 descriptor split, use **composition (artistic arrangement)** + **studies (visual works)**

composition, typewriter
USE strike-on composition

<compositional elements>
BM.55

compositors
HG.673
HN December 1992 related term added
December 1992 alternate terms added
ALT compositor
compositor's
compositors'
SN Persons who assemble, set, proof, and generally prepare type and illustrations for printing. (W)
RT composition (printing preparation)

compotes
　　TQ.331　　　　　　　　　　(N)
ALT　compote
SN　Bowls, usually set on a high footed stem and sometimes having a cover, used to serve fruit, compotes, nuts, or sweets.
UF　comports
　　compotiers
RT　bowls (vessels)
　　dessert services
　　fruit bowls

compotiers
USE　compotes

compound, antifreeze
USE　antifreeze

compound beams
USE　built-up beams

compound, calking
USE　caulking compound

compound, caulking
USE　caulking compound

compound, cleaning
USE　cleaning compound

compound, organometallic
USE　organometallic compound

compound, parting
USE　release agent

compound piers
　　PJ.1556
HN　March 1993 descriptor moved
　　April 1991 scope note added
　　April 1991 lead-in terms added
ALT　compound pier
SN　Use for piers composed of several engaged columns or pilasters grouped around a central core.
UF　clustered piers
　　compound pillars
　　piers, clustered
　　piers, compound
　　pillars, compound

compound pillars
USE　compound piers

compound, priming
USE　priming powder

compound, sealing
USE　sealing compound

compound vaults
　　PJ.1860
HN　March 1993 descriptor moved
ALT　compound vault
SN　Use for vaults formed by the intersection of two or more simple vaults. (RS)
UF　vaults, compound

<compound vaults by form>
　　PJ.1861
HN　March 1993 guide term moved

<compound vaults by form: number of compartments>
　　PJ.1862
HN　March 1993 guide term moved

<compound vaults by form: profile>
　　PJ.1867
HN　March 1993 guide term moved

compreg
USE　impregnated wood

compregnated wood
USE　impregnated wood

comprehensive layouts
USE　comprehensives

comprehensive plans
　　VW.927　　　　　　　　　　(A)
HN　November 1992 descriptor moved
ALT　comprehensive plan
SN　Use with reference to land use control law, zoning, and urban redevelopment to describe the omnibus plans of cities or towns for housing, industry, commercial, and recreational facilities and their impact on environmental factors. (BLACKS)
UF　general plans
　　master plans (reports)
　　plans, comprehensive
　　plans, general
　　plans, master

comprehensive record schedules
USE　records schedules

comprehensives
　　VW.1192
HN　March 1993 descriptor added
ALT　comprehensive
SN　Highly detailed or finished layouts, especially for one-page pieces; for more extensive detailed layouts, including representation of the arrangement of pages, use **dummies (printed matter).**
UF　comprehensive layouts
　　comps
　　layouts, comprehensive

compressed charcoal
USE　charcoal sticks

compressed wood
　　MT.3008　　　　　　　　　(L)
HN　March 1992 descriptor moved
SN　Wood which has been impregnated with resin and subjected to a high pressure to increase its density and strength. (DAC)
UF　densified wood
　　pressed wood
　　wood, compressed
　　wood, densified
　　wood, pressed

compressibility
　　DC.175　　　　　　　　　　(L)
HN　October 1992 descriptor moved
　　June 1992 alternate term added
ALT　compressible

SN　Property by which a decrease of volume results when an external pressure is applied. (STEIN)

compressing
USE　compression

compression
　　BM.630　　　　　　　　　　(L)
HN　June 1992 descriptor added
SN　The dimensional response of a material subject to crushing forces and the action that leads to it. (AITSTP)
UF　compressing

compression molding
　　KT.329
UK　compression moulding
SN　Molding process used especially for plastics in which heat and pressure are brought to bear on the materials in the mold. (W)
UF　molding, compression
　　moulding, compression

compression moulding
SEE　compression molding

compressors
　　TH.931　　　　　　　　　(L,N)
ALT　compressor
SN　Machines that compress a refrigerant gas; used in air conditioning and refrigeration. (MEANS)

comps
USE　comprehensives

compters
USE　debtors' prisons

comptrollers
　　HG.614
HN　December 1992 alternate terms added
ALT　comptroller
　　comptroller's
　　comptrollers'
UK　controllers
UKA　controller
SN　Controllers of accounts or finances. (W)

computation laboratories
USE　computer centers

computational linguistics
　　KD.46　　　　　　　　　　(L)
HN　April 1990 scope note added
SN　Branch of linguistics concerned with the use of computers for the analysis and synthesis of language data, as in translation, word frequency counts, and speech recognition and synthesis. (ERIC9)
UF　linguistics, computational

computations
USE　calculations

computer-aided
USE　computer-assisted

computer-aided design
  KT.355   (A,L)
  HN February 1993 descriptor moved
      March 1991 descriptor moved
  UF CAD
      computer drawing
      design, computer-aided
      drawing, computer

computer-aided typesetting
  USE computerized composition

computer animation
  KT.349   (L)
  HN February 1993 related term added
  UF animation, computer
  RT *<computer image-making processes and
       techniques>*

computer art
  BM.181   (L,R)
  HN May 1993 related term added
      February 1993 scope note added
      April 1992 lead-in term added
      October 1991 descriptor moved
  SN Use generally for art produced us-
      ing computers at some step in the
      process.
  UF art, computer
      dataism
  RT *<computer image-making processes and
       techniques>*

computer-assisted
  DC.208   (L)
  HN February 1993 descriptor added
  SN Use to describe an activity or some-
      thing produced by an activity that
      employs a computer to expedite
      some of the steps or operations re-
      quired. When programming gener-
      ates automatically a relatively large
      number of the steps between what
      is input and what is produced, use
      computer-generated.
  UF computer-aided

computer-assisted maps
  VW.88
  HN November 1992 descriptor moved
  ALT computer-assisted map
  UF maps, computer-assisted

computer buildings
  USE computer centers

computer centers
  RK.201   (A,L,B)
  ALT computer center
  UF buildings, computer
       centers, computer
       centers, data processing
       centers, data processing service
       computation laboratories
       computer buildings
       computer laboratories
       computing centers
       computing laboratories
       data processing centers
       data processing service centers
       departments, electronic data pro-
         cessing

electronic data processing departments
laboratories, computation

<computer components>
  PJ.2599

computer controlled typesetting
  USE computerized composition

computer drawing
  USE computer-aided design

computer drawings
  VC.203
  HN April 1992 descriptor moved
  ALT computer drawing
  UF computer-generated drawings
       drawings, computer
       drawings, computer-generated

computer enhancement
  KT.362
  HN February 1993 descriptor added
  ALT computer-enhanced
  SN Computerized process of accentuat-
      ing or exaggerating forms in an im-
      age, often used to clarify indistinct
      forms, as for example in photo-
      graphs.
  UF computer image enhancement
       enhancement, computer
       enhancement, image
       image enhancement

<computer equipment>
  TH.552
  HN January 1993 guide term added

computer-generated
  DC.209
  HN February 1993 descriptor added
  SN Use to describe something, as an ar-
      rangement of visible forms or of
      data, that is produced by a com-
      puter, especially when the program-
      ming generates automatically a rela-
      tively large number of the steps
      between what is input and what is
      produced.

computer-generated drawings
  USE computer drawings

computer graphics
  KT.356   (A,L)
  HN February 1993 descriptor moved
  SN Use generally for computer pro-
      cessing in which the output is in pic-
      torial form. (DOC)
  UF graphics, computer

computer image enhancement
  USE computer enhancement

*<computer image-making processes and
  techniques>*
  KT.354
  HN February 1993 guide term added
  RT computer animation
       computer art

computer imaging
  USE electronic imaging

computer laboratories
  USE computer centers

computer modeling
  KG.127   (L)
  HN March 1993 descriptor added
  UK computer modelling
  SN Use for the development of com-
      puter models to represent concepts
      or dynamic systems.
  UF modeling, computer
       modelling, computer

computer modelling
  SEE computer modeling

computer operating systems
  USE operating systems

computer-output microfiche
  VW.1049
  HN November 1992 descriptor moved
  SN Computer output produced directly
      onto microfiche, without paper
      printout as an intermediary. (ICA)
  UF COM
       microfiche, computer-output

computer-output microfilms
  VW.1050   (L)
  HN November 1992 descriptor moved
  ALT computer-output microfilm
  SN Computer output produced directly
      onto microfilm, without paper
      printout as an intermediary. (ICA)
  UF COM
       microfilms, computer-output

computer-output microforms
  VW.1048
  HN November 1992 descriptor moved
  ALT computer-output microform
  SN Computer output produced directly
      onto microform, without paper
      printout as an intermediary. (ICA)
  UF COM
       microforms, computer-output

computer peripherals
  USE peripherals

computer printouts
  USE printouts

computer programmers
  HG.579   (L)
  HN April 1993 related term added
      December 1992 alternate terms
        added
      September 1990 lead-in term added
  ALT computer programmer
       computer programmer's
       computer programmers'
  UF programmers
       programmers, computer
  RT computer programming

computer programming
  KG.128   (L,B)
  HN April 1993 related term added
      March 1993 descriptor moved
      January 1991 scope note added
  SN Composing precise, logical se-

quences of instructions that direct the actions of a computer or computer system.
UF programming (computers)
RT computer programmers

computer programs
USE software

computer rooms
PJ.1083
HN March 1993 descriptor moved
ALT computer room
UF rooms, computer

computer science
KD.107 (L)
HN February 1993 related term added
SN Study of phenomena related to computers; it emphasizes the creation, analysis, and implementation of algorithms at all levels in the computer hierarchy, from circuits at the binary representation level to the more macroscopic description of algorithms by programming languages. (PG)
UF science, computer
RT computer scientists

<computer science concepts>
BM.593
HN March 1993 guide term added

computer scientists
HG.534 (L)
HN January 1993 descriptor added
ALT computer scientist
computer scientist's
computer scientists'
SN Scientists trained or working in the field of computer science.
UF scientists, computer
RT computer science

computer searching
USE online searching

computer simulation
USE simulation

computer storage devices
USE storage devices

computer terminals
TH.553 (L,N)
HN January 1993 descriptor moved
ALT computer terminal
SN Computer peripherals composed of a monitor or printing device and a keyboard, which are linked together to function as a single input/output unit.
UF terminals (computers)
terminals, computer

computer typesetting
USE computerized composition

<computer-use functions>
KG.126
HN March 1993 guide term added

computer visualization
USE visualization

computerization
KG.234 (L)
HN November 1992 descriptor added
ALT computerized

computerized composition
KT.631 (L)
HN February 1993 descriptor added
SN Use generally for methods of character assembly for printing that employ a computer. Can be directed toward exposure of the characters on photosensitive film or paper, or output from a computer printer.
UF automated typesetting
composition, computerized
computer-aided typesetting
computer controlled typesetting
computer typesetting
computerized typesetting
controlled typesetting, computer
typesetting, automated
typesetting, computer
typesetting, computer-aided
typesetting, computer controlled
typesetting, computerized
RT computers
desktop publishing
photocomposition

computerized typesetting
USE computerized composition
photocomposition

computers
TH.554 (A,L,B,R)
HN January 1993 descriptor moved
December 1992 related term added
ALT computer
SN Devices or systems capable of carrying out a sequence of operations in a distinctly and explicitly defined manner. (DOC)
UF hardware (computers)
RT computerized composition

computers, home
USE microcomputers

computers, laptop
USE laptop computers

computers, mainframe
USE mainframes

computers, micro
USE microcomputers

computers, personal
USE microcomputers

computers, portable
USE portable computers

computing centers
USE computer centers

computing laboratories
USE computer centers

computus manuscripts
VW.7 (H)
HN November 1992 descriptor moved
ALT computus manuscript
UF manuscripts, computus

concave
DC.64
HN January 1993 lead-in term added
October 1992 descriptor moved
SN Hollowed out like the inner curve of a circle or sphere. (PUTNAM)
UF dished

<concave-back chairs>
TC.554
HN January 1993 guide term moved

concave glasses
USE concave mirrors

concave joints
PJ.668
HN April 1993 descriptor moved
ALT concave joint
SN Recessed masonry joints formed in mortar by the use of a curved steel jointing tool; effective in resisting rain penetration.
UF joints, concave
joints, rodded
rodded joints

concave mirrors
TC.1465
ALT concave mirror
SN Use for mirrors in which the center is farther away from the object than the edges and that reflect enlarged or reduced images.
UF concave glasses
glasses, concave
mirrors, concave

concave relief
USE intaglio

concave seats
USE hollowed seats

concealed beds
USE deception beds

concealed doors
USE jib doors

concealed hinges
PJ.417
HN April 1993 descriptor moved
ALT concealed hinge
SN Use for door hinges that are visible when the door is open but concealed when the door is closed. Distinguished from **invisible hinges** which are completely concealed, from the outside, whether the door is open or closed.
UF blind hinges
hinges, blind
hinges, concealed

concentrated loads
BM.602

HN November 1992 descriptor moved
January 1991 alternate term added
ALT concentrated load
SN Loads acting on a very small area of
a structure. (DAC)
UF loads, concentrated

concentration
DC.15
HN October 1992 descriptor added
SN Quantity of a substance contained in
a unit quantity sample. (NASATH)

concentration camps
RG.49   (A,L,B,R)
HN April 1991 scope note added
ALT concentration camp
SN Designates internment centers established outside ordinary detention
systems in which persons are confined for military or political security or for punishment or exploita-
tion; persons are generally
imprisoned by decree or military order, often including classes or
groups of people without regard for
their individual culpability. (ENCYB)
UF camps, concentration
camps, detention
camps, internment
detention camps
internment camps

concentric
DC.321
HN October 1992 descriptor moved

concentric arches
HN March 1991 descriptor split, use
concentric + arches

Concept art
USE Conceptual

concept drawings
USE conceptual drawings

concept sketches
USE conceptual drawings

Conception, Immaculate
USE Immaculate Conception

<concepts in the arts>
BM.1

<concepts relating to the creative process>
BM.25

Conceptual
FL.3858   (L,R)
UF Concept art
Conceptualist
Idea art
Possible art
Post-object art

conceptual artists
HG.274
HN February 1993 descriptor moved
November 1992 alternate terms
added
ALT conceptual artist

conceptual artist's
conceptual artists'
UF artists, conceptual

conceptual drawings
VC.177
HN April 1992 descriptor moved
ALT conceptual drawing
SN Designates architectural drawings
done early in the design process; often not to scale and may include diagrammatic elements.
UF concept drawings
concept sketches
conceptual sketches
drawings, conceptual
sketches, conceptual

conceptual sketches
USE conceptual drawings

Conceptualist
USE Conceptual

concert grand pianos
TT.413
ALT concert grand piano
SN Grand pianos of the largest size,
about 9 feet or more in length,
adapted in volume, timbre, and bril-
liancy of tone to concert use.
UF concert grands
grand pianos, concert
grands, concert
pianos, concert grand

concert grands
USE concert grand pianos

concert halls
RK.882   (A,L,B,R)
HN September 1990 scope note added
ALT concert hall
SN Use for buildings designed for mu-
sical performances.
UF halls, concert
halls, symphony
symphony halls

concert horns
USE mellophones

concertina doors
USE folding doors

concertina fold books
USE folded books

concertinas
TT.130   (L,N)
ALT concertina
SN Portable free-reed instruments having two hexagonal casings connected by an expandable bellows,
each of which has a small button
keyboard.

concerts
KM.81   (L,R)
HN May 1991 alternate term added
ALT concert

conch
MT.1332

HN February 1992 descriptor added
SN The spiral shell of gastropods, often
blown as sounding horns.
UF conch shell
shell, conch
RT marine shell trumpets

conch domes
USE umbrella domes

conch shell
USE conch

conch shell trumpets
USE marine shell trumpets

Conchas
FL.1046

conches
USE semidomes

Concho
FL.1472

conchs
PJ.1987
HN March 1993 descriptor moved
ALT conch
SN Semicircular niches which are cov-
ered with a semidome. (RK)

conchs (trumpets)
USE marine shell trumpets

concinnity
BM.98   (L)
SN Harmony or fitness in the adaptation of the parts of a whole to each
other; often, studied elegance of design or arrangement. (W)
UF eurythmy

concord
USE harmony

concord coaches
TX.169   (N)
ALT concord coach
SN Use for public coaches with sturdy,
large, ovoid bodies with curved panels set on three-perch, throughbrace
suspension and having large
amounts of baggage space, seating
six, nine, or twelve passengers, and
often having additional seating on
the roof; designed in the United
States from the 1820s until the early
20th century.
UF coaches, concord
concords

concordances
VW.817   (L)
HN November 1992 descriptor moved
ALT concordance
SN Includes indexes to the location of
words or phrases in a text and finding aids, in two columns, establishing the relationship between the
past and present reference numbers
of individual items.

concords
USE concord coaches

concourses
PJ.1025   (A)
HN March 1993 descriptor moved
ALT concourse
SN Use for open spaces or halls where crowds may gather, especially by chance coming together, as in a large railroad station.

concrete
MT.195   (A,L,B,R)
HN April 1992 descriptor moved
December 1991 scope note changed
SN A mixture of sand, gravel, crushed rock, or other aggregate, held together by a hardened paste of cement. (HORNB)

concrete, aerated
USE air-entrained concrete

concrete, air-entrained
USE air-entrained concrete

<concrete and concrete products>
MT.194
HN April 1992 guide term moved

Concrete art
FL.3381   (L,R)
UF Art Concret
art, Concrete
Konkrete Kunst

concrete, asphalt
USE asphalt concrete

concrete block
HN April 1993 descriptor split, use concrete + block (shaped mass) (ALT of blocks (shaped masses))

<concrete by composition or origin>
MT.196
HN April 1992 guide term moved

<concrete by function>
MT.207
HN April 1992 guide term moved

<concrete by property>
MT.222
HN April 1992 guide term moved

<concrete by technique>
MT.210
HN April 1992 guide term moved

concrete carts
USE buggies (equipment)

concrete, cast
USE cast-in-place concrete

concrete, cast-in-place
USE cast-in-place concrete

concrete, cellular
USE air-entrained concrete

concrete, cinder
USE cinder concrete

concrete coating
MT.1981   (L)
HN April 1993 descriptor changed, was concrete coatings
UF coating, concrete

concrete, colloidal
USE colloidal concrete

concrete, cyclopean
USE cyclopean concrete

concrete, expanding
USE expansive concrete

concrete, expansive
USE expansive concrete

concrete finishing machines
TH.1126   (N)
ALT concrete finishing machine
SN Used both for large power-driven machines mounted on wheels that ride on steel pavement forms and for portable machines with large paddles used to float and finish concrete floors and slabs. (MEANS)
UF finishing machines, concrete
machines, concrete finishing

concrete, foamed
USE foamed concrete

concrete, foamed sand
USE foamed sand concrete

concrete, foamed slag
USE foamed slag concrete

concrete, frost-resistant
USE frost-resistant concrete

concrete, heat-resistant
USE heat-resistant concrete

concrete, high-strength
USE high-strength concrete

concrete inserts
PJ.139
HN April 1993 descriptor moved
ALT concrete insert
SN Devices such as pipe sleeves, threaded bolts, or nailing blocks that are attached to a concrete form before pouring the concrete. When the forms are removed, the inserts remain embedded in the concrete. (MEANS)
UF inserts, concrete

concrete, insulating
USE insulating concrete

<concrete joints>
PJ.654
HN April 1993 guide term moved

concrete joist systems, one-way
USE one-way joist systems

concrete laying
USE placing (concrete process)

concrete, lime
USE lime concrete

concrete mixers
TH.1127   (L,N,B)
ALT concrete mixer
SN Machines that mix cement, aggregate, and water in a rotating drum to make concrete. (MEANS)
UF cement mixers
mixers, cement
mixers, concrete

concrete nails
PJ.189
HN April 1993 descriptor moved
ALT concrete nail
SN Steel nails each having a diamond point that has been hardened so that it can be driven into concrete without bending. (MEANS)
UF nails, concrete

concrete, no-fines
USE no-fines concrete

concrete, normal-weight
USE normal-weight concrete

concrete paint
MT.1962
SN Paint used on concrete.
UF paint, concrete

concrete pavers
TH.1128
ALT concrete paver
SN Concrete mixers, usually mounted on crawler tracks, that mix and place concrete pavement on the subgrade. (STEIN)
UF pavers
pavers, concrete

concrete placing
USE placing (concrete process)

concrete, plastic
USE polymer-impregnated concrete

concrete poetry
BM.215   (H,L)
HN September 1991 scope note changed
July 1991 descriptor moved
SN Works of visual poetry from the 1950s and 1960s associated with the concrete poetry movement; employ language elements but often out of syntax, to be seen but not read.
UF poetry, concrete

concrete, polymer-cement
USE polymer-impregnated cement

concrete, polymer-impregnated
USE polymer-impregnated concrete

concrete, post-tensioned pre-stressed
SEE post-tensioned prestressed concrete

concrete, post-tensioned prestressed
USE post-tensioned prestressed concrete

concrete, poured
USE cast-in-place concrete

concrete, poured-in-place
USE cast-in-place concrete

concrete, pouring
USE placing (concrete process)

concrete, pre-cast
SEE precast concrete

concrete, pre-stressed
SEE prestressed concrete

concrete, precast
USE precast concrete

concrete, prestressed
USE prestressed concrete

<concrete processing and fabricating equipment>
TH.1122

<concrete processing and fabricating machines>
TH.1125

<concrete processing and fabricating tools>
TH.1131

concrete products
HN April 1993 descriptor deleted

<concrete products>
MT.230
HN April 1993 guide term added

concrete pumps
TH.1129 (L)
ALT concrete pump
SN Pumps that force premixed concrete through a hose to a desired location. (MEANS)
UF pumps, concrete

concrete, ready-mixed
USE ready-mixed concrete

concrete, reinforced
USE reinforced concrete

concrete, resin
USE polymer-impregnated concrete

concrete, rubble
USE rubble concrete

concrete saws
TH.1132 (N)
ALT concrete saw
SN Power-operated saws used in grooving uncured concrete, to prevent cracking, or in cutting hard concrete slabs. (DAC)
UF saws, concrete

concrete slab systems, waffle
USE waffle slabs

concrete slabs
USE slabs (structural elements)

concrete, slag
USE slag concrete

concrete, sprayed
USE gunite

concrete spreaders
TH.1130
ALT concrete spreader
SN Machines, usually carried on side forms or on rails parallel thereto, designed to spread concrete from heaps or to receive and spread concrete in a uniform layer. (STEIN)
UF spreaders, concrete

concrete, sulfate-resistant
USE sulfate-resistant concrete

concrete, sulphate-resistant
SEE sulfate-resistant concrete

concrete-work
SEE concretework

concrete, Zonolite (TM)
USE Zonolite concrete (TM)

concreters
HG.819
HN December 1992 alternate terms added
ALT concreter
concreter's
concreters'
SN Persons who build or work with concrete. (W)

concretework
PE.124
HN October 1992 descriptor moved
UK concrete-work

concreting
USE placing (concrete process)

concretion
MT.911
HN April 1992 descriptor moved
March 1992 lead-in term changed, was concretion
March 1992 descriptor changed, was concretionary stone
UF concretionary stone
stone, concretionary

concretionary stone
USE concretion

concretions, humor
USE biomorphic abstraction

concussion idiophones
USE clappers (idiophones)

concussion sticks
TT.456
ALT concussion stick
SN Concussion idiophones consisting of sticks, usually used in pairs, played by being struck together. Known in ancient Egypt, they are distributed worldwide today. (MARCUS)
UF clappers, stick
stick clappers
sticks, concussion

concussion vessels
TT.458
ALT concussion vessel

SN Concussion idiophones made of hollowed-out objects.
UF clappers, vessel
vessel clappers
vessels, concussion

condemnation
USE condemning

condemning
KG.267 (L,B)
HN April 1993 lead-in term added
April 1993 related term added
ALT condemned
SN Use when real estate is legally declared unfit for habitation or use, usually accompanied by the appropriation of that property under the power of eminent domain. For the appropriating of real estate or other property as a punishment for breach of the law, use confiscating.
UF condemnation
RT confiscating

condensation
KT.822 (L,B)
HN March 1993 descriptor moved
March 1993 scope note added
March 1993 lead-in terms added
March 1993 alternate term added
ALT condensed
SN The act or process of reducing a gas or vapor to a liquid or solid form. (RHDEL2)
UF condensing
gas liquefaction

condensations
USE abridgements

condensed typefaces
PJ.3494
ALT condensed typeface
SN Typefaces whose characters are especially narrow in proportion to their height.
UF typefaces, condensed

condensers
PJ.804 (L)
HN March 1993 descriptor moved
ALT condenser
SN In refrigeration systems, the heat exchangers that remove heat from the refrigerant and transform a hot gas under pressure into a cool liquid. (MEANS)

condensing
USE condensation

<condiment vessels>
TQ.332
RT dredgers (containers)

<condition changing processes>
KT.224
HN November 1992 guide term added
SN Collocates descriptors for processes that alter the condition of an object or structure; some descriptors collo-

cated here are both such a process and the resultant effect on the item.

conditioners, air
USE air conditioners

<conditions and effects>
DE.1
HN November 1992 guide term moved

<conditions and effects: architecture>
DE.26
HN November 1992 guide term moved
October 1990 guide term added

<conditions and effects: glass>
DE.28

<conditions and effects: leather>
DE.30

<conditions and effects: metals>
DE.32

<conditions and effects: paper>
DE.36

<conditions and effects: photography>
DE.38
HN November 1992 guide term moved
October 1990 guide term added

<conditions and effects: printing>
DE.42
HN November 1992 guide term moved
November 1992 guide term changed, was *<conditions and effects: printing and printmaking>*
October 1990 guide term added

<conditions and effects: textiles>
DE.49
HN November 1992 guide term moved
June 1991 guide term added

<conditions and effects: wood>
DE.52

condominiums (dependencies)
HN.6   (L)
HN January 1993 descriptor added
ALT condominium (dependency)
SN Politically dependent territories administered jointly by two or more foreign powers.

condominiums (housing)
RG.95   (A,L)
HN March 1993 descriptor changed, was **condominiums**
March 1993 alternate term changed, was **condominium**
ALT condominium (housing)
SN Multifamily dwellings in which each unit is individually owned and ownership of common areas and facilities is shared. (MEANS)
UF condos

condos
USE condominiums (housing)

condottieri
HG.135   (H,L)
HN January 1993 descriptor added
ALT condottiere
condottiere's
condottieri's
SN Commanders of private bands of mercenaries who sell their services to warring states or rulers, especially those active in Italy and other regions of Europe from the 14th to the 16th century.
RT commanding officers

conducting material
USE conductor

conductivity
DC.247   (L)
HN October 1992 descriptor added
SN The ability of a material to conduct electricity, heat, or sound.
UF specific conductance

conductivity, electrical
USE electrical conductivity

conductivity, thermal
USE thermal conductivity

conductor
MT.2307
HN April 1993 descriptor changed, was **conductors (materials)**
April 1993 lead-in term changed, was **conducting materials**
May 1991 descriptor changed, was **conductors**
UF conducting material
material, conducting

conductor, electric
USE electric conductor

conductors
HG.218
HN April 1993 descriptor changed, was **conductors (musicians)**
April 1993 alternate term changed, was **conductor (musician)**
February 1993 descriptor moved
November 1992 alternate terms added
May 1992 lead-in term deleted, was **directors (music)**
May 1991 descriptor changed, was **conductors (music)**
May 1991 alternate term changed, was **conductor (music)**
ALT conductor
conductor's
conductors'
SN Persons who conduct an orchestra, chorus, or other group of musical performers. (W)
UF directors, music
music directors

conductors (downspouts)
USE downspouts

conductors' batons
USE batons (music equipment)

conductors, lightning
USE lightning rods

conduits
RK.541   (A,L,R)
ALT conduit

conduits (electric)
USE electric conduits

conduits, electric
USE electric conduits

cone flutes
TT.15
ALT cone flute
SN Conical end-blown flutes made of wood, horn, clay, or gourd, common among the Nilotes of Uganda. (NGDMI)
UF flutes, cone

cone hip tile
USE bonnet hip tile

cone tile
USE bonnet hip tile

cones
BM.683
HN January 1991 alternate term added
ALT cone
conical

Conestoga
FL.1303   (L)

Conestoga wagons
TX.111   (N)
ALT Conestoga wagon
SN Use for large, covered freight wagons distinguished by their curving boat-shaped profile with flaring endgates and side panels of planking with a series of short uprights; usually pulled by six horses and used between the mid-18th and mid-19th century in the areas of Ohio, Virginia, Maryland, and Pennsylvania. For similar wagons but characterized by mostly straight lines and linen tops and used across the western prairies and plains to carry freight and emigrants, use **prairie schooners.**
UF Conestogas
wagons, Conestoga
RT prairie schooners

Conestogas
USE Conestoga wagons

confectioneries
RK.158   (A)
ALT confectionery
UF confectionery stores
confiseries
stores, confectionery

confectionery stores
USE confectioneries

confederations
USE federations

conference centers
USE convention centers

conference centres
SEE convention centers

conference facilities
USE convention centers

conference proceedings
USE proceedings

conference reports
USE proceedings

conference rooms
PJ.999 (A,L,B)
HN March 1993 descriptor moved
ALT conference room
UF committee rooms
meeting rooms
rooms, committee
rooms, conference
rooms, meeting

conferences
KM.121 (A,L,B,R)
HN May 1991 alternate term added
ALT conference
UF congresses
conventions

confessionals
PJ.2522 (L,R)
HN March 1993 descriptor moved
ALT confessional
SN Small booths furnished with a seat
for a priest and with a screen or lat-
ticed window through which the
penitent may talk to the priest, who
is hidden. (HAS)
UF shriving-seats

confessionals (chairs)
USE bergères en confessional

confessors
HG.398 (L,R)
HN April 1993 scope note changed
February 1993 descriptor moved
December 1992 alternate terms
added
ALT confessor
confessor's
confessors'
SN Christian clergy whose defining of-
ficial function is to hear the confes-
sions of others.

confidantes
TC.743 (N)
HN May 1993 related term added
March 1993 scope note added
March 1993 lead-in terms added
March 1993 lead-in term deleted,
was vis-à-vis
March 1993 lead-in term deleted,
was tête-à-têtes
March 1993 lead-in term deleted,
was têtes (confidantes)
January 1993 descriptor moved
ALT confidante
SN Use for straight-fronted sofas with

small triangular seats (sometimes
detachable) set outside the arms at
either end. For S-shaped sofas with
ends curving inward so two people
could sit face to face use **canapés à
confident.**
UF canapés à confident (confidantes)
canapés à la maintenon
canapés en confident
confidents
RT canapés à confident

confidents
USE canapés à confident
confidantes

confidents à deux place
USE canapés à confident

confidents à trois places
USE indiscrets

confirmations
KM.42 (H,L,R)
HN February 1991 alternate term added
February 1991 descriptor changed,
was **confirmation**
ALT confirmation

confirmed credit
USE letters of credit

confirmed letters of credit
USE letters of credit

confiscating
KG.268 (L)
HN April 1993 lead-in term added
April 1993 related term added
SN Seizing and appropriating real estate or other property to the public
domain as a punishment for breach
of the law. For the appropriation of
real estate accompanying the declaration of its unfitness for habitation
or use, use **condemning.**
UF confiscation
RT condemning

confiscation
USE confiscating

confiseries
USE confectioneries

conflagrations
USE fires

conflict, social
USE social conflict

confraternities
HN.83 (L,R)
HN February 1993 descriptor moved
ALT confraternity
SN Groups of people united for a reli-
gious, charitable, or other purpose,
or in a profession or occupation.
(W)
UF sodalities

Confucianism
BM.498 (L)
ALT Confucian

congas
TT.613 (L)
ALT conga
SN Afro-Cuban drums having a long tapered or barrel-shaped shell up to
about 90 cm deep and a single head
about 25 to 30 cm in diameter, usually played with the hands. (NGDMI)

Congdon
FL.940

congés
USE apophyges

conglomerate
MT.917 (L)
HN March 1992 descriptor moved
SN Elastic sedimentary rock composed
of rounded fragments varying from
small pebbles to large boulders in a
cement of calcareous material, iron
oxide, silica, or hardened clay. (W)

Congo copal
MT.1250
HN April 1992 descriptor moved
June 1990 scope note added
SN A general name for fossil and other
hard resins found in nearly all tropical countries and used in making
varnishes and lacquers, adhesives,
and coatings, though now largely
replaced by synthetic resins. (MH)
UF copal, Congo

Congo Kingdom
USE Kongo Kingdom

congo-wood
USE African blackwood

Congregational
BM.473 (L,B)
HN July 1991 lead-in term added
UF Congregationalist

Congregationalist
USE Congregational

congress facilities
USE convention centers

Congress, Members of
USE Members of Congress

congresses
USE conferences

congressional committee records
VW.773 (L)
HN November 1992 descriptor moved
ALT congressional committee record
UF records, congressional committee

congressional committee reports
VW.774 (L)
HN November 1992 descriptor moved
ALT congressional committee report
UF reports, congressional committee

congressional districts
RG.262
ALT congressional district
UF districts, congressional

congressional records
VW.772
HN November 1992 descriptor moved
ALT congressional record
UF records, congressional

Congressmen
USE Members of the House of Representatives

Congresspersons
USE Members of the House of Representatives

Congresswomen
USE Members of the House of Representatives

Coniagui
USE Koniagui

Conibo
FL.1594

conical drums, double
USE double-conical drums

conical mounds
USE burial mounds

conical vaults
USE expanding vaults

conimeters
USE konimeters

connected barns
RK.57
ALT connected barn
SN Use for barns connected, often via intermediate outbuildings, to the main farmhouse.
UF barns, connected
barns, continuous
barns, New England connected
connected barns, New England
continuous barns
New England connected barns

connected barns, New England
USE connected barns

Connecticut barns
USE English barns

connecting-door locks
USE communicating-door locks

connections
USE joints (connections)

connelly feet
USE therm feet

Connemara marble
MT.734
HN April 1992 descriptor moved
UF marble, Connemara

connoisseurship
BM.223   (L,R)
HN February 1992 scope note added
SN Expertise in matters of taste and discrimination, particularly in relation to art or art objects.

conoidal vaults
PJ.1881
HN March 1993 descriptor moved
ALT conoidal vault
SN Use for expanding vaults in which the smaller base is semicircular, the larger base semielliptical.
UF vaults, conoidal

consecrations
KM.43   (L)
HN February 1991 alternate term added
February 1991 descriptor changed, was **consecration**
ALT consecration

consents
VW.499   (B)
HN November 1992 descriptor moved
ALT consent

conservation
KD.316   (A,L,B,R)
HN April 1993 related terms added
January 1993 descriptor moved
January 1993 scope note changed
SN Use for the discipline involving treatment, preventive care, and research directed toward the long-term safekeeping of cultural and natural heritage. For actions taken to prevent further changes or deterioration in objects, sites, or structures, use **preservation,** and for changes made to an object or structure so that it will closely approximate its state at a specific past time, use **restoration (process).**
RT conservators
preservation
restoration (process)

conservation board
MT.1446
HN February 1992 descriptor moved
July 1990 descriptor added
SN Board composed of purified cellulose pulp from wood where lignin has been removed and to which an alkaline buffer has been added. (SAITZY)
UF board, chemical wood pulp
board, conservation
chemical wood pulp board

conservation, energy
USE energy conservation

conservation laboratories
HN April 1993 descriptor split, use conservation + laboratories

conservation, preventive
USE preventive conservation

conservation quality
USE archival quality

conservation scientists
HG.535
HN January 1993 scope note changed
December 1992 alternate terms added
August 1991 descriptor added

ALT conservation scientist
conservation scientist's
conservation scientists'
SN Scientists who apply their knowledge to problems of conservation.
UF scientists, conservation

conservationists
HG.973   (A,L)
HN February 1993 descriptor moved
January 1993 alternate terms added
ALT conservationist
conservationist's
conservationists'
SN Persons who advocate conservation of natural resources. (W)

conservatism
BM.970   (L)
HN February 1993 descriptor moved
January 1991 alternate term added
ALT conservative

Conservative Judaism
BM.509   (L)
ALT Conservative Jewish

conservatories
PJ.1038   (L,B)
HN March 1993 descriptor moved
ALT conservatory
SN Greenhouses or mostly glazed rooms, devoted to growing and displaying plants and attached to a residence.

conservatories (greenhouses)
USE greenhouses

conservatories, music
USE music conservatories

conservatories of music
USE music conservatories
music schools

conservators
HG.906
HN April 1993 related term added
January 1993 descriptor moved
January 1993 scope note changed
December 1992 alternate terms added
November 1991 lead-in term deleted, was **conservation technicians**
October 1991 lead-in term deleted, was **conservation scientists**
August 1991 descriptor moved
ALT conservator
conservator's
conservators'
SN People responsible for treatment, preventive care, and research directed toward the long-term safekeeping of cultural and natural heritage.
RT conservation

console dessertes
TC.1005
HN January 1993 descriptor moved

ALT console desserte
SN French sideboards with a drawer or drawers beneath the top and a shelf between the legs. Usually D-shaped in plan, but sometimes rectangular. Used for the serving of food.
UF dessertes

console tables
TC.1103
HN January 1993 descriptor moved
ALT console table
SN Side tables with tops supported by a substructure consisting of two or more legs of console form, sometimes having marble tops and heavily carved substructures.
UF bracket tables
   clap tables
   consoles (tables)
   tables, bracket
   tables, clap
   tables, console

console tables, eagle
USE eagle console tables

consoles
PJ.1667   (R)
HN March 1993 descriptor moved
   January 1992 scope note changed
   January 1992 lead-in terms added
ALT console
SN Use for projecting, scroll-shaped members serving as brackets or corbels. Often used to support entablatures and cornices over doorways and windows.
UF ancones
   brackets (consoles)
   elbows

consoles (tables)
USE console tables

consoles en acajou
USE pier tables

consoles, key
USE key consoles

consolidated schools
RK.765   (L)
HN September 1990 scope note added
ALT consolidated school
SN Use for schools formed by the merging of two or more public schools, usually at the elementary level and often in rural areas. (W)
UF schools, consolidated

consolidation
KT.890   (L)
HN January 1993 descriptor moved
   August 1992 scope note changed
   August 1992 alternate term added
   August 1992 descriptor changed, was **consolidation (masonry)**
ALT consolidated
SN Stabilizing degraded or weakened areas by introducing or attaching

materials capable of holding them together. (FCAC)

consortia
HN.72   (L,B)
HN January 1993 scope note changed
   January 1993 lead-in term added
ALT consortium
SN Associations of independent institutions, commonly financial or educational, formed to undertake an enterprise or project involving the sharing of resources such as funds, services, manpower, and markets.
UF consortiums

consortiums
USE consortia

consorts
HG.28
HN March 1992 descriptor added
ALT consort
SN Ensembles of voices and/or instruments in English music from about 1570 to 1720; also used for present-day ensembles of like nature which play music of that period.

conspirators
HG.907
HN January 1993 descriptor added
ALT conspirator
   conspirator's
   conspirators'
SN Those who take part in a conspiracy. (RHDEL2)

constables
HG.155   (L)
HN January 1993 descriptor moved
   December 1992 alternate terms added
ALT constable
   constable's
   constables'
SN Public officers responsible for keeping the public peace and for certain petty judicial duties. (W)

constancy
DL.24
HN February 1992 descriptor moved
SN The relative independence of perceived object color from changes in color of the light source. (GCT)
UF color constancy
   constancy, color

constancy, color
USE constancy

constant white
USE barium sulfate
   zinc white

Constantinian
FL.2811

Constantinopolitan
FL.3170
UF Metropolitan (Byzantine)

constituencies
USE election districts

Constitution mirrors
TC.1474
ALT Constitution mirror
SN Modern term for mirrors with a carved eagle surmounting the frame.
UF Martha Washington mirrors
   mirrors, Constitution
   mirrors, Martha Washington
   mirrors, tabernacle
   tabernacle mirrors

constitutions
VW.522   (L)
HN November 1992 descriptor moved
ALT constitution
SN Documents embodying the fundamental organic law of government of a nation, state, society, or other organized body; laying down fundamental rules and principles for the conduct of affairs. (GAHLM)

constructed sculpture
USE constructions (sculpture)

construction
KT.11   (A,L,B,R)
HN January 1993 descriptor moved
ALT constructed
SN Use for the process of creating something by combining parts or elements, and also for the manner in which the thing has been put together.
UF building

construction, balloon frame
USE balloon frames

construction, bombproof
USE bombproof construction

<construction by form>
KT.12
HN January 1993 guide term moved

<construction by function>
KT.28
HN January 1993 guide term moved

construction, cantilever
USE cantilever construction

construction, carvel
USE carvel-built

construction, composite
USE composite construction

construction, cross-wall
USE box frames

construction drawings
VC.197
HN April 1992 descriptor moved
ALT construction drawing
UF construction plans
   drawings, construction
   drawings, operational

operational drawings
plans, construction

construction, drywall
USE drywall construction

construction, earthquake-resistant
USE earthquake-resistant construction

construction equipment
TH.422 (A,L,N,B)
HN April 1991 lead-in terms added
UF building equipment
building machinery
construction machinery
equipment, building
equipment, construction

construction, fast-track
USE fast-track method

construction, fire-resistive
USE fire-resistive construction

construction, fireproof
USE fire-resistive construction

construction, flat slab
USE flat slab systems

construction, frame
USE frame construction

construction, half-timber
USE half-timber construction

construction, incremental self-help
USE incremental housing

construction joints
PJ.656 (L)
HN April 1993 descriptor moved
ALT construction joint
SN Interfaces or meeting surfaces between two successive pours of concrete. (MEANS)
UF joints, construction

construction, light-weight
SEE lightweight construction

construction, lightweight
USE lightweight construction

construction loads
BM.603
HN March 1993 scope note added
November 1992 descriptor moved
January 1991 alternate term added
ALT construction load
SN The loads to which a structure is subjected during construction. (DAC)
UF loads, construction

construction, log
USE log construction

construction, log-end
USE stovewood construction

construction machinery
USE construction equipment

construction materials
USE building materials

construction, metal pan
USE one-way joist systems

construction, modular
USE modular construction

construction, monocoque
USE monocoque construction

construction, one-way joist
USE one-way joist systems

construction paper
MT.1469 (N)
HN February 1992 descriptor moved
July 1990 descriptor added
SN Inexpensive colored paper suitable for crayon and ink drawings, watercolors, and for making paper cutouts. (W)
UF paper, construction

construction, phased
USE fast-track method

construction, plank-and-beam
USE post-and-beam structures

construction plans
USE construction drawings

construction, platform frame
USE platform frames

construction, post-and-beam
USE post-and-beam structures

construction, post-and-lintel
USE post-and-beam structures

construction, poteaux sur solle
USE poteaux sur solle construction

construction, reinforced monocoque
USE monocoque construction

construction, sandwich
USE sandwich construction

construction, semi-monocoque
USE monocoque construction

construction sets
USE construction toys

construction, shell
USE shell structures

construction sites
USE building sites

construction, slab (pottery technique)
USE slab method

construction, stackwood
USE stovewood construction

construction, storm-proof
SEE stormproof construction

construction, stormproof
USE stormproof construction

construction, stove-wood
SEE stovewood construction

construction, stovewood
USE stovewood construction

construction, stressed-skin
USE stressed-skin construction
stressed-skin structures

construction, thesaurus
USE thesaurus construction

construction toys
TV.144 (N)
ALT construction toy
SN Use for toys with or without interlocking pieces that are designed to be put together to create various structures or other forms.
UF construction sets
sets, construction
toys, construction
RT building blocks

construction, tube-in-tube
USE tube structures

construction, two-way
USE two-way structural systems

construction, two-way flat slab
USE flat slab systems

construction, unit
USE modular construction

construction, wood frame
USE frame construction

construction workers
HG.812 (A,L)
HN December 1992 alternate terms added
ALT construction worker
construction worker's
construction workers'
SN Use for all types of laborers employed in building construction, including skilled and unskilled workers.
UF workers, construction

constructional steel, alloy
USE high-strength low-alloy steel

Constructionist
FL.3859 (R)
ALT Constructionism
SN Use especially with reference to certain work in Britain in the 1950s; can also refer to certain American and European works of the 1930s and 1940s.
UF Structurist

constructions (assemblages)
USE assemblages

constructions (sculpture)
VC.555
ALT construction (sculpture)
SN Sculpture fabricated by assembling and joining a number of separate parts rather than by traditional sculptural processes such as modeling, casting, or carving. (THDAT)
UF constructed sculpture
sculpture, constructed

constructions, beam-and-girder
USE one-way beam and slab systems

constructions, beam-and-slab floor
USE one-way beam and slab systems
two-way beam and slab systems

constructions, direct metal
USE direct metal sculpture

constructions, junk
USE junk sculpture

constructions, one-way
USE one-way structural systems

constructions, soft
USE soft sculpture

constructions, waffle flat plate
USE waffle slabs

Constructivist
FL.3507   (A,L,B,R)
ALT Constructivism
UF Productivist

constructors
HG.840   (L)
HN December 1992 alternate terms
added
ALT constructor
constructor's
constructors'
SN Naval officers supervising the construction and repair of ships. (W)

consular diptychs
VC.513   (R)
ALT consular diptych
SN Ivory diptychs with relief images
presented by ancient Roman consuls
to the emperor, Senate, and influ-
ential friends, to mark the com-
mencement of their term of office.
(OCA)
UF diptychs, consular

Consulat
FL.3449   (R)

consulates
RK.927   (A,L,B)
HN March 1993 related terms added
ALT consulate
SN Use for the official headquarters of
foreign ministers appointed primarily to oversee and protect the home
country's economic interests in a
host country; when such headquarters are for ministers called ambassadors appointed to transact matters
of international policy and business
with a foreign government, use **embassy buildings**. For the official residences of foreign ministers in general, use **legations**.
RT embassy buildings
legations

consuls
HG.156   (L)
HN January 1993 descriptor moved

December 1992 alternate terms
added
ALT consul
consul's
consuls'
SN Officials appointed by or with the
authority of a government to reside
in a foreign country in order to represent the interests of citizens of the
appointing country. (W)

consultants
HG.908   (L)
HN April 1993 related term added
December 1992 alternate terms
added
ALT consultant
consultant's
consultants'
SN Use for persons called on for professional advice or services regarding matters in the field of their special knowledge or training, usually
for specific projects or problems.
For persons who give advice either
professionally or nonprofessionally,
usually on an ongoing basis, use advisors.
RT advisors

consulting
KG.47
SN Providing professional or expert ad-
vice. (WCOL9)

consumers
HG.632   (L,R)
HN December 1992 alternate terms
added
ALT consumer
consumer's
consumers'

consumption, energy
USE energy consumption

consumption, fuel
USE fuel consumption

contact frames
USE contact printing frames

contact frames, photographic
USE contact printing frames

contact lenses
TH.365   (L,N)
HN January 1993 descriptor added
ALT contact lens
SN Thin lenses of glass or plastic which
fit over the cornea and correct vi-
sion defects.
UF lenses, contact
RT opticians

contact photoprints
USE contact prints

contact print frames
USE contact printing frames

contact printers
USE contact printing frames

contact printing
KT.614
HN March 1993 descriptor moved
January 1993 related terms added
SN Making photographic prints by
placing a negative in contact with
sensitized paper and exposing the
sandwich to strong light, giving a
print the same size as the negative.
Many 19th-century printing processes employed contact printing because they required exposure to intense light.
UF printing, contact
RT contact printing frames
contact prints

contact printing frames
TH.791   (N)
HN January 1993 lead-in terms added
January 1993 related term added
January 1993 descriptor changed,
was **contact printers**
January 1993 alternate term
changed, was **contact printer**
January 1993 lead-in term changed,
was **contact printing frames**
ALT contact printing frame
SN Devices used for making contact
prints, having a frame for holding
printing paper and negatives together and a light source for making an exposure. (RHDEL2)
UF contact frames
contact frames, photographic
contact print frames
contact printers
contact units, photographic
frames, contact
frames, contact print
frames, contact printing
frames, photographic contact
frames, printing
photographic contact frames
photographic contact units
print frames, contact
printers, contact
printing frames
printing frames, contact
units, photographic contact
RT contact printing

contact prints
VC.385   (L)
HN January 1993 related term added
April 1992 descriptor moved
ALT contact print
SN Photographic prints made by in-
terfacing a negative and a sheet of
photographic paper and exposing
the paper with raw light. (SWED)
UF contact photoprints
lumiprints
photoprints, contact
prints, contact
RT contact printing

contact sheets
VC.386
HN April 1992 descriptor moved
May 1991 related term added

ALT   contact sheet
SN   Use for contact prints containing prints from more than one negative, usually from all the negatives on a roll of film.
UF   prints, proof
      proof prints
      proof sheets
      sheets, contact
      sheets, proof
RT   proofs

contact units, photographic
USE   contact printing frames

contadores
      TC.838
HN   January 1993 descriptor moved
ALT   contador
SN   Portuguese paneled cabinets on stands. (PAYNE)

contained crazy quilts
      TC.246
ALT   contained crazy quilt
SN   Crazy quilts constructed of square blocks, long strips, stars, or diamonds, or having some other regular format.
UF   crazy quilts, contained
      quilts, contained crazy
RT   blocks (quilt components)

container cars
      TX.257
ALT   container car
SN   Use for railroad freight cars, usually flatcars or gondola cars, equipped to transport one or more standardized removable containers.
UF   cars, container

<container components>
      PJ.3086

<container groupings>
      PC.50

container ships
      TX.393
ALT   container ship
SN   Use for vessels designed to carry cargo packed in standardized, sealable, and reusable containers, that are made to fixed dimensions and designed to stack and lock together.
UF   ships, container

containers
      TQ.1   (H,L)
ALT   container
SN   Receptacles or formed or flexible coverings designed to hold, store, or ship objects or substances.
RT   case furniture
      <coverings and hangings for containers>

<containers by form>
      TQ.2

<containers by function or context>
      TQ.114

<containers by location>
      TQ.666

<containers for cooking food>
      TQ.280
RT   *<cooking tools and equipment>*

<containers for exchange media>
      TQ.164
RT   money belts

<containers for health care>
      TQ.172

<containers for personal gear>
      TQ.184

<containers for personal grooming and hygiene>
      TQ.219

<containers for personal use>
      TQ.171
RT   *<equipment for personal use>*

<containers for preparing food>
      TQ.269

<containers for priming powder or gunpowder>
      TQ.250

<containers for serving and consuming food>
      TQ.320
RT   *<culinary equipment for serving and consuming food>*

<containers for smoking and tobacco use>
      TQ.237

<containers for storing or transporting food>
      TQ.572

<containers for textiles and needlework>
      TQ.253

<containers for writing equipment>
      TQ.260
RT   *<drafting, drawing and writing equipment>*

containers, incense
USE   incense burners

containers, plant
USE   planters

containers, toothpick
USE   toothpick holders

containment buildings
USE   reactor containment buildings

containment buildings, reactor
USE   reactor containment buildings

containment, cost
USE   cost control

conté
USE   Conté crayon (TM)

Conté crayon (TM)
      TH.662

HN   March 1992 scope note changed February 1992 descriptor moved
SN   Mixture of graphite and clay in white, sepia, sanguine, and three grades of black; used by artists in the form of a hard crayon. (W)
UF   conté
      crayon, Conté (TM)

Conte Polychrome
      FL.1105
UF   Cocle, Early
      Early Cocle
      Polychrome, Conte

content analysis
USE   subject analysis

contents
USE   tables of contents

contents, tables of
USE   tables of contents

contests
      KM.50   (L)
HN   May 1991 alternate term added
ALT   contest

contests, invited
USE   invited competitions

contextualism
      BM.251   (A,H)
HN   January 1991 alternate term added
ALT   contextualist

Continental currency
      VK.149   (L)
SN   Use for the first national paper money of the United States, authorized for issue in 1775.

continental displacement
USE   continental drift

continental drift
      KM.128   (L)
UF   continental displacement
      displacement, continental
      drift, continental

continental log house
USE   log houses

continental masses
USE   continents

continental quilts
SEE   duvets

continents
      RD.146   (L,R)
HN   April 1993 lead-in term added
ALT   continent
UF   continental masses
      masses, continental

continuing education
      KD.258   (A,L)
UF   education, continuing
      education, lifelong
      learning, lifelong
      lifelong education
      lifelong learning

continuing education centers
RK.810 (L)
HN September 1990 scope note added
ALT continuing education center
SN Use for buildings designed to meet the needs of a continuing education program.
UF adult education centers
centers, adult education
centers, continuing education

continuity
USE rhythm

continuous
USE unbroken

continuous-arm armchairs, Windsor
USE continuous-bow Windsor armchairs

continuous arm chairs
USE continuous-bow Windsor armchairs

continuous arm Windsor chairs
USE continuous-bow Windsor armchairs

continuous barns
USE connected barns

continuous beams
PJ.1663
HN March 1993 descriptor moved
ALT continuous beam
SN Use for beams with three or more supports.
UF beams, continuous

continuous-bow Windsor armchairs
TC.528
HN January 1993 descriptor moved
ALT continuous-bow Windsor armchair
SN Windsor armchairs having a back of medium height consisting of back spindles contained within a bent bow that continues forward to form arms; frequently with a back brace. (EVANS)
UF arm chairs, continuous
armchairs, continuous-bow Windsor
armchairs, Winsor continuous-bow
chairs, continuous arm
chairs, continuous arm Windsor
continuous-arm armchairs, Windsor
continuous arm chairs
continuous arm Windsor chairs
Windsor armchairs, continuous-bow
Windsor chairs, continuous arm
Windsor continuous-arm armchairs

continuous bridges
RK.1216 (L)
ALT continuous bridge
UF bridges, continuous
continuous span bridges

continuous casting
KT.306 (L)
HN March 1991 alternate term added
ALT continuous-cast
UF casting, continuous

continuous curve amphorae
TQ.650
ALT continuous curve amphora

SN Amphorae in which the neck and body merge into a continous, unbroken curve.
UF amphorae, belly
amphorae, continuous curve
amphorae, type I
belly amphorae
type I amphorae

continuous footings
PJ.1544
HN March 1993 descriptor moved
December 1990 scope note changed
ALT continuous footing
SN Use for footings that support a wall or a number of columns in a line.
UF footings, continuous
footings, strap
footings, strip
strap footings
strip footings

continuous girders
PJ.1650 (L)
HN March 1993 descriptor moved
ALT continuous girder
SN Girders with more than two supports. (DAC)
UF girders, continuous

continuous hinges
PJ.383
HN April 1993 descriptor moved
ALT continuous hinge
UF hinges, continuous
hinges, piano
piano hinges

continuous inserts
USE channel inserts

continuous kilns
USE tunnel kilns

continuous linear pattern
USE running ornament

continuous narration
USE continuous representation

continuous representation
BM.103
SN Pictorial narrative featuring two or more successive actions from the same story within one setting. A character may, therefore, appear more than once in the same painting or sculpture. (RHLPS)
UF continuous narration
narration, continuous
representation, continuous

continuous span bridges
USE continuous bridges

continuous tone
DL.29
HN February 1993 descriptor added
SN Use to describe an image, or to denote the effect itself, when the image is composed of a smooth gradation of tones. Often used to designate copy that will need to be

photographed with a halftone screen in order to be printed.
UF tone, continuous

contour
BM.69
HN January 1993 descriptor moved
SN The outer boundary of an object or shape, especially when it suggests volume or mass. (A-Z)
UF edge (contour)

contour drawing
KT.393
UF contour line drawing
drawing, contour

contour drawing, blind
USE blind contour drawing

contour drawing, cross
USE cross-contour drawing

contour drawings
VC.210
HN April 1992 descriptor moved
ALT contour drawing
SN Distinct from **outline drawings** in that the lines in contour drawings also follow major spatial edges within an outline; distinct from **contour maps**, which delineate contours at regular intervals of elevation; distinct from **cross-countour drawings**, in which the lines follow contours across the surface of the form.
UF drawings, contour
line drawing, contour

contour drawings, blind
USE blind contour drawings

contour line drawing
USE contour drawing

contour maps
VW.76
HN November 1992 descriptor moved
ALT contour map
SN Maps showing elevation and the configuration of the ground by the use of contour lines and usually lacking other detail.
UF maps, contour

contour sanders
TH.1084
ALT contour sander
SN Sanders shaped so that they can be used to smooth complex moldings. (HAND)
UF sanders, contour
sanding slips
slips, sanding

contour sheets
USE fitted sheets

contrabass
DC.205
HN October 1992 descriptor added

contrabass players
USE bassists

contrabasses
USE double basses

contrabassists
USE bassists

contrabassoons
 TT.181   (L,N)
ALT contrabassoon
 SN Bassoons pitched an octave below
      the regular bassoon, with the tube
      bent back upon itself several times
      in order to reduce the overall length
      and bring the keys within conve-
      nient playing position. (MARCUS)
 UF bassoons, double
      double bassoons

contract awards
 VW.611
HN November 1992 descriptor moved
ALT contract award
 UF awards, contract

contract documents
 VW.538   (B)
HN November 1992 descriptor moved
ALT contract document
 SN Use with specific reference to docu-
      ments, such as drawings and speci-
      fications, associated with a construc-
      tion project.
 UF documents, contract

contract drawings
 VC.174
HN April 1992 descriptor moved
ALT contract drawing
 SN Use for drawings that form part of
      a contractual agreement and on the
      basis of which the contractor, archi-
      tect, or artist is legally obliged to
      produce the drawings, building,
      painting, or other commissioned
      work.
 UF drawings, contract

contracting
 KG.281
HN February 1991 scope note changed
      February 1991 lead-in term deleted,
      was **contracting out**
 SN The entering of two or more legally
      competent parties into a binding
      agreement to do or not to do some-
      thing, subject to specified terms
      and conditions.

contraction
 KT.239
HN January 1993 descriptor moved
      March 1991 alternate term added
ALT contracted
 SN The action or process of becoming
      smaller, shorter, or pressed to-
      gether. (W)

contraction joints
 PJ.647
HN April 1993 descriptor moved
ALT contraction joint

 SN Joints that allow for contraction of
      two adjacent parts of a structure.
 UF joints, contraction

contraction rules
USE shrinkage rules

contractors
 HG.846   (H,L,B)
HN December 1992 alternate terms
      added
ALT contractor
      contractor's
      contractors'
 SN Persons who perform work or pro-
      vide supplies on a large scale ac-
      cording to a contractual agreement.
      (W)

contractors, general
USE general contractors

contractors, main
USE general contractors

contractors, prime
USE prime contractors

contracts
 VW.619   (L,N,B,R)
HN November 1992 descriptor moved
ALT contract
 SN Documents, enforceable by law, em-
      bodying agreements between two or
      more competent parties to do or not
      to do something, and specifying the
      terms   and   conditions   of   the
      agreement.

contracts, architect-consultant
USE architect-consultant contracts

<contracts by form or function>
 VW.620
HN November 1992 guide term moved

<contracts by manner of payment>
 VW.628
HN November 1992 guide term moved

<contracts by party>
 VW.632
HN November 1992 guide term moved

contracts, cost plus fee
USE cost plus fee agreements

contracts, cost reimbursement
USE cost reimbursement contracts

contracts, discharges of
USE discharges of contracts

contracts, divided
USE divided contracts

contracts, firm price
USE fixed-price contracts

contracts, fixed-price
USE fixed-price contracts

contracts, government
USE government contracts

contracts, lump sum
USE fixed-price contracts

contracts, public
USE government contracts

contracts, separate
USE separate contracts

contracts, single
USE single contracts

contracts, turnkey
USE turnkey contracts

contrapposto
 BM.125   (R)
 SN Position of the depicted human
      body, balanced but asymmetrical, in
      which twisting or bending of the
      body's vertical axis results in hips,
      shoulders, and head turned or
      tipped in different directions. (W)

contrast, simultaneous
USE simultaneous contrast

contrasted arches
USE ogee arches

contributions
USE donations

control, authority
USE authority control

control, avalanche
USE avalanche protection

control, cost
USE cost control

control, environmental
USE environmental control

control, eviction
USE rent control

control, flood
USE flood control

control, humidity
USE humidity control

control, inventory
USE inventorying

control joints
 PJ.648
HN April 1993 descriptor moved
ALT control joint
 SN Shallow grooves in masonry or con-
      crete designed to control and guide
      stresses and resultant cracking or
      separation.
 UF joints, control

control, landslide
USE landslide protection

control, mold
USE mold control

control, mould
SEE mold control

control, noise
USE noise control

control, pest
USE pest control

control, pollution
USE pollution control

control, quality
USE quality control

control, rent
USE rent control

control, rent and eviction
USE rent control

control rooms
PJ.1168 (A)
HN March 1993 descriptor moved
June 1990 scope note changed
ALT control room
SN Use for rooms containing control
equipment, common examples be-
ing in broadcasting stations, audito-
riums, and theaters.
UF rooms, control

control signals, traffic
USE traffic signals

control, terminological
USE authority control

control towers
RK.1175 (A,L,N,B)
HN March 1993 lead-in terms added
ALT control tower
UF airport control towers
control towers, airport
control towers, traffic
towers, airport control
towers, control
towers, traffic control
traffic control towers

control towers, airport
USE control towers

control towers, traffic
USE control towers

control, vocabulary
USE authority control

controlettes
USE corselets

controlled access highways
USE limited access highways

controlled typesetting, computer
USE computerized composition

controllers
SEE comptrollers

conurbations
RD.18 (L,B)
HN March 1993 related term added
ALT conurbation
SN Extensive built-up urban areas that
contain some isolated rural areas
and are formed by the merging to-
gether of cities or towns that for-

merly were separate. For more extensive or comprehensive clusters of
urban areas, use **megalopolises.**
RT megalopolises

convalescent homes
USE convalescent hospitals

convalescent hospitals
RK.730 (A,L,B,R)
ALT convalescent hospital
UF convalescent homes
homes, convalescent
hospitals, convalescent

convection crackle
USE age cracks

convection heaters
USE convectors

convectors
PJ.809
HN March 1993 descriptor moved
December 1990 scope note added
ALT convector
SN Use for room heating units consisting of a heating device, often a
finned tube, mounted in a metal enclosure with openings to allow the
transfer of heat to the air, principally by convection.
UF convection heaters
heaters, convection

convenience stores
RK.171 (A,L)
ALT convenience store
UF stores, convenience

conveniences, public
SEE rest rooms

conventicles
PJ.1263
HN March 1993 descriptor moved
ALT conventicle
SN Rooms or buildings used for secret
or nonconformist worship.

convention centers
RK.1133 (A,H,L,B)
ALT convention center
UK conference centres
UKA conference centre
UF centers, conference
centers, convention
centres, conference
conference centers
conference facilities
congress facilities
convention facilities
convention halls
facilities, conference
facilities, congress
halls, convention

convention facilities
USE convention centers

convention halls
USE convention centers

conventional locks
USE mortise locks

conventions
USE conferences

convents
RG.203 (A,L,B,R)
ALT convent
UF buildings, conventual
conventual buildings
nunneries

conventual buildings
USE convents

conventual churches
USE abbey churches

conversation chairs
USE voyeuses

conversation pieces
VC.618 (L,R)
ALT conversation piece
SN Group portraits in a domestic or
landscape setting in which the sitters
are engaged in casual conversation
or social activity; especially popular
in Britain in the 18th century.
(OCA)

conversation-seats
USE voyeuses

conversion, data
USE data conversion

conversion of buildings
USE adaptive reuse

conversion plants, ocean thermal energy
USE ocean thermal energy conversion
plants

conversion, retrospective
USE retrospective conversion

conversion tables
VW.157 (L)
HN November 1992 descriptor moved
ALT conversion table
UF tables, conversion

convertible automobiles
USE convertibles

convertible bedroom pianos
USE piano beds

convertible beds
USE sofa beds

convertible fixtures
TC.1411
ALT convertible fixture
UF fixtures, convertible

convertible furniture
USE folding + furniture

convertible lenses
TH.774
ALT convertible lens
SN Camera lenses that consist of several
elements which can be used in vari-

ous combinations to provide different focal lengths. (QCKAIE)
UF lenses, convertible
lenses, separable
separable lenses

convertible sofas
USE sofa beds

convertibles
TX.146 (L)
ALT convertible
SN Use for automobiles with tops that may be removed or folded open. (DOFAE)
UF automobiles, convertible
convertible automobiles

convex
DC.65
HN October 1992 descriptor moved
SN Curved or rounded outward like the exterior curve of a circle or sphere.

convex conoidal vaults
HN December 1990 descriptor split, use convex + conoidal vaults

convex glasses
USE convex mirrors

convex looking glasses
USE convex mirrors

convex mirrors
TC.1466
ALT convex mirror
SN Use for mirrors in which the center is closer to the object than the edges and that reflect reduced images.
UF bull's eye mirrors
convex glasses
convex looking glasses
convex spherical mirrors
glasses, convex
looking glasses, convex
mirrors, bull's eye
mirrors, convex

convex planes
USE guttering planes

convex spherical mirrors
USE convex mirrors

conveyances
VW.665
HN November 1992 descriptor moved
ALT conveyance
SN Documents, such as deeds, by which title to property is conveyed from one person to another. (W)
UF conveyances, property
property conveyances

conveyances, property
USE conveyances

conveying machinery
USE conveyors

<conveying system components>
HN March 1993 guide term deleted

conveying systems
PC.111
HN March 1993 descriptor moved
December 1990 scope note added
ALT conveying system
SN Use for building systems designed to move people, equipment, or goods through a building or complex; for networks of equipment designed to move similar items through and between settlements, use transit systems; for machinery designed for the continuous transport of material, use conveyors.
UF systems, conveying

<conveying systems and conveying system components>
HN March 1993 guide term deleted

conveyors
TH.909 (L,N,B)
ALT conveyor
SN Motor-driven machines, such as endless belts or a series of rollers, used for the continuous transport of material. (DAC)
UF conveying machinery
machinery, conveying

conveyors, belt
USE belt conveyors

conveyors, chain
USE chain conveyors

conveyors, passenger
USE moving walkways

conveyors, roller
USE roller conveyors

conveyors, slat
USE slat conveyors

conveyors, vibrating
USE vibrating conveyors

convicting
KG.290
HN April 1993 lead-in term added
SN Proving, finding, or judging a person guilty of an offense or crime. (W)
UF conviction

conviction
USE convicting

convicts
HG.1002 (H,L)
HN January 1993 alternate terms added
February 1991 descriptor added
ALT convict
convict's
convicts'
SN Use for those serving a prison sentence following conviction for a criminal offense. For those involuntarily confined in prison or kept in custody, use prisoners. For those confined to an institutional facility voluntarily or involuntarily, use inmates.

RT inmates
prisoners

convocations
KM.22
HN May 1991 alternate term added
ALT convocation
SN Assemblies of members of a college or university to observe a particular ceremony, such as the opening of the academic year or the announcing of prizes, awards, and honors. (W)

convoys
PC.65 (L)
ALT convoy
SN Use both for groups of merchant or naval auxilliary ships traveling under armed escort and for groups of motor vehicles organized for the purpose of control and orderly movement, with or without escort protection. (DODDIC)

Cook Island
FL.3826 (L,B)
UF Hervey Island
Tarawa Atoll

cook knives
USE cooks' knives

cook knives, French
USE cooks' knives

cookbooks
VW.450 (L,R)
HN November 1992 descriptor moved
May 1992 lead-in term added
November 1991 lead-in term changed, was books, receipt
August 1990 lead-in term changed, was receipt books
ALT cookbook
UF books, receipt (cookbooks)
books, recipe
cookery books
receipt books (cookbooks)
recipe books

cookers, egg
USE egg coddlers

cookers, pressure
USE pressure cookers

cookers, steam
USE steamers

cookery books
USE cookbooks

cookie cutters
TH.111 (L,N)
HN April 1993 descriptor added
ALT cookie cutter
SN Devices, usually of sheet metal, for cutting shaped forms for cookies, such as circles or stars, from rolled dough. (RHDEL2)
UF cake cutters
cutters, cake
cutters, cookie

cookie jars
TQ.591 (L,N)
ALT cookie jar
SN Covered containers of varying form intended primarily for storing cookies.
UF jars, cookie

cookie presses
TH.200
HN April 1993 descriptor added
ALT cookie press
SN Devices in which dough is inserted in a chamber and extruded by means of a plunger, through one of a number of interchangeable plates to form shaped cookies. (W)
UF presses, cookie

cookie sheets
TQ.295 (N)
ALT cookie sheet
SN Large flat pans on which cookies are baked. (RHDEL2)
UF sheets, cookie

<cooking and heating devices>
TH.52
HN April 1993 guide term added
RT *<heating equipment>*

cooking baskets
TQ.281 (N)
ALT cooking basket
SN Relatively large, deep, globular-shaped baskets, tightly twined and intended primarily for cooking food.
UF baskets, cooking
RT baskets

<cooking tools and equipment>
TH.51
HN April 1993 guide term added
RT *<containers for cooking food>*

<cooking utensils>
TH.86
HN April 1993 guide term added

cooks' knives
TH.112 (N)
HN April 1993 descriptor added
ALT cook's knife
SN Large, fairly broad-bladed knives of generally triangular profile with a sharply pointed end. Designed especially for use on cutting boards.
UF chefs' knives
cook knives
cook knives, French
cooks' knives, French
French cook knives
French cooks' knives
knives, chefs'
knives, cooks'
knives, French cook
knives, French cooks'
RT cutting boards

cooks' knives, French
USE cooks' knives

cookstoves
USE stoves

cookware
TQ.299 (L)
SN Containers intended primarily for cooking.
RT terrines

cool colors
DL.339
HN February 1992 descriptor moved
January 1991 alternate term added
ALT cool color
UK cool colours
UKA cool colour
SN Colors commonly associated with air, sky, and water, such as green, greenish blue, and violet, which suggest coolness and which normally appear to recede.
UF colors, cool
colours, cool

cool colours
SEE cool colors

Cool Realist
USE Photorealist

coolant
MT.2311
HN April 1993 descriptor changed, was coolants

coolers
USE wine coolers

coolers, bread
USE cooling racks

coolers, butter
USE butter coolers

coolers, cold storage
USE cold storage rooms

coolers, water
USE water coolers

coolers, wine
USE wine coolers

cooling
KT.850 (L)
HN January 1993 descriptor moved
ALT cooled

cooling coils
PJ.801
HN March 1993 descriptor moved
May 1991 scope note added
ALT cooling coil
SN Designates coiled arrangements of piping or tubing used to cool by transferring heat between one fluid and another or between a space and a refrigerant.
UF air-cooling coils
coils, air cooling
coils, cooling

<cooling, heating and humidifying components>
PJ.789
HN March 1993 guide term moved

<cooling, heating and humidifying equipment>
TH.489
HN April 1993 related term added
RT *<culinary equipment for cooling food>*

cooling racks
TH.45 (N)
HN April 1993 descriptor added
ALT cooling rack
SN Wire racks used for cooling baked foods such as bread and cakes. (HEARTH)
UF bread coolers
coolers, bread
racks, cooling

cooling systems
USE air cooling

cooling towers
PJ.794 (L,B)
HN March 1993 descriptor moved
ALT cooling tower
SN Outdoor structures frequently placed on roofs, through which warm water is circulated to cool it by evaporation and exposure to the air. (MEANS)
UF towers, cooling

cooperage
USE coopering

cooperative apartment houses
RK.356 (A,L)
ALT cooperative apartment house
SN Apartment houses owned and managed by a corporation in which shares are sold entitling shareholders to occupy individual units in the building. (RHDEL2)
UF apartment houses, cooperative
apartments, cooperative
co-ops
cooperative apartments
cooperatives

cooperative apartments
USE cooperative apartment houses

cooperative housing
RG.96 (A,L,B)
UK co-operative housing
SN Housing owned by a legal entity that permits a group of members to mutually own all, or agreed-upon parts, of the complex and to share mutually in the benefits derived by the group under provisions of the entity's rules. (DDT)
UF co-ops
housing, co-operative
housing, cooperative

cooperative stores
RK.172 (L,B)

ALT   cooperative store
UF   co-ops
    stores, cooperative

cooperatives
USE   cooperative apartment houses

coopered joints
    PJ.627
HN   April 1993 descriptor moved
ALT   coopered joint
SN   Joints made on a curved surface similar to the joints made between the staves of a barrel. (MEANS)
UF   joints, coopered

coopering
    KT.790   (H,L)
HN   April 1993 related term added
SN   The construction of barrels or casks.
UF   cooperage
RT   coopers

coopers
    HG.777   (L)
HN   April 1993 related term added
    February 1993 descriptor moved
    December 1992 alternate terms added
ALT   cooper
    cooper's
    coopers'
SN   Persons who make or repair wooden casks or tubs; also shipboard artisans who repair casks and other vessels. (W)
RT   coopering

coopers' adzes
    TH.1391   (N)
HN   March 1993 descriptor changed, was cooper's adzes
    March 1993 lead-in term changed, was adzes, cooper's
ALT   cooper's adz
SN   Short handled tools where the handle is often wedged into the head to lean sharply towards the blade. (SALAM)
UF   adzes, coopers'

coopers' jointer planes
    TH.1522
HN   March 1993 descriptor changed, was cooper's jointer planes
    March 1993 lead-in term changed, was jointer planes, cooper's
    March 1993 lead-in term changed, was planes, cooper's jointer
ALT   cooper's jointer plane
SN   Planes as large as 5 to 6 feet in length which are turned upside down and mounted on legs. The wood to be planed is slid over the plane.
UF   jointer planes, coopers'
    long-jointer planes
    planes, coopers' jointer
    planes, long-jointer

coopers' levellers
USE   sun-planes

coopers' stoup planes
    TH.1529   (N)
HN   March 1993 descriptor changed, was cooper's stoup planes
    March 1993 lead-in term changed, was planes, cooper's stoup
ALT   cooper's stoup plane
SN   Coffin-shaped planes, similar to smoothing planes except that they are round in both planes on the bottom, with a 2-inch single or double iron made in different sizes to fit the barrel it is cleaning and smoothing. (SALAM)
UF   cleaning-out planes
    inside planes
    planes, cleaning-out
    planes, coopers' stoup
    planes, inside
    planes, round-both-ways
    round-both-ways planes

coops, chicken
USE   chicken houses

coordinating
    KG.211
HN   April 1993 lead-in term added
SN   Causing discrete agents or agencies to work together. (RLG7)
UF   coordination

coordination
USE   coordinating

coordination, dimensional
USE   modular coordination

coordination, modular
USE   modular coordination

Coos
    FL.1353   (L)
UF   Kusan

Copador
    FL.1095

copaiba balsam
    MT.1239   (L)
HN   April 1992 descriptor moved
SN   A viscous fluid oleoresin obtained from several species of tropical trees. (MAYER)
UF   balsam, copaiba

copal
    MT.1249   (L)
HN   April 1992 descriptor moved
SN   A general name for fossil and other hard resin found in nearly all tropical countries and used in making varnish, lacquer, adhesive, and coatings. (MH)

copal, Congo
USE   Congo copal

copal, East African
USE   East African copal

copal, kauri
USE   kauri

copal, Manila
USE   Manila copal

copal, Manilla
SEE   Manila copal

copal, Sierra Leone
USE   Sierra Leone copal

copal varnish
    MT.1892
HN   December 1992 descriptor changed, was copal varnishes
    March 1992 descriptor moved
UF   varnish, copal

copal, Zanzibar
USE   Zanzibar copal

cope chisels
USE   cape chisels

copecks
USE   kopecks

coped joints
    PJ.714
HN   April 1993 descriptor moved
ALT   coped joint
SN   Intersections consisting of two pieces of molding where one is cut to fit the contour of the other. (MEANS)
UF   joints, coped
    joints, scribed
    scribed joints

copen blue
USE   light blue
    moderate blue
    strong blue

copen blue, bright
USE   strong blue

copen blue, light
USE   light blue

Copena
    FL.904

copes
    TE.137   (H,L,N)
ALT   cope
SN   Long, semi-circular cloaklike garments fastened at the neck with a morse; worn by ecclesiastics in processions and on other ceremonial occasions. Also, similar garments worn as coronation or processional robes by laymen.
RT   <ceremonial costume>
    morses
    robes

copier art
USE   copy art

copies
    PE.16   (R)
HN   January 1993 descriptor moved
    May 1991 scope note changed
    March 1991 related terms added
    November 1990 descriptor moved
ALT   copy

SN Use for objects, images, or documents made to resemble other, existing objects, images, or documents. Implies less precise and faithful imitation than does the term **reproductions**. When copies are presented with intent to deceive, use **forgeries** or **counterfeits**. When more than one similar work is produced by the same maker, use **replicas** or **versions**.
UF imitations
RT copy prints
   <reprographic copies>

copies (photographic prints)
USE copy prints

copies, carbon
USE carbon copies

copies, electrostatic
USE xerographic copies

copies, letterpress
USE letterpress copies

copies, master
USE master copies

copies, mimeograph
USE mimeograph copies

copies, multilith
USE multigraphs

copies, presentation
USE presentation copies

copies, xerographic
USE xerographic copies

coping brick
USE capping brick

coping saws
   TH.1582   (N)
ALT coping saw
SN Light hand saws with a narrow blade mounted in a U-shaped frame with a handle; used to cut curves in wood. The blade may be rotated to keep the frame away from the work. (MEANS)
UF saws, coping
   saws, scribing
   scribing saws

copings
   PJ.2061
HN March 1993 descriptor moved
   December 1990 alternate term added
   December 1990 descriptor changed, was **coping**
ALT coping
SN Protective caps, tops, or covers of walls, parapets, or other structures, often of stone, terracotta, or metal. (DAC)

copolymer, acrylonitrile-butadiene-styrene
USE acrylonitrile-butadiene-styrene copolymer

copolymer, furfurane
USE furan

copolymer, sytrene-butadiene
USE styrene-butadiene rubber

copolymer, tetrole
USE furan

copolymer, vinyl
USE vinyl

copotain hats
USE copotains

copotains
   TE.585
ALT copotain
SN Hats with a tall conical crown and a moderate brim, especially fashionable from 1560 to 1620. (HFC)
UF copotain hats
   hats, copotain
   sugarloaves

copper
   MT.385   (A,L,B,R)
HN March 1993 scope note added
   March 1993 descriptor moved
   December 1992 lead-in term added
SN Use for the pure metallic element having the symbol Cu and atomic number 29; a reddish metal that is very malleable and ductile. Use also for this metal as processed and formed, usually in combination with other substances, to make various objects and materials.
UF Cu

copper (color)
USE grayish reddish orange
   moderate orange
   moderate reddish orange

Copper Age
USE Chalcolithic

copper alloy
   MT.386   (L,B)
HN March 1993 descriptor changed, was **copper alloys**
   March 1993 descriptor moved
UF alloy, copper

<copper-aluminum alloy>
   MT.405
HN March 1993 guide term added

<copper and copper alloy>
   MT.384
HN March 1993 guide term added

copper arsenate, ammoniacal
USE ammoniacal copper arsenate

copper arsenate, chromated
USE chromated copper arsenate

copper basic acetate
USE verdigris

copper, beryllium
USE copper-beryllium alloy

copper-beryllium alloy
   MT.407   (L)
HN March 1993 descriptor changed, was **copper-beryllium alloys**
   March 1993 descriptor moved
SN Alloy of copper and beryllium containing usually not more than 3% beryllium. The alloy has a bronzelike, crystalline structure and is unsurpassed in its ability to withstand fatigue, wear, and corrosion and in its electrical conductivity at high temperatures.
UF alloy, copper-beryllium
   beryllium bronze
   beryllium copper
   bronze, beryllium
   copper, beryllium

copper blue
USE azurite
   blue verditer

copper brick
   MT.108   (B)
HN April 1992 descriptor moved
UF brick, copper

copper brown, light
USE strong brown

copper chromate, acid
USE acid copper chromate

Copper Culture, Old
USE Old Copper Culture

copper enameling
   KT.98   (L)
HN March 1993 descriptor moved
UK copper enamelling
UF enameling, copper
   enamelling, copper

copper enamelling
SEE copper enameling

copper engraving
   KT.673   (L,R)
HN March 1991 descriptor added
SN Process of engraving for printing using copper plates; replaced in the early 19th century by the use of more durable plates, either of steel or steel-faced copper.
UF chalcography
   copperplate engraving
   engraving, copper
   engraving, copperplate

copper engravings
   VC.463
ALT copper engraving
SN Prints made by the process of copper engraving.
UF copperplate engravings
   engravings, copper

Copper Eskimo
USE Copper Inuit

copper frit
USE Egyptian blue

copper green
USE malachite (pigment)

Copper Inuit
FL.1223
HN June 1990 lead-in terms added
UF Copper Eskimo
Eskimo, Copper
Inuit, Copper

copper mines
RG.103   (L)
ALT copper mine
UF mines, copper

copper-nickel alloy
MT.408   (L)
HN March 1993 descriptor changed,
was **copper-nickel alloys**
March 1993 lead-in term changed,
was **nickel-copper alloys**
March 1993 descriptor moved
UF alloy, copper-nickel
alloy, nickel-copper
nickel-copper alloy

copper ore, green
USE malachite (mineral)

copper points
TH.676
ALT copper point
SN Points or styluses of copper used as
drawing instruments. (GETTEN)
UF points, copper

copper pyrite
USE chalcopyrite

copper resinate
MT.2152
HN April 1992 descriptor moved
UF resinate, copper

copper ruby glass
MT.253
HN January 1992 descriptor added
SN Glass with a red color due to the
presence of copper.
UF glass, copper ruby
ruby glass, copper

copper-silicon alloy
MT.413
HN March 1993 descriptor changed,
was **copper-silicon alloys**
March 1993 descriptor moved
UF alloy, copper-silicon

copper-smiths
SEE coppersmiths

copper-tin alloy
USE bronze

copper-tin alloys
HN March 1993 descriptor deleted

copper-work
SEE copperwork

copper-zinc alloy
USE brass (alloy)

copper-zinc alloys
HN March 1993 descriptor deleted

copperplate (script)
PJ.3447   (L)
SN An elegant style of handwriting
originally derived from cursive
script engraved in copper with a
burin.

copperplate engraving
USE copper engraving

copperplate engravings
USE copper engravings

copperplate presses
USE rolling presses

coppers, soldering
USE soldering irons

coppersmithing
KT.1067   (L)
HN May 1993 related term added
RT coppersmiths

coppersmiths
HG.712   (L)
HN April 1993 related term added
December 1992 alternate terms
added
ALT coppersmith
coppersmith's
coppersmiths'
UK copper-smiths
UKA copper-smith
SN Persons who work in copper, espe-
cially those who make objects such
as kettles, coils, tubing, and fittings.
(W)
RT coppersmithing

copperwork
PE.134   (L)
HN October 1992 descriptor moved
UK copper-work

cops, elbow
USE cowters

cops, knee
USE poleyns

Coptic (Christian sect)
BM.482   (A,L,B,R)
HN May 1991 descriptor changed, was
Coptic
SN Use with reference to the Egyptian
Christian church; with reference
specifically to the Early Medieval pe-
riod in Egypt, use **Coptic (period)**.

Coptic (period)
FL.2923   (A,L,B,R)

copy
VW.1188
HN March 1993 descriptor added

SN Matter prepared or to be prepared
for printing, often referring to both
text and images, sometimes to the
text as distinguished from the
images.
RT copyediting

copy (camera ready)
USE camera ready copy

copy art
VC.81   (L,R)
HN May 1991 scope note added
April 1991 descriptor moved
March 1991 lead-in term added
SN Use for works of art produced using
the technology of copying machines.
UF art, copy
art, reprographic
art, xerographic
art, Xerox
copier art
generative systems (copy art)
reprographic art
systems, generative (copy art)
xerographic art
Xerox art

copy, camera
USE camera ready copy

copy cameras
USE process cameras

copy-editing
SEE copyediting

copy editors
SEE copyeditors

copy, line
USE line copy

copy photographs
USE copy prints

copy photoprints
USE copy prints

copy prints
VC.311
HN April 1992 descriptor moved
December 1990 descriptor added
ALT copy print
SN Photographic prints produced by
photographing a two-dimensional
work, such as a drawing or painting,
or by rephotographing another
photograph.
UF copies (photographic prints)
copy photographs
copy photoprints
copyprints
photographs, copy
photoprints, copy
prints, copy
RT copies

copybooks
VW.451   (L)
HN November 1992 descriptor moved
ALT copybook
SN Books in which copies, especially of

penmanship, are written or printed
for learners to imitate. (GAHLM)
UF books, penmanship
penmanship books

copybooks (pattern books)
USE pattern books

copybooks, letterpress
USE letterpress copybooks

copyediting
KG.138 (L)
HN November 1992 related term added
November 1992 related term de-
leted, was **documents**
January 1991 descriptor added
UK copy-editing
SN Editing a document for correctness
and consistency in such matters as
punctuation, spelling, grammar, or
style prior to publication. (RHDEL2)
UF copyreading
RT copy
copyeditors

copyeditors
HG.378
HN December 1992 alternate terms
added
January 1991 descriptor added
ALT copy editor's
copy editors'
copyeditor
UK copy editors
UKA copy editor
SN Those who edit a document for cor-
rectness and consistency in such
things as punctuation, spelling,
grammar, or style prior to publica-
tion. (RHDEL2)
RT copyediting

copying
KT.363 (L,B)
ALT copied
SN Use for any of various processes involved in the reproduction of documents or other artifacts. Use a more
specific term if possible.
UF duplicating
duplicating processes

copying, electrostatic
USE xerography

copying, heat
USE thermal copying

copying processes, fluid
USE spirit duplicating

copying, thermal
USE thermal copying

copying, thermic
USE thermal copying

copyists
HG.909 (H,L,R)
HN December 1992 alternate terms
added
April 1991 descriptor moved

April 1991 scope note changed
April 1991 related term added
ALT copyist
copyist's
copyists'
SN Use for people who make copies, especially those who copy manuscripts, music notation, or other
documents by hand.
RT scribes

copyprints
USE copy prints

copyreading
USE copyediting

copyright
BM.927 (A,L,B,R)
HN February 1993 descriptor moved
SN Exclusive, legally secured right to
reproduce (as by writing or printing), publish, and sell the matter
and form of a literary, musical, or
artistic work. (W)

copyright certificates
VW.337
HN November 1992 descriptor moved
ALT copyright certificate
UF certificates, copyright

coquetières
USE eggcups

coquillage
DG.16
SN Use for shell-like ornament, espe-
cially of the Rococo period.

coquille board
MT.1449
HN February 1992 descriptor moved
SN An artist's white drawing board with
stippled texture that produces a dot-
ted drawing. (W)
UF board, coquille

coquilliers
TC.847
HN January 1993 descriptor moved
ALT coquillier
SN 18th-century French cabinets with
small drawers designed to house a
collection of shells; fashionable be-
tween 1730 and 1750. (HAYWAR)

coquina
MT.850
HN April 1992 descriptor moved
March 1992 lead-in term changed,
was **coquina**
March 1992 descriptor changed,
was **coquina rock**
SN Limestone composed of loosely co-
hering shell fragments cemented together by an infiltration of carbonate of lime. (STEIN)
UF coquina rock
rock, coquina
shellstone

coquina rock
USE coquina

Cor-Ten steel (TM)
MT.362
HN March 1993 descriptor moved
April 1990 descriptor added
UF steel, Cor-Ten (TM)

Cora
FL.1505 (L)
UF Nayarit (Cora)

coracles
TX.510 (N)
ALT coracle
SN Small, broad round or roundish skin
boats of various constructions used
for river or coastal transport in
ports of the Near East and Great
Britain in ancient and modern
times.

coral
MT.1325 (L,R)
HN May 1992 related term added
March 1992 scope note added
February 1992 descriptor moved
SN Hard material consisting of calcium
carbonate; the skeletal deposit of
certain marine animals.
RT <calcium carbonate white pigment>

coral limestone
MT.845
HN April 1992 descriptor moved
UF bird's eye marble
coral rag
coral rock
coral stone
coraliferous limestone
corallian oolite
limestone, coral
limestone, coraliferous
marble, bird's eye
oolite, corallian
rag, coral
rock, coral
stone, coral

coral rag
USE coral limestone

coral rock
USE coral limestone

coral, star
USE star coral

coral stone
USE coral limestone

Coralene glass
MT.287
HN March 1992 descriptor added
SN Use to describe glassware decorated
with coral-like sprays created with
enamel and applied glass beads
fused to the object.
UF glass, Coralene

coraliferous limestone
USE coral limestone

corallian oolite
USE coral limestone

corantos
　　VW.971
HN June 1992 descriptor added
ALT coranto
SN Use for single-leaf forerunners of newspapers. For similar items consisting of more than one leaf, use newsbooks. (RBGENR)
UF courants

coras
USE koras

corbel arches
　　PJ.1608
HN March 1993 descriptor moved
　　December 1990 scope note changed
ALT corbel arch
UK false arches
UKA false arch
SN Masonry constructions whose arch-like form is created by cantilevering successive courses inward beyond the preceding until they meet at the span's midpoint; thus the courses are set horizontally, not radially; not true arches.
UF arches, corbel
　　arches, false

corbel courses
USE corbel tables

corbel gables
USE corbie gables

corbel rings
USE shaft rings

corbel steps
USE corbiesteps

corbel tables
　　PJ.1948
HN March 1993 descriptor moved
　　January 1991 scope note changed
ALT corbel table
SN May designate projecting masonry courses supported by a range of corbels, or ranges of corbels supporting cornices or other projecting courses, or ensembles of corbels and projecting courses; found especially in Medieval architecture.
UF corbel courses
　　courses, corbel
　　tables, corbel

corbel vaults
　　PJ.1883
HN March 1993 descriptor moved
　　March 1991 descriptor moved
　　December 1990 scope note changed
ALT corbel vault
SN Use for vaults constructed by corbeling, or cantilevering, successive courses inward beyond the preceding one, until they meet and are capped at the vault's midpoint.
UF vaults, corbel

corbelling
USE corbels

corbels
　　PJ.1669　　　　　　　　(A,L,B,R)
HN March 1993 descriptor moved
　　December 1990 scope note changed
ALT corbel
SN Cantilevered masonry blocks used singly or in ranges to support architectural or ornamental features or used in successive courses to form arches, domes, or vaults; when referring generally to the projecting courses of masonry, prefer oversailing courses.
UF corbelling

corbie gables
　　PJ.1965　　　　　　　　(B)
HN March 1993 descriptor moved
　　November 1991 scope note changed
　　November 1991 lead-in term changed, was corbie gables
　　November 1991 lead-in term changed, was gables, crow-stepped
　　December 1990 lead-in terms added
　　December 1990 lead-in term changed, was step gables
　　December 1990 lead-in term changed, was gables, step
　　December 1990 lead-in term deleted, was catsup gables
　　December 1990 lead-in term deleted, was gables, catsup
　　December 1990 descriptor changed, was crow-stepped gables
　　December 1990 lead-in term changed, was corbiestepped gables
　　December 1990 alternate term changed, was crow-stepped gable
　　December 1990 lead-in term changed, was gables, corbie-stepped
ALT corbie gable
SN Gables having stepped edges.
UF corbel gables
　　corbiestep gables
　　crow gables
　　crowstepped gables
　　gables, corbel
　　gables, corbie
　　gables, corbiestep
　　gables, crow
　　gables, crowstepped
　　gables, stepped
　　stepped gables

corbiestep gables
USE corbie gables

corbiesteps
　　PJ.1973
HN March 1993 descriptor moved
　　December 1990 scope note changed
　　December 1990 descriptor changed, was crowsteps
　　December 1990 alternate term changed, was crowstep

　　December 1990 lead-in term changed, was corbiesteps
ALT corbiestep
SN The component projections of corbie gables.
UF catsteps
　　corbel steps
　　crowsteps
　　steps, corbel

corbitae
　　TX.314
ALT corbita
SN Use for ancient Roman merchant vessels having a full hull with curved stem and sternpost; generally shorter and wider than pontones, the other major Roman merchant craft.
RT merchant vessels
　　pontones

cord
　　MT.1408
HN April 1993 related term added
　　March 1993 scope note added
　　March 1993 descriptor moved
SN Long, slender, flexible, roughly cylindrical construction of fibrous material, usually made of several strands twisted together.
RT thread

cord marking
　　KT.1156
HN March 1991 alternate term changed, was cord marked
ALT cord-marked
SN A ceramic technique in which fine cord is wrapped around a paddle and pressed against an unfired clay vessel, leaving the cord imprint. (MUSER)
UF marking, cord

cord quilting
　　KT.1231
HN December 1992 descriptor added
ALT cord-quilted
SN Quilting technique in which two parallel lines of stitching are made through two layers of cloth, then heavy yarn or soft cord is inserted between the layers within the lines of stitching, making a raised linear pattern on an otherwise flat ground.
UF corded quilting
　　Italian quilting
　　quilting, cord
　　quilting, corded
　　quilting, Italian

Corded
　　FL.2577　　　　　　　　(L)
HN April 1993 descriptor added
UF Battle-ax (pottery style)

corded quilting
USE cord quilting

corded velveteen
USE corduroy

Corded ware
HN April 1993 descriptor split, use Corded + ware

cordial glasses
TQ.430 (N)
ALT cordial glass
SN Small drinking glasses, generally of 1- to 1 1/2-ounce capacity, intended for drinking cordials, liqueurs, and eaux-de-vie. They are usually in the form of wine glasses but smaller with a bowl resting on a tall stem or in the form of a beaker.
UF cordials
glasses, cordial
glasses, liqueur
glasses, Schnapps
liqueur glasses
Schnapps glasses
RT toastmasters' glasses
wine glasses

cordials
USE cordial glasses

cordials, flute
USE ratafia glasses

Cordilleran, Old
USE Old Cordilleran

cording
USE piping (trimming)

cordonata cascades
USE water chains

cordonate
USE water chains

cordons
USE stringcourses

cords, lamp
USE lamp cords

cords, sash
USE sash cords

corduroy
MT.1609 (L)
HN March 1993 scope note added
March 1993 lead-in terms added
March 1993 descriptor moved
SN Weft pile weave with cut pile ribbed in the direction of the warp, usually made of cotton. (WRPWFT)
UF corded velveteen
velveteen, corded

core-forming
KT.1030
HN March 1993 descriptor added
ALT core-formed
SN Process of manufacturing glass vessels around a core of material made in the shape of the desired vessel.
UF core-made
core technique

core-made
USE core-forming

core-makers
SEE coremakers

core technique
USE core-forming

Corean
USE Korean

coremakers
HG.733 (L)
HN December 1992 alternate terms added
ALT coremaker
coremaker's
coremakers'
UK core-makers
UKA core-maker
SN Persons who make sand cores for metal castings, clay cores for iron pipe, or metal cores for building tile. (W)

corers
TH.156 (N)
HN April 1993 descriptor added
ALT corer
SN Specially designed curved or cylindrical knives or other circular multi-bladed devices for removing the core of a fruit or vegetable.
UF apple corers
corers, apple
corers, fruit
corers, pineapple
fruit corers
pineapple corers

corers, apple
USE corers

corers, fruit
USE corers

corers, pineapple
USE corers

cores
USE service cores

coretti
PJ.1264
HN March 1993 descriptor moved
ALT coretto
SN Small galleries like the boxes of a theater, often inserted into the choir wall of Baroque churches. (BLUNT)

Corinthian (architectural style)
FL.2677

Corinthian (pottery style)
FL.2714

Corinthian, Early
USE Early Corinthian

Corinthian helmets
TE.281
ALT Corinthian helmet
SN Helmets consisting of a single plate of bronze, shaped to cover the cranium, nose, cheeks, and chin. The most widely used type of military helmet of Classical Greece, it had spread to Italy by the beginning of the 6th century BCE.
UF helmets, Corinthian

Corinthian kraters
USE column kraters

Corinthian, Late
USE Late Corinthian

Corinthian, Middle
USE Middle Corinthian

Corinthian order
PJ.1426 (A,B,R)
HN March 1993 descriptor moved
December 1990 scope note added
SN Use for the architectural order characterized by a capital having a bell-shaped echinus decorated with a combination of spiral and plant, usually acanthus, motifs. (FOFDA)
UF order, Corinthian

corium
MT.2548 (L)
HN May 1993 descriptor added
SN Part of hide or skin consisting of fibrous connective tissue. The layer of hide or skin from which leather is made.
UF cutis vera
dermis
enderon
skin, true
true skin

cork (bark)
MT.2614 (A,L,B)
HN March 1992 descriptor moved
May 1991 descriptor changed, was cork

cork (blue pigment)
MT.2092 (L)
HN April 1992 descriptor moved

cork black
USE vine black

cork-board
SEE corkboard

cork disc burners
PJ.2923
ALT cork disc burner
SN Burners for oil lamps consisting of a thin metal disc mounted on a cork through which one or more wick tubes protrude.
UF burners, cork disc

cork rumps
USE bustles

cork stoppers
USE corks

corkboard
MT.3054
HN March 1992 descriptor moved
UK cork-board
SN Construction board made by com-

pressing granulated cork and subjecting it to heat so that the particles cement themselves together. (MH)

corks
PJ.3102 (L,N)
ALT cork
SN Usually tapering or cylindrical pieces of cork used as stoppers.
UF cork stoppers
stoppers, cork

corks, crown
USE crowns (closures)

corkscrew stairs
USE spiral stairs

corkscrews
TH.176 (L,N)
HN April 1993 descriptor added
ALT corkscrew
SN Tools with a pointed spiral piece of metal attached to a handle, used for drawing corks from bottles. (W)

corn
MT.2654 (L)
HN March 1992 descriptor moved

corn dryers
TH.96
HN April 1993 descriptor added
ALT corn dryer
SN Utensils, often wire or iron, which hold ears of corn for the process of drying.
UF corn hands
dryers, corn
dryers, herb
hands, corn
herb dryers
seed-corn trees
trees, seed-corn

corn hands
USE corn dryers

corn houses
USE corncribs

corn oil
MT.1072
HN April 1992 descriptor moved
July 1990 descriptor changed, was maize oil
July 1990 lead-in term changed, was corn oil
UF maize oil
oil, corn
oil, maize

corn palaces
RK.371 (L,R)
ALT corn palace
UF palaces, corn

corn poppers
TH.64 (N)
HN April 1993 descriptor added
ALT corn popper
SN Any of various utensils used in popping corn. (W)

UF poppers
poppers, corn

corn-stalk
SEE cornstalk

corn stalk, guinea
USE guinea corn stalk

corncribs
RK.98 (A,L,N)
ALT corncrib
SN Structures for storing corn, usually with slotted boards for ventilation, slanted walls for weather protection, and set on stilts to deter rodents. (BIGHSE)
UF corn houses
houses, corn

cornelian
USE carnelian

corner
DC.311
HN October 1992 descriptor moved
October 1992 scope note added
SN Use to describe something situated at or near a corner. To refer to those parts of things where converging lines or surfaces meet, use corners from the Components hierarchy.

corner basin stands
TC.1071
HN January 1993 descriptor moved
ALT corner basin stand
UF basin stands, corner
stands, corner basin

corner-block frames
TC.406
ALT corner-block frame
SN Use for frames with protrusions, often disc-shaped, from the face at each corner.
UF frames, corner-block

corner blocks
PJ.2760
HN March 1993 descriptor moved
ALT corner block
SN Reinforcing blocks glued, nailed, or screwed into the corner of a chair or sofa frame to hold the leg and seat rail together. (FAIRB)
UF blocks, corner

corner boards
PJ.1998
HN March 1993 descriptor moved
December 1990 descriptor moved
ALT corner board
SN Boards which are used as trim on the external corner of a wood frame structure and against which the ends of the siding are fitted. (HAS)
UF boards, corner

<corner buttresses>
PJ.1448
HN March 1993 guide term moved

corner cabinets
TC.839 (N)
HN January 1993 descriptor moved
ALT corner cabinet
SN Cabinets designed to fit into a corner of a room, usually by being triangular.
UF cabinets, corner
meubles de coin

corner capitals
USE angle capitals

corner chairs
TC.483 (N)
HN May 1993 lead-in term changed, was barber's chairs (corner chairs)
May 1993 lead-in term changed, was chairs, barber's (corner chairs)
January 1993 descriptor moved
ALT corner chair
UF angle chairs
barbers' chairs (corner chairs)
burgomaster chairs
burgomeister chairs
chairs, angle
chairs, barbers'
chairs, burgomeister
chairs, corner
chairs, half-round
chairs, round
chairs, roundabout
chairs, shaving
chairs, writing
fauteuils en encoignures
half-round chairs
round chairs
roundabout chairs
roundabouts
shaving chairs
writing chairs

corner chisels
TH.1431 (N)
ALT corner chisel
SN Chisels having two cutting edges which meet at right angles; used to cut corners of mortises. (DAC)
UF bruzz chisels
chisels, bruzz
chisels, corner
chisels, dogleg
dogleg chisels

corner clamps
TH.1627 (N)
ALT corner clamp
SN Clamps used to join corners during gluing.
UF clamps, corner
clamps, picture-framing
picture-framing clamps

corner clips
PJ.80
HN April 1993 descriptor moved
ALT corner clip
UF clips, corner

corner commodes
TC.904

HN   January 1993 descriptor moved
ALT   corner commode
UF   commodes, corner

corner cupboards
   TC.917   (L,N)
HN   May 1993 related term added
   January 1993 descriptor moved
ALT   corner cupboard
SN   Freestanding, built-in, or hanging
   cupboards made to fit the shape of
   a room's corner. (PAIN)
UF   corner dish dressers
   corners (cupboards)
   cupboards, corner
   dish dressers, corner
   dressers, corner dish
RT   built-in furniture

corner dish dressers
USE   corner cupboards

corner double seams
   PJ.696
HN   April 1993 descriptor moved
ALT   corner double seam
UF   double seams, corner
   seams, corner double

corner drills
USE   hand drills

corner enclosed basin stands
   TC.1072
HN   January 1993 descriptor moved
ALT   corner enclosed basin stand
UF   basin stands, corner enclosed
   enclosed basin stands, corner
   stands, corner enclosed basin

corner saws
USE   dovetail saws

corner shelves
   TC.911
HN   January 1993 descriptor moved
ALT   corner shelf
UF   corner stands
   shelves, corner
   stands, corner

corner stands
USE   corner shelves

corner tables
USE   handkerchief tables

corner trowels
   TH.1176
HN   December 1992 descriptor moved
ALT   corner trowel
SN   Plasterers' trowels having a V-
   shaped blade made for working cor-
   ners. (PUTNAM)
UF   trowels, corner

corner trowels, inside
USE   inside corner trowels

corner trowels, outside
USE   outside corner trowels

corners
   PJ.757

HN   April 1993 related term added
ALT   corner
SN   Use for areas of objects where converging lines or surfaces meet. For
   the adjective describing the location
   of something at or near the corner
   of something, use **corner** from the
   Attributes and Properties hierarchy.
RT   *<corners: furniture components>*

corners (cupboards)
USE   corner cupboards

corners (encoignures)
USE   encoignures

corners, canted
USE   canted corners

corners, chimney
USE   inglenooks

<corners: furniture components>
   PJ.2761
HN   April 1993 related term added
   March 1993 guide term moved
RT   corners

corners, hollow
USE   hollow corners

corners, ovolo
USE   ovolo corners

corners, sash plan
USE   ovolo corners

cornerstones
   PJ.1999   (N,B)
HN   March 1993 descriptor moved
ALT   cornerstone
SN   Stones forming part of corners or
   angles in walls, especially lying at
   the foundation of a principal angle.
   (W)
UF   pillar-stones

cornetas
USE   cornetts

cornets (aerophones)
   TT.81   (L,N)
ALT   cornet (aerophone)
SN   Valved brass instruments of me-
   dium conical bore, played with a
   cup mouthpiece. (MARCUS)
UF   cornettas
   cornopeans

cornets (headdresses)
   TE.621   (N)
ALT   cornet (headdress)
SN   Term applied to women's headdresses which vary in style from the
   14th to the 18th century, but which
   are often of conical shape and usually made of delicate materials with
   lappets of lace or ribbon.
RT   lappets

cornets (lappets)
USE   lappets

cornets, alto
USE   althorns

cornettas
USE   cornets (aerophones)

cornettos
USE   cornetts

cornetts
   TT.66   (L)
ALT   cornett
SN   European lip-vibrated aerophones
   of conical bore, consisting of a long
   wood tube, straight or gently
   curved, with fingerholes; they were
   made in three main sizes: treble,
   small treble, and tenor.
UF   cornetas
   cornettos
   zinks

cornetts, black
USE   curved cornetts

cornetts, curved
USE   curved cornetts

cornetts, mute
USE   mute cornetts

cornetts, straight
USE   straight cornetts

cornetts, straight treble
USE   straight cornetts

cornetts, white
USE   straight cornetts

cornflower blue
   MT.2093
HN   April 1992 descriptor moved
UF   blue, cornflower

cornflower blue (color)
USE   moderate purplish blue

cornflower blue, light
USE   light purplish blue
   light violet
   moderate purplish blue
   moderate violet

cornhusk dolls
   TV.162   (L)
ALT   cornhusk doll
SN   Use for folk or craft dolls of which
   the full figure or the head is hand-
   crafted from cornhusks.
UF   cornshuck dolls
   dolls, cornhusk
   dolls, cornshuck

<cornice components>
   PJ.1684
HN   March 1993 guide term moved

cornice lighting
   PC.213
HN   March 1993 descriptor moved
   April 1991 scope note added
SN   Lighting systems comprising light
   sources shielded by a panel set par-
   allel to the wall and attached to the
   ceiling to distribute light over the

wall; generally used for visual effect. (IESREF)
UF lighting, cornice

cornice planes
TH.1549   (N)
ALT cornice plane
SN General term for wide molding planes with a simple or complicated profile. (SALAM)
UF bed mold planes
cornish planes
crown mold planes
crown planes
mold planes, bed
mold planes, crown
planes, bed mold
planes, cornice
planes, cornish
planes, crown
planes, crown mold

cornices
PJ.1680   (A,L,N,B,R)
HN March 1993 descriptor moved
December 1990 lead-in term added
ALT cornice
SN The projecting, uppermost features of classical entablatures; use also for similar features crowning a wall, in any style.
UF geisons

<cornices and cornice components>
PJ.1679
HN March 1993 guide term moved

cornices, architrave
USE architrave cornices

cornices, block
USE block cornices

cornices, cavetto
USE cavetto cornices

cornices, gorge
USE cavetto cornices

cornices, open
USE open eaves

cornices, raking
USE raking cornices

cornicylls
USE pibgorns

Cornish granite
MT.638
HN April 1992 descriptor moved
UF granite, Cornish

cornish planes
USE cornice planes

cornopeans
USE cornets (aerophones)

cornshuck dolls
USE cornhusk dolls

cornstalk
MT.2660   (L)

HN March 1992 descriptor moved
UK corn-stalk

corona discharge photography
USE Kirlian photography

coronary care units
PJ.1239   (L)
HN March 1993 descriptor moved
ALT coronary care unit
UF CCUs

coronas (cornice components)
PJ.1685
HN March 1993 descriptor moved
July 1991 descriptor changed, was **coronas**
July 1991 alternate term changed, was **corona**
December 1990 scope note changed
ALT corona (cornice component)
SN Overhanging vertical members of a cornice in classical architecture, supported by bed moldings and crowned by cymatia, usually with a drip to throw rainwater clear of the building. (DAC)

coronas (lighting devices)
TC.1262
ALT corona (lighting device)

Coronation carpets
TC.95
ALT Coronation carpet
SN Term of convenience for Polonaise carpets used in the ointment ceremonies of Danish kings.
UF carpets, Coronation

coronation chairs
USE thrones

coronations
KM.27   (L,R)
HN May 1991 alternate term added
ALT coronation

Corondá
FL.1710

coronets (architectural elements)
PJ.1961
HN March 1993 descriptor moved
July 1991 scope note changed
ALT coronet (architectural element)
SN Use for ornamental features, usually in relief and triangular in form, resembling pediments and located over doors or windows.

coronets (crowns)
TE.623   (H)
ALT coronet (crown)
SN Smaller or lesser crowns usually signifying a high rank below that of a sovereign. (W)

corporal art
USE body art

corporal-cloths
SEE corporals

corporals
TC.347   (H,N)
ALT corporal
SN Linen cloths on which the consecrated elements are placed and with which the elements, or the remnants of them, are covered.
UF cloths, communion
communion cloths
corporal-cloths

corporate aircraft
USE business aircraft

corporate airplanes
USE business aircraft

corporate collections
PC.4   (A,L,R)
HN March 1993 descriptor moved
ALT corporate collection
UF collections, corporate

corporate files
USE corporation records

corporate headquarters
RK.876   (A,L)
HN May 1990 lead-in terms added
UF headquarters, corporate
home offices (corporate headquarters)
offices, home

corporate identity
USE corporate image

corporate image
BM.861   (L)
HN February 1993 descriptor added
SN The impression imparted to the public and employees by a corporation, especially as shaped by public relations programs.
UF company image
corporate identity
identity, corporate
image, company
image, corporate

corporate libraries
RK.673   (L)
ALT corporate library
UF libraries, corporate

corporate plazas
USE shopping plazas

corporation records
VW.720   (L)
HN November 1992 descriptor moved
ALT corporation record
SN Records evidencing the creation or existence of a corporate body, such as charters or articles of incorporation; also used generally to refer to records growing out of a corporate enterprise. (GAHLM)
UF corporate files
files, corporate
records, corporation

corporation reports
VW.916   (L)

HN November 1992 descriptor moved
ALT corporation report
UF annual reports of corporations
corporations, annual reports of
reports, corporation

corporations
HN.105 (L)
HN April 1993 related term added
ALT corporation
SN Groups of persons, commonly formed as business enterprises, considered in law as legal persons having an existence and rights and duties distinct from those of the individuals who form it. For unincorporated groups of persons contractually associated as joint principals in business, use **partnerships**.
UF companies, incorporated
incorporated companies
RT partnerships

corporations, annual reports of
USE corporation reports

corporations, directors of
USE boards of directors

corps
USE corsets

corps de logis
PJ.948
HN March 1993 descriptor moved
June 1990 alternate term deleted, was **corp de logis**
SN Use to designate the central portions of a building as opposed to the terminal or end pavilions or other outlying portions, especially found in French architecture or in buildings closely derived from French architecture.

corpses, exquisite
USE cadavres exquis

corrals
RK.84
ALT corral

correction, optical
USE optical correction

correctional facilities
USE correctional institutions

correctional institutions
RK.680 (A,L)
ALT correctional institution
SN Use to denote any buildings or groups of buildings in which people accused or convicted of breaking the law may be confined and which may or may not attempt some form of reform or rehabilitative correction of offenders.
UF correctional facilities
facilities, correctional
houses of correction
institutions, correctional

institutions, penal
penal institutions

correctional institutions, medium-security
USE medium-security prisons

correctional institutions, minimum-security
USE minimum-security prisons

correlation
BM.709 (L)
HN February 1992 scope note added
SN Degree to which two or more attributes or measurements on the same group of elements show a tendency to vary together. (RHDEL2)

correspondence
VW.341 (L,R)
HN November 1992 descriptor moved
November 1992 scope note changed
September 1992 related term added
SN Any forms of addressed and written communication sent and received, including letters, postcards, memorandums, notes, telegrams, or cables. (ICA)
RT correspondents (correspondence writers)

correspondence art
USE mail art

<correspondence artifacts>
VW.1109
HN January 1992 guide term added

<correspondence by function>
VW.363
HN November 1992 guide term moved

<correspondence by internal form>
VW.342
HN November 1992 guide term moved
September 1992 scope note added
September 1992 guide term changed, was *<correspondence by form>*
SN Collocates descriptors for types of correspondence that are distinguished by some aspect of their content. Other terms for physical forms that are relevant specifically to correspondence are found under *<correspondence artifacts>*.

<correspondence by method of transmission>
VW.367
HN September 1992 guide term added

correspondence, commercial
USE commercial correspondence

correspondence, legal
USE legal correspondence

correspondence, personal
USE personal correspondence

correspondence, private
USE personal correspondence

correspondents (correspondence writers)
HG.910
HN September 1992 descriptor added
ALT correspondent (correspondence writer)
correspondent's (correspondence writer)
correspondents' (correspondence writers)
SN Use for those people or organizations who communicate with others by correspondence. For people employed by a newspaper or broadcasting company to contribute regular news reports or interpretations from a location distant from the home office, use **correspondents (reporters)**.
RT correspondence
correspondents (reporters)

correspondents (reporters)
HG.482 (L)
HN January 1993 alternate terms added
September 1992 related term added
September 1992 descriptor changed, was **correspondents**
September 1992 alternate term changed, was **correspondent**
ALT correspondent (reporter)
correspondent's (reporter)
correspondents' (reporters)
SN Use for people employed by a newspaper or broadcasting company to contribute regular news reports or interpretations from a location distant from the home office. For those people or organizations who communicate with others by correspondence, use **correspondents (correspondence writers)**.
RT correspondents (correspondence writers)

correspondents, foreign
USE foreign correspondents

corridors
PJ.1028 (A,L,B)
HN March 1993 descriptor moved
ALT corridor
SN Use for passages affording entrance to the rooms of a building.
UF halls (corridors)
hallways

corrosion
KT.252 (A,L,B)
HN January 1993 descriptor moved
ALT corroded
SN The deterioration of metal or other substances by chemical or electrochemical reaction resulting from exposure to weathering, moisture, chemicals, or other agents. (DAC)

corrosion, biological
USE biodeterioration

corrosion, electrochemical
USE electrochemical corrosion

corrosion, electrolytic
USE electrochemical corrosion

corrosion, galvanic
USE electrochemical corrosion

corrosion inhibitors
HN April 1993 descriptor split, use corrosion + inhibitor

corrosive material
MT.3085
HN April 1993 descriptor changed, was corrosive materials
UF material, corrosive

corrugated board
MT.1447 (L)
HN February 1992 descriptor moved
July 1990 descriptor added
SN Cardboard consisting of a sheet of corrugated paper with an adherent flat board on one or both sides. (W)
UF board, corrugated
cardboard, corrugated
corrugated cardboard
corrugated paperboard
paperboard, corrugated

corrugated cardboard
USE corrugated board

corrugated, Mimbres
USE Mimbres corrugated

corrugated paper
HN May 1992 descriptor split, use corrugated (ALT of corrugating) + paper

corrugated paperboard
USE corrugated board

corrugating
KT.316 (A,L)
HN May 1992 descriptor added
ALT corrugated
SN Drawing or bending into folds or alternate furrows and ridges. (RHDEL2)
UF corrugation

corrugation
USE corrugating

cors anglais
USE English horns

cors de chasse
USE hunting horns

cors omnitoniques
USE omnitonic horns

cors, tenor
USE mellophones

corsages (costume accessories)
TE.429 (L,N)
ALT corsage (costume accessory)
SN Arrangements of flowers to be worn as costume accessories, as on the bodice or at the wrist. (W)

corsages (costume components)
PJ.3038
ALT corsage (costume component)
SN Term used in the 18th and 19th centuries for a woman's bodice or upper portion of a dress or garment.

corselets
TE.202
ALT corselet
SN One-piece garments combining a brassiere and a corset or girdle.
UF controlettes
corsets, foundation
corsets, one-piece
foundation corsets
one-piece corsets
RT brassieres
corsets
girdles (underwear)

corselets (half armor)
USE corslets

corsescas
TK.37
ALT corsesca
SN Staff weapons having a three-pronged head with a central triangular double-edged blade, often with a strong medial ridge, with two shorter blades radiating from its base or curving up like the prongs of a trident. They were used from the 15th to the 17th century, mainly in France and Italy.
UF chauve-souris

corset covers
TE.219 (N)
ALT corset cover
SN Underbodices worn over a corset with sleeves or built-up straps.
UF covers, corset

corset waists
USE waists

corsets
TE.203 (H,L,N)
ALT corset
SN Smoothly fitted undergarments extending from or below the bust down to waist or below; stiffened by strips of steel or whalebone, or with casing for busk; sometimes limbered by elastic goring; sometimes tightened by lacing, and fastened by hooks. Worn by women for support and molding of figure including ribcage and possibly hips. (NMAHDC)
UF corps
RT basquines
bust forms
corselets

corsets, foundation
USE corselets

corsets, one-piece
USE corselets

corsets, pantee
USE panty girdles

Corsican pine
MT.2963 (L)
HN March 1992 descriptor moved
UF pine, Corsican

corslets
PC.33 (H)
ALT corslet
SN Light half armor worn by heavy infantry from the early 16th to the mid-17th century in Europe, at first comprised of a gorget, spaudlers, breastplate, backplate, tassets, vambraces, gauntlets, and an open helmet, but no legharness. In the 17th century, arm defenses were usually omitted. (TARA)
UF corslets (half armor)

corslets, bell
USE bell corslets

corslets, bell-shaped
USE bell corslets

corthols
USE dulcians

cortili
USE courtyards

corundum
MT.535 (L)
HN April 1992 descriptor moved
February 1992 lead-in term added
February 1992 related term added
SN A very hard crystalline mineral made of aluminum oxide, used chiefly as an abrasive. (MH)
UF aluminum oxide
oxide, aluminum
RT gemstone

corvettes
USE sloops (warships)

cosies, tea
SEE tea cozies

Cosmati work
KT.128
HN January 1993 descriptor moved
SN A type of decoration in mosaic and marble inlay, found especially in Rome from the 12th to the 14th centuries. (THDAT)

cosmetics
TH.378 (H,L,R)
HN January 1993 descriptor added
ALT cosmetic
SN Powders, lotion, lipstick, rouge, or other preparations to be applied to the human body for the beautifying, preserving, or altering the appearance of a person. (W)
RT compacts

cosmographers
HG.536
HN January 1993 descriptor added
ALT cosmographer
cosmographer's
cosmographers'

SN Scientists trained or working in the field of cosmography.
RT cosmography

cosmography
KD.173 (L)
HN February 1993 related term added
January 1993 descriptor moved
January 1993 scope note changed
SN Term originating in the 16th century for the general science that describes and maps the overall features of the universe, both the heavens and the earth, encompassing what is now considered to fall within astronomy, geography, and geology.
RT cosmographers

cosmology
KD.79 (L,R)
SN Branch of systematic philosophy that deals with the character of the universe as a cosmos, combining speculative metaphysics and scientific knowledge. (W)

cossies
SEE bathing suits

cost accounting
KG.243 (L,B)
HN January 1991 scope note added
SN Accounting that deals with systematically classifying, recording, analyzing, and summarizing the costs incident to production or the rendering of a service. (W)
UF accounting, cost

cost analysis
USE cost benefit analysis

cost benefit analysis
KG.6 (A,L,B)
SN Systematic, quantitative appraisal of a project to determine whether its benefits justify its costs. (MHDME)
UF analysis, cost benefit
cost analysis
engineering, value
value analysis
value engineering

cost containment
USE cost control

cost control
KG.91 (L,B)
SN Using corrective measures through management and interpretation of cost benefit analyses to increase efficiency and economy of operation. (W)
UF containment, cost
control, cost
cost containment
cost reduction
reduction, cost

cost estimates
USE estimates

cost plus contracts
USE cost plus fee agreements

cost plus fee agreements
VW.629
HN November 1992 descriptor moved
ALT cost plus fee agreement
SN Agreements or contracts under which the contractor or the architect is reimbursed for the direct and indirect costs of performance of the agreement and in addition is paid a fee for services. (GCIT)
UF agreements, cost plus fee
contracts, cost plus fee
cost plus contracts
cost plus fee contracts

cost plus fee contracts
USE cost plus fee agreements

cost reduction
USE cost control

cost reimbursement contracts
VW.630
HN November 1992 descriptor moved
ALT cost reimbursement contract
UF contracts, cost reimbursement

Costanoan
FL.1265 (L)

costrels
USE pilgrim bottles

costruzione legittima
USE linear perspective

costs
BM.870 (L,B)
HN February 1993 descriptor moved
January 1991 alternate term added
ALT cost
SN Amount paid, given, or charged, or engaged to be paid or given, for anything bought or taken in barter or for service rendered. (W)

costume
TE.1 (H,L,N,B,R)
SN Artifacts worn or carried for warmth, protection, embellishment, or symbolic purposes.
UF clothes
clothing
garments
RT <costume components>

<costume accessories>
TE.407
RT trousseaux

<costume accessories carried>
TE.408
RT attaché cases
briefcases
crops
fans
knapsacks
riding whips
umbrellas
walking sticks

<costume accessories worn>
TE.428
RT aprons (costume)
pinafores
shawls
stoles (outerwear)

costume, afternoon
USE afternoon dress

<costume by form>
TE.2

<costume by function>
TE.237

costume, church
USE vestments

<costume components>
PJ.2999
RT bibs
bodices
buckles
buttons (fasteners)
clasps (fasteners)
collars (neckwear)
costume
cuffs (costume accessories)
hoods (headgear)
hooks and eyes
insoles
plumes
shoulder pads
skirts
sleeves
snaps
veils
visors

costume design
KD.28 (L)
HN April 1993 related term added
March 1991 descriptor moved
SN Designing clothing, accessories, and ensembles intended to create an appearance characteristic of a particular period, person, place, or thing, especially (but not exclusively) for theatrical performances. For the design of clothing and accessories for personal wear, use **fashion design**.
UF design, costume
design, dress
dress design
RT fashion design

costume designers
HG.320 (L)
HN February 1993 descriptor moved
December 1992 alternate terms added
ALT costume designer
costume designer's
costume designers'
SN Persons engaged in costume design.
UF costumers, theatrical
designers, costume
designers, dress
dress designers
theatrical costumers

costume dolls
VC.575 (L)
ALT costume doll
SN Use for dolls outfitted in traditional national or ethnic dress.
UF dolls, costume

costume, ecclesiastical
USE vestments

<costume groupings>
PC.29
RT suits

costume jewelry
TE.497 (L)
SN Jewelry for wear with current fashions usually made of inexpensive materials (metals, shells, plastic, wood) often set with imitation or semiprecious stones. (W)
UF jewelry, costume

costume museums
HN March 1993 descriptor split, use
costume + museums

costumers (furniture)
TC.1048
HN January 1993 descriptor moved
September 1991 descriptor changed, was costumers
September 1991 alternate term changed, was costumer
ALT costumer (furniture)

costumers (people)
HG.209
HN November 1992 alternate terms added
ALT costumer (person)
costumer's
costumers'
SN Persons who make, sell, or rent costumes, as for stage or fancy dress events. (W)

costumers, theatrical
USE costume designers

costumes, ski
USE ski suits

cot bedsteads
USE cots

cotes
USE cottages

cotes, bell
USE bell cotes

cothurni
TE.710
ALT cothurnus
SN Thick-soled laced boots reaching halfway to the knees worn by actors in Greek and Roman tragic drama. (W)
UF buskins (boots)
cothurns

cothurns
USE cothurni

cots
TC.770
HN May 1993 related term added
January 1993 descriptor moved
ALT cot
SN Light beds, often collapsible and typically used for camping or by a child; generally made of canvas stretched on a frame. (W)
UF bedsteads, cot
cot bedsteads
RT camp furniture

cottage courts
USE motor courts

cottage curtains
TC.307
ALT cottage curtain
SN A combination of café curtains across the lower part of an opening and tieback curtains, usually ruffled, across the top.
UF curtains, cottage
RT café curtains
tieback curtains

cottage hospitals
RK.725 (B)
ALT cottage hospital
SN Use for health care facilities which, by their design, layout, or plan, are made to resemble cottages or a group of cottages rather than elaborate public buildings.
UF hospitals, cottage

cottage industries
HN.115 (L)
ALT cottage industry
SN Use for industries carried on in the home by a self-employed worker and his/her family, often with the aid of a few apprentices.
UF industries, cottage
industries, village
village industries

cottage latches
PJ.477
HN April 1993 descriptor moved
ALT cottage latch
UF latches, cottage

cottage roofs
USE single-framed roofs

Cottage Style
FL.1768
SN Mid-19th-century furniture style, characterized by simplicity of design with natural woods, unpolished or painted in pale colors. (IDO)

cottages
RK.232 (A,L,N,B,R)
ALT cottage
UF cotes

cottages, Creole
USE Creole cottages

cottages, elder
USE ECHO houses

cottages ornés
RK.233 (A,B)
ALT cottage orné
SN Use for certain picturesque, small rustic houses, primarily of the late 18th and early 19th centuries in England, with an asymmetrical plan and wood siding.
UF fermes ornées

cottages, summer
USE summer houses

cottanello
MT.748
HN April 1992 descriptor moved

cottas
TE.255 (N)
ALT cotta
SN Short-sleeved, waist-length version of the surplice with a square-cut yoke at the neck. (LITG)

cotter pin hinges
PJ.384
HN April 1993 descriptor moved
March 1993 alternate term added
ALT cotter pin hinge
UF hinges, cotter pin
hinges, snipe
hinges, snipe-bill
snipe-bill hinges
snipe hinges

cotter pins
PJ.216 (N)
HN April 1993 descriptor moved
ALT cotter pin
SN Half-round metal strips bent into a pinlike shape whose ends can be flared after insertion through a slot or hole. (W)
UF kotter pins
pins, cotter
pins, kotter

cotton (fiber)
MT.1386
HN April 1993 related term added
April 1993 descriptor changed, was cotton fiber
August 1992 lead-in term changed, was cotton (fiber)
February 1992 descriptor moved
July 1990 descriptor added
UK cotton fibre
SN White-to-yellowish fiber of the calyx, or blossom, of several species of plant of the genus Gossypium of the mallow family; used especially for making textile, cord, and padding, and for producing cellulose for plastic and rayon. (MH12)
UF cotton fiber
fiber, cotton
fibre, cotton
RT cotton (textile)

cotton (textile)
MT.1518   (H,L,R)
HN April 1993 related term added
April 1993 descriptor changed, was **cotton**
March 1993 scope note changed
March 1993 descriptor moved
May 1991 scope note changed
SN Textile made from cotton fiber.
RT cotton (fiber)

cotton carpets
USE dhurries

cotton cloths, Indian
USE dhurries

cotton fiber
USE cotton (fiber)

cotton fibre
SEE cotton (fiber)

cotton gum
USE tupelo

cotton, java
USE kapok

cotton linter
USE linter

cotton mills
RK.628   (L)
ALT cotton mill
UF mills, cotton

cotton, padding
USE batting

cotton rag board, 100%
USE museum board

cotton-seed oil
SEE cottonseed oil

cotton, silk
USE kapok

cottons, lamp
USE wicks

cottonseed oil
MT.1073   (L)
HN August 1992 lead-in term added
April 1992 descriptor moved
October 1990 descriptor moved
UK cotton-seed oil
UF oil, cotton-seed
oil, cottonseed

cottonwood
MT.2866   (L)
HN March 1992 descriptor moved

cottonwood, black
USE black cottonwood

cottonwood, eastern
USE eastern cottonwood

Cotzumalhuapa
FL.1051

couch beds
TC.813

HN May 1993 related term added
January 1993 descriptor moved
ALT couch bed
SN Term used by Chippendale for double-headed couches with a canopy. (GILBR2)
UF beds, couch
RT beds (furniture)

couch grass
MT.2624   (L)
HN March 1992 descriptor moved
February 1991 lead-in terms added
February 1991 descriptor changed, was **cutch-grass**
UF cutch-grass
grass, quitch
quack grass
quitch grass

couches
TC.811   (N)
HN May 1993 related term added
January 1993 descriptor moved
ALT couch
SN Long seating forms with a back support and one end; primarily used for reclining rather than sitting. Distinct from **sofas** which have a back and two ends and are primarily used for sitting rather than reclining.
UF lounges (couches)
RT sofas

couches (sofas)
USE sofas

couches à l'antique
USE lits à l'antique

couches, Grecian
USE Grecian couches

couching (embroidering)
KT.1225
HN March 1993 alternate term changed, was **couched**
March 1993 descriptor changed, was **couching (embroidery)**
March 1993 descriptor moved
May 1991 descriptor changed, was **couching**
ALT couched (embroidering)
SN Embroidering a design by laying down a thread and fastening it with small stitches at regular intervals. (W)

couching (papermaking)
KT.1153
HN March 1993 alternate term changed, was **couched**
ALT couched (papermaking)
SN Use for the pressing of a wet sheet of newly made paper still on the mold onto a felt.

coudes
USE cowters

Coula
USE Kula

coulées
SEE coulees

coulees
RD.161   (L)
ALT coulee
UK coulées
UKA coulée

coulisses
BM.57
HN January 1991 alternate term added
ALT coulisse
SN Elements in a pictorial composition like side-pieces in a stage set that lead the eye step-by-step back into depth.

council housing
USE public housing

counseling
KG.48   (L)
UK counselling
SN Providing professional assistance to people in making decisions and coping with adjustment problems.
UF advising

counselling
SEE counseling

counsellors
SEE counselors

counselors
HG.489
HN December 1992 alternate terms added
ALT counselor
counselor's
counselors'
UK counsellors
UKA counsellor
SN Persons whose profession is counseling.

counselors, investment
USE investment advisors

counter apses
PJ.1200
HN March 1993 descriptor moved
ALT counter apse
SN Use for apses opposite other apses.
UF apses, counter

counter arches
PJ.1628
HN March 1993 descriptor moved
ALT counter arch
SN Use for arches that counteract the thrust of another arch.
UF arches, counter

counter boards
USE counters

counter culture
USE radicalism

counter-enameling
KT.99

HN March 1993 descriptor moved
March 1991 alternate term added
ALT counter-enameled
UK counter-enamelling
UKA counter-enamelled
SN A technique invented in the late 15th century in which both sides of an object are covered with enamel of the same thickness, which prevents the object from curling. (THDAT)

counter-enamelling
SEE counter-enameling

counter-proofs
SEE counterproofs

Counter-Reformation
FL.3260   (L,R)
UF Catholic Reformation

counter scales, platform
USE platform scales

counter stools
TC.691
HN January 1993 descriptor moved
ALT counter stool
SN High stools that are usually one of a row of such stools fixed in front of a counter; often backless and having a revolving seat.
UF lunch counter stools
lunch stools
stools, counter
stools, lunch
stools, lunch counter

counter tables
USE counters

counterbores
TH.596   (N)
ALT counterbore
SN Drills used to enlarge holes for the reception of a bolt or nut.

counterchange
DG.117
SN Interlocking patterns of similar shapes with alternating colors or tones; both figures and ground may be read as coherent patterns.
UF counterchange patterns
patterns, counterchange

counterchange patterns
USE counterchange

counterfeiters
HG.913   (L)
HN December 1992 alternate terms added
ALT counterfeiter
counterfeiter's
counterfeiters'

counterfeits
PE.21   (L)
HN January 1993 descriptor moved
ALT counterfeit
SN Use for reproductions of whole objects when the intention is to de-

ceive; includes sculptures cast without the artist's permission.

counterflashing
PJ.2133
HN March 1993 descriptor moved
December 1990 descriptor changed, was **counter flashing**
SN Strips of sheet metal, often built into masonry and turned down over other flashing; used to prevent water from entering the joints and exposed upturned edges of base flashing on a roof. (DAC)
UF cap flashing
cover flashing
flashing, cap
flashing, counter
flashing, cover

counterfoils
USE check stubs

countermarks
VW.417   (L)
HN November 1992 descriptor moved
January 1991 descriptor added
ALT countermark
SN Additional marks added to something to substantiate or supersede the information given by the first marks, as a second watermark on paper, a second hallmark on gold or silver, or a mark added to a coin after issue to denote a change of value.
UF counterstamps

countermine galleries
USE countermines

countermines
PJ.2499
HN March 1993 descriptor moved
April 1990 descriptor added
ALT countermine
SN Designates horizontal tunnels constructed in order to listen for and intercept and destroy attackers' undermining efforts.
UF countermine galleries
galleries, countermine

counterpanes
TC.205   (N)
ALT counterpane
SN Term formerly used for a variety of bedcovers, especially those woven of cotton or wool; from the mid-19th century onwards generally replaced by the term **bedspreads**.
UF counterpoints
RT bedspreads

counterpoints
USE counterpanes

counterpoises
PJ.2636
ALT counterpoise
SN Use for the compensating or counterbalancing weights on scales.

counterproofs
PE.17   (R)
HN February 1991 descriptor added
ALT counterproof
UK counter-proofs
UKA counter-proof
SN Impressions taken from a print or drawing by pressing it against a sheet of damp paper; the image appears in reverse. For images or marks that result from an unintentional transfer of ink or other medium, use **offsets**.

counterpunches
TH.1212
ALT counterpunch
SN Supports beneath metal being hammered or punched from above. (W)

counters
TC.912   (N)
HN May 1993 scope note changed
May 1993 related term added
January 1993 descriptor moved
ALT counter
SN Originally small tables or chests with the top marked for counting money, sometimes with a cupboard below. Term later applied to cases or shelflike surfaces usually of a height convenient for a person standing before them, as in a kitchen or store, or sitting on stools in front of them, as in a restaurant or bar.
UF boards, counter
counter boards
counter tables
tables, counter
RT built-in furniture

counters (tokens)
USE jettons

counters, gaming
USE gaming counters

counters, Geiger
USE Geiger counters

counters, Geiger-Müller
USE Geiger counters

counters, reckoning
USE jettons

counterscarps
PJ.2500
HN March 1993 descriptor moved
ALT counterscarp
SN Use for the outer slopes of encircling defensive ditches; for the inner slopes, use **scarps**.

countersink bits
PJ.2580   (N)
HN March 1993 descriptor moved
ALT countersink bit
SN Bits used to cut a conical depression for recessing the head of a bolt, nut, or screw, so that it is flush with the surface.
UF bits, countersink

countersinks
TH.1072 (N)
ALT countersink
SN Hand tools that usually take the form of a triangular blade at the end of a shaft; used to make conical depressions for recessing the head of a bolt, nut, or screw so that it is flush with the surface.
UF bob punches
punches, bob

counterstamps
USE countermarks

countervaults
USE inverted arches

counterweights
PJ.9 (N)
HN March 1993 descriptor moved
ALT counterweight

counterweights, sash
USE sash weights

counties
HN.18
HN February 1993 descriptor moved
ALT county

counting
KT.179 (L)
HN November 1992 descriptor added

counting coins
USE jettons

counting desks
USE counting-house desks

counting-house bookcases
TC.827
HN January 1993 descriptor moved
ALT counting-house bookcase
SN Term used in the late 18th and early 19th centuries for relatively small and narrow bookcases, generally 3 feet wide and 3 feet high.
UF bookcases, counting-house

counting-house chairs
USE tall chairs

counting-house desks
TC.938
HN January 1993 descriptor moved
ALT counting-house desk
SN 18th-century term for desks on frames set on high legs.
UF counting desks
counting-house desks, single
desks, counting
desks, counting-house
desks, single counting-house
single counting-house desks

counting-house desks, double
USE double counting-house desks

counting-house desks, single
USE counting-house desks

countries
USE nations

country clubs
RG.174 (A,L,B)
HN November 1991 descriptor moved
ALT country club
UF clubs, country

country elevators
USE grain elevators

country homes
USE country houses

country houses
RK.291 (A,L,B,R)
ALT country house
UF country homes
country residences
country seats
estates (country houses)
homes, country
houses, country
residences, country
seats, country

country maps
USE national maps

country of origin marks
VW.425
HN November 1992 descriptor moved
ALT country of origin mark
UF marks, country of origin

country planning
USE rural planning

country printers
USE job printers

country residences
USE country houses

country seats
USE country houses

country stores
USE general stores

countships
HN.40
HN January 1993 descriptor added
ALT countship
SN Administrative bodies subject to a count or countess.

county atlases
HN April 1993 descriptor split, use county (ALT of counties) + atlases

county courthouses
RK.935 (L,B)
HN March 1993 related term added
September 1990 scope note added
ALT county courthouse
UK county courts
UKA county court
SN Use for public buildings in the United States that house county-level judicial and administrative facilities; for structures that house similar functions in the United Kingdom, use **county halls.**

UF courthouses, county
courts, county
RT county halls

county courts
SEE county courthouses

county directories
HN March 1991 descriptor split, use county (ALT of counties) + directories

county government records
VW.783 (L)
HN November 1992 descriptor moved
March 1991 descriptor moved
ALT county government record
UF records, county government

county halls
RK.952 (A,B)
HN March 1993 related term added
September 1990 scope note added
ALT county hall
SN Use for public buildings in the United Kingdom that house various county functions, often comprising a large hall for public meetings and rooms for county courts and administration; for structures housing similar judicial functions in the United States, use **county courthouses.**
UF halls, county
RT county courthouses

county maps
HN July 1991 descriptor split, use county (ALT of counties) + maps

county museums
RK.398
ALT county museum
UF museums, county

county seats
RD.26
ALT county seat
UF seats, county

coupés (carriages)
TX.170
ALT coupé (carriage)
SN Use for reduced-size coaches, generally having curved fronts, designed for compactness or to improve appearance yet retaining the elegance of the original, larger enclosed vehicles. For smaller, low-hung coaches, built generally with straight fronts and not based on larger prototypes, especially in the United States in the late 19th century, use **broughams.**
RT broughams

coupes (champagne glasses)
USE champagne glasses

coupes (dessert dishes)
TQ.352
ALT coupe (dessert dish)
SN Footed dessert dishes having a wide but shallow bowl.

coupettes
TQ.353
ALT coupette
SN Small coupes.

couple roofs
PJ.1792
HN March 1993 descriptor moved
ALT couple roof
SN Use for roofs without tie or collar beams, and depending on walls to resist thrust.
UF roofs, couple

coupled-column rugs
TC.73
ALT coupled-column rug
SN Use for prayer rugs with a columnar motif on either side of the mirhab.
UF columnar prayer rugs
rugs, columnar prayer
rugs, coupled-column
rugs, Tintoretto
Tintoretto rugs

coupled columns
PJ.1473
HN March 1993 descriptor moved
December 1990 scope note changed
December 1990 lead-in terms added
ALT coupled column
SN Use for groups of two columns set closer together than others in a line, or otherwise forming a visual unit; for columns with interpenetrating shafts, use **doubled columns**.
UF columns, coupled
columns, paired
paired columns

coupled windows
PJ.2228
HN March 1993 descriptor moved
January 1991 lead-in terms added
ALT coupled window
SN Two closely spaced windows which form a pair. (DAC)
UF gemel windows
paired windows
twin-lights
two-lights
windows, coupled
windows, gemel
windows, paired

coupler prints, color
USE chromogenic color prints

coupler prints, dye
USE chromogenic color prints

coupons
VK.1   (L,N)
ALT coupon
SN Use for slips or sections of paper redeemable for specifically named articles, services, or funds and often attached as a group in book form or incorporated individually within larger printed matter.

courants
USE corantos

Couri
FL.1119

courie shell
USE cowrie shell

cours d'honneur
USE forecourts

course, damp
USE damp course

course, damp-proof
SEE damp course

course, dampproof
USE damp course

course lights
RM.222
HN April 1993 descriptor moved
May 1990 descriptor added
ALT course light
SN Aeronautical ground lights supplementing an airway beacon, used to indicate the direction of the airway and to identify by coded signal the location of the airway beacon with which it is associated. (STEIN)
UF lights, course

<course sports>
KQ.49
RT sports

courses
PJ.1944
HN March 1993 descriptor moved
October 1992 related term added
ALT course
SN Layers of masonry units running horizontally in a wall or, much less commonly, curved over an arch. (HAS)
RT layers

courses, belt
USE stringcourses

courses, bond
USE bond courses

courses, chain
USE chain courses

courses, corbel
USE corbel tables

courses, dogtooth
USE dogtooth courses

courses, golf
USE golf courses

courses, lacing
USE lacing courses

courses, lintel
USE lintel courses

courses, melody
USE melody strings

courses, obstacle
USE obstacle courses

courses, oversailing
USE oversailing courses

courses, plinth
USE plinth courses

courses, putt-putt
USE miniature golf courses

courses, sill
USE sill courses

courses, Tom Thumb
USE miniature golf courses

courses, vaulting
USE vaulting courses

court art
BM.182   (R)
SN Includes both art created by court artists and art produced for a royal court.
UF art, court

<court ball games>
KQ.53

court calendars
USE dockets

court carpets
TC.159
ALT court carpet
SN Rugs of any design made by commission on royal or court looms, such as Moghul, Ottoman, or Safavid.
UF carpets, court

court chapels
USE royal chapels

court cupboards
TC.919
HN May 1993 related term added
January 1993 descriptor moved
ALT court cupboard
SN Large but fairly low cupboards with an enclosed storage cabinet above and an open shelf or shelves below; a type made in 16th- and 17th-century England and 17th-century America. Distinct from **press cupboards** which have both the upper and lower sections enclosed.
UF cupboards, court
cupboards, plate
plate cupboards
RT press cupboards

court decisions
USE decisions

<court games>
KQ.52
RT courts (built works)
games

court records
USE judicial records

court reporters
USE law reporters

court rolls
USE judicial records

court-rooms
SEE courtrooms

court shoes
SEE pumps (shoes)

court style
    BM.240
SN Official or approved style, as of art, architecture, or costume, established at a ruler's court.
UF palace style (court style)
    style, court
    style, palace

Court Style, Kuba
USE Kuba Court Style

court-swords
SEE court swords

court swords
    TK.93   (N)
ALT court sword
UK court-swords
UKA court-sword
SN Light swords, usually of the small-sword type, worn as part of a man's court dress.
UF swords, court

court-yards
SEE courtyards

courtesans
    HG.104   (H,L)
HN January 1993 descriptor added
ALT courtesan
    courtesan's
    courtesans'
SN Prostitutes who draw their clientele from a court or from the upper classes, and whose services often include social entertaining as well as sexual activity.

courtesy books
    VW.452
HN June 1992 descriptor added
ALT courtesy book
SN Use for books outlining the education, conduct, duties, and training of noble or royal persons, or persons serving at court. (RBGENR)
UF books, courtesy
    books of courtesy
    courtesy, books of

courtesy, books of
USE courtesy books

courthols
USE dulcians

courthouses
    RK.934   (A,L,N,B,R)
ALT courthouse
SN Use to designate buildings which contain rooms for courts of law and often judges' chambers and other offices.

UF courts, law
    law courts

courthouses, county
USE county courthouses

courtiers
    HG.173   (L,R)
HN December 1992 alternate terms added
ALT courtier
    courtier's
    courtiers'
SN Persons who frequent the court of a sovereign or are attendants at court. (OED)

courting chairs
USE love seats

courting flutes
    TT.26
ALT courting flute
SN Native American duct flutes traditionally made of wood or cane. The bore is divided in to two chambers and a plate and block are laid over two holes in the bore. The airstream vibrates as it passes under the block, is divided by the plate, and part of it enters the lower chamber. Its traditional use was as a man's solo courting instrument.
UF flutes, courting

courtroom art
USE courtroom illustrations

courtroom illustrations
    PJ.3426   (L)
HN March 1993 descriptor moved
ALT courtroom illustration
UF courtroom art
    illustrations, courtroom

courtrooms
    PJ.1001
HN March 1993 descriptor moved
ALT courtroom
UK court-rooms
UKA court-room

courts (built works)
    RK.963   (A,L,B,R)
HN March 1993 descriptor changed, was **courts**
    March 1993 alternate term changed, was **court**
    March 1993 related term added
ALT court (built work)
SN Quadrangular spaces either walled or otherwise marked off for playing one of various games usually with a ball. (W)
RT <court games>

courts (courtyards)
USE courtyards

courts (social groups)
    HG.7   (H,L)
HN January 1993 descriptor added
ALT court (social group)

SN The collective body of courtiers, family members, counselors, officers, and attendants constituting the retinue of a sovereign or high dignitary.

courts, auto
USE motor courts

courts, badminton
USE badminton + courts (built works)

courts, ball
USE ball courts

courts, basketball
USE basketball + courts (built works)

courts, cottage
USE motor courts

courts, county
SEE county courthouses

courts, croquet
USE croquet + courts (built works)

courts, district
USE district courts

courts, fives
USE fives + courts (built works)

courts, handball
USE handball courts

courts, indoor tennis
USE indoor tennis courts

courts, jai alai
USE canchas

courts, law
USE courthouses

courts, lawn tennis
USE tennis + courts (built works)

courts, light
USE light courts

courts, motor
USE motor courts

courts, pelota
USE canchas

courts, racquetball
USE racquetball + courts (built works)

courts, shuffleboard
USE shuffleboard + courts (built works)

courts, squash
USE squash courts

courts, squash racquet
USE squash courts

courts, tennis
USE tennis + courts (built works)

courts, tourist
USE motor courts

courts, trailer
USE trailer camps

courts, volleyball
USE volleyball + courts (built works)

courtyard houses
    RK.257   (A,L,B)
ALT courtyard house
SN   Houses with internal courtyards of
     any configuration or design. For
     houses with internal courtyards hav-
     ing impluvia but no colonnades, use
     atrium houses; for houses with in-
     ternal courtyards with colonnades,
     use **peristyle houses.**
UF   houses, courtyard
     houses, patio
     patio houses

courtyards
    PJ.976   (A,L,B,R)
HN   March 1993 descriptor moved
     June 1990 lead-in term deleted,
         was **cortiles**
ALT courtyard
UK   court-yards
UKA court-yard
SN   Use for uncovered areas, sur-
     rounded or partially surrounded by
     the walls of a building.
UF   cortili
     courts (courtyards)

couteaux-de-chasse
USE cuttoes

couters
SEE cowters

couturiers
USE fashion designers

cove ceilings
    PJ.2058
HN   March 1993 descriptor moved
     July 1991 scope note changed
ALT cove ceiling
SN   Designates ceilings having a large
     concave curve at the wall-to-ceiling
     transition instead of a sharp angle
     intersection. (CHAMBD)
UF   ceilings, cove

cove lighting
    PC.214
HN   March 1993 descriptor moved
     April 1991 scope note changed
SN   Indirect lighting systems comprising
     light sources shielded by vertical or
     horizontal   ledges   or   recesses
     attached to walls and distributing
     light over the ceiling and upper and
     side walls. (STEIN)
UF   lighting, cove

cove molding planes
USE cove planes

cove moldings
USE cavetto moldings

cove planes
    TH.1542
ALT cove plane
SN   Planes whose blades cut a quarter of

a circle, or a cove; used for cutting
the under edge of a table leaf or to
produce   decorative   moldings.
(HUMMEL)
UF   cove molding planes
     molding planes, cove
     planes, cove
     planes, cove molding

coved vaults
USE cloister vaults

covenants
    BM.911   (L,B)
HN   February 1993 descriptor moved
     January 1991 alternate term added
ALT covenant
SN   Promises or undertakings of legal
     validity embodied in a contract un-
     der seal; also particular agreements
     contained in a deed or contract un-
     der seal which are incidental to the
     main purpose of the document. (W)

covenants, restrictive
USE restrictive covenants

cover fabric (upholstery components)
USE top covers (upholstery components)

cover fillets
USE cover moldings

cover flashing
USE counterflashing

cover lifters
USE stove lifters

cover linen
USE undercovers

cover moldings
    PJ.745
HN   April 1993 descriptor moved
     April 1991 scope note added
ALT cover molding
SN   Use for wooden strips, plain or
     molded, that cover joints, as in pan-
     eling.
UF   cover fillets
     cover strips
     fillets, cover
     moldings, cover
     strips, cover

cover strips
USE cover moldings

cover tile
    MT.177
HN   April 1992 descriptor moved
UF   covering tile
     tile, cover
     tile, covering

cover towels
USE show towels

coveralls
    TE.375   (N)
UK   boiler suits
UKA boiler suit
SN   One-piece garments consisting of a

trouserlike portion and a full top
with or without sleeves worn over
other garments for protection. For
one-piece garments consisting of
trousers with a bib use **overalls.**
UF   overalls (boiler suits)
     suits, boiler
RT   overalls (main garments)
     trousers

covered bowls
    TQ.67
ALT covered bowl
UF   bowls, covered

covered bridges
    RK.1217   (A,H,L,N,B)
ALT covered bridge
UF   bridges, covered

covered cups
    TQ.398
ALT covered cup
UF   cups, covered

covered hopper cars
    TX.253
ALT covered hopper car
SN   Hopper cars with a permanent roof,
     roof hatches, and bottom openings
     for unloading bulk commodities.
UF   cars, covered hopper
     hopper cars, covered

covered joints
    PJ.628
HN   April 1993 descriptor moved
ALT covered joint
UF   joints, covered
     joints, shiplap
     shiplap joints

‹covered wagons›
    TX.110

covered walkways
    RM.180   (A,B)
HN   April 1993 descriptor moved
ALT covered walkway
UF   covered ways (covered walkways)
     walkways, covered
     ways, covered

covered ways
    PJ.2501
HN   March 1993 descriptor moved
     March 1993 descriptor changed,
         was **covered ways (fortification el-
         ements)**
     March 1993 alternate term changed,
         was **covered way (fortification el-
         ement)**
ALT covered way
SN   Corridors running along the tops of
     counterscarps and protected by em-
     bankments whose outer slopes form
     glacis. (W)
UF   covert-ways
     ways, covered

covered ways (covered walkways)
USE covered walkways

covering canvas
USE undercovers

covering power
DC.239
SN The ability of a paint or varnish to cover a surface in one coat.
UF power, covering

covering tile
USE cover tile

coverings
TC.5
ALT covering
SN Artifacts, usually flexible, often textiles, used to cover or conceal interior spaces, surfaces, or furnishings, especially for protection, warmth, or embellishment.

<coverings and hangings>
TC.3

<coverings and hangings by form>
TC.8

<coverings and hangings by function>
TC.165

<coverings and hangings by general type>
TC.4

<coverings and hangings by location or context>
TC.176
RT covers (overlying objects)

<coverings and hangings by specific type>
TC.7

<coverings and hangings components>
PJ.2672

<coverings and hangings for containers>
TC.177
RT containers

<coverings and hangings for documents>
TC.186

<coverings and hangings for furniture>
TC.189
RT furniture

<coverings and hangings for musical instruments>
TC.295

<coverings and hangings for openings>
TC.297
RT engsis

<coverings and hangings for religious building fixtures>
TC.344
RT *<religious building fixtures>*

<coverings and hangings for seating furniture>
TC.190

<coverings and hangings for sleeping and reclining furniture>
TC.194

<coverings and hangings for storage and support furniture>
TC.274
RT coasters (containers)

<coverings and hangings for surface elements>
TC.360
RT *<surface elements>*

coverings, bed
USE bed coverings

coverings, floor
USE floor coverings

<coverings for food>
TC.166

<coverings for gathered matter>
PJ.3372
SN Collocates descriptors for detachable, flexible coverings for books. For the outer constituent parts of gathered matter, whether attached or simply the front surface designed separately from the body of the document, use covers (gathered matter components) or, for example, pamphlet (ALT of pamphlets) + covers (gathered matter components).

<coverings for liturgical vessels>
TC.180

<coverings for soft furnishings>
TC.290

coverings, wall
USE wall coverings

coverlets
TC.206   (H,L,N)
ALT coverlet
SN Woven bedcovers, especially those made of a single piece of fabric, usually of wool and cotton.
UF coverlids
overblankets

coverlets, Bolton
USE Bolton coverlets

coverlets, boutonné
USE boutonné coverlets

coverlets, rag
USE rag coverlets

coverlids
USE coverlets

covers (closures)
PJ.3092
ALT cover (closure)

covers (gathered matter components)
PJ.3375   (H,L)
ALT cover (gathered matter component)
SN Use for outer sheets or boards that are part of, or are attached to, groups of leaves, whether a substantial block or a single gathering; sometimes simply the first page of a document, as for example of a

leaflet, if it is designed as distinct from the body of the document.

covers (lock components)
USE caps (lock components)

covers (overlying objects)
PE.71
HN May 1993 descriptor added
ALT cover (overlying object)
SN Articles that overlie other articles with the effect of protecting, enclosing, or hiding them, especially those designed to have this function.
RT *<coverings and hangings by location or context>*

covers, bed
USE bedcovers

covers, bed bolt
USE bed bolt covers

covers, book match
USE matchbooks

covers, canvas
USE undercovers

covers, cap
USE cap covers

covers, case
SEE slipcovers

covers, chalice
USE palls (chalice covers)

covers, coffin
USE funeral palls

covers, corset
USE corset covers

covers, cupboard
USE cupboard cloths

covers, dome
USE dome covers

covers, domed
USE dome covers

covers, dust
USE book jackets
dust covers

covers, first day
USE first day covers

covers, floor
USE floor coverings

covers, furniture
USE slipcovers

covers, hallah
USE hallah covers

covers, Kaaba
USE kiswas

covers, loose
USE slipcovers

covers, man-hole
SEE manhole covers

covers, manhole
USE manhole covers

covers, matchbook
USE matchbooks

covers, matzah
USE matzah covers

covers, pull-off
USE cap covers

covers, screw
USE screw caps

covers, self
USE self covers

covers, show
USE top covers (upholstery components)

covers, slip
USE slipcovers

covers, slip-over
USE slipcovers

covers, strut pole
USE okbashes

covers, tea-table
USE tea cloths

covers, top
USE top covers (upholstery components)

covers, top linen
USE undercovers

covers, towel
USE show towels

covers, under
USE undercovers

covers, upholstery
USE top covers (upholstery components)

covert-ways
USE covered ways

coverups
TE.257
ALT coverup
SN Any of various garments, as loose blouses, jump suits, caftans, or sarongs, worn over a swimsuit, exercise clothing, or the like. (RHDEL2)

coves
RD.112
ALT cove
SN Denotes small rounded indentations in a coastline, smaller than bays and generally characterized by a narrow entrance.

coves (coving)
USE coving

coving
PJ.1979
HN March 1993 descriptor moved
April 1991 scope note changed
SN Concave surfaces located at the junction of a wall and ceiling.
UF coves (coving)

cow barns
USE dairy barns

cow bells
USE cowbells

cow cream jugs
USE cow creamers

cow creamers
TQ.523
ALT cow creamer
SN Containers for cream and other liquids in the form of a cow, with an opening in the back for filling, a spout in the form of a mouth, and a curved tail as a handle.
UF cow cream jugs
cow milk jugs
cream cows
creamers, cow
jugs, cow cream
jugs, cow milk

cow manure
HN April 1991 descriptor deleted

cow milk jugs
USE cow creamers

cow planes
USE roughing planes

cow sheds
RK.85 (B)
HN March 1993 related terms added
ALT cow shed
SN Use for open-sided structures, set against a barn or other large farm building, for sheltering bovines and for protecting manure piles from the weather to preserve their nutrients; for buildings designed for the housing of bovines, use either **cattle barns** or **dairy barns.**
UF cattle sheds
sheds, cattle
sheds, cow
RT cattle barns
dairy barns

cowbells
TT.471 (N)
ALT cowbell
SN Orchestral bells resembling the clapper bells hung around the necks of cows and other herd animals, but without a clapper, sounded by being struck with a drumstick.
UF bells, cow
cow bells

cowboy boots
TE.711 (L,N)
ALT cowboy boot
SN High-heeled boots of leather or leatherlike material often having decorative stitching or tooling, generally extending to mid-calf and usually having external boot straps of a type traditionally worn by ranch hands, especially in the American West.
UF boots, cowboy

cowboy hats
TE.586 (N)
ALT cowboy hat
SN Wide-brimmed hats with a large soft crown of the type worn by ranch hands in the American West. (W)
UF hats, cowboy

Cowichan
FL.1372 (L)

Cowlitz
FL.1354 (L)

cowls
PJ.820
HN March 1993 descriptor moved
December 1990 descriptor moved
December 1990 scope note changed
ALT cowl
SN Use for caps or hoodlike devices which cover and protect the open top of pipes, stacks, or shafts while permitting the free passage of air. (RS)
UF cowls, ventilating
ventilating cowls

cowls, ventilating
USE cowls

cowrie shell
MT.1333 (L)
HN April 1993 lead-in term added
March 1992 descriptor changed, was **cowrie**
March 1992 lead-in term changed, was **courie**
February 1992 descriptor moved
SN Shell of any of numerous marine gastropod mollusks of a family widely distributed in warm seas; beautifully polished, often brightly colored, and much used for ornament or as money. (W)
UF courie shell
cowry shell
shell, courie
shell, cowrie
shell, cowry

cowry shell
USE cowrie shell

cowters
PJ.3030
ALT cowter
UK couters
SN Plate armor to protect the elbow joints, attached by screws between the upper and lower cannons of the right and left vambraces; originally a single inarticulated curved plate in the 14th century, they evolved into a set of mobile lames loosely riveted together, remaining in use until the mid-17th century.

UF cops, elbow
coudes
elbow cops

coyns
USE quoins

Coyotlatelco
FL.1008
UF Xometla

cozies
TC.167 (N)
ALT cozy
SN Padded coverings for food, used to retain heat.

cozies, tea
USE tea cozies

Cr
USE chromium

crab-apple, prairie
SEE prairie crabapple

crab scrapers
TX.365
ALT crab scraper
SN Use for small half-decked skipjacks in the 24- to 30-foot range, from the lower eastern shore of Chesapeake Bay; may also be used for recent motorized versions.
UF crab scrapes
scrapers, crab
scrapes, crab

crab scrapes
USE crab scrapers

crab skiffs
USE crabbing skiffs

crabapple, prairie
USE prairie crabapple

crabbing skiffs
TX.367 (N)
ALT crabbing skiff
SN Use for small (under about 25 feet) V-bottomed boats, both power and sail, chiefly used for crabbing on Chesapeake Bay, with handliners or trotlines in summer; may be used for oyster tonging in winter.
UF Chesapeake Bay skiffs
crab skiffs
skiffs, Chesapeake Bay
skiffs, crab
skiffs, crabbing

crackers, lobster
USE nutcrackers

crackers, nut
USE nutcrackers

crackers, skull
USE wrecking balls

cracking
KT.255 (A,L)
HN January 1993 descriptor moved
ALT cracked

SN Use for the fracturing in a material or object, usually along a single or branched path.
UF fissuring

cracking, age
USE age cracks

cracking, drying
USE traction crackle

cracking, mechanical
USE mechanical cracks

cracking off
KT.1031
HN January 1993 descriptor added
ALT cracked-off
SN The severing of a glass object from the blowpipe or pontil rod. (JSSG)

crackle
DE.8 (H,L)
SN A network of fine fracture lines in a coating layer, such as a ground, paint layer, varnish, or glaze.
UF crackle pattern
craquelure
pattern, crackle

crackle, age
USE age cracks

crackle, alligator
USE traction crackle

crackle, branching
USE traction crackle

crackle, convection
USE age cracks

crackle glass
MT.288 (L)
HN January 1992 descriptor added
SN Use to describe glassware with a surface resembling cracked ice; produced either by plunging the vessel into cold water during its forming or by rolling the hot glass on a table covered with glass fragments and then blowing the form.
UF craquelé
glass, crackle
ice glass

crackle pattern
USE crackle

crackle, traction
USE traction crackle

crackle, youth
USE traction crackle

crackling
KT.256
HN January 1993 descriptor added
ALT crackled
SN Developing a network of fine cracks in a coating layer, such as a ground, paint layer, varnish, or glaze.

cracks
DE.7

SN Fissures or systems of fissures without complete separation into pieces.

cracks, age
USE age cracks

cracks, alligator
USE traction crackle

cracks, drying
USE traction crackle

cracks, early
USE traction crackle

cracks, late
USE age cracks

cracks, mechanical
USE mechanical cracks

cracks, nut
USE nutcrackers

cracks, shrinkage
USE traction crackle

cracks, traction
USE traction crackle

cradle benches
TC.708 (N)
HN March 1993 lead-in term added
March 1993 lead-in term changed, was **mamma's benches**
March 1993 lead-in term changed, was **mammy's benches**
March 1993 lead-in term changed, was **mammy's rockers**
March 1993 lead-in term changed, was **benches, mammy's**
March 1993 lead-in term changed, was **rockers, mammy's**
January 1993 descriptor moved
ALT cradle bench
SN Popular American term for mid-19th-century benches on rockers, with detachable fences two thirds of their length so that a baby could lie on the seat without rolling off, while the mother sat beside it.
UF benches, cradle
benches, mammas'
benches, mammies'
benches, rocking
mammas' benches
mammies' benches
mammies' rockers
rockers, mammies'
rocking benches
rocking settees
settees, rocking

cradle books
USE incunabula

cradle roofs
USE barrel roofs
compass roofs

cradle spits
USE basket spits

cradle vaults
USE barrel vaults

cradles (children's beds)
　　TC.765　　　　　　　　　　(L,N,R)
HN　May 1993 scope note changed
　　March 1993 descriptor changed,
　　　was **cradles**
　　March 1993 alternate term changed,
　　　was **cradle**
　　January 1993 descriptor moved
ALT　cradle (child's bed)
SN　Small beds for infants, usually on
　　bends. (RHDEL2)

cradles (framing and mounting
equipment)
　　TH.618
HN　February 1993 descriptor added
ALT　cradle (framing and mounting
　　　equipment)
SN　Devices used to prevent wood pan-
　　els from warping and cracking, con-
　　sisting of a system of wooden ribs
　　attached to the back of the panel.
　　(TAUB)

cradles and carriages
USE　carriage cradles

cradles, carriage
USE　carriage cradles

cradles, swing
USE　swinging cradles

cradles, swinging
USE　swinging cradles

craft
USE　aircraft
　　spacecraft
　　watercraft

craft, fishing
USE　fishing vessels

craft, heavier than air
USE　heavier than air aircraft

craft knives
USE　utility knives

craft, lighter than air
USE　lighter than air aircraft

craft, passenger
USE　passenger vessels

craft, pleasure
USE　yachts

craft, sailing
USE　sailing vessels

craft, small
USE　boats

crafts
　　BM.183　　　　　　　　　(H,L,B,R)
SN　The activity, and its products, of
　　forming handmade articles.
UF　handicrafts

Craftsman
　　FL.1748　　　　　　　　　　(A)
HN　July 1991 related term added
RT　Arts and Crafts

craftsmanship
　　BM.27　　　　　　　　　　(A,L,B)
HN　February 1992 scope note added
SN　Skill of producing work of high
　　quality.
UF　workmanship

craftsmen
　　HG.657　　　　　　　　　(A,L,B,R)
HN　December 1992 alternate terms
　　added
ALT　craftsman
　　craftsman's
　　craftsmen's
SN　Persons who practice or are highly
　　skilled in a craft. (RHDEL2)
UF　artisans

crakows
　　TE.720　　　　　　　　　　(N)
ALT　crakow
SN　Shoes, boots, or slippers made with
　　an extremely pointed toe and worn
　　in Europe in the 14th and 15th cen-
　　turies. (W)
UF　pikes (footwear)
　　poulaines
RT　boots
　　shoes (footwear)
　　slippers

cramps
USE　clamps

crandall hammers
　　TH.1354　　　　　　　　　(N)
HN　December 1992 descriptor moved
ALT　crandall hammer
SN　Hand tools consisting of several
　　sharp pointed bars fixed to the end
　　of a handle in a hammerlike con-
　　figuration: used for dressing stone.
　　(MEANS)
UF　hammers, crandall

cranemen
　　HG.820
HN　December 1992 alternate terms
　　added
ALT　craneman
　　craneman's
　　cranemen's

cranes
　　TH.466　　　　　　　　　(L,N,B)
ALT　crane
SN　Machines for raising, shifting, or
　　lowering heavy weights, usually by
　　means of a projecting swinging
　　arm. (MEANS)

cranes, bridge
USE　bridge cranes
　　gantry cranes

cranes, climbing
USE　climbing cranes

cranes, crawler
USE　crawler cranes

cranes, gantry
USE　gantry cranes

cranes, locomotive
USE　locomotive cranes

cranes, tower
USE　tower cranes

cranes, traveling
USE　traveling cranes

cranes, truck
USE　truck cranes

cranes, truck-mounted
USE　truck cranes

cranes, wall
USE　wall cranes

cranes, wheel-mounted
USE　wheel-mounted cranes

craniometers
　　TN.79　　　　　　　　　　(N)
ALT　craniometer
SN　Instruments for measuring the ex-
　　ternal dimensions of the skulls of
　　deceased beings; for devices to mea-
　　sure the skulls of living beings, use
　　cephalometers.
RT　cephalometers

crannogs
　　RK.312　　　　　　　　　　(L,R)
ALT　crannog
SN　Use for ancient dwellings built on
　　artificial islands in lakes, common in
　　Ireland, Scotland, and Britain.

crapauds
　　TC.484
HN　January 1993 descriptor moved
ALT　crapaud
SN　Heavily upholstered low armchairs,
　　generally with fringe hiding the legs
　　and woodwork; of a type first made
　　in France in the 1840s.

craps
　　KQ.33　　　　　　　　　　(L)

craquelé
USE　crackle glass

craquelure
USE　crackle

craquelure, youth
USE　traction crackle

crash helmets
　　TE.379　　　　　　　　　　(N)
ALT　crash helmet
SN　Helmets worn by motorcyclists, au-
　　tomobile racers, and the like, for
　　protection of the head in the event
　　of an accident.
UF　helmets, crash

crassets
USE　crusies

Crataegus
USE　hawthorn

Crataegus monogyna
USE　hawthorn

crate furniture
TC.1209
HN January 1993 descriptor moved
SN Precut furniture parts, made of wood generally used for crates, sold in kits to be assembled by the purchaser into tables, chairs, and bookcases at low cost. Designed by Gerrit Rietveld in 1934. (PAGE)
UF furniture, crate

craters, volute
USE volute kraters

crates
TQ.26   (L,N)
ALT crate
SN Large or strong containers used especially for transporting goods.
UF crates, shipping
shipping crates

crates, shipping
USE crates

cravat pins
USE stickpins

cravats
TE.657   (L,N)
ALT cravat
SN Formal neckcloths folded or tied at front with ends tucked inside the coat. Also, pieces of lace, silk, or other fine cloth worn about the neck by men, especially fashionable in the 17th century. For long, narrow bands of cloth worn around the neck, under the collar, and tied in a knot, loop, or bow, use **neckties**.
RT neckties

crawl spaces
PJ.1157   (L)
HN March 1993 descriptor moved
ALT crawl space
SN Small spaces provided in a building in order to be able to gain access to plumbing, wiring, and other equipment.
UF spaces, crawl

crawler cranes
TH.469
HN November 1992 related term added
ALT crawler crane
SN Cranes consisting of a rotating superstructure with power plant, operating machinery, and boom mounted on a base equipped with crawler treads for travel; used to hoist and swing loads at various radii. (STEIN)
UF cranes, crawler
RT tracklaying vehicles

crawler tractors
TH.444   (L)
HN November 1992 related term added
ALT crawler tractor
SN Engine-driven vehicles that travel on segmented roller-chain tracks designed to reduce ground pressure

and increase traction in loose footing. (DAC)
UF track-type tractors
tracklaying tractors
tractors, crawler
tractors, track-type
tractors, tracklaying
RT tracklaying vehicles

crayon, Conté (TM)
USE Conté crayon (TM)

crayon daguerreotypes
USE cameotypes

crayon engraving
USE crayon manner

crayon engravings
USE crayon manner prints

crayon enlargements
VC.387
HN April 1993 scope note changed
April 1992 descriptor moved
March 1991 descriptor moved
ALT crayon enlargement
SN A term for a type of photographic portrait popular in the years before the First World War. Usually oval, finished with liberal airbrushing and colored with pastels. (HCOP)
UF enlargements, crayon

crayon holders
USE portcrayons

crayon manner
KT.671   (L)
HN April 1990 descriptor added
SN 18th-century printmaking process that imitates the appearance of chalk lines; employs etching, with the ground having been marked with a roulette, and sometimes the addition of directly engraved stippling. (OCA)
UF à trois crayons (printmaking)
chalk engraving
chalk manner
chalk method
crayon engraving
crayon method
engraving, chalk
engraving, crayon
manner, chalk
manner, crayon
method, chalk
method, crayon

crayon manner prints
VC.461
ALT crayon manner print
SN Prints made by the process of crayon manner.
UF crayon engravings
engravings, crayon
engravings, pastel
pastel engravings
prints, crayon manner

crayon method
USE crayon manner

crayons
TH.660   (L,N)
ALT crayon
SN A generic term for any drawing material made in stick form. (MAYER)

crayons, charcoal
USE charcoal sticks

crayons, grease
USE grease pencils

crayons, litho
USE lithographic crayons

crayons, lithographic
USE lithographic crayons

crayons, pastel
USE pastels (crayons)

crayons, wax
USE wax crayons

crazing
DE.12
HN November 1992 descriptor moved
August 1992 scope note changed
ALT crazed
SN Use for fine, random cracks or fissures in the surface of hardened or dried material, such as concrete, plaster, paint, or ceramic glazes; sometimes appearing opaque; usually not exposing the underlying surface.

crazy quilts
TC.245   (L)
ALT crazy quilt
SN Quilts composed of pieces cut from many different textiles, often including rich velvets, satins, or brocades, usually in irregular shapes and sizes, and often embellished with fancy embroidery stitches. Done in press piecing, usually tied rather than quilted, and rarely contain batting.
UF quilts, crazy

crazy quilts, contained
USE contained crazy quilts

CRC
USE camera ready copy

cream
USE pale yellow
yellowish white

cream blanc marble
MT.762
HN April 1992 descriptor moved
UF marble, cream blanc

cream buff
USE moderate yellow
pale yellow

cream color
USE light yellow

cream-colored earthenware
USE creamware

cream cows
USE cow creamers

cream jugs
USE creamers

cream ladles
TH.267
HN April 1993 descriptor added
ALT cream ladle
SN Small ladles intended primarily for serving cream; generally smaller than gravy ladles. Sometimes made en suite with a cream pail.
UF ladles, cream
RT cream pails

cream marble, Alabama
USE Alabama cream marble

cream marble, madre
USE madre cream marble

cream pails
TQ.524
ALT cream pail
SN Small pail-like vessels used for holding and serving cream, generally made of porcelain or silver, the latter sometimes having a glass liner.
UF pails, cream
piggins (cream pails)
RT cream ladles

cream pitchers
USE creamers

cream pots
USE creamers

cream scoops
USE cream skimmers

cream skimmers
TH.190   (N)
HN April 1993 descriptor added
ALT cream skimmer
SN Skimmers specifically used to remove cream from the surface of milk.
UF cream scoops
dishes, skimming
milk skimmers
scoops, cream
skimmers, cream
skimmers, milk
skimming dishes

cream soup spoons
TH.332
HN April 1993 descriptor added
ALT cream soup spoon
SN Round-bowled spoons similar to but larger than bouillon spoons and intended to be used to consume cream soups.
UF soup spoons, cream
spoons, cream soup

cream strainers
USE milk strainers

cream-ware
SEE creamware

creameries
USE dairy plants

creamers
TQ.522   (L,N)
ALT creamer
SN Containers for holding and serving cream, especially a small pitcher which may be accompanied by a sugar bowl. Sometimes made as part of a tea or coffee service.
UF cream jugs
cream pitchers
cream pots
jugs, cream
pitchers, cream
pots, cream
RT breakfast services
coffee services
sugar bowls
tea services

creamers, cow
USE cow creamers

creamware
PE.106   (L,R)
HN January 1993 descriptor added
UK cream-ware
UF cream-colored earthenware
earthenware, cream-colored

crease tile
USE crest tile

creases
DE.13
SN Ridges or grooves produced in flexible materials by, for example, folding or pressure against a hard edge. For the parts of something that fold onto themselves, use **folds.**
UF fold lines
lines, fold

creases (pleats)
USE pleats

creasing
KT.258   (L)
HN January 1993 descriptor moved
SN The process of creating a crease or creases.

creasing stakes
TH.1226   (N)
ALT creasing stake
SN T-shaped stakes with a grooved surface on one side and square end on the other; used in metalworking to shape corners and edges.
UF stakes, creasing

creation
BM.520   (L,R)

Creationist
FL.1784
ALT Creationism

creative ability
USE creativity

creative abstraction
USE biomorphic abstraction

creative arts therapy
USE art therapy

creativity
BM.28   (L,R)
HN January 1991 alternate term added
ALT creative
UF creative ability

creches
USE day care centers

credence cloths
TC.283
ALT credence cloth
SN Linen coverings for the credence, often matching the altar cloth.
UF cloths, credence

credence tables
USE credences

credences
TC.1131
HN January 1993 descriptor moved
ALT credence
SN Collector's term for small tables or shelves near the altar in a church, used for the eucharistic elements before consecration; obsolete term for a sideboard or side table. (DDA)
UF credence tables
credenzas (credences)
tables, credence

credences (credenzas)
USE credenzas

credences (cupboards)
USE cupboards

credentials
VW.370
HN March 1993 alternate term deleted, was **credential**
November 1992 descriptor moved
SN Use to designate evidence of authority, status, rights, entitlement to privileges, or the like. (RHDEL2)

credenzas
TC.1006   (N)
HN May 1993 scope note changed
January 1993 descriptor moved
ALT credenza
SN Sideboards, especially Italian or Italian-styled sideboards, generally having two or three cupboard doors and drawers in the frieze; the bases are often molded and rest directly on the floor or on lion feet.
UF credences (credenzas)

credenzas (credences)
USE credences

credit
BM.871   (L)
HN February 1993 descriptor moved
SN The extent to which a person can

receive money or goods for payment in the future. (W)

credit cards
VW.1027 (L,N)
HN November 1992 descriptor moved
ALT credit card
SN Cards used to obtain money, goods, or services on credit. (BLACKS)
UF cards, credit
charge plates
plates, charge

credit, circular letters of
USE letters of credit

credit, commercial letters of
USE letters of credit

credit, confirmed
USE letters of credit

credit, confirmed letters of
USE letters of credit

credit instruments
VK.162
ALT credit instrument
SN Use for negotiable documents other than paper money that are supported by coin reserves and provide evidence of current or long-term debt. (ENCYBF)
UF instruments, credit
RT acceptances
bonds (negotiable instruments)
<orders to pay>
promissory notes

credit, letters of
USE letters of credit

credit records
VW.595
HN November 1992 descriptor moved
ALT credit record
UF records, credit

credit, travelers' letters of
USE letters of credit

credit unions
HN.73 (L)
ALT credit union
SN Cooperative associations that make small loans to their members at low interest rates. (W)
UF unions, credit

Cree
FL.1234 (L,R)

Cree, Plains
USE Plains Cree

Creek
FL.1451 (L)
HN June 1990 lead-in term added
UF Maskoki
Muskogee

creeks
RD.107 (L)
ALT creek

creels
TQ.119 (N)
ALT creel
SN Lidded baskets, flat on one side and bulging on the other, intended primarily for holding fish, lobster, tackle, or the like; used especially with reference to those worn on the back or suspended from the shoulder by anglers.
UF baskets, trout
creels, fishing
fishing creels
trout baskets
RT baskets

creels, fishing
USE creels

creep
DC.176 (L)
HN October 1992 descriptor moved
SN Slow, continuous deformation or movement of structures and landscape features under sustained pressure or downward pull, such as by gravity. (MEANS)

creepers
TE.15
ALT creeper
UK bodygros
UKA bodygro
SN Combination bifurcated garments for infants and toddlers, close-fitting, usually of knit, extending to the hip. May be made with or without sleeves.
UF bodysuits
RT combinations

creepie stools
USE cutty stools

creepies
USE cutty stools

creeping bite
KT.712
HN April 1990 descriptor added
SN Technique of submerging a printing plate in acid in stages to produce subtle tonal gradations or other effects. (SAFF)
UF bite, creeping

Cremation, Late
USE Late Cremation

cremation urns
TQ.145 (L,N,R)
ALT cremation urn
SN Vessels holding or intended to hold the ashes of cremated bodies. (RHDEL2)
UF ash urns
cinerary urns
funerary urns
mortuary jars
sepulchral urns
urns, ash
urns, cinerary
urns, cremation

urns, funerary
urns, sepulchral
RT urns

crematories
RK.429 (A,L,B)
ALT crematory

Cremnitz white
USE lead white

cremorne bolts
PJ.526
HN April 1993 descriptor moved
ALT cremorne bolt
UF bolts, cremorne

crenelated parapets
USE battlements

crenelets
USE embrasures (battlement components)

crenellations
USE battlements

crenels
USE embrasures (battlement components)

Creole
FL.1721 (L)
HN October 1991 descriptor added

Creole cottages
RK.234
ALT Creole cottage
SN Side-gabled vernacular buildings of simple massing, normally having their front walls moved inward to make an integral porch under a single steep roofline; the form was originally brought to Louisiana by French Canadian (Acadian) immigrants with a knowledge of long-span roof framing techniques.
UF Acadian houses
cottages, Creole
Creole houses
grenier houses
houses, Acadian
houses, Creole
houses, grenier

Creole houses
USE Creole cottages

creosote
MT.2389 (L,B)
UF dead oil
oil, dead
oil, pitch
pitch oil

creosote, coal tar
USE coal tar creosote

crêpe
SEE crepe

crepe
MT.1570 (L)
HN March 1993 descriptor moved

March 1993 scope note changed
July 1990 descriptor added
UK crêpe
SN Lightweight textile made of various types of fiber, having a crinkled surface obtained by using hard twisted thread or yarn, by printing with caustic soda, by weaving with varied tensions, or by embossing. (W)

crêpe paper
SEE crepe paper

crepe paper
MT.1431 (L)
HN February 1992 descriptor moved
UK crêpe paper
UF paper, crêpe
paper, crepe

crepidomas
PJ.954
HN March 1993 descriptor moved
ALT crepidoma
SN Use for the stepped platforms of Classical temples.
UF krepidomas

crepitaculi
USE sistra

crescent arches
USE horseshoe arches

crescent moons
USE crescents (shapes)

crescent stretchers
HN March 1993 descriptor split, use crescent (shape) (ALT of crescents (shapes)) + stretchers (furniture components)

crescent trusses
PJ.1705
HN March 1993 descriptor moved
March 1991 descriptor moved
ALT crescent truss
SN Use for trusses whose upper and lower chords are both curved in the same direction but with different radii of curvature, so that they meet at the ends, giving a crescentlike appearance.
UF camelback trusses
curved trusses
trusses, camelback
trusses, crescent
trusses, curved

crescent wrenches
USE adjustable wrenches

crescents (row houses)
RK.270 (B)
ALT crescent (row house)
SN Use for row houses whose facades in plan follow the concave arc of a circle or ellipse.

crescents (shapes)
DG.57 (H)
HN May 1991 lead-in terms added

May 1991 descriptor changed, was crescents
May 1991 alternate term changed, was crescent
ALT crescent (shape)
SN Motifs consisting of a curved segment of a circle, often suggesting a crescent moon.
UF crescent moons
moons, crescent

crescents, Turkish
USE jingling Johnnies

cress tile
USE crest tile

cressets
TC.1263 (N)
ALT cresset
SN Vessels, usually made of iron or earthware, used for holding burning oil, pitch, or other flammable substances for lighting.
UF basket torches
baskets, fire
fire baskets
torches, basket

cressets (crusies)
USE crusies

crest pieces
USE crest rails

crest rails
PJ.2727
HN March 1993 descriptor moved
ALT crest rail
UF crest pieces
cresting rails
crossrails
pieces, crest
rails, crest
top-rails (crest rails)

crest tile
MT.180
HN April 1992 descriptor moved
UF crease tile
cress tile
tile, crease
tile, cress
tile, crest

cresting
PJ.12
HN March 1993 descriptor moved
March 1993 related terms added
December 1990 scope note changed
SN Ornamental finish, usually rhythmic and highly decorative, consisting of a regular series of motifs applied to the top of walls, roof ridges, and the like; may also be used for similar decoration on furniture or glass objects.
UF crests (culminating and edge ornaments)
RT brattishing
cheneaux

cresting rails
USE crest rails

crests
DG.52
HN December 1992 descriptor added
ALT crest
SN Heraldic motifs forming part of a coat of arms sometimes displayed or inscribed to indicate ownership; a crest may be common to more than one family.

crests (culminating and edge ornaments)
USE cresting

Cretan
FL.2673 (L)

Creto-Mycenaean
FL.2674

cretonne appliqué
USE broderie perse

cretonne work
USE broderie perse

crevé
DE.43
HN November 1992 descriptor moved
April 1990 descriptor added
SN Use when, in etching, an area of the printing plate is too deeply bitten and lines fuse together.

crew neck sweaters
TE.76
ALT crew neck sweater
SN Pullover sweaters with a collarless neckline that fits snugly at the base of the neck.
UF crew necks
sweaters, crew neck

crew necks
USE crew neck sweaters

crewed spacecraft
USE manned spacecraft

crewel
USE crewel wool

crewel embroidery
USE crewelwork

crewel wool
MT.1543
HN November 1992 descriptor added
SN Fine, loosely twisted, two-ply, worsted yarn used in embroidering. (IWINGT)
UF crewel
crewel yarn
cruel wool
wool, crewel
wool, cruel
yarn, crewel

crewel-work
SEE crewelwork

crewel yarn
USE crewel wool

crewelwork
KT.1226 (L,R)
HN March 1993 descriptor moved
January 1993 scope note changed
February 1992 lead-in term added
March 1990 lead-in term added
UK crewel-work
SN Embroidery utilizing simple stitches
and crewel wool, usually worked
into floral and scroll patterns on
plain cloth.
UF crewel embroidery
embroidery, crewel

crewets
USE cruets

criardes
TE.234
ALT criarde
SN Petticoats of linen stiffened by gum
or paste; worn in the early 18th
century.

crib barns
RK.45
ALT crib barn
UF barns, crib

crib beds
USE cribs

crib beds, swinging
USE swinging cribs

crib bedsteads
USE cribs

crib retaining walls
USE cribbing

cribbage
KQ.25 (L,N)
RT cribbage boards

cribbage boards
TV.22 (N)
ALT cribbage board
SN Boards, normally long narrow rectangles of wood, for keeping score
during the game of cribbage and
having holes in the upper surface
into which pegs are placed to mark
the score and progress of the
players.
UF boards, cribbage
RT cribbage

cribbing
PJ.1521 (A,L)
HN March 1993 descriptor moved
SN Designates a framework of open
bins filled with rocks or other pervi-
ous materials and used as retaining
walls or to support a construction.
UF crib retaining walls
cribwork
retaining walls, crib
walls, crib retaining

criblé
USE dotted manner

criblé prints
USE dotted prints

cribs
TC.768 (L,N)
HN January 1993 descriptor moved
ALT crib
SN Small bedsteads with a high enclosure and usually slatted sides for a
child. (W)
UF beds, crib
bedsteads, crib
crib beds
crib bedsteads

cribs, swing
USE swinging cribs

cribs, swinging
USE swinging cribs

cribwork
USE cribbing

cricket
KQ.70 (H,L)
RT balls (recreational artifacts)
bats
wickets

cricket bowls
USE cricket fields

cricket fields
RM.88 (A,L,B)
HN April 1993 descriptor moved
ALT cricket field
SN Use for the entire playing areas
upon which the game of cricket is
played.
UF bowls, cricket
cricket bowls
cricket grounds
cricket pitches
fields, cricket
grounds, cricket
pitches, cricket

cricket grounds
USE cricket fields

cricket pitches
USE cricket fields

cricket stools
TC.669
HN May 1993 related term added
January 1993 descriptor moved
ALT cricket stool
SN Applies to a variety of small stools,
such as footstools, generally having
splayed legs. (DADA)
UF splayed-leg stools
stools, cricket
RT footstools

cricket stools (buffet stools)
USE buffet stools

cricket tables
TC.1077
HN January 1993 descriptor moved
ALT cricket table
SN Joined tables with three legs; of a

type made in 17th-century England. (CHINNE)
UF splay-leg tables
tables, cricket
tables, splay-leg

crickets
USE chimney crickets

crickets, chimney
USE chimney crickets

cricris
USE clack idiophones

Crideb
USE Sri Deb

cries
VW.304 (H,L)
HN June 1992 descriptor added
ALT cry
SN Those rhymes used by peddlers to
announce their wares, sometimes
printed up with illustrations for distribution.
UF cries, street
songs, street
street cries
street songs

cries, street
USE cries

crime
BM.1062 (L,R)
HN February 1993 descriptor moved
May 1991 related terms added
January 1991 scope note added
SN The commission of acts that are forbidden by, or the omission of duties
that are required by, public law and
that make the offender liable to
punishment by that law. (WCOL9)
RT crime prevention
criminal law
prostitution

crime laboratories
RK.1106 (A,L)
ALT crime laboratory
UF laboratories, crime

crime prevention
KG.169 (A,L,B)
HN December 1992 descriptor moved
May 1991 scope note added
May 1991 related term added
SN Measures taken to forestall criminal
or delinquent acts. (ERIC12)
UF prevention, crime
prevention of crime
RT crime

criminal court records
VW.763 (L)
HN November 1992 descriptor moved
ALT criminal court record
UF records, criminal court

criminal law
KD.297 (L,R)
HN May 1991 related term added

SN Branch of jurisprudence that relates to crimes. (W)
UF law, criminal
law, penal
penal law
RT crime

criminals
HG.911 (L,R)
HN December 1992 alternate terms added
ALT criminal
criminal's
criminals'

criminology
KD.245
HN February 1991 alternate term added
ALT criminological
SN Scientific study of offenders, of crime as a social phenomenon, and of the criminal justice system. (PG)

crimp warp
USE binding warp

crimping
KT.317 (L)
HN March 1993 scope note changed
February 1993 related term added
ALT crimped
SN Pinching together, often to make wavy or bent; also the process of drawing molten glass to form the neck of a vessel.
RT goffering

crimson
USE carmine
deep purplish red
madder
vivid purplish red
vivid red

crimson, alizarin
USE alizarin madder

crimson lake
MT.2189
HN April 1992 descriptor moved
SN Deep, transparent, ruby-red lake pigment with bluish undertone, made from kermes, a natural dyestuff of insect origin; carmine, a better pigment introduced in the 16th century, became its chief competitor. (MAYER)
UF Florentine lake
lake, crimson
lake, Florentine

crimson lake (color)
USE moderate red

crimson madder
USE madder
vivid red

crinets
TH.22
HN February 1993 descriptor added
ALT crinet
SN Armor for the horse's neck, made of

narrow lames articulated together, or of lames alternating with bands of mail.

crinkling
USE wrinkling

crinoidal limestone
MT.846
HN April 1992 descriptor moved
UF limestone, crinoidal

crinolines
TE.205 (L,N)
ALT crinoline
SN Petticoats originally made with a stiff, woven fabric of horsehair, linen, cotton, or wool. Later often used in conjunction with hoops of whalebone or steel.

crinolines, artificial
USE cage crinolines

crinolines, cage
USE cage crinolines

cripple jacks, valley
USE valley jacks

cripple rafters
USE jack rafters

Cris
FL.2578
UF Cris-Körös

Cris-Körös
USE Cris
Körös

crisis centers
USE crisis shelters

crisis shelters
RK.754 (L)
HN February 1991 descriptor added
ALT crisis shelter
SN Denotes facilities that provide emergency social services and temporary housing in times of personal or family crisis.
UF battered women's shelters
centers, crisis
crisis centers
shelters, battered women's
shelters, crisis
shelters, women's
women's shelters
women's shelters, battered
RT emergency housing

crisselling
USE crizzling

cristallo
MT.239
HN January 1992 descriptor added
SN General term for Venetian glass often yellow or smoky gray in color unless formulated with the decolorizing agent manganese, which gives the glass the appearance of rock crystal.

critical bibliography
USE analytical bibliography

critical care units
USE intensive care units

<critical theories>
BM.224

critical theory
BM.1054 (L)
HN February 1993 descriptor moved
UF Frankfurt school of sociology
sociology, Frankfurt school of
theory, critical

criticism
KG.13 (A,L)
HN April 1993 related terms added
April 1993 lead-in term added
April 1993 alternate term changed, was **criticizing**
April 1993 scope note changed
January 1991 scope note added
January 1991 alternate term added
October 1990 descriptor moved
ALT criticized
SN Activity of analyzing and judging the quality of a man-made object, action, or plan. For critical descriptions or analyses of relatively recent works or events, use **reviews**.
UF criticizing
RT critics
reviews

criticism, architectural
USE architectural criticism

criticism, art
USE art criticism

criticism, historical
USE historiography

criticism, literary
USE literary criticism

criticism of literature
USE literary criticism

criticizing
USE criticism

critics
HG.375 (L,R)
HN April 1993 related term added
December 1992 alternate terms added
ALT critic
critic's
critics'
SN Persons who write critical reviews of literary, musical, or artistic works and performances for broadcast or publication. (DOT)
RT criticism

critics, architectural
USE architectural critics

critics, art
USE art critics

critics, literary
USE literary critics

critiques
KM.71
HN May 1991 alternate term added
ALT critique

Crivelli carpets
TC.102
ALT Crivelli carpet
SN Rugs with a large, complex star motif, so named because they appeared in a painting by the Italian Renaissance painter Carlo Crivelli.
UF carpets, Crivelli
Crivelli pattern (rugs)
Crivelli rugs
rugs, Crivelli
Turkish crivelli pattern (rugs)

Crivelli pattern (rugs)
USE Crivelli carpets

Crivelli rugs
USE Crivelli carpets

crizzled glass
USE crizzling

crizzling
DE.29
ALT crizzled
SN A basic defect in glass caused by an imperfect proportion of ingredients, particularly an excess of alkali, and consisting of a fine network of cracks and the formation of moisture on the surface.
UF crisselling
crizzled glass
disease, glass
diseased glass
glass, crizzled
glass disease
glass, diseased
glass, sick
sick glass

croats
VK.69   (L)
ALT croat
SN Silver Catalonian coins, a form of the gros tournois, struck between the late 13th and the early 18th century. (DOTY)

crocheting
KT.1174   (L)
HN March 1993 descriptor changed, was **crochet**
March 1993 lead-in term deleted, was **crocheting**
March 1993 descriptor moved
ALT crocheted
SN Textile construction involving the interlocking of looped stitches, employing a single cord or strand of yarn and a single hooked needle.

crocket capitals
PJ.1496

HN March 1993 descriptor moved
ALT crocket capital
SN Capitals having a series of crockets.
UF capitals, crocket

crockets
DG.70
HN July 1991 scope note changed
March 1991 descriptor moved
ALT crocket
SN In Gothic architecture and derivatives, projecting ornaments usually vegetal in form, often regularly spaced along edges of larger features, such as gables, or used on capitals.

crockpots
TH.65   (N)
HN April 1993 descriptor added
ALT crockpot
SN Any ceramic or metal pots or utensils used in the slow cooking of food, such as beans.

crocks
TQ.71   (N)
ALT crock
SN Earthenware vessels, with or without a cover, of cylindrical shape.

crocodile shears
USE lever shears

crocus cloth
TH.1073
SN Fabric coated with red iron oxide marketed in sheets and used for polishing metal. (MH)
UF cloth, crocus

crofts
TC.987
HN May 1993 scope note changed
January 1993 descriptor moved
ALT croft
SN Small writing cabinets of table height with drawers in the support and a flap top with drop leaves; of a type invented in late 18th-century England by the Reverend Sir Herbert Croft.

croisettes
USE crossettes

crokinole
KQ.99   (N)

cromlechs
RK.850   (A,L,B,R)
ALT cromlech
SN Use only for prehistoric circular enclosures of well-spaced large upright stones; if the ring of stones is bordered by a circular ditch and bank of earth, use **henges**. Use **megalithic chamber tombs** if the stone enclosure is capped by stones and covered by a mound of earth or stones.
UF circles, stone
peristaliths
stone circles

Cromwellian chairs
TC.485
HN January 1993 descriptor moved
ALT Cromwellian chair
SN Collector's term for square low-back chairs, often without arms, having turned legs and stretchers; this type, covered in leather or turkey work, long antedated the period of Cromwell but became widely popular in England in the mid-1600s.
UF chairs, Cromwellian
chairs, leather-upholstered (Cromwellian chairs)
chairs, turkey work (Cromwellian chairs)
leather-upholstered chairs (Cromwellian chairs)
turkey work chairs (Cromwellian chairs)

crook-bit tongs
TH.1293   (N)
SN Tongs with one straight jaw and one crooked jaw; used by blacksmiths.
UF bits, crook
crook bits
tongs, crook-bit

crook bits
USE crook-bit tongs

crook'd-back leather chairs
USE Boston chairs

crooked-back chairs
USE Boston chairs

crooks
PJ.3225
ALT crook
SN Detachable lengths of tubing inserted into aerophones, either permanently or for a specific playing occasion, for the purpose of either changing the sounding tube length, or to carry the mouthpiece where it is within easier reach of the player.
RT brass instruments
Inventionshorns
trumpets

cropland
RD.253

cropping
KT.943
HN January 1993 descriptor moved
ALT cropped
SN The trimming or cutting away of edges, as portions of a photograph or printed page.

crops
TH.362   (N)
HN June 1992 descriptor added
ALT crop
UK hunting-crops
SN Short, straight whips consisting of a stock with a loop instead of a lash.
UF crops, hunting
crops, riding

hunting crops
riding crops
RT *<costume accessories carried>*

crops, hunting
USE   crops

crops, riding
USE   crops

croquet
KQ.50   (A,H,L)
RT   croquet sets

croquet courts
HN   March 1993 descriptor split, use
croquet + courts (built works)

croquet sets
PC.58   (N)
ALT   croquet set
SN   Use for the ensembles of balls, mal-
lets, and wickets needed to play the
game of croquet.
UF   sets, croquet
RT   croquet
mallets (sports equipment)
wickets

croquis
USE   preliminary sketches

crosettes
USE   crossettes

crosiers
VW.1178   (H,L,N)
HN   June 1992 descriptor added
ALT   crosier
SN   Staffs resembling shepherds' crooks
borne by bishops, abbots, or abbesses, as symbols of the pastoral
office.
UF   croziers
episcopal staffs
pastoral staffs
staffs, episcopal
staffs, pastoral
RT   staffs (walking sticks)

<cross- and interdisciplinary fields>
KD.315
HN   January 1993 guide term changed,
was *<cross-disciplinary studies>*

cross axes
USE   twivels

cross-band
USE   S-twist

cross banding
DG.4
HN   March 1993 descriptor moved
SN   Decorative border of contrasting
types of wood cut straight across the
grain, generally used to finish edges
and rims of furniture.
UF   banding, cross

cross-blown flutes
USE   transverse flutes

cross-bows
SEE   crossbows

cross bridging
PJ.1441
HN   March 1993 descriptor moved
SN   Diagonal bracing in pairs between
adjacent floor joists to prevent the
joists from twisting. (DAC)
UF   bridging, cross
bridging, diagonal
diagonal bridging
herringbone strutting
strutting, herringbone

cross chairs, Savonarola
USE   Savonarola chairs

cross-contour drawing
KT.395
SN   Drawing technique in which lines
move in any direction across the
form rather than along the edge of
it. (KAUP)
UF   contour drawing, cross
drawing, cross-contour

cross-contour drawings
VC.212
HN   April 1992 descriptor moved
ALT   cross-contour drawing
SN   Use for drawings in which lines fol-
low contours of the form across the
surface of the form; distinct from
contour drawings, in which lines fol-
low edges of the form.
UF   drawings, cross-contour

cross-country skiing
KQ.96   (L)
UF   ski touring
skiing, cross-country
touring, ski

cross-cultural psychology
USE   ethnopsychology

cross-dating
KT.187
HN   November 1992 descriptor added
SN   Inferring the date of one thing, as
an artifact, a pollen deposit, or a
tree ring, from the age of a similar
one that has been more firmly
dated.

cross flutes
USE   transverse flutes

cross gables
PJ.1966
HN   March 1993 descriptor moved
ALT   cross gable
SN   Gables set parallel to the roof ridge.
(HAS)
UF   gables, cross

cross-guards
SEE   cross guards

cross guards
PJ.3136
ALT   cross guard
UK   cross-guards
UKA   cross-guard
SN   The simplest form of guard on

edged weapons, known since antiquity, consisting basically of a bar positioned crosswise to the blade and
the grip.
UF   crosses (guards)
guards, cross
RT   quillons

cross-hatching
KT.463
HN   March 1991 alternate term added
ALT   cross-hatched
SN   Hatching in which a network of
lines creating a darker value is made
by drawing one set of hatchings
over another at a different angle.
(A-Z)

cross hilts
PJ.3141
ALT   cross hilt
SN   Simple hilts in which the grip and
quillons, together with the blade of
the weapon, form the outline of a
Latin cross.
UF   cruciform hilts
hilts, cross
hilts, cruciform

cross-legged stools
USE   folding + stools

cross legs, Grecian
USE   curule legs

cross-lighting
SEE   crosslighting

cross-line screens
TH.807
HN   February 1993 descriptor added
ALT   cross-line screen
SN   Halftone screens consisting of a grid
of fine lines.
UF   screens, cross-line

cross-lined, white
USE   white cross-lined

<cross monuments>
RK.842

cross-peen hammers
TH.1023   (N)
ALT   cross-peen hammer
SN   Hammers having a wedge-shaped
peen. (DAC)
UF   hammers, cross-peen

cross ribs
USE   transverse ribs

<Cross River region>
FL.233

cross-section paper
USE   graph paper

cross sections
VC.150
HN   April 1992 descriptor moved
ALT   cross section
UF   sections, cross

sections, transverse
transverse sections

cross shaped stretchers, diagonal
USE   cross stretchers

cross springers
USE   diagonal ribs

cross-staffs
    TN.27   (N)
ALT   cross-staff
SN   Calibrated wooden rods with sliding
    crosspieces used for measuring the
    altitude of celestial bodies; fore-
    runnners of modern sextants.
UF   forestaffs
    Jacob's staffs
    staffs, Jacob's
RT   astronomical instruments

cross stretchers
    PJ.2892
HN   March 1993 descriptor moved
ALT   cross stretcher
SN   X-shaped horizontal braces or rails
    connecting and supporting the legs
    of chairs, tables, and case pieces.
    (FAIRB)
UF   cross shaped stretchers, diagonal
    cruciform stretchers
    diagonal cross shaped stretchers
    diagonal-shaped stretchers
    diagonal stretchers
    stretchers, cross
    stretchers, cruciform
    stretchers, diagonal
    stretchers, diagonal cross shaped
    X-stretchers

cross vaults
USE   groined vaults

cross vaults, domical
USE   domical vaults

cross-wall construction
USE   box frames

crossbeams
    PJ.1656
HN   March 1993 descriptor moved
ALT   crossbeam
SN   Use for large beams that span be-
    tween the two walls or sides of a
    structure.

crossbows
    TK.225   (H,L,N,R)
ALT   crossbow
UK   cross-bows
UKA   cross-bow
SN   Bows basically consisting of a curved
    stave mounted crosswise on a center
    shaft by means of a system of cord
    or gut bindings or metal bands, the
    string being drawn back, held, and
    released by some mechanical means
    such as a windlass or a rotatable nut.
    They were in use as early as the
    11th century and continue in use in

the 20th century for hunting and
recreation.
RT   bolts (arrows)

crosscloths
USE   forehead cloths

crosscut saws
    TH.1597   (L,N)
ALT   crosscut saw
SN   Large saws whose teeth are filed and
    set to cut across the grain of wood,
    providing more of a knife action in
    the cutting than ripsaws; designed
    for either one or two people.
UF   long saws
    saws, crosscut
    saws, long

crosscut saws, one-man
USE   one-man crosscut saws

crosses (guards)
USE   cross guards

crosses (motifs)
    DG.17   (A,L,R)
HN   January 1993 scope note changed
    January 1993 related term added
    January 1993 descriptor changed,
    was **crosses**
    January 1993 alternate term
    changed, was **cross**
ALT   cross (motif)
SN   Use to describe motifs consisting of
    two intersecting lines or bars, with
    many variations in the shapes of the
    arms. For structures or objects of
    cross shape, especially those used as
    Christian symbols, use **crosses (ob-
    jects)**.
RT   crosses (objects)

crosses (objects)
    PE.41   (B)
HN   January 1993 descriptor added
ALT   cross (object)
SN   Use for structures or objects com-
    posed of two intersecting bars, usu-
    ally an upright one traversed by a
    horizontal one, especially those used
    as Christian symbols. For motifs
    consisting of two intersecting lines,
    with many variations in the shapes
    of the arms, use **crosses (motifs)**.
RT   crosses (motifs)

crosses (quillons)
USE   quillons

crosses (sports equipment)
    TV.30   (N)
ALT   crosse (sports equipment)
SN   Use for long-handled wooden sticks
    with meshwork heads, generally 3 to
    6 feet long and 7 to 12 inches wide
    across the head, for catching, car-
    rying, and throwing balls during the
    game of lacrosse.
UF   lacrosse sticks
    sticks, lacrosse
RT   lacrosse

crosses, ansate
USE   ankhs

crosses, Calvary
USE   Calvary crosses

crosses, Celtic
USE   Celtic crosses

crosses, city
USE   market crosses

crosses, dish
USE   dish crosses

crosses, Egyptian
USE   ankhs

crosses, Greek
USE   Greek crosses

crosses, Iona
USE   Celtic crosses

crosses, Irish
USE   Celtic crosses

crosses, Latin
USE   Latin crosses

crosses, long
USE   Latin crosses

crosses, Lorraine
USE   crosses of Lorraine

crosses, Maltese
USE   Maltese crosses

crosses, market
USE   market crosses

crosses of eight points
USE   Maltese crosses

crosses of Iona
USE   Celtic crosses

crosses of Lorraine
    DG.20   (L)
ALT   cross of Lorraine
SN   Crosses having two crossbars, a
    shorter one crossing above the cen-
    ter and a longer one below the
    center.
UF   crosses, Lorraine
    Lorraine crosses

crosses, papal
USE   papal crosses

crosses, passion
USE   Calvary crosses

crosses, patriarchal
USE   patriarchal crosses

crosses, pope's
USE   papal crosses

crosses, popes'
USE   papal crosses

crosses, preaching
USE   preaching crosses

crosses, ring
USE   Celtic crosses

crosses, roadside
USE wayside crosses

crosses, Saint Andrew's
USE Saint Andrew's crosses

crosses, St. Anthony's
USE tau crosses

crosses, table
USE dish crosses

crosses, tau
USE tau crosses

crosses, wayside
USE wayside crosses

crosses, weeping
USE preaching crosses

crosses, wheel
USE Celtic crosses
     wheel crosses

crosses, wheel-head
USE Celtic crosses

crossettes
PJ.2121
HN April 1993 descriptor moved
ALT crossette
SN Elaborated details projecting later-
     ally at the corners of door and win-
     dow frames.
UF croisettes
     crosettes
     elbows

crossing
USE transverse

crossing towers
PJ.1364   (A)
HN March 1993 descriptor moved
ALT crossing tower
SN Use for towers over the crossings of
     churches.
UF central towers
     lantern towers
     rood spires
     rood steeples
     rood towers
     spires, rood
     steeples, rood
     towers, central
     towers, crossing
     towers, lantern
     towers, rood

crossings
PJ.1265   (L,B)
HN March 1993 descriptor moved
ALT crossing
SN Places in churches where a transept
     crosses the nave. (W)

crossings (grade crossings)
USE grade crossings

crossings, level
USE grade crossings

crossings, railroad
USE grade crossings

crosslap joints
PJ.728
HN April 1993 descriptor moved
ALT crosslap joint
SN Wood joints in which two pieces are
     each cut to half their thickness at
     the overlap, so that the total thick-
     ness of the system does not change.
     (MEANS)
UF joints, crosslap

crosslight
USE crosslighting

crosslighting
KT.747
HN April 1991 descriptor added
UK cross-lighting
SN Method of lighting providing illumi-
     nation from two directions at sub-
     stantially equal and opposite angles
     from each other. (IESREF)
UF crosslight

crosslinking
KT.823   (L)
HN November 1992 descriptor added
ALT crosslinked
SN Joining, by comparatively short con-
     necting units, neighboring chains of
     atoms in a complex chemical mole-
     cule. (W)

crossrails
USE crest rails

crossroads
USE intersections

crosswalks
PJ.855
HN March 1993 descriptor moved
     December 1990 descriptor moved
ALT crosswalk
UK pedestrian crossings
UKA pedestrian crossing
SN Specially paved or marked paths for
     pedestrians crossing a street or
     road. (W)

crosswise
USE transverse

crotales
TT.461
ALT crotale
SN Small metal cymbals, attached in
     pairs to a hinged fork or forked
     sticks that can be tuned to a definite
     pitch. They were known in ancient
     Egypt, Greece, and Rome and con-
     tinue in use in present-day Burma.
UF crotals

crotals
USE crotales

crotch mahogany
MT.2801
HN March 1992 descriptor moved
UF branch mahogany
     mahogany, branch
     mahogany, crotch

croton oil
MT.1074   (L)
HN April 1992 descriptor moved
     October 1990 descriptor moved
UF oil, croton

crots
USE crwths

crouths
USE crwths

Crow
FL.1396   (L)
UF Absaroke

crow gables
USE corbie gables

crowbars
TH.962   (L,N)
ALT crowbar
SN Steel bars with a flattened, forked,
     or chisel-shaped end which is some-
     times slightly bent; used for heavy
     prying, and as a lever for moving
     heavy objects.
UF bars, pry
     crows
     pry bars

crowding
USE overcrowding

crowding stress
USE overcrowding

crowds
USE crwths

crown caps
USE crowns (closures)

crown corks
USE crowns (closures)

crown glass
MT.289
HN March 1993 descriptor moved
UF disc-blown glass
     glass, crown
     glass, disc-blown

crown jewels
PE.83   (L)
HN December 1992 descriptor added
SN Objects of precious materials and
     symbolic value, such as jeweled
     scepters or crowns, appendant to
     the office of a sovereign. (W)
UF jewels, crown

crown land
RD.279   (L)
SN Land in some countries and regions
     belonging to the British Common-
     wealth and held in the name of the
     sovereign.
UF land, crown

Crown Milano
MT.273
HN January 1992 descriptor added
SN Term used in the glass trade for an
     opal glass which has been acid fin-

ished and had various ornate designs embedded in the glass in shades of brown and beige. A type of art glass, developed by the Mt. Washington Glass Company.
UF Crown Milano glass
glass, Crown Milano

Crown Milano glass
USE Crown Milano

crown mold planes
USE cornice planes

crown moldings
PJ.747
HN April 1993 descriptor moved
ALT crown molding
SN The uppermost moldings, as on an interior wall, the top of a cornice, or a piece of furniture.
UF moldings, crown

crown planes
USE cornice planes

crown posts
PJ.1850
HN March 1993 descriptor moved
ALT crown post
SN Any vertical members in a roof truss, especially a king post or a queen post. (RHDEL2)
UF posts, crown

crown saws
TH.544   (N)
ALT crown saw
SN Metal cylinders with teeth cut on one end; used for cutting cylindrical objects or discs from wood, horn, metal, and other materials. (SALAM)
UF cylinder saws
hole saws
round saws
saws, crown
saws, cylinder
saws, hole
saws, round
saws, sheave
saws, trepan
sheave saws
trepan saws

crown seals
USE crowns (closures)

crown steeples
PJ.1349
HN March 1993 descriptor moved
June 1990 scope note changed
June 1990 lead-in term added
ALT crown steeple
SN Openwork spires, the upper portion being carried over an open area by crossed arches or buttresses, thus resembling a crown.
UF crowns (spires)
steeples, crown

crown tile
USE ridge tile

crown wheel escapements
USE verge escapements

crown wheels
PJ.2651
ALT crown wheel
SN Short cylinders with a serrated edge, resembling a crown, used as the escape wheel in verge escapements.
UF wheels, crown

crowns (architectural elements)
PJ.2012
HN March 1993 descriptor moved
ALT crown (architectural element)
SN The highest points of arches or vaults.

crowns (closures)
PJ.3095
ALT crown (closure)
SN Crimped metal bottle caps. (RHDEL2)
UF caps, crown
corks, crown
crown caps
crown corks
crown seals
seals, crown

crowns (coins)
VK.111   (L)
ALT crown (coin)
SN Use only for those British large silver coins struck sporadically from 1551 to 1937 and valued at five shillings, and for British cupronickel coins of the same value issued from 1937 to 1965. (DOTY)

crowns (costume components)
PJ.3039
ALT crown (costume component)
SN The part of a hat or other headgear covering the crown of the head. (W)

crowns (headdresses)
TE.622   (H,L,N,R)
ALT crown (headdress)
SN Ornamental fillets, wreaths, or similar encircling ornaments for the head worn for personal adornment or as a mark of honor or achievement; also, coronal wreaths of leaves or flowers.
RT <ceremonial costume>
tiaras
wreaths (costume accessories)

crowns (spires)
USE crown steeples

crowns, half
USE half crowns

crowns, steeple
USE steeple crowns

crows
USE crowbars

crowstepped gables
USE corbie gables

crowsteps
USE corbiesteps

croziers
USE crosiers

CRT's
USE monitors (data processing equipment)

CRTs
USE monitors (data processing equipment)

Crucero
FL.1047

cruces ansatae
USE ankhs

cruces capitatae
USE Latin crosses

cruces commissae
USE tau crosses

cruces decussatae
USE Saint Andrew's crosses

cruces immissae
USE Latin crosses

crucibles
TQ.72   (L,N)
ALT crucible
SN Vessels or melting pots made of a refractory material (such as clay, graphite, porcelain, or a relatively infusible metal) that may vary in size and that are used for melting and calcining a substance at high temperatures. (W)

cruciform hilts
USE cross hilts

cruciform-plan
USE Greek cross-plan
Latin cross-plan

cruciform stretchers
USE cross stretchers

crucks
PJ.1413   (A,L,R)
HN March 1993 descriptor moved
July 1991 scope note changed
January 1991 descriptor moved
ALT cruck
SN Pairs of naturally curved timbers that rise from the ground or outer walls of buildings to support a ridge beam; joined at the top and connected by tie beams. (DAC)
UF crutches (frame components)

cruel wool
USE crewel wool

cruet bottles
USE cruets

cruet frames
USE cruet stands

cruet sets
 PC.53
 ALT cruet set
 SN Sets of two to five cruets generally accompanied by a cruet stand or a small tray.
 UF sets, cruet
 RT cruets

cruet stands
 TQ.552 (N)
 ALT cruet stand
 SN Receptacles for holding two or more small bottles or other vessels for oil, vinegar, spices, mustard, or other condiments.
 UF cruet frames
  frames, cruet
  stands, cruet
 RT cruets
  dinner services
  mustard casters
  mustard pots

cruets
 TQ.338 (H,L,N,R)
 ALT cruet
 SN Vessels, usually with a handle and a stopper, used to serve condiments; generally of glass and often made in sets of two or more.
 UF bottles, cruet
  crewets
  cruet bottles
  vinaigrettes (cruets)
 RT altar cruets
  bottles
  cruet sets
  cruet stands

cruets, altar
 USE altar cruets

cruets, double
 USE gemel bottles

cruise liners
 USE cruise ships

cruise ships
 TX.399 (L)
 ALT cruise ship
 SN Use for passenger ships taking extended cruises, often with intermediary stops along the way. (RHDEL2)
 UF cruise liners
  liners, cruise
  ships, cruise

cruisers
 TX.431 (L,N)
 ALT cruiser
 SN Use for fast moderately sized warships designed to provide fleet reconnaissance and protection, able to roam independently in search of enemy craft.

cruisers, raised deck
 USE raised deck boats

crumb knives
 USE crumbers

crumbcloths
 TC.363
 ALT crumbcloth
 SN Use for coverings laid under a table to catch crumbs and protect the carpet.
 RT art squares

crumbers
 TH.341 (N)
 HN April 1993 descriptor added
 ALT crumber
 SN Knifelike utensils with one long straight edge shaped like a sharp-edged half-cylinder, or fitted with a friction-driven rotating brush inside a housing, used to remove crumbs from a tablecloth or similar surface.
 UF crumb knives
  knives, crumb

crumbling
 KT.259
 HN January 1993 descriptor moved
 ALT crumbled

crumhorns
 TT.184 (L,N)
 ALT crumhorn
 SN Reedpipes with double reed and cylindrical bore, with a wind cap covering the reed, a body curved at the lower end and slightly flared at the opening, one thumbhole, seven fingerholes, and one or more ventholes in the curved lower section.
 UF Krummhorns
 RT wind caps

cruppers (horse armor)
 TH.23
 HN February 1993 descriptor added
 ALT crupper (horse armor)
 SN Use for plate metal or leather armor protecting a horse's hindquarters, in complete form consisting of three heavy oblong plates covering the top of the rump and sides and back of the hind legs. Lighter versions consist of several leather straps, often metal plated, which run along the spine to the tail guard, down either side of the horse's flanks, and horizontally below the root of the tail. For the leather straps looping around the root of a horse's tail and fastened to the saddle to keep it from slipping forward, use **cruppers (tail straps)**.
 RT cruppers (tail straps)

cruppers (tail straps)
 TH.18 (N)
 HN March 1993 descriptor added
 ALT crupper (tail strap)
 SN Use for the leather straps that loop around the root of a horse's tail and fasten to the saddle to keep it from slipping forward. For the armor protecting a horse's hind quarters, use **cruppers (horse armor)**.
 RT cruppers (horse armor)

Crusader
 FL.3190 (A,R)
 HN October 1991 scope note changed
 SN European-influenced art and architecture of the eastern Mediterranean, from the 12th to the 15th century.

crusaders
 HG.916 (H)
 HN January 1993 descriptor added
 ALT crusader
  crusader's
  crusaders'
 SN Those who engage in aggressive movements or enterprises against some public evil or some institution or group considered an evil. Includes specifically those who take part in wars or fighting expeditions instigated and blessed by the Church.

crushed relief
 USE rilievo schiacciato

crushed rock
 USE crushed stone

crushed stone
 MT.927 (L)
 HN April 1992 descriptor moved
 UF broken stone
  crushed rock
  rock, crushed
  stone, broken
  stone, crushed

crushers, ice
 USE ice crushers

crushing
 KT.276
 ALT crushed

<crushing equipment>
 TH.517

crushing machinery
 TH.518 (L)
 UF machinery, crushing

crushing plants
 RK.596 (B)
 ALT crushing plant
 UF plants, crushing

crusie lamps
 USE crusies

crusie lamps, double valve
 USE double crusies

crusies
 TC.1317
 ALT crusie
 SN Shallow pans, usually open, with the reservoir narrowed at one point to form a channel or slot for the wick; often have an attached curved half bail ending in a hook opposite the wick channel.
 UF chills
  collies

crassets
cressets (crusies)
crusie lamps
crusies, single
lamps, crusie
lamps, witch
single crusies
witch lamps

crusies, double
USE double crusies

crusies, single
USE crusies

crust
   MT.1374
HN June 1992 descriptor added
SN A hard or brittle external coating or covering on a material or object. (W)

crusted (pottery style)
   FL.2743
HN April 1993 descriptor added

crusted ware
HN April 1993 descriptor split, use crusted (pottery style) + ware

crutches
   TH.363   (L,N)
HN January 1993 descriptor added
ALT crutch
SN Staffs or supports to assist a lame or infirm person in walking, especially those with a cross-piece at one end to fit under the armpit. (RHDEL2)

crutches (frame components)
USE crucks

cruths
USE crwths

crwths
   TT.340   (L,N)
ALT crwth
SN Bowed or plucked box lyres of ancient Wales, surviving into the early 19th century.
UF chorus
choruses
crots
crouths
crowds
cruths
crythau

cryolite glass
USE opaque white glass

cryometers
   TN.320   (N)
ALT cryometer
SN Thermometers for measuring low temperatures. (MHDSTT)

cryptographers
   HG.352   (L)
HN December 1992 alternate terms added

ALT cryptographer
cryptographer's
cryptographers'

cryptoportici
   PJ.1029   (H,L)
HN March 1993 descriptor moved
ALT cryptoporticum
SN Use for corridors or galleries in Roman architecture with windowlike openings, whether subterranean or above ground.

crypts
   PJ.1266   (A,L,B,R)
HN March 1993 descriptor moved
ALT crypt
SN Use for subterranean rooms or entire stories in churches, often serving as places of burial.

crystal (lead glass)
   MT.245   (H,L,R)
HN March 1993 descriptor moved
March 1993 descriptor changed, was crystal
UF crystal glass
crystal glass, high-lead
crystal, lead
glass, crystal
glass, high-lead crystal
high-lead crystal glass
lead crystal

crystal (material by form)
   MT.1375   (H,L,B)
HN June 1992 descriptor added
SN A solid body having a characteristic internal structure and enclosed by systematically arranged plane surfaces. (RHDEL2)

crystal glass
USE crystal (lead glass)

crystal glass, high-lead
USE crystal (lead glass)

crystal, lead
USE crystal (lead glass)

crystal, quartz
USE quartz crystal

crystal, rock
USE quartz crystal

crystal, soda
USE sodium carbonate

crystalline glaze
   MT.1998   (L)
UF glaze, crystalline

crystallinity
   DC.248
HN October 1992 descriptor added
ALT crystalline
SN The state or quality of being composed of or like crystals.

crystallization
   KT.824   (L)

HN November 1992 descriptor added
ALT crystallized
UF crystallizing

crystallizing
USE crystallization

crystallographers
   HG.537   (L)
HN December 1992 alternate terms added
ALT crystallographer
crystallographer's
crystallographers'

crystals, snow
USE snowflakes

crythau
USE crwths

Cu
USE copper

Cuadros
   FL.1044

Cuautepec
   FL.997

Cuban
   FL.722   (L,B)

Cuban mahogany
USE South American mahogany

Cuban pine
   MT.2964   (L)
HN March 1992 descriptor moved
June 1990 lead-in term added
UF Caribbean pine
ocote
pine, Cuban
pine, pitch
pine, slash
pine, spruce
pine, swamp
Pinus caribaea
pitch pine
slash pine
spruce pine
swamp pine

cube capitals
USE cushion capitals

Cubeo
   FL.1595   (L)
UF Cobbeos

cubes
   BM.687   (L,R)
HN July 1991 alternate term added
ALT cube
cubic

cubes, flash
USE flash cubes

cubicles, toilet
USE toilet compartments

cubicula
   PJ.1103

HN March 1993 descriptor moved
ALT cubiculum
SN Ancient Roman bedrooms.

cubiform capitals
USE cushion capitals

Cubist
    FL.3382   (A,L,R)
ALT Cubism

Cubist, Analytical
USE Analytical Cubist

Cubist, Collage
USE Synthetic Cubist

Cubist, Facet
USE Analytical Cubist

Cubist-Realist
USE Precisionist

Cubist, Synthetic
USE Synthetic Cubist

Cubo-Futurist
    FL.3509   (L,R)
ALT Cubo-Futurism

Cubo-Realist
USE Precisionist

cuckoo clocks
    TN.177
ALT cuckoo clock
SN Wall clocks elaborately carved and decorated, usually with floral motifs, that announce the hours by a sound like the call of the cuckoo; often with exposed weights and pendulum. Introduced in the mid-18th century in the Black Forest region, the earliest examples had wooden movements.
UF clocks, cuckoo

Cucuteni-Tripolye
USE Tripolye

cudbear
USE orchil

cudgels
USE froe clubs

cue sticks
USE cues

cuenas
USE quenas

cuenca (pottery technique)
    KT.1167
HN April 1993 descriptor changed, was cuenca
    January 1993 descriptor moved
SN A technique of decoration employed in Spain for tiles and other wares which superseded the cuerda seca method. It involved impressing the pattern on tiles to form ridges which prevented the colored glazes from intermingling. (IDC74)

Cuenca (textile style)
    FL.3542
HN April 1993 descriptor added

cuerda seca
    KT.1168
HN January 1993 descriptor moved
SN Tile decoration technique found in Spain in which outlines were drawn on the surface of the ware with a greasy substance colored with manganese, allowing glazes of several colors to be used without intermingling. The grease would disappear during firing. (IDC74)

cues
    TV.46   (N)
ALT cue
SN Long, usually wooden, sticks with various types of heads used to propel balls or disks in some games, such as billiards and shuffleboard.
UF cue sticks
     sticks, cue
RT billiards
     shuffleboard

Cueva-Cuna
    FL.1566

cuff links
    TE.484   (L,N)
ALT cuff link
SN Linked ornamental buttons or buttonlike devices for fastening a shirt cuff. (RHDEL2)
UF links, cuff
RT buttons (fasteners)

cuff ruffs
USE sleeve ruffs

cuffs (costume accessories)
    TE.430   (L,N)
ALT cuff (costume accessory)
SN Any of various folds or bands serving as a trimming or finish for the bottom of a sleeve, trousers, the top of a boot, or the like; includes those made as separate items and worn with or attached to garments or costume accessories and those made as component parts of garments or costume accessories.
RT *<costume components>*

cuffs (leg components)
    PJ.2852
HN March 1993 descriptor moved
ALT cuff (leg component)

cuffs, boot
USE boot cuffs

Cufic
USE Kufic

cuícas
    TT.565
ALT cuíca
SN Friction drums of Brazil, the membrane of which is perforated by a

stick which is rubbed with either the player's wetted hands or a damp cloth.
UF puícas

Cuicatec
    FL.1531   (L)

Cuicuilco
USE Ticomán

Cuicuru
USE Kuikuru

Cuilcuilco-Ticomán
USE Ticomán

cuir bouilli
    MT.2595
HN February 1992 descriptor added
SN Strong, rigid leather used for durable items such as powder flasks, pots, or armor, made by tanning skin in a hot tanning solution and molding, pressing, or stamping it to shape.

cuirasses
    TE.312   (H,N,R)
ALT cuirass
SN Armor protecting the front and back of the torso, variously made throughout their history of layers of linen or leather, metal scales, lames, or plates, or combinations of leather and metal.

cuirasses, waistcoat
USE waistcoat cuirasses

cuisses
    TE.340
ALT cuisse
SN Plate armor for the thighs, usually attached to the poleyns at their lower end. Introduced during the 14th century, they evolved from a single plate covering the front of the thigh to articulated lames encircling the entire thigh.
UF quissers

cuisses, tilting
USE tilting sockets

cul de fours
USE semidomes

culets
    TE.342
ALT culet
SN Armor pieces worn in both foot and mounted combat to protect the upper part of the buttocks, consisting of one or more articulated lames.
UF garde-reins
     guards, rump
     hoguines
     rump guards

Culhucán
USE Aztec I

<*culinary containers*>
TQ.268
RT <*culinary equipment*>
kitchenware

<*culinary equipment*>
TH.31
HN April 1993 guide term added
RT <*culinary containers*>
<*culinary tool components*>

<*culinary equipment by form*>
TH.32
HN April 1993 guide term added

<*culinary equipment by function*>
TH.43
HN April 1993 guide term added

<*culinary equipment for cooling food*>
TH.44
HN April 1993 guide term added
RT <*cooling, heating and humidifying equipment*>

<*culinary equipment for preparing and cooking food*>
TH.48
HN April 1993 guide term added

<*culinary equipment for serving and consuming food*>
TH.245
HN April 1993 guide term added
RT <*containers for serving and consuming food*>

<*culinary equipment: textiles*>
TH.33
HN April 1993 guide term added

<*culinary molds*>
TH.201
HN April 1993 guide term added
RT molds

<*culinary tool components*>
PJ.2602
RT <*culinary equipment*>
grills
spits

<*culinary tools and equipment for cutting*>
TH.97
HN April 1993 guide term added
RT <*cutting equipment*>
grape shears
knives (culinary tools)

<*culinary tools and equipment for mixing*>
TH.134
HN April 1993 guide term added

<*culinary tools for extracting*>
TH.155
HN April 1993 guide term added

<*culinary tools for handling food or culinary equipment*>
TH.166
HN April 1993 guide term added

<*culinary tools for opening*>
TH.173
HN April 1993 guide term added

<*culinary tools for separating*>
TH.178
HN April 1993 guide term added

<*culinary tools for shaping and decorating*>
TH.197
HN April 1993 guide term added

cullenders
USE colanders

Cullens earth
USE Vandyke brown

cullet
MT.333
HN January 1992 descriptor added
SN Scrap glass intended for reuse or recycling.

cullonen
USE white beech

<*culminating and edge ornaments*>
PJ.10
HN May 1993 guide term moved
RT <*culminating and edge ornaments: architectural*>

<*culminating and edge ornaments: architectural*>
PJ.2353
HN March 1993 guide term added
RT <*culminating and edge ornaments*>

culots
USE husks (motifs)

culotte skirts
USE culottes

culottes
TE.83 (N)
SN Exposed, bifurcated garments which hang and have an exterior silhouette of a skirt. May have a panel to cover the joint between the legs. (NMAHDC)
UF culotte skirts
skirts, culotte
RT skirts

culs-de-sac
RM.143 (A,L)
HN April 1993 descriptor moved
ALT cul-de-sac
SN Use for dead-end streets that have circular turn-around areas at their ends.

culs postiches
USE bustles

cult images
VC.56 (L,R)
ALT cult image
SN Pictorial or sculptural images that are venerated within a particular system of worship. For objects used similarly but containing no images, use **religious objects** or **cult objects**.

UF idols
images, cult
RT cult objects

cult objects
PE.65
HN December 1992 descriptor added
ALT cult object
SN Objects that are venerated within a particular system of worship; for those that are, or contain, images, use **cult images**. Use especially with regard to extinct cultures and religions; for objects venerated in still-living religions, prefer **religious objects**, and if those objects retain their sacredness in their present context, use **sacred objects**.
UF objects, cult
RT cult images

cultural anthropologists
USE social anthropologists

cultural anthropology
USE social anthropology

cultural buildings
USE cultural centers

cultural centers
RK.1134 (A,N,B,R)
ALT cultural center
UF buildings, cultural
centers, cultural
cultural buildings

<*cultural ceremonies*>
KM.25

cultural diffusion
BM.1055 (L)
HN December 1992 descriptor added
SN The spread of cultural traits and institutions from one human community, society, or generation to another via contact and interaction.
UF cultural transmission
diffusion, cultural
dissemination of culture
transmission, cultural

cultural landscapes
RD.248
HN March 1993 related term added
ALT cultural landscape
SN Designates land and water areas significantly altered or modified by human actions; used in contrast to **natural landscapes**, that designate areas where human effects, if present, are not ecologically significant to the regions as a whole.
UF landscapes, cultural
RT natural landscapes

<*cultural landscapes by development practice*>
RD.271

<*cultural landscapes by function*>
RD.249

<cultural landscapes by location or context>
RD.259

<cultural landscapes by ownership>
RD.277

<cultural movements and attitudes>
BM.281

cultural patrimony
USE cultural property

cultural pluralism
USE multiculturalism

cultural property
BM.921 (A,L)
HN February 1993 descriptor moved
UF cultural patrimony
heritage property
national treasure
patrimony, cultural
property, cultural
property, heritage
treasure, national

cultural transmission
USE cultural diffusion

culturally sensitive materials
USE culturally sensitive objects

culturally sensitive objects
PE.8
HN December 1992 descriptor added
ALT culturally sensitive object
SN Use broadly for objects or types of objects about which people of the culture from which the objects originate have concerns about the objects' present and future use, care, and possession.
UF culturally sensitive materials
materials, culturally sensitive
materials, sensitive
objects, culturally sensitive
objects, sensitive
sensitive materials
sensitive objects

culture
BM.262 (L,R)
HN February 1992 scope note added
ALT cultural
SN The sum total of ways of living built up by a group of people and transmitted from one generation to another. (RHDEL2)

<culture and related concepts>
BM.261

culture, counter
USE radicalism

culture, mass
USE popular culture

culture, material
USE material culture

culture, popular
USE popular culture

culture, punk
USE punk culture

<culture-related concepts>
BM.263

culverins
TK.141 (N)
ALT culverin
SN Term used from the 15th to the 17th century for cannons especially long in proportion to their bore.

culverins, bastard
USE serpentines (cannons)

culverts
RK.510 (L,B)
ALT culvert
SN Use for drainage structures that extend across and beneath roadways, canals, embankments, or traveled ways other than bridges.

cum ceilings
USE camp ceilings

Cumberland Fluted
FL.747
UF Fluted, Cumberland

cummerbunds
TE.686 (N)
ALT cummerbund
SN Wide sashes worn at the waist, especially horizontally pleated ones worn with tuxedoes. (RHDEL2)
UF kummerbunds
RT tuxedoes

cumulative indexes
VW.866
HN November 1992 descriptor moved
ALT cumulative index
SN Indexes which combine separately published indexes into one sequence. (LG)
UF indexes, cumulative

Cuna
FL.1565 (L)

cunei
PJ.1298
HN March 1993 descriptor moved
ALT cuneus
SN Use for wedgeshaped sections of seats in ancient theaters.

cuneiform
PJ.3440 (L)
SN Script originally developed for the Sumerian language in the 3rd millennium BCE, consisting of characters made in clay with a wedge-shaped stylus. (FOFDA)
UF cuneiform script
cuneiform writing
script, cuneiform
writing, cuneiform

cuneiform script
USE cuneiform

cuneiform writing
USE cuneiform

cup-and-ball games
USE cup-and-ball toys

cup-and-ball toys
TV.146 (N)
ALT cup-and-ball toy
SN Use for toys consisting of a stick with a cuplike top and a ball attached to the stick by a string long enough for the ball to swing freely and be swung up and caught in the cup.
UF balls, cup and
bilboquets
cup-and-ball games
cup and balls
cups and balls
games, cup-and-ball
toys, cup-and-ball
RT mechanical puzzles

cup and balls
USE cup-and-ball toys

cup escutcheons
PJ.440
HN April 1993 descriptor moved
ALT cup escutcheon
UF escutcheons, cup

cup-hilts
PJ.3142
ALT cup-hilt
SN Hilts characterized by a cup- or bowl-shaped guard in front of the quillons, covering the user's hand and the arms of the hilt, developed in 17th-century Spain and those parts of Italy under Spanish influence. They are most often found on rapiers.

cup joints
PJ.689
HN April 1993 descriptor moved
ALT cup joint
SN In plumbing, a socket joint formed between two similar pipes in the same line, by opening out the end of one pipe to receive the tapered end of the other. (PUTNAM)
UF joints, cup

cup plates
TQ.363 (L,N)
ALT cup plate
SN Small plates, generally 3 to 4 inches in diameter, made in pressed glass and used to hold ceramic teacups while tea is being drunk from the saucer.
UF plates, cup
saucers, tea
tea saucers
RT saucers
teacups

cupboard beds
USE box beds
press beds (deception beds)

cupboard catches
PJ.325
HN April 1993 descriptor moved
ALT cupboard catch
UF catches, cupboard

cupboard cloths
TC.276
ALT cupboard cloth
SN Period term for textile coverings for cupboards.
UF cloths, cupboard
covers, cupboard
cupboard covers

cupboard covers
USE cupboard cloths

cupboard knobs
USE cabinet knobs

cupboard locks
PJ.542
HN April 1993 descriptor moved
ALT cupboard lock
UF locks, cupboard

cupboard turns
PJ.330
HN April 1993 descriptor moved
ALT cupboard turn
UF turns, cupboard

cupboards
TC.913   (A,L,N,B,R)
HN May 1993 scope note changed
May 1993 related terms added
January 1993 descriptor moved
August 1992 lead-in term deleted, was **huches**
ALT cupboard
SN Originally boards or open structures of shelves on which cups, especially silver, might be placed for storage or display; often used interchangeably with buffets and dressers in the Middle Ages. Beginning in the 15th century, doors were added. Today a generic term for all such receptacles enclosed by doors, sometimes built-in.
UF credences (cupboards)
hutches
vaisseliers
RT aumbries
buffets
built-in furniture
dressers (cupboards)

cupboards, almoners
USE livery cupboards

cupboards, bedside
USE night tables

cupboards, book
USE book cupboards

cupboards, bread and cheese
USE livery cupboards

cupboards, broom
SEE broom closets

cupboards, butter
USE livery cupboards

cupboards, close
USE aumbries

cupboards, clothes
USE wardrobes (case furniture)

cupboards, clothes
SEE clothes closets

cupboards, corner
USE corner cupboards

cupboards, court
USE court cupboards

cupboards, dole
USE dole cupboards

cupboards, food
USE livery cupboards

cupboards, hanging
USE hanging cupboards

cupboards, linen
USE linen presses

cupboards, linen
SEE linen closets

cupboards, livery
USE livery cupboards

cupboards, plate
USE court cupboards

cupboards, press
USE press cupboards

cupboards, spice
USE spice cupboards

cupboards, tridarn
USE tridarns

cupboards, wall
USE hanging cupboards

cupboards, Welsh
USE tridarns

Cupeño
FL.1266   (L)

Cupisnique
FL.1158   (L)
UF Coast Chavin

cupolas
PJ.1813   (N,R)
HN March 1993 descriptor moved
July 1991 scope note changed
ALT cupola
SN Use for small structures built on the ridges of roofs, particularly common in American architecture; when these structures are intended to be used as lookouts, prefer **belvederes**; for windowed superstructures on roofs or domes used to admit light or air to the space below, use **lanterns (roof appendages)**; for hemispherical roofs, use **domes**.

cupolas (domes)
USE domes

cupped nails
PJ.166
HN April 1993 descriptor moved
ALT cupped nail
UF nails, cupped

cupping
KT.257
HN January 1993 descriptor added
ALT cupped
SN Formation of a concavity or cuplike hollow in a paint layer. (GRCA)
UF curling (cracking)

cupping bowls
USE bleeding bowls

Cupressus
USE cypress

Cupressus lawsoniana
USE Port Orford cedar

Cupressus sempervirens
USE classic cypress

cupro-nickel
SEE cupronickel

Cuprolithic
USE Chalcolithic

cupronickel
MT.409
HN March 1992 descriptor added
UK cupro-nickel
SN Alloy of copper, nickel, iron, and manganese in which copper is dominant; the metal of choice for late-20th-century coins, also used for condenser plates and heat exchangers.

cups
TQ.395   (H,L,N,R)
ALT cup
SN Open bowl-shaped vessels, used chiefly for drinking, often having one handle, but sometimes two handles or none, generally on a low foot-ring; also includes similar bowl-shaped vessels, generally without handles, resting on a stem and supported by a spreading foot. Occasionally made with a lid.
UF cups, drinking
drinking cups
RT bouillon cups
canns
custard cups
fuddling cups
kylikes
mugs
palette cups
saucers
tableware
tazzas
trembleuses
wager cups
zarfs

cups, acorn
USE   acorn cups

cups and balls
USE   cup-and-ball toys

cups, band
USE   band cups

cups, bouillon
USE   bouillon cups

cups, bridal
USE   wager cups

<cups by form>
TQ.396

<cups by function>
TQ.414

cups, cassel
USE   cassel cups

cups, caudle
USE   caudle cups

cups, chocolate
USE   chocolate cups

cups, coconut
USE   coconut cups

cups, coffee
USE   coffee cups

cups, columbine
USE   columbine cups

cups, communion
USE   communion cups

cups, covered
USE   covered cups

cups, custard
USE   custard cups

cups, demitasse
USE   demitasses

cups, depas
USE   depas

cups, dipper
USE   palette cups

cups, double
USE   double cups

cups, dram
USE   dram cups

cups, drinking
USE   cups

cups, droop
USE   droop cups

cups, flat-bowl
USE   font-shaped cups

cups, font-shaped
USE   font-shaped cups

cups, force
USE   plungers

cups, fuddling
USE   fuddling cups

cups, gordion
USE   gordion cups

cups, grace
USE   loving cups

cups, kiddush
USE   kiddush cups

cups, lemonade
USE   punch cups

cups, lip
USE   lip cups

cups, little master
USE   little master cups

cups, loving
USE   loving cups

cups, marriage
USE   wager cups

cups, mastoid
USE   mastoid cups

cups, measuring
USE   measuring cups

cups, merrythought
USE   merrythought cups

cups, mint julep
USE   beakers (drinking vessels)

cups, mustache
USE   mustache cups

cups, mustard
USE   mustard pots

cups, nautilus
USE   nautilus shell cups

cups, nautilus shell
USE   nautilus shell cups

cups, oil
USE   palette cups

cups, orange
USE   orange cups

cups, ostrich-egg
USE   ostrich-egg cups

cups, palette
USE   palette cups

cups, posset
USE   posset pots

cups, punch
USE   punch cups

cups, puzzle
USE   wager cups

cups, quaffing
USE   wine cups

cups, shaving
USE   shaving mugs

cups, siana
USE   siana cups

cups, slip
USE   slip cups

cups, slip-trailing
USE   slip cups

cups, soup
USE   bouillon cups

cups, spout
USE   spout cups

cups, standing
USE   standing cups

cups, stirrup
USE   stirrup cups

cups, tea
USE   teacups

cups, thistle
USE   thistle cups

cups, tumbler
USE   tumblers (drinking glasses)

cups, two-handled
USE   two-handled cups

cups, vodka
USE   charkas

cups, wager
USE   wager cups

cups, wine
USE   wine cups

curating
KG.121
SN Superintending or managing the collections, exhibits, research activities, and personnel of a museum, art gallery, zoo, or other place of exhibit; also, the superintending or managing of a single collection or subject of study in such an institution. (W)
UF curatorship

curators
HG.381   (L)
HN December 1992 alternate terms added
ALT curator
curator's
curators'
SN Persons engaged in curating.
UF keepers

curatorship
USE   curating

curb joints
USE   knuckle joints

curb rolls
USE   knuckle joints

curb roofs
PJ.1764

HN March 1993 descriptor moved
ALT curb roof
SN Roofs in which the slope is broken, the lower slope being steeper than the upper slope; may be two-sided or four-sided roofs.
UF dual-pitched roofs
roofs, curb
roofs, dual-pitched

curbing
MT.944 (B)
HN April 1992 descriptor moved
UF curbstone

curbs
PJ.836 (L,B)
HN March 1993 descriptor moved
ALT curb
SN Raised edgings, as of stone or concrete, built along driveways, roads, or roofs, usually forming part of a gutter.

curbs, seat
USE fender stools

curbstone
USE curbing

curcas oil
MT.1075
HN April 1992 descriptor moved
October 1990 descriptor moved
UF oil, curcas

curcuma
USE turmeric

curd baskets
USE cheese baskets

curd cutters
USE curd knives

curd knives
TH.113 (N)
HN April 1993 descriptor added
ALT curd knife
SN Tools of various forms used to cut soft curd into cubes to facilitate drainage of whey. Prefer **cheese knives (food preparation tools)** for large spatulas used to break up the curd for cheesemaking.
UF cheese knives (curd knives)
curd cutters
cutters, curd
knives, cheese
knives, curd
RT cheese knives (food preparation tools)

curiae
RK.940
ALT curia
SN Council houses in Roman municipalities. (HAS)

curing
KT.860 (L)
HN November 1992 descriptor moved
October 1991 descriptor moved
October 1991 scope note added

October 1991 descriptor changed, was **curing (leather)**
ALT cured
SN A process or method involving aging, seasoning, washing, drying, heating, smoking, or otherwise treating whereby a product is preserved, perfected, or readied for use. (W)

curing agent
MT.1689
HN April 1993 descriptor changed, was **curing agents**
UF agent, curing

curlers
TH.380 (N)
HN January 1993 descriptor added
ALT curler
SN Any of various pins, clasps, rollers, or appliances on which locks of hair are wound or clamped for curling. (RHDEL2)

curlers, butter
USE butter curlers

curling (cracking)
USE cupping

curling (game)
KQ.90 (H,L)
RT curling brooms
curling stones

curling (structural change)
KT.260
HN March 1993 scope note changed
March 1993 descriptor changed, was **curling**
January 1993 descriptor moved
ALT curled
SN The distortion of an object originally linear or planar so that it is curved or coiled in shape.

curling brooms
TV.87 (N)
ALT curling broom
SN Specially designed brooms used to sweep the ice in the game of curling.
UF besoms
brooms (curling equipment)
brooms, curling
RT curling (game)

curling-irons
SEE curling irons

curling irons
TH.381 (N)
HN January 1993 descriptor added
ALT curling iron
UK curling-irons
UKA curling-iron
SN Rod-shaped, usually metal instruments around which locks of hair are wound for curling by means of heat.
UF curling sticks
curling tongs

irons, curling
sticks, curling
tongs, curling

curling sticks
USE curling irons

curling stones
TV.88 (N)
ALT curling stone
SN Use for large, heavy, ellipsoidal stone or iron disks usually having one rough side and one smooth side with a hole in the center of each into which can be screwed a short gooseneck handle by which the disks are released across the ice in the game of curling.
UF stones
stones, curling
RT curling (game)

curling tongs
USE curling irons

curraghs
TX.511
ALT curragh
SN Use for vessels constructed of skin, or later of tarred canvas, over a substantial wooden frame and having a distinctive narrow shape, with the bottom rising forward and a definite knuckle or break in the sheer; sometimes as large as 10m long, built in Ireland, particularly on the west coast.

currency
USE money

currency, emergency
USE emergency currency

currency, fractional
USE fractional currency

currency, occupation
USE occupation currency

currency, paper
USE paper money

currency, spade
USE spade money

curricles (carriages)
TX.190 (N)
ALT curricle (carriage)
SN Use for light, two-wheeled carriages, open or hooded, akin to gigs and chaises but, instead of having shafts, equipped with traces and a center pole to be drawn by two horses abreast; popular in England and the United States from the mid-18th to the mid-19th century, although production continued into the early 20th century.

curricles (chairs)
TC.486
HN May 1993 related term added

March 1993 descriptor changed, was **curricles**
March 1993 alternate term changed, was **curricle**
January 1993 descriptor moved
ALT curricle (chair)
SN Term used by Sheraton to describe armchairs having a semicircular back and elongated seat, whose shape suggests an open carriage.
UF chairs, cirricule
     cirricule chairs
     currieles
RT armchairs

curricula
VW.802   (L)
HN November 1992 descriptor moved
ALT curriculum

curricula vitae
USE resumes

currieles
USE curricles (chairs)

Currier and Ives frames
TC.407
ALT Currier and Ives frame
SN Use for frames with overlapping moldings and corner embellishment, often carved to imitate wood bark, popular in the 19th century and named for American artists Nathaniel Currier and James M. Ives. (ADAIR)
UF frames, Currier and Ives

curriers
HG.704
HN December 1992 alternate terms added
ALT currier
     currier's
     curriers'
SN Persons who dress and color leather after it has been tanned. (RHDEL2)

currying
KT.1047
HN January 1993 descriptor moved
     October 1992 scope note changed
     October 1991 descriptor moved
ALT curried
SN Incorporating a fatty substance into heavy leather, such as belting leather, to increase its strength, pliability, and water repellency; distinguished from **fat-liquoring**, which is the introduction of a fatty substance into light leather.

cursive
FL.1190
UF Abigarrado
     cursive modeled
     modeled, cursive

cursive, capitalis
USE older Roman cursive

cursive, earlier Roman
USE older Roman cursive

cursive, Gothic
USE Gothic cursive

cursive, humanistic
USE humanistic cursive

cursive, later Roman
USE later Roman cursive

cursive, majuscule
USE older Roman cursive

cursive, minuscule
USE later Roman cursive

cursive modeled
USE cursive

cursive, new Roman
USE later Roman cursive

cursive, newer Roman
USE later Roman cursive

cursive, older Roman
USE older Roman cursive

cursive typefaces
USE italic (typeface group)
     script (typeface group)

curtain papers
TC.335
ALT curtain paper
SN Wallpapers made to be hung as window shades.
UF curtain wallpapers
     papers, curtain
     wallpapers, curtain
RT wallpapers

curtain straps
USE tiebacks

curtain wallpapers
USE curtain papers

curtain walls (fortification elements)
PJ.2479
HN March 1993 descriptor moved
ALT curtain wall (fortification element)
SN Use for the enclosing walls connecting bastions or towers in fortifications.
UF walls, curtain

curtain walls (nonbearing walls)
PJ.1915   (A,L,B)
HN March 1993 descriptor moved
     May 1991 descriptor changed, was **curtain walls**
     May 1991 alternate term changed, was **curtain wall**
ALT curtain wall (nonbearing wall)
SN Nonbearing walls supported by the members of a rigid frame structure, such as a reinforced concrete or steel frame, and therefore serving to enclose but not to support.
UF enclosure walls
     walls, curtain
     walls, enclosure
     walls, window
     window walls

curtains
TC.302   (A,L,N,R)
ALT curtain
SN Cloth hangings for windows, doorways, or other openings that are generally finished with hems, casings, pleats, or ruffles and hung by the top edge; used for privacy, control of light and drafts, or decoration.
UF curtains, outer
     outer curtains
     over-curtains
     overcurtains
RT bed curtains
     dossals
     Lenten veils
     parokhets
     riddels

curtains, ark
USE parokhets

curtains, asbestos
USE asbestos curtains

curtains, bed
USE bed curtains

<curtains by form>
TC.303

<curtains by form: length>
TC.316

<curtains by location or context>
TC.319

<curtains by mode of operation>
TC.328

curtains, café
USE café curtains

curtains, case
USE case curtains

curtains, cottage
USE cottage curtains

curtains, divided
USE divided curtains

curtains, dossal
USE dossals

curtains, drapery
USE festoon curtains

curtains, draw
USE draw curtains

curtains, draw-up
USE pull-up curtains

curtains, dress
USE dress curtains

curtains, drop
USE drop curtains

curtains, festoon
USE festoon curtains

curtains, fire
USE asbestos curtains

curtains, floor-length
USE floor-length curtains

curtains, foot
USE foot curtains

curtains, full
USE straight hanging curtains

curtains, full-length
USE floor-length curtains

curtains, glass
USE glass curtains

curtains, half
USE café curtains
sash curtains

curtains, head
USE head curtains

curtains, inner
USE undercurtains

curtains, Lenten
USE Lenten veils

curtains, outer
USE curtains

curtains, priscilla
USE priscilla curtains

curtains, pull-up
USE pull-up curtains

curtains, reefed
USE festoon curtains

curtains, riddel
USE riddels

curtains, safety
USE asbestos curtains

curtains, sash
USE sash curtains

curtains, sheer
USE sheer curtains

curtains, shower
USE shower curtains

curtains, sill
USE sill-length curtains

curtains, sill-length
USE sill-length curtains

curtains, sliding
USE draw curtains

curtains, straight
USE straight hanging curtains

curtains, straight hanging
USE straight hanging curtains

curtains, swag
USE festoon curtains

curtains, tableau
USE tableau curtains

curtains, tailed
USE festoon curtains

curtains, tieback
USE tieback curtains

curtains, Torah
USE parokhets

curtains, Torah ark
USE parokhets

curtains, traverse
USE draw curtains

curtains, Venetian
USE festoon curtains

curtals
USE dulcians

curule chairs
USE sellae curulis

curule legs
PJ.2841
HN March 1993 descriptor moved
ALT curule leg
SN X-shaped legs based on Roman chair design, used on Federal and other classically inspired furnishings. (CTSB)
UF cross legs, Grecian
Grecian cross legs
legs, curule
legs, Grecian cross
legs, X-shaped
X-shaped legs

curvature
USE curved

curve tracers
USE flexible curves

curved
DC.63   (L)
HN October 1992 descriptor moved
May 1991 lead-in term added
UF curvature

curved-back chairs en gondola
USE gondola chairs

curved cornetts
TT.67
ALT curved cornett
SN The most common type of cornett, made of a long section of wood, split in two and glued together after the conical tube was carved out, finished to an octagonal exterior cross-section, and covered in thin black leather. Usually the instruments curved to the right, accommodating right-handed players, but left-curving models were also made.
UF black cornetts
cornetts, black
cornetts, curved

curved dormers
HN April 1991 descriptor deleted

<curved mirrors>
TC.1463
SN Collocates descriptors for mirrors having curved, rather than flat, reflective surfaces.

curved trusses
USE crescent trusses

curved windows
USE bow windows

curves
TH.993   (N,B)
HN November 1992 descriptor moved
ALT curve
SN Tools which take a variety of forms; used to guide draftsmen in drawing curved lines.
UF curves, drawing
drawing curves

curves, Brook's
USE Brook's curves

curves, drawing
USE curves

curves, flexible
USE flexible curves

curves, French
USE French curves

curves, irregular
USE French curves

curves, snake
USE flexible curves

curves, whiplash
USE whiplash curves

curvilinear
DC.66   (A)
HN April 1993 related terms added
October 1992 descriptor moved
SN Consisting of or bounded by curved lines. With reference to furniture pieces, the fronts of which have alternating concave and convex curves, use **serpentine (shape)**. For other features, such as arches or moldings, composed of flowing, wavelike curves, use **undulating**.
RT serpentine (shape)
undulating

Curvilinear Decorated
FL.3215
UF Curvilinear Style (architecture style)
Decorated, Curvilinear

Curvilinear Style
FL.2682
UF Naturalistic Style

Curvilinear Style (architecture style)
USE Curvilinear Decorated

curvilinear tracery
PJ.2327
HN March 1993 descriptor moved
March 1991 scope note added
March 1991 descriptor changed, was **flowing tracery**
March 1991 lead-in term changed, was **curvilinear tracery**

SN Use for tracery in which continuous compound or ogee curves predominate.
UF flowing tracery
tracery, curvilinear
tracery, flowing
tracery, undulating
undulating tracery

cushion capitals
PJ.1497
HN March 1993 descriptor moved
December 1990 scope note changed
December 1990 lead-in terms added
ALT cushion capital
SN Cubic capitals with their lower angles rounded off, to make the transition to a round column; found in Medieval architecture.
UF block capitals
capitals, block
capitals, cube
capitals, cushion
capitals, pillow
cube capitals
cubiform capitals
pillow capitals

cushion lace
USE bobbin lace

cushioned friezes
USE pulvinated friezes

cushions
TC.1486   (L,N)
ALT cushion
SN Bags or similar containers made typically of cloth, leather, or rubber stuffed with a resilient material and used to give support or ease to the body while sitting, reclining, or kneeling.

Cushite
USE Kushite

cusped arches
PJ.1584
HN March 1993 descriptor moved
ALT cusped arch
SN Arches which have cusps or foliations worked on the intrados. (RS)
UF arches, cusped
arches, foiled
arches, lobed
foiled arches
lobed arches

cuspidors
USE spittoons

cusps
PJ.2358
HN March 1993 descriptor moved
December 1990 scope note changed
ALT cusp
SN The intersection of two arcs or foils, as in Gothic tracery.

custard cups
TQ.350   (N)
ALT custard cup

SN Small cups for serving, and sometimes also baking, an individual portion of custard or similar food. Generally made in sets; may have a cover or one or more handles.
UF cups, custard
RT cups
dinner services
ramekins

custard glasses
TQ.356
ALT custard glass
SN Dessert glasses for serving an individual portion of custard, sometimes set on a stem and may have a single handle.
UF glasses, custard

custard kettles
USE double boilers

custodians
HG.90   (L)
HN November 1992 alternate terms added
ALT custodian
custodian's
custodians'
SN Persons officially entrusted with guarding and keeping things, such as property, artifacts, or records, or with custody or guardianship of people, such as prisoners, inmates, or wards. (W)

custom-made
DC.32
HN November 1992 descriptor added
SN Use to describe items made to an individual's specific order, especially items of clothing.

customhouses
RK.930   (A,B,R)
HN September 1990 scope note added
ALT customhouse
SN Use for government office buildings where customs and duties are paid or collected and where vessels are recorded and cleared. (W)
UF customs posts
posts, customs

customs
BM.265   (L,R)
HN January 1991 alternate term added
ALT custom
SN Usages, practices, or conventions that regulate social life. (W)
UF social customs

customs posts
USE border inspection stations
customhouses

customs records
VW.726
HN November 1992 descriptor moved
ALT customs record
UF records, custom

cut and straight hangers
PJ.103
HN April 1993 descriptor moved
ALT cut and straight hanger
UF hangers, cut and straight

cut-card ornament
USE cut-card work

cut-card work
DG.7
HN February 1993 descriptor added
SN Use for applied decoration consisting of a thin sheet of metal, usually silver, cut from a rolled sheet to produce a border or surface silhouette design and affixed by soldering to an object.
UF cardwork
cut-card ornament

cut edges
PJ.3379
SN Book edges that have been smoothly cut with a guillotine.
UF edges, cut

cut film
MT.2375
HN April 1992 descriptor moved
UF film, cut
film, sheet
sheet film

cut glass
MT.290   (H,L)
HN January 1992 descriptor added
SN Use generally to describe glassware with facets, grooves, and depressions produced by cutting with a rotating wheel of metal or stone.
UF glass, cut

cut-in indexes
USE thumb indexes

cut nails
PJ.151
HN April 1993 descriptor moved
ALT cut nail
SN Hard, wedge-shaped nails used for nailing hardwoods such as oak flooring. (MEANS)
UF clasp nails
nails, clasp
nails, cut

cut-out chintz appliqué
USE broderie perse

cut pile
USE pile-woven carpets

cut-pile cloth
HN March 1993 descriptor deleted

cut slating nails
PJ.190
HN April 1993 descriptor moved
ALT cut slating nail
UF nails, cut slating
slating nails, cut

cut stone
USE dimension stone

cut strings
USE open strings

cut velvet
MT.1604
HN November 1992 descriptor added
SN Velvet in which the loops formed by the pile warp are cut to form tufts. (WRPWFT)
UF velvet, cut

cutaway coats
USE cutaways

cutaway drawings
VC.86
HN April 1992 descriptor moved
ALT cutaway drawing
SN Use for drawings in which part of an object or structure is removed to show the interior. For orthographic drawings specifically, use **broken-out sections, half sections** (for objects), or **sectional elevations** (for structures).
UF cutaways (drawings)
drawings, cutaway

cutaways
TE.10   (N)
ALT cutaway
UK morning coats
UKA morning coat
SN Suit coats having tails extending to near the back of the knee; the front is cut away on a curved line from the waist in front to the rear; originally derived from riding coats.
UF coats, cutaway
coats, morning
cutaway coats

cutaways (drawings)
USE cutaway drawings

cutch
MT.2120   (L)
HN April 1992 descriptor moved
SN Natural, nearly permanent dye obtained chiefly from various species of acacia and mimosa, used to produce shades of brown, black, and olive; also employed in tanning leather. (MAYER)
UF Bengal cutch
cachou
catechu
cutch, Bengal
earth, Japan
Japan earth
katechu

cutch, Bengal
USE cutch

cutch-grass
USE couch grass

cutflower baskets
USE flower baskets

cutis vera
USE corium

cutlasses
TK.72   (H,N)
ALT cutlass
SN Short, heavy cutting swords with a curved, single-edged blade. From the late 17th century onwards, the term has been used specifically for this type of sword as worn and used by navy personnel.
RT cutting swords

cutlers
HG.778   (L)
HN January 1993 descriptor added
ALT cutler
cutler's
cutlers'
SN Those who make, sell, or repair knives and other cutting implements. (RHDEL2)
RT cutlery

cutlery
TH.38   (H,L)
HN April 1993 descriptor added
SN Culinary utensils that have a cutting edge, especially various forms of knives used for cutting, carving, dividing, or serving food. Sometimes used to embrace all types of flat culinary utensils; however, prefer **flatware** when referring to forks, spoons, and similar culinary tools without a cutting edge.
RT breakfast services
cutlers
<cutting tools>
flatware
hollowware
kitchenware
place settings
shears

cutouts, paper
USE paper cutouts

cuts
RK.1289
ALT cut

cuts, cardboard
USE cardboard relief prints

cuts, linoleum
USE linocuts

cuts, metal
USE metal cuts

cuts, thumb
USE thumb indexes

cuts, white line
USE white line engravings

cutter
MT.79
HN April 1992 descriptor moved
UF rubber (brick)

cutters (sailing vessels)
TX.553
ALT cutter (sailing vessel)
SN Relatively small, decked sailing vessels similar to sloops, with a single mast and a bowsprit with, often two, headsails, but with the mast stepped farther aft.

cutters (ships' boats)
TX.463
ALT cutter (ship's boat)
SN Use for clinker built ships' boats, usually 24 to 36 feet long, generally rowed double banked.

cutters (sleighs)
TX.289   (N)
ALT cutter (sleigh)
SN Use for light one-horse sleighs with a single seatboard for two or three passengers; developed in the United States around 1800. (MSBTCC)

cutters, albany
USE albany cutters

cutters, anvil
USE hardies

cutters, biscuit
USE biscuit cutters

cutters, block
USE wood engravers

cutters, bolt
USE bolt cutters

cutters, butter
USE butter cutters

cutters, cabbage
USE cabbage cutters

cutters, cake
USE cookie cutters

cutters, cheese
USE cheese slicers

cutters, cider cheese
USE cider cheese cutters

cutters, clinch
USE buffers (cutters)

cutters, cookie
USE cookie cutters

cutters, curd
USE curd knives

cutters, doughnut
USE doughnut cutters

cutters, dovetail
USE dovetail cutters

cutters, dowel
USE peg cutters

cutters, gould
USE albany cutters

cutters, kimball
USE portland cutters

<cutters: metalworking tools>
TH.1247

cutters, milling
USE milling cutters

cutters, peg
USE peg cutters

cutters, pinion
USE pinion cutters

cutters, pipe
USE pipe cutters

cutters, plug
USE plug cutters

cutters, portland
USE portland cutters

cutters, revenue
USE revenue cutters

cutters, rotary
USE milling cutters

cutters, side
USE side cutters

cutters, slaw
USE cabbage cutters

cutters, sprue
USE sprue cutters

cutters, stencil
USE stencil knives

cutters, sugar
USE sugar cutters

cutters, swell-body
USE albany cutters

cutters, swell-side
USE albany cutters

cutters, vegetable
USE vegetable slicers

cutters, wick
USE wick trimmers

cutters, wire
USE wire cutters

<cutters: woodworking tools>
TH.1446

cutting (dividing)
KT.933   (L)
HN March 1993 alternate term changed,
   was cut
   March 1993 descriptor changed,
   was cutting
   November 1992 descriptor moved
   August 1992 scope note added
ALT cut (divided)
SN Making an incision with a sharp-
   edged instrument, thus removing
   material or dividing an object into
   parts.

cutting (glassworking)
KT.1032   (L)

HN December 1992 descriptor added
ALT cut (glassworking)
SN The process of shaping glass, making facets, grooves, and depressions,
   by grinding using rotating disks of
   various materials, sizes, and shapes
   and a stream of water with an
   abrasive.

cutting baskets
USE flower baskets

cutting boards
TH.114   (N)
HN April 1993 descriptor added
ALT cutting board
SN Boards often of wood and sometimes of plastic or other synthetic
   material, used as firm surfaces for
   cutting food.
UF boards, chopping
   boards, cutting
   chopping boards
RT breadboards
   cooks' knives

cutting, bright
USE bright cutting

cutting, cold
USE cold cutting

cutting, die
USE die cutting

cutting, electrochemical
USE electrochemical cutting

<cutting equipment>
TH.519
RT *<culinary tools and equipment for
   cutting>*

cutting, gem
USE lapidary

cutting, laser beam
USE laser beam cutting

<cutting machinery>
TH.520

cutting oil
MT.1105
HN April 1992 descriptor moved
SN An oil or oily preparation used on
   cutting tools or on work being ma-
   chined to aid in the cutting action.
UF oil, cutting

cutting swords
TK.96
ALT cutting sword
SN Swords designed primarily for cutting blows.
UF swords, cutting
RT backswords
   broadswords
   cutlasses
   falchions
   hangers (swords)
   sabers

cutting, thermal
USE thermal cutting

<cutting tools>
TH.522
HN February 1993 related terms added
RT cutlery
   nail clippers

cuttings
USE clippings

cuttings files
USE clippings files

cuttings, press
USE clippings

cuttlefish ink
USE sepia

cuttoes
TK.78
ALT cuttoe
SN Short swords, hangers, with short
   cross hilts, often elaborately decorated and made of fine materials
   such as carved bone or ivory or cast
   silver, sometimes with a chain linking the forward quillon to the pommel; some but not all were designed
   for hunting. They first appeared in
   the second quarter of the 17th century and became quite common in
   the 18th.
UF couteaux-de-chasse

cutty stools
TC.670
HN January 1993 descriptor moved
ALT cutty stool
SN Low stools used in churches in Scot-
   land before pews were introduced.
   (OCDA)
UF creepie stools
   creepies
   stools, creepie
   stools, cutty

cutwaters
PJ.834
HN March 1993 descriptor moved
ALT cutwater
SN Structures built around or upstream
   from a bridge pier with an angle or
   edge to resist better the action of
   water, ice, or flotsam. (W)

cuvals
TQ.669
ALT cuval
SN Large, deep wall bags, used pri-
   mairly in tents, suspended from the
   trellis structure. The fronts are pile
   woven and the backs done in a weft-
   faced plain weave. (TURKMN)
UF chovals
   chuvals
   jovals
   juvals
   tschovals
   tschowals
RT rugs

Cuzco
  FL.1735   (L)
  HN June 1991 descriptor moved
  UF Cuzco Circle

Cuzco Circle
  USE Cuzco

cyan blue
  USE moderate bluish green
       moderate greenish blue

Cyanine
  USE Prussian blue

cyanine blue
  USE dark purplish blue
       moderate purplish blue

cyanotype
  USE blueprint process

cyanotypes
  VC.324   (L)
  HN April 1992 descriptor moved
  ALT cyanotype
  SN Use for blue-toned photographic
       prints produced by the blueprint
       process, not including reproductive
       prints of architectural or other tech-
       nical drawings; for these, use **blue-
       prints** or **blueline prints.**
  UF blueprints (photographs)

cyanotypes (photocopies)
  USE blueprints

cyberart
  USE cybernetic art

cybernetic art
  BM.184   (R)
  SN Mechanical sculpture and other
       works of art capable of responding
       to external stimuli. (THDAT)
  UF cyberart
       post-kinetic art

cyberneticians
  HG.538
  HN December 1992 alternate terms
       added
  ALT cybernetician
       cybernetician's
       cyberneticians'
  UF cyberneticists

cyberneticists
  USE cyberneticians

cybernetics
  KD.108   (A,R)
  SN Comparative study of control and
       communication processes of organ-
       isms and machines. (ERIC9)

Cycladic
  FL.2625   (L,B,R)

Cycladic, Early
  USE Early Cycladic

Cycladic, Late
  USE Late Cycladic

Cycladic, Middle
  USE Middle Cycladic

<Cycladic pottery styles>
  FL.2681

<Cycladic sculpture styles>
  FL.2765

Cycladic white
  FL.2683
  HN April 1993 descriptor added
  UF white, Cycladic

Cycladic white ware
  HN April 1993 descriptor split, use
       Cycladic white + ware

cycle racing tracks
  USE velodromes

cycle sheds
  USE bicycle sheds

cycle tracks
  USE velodromes

cyclecars
  TX.147   (L)
  ALT cyclecar
  SN Use for small, light, open automo-
       biles powered by motorcycle engines
       and usually with four wheels, al-
       though some had three wheels; for
       three-wheeled closed automobiles,
       usually with larger engines, use
       three-wheelers.
  RT three-wheelers

cycles, narrative
  USE narrative cycles

cycleways
  USE cycling paths

cycling paths
  RM.184   (A,L,B)
  HN April 1993 descriptor moved
       July 1992 lead-in terms added
  ALT cycling path
  UF bicycle paths
       bicycle tracks
       bicycle trails
       bike paths
       bikeways
       cycleways
       cycling tracks
       paths, bicycle
       paths, cycling
       tracks, bicycle
       tracks, cycling
       trails, bicycle

cycling tracks
  USE cycling paths

cyclometers
  TN.34   (N)
  ALT cyclometer
  SN Instruments for measuring circular
       arcs or for recording the revolutions
       of a wheel and thus measuring the
       distance traversed. (RHDEL2)

cyclone cellars
  USE storm cellars

cyclones
  KM.136   (L,B)
  HN May 1991 alternate term added
  ALT cyclone

cyclopean concrete
  MT.201
  HN April 1992 descriptor moved
  UF concrete, cyclopean

cyclopean masonry
  MT.1822
  HN October 1992 descriptor moved
  SN Stonework using large, irregular
       block of stone fitted closely to-
       gether. (FOFDA)
  UF masonry, cyclopean

cyclopedias
  USE encyclopedias

cyclotrons
  RK.1101   (L,N,B)
  ALT cyclotron
  SN Designates structures in which
       charged atomic particles are acceler-
       ated along a spiral path by means of
       alternating electric currents with a
       constant magnetic field.
  UF accelerators, circular
       accelerators, magnetic resonance
       circular accelerators
       magnetic resonance accelerators
       phasotrons

cylinder augers
  TH.1401
  ALT cylinder auger
  UF augers, cylinder
       borers, cylindrical bung
       bung borers, cylindrical
       cylindrical bung borers

cylinder bookcases, sisters'
  USE cylinder desks and bookcases

cylinder bureaus
  USE bureaux à cylindre

cylinder desks
  USE cylinder fall desks

cylinder desks and bookcases
  TC.945
  HN May 1993 scope note changed
       May 1993 related term added
       March 1993 lead-in term changed,
         was **sister's cylinder bookcases**
       March 1993 lead-in term changed,
         was **bookcases, sister's cylinder**
       March 1993 lead-in term changed,
         was **cylinder bookcases, sister's**
       January 1993 descriptor moved
  ALT cylinder desk and bookcase
  SN Desks and bookcases with a hinged
       one-piece round lid or cover that re-
       sembles a section of a cylinder and
       which rolls up into the desk top;
       chiefly made in the late 18th and
       early 19th centuries. For similar

desks without a bookcase use cylinder fall desks.
UF bookcases, sisters' cylinder
    cylinder bookcases, sisters'
    cylinder-fall desks and bookcases
    cylinder secretaries and bookcases
    desks and bookcases, cylinder
    desks and bookcases, cylinder-fall
    secretaries and bookcases, cylinder
    sisters' cylinder bookcases
RT cylinder fall desks

cylinder desks, rotary
USE rotary desks

cylinder fall desks
    TC.940   (H)
HN May 1993 scope note changed
    May 1993 related term added
    January 1993 descriptor moved
ALT cylinder fall desk
SN Desks with a hinged one-piece
    round lid or cover that resembles a
    section of a cylinder and which rolls
    up into the desk top. For similar
    desks surmounted by a bookcase use
    cylinder desks and bookcases.
UF cylinder desks
    cylinder fall writing tables
    cylinder-front desks
    cylinder-top desks
    cylindrical writing tables
    desks, cylinder
    desks, cylinder fall
    writing tables, cylinder fall
RT cylinder desks and bookcases

cylinder-fall desks and bookcases
USE cylinder desks and bookcases

cylinder fall writing tables
USE cylinder fall desks

cylinder-front desks
USE cylinder fall desks

cylinder glass
    MT.292
HN March 1993 descriptor moved
UF broad glass
    glass, broad
    glass, cylinder
    glass, muff
    muff-blown glass
    muff glass

cylinder locks
    PJ.491
HN April 1993 descriptor moved
ALT cylinder lock
SN Locks in which the keyhole and
    tumbler mechanism are contained
    in a cylinder or escutcheon separate
    from the lock case. (MEANS)
UF locks, cylinder

cylinder locks, mortise
USE mortise locks

cylinder pianos
USE barrel pianos

cylinder presses
    TH.815   (N)
HN February 1993 descriptor added
ALT cylinder press
SN Presses in which the type or the
    plates are held on a horizontal or
    vertical plane, and ink rollers and
    sheets of paper, carried by a cylinder, alternately pass over them.
    (LEEBK)
UF presses, cylinder

cylinder presses, flat-bed
USE flat-bed cylinder presses

cylinder saws
USE crown saws

cylinder scales
    TN.288   (N)
ALT cylinder scale
SN Automatic indicating scales in which
    the graduations are on a rotatable
    cylindrical chart. (W)
UF barrel scales
    drum scales
    scales, barrel
    scales, cylinder
    scales, drum

cylinder screws
    PJ.234
HN April 1993 descriptor moved
ALT cylinder screw
SN Set screws that hold a cylinder in
    place to prevent the cylinder from
    being turned after installation.
    (BROWNL)
UF screws, cylinder

cylinder seals
    VW.1175   (L)
HN June 1992 descriptor added
ALT cylinder seal
SN Cylinders of hard material engraved
    in intaglio upon the curved surface,
    used especially in ancient Mesopotamia to roll an identifying impression
    on wet clay. (W)
UF cylinders (seals)
    cylindrical seals
    roll seals
    seals, cylinder
    seals, cylindrical
    seals, roll

cylinder secretaries and bookcases
USE cylinder desks and bookcases

cylinder-top desks
USE cylinder fall desks

cylinder writing tables, ladies'
USE ladies' writing tables

cylinders (lock components)
    PJ.565
HN May 1993 descriptor moved
ALT cylinder (lock component)
SN The housing containing the tumbler
    mechanism and the key way, which
    can be actuated only by the correct
    key. (BROWNL)

cylinders (seals)
USE cylinder seals

cylinders (solids)
    BM.684   (L,R)
HN May 1991 descriptor changed, was
    cylinders
    January 1991 alternate term added
ALT cylinder (solid)
    cylindrical

cylinders, graduated
USE graduates

cylinders, measuring
USE graduates

cylinders, phonograph
USE phonograph cylinders

cylindrical bung borers
USE cylinder augers

cylindrical seals
USE cylinder seals

cylindrical writing tables
USE cylinder fall desks

cyma rectas
    PJ.2096
HN April 1993 descriptor moved
    April 1991 lead-in terms added
ALT cyma recta
SN Moldings of double curvature where
    the uppermost surface is concave
    and the lowermost is convex.
UF cymas, Doric
    Doric cymas
    moldings, ogee
    ogee moldings
    rectas, sima
    sima rectas

cyma reversas
    PJ.2097
HN April 1993 descriptor moved
    April 1991 lead-in terms added
ALT cyma reversa
SN Moldings of double curvature where
    the uppermost surface is convex
    and the lowermost is concave.
UF cymas, Lesbian
    Lesbian cymas
    moldings, reverse ogee
    ogee moldings, reverse
    reversas, sima
    reverse ogee moldings
    sima reversas

cymas
    PJ.2095
HN April 1993 descriptor moved
    November 1991 lead-in term deleted, was **moldings, ogee**
    November 1991 lead-in term deleted, was **moldings, talon**
    April 1991 lead-in term deleted, was **ogee moldings**
    April 1991 lead-in term deleted, was **talon moldings**
ALT cyma

SN Moldings having a profile of double curvature. (HAS)
UF cimas
doucines
simas

cymas, Doric
USE cyma rectas

cymas, Lesbian
USE cyma reversas

cymatia
PJ.1686
HN March 1993 descriptor moved
April 1991 lead-in term changed, was **scimatia**
ALT cymatium
SN Crowning moldings of a classical cornice, especially when in the form of a cyma, though they may also be an ovolo or cavetto molding. (HAS)
UF simas

cymbaloms
USE cimbaloms

cymbals
TT.460   (L,N)
ALT cymbal
SN Concussion vessels of great antiquity, occurring in many sizes and grades of sound throughout their history. Traditionally they have consisted of a pair of round metal plates, usually slightly convex to create a resonant hollow, sounded by striking together. In modern orchestral and jazz music, cymbals are often played as percussion instruments, suspended and struck with drumsticks or wire brushes.

cymographs
USE kymographs

cypher-back chairs
TC.573
HN January 1993 descriptor moved
ALT cypher-back chair
SN Chairs whose splats are pierced to form a cypher with the initials of their owners. (KANE)
UF chairs, cypher-back

cyphers
USE monograms

cypress
MT.2933   (L)
HN March 1992 descriptor moved
UF Cupressus

cypress, classic
USE classic cypress

cypress, lawson
USE Port Orford cedar

cypress, Mediterranean
USE classic cypress

cypress, white
USE white cypress

cypress, yellow
USE yellow cypress

Cypressus nootkatensis
USE yellow cypress

Cyprian green earth
MT.2139
HN April 1992 descriptor moved
UF green earth, Cyprian

Cypriote
FL.2979   (L)

Cypriote, Early
USE Early Cypriote

Cypriote, Late
USE Late Cypriote

Cypriote, Middle
USE Middle Cypriote

<Cypriote periods>
FL.2980

<Cypriote pottery styles>
FL.2988

<Cypriote styles>
FL.2986

Cypro-Phoenician
FL.2987

Cyprus umber
USE umber

Cyrenaic
USE Laconian

Cyrenaican
FL.694

cyrtostyles
PJ.1196
HN March 1993 descriptor moved
June 1990 scope note changed
ALT cyrtostyle
SN Circular, projecting porticoes. (W)
UF sigmas

Cyzican marble
USE Proconnesian marble

czars
HG.190
HN January 1993 descriptor moved
December 1992 alternate terms added
ALT czar
czar's
czars'
UK tzars
UKA tzar
SN Rulers of Russia before the 1917 revolution. (W)
UF tsars

Czech
FL.3133   (L,B)

Dabban
FL.39

dabbers
TH.836   (N)
HN February 1993 descriptor added
ALT dabber
SN Tools used for inking a plate or laying an etching ground, usually a cotton pad covered with silk or leather, sometimes a piece of rolled felt or other material. (PRTT)
UF daubers
daubers, inking
inking daubers

dachas
RK.293
ALT dacha
SN Country houses, summer houses, or villas in Russia. (W)

dacite
MT.627   (L)
HN April 1992 descriptor moved

Dacron (TM)
MT.1404   (L)
HN April 1993 descriptor moved
UF fiber V
terylene

Dada
FL.3385   (L,R)
ALT Dadaism

daders
USE twivels

dado and rabbet joints
PJ.711
HN April 1993 descriptor moved
ALT dado and rabbet joint
UF joints, dado and rabbet

dado grooving planes
USE dado planes

dado joints
PJ.710
HN April 1993 descriptor moved
ALT dado joint
SN Joints which are created by the end of a piece of wood fitting, usually at right angles, into a groove cut across the width of another piece to a depth of half its thickness. (MEANS)
UF joints, dado

dado planes
TH.1501   (N)
ALT dado plane
SN Planes whose iron is set on a skew; used to cut grooves across the grain of wood.
UF carcase grooving planes
dado grooving planes
grooving planes, carcase
grooving planes, dado
housing planes
planes, carcase grooving
planes, dado
planes, dado grooving
planes, housing
planes, trenching

raglets
trenching planes

dado, tongue and rabbet joints
PJ.712
HN April 1993 descriptor moved
ALT dado, tongue and rabbet joint
UF joints, dado, tongue and rabbet

dadoes
PJ.1551
HN March 1993 descriptor moved
ALT dado
SN Use for the middle portion of a pedestal, between the base and the cap. Use also for the lower zone of an interior wall, when given a distinct treatment, as this treatment often resembles a pedestal in appearance.
UF dies (dadoes)

Daedalic
FL.2774

daffodil
USE cadmium yellow

daffs
USE duffs

daga
MT.1346
HN April 1992 descriptor moved
SN Coarse, granular, sandlike substance that consists chiefly of clay, made into a mortar used in African building construction.
UF dagga

daga, burnt
USE burnt daga

Dagestan
FL.1805
HN April 1993 descriptor added
UF Daghestan

Dagestan carpets
USE Dagestan + rugs

Dagestans
USE Dagestan + rugs

dagga
USE daga

Dagger period
FL.2598

daggers (tracery components)
PJ.2334
HN March 1993 descriptor moved
January 1991 lead-in term added
ALT dagger (tracery component)
SN In late 13th- and early 14th-century Gothic tracery, lancet-shaped openings pointed at the foot, rounded or pointed at the head, and cusped inside.
UF soufflets

daggers (weapons)
TK.16   (H,L,N,R)
ALT dagger (weapon)
SN Weapons with a short, double-edged, sharp-pointed blade and a grip, used for stabbing or parrying.
RT dirks

daggers, ballock
USE ballock daggers

daggers, eared
USE eared daggers

daggers, kidney
USE ballock daggers

daggers, Landsknecht
USE Landsknecht daggers

daggers, left-hand
USE left-hand daggers

daggers, parrying
USE left-hand daggers

Daghestan
USE Dagestan

Daghestan rugs
USE Dagestan + rugs

Daghestans
USE Dagestan + rugs

dagobas
RK.1095   (A,L)
ALT dagoba
SN Use for Ceylonese and Singhalese stupas, generally with a tripartite base and a dome surmounted by a small pavilionlike structure and a spire.

dags, pocket
USE pocket pistols

daguerreotype
KT.521   (L)
SN An early photographic process producing a direct positive image on a silver-coated copper plate.
UF daguerreotypy

daguerreotype prints
USE etched daguerreotype prints

daguerreotype prints, etched
USE etched daguerreotype prints

daguerreotypes
VC.302   (L,N,R)
HN April 1992 descriptor moved
ALT daguerreotype
SN Use for photographs made by the process called daguerreotype, usually mounted in cases.

daguerreotypes, crayon
USE cameotypes

daguerreotypes, vignette
USE cameotypes

daguerreotypists
HG.301
HN January 1993 descriptor added
ALT daguerreotypist
daguerreotypist's
daguerreotypists'
SN Photographers who use the daguerreotype process.

daguerreotypy
USE daguerreotype

Dai Co Viet
USE Vietnamese

Dai-La
FL.2514

Dai Viet
USE Vietnamese

Daibutsuyo
FL.2071
HN June 1990 lead-in term deleted, was Tenjiku yo
June 1990 lead-in term deleted, was Tenjiku-yo
UF Great Buddha Style
Indian Style
Tenjikuyo

daiko
USE taiko

daily reports
VW.919
HN November 1992 descriptor moved
ALT daily report
UF reports, daily

Daima
FL.96

dairies
RK.58   (A,B,R)
HN March 1993 related term added
ALT dairy
SN Use for farm buildings, generally of the 18th to early 19th century, where country ladies supervised the making and storing of dairy products. Distinguished from **dairy plants** by their lack of mechanization.
RT dairy plants

dairies (mechanized)
USE dairy plants

dairy barns
RK.50   (L,B)
HN March 1993 related terms added
ALT dairy barn
SN Barns for dairy cows; for beef cattle housing, use **cattle barns**; for primarily open shelters, use **cow sheds**.
UF barns, cow
barns, dairy
byres
cow barns
RT cattle barns
cow sheds

dairy farms
RG.8   (L,B)
ALT dairy farm
UF farms, dairy

dairy plants
RK.599   (A,L,B)

HN March 1993 related term added
ALT dairy plant
SN Use for buildings built after the early 19th century, not found only on farms, for the mechanized processing, storing, or selling of milk and milk products. Distinguished from **dairies** by the use of mechanization.
UF creameries
dairies (mechanized)
plants, dairy
RT dairies

daisywheel printers
TH.580
HN January 1993 descriptor moved
ALT daisywheel printer
SN Serial impact printers in which the font is formed on the end of spring fingers that extend radially from a central hub. (DOC)
UF printers, daisywheel

Dakota
FL.1412 (L,R)
UF Nadowessioux
Wahpekute

Dakota, Santee
USE Santee Dakota

dala-fandïrs
USE fandurs

Dalbergia
MT.2890 (L)
HN March 1992 descriptor moved

Dalbergia latifolia
USE East Indian rosewood

Dalbergia melanoxylin
USE African blackwood

Dalbergia nigra
USE Brazilian rosewood

Dalbergia retusa
USE cocobolo

dalmaticas
USE dalmatics

dalmatics
TE.247 (H,N)
ALT dalmatic
SN Long-sleeved tuniclike upper garments worn as ecclesiastical vestments. Also, similar garments worn as secular dress in the Roman Empire or by English kings, especially at coronations.
UF dalmaticas

Dalton
FL.748

d'Alva bottles
USE bellarmines

Dalverzin
USE Dalverzin-Tepe

Dalverzin-Tepe
FL.1795
HN April 1993 descriptor moved
UF Dalverzin

<dam elements>
PJ.826
HN March 1993 guide term moved

damage
DE.14 (A,L,B)
HN November 1992 descriptor moved
ALT damaged

damage, insect
USE insect damage

damage reports
VW.917 (A)
HN November 1992 descriptor moved
ALT damage report
UF reports, damage

damar, cat's eye
USE Mata Kuching dammar

damar, gum
USE dammar

damarus
TT.606
ALT damaru
SN Hourglass rattle drums of the Indian subcontinent, the Himalayas, and Mongolia, with a wood body with two thin skins wrapped around wood hoops tightened by V-lacings and a central crosslacing. Two cords knotted at the ends or with pellets of wood, clay, or other hard material threaded on their ends, are attached to the central lacing; the knots or pellets strike the drum heads when the drum is twirled.
UF dambarus
damrus
RT hourglass drums

damascening
KT.1127 (H,L)
ALT damascened
SN Decorating metal, usually iron, with flat ornaments of precious metal, such as gold or silver.

damasco
USE damask

Damascus
FL.3650
HN April 1993 descriptor added
UF Damascus style Iznik
Iznik, Damascus style

Damascus style Iznik
USE Damascus

Damascus style Iznik pottery
USE Damascus + ware

Damascus ware
HN April 1993 descriptor split, use Damascus + ware

damask
MT.1591 (R)
HN March 1993 scope note changed
March 1993 related term added
March 1993 descriptor moved
March 1993 lead-in term added
SN Woven figured textile with one warp and one weft in which the pattern is formed by a contrast of binding systems, and appears on the face and the back in reverse positions. By extension, used also for any textile woven with the use of two distinct binding systems.
UF damasco
RT damassé

damask diaper
MT.1592
HN December 1992 descriptor added
SN A simple form of damask having a rectilinear pattern formed by the contrast of warp and weft faces, with numerous warp floats on the surface as in satin; much used for simple linens.
UF diaper, damask
RT diaper

damassé
MT.1593
HN December 1992 descriptor added
SN Figured woven textile having a damasklike appearance, with contrasting luster in the pattern and ground.
UF pseudo-damask
RT damask

dambarus
USE damarus

dammar
MT.1255
HN April 1992 descriptor moved
March 1992 descriptor changed, was **damar**
UF damar, gum
gum damar

dammar, Batavia
USE Batavia dammar

dammar, Singapore
USE Singapore dammar

damp check
USE damp course

damp course
MT.1785 (B)
HN April 1993 lead-in terms added
April 1993 descriptor changed, was **damp courses**
April 1993 lead-in term changed, was **dampproof courses**
February 1991 descriptor moved
UK damp-proof course
SN In masonry walls, impervious horizontal layer of material used to prevent upward capillary movement or downward seepage of water.
UF check, damp

course, damp
course, damp-proof
course, dampproof
damp check
dampproof course

damp-proof course
SEE   damp course

damp-proofing paint
SEE   dampproofing paint

damp, rising
USE   rising damp

dampers (HVAC components)
PJ.821   (B)
HN   March 1993 descriptor moved
       March 1993 descriptor changed,
          was **dampers**
       March 1993 alternate term changed,
          was **damper**
ALT   damper (HVAC component)
SN   Use for devices, such as valves or
       gates, for controlling the flow of air
       in a ventilation system, or the flow
       of combustion gases in a chimney
       flue.

dampers (mutes)
PJ.3265
ALT   damper (mute)
SN   Mutes incorporated into the piano
       actions, consisting of felted blocks
       resting on the strings to keep them
       silent except when their keys are
       pressed or when the entire set is
       lifted by a pedal.

dampness
DE.16   (A,L,B)
HN   November 1992 descriptor moved
       November 1992 scope note added
ALT   damp
SN   The state of an artifact, structure, or
       atmosphere when it contains mois-
       ture, usually meaning more than a
       desirable amount of moisture.

dampproof course
USE   damp course

dampproofing
USE   waterproofing

dampproofing paint
MT.1969
HN   August 1992 lead-in term added
UK   damp-proofing paint
UF   paint, damp-proofing
       paint, dampproofing
       paint, vapor barrier
       vapor barrier paint

damrus
USE   damarus

dams
RK.488   (A,L,N,B,R)
ALT   dam

dams, arch
USE   arch dams

dams, buttress
USE   buttress dams

<dams by construction>
RK.502

<dams by form>
RK.489

<dams by function>
RK.493

dams, check
USE   check dams

dams, diversion
USE   diversion dams

dams, earth-fill
USE   earth-fill dams

dams, flood
USE   flood dams

dams, flood control
USE   flood dams

dams, gravity
USE   gravity dams

dams, hydraulic fill
USE   earth-fill dams

dams, hydroelectric
USE   hydroelectric dams

dams, power
USE   hydroelectric dams

dams, reinforced earth
USE   zoned earth dams

dams, rock-fill
USE   rock-fill dams

dams, rolled-fill
USE   rolled-fill dams

dams, wing
USE   wing dams

dams, zoned earth
USE   zoned earth dams

Dan
FL.320   (L)
HN   June 1990 lead-in term added
UF   Gere
       Gio
       Yakuba

Dan Day chairs
USE   Mendlesham chairs

Danakil
USE   Afar

dance
KD.6   (L,R)
HN   February 1993 related term added
RT   dancers

dance cards
VW.1028
HN   November 1992 descriptor moved
       June 1992 lead-in terms added

ALT   dance card
UK   dance programmes
UKA   dance programme
SN   Cards listing, in order, the names of
       the partners with whom a woman
       has agreed to dance at a formal ball
       or party. (RHDEL2)
UF   cards, dance
       dance programs
       programmes, dance
       programs, dance

dance grounds
RG.218
ALT   dance ground
SN   Use for cleared and bounded areas,
       devoid of artifacts, and of unknown
       function found associated with
       hunter-gatherer camps, especially
       those of the North American Great
       Basin.
UF   grounds, dance

dance halls
RK.982   (A,B)
ALT   dance hall
SN   Use for large rooms or buildings set
       aside for dancing, but which may be
       used for other social functions. Dis-
       tinguished from **ballrooms** by their
       less formal nature.
UF   halls, dance

dance programmes
SEE   dance cards

dance programs
USE   dance cards

dance, tap
USE   tap dance

dancers
HG.249   (L,R)
HN   February 1993 related term added
       November 1992 alternate terms
          added
ALT   dancer
       dancer's
       dancers'
RT   dance

dancers, ballet
USE   ballet dancers

dancettes
USE   chevrons

dancing sandals
SEE   ballet slippers

dancing steps
USE   balanced steps

dancing winders
USE   balanced steps

Dandan Oilik
FL.1820
HN   April 1993 descriptor moved

dandyism
BM.289   (L,R)
SN   Literary or artistic style often associ-

ated with the English and French decadents of the late 19th century, marked especially by precocity of language and refined emotionalism of subject matter. (W)

danger
USE hazards

Danger Cave
FL.922

danger signs
USE warning signs

Dani
FL.3767 (L)
UF Ndani

Danish
FL.3147 (L,B)

dankos
USE kalangus

Dante chairs
TC.546
HN January 1993 descriptor moved
ALT Dante chair
SN Collector's term for Italian Renaissance X-chairs with crossing assemblies only in the front and back. Their name is derived from association with the 14th-century poet Dante, although it is questionable that such chairs were actually used by him.
UF chairs, Dante
chairs, Dantesca
Dantesca chairs
sedia Dantesca

Dantesca chairs
USE Dante chairs

Dantesque
FL.3493

Danubian
FL.2579

Danzig fir
USE Scotch pine

Danzig pine
USE Scotch pine

Daoguang
FL.1987 (L)
UF Tao-kuang

dap joints
PJ.629
HN April 1993 descriptor moved
ALT dap joint
UF joints, dap

Daphne
FL.2697
HN April 1993 descriptor added

Daphne ware
HN April 1993 descriptor split, use
Daphne + ware

daphs
USE duffs

dapping blocks
TH.1195
ALT dapping block
SN Anvils used in conjunction with dapping punches for depressing metal.
UF blocks, dapping

dapping punches
TH.1213
ALT dapping punch
SN Punches used in conjunction with dapping blocks for depressing metal.
UF punches, dapping

darabukes
USE darabukkas

darabukkas
TT.593 (L)
ALT darabukka
SN Single-headed goblet drums of the Islamic Near East and North Africa, made of pottery, wood, or metal, with the bottom open and the skin head directly attached by nails or glue. They are played with the fingers and palms of both hands, held under the arm or resting on the thigh.
UF darabukes
darboukkas
darbukat
derboukas

Darband
USE Derbent

Darbands
USE Derbent + rugs

darbies
TH.1152 (N)
HN December 1992 descriptor moved
ALT darby
SN Float tools which are about 4 feet long, usually made of wood or aluminum and having either one or two handles; used by concrete finishers and plasterers in preliminary floating and leveling operations. (MEANS)
UF derby slickers
floats, long
long floats
slickers, derby

darboukkas
USE darabukkas
tarabukas

darbukat
USE darabukkas

darbuks
USE tarabukas

Darby and Joan settees
USE chair-back settees

Darfur
FL.167

darics
VK.30
ALT daric
SN Ancient Persian gold coins possibly introduced by Darius I in the late 6th century BCE and in use until the early 4th century BCE. (DOTY)

Darién
FL.1112

Dark Ages
FL.3
SN Can be used for substantial periods of any cultures from which little reliable data are available.
UF Ages, Dark

Dark Ages (Medieval)
USE Migration period

dark aniline blue
USE dark grayish blue
dark grayish purple

dark anthracene violet
USE dark grayish purple
dark purple

dark blue
DL.251
UF Antwerp blue (color)
Berlin blue
blue, Antwerp
blue, Berlin
blue, dark
blue, deep royal
blue, deep sapphire
blue, delft
blue, medium
blue, Monastral
blue, royal
blue, sapphire
bluish slate black
bright navy
centroid color 183
dark green blue slate
dark navy
deep royal blue
deep sapphire blue
delft blue
green blue slate, dark
greenish navy
indigo (color)
kingfisher
light navy
medium blue
Monastral blue
navy
navy, bright
navy, dark
navy, greenish
navy, light
royal blue
royal blue, deep
sapphire blue
sapphire blue, deep
slate black, bluish
slate, dark green blue

dark blue green
USE blackish green
dark grayish green
dark green
light bluish green
moderate bluish green
moderate greenish blue
strong bluish green
strong green
very dark green

dark bluish gray
DL.260
UF black, blue
black, ink
blue black
blue, dull
blue, logwood
blue, midnight
blue, slate
bluish gray, dark
centroid color 192
dark navy
dark Payne's gray
dull blue
dull violet black
gray, dark bluish
gray, dark Payne's
gray, teal
indigo (color)
ink black
logwood blue
midnight blue
navy, dark
Payne's gray, dark
slate (color)
slate blue
teal gray
violet black, dull

dark bluish gray green
USE dark bluish green
dark grayish green
grayish green
moderate bluish green

dark bluish green
DL.234
UF blue, deep teal
bluish gray green, dark
bluish green, dark
centroid color 165
dark bluish gray green
dark jade gray
dark jade green
dark teal
dark teal green
deep teal
deep teal blue
deep teal green
gray, dark jade
gray green, dark bluish
green, dark bluish
green, dark jade
green, dark teal
green, deep teal
green, teal
jade gray, dark
jade green, dark
teal
teal blue, deep

teal, dark
teal, deep
teal green
teal green, dark
teal green, deep

dark bluish violet
USE dark violet
grayish purple
grayish violet

dark brown
DL.112
UF brown, dark
brown, very dark
centroid color 59
very dark brown

dark-burnished
FL.2684
HN April 1993 descriptor added

dark-burnished ware
HN April 1993 descriptor split, use
dark-burnished + ware

dark carmine
USE moderate red
vivid red

dark cerulean blue
USE dark greenish blue
grayish blue

dark delft blue
USE dark grayish blue

dark dull bluish violet
USE dark purple
grayish violet
moderate violet

dark dull violet blue
USE grayish purplish blue
grayish violet

dark dull yellow green
USE grayish olive green
moderate olive green

dark eggplant
USE blackish purple

dark emerald green
USE deep green
moderate bluish green

dark-faced burnished
FL.3026
HN April 1993 descriptor added
UF burnished, dark-faced

dark-faced burnished ware
HN April 1993 descriptor split, use
dark-faced burnished + ware

dark-faced incised
FL.2685
HN April 1993 descriptor added
UF incised, dark-faced

dark-faced incised ware
HN April 1993 descriptor split, use
dark-faced incised + ware

dark fuchsia
USE strong reddish purple

dark glasses
SEE sunglasses

dark gray
DL.335
HN November 1991 lead-in terms
added
August 1990 lead-in term deleted,
was **slate color**
UF black, blue violet
black, dull greenish
blackish slate
blackish violet gray
blue green, dark grayish
blue, iron
blue violet black
brown, ebony
centroid color 266
charcoal gray
dark gray, medium
dark grayish blue green
dark neutral gray
dark purplish gray (dark gray)
dark violet gray
deep navy gray
deep neutral gray
deep violet gray
dull greenish black
dull violet black
ebony (color)
ebony brown
gray, charcoal
gray, dark
gray, dark neutral
gray, dark purplish
gray, deep navy
gray, deep neutral
gray, iron
gray, lead
gray, medium dark
gray, navy
gray, steel
gray, teal
gray, very dark
grayish blue green, dark
greenish black, dull
greenish slate black
gunmetal (color)
gunmetal, light
india ink (color)
ink, india
iron blue
iron gray
lead (color)
lead gray
light gunmetal
medium dark gray
navy gray
navy gray, deep
neutral gray, dark
neutral gray, deep
pewter (color)
purplish gray, dark
rose taupe
slate (color)
slate black, greenish
slate, blackish
slate gray

steel (color)
steel gray
taupe, rose
teal gray
very dark gray
violet black, dull
violet gray, blackish
violet gray, dark
violet gray, deep
wrought iron (color)

dark gray, medium
USE dark gray

dark grayish blue
DL.255
UF aniline blue, dark
black, dull blue green
blue, dark aniline
blue, dark delft
blue, dark grayish
blue, dark teal
blue, dull
blue, dull greenish
blue, dull reddish
blue, graphite
blue green black, dull
blue, indigo
blue, ink
blue, teal
centroid color 187
charcoal (color)
dark aniline blue
dark delft blue
dark green blue slate
dark navy
dark Payne's gray
dark teal
dark teal blue
delft blue, dark
dull blue
dull blue green black
dull greenish blue
dull reddish blue
dull violet black
graphite (color)
graphite blue
gray, dark Payne's
gray, Payne's
grayish blue, dark
green blue slate, dark
greenish blue, dull
indigo (color)
indigo blue
ink blue
midnight
navy
navy, dark
Payne's gray
Payne's gray, dark
reddish blue, dull
slate (color)
slate, dark green blue
teal blue
teal blue, dark
teal, dark
violet black, dull

dark grayish blue green
USE dark gray
dark greenish gray

dark grayish blue violet
USE grayish violet

dark grayish brown
DL.115
UF black brown
blackish brown
brown, black
brown, blackish
brown, dark grayish
brown, dull
centroid color 62
charcoal (color)
dull brown
grayish brown, dark

dark grayish green
DL.207
UF black, green
blackish green, dull
blue green, dark
bluish gray green, dark
bluish green, dull
centroid color 151
dark blue green
dark bluish gray green
dark slate green
dull blackish green
dull bluish green
dull green
gray green, dark bluish
grayish green, dark
green black
green, dark grayish
green, dark slate
green, dull
green, dull blackish
green, dull bluish
green, hemlock
green, slate
hemlock green
slate (color)
slate green
slate green, dark

dark grayish lavender
USE pale violet

dark grayish olive
DL.181
UF centroid color 111
grayish olive, dark
olive, dark grayish

dark grayish olive green
DL.242
UF bluish olive
centroid color 128
grayish olive green, dark
green, dark grayish olive
green, ivy
ivy green
olive, bluish
olive green, dark grayish

dark grayish purple
DL.311
UF aniline black (color)
aniline blue, dark
anthracene purple
anthracene violet, dark
black, aniline

black plum
black violet
blue, dark aniline
blue, diamin azo
blue plum
bluish violet, dull
brown, dark violet
brown, taupe
centroid color 229
charcoal (color)
dark aniline blue
dark anthracene violet
dark madder violet
dark naphthalene violet
dark orchid taupe
dark violet brown
deep plum
diamin azo blue
dull bluish violet
dull reddish violet
dull violet
dull violet black
graphite (color)
grayish purple, dark
indigo (color)
madder violet, dark
Mars violet (color)
mauve, rose
mauve taupe
midnight
naphthalene violet, dark
navy
orchid taupe
orchid taupe, dark
plum (color)
plum, black
plum, deep
plum, red
purple, anthracene
purple, dark grayish
red plum
reddish violet, dull
rose mauve
slate purple
slate violet
taupe brown
taupe, dark orchid
taupe, mauve
taupe, orchid
violet, black
violet black, dull
violet brown, dark
violet, dark anthracene
violet, dark madder
violet, dark naphthalene
violet, dull
violet, dull bluish
violet, dull reddish
violet, Mars

dark grayish red
DL.74
UF black, violet
brown, dark rose
brown, dull reddish
brown, light rose
brown, rose
centroid color 20
dark Indian red
dark mauve taupe
dark rose brown

deep maroon
dull reddish brown
grayish red, dark
haematite red
Indian red, dark
light rose brown
maroon
maroon, deep
mauve taupe, dark
red, dark grayish
red, dark Indian
red, haematite
reddish brown, dull
rose brown
rose brown, dark
rose brown, light
taupe, dark mauve
violet black

dark grayish reddish brown
DL.128
UF brown, dark grayish reddish
brown, dull reddish
centroid color 47
deep maroon
dull reddish brown
grayish reddish brown, dark
maroon, deep
reddish brown, dark grayish
reddish brown, dull

dark grayish yellow
DL.152
UF centroid color 91
dull reddish yellow
dull yellow
grayish yellow, dark
parchment (color)
reddish yellow, dark
yellow, dark grayish
yellow, dull reddish

dark grayish yellowish brown
DL.137
UF asphaltum (color)
bitumen (color)
brown, dark grayish yellowish
brown, dull yellowish
brown, sepia
brown, very dark grayish
centroid color 81
dull yellowish brown
grayish brown, very dark
grayish yellowish brown, dark
mummy (color)
sepia (color)
sepia brown
very dark grayish brown
yellowish brown, dark grayish
yellowish brown, dull

dark green
DL.202
UF blue green, dark
centroid color 146
chrome green, medium
dark blue green
dark hunter green
dark jade green
dark slate green
forest green

green, dark
green, dark hunter
green, dark jade
green, dark slate
green, forest
green, hunter
green, medium chrome
hunter green
hunter green, dark
jade green, dark
medium chrome green
mint
slate green, dark

dark green blue slate
USE dark blue
dark grayish blue

dark greenish blue
DL.271
UF blackish green blue
blue, bright teal
blue, dark cerulean
blue, dark greenish
blue, dark peacock
blue, dark teal
blue, deep cerulean
blue, deep peacock
blue, deep teal
blue, medium
blue, peacock
blue, Prussian
blue, teal
blue, Thalo (color)
bright teal blue
centroid color 174
cerulean blue, dark
cerulean blue, deep
dark cerulean blue
dark peacock blue
dark teal blue
deep cerulean blue
deep peacock blue
deep teal blue
green blue, blackish
greenish blue, dark
medium blue
peacock blue
peacock blue, dark
peacock blue, deep
Prussian blue (color)
teal blue
teal blue, bright
teal blue, dark
teal blue, deep
Thalo blue (color)

dark greenish gray
DL.212
HN April 1990 lead-in terms added
UF black, dull greenish
black, green
blue green, dark grayish
centroid color 156
dark grayish blue green
dark ivy
deep slate green
deep slate olive
dull greenish black
gray, dark greenish
gray, olive

grayish blue green, dark
green black
greenish black, dull
greenish gray, dark
greenish slate black
ivy
ivy, dark
olive gray (dark greenish gray)
slate (color)
slate black, greenish
slate green
slate green, deep
slate olive
slate olive, deep

dark greenish olive
USE grayish olive
moderate olive

dark greenish yellow
DL.172
UF centroid color 103
chartreuse green
green, chartreuse
green, lime
greenish yellow, dark
light yellowish olive
lime green
olive, light yellowish
olive yellow
yellow, dark greenish
yellow, olive
yellowish olive, light

dark header
USE glazed header

dark hunter green
USE dark green
very dark yellowish green

dark Indian red
USE dark grayish red
grayish red

dark ivy
USE dark greenish gray

dark jade gray
USE dark bluish green

dark jade green
USE dark bluish green
dark green
light bluish green
moderate bluish green

dark lanterns
TC.1398
ALT dark lantern
SN Any lantern with means of closing
off light without extinguishing the
flame.
UF lanterns, dark

dark lanterns (bull's eye lanterns)
USE bull's eye lanterns

dark lavender
USE light purple

dark madder violet
USE dark grayish purple

dark maroon purple
USE dark reddish purple

dark mauve taupe
USE dark grayish red
dark purplish gray

dark naphthalene violet
USE dark grayish purple

dark navy
USE black
blackish blue
blackish purple
bluish black
dark blue
dark bluish gray
dark grayish blue
dark purplish blue
dark purplish gray
grayish blue

dark neutral gray
USE dark gray

dark nigrosin violet
USE dark purple

dark ocher
USE light olive brown

dark olive
DL.178
UF black olive
centroid color 108
drab, olive
ebony (color)
olive, black
olive, dark
olive drab

dark olive brown
DL.141
UF brown, dark olive
brown, sepia
brownish olive, dull
centroid color 96
dull brownish olive
olive brown, dark
olive, dull brownish
sepia (color)
sepia brown

dark olive gray
USE grayish olive
grayish olive green
olive gray

dark olive green
DL.240
UF bluish olive
centroid color 126
green, dark olive
olive, bluish
olive green, dark

dark-on-light painted
FL.2744
HN April 1993 descriptor added
UF painted, dark-on-light

dark-on-light painted ware
HN April 1993 descriptor split, use
dark-on-light painted + ware

dark orange yellow
DL.163
UF amber (color)
amber, light
bistre
brown, yellow
brownish yellow
buff
centroid color 72
dark yellowish orange
golden yellow
light amber
Mars yellow (color)
ocher, yellow
orange, dark yellowish
orange yellow, dark
orange, yellowish
raw sienna (color)
reddish yellow
sienna, raw
topaz (color)
yellow brown
yellow, brownish
yellow, dark orange
yellow, golden
yellow, Mars
yellow ocher (color)
yellow, reddish
yellowish orange
yellowish orange, dark

dark orchid taupe
USE dark grayish purple
dark purplish gray

dark Payne's gray
USE dark bluish gray
dark grayish blue

dark peacock blue
USE dark greenish blue

dark pink
DL.40
UF carmine (color)
centroid color 6
pink, dark
rose
vermilion (color)

dark plum
USE blackish purple
dark purplish gray

dark purple
DL.306
UF amethyst (color)
anthracene violet, dark
bluish violet, dark dull
centroid color 224
dark anthracene violet
dark dull bluish violet
dark nigrosin violet
dull bluish violet, dark
litho purple
nigrosin violet
nigrosin violet, dark
plum (color)
purple, dark
purple, litho
violet, dark anthracene
violet, dark dull bluish

violet, dark nigrosin
violet, nigrosin

dark purple, dull
USE deep reddish purple

dark purplish blue
DL.281
UF blue, cyanine
blue, dark purplish
blue, graphite
blue, midnight
blue, navy
blue, reddish
centroid color 201
cyanine blue
dark navy
graphite blue
light navy
midnight blue
navy
navy blue
navy, dark
navy, light
purplish blue, dark
reddish blue
slate (color)

dark purplish gray
DL.316
UF aniline black (color)
black, aniline
black, blue violet
black, deep purplish
black plum
black, violet
blackish violet gray
blue violet black
centroid color 234
charcoal (color)
dark mauve taupe
dark navy
dark orchid taupe
dark plum
dark slate violet
deep purplish black
deep violet gray
dull violet black
gray, dark purplish
gray, taupe
mauve taupe
mauve taupe, dark
midnight blue
navy, dark
orchid taupe, dark
plum, black
plum, dark
purplish black, deep
purplish gray, dark
slate (color)
slate violet
slate violet, dark
taupe, dark mauve
taupe, dark orchid
taupe gray
taupe, mauve
violet black
violet black, dull
violet gray, blackish
violet gray, deep

dark purplish gray (dark gray)
USE dark gray

dark purplish pink
DL.52
UF bluish pink
centroid color 251
lilac, rose
mauve, orchid
orchid mauve
pink, bluish
pink, dark purplish
purplish pink, dark
rose
rose lilac

dark purplish red
DL.87
UF anthracene purple
black violet
blackish red purple
bluish red, dull
brown, dark violet
brown violet
brown, violet
carmine, violet
centroid color 259
dark violet brown
deep lake
dull bluish red
dull violet
garnet (color)
lake, deep
lake, purple
lake, rose
magenta (color)
magenta rose
maroon
mauve, rose
plum, red
plum, rose
plum violet
purple, anthracene
purple lake
purple, red
purplish red, dark
red, dark purplish
red, dull bluish
red plum
red purple
red purple, blackish
rose lake
rose, magenta
rose mauve
rose plum
violet, black
violet brown
violet, brown
violet brown, dark
violet carmine (color)
violet, dull
violet, plum

dark putty
USE olive gray

dark red
DL.71
UF brick red
brown carmine
brown, dull reddish

brown, garnet
brown, orange
brown, red
carmine, brown
centroid color 16
dull red
dull reddish brown
garnet (color)
garnet brown
garnet, light
garnet red
haematite red
lake (color)
light garnet
madder, purple
maroon
orange brown
purple madder
red, brick
red brown
red, dark
red, dull
red, garnet
red, haematite
red, rose
reddish brown, dull
rose red
ruby (color)

dark red brown
USE grayish reddish brown

dark reddish brown
DL.125
UF brown, dark reddish
brown, dull reddish
centroid color 44
dull reddish brown
maroon
reddish brown, dark
reddish brown, dull

dark reddish gray
DL.78
UF blackish brown
brown, blackish
brown, dark rose
brown, ebony
centroid color 23
dark rose brown
dark rose taupe
ebony brown
gray, dark reddish
mauve taupe
reddish gray, dark
rose brown, dark
rose taupe
rose, taupe
rose taupe, dark
taupe, dark rose
taupe, mauve
taupe rose
taupe, rose

dark reddish orange
DL.104
UF brown, red
brown, yellow
burnt Italian earth
burnt Italian ocher
burnt sienna (color)

centroid color 38
Indian red (color)
Mars orange
Mars red
ocher, burnt Italian
orange, dark reddish
orange, Mars
red brown
red, Indian
red, Mars
red, yellowish
reddish orange, dark
sienna, burnt
terra cotta
vermilion (color)
yellow brown
yellowish red

dark reddish purple
DL.326
HN April 1990 lead-in terms added
UF carmine, violet
centroid color 242
dark maroon purple
dark slate purple
fuchsia purple
magenta (color)
maroon purple, dark
naphthalene violet
purple, dark maroon
purple, dark reddish
purple, dark slate
purple, fuchsia
reddish purple, dark
reddish violet
slate purple
slate purple, dark
violet carmine (color)
violet, naphthalene
violet, reddish

dark-rooms
SEE darkrooms

dark rose
USE moderate purplish red
moderate red

dark rose brown
USE dark grayish red
dark reddish gray

dark rose taupe
USE brownish gray
dark reddish gray

dark slate green
USE blackish green
dark grayish green
dark green
very dark green

dark slate purple
USE dark reddish purple

dark slate violet
USE dark purplish gray
grayish purple

dark steel blue
USE grayish blue

dark teal
USE dark bluish green
dark grayish blue
grayish blue
very dark bluish green

dark teal blue
USE dark grayish blue
dark greenish blue

dark teal green
USE dark bluish green

dark terre verte
USE grayish green

dark violet
DL.293
UF blackish violet
blue plum
bluish violet
bluish violet, dark
centroid color 212
dark bluish violet
navy, reddish
plum (color)
plum, blue
plum purple
purple, plum
reddish navy
violet, blackish
violet, bluish
violet, dark
violet, dark bluish

dark violet brown
USE blackish purple
dark grayish purple
dark purplish red
very dark purplish red

dark violet gray
USE dark gray

dark violet slate
USE grayish blue

dark viridian green
USE moderate green

dark yellow
DL.149
UF bistre
brass (color)
centroid color 88
mustard
olive yellow
reddish yellow
yellow, dark
yellow, olive
yellow, reddish

dark yellowish brown
DL.134
UF brown, dark yellowish
brown, dull yellowish
brown, mummy
brown, sepia
brown, very dark
centroid color 78
dull yellowish brown
mummy brown
raw umber (color)

sepia brown
umber, raw
very dark brown
yellowish brown, dark
yellowish brown, dull

dark yellowish green
DL.224
UF centroid color 137
chrome green, deep
chrome green, light
chrome green, medium
deep chrome green
deep dull yellow green
dull green
dull yellow green, deep
green, dark yellowish
green, deep chrome
green, dull
green, light chrome
green, medium chrome
light chrome green
medium chrome green
yellow green, deep dull
yellowish green, dark

dark yellowish orange
USE dark orange yellow

dark yellowish pink
DL.61
HN April 1990 lead-in terms added
UF centroid color 30
light red
pink, dark yellowish
red, light
rose
vermilion (color)
yellowish pink, dark

darkness
BM.803 (R)
HN April 1993 descriptor moved

darkrooms
PJ.1343 (L,B)
HN March 1993 descriptor moved
ALT darkroom
UK dark-rooms
UKA dark-room
SN Rooms freed from light or lighted by a safelight for handling and processing light-sensitive materials. (W)
UF darkrooms, photographic
photographic darkrooms

darkrooms, photographic
USE darkrooms

darning baskets
USE sewing baskets

dart boards
TV.72 (L,N)
ALT dart board
SN Large circular boards, usually of cork and having numbered compartments, used as targets during the game of darts.
UF boards, dart

darts
TK.239

ALT dart
SN Use for the light, pointed projectiles resembling arrows or short javelins, often with flights on the butt of the shaft, hand-thrown or projected through blowguns. Use also for the small projectiles of similar form used in the game of darts.
RT edged weapons
<sports and athletic equipment>

Darwinism, Social
USE Social Darwinism

dash, pebble
USE pebble dash

dash, rock
USE pebble dash

dasymeters
TN.118 (N)
ALT dasymeter
SN Thin glass globes used to measure the density of gases by weighing the globe in the gases. (MHDSTT)

data conversion
KG.130
HN March 1993 descriptor moved
SN Changing the representation of data in a database from one form to another, as for instance changing the storage medium, data format, or the code in which the data is held.
UF conversion, data

data dictionaries
VW.476 (L)
HN November 1992 descriptor moved
ALT data dictionary
UF dictionaries, data

data disk drives
USE disk drives

data files
USE databases

data processing
KG.129 (L)
HN March 1993 descriptor moved
February 1992 lead-in terms added
February 1991 scope note added
January 1991 lead-in term added
SN Creating and manipulating data in machine-readable form by means of computers, including inputting, storage, conversion, editing, and printing.
UF automatic data processing
data processing, automatic
data processing, electronic
electronic data processing
processing, automatic data
processing, data
processing, electronic data

data processing, automatic
USE data processing

data processing centers
USE computer centers

data processing, electronic
USE data processing

<data processing equipment>
TH.548

data processing service centers
USE computer centers

data retrieval
USE information retrieval

data search services
USE information retrieval services

data tape drives
USE tape drives

database search services, online
USE information retrieval services

database searching
USE online searching

database vendors
USE online vendors

databases
VW.35   (A,L)
HN November 1992 descriptor moved
ALT database
SN Structured assemblies of logically related data, usually machine-readable
data, designed to meet various applications but managed independently of them. (ICA)
UF data files
files, data

databases, bibliographic
USE bibliographic databases

databases, electronic image
USE image databases

databases, image
USE image databases

dataism
USE computer art

date books
USE appointment books

date hallmarks
USE date letters

date letters
VW.419
HN February 1993 descriptor added
ALT date letter
SN The letter of the alphabet stamped
on silver to indicate the year in
which it was made or assayed, especially in England. (MGFEAS)
UF date hallmarks
hallmarks, date
letters, date
marks, wardens'
wardens' marks

date marks
VW.418
HN February 1993 lead-in term added
November 1992 descriptor moved

ALT date mark
UF datemarks
marks, date

datemarks
USE date marks

dates
USE dating

dates, absolute
USE absolute dating

Datia
FL.2349

dating
KT.180   (A,L)
HN January 1993 descriptor moved
September 1992 lead-in term added
ALT dated
SN Determining or fixing a date of
origination, fabrication, composi-
tion, or occurrence. (W)
UF dates

dating, absolute
USE absolute dating

dating, amino acid
USE amino acid dating

dating, archaeomagnetic
USE archaeomagnetic dating

dating, archaeomagnetism
USE archaeomagnetic dating

dating, C-14
USE radiocarbon dating

dating, carbon-14
USE radiocarbon dating

dating, chronometric
USE absolute dating

dating, epimerization
USE amino acid dating

dating, fission track
USE fission track dating

dating, fluorine
USE fluorine dating

dating, growth ring
USE dendrochronology

dating, hydration ring
USE neutron activation analysis

dating, K-Ar
USE potassium-argon dating

dating, nitrogen
USE nitrogen dating

dating, obsidian hydration
USE obsidian hydration dating

dating, paleomagnetic
USE paleomagnetic dating

dating, potassium-argon
USE potassium-argon dating

dating, racemization
USE amino acid dating

dating, radioactive
USE radioactive dating

dating, radiocarbon
USE radiocarbon dating

dating, radiometric
USE radioactive dating

dating, relative
USE relative dating

dating, thermoluminescence
USE thermoluminescence dating

dating, tree ring
USE dendrochronology

daub
MT.1786
SN Material, such as plaster or mud,
used with wattle as a building material.

daub, wattle and
USE wattle and daub

daubers
USE dabbers

daubers, inking
USE dabbers

daughters
HG.56   (L)
HN March 1992 alternate terms added
ALT daughter
daughter's
daughters'

Daulatabad
FL.2304
HN February 1991 descriptor moved
UF Devagiri

davenport beds
USE davenports (sofas)

davenport desks
USE davenports (desks)

davenport tables
USE sofa tables

davenports (desks)
TC.942   (R)
HN January 1993 descriptor moved
ALT davenport (desk)
UF davenport desks
desks, davenport
devonports

davenports (sofas)
TC.745   (N)
HN January 1993 descriptor moved
May 1991 descriptor changed, was
davenports
May 1991 alternate term changed,
was **davenport**
ALT davenport (sofa)
SN Large upholstered sofas, often con-
vertible into beds. (W)

UF beds, davenport
davenport beds

davids
TX.432
ALT david
SN Use for semisubmersible torpedo boats built and used by Confederate forces during the American Civil War; steam driven, with a small, protected opening at the top of a long, spindle-shaped hull.
RT semisubmersibles
steamboats

David's shields
USE Stars of David

davits
TH.470   (L,N)
ALT davit
SN Fixed or moveable cranes that project over the side of a ship or over a hatchway; used especially for hoisting ships' boats, anchors, or cargo. (W)
UF anchor davits
boat davits
davits, anchor
davits, boat
davits, hatch
hatch davits

davits, anchor
USE davits

davits, boat
USE davits

davits, hatch
USE davits

Davolder
USE Chodor

dawn, gray
USE purplish gray

dawn redwood
MT.2983
HN March 1992 descriptor moved
UF Metasequoia glyptostroboides
redwood, dawn

Dawu
FL.76

day
BM.722   (L,R)
HN November 1992 descriptor moved

day camps
RG.164   (L)
ALT day camp
UF camps, day

day care
BM.1069   (L)
HN February 1993 descriptor moved
SN Care of children or others unable to be left by themselves by persons other than their parents, family, or

guardians on a partial or full day basis. (ERIC12)
UF care, day

day care centers
RK.794   (A,L,B)
HN September 1990 scope note added
ALT day care center
SN Designates professionally run facilities that care for groups of pre-school children on a partial or full-day basis. (ERIC9)
UF centers, child care
centers, day care
child care centers
creches
day nurseries
nurseries, day

day care centers, adult
USE adult day care centers

day coaches
USE coaches (railroad cars)

day nurseries
USE day care centers

Day of Atonement
USE Yom Kippur

day sailers
USE daysailers

day schools
RK.766
ALT day school
SN Use for schools, usually elementary or secondary, where classes are held only on weekdays and that do not provide any boarding facilities.
UF schools, day

daybeds
TC.817   (N)
HN May 1993 scope note changed
May 1993 related term added
January 1993 descriptor moved
ALT daybed
SN Extended chairs, generally without arms, used for lounging with one backed end usually made to tilt; often supported on a stretcher frame with six or eight legs. Also, long, wide, sofalike seats, often with two low ends that somewhat resemble headboards or footboards, that can be use for sitting or sleeping.
UF beds, rest
lits de repos
reading seats
rest beds
seats, reading
sultanes (lits de repos)
RT chairs

daybooks
VW.587   (N)
HN November 1992 descriptor moved
May 1991 descriptor moved
ALT daybook
SN Volumes used in bookkeeping containing daily records of receipts and

expenditures in the order of their occurrence. (GAHLM)

daylight
BM.780   (A,L,B)
HN April 1993 descriptor moved
SN Use with reference to the natural light of day; for the direct light of the sun specifically, use **sunlight.**
UF daylighting
light, natural
lighting, natural
natural light
natural lighting

daylight lamps
PJ.2968
ALT daylight lamp
UF lamps, daylight

daylighting
USE daylight

daysailers
TX.351
ALT daysailer
SN Use for small open sailboats without any or with very limited accommodations designed primarily for day sailing, although many are also class boats used for racing.
UF day sailers
sailers, day
RT sailboats

De
FL.317

De Stijl
FL.3439   (A,B,R)
UF Stijl, De

deaccessioning
KG.122
ALT deaccessioned
SN Permanently removing an object from a collection.

deacidification
KT.825   (L)
HN November 1992 descriptor added
ALT deacidified
SN The removal or reduction of acid content, as by neutralization, including the treatment of paper with a buffering substance to protect it from acid attack.
UF deacidifying

deacidification, nonaqueous
USE nonaqueous deacidification

deacidifying
USE deacidification

deacons
HG.399   (L,R)
HN February 1993 descriptor moved
December 1992 alternate terms added
ALT deacon
deacon's
deacons'

SN Subordinate officers in a Christian church. (W)

deacons' benches
TC.709
HN March 1993 descriptor changed, was **deacon's benches**
March 1993 lead-in term changed, was **deacon's seats**
March 1993 lead-in term changed, was **seats, deacon's**
January 1993 descriptor moved
ALT deacon's bench
UF benches, deacons'
benches, meeting house
deacons' seats
meeting house benches
meeting house seats
seats, deacons'
seats, meeting house

deacons' seats
USE deacons' benches

dead-blow mallets
TH.1665
ALT dead-blow mallet
SN Mallets whose heads are filled with lead shot so that there is no rebound to the blow. (HAND)
UF mallets, dead-blow

dead bolts
PJ.556
HN March 1993 descriptor moved
ALT dead bolt
SN Door locks that must be operated actively in both directions by turning a key or a thumb bolt. (MEANS)
UF bolts, dead

dead bolts, split
USE split dead bolts

dead color
USE lay-in

dead-end streets
RM.142   (L)
HN April 1993 descriptor moved
ALT dead-end street
UF streets, dead-end

dead latches
USE night latches

dead latches, auxiliary
USE auxiliary dead latches

dead loads
BM.604   (L)
HN November 1992 descriptor moved
January 1991 alternate term added
ALT dead load
SN Constant loads in structures that are due to the combined weight of its members, the supported structures, and permanent attachments or accessories. (W)
UF loads, dead
loads, static
static loads

dead oil
USE creosote

dead walls
USE blank walls

deadbeat escapements
PJ.2655
ALT deadbeat escapement
SN Use for escapements in which there is no recoil from the shock of contact among the locking parts; introduced in the early 18th century and best suited for expensive or precise timekeepers.
UF escapements, deadbeat
escapements, Graham
Graham escapements

deadlights
USE fixed windows

deadlocking latch bolts
USE auxiliary dead latches

deadlocking latches
USE auxiliary dead latches

deadlocks
PJ.492
HN April 1993 descriptor moved
ALT deadlock
SN Use for locks with dead bolts only.

deadrise boats
TX.332
ALT deadrise boat
SN Use for Chesapeake Bay watercraft with V-bottom hulls.
UF boats, deadrise
RT skipjacks

deaf
HG.42   (L,B)
HN February 1993 descriptor moved
SN People deprived of the functional use of the sense of hearing. (ERIC9)

deal, white
USE common spruce

deal, yellow
USE Scotch pine

dealers
HG.633   (L,R)
HN December 1992 alternate terms added
ALT dealer
dealer's
dealers'
SN Persons who buy and sell. (W)

dealers' marks
VW.420
HN November 1992 descriptor moved
ALT dealer's mark
UF marks, dealers'

dealerships, automobile
USE automobile showrooms

deambulatories
USE ambulatories

deaneries
RK.330   (A,H,L,B,R)
ALT deanery

deans
HG.491   (L)
HN December 1992 alternate terms added
ALT dean
dean's
deans'
SN Persons who head one of the divisions, faculties, colleges, or schools of a university. (W)

death certificates
VW.694   (L,N)
HN November 1992 descriptor moved
ALT death certificate
SN Certificates issued by public officials stating that a person has died; often include the cause of death and the signature of the attending or examining physician. (BLACKS)
UF certificates, death

death masks
VC.566   (L,R)
ALT death mask
SN Casts taken of a person's face after death. (RHDEL1)
UF masks, death

death notices
USE obituaries

death records
VW.692
HN November 1992 descriptor moved
ALT death record
SN Official records of deaths kept by public officials charged with registering deaths. (BLACKS)
UF records, death

death registers
VW.695   (L,R)
HN November 1992 descriptor moved
ALT death register
UF necrologies
registers, death

deaths
KM.159   (H,L,R)
HN February 1991 alternate term added
February 1991 descriptor changed, was **death**
ALT death

debarkers
USE barkers

debates
KM.56   (L)
HN October 1992 descriptor added
ALT debate
SN Use for formal contests in which the affirmative and negative sides of a proposition are advocated by opposing speakers.

debtors' prisons
RK.687   (A)

HN January 1993 descriptor changed, was **debtor's prisons**
ALT debtor's prison
SN Use for local places of detention primarily for debtors.
UF compters
prisons, debtors'

Decadence (artistic and literary movement)
USE Decadent Movement

Decadent Movement
FL.3347 (L,R)
UF Decadence (artistic and literary movement)

Decadent period
USE Late Postclassic

decadrachms
VK.37 (L)
ALT decadrachm
SN Ancient Greek silver coins worth ten drachmas, struck in the 5th and 4th centuries BCE, primarily in Sicily.

decagons
BM.676
HN January 1991 alternate term added
ALT decagon
decagonal

decalcomania
KT.1007 (L,R)
SN Technique of transferring pictures and designs from specially prepared paper onto a surface, such as glass, and the Surrealist painting technique in which one freshly painted or inked surface is pressed against another to form an image.

decals
VC.82 (L,N)
ALT decal
SN Images made on paper specially treated so the image can be transferred to another surface. (GMGPC)

decanter bottles
TQ.525
ALT decanter bottle
SN Type of bottle that preceded the decanter and was used to bring wine to the table from the cask; made in a variety of forms and materials such as stoneware, delftware, and glass.
UF bottle decanters
bottle-decanters
bottles, decanter
bottles, serving
serving bottles
RT bottles
decanters

decanter jugs
TQ.527
ALT decanter jug
SN Decanters in the form of a jug with a long neck and a loop handle extending from the rim to the shoulder.
UF jugs, decanter
RT jugs

decanter labels
USE bottle tickets

decanter stands
USE wine coasters

decanters
TQ.526 (H,L,N,R)
ALT decanter
SN Decorative bottles, often with a stopper, used to store or serve beverages, especially wine or liquor.
RT bottles
carafes
claret jugs
decanter bottles
jolly-boat decanter wagons
tantaluses
toddy lifters
whiskey jugs
wine bottles

decastyle
DC.146
HN October 1992 descriptor moved

decay
HN November 1992 descriptor deleted, made lead-in to **deterioration**

decay
USE deterioration

decay, red
USE red rot

Deccani
FL.2300 (L)
HN February 1991 descriptor moved
UF Deccani School
Dekkhan

Deccani School
USE Deccani

decentralization
KG.212 (L)
HN April 1993 lead-in term added
January 1991 scope note added
October 1990 descriptor moved
January 1990 alternate term added
ALT decentralized
SN Distributing the functions and powers of an organization, governing body, or other authority over a less centralized area or among a large number of parties.
UF decentralizing

decentralizing
USE decentralization

deception beds
TC.772
HN January 1993 descriptor moved
ALT deception bed
SN Any of various kinds of concealed or disguised beds first designed in the 18th century. Such beds were among the many ingenious forms of late 19th-century patent furniture.
UF beds, concealed
beds, deception
concealed beds

deciduous trees
RD.243
ALT deciduous tree
UF trees, deciduous

decision making
KG.14 (L)
HN January 1991 scope note added
SN Process of making choices between or among alternatives.

decisions
VW.751
HN November 1992 descriptor moved
ALT decision
UF court decisions
determinations
judgements

deck boats, raised
USE raised deck boats

deck bridges
USE deck truss bridges

deck chairs
TC.635 (N)
HN May 1993 related terms added
January 1993 descriptor moved
ALT deck chair
SN Chairs usually with arms and having full-length leg rests, designed for lounging outdoors. Use **chaises longues** for similar forms used indoors.
UF chairs, deck
chairs, steamer
steamer chairs
RT chaises longues
outdoor furniture

deck cruisers, raised
USE raised deck boats

deck dowelling bits
USE tenon-cutting bits

deck nails
PJ.191
HN April 1993 descriptor moved
ALT deck nail
UF nails, deck

deck paint
MT.1963
SN Enamel with a high degree of resistance to mechanical wear, for use on such surfaces as porch floors. (STEIN)
UF paint, deck

deck plans
VC.139
HN April 1992 descriptor moved
ALT deck plan
SN In shipbuilding, drawings showing layouts of decks.
UF plans, deck

deck span bridges
USE   deck truss bridges

deck truss bridges
RK.1244
ALT   deck truss bridge
SN   Truss bridges having the roadway or track on top of the trusses. (WB)
UF   bridges, deck
bridges, deck truss
deck bridges
deck span bridges

decking
PJ.1670
HN   March 1993 descriptor moved
SN   Self-supporting flooring or roofing units that span between structural members. (HORNB)
UF   planking
planks

deckle edges
DE.37
ALT   deckle edge
SN   Feathery edge at the border of a sheet of hand- or mold-made paper, caused by the deckle or frame which confines the pulp to the mold; also on some machine-made papers, caused by the rubber deckle straps at the sides of the paper machine, or made by artificial means. (LG)
UF   deckled edges
edges, deckle
edges, deckled
edges, feathered
feathered edges
RT   edges

deckled edges
USE   deckle edges

deckling
HN   August 1992 descriptor deleted

decks
PJ.984   (A,L)
HN   March 1993 descriptor moved
June 1990 scope note changed
ALT   deck
SN   Use for uncovered wood or metal platforms, usually attached to structures and often raised off the ground or on rooftops.

decks (packs of cards)
USE   packs of cards

decks, observation
USE   observation decks

decks, sun
USE   sun decks

Deckweiss
USE   lithopone

declarations
VW.381   (L)
HN   November 1992 descriptor moved
ALT   declaration
SN   Documents conveying formal state-

ments intended to create, preserve, assert, or testify to a right. (BOCLD)

<declaratory and advertising artifacts>
VW.1119
HN   June 1992 guide term added
SN   Collocates descriptors for items whose purpose is to be distributed or posted in order to give public notice of information.

<declaratory document genres>
VW.372
HN   November 1992 guide term moved
November 1992 guide term changed, was <declaratory documents>

decline, population
USE   population decline

declinometers
TN.233   (N)
ALT   declinometer
SN   Devices for measuring the direction of a magnetic field relative to astronomical or survey coordinates. (STEIN)

décollage
KT.385   (R)
HN   July 1991 scope note changed
SN   The tearing away of parts of posters, or other materials, that have been applied in layers, so that selected portions of the underlayers contribute to the total image. To designate the resulting works, use **affiches lacerérées.**

décollages
USE   affiches lacérées

decomposing
USE   decomposition

decomposition
KT.233   (L)
HN   January 1993 descriptor added
ALT   decomposed
SN   Dissolution into separate parts, used especially of organic materials or of such changes at a molecular level.
UF   decomposing

deconsecrations
KM.44
HN   March 1993 descriptor moved
February 1991 alternate term added
February 1991 descriptor changed, was **deconsecration**
ALT   deconsecration
SN   Acts or ceremonies of removing the sacred character of a thing or place. (OED)

deconstruction
BM.225   (L,R)
HN   January 1991 alternate term added
ALT   deconstructive
SN   Strategy of critical analysis arising in the mid-20th century, directed toward exposing unquestioned as-

sumptions and internal contradictions in philosophical and literary language. (OED)

Deconstructivist
FL.3844   (A)
ALT   Deconstructivism

Decorated, Curvilinear
USE   Curvilinear Decorated

Decorated, Early
USE   Early Decorated

Decorated, Geometrical
USE   Early Decorated

Decorated Style
FL.3213   (R)
UF   Pointed, Second
Second Pointed

decorated typefaces
USE   ornate (typeface group)

decorating
USE   decoration

decoration
KT.271   (A,L,B,R)
ALT   decorated
SN   Use for the overall approach to and techniques of embellishing architecture, furniture, or other objects. Use **ornament** in reference to specific forms, such as fluting, finials, or monograms, that embellish and are part of the building or object, but are not structurally essential to it.
UF   decorating

decoration, applied
USE   applied decoration

decoration, encaustic
USE   encaustic decoration

decoration, foliate
USE   foliation (pattern)

decoration, graffito
USE   sgraffito

decoration, interior
USE   interior decoration

decoration, knulled
USE   gadrooning

decoration, lobed
USE   gadrooning

decoration, nulled
USE   gadrooning

decoration, running
USE   running ornament

Decorationist
USE   Pattern painting

decorative arts
KD.19   (L,B,R)
SN   Traditional Western designation for those arts involving the creation of works that serve utilitarian as well as

aesthetic purposes, or involving the decoration and embellishment of utilitarian objects.

UF applied arts
arts, applied
arts, decorative
arts, minor
minor arts

decorative arts museums
HN March 1993 descriptor split, use decorative arts + museums

decorative glass
USE figured glass

decorative lighting
PC.207 (A,L)
HN March 1993 descriptor moved
April 1991 descriptor added
SN System of lights arranged for decorative purposes, as in store window displays, on Christmas trees, or on bushes.
UF lighting, decorative

decorative motifs
USE motifs

decorative typefaces
USE ornate (typeface group)

<decorative wall components>
PJ.1958
HN March 1993 guide term moved

decorators, interior
USE interior decorators

decorators' show houses
RK.277
ALT decorators' show house
UF houses, show
show houses

decorum
BM.228 (R)
SN A critical concept concerning the qualities of congruence among the elements of a work of visual art, literature, or theater, and good taste in the work's relationship to external reality.
UF propriety

découpé
USE reverse appliqué

decrees
VW.382 (L)
HN November 1992 descriptor moved
ALT decree
SN Includes judicial decisions issued in an equity or probate court and doctrinal or disciplinary religious orders applying or interpreting articles of canon law.
UF edicts

decretals
VW.383 (R)
HN November 1992 descriptor moved
ALT decretal
SN Letters of the pope determining

some point or question in ecclesiastical law and possessing the force of law within the Roman Catholic Church. (BLACKS)

decumani
RM.154
HN April 1993 descriptor moved
ALT decumanus
SN Designates the east-west streets used in laying out ancient Roman countryside tracts and associated towns and thus, by extension, the main east-west streets, distinguished by greater width and scale of appointments, of planned Roman towns.

Dedi Paca Gördes
USE Gördes + rugs

dedicatees
HG.1004
HN January 1993 alternate terms added
ALT dedicatee
dedicatee's
dedicatees'
SN Persons to whom anything is dedicated. (OED)

Dedication, Feast of
USE Hanukkah

dedication to public use
BM.906 (L)
HN February 1993 descriptor moved
SN An appropriation or giving up of property to public use that precludes the owner from asserting any right of ownership inconsistent with the use for which the property is dedicated. (W)
UF public use, dedication to
use, dedication to public

dedications (ceremonies)
KM.28 (L)
HN May 1991 alternate term added
ALT dedication (ceremony)
SN Acts or rites of dedicating something or someone to a special use or purpose, or to the memory of particular people or events.

dedications (documents)
VW.389 (L)
HN November 1992 descriptor moved
May 1991 descriptor changed, was dedications
May 1991 alternate term changed, was dedication
ALT dedication (document)
SN Authors' notes prefixed to works, offering them to friends or patrons as marks of esteem, affection, or gratitude, or as pleas for patronage. (GAHLM)

deed books
VW.666
HN November 1992 descriptor moved
June 1992 scope note added
ALT deed book

SN Use for books in which official copies of deeds are collected.
UF books, deed

deed registers
VW.667
HN November 1992 descriptor moved
ALT deed register
UF registers, deed

deeds
VW.669 (L,N)
HN November 1992 descriptor moved
ALT deed
SN Documents, usually executed under seal, containing a conveyance, especially of real estate. (RHDEL2)
UF deeds, title
title deeds

deeds, mortgage
USE mortgage deeds

deeds, title
USE deeds

deep bistre
USE light olive brown

deep bite
USE deep etching

deep blue
DL.247
UF blue, deep
blue, deep royal
blue, deep sapphire
blue, dull
blue, lapis lazuli
blue, powder
blue, royal
bright navy
centroid color 179
deep royal blue
deep sapphire blue
dull blue
indigo (color)
lapis lazuli blue
navy, bright
powder blue
royal blue
royal blue, deep
sapphire blue, deep
smalt (color)
ultramarine

deep blue violet
USE vivid purplish blue
vivid violet

deep bluish gray green
USE grayish green

deep bluish green
DL.230
UF bluish green, deep
centroid color 161
deep turquoise green
green, deep bluish
green, deep turquoise
green, Prussian
Prussian green
turquoise green, deep

deep brown
  DL.109
 UF brown, deep
     brown, metallic
     centroid color 56
     metallic brown

deep buttoning
  KT.1245
 HN December 1992 descriptor added
 ALT deep-buttoned
 SN Form of buttoning originating in
     the Victorian period, producing
     deeply puckered, comfortable up-
     holstery.
 UF buttoning, deep

deep cadmium yellow
  MT.2273
 HN April 1992 descriptor moved
 UF cadmium yellow, deep
     jaune de cadmium foncé
     Kadmiumgelb dunkel
     orient yellow
     yellow, deep cadmium
     yellow, orient

deep cerulean blue
 USE dark greenish blue
     deep greenish blue
     moderate blue
     moderate greenish blue

deep chrome
 USE strong orange yellow

deep chrome green
 USE dark yellowish green

deep chrome yellow
 USE moderate orange yellow

deep cobalt phosphate
  MT.2216
 HN April 1992 descriptor moved
 UF cobalt phosphate, deep
     phosphate, deep cobalt

deep delft blue
 USE grayish blue

deep dull bluish violet
 USE grayish purplish blue
     moderate violet
     pale purplish blue
     pale violet
     strong violet

deep dull lavender
 USE pale purple

deep dull yellow green
 USE dark yellowish green
     moderate olive green
     moderate yellow green

deep emerald green
 USE moderate bluish green
     moderate green

deep etch
 USE deep etching

deep etching
  KT.713

 HN October 1991 descriptor moved
     March 1991 alternate term added
     October 1990 scope note changed
     October 1990 lead-in terms added
 ALT deep-etched
 SN The biting of a printing plate to
     such a degree that the printing area
     becomes substantially recessed and
     thereby productive of sharper defi-
     nition and longer runs. (W)
 UF bite, deep
     deep bite
     deep etch
     etch, deep
     etching, deep

deep fat fryers
 USE deep fryers

deep fryers
  TQ.301   (L,N)
 ALT deep fryer
 SN Containers suitable for deep frying;
     usually deep and often with a mesh
     or perforated compartment in
     which the food is exposed to the
     fat. (W)
 UF deep fat fryers
     fryers, deep
     fryers, deep fat

deep grayish blue green
 USE grayish green

deep grayish lavender
 USE pale purple
     pale violet

deep grayish olive
 USE olive gray

deep green
  DL.198
 UF bright green
     centroid color 142
     dark emerald green
     emerald green, dark
     green, bright
     green, dark emerald
     green, deep

deep green blue gray
 USE grayish blue

deep greenish blue
  DL.267
 UF blue, deep cerulean
     blue, deep greenish
     blue, Prussian
     centroid color 170
     cerulean blue, deep
     deep cerulean blue
     green, Prussian
     greenish blue, deep
     Prussian blue (color)
     Prussian green

deep greenish yellow
  DL.169
 UF centroid color 100
     greenish yellow, deep
     lemon yellow
     olive yellow

     yellow, deep greenish
     yellow, lemon
     yellow, olive

deep lake
 USE dark purplish red

deep lavender
 USE light violet

deep lavender blue
 USE brilliant purplish blue

deep magenta
 USE vivid purplish red

deep malachite green
 USE moderate yellowish green

deep maroon
 USE dark grayish red
     dark grayish reddish brown

deep mourning
  BM.269
 HN September 1992 descriptor added
 SN Attire worn during the period of
     full mourning; generally refers to
     dress which is not only black but
     also of drab and lusterless materials.
 UF full mourning
     mourning, deep
     mourning, full
 RT mourning

deep navy gray
 USE dark gray

deep neutral gray
 USE dark gray

deep olive
 USE grayish olive
     moderate olive

deep olive gray
 USE light olive gray

deep olive green
  DL.238
 UF bluish olive
     centroid color 124
     green, deep olive
     olive, bluish
     olive green, deep

deep orange
  DL.95
 UF brown orange
     brown, orange
     brown, red
     centroid color 51
     ocher (color)
     orange brown
     orange, brown
     orange, deep
     orange vermilion (color)
     orange, xanthine
     red brown
     terra cotta
     vermilion, orange
     xanthine orange

deep orange yellow
  DL.160

UF amber (color)
centroid color 69
Mars yellow (color)
orange yellow, deep
orange, yellowish
reddish yellow
yellow, deep orange
yellow, Mars
yellow, reddish
yellowish orange

deep Payne's gray
USE grayish blue

deep peacock blue
USE dark greenish blue
moderate greenish blue

deep pink
DL.37
UF alizarine pink
bright rose
centroid color 3
deep rose
pink, alizarine
pink, deep
rose, bright
rose, deep
scarlet

deep plum
USE dark grayish purple
moderate purplish red
very dark reddish purple

deep purple
DL.301
UF centroid color 219
purple, deep
red violet
violet, red

deep purplish black
USE dark purplish gray

deep purplish blue
DL.277
UF blue, deep purplish
blue, deep royal
blue, reddish
blue, royal
blue, sapphire
centroid color 197
deep royal blue
purplish blue, deep
reddish blue
royal blue
royal blue, deep
sapphire blue

deep purplish pink
DL.49
UF bluish pink
bright rose
bright rose violet
carmine rose
centroid color 248
fuchsia pink
light orchid rose
lilac rose
orchid
orchid rose
orchid rose, light

pink, bluish
pink, deep purplish
pink, fuchsia
purplish pink, deep
rose
rose, bright
rose, carmine
rose, light orchid
rose, lilac
rose, orchid
rose violet, bright
violet, bright rose

deep purplish red
DL.84
UF bluish red
bright fuchsia purple
brown, rose
carmine (color)
centroid color 256
cerise
crimson
fuchsia purple
fuchsia purple, bright
fuchsia red
magenta (color)
magenta rose
plum (color)
purple, bright fuchsia
purple, fuchsia
purplish red, deep
red, bluish
red, deep purplish
red, fuchsia
rose brown
rose, magenta
rose violet
ruby (color)
violet, rose

deep red
DL.68
HN April 1990 lead-in term added
UF brown, garnet
brown, rose
cadmium purple
carmine (color)
centroid color 13
garnet brown
garnet red
lake, purple
purple, cadmium
purple lake
red, deep
red, garnet
red, rose
red, ruby
rose
rose brown
rose red
ruby (color)
ruby red

deep red brown
USE grayish reddish brown

deep reddish brown
DL.122
UF brown, deep reddish
brown, metallic
centroid color 41

dull red
garnet (color)
maroon
Mars violet (color)
metallic brown
metallic red
red, dull
red, metallic
red oxide
red, Venetian
reddish brown, deep
Venetian red (color)
violet, Mars

deep reddish orange
DL.102
UF centroid color 36
lacquer red
lead, red
orange, deep reddish
quinacridone red (color)
red, lacquer
red lead (color)
red, quinacridone
red, yellowish
reddish orange, deep
vermilion (color)
yellowish red

deep reddish purple
DL.322
HN April 1990 lead-in terms added
UF bright fuchsia purple
centroid color 238
dark purple, dull
dull dark purple
fuchsia purple
fuchsia purple, bright
plum (color)
purple, bright fuchsia
purple, deep reddish
purple, dull dark
purple, fuchsia
purple, red
purple, violet
red purple
red violet
reddish purple, deep
reddish violet
rose violet
violet purple
violet, red
violet, reddish
violet, rose

deep relief
USE high relief

deep rose
USE deep pink
moderate purplish red
moderate red

deep rose pink
USE strong purplish pink

deep royal blue
USE dark blue
deep blue
deep purplish blue
moderate purplish blue

deep sapphire blue
USE dark blue
    deep blue
    moderate purplish blue

deep-sea moorings
USE moorings

deep slate blue
USE grayish blue

deep slate green
USE dark greenish gray

deep slate olive
USE dark greenish gray

deep slate violet
USE grayish purple

deep space probes
USE space probes

deep teal
USE dark bluish green

deep teal blue
USE dark bluish green
    dark greenish blue
    moderate greenish blue

deep teal green
USE dark bluish green

deep turquoise green
USE deep bluish green
    moderate bluish green

deep ultramarine
USE moderate blue
    vivid blue
    vivid purplish blue

deep violet
    DL.289
UF bluish violet
    centroid color 208
    violet, bluish
    violet, deep

deep violet gray
USE dark gray
    dark purplish gray
    medium gray
    purplish gray

deep yellow
    DL.146
UF aniline yellow
    bistre
    bright gold
    centroid color 85
    gold, bright
    lemon yellow
    reddish yellow
    yellow, aniline
    yellow, deep
    yellow, lemon
    yellow, reddish

deep yellow green
    DL.189
UF centroid color 118
    green, deep yellow
    yellow green, deep

deep yellowish brown
    DL.131
UF brown, deep yellowish
    brown, golden
    centroid color 75
    golden brown
    yellowish brown, deep

deep yellowish green
    DL.219
UF bright green
    centroid color 132
    emerald (color)
    green, bright
    green, deep yellowish
    green, kelly
    kelly green
    yellowish green, deep

deep yellowish pink
    DL.58
UF centroid color 27
    light red
    pink, deep yellowish
    red, light
    rose
    vermilion (color)
    yellowish pink, deep

deer-hoof feet
USE hoof feet

deerstalker caps
    TE.532
ALT deerstalker cap
SN Caps, often made of wool, with a visor in the front and in the back, and with earflaps usually raised and tied on the top of the hat; use especially for those worn as hunting caps.
UF caps, deerstalker
    deerstalkers

deerstalkers
USE deerstalker caps

defacement
    KT.277   (A,L)
HN January 1993 descriptor moved
    November 1992 scope note changed
    January 1991 alternate term added
    December 1990 descriptor moved
ALT defaced
SN The act or result of intentionally inflicting damage on the surface or outer appearance of buildings or objects.

defects
    DE.18   (A,L,B)
HN November 1992 descriptor moved
ALT defect
SN Irregularities in the surface or structure of something that spoil appearance or cause weakness or failure. (W)

defenders, public
USE public defenders

defense guns, coast
USE coastal artillery

defensible space
    BM.1056
HN February 1993 descriptor moved
SN Use for the concept of a residential environment in which inhabitants can enhance the quality of their lives, while providing security for their families, neighbors, and friends. (NEWMAN)
UF space, defensible

defensive grenades
USE antipersonnel grenades

<defensive towers>
    RK.827

<defensive wall components>
    PJ.2482
HN March 1993 guide term moved

defensive walls
    PJ.2477
HN March 1993 descriptor moved
ALT defensive wall
SN Use broadly for all sorts of walls constructed to resist attack.
UF walls, defensive

<defensive walls and defensive wall components>
    PJ.2476
HN March 1993 guide term moved

deficiency, mental
USE mental retardation

defining
    KG.16   (H,L)
HN August 1992 descriptor added
SN Providing statements of the meanings of words or phrases.
UF definition

definition
USE defining

definitive drawings
USE design development drawings

deflection
    BM.632
HN March 1993 scope note added
    January 1993 descriptor changed, was **deflections**
    January 1993 alternate term deleted, was **deflection**
    November 1992 descriptor moved
    January 1991 alternate term added
SN The deformation or movement of a structure and its flexural members (such as beams or trusses) from their original positions, due to loads and forces acting on that structure.

deflectors
    PJ.2931   (L)
ALT deflector
SN Burner components consisting of discs, cones, or domes, usually of metal, that direct a current of air onto the flame.
UF deflectors, light
    light deflectors

deflectors, light
USE deflectors

defleshing
USE fleshing

deformation
BM.631 (L)
HN January 1993 descriptor changed, was **deformations**
January 1993 alternate term deleted, was **deformation**
November 1992 descriptor moved
January 1991 alternate term added
SN Any change of form, shape, or dimensions produced in a body by a stress or force without a breach of the continuity of its parts. (DAC)

deformed bars
MT.1779
HN April 1993 alternate term added
ALT deformed bar
SN Reinforcing bars made with lugs or ridges to produce a better bond between with the concrete.
UF bars, deformed

deformed joints
PJ.630
HN April 1993 descriptor moved
ALT deformed joint
SN Joints made by deforming the members in order to make the connection. (DS)
UF joints, deformed

defrosting
USE thawing

Degenerate art
USE Entartete Kunst

degeneration
USE deterioration

degradation
KT.234
HN January 1993 descriptor added
ALT degraded
SN Gradual loss of quality; can be without structural change.
UF degrading

degradation, biological
USE biodeterioration

degrading
USE degradation

dehumidification
KT.827 (B)
HN January 1993 descriptor moved
March 1991 alternate term added
ALT dehumidified
SN Removal of water vapor from air by chemical or physical methods. (CUT)

dehumidifying coils
PJ.802
HN March 1993 descriptor moved
May 1991 scope note added
ALT dehumidifying coil
SN Use for coils designed to remove

moisture from the air by condensation.
UF coils, dehumidifying

dehydrating
USE dehydration

dehydration
KT.835 (L)
HN November 1992 descriptor added
ALT dehydrated
SN The act or process of removing or depriving of water; though other liquids may remain. For the process of making free, or nearly free, of liquids, use **drying**.
UF dehydrating

deinstallation
USE dismantling

deionization
KT.828
HN November 1992 descriptor added
ALT deionized
SN The removal of ions from a solution by ion exchange. (NASATH)
UF deionizing

deionized water
MT.981
HN February 1992 descriptor added
SN Water from which dissolved ions have been removed by passing the water through cationic and anionic ion exchange.
UF water, deionized

deionizing
USE deionization

déjeuner tables
TC.1121
HN January 1993 descriptor moved
ALT déjeuner table
SN Period term for small breakfast tables, made in early 19th century, intended to be used in ladies' boudoirs or morning rooms.
UF tables, déjeuner

Dekkhan
USE Deccani

delamination
KT.263
HN January 1993 descriptor moved
March 1991 alternate term added
February 1991 scope note changed
ALT delaminated
SN Separation into constituent layers. (GRIMMR)

Delaware
FL.1304 (L,R)
UF Lenape
Lenni Lenape

Delft
FL.3330

delft blue
USE dark blue
grayish blue

grayish purplish blue
moderate blue
pale purplish blue

delft blue, dark
USE dark grayish blue

delft blue, deep
USE grayish blue

Delft ware
SEE delftware

delftware
PE.107 (H)
HN January 1993 descriptor moved
UK Delft ware
UF ware, Delft

Delhi Sultanate
FL.2307
UF Sultanate of Delhi

delicatessens
RK.159 (A,L)
ALT delicatessen
SN Use for stores selling foods already prepared or requiring little preparation for serving, such as cooked meats, cheeses, and salads, to be taken out or to be eaten on the premises.

delineators
HG.852
HN December 1992 alternate terms added
ALT delineator
delineator's
delineators'
SN Use for draftsmen who execute technical drawings from others' designs.

delivery of documents
USE document delivery

delivery stamps, special
USE special delivery stamps

della robbia
USE strong purplish blue

della robbia blue
USE light blue
moderate blue

deltas
RD.157 (L)
ALT delta
SN Alluvial deposits at the mouths of rivers commonly forming nearly flat, fan-shaped plains of considerable area traversed by many separate branches of water. (W)

demand responsive service
USE paratransit

demand responsive transportation
USE paratransit

demesnes
RD.280 (L)
ALT demesne

SN Land portions of estates kept in possession by the owner for personal use or the use of servants; manorial land not granted out or held by tenants.

demi-canapés
USE marquises

demi-cannons
TK.146 (N)
ALT demi-cannon
SN One of the common types of cannons in the 16th and 17th centuries, varying in weight and in the size and weight of shot fired from it, but generally of a bore between 6 and 7 inches in diameter.

demi-castors
TE.579
ALT demi-castor
SN Men's hats made from beaver-fur felt; worn from the 17th to the 19th century. (HFC)

demi-chanfrons
USE half shaffrons

demi-commodes
TC.905
HN January 1993 descriptor moved
ALT demi-commode
SN Small and narrow commodes.

demi-culverins
TK.142 (N)
ALT demi-culverin
SN One of the common types of culverins in the 16th and 17th centuries, having a bore between 4 1/4 and 4 3/4 inches in diameter and firing balls of from 9 to 13 pounds in weight.

demi-landaus
USE landaulets

demi-lune
DC.84
HN October 1992 descriptor moved

demi-relief
USE mezzo rilievo

demi-shaffrons
USE half shaffrons

demicolumns
USE half columns

demigreaves
USE schynbalds

demijohns
TQ.50 (N)
ALT demijohn
SN Bottles covered with wicker and holding from 1 quart to 10 gallons; intended to contain noncorrosive and bland liquids. For similar large bottles covered with wicker, wood, or other protective material and in-

tended for corrosive liquids, acids or distilled water, use **carboys**.
UF basketry-covered bottles
bottles, basketry-covered
jimmy-johns
RT carboys

demilitarized zones
RG.298
ALT demilitarized zone
SN Defined areas in which the stationing or concentrating of military forces, or the retention or establishment of military installations of any description, is prohibited. (DODDIC)
UF zones, demilitarized

demilunes
USE ravelins

demimetopes
PJ.1697
HN March 1993 descriptor moved
March 1991 scope note changed
March 1991 lead-in term added
ALT demimetope
SN Half or incomplete metopes in Doric friezes, usually found at corners. (RS)
UF semi-metopes

demineralisation
USE demineralization

demineralization
KT.829 (L)
HN November 1992 descriptor added
ALT demineralized
SN The removal of minerals, usually from water.
UF demineralisation
demineralizing

demineralizing
USE demineralization

Demirci
FL.3657
HN April 1993 descriptor added
UF Dermici Kula

demitasse cups
USE demitasses

demitasse spoons
USE coffee spoons

demitasses
TQ.418 (N)
ALT demitasse
SN Small coffee cups for serving strong coffee.
UF cups, demitasse
demitasse cups
RT coffee spoons

democracy
BM.956 (L,R)
HN February 1993 descriptor moved
January 1991 alternate term added
ALT democratic

democrat wagons
TX.178
ALT democrat wagon
SN Square, boxlike, unassuming buggies having two or more movable seatboards set at the same level as the driver's seat.
UF democrats
wagons, democrat

democrats
USE democrat wagons

demographers
HG.448 (L)
HN April 1993 related term added
December 1992 alternate terms added
ALT demographer
demographer's
demographers'
UF population specialists
specialists, population
RT demography

demographic anthropology
KD.211 (L)
HN September 1991 descriptor moved
UF anthropology, demographic

demographic maps
USE population maps

demographics
BM.1038
HN February 1993 descriptor moved
February 1992 scope note added
January 1991 alternate term added
ALT demographic
SN Statistical data of a population, especially relating to density, growth, distribution, and vital statistics.

demography
KD.246 (L,B,R)
HN April 1993 related term added
February 1991 alternate term added
ALT demographical
SN Statistical study of the characteristics of human populations especially with reference to size and density, growth, distribution, migration, and vital statistics, and the effect of all these on social and economic conditions. (W)
UF population studies
studies, population
RT demographers

demolishers
USE wreckers (people)

demolishing
USE demolition

demolition
KT.278 (A,L,B)
ALT demolished
UF demolishing
wrecking

demolition permits
VW.504

HN November 1992 descriptor moved
ALT demolition permit
SN Permits granted by public officials authorizing the wrecking or destruction of property, especially by the use of explosives.
UF permits, demolition

demonstration houses
USE model houses

demotic
PJ.3442 (L)
SN A script of ancient Egypt, derived from hieratic and used from about 700 BCE to 500 CE.
UF demotic script
demotic writing
script, demotic
writing, demotic

demotic script
USE demotic

demotic writing
USE demotic

demountable buildings
RK.1321 (A,L,B)
ALT demountable building
UF buildings, demountable

demountable partitions
PJ.1937 (B)
HN March 1993 descriptor moved
ALT demountable partition
SN Nonloadbearing partitions made of prefabricated sections that can be readily disassembled and relocated.
UF partitions, demountable
partitions, relocatable
relocatable partitions

denarii
VK.27 (L)
ALT denarius
SN Roman silver coins originally valued at ten asses, later debased in value and purity; in use from the late 3rd century BCE until the mid-3rd century CE.

denarius aureus
USE aurei

denatured alcohol
MT.2447 (L)
HN May 1990 lead-in term changed, was **synasol**
SN Ethyl alcohol which has been rendered unfit for drinking; used as a diluent and cleaner. (MAYER)
UF alcohol, denatured
Synasol (TM)

Denbigh
FL.821

dendrochronology
KT.188 (A,L,R)
HN January 1993 descriptor moved
February 1992 lead-in term added
April 1991 lead-in term added
SN The technique of dating events, in-

tervals of time, and variations in environment understood by studying the sequence of and differences between rings of growth in trees and aged wood. (W)
UF dating, growth ring
dating, tree ring
growth ring dating
tree ring dating

dendrometers
TN.80 (L,N)
ALT dendrometer
SN Devices used for measuring the height and diameter of trees using principles based on the relation of the sides of similar triangles. (W)

Dengese
USE Ndengese

deniers
VK.70
ALT denier
SN Widely circulated small, silver French coins introduced in the mid-8th century; appear in debased form until the French Revolution. For comparable English coins, also derived from Roman denarii, use **pennies.**
RT pennies

denim
MT.1617 (L)
HN March 1993 descriptor moved
SN A heavy, twill-woven, warp-flush textile. (MH)

denim jackets
SEE jean jackets

denim jackets, blue
USE jean jackets

denominational schools
USE parochial schools

dens
PJ.1110
HN March 1993 descriptor moved
ALT den
SN Small, private, informal rooms in houses or apartments used for work, reading, or relaxation.

densified wood
USE compressed wood

densimeters
TN.117 (N)
ALT densimeter
SN Any of several instruments that measure the density or specific gravity of liquids, solids, or gases. (STEIN)

densitometers
TN.329 (L,N)
ALT densitometer
SN Instruments that measure optical density of materials or objects by measuring the intensity of transmitted or reflected light; used, for ex-

ample, in photography to measure the opacity of images or to determine film speed.

density
DC.20 (L,B)
HN October 1992 descriptor moved
October 1992 scope note changed
July 1991 scope note added
January 1991 alternate term added
ALT dense
SN The distribution of something per unit area; can be, for example, the measure of the mass of a substance per unit volume, or the number of dwelling units per acre.

density of population
USE population density

density, population
USE population density

dental cabinets
TC.848
HN January 1993 descriptor moved
ALT dental cabinet
UF cabinets, dental

dental clinics
RK.707 (A,L,B)
ALT dental clinic
UF clinics, dental

dental colleges
USE dental schools

dental enamel
MT.1320 (L)
HN February 1992 descriptor added
SN Intensely hard calcareous substance that forms a thin layer capping or partly covering the teeth of most mammals. (W)
UF enamel, dental

dental lights
TC.1326
ALT dental light
UF lights, dental

dental offices
PJ.1174 (A,L)
HN April 1993 descriptor moved
ALT dental office
UF dentists' offices
offices, dental

dental prosthesis
USE dentures

dental schools
RK.774 (L,B)
HN September 1990 scope note added
ALT dental school
SN Schools devoted to training dentists.
UF colleges, dental
dental colleges
schools, dental

dental sinks
HN February 1991 descriptor deleted

dentils
PJ.1687
HN March 1993 descriptor moved
March 1991 scope note changed
ALT dentil
SN Bands of small, rectangular, toothlike blocks, usually along the underside of a cornice; a characteristic ornament of classical and classicizing styles.

dentin
MT.1321 (L)
HN February 1992 descriptor added
SN Calcareous materials similar to bones but harder and denser that compose the principal parts of teeth. (W)
UF dentine

dentine
USE dentin

dentistry
KD.133 (L)
HN April 1993 related term added
RT dentists

dentists
HG.583 (L,R)
HN April 1993 related term added
December 1992 alternate terms added
ALT dentist
dentist's
dentists'
RT dentistry

dentists' chairs
TC.604 (N)
HN May 1993 related term added
March 1993 descriptor changed, was dentist's chairs
January 1993 descriptor moved
ALT dentist's chair
UF chairs, dentists'
RT mechanical furniture

dentists' offices
USE dental offices

D'Entrecasteaux
FL.3776 (L)

dentures
TH.382 (L,N)
HN January 1993 descriptor added
ALT denture
SN Artificial replacements of one, several, or all of the natural teeth especially ones not permanently anchored in the mouth. (W)
UF artificial teeth
dental prosthesis
false teeth
prosthesis, dental
teeth, artificial
teeth, false

deodar
MT.2926
HN March 1992 descriptor moved
UF cedar, Himalayan

Cedrus deodara
Himalayan cedar

Deogarh
FL.2370

department stores
RK.173 (A,L,B,R)
ALT department store
UF stores, department

departments
HN.19
HN February 1993 descriptor moved
ALT department

departments, electronic data processing
USE computer centers

departments, maternity
USE maternity wards

departments, out-patient
USE clinics

depas
TQ.413 (L)
UF cups, depas
depas amphikypellon
depas cups

depas amphikypellon
USE depas

depas cups
USE depas

dependencies
HN.5
HN January 1993 descriptor added
ALT dependency
SN Administrative bodies subject to domination or a high degree of political control by one or more foreign powers while yet remaining outside the official boundaries of those powers.

dependency, alcohol
USE alcoholism

dependency, drug
USE drug addiction

dependency, narcotics
USE drug addiction

depiction
USE representation

depilation
KT.1051 (L)
HN January 1993 descriptor added
ALT depilated
SN The removal, by chemical or mechanical means, of epidermal structures such as hair from flayed skin or hide; also serves to loosen and expand dermal fiber network and alters the swelling characteristics of the hide or skin.
UF unhairing

deposit, certificates of
USE certificates of deposit

depositions
VW.943 (L)
HN November 1992 descriptor moved
ALT deposition
SN Testimonies of witnesses, under oath or affirmation, before a person empowered to administer oaths. (GAHLM)

depositories
USE repositories

depository libraries
RK.677 (L)
ALT depository library
SN In Canada and the United States, libraries designated to receive all or selected government publications, with the provision that public access to the collections be provided.
UF libraries, depository

deposits, fluvial
USE fluvial landforms

depots
USE railroad stations
stations

depots, ordnance
USE ordnance depots

depots, railway
USE railroad stations

depots, tram
USE tram depots

depreciation
BM.872 (L)
HN February 1993 descriptor moved
January 1991 alternate term added
ALT depreciated
SN A decline in value or reduction of worth. (PUTNAM)

depressed arches
USE drop arches

depressed center cars
USE depressed center flatcars

depressed center flatcars
TX.248
ALT depressed center flatcar
SN Use for flatcars having a portion of the floor set lower than the deck to accommodate special loads with oversized vertical dimensions; in use since the early 20th century. For flatcars in use since the mid-20th century with larger depressed central sections designed primarily to accommodate intermodal containers, use well cars.
UF cars, depressed center
center cars, depressed
center flatcars, depressed
depressed center cars
flatcars, depressed center
RT well cars

depression glass
MT.293 (L)

HN March 1992 descriptor added
UF glass, depression
glass, oatmeal
oatmeal glass

Deptford
FL.905

depth
DC.94
HN October 1992 descriptor moved
September 1992 scope note added
January 1991 alternate term added
ALT deep
SN Perpendicular measurement downward from a surface. (W)

depth bombs
USE depth charges

depth charges
TK.105 (L,N)
ALT depth charge
SN Bombs fired by ships or aircraft at underwater targets such as submarines, installations, and the underwater part of unarmored hulls, detonated by water pressure, on impact, or magnetically.
UF bombs, depth
charges, depth
depth bombs

depth finders
TN.103 (N)
ALT depth finder
SN Radar or ultrasonic instruments using echo location to measure the depth of the sea.
UF depth finders, sonic
Fathometers (TM)
finders, depth
finders, sonic depth
sonic depth finders

depth finders, sonic
USE depth finders

depth gauges
TN.81 (L,N)
ALT depth gauge
SN Instruments consisting of a rule that slides through a crosspiece and is inserted to measure the depth of holes, grooves, or other similar small depressions.
UF gages, depth
gauges, depth

depth of field
BM.104 (L)
SN Range of distances, near and far, within which objects appear in sharp focus. (A-Z)

Derbend
USE Derbent

Derbends
USE Derbent + rugs

Derbent
FL.1806

HN April 1993 descriptor added
UF Darband
Derbend

Derbents
USE Derbent + rugs

derbies
TE.587 (N)
ALT derby
UK bowlers
UKA bowler
SN Men's hard, round-crowned, felt hats with a narrow brim, slightly rolled in. (HFC)
UF billy-cocks
billycock hats
billycocks
bowler hats
derby hats
hats, billycock
hats, bowler
hats, derby

derboukas
USE darabukkas

derby hats
USE derbies

Derby red
USE chrome red

derby slickers
USE darbies

derelict buildings
RK.1333 (A)
ALT derelict building
SN Designates abandoned or unoccupied buildings or groups of buildings that constitute potential public hazards.
UF abandoned buildings
buildings, abandoned
buildings, derelict

Deringer pistols
USE deringers

deringers
TK.178 (L)
ALT deringer
SN Use for those derringers actually made by Henry Deringer, the Philadelphia gunsmith who first developed the type.
UF Deringer pistols
pistols, Deringer

<derivative objects>
PE.14
HN November 1990 guide term moved

Dermici Kula
USE Demirci

dermis
USE corium

derrick-men
SEE derrickmen

derrickmen
HG.822

HN December 1992 alternate terms added
ALT derrickman
derrickman's
derrickmen's
UK derrick-men
UKA derrick-man

derricks
TH.479 (L,N)
ALT derrick
SN Devices consisting of a vertical mast and a horizontal or sloping boom operated by cables to a separate engine or motor; used for hoisting and moving heavy loads or objects. (MEANS)

derricks, gin pole
USE gin poles

derricks, guy
USE guy derricks

derricks, pole
USE pole derricks

Derringer pistols
USE derringers

derringers
TK.177 (L,N)
ALT derringer
SN Small single-shot muzzleloading percussion pocket pistols of large bore, first made by the Philadelphia gunsmith Henry Deringer in the 1840s and subsequently widely copied throughout the United States. Specifically for those actually made by Henry Deringer himself, use deringers.
UF Derringer pistols
pistols, Derringer

dervishes
HG.418 (L)
HN May 1992 alternate terms added
ALT dervish
dervishes'
dervish's
SN Friars or monks of Islam.

desalination
KT.830
HN January 1993 descriptor moved
SN Removal of salts, as from water or soil.

desalination facilities
USE desalination plants

desalination plants
RK.554
ALT desalination plant
UF desalination facilities
facilities, desalination
plants, desalination

describing
KG.17
HN January 1991 scope note added
SN Representing in spoken, written, or

signed language the attributes or qualities of something or someone. (RHDEL2)

UF description

description
USE describing

descriptive bibliography
USE analytical bibliography

descriptive cataloging
    KG.116 (L)
HN August 1992 lead-in term added
UK descriptive cataloguing
SN Identifying and describing items in a library or other collection, and recording this information in the form of a catalog entry. (WYNAR)
UF cataloging, descriptive
    cataloguing, descriptive

descriptive cataloguing
SEE descriptive cataloging

desemers
    TN.289 (L)
ALT desemer
SN Scales with fixed counterweights at one end of a horizontal bar, a movable fulcrum which allows for changes in the ratio of the lengths of the arms, and a single hook from which to attach the item to be weighed; for scales of similar form, but with a fixed fulcrum and a movable counterweight, use steelyards.
UF besems
    bismars
RT steelyards

Desert Archaic
USE Desert Tradition

desert climate
    BM.735 (L,B,R)
HN November 1992 descriptor moved
SN Climate characterized by very little precipitation and extreme hot to cold temperatures, with great changes in daily temperature except in coastal areas. (WB)
UF climate, desert

Desert Tradition
    FL.772
UF Archaic, Desert
    Desert Archaic

deserted medieval villages
USE deserted villages

deserted villages
    RD.44
HN April 1993 lead-in terms added
ALT deserted village
SN Use for western European abandoned settlements from the Middle Ages, usually buried and visible only on aerial photographs.
UF deserted medieval villages
    medieval villages, deserted

    villages, deserted
    villages, deserted medieval

deserts
    RD.133 (A,L,R)
ALT desert
SN Dry, barren, treeless regions, so arid because of little rainfall that they support only sparse and widely spaced vegetation or no vegetation at all; usually sandy. (RHDEL2)

deshabille
USE undress

desiccation
    DC.250 (L)
HN February 1993 descriptor added
ALT desiccated
SN Extreme dryness.

design
    KD.27 (A,L,B,R)
HN March 1991 descriptor moved

design-and-build
USE design-build

design, aseismic
USE earthquake-resistant construction

design, barrier-free
USE barrier-free design

design books
HN June 1991 descriptor split, use **design** (ALT of **designs**) + **books**

design-build
    KG.282 (A,B)
SN A contracting arrangement in which a person or organization assumes responsibility under a single contract for both the design and construction of a project. (GCIT)
UF design-and-build
    package deal

design centers
    RK.142 (A,B)
ALT design center
SN Use for buildings providing permanent showrooms, galleries, or other display spaces for designers' work or for vendors of products for the design professions.
UF centers, design

design centers, community
USE community design centers

design centres, community
SEE community design centers

design, chintamani
USE chintamani

design, civic
USE city planning

design, collapse
USE plastic design

design, computer-aided
USE computer-aided design

design, costume
USE costume design

design development drawings
    VC.178
HN April 1992 descriptor moved
ALT design development drawing
SN Use for drawings done when an architectural design is more developed than at the stage of conceptual and schematic drawings but is not yet to the stage of working drawings.
UF definitive drawings
    developed sketches
    drawings, definitive
    drawings, design development
    sketches, developed

design drawings
    VC.176
HN April 1992 descriptor moved
ALT design drawing
SN Use for drawings intended to work out the scheme of a project, whether the project is expected to be executed or not; more finished than sketches.
UF designs (drawings)
    drawings, design

design drawings, schematic
USE schematic drawings

design, dress
USE costume design
    fashion design

design, earthquake-resistant
USE earthquake-resistant construction
    seismic design

<design elements>
    DG.1

design, fashion
USE fashion design

design, graphic
USE graphic design

design, green
USE green design

design guidelines
HN April 1993 descriptor split, use design + guidelines

design, industrial
USE industrial design

design, interior
USE interior design

design, landscape
USE landscape architecture

design, limit-load
USE plastic design

design, limit-states
USE plastic design

design, modular
USE modular coordination

design, participatory
USE participatory design

design patents
　　VW.739　　　　　　　　　　　　(L)
HN November 1992 descriptor moved
ALT design patent
UF patents, design

design, plastic
USE plastic design

design review
　　KG.35　　　　　　　　　　　　(A)
UF review, design

design, scene
USE theater design

design, seismic
USE seismic design

design, stage
USE theater design

design, theater
USE theater design

design, theatre
SEE theater design

design, ultimate-load
USE plastic design

design, urban
USE urban design

designers
　　HG.319　　　　　　　　　(A,L,B,R)
HN February 1993 descriptor moved
　　December 1992 alternate terms
　　　added
ALT designer
　　designer's
　　designers'

designers, clothes
USE fashion designers

designers, costume
USE costume designers

designers, display
USE display designers

designers, dress
USE costume designers
　　fashion designers

designers, exhibit
USE exhibit designers

designers, exhibition
USE exhibit designers

designers, fashion
USE fashion designers

designers, floral
USE floral designers

designers, graphic
USE graphic designers

designers, industrial
USE industrial designers

designers, interior
USE interior designers

designers, landscape
USE landscape architects

designers, scene
USE theater designers

designers, scenic
USE theater designers

designers, stage
USE theater designers

designers, theater
USE theater designers

designs
　　BM.32　　　　　　　　　　　　(L)
HN May 1993 related term added
　　January 1991 alternate term added
ALT design
SN Specific conceptual schemes for the
　　organization or appearance of
　　graphic works, objects, structures,
　　or systems. For proposed undertak-
　　ings or creations in general, includ-
　　ing works of art or architecture, or
　　for the actual carrying out of such
　　proposals, use **projects.**
RT projects

designs (drawings)
USE design drawings

designs, competition
USE competition drawings

designs, geometric
USE geometric patterns

designs, preliminary
USE preliminary drawings

designs, presentation
USE preparatory drawings
　　presentation drawings (proposals)

designs, proposed
USE preparatory drawings
　　presentation drawings (proposals)

designs, theoretical
USE theoretical drawings

designs, unbuilt
USE unbuilt projects

designs, unexecuted
USE unexecuted designs

desk articles
USE desk sets

desk boxes
USE Bible boxes

desk calculators
USE calculators

desk chairs
　　TC.605　　　　　　　　　　　(N)
HN January 1993 descriptor moved
ALT desk chair
UF chairs, desk

desk furnishings
USE desk sets

desk lamps
　　TC.1354
ALT desk lamp
SN Lamps designed to be used on a
　　desk, usually having some means of
　　adjusting the light source.
UF lamps, desk

desk locks
　　PJ.543
HN April 1993 descriptor moved
ALT desk lock
UF locks, desk

desk sets
　　PC.15　　　　　　　　　　　(H,N)
ALT desk set
SN Sets of matching articles such as pen
　　trays, stampboxes, paperweights, or
　　the like intended primarily for use
　　on a desk.
UF articles, desk
　　desk articles
　　desk furnishings
　　furnishings, desk
　　library sets
　　sets, desk
　　sets, library
RT inkstands
　　inkwells
　　paperweights
　　pen trays
　　pens
　　pounce boxes
　　pounce pots
　　stamp boxes
　　tapersticks

desk trays
USE pen trays

desks
　　TC.936　　　　　　　　　　(L,N,R)
HN January 1993 descriptor moved
ALT desk
SN Various forms of furniture for read-
　　ers or writers, generally having a flat
　　writing surface and often drawers
　　and other compartments.
UF scriptoires
　　scrutoires
　　scrutoirs

desks and bookcases
　　TC.943　　　　　　　　　　　(R)
HN May 1993 related term added
　　January 1993 descriptor moved
ALT desk and bookcase
SN Desks surmounted by a bookcase
　　with glazed or paneled doors. For
　　similar English forms which have a
　　steeply sloping lid, use **bureau-**
　　bookcases.
UF bookcases, desks and
　　bookcases, secretary
　　desks, secretary
　　escritoires (desks and bookcases)
　　secretary bookcases (desks and
　　　bookcases)

secretary-cabinets
secretary desks
RT bureau-bookcases

desks and bookcases, cylinder
USE cylinder desks and bookcases

desks and bookcases, cylinder-fall
USE cylinder desks and bookcases

desks, butlers'
USE butlers' desks

desks, Carlton House
USE Carlton House tables

desks, counting
USE counting-house desks

desks, counting-house
USE counting-house desks

desks, cylinder
USE cylinder fall desks

desks, cylinder fall
USE cylinder fall desks

desks, davenport
USE davenports (desks)

desks, double
USE partners' desks

desks, double counting-house
USE double counting-house desks

desks, drop-front
USE fall-front desks

desks, fall-front
USE fall-front desks

desks, gentlemen's portable
USE portable desks

desks, Governor Winthrop
USE Governor Winthrop desks

desks, kneehole
USE bureau tables
kneehole desks

desks, ladies'
USE ladies' desks

desks, ladies' small writing
USE ladies' writing tables

desks, larkin
USE desks-over-bookcases

desks, music
USE reading desks

desks-on-frames
TC.946
HN January 1993 descriptor moved
ALT desk-on-frame
SN Slant-front desks supported on low removable frames, popular in the Queen Anne period. (KETCH)
UF box stretcher desks-on-frames

desks-over-bookcases
TC.947

HN January 1993 descriptor moved
ALT desk-over-bookcase
SN Shallow desks with a slant front over a bookcase base. (CTSB)
UF desks, larkin
larkin desks

desks, partners'
USE partners' desks

desks, pedestal
USE pedestal desks

desks, portable
USE portable desks

desks, portable writing
USE portable desks

desks, reading
USE reading desks

desks, rolltop
USE rolltop desks

desks, rotary
USE rotary desks

desks, rotary cylinder
USE rotary desks

desks, screen
USE ladies' screen writing tables

desks, secretary
USE bureau-bookcases
desks and bookcases

desks, single counting-house
USE counting-house desks

desks, slant-front
USE slant-front desks

desks, spinet
USE spinet desks

desks, standing
USE standing desks

desks, straight-front
USE fall-front desks

desks, table
USE Bible boxes
portable desks

desks, tambour
USE tambour desks

desks, traveling
USE traveling desks

desks, wall
USE wall desks

desks, Winthrop
USE Governor Winthrop desks

desks, Wooton
USE Wooton desks

desks, writing
USE portable desks
writing desks

desktop publishing
KG.152   (L)

HN December 1992 descriptor added
SN The writing, assembling, and design of publications using microcomputers and word processing, graphics, and page layout software.
UF publishing, desktop
RT computerized composition

despotism
BM.971   (L,R)
HN February 1993 descriptor moved
June 1991 related term added
January 1991 alternate term added
ALT despotic
UF absolutism
tyranny
RT <government by form>

dessert dishes
TQ.351   (N)
ALT dessert dish
SN Dishes of varying form intended primarily for serving dessert.
UF dishes, dessert
RT dessert services

dessert forks
TH.305   (N)
HN April 1993 descriptor added
ALT dessert fork
SN Forks smaller than a dinner fork intended primarily for eating desserts; generally having a short handle and three or four, but sometimes two, tines. May be accompanied by a dessert spoon; sometimes a part of a dessert service.
UF forks, dessert
forks, luncheon
luncheon forks
RT dessert services
dessert spoons
dinner forks

dessert glasses
TQ.355   (N)
ALT dessert glass
SN Term generally applied to individual serving dishes made of glass and used for various types of desserts. In the 18th century the term also referred to large glass receptacles for serving sweetmeats and fruit.
UF glasses, dessert
RT syllabub glasses

dessert knives
TH.316   (N)
HN April 1993 descriptor added
ALT dessert knife
SN Knives smaller than a dinner knife intended for eating desserts; generally having a shorter handle and may have a curved and pointed blade; sometimes a part of a dessert service. Use **fruit knives** for knives with a sharp, sometimes serrated blade and often an ornamental handle used to pare and cut fruit at the table.
UF knives, dessert

knives, luncheon
luncheon knives
RT dessert services
dinner knives
fruit knives

dessert plates
TQ.364 (N)
ALT dessert plate
SN Plates for holding an individual portion of the dessert course of a meal, similar to but smaller than dinner plates.
UF cake plates (dessert plates)
plates, dessert
RT bread-and-butter plates
coffee services
dessert services
place settings
tea services

dessert pyramids
USE pyramids (containers)

dessert services
PC.21 (N)
ALT dessert service
SN A type of service for the dessert course served as the last course of a meal, usually consisting of dessert plates, dessert dishes, dessert forks, dessert knives, dessert spoons, and sometimes a serving spoon and finger bowls.
UF services, dessert
RT compotes
dessert dishes
dessert forks
dessert knives
dessert plates
dessert spoons
finger bowls
ice buckets

dessert spoons
TH.325 (N)
HN April 1993 descriptor added
ALT dessert spoon
SN Spoons intended for eating desserts, intermediate in size between a teaspoon and a tablespoon. May be accompanied by a dessert fork; sometimes a part of a dessert service.
UF spoons, dessert
RT dessert forks
dessert services

dessertes
USE console dessertes

dessus-de-portes
USE overdoors

destitution
USE poverty

destroyers
TX.433 (L,N)
ALT destroyer
SN Use for light, fast warships designed to operate offensively as attack craft with antisubmarine weapons; originally developed at the end of the

19th century to counter torpedo boats.
UF destroyers, torpedoboat
torpedoboat destroyers

destroyers, torpedoboat
USE destroyers

destroying
USE destruction

destruction
KT.272
HN August 1992 scope note added
ALT destroyed
SN Process of ruining the structure, organic existence, or condition of a material or immaterial object. (W)
UF destroying

destruction of property
USE vandalism

Destructive Art
FL.3886 (R)
HN May 1990 scope note added
May 1990 lead-in term added
May 1990 descriptor changed, was **Auto-destructive**
SN Use for art done around the early 1960s in which the process of destruction of objects or materials within the work is regarded as the work; usually associated theoretically with artists' concerns about social violence.
UF Auto-destructive
Self-destructive

detachable keys
PJ.598
HN March 1993 descriptor moved
ALT detachable key
SN Keys so constructed that the bit or portion that actuates the tumblers may be detached from the shank or handle of the key for convenience in carrying. (STEIN)
UF keys, detachable

detachable legs
PJ.2848
HN March 1993 descriptor moved
ALT detachable leg
UF legs, detachable

detachable linings
SEE liners (costume components)

detached
DC.322 (B)
HN October 1992 descriptor moved
UF separate

detached houses
RK.260 (A)
ALT detached house
UF houses, detached

detail assemblies
USE subassembly drawings·

detail drawings
VC.230 (L)

HN April 1992 descriptor moved
ALT detail drawing
SN Use for drawings of construction or design details. For minute parts of a larger structure, object, or image, use **details**. For preparatory studies of pictorial or design details, use **detail studies**.
UF details (drawings)
drawings, detail

detail drawings (studies)
USE detail studies

detail drawings, standard
USE standard detail drawings

detail sketches
USE detail studies

detail studies
VC.65
HN April 1991 descriptor moved
ALT detail study
SN Use for preparatory studies of pictorial or design details. For minute parts of a larger structure, object, or image, use **details**. For drawings of architectural construction or design details, use **detail drawings**.
UF detail drawings (studies)
detail sketches
drawings, detail
sketches, detail
studies, detail

detailing, architectural
USE architectural drawing

details
PJ.16 (A,L,B)
HN March 1993 descriptor moved
ALT detail
SN Use for minute parts of a larger structure, object, or image. For architectural drawings of design or construction details, use **detail drawings**. For preparatory studies of pictorial or design details, use **detail studies**.

details (drawings)
USE detail drawings

detection systems, fire
USE fire detectors

detective cameras
TH.752
HN October 1992 descriptor added
ALT detective camera
SN Cameras made in forms that disguise them, such as looking like a book or opera glasses.
UF cameras, detective

detectives
HG.917 (L)
HN December 1992 alternate terms added
ALT detective
detective's
detectives'

detectors, fire
USE fire detectors

detectors, flame
USE flame detectors

detectors, heat-actuated
USE temperature detectors

detectors, heat-sensing
USE temperature detectors

detectors, ionization
USE ionization detectors

detectors, photoelectric smoke
USE photoelectric smoke detectors

detectors, smoke
USE smoke detectors

detectors, temperature
USE temperature detectors

detectors, thermal
USE temperature detectors

detectors, thermostatic
USE temperature detectors

detention camps
USE concentration camps

detention centers
RK.697   (A,L,B)
ALT detention center
UK   detention centres
UKA detention centre
SN   Use for places of relatively short
     confinement for youthful offenders
     pending transfer or trial.
UF   centers, detention
     centers, juvenile detention
     centres, detention
     centres, remand
     detention centers, juvenile
     detention facilities
     detention homes
     detention homes, juvenile
     facilities, detention
     homes, detention
     homes, juvenile detention
     juvenile detention centers
     juvenile detention homes
     remand centres

detention centers, juvenile
USE detention centers

detention centres
SEE detention centers

<detention complexes>
RG.48

detention facilities
USE detention centers

detention homes
USE detention centers

detention homes, juvenile
USE detention centers

detergency
DC.16

HN   October 1992 descriptor added
ALT detergent
SN   The cleansing quality or power of a
     substance.

detergent
MT.1842   (L)
HN   April 1993 descriptor changed, was
        detergents
     April 1993 lead-in term changed,
        was synthetic detergents
     February 1993 related term added
     December 1991 scope note changed
SN   Generally any cleaning agent al-
     though it usually refers to a clean-
     ing agent other than soap but re-
     sembling soap in its ability to
     emulsify oil and hold dirt.
UF   detergent, synthetic
     synthetic detergent
RT   surface active agent

detergent, nonionic
USE nonionic detergent

detergent, synthetic
USE detergent

deteriorating
USE deterioration

deterioration
KT.231   (A,L)
HN   January 1993 descriptor moved
     November 1992 lead-in terms
        added
ALT deteriorated
SN   Use broadly for the action or pro-
     cess of growing worse or becoming
     impaired in quality, state, or condi-
     tion. (W)
UF   decay
     degeneration
     deteriorating

deterioration, oxidative-reductive
USE oxidative-reductive deterioration

determinate structures
USE statically determinate structures

determinations
USE decisions

determinism
BM.421   (L)
HN   January 1991 alternate term added
ALT deterministic
SN   Doctrine that all acts of will result
     from causes which determine them
     either in such a manner that people
     have no alternative course of action,
     or that the will is still free in the
     sense of being uncompelled. (W)

detonating powder
USE fulminate

detoxification
KT.923
HN   January 1993 descriptor moved
ALT detoxified

SN   The act of removing the poison or
     effect of poison from something.
     (W)

deux crayons
USE à deux crayons

Devagiri
USE Daulatabad

Developed Orientalizing
FL.2664
UF   Orientalizing, Developed

developed sketches
USE design development drawings

developers
HG.850   (A,L)
HN   December 1992 alternate terms
        added
ALT developer
     developer's
     developers'
SN   Individuals, companies, or corpora-
     tions engaged in the development
     and improvement of land for con-
     struction purposes. (STEIN)

developing (photography)
KT.601   (L)
ALT developed
SN   Procedures for making a latent pho-
     tographic image visible and then
     fixing it (making it insensitive to
     further changes from light).
UF   development (photography)

developing, collection
USE collection development

developing-out paper
MT.1483
HN   February 1992 descriptor moved
SN   Photographic paper on which the
     image is brought out by develop-
     ment after exposure. (JCCOP)
UF   development paper
     DOP
     paper, developing-out
     paper, development

developing tanks
TH.792
ALT developing tank
UF   tanks, developing

development
KG.59
HN   December 1990 descriptor added
ALT developed
SN   Change over time in human activi-
     ties, institutions, or settlements, usu-
     ally in the sense of improvement or
     expansion.
RT   land use

development (photography)
USE developing (photography)

development areas
RG.313
ALT development area
UF   areas, development

development class boats
TX.347
ALT development class boat
SN Use for racing sailboats built to a rule which allows hull and rig variations, but still allows boats built to the rule to race without handicap.
UF boats, development class
boats, measurement-class
boats, restricted class
class boats, development
class boats, restricted
measurement-rule boats
restricted class boats

development, collection
USE collection development

development, community
USE community development

<development concepts>
HN November 1991 guide term deleted

development, economic
USE economic development

development, industrial
USE industrialization

development, infill
USE infill

development, land
USE real estate development

development, linear
USE ribbon development

development paper
USE developing-out paper

development parks, research and
USE research parks

development, real estate
USE real estate development

development, regional
USE community development

development, ribbon
USE ribbon development

development rights transfer
BM.907   (A,L)
HN February 1993 descriptor moved
SN Use for the transfer, usually by sale, of the right to construct a certain amount of building space, from one piece of property to another, adjacent or in the same area; often as a means of subsidizing the preservation of landmark buildings in built-up areas.
UF rights transfer, development
transfer of development rights

development, rural
USE rural development

development, string
USE ribbon development

development, strip
USE ribbon development

development, sustainable
USE sustainable development

development, urban
USE urban development

development, urban economic
USE urban development

development, water resources
USE water resources development

<developmental concepts>
BM.563
HN February 1991 guide term added

developmental sketches
USE preliminary sketches

developments
USE housing developments

developments, housing
USE housing developments

developments, mixed-use
USE mixed-use developments

developments, multiuse
USE mixed-use developments

developments, planned unit
USE planned unit developments

deversoria
RK.914
ALT deversorium
SN Use for private ancient Roman residences providing food and lodging for travelers en route to rural estates.

deviancy, social
USE deviant behavior

deviant behavior
BM.1010   (L)
HN February 1993 descriptor moved
December 1990 scope note added
SN Conduct that departs from a society's established norms, rules, standards, or expectations. (TSIT)
UF behavior, deviant
deviancy, social
social deviancy

deviation, standard
USE standard deviation

devices
VW.396   (A,L,R)
HN November 1992 descriptor moved
ALT device
SN Use for representations, designs, or mottoes, or combinations of these, used to signify an individual, a group, or sometimes a commercial concern, and intended to convey a sense of lineage or quality.

devices (motifs)
USE motifs

devices, computer storage
USE storage devices

devices, input
USE input devices

devices, lighting
USE lighting devices

devices, measuring
USE measuring devices

devices, output
USE output devices

devices, step-and-hook
USE stepped frets

devices, storage
USE storage devices

devices, weighing
USE weighing devices

devil floats
TH.1170
HN December 1992 descriptor moved
ALT devil float
SN Hand-held flat tools with nails in each edge; used to scratch a coat of plaster prior to applying the next coat. (MEANS)
UF devils
floats, devil
floats, nail
nail floats

devils
USE devil floats
jumpers (tools)

devils' tails
USE jumpers (tools)

devitrification
KT.236   (L)
HN January 1993 descriptor moved
ALT devitrified
SN In glass, the loss of transparency caused by crystallization or deposition of one or more of its ingredients.

devonports
USE davenports (desks)

Devonshire clay
USE kaolin

devotional art
USE devotional images

devotional calendars
VW.10   (L)
HN November 1992 descriptor moved
ALT devotional calendar
UF calendars, devotional

devotional chairs
USE prie-dieus

devotional images
VC.57   (R)
ALT devotional image
SN Images used in private piety in the church or home, intended as recipients of prayer or aids to meditation;

distinct from images that serve the liturgy or are primarily didactic. (RINGBO)

UF art, devotional
 devotional art
 devotional pictures
 images, devotional
 pictures, devotional
RT devotional objects

devotional objects
 PE.66   (H,L)
HN December 1992 descriptor added
ALT devotional object
SN Use broadly for articles associated with or used in private religious devotions.
UF objects, devotional
RT devotional images

devotional pictures
USE devotional images

dew
 BM.739
HN November 1992 descriptor moved

dew point
 BM.740   (L)
HN March 1993 scope note added
 November 1992 descriptor moved
SN The temperature at which air becomes saturated when cooled, without the addition of moisture or any change in pressure; further cooling causes condensation.
UF point, dew

dewatering
 KT.831
HN January 1993 descriptor moved
SN Use for the removal of water from a site to maintain a dry and stable condition during construction.

dextrin
SEE dextrine

dextrine
 MT.1733   (L)
HN March 1992 descriptor moved
UK dextrin
SN A type of compound obtained from starch by the action of heat, acid, or enzyme. Have strong adhesive properties and are used as paste, particularly for envelopes, gummed paper, and postage stamps, for blending with gum arabic, in pyrotechnic compositions, and in textile finishing.
UF amylin
 gum, starch
 starch gum

DGEBA
USE basic liquid epoxy

Dharanindravarman I
 FL.2424

Dharanindravarman II
 FL.2426

dharmsalas
USE caravanserais

Dhlo Dhlo
 FL.137

dhows
 TX.554   (L,N)
ALT dhow
SN Use for a wide variety of lateen-rigged watercraft used for trading along the East African, Arabian, and Indian coasts; generally having long raking bows and fuller sterns. This is a European term derived from the Swahili and is not used by most of the people who sail such vessels.
RT lateen rigs

dhurries
 TC.124
ALT dhurrie
SN A type of flat-woven rug usually made of cotton, produced in India.
UF carpets, cotton
 cotton carpets
 cotton cloths, Indian
 durries
 Indian cotton cloths
 suttrangis

di-acetone alcohol
SEE diacetone alcohol

di sotto in su
USE sotto in su

diabase
 MT.652   (L)
HN April 1992 descriptor moved
 March 1992 lead-in term deleted, was **dolerite**
UK dolerite
SN Coarsely crystalline variety of basalt. (STEIN)
UF black granite
 granite, black
 traprock

diabolos
 TV.186   (L,N)
ALT diabolo
SN Use for inertial toys of skill consisting of a double-cone-shaped object and two sticks, one attached to each end of a length of string on which the double cone rolls.

diacetate, cellulose
USE cellulose diacetate

diacetone alcohol
 MT.2444
UK di-acetone alcohol
SN Solvent for nitrocellulose, cellulose acetate, gum, and resin; also used in lacquer, thinner, and ink remover. (MH)
UF alcohol, di-acetone
 alcohol, diacetone

diachronic linguistics
USE historical linguistics

Diacon lamps
 TC.1285
ALT Diacon lamp
SN Mechanical lamps similar to Carcel lamps in that they contain a clockwork movement in the base actuating a pump which forces oil through a tube from the reservoir to the wick. The distinction between Diacon and Carcel lamps is unclear.
UF lamps, Diacon

diaconica
 PJ.1276   (A)
HN March 1993 descriptor moved
ALT diaconicon
SN Sacristies in Orthodox Eastern and Byzantine churches.
UF parabemata
 sceuophylacia

diadems
 TE.606   (H,N,R)
ALT diadem
SN Ornamental headbands of metal or cloth; use especially for those worn as a sign of royalty.
RT jewelry

diagnosing
 KG.18   (L)
HN April 1993 lead-in term added
SN Identifying the condition of a person, object, or structure.
UF diagnosis

diagnosis
USE diagnosing

diagnostics, building
USE building diagnostics

diagonal
 DC.303
HN October 1992 descriptor moved

<diagonal and multidirectional conveying systems>
 PC.112
HN March 1993 guide term moved

diagonal bridging
USE cross bridging

diagonal buttresses
 PJ.1451
HN March 1993 descriptor moved
ALT diagonal buttress
SN Use for buttresses extending at about a 45-degree angle from the corner of a building.
UF buttresses, diagonal

diagonal cross shaped stretchers
USE cross stretchers

diagonal ribs
 PJ.2016
HN March 1993 descriptor moved
 January 1991 scope note changed

January 1991 lead-in term changed, was **cross-springers**
ALT diagonal rib
SN Ribs crossing a vault bay diagonally, used either to mask the groins or to support the vault.
UF cross springers
groin ribs
ogives
ribs, diagonal
ribs, groin

diagonal-shaped stretchers
USE cross stretchers

diagonal stretchers
USE cross stretchers

diagonal views
USE oblique views

diagrams
VW.148
HN November 1992 descriptor moved
ALT diagram
SN Graphic designs that explain rather than represent. (W)
UF diagrams, graphic
graphic diagrams

diagrams, block
USE block diagrams

diagrams, color
USE color charts

diagrams, flow
USE flowcharts

diagrams, graphic
USE diagrams

diagrams, plan
USE plans (drawings)

diagrams, planting
USE planting plans

diagrams, Venn
USE Venn diagrams

diagrams, wireframe
USE wireframe drawings

Diaguita
FL.1198   (L)
UF Calchaqui

Diaguita, Northern
USE Santa Maria (pottery style)

<Diaguita pottery styles>
FL.1199

Diaguite, Chilean
USE Chilean Diaguite

dial locks
USE combination locks

dial scales
TN.290
ALT dial scale
SN Use for scales generally characterized as having a large dial on the front of a box containing the mech-

anism, on top of which is mounted the weighing surface.
UF family scales
scales, dial
scales, family

dialectic
BM.414   (A,L,R)
HN January 1991 alternate term added
ALT dialectical

dialectical materialism
BM.1058   (L)
HN February 1993 descriptor moved
UF materialism, dialectical

dialogues
VW.268   (L)
HN November 1992 descriptor moved
ALT dialogue
SN Written compositions in which two or more characters are represented as conversing. (WCOL9)

dials
PJ.2605
HN January 1993 descriptor added
ALT dial
SN Plates, disks, faces, or other surfaces with markings or figures for indicating such information as time, measurement, or frequency, usually by means of pointing devices.

dials, equatorial
USE equatorial sundials

dials, horizontal
USE horizontal (ALT of horizontality) + sundials

dials, horizontal sun
USE horizontal (ALT of horizontality) + sundials

dials, sun
USE sundials

dials, vertical
USE vertical (ALT of verticality) + sundials

diameter
DC.95
HN October 1992 descriptor moved
September 1992 scope note added
SN The measurement taken across an object or along a straight line passing through the center of a circle or sphere from one side to the other. (DUDWIL)

<diameter measuring devices>
TN.82

diamin azo blue
USE dark grayish purple
grayish violet

diamond
MT.539   (L)
HN April 1992 descriptor moved
February 1992 scope note changed
February 1992 related term added

SN A highly transparent and exceedingly hard mineral of carbon; it is the hardest known substance.
RT gemstone

diamond black
USE carbon black

diamond chairs
TC.487
HN January 1993 descriptor moved
ALT diamond chair
UF Bertoia chairs
chairs, Bertoia
chairs, diamond
chairs, shell
shell chairs

diamond mesh lath
MT.1810
UF expanded metal lath, flat
flat expanded metal lath
lath, diamond mesh
lath, flat expanded metal
mesh lath, diamond
metal lath, flat expanded

diamond mines
RG.104   (L)
ALT diamond mine
UF mines, diamond

diamond nails
PJ.182
HN April 1993 descriptor moved
ALT diamond nail
UF nails, diamond

diamond, paste
USE paste (glass)

diamond-point engraving
KT.949
HN January 1993 descriptor moved
October 1990 descriptor moved
SN A technique for decorating glass, and sometimes porcelain, by scratching or stippling it with a diamond-tipped stylus. (THDAT)
UF engraving, diamond-point

diamond tufting
KT.1207
HN December 1992 descriptor added
ALT diamond-tufted
SN Pleated tufting done in a diamond pattern.
UF tufting, diamond

diamond twill
USE lozenge twill

Diamond Vehicle
USE Vajrayana

diamonds (motifs)
USE lozenges

diaper
MT.1594
HN December 1992 descriptor added
SN Self-patterned textile with a small rectilinear pattern formed by con-

trasting the weave's warp and weft faces.
RT damask diaper
twill diaper

diaper (patterns)
USE diaper patterns

diaper, damask
USE damask diaper

diaper pattern, petal
USE scale pattern

diaper patterns
DG.115
ALT diaper pattern
UK diaper-work
SN Designs consisting of repeated geometric allover patterning often forming a framework filled by such motifs as lozenges or formalized leaves. (LDDO)
UF diaper (patterns)
diaper work
patterns, diaper

diaper, twill
USE twill diaper

diaper-work
SEE diaper patterns

diaper work
USE diaper patterns

diapers
TE.191   (L,N)
ALT diaper
UK nappies
UKA nappy
SN Square, oblong, or triangular cloths, usually without fastenings, worn by infants. (NMAHDC)
UF baby napkins
napkins, baby

diaphragm arches
PJ.1634
HN March 1993 descriptor moved
October 1991 scope note changed
ALT diaphragm arch
SN Use for arches built across a nave or hall that support walls rather than vaults; for such arches when they support vaults, use **transverse arches.**
UF arches, diaphragm

diaphragm walls
PJ.1919   (A)
HN March 1993 descriptor moved
June 1990 scope note added
ALT diaphragm wall
SN Designates walls erected around a site to hold back wet earth to permit the construction of, for example, basements, in areas of high groundwater.
UF slurry-trenches
slurry-walls
walls, diaphragm

diapositives
USE transparencies

diaries
VW.166   (L,N,R)
HN November 1992 descriptor moved
ALT diary
SN Use for books containing the daily, personal accounts of the writer's own experiences, attitudes, and observations. Use journals (accounts) when referring to an individual's or an organization's account of occurrences or transactions.

diaries, weather
USE weather diaries

diarists
HG.360
HN December 1992 alternate terms added
ALT diarist
diarist's
diarists'
SN Persons who keep a diary. (W)

diatomaceous earth
MT.2246   (L)
HN May 1992 lead-in terms added
January 1992 descriptor moved
UF celite
diatomite
diatomite earth
earth, diatomaceous
earth, diatomite
earth, infusorial
infusorial earth

diatomite
USE diatomaceous earth

diatomite earth
USE diatomaceous earth

diatonic harps
TT.218
ALT diatonic harp
SN Harps in which the strings are all tuned to the notes of a single key.
UF harps, diatonic

diatretae vasae
USE cage-cups

diatretons
USE cage-cups

diazo photoprints
USE diazotypes

diazo prints
USE diazotypes

diazo process
KT.370   (L)
HN March 1993 descriptor moved
February 1993 lead-in terms added
SN Printing processes based on light-sensitive diazonium compounds, most often used to reproduce technical drawings.
UF diazotype (process)
diazotypy

Ozalid process
whiteprinting

diazo process, dry
USE ammonia process

diazo process, moist
USE moist diazo process

diazo process prints
USE diazotypes

diazo process, semi-dry
USE moist diazo process

diazo process, thermal
USE thermal diazo process

diazo process, vapor
USE ammonia process

diazomata
PJ.1299
HN March 1993 descriptor moved
July 1991 scope note changed
ALT diazoma
SN Passages or aisles in Greek theaters concentric with the outer wall. For similar features in Roman theaters, use **praecinctiones.** (RS)

diazotype (process)
USE diazo process

diazotypes
VW.1070   (L)
HN March 1993 descriptor moved
March 1993 lead-in term added
November 1992 scope note changed
ALT diazotype
SN Prints produced using a duplicating process in which images are produced by the effect of light on diazonium-sensitized materials, most often architectural or other technical drawings.
UF Brunings
diazo photoprints
diazo prints
diazo process prints
ozalids
prints, diazo

diazotypy
USE diazo process

dice
TV.14   (L,N)
ALT die
SN Use for small cubes necessary to the play of many games, marked on each face distinctively with from one to six dots such that opposite faces add to seven; may also be used for similar cubes marked with other numbers or symbols specially created for certain other games.
RT dice games

dice games
KQ.32
UF games, dice
RT dice
games

dichloromethane
USE methylene chloride

dichromate processes
USE bichromate processes

dichromatic glass
MT.315
HN January 1992 descriptor added
SN Glass which appears to be a different color when viewed in transmitted or reflected light; often achieved by the addition of colloidal gold to the glass batch.
UF glass, dichromatic

dichromatic processes
USE two-color processes

dickeys
TE.645   (N)
ALT dickey
SN Separate or detachable shirt fronts, often with a collar, worn under another garment.
UF bosoms, shirt
      shirt bosoms
      shirtfronts
RT shirts

dictators
HG.187   (L)
HN January 1993 descriptor added
ALT dictator
      dictator's
      dictators'
SN Use for nonhereditary rulers who exercise absolute, unrestricted power over the government of a nation. Originally the title of officials of ancient Rome and other Italian states elected in times of crisis and invested with absolute authority for the duration.

dictatorship
BM.957
HN February 1993 descriptor moved
SN A form of government in which a person or small clique has absolute power without effective constitutional limitations. (W)

dictionaries
VW.818   (A,L,B,R)
HN November 1992 descriptor moved
ALT dictionary
SN Reference sources containing alphabetical lists of words with information given for each word; generally including meanings, pronunciation, etymology, and often usage guidance. (AHD)

dictionaries, bilingual
USE foreign-language dictionaries

dictionaries, biographical
USE biographical dictionaries

<dictionaries by form>
VW.819
HN November 1992 guide term moved

<dictionaries by subject>
VW.823
HN November 1992 guide term moved

dictionaries, data
USE data dictionaries

dictionaries, etymological
USE etymological dictionaries

dictionaries, foreign-language
USE foreign-language dictionaries

dictionaries, heraldic
USE heraldic dictionaries

dictionaries, multilingual
USE polyglot dictionaries

dictionaries of heraldry
USE heraldic dictionaries

dictionaries of synonyms
VW.825   (L)
HN November 1992 descriptor moved
ALT dictionary of synonyms
UF synonyms, dictionaries of

dictionaries, pictorial
USE picture dictionaries

dictionaries, picture
USE picture dictionaries

dictionaries, polyglot
USE polyglot dictionaries

dictionaries, technical
USE technical dictionaries

dictionary catalogs
VW.17   (L)
HN November 1992 descriptor moved
ALT dictionary catalog
UF catalogs, dictionary

dictionary stands
USE bookstands

didactic art
BM.185
UF art, didactic

diddley bows
TT.348
ALT diddley bow
SN Single-string musical bows of the southern United States, consisting of a length of wire attached to the wall of a frame house, which acts as a resonator; a cotton reel is often used as a bridge. They are plucked with glass bottlenecks or nails. A more portable version replaces the house with a fence picket.
UF bows, diddley

didjeridus
TT.101
ALT didjeridu
SN End-blown, straight natural trumpets of more or less conical bore of northern Australia, traditionally consisting of a hollowed eucalyptus branch over three feet in length,

stripped of outer bark and often decorated with totemic symbols. They are played by men, standing or seated on the ground, employing a complex technique involving lip vibration, tongue movements, voiced sounds, circular breathing, and changing the shape of the mouth cavity.

didrachms
VK.33
ALT didrachm
SN Ancient Greek and Roman silver coins valued at two drachmas.

die casting
KT.307   (L)
HN March 1991 alternate term changed, was **die cast**
ALT die-cast
SN Metal casting technique in which a molten metal (as a zinc, lead, or aluminum alloy) is forced into a die. (W)
UF casting, die

die cutting
KT.934
HN December 1992 descriptor added
ALT die-cut
SN Cutting, as metal or paper, with dies.
UF cutting, die

die stamping
KT.340
HN March 1991 alternate term added
      October 1990 descriptor moved
      October 1990 scope note changed
ALT die-stamped
SN Shaping material, such as paper or sheet metal, between two plates, one with the design in relief and the other with the corresponding design recessed.
UF stamping, die

Diegueño
FL.1289   (L)
UF Yahano

dielectric
MT.3086   (L)
HN August 1992 descriptor added
SN Material which is an electrical insulator or in which an electric field can be sustained with a minimum of dissipation in power. (MHDSTT)
UF dielectric material
      material, dielectric

dielectric material
USE dielectric

dielectric properties
DC.25   (L)
HN October 1992 descriptor added
SN Properties relating to or resembling those of dielectrics.
UF properties, dielectric

diereis
USE biremes

dies (dadoes)
USE dadoes

dies (metalwork)
TH.1272 (L,N,R)
ALT die (metalwork)
SN Tools used for cutting the threads of bolts, pipes, or other metal objects.

dies (tools)
TH.1008 (H,L,N)
HN March 1992 descriptor added
ALT die (tool)
SN Stamps, usually engraved, used for impressing a design upon a softer material, as in coining money. (RHDEL2)

dies, anvil
USE anvil dies

dies, pile
USE anvil dies

dies, punch
USE trussells

diesel-electric locomotives
TX.238 (L,N)
ALT diesel-electric locomotive
SN Use for locomotives in which power is developed by oil-burning internal combustion engines driving electric generators that supply power to electric traction motors for propulsion.
UF diesel-electrics
diesel locomotives
diesels
electric locomotives, diesel
locomotives, diesel
locomotives, diesel-electric

diesel-electrics
USE diesel-electric locomotives

diesel-hydraulic locomotives
TX.239 (N)
ALT diesel-hydraulic locomotive
SN Use for locomotives in which power developed by oil-burning internal combustion engines is delivered through hydraulic transmissions to driving rods and axles by means of shafts and gears.
UF diesels
locomotives, diesel-hydraulic

diesel locomotives
USE diesel-electric locomotives

diesels
USE diesel-electric locomotives
diesel-hydraulic locomotives

dietitians
HG.584 (L)
HN December 1992 alternate terms added
ALT dietitian

dietitian's
dietitians'

differences, class
USE social stratification

differential thermal analysis
KT.222 (L)
HN November 1992 descriptor added
SN A technique for observing the temperature, direction, and magnitude of thermally induced transitions in a material by heating or cooling a sample and comparing its temperature with that of an inert reference material under similar conditions. (CTRRH)
UF DTA

diffraction
BM.718 (L)
HN November 1992 descriptor added
SN The changing or bending of waves, especially sound and light waves, as they pass by and around obstacles in their path.

diffraction, electron
USE electron diffraction

diffractometers
TN.5 (L)
ALT diffractometer
SN Instruments that measure the angles at which x-rays, neutrons, or electrons are diffracted by matter; used to study atomic crystal structure. (RHDEL2)

diffuse lighting, general
USE general diffuse lighting

diffuse reflectance
BM.814
HN April 1993 descriptor moved
April 1990 descriptor added
SN Reflectance that is not specular.
UF reflectance, diffuse

diffuse reflection
BM.855
HN November 1992 descriptor moved
April 1990 descriptor added
SN Reflection in which a significant portion of the light is reflected in many different directions. (ICPEP)
UF reflection, diffuse

diffusers
PJ.2932 (L)
ALT diffuser
SN Devices to redirect or scatter light from a source, primarily by the process of diffuse transmission. (STEIN)

diffusers, air
USE air diffusers

diffusion
KT.886 (L)
ALT diffused
SN Use for the process whereby particles intermingle and move from a region of higher to one of lower

concentration, and for the transmission or reflection of light. Includes the effect of such processes, such as the softening of sharp outlines in a photograph.

diffusion, cultural
USE cultural diffusion

diffusion transfer, dye
USE dye diffusion transfer process

diffusion transfer prints
USE instant camera photographs

diffusion transfer prints, dye
USE dye diffusion transfer prints

diffusion transfer process
KT.516
SN Photographic process used primarily for instant or self-developing photographs in which the positive image is formed from undeveloped silver halides in the negative. The negative is placed in contact with a support in the presence of a developing agent, and the unexposed silver diffuses to the support to form the positive image. For making color instant camera photographs, it is dye couplers that are in the negative, in which case use dye diffusion transfer process or internal dye diffusion transfer process.
UF instant photography
photography, instant

diffusion transfer process, internal dye
USE internal dye diffusion transfer process

diffusion transfer reversal
KT.374
HN March 1993 descriptor added
SN Copying process employing silver halides in which both a positive and a negative copy are produced simultaneously. (CMM)
UF DTR
reversal, diffusion transfer

digests (compendiums)
USE compendiums

digests (legal documents)
VW.612 (L)
HN November 1992 descriptor moved
ALT digest (legal document)
SN Systematically arranged summaries of laws, reported cases, decisions, and other legal documents. (GAHLM)

digests (periodicals)
VW.978 (L)
HN November 1992 descriptor moved
ALT digest (perdiodical)

diggers, post-hole
USE post-hole diggers

digging
USE excavation

digital clocks
TN.193 (L)
ALT digital clock
SN Clocks that indicate the time by a display of figures rather than by a dial. (IDOFC)
UF clocks, digital
clocks, digital electronic
digital electronic clocks
electronic clocks, digital

digital electronic clocks
USE digital clocks

digital image processing
USE digital imaging

digital images
VC.239
ALT digital image
SN Electronic images stored in the form of electronically encoded picture elements.
UF digital photographs
digitized images
images, digital
images, digitized
photographs, digital
RT digital imaging

digital imaging
KT.360 (L)
HN February 1993 descriptor added
SN The recording, storage, and manipulation of images in computer systems in the form of electronically encoded picture elements.
UF digital image processing
digital photography
electronic digital imaging
image processing, digital
imaging, digital
imaging, electronic digital
photography, digital
RT digital images

digital maps
VW.89
HN November 1992 descriptor moved
ALT digital map
UF maps, digital

digital photographs
USE digital images

digital photography
USE digital imaging

digitization
USE digitizing

digitized images
USE digital images

digitizers
TH.562
HN January 1993 descriptor moved
ALT digitizer
SN Devices used to convert data to digital form for use in a computer. (RHDEL2)
UF quantizers

digitizing
KG.132 (L)
HN March 1993 descriptor added
ALT digitized
SN Converting data to digital form for use in a computer.
UF digitization

digitizing tablets
USE graphics tablets

Digo
FL.602 (L)

digs
USE excavations

dihydroxy anthraquinone
USE alizarin

dikes
RK.535 (A,H,L,B)
HN March 1993 related term added
ALT dike
SN Use for embankments built along a river or sea and set at some distance from it to control or retain flood waters. For embankments built only to prevent flooding of low-lying land use **levees.**
UF dykes
RT levees

dikes, spur
USE wing dams

dikkas
PJ.2549
HN March 1993 descriptor moved
June 1991 alternate term added
June 1991 descriptor changed, was **dikka**
ALT dikka
SN In mosques, high podiums on columns from which the celebrant's assistant repeats his Koran readings and gestures for the more distant worshippers. (AK)

dilatometers
TN.86 (L,N)
ALT dilatometer
SN Devices for measuring thermal expansion and dilation of liquids or solids. (MHDSTT)

dilettantism
BM.283 (L,R)
SN The quality or procedure characteristic of a person who cultivates an art or a branch of knowledge as a pastime without pursuing it professionally. (W)

Dilgen
USE tilting sockets

dill axes
USE froes

dilla
USE dillis

dillis
TT.226
ALT dilli
SN Five-string arched harps of the Masa people of central Chad, having a skin-covered soundbox and tuning pegs; played resting either on the ground or on the shoulder of the player. (NGDMI)
UF dilla

Dilmun
FL.2971

Dilmun, Early
USE Early Dilmun

Dilmun, Late
USE Late Dilmun

Dilmun, Middle
USE Middle Dilmun

diluent
USE thinner

diluting
USE dilution

dilution
KT.832 (L)
HN November 1992 descriptor added
SN Act or process of making thinner, more liquid, or less concentrated, as by admixture of water. (W)
UF diluting

dime stores
USE variety stores

dimension lumber
MT.3033
HN March 1992 descriptor moved
SN Lumber cut to a particular size and stocked for the building industry; usually 2 to 5 inches thick and 5 to 12 inches wide. (DAC)
UF common dimension lumber
dimension lumber, common
dimension parts
dimension stock
dimension stuff
lumber, common dimension
lumber, dimension
parts, dimension
stock, dimension
stuff, dimension

dimension lumber, common
USE dimension lumber

dimension parts
USE dimension lumber

dimension stock
USE dimension lumber

dimension stone
MT.939 (L)
HN April 1992 descriptor moved
SN Stone finished to a specific size and squared to specific dimensions and thickness. (HORNB)
UF cut stone

stone, cut
stone, dimension

dimension stuff
USE dimension lumber

dimensional coordination
USE modular coordination

dimensioning
KT.735
ALT dimensioned
SN Indicating on a drawing the actual dimensions of whatever is represented in the drawing.

dimensions
USE size (extent)

dimes
VK.64   (L)
ALT dime
SN Silver and cupronickel decimal coins of the United States and certain other former British colonies issued since 1796 and valued at one tenth of a dollar. (W)

dimes, half
USE half dimes

dimethyl ketone
USE acetone

dimetric drawings
VC.93
HN April 1992 descriptor moved
ALT dimetric drawing
SN Use for drawings in which all three spatial axes are inclined, and two of those are equally inclined, to the plane of projection (drawing surface).
UF dimetric projections
drawings, dimetric
projections, dimetric

dimetric projection
KT.479
SN Axonometric projection in which only two spatial axes are equally inclined to the plane of projection (drawing surface).
UF projection, dimetric

dimetric projections
USE dimetric drawings

Dimini
FL.2623

diminishing columns
PJ.1464
HN March 1993 descriptor moved
ALT diminishing column
SN Use for columns with shafts smaller in radius at the top than at the bottom, particularly when the inward taper is a straight line, as opposed to exhibiting entasis.
UF columns, diminishing

dimity
MT.1519

HN March 1993 descriptor moved
SN Cotton with corded stripes or check effects. (NYLAN)

dimmer switches
USE dimmers

dimmers
PJ.2933   (N)
ALT dimmer
UF dimmer switches
switches, dimmer

dimple based
FL.145
HN April 1993 descriptor added

dimple based ware
HN April 1993 descriptor split, use dimple based + ware

dinars
VK.133   (L)
ALT dinar
SN Islamic gold coins issued from the 7th to the 18th century; originally struck with legends on both sides and in the same size and weight as Byzantine solidi. (DOTY)

diners
RK.117   (A,L,B,R)
ALT diner

diners (railroad cars)
USE dining cars

dinettes
PJ.1052
HN March 1993 descriptor moved
ALT dinette
SN Use for small dining areas, usually extensions of kitchens or pantries; for such areas when they are extensions of living rooms, use **dining alcoves.**

Ding
FL.2002
HN April 1993 descriptor added
UF Ting

Ding ware
HN April 1993 descriptor split, use **Ding** + **ware**

dingbats
PJ.3416
ALT dingbat
SN Typographical ornaments (as bullets or stars) used typically to call attention to an opening sentence or to make a break between paragraphs. (W)

dinghies
TX.464   (L,N)
ALT dinghy
SN Use for small open boats carried on or towed by larger watercraft as lifeboats, tenders, or workboats; may be rowed, sailed, or driven by outboard motors.
UF dinks

Dingler's green
USE chromium oxide green

dining alcoves
PJ.1053   (B)
HN March 1993 descriptor moved
ALT dining alcove
SN Use for small dining areas when they are extensions of living rooms. Use **dinettes** when referring to similar structures that are extensions of kitchens or pantries.
UF alcoves, dining
dining recesses
recesses, dining

dining cars
TX.272   (L)
ALT dining car
UK restaurant cars
UKA restaurant car
SN Use for railroad passenger cars equipped with facilities for serving meals, usually fitted with seating and tables or counters.
UF cars, dining
cars, restaurant
diners (railroad cars)

dining chairs
TC.640   (N)
HN May 1993 related term added
January 1993 descriptor moved
ALT dining chair
UF chairs, dining
dining-room chairs
RT dining tables

dining halls
PJ.1054   (A,B,R)
HN March 1993 descriptor moved
ALT dining hall
SN Use both for large dining rooms, as in a college, and for buildings containing a dining hall.
UF halls, dining

dining recesses
USE dining alcoves

dining-room chairs
USE dining chairs

dining-room tables
USE extension dining tables

dining rooms
PJ.1057   (A,L,B,R)
HN March 1993 descriptor moved
June 1990 scope note added
ALT dining room
SN Rooms in private houses or public establishments in which dinner and other principal meals are taken and which are furnished for this purpose. (OED)
UF rooms, dining

dining tables
TC.1132   (N)
HN May 1993 related terms added
January 1993 descriptor moved

ALT dining table
UF banquet tables
   tables, banquet
   tables, dining
RT armchairs
   dining chairs
   perroquets

dining tables, expandable
USE extension dining tables

dining tables, extension
USE extension dining tables

dining tables, horseshoe
USE horseshoe dining tables

dining tables, imperial
USE extension dining tables

dining tables, long
USE refectory tables

dining tables, pillar and claw
USE pillar and claw dining tables

dining tables, telescope
USE telescope tables

dining tables, three-part
USE three-part dining tables

dining Windsor chairs
USE bow-back Windsor chairs

Dinka
   FL.621   (L)

dinks
USE dinghies

dinner buckets
USE lunchboxes

dinner coats
USE dinner jackets

dinner forks
   TH.306   (N)
HN April 1993 descriptor added
ALT dinner fork
SN The largest of the individual dining
   forks used to eat the main course of
   meals; generally having three or
   four, but sometimes two, tines of
   equal size. May be accompanied by
   a dinner knife.
UF forks, dinner
RT dessert forks
   dinner knives
   salad forks

dinner-jackets
SEE dinner jackets

dinner jackets
   TE.11
ALT dinner jacket
UK dinner-jackets
UKA dinner-jacket
SN Men's suit coats cut sack-style, usu-
   ally with satin- or faille-faced lapels.
   Worn with trousers having a stripe
   down the outside of the leg to form
   a tuxedo. (NMAHDC)

UF coats, dinner
   dinner coats
   jackets, dinner
   jackets, tuxedo
   tuxedo jackets
RT jackets
   tuxedoes

dinner knives
   TH.317   (N)
HN April 1993 descriptor added
ALT dinner knife
SN The largest of individual dining
   knives used in eating the main
   course of meals; usually having a silver or steel blade and a handle of
   varying form and material. May be
   accompanied by a dinner fork.
UF knives, dinner
RT dessert knives
   dinner forks

dinner pails
USE lunchboxes

dinner plates
   TQ.365   (N)
ALT dinner plate
SN Plates for holding an individual por-
   tion of the main course of a meal;
   often circular, but sometimes oval,
   octagonal, or other form.
UF plates, dinner
RT place settings

dinner pots
USE Dutch ovens

dinner services
   PC.22
ALT dinner service
SN Services intended for use at a dinner table by a number of diners,
   generally consisting of dishes,
   plates, and cups of different size,
   and sometimes other vessels such as
   tureens, platters, casters, or decorative articles such as vases and
   épergnes.
UF services, dinner
   services, table
   table services
RT bowls (vessels)
   casters (vessels)
   centerpieces
   cruet stands
   custard cups
   dishes
   epergnes
   ice buckets
   mustard pots
   platters
   saltcellars
   sauceboats
   tureens

dinnerware
   PE.89
HN March 1993 descriptor added
RT place settings

diocesan records
   VW.716   (L)

HN November 1992 descriptor moved
ALT diocesan record
SN Records of districts or churches un-
   der the jurisdiction of a bishop.
   (AHD)
UF records, diocesan

diocesan schools
USE parochial schools

dioceses
   HN.30   (L)
HN February 1993 descriptor moved
   February 1993 scope note added
ALT diocese
SN Administrative divisions of church
   government under the authority of
   a bishop.
UF bishoprics

Diocletian windows
   PJ.2241
HN March 1993 descriptor moved
   January 1991 lead-in terms added
ALT Diocletian window
SN Semicircular windows divided by
   two upright mullions. (IGA)
UF thermal windows
   windows, Diocletian
   windows, thermal

Diola
   FL.337   (L)

dioptrics
USE refraction

dioramas
   VC.3   (L,N,B,R)
ALT diorama
SN Works in which three-dimensional
   objects, often figural sculpture, in
   the foreground blend with a realistic
   painted background. The entire
   work is usually enclosed in a case or
   niche and is viewed from a distant,
   darkened vantage point.

diorite
   MT.656   (L)
HN April 1992 descriptor moved
UF black granite
   granite, black

diorite, mica
USE mica diorite

diorite, porphyritic
USE red antique porphyry

diorite, quartz
USE quartz diorite

Diospyros
USE ebony

Diospyros dendo
USE black ebony

Diospyros ebenum
   MT.2727
HN March 1992 descriptor moved

Diospyros kurzii
USE marblewood

Diospyros melanoxylos
MT.2728 (L)
HN March 1992 descriptor moved

Diospyros virginiana
USE common persimmon

diotae
TQ.655
ALT diota
SN Ancient Greek storage vessels for wine, water, or oil, similar to amphorae but with a pointed bottom and characterized by two side handles.
UF amphorae, pointed
pointed amphorae

dioxide, sulfur
USE sulfur dioxide

dioxide, sulphur
SEE sulfur dioxide

dióxido de titanio
USE titanium dioxide white

dip brazing
KT.1078
HN March 1993 descriptor moved
SN Process whereby the metals to be joined are dipped into a bath of molten salt, which acts as both flux and a source of heat. (HORNB)
UF brazing, dip

dip molds
TH.986 (N)
HN December 1992 descriptor added
ALT dip mold
UK dip-moulds
UKA dip-mould
SN Open-top one-piece molds used to make pattern molded glassware. (W)
UF dip moulds
molds, dip

dip-moulds
SEE dip molds

dip moulds
SEE dip molds

dipentene
MT.2462
SN Liquid terpene hydrocarbon found in many essential oils, usually obtained along with other types of terpenoid from certain kinds of terpentine and used chiefly as a solvent and dispersing agent, such as for resin and varnish. (W)

diphroi
TC.671
HN January 1993 descriptor moved
ALT diphros
SN Ancient Greek stools without a back and having four turned legs, sometimes connected by stretchers.

diphroi okladias
TC.696

HN April 1993 descriptor moved
ALT diphros okladias
SN Ancient Greek folding stools without a back and having crossed legs.

diples
TT.155
ALT diple
SN Any of a group of single pipes or sets of pipes having an idioglot single reed and a very narrow cylindrical bore. Some terminate in bells or are attached to bags. (NGDMI)
UF diplyes

diploma pictures
USE reception pieces

diploma pieces
USE reception pieces

diplomas
VW.803 (L,N)
HN November 1992 descriptor moved
ALT diploma
SN Formal documents conferring some honor, degree, or privilege, especially those bearing record of graduation from or a degree conferred by an educational institution.

<diplomatic buildings>
RK.926

diplomats
HG.174 (L,R)
HN January 1993 descriptor moved
December 1992 alternate terms added
November 1990 scope note added
ALT diplomat
diplomat's
diplomats'
SN People employed by a national government or ruler to conduct official negotiations and maintain political, economic, and social relations with other nations or international organizations. (RHDEL2)

diplyes
USE diples

dipped seats
USE hollowed seats

dipper buckets
USE dippers (construction equipment)

dipper cups
USE palette cups

dippers (construction equipment)
TH.463
HN March 1993 descriptor changed, was **dippers**
March 1993 alternate term changed, was **dipper**
ALT dipper (construction equipment)
SN Type of bucket used on any of several kinds of excavating equipment.
UF buckets, dipper
dipper buckets

dippers (palette cups)
USE palette cups

dippers (serving utensils)
TH.248 (N)
HN April 1993 descriptor added
ALT dipper (serving utensil)
SN Utensils consisting of concave containers fitted with long handles intended primarily for lifting liquids, such as drinking water.
RT ladles

dippers, ice cream
USE ice-cream scoops

dippers, ice-cream
USE ice-cream scoops

dippers, palette
USE palette cups

dipteral
DC.147
HN October 1992 descriptor moved
SN Describes buildings surrounded by two rows of columns on all sides.

diptychs
VC.4 (L,N)
ALT diptych
SN Pairs of panels hinged together; used by ancient Romans for writing tablets, often having images on the outer surfaces. In Medieval and later times, used primarily to support images, especially on the interior surfaces. Most often composed of carved ivory or of painted wood panels. Also used of other works having two related images side by side.

diptychs, consular
USE consular diptychs

Diquis
FL.1113

direct advertising
USE direct mail + advertising

Direct art
FL.3860
UF art, Direct

direct carving
KT.915
HN January 1993 descriptor moved
November 1990 descriptor moved
SN Sculptural process in which the sculptor forms the image by cutting away from the block of stone, generally without working from a model. The concept of the work evolves and develops during the carving process and adaptation may be made according to the character of the stone found within the block.
UF carving, direct

direct image photographs
USE direct positives

direct impression composition
USE   strike-on composition

direct lighting
KT.753
HN   April 1991 lead-in terms added
April 1991 descriptor moved
April 1991 scope note added
SN   Use for lighting techniques in which
90 to 100% of the light is directed
toward the surface to be illumi-
nated; usually downward light.
(IESREF)
UF   direct lighting system
lighting, direct
lighting system, direct

direct lighting system
USE   direct lighting

direct mail
VW.1111   (L)
HN   February 1993 descriptor added
SN   Printed matter prepared to solicit
trade or contributions and sent directly through the mail to individuals. (W)
UF   advertising mail
direct mailers
junk mail
mail, advertising
mail, direct
mail, junk
mailers, direct

direct mail campaigns
USE   direct mail + advertising

direct mailers
USE   direct mail

direct metal constructions
USE   direct metal sculpture

direct metal sculpture
VC.557
SN   Sculpture that is constructed of
metal using such processes as welding, hammering, and soldering as
opposed to casting.
UF   constructions, direct metal
direct metal constructions
sculpture, direct metal

direct painting
USE   alla prima

direct positive processes
KT.519
HN   March 1993 related term added
SN   Use for processes in which a positive-image photograph is formed in
the camera without an intermediate
negative, or for positive-to-positive
processes.
RT   autopositive printing

direct positives
VC.300
HN   April 1992 descriptor moved
ALT   direct positive
SN   Use for positive-image photographs
produced in the camera without the

intervening use of a negative, or
produced by a positive-to-positive
process.
UF   camera originals
direct image photographs
originals, camera
photographs, direct image
photographs, unique image
positives, direct
unique image photographs

direct printing presses
USE   lithographic presses

direction indicators, landing
USE   landing direction indicators

direction signs
VW.1147
HN   June 1992 descriptor added
ALT   direction sign
SN   Use for signs that guide users to
destinations.
UF   guide signs
orientation signs
signs, direction
signs, guide
signs, orientation

direction words
USE   catchwords

directional lighting
KT.745
HN   April 1991 descriptor moved
April 1991 scope note added
April 1991 lead-in term deleted, was
accent lighting
SN   Use for the lighting of an object or
work plane primarily from a specific
and preferred direction. (IESREF)
UF   lighting, directional

directional signage
USE   signage

directives
USE   guidelines

<directly struck idiophones>
TT.451

Directoire
FL.3448   (L)

Director Style
USE   Chippendale

directorial photographs
USE   staged photographs

directories
VW.832   (A,L,R)
HN   November 1992 descriptor moved
February 1991 scope note changed
ALT   directory
SN   Enumerations of names, addresses,
and other data about specific groups
of persons or organizations; may ap-
pear in alphabetic or graphic for-
mat. (AHD)

directories, alumni
USE   alumni directories

directories, building
USE   building directories

directories, business
USE   commercial directories

<directories by subject>
VW.833
HN   November 1992 guide term moved

<directories by subject: location>
VW.841
HN   November 1992 guide term moved

directories, city
USE   city directories

directories, commercial
USE   commercial directories

directories, elite
USE   social registers

directories, international
USE   international directories

directories, local
USE   city directories

directories, manufacturers'
USE   manufacturers' registers

directories, national
USE   national directories

directories, post office
USE   post office directories

directories, professional
USE   professional directories

directories, regional
USE   regional directories

directories, state
USE   state directories

directories, street
USE   street directories

directories, telephone
USE   telephone directories

directories, trade
USE   commercial directories

directors (administrators)
HG.140   (A,L)
HN   April 1993 related term added
January 1993 alternate terms added
September   1991   descriptor
changed, was **directors**
September 1991 alternate term
changed, was **director**
ALT   director (administrator)
director's (administrator)
directors' (administrators)
SN   Use for the official heads of organizations such as schools, institutions,
or government bureaus, or those
named to control a business. Distinct from **managers,** who control a
portion of an institution or business.
RT   managers

directors (layout features)
USE guide letters

directors (performing arts)
HG.210 (L)
HN November 1992 alternate terms added
ALT director (performing arts)
director's (performing arts)
directors' (performing arts)
SN People who supervise the production of a stage show or motion picture. (WCOL9)

directors, art
USE art directors

directors, boards of
USE boards of directors

directors' chairs
TC.488
HN March 1993 descriptor changed, was director's chairs
March 1993 lead-in term changed, was chairs, director's
January 1993 descriptor moved
ALT director's chair
UF chairs, directors'
chairs, safari
safari chairs

directors, gallery
USE gallery directors

directors, music
USE conductors

directors of corporations
USE boards of directors

dirhams
VK.134 (L)
ALT dirham
SN Islamic silver coins struck from the 7th to the 14th century. (DOTY)

dirigible balloons
USE airships

dirigibles
USE airships

dirks
TK.33 (N)
ALT dirk
SN Use for the Highland Scottish sheath knives, daggerlike in appearance, having a blade with a single full-length cutting edge and a back which has a sharpened edge extending up for a short distance from the point, and a grip swelling in the center with a disc-shaped pommel. Use also for the short swords or daggers carried by navy officers in the 18th and 19th centuries.
RT daggers (weapons)

dirndls
TE.93 (N)
ALT dirndl
SN Fulls skirts gathered or pleated on a tight waistband. Also, similar parts of dresses.

dirt
USE earth

disabled
USE handicapped

disabled, housing for
USE housing for the handicapped

disadvantaged, economically
USE poor

disappearing stairs
PJ.2372
HN March 1993 descriptor moved
ALT disappearing stair
SN Specially constructed stairs which can be folded and swung upward into a space in the ceiling when not in use. (PUTNAM)
UF disappearing stairways
stairs, disappearing
stairways, disappearing

disappearing stairways
USE disappearing stairs

disaster housing
USE emergency housing

disasters
KM.65 (A,L,R)
HN July 1990 descriptor added
ALT disaster
SN Sudden calamitous events producing great material damage, loss, or distress. (W)
UF calamities
cataclysms
catastrophes

disasters, man-made
USE man-made disasters

disasters, natural
USE natural disasters

disbursement
USE disbursing

disbursing
KG.92
HN April 1993 lead-in term added
January 1991 scope note added
SN Paying out money or provisions, especially from a public fund. (RLG7)
UF disbursement

disc-blown glass
USE crown glass

disc brooches
TE.488
ALT disc brooch
SN Brooches made in the form of a flat disc, to the back of which is attached a fastening pin. (HNDOJ)
UF brooches, disc

discharge lamps
USE electric discharge lamps

discharge lamps, electric
USE electric discharge lamps

discharge photography, corona
USE Kirlian photography

discharge tubes
USE electric discharge lamps

discharges
VW.613
HN November 1992 descriptor moved
ALT discharge
SN Documents effecting the release of a right or obligation from its binding force; used especially in military and legal contexts.
UF releases (discharges)

discharges of contracts
VW.614 (L)
HN November 1992 descriptor moved
ALT discharge of contract
SN Documents attesting to the fulfillment of the terms or conditions of a contract.
UF contracts, discharges of

discharging
USE releasing

discharging arches
USE relieving arches

disciplinary barracks
USE military prisons

disciplines
KD.1
HN February 1991 alternate term added
ALT discipline
SN Branches of learning, professions, and areas of professional specialization.

disciplining
USE punishing

discographies
VW.182 (L)
HN November 1992 descriptor moved
March 1991 descriptor moved
March 1991 related term added
ALT discography
SN Selective or complete lists of phonographic recordings, typically of one composer, performer, or group of performers. (RHDEL2)
RT sound recordings

discoloration
KT.227
HN January 1993 descriptor moved
ALT discolored
UK discolouration
UKA discoloured
SN Any change in the color of an object. (W)

discolouration
SEE discoloration

discontinuous
USE broken

discos
USE discotheques

discotheques
RK.983 (A,L,B,R)
HN September 1990 scope note added
ALT discotheque
SN Entertainment buildings for dancing to recorded music or music videos and often featuring sophisticated sound systems, elaborate lighting, and other effects. (RHDEL2)
UF discos

discount houses
RK.175 (L)
ALT discount house
SN Stores that sell merchandise at a price below the usual price. (RHDEL2)
UF discount stores
houses, discount
stores, discount

discount stores
USE discount houses

discourse
USE pragmatics

discourse analysis
USE pragmatics

discourse grammar
USE pragmatics

discrimination
BM.1070 (L)
HN February 1993 descriptor moved
July 1991 scope note changed
February 1991 lead-in terms added
January 1991 alternate term added
ALT discriminatory
SN Biased or differential attitudes toward or treatment of people on the basis of the group, class, or category to which they belong.
UF bigotry
social discrimination

discrimination, age
USE age discrimination

discrimination, housing
USE housing discrimination

discrimination in housing
USE housing discrimination

discrimination, race
USE racial discrimination

discrimination, racial
USE racial discrimination

discrimination, sex
USE sex discrimination

discs (foot components)
PJ.2828
HN March 1993 descriptor moved
ALT disc (foot component)

discs, compact
USE compact disks

discs, magnetic
USE magnetic disks

discs, optical
USE optical disks

discs, video
USE videodiscs

discuses
TV.75 (L,N)
ALT discus
SN Disk-shaped objects, over 7 inches in diameter, thicker at the center than at the edges and having a metal rim permanently attached to a wooden body and with a central weight; to be thrown for distance in a field event.

disease
BM.565 (L,R)
HN March 1991 descriptor moved
February 1991 scope note added
February 1991 lead-in term added
SN Abnormal functioning of one or more of an organism's systems, parts, or organs. (IDMB)
UF diseases

disease, bronze
USE bronze disease

disease, glass
USE crizzling

diseased glass
USE crizzling

diseases
USE disease

diseases, mental
USE mental disorders

disegno
BM.254 (R)

dish antennas
USE satellite home antennas

dish cloths
USE dishcloths

dish crosses
TH.342
HN April 1993 descriptor added
ALT dish cross
SN Receptacles with crossed arms, often adjustable and usually with a spirit lamp in the center, used to support dishes and keep them warm while protecting the surface below from the heat.
UF crosses, dish
crosses, table
table crosses

dish dressers
USE dressers (cupboards)

dish dressers, corner
USE corner cupboards

dish rings
TH.343
HN April 1993 descriptor added
ALT dish ring
SN Cylindrical, or spool-shaped rings with pierced or openwork sides, or stands used to support hot dishes and protect the surface below.
UF potato rings
rings, dish
rings, potato

dish towels
TH.34 (N)
HN April 1993 descriptor added
ALT dish towel
UF tea towels
towels, dish
towels, tea
RT towels

dish warmers
TH.66
HN April 1993 descriptor added
ALT dish warmer
SN Table or sideboard accessories used to keep food warm.
UF warmers, dish
RT <accessory table equipment>

dishcloths
TH.35
HN April 1993 descriptor added
ALT dishcloth
UF cloths, dish
dish cloths
dishrags

dished
USE concave

dished adzes
USE hollowing adzes

dished-top tables
USE china tables

dished tops
USE china tables

dishers, ice cream
USE ice-cream scoops

dishers, ice-cream
USE ice-cream scoops

dishes
TQ.347 (H,L,N,R)
ALT dish
SN Open, often shallow, containers, sometimes having a cover; made of pottery, glass, metal, wood or the like and used for various purposes, especially for holding or serving food.
RT baking dishes
bone dishes
bowls (vessels)
chafing dishes
dinner services
soap dishes

dishes (satellite antennas)
USE satellite home antennas

dishes, alms
USE alms dishes

dishes, altar
USE alms dishes

dishes, baking
USE baking dishes

dishes, banana
USE banana boats

dishes, bonbon
USE bonbon dishes

dishes, bone
USE bone dishes

dishes, butter
USE butter dishes

dishes, casserole
USE casseroles

dishes, celery
USE celery dishes

dishes, chafing
USE chafing dishes

dishes, cheese
USE cheese dishes

dishes, dessert
USE dessert dishes

dishes, fern
USE ferneries

dishes, salad
USE salad plates

dishes, satellite
USE satellite home antennas

dishes, sauce
USE sauce dishes

dishes, sideboard
USE chargers

dishes, skimming
USE cream skimmers

dishes, soap
USE soap dishes

dishes, soufflé
USE soufflé dishes

dishes, strawberry
USE strawberry dishes

dishes, sweetmeat
USE sweetmeat dishes

dishes, toasted-cheese
USE cheese toasters

dishes, vegetable
USE vegetable dishes

dishrags
USE dishcloths

disinfectant
MT.1766 (L)
HN April 1993 lead-in term changed, was **germicides**
April 1993 descriptor changed, was **disinfectants**
ALT disinfectant
SN Material used for killing germs, bacteria, or spores. (MH)
UF germicide

disinfecting
KT.924
HN April 1993 scope note changed
January 1993 descriptor moved
June 1992 lead-in term added
March 1991 alternate term added
ALT disinfected
SN Freeing from infection especially by destroying harmful microorganisms. (W)
UF disinfection

disinfection
USE disinfecting

disintegrating
USE disintegration

disintegration
KT.235 (L)
HN January 1993 descriptor added
ALT disintegrated
SN Dissolution into separate parts, losing intactness or solidity.
UF disintegrating

disk drives
PJ.2600 (L)
ALT disk drive
SN Devices that, using an access mechanism under program control, enable data to be read from or written on a spinning magnetic disk, magnetic disk pack, floppy disk, or optical disk. (RHDEL2)
UF data disk drives
disk drives, data
drives, disk

disk drives, data
USE disk drives

disk feet
USE pad feet

disk film
MT.2376
HN April 1992 descriptor moved
UF film, disk

disk operating systems
USE operating systems

disk sanders
TH.1085 (N)
ALT disk sander
SN Power hand tools that have a rotating, circular abrasive disk; used for smoothing or polishing a surface. (MEANS)
UF sanders, disk

diskettes
USE floppy disks

disks
USE magnetic disks
shuffleboard disks

disks, compact
USE compact disks

disks, floppy
USE floppy disks

disks, laser
USE optical disks

disks, magnetic
USE magnetic disks

disks, optical
USE optical disks

disks, sanding
USE sanding disks

disks, shuffleboard
USE shuffleboard disks

disks, video
USE videodiscs

Dismal River
FL.933

dismantling
KT.944 (H)
HN January 1993 descriptor moved
August 1992 scope note added
March 1991 alternate term added
ALT dismantled
SN Taking apart or removing significant pieces, especially to reduce or disable the function.
UF deinstallation

dismissal
USE firing (managing)

disorder, mental
USE mental disorders

disorders, behavior
USE behavior disorders

disorders, mental
USE mental disorders

dispatch systems, pneumatic
USE pneumatic tubes

dispatches
VW.343
HN November 1992 descriptor moved
ALT dispatch
SN Messages, intended usually for special or expeditious transmittal or delivery, such as important official messages, or news items sent with promptness by correspondents to newspapers or news agencies. (GAHLM)

dispensaries (furniture)
TC.997

HN April 1993 alternate term added
    January 1993 descriptor moved
ALT dispensary (furniture)

dispensaries (health facilities)
   RK.708   (L,B)
  HN May 1991 descriptor changed, was
      dispensaries
     May 1991 alternate term changed,
     was **dispensary**
  ALT dispensary (health facility)

dispensers
   TQ.596   (N)
  ALT dispenser
  SN Containers or devices that hold and
     dispense something in small
     amounts.

dispensers, hand towel
  USE hand towel dispensers

dispensers, soap
  USE soap dispensers

dispensers, tape
  USE tape dispensers

dispersant
   MT.3100
  HN April 1993 descriptor changed, was
     dispersants
     March 1992 descriptor moved
  SN Material that deflocculates or dis-
     perses finely ground materials by
     satisfying the surface energy re-
     quirements of the particles; used as
     slurry thinner or a grinding agent.
     (STEIN)

dispersing agent
   MT.1690   (L)
  HN April 1993 descriptor changed, was
     dispersing agents
  UF agent, dispersing

dispersion (material)
   MT.1376
  HN February 1992 descriptor added
  SN A suspension in a liquid of relatively
     fine particles of matter, which have
     no particular propensity to dissolve
     or combine with the liquid.
     (ABMVAA)

dispersion (process)
   KT.885   (L)
  HN May 1993 descriptor changed, was
     dispersion
  ALT dispersed

displacement, continental
  USE continental drift

<displacement vessels>
   TX.476

display artists
  USE display designers

display cards
  USE lobby cards

display cases
  USE showcases

display designers
   HG.321
  HN February 1993 descriptor moved
     December 1992 alternate terms
     added
  ALT display designer
     display designer's
     display designers'
  SN Persons who plan and design dis-
     plays to decorate streets, fair-
     grounds, buildings, and other places
     for celebrations, fairs, and special
     occasions. (DOT)
  UF artists, display
     designers, display
     display artists

display domes
  USE bell jars

display drawings
  USE presentation drawings (proposals)

display faces
  USE display type

display pieces
  USE point-of-purchase displays

<display rooms and spaces>
   PJ.1036
  HN March 1993 guide term moved

display scripts
   PJ.3476
  ALT display script
  SN Scripts used for titles or other head-
     ings, especially when different from
     that used for the body of the text.
  UF scripts, display

display type
   PJ.3498   (L)
  SN Typefaces used for such elements as
     headlines, title pages, or advertise-
     ments, often defined as type of 24
     points or larger.
  UF display faces
     display typefaces
     display types
     type, display
     typefaces, display

display typefaces
  USE display type

display types
  USE display type

display, vector
  USE vector graphics

display windows
  USE show-windows

displaying
  USE exhibiting

displays
  USE monitors (data processing equip-
     ment)

displays, point-of-sale
  USE point-of-purchase displays

displays, POP
  USE point-of-purchase displays

disposal fields
  USE leaching fields

disposal of refuse
  USE refuse disposal

disposal, refuse
  USE refuse disposal

disposal, sewage
  USE sewage disposal

disposal, solid waste
  USE refuse disposal

disposal, waste
  USE waste disposal

disposition schedules
  USE records schedules

disposition schedules, records
  USE records schedules

disproportion
   BM.62
  SN A lack of symmetry or proper rela-
     tion. (W)

dissected maps
   TV.133
  ALT dissected map
  SN Use only for puzzles consisting of
     maps mounted on pasteboard or
     wood and cut out into irregularly
     shaped pieces to be reassembled as
     an educational exercise; invented in
     the mid-18th century and popular
     through the early 19th century, es-
     pecially in England and the United
     States.
  UF maps, dissected
  RT educational toys
     picture puzzles

dissected pictures
  USE dissection puzzles

dissected puzzles
  USE dissection puzzles

dissection puzzles
   TV.132
  ALT dissection puzzle
  SN Use for mechanical puzzles con-
     sisting of plane or solid figures cut
     into various shapes, the goal of
     which is to reassemble the pieces
     into a prespecified form; known
     since the 3rd century BCE in
     Greece.
  UF dissected pictures
     dissected puzzles
     pictures, dissected
     puzzles, dissected
     puzzles, dissection

disseminating
  USE publicizing

dissemination of culture
  USE cultural diffusion

dissenters
HG.974 (L,R)
HN February 1993 descriptor moved
January 1993 alternate terms added
ALT dissenter
dissenter's
dissenters'
SN People who disagree with or take an opposing view to established, orthodox, or majority values or opinions, especially those of a church or political party. (RHDEL2)
UF nonconformists

dissenters, artistic
USE dissident artists

dissertations
VW.810 (L,B,R)
HN November 1992 descriptor moved
ALT dissertation
SN Written treatises, or the records of a discourse on a subject, usually prepared and presented as the final requirement for a degree or diploma and typically based on independent research and giving evidence of the candidate's mastery of the subject and of scholarly method. (GAHLM)

dissident art
BM.186 (L,R)
UF art, dissident
art, nonconformist
art, unofficial
nonconformist art
unofficial art

dissident artists
HG.275 (L)
HN February 1993 descriptor moved
November 1992 alternate terms added
ALT dissident artist
dissident artist's
dissident artists'
UF artistic dissenters
artists, dissident
dissenters, artistic

distance
BM.657 (L)
HN February 1992 scope note added
SN Degree or amount of separation between two points, lines, surfaces, or objects in geometrical space. (W)

<distance measuring devices>
TN.3

distance, middle
USE middle ground

distant views
VC.24
HN April 1991 descriptor moved
ALT distant view
UF views, distant

distemper
MT.1946 (L,B)
HN February 1993 lead-in term added

February 1993 descriptor changed, was **distemper paint**
February 1993 scope note added
August 1992 descriptor moved
August 1991 descriptor moved
July 1990 lead-in terms added
SN Paint made with a glutinous vehicle. (GETTEN)
UF color, scenic
color, size
distemper paint
glue paint
paint, distemper
paint, glue
paint, size
scenic color
size color
size paint

distemper paint
USE distemper

distillation
KT.833 (L)
HN November 1992 descriptor added
ALT distilled
SN The volatilization or evaporation and subsequent condensation of a liquid, as when water is boiled and the steam is condensed, for such purposes as purification, concentration, or separation of substances.
UF distilling

distilled water
MT.982 (L)
HN April 1992 descriptor moved
UF water, distilled

distilleries
RK.592 (A,L,N,B)
ALT distillery
UF stills

distilling
USE distillation

distortion
BM.105

distributed loads
BM.605 (B)
HN November 1992 descriptor moved
January 1991 alternate term added
ALT distributed load
UF loads, distributed

distributing
KG.93 (L)
HN March 1993 lead-in term added
January 1991 scope note added
SN Sending out or apportioning something from a central source to a group, community, or individuals.
UF distribution (function)

distribution
BM.710 (L)
HN March 1993 descriptor changed, was **distribution (statistics)**

distribution (function)
USE distributing

distribution centers
RK.143
HN February 1991 descriptor added
ALT distribution center
SN Use for commercial buildings located regionally that combine large warehouse facilities with sales and office spaces.
UF centers, distribution
RT warehouses

distribution, downfeed
USE downfeed systems

distribution equipment, heat
USE heat-distributing units

distributional art
USE floor pieces

district courts
RK.936 (L)
HN September 1990 scope note added
ALT district court
SN Use for courthouses housing a court of general jurisdiction within a judicial district; may designate Federal or state courts.
UF courts, district

districts
RG.254 (A,L)
ALT district
SN Territorial divisions as for administrative or electoral purposes, or settlement areas with distinguishing characteristics. (WCOL9)

districts, assessment
USE assessment districts

districts, business
USE business districts

<districts by condition>
RG.312

<districts by function>
RG.255

<districts by function: administrative>
RG.256

<districts by function: land use>
RG.275

<districts by location or context>
RG.300

districts, census
USE census tracts

districts, central business
USE central business districts

districts, commercial
USE business districts

districts, congressional
USE congressional districts

districts, election
USE election districts

districts, frontier
USE marches

districts, historic
USE historic districts

districts, historic preservation
USE historic districts

districts, industrial
USE industrial districts

districts, legislative
USE legislative districts

districts, park
USE park districts

districts, planning
USE planning districts

districts, preservation
USE historic districts

districts, red-light
USE red-light districts

districts, residential
USE residential districts

districts, retailing
USE shopping districts

districts, school
USE school districts

districts, shopping
USE shopping districts

districts, voting
USE election districts

districts, water
USE water districts

distyle in antis
DC.148
HN October 1992 descriptor moved

ditchers
USE trenching machines

ditches
RK.1290 (A,L)
ALT ditch
SN Long narrow excavations dug in the earth for defense, drainage, or irrigation. (WCOL9)

ditching machines
USE trenching machines

ditty bags
TQ.192 (L,N)
ALT ditty bag
SN Small bags used especially by sailors to hold thread, needles, tape, or other small articles of gear. (W)
UF bags, ditty

ditty boxes
TQ.193
ALT ditty box
SN Small boxes used especially by sailors to hold thread, needles, tape, or other small articles of gear.
UF boxes, ditty
RT boxes (containers)

divans
TC.723 (N)
HN January 1993 descriptor moved
ALT divan
SN Long, low, upholstered seats of Turkish origin usually without backs or arms. (GLOAG)

divans, club
USE club chairs

divergent spirals
USE trumpet spirals

divers' suits
USE wetsuits

diversification
USE diversifying

diversifying
KG.94 (L)
HN April 1993 lead-in term added
    July 1990 descriptor added
ALT diversified
SN Act or practice of manufacturing a variety of products, selling a variety of merchandise, or investing in a variety of securities, for example, so that failure in or economic slump affecting one of them will not be disastrous. (RHDEL2)
UF diversification

diversion dams
RK.497 (L)
ALT diversion dam
SN Use for barriers built across waterways to turn aside all or some of the flow from its usual course into a pipe, trench, or channel, as to bypass construction work.
UF dams, diversion

divided contracts
VW.621
HN November 1992 descriptor moved
ALT divided contract
SN Contracts in which the work of the job is divided into several prime contracts, such as general, mechanical, and electrical, rather than awarded to one contractor. (STEIN)
UF contracts, divided

divided curtains
TC.308
ALT divided curtain
SN Symmetrical pairs of curtains.
UF curtains, divided

divided highways
RM.126
HN April 1993 descriptor moved
ALT divided highway
UF dual highways
    highways, divided
    highways, dual

dividers
TN.87 (N)
SN Measuring devices with two legs movable on a joint or pivot, similar in form to drawing compasses but with two metal points and used, for example, to divide lines, transfer dimensions, or lay off circles or arcs.
UF compasses (measuring devices)
    compasses, dividing
    dividing compasses
RT compasses (drawing instruments)

dividers (froes)
USE froes

dividers (interior walls)
USE room dividers

dividers, carpenters'
USE wing dividers

dividers, proportional
USE proportional dividers

dividers, room
USE room dividers

dividers, space
USE room dividers

dividers, wing
USE wing dividers

dividing compasses
USE dividers

dividing engines
TH.975 (L,N)
ALT dividing engine
SN Machines for graduating or dividing a circle into a number of equal parts, or for cutting the circumference of a wheel into a number of teeth. (OED)
UF dividing machines
    engines, dividing
    machines, dividing

dividing machines
USE dividing engines

divination
KD.329 (L)
HN January 1992 descriptor added
SN Art or practice of foreseeing future events or obtaining secret knowledge through divine sources, omens, or oracles; it is based on the belief that revelations are offered to humans in extrarational forms of knowledge. (CCE)
RT diviners

diviners
HG.606
HN January 1992 descriptor added
ALT diviner
    diviner's
    diviners'
SN Those who practice divination.
RT divination

divining mirrors
USE magic mirrors

divinity
BM.521

HN January 1991 alternate term added
ALT divine
SN The quality or state of being divine; the nature or essence of God. (W)

divinity schools
USE theological seminaries

division viols
TT.266
ALT division viol
SN English form of bass viol, developed around the middle of the 17th century, used primarily for the performance of free ornamentation by way of varying given melodies. (NGDMI)
UF viols, division

divisionism
USE pointillism

Divisionist
USE Neo-Impressionist

divisions
HN.13
HN December 1992 descriptor added
ALT division
SN Administrative sections of larger nations, territories, or other districts as defined for political, religious, military, judicial, or other purpose.
RT satrapies

divorce records
VW.697   (L)
HN November 1992 descriptor moved
ALT divorce record
SN Records documenting the legal separation of husband and wife, effected by the judgment or decree of a court, and either totally dissolving the marriage relation, or suspending its effects so far as concerns the cohabitation of the parties. (BLACKS)
UF records, divorce

diyugis
TE.180
ALT dyugie
SN Soft, loosely woven, weft-banded Navajo shoulder blankets for everyday, all-purpose use.
UF dougies
RT shoulder blankets
utility blankets

dizi
TT.7
SN Transverse bamboo flutes of China, having in addition to regular finger holes, an extra one next to the mouthpiece, covered by a membrane which vibrates during play, creating a characteristic buzzing timbre.
UF ti
ti tse
ti-tze
ti-tzu
RT mirlitons

Djaba
USE Jaba

djamis
USE jamis

Djebel
USE Dzhebel Cave

Djeitun
USE Dzheytun

Djemdet Nasr
USE Jamdat Nasr

Djenne
USE Jenne

Djibu
USE Jibu

djidjims
USE cicims

Djubu
USE Jibu

djufti
USE jufti knots

djufti knots
USE jufti knots

Djukun
USE Jukun

do-it-yourself manuals
VW.483
HN November 1992 descriptor moved
ALT do-it-yourself manual
UF manuals, do-it-yourself

docents
HG.382   (L)
HN December 1992 alternate terms added
ALT docent
docent's
docents'
SN Persons who conduct guided groups through a museum or art gallery and discuss and comment on the exhibits. (W)
UF guides (docents)
interpreters (docents)

dockets
PC.98
HN March 1993 descriptor moved
ALT docket
SN Lists or registers of cases before a tribunal, usually kept by the clerk of the court, identifying the cases, with entries of action taken; used originally in connection with judicial proceedings, now also used in connection with quasi-judicial or administrative proceedings. (GAHLM)
UF calendars, court
calendars, trial
court calendars
trial calendars

docking plans
VC.235

HN April 1992 descriptor moved
ALT docking plan
SN Use for drawings giving the information necessary for preparing a dry dock for reception of a ship. May include profiles and sections.
UF plans, docking

docks
RM.210   (A,L,N,B,R)
HN April 1993 descriptor moved
March 1993 related terms added
ALT dock
SN Use for the open water spaces occupied by vessels made fast to landing places. When such open spaces are unoccupied and are alongside a landing place, use **berths (waterfront spaces)**; use **slips (waterfront spaces)** when such water spaces are unoccupied and set between adjacent piers or perpendicular to landing places. Use **dockyards** for the group of landing places in ports or for port facilities as a whole.
RT berths (waterfront spaces)
slips (waterfront spaces)

docks, dry
USE dry docks

docks, floating
USE floating docks

docks, graving
USE dry docks

docks, loading
USE loading docks

docks, wet
USE wet docks

dockyards
RG.239   (A,L,R)
ALT dockyard

doctors
USE physicians

doctors, medical
USE physicians

doctors' offices
USE medical (ALT of medicine) + offices

doctors' surgeries
USE medical (ALT of medicine) + offices

<doctrinal concepts>
BM.519

<document containers>
TQ.599

document delivery
KG.135
SN Providing documents, published or unpublished, in hard copy or microform, upon request, either free of charge or for a fee. (ALAG)
UF delivery of documents

document drawers
PJ.2775

HN March 1993 descriptor moved
ALT document drawer
UF drawers, document

\<document genres\>
VW.2
HN November 1992 guide term moved

\<document genres by conditions of production\>
VW.949
HN June 1992 guide term added
SN Collocates descriptors that emphasize the way in which a document was formulated, prepared, or produced.

\<document genres by form\>
VW.3
HN June 1992 guide term moved
June 1992 scope note added
SN Collocates descriptors for documents that emphasize some particular manner in which the textual or visual content of the document has been arranged.

\<document genres by form: arrangement of data\>
HN June 1992 guide term deleted

\<document genres by form: partial documents\>
VW.238
HN June 1992 guide term added

\<document genres by function\>
VW.331
HN June 1992 guide term moved
June 1992 scope note added
SN Collocates descriptors for documents that emphasize a specific purpose for which the document was created.

\<document genres for literary works\>
VW.259
HN June 1992 guide term added
SN Collocates descriptors for texts that communicate ideas through particular forms or formats that may be associated with literature.

\<document genres for music\>
VW.305
HN November 1992 guide term moved
November 1992 guide term changed, was \<music documents\>

\<document genres for oral or performed works\>
VW.302
HN June 1992 guide term added

\<documentary artifacts by form: medium\>
HN June 1992 guide term deleted

documentary papyri
VW.1062
HN June 1992 descriptor added
ALT documentary papyrus
SN Use for Greek and Latin papyri that contain text concerning aspects of

everyday life, such as letters, contracts, and records. (GALLO)
UF papyri, documentary

documentary photography
KT.492   (L,R)
SN Use for an approach to photography in which the subject is recorded with an emphasis on factual accuracy and with a high degree of objectivity by the photographer; often of a newsworthy event. May be intended to record, and ultimately influence, social conditions. (ICPEP)
UF photography, documentary

documentary scripts
PJ.3477
ALT documentary script
SN Those scripts developed in contexts of writing or transcribing documents, often tending toward cursive and informality and sometimes characterized by special stylization or ornamentation.
UF charter hands
charter scripts
scripts, charter
scripts, documentary

documentation
USE documenting

documentation centers
RK.658   (B)
ALT documentation center
UK documentation centres
UKA documentation centre
SN Use for places where publications are received, preserved, abstracted, and indexed for bulletins and bibliographies which are produced for distribution. (LG)
UF centers, documentation

documentation centres
SEE documentation centers

documenting
KG.136   (A,L,B)
HN April 1993 lead-in term added
March 1991 alternate term added
ALT documented
SN Use broadly for the gathering and recording of information. For the organizing and controlling of information, use **information management**.
UF documentation

documents
PE.9   (L,R)
HN December 1992 descriptor moved
November 1992 scope note changed
November 1992 related term deleted, was **copyediting**
January 1991 related term added
ALT document
SN Use especially for recorded information regardless of medium or characteristics. In its broadest sense, however, can include any item ame-

nable to cataloging and indexing, that is, not only written and printed materials in paper or microform versions but also nonprint media and, in some circumstances, three-dimensional objects or realia.

documents, base bid
USE base bid specifications

documents, bidding
USE bidding documents

documents, chancery
USE chancery documents

documents, contract
USE contract documents

documents in machine-readable form
USE machine-readable + documents

documents, legal
USE legal documents

documents, manorial
USE manorial records

documents, notarial
USE notarial documents

documents, official
USE official documents

documents, public
USE government records

dodecagons
BM.677
HN January 1991 alternate term added
ALT dodecagon
dodecagonal
SN Polygons having 12 angles and 12 sides. (WCOL9)
UF duodecagons

dodgers
TH.793
ALT dodger
SN Tools used for photographic dodging.

dodging
KT.615
HN March 1993 descriptor moved
SN Use for photographic printing techniques in which light is obstructed or reduced in selective portions of the image, lessening exposure (and resulting density) in those areas.

dods
TH.1119
HN December 1992 descriptor added
ALT dod
SN Perforated metal plates through which clay is forced to mold it into a desired shape. (W)

Doe
FL.595

dog anchors
USE dogs

dog catches
PJ.3200
ALT dog catch
SN Firearm safety catches found on dog locks, consisting of small pivoted hooks located behind the cock which engage in a notch in the cock's heel to hold it at half cock, enabling the firearm to be safely carried ready-loaded and primed.
UF back catches (dog catches)
catches, back
catches, dog
RT dog locks

dog collars
TE.459   (H)
ALT dog collar
SN Wide, close-fitting necklaces worn tightly around the neck, often ornamented with precious or semiprecious stones. For short, narrow necklaces worn close to the throat use **chokers.**
UF collars, dog
colliers de chien
RT chokers

dog-eared fold joints
PJ.690
HN April 1993 descriptor moved
ALT dog-eared fold joint
UF fold joints, dog-eared
joints, dog-eared fold

dog gates
PJ.2208   (A)
HN March 1993 descriptor moved
ALT dog gate
SN Swinging doors or flexible barriers which may be closed across stairs, doorways, or other indoor circulation points to restrain the free movement of dogs.
UF gates, dog

dog irons
USE dogs

dog kennels
USE kennels

dog-leg brick
SEE dogleg brick

dog-locks
SEE dog locks

dog locks
PJ.3185
ALT dog lock
UK dog-locks
UKA dog-lock
SN English firearm locks incorporating a dog catch, enabling them to be placed at half cock.
UF locks, dog
RT dog catches

dog nails
PJ.152
HN April 1993 descriptor moved
ALT dog nail

SN Large nails or spikes whose heads project over one side. (MEANS)
UF nails, dog

dog racetracks
USE dog tracks

dog sledges
USE dogsleds

dog tracks
RG.193   (B)
ALT dog track
UF dog racetracks
tracks, dog

dog-trots
SEE dogtrots

doges
HG.188   (R)
HN December 1992 alternate terms added
ALT doge
doge's
doges'
SN Rulers and chief magistrates of the former republics of Venice and Genoa. (W)

doghouses
RK.86   (A,L,N)
ALT doghouse

dogleg brick
MT.80
HN April 1992 descriptor moved
UK dog-leg brick
UF brick, dog-leg
brick, dogleg

dogleg chisels
USE corner chisels

dogleg stairs
PJ.2384   (B)
HN March 1993 descriptor moved
January 1991 scope note changed
ALT dogleg stair
SN Halfpace stairs which have no well hole between successive flights; the rail and balusters of the upper and under flights fall in the same vertical plane. (DAC)
UF stairs, dogleg

Dogon
FL.351   (L)
UF Habe

Dogrib
FL.1245   (L)
UF Thlingchadine

dogs
TH.1635   (N)
HN May 1993 descriptor changed, was **dogs (woodworking tools)**
May 1993 alternate term changed, was **dog (woodworking tool)**
ALT dog
SN Simple metal devices, usually a bar with hooks at each end, used for binding two pieces of timber to-

gether. Also a general term for any device used for gripping, holding, or fastening an object.
UF anchors, dog
dog anchors
dog irons
irons, dog

dogs, bench
USE bench dogs

dog's paw feet
PJ.2814
HN March 1993 descriptor moved
ALT dog's paw foot
UF feet, dog's paw
paw feet, dog's

dogs, ring
USE ring dogs

dogs, shutter
USE shutter dogs

dogs, spoke
USE spoke dogs

dogsleds
TX.285   (N)
ALT dogsled
SN Runnered vehicles pulled by dogs, especially those used by various Arctic peoples. For similar runnered vehicles operated by hand or by gravity, use **sleds.**
UF dog sledges
sledges, dog
RT sleds

dogtooth courses
PJ.1954
HN March 1993 descriptor moved
ALT dogtooth course
SN Stringcourses of bricks laid diagonally so that one corner projects from the face of the wall. (DAC)
UF courses, dogtooth

dogtooth moldings
PJ.2084
HN April 1993 descriptor moved
ALT dogtooth molding
SN Moldings enriched with a series of starlike, raised pyramidal forms; common especially in Early English Gothic architecture. (PDARC)
UF moldings, dogtooth

dogtrot houses
RK.262
ALT dogtrot house
SN Use for houses, generally of logs, in which two pens are separated by a passageway, and the whole is covered by a single roof.
UF dogtrot plan houses
houses, dogtrot
houses, possum-trot plan
possum-trot plan houses

dogtrot plan houses
USE dogtrot houses

dogtrots
PJ.1189
HN March 1993 descriptor moved
ALT dogtrot
UK dog-trots
UKA dog-trot
SN Use for passages, sharing a roof common with the rest of the building, connecting two parts of a log house of the American folk architecture tradition. Distinguished from **breezeways** by its folk architecture and log house context and its common roof.

dogwood
MT.2724   (L)
HN March 1992 descriptor moved

doilies
TC.278   (N)
ALT doily
SN Small mats, often crocheted, laid on furniture for protection or decoration, used especially to keep heat or scratches from polished surfaces.

Dokathismata type
FL.2766

dokhmas
USE towers of silence

dolcians
USE dulcians

dole cupboards
TC.920
HN January 1993 descriptor moved
ALT dole cupboard
UF cupboards, dole

dolerite
SEE diabase

doll artists
USE dollmakers

doll buggies
USE doll carriages

doll carriages
TV.148   (N)
ALT doll carriage
SN Children's scale baby carriages for use with dolls.
UF buggies, doll
carriages, doll
doll buggies

doll-makers
SEE dollmakers

doll-making
SEE dollmaking

<doll-playing accessories>
TV.147

<dollar coins>
VK.71

dollar mats
USE button rugs

dollar rugs
USE button rugs

dollars (coins)
VK.72   (L)
ALT dollar (coin)
SN Silver or cupronickel coins valued at 100 cents.

dollars, half
USE half dollars

dollars, holey
USE holey dollars

dollars, Levant
USE Maria Theresa dollars

dollars, Maria Theresa
USE Maria Theresa dollars

dollars, quarter
USE quarter dollars

dollars, ring
USE holey dollars

dollars, trade
USE trade dollars

dollhouses
TV.149   (A,H,L,N,B,R)
ALT dollhouse
SN Use for miniature scale houses or sets of rooms designed to hold or display miniature furniture and furnishings and usually to be used in conjunction with like-sized dolls; known since the 16th century.
UF baby houses
dolls' houses
houses, baby
houses, dolls'
houses, miniature
miniature houses

dollmakers
HG.779   (L)
HN February 1993 related terms added
December 1992 alternate terms added
ALT dollmaker
dollmaker's
dollmakers'
UK doll-makers
UKA doll-maker
UF artists, doll
doll artists
RT dollmaking
dolls

dollmaking
KT.791   (L)
HN April 1993 related terms added
February 1993 descriptor moved
UK doll-making
RT dollmakers
dolls

dolls
VC.574   (H,L,N)
ALT doll
SN Human or humanoid figurines, especially those used for play, and certain ones used for ceremonial, religious, or decorative purposes.
UF action figures
figures, action
RT dollmakers
dollmaking
<recreational dolls>

dolls, baby
USE baby dolls

dolls, bisque
USE bisque dolls

dolls, character
USE character dolls

dolls, character-faced
USE character dolls

dolls, cloth
USE cloth dolls

dolls, cornhusk
USE cornhusk dolls

dolls, cornshuck
USE cornhusk dolls

dolls, costume
USE costume dolls

dolls, dummy
USE ventriloquial figures

dolls, fashion
USE fashion dolls

dolls' houses
USE dollhouses

dolls, kachina
USE kachina dolls

dolls, Kewpie
USE Kewpie dolls

dolls, ladies of fashion
USE fashion dolls

dolls, mechanical
USE mechanical dolls

dolls, paper
USE paper dolls

dolls, pedlar
USE pedlar dolls

dolls, rag
USE cloth dolls

dolls, walking
USE walking dolls

dolly method
USE à la poupée

dolmans
TE.145
ALT dolman
SN Mantles with a sleeve cut all in one with the side piece and hanging loose; sometimes made in the form of a sling. (CDC)

dolmens
USE megalithic chamber tombs

dolomite
MT.540 (L)
HN April 1992 descriptor moved
March 1992 scope note changed
SN A common rock-forming mineral. (AGI)

dolomite (limestone)
USE dolostone

dolomitic limestone
USE magnesian limestone

dolostone
MT.853 (L)
HN March 1992 descriptor added
SN A type of limestone whose calcium carbonate content approaches 45%; employed as a flux in melting iron, as a lining for basic steel furnaces, for the production of magnesium metal, for filtering, and as a construction stone. (MH)
UF dolomite (limestone)

dolphin feet
PJ.2810
HN March 1993 descriptor moved
ALT dolphin foot
SN Popular motif used as the terminal ornament on chair feet and table legs in the 17th, 18th, and 19th centuries. (IDO)
UF feet, dolphin

dolphin supports
PJ.2884
HN March 1993 descriptor moved
ALT dolphin support
UF supports, dolphin

dolphins
RK.1256
ALT dolphin
SN Use for multipurpose boating structures consisting of a group of piles driven close together into the sea bottom and bound firmly into a single cluster.

domain, eminent
USE eminent domain

domain, national
USE public domain

domain, public
USE public domain

domain, state
USE public domain

dombaks
TT.594 (L)
ALT dombak
SN Goblet drums of Iran, made of clay. (NHDM)
UF dumbaks
dumbalaks
dunbaks
tombaks

tunbaks
zarbs

dome beds
TC.760
HN January 1993 descriptor moved
July 1992 lead-in term added
ALT dome bed
UF beds, dome
doom canopies

dome beds, French
USE French beds

dome cars
TX.268
ALT dome car
SN Railroad passenger cars constructed with raised areas in the center of the car with a transparent roof for passenger observation. (RRDICT)
UF cars, dome

<dome components>
PJ.1744
HN April 1993 related term added
March 1993 guide term moved
RT *<structural element components>*

dome covers
PJ.3097
ALT dome cover
SN Container covers which are circular and have a dome-shaped profile.
UF covers, dome
covers, domed
domed covers
domes (dome covers)

domed
DC.50 (A)
HN October 1992 descriptor added
SN Use to describe things shaped like domes, or things having domes.
UF domic
domical

domed ceilings
HN April 1993 descriptor split, use domed + ceilings

domed covers
USE dome covers

domed groin vaults
USE domical vaults

domes
PJ.1733 (A,L,B,R)
HN March 1993 descriptor moved
January 1991 scope note changed
January 1991 lead-in term added
ALT dome
SN Structural elements, usually resembling spheres or portions of spheres, constructed such that they exert equal thrust in all directions.
UF cupolas (domes)

domes (dome covers)
USE dome covers

domes (furniture components)
USE hoods (furniture components)

domes, alveated
USE beehive domes

<domes and dome components>
PJ.1732
HN March 1993 guide term moved

domes, beehive
USE beehive domes

domes, bulbous
USE onion domes

domes, conch
USE umbrella domes

domes, display
USE bell jars

domes, geodesic
USE geodesic domes

domes, half
USE semidomes

domes, melon
USE umbrella domes

domes, onion
USE onion domes

domes, parachute
USE umbrella domes

domes, pendentive
USE pendentive domes

domes, pumpkin
USE umbrella domes

domes, ribbed
USE ribbed domes

domes, saucer
USE saucer domes

domes, Schwedler
USE Schwedler domes

domes, segmental
USE saucer domes

domes, Turkish
USE onion domes

domes, umbrella
USE umbrella domes

domestic architecture
USE dwellings

domestic architecture, grouped
USE cluster housing

domestic chapels
USE private chapels

domestic facilities
USE dwellings

domestic science
USE home economics

domestic stylebooks
HN March 1991 descriptor deleted

domestic wings
USE apartments

domestics
HG.107 (L)
HN February 1993 descriptor moved
November 1992 alternate terms added
ALT domestic
domestic's
domestics'
SN Hired household servants. (RHDEL2)

domic
USE domed

domical
USE domed

domical cross vaults
USE domical vaults

domical vaults
PJ.1873
HN March 1993 descriptor moved
January 1992 scope note changed
January 1992 lead-in terms added
ALT domical vault
SN Use for vaults in which the crown of the vault is higher than the crown of the transverse arches so that the ridge line is curved in elevation often having a transverse of a semicircle.
UF cross vaults, domical
domed groin vaults
domical cross vaults
groin vaults, domed
vaults, domical

domiciles
USE dwellings

Dominican
BM.495 (A,L)

domino papers
TC.382
ALT domino paper
SN Crudely printed and hand-colored papers made by dominotiers and used as wallpapers, as endpapers in books, or to line boxes.
UF domino wallpapers
dominos
papers, domino
wallpapers, domino

domino wallpapers
USE domino papers

dominoes (cloaks)
TE.138
ALT domino (cloak)
SN Large hooded cloaks; use especially for those with a mask covering the eyes and worn at masquerades.

dominoes (game pieces)
TV.15 (L,N)
ALT domino (game piece)
SN Flat, rectangular, thumb-sized blocks, usually of bone, ivory, or wood, the top face of each being divided transversely into two equal parts by a line; each part is either blank or bears from one to six dots.
UF bones (dominoes)

dominos
USE domino papers

dominotiers
HG.743
HN December 1992 alternate terms added
ALT dominotier
dominotier's
dominotiers'
SN Workmen in 15th-century France who made wallpapers printed from wood blocks and colored by hand. (MCCLEL)

domus
RK.235
SN Use for ancient Roman single-family dwellings.

domus ecclesiae
RK.1057 (R)
SN Use for the Early Christian meeting house and community center, derived from utilitarian domestic structures, serving the religious, administrative, and charitable needs of the congregation.
UF oikos ekklesias
tituli

donations
BM.925
HN February 1993 descriptor moved
January 1991 alternate term added
ALT donation
SN Gifts or contributions to public or charitable causes. (WCOL9)
UF contributions

Dondo
FL.477

Dong-duong
FL.2528

Dong-Ju
FL.2016

Dông-Son (Indonesian)
FL.2456
HN May 1991 descriptor changed, was Dông-Son

Dông-Son (Vietnamese)
FL.2515
UF Dongsonian

Dongsonian
USE Dông-Son (Vietnamese)

donjons
USE keeps

donkey saws
USE felloe saws

donor lists
VW.195
HN November 1992 descriptor moved
ALT donor list
SN Lists documenting persons or organizations from which a repository or institution has received gifts or donations.
UF lists, donor

donors
HG.918
HN December 1992 alternate terms added
ALT donor
donor's
donors'

doodles
VC.206 (L)
HN April 1992 descriptor moved
ALT doodle
UF scribbles

doodling
KT.396
ALT doodled

doom canopies
USE dome beds

door bells
USE doorbells

door bolts
PJ.456
HN April 1993 descriptor moved
ALT door bolt
SN Sliding bars or rods used for locking a door. (MEANS)
UF bolts, door

door bucks
PJ.2157
HN March 1993 descriptor moved
May 1991 descriptor moved
May 1991 scope note changed
ALT door buck
SN Rough wood or metal subframes, set in a wall, to which finished doorframes are attached. (DAC)
UF bucks, door
bucks, rough
rough bucks
sub-bucks

door bumpers
PJ.287 (N)
HN April 1993 descriptor moved
ALT door bumper
SN Devices placed on the wall or floor behind a door to limit the swing of the door. (MEANS)
UF bumpers, door
bumpers, door

door casings
USE doorframes

door checks
PJ.288
HN April 1993 descriptor moved
ALT door check
SN Devices used to retard the movement of a closing door and to guard

against its slamming or banging, but also insures the closing of the door. (PUTNAM)
UF back checks
     checks, back
     checks, door
     closers, door
     door closers

door cheeks
USE doorjambs

door chimes
USE doorbells

door closers
USE door checks

<door components>
PJ.2192
HN March 1993 guide term moved

door curtain rugs
USE door rugs

door edge pulls
PJ.365
HN April 1993 descriptor moved
ALT door edge pull
UF edge pulls, door
     pulls, door edge

door fasteners, chain
USE chain door fasteners

door fittings
USE door hardware

door fixtures
USE door hardware

door frames
USE doorframes

door hardware
PJ.588   (A,B)
HN April 1993 descriptor moved
UF door fittings
     door fixtures
     fittings, door
     fixtures, door
     hardware, door

door heads
USE doorheads

door hinges, gravity
USE rising hinges

door holders
PJ.289
HN April 1993 descriptor moved
ALT door holder
SN Devices used for holding a door open. (MEANS)
UF holders, door

door holders, overhead
USE overhead door holders

door hoods
USE doorheads

door hooks, cabin
USE cabin door hooks

door jacks
TH.1638
ALT door jack
SN Frames for holding a wood door in place while it is off its hinges and being planed. (DAC)
UF jacks, door

door jambs
USE doorjambs

door knobs
USE doorknobs

door knockers
PJ.291   (L,N,R)
HN April 1993 descriptor moved
ALT door knocker
UF knockers
     knockers, door

door leaves
PJ.2193
HN March 1993 descriptor moved
     February 1991 lead-in term added
     February 1991 lead-in term deleted, was *fores*
ALT door leaf
SN The separate elements that make up a folding or double door.
UF leaves (door components)
     leaves, door
     panels (door components)

door linings
USE doorframes

door locks
PJ.522   (N)
HN April 1993 descriptor moved
ALT door lock
UF locks, door

door locks, surface
USE rim locks

door plates
USE doorplates

door posts
USE doorjambs

door pulls
PJ.364
HN April 1993 descriptor moved
ALT door pull
UF pulls, door

door rails
PJ.2194
HN March 1993 descriptor moved
     February 1991 scope note added
     February 1991 lead-in term added
ALT door rail
SN Use for the horizontal members that connect the stiles of doors. (MEANS)
UF rails (door components)
     rails, door

door rings
PJ.292
HN April 1993 descriptor moved
ALT door ring
SN Entrance doorbell devices activated

by turning a bar or thumb piece located on the outside of an exterior door frame that communicates with a bell located somewhere inside the door frame. (DITTRI)
UF rings, door

door rugs
TC.47
ALT door rug
SN Rugs intended for use as door curtains.
UF door curtain rugs

door rugs, Afghan
USE Afghan + rugs

door silencers
PJ.293
HN April 1993 descriptor moved
ALT door silencer
UF silencers, door

door sills
USE doorsills

door stones
USE doorstones

door trees
USE doorjambs

door windows
USE French doors

doorbells
PC.107   (N)
HN March 1993 descriptor moved
     January 1991 scope note added
     January 1991 lead-in terms added
ALT doorbell
SN Bells, gongs, buzzers, or sets of chimes that ring inside a building when their control, usually a button located adjacent to an entrance, is activated. (PUTNAM)
UF bells, door
     chimes, door
     door bells
     door chimes

doorcheeks
USE doorjambs

<doorframe components>
PJ.2160
HN March 1993 guide term moved
     March 1993 guide term changed, was *<door frame components>*

doorframes
PJ.2159   (A,N,B)
HN March 1993 descriptor moved
ALT doorframe
SN Assemblies built into a wall, consisting of two upright members (doorjambs) and a horizontal member (doorhead) and providing support on which to hang the door. (DAC)
UF casings, door
     door casings
     door frames
     door linings

doorway frames
frames, door
frames, doorway
linings, door

<doorframes and doorframe components>
PJ.2158
HN March 1993 guide term moved

doorheads
PJ.2161 (B)
HN March 1993 descriptor moved
October 1991 lead-in terms added
ALT doorhead
SN Uppermost, horizontal member of a doorframe; also horizontal projections above a door. (DAC)
UF door heads
door hoods
heads, door
hoods, door

doorjambs
PJ.2162 (B)
HN March 1993 descriptor moved
November 1991 lead-in terms added
February 1991 scope note changed
February 1991 descriptor changed, was **door jambs**
February 1991 alternate term changed, was **door jamb**
ALT doorjamb
SN The vertical members forming the sides of doorways. (HAS)
UF cheeks, door
door cheeks
door jambs
door posts
door trees
doorcheeks
doorposts
jambs, door
posts, door
trees, door

doorknobs
PJ.294 (L,N)
HN April 1993 descriptor moved
ALT doorknob
SN A form of door hardware that consists of a pair of knobs on opposite ends of a spindle used to release a door latch. Distinguished from **closet knobs**, which have a knob on one end of the spindle and a rose or plate on the other.
UF door knobs
knobs, door

doormats
TC.367 (N)
HN May 1993 descriptor moved
ALT doormat
SN Use for mats placed before or just inside a door for wiping mud and dirt from shoes. (W)
UF mats, door

doornails
PJ.167

HN April 1993 descriptor moved
ALT doornail
UF nails, door

doorplates
PJ.295 (N)
HN April 1993 descriptor moved
ALT doorplate
SN Plates that serve as a mount for a doorknob or lever door handle and intervene between them and the door. (DITTRI)
UF door plates
plates, door

doorposts
USE doorjambs

doors
PJ.2164 (A,L,N,B,R)
HN April 1993 related term added
March 1993 descriptor moved
February 1993 scope note changed
ALT door
SN Barriers which swing, slide, tilt, or fold to close a doorway, usually of solid and finished construction and usually leading to or separating interior spaces. Use also for similar features that close a container or a piece of case furniture. For barriers of less solid or finished construction, and usually separating two exterior spaces, use **gates.**
RT prospect doors

doors, access
USE access doors

doors, accordion
USE folding doors

doors, air
USE air curtains

<doors and door components>
PJ.2163
HN March 1993 guide term moved

doors, automatic
USE automatic doors

doors, barn
USE barn doors

doors, blank
USE false doors

doors, blind
USE false doors

<doors by form>
PJ.2165
HN March 1993 guide term moved

<doors by form: construction>
PJ.2170
HN March 1993 guide term moved

<doors by function>
PJ.2178
HN March 1993 guide term moved

<doors by location or context>
HN April 1993 guide term deleted

<doors by mode of operation>
PJ.2182
HN March 1993 guide term moved

doors, casement
USE French doors

doors, concealed
USE jib doors

doors, concertina
USE folding doors

doors, double
USE double doors

doors, double-acting
USE swinging doors

doors, Dutch
USE Dutch doors

doors, false
USE false doors

doors, fire
USE fire doors

doors, fire-resistant
USE fire doors

doors, flush
USE flush doors

doors, folding
USE folding doors

doors, French
USE French doors

<doors: furniture components>
PJ.2765
HN March 1993 guide term moved

doors, garage
USE garage doors

doors, gib
USE jib doors

doors, hatchet
USE Dutch doors

doors, hinged
USE hinged doors

doors, hollow-core
USE hollow-core doors

doors, jib
USE jib doors

doors, louver
USE louver doors

doors, mechanically operated
USE automatic doors

doors, overhead
USE overhead doors

doors, panel
USE panel doors

doors, pivoted
USE pivoted doors

doors, pocket
USE pocket doors

doors, prospect
USE prospect doors

doors, roll-up
USE roll-up doors

doors, rolling
USE roll-up doors

doors, screen
USE screen doors

doors, sham
USE false doors

doors, shutter
USE louver doors

doors, slat
USE louver doors

doors, sliding
USE sliding doors

doors, solid
USE solid-core doors

doors, solid-core
USE solid-core doors

doors, soot
USE soot doors

doors, storm
USE storm doors

doors, swing
USE swinging doors

doors, swinging
USE swinging doors

doors, trap
USE trap doors

doors, weather
USE storm doors

doorsills
PJ.2196
HN March 1993 descriptor moved
May 1991 descriptor moved
May 1991 scope note changed
May 1991 lead-in terms added
ALT doorsill
SN Designates the lower sides and bottom of doorways; for strips fastened to the floor beneath doors to cover joints or provide weather protection, use **thresholds**. (DAC)
UF door sills
saddles
sills, door

doorstones
PJ.2197
HN March 1993 descriptor moved
May 1991 descriptor moved
February 1991 lead-in terms added
ALT doorstone
SN Stepstones at the threshold of a door. (DAC)

UF door stones
stones, door

doorstops
PJ.302   (N)
HN April 1993 descriptor moved
ALT doorstop
SN Strips on the door frame against which the door closes.

<doorway components>
PJ.2155
HN April 1993 related term added
March 1993 guide term moved
RT *<opening components>*

doorway frames
USE doorframes

doorways
PJ.2154   (A,L,B,R)
HN March 1993 descriptor moved
August 1991 scope note changed
ALT doorway
SN Denotes openings, which contain or could contain a door, that provide access into or out of building spaces.

<doorways and doorway components>
PJ.2153
HN March 1993 guide term moved

dooryards
RM.214
HN April 1993 descriptor moved
ALT dooryard
SN Use for the outside areas of farms adjacent to the main house, kitchen, and the main barn door.

DOP
USE developing-out paper

dope addicts
USE drug addicts

Dorasque
FL.1568   (L)

dorcers
USE dossals

Doric
FL.2678

Doric chitons
USE peploses

Doric cymas
USE cyma rectas

Doric order
PJ.1427   (A,B,R)
HN March 1993 descriptor moved
March 1991 scope note added
SN Architectural order characterized by columns generally without bases, relatively simple capitals, and a frieze composed of alternating triglyphs and metopes.
UF order, Doric

dories
TX.497   (L,N)
ALT dory

SN Use for relatively small simple boats with flat, rockered, keel-less bottoms, high bows, and flaring clinker or plywood sides, widely used by fishermen.

dormer windows
USE dormers

dormers
PJ.1814   (N)
HN March 1993 descriptor moved
February 1991 lead-in terms added
ALT dormer
SN Structures projecting from a sloping roof usually housing a window or ventilating louver. (DAC)
UF dormer windows
dormers, roof
lucarnes
lutherns
roof dormers
windows, dormer

dormers, eyebrow
USE eyebrow dormers

dormers, gable
USE gable dormers

dormers, gable-roof
USE gable dormers

dormers, hipped
USE hipped dormers

dormers, hipped-roof
USE hipped dormers

dormers, pedimented
USE pedimented dormers

dormers, roof
USE dormers

dormers, shed
USE shed dormers

dormers, swept
USE eyebrow dormers

dormeuses
TE.533
ALT dormeuse
SN Soft, cloth caps with a gathered crown, worn indoors by women in the 18th century.
UF dormouses
French night caps
night caps, French
RT nightcaps

dormeuses (chaises longues)
USE chaises longues

dormitories (buildings)
RK.221   (A,H,L,B,R)
HN May 1991 descriptor changed, was **dormitories**
May 1991 alternate term changed, was **dormitory**
ALT dormitory (building)
UF halls, residence
residence halls

dormitories (rooms)
PJ.1104
HN March 1993 descriptor moved
ALT dormitory (room)
SN Rooms containing a number of beds and serving as communal sleeping quarters, as in an institution, fraternity house, or passenger ship. (RHDEL2)

dormouses
USE dormeuses

Dorobo
FL.645 (L)
UF Andorobo
Ndorobo
Ogiek
Okiek
Torobo
Wandorobo

dorsals
USE dossals

dorsers
USE dossals

Dorset
FL.807

dory hand-liners
TX.369
ALT dory hand-liner
SN Use for fishing craft in which hand-lining is carried out from dories. (IMD)
UF hand-liners, dory

dos-à-dos
USE boudeusses

dosars
USE dozars

dosimeters
TN.237 (L,N)
ALT dosimeter
SN Instruments that measure and record the amount of exposure to nuclear radiation over a given period.

dosimetry
KT.197 (L)
HN November 1992 descriptor added
SN Use for the process or method of measuring the dosage of ionizing radiation received over a given period, whether by individuals or materials and whether to assess a health hazard or to date archaeological materials.

dossal curtains
USE dossals

dossals
TC.351
ALT dossal
SN Originally a term for hangings behind or on the backs of either seats or altars. Today a term referring to curtains behind or on the backs of altars. For wall hangings above and

behind an altar and containing religious images, use **altarpieces.**
UF curtains, dossal
dorcers
dorsals
dorsers
dossal curtains
dossers
RT altarpieces
curtains
riddels

dosserets
USE impost blocks

dossers
USE dossals

dossiers
USE case files
hooded settles

dot maps
VW.62
HN November 1992 descriptor moved
ALT dot map
SN Maps that indicate density of distribution by dots of uniform size, each dot representing a given quantity. (LG)
UF maps, dot

dot matrix printers
TH.581
HN January 1993 descriptor moved
ALT dot matrix printer
SN Printers that create each character from an array of dots that are usually formed by transferring ink by mechanical impact. (DOC)
UF matrix printers
printers, dot matrix

dotaku
TT.474
SN Ancient Japanese bronze bells of the Yayoi period, elliptical in cross-section with pointed ends, and in profile a tall trapezoid with a flat top, surmounted by a wide metal loop for suspension. They were cast in one piece, were highly decorated, and are believed to have served a ritual or symbolic rather than strictly musical function. A few surviving examples show signs of having held clappers.

dots
DG.38 (L)

dotted line pens
USE dotting wheels

dotted manner
KT.695
HN April 1990 descriptor added
SN Printmaking process for making relief engravings on metal, called dotted prints, using dots from punches of various shapes and sometimes including burin lines; common in the second half of the 15th century. For

later, intaglio processes employing directly engraved flicks or dots for tonal areas, use **stipple engraving.** (OCA)
UF criblé
manière criblée
manner, dotted

dotted prints
VC.486 (L)
ALT dotted print
SN Prints made using the process of dotted manner.
UF criblé prints
prints, criblé
prints, dotted

dotting wheels
TH.700
ALT dotting wheel
SN Instruments composed of a pen attached to a wheel with interchangeable cogs used in conjunction with a straightedge to produce a stippled line of dots, dashes, or both; used for technical and working drawings.
UF dotted line pens
pens, dotted line
wheels, dotting

double-acting doors
USE swinging doors

double-acting hinges
PJ.385
HN April 1993 descriptor moved
ALT double-acting hinge
SN Hinges used on a swinging door that swings both ways. (MEANS)
UF hinges, double-acting

double-acting spring hinges
PJ.404
HN April 1993 descriptor moved
ALT double-acting spring hinge
SN Double-acting hinges equipped with a spring to bring the door back in line with the frame. (DITTRI)
UF hinges, double-acting spring
spring hinges, double-acting

double action
DC.216
HN November 1992 descriptor added
SN Use to describe firearms, usually pistols or revolvers, in which a single pull of the trigger first cocks the firearm and then releases the hammer to fire it.
UF action, double

double-action harps
TT.215
ALT double-action harp
SN Harps equipped with a double-action pedal mechanism to raise the pitch of the strings by either a semitone or a whole tone during performance.
UF harps, double-action
pedal harps, double-action

double-arched prayer rugs
USE double-niche Ushaks

double-barreled
DC.160 (N)
HN November 1992 descriptor added
UK double-barrelled
SN Use to describe firearms having two barrels.

double-barrelled
SEE double-barreled

double bass players
USE bassists

double basses
TT.254 (L,N)
ALT double bass
SN Largest and lowest-pitched instruments of the violin family, having four, or more rarely, five strings, and varying considerably in size and shape. (NGDMI)
UF basses
basses, double
basses, stand-up
basses, string
contrabasses
stand-up basses
string basses
violones
RT bassists

double bassists
USE bassists

double bassoons
USE contrabassoons

double beds
TC.754
HN January 1993 descriptor moved
ALT double bed
SN Beds which are 54 inches wide; large enough to accommodate two adults.
UF beds, double
beds, full
full beds
full size beds

double-bitted keys
PJ.599
HN March 1993 descriptor moved
ALT double-bitted key
UF keys, double-bitted

double boilers
TQ.302 (N)
ALT double boiler
SN Containers consisting of two pots, one of which fits partway into the other; water is boiled in the lower pot to warm, melt, or cook the substance in the other. (RHDEL2)
UF boilers, double
custard kettles
kettles, custard

double bow-back Windsor chairs
USE double rod-back Windsor chairs

double-cable structures
PJ.1392
HN March 1993 descriptor moved
August 1991 descriptor moved
August 1991 scope note changed
August 1991 lead-in terms added
ALT double-cable structure
SN Use for structures supported by a series of double cables of different curvature used in the same vertical plane and held apart by struts in compression.
UF bicycle-wheel roofs
cable-beam structures
cable-supported roofs, double-layer
double-layer cable-supported roofs
roofs, bicycle wheel
roofs, double-layer cable-supported
structures, cable beam
structures, double-cable

double calipers
TN.74 (N)
ALT double caliper
SN Calipers that may be used as either inside or outside calipers or as dividers.
UF calipers, double

double cathedrals
USE double churches

double chairs
USE chair-back settees

double chests
USE chests-on-chests

double chests of drawers
USE chests-on-chests

double churches
RK.1040 (H)
ALT double church
SN Use for churches comprised of two complete sanctuaries, either placed one above the other or attached side by side.
UF cathedrals, double
cathedrals, twin
churches, double
churches, twin
double cathedrals
twin cathedrals
twin churches

double clarinets
TT.153
ALT double clarinet
SN Reedpipes of great antiquity, consisting of two pipes, normally glued or tied together, whose air columns are each set in vibration by a single reed; in some cases both pipes have fingerholes, in others only one does, the other serving as a drone. (NGDMI)
UF clarinets, double

double-cleat ladders
TH.1041
ALT double-cleat ladder
SN Similar to the single-cleat ladders,

but wider, with an additional center rail which allows for two-way traffic of workmen ascending and descending. (DAC)
UF ladders, double-cleat

double cloth
USE double weave

double-conical drums
TT.582
ALT double-conical drum
SN Drums whose diameter is larger at the middle than at the ends and whose body is rectilinear with an angular profile. (NGDMI)
UF biconical drums
conical drums, double
drums, biconical
drums, double-conical

double counting-house desks
TC.939
HN January 1993 descriptor moved
ALT double counting-house desk
UF counting-house desks, double
desks, double counting-house

double-creasing stakes
TH.1227 (N)
ALT double-creasing stake
UF stakes, double-creasing

double cruets
USE gemel bottles

double crusies
TC.1318
ALT double crusie
SN Crusies incorporating two pans, the upper pan to hold the fuel and wick and the lower pan to serve as a drip catcher.
UF crusie lamps, double valve
crusies, double
double pan lamps
double valve crusie lamps
lamps, double pan
lamps, double valve crusie
lamps, Phoebe
pan lamps, double
Phoebe lamps

double cups
TQ.405
ALT double cup
SN Cups of identical form which fit together, rim to rim, sometimes having, when joined, the appearance of a barrel, its staves bound with hoops of wire bands. (HNSIL)
UF cups, double

double curvature net structures
USE cable net structures

double-deck buses
TX.155
ALT double-deck bus
SN Buses with two levels of seating, one above the other, connected by one or two stairways.

UF buses, double-deck
    double-deckers

double-deck elevators
PC.124
HN March 1993 descriptor moved
    February 1991 scope note added
ALT double-deck elevator
SN Use for tandem elevators with one
    car above the other riding in the
    same hoistway and serving two con-
    secutive floors simultaneously.
UF elevators, double-deck

double-deckers
USE double-deck buses

double desks
USE partners' desks

double-door bolts
PJ.458
HN April 1993 descriptor moved
ALT double-door bolt
UF bolts, double-door

double doors
PJ.2166
HN March 1993 descriptor moved
ALT double door
SN Two single doors or door leaves
    hung in the same frame. (DAC)
UF doors, double

double draperies
USE double festoons

double dwellings
USE double houses

double eagles
VK.77
ALT double eagle
SN United States gold coins issued be-
    tween 1849 and 1933 and valued at
    twenty dollars.
UF eagles, double
    gold pieces, twenty-dollar
    twenty-dollar gold pieces

double end anchors
PJ.34
HN April 1993 descriptor moved
ALT double end anchor
UF anchors, double end

double-ended niche rugs
USE double-niche Ushaks

double-enders
TX.312
ALT double-ender
SN Use for watercraft with both ends
    coming to a point or ending in a full
    stem and sternpost.
RT gundalows
    whaleboats

double-faced hammers
USE framing hammers

double festoons
TC.312
ALT double festoon

SN Curtains, often in pairs, made of
    straight pieces of cloth with rings
    and cords running diagonally on the
    back of each from bottom center to
    outer top. When the cords are
    pulled, the cloth is gathered up and
    to the side in two swags, with points
    or tails hanging down to either side.
UF double draperies
    draperies, double
    festoons, double

double frame windows
USE double windows

double-framed roofs
PJ.1790
HN March 1993 descriptor moved
ALT double-framed roof
SN Use for roofs in which the common
    rafters rest on purlins which trans-
    fer the loads to principal rafters or
    trusses.
UF double roofs
    principal rafter roofs
    roofs, double
    roofs, double-framed
    roofs, principal rafter

double-gable roofs
PJ.1771
HN March 1993 descriptor moved
    February 1991 scope note changed
ALT double-gable roof
SN Roofs formed by the junction of two
    gable roofs with a valley between
    them, resembling the letter M in
    section. (DAC)
UF gable roofs, parallel
    M-roofs
    parallel gable roofs
    roofs, double-gable
    roofs, parallel gable
    roofs, trough
    trough roofs

double glazing, sealed
USE double windows

double-headed nails
PJ.168
HN April 1993 descriptor moved
ALT double-headed nail
SN Nails having two heads, one above
    the other, used for temporary con-
    struction such as concrete forms and
    scaffolds. The nail can secure the
    work but still be easily extracted.
    (MEANS)
UF duplex nails
    form nails
    nails, double-headed
    nails, duplex
    nails, form
    nails, scaffold
    scaffold nails

double helix stairs
USE double spiral stairs

double hip roofs
USE mansard roofs

double houses
RK.361   (A)
HN March 1993 related term added
ALT double house
SN Use for houses with separate dwell-
    ing units for two individual families
    placed side by side and separated
    horizontally by party walls. When
    the units are set one above the other
    use **duplex houses.**
UF double dwellings
    duplexes, horizontal
    dwellings, double
    horizontal duplexes
    houses, double
    houses, semidetached
    houses, two-family
    semidetached houses
    two-family houses
RT duplex houses

double-hung windows
PJ.2251
HN March 1993 descriptor moved
ALT double-hung window
SN Windows having two vertically slid-
    ing sashes, each closing a different
    part of the window; the weight of
    each sash is counter-balanced for
    ease of opening and closing. (DAC)
UF windows, double-hung

double-layer cable-supported roofs
USE double-cable structures

double leaf books
USE folded books

double-lens cameras
USE stereoscopic cameras

double-lens reflex cameras
USE twin-lens reflex cameras

double monasteries
RG.210
ALT double monastery
UF monasteries, double

double nailing
KT.1247
HN December 1992 descriptor added
ALT double-nailed
SN Close nailing in which the nails are
    set in two parallel rows.
UF nailing, double

double-niche prayer rugs
USE double-niche Ushaks

double-niche Ushaks
TC.111
ALT double-niche Ushak
SN Small Ushak rugs with opposed
    niches in the central field.
UF double-arched prayer rugs
    double-ended niche rugs
    double-niche prayer rugs
    opposed arch rugs
    rugs, double-arched prayer
    rugs, double-ended niche
    rugs, double-niche prayer
    rugs, opposed arch

rugs, Ushak prayer
small medallion Ushaks
Ushak prayer rugs
Ushaks, double-niche
Ushaks, small medallion

double organs
TT.116
ALT double organ
SN Use for 17th-century British organs having two manual keyboards.
UF organs, double

double page spreads
USE double spreads

double pan lamps
USE double crusies

double-pen houses
RK.261
ALT double-pen house
UF double-pens
houses, double-pen

double-pens
USE double-pen houses

double pieces
TE.366
ALT double piece
SN Supplementary pieces of armor attached to pieces of a basic set in order to reinforce the protection and suit it for other purposes.
UF advantage, pieces of
pieces, double
pieces of advantage
pieces, reinforcing
reinforcing pieces
RT <armor components>
close gauntlets
grandguards
plackarts
tilting targets

double-pile houses
RK.264
ALT double-pile house
UF houses, double-pile

double pitch roofs
USE gable roofs

double pointed tacks
PJ.259
HN April 1993 descriptor moved
ALT double pointed tack
UF tacks, double pointed

double printing
KT.707
HN April 1993 alternate term changed, was **double printed**
February 1992 lead-in term added
October 1991 descriptor moved
July 1990 scope note changed
July 1990 lead-in term added
July 1990 alternate term added
July 1990 descriptor changed, was **double-printing**
ALT double-printed
SN Process of reprinting a plate or

block to ensure a strong, fully printed image.
UF double run
printing, double
printing, second
run, double
second printing

double rabbet joints
PJ.639
HN April 1993 descriptor moved
ALT double rabbet joint
UF joints, double rabbet
rabbet joints, double

double refraction
USE birefringence

double return stairs
PJ.2388
HN March 1993 descriptor moved
ALT double return stair
SN Stairs with one flight up from the lower floor to the landing and two flights from the landing to the next floor. (SCOTT)
UF stairs, double return

double rod-back Windsor chairs
TC.536
HN January 1993 descriptor moved
ALT double rod-back Windsor chair
SN Square-back Windsor chairs with two turned rods across the top, the upper rod either capping the back posts or framed between them. (EVANS)
UF chairs, double bow-back Windsor
chairs, double rod-back Windsor
double bow-back Windsor chairs
Windsor chairs, double bow-back
Windsor chairs, double rod-back

double roofs
USE double-framed roofs

double run
USE double printing

double seamers
TH.1221
ALT double seamer
SN Closing machines that roll together the rims and lids of metal cans to make a hermetic seal. (W)
UF seamers, double

double seams, bottom
USE bottom double seams

double seams, corner
USE corner double seams

double sliding fire screens
TC.442
HN April 1993 alternate term added
January 1993 descriptor moved
ALT double sliding fire screen
SN Fire screens constructed of two folding leaves with sliding panels. (GILBR2)

double spiral stairs
PJ.2378

HN March 1993 descriptor moved
February 1991 lead-in terms added
ALT double spiral stair
SN Stairs in which two spiral stairs are intertwined, one of the most famous examples being the central staircase at the Château of Chambord.
UF double helix stairs
spiral stairs, double
stairs, double helix
stairs, double spiral

double spreads
PJ.3395
ALT double spread
SN Images or texts designed to occupy two facing pages.
UF double page spreads
double tricks
spreads
spreads, double
spreads, double page
spreads, two-page
tricks, double
two-page spreads

double strength window glass
MT.262
HN March 1993 descriptor moved
UF glass, double strength window
window glass, double strength

double-struck coins
VK.10
ALT double-struck coin
SN Use for coins that have two or more impressions of the same design on either the obverse or reverse, generally caused by movement of the coins in the die between successive hammer blows.
UF coins, double-struck

double style hangers
PJ.122
HN April 1993 descriptor moved
ALT double style hanger
UF hangers, double style

double sun snakes
USE swastikas

double throw bolts
PJ.558
HN March 1993 descriptor moved
ALT double throw bolt
SN Bolts that can be projected beyond their normal position, thus giving extra security. (BROWNL)
UF bolts, double throw
throw bolts, double

double tricks
USE double spreads

double valances
TC.268
ALT double valance
SN Inner and outer bed valances which allow curtains to be drawn between them, thus concealing curtain hardware both to the interior and exterior of the bed.

UF   paired valances
      valances, double
      valances, paired

double valve crusie lamps
USE   double crusies

double weave
      MT.1595   (R)
HN   November 1992 descriptor added
SN   Weaving technique that produces
      two textiles simultaneously, one
      above the other. The warp is com-
      posed of two series of ends, and
      each interlaces with its own weft, or
      with a common weft which works
      with each series in turn. In pat-
      terned double weave, the two tex-
      tiles change position as required by
      the pattern. (WRPWFT)
UF   cloth, double
      double cloth
      doublecloth
      weave, double

double whole plate
      DC.112
HN   October 1992 descriptor moved
SN   A photographic plate size, about 8
      1/2 by 13 inches.

double windows
      PJ.2229   (L,B)
HN   March 1993 descriptor moved
      November 1991 lead-in term added
      February 1991 lead-in term deleted,
         was **heat insulation windows**
ALT   double window
SN   Two windows, one outside the
      other, as storm windows, used to
      provide improved thermal and
      noise insulation. (DAC)
UF   double frame windows
      double glazing, sealed
      frame windows, double
      glazing, sealed double
      sealed double glazing
      windows, double
      windows, double frame

double wine glasses
      TQ.452
ALT   double wine glass
SN   Wine glasses with a foot shaped to
      form another drinking vessel when
      reversed.
UF   glasses, double wine
      wine glasses, double

doublecloth
USE   double weave

doubled columns
      PJ.1474
HN   March 1993 descriptor moved
ALT   doubled column
SN   Use for pairs of columns which in-
      terlock as if the shaft of one were
      gripping the shaft of the other; for
      pairs of columns set close together

so as to form a visual unit, use coupled columns.
UF   columns, doubled

doublés
USE   doublures

doublets
      TE.52   (H,N)
ALT   doublet
SN   Close-fitting waist-length or hip-
      length garments with or without
      sleeves worn by men from the 15th
      to the 17th century. Also, similar
      garments reinforced by mail and
      worn under armor.
UF   gipons
      jerkins (doublets)
      pourpoints (doublets)
RT   armor

doublets, arming
USE   arming doublets

doubloons
      VK.122   (L)
ALT   doubloon
SN   Designates various Spanish and
      Spanish-American gold coins issued
      between the 15th and the 19th cen-
      turies.

doublures
      PJ.3365
ALT   doublure
SN   Ornamental inside linings of book
      covers, sometimes leather, which
      take the place of the regular fly-
      leaves or pastedowns.
UF   doublés

doucines
USE   cymas

dough baskets
      TQ.272   (N)
ALT   dough basket
SN   Coiled baskets in which dough is set
      to rise.
UF   baskets, bread-raising
      baskets, dough
      baskets, dough-rising
      bread baskets (dough baskets)
      bread-raising baskets
      dough-rising baskets
RT   baskets

dough blenders
USE   pastry blenders

dough boards
USE   breadboards

dough boxes
USE   dough troughs

dough brakes
USE   bread makers

dough-brakes
USE   bread makers

dough cutters
USE   jagging wheels

dough hooks
      PJ.2603
ALT   dough hook
SN   Attachments for a food processor or
      electric mixer, for kneading dough.
      (RHDEL2)
UF   hooks, dough
RT   food processors
      mixers (culinary equipment)

dough kneaders
USE   bread makers

dough-kneaders
USE   bread makers

dough makers
USE   bread makers

dough-makers
USE   bread makers

dough mixers
USE   bread makers
      cake mixers

dough-rising baskets
USE   dough baskets

dough spurs
USE   jagging wheels

dough trays
USE   dough troughs

dough troughs
      TQ.273   (N)
ALT   dough trough
SN   Boxes or troughs, usually having a
      lid, in which dough is mixed and
      kneaded.
UF   boxes, dough
      boxes, kneading
      bread-brakes
      bread troughs
      dough boxes
      dough trays
      kneading boxes
      kneading troughs
      kneeding troughs
      trays, dough
      troughs, bread
      troughs, dough
      troughs, kneading
      troughs, kneeding

doughnut cutters
      TH.115   (N)
HN   April 1993 descriptor added
ALT   doughnut cutter
SN   Sheet tin utensils with vertical sides
      and an inner and outer ring used to
      shape doughnuts, often with an
      attached handle.
UF   cutters, doughnut

dougies
USE   diyugis

Douglas fir
      MT.2942   (L)
HN   March 1992 descriptor moved
UF   Douglas pine
      Douglas spruce

fir, Douglas
fir, red
fir, yellow
Oregon pine
pine, Douglas
pine, Oregon
pine, Puget Sound
Puget Sound pine
red fir
spruce, Douglas
yellow fir

Douglas pine
USE Douglas fir

Douglas spruce
USE Douglas fir

Dourour
USE Aua

dousing cones
USE extinguishers

douters
PJ.2934
ALT douter
SN Scissorlike devices, usually with flat disc-shaped ends, used for pinching out a flame. For scissorlike devices with a boxlike receptacle attached to one blade, use **candle snuffers.** For cone-shaped devices used to extinguish flames, use **extinguishers.**
UF out-quenchers

dovecotes
RK.83   (A,L,B,R)
ALT dovecote
UF columbaria (dovecotes)
columbariums
houses, pigeon
pigeon houses

dovetail clamps
TH.635
ALT dovetail clamp
SN Devices, usually of iron, bent at the ends, or of dovetail form; used to hold together structural timbers or stone. (PUTNAM)
UF clamps, dovetail

dovetail cutters
TH.1447
ALT dovetail cutter
SN Rotary cutting tools used to shape dovetails. (DAC)
UF cutters, dovetail

dovetail joints
PJ.715
HN April 1993 descriptor moved
ALT dovetail joint
SN Interlocking joints formed by a flaring or fanlike tenon and a mortise into which it fits tightly. (WCOL9)
UF joints, dovetail

dovetail joints, blind
USE blind dovetail joints

dovetail joints, shouldered
USE shouldered dovetail joints

dovetail saws
TH.1564   (N)
ALT dovetail saw
SN Small backsaws, about 9 inches in length, with thin blades, fine teeth, and straight handles; used for accurate work, as in cabinetmaking and patternmaking.
UF angle saws
corner saws
saws, angle
saws, corner
saws, dovetail

dovetail seams
USE plain dovetail seams

dovetail seams, beaded
USE beaded dovetail seams

dovetail seams, flange
USE flange dovetail seams

dovetail templates
TH.1015
ALT dovetail template
UF templates, dovetail

dovetail wire anchors
PJ.35
HN April 1993 descriptor moved
ALT dovetail wire anchor
UF anchors, dovetail wire
wire anchors, dovetail

dovetailed tapestry
KT.1192
HN November 1992 descriptor added
SN Tapestry weaving technique in which the weft threads of two adjacent areas are turned alternately around a common end in groups of two or more. (WRPWFT)

dowel anchors
PJ.26
HN April 1993 descriptor moved
ALT dowel anchor
UF anchors, dowel

dowel bits
USE spoon bits

dowel cutters
USE peg cutters

dowel pins
PJ.217
HN April 1993 descriptor moved
November 1992 related term added
ALT dowel pin
SN Special nails that are pointed at both ends and are used to fasten mortise-and-tenon joints. (MEANS)
UF pins, dowel
RT dowels

dowel pins, barbed
USE barbed dowel pins

dowel plates
USE peg cutters

doweling
KT.36
HN March 1993 descriptor moved
November 1992 related term added
November 1990 descriptor added
ALT doweled
SN Fastening together two pieces of wood by means of dowels.
RT dowels

dowels
PE.42   (L,N)
HN November 1992 descriptor moved
November 1992 related terms added
November 1992 alternate term added
November 1992 descriptor changed, was **dowel**
November 1990 scope note changed
ALT dowel
SN Pins of wood or metal used to hold or strengthen two pieces of wood where they join; also, thin round rods of wood.
RT dowel pins
doweling

dower chests
TC.876   (N)
HN May 1993 related terms added
January 1993 descriptor moved
ALT dower chest
SN Chests made to commemorate or anticipate a wedding; usually incorporating names and dates in their decoration. (PAIN)
UF bridal chests
chests, bridal
chests, dower
chests, hope
chests, marriage
chests, wedding
hope chests
marriage chests
wedding chests
RT cassoni
commemoratives

down
MT.2580   (H,L)
HN March 1992 scope note added
February 1992 descriptor moved
SN The small fluffy feathers that lie next to the body of an adult bird and that are notably developed and fine in texture, found on ducks, geese, and other waterfowl.

down pipes
USE downspouts

downcutting augers
USE nose augers

downfeed distribution
USE downfeed systems

downfeed systems
PC.224
HN March 1993 descriptor moved

February 1991 lead-in term added
February 1991 scope note added
ALT downfeed system
SN Water distribution systems in which water is pumped to holding tanks above the points of use, thereby increasing water pressure through gravity; most often employed in tall buildings where municipal water supply lacks the pressure necessary for an upfeed system.
UF distribution, downfeed
downfeed distribution
systems, downfeed

downhill skiing
KQ.94 (L)
UF skiing, downhill

downlighters
USE downlights

downlights
TC.1439
ALT downlight
SN Any lamp whose light is directed downwards.
UF downlighters

downspouts
PJ.898
HN March 1993 descriptor moved
July 1991 scope note changed
December 1990 lead-in terms added
December 1990 descriptor changed, was **conductors (piping)**
December 1990 alternate term changed, was **conductor (piping)**
ALT downspout
SN Any vertical pipes, including those within a building, that convey rainwater to sewers, drains, or the ground.
UF conductors (downspouts)
down pipes
leader pipes
leaders (downspouts)
leaders, rainwater
pipes, down
pipes, leader
pipes, rainwater
rainwater leaders
rainwater pipes

downtowns
USE central business districts
inner cities

downy birch
MT.2702
HN March 1992 descriptor moved
UF Betula pubescens
birch, downy

downy calves
TE.703
ALT downy calf
SN Pads woven into the calves of stockings to exaggerate and produce manly looking calves; patented in 1788. (EMAEA)
UF calves, downy

calves, false
false calves

dowsing
KT.281 (L,B)
SN Use for the technique of detecting underground water or other substances or objects by feeling the motion of a divining rod.

dozars
TC.39
ALT dozar
SN A Persian term for long, relatively narrow rugs measuring approximately 6 by 4 feet, or 2 zars.
UF dosars

dozers
USE bulldozers

dozers, angle
USE angle dozers

dozers, angling
USE angle dozers

dozers, shovel
USE shovel dozers

dozers, tilting
USE tilting dozers

drab gray
USE yellowish gray

drab gray, pale
USE light gray
white (neutral)

drab, light olive
USE olive gray

drab, olive
USE dark olive
grayish olive
olive gray

<drachma coins>
VK.31

drachmas
VK.32 (L)
ALT drachma
SN Small, silver Greek coins originally equivalent to six obols and issued from the 6th century BCE; usage continued by the Parthians and Sassanians until the 7th century CE. (DOTY)

Draconian
FL.1202

draft shaves
USE drawknives

drafting
KT.397 (A,L)
ALT drafted
UF drawing, mechanical
drawing, precision
mechanical drawing
precision drawing

drafting cloth
MT.1556
HN March 1993 descriptor moved
SN Linen or cotton coated on one or both sides with starch or a mixture of starch and gelatine, producing a support of even transparency and strength. (ADAG)
UF cloth, drafting

<drafting, drawing and writing equipment>
TH.648
HN January 1993 related terms added
RT <containers for writing equipment>
drawing (image-making)

<drafting, drawing and writing equipment by general type>
TH.649

<drafting, drawing and writing equipment by specific type>
TH.653

drafting equipment
TH.650 (N)
HN November 1992 related term added
UF equipment, drafting
RT parallel rules

drafting lamps
USE architects' lamps

drafting machines
TH.667 (N)
ALT drafting machine
SN Devices which attach to a drawing table and combine the functions of a straightedge, T-square, triangle, and protractor; used by draftsmen, designers, architects, and engineers.
UF machines, drafting

drafting paper
USE drawing paper

drafting tables
USE drawing tables

drafts (documents)
VW.227
HN November 1992 descriptor moved
June 1992 alternate term changed, was **draft**
ALT draft (document)
SN Preliminary or tentative versions of documents.

drafts (negotiable instruments)
VK.168 (L)
ALT draft (negotiable instrument)
SN Written orders drawn by one party ordering a second party to pay a specified sum of money to a third party (who may be the first party); usually restricted to domestic transactions. For similar orders to pay used for foreign transactions, prefer **bills of exchange**. (ENCYBF)
UF bank drafts
drafts, bank

RT bills of exchange
commercial paper

drafts, bank
USE drafts (negotiable instruments)

drafts, first
USE first drafts

drafts, rough
USE first drafts

draftsmen (artists)
HG.276
HN May 1993 lead-in term changed, was **graphic artists (draftsmen)**
March 1993 lead-in term changed, was **artists, graphic (draftsmen)**
February 1993 descriptor moved
January 1993 alternate terms added
May 1991 descriptor changed, was **draftsmen**
May 1991 alternate term changed, was **draftsman**
ALT draftsman (artist)
draftsman's (artist)
draftsmen's (artists)
UK draughtsmen
UKA draughtsman
SN Persons skilled in drawing.
UF artists, graphic
graphic artists

draftsmen (technical)
HG.851
HN January 1993 alternate terms added
ALT draftsman (technical)
draftsman's (technical)
draftsmen's (technical)
UK draughtsmen
UKA draughtsman
SN Persons skilled in the creation of technical drawings, as of structures or machines. (W)

draftsmen's scales
USE architects' scales

drag shovels
USE backhoes

drag strips
RG.192
ALT drag strip
UF dragways

draggers
TX.374
ALT dragger
SN Use for small otter trawlers of various types and sizes, which engage in shore fishing along the Atlantic Coast of the United States, usually within 50 miles of the coastline; introduced in the mid-20th century.

dragging
KT.419
HN July 1990 scope note changed
ALT dragged
SN A technique of stroking paint lightly over a rough surface so that it covers the high spots and leaves the de-

pressions untouched, thus creating a broken area of color with irregular spots of the color underneath showing through.
UF scruffing
scuffing

dragging beams
USE dragon beams

dragging pieces
USE dragon beams

dragging ties
USE dragon beams

dragline buckets
TH.464 (N)
ALT dragline bucket
SN Bucket attachments for cranes; used for removing earth by pulling the bucket toward the crane. (DAC)
UF buckets, dragline

dragon beams
PJ.1657
HN March 1993 descriptor moved
March 1991 scope note changed
March 1991 lead-in terms added
ALT dragon beam
SN Use for short horizontal timbers bisecting the angle of a corner of a structure, at the level of the roof plate, reaching to an angle brace, and serving to support the foot of a hip rafter.
UF beams, dragging
beams, dragon
dragging beams
dragging pieces
dragging ties
dragon pieces
pieces, dragging
pieces, dragon
ties, dragging

dragon feet
PJ.2811
HN March 1993 descriptor moved
ALT dragon foot
UF feet, dragon

dragon Kuba
USE dragon rugs

dragon pieces
USE dragon beams

dragon rugs
TC.78
ALT dragon rug
SN Late-17th- and 18-century rugs, thought to have originated in the Caucasus, frequently characterized by a depressed two-level natural wool warp, wool wefts often dyed red, and knotted with symmetrical knots; the field pattern consists of a drop repeat directional lattice pattern made up of jagged leaf forms enclosing stylized dragons.
UF carpets, dragon
dragon Kuba

Kuba, dragon
rugs, dragon

dragon ties
PJ.1443
HN March 1993 descriptor moved
November 1990 descriptor moved
ALT dragon tie
SN Angle braces which support one end of a dragon beam. (DAC)
UF ties, dragon

dragon's blood
MT.1259 (L)
HN May 1992 scope note changed
May 1992 lead-in term added
February 1992 descriptor moved
SN Type of red resin used in fine lacquer, dye, and varnish; also used infrequently as a pigment. (MH)
UF blood, dragon's
cinnaharis

dragon's blood (color)
USE grayish red

drags (scratch tools)
TH.1171
HN December 1992 descriptor moved
ALT drag (scratch tool)
SN Long serrated plates used to level and score plaster in preparation for the next coat. (MEANS)

<drags, litters and pedestrian land vehicles>
TX.81
SN Land vehicles pulled along the ground or carried, or devices used directly on the feet to move around.

dragsters
TX.122
ALT dragster
SN Use for automobiles designed and built especially for straight line sprinting or drag racing.

dragways
USE drag strips

drain tile
MT.163 (L)
HN March 1993 scope note added
March 1993 lead-in term added
March 1993 descriptor changed, was **draintile**
March 1993 lead-in term changed, was **drain tile**
April 1992 descriptor moved
SN Ceramic tile, usually in short-length sections, used for constructing water drains.
UF drainage tile
draintile
field tile
tile, drain
tile, drainage
tile, field

drainage
BM.314 (A,L,B)
HN February 1992 scope note added

SN Removal of ground or surface water by artificial or natural means.

drainage, land
USE land drainage

drainage networks
USE drainage systems

drainage piping
　　PJ.899　　　　　　　　　　(L)
HN March 1993 descriptor moved
SN The piping comprising the plumbing of a drainage system. (MEANS)
UF piping, drainage

drainage, sanitary
USE sanitary drainage systems

drainage, soil
USE land drainage

<drainage structures>
　　RK.509

drainage systems
　　PC.169　　　　　　　　　　(B)
HN March 1993 descriptor moved
ALT drainage system
UF drainage networks
　　networks, drainage
　　systems, drainage

drainage systems, sanitary
USE sanitary drainage systems

drainage systems, storm
USE stormwater systems

drainage tile
USE drain tile

drainage, waste and vent piping
USE DWV piping

drainers, cheese
USE cheese baskets

drainers, fish
USE mazarines

drains
　　PJ.884
HN March 1993 descriptor moved
ALT drain
SN Artificial channels by means of which liquid or other matter is drained or carried off. (W)

drains, area
USE area drains

drains, fixture
USE fixture drains

drains, French
USE French drains

drains, storm
USE storm drains

drains, storm water
USE storm drains

draintile
USE drain tile

drake feet
USE trifid feet

dram cups
　　TQ.419
ALT dram cup
SN Small shallow cups, usually with two loop handles and often flat bottoms and slightly rounded sides, used for drinking a draught (dram) of distilled spirits.
UF cups, dram
RT brandy bowls
　　wine tasters

dram glasses
　　TQ.431
ALT dram glass
SN Small drinking glasses for spirits, generally of 2- or 3-ounce capacity, with a funnel or conical bowl and a short rudimentary stem resting on a heavy foot.
UF glasses, dram
　　glasses, joey
　　joey glasses
RT toastmasters' glasses

drama
　　KD.66　　　　　　　　　　(L,R)
HN April 1993 related term added
SN Use for the academically oriented study of theater, comprising theater criticism, history, aesthetics, and the study of drama as a specialized form of literature. For the professionally oriented study and practice of theater, use **theater**.
UF arts, dramatic
　　dramatic arts
RT theater

drama, religious
USE religious drama

drama, sacred
USE religious drama

dramatic arts
USE drama

dramatists
USE playwrights

draped valances
　　TC.341
ALT draped valance
SN Valances consisting of lengths of fabric draped around or from a rod, pole, or mounting board; used either with curtains or alone.
UF draperies (valances)
　　draperies, upper
　　overdraperies
　　upper draperies
　　valances, draped

draperies
　　TC.309　　　　　　　　　　(N)
ALT drapery
SN Curtains, especially long curtains of heavy fabric, usually hung in carefully arranged folds at the sides of openings, either in a straight or draped fashion, and often used over sheer curtains.
UF draperies, window
　　drapes
　　drapes, outer
　　outer drapes
　　overdraperies
　　overdrapes
　　window draperies
RT draw curtains

draperies (valances)
USE draped valances

draperies (wallpapers)
USE drapery papers

draperies, double
USE double festoons

draperies, festoon
USE festooned valances

draperies, floor-length
USE floor-length curtains

draperies, full-length
USE floor-length curtains

draperies, upper
USE draped valances

draperies, window
USE draperies

drapers
　　HG.331
HN February 1993 descriptor moved
　　December 1992 alternate terms added
ALT draper
　　draper's
　　drapers'

drapery curtains
USE festoon curtains

drapery figures
USE drapery papers

drapery holdbacks
HN April 1993 descriptor deleted, made lead-in to **tiebacks**

drapery holdbacks
USE tiebacks

drapery panels
USE drapery papers

drapery papers
　　TC.383
ALT drapery paper
SN Wallpapers with patterns that simulate draped textiles.
UF draperies (wallpapers)
　　drapery figures
　　drapery panels
　　drapery wallpapers
　　figures, drapery
　　panels, drapery
　　papers, drapery
　　wallpapers, drapery

drapery studies
VC.63
HN May 1991 scope note added
April 1991 descriptor moved
ALT drapery study
SN Studies, usually drawings, that concentrate on the depiction of cloth or a detail of cloth.
UF studies, drapery

drapery, swag
USE swags

drapery wallpapers
USE drapery papers

drapes
USE draperies

drapes, outer
USE draperies

draught chairs
USE easy chairs

draught screens
USE folding + screens (furniture)

draughts
SEE checkers (game pieces)

draughtsmen
SEE draftsmen (artists)
draftsmen (technical)

Dravidian
FL.2334 (A,L)

draw curtains
TC.329
ALT draw curtain
SN Curtains that can be drawn to the side, especially those that slide back and forth on a rod or track through a system of cords and pulleys operated either by hand or electrically. (JWDD)
UF curtains, draw
curtains, sliding
curtains, traverse
sliding curtains
traverse curtains
RT draperies

draw leaf tables
USE draw tables

draw-out tables
USE draw tables

draw runners
USE lopers

draw slips
USE lopers

draw tables
TC.1078
HN January 1993 descriptor moved
ALT draw table
SN Tables with flaps which may be drawn out from beneath the top to extend the length. Late 16th-century and early 17th-century hall tables are often of this type. (DDA)
UF draw leaf tables
draw-out tables
draw-top tables
drawer tables
drawing tables (draw tables)
tables, draw
tables, draw leaf
tables, draw-out
tables, draw-top
tables, drawer
tables, drawing (draw tables)

draw tongs
USE clip tongs

draw-top tables
USE draw tables

draw-up curtains
USE pull-up curtains

drawbenches
TH.1283 (L)
ALT drawbench
SN Benches used in conjunction with drawplates for drawing long or tough lengths of wire. (HAND)

drawbridges
RK.1220 (A,L,R)
ALT drawbridge
SN Use for movable bridges in which one or more span sections can be pivoted upward by means of chains, cables, or other ropelike devices; if the sections are pivoted by counterweights, use bascule bridges.

<drawer components>
PJ.2782
HN March 1993 guide term moved

drawer knobs
USE cabinet knobs

drawer locks
PJ.544
HN April 1993 descriptor moved
ALT drawer lock
UF locks, drawer
locks, till
till locks

drawer pulls
PJ.367
HN April 1993 descriptor moved
ALT drawer pull
UF chest lifts
chest pulls
lifts, chest
pulls, chest
pulls, drawer

drawer pulls, drop
USE drop pulls

drawer supports
PJ.2888
HN March 1993 descriptor moved
ALT drawer support
UF supports, drawer

drawer tables
USE draw tables

drawers (furniture components)
PJ.2768
HN March 1993 descriptor moved
March 1993 descriptor changed, was **drawers**
March 1993 alternate term changed, was **drawer**
ALT drawer (furniture component)
UF furniture drawers

drawers (underpants)
TE.226 (N)
SN Trouserlike undergarments extending from the waist to the top of the knee or below. For similar garments with elastic or a band near the knee or below use **bloomers**.
UF underdrawers
RT bloomers

<drawers and drawer components>
PJ.2767
HN March 1993 guide term moved

drawers, blind
USE blind drawers

drawers, bottle
USE celleret drawers

<drawers by form>
PJ.2769
HN March 1993 guide term moved

<drawers by function>
PJ.2773
HN March 1993 guide term moved

<drawers by location or context>
PJ.2780
HN March 1993 guide term moved

drawers, cabinets of
USE cabinets of drawers

drawers, cellarette
USE celleret drawers

drawers, celleret
USE celleret drawers

drawers, chests of
USE chests of drawers

drawers, chests with
USE chests with drawers

drawers, document
USE document drawers

drawers, double chests of
USE chests-on-chests

drawers, dressing
USE dressing drawers

drawers, high chests of
USE high chests of drawers

drawers, kneehole chests of
USE kneehole desks

drawers, lipped
USE lipped drawers

drawers, low chests of
USE low chests

drawers, nests of
USE nests of drawers

drawers, pedestals with
USE cabinets of drawers

drawers, quadrant
USE quadrant drawers

drawers, secret
USE secret drawers

drawers, secretary
USE secretary drawers

drawers, tall chests of
USE chiffoniers (chests of drawers)

drawers, writing
USE secretary drawers

drawing (image-making)
KT.387   (A,L,R)
HN March 1993 lead-in term added
January 1993 related terms added
May 1991 descriptor changed, was
drawing
April 1991 scope note added
January 1991 related term added
SN Producing visible forms primarily by
delineation, usually by the direct ap-
plication of material or instrument
to the surface of the support.
UF arts, graphic
graphic arts
RT *<drafting, drawing and writing
equipment>*
drawings
sketching

drawing (metal-working)
SEE drawing (metalworking)

drawing (metalworking)
KT.1140   (L)
HN March 1991 alternate term added
ALT drawn
UK drawing (metal-working)
SN The stretching, spreading, or shap-
ing of metal by passing through dies
or by stamping successively, as with
a series of dies or by hammering.
(W)

<drawing and drawing techniques>
KT.386

drawing and writing tables, ladies'
USE Carlton House tables

drawing, architectural
USE architectural drawing

drawing, blind contour
USE blind contour drawing

drawing, blot
USE blot drawing

drawing books
HN June 1991 descriptor split, use
drawing + books

drawing chambers
USE drawing rooms

drawing, computer
USE computer-aided design

drawing, contour
USE contour drawing

drawing, cross-contour
USE cross-contour drawing

drawing curves
USE curves

drawing, fashion
USE fashion illustration

drawing, free-hand
SEE freehand drawing

drawing, freehand
USE freehand drawing

drawing, gesture
USE gesture drawing

drawing instruments
TH.651   (A,L,B)
ALT drawing instrument
UF drawing tools
instruments, drawing
tools, drawing

drawing, mechanical
USE drafting

drawing paper
MT.1470
HN February 1992 descriptor moved
July 1990 lead-in terms added
UF drafting paper
paper, drafting
paper, drawing
paper, sketching
sketching paper

drawing, photogenic
USE photogenic drawing

drawing, precision
USE drafting

drawing rooms
PJ.1111   (A)
HN March 1993 descriptor moved
June 1990 lead-in terms added
ALT drawing room
SN Formal reception rooms, as in a
home or hotel, or rooms to which
one may retire for privacy or rest.
(W)
UF chambers, drawing
chambers, withdrawing
drawing chambers
rooms, drawing
rooms, withdrawing
withdrawing chambers
withdrawing rooms

drawing tables
TC.1138   (N)
HN March 1993 lead-in term changed,
was **artist's tables**
March 1993 lead-in term changed,
was **tables, artist's**
March 1993 lead-in term deleted,
was **architect's tables**
March 1993 lead-in term deleted,
was **tables, architect's**
January 1993 descriptor moved
ALT drawing table
SN Tables with surfaces adjustable for
elevation and angles of incline.
UF artists' tables
drafting tables
tables, artists'
tables, drafting
tables, drawing

drawing tables (draw tables)
USE draw tables

drawing techniques
KT.389   (L,R)

drawing tools
USE drawing instruments

drawings
VC.83   (A,L,N,B)
HN April 1993 lead-in term added
January 1993 related term added
April 1992 descriptor moved
April 1991 scope note changed
ALT drawing
SN Use for images produced by
drawing.
UF pictures
RT drawing (image-making)

drawings, addendum
USE clarification drawings

drawings, architectural
USE architectural drawings

drawings, as-built
USE as-built drawings

drawings, assembly
USE assembly drawings

drawings, auxiliary
USE auxiliary views

drawings, axonometric
USE axonometric drawings

drawings, blind contour
USE blind contour drawings

drawings, blot
USE blot drawings

<drawings by function>
VC.171
HN April 1992 guide term moved

<drawings by location or context>
HN October 1990 guide term deleted

<drawings by maker>
VC.220
HN April 1992 guide term moved

<drawings by method of projection>
VC.91
HN   April 1992 guide term moved

<drawings by method of representation>
VC.84
HN   April 1992 guide term moved

<drawings by subject type>
VC.224
HN   April 1992 guide term moved

<drawings by technique>
VC.200
HN   April 1992 guide term moved

drawings, cabinet oblique
USE   cabinet oblique drawings

drawings, cavalier oblique
USE   cavalier oblique drawings

drawings, cave
USE   cave paintings

drawings, chiaroscuro
USE   three-tone drawings

drawings, clarification
USE   clarification drawings

drawings, competition
USE   competition drawings

drawings, component
USE   minor assembly drawings

drawings, composite
USE   composite drawings

drawings, composition
USE   composition drawings

drawings, computer
USE   computer drawings

drawings, computer-generated
USE   computer drawings

drawings, conceptual
USE   conceptual drawings

drawings, construction
USE   construction drawings

drawings, contour
USE   contour drawings

drawings, contract
USE   contract drawings

drawings, cross-contour
USE   cross-contour drawings

drawings, cutaway
USE   cutaway drawings

drawings, definitive
USE   design development drawings

drawings, design
USE   design drawings

drawings, design development
USE   design development drawings

drawings, detail
USE   detail drawings
        detail studies

drawings, dimetric
USE   dimetric drawings

drawings, display
USE   preparatory drawings
        presentation drawings (proposals)

drawings, electrical
USE   electrical drawings

drawings, elevation
USE   elevations (drawings)

drawings, elevation oblique
USE   elevation oblique drawings

drawings, engineering
USE   technical drawings

drawings, erection
USE   erection drawings

drawings, exploded
USE   exploded drawings

drawings, facade oblique
USE   elevation oblique drawings

drawings, freehand
USE   freehand drawings

drawings, full-scale
USE   full-scale drawings

drawings, full-size
USE   full-scale drawings

drawings, general oblique
USE   general oblique drawings

drawings, gesture
USE   gesture drawings

drawings, gouache
USE   gouaches

drawings, hard-line
USE   mechanical   drawings   (tool-aided
        drawings)

drawings, HVAC
USE   HVAC drawings

drawings, isometric
USE   isometric drawings

drawings, layout
USE   site plans

drawings, life
USE   life drawings

drawings, line
USE   line drawings

drawings, lines
USE   lines drawings

drawings, master
USE   master drawings

drawings, measured
USE   measured drawings

drawings, mechanical
USE   mechanical drawings (building sys-
        tems drawings)
        mechanical   drawings   (tool-aided
        drawings)

drawings, minor assembly
USE   minor assembly drawings

drawings, multiview
USE   multiview drawings

drawings, oblique
USE   oblique drawings

drawings of record
USE   record drawings

drawings, old master
USE   master drawings

drawings, operational
USE   construction drawings

drawings, orthogonal
USE   orthographic drawings

drawings, orthographic
USE   orthographic drawings

drawings, outline
USE   outline drawings

drawings, paraline
USE   axonometric drawings

drawings, pastel
USE   pastels (visual works)

drawings, pattern
USE   pattern drawings

drawings, perspective
USE   perspective drawings

drawings, photogenic
USE   photogenic drawings

drawings, pictorial
USE   pictorial drawings

drawings, plan
USE   plans (drawings)

drawings, plan oblique
USE   plan oblique drawings

drawings, planometric
USE   plan oblique drawings

drawings, plumbing
USE   plumbing drawings

drawings, preliminary
USE   preliminary drawings
        underdrawings

drawings, preparatory
USE   preparatory drawings

drawings, presentation
USE   presentation drawings (gifts)
        presentation drawings (proposals)

drawings, production
USE   working drawings

drawings, record
USE record drawings

drawings, rock
USE rock engravings
    rock paintings

drawings, scale
USE scale drawings

drawings, schematic
USE schematic drawings

drawings, section
USE sections

drawings, ships
USE ships plans

drawings, shop
USE shop drawings

drawings, single-view
USE pictorial drawings

drawings, standard detail
USE standard detail drawings

drawings, structural
USE structural drawings

drawings, student
USE student drawings

drawings, subassembly
USE subassembly drawings

drawings, subcomponent
USE subassembly drawings

drawings, subcontractors'
USE shop drawings

drawings, survey
USE measured drawings

drawings, technical
USE technical drawings

drawings, theoretical
USE theoretical drawings

drawings, thesis
USE student drawings

drawings, three-tone
USE three-tone drawings

drawings, tone
USE tone drawings

drawings, trimetric
USE trimetric drawings

drawings, value
USE tone drawings

drawings, wire frame
USE wireframe drawings

drawings, wireframe
USE wireframe drawings

drawings, working
USE working drawings

drawknives
TH.1476 (N)

ALT drawknife
SN Two-handled curved knives used in woodworking which are utilized by pulling them toward the user. (MEANS)
UF draft shaves
    drawshaves
    knives, shaving
    shaves, draft
    shaving knives

drawknives, backing
USE backing drawknives

drawknives, barking
USE barking drawknives

drawknives, heading
USE heading drawknives

drawknives, mast
USE mast drawknives

drawn glass
MT.294
HN March 1993 descriptor moved
SN Glass that is made by continuous drawing of the molten glass by a series of rolls on automatic machinery. (W)
UF glass, drawn

drawplates
TH.1200 (N)
HN April 1991 lead-in term added
ALT drawplate
SN Plates with holes through which wire is drawn and shaped. (HAND)
UF plates, wire
    wire plates
    wiredrawing dies

draws
USE gullies

drawshaves
USE drawknives

drays
TX.96 (N)
ALT dray
SN Heavy, two- or four-wheeled, horse-drawn freight carriers, generally without sides, having flat, level floors or loading beds, with or without springs; primarily for use by industry in and around cities; distinguished from horse-drawn trucks by having straight and level loading areas and rear wheels smaller than trucks so that they fall below the floor level to allow the hauling of large items.
UF drays, transfer
    transfer drays
RT horse-drawn vehicles
    trucks

drays, transfer
USE drays

dread
USE fear

dreadnoughts
USE battleships

dredgers (containers)
TQ.385 (N)
ALT dredger (container)
SN Cylindrical containers, often metal, with a close lid perforated with a number of coarse or fine holes for sprinkling flour, sugar, or spices especially when cooking. Typically undecorated, except for some horizontal molding, and often having one simple scroll or ring handle.
UF boxes, dredging
    boxes, drudging
    dredging boxes
    drudgers
    drudging boxes
RT casters (vessels)
    <condiment vessels>

dredgers (watercraft)
TX.452 (L,N)
ALT dredger (watercraft)
SN Use for vessels fitted with machinery for deepening or cleaning and improving waterways, especially harbors and river channels.
UF dredges

dredgers, clam
USE clam dredgers

dredgers, pounce
USE pounce pots

dredges
HN May 1993 descriptor deleted, made lead-in to **dredgers (watercraft)**

dredges
USE dredgers (watercraft)

dredging
KT.945 (L)
HN March 1991 alternate term added
ALT dredged
SN Digging or pulling out with a dredge, especially for the purpose of deepening a body of water, searching for foreign objects in a body of water, or for keeping waterways clean.

dredging boxes
USE dredgers (containers)

<dredging vessels>
TX.362

dreidels
TV.190 (L)
ALT dreidel
SN Four-sided tops with the Hebrew letters non, gimmel, hé, and shin one on each side and used in a children's game traditionally played during the Jewish festival of Hanukkah. (RHDEL2)

dress
BM.267 (H,L)
HN February 1993 descriptor added

SN Manner of dressing required by custom or etiquette for certain occasions or times of day.

dress, afternoon
USE afternoon dress

dress coats
USE tail coats

dress curtains
TC.310
ALT dress curtain
SN Narrow curtains fixed at the side of an opening, used purely for decoration as they do not have enough width to be drawn across to cover the intervening space.
UF curtains, dress

dress design
USE costume design
fashion design

dress designers
USE costume designers
fashion designers

dress, evening
USE evening dress

dress, fancy
USE fancy dress

dress-makers
SEE dressmakers

dress-making
SEE dressmaking

dress protectors
USE dress shields

dress shields
TE.646
ALT dress shield
SN Shaped pieces of absorbent and rubberized or plastic-coated materials often padded or occasionally filled with deodorizing herbs; attached to or placed inside a garment, as in the underarm of a dress or blouse, to prevent the garment from being soiled by perspiration.
UF dress protectors
protectors, dress
shields (dress shields)
shields, dress
RT <protective wear>

dress shirts
TE.68   (N)
ALT dress shirt
SN Men's or boys' shirts buttoning down the front and typically having long sleeves with barrel or french cuffs, and a soft or starched collar. Those worn for formal or semiformal wear usually have a stiff or pleated front fastened with studs.
UF shirts, dress

dress swords
TK.94

ALT dress sword
SN Light swords worn by European and American military officers as part of dress uniform, beginning in the 18th century.
UF swords, dress

dressed lumber
MT.3018
HN March 1992 descriptor moved
SN Lumber machined and surfaced at a mill. (PUTNAM)
UF lumber, dressed
lumber, surfaced
surfaced lumber

dressed stone
MT.941
HN April 1992 descriptor moved
SN Dimension stone with a smooth exposed face.
UF stone, dressed

dresser sets
USE toilet sets (dresser sets)

dressers (chests of drawers)
USE chests of drawers

dressers (cupboards)
TC.921
HN May 1993 related term added
January 1993 descriptor moved
May 1991 descriptor changed, was
dressers
May 1991 alternate term changed,
was **dresser**
ALT dresser (cupboard)
UF armoires dressoirs
dish dressers
dressers, dish
RT cupboards

dressers (leatherworkers)
HG.705
HN January 1993 alternate terms added
ALT dresser (leatherworker)
dresser's
dressers'
SN Persons that finish leather. (W)

dressers (sideboards)
USE sideboards

dressers, cheval
USE cheval dressers

dressers, corner dish
USE corner cupboards

dressers, dish
USE dressers (cupboards)

dressers, window
USE window dressers

dresses
TE.16   (H,L,N,R)
ALT dress
SN Main garments for women, children, or infants consisting of a bodice and skirt made in one or more pieces.

RT bodices
skirts

dresses, after-five
USE cocktail dresses

<dresses by form>
TE.17

<dresses by function>
TE.27

dresses, chemise
USE chemise dresses

dresses, coat
USE coatdresses

dresses, cocktail
USE cocktail dresses

dresses, evening
USE evening dresses

dresses, night
SEE nightgowns

dresses, pinafore
SEE jumpers (dresses)

dresses, sheath
USE sheath dresses

dressing (leather)
KT.1046   (L)
HN January 1993 descriptor moved
June 1992 scope note added
ALT dressed
SN Processes that follow the tanning or tawing of hide or skin in order to modify it to meet specific needs.

dressing, alum
USE tawing

dressing boxes
USE dressing cases

dressing bureaux
USE dressing tables

dressing cases
TQ.194
ALT dressing case
SN Boxes fitted with drawers, trays, or partitions and usually a mirror; intended for toilet articles and sometimes writing materials, especially for travel.
UF boxes, dressing
cases, dressing
cases, toilet
dressing boxes
toilet cases
RT boxes (containers)

dressing chairs
TC.608
HN January 1993 descriptor moved
ALT dressing chair
UF chairs, dressing

dressing chests
USE   chests of drawers

dressing chests, French commode
USE   commode dressing tables

dressing chests, Rudd
USE   Rudd dressing chests

dressing drawers
    PJ.2776
HN   March 1993 descriptor moved
ALT   dressing drawer
SN   Term used by Hepplewhite for a specially designed top drawer equipped with compartments for such items as combs, powders, and essences. (MONTGO)
UF   drawers, dressing

dressing glasses
    TC.1477   (N)
ALT   dressing glass
SN   Small freestanding mirrors, usually supported on a standing frame within which the glass can be adjusted, designed to be used on a dressing table; sometimes made with a boxlike base fitted with small drawers.
UF   dressing looking glasses
    dressing mirrors
    dressing table mirrors
    glasses, dressing
    glasses, toilet
    looking glasses, dressing
    mirrors, dressing
    mirrors, dressing table
    mirrors, standing
    mirrors, toilet
    standing mirrors
    swingers (looking glasses)
    toilet glasses
    toilet mirrors
RT   dressing tables

dressing glasses, horse
USE   cheval glasses

dressing glasses, screen
USE   cheval glasses

dressing-gowns
SEE   dressing gowns

dressing gowns
    TE.263   (H,N)
ALT   dressing gown
UK   dressing-gowns
UKA   dressing-gown
SN   Loose, informal garments worn when partly or fully undressed, generally warm and often full-length with a rope belt. (CDC)
UF   gowns, dressing
RT   gowns

dressing jackets
    TE.264   (N)
ALT   dressing jacket
SN   Hip- to knee-length garments made in jacket or mantle form, worn while dressing.

UF   combing jackets
    dressing sacks
    dressing sacques
    jackets, combing
    jackets, dressing
    jackets, tea
    matinees
    nightingales
    sacks, dressing
    sacques, dressing
    tea jackets
RT   jackets

dressing looking glasses
USE   dressing glasses

dressing mirrors
USE   dressing glasses

dressing mirrors, cheval
USE   cheval glasses

dressing, oil
USE   fat-liquoring
    oil tanning

dressing rooms
    PJ.1005   (A,H,B)
HN   March 1993 descriptor moved
ALT   dressing room
UF   changing rooms
    rooms, changing
    rooms, dressing

dressing sacks
USE   dressing jackets

dressing sacques
USE   dressing jackets

dressing stands
    TC.1049
HN   January 1993 descriptor moved
ALT   dressing stand
UF   stands, dressing

dressing stands, ladies'
USE   ladies' dressing stands

dressing stools
    TC.685
HN   January 1993 descriptor moved
ALT   dressing stool
SN   Stools designed as seats at dressing tables; introduced in the 18th century.
UF   stools, dressing
    stools, vanity
    vanity stools

dressing table mirrors
USE   dressing glasses

dressing tables
    TC.1139   (H,N)
HN   May 1993 related terms added
    January 1993 descriptor moved
ALT   dressing table
SN   Generally applied to a variety of tables used for dressing, usually fitted with a mirror and having drawers to hold toilet articles such as brushes and combs.
UF   bureaux, dressing

    dressing bureaux
    tables, dressing
    tables, toilet
    toilet tables
    vanities
RT   bureau tables
    bureaux Mazarins
    dressing glasses
    kidney tables

dressing tables and desks, combined
USE   bureau tables

dressing tables, Beau-Brummel
USE   Beau-Brummel dressing tables

dressing tables, bureau
USE   bureau tables

dressing tables, commode
USE   commode dressing tables

dressing tables, gentlemen's
USE   gentlemen's dressing tables

dressing tables, ladies'
USE   ladies' dressing tables

dressing tables, ladies' cabinet
USE   ladies' cabinet dressing tables

dressing tables, reflecting
USE   Rudd tables

dressing tables, Rudd
USE   Rudd tables

dressmakers
    HG.756   (L)
HN   April 1993 related term added
    December 1992 alternate terms added
ALT   dressmaker
    dressmaker's
    dressmakers'
UK   dress-makers
UKA   dress-maker
RT   dressmaking

dressmaking
    KT.792   (L)
HN   May 1993 related term added
UK   dress-making
RT   dressmakers

drier
    MT.1691   (L)
HN   April 1993 descriptor changed, was **driers**
    April 1993 lead-in term changed, was **siccatives**
SN   Material, often a compound of lead, iron, manganese, or cobalt, used for increasing the rapidity of the drying of paint and varnish. (MH)
UF   siccative

driers
USE   dryers

drift, continental
USE   continental drift

drift pins
USE   driftpins

drift punches
TH.1214 (N)
ALT drift punch
SN Tapered punches used to align holes for bolting and riveting.
UF aligning punches
punches, aligning
punches, drift

driftpins
PJ.219 (N)
HN April 1993 descriptor moved
ALT driftpin
SN Tapered pins used in steel erection to align holes for bolting or riveting. (MEANS)
UF drift pins
pins, drift

drifts
TH.1201
HN March 1993 descriptor changed, was **drifts (metalworking tools)**
March 1993 alternate term changed, was **drift (metalworking tool)**
ALT drift
SN Tools similar to punches; used to open up punched holes, smoothing and shaping them at the same time. (ALMEID)

driftwood
MT.3001
HN March 1992 descriptor moved

drill ammunition
TK.274
SN Inert cartridges containing no explosive components, used in the armed forces for practice loading and manipulation of firearms. (HOGGAM)
UF ammunition, drill
ammunition, dummy
cartridges, drill
drill cartridges
drill rounds
dummy ammunition
rounds, drill

drill bits
USE bits (tool components)

drill braces
USE hand drills

drill cartridges
USE drill ammunition

drill clamps
TH.636
ALT drill clamp
SN Clamp-shaped tools used to put pressure on a drill when boring through metal.
UF clamp drills
clamps, drill
drills, clamp
drills, smiths'
smiths' drills

drill halls
RK.836 (A,B)

ALT drill hall
UF halls, drill

drill presses
TH.589 (L,N)
ALT drill press
SN Rotary drills, mounted on a permanent stand, that operate along a vertical shaft. (MEANS)
UF presses, drill

drill rounds
USE drill ammunition

drill-work
SEE drillwork

drill work
USE drillwork

drillers
HG.823 (L)
HN December 1992 alternate terms added
ALT driller
driller's
drillers'

drilling
KT.946 (L,B)
ALT drilled
SN Use for the making of holes in metal, wood, or other materials, and for making holes in the earth, as for drilling a well or for oil.
UF boring

drilling (sculpture technique)
USE drillwork

<drilling equipment>
TH.586

drilling machinery
TH.587 (L)
UF machinery, drilling

drilling platforms, offshore
USE offshore drilling platforms

drilling rigs
RK.570
ALT drilling rig
UF rigs, drilling

<drilling structures>
RK.569

<drilling tools>
TH.590

drills
TH.591 (N)
ALT drill
SN Large machines or hand tools used for making holes in a variety of materials.

drills, air
USE pneumatic drills

drills, automatic
USE push drills

drills, barrel
USE barrel drills

drills, bow
USE bow drills

drills, breast
USE breast drills

<drills by form>
TH.592

<drills by mode of operation>
TH.600

drills, clamp
USE drill clamps

drills, corner
USE hand drills

drills, electric
USE electric drills

drills, electric-portable
USE electric drills

drills, fiddle
USE bow drills

drills, gimlet
USE gimlets

drills, hammer
USE hammer drills

drills, hand
USE hand drills

drills, percussion
USE jackhammers

drills, percussive
USE jackhammers

drills, plugging
USE plugging chisels

drills, pneumatic
USE pneumatic drills

drills, pump
USE pump drills

drills, push
USE push drills

drills, reciprocating
USE push drills

drills, smiths'
USE drill clamps

drills, star
USE plugging chisels

<drills: stone and masonry working equipment>
TH.1344
HN December 1992 guide term moved
December 1992 guide term changed, was *<drills: masonry and plastering tools>*

drills, thong
USE bow drills

drills, twist
USE twist drills

drillwork
KT.916
HN January 1993 descriptor moved
November 1990 descriptor added
UK drill-work
UF drill work
drilling (sculpture technique)
work, drill

drink stands
USE drinking stands

drink tables
USE drinking tables

drinking cups
USE cups

drinking fountains
PJ.911   (A,L,N,B)
HN March 1993 descriptor moved
February 1991 scope note added
ALT drinking fountain
SN Plumbing fixtures consisting of a
water jet and often a shallow basin
designed to provide potable water
for human consumption. (DAC)
UF fountains, drinking

drinking glasses
TQ.424   (H,L,N,R)
ALT drinking glass
SN Vessels intended for an individual to
use for drinking wine, water, or
other beverage.
UF glasses (drinking glasses)
glasses, drinking
RT stemware

drinking horns
TQ.458   (L,N,R)
ALT drinking horn
SN Drinking vessels made of horn, es-
pecially those elaborately mounted
in bronze or silver. (CHAES)
UF horns, drinking

drinking stands
TC.1052
HN January 1993 descriptor moved
ALT drinking stand
SN Stands fitted for bottles and glasses.
(MONTGO)
UF drink stands
social tables
stands, drinking
tables, social
tables, toddy
tables, wine
toddy tables
wine tables

drinking tables
TC.1157
HN January 1993 descriptor moved
ALT drinking table
SN Small plank top tables supported on
a triangular frame with three legs.
(COMMFR)
UF drink tables
tables, drinking

drinking tables (slab tables)
USE slab tables

drinking vessels
TQ.386   (H,L,R)
ALT drinking vessel
SN Vessels used for drinking liquids.
RT chalices
communion cups
loving cups
nefs
phialae
rhyta

drinking water
MT.983   (L)
HN April 1992 descriptor moved
UF potable water
water, drinking
water, potable

drip and pour technique
USE drip painting

drip catchers
USE bobeches

drip painting
KT.420
HN July 1990 scope note changed
July 1990 lead-in terms added
July 1990 lead-in term deleted, was
dripping
SN Use for the technique of creating
paintings by dripping or pouring
paint in a semi-controlled manner
onto the support.
UF drip and pour technique
drip technique
painting, drip

drip pans
USE bobeches
dripping pans

drip technique
USE drip painting

dripping pans
TQ.298
ALT dripping pan
SN Shallow metal pans used under
roasting meats to catch the drip-
pings. (RHDEL2)
UF drip pans
pans, drip
pans, dripping
RT pans (containers)

dripstones
USE hood moldings

drive anchors
PJ.27
HN April 1993 descriptor moved
ALT drive anchor
UF anchors, drive

drive-in banks
RK.132   (A,B)
ALT drive-in bank
UF banks, drive-in
drive-through banks

drive-in cinemas
USE drive-in theaters

drive-in restaurants
RK.119   (B)
ALT drive-in restaurant
UF drive-ins
restaurants, drive-in

drive-in theaters
RK.895   (A,L,B)
HN September 1990 scope note added
September 1990 lead-in term added
ALT drive-in theater
SN Designates outdoor movie theaters
designed to accommodate patrons
viewing from their automobiles.
UF cinemas, drive-in
drive-in cinemas
drive-ins
theaters, drive-in

drive-ins
USE drive-in restaurants
drive-in theaters

drive screws
USE drivescrews

drive-through banks
USE drive-in banks

drive type hangers
PJ.94
HN April 1993 descriptor moved
ALT drive type hanger
UF hangers, drive type

driven piles
PJ.1534
HN March 1993 descriptor moved
ALT driven pile
SN Use for piles driven into position at
the site.
UF piles, driven

driven wells
RK.566   (L)
ALT driven well
UF tube wells
wells, driven
wells, tube

drivers, pile
USE pile drivers

drivers, stud
USE stud drivers

drives
USE driveways

drives, data tape
USE tape drives

drives, disk
USE disk drives

drives, tape
USE tape drives

drivescrew nails
USE drivescrews

drivescrews
PJ.183
HN April 1993 descriptor moved
ALT drivescrew
SN Screws that are driven with a hammer and removed with a screw-
driver. (MEANS)
UF drive screws
drivescrew nails
nails, screw
screw nails
screws, drive

driveway lights
TC.1363
ALT driveway light
UF lights, driveway

driveways
RM.160   (A,L,B)
HN April 1993 descriptor moved
ALT driveway
UF drives

driving
KQ.3   (L)

driving machines
HN February 1991 descriptor deleted

driving, pile
USE pile driving

driving punches
USE nail sets

driving ranges
RM.98   (A)
HN April 1993 descriptor moved
ALT driving range
SN Areas equipped with distance mark-
ers, clubs, balls, and tees for practic-
ing golf drives. (W)
UF driving ranges, golf
golf driving ranges
ranges, driving

driving ranges, golf
USE driving ranges

drôleries
USE drolleries

drolleries
DG.30
ALT drollery
SN Humorous designs in the margins
of Medieval manuscripts or in in-
conspicuous parts of wood or stone
carving in Medieval buildings.
(THDAT)
UF drôleries

dromoi
PJ.1331
HN March 1993 descriptor moved
ALT dromos
SN Long, narrow passages leading into
chamber tombs and tholoi.

dromons
TX.434
ALT dromon
SN Use for large, Byzantine two-banked

galleys, with one or two sails and
usually equipped with flamethrow-
ers for use with Greek fire.
RT galleys (watercraft)

drone pipes
PJ.3241
ALT drone pipe
SN Use for pipes that are constituent
parts of other aerophones, have no
fingerholes, and are used to sustain
single notes.
UF drones
pipes, drone
RT arghuls
bagpipes

drone strings
PJ.3256
ALT drone string
SN Strings which produce a single low
tone when played.
UF drones
strings, drone
RT épinettes des Vosges
hurdy-gurdies
liras da braccio
sarods

drones
USE drone pipes
drone strings

droop cups
TQ.464
ALT droop cup
SN Kylikes with a handle zone decorated with a chain of buds, the next
zone usually decorated with upside
down silhouettes of animals or other
figures, and the base of the bowl
decorated with rays and separated
from the zone above by stripes.
UF cups, droop

drop arches
PJ.1590
HN March 1993 descriptor moved
November 1991 lead-in terms
added
February 1991 descriptor moved
February 1991 scope note changed
ALT drop arch
SN Use for pointed arches whose radii
are located within the span of the
arch, whether or not the centers are
above, at, or below the springing.
UF angle arches, obtuse
arches, blunt
arches, depressed
arches, drop
arches, obtuse angle
blunt arches
depressed arches
obtuse angle arches

drop black
USE bone black
vine black

drop burners
PJ.2924

ALT drop burner
SN Metallic discs perforated by one or
two wick tubes, which rest on the
opening into the font; such burners
often have a small tab on the edge
by which they can be lifted.
UF burners, drop

drop ceilings
USE suspended ceilings

drop chutes
TH.1124
ALT drop chute
UF chutes, drop

drop curtains
TC.321
ALT drop curtain
SN Stage curtains that are lowered in-
stead of drawn. (W)
UF curtains, drop

drop drawer pulls
USE drop pulls

drop escutcheons
PJ.441
HN April 1993 descriptor moved
ALT drop escutcheon
SN Key plates with a pivoting pendant
attached that drops to cover the keyhole. (DITTRI)
UF drop key plates
escutcheons, drop
key plates, drop
plates, drop key

drop forges
USE drop hammers

drop-front cabinets
USE fall-front desks

drop-front desks
USE fall-front desks

drop-front secrétaires
USE secrétaires à abattant

drop hammers
TH.1019   (N)
ALT drop hammer
SN Heavy weights for driving piles into
the ground; dropped by gravity
along a set of guide rails onto the
head of the pile. (DAC)
UF board hammers
drop forges
forges, drop
hammers, board
hammers, drop

drop handles
USE drop pulls

drop handles, pear
USE pear drop handles

drop hangers
PJ.111
HN April 1993 descriptor moved
ALT drop hanger
UF hangers, drop

drop-in seats
USE slip seats

drop key plates
USE drop escutcheons

drop keys
PJ.600
HN March 1993 descriptor moved
ALT drop key
SN Keys having a bow or handle pivoted to the shank so that it may drop or fall parallel with the surface of the door. (STEIN)
UF keys, drop

drop moldings
PJ.2122
HN April 1993 descriptor moved
ALT drop molding
SN Panel moldings recessed below the surface of the surrounding stiles and rails. (DAC)
UF moldings, drop

drop ornament
USE drops

drop panels
PJ.1408
HN March 1993 descriptor moved
ALT drop panel
SN The structural portion of a flat slab which is thickened (by lowering the form) throughout an area surrounding a column, column capital, or bracket. (PUTNAM)
UF panels, drop

drop pigment
MT.2303
HN April 1992 descriptor moved
UF pigment, drop

drop pulls
PJ.350
HN April 1993 descriptor moved
ALT drop pull
SN In furniture making, any type of handle, or drawer pull, which hangs like a pendant. (PUTNAM)
UF drawer pulls, drop
    drop drawer pulls
    drop handles
    handles, drop
    pulls, drop

drop testers
PJ.2753
HN March 1993 descriptor moved
ALT drop tester
SN Folding testers, such as those found on a press bed. (GILBR2)
UF testers, drop

drop tracery
PJ.2331
HN March 1993 descriptor moved
    February 1991 scope note changed
SN Tracery hanging from the intrados of an arch. (HAS)
UF tracery, drop

dropleaf tables
TC.1079   (N)
HN January 1993 descriptor moved
ALT dropleaf table
SN Generic term for various types of space-saving tables with leaves hinged to the top so that they can be raised to extend the surface. (DDA)
UF fall-leaf tables
    flap tables
    tables à abattant
    tables, dropleaf
    tables, fall-leaf
    tables, flap

dropout
DL.31
HN February 1993 descriptor added
SN An area of a halftone image in which dots are eliminated, thus printing white.
UF dropout halftone
    dropouts
    halftone, dropout
    halftone, highlight
    highlight halftone

dropout halftone
USE dropout

dropouts
USE dropout

dropped seats
USE hollowed seats

drops
PJ.2359
HN March 1993 descriptor moved
ALT drop
SN Use for pendant ornament, such as on a furniture apron or rail, or within an arch and more loosely hanging than drop tracery.
UF drop ornament
    ornament, drop

drops (prisms)
USE prisms

drops, newel
USE newel drops

droshkies
TX.173   (N)
ALT droshky
SN Use for four-wheeled carriages of simple construction in which passengers sit astride a narrow bench extending between axles; found primarily in Russia.

drosometers
TN.135   (N)
ALT drosometer
SN Instruments used to measure the amount of dew formed on a given surface. (STEIN)

drought
BM.741   (L,B)

HN March 1993 scope note added
    November 1992 descriptor moved
SN A period of abnormally dry weather sufficiently prolonged that a serious hydraulic imbalance occurs, such as crop damage or reduced water supply.

drought-resistant gardens
USE xeriscapes

drought-tolerant gardens
USE xeriscapes

drudgers
USE dredgers (containers)

drudging boxes
USE dredgers (containers)

drug abuse
BM.992   (L)
HN February 1993 descriptor moved
    January 1991 descriptor added
SN Excessive use or misuse of drugs, causing physical, emotional, mental, or sensory injury or impairment. For addiction to narcotics or other drugs, use **drug addiction**. (ERIC9)
UF abuse, drug
RT drug addiction

drug addiction
BM.568   (L)
HN January 1991 descriptor added
SN Addiction to narcotics or other drugs. For excessive use or misuse of drugs, use **drug abuse**.
UF addiction, drug
    addiction, narcotic
    dependency, drug
    dependency, narcotics
    drug dependence
    habit, narcotic
    narcotic dependence
    narcotic habit
    narcotics addiction
RT drug abuse

drug addicts
HG.993   (L)
HN January 1993 alternate terms added
    January 1991 descriptor added
ALT drug addict
    drug addict's
    drug addicts'
SN Those who are addicted to narcotics or other drugs.
UF addicts, dope
    addicts, drug
    addicts, narcotic
    dope addicts
    narcotic addicts

drug dependence
USE drug addiction

druggets
TC.364   (N)
ALT drugget
SN Use for coarse textiles which were used as inexpensive floor coverings by themselves or on top of a carpet.

UF druggets, milled
milled druggets

druggets, milled
USE druggets

druggists
USE pharmacists

druggists' scales
USE prescription scales

drugstores
RK.160   (A,L,B,R)
HN March 1993 lead-in term changed,
was **chemist's shops**
March 1993 lead-in term changed,
was **shops, chemist's**
ALT drugstore
UF apothecaries
chemists' shops
pharmacies
shops, chemists'

druid stone
USE sarsen

<drum components>
PJ.3268
RT drums (membranophones)

drum players
USE drummers

drum sanders
USE sanding disks

drum scales
USE cylinder scales

drum skins
USE drumheads

drum sticks
USE drumsticks

drum tables
USE capstan tables
rent tables

drumheads
PJ.3269
ALT drumhead
SN Membranes stretched over the
frames or shells of drums and
sounded by being rubbed, plucked,
or, most commonly, struck with the
hands or beaters. (MARCUS)
UF drum skins
heads (drumheads)
heads, playing
playing heads
skins
skins, drum

drumlins
RD.151   (L)
ALT drumlin
SN Use for long, smooth, cigar-shaped
hills of glacial origin.

drummers
HG.241   (L)
HN January 1993 descriptor added
ALT drummer

drummer's
drummers'
SN Those who play the drum.
(RHDEL2)
UF drum players
players, drum
RT drums (membranophones)

drums (column components)
PJ.1519
HN March 1993 descriptor moved
April 1991 scope note changed
ALT drum (column component)
SN Use for the cylinders of stone which
form the shaft of a column.

drums (membranophones)
TT.563   (L,N,R)
ALT drum (membranophone)
SN Membranophones with a resonating
cavity covered at one or both ends
by a membrane which is sounded by
striking, rubbing, or plucking.
RT <drum components>
drummers
drumsticks

drums (walls)
PJ.1924
HN March 1993 descriptor moved
ALT drum (wall)
SN The vertical wall, circular or polygo-
nal in plan, which carries a dome.

drums, barrel
USE barrel drums

drums, barrel-shaped
USE barrel drums

drums, bass
USE bass drums

drums, biconical
USE double-conical drums

drums, bongo
USE bongos

drums, double-conical
USE double-conical drums

drums, field
USE snare drums

drums, footed
USE footed drums

drums, frame
USE frame drums

drums, friction
USE friction drums

drums, goblet
USE goblet drums

drums, gong
USE gong drums

drums, gong bass
USE gong drums

drums, ground
USE ground drums

drums, hourglass
USE hourglass drums

drums, hourglass pressure
USE hourglass pressure drums

drums, log
USE slit drums

drums, machine
USE machine drums

drums, metal
USE kettle gongs

drums, plucked
USE plucked drums

drums, pot
USE pot drums

drums, pressure
USE hourglass pressure drums

drums, rattle
USE rattle drums

drums, side
USE snare drums

drums, slit
USE slit drums

drums, snare
USE snare drums

drums, steel
USE steel drums

drums, talking
USE talking drums

drums, tension
USE hourglass pressure drums

drums, tubular
USE tubular drums

drums, Uganda
USE Uganda drums

drums, variable tension
USE hourglass pressure drums

drums, waisted
USE hourglass drums

drums, water
USE water drums

drumsticks
PJ.3274   (N)
ALT drumstick
SN Sticks, usually of wood, either padded with fabric or some other soft
material on one end or plain, used
to strike drums.
UF drum sticks
sticks (drumsticks)
sticks, drum
RT drums (membranophones)

drunken saws
TH.1573
ALT drunken saw.
SN Circular saws designed to operate
with a built-in wobble so that the

kerf it makes is greater than the thickness of the saw; used for grooving and for other special purposes in carpentry. (MEANS)
UF saws, drunken
    saws, wobble
    wobble saws

dry-air filters
USE dry filters

dry-brush painting
KT.421
SN The technique of creating a broken or mottled effect with paint or ink on a relatively dry brush, allowing traces of the paper or underpainting to show through. (MAYER)
UF painting, dry-brush

dry cleaning
KT.925   (L,B)
HN November 1992 descriptor added
ALT dry-cleaned
SN Any of various nonaqueous cleaning methods such as the removal of surface dirt by brushing, using appropriate erasers on paper, or the use of nonaqueous organic solvents on fabrics.
UF cleaning, dry

dry collodion glass negatives
USE dry collodion negatives

dry collodion negatives
VC.294
HN March 1993 descriptor added
ALT dry collodion negative
SN Use for negatives produced by the dry collodion process.
UF collodion dry plate photonegatives
    collodion dry plates
    collodion negatives
    collodion negatives, dry
    collodion photonegatives
    dry collodion glass negatives
    dry collodion plates
    dry plate negatives
    dry plate photonegatives
    dry plates, collodion
    glass negatives, dry collodion
    negatives, collodion
    negatives, collodion dry plate
    negatives, dry collodion
    negatives, dry plate
    plates, collodion dry

dry collodion plates
USE dry collodion negatives

dry collodion process
KT.512
SN A type of collodion process in which the binder was dried before exposure or contained a hygroscopic agent to retain sufficient moisture to allow processing after an extended period of time; an improvement on the wet collodion process because it alleviated the need for a portable

darkroom. Used to produce negatives and lantern slides.
UF collodion dry-plate process
    dry plate process (collodion)

dry color
MT.2304
HN April 1992 descriptor moved
UK dry colour
UF color, dry
    colour, dry
    pigment, powdered
    powdered pigment

dry colour
SEE dry color

dry construction
USE drywall construction

dry diazo process
USE ammonia process

dry docks
RK.1257   (A,L,B)
ALT dry dock
UF docks, dry
    docks, graving
    graving docks

dry docks, floating
USE floating docks

dry filters
PJ.816
HN March 1993 descriptor moved
ALT dry filter
SN Devices for removing pollutants from the air in a system by passing it through various screens and dry porous materials. (MEANS)
UF dry-air filters
    dry-type filters
    filters, dry
    filters, dry-air
    filters, dry-type

dry fresco
USE secco

dry kilns
TH.505
ALT dry kiln
SN Ovens for drying and seasoning cut lumber. (DAC)
UF kilns, dry

dry lumber
USE air-dried lumber

dry masonry
USE dry walls

dry mortar
MT.2344
SN In masonry, mortar which contains enough moisture to cause it to set properly but is not wet enough to cause it to be sticky. (PUTNAM)
UF mortar, dry

dry mounting
KT.903
ALT dry-mounted

SN Attaching a drawing, print, photograph, or other work of art done on paper to a cardboard or other backing by using a thermoplastic tissue as an adhesive.
UF mounting, dry

dry-mounting tissue
USE mounting tissue

dry mustard jars
USE mustard casters

dry plate, gelatin
USE gelatin dry plate process

dry plate negatives
USE dry collodion negatives

dry plate negatives, gelatin
USE gelatin dry plate negatives

dry plate photonegatives
USE dry collodion negatives

dry plate process (collodion)
USE dry collodion process

dry plate process (gelatin)
USE gelatin dry plate process

dry plate, silver gelatin
USE gelatin dry plate process

dry plates, collodion
USE dry collodion negatives

dry-points
SEE drypoints

dry rot
DE.54   (L,B)
HN November 1992 descriptor moved
    December 1990 descriptor added
SN Use for a type of decomposition of timber by fungi.
UF rot, dry

dry sgraffito
KT.722
SN The technique of scratching designs or images into a dry plaster surface which has been covered with a thin or moderately thick lime wash layer. (WEHLTE)
UF sgraffito, dry

dry sinks
TC.922
HN January 1993 descriptor moved
ALT dry sink
SN Wooden kitchen sinks, especially of the 19th century, not connected to an external water supply, with a shallow zinc or tin-lined well on top in which a dishpan can be placed, and usually a cupboard below. (RHDEL2)
UF sinks, dry

dry stone walls
USE dry walls

dry-type filters
USE dry filters

dry wall
USE   wallboard

dry walls
PJ.1906   (B)
HN   March 1993 descriptor moved
January 1992 lead-in terms added
January 1992 descriptor changed,
was **dry laid walls**
January 1992 lead-in term deleted,
was **walls, dry laid**
January 1992 alternate term
changed, was **dry laid wall**
ALT   dry wall
SN   Masonry walls constructed without
mortar.
UF   dry masonry
dry stone walls
masonry, dry
mortarless walls
walls, dry
walls, dry stone
walls, mortarless

dry wood
USE   air-dried lumber

dryers
TH.491   (L,N)
HN   April 1991 lead-in term added
ALT   dryer
UF   apparatus, drying
driers
drying apparatus

dryers (film)
USE   film dryers

dryers, blow
USE   blow dryers

dryers, corn
USE   corn dryers

dryers, film
USE   film dryers

dryers, hair
USE   hair dryers

dryers, herb
USE   corn dryers

dryers, print
USE   print dryers

drying
KT.834   (A,L)
HN   January 1993 descriptor moved
October 1992 scope note added
ALT   dried
SN   Making free or nearly free of liq-
uids. For the removal or deprivation
of water, though other liquids may
remain, use **dehydration.**

drying apparatus
USE   dryers

drying cabinets
USE   print dryers

drying cracking
USE   traction crackle

drying cracks
USE   traction crackle

drying oil
MT.1121   (L)
HN   April 1992 descriptor moved
SN   Any oil that will solidify to a tough,
leathery film when spread out in
thin layers, either alone or with the
assistance of a drier. (MAYER)
UF   oil, drying
oil, paint
paint oil

drying racks
USE   clotheshorses
drying trays

drying sheds
RK.1156
ALT   drying shed
SN   Use for structures of various designs
erected to aid in the drying by flow-
ing air of, for example, paper and
textiles.
UF   sheds, drying

drying trays
TQ.274   (H,N)
ALT   drying tray
UF   baskets, food drying
baskets, fruit-drying
drying racks
food drying baskets
fruit-drying baskets
fruit-drying platters
fruit-drying trays
platters, fruit-drying
racks, drying
trays, drying
trays, fruit-drying
RT   trays

dryness
DC.249
HN   November 1992 descriptor added
ALT   dry
SN   The state or condition of having low
moisture content.

drypoint
KT.674   (L,R)
HN   October 1991 descriptor moved
SN   Intaglio process in which a sharp
needle scratches the plate creating a
burr that yields a characteristically
soft and velvety line in the final
print. (SAFF)

drypoints
VC.464   (R)
ALT   drypoint
UK   dry-points
UKA   dry-point
SN   Prints made using the drypoint
process.

drywall
USE   wallboard

drywall (construction)
USE   drywall construction

drywall construction
KT.15   (L)
HN   January 1993 descriptor moved
SN   Use for a construction technique
that employs dry materials such as
wallboard, plywood, or other prefabricated materials, without the use
of plaster or mortar. (DAC)
UF   construction, drywall
dry construction
drywall (construction)

DTA
USE   differential thermal analysis

DTR
USE   diffusion transfer reversal

dual highways
USE   divided highways

dual-pitched roofs
USE   curb roofs

dual spectrum process
KT.375
HN   March 1993 descriptor added
SN   Copying process that uses visible
light from one band of the electromagnetic spectrum to form a latent
image and infrared radiation to
make the image visible on the copy
paper. (CMM)

Duala
FL.424   (L)

dualism
BM.422   (L)
HN   January 1991 alternate term added
ALT   dualistic
SN   Doctrine that the universe is under
the dominion of two opposing prin-
ciples, one of which is good and the
other evil. (WCOL9)

dubbing adzes
USE   lipped adzes

ducal palaces
RK.345
ALT   ducal palace
SN   Use for the official residences of
sovereigns bearing the title of duke.
UF   palaces, ducal

ducato d'oro
USE   ducats

ducats
VK.78   (L)
ALT   ducat
SN   Use only for gold coins struck in
Venice from the late 13th through
the 19th century and for similar
Austrian and Czechoslovakian coins
issued in the early 20th century.
UF   ducato d'oro
sequins
zecchinos

duchesse
MT.1579
HN   December 1992 descriptor added

SN Type of bobbin lace without a mesh ground made in Belgium in the second half of the 19th century.
UF duchesse lace
Duchesse, point
lace, duchesse
point Duchesse

duchesse beds
USE lits à la duchesse

duchesse lace
USE duchesse

Duchesse, point
USE duchesse

duchesses (aristocrats)
HG.999
HN February 1993 descriptor moved
February 1993 descriptor changed, was **duchesses (people)**
January 1993 alternate terms added
ALT duchess (aristocrat)
duchesses'
duchess's

duchesses (chaise longues)
TC.478
HN January 1993 descriptor moved
May 1991 descriptor changed, was **duchesses**
May 1991 alternate term changed, was **duchesse**
ALT duchesse (chaise longue)
SN French chaise longues whose foot end is surrounded on three sides by a low curving back.

duchesses brisées
TC.479
HN January 1993 descriptor moved
ALT duchesse brisée
SN Duchesses made in two or three parts, each of which can be used separately as a seat.
UF duchesses en trois

duchesses en trois
USE duchesses brisées

duchies
HN.41   (L)
HN January 1993 descriptor added
ALT duchy
SN Administrative bodies subject to a duke or duchess.
UF dukedoms

duck
MT.1571   (L)
HN March 1993 scope note changed
March 1993 descriptor moved
SN Durable, closely woven textile of plain weave, made formerly of linen but now usually of cotton, made in various weights; very similar to canvas but finer and lighter. Common uses are for tents, belts, and clothing.

duck bill nails
PJ.184

HN April 1993 descriptor moved
ALT duck bill nail
UF nails, duck bill

duck-billed solerets
USE bear-paw sabatons

duck boats
USE gunning boats

duck feet
USE trifid feet

duckpin bowling
KQ.43   (L)
UF bowling, duckpin
duckpins

duckpins
USE duckpin bowling

Duco (TM)
USE lacquer

duct flutes
TT.24
ALT duct flute
SN Flutes in which the air stream is directed through a narrow duct against the sharp edge of a lateral aperture. (MARCUS)
UF flutes, duct
RT dvojnices

ductile iron
MT.350   (L)
HN March 1993 descriptor moved
UF iron, ductile
iron, nodular
nodular iron

ductility
DC.177   (L)
HN October 1992 descriptor moved
ALT ductile
SN The property of being permanently deformed by tension without rupture, that is, the ability to be drawn from a large to a small size. (MH)

ducts, air
USE air ducts

dudas
TT.191   (L)
ALT duda
SN Bellows-blown bagpipes of Hungary, Poland, the Ukraine, and Yugoslavia, with kidskin bag, a double melody pipe set in a stock carved to resemble a goat's head, and a bass drone pipe. (MARCUS)
UF bagpipes, Polish
dudy
Polish bagpipes

dude ranches
RG.178   (L)
ALT dude ranch
UF guest ranches
ranches, dude
ranches, guest

dudgeon-daggers
SEE ballock daggers

dudy
USE dudas

dueling gauntlets
TE.325
ALT dueling gauntlet
UK duelling gauntlets
UKA duelling gauntlet
SN Gauntlets worn by duelists, often reinforced over the palm by mail.
UF gauntlets, dueling
gauntlets, duelling

dueling pistols
TK.181   (N)
ALT dueling pistol
SN Pistols made expressly for formal personal combat, usually in pairs and furnished with a case, and generally characterized by high technical quality with only modest decoration. They commonly date from the late 18th to the mid-19th century.
UF pistols, dueling

duelling gauntlets
SEE dueling gauntlets

duels
KM.4   (H,L)
HN December 1992 descriptor added
ALT duel
SN Use for occurrences of prearranged combat between two people, fought with deadly weapons according to an accepted code or procedure, especially to settle a private quarrel. (RHDEL2)

Dufaycolor
KT.507
UF Dufay's screen plate process
screen plate process, Dufay's

Dufay's screen plate process
USE Dufaycolor

duffel bags
TQ.195   (N)
ALT duffel bag
SN Large cylindrical bags, often of canvas or rubberized fabric, used to carry personal belongings.
UF bags, duffel
RT traveling bags

duffs
TT.587   (L)
ALT duff
SN Use generally for single- or double-headed frame drums of the Near East, Central Asia, southern Europe, and parts of Africa, South Asia, and Latin America. The various types are round, square, or octagonal in shape, and may have jingles or snares.
UF daffs
daphs
dufuf

dufuf
USE duffs

dug-out chests
TC.879
HN January 1993 descriptor moved
ALT dug-out chest
UF chests, dug-out

dug-outs
SEE dugouts

dug wells
RK.567
ALT dug well
SN Wells excavated by hand tools or dredging machinery as distinguished from ones put down by drills or augers. (STEIN)
UF wells, dug

<dugout-based watercraft>
TX.503

dugout canoes
USE dugouts

dugouts
TX.502 (L,N)
ALT dugout
UK dug-outs
UKA dug-out
SN Use for simple watercraft constructed by hollowing out and carving a single log; found in cultures all over the world and developed at least during the Paleolithic era.
UF canoes, dugout
dugout canoes
logboats
monoxylons

<dugouts and dugout-based watercraft>
TX.501

dugouts, expanded
USE expanded dugouts

dugouts, extended
USE extended dugouts

dukedoms
USE duchies

dukes
HG.1000
HN February 1993 descriptor moved
December 1992 alternate terms added
ALT duke
duke's
dukes'

dulcians
TT.182 (N)
ALT dulcian
SN English reedpipes, well-known from the late 16th to the early 18th century and considered to be the precursor of the bassoon, having a body made of a single piece of wood with two parallel conical channels bored down and up within it, a slightly flared bell set on top of the

body, and a short crook carrying a double reed.
UF corthols
courthols
curtals
dolcians

dulcimers
TT.405 (L,N)
ALT dulcimer
SN Zitherlike chordophones with a box resonator and multiple strings but no keyboard, played by being struck with hammers.
UF hackbretts
haskbretts

dulcimers, American
USE Appalachian dulcimers

dulcimers, American hammer
USE hammer dulcimers

dulcimers, Appalachian
USE Appalachian dulcimers

dulcimers, hammer
USE hammer dulcimers

dulcimers, Kentucky
USE Appalachian dulcimers

dulcimers, mountain
USE Appalachian dulcimers

dull blackish green
USE dark grayish green

dull blue
USE blackish blue
dark bluish gray
dark grayish blue
deep blue
grayish blue
grayish purplish blue
light blue
moderate blue
pale blue
pale purplish blue
strong blue
very pale blue
very pale purplish blue

dull blue green black
USE blackish blue
bluish black
dark grayish blue

dull blue violet
USE brilliant violet
moderate violet
strong purplish blue
strong violet

dull bluish green
USE blackish green
dark grayish green
grayish green
pale green
very pale green

dull bluish red
USE dark purplish red

moderate purplish red
very dark purplish red

dull bluish violet
USE blackish purple
brilliant violet
dark grayish purple
grayish violet
light violet
moderate violet
pale purple
pale violet
strong violet
very pale purple
very pale violet

dull bluish violet, dark
USE dark purple

dull bluish violet, deep
USE grayish purplish blue

dull bluish violet, light
USE light violet

dull brown
USE brownish pink
dark grayish brown
grayish brown
light grayish brown

dull brownish olive
USE dark olive brown

dull buff
USE grayish yellowish pink
moderate orange yellow
pale orange yellow
pale yellowish pink

dull dark purple
USE deep reddish purple
strong reddish purple

dull gold
USE light olive
light olive brown
moderate olive

dull green
USE blackish green
dark grayish green
dark yellowish green
grayish green
grayish olive green
light bluish green
light green
light yellowish green
pale green
very pale green

dull greenish black
USE dark gray
dark greenish gray

dull greenish blue
USE blackish blue
dark grayish blue
grayish blue
pale blue
very pale blue

dull greenish yellow
USE grayish greenish yellow

light olive
pale greenish yellow

dull lavender
USE grayish purplish pink

dull lilac
USE grayish purplish red
moderate violet
pale purple

dull magenta purple
USE strong reddish purple

dull orange
USE moderate yellowish pink

dull red
USE dark red
deep reddish brown
grayish red
moderate red
moderate reddish brown
strong reddish orange
very dark red

dull reddish blue
USE blackish blue
dark grayish blue
grayish blue
grayish purplish blue
pale blue
pale purplish blue
very pale blue
very pale purplish blue

dull reddish brown
USE blackish red
dark grayish red
dark grayish reddish brown
dark red
dark reddish brown
grayish red
grayish reddish brown
light grayish reddish brown
light reddish brown
very dark red

dull reddish orange
USE grayish reddish orange

dull reddish violet
USE blackish purple
dark grayish purple
grayish purple
grayish reddish purple
pale purple
pale reddish purple

dull reddish yellow
USE dark grayish yellow
grayish yellow
pale orange yellow
pale yellow

dull rose
USE light grayish red
moderate purplish pink

dull vermilion
USE moderate reddish orange

dull violet
USE blackish purple

dark grayish purple
dark purplish red
grayish purple
grayish purplish red
grayish reddish purple
light grayish purplish red
pale purple
very pale purple

dull violet black
USE black
dark bluish gray
dark gray
dark grayish blue
dark grayish purple
dark purplish gray

dull violet blue, dark
USE grayish purplish blue

dull yellow
USE dark grayish yellow
grayish yellow
light orange yellow
pale yellow

dull yellow green, dark
USE grayish olive green

dull yellow green, deep
USE dark yellowish green

dull yellowish brown
USE dark grayish yellowish brown
dark yellowish brown
grayish yellowish brown
light grayish yellowish brown
light yellowish brown
moderate yellowish brown

dull yellowish green
USE grayish yellow green
pale yellow green

dull yellowish orange
USE pale orange yellow

dull yellowish red
USE grayish reddish orange

Duma
FL.412   (L)
UF Aduma

dumb
USE mute

dumb waiters
USE dumbwaiters (stands)

dumb waiters, sweetmeat
USE pyramids (containers)

dumbaks
USE dombaks

dumbalaks
USE dombaks

dumbbell tenements
RK.360
ALT dumbbell tenement
SN Use for apartment houses offering an improvement over standard long, narrow tenements by includ-

ing air and light shafts between adjacent buildings resulting in characteristic dumbbell-shaped plans; common in New York City between 1879 and 1901, after which their construction was banned.
UF tenements, dumbbell

dumbbells
TV.94   (L,N)
ALT dumbbell
SN Weights consisting of two spherical ends firmly attached to a short bar serving as a handle; used as exercise and fitness apparatus.

Dumbo
FL.675
UF Wadumbo

dumbwaiters (conveying systems)
PC.121   (N)
HN March 1993 descriptor moved
May 1991 descriptor changed, was **dumbwaiters**
May 1991 alternate term changed, was **dumbwaiter**
February 1991 scope note added
ALT dumbwaiter (conveying system)
SN Hoisting or lowering mechanisms equipped with a car or platform used in buildings exclusively for carrying materials.

dumbwaiters (stands)
TC.1035
HN January 1993 descriptor moved
ALT dumbwaiter (stand)
SN Term used by Sheraton for three-tiered stands intended for use in the dining room on which to place glasses and plates, both clean and used. (MONTGO)
UF dumb waiters
serviteurs-muets
tables servantes

dumdum bullets
USE dumdums

dumdums
TK.265
ALT dumdum
SN Type of expanding bullet developed at the western Bengal town of Dum Dum, derived from a rifle cartridge. The metal envelope encasing the bullet is removed at the tip, exposing the interior lead which then expands upon impact.
UF bullets, dumdum
dumdum bullets

dummies (mallets)
TH.1348   (N)
HN December 1992 descriptor moved
ALT dummy (mallet)
SN Small mallets with heads of malleable iron. (HAND)

dummies (printed matter)
VW.1190   (L)

HN March 1993 descriptor added
ALT dummy (printed matter)
SN Unprinted, partially printed, or sketched samples of projected publications to suggest the appearance of the completed work. (ALAG)
UF maquettes (printed matter)
roughs
scratches
tissues

dummies, ventriloquists'
USE ventriloquial figures

dummy ammunition
USE drill ammunition

dummy board figures
VC.255   (L)
ALT dummy board figure
SN Use for life-size paintings of figures, usually people, occasionally animals, on thin panel cut out to give a lifelike effect; popular in the 17th and 18th centuries.
UF board figures, dummy
boards, dummy
companions, silent
dummy boards
figures, dummy board
silent companions

dummy boards
USE dummy board figures

dummy cartridges
TK.273   (N)
ALT dummy cartridge
SN Inoperative cartridges or facsimiles used for training in the handling of firearms or to test a firearm's functioning. (FOFSF)
UF cartridges, dummy

dummy dolls
USE ventriloquial figures

dummy knobs
PJ.340
HN April 1993 descriptor moved
ALT dummy knob
UF dummy levers
knobs, dummy
levers, dummy

dummy levers
USE dummy knobs

dumont blue
USE smalt

dump cars
TX.262   (L)
ALT dump car
SN Freight cars whose bodies can be tipped for discharging loads.
UF cars, dump

dump trucks
TX.102   (L,N)
ALT dump truck
SN Use for open-topped motor trucks having a body that can be tilted to

discharge its contents, usually loose materials, through an open tailgate. (RHDEL2)
UF dumpers
trucks, dump

dumpers
USE dump trucks

dumping-grounds
USE dumps (refuse areas)

dumps (coins)
VK.7
ALT dump (coin)
SN Use for small, usually thick coins; may have been created by removing circular pieces from other, larger coins, as in the case of holey dollars. (DOTY)

dumps (refuse areas)
RM.77
HN April 1993 descriptor moved
January 1992 descriptor changed, was **dumps**
January 1992 alternate term changed, was **dump**
ALT dump (refuse area)
UF dumping-grounds
dumps, garbage
dumps, rubbish
dumpsites
garbage dumps
rubbish dumps

dumps, garbage
USE dumps (refuse areas)

dumps, rubbish
USE dumps (refuse areas)

dumpsites
USE dumps (refuse areas)

dumpy levels
TN.109
ALT dumpy level
SN Surveying instruments used to determine relative elevation, generally comprised of a telescope rigidly attached to a vertical spindle, thus capable of only horizontal rotary movement.
UF levels, dumpy

dunbaks
USE dombaks

dunduns
TT.599
ALT dundun
SN Use for the double-headed hourglass pressure drums of the Yoruba people, held under the arm and beaten with a hooked stick. Use also for the sets of Yoruba hourglass pressure drums of which the dundun constitutes the largest member.

dunes
RD.166   (L,R)

HN March 1993 lead-in term added
ALT dune
UF dunes, sand
sand dunes

dunes, sand
USE dunes

dung
MT.2526
HN March 1992 scope note added
February 1992 descriptor moved
SN Excrement of animals. (W)

dung-chen
TT.49
SN Long straight metal end-blown trumpetlike instruments of Tibet, of conical bore, made of several sections which can be telescoped together when not in use, and with a large bell which usually rests on the ground or some other support during play. They are traditionally played in pairs in Buddhist ritual.

dung-dkar
TT.56
SN End-blown marine shell trumpets of Tibet, made from a conch shell with a metal mouthpiece and mountings, usually played in pairs during Buddhist rituals.
RT <end-blown trumpets>

Dunhuang
USE Tun-huang

Dunn County sandstone
USE Dunville sandstone

Dunville sandstone
MT.903
HN April 1992 descriptor moved
UF Dunn County sandstone
sandstone, Dunn County
sandstone, Dunville

duochromatic processes
USE two-color processes

duodecagons
USE dodecagons

duplex apartments
PJ.1209   (B)
HN March 1993 descriptor moved
June 1990 lead-in term added
ALT duplex apartment
UK duplexes
UKA duplex
SN Use for apartments with rooms on two levels.
UF apartments, duplex
maisonettes

duplex burners
PJ.2906
ALT duplex burner
SN Burners designed to hold two wicks.
UF burners, duplex

duplex houses
RK.362   (A,N)

HN March 1993 related term added
ALT duplex house
SN Use for houses with separate dwelling units for two individual families placed one above the other. When the units are placed side by side use **double houses.**
UF duplexes, vertical
  houses, duplex
  houses, two-family
  two-family houses
  vertical duplexes
RT double houses

duplex locks
  PJ.499
HN April 1993 descriptor moved
ALT duplex lock
UF locks, duplex

duplex nails
USE double-headed nails

duplexes
SEE duplex apartments

duplexes, horizontal
USE double houses

duplexes, vertical
USE duplex houses

duplicates
  PE.18
HN January 1993 descriptor moved
ALT duplicate
SN In the context of a collection of images or printed matter, use for additional copies in the same format and medium.

duplicating
USE copying

duplicating, fluid
USE spirit duplicating

duplicating, offset
USE offset printing

duplicating processes
USE copying

duplicating, spirit
USE spirit duplicating

duplicating, stencil
USE stencil duplicating

dupondii
  VK.24
ALT dupondius
SN Roman bronze or brass coins worth two asses minted from the early third century BCE until the mid-3rd century CE.

durability
  DC.280   (L,B)
HN October 1992 descriptor added
ALT durable
SN The ability of a material or object to resist mechanical wear or decay and to last over time. With regard to long-term situations or to nonme-

chanical properties existing over a long period of time without significant change, prefer **permanence.**
UF durableness
  endurability
  endurableness
  endurance
  longevity
  service life
RT permanence

durableness
USE durability

dural
USE duralumin

duralumin
  MT.377   (L)
HN March 1993 descriptor moved
SN An alloy consisting of 95.5 parts of aluminum to 3 parts of copper, 1 of manganese, and 0.5 of magnesium that after age-hardening is comparable in strength and hardness to soft steel. (W)
UF dural

duranga
USE primavera

durmast oak
  MT.2828   (L)
HN March 1992 descriptor moved
UF oak, durmast
  Quercus petraea

durometers
  TN.119
ALT durometer
SN Devices consisting of a small drill or blunt indenter point under pressure and used to measure the hardness of materials, especially metals and rubber.
UF hardness testers
  testers, hardness

duros
USE pesos
  Pieces of Eight

Durour
USE Aua

durries
USE dhurries

Duruma
  FL.603

dust
  MT.1645   (L)
HN April 1993 descriptor moved

dust bags
  TH.841
HN February 1993 descriptor added
ALT dust bag
SN Small mesh bags used to dust aquatint plates with powdered rosin. (SAFF)
UF aquatint bags
  bags, aquatint

bags, dust
  bags, resin
  bags, rosin
  dust-bags, rosin
  resin bags
  rosin bags
  rosin dust-bags

dust-bags, rosin
USE dust bags

dust boxes
  TH.833
HN February 1993 descriptor added
ALT dust box
SN Box constructions enabling the artist to control the even distribution of rosin particles onto the aquatint plate. (COMPRI)
UF aquatint boxes
  aquatint chambers
  aquatint dust boxes
  boxes, aquatint
  boxes, aquatint dust
  boxes, dust
  boxes, rosin
  boxes, rosin dust
  chambers, aquatint
  dust boxes, aquatint
  dust boxes, rosin
  rosin boxes
  rosin dust boxes

dust boxes, aquatint
USE dust boxes

dust boxes, rosin
USE dust boxes

dust cloaks
USE dusters

dust coats
USE dusters

dust covers
  TC.171   (N)
ALT dust cover
SN Cloth or plastic coverings used to protect furniture and equipment, as during a period of nonuse. (RHDEL2)
UF covers, dust

dust covers (book jackets)
USE book jackets

dust ground
USE rosin ground

dust jackets
USE book jackets

dust, marble
USE marble dust

dust masks
  TH.955
ALT dust mask
UF masks, dust

dust ruffles
  TC.267   (N)
ALT dust ruffle

SN Base valances with floor-length ruffles.
UF bed flounces
flounces, bed
petticoat valances
petticoats (bed valances)
plateau ruffles
ruffles, dust
ruffles, plateau
skirts (bed valances)
valances, petticoat

dust, stone
USE stone dust

dust-storms
SEE duststorms

dust wrappers
USE book jackets

dust wraps
USE dusters

dustboards
    PJ.2784
HN March 1993 descriptor moved
ALT dustboard
SN Horizontal boards between drawers. (FAIRB)

dusters
    TE.376
ALT duster
SN Long, lightweight coatlike overgarments worn in the early 20th century to protect the wearer from dust, especially while riding in automobiles.
UF cloaks, dust
coats, dust
dust cloaks
dust coats
dust wraps
wraps, dust
RT coats

dusters (housecoats)
USE housecoats

Dustin
    FL.830

dusting brushes
    TH.893   (A,N,B)
ALT dusting brush
SN Flat brushes with long coarse bristles set in a wood handle; used by artists and draftsmen to sweep away eraser crumbs from work being done on a drawing board. (MAYER)
UF brushes, dusting

dusting brushes
USE fan brushes

dusting-on
USE dusting-on process

dusting-on process
    KT.542
SN Photographic process in which the image is formed by dusting a pigment onto a surface of bichromated colloid that has been exposed through a transparency. Areas exposed to light lose their tackiness and hold less pigment. Generally for prints on glass or ceramic, where the pigment is fired as a glaze.
UF dusting-on
powder process

dustproof strikes
    PJ.65
HN March 1993 descriptor moved
ALT dustproof strike
SN Strikes with a spring plunger that completely fills the hole when the door is open. (BROWNL)
UF strikes, dustproof

duststorms
    KM.140   (L)
HN May 1991 alternate term added
ALT duststorm
UK dust-storms
UKA dust-storm

Dutch
    FL.3140   (L,B)

Dutch arches
USE French arches

Dutch barns
    RK.46
ALT Dutch barn
SN Designates squarish barns found in the northeast United States and characterized by one main floor, steeply pitched gables, primary entrances located under each gable end, wide central interior spaces spanned by massive anchor beams, and narrow flanking aisles.
UF barns, Dutch
barns, New World Dutch
New World Dutch barns

Dutch brick
USE clinker brick

Dutch clinker
USE clinker brick

Dutch Colonial
    FL.3328   (A)
UF Colonial, Dutch

Dutch-door bolts
    PJ.459
HN April 1993 descriptor moved
ALT Dutch-door bolt
SN Devices for locking together upper and lower leaves of a Dutch door. (STEIN)
UF bolts, Dutch-door

Dutch-door quadrants
    PJ.478
HN April 1993 descriptor moved
ALT Dutch-door quadrant
UF quadrants, Dutch-door

Dutch doors
    PJ.2167
HN March 1993 descriptor moved
ALT Dutch door
SN Doors consisting of two separate leaves, one above the other; the leaves may operate independently or together. (HAS)
UF doors, Dutch
doors, hatchet
hatchet doors

Dutch feet
USE pad feet
trifid feet

Dutch foil
USE Dutch metal

Dutch gables
    PJ.1967
HN March 1993 descriptor moved
ALT Dutch gable
SN Gables with curving sides and surmounted by a pediment. (HAS)
UF gables, Dutch

Dutch gilding
USE Dutch metal

Dutch gilt
USE Dutch metal

Dutch gold
USE Dutch metal

Dutch leaf
USE Dutch metal

Dutch metal
    MT.481
HN February 1993 descriptor added
SN An alloy of copper and zinc, often used as a substitute for gold leaf.
UF composition leaf
Dutch foil
Dutch gilding
Dutch gilt
Dutch gold
Dutch leaf
Dutch metal leaf
foil, Dutch
gilding, Dutch
gilt, Dutch
gold, Dutch
leaf, composition
leaf, Dutch
leaf, Dutch metal
metal, Dutch
metal leaf, Dutch

Dutch metal leaf
USE Dutch metal

Dutch mordant
    MT.2481
SN A compound solution of potassium chlorate and hydrochloric acid used as a mordant in etching. (MAYER)
UF mordant, Dutch

Dutch New Guinea
USE Irian Jaya

Dutch ovens
    TQ.303   (L,N)

ALT Dutch oven
SN Cast iron kettles, usually set on three legs, with a tight-fitting lid on which coals may be placed when baking in an open fire.
UF bake kettles
bake ovens (Dutch ovens)
dinner pots
Dutch pots
gypsy pots
kettles, bake
ovens, Dutch
pots, dinner
pots, Dutch
pots, gypsy
pots, stew
stew pots
RT kettles

Dutch ovens (bake ovens)
USE bake ovens

Dutch ovens (reflector ovens)
USE reflector ovens

Dutch ovens, tin
USE tin kitchens

Dutch, Pennsylvania
USE Pennsylvania German

Dutch pink
MT.2260
HN April 1992 descriptor moved
UF brown pink
English pink
Italian pink
pink, brown
pink, Dutch
pink, English
pink, Italian
stil de grain brun
stil de grain vert

Dutch pots
USE Dutch ovens
Zischäggen

Dutch process white lead
MT.2230
HN April 1992 descriptor moved
UF white lead, Dutch process

Dutch ripple molding frames
TC.418
ALT Dutch ripple molding frame
SN Use for frames with moldings which have undulating surfaces.
UF frames, Dutch ripple molding
frames, Rembrandt
Rembrandt frames

Dutch vermilion
USE vivid reddish orange

Dutch white metal
MT.460
HN March 1993 descriptor moved
UF metal, Dutch white
white metal, Dutch

duvets
TC.203

ALT duvet
SN Down-filled comforters.
UF continental quilts
quilts, continental

Dvaravati
FL.2490

dvojnices
TT.39
ALT dvojnice
SN Double-duct flutes of Yugoslavia, consisting of two slightly divergent pipes bored in one piece of wood, with a beak-shaped double mouthpiece. (NGDMI)
RT duct flutes

dwarf ale glasses
TQ.426   (L)
ALT dwarf ale glass
SN Term applied to small short-stemmed ale glasses of 3- to 4-ounce capacity, especially those made in England from the early 17th until the early 19th century.
UF ale glasses, dwarf
ales, dwarf
dwarf ales
glasses, dwarf ale

dwarf ales
USE dwarf ale glasses

dwarf birch
MT.2703
HN March 1992 descriptor moved
UF Betula nana
birch, dwarf

dwarf bookcases
TC.828
HN January 1993 descriptor moved
ALT dwarf bookcase
SN Low bookcases deliberately designed so as to leave the wall above free for paintings or pier glasses; generally having open shelves or doors with open grilles, instead of solid or silk-paneled doors.
UF bookcases, dwarf

dwarf buck-eye
SEE dwarf buckeye

dwarf buckeye
MT.2676
HN August 1992 lead-in term added
March 1992 descriptor moved
UK dwarf buck-eye
UF Aesculus pavia
buck-eye, dwarf
buckeye, dwarf

dwarf galleries
PJ.1030
HN March 1993 descriptor moved
June 1990 scope note changed
ALT dwarf gallery
SN Passageways through the exterior walls of buildings and open to the outside through small-scale or slen-

der arcades; found in Italian and German Romanesque architecture.
UF galleries, dwarf

dwarf tall case clocks
USE dwarf tall clocks

dwarf tall clocks
TN.159   (N)
ALT dwarf tall clock
SN Use for scaled-down versions of tall case clocks, usually 2 to 5 feet high, with 8-day brass movements, and having pendulums; popular in the United States in the early 18th century.
UF case clocks, dwarf tall
case clocks, miniature tall
clocks, dwarf tall
clocks, dwarf tall case
clocks, grandmother
clocks, miniature tall case
dwarf tall case clocks
grandmother clocks
miniature tall case clocks
tall case clocks, dwarf
tall case clocks, miniature
tall clocks, dwarf

dwarfs
HG.1005   (H,L)
HN January 1993 descriptor added
ALT dwarf
dwarf's
dwarfs'
SN People who are abnormally small in stature.

dwelling terraces
USE terrace houses

dwelling units
USE apartments

dwellings
RK.217   (A,L,N,R)
HN March 1993 scope note changed
February 1993 related terms added
ALT dwelling
SN Use for buildings or portions of a building designed exclusively for human residential occupancy, but not including hotels or other buildings intended for use by transients. For the locale which constitutes the center of an individual's domestic life, affectional relationships, and interests, together with the feeling of comfort and satisfaction that it conveys, use **home**.
UF architecture, domestic
buildings, residential
domestic architecture
domestic facilities
domiciles
facilities, domestic
facilities, residential
habitations
homes
housing, residential
residences
residential buildings

residential facilities
residential housing
RT home
   houseboats

dwellings, beehive
USE beehive houses

dwellings, cave
USE cave dwellings

dwellings, cliff
USE cliff dwellings

dwellings, double
USE double houses

dwellings, ECHO
USE ECHO houses

dwellings, lake
USE lake dwellings

dwellings, log
USE log cabins
   log houses

dwellings, multiple
USE multiple dwellings

dwellings, pit
USE pit dwellings

dwellings, row
USE row houses

dwellings, seasonal
USE seasonal dwellings

dwellings, single-family
USE single-family dwellings

dwellings, slave
USE slave quarters

dwellings, spirit
USE spirit houses

dwellings, tree
USE tree houses

DWV piping
PJ.900
HN March 1993 descriptor moved
UF drainage, waste and vent piping
   piping, drainage, waste, and vent
   piping, DWV

dye
MT.2022   (H,L,R)
HN March 1993 scope note changed
   January 1992 descriptor moved
SN A colored substance that dissolves or
   is suspended in a liquid and imparts
   its color by staining or being ab-
   sorbed, or by serving as a pigment.

dye, aniline
USE aniline dye

dye bleach process
USE silver-dye bleach process

dye bleaching process
USE silver-dye bleach process

<dye by composition or origin>
MT.2023
HN April 1992 guide term moved

<dye by property>
MT.2048
HN April 1992 guide term moved

dye, coal-tar
USE synthetic organic pigment

dye coupler photoprints
USE chromogenic color prints

dye coupler prints
USE chromogenic color prints

dye coupler processes
USE chromogenic processes

dye coupling processes
USE chromogenic processes

dye destruction process
USE silver-dye bleach process

dye diffusion transfer
USE dye diffusion transfer process

dye diffusion transfer photoprints
USE dye diffusion transfer prints

dye diffusion transfer prints
VC.305
HN April 1992 descriptor moved
ALT dye diffusion transfer print
SN Color instant camera photographs.
   (GMGPC)
UF diffusion transfer prints, dye
   dye diffusion transfer photoprints
   Kodak (TM) instant color pho-
    toprints
   Kodak (TM) instant prints
   photographs, Polaroid (TM) instant
    color
   photoprints, dye diffusion transfer
   Polaroid (TM) instant color photo-
    graphs
   prints, dye diffusion transfer
   prints, Kodak (TM) instant
   transfer prints, dye diffusion

dye diffusion transfer process
KT.517
SN Diffusion transfer process that uses
   dye couplers rather than silver and
   produces color instant camera photographs.
UF diffusion transfer, dye
   dye diffusion transfer

dye diffusion transfer process, internal
USE internal dye diffusion transfer
   process

dye imbibition process
USE dye transfer process

dye, methyl
USE methyl dye

dye mordant process
USE dye toning

dye mordanting
USE dye toning

dye, natural
USE natural dye

dye, oil soluble
USE oil soluble dye

dye, synthetic
USE synthetic dye

dye toning
KT.619
ALT dye-toned
UF dye mordant process
   dye mordanting
   mordant dye process
   mordanting
   toning, dye

dye transfer
USE dye transfer process

dye transfer photoprints
USE dye transfer prints

dye transfer prints
VC.408
HN April 1993 scope note changed
   April 1992 descriptor moved
ALT dye transfer print
SN Use for photomechanical prints
   made by the dye transfer process.
UF dye transfer photoprints
   photoprints, dye transfer
   prints, dye transfer
   transfer prints, dye

dye transfer process
KT.653   (L)
HN April 1993 descriptor moved
SN Photomechanical process in which
   gelatin relief matrices are made by a
   bichromate process from color separation negatives or positives; a full-
   color print is then made by transferring dye from the matrices, in
   register, to a support.
UF dye imbibition process
   dye transfer
   imbibition printing
   imbibition process
   imbibition process, dye
   printing, imbibition
   transfer process, dye

dye transfer process, gelatin
USE gelatin dye transfer process

dye, vegetable
USE vegetable dye

dyehouses
USE dyeworks

dyeing
KT.51   (L,R)
HN January 1993 descriptor moved
   August 1992 scope note added
ALT dyed
SN Process of applying a coloring mat-
   ter that is in a solution or fine dis-
   persion so that at least some of the

coloring matter is taken up by the substance.

dyeing, resist
USE   resist dyeing

dyers
  HG.746
HN December 1992 alternate terms
   added
ALT dyer
   dyer's
   dyers'

dyestuff, natural
USE   natural dye

dyeworks
  RK.629   (H,B)
UF dyehouses

dykes
USE   dikes

dynamic analysis
  KT.175   (L)
HN November 1992 descriptor added
SN Analysis under dynamic conditions.
UF dynamic testing

dynamic symmetry
USE   approximate symmetry

dynamic testing
USE   dynamic analysis

dynamics
  BM.821   (L)
HN November 1992 descriptor moved
SN Physical forces which affect the motion or equilibrium of material bodies.
UF structural dynamics

dynamism
  BM.152
SN A key concept for Futurist artists concerning the representation of movement and the persistence of images.
UF universal dynamism

dynamite
  MT.2317   (L)
HN January 1993 descriptor moved

dynamos
USE   generators

Dynastic, Early
USE   Early Dynastic (Egyptian)
   Early Dynastic (Mesopotamian)

Dynasties, Southern
USE   Southern Dynasties

Dynasty, Eighteenth
USE   Eighteenth Dynasty

Dynasty, Eighth
USE   Eighth Dynasty

Dynasty, Eleventh
USE   Eleventh Dynasty

Dynasty, Fifteenth
USE   Fifteenth Dynasty

Dynasty, Fifth
USE   Fifth Dynasty

Dynasty, First
USE   First Dynasty

Dynasty, Fourteenth
USE   Fourteenth Dynasty

Dynasty, Fourth
USE   Fourth Dynasty

Dynasty, Nineteenth
USE   Nineteenth Dynasty

Dynasty, Ninth
USE   Ninth Dynasty

Dynasty, Second
USE   Second Dynasty

Dynasty, Seventeenth
USE   Seventeenth Dynasty

Dynasty, Seventh
USE   Seventh Dynasty

Dynasty, Sixteenth
USE   Sixteenth Dynasty

Dynasty, Sixth
USE   Sixth Dynasty

Dynasty, Tenth
USE   Tenth Dynasty

Dynasty, Third
USE   Third Dynasty

Dynasty, Thirteenth
USE   Thirteenth Dynasty

Dynasty, Thirtieth
USE   Thirtieth Dynasty

Dynasty, Thirty-first
USE   Thirty-first Dynasty

Dynasty, Twelfth
USE   Twelfth Dynasty

Dynasty, Twentieth
USE   Twentieth Dynasty

Dynasty, Twenty-eighth
USE   Twenty-eighth Dynasty

Dynasty, Twenty-fifth
USE   Twenty-fifth Dynasty

Dynasty, Twenty-first
USE   Twenty-first Dynasty

Dynasty, Twenty-fourth
USE   Twenty-fourth Dynasty

Dynasty, Twenty-ninth
USE   Twenty-ninth Dynasty

Dynasty, Twenty-second
USE   Twenty-second Dynasty

Dynasty, Twenty-seventh
USE   Twenty-seventh Dynasty

Dynasty, Twenty-sixth
USE   Twenty-sixth Dynasty

Dynasty, Twenty-third
USE   Twenty-third Dynasty

Dzalamo
USE   Zaramo

Dzhanbas-Kala
  FL.1853
HN April 1993 descriptor moved

Dzhebel Cave
  FL.1854
HN April 1993 descriptor moved
UF Djebel

Dzheytun
  FL.1855
HN April 1993 descriptor moved
UF Djeitun

E-boats
USE   motor torpedo boats

e-mail
USE   electronic mail

e-tsuzumi
USE   otsuzumi

eagle bracket tables
USE   eagle console tables

eagle Chelaberds
USE   sunburst Kazaks

eagle console tables
  TC.1104
HN January 1993 descriptor moved
ALT eagle console table
SN Console tables supported by an eagle bracket.
UF bracket tables, console
   console tables, eagle
   eagle bracket tables
   eagle tables
   tables, eagle
   tables, eagle bracket
   tables, eagle console

eagle Kazak rugs
USE   sunburst Kazaks

eagle Kazaks
USE   sunburst Kazaks

eagle tables
USE   eagle console tables

eagles
  VK.76
ALT eagle
SN United States gold coins issued between 1795 and 1933 and valued at ten dollars.
UF gold pieces, ten-dollar
   ten-dollar gold pieces

eagles, double
USE   double eagles

eagles' feet
USE   claw-and-ball feet

eagles, half
USE   half eagles

eagles, quarter
USE   quarter eagles

ear clips
TE.448
ALT   ear clip
SN   Earrings with clip fasteners. (W)
UF   clip-on earrings
   clips, ear
   earrings, clip-on
   earrings, snap
   snap earrings

ear-daggers
SEE   eared daggers

ear ornaments
TE.446
ALT   ear ornament
SN   Decorative items worn in, on, or about the ear.
UF   ornaments, ear

ear-plugs
SEE   earplugs

eared daggers
TK.20
ALT   eared dagger
UK   ear-daggers
UKA   ear-dagger
SN   European daggers characterized by a pommel formed by two disc-shaped appendages splayed outwards from the bottom of the grip.
UF   daggers, eared

earflaps
PJ.3041
ALT   earflap
SN   Side extensions to a cap which may be worn either turned up and secured to the crown or turned down to cover the ears. (FDOF)
UF   earlaps

earlaps
USE   earflaps
   earmuffs

earlier Roman cursive
USE   older Roman cursive

<Earlier Stone Age>
FL.46

Early American
USE   American Colonial

Early American Hunter
USE   Paleo-Indian (Pre-Columbian North American)

Early Andhra
FL.2272
HN   November 1991 descriptor changed, was **Early Andra**

November 1991 lead-in term changed, was **Andra, Early**
UF   Andhra, Early

Early Archaic
FL.2653
UF   Archaic, Early

Early Babylonian
USE   Old Babylonian

Early Baroque
FL.3262
UF   Baroque, Early

Early Benin
FL.93
UF   Benin, Early
   Ogiso period

Early Bronze Age
FL.26
UF   Bronze Age, Early

Early Byzantine
FL.3158
UF   Byzantine, Early

Early Chalcolithic
FL.20
UF   Chalcolithic, Early

early childhood
USE   infancy

early childhood education
KD.252
SN   Includes activities and experiences that are intended to effect developmental changes in children from birth through the early years of elementary school.
UF   education, early childhood
   education, nursery school
   nursery school education

Early Chiripa
FL.1152
UF   Chiripa, Early

Early Christian
FL.3156   (A,L,B,R)
UF   Christian, Early

<Early Christian-Byzantine styles and periods>
FL.3155

Early Classic
FL.983
UF   Classic, Early

Early Classical
FL.2667
UF   Classical, Early

Early Cocle
USE   Conte Polychrome

Early Corinthian
FL.2716
UF   Corinthian, Early

early cracks
USE   traction crackle

Early Cycladic
FL.2626
UF   Cycladic, Early

Early Cypriote
FL.2981
UF   Cypriote, Early

Early Decorated
FL.3214
UF   Decorated, Early
   Decorated, Geometrical
   Geometrical Decorated

Early Dilmun
FL.2972
UF   Dilmun, Early

Early Dynastic (Egyptian)
FL.2876
HN   June 1990 lead-in term added
UF   Archaic period
   Dynastic, Early
   Protodynastic
   Semainean period

Early Dynastic (Mesopotamian)
FL.3049
HN   May 1991 lead-in term added
   May 1991 descriptor changed, was **Early Dynastic**
UF   Dynastic, Early

Early Edo
FL.2061
UF   Early Tokugawa
   Edo, Early
   Tokugawa, Early

Early Elamite
USE   Old Elamite

Early English
FL.3216   (B)
UF   Early English Gothic
   English, Early
   English Gothic, Early
   First Pointed
   Gothic, Early English
   Lancet
   Pointed, First

Early English Gothic
USE   Early English

Early Etruscan
FL.2814
UF   Etruscan, Early

Early Formative
USE   Early Preclassic

Early Free Style
FL.2705
UF   Free Style, Early

Early Geometric
FL.2658
UF   Geometric, Early

Early Gerzean
FL.2874
UF   Gerzean, Early

Early Gothic
FL.3182 (L,B)
UF 1200 Style
Gothic, Early
Primaire
Style 1200
Transitional Style

Early Han
USE Western Han

Early Heian
FL.2057
UF Heian, Early
Jogan
Konin

Early Helladic
FL.2638
UF Helladic, Early

<early historical Japanese periods>
FL.2051

Early horizon
FL.1154

Early Imperial
FL.2797
UF Imperial, Early

Early Intermediate period
FL.1165
UF Intermediate period, Early

Early Iron Age
FL.30
UF Iron Age, Early

Early Jomon
FL.2039
UF Jomon, Early

Early Kerma
FL.157
UF Kerma, Early

Early Khmer
USE Pre-Angkorean

Early Malla
FL.2238
UF Malla, Early

Early Medieval
FL.3177 (A)
UF Medieval, Early

Early Minoan
FL.2645
UF Minoan, Early

<early modern Japanese periods>
FL.2059

Early Naqada
USE Amratian

Early Nara
FL.2054
UF Hakuho
Nara, Early

Early Neolithic
FL.15
UF Neolithic, Early

Early Nomads Age
FL.2201
UF Nomads Age, Early

Early Orientalizing
FL.2663
UF Orientalizing, Early

Early Palace period
USE Old Palace period

Early Palaeologan
FL.3167
UF Palaeologan, Early

Early period Californian
FL.786
UF Californian, Early period

Early period Plateau
FL.792
UF Plateau, Early period

Early Postclassic
FL.987
UF Postclassic, Early

Early Preclassic
FL.978
UF Early Formative
Formative, Early
Preclassic, Early

early red
FL.3115
HN April 1993 descriptor added
UF red (pottery style)
red, early

early red ware
HN April 1993 descriptor split, use **early red** + **ware**

Early Renaissance
FL.3256
UF Renaissance, Early

Early Style
FL.2613

Early Tokugawa
USE Early Edo

Early Victorian
FL.3408
UF Victorian, Early

<Early Western World>
FL.2536

<Early Western World coins>
VK.19
SN Collocates descriptors for coins of the ancient Western world from the 6th century BCE until the financial restructuring undertaken by the Franks and Arabs in the 7th and 8th centuries CE; includes Greece, Rome, and the Near East through the Sassanians.

<Early Western World coins by denomination name>
VK.20

<Early Western World coins by descriptive name>
VK.52

early works
PE.162 (H)
HN May 1993 lead-in term added
May 1991 descriptor added
ALT early work
SN Works, particularly artistic or written works, produced relatively early in the maker's career.
UF works, early

earmuffs
TE.565 (N)
ALT earmuff
SN Ear coverings worn as protection against the cold.
UF earlaps
eartabs

earplugs
TH.383 (N)
HN January 1993 descriptor added
ALT earplug
UK ear-plugs
UKA ear-plug
SN Devices of soft, pliable material for insertion into the opening of the outer ear, especially to keep out water or noise. (RHDEL2)

earrings
TE.447 (H,L,N,R)
ALT earring
SN Ear ornaments worn suspended from a bent wire or a thin loop passed through a hole pierced in the lobe of the ear or clipped or screwed to the lobe. (HNDOJ)

earrings, clip-on
USE ear clips

earrings, pierced
USE pierced earrings

earrings, snap
USE ear clips

ears (furniture components)
PJ.2728
HN March 1993 descriptor moved
ALT ear (furniture component)
SN Up-curved ends of a crest rail; usually on Chippendale chairs. (CTSB)

earspools
TE.450 (N)
ALT earspool
SN Spool-shaped ear ornaments worn through an enlarged hole in the earlobe. (W)

eartabs
USE earmuffs

earth
MT.1348
HN April 1992 descriptor moved
SN Use for soil as a building material.
UF dirt

earth art
USE   earthworks (sculpture)

earth, bituminous
USE   Vandyke brown

earth, Bohemian
USE   Bohemian earth

earth bows
USE   ground bows

earth, Cassel
USE   Vandyke brown

earth, Cologne
USE   Vandyke brown

earth color
USE   natural inorganic pigment

earth dams
USE   earth-fill dams

earth dams, reinforced
USE   zoned earth dams

earth dams, zoned
USE   zoned earth dams

earth, diatomaceous
USE   diatomaceous earth

earth, diatomite
USE   diatomaceous earth

earth-fill dams
RK.503   (L)
ALT   earth-fill dam
SN   Use for dams built of fine earth near the center, coarser earth or rock on the outside, and a waterproof core. (EAA)
UF   dams, earth-fill
dams, hydraulic fill
earth dams
hydraulic fill dams

earth, green
USE   green earth

earth houses
USE   earth lodges

earth, infusorial
USE   diatomaceous earth

earth, Japan
USE   cutch

earth lodges
RK.316   (A,L,B)
ALT   earth lodge
SN   Designates certain Native North American dwellings framed by heavy timbers and covered with earth or sod and a dome-shaped arrangement of branches.
UF   earth houses
houses, earth
lodges, earth

earth movements
KM.127   (A,L)
HN   May 1991 alternate term added
ALT   earth movement

SN   Differential movements of the earth's crust or parts of its surface, or elevations or subsidences of land. (W)
UF   movements, earth

earth of cullen
USE   Vandyke brown

earth, potter's
USE   potter's clay

earth pressure
BM.849   (L)
HN   November 1992 descriptor moved
February 1992 scope note added
SN   Pressure exerted by soil or other sub-surface material, as on a wall located below ground level.
UF   pressure, earth

earth, rammed
USE   rammed earth

earth red
USE   moderate brown

earth, red
USE   moderate reddish brown

earth sciences
KD.174   (L)
HN   December 1992 descriptor moved
UF   sciences, earth

<earth sciences concepts>
BM.721
HN   November 1992 guide term moved

earth sculpture
USE   earthworks (sculpture)

earth sheltered buildings
RK.1312   (A,L)
ALT   earth sheltered building
UF   buildings, earth sheltered

earth stations
USE   satellite tracking stations

earth, tamped
USE   rammed earth

earth wax
USE   ozokerite

earth yellow
USE   light yellowish brown

earth, yellow
USE   moderate orange yellow
yellow ocher

earthenware
PE.105   (L,B,R)
HN   January 1993 descriptor moved

earthenware, cream-colored
USE   creamware

earthmovers
USE   earthmoving equipment

earthmoving equipment
TH.439   (L)

UF   earthmovers
equipment, earthmoving

earthquake design
USE   seismic design

earthquake loads
BM.609
HN   March 1993 scope note added
November 1992 descriptor moved
January 1991 alternate term added
April 1990 lead-in terms added
ALT   earthquake load
SN   Dynamic loads created in a structure caused by the rapid movement of structural members due to seismic vibrations.
UF   loads, earthquake
loads, seismic
seismic loads

earthquake-resistant construction
KT.30   (L,B)
HN   January 1993 descriptor moved
ALT   earthquake-resistant
UF   aseismic design
construction, earthquake-resistant
design, aseismic
design, earthquake-resistant
earthquake-resistant design
earthquake-resisting construction

earthquake-resistant design
USE   earthquake-resistant construction
seismic design

earthquake-resisting construction
USE   earthquake-resistant construction

earthquake stations
USE   seismological stations

earthquakes
KM.129   (L,B,R)
HN   May 1991 alternate term added
ALT   earthquake
SN   Occasions of shaking or trembling of earth, divisible into two major types, volcanic or tectonic, according to the major precipitating factor.

earthworks (art)
USE   earthworks (sculpture)

earthworks (engineering works)
RK.1288   (A,L,N,B,R)
HN   September 1991 scope note changed
September 1991 descriptor changed, was **earthworks**
September 1991 alternate term changed, was **earthwork**
ALT   earthwork (engineering work)
SN   Use generally for the results of grading, trenching, or embanking earth, for utilitarian purposes; when earth construction has more of an artistic, rather than functional, purpose, use **earthworks (sculpture)**.

earthworks (sculpture)
VC.242   (A,L,N,R)

ALT earthwork (sculpture)
SN Use for works that manipulate natural earth and stone, altering the terrain of the land itself for artistic purposes. For large-scale outdoor works that otherwise exploit or incorporate aspects of their sites, use the more general term **environmental art.**
UF art, earth
art, eco
art, ecological
art, land
earth art
earth sculpture
earthworks (art)
ecological art
land art
landscape sculpture
sculpture, earth
sculpture, landscape

easel painting
KT.412
HN April 1990 descriptor added
SN Use to distinguish the activity of painting portable, relatively small paintings from the painting of other types, such as mural paintings, manuscript illuminations, or decorative painting on objects.
UF painting, easel

easel paintings
VC.256
ALT easel painting
SN Use for portable, relatively small paintings, especially when distinguishing them from mural paintings or manuscript illuminations.
UF easel pictures
paintings, easel
pictures, easel

easel pictures
USE easel paintings

easels
TC.1018   (L,N)
HN January 1993 descriptor moved
ALT easel
SN Stands or frames for supporting or displaying at an angle an artist's canvas, a blackboard, china plate, or other object. (RHDEL2)

easels, studio
USE studio easels

easels, table
USE table easels

easement
BM.908   (A,L,B)
HN February 1993 descriptor moved
SN Usually nonprofitable interest granted by deed or will that is held by one person in land owned by another and that entitles the holder to a specific limited use. (W)
UF servitude

east
DC.338
HN October 1992 descriptor moved

East African copal
MT.1251
HN April 1992 descriptor moved
May 1990 lead-in term changed, was **anime**
UF animé
copal, East African

<East African styles>
FL.580

East Asian
FL.1903   (L)
UF Asian, East

<East Caucasian textile styles>
FL.1803
HN April 1993 guide term added

East Gravettian
FL.2550
UF Gravettian, East

East Greek
FL.2690
UF Greek, East

East India
USE Compagnie des Indes

East India porcelain
USE Compagnie des Indes + ware

East India walnut
MT.2910
HN March 1992 descriptor moved
UF Albizia lebbeck
walnut, East India

East Indian rosewood
MT.2894   (L)
HN March 1992 descriptor moved
UF Dalbergia latifolia
Indian rosewood
rosewood, East Indian
rosewood, Indian

East Javanese
FL.2467
UF Javanese, East

<East Javanese periods>
FL.2468

<East Turkestani historic painting styles>
FL.1817
HN April 1993 guide term added

<East Turkestani historic styles and periods>
FL.1814
HN April 1993 guide term added

<East Turkestani historic textile styles>
FL.1832
HN April 1993 guide term added

Easter
KM.105   (L,R)

Easter candles
USE paschal candles

Easter cards
VW.347
HN November 1992 descriptor moved
ALT Easter card
SN Cards imprinted with greetings or messages and often suitable illustrations that are sent or given to celebrate Easter.
UF cards, Easter

Easter Island
FL.3828   (L)

Easter sepulchers
PJ.2523
HN March 1993 descriptor moved
August 1991 scope note changed
ALT Easter sepulcher
SN Recesses with tomb chests, usually placed in the north wall of a chancel, to hold the reserved consecrated wafers and sometimes a cross or effigy of Christ.
UF sepulchers, Easter

Eastern Apache
FL.1466
UF Apache, Eastern

Eastern Archaic
FL.770
UF Archaic, Eastern

Eastern Chin
USE Eastern Jin

Eastern Chou
USE Eastern Zhou

eastern cottonwood
MT.2861   (L)
HN March 1992 descriptor moved
UF cottonwood, eastern
Populus deltoides

<Eastern European Renaissance-Baroque ceramics styles>
FL.3294
HN March 1993 guide term changed, was *<Eastern European Renaissance-Baroque pottery styles>*

<Eastern European Renaissance-Baroque styles>
FL.3293

<Eastern European Upper Paleolithic styles and periods>
FL.2549

Eastern Hamitic
FL.614   (L)
UF Hamitic, Eastern
Nilo-Hamitic
Nilotes

Eastern Han
FL.1921
UF Han, Eastern
Han, Later
Later Han (Eastern Han)

eastern hemlock
MT.2945   (L)

HN March 1992 descriptor moved
UF Canada hemlock
common hemlock
hemlock, Canada
hemlock, common
hemlock, eastern
hemlock, New England
hemlock spruce
New England hemlock
pine, spruce
spruce, hemlock
spruce pine
Tsuga canadensis

Eastern Indian
FL.2339
UF Indian, Eastern

Eastern Jin
FL.1953
UF Chin, Eastern
Eastern Chin
Jin, Eastern

Eastern Luba
USE Hemba

Eastern Mono
FL.1324
UF Mono, Eastern

Eastern Nahane
USE Kaska

<Eastern North American Paleo-Indian periods>
FL.745

Eastern Orthodox
USE Orthodox Eastern

<Eastern Subarctic Native American>
FL.1231

Eastern Wei
FL.1942
UF Wei, Eastern

<Eastern Woodland and Eastern Great Lake Native American styles>
FL.1301

<Eastern Zambian, Zimbabwe, and Western Mozambique styles>
FL.541

Eastern Zhou
FL.1933
UF Chou, Eastern
Eastern Chou
Zhou, Eastern

Eastlake
FL.1769

Eastman Wash-off Relief (TM)
KT.654
HN April 1993 descriptor moved
UF relief, Eastman wash-off
relief process, wash-off
wash-off relief process

easy chairs
TC.489   (N,B)

HN March 1993 lead-in term changed,
was **grandfather's chairs**
March 1993 lead-in term changed,
was **chairs, grandfather's**
January 1993 descriptor moved
ALT easy chair
SN Armchairs with an upholstered
frame and projecting wings for protection against drafts.
UF chairs, draught
chairs, easy
chairs, grandfathers'
chairs, lug
chairs, saddle cheek
chairs, wing
chairs, wing-back
draught chairs
grandfathers' chairs
lug chairs
saddle cheek chairs
wing-back chairs
wing chairs

easy chairs, circular
USE circular easy chairs

easy chairs, egg
USE egg chairs

easy chairs, square
USE square easy chairs

easy chairs, straight-back
USE square easy chairs

easy chairs, swan
USE swan chairs

easy chairs, tub-back
USE circular easy chairs

<eating and drinking buildings>
RK.103

<eating and drinking spaces>
PJ.1046
HN March 1993 guide term moved

<eave components>
PJ.1803
HN March 1993 guide term moved

eaves
PJ.1800   (B,R)
HN March 1993 descriptor moved
February 1991 alternate term added
ALT eave
SN Use for those horizontal portions of
a sloping roof that project beyond
the walls. For portions of the roof
projecting beyond the gable, use
verges.

<eaves and eave components>
PJ.1799
HN March 1993 guide term moved

eaves boards
PJ.1804
HN March 1993 descriptor moved
October 1991 lead-in term added
February 1991 scope note added
ALT eaves board
SN Use for wedgeshaped boards placed

at the lower edges of sloping roofs
to raise slightly the lowest course of
tiles or slate in order to give that
course the same pitch as the
courses above.
UF boards, eaves
catches, eaves
eaves catches
eaves laths
fillets, tilting
tilting fillets

eaves catches
USE eaves boards

eaves, closed
USE closed eaves

eaves fascias
USE fascia boards

eaves gutters
PJ.892
HN March 1993 descriptor moved
February 1991 scope note added
February 1991 lead-in terms added
ALT eaves gutter
SN Long shallow channels positioned
under and paralleling the eaves of a
building for the purpose of collect-
ing and directing water from a
roof. (MEANS)
UF eaves troughs
gutters, eaves
troughs, eaves

eaves laths
USE eaves boards

eaves, open
USE open eaves

eaves tile
MT.181
HN April 1992 descriptor moved

eaves troughs
USE eaves gutters

ébano
USE brazilwood

ebauches
VC.587
ALT ébauche
SN Use for abbozzi when in the context
of French painting.

ebenaceae
USE ebony

ébénistes
HG.782
HN December 1992 alternate terms
added
ALT ébéniste
ébéniste's
ébénistes'
SN Skilled French craftsmen of luxury
furniture; also French cabinetmakers specializing in veneered furniture.
UF ebonists

menuisiers-ébéniste
menuisiers en ébène

Ebira
    FL.256   (L)
  UF Igbira

ebonists
  USE ébénistes

ebony
    MT.2725   (R)
  HN March 1992 descriptor moved
  SN A hard, heavy, durable wood yielded by various trees of the genus diospyros in tropical Asia and Africa. (W)
  UF Diospyros
        ebenaceae

ebony (color)
  USE dark gray
        dark olive
        olive gray

ebony, black
  USE black ebony

ebony brown
  USE dark gray
        dark reddish gray
        reddish black

ebony, Senegal
  USE African blackwood

ebony, West Indian
  USE granadilla

Ebrie
    FL.294
  UF Kyama

ebulliometers
    TN.307   (N)
  ALT ebulliometer
  SN Instruments for the precise measurement of the absolute or differential boiling points of solutions. (MHDSTT)
  UF ebullioscopes

ebullioscopes
  USE ebulliometers

EC
  USE ethyl cellulose

Eccentric Abstraction
    FL.3861
  HN May 1991 descriptor added
  UF Abstraction, Eccentric

eccentric loads
    BM.606   (L)
  HN November 1992 descriptor moved
      January 1991 alternate term added
  ALT eccentric load
  SN Load on a column or pile which is nonsymmetric with respect to the central axis, therefore producing a bending moment. (DAC)
  UF loads, eccentric
        loads, unsymmetrical
        unsymmetrical loads

ecclesiastical architecture
  USE religious buildings

ecclesiastical costume
  USE vestments

ecclesiastical plate
  USE church plate

ecclesiology
    KD.93   (R)
  SN Study of the doctrines of the church, including the study of ecclesiastical art, antiquities, and the adornment and equipment of churches. (W)

echini
    PJ.1508
  HN March 1993 descriptor moved
      September 1991 scope note changed
  ALT echinus
  SN The convex moldings supporting the abaci of Doric capitals and appearing between the volutes on Ionic capitals. (DINSMR)

echo
    BM.766   (H,L,B)
  HN April 1993 descriptor moved
      March 1993 scope note added
  SN A packet of sound waves that has been reflected or otherwise returned with a sufficient delay and magnitude to be perceived as a signal distinct from the original transmission.
  UF sound reverberation

ECHO dwellings
  USE ECHO houses

ECHO homes
  USE ECHO houses

ECHO houses
    RK.335
  HN February 1991 descriptor added
  ALT ECHO house
  SN Designates small, free-standing, barrier-free, energy-efficient, and removable dwellings that are installed adjacent to single-family homes as residences for elderly relatives, usually parents. (AARP)
  UF cottages, elder
        dwellings, ECHO
        ECHO dwellings
        ECHO homes
        ECHO units
        Elder Cottage Housing Opportunity units
        elder cottages
        flats, granny
        granny flats
        homes, ECHO
        houses, ECHO
        units, ECHO
  RT temporary housing

echo ranging
  USE sonar

echo sounding
  USE sonar

ECHO units
  USE ECHO houses

echoppes
    TH.844   (N)
  HN February 1993 descriptor added
  ALT echoppe
  SN Etching needles ground to an oblique face to obtain swelling lines; first used by 17th-century artist Jacques Callot.
  UF échoppes

échoppes
  USE echoppes

Eclectic Style
  USE Setchuyo

eclecticism
    BM.135   (A,L,R)
  HN January 1991 alternate term added
  ALT eclectic
  SN Approach or practice of selecting the best elements from different doctrines, methods, or styles to apply them in a new creation. In the specific context of art or architectural criticism, use to mean borrowing from a variety of visual sources in the creation of a work. (PDAT)

ecological art
  USE earthworks (sculpture)

ecological psychology
  USE environmental psychology

ecologists
    HG.539   (L)
  HN April 1993 related term added
      December 1992 alternate terms added
  ALT ecologist
        ecologist's
        ecologists'
  RT ecology

ecology
    KD.158   (A,L,B,R)
  HN April 1993 related term added
      December 1992 descriptor moved
      July 1991 scope note changed
      July 1991 related terms added
      February 1991 alternate term added
  ALT ecological
  SN Use for the branch of biology dealing with the relations and interactions between organisms and their habitat, including other organisms. For the aggregate of physical things, conditions, and influences surrounding and affecting a given organism or community of organisms at any time, use **environment**. For the concept of the external world, including the forces at work in it and the nonhuman life inhabiting it, perceived by human beings as sepa-

rate and independent from themselves, their activities and civilization, use **Nature**.
RT ecologists
environment
Nature

ecology, human
USE human ecology

ecology, social
USE human ecology

<economic and financial functions>
KG.81

<economic concepts>
BM.862
HN February 1993 guide term moved

economic development
KG.70 (L)
UF development, economic

economic development, rural
USE rural development

<economic ideologies>
BM.873
HN February 1993 guide term moved

economic rent
BM.898
HN February 1993 descriptor moved
SN Rate of rent which is sufficient to cover all costs of maintenance and operation of a building and, in addition, yield a reasonable return on the investment of the owner. (PUTNAM)
UF rent, economic

economic value
USE value (economic concept)

economically disadvantaged
USE poor

economics
KD.247 (L,B,R)
HN August 1991 related term added
July 1991 scope note changed
February 1991 alternate term added
ALT economic
SN Study concerned with the production, distribution, and consumption of money, goods, and services. (RHDEL2)
RT money

economists
HG.449 (L)
HN December 1992 alternate terms added
ALT economist
economist's
economists'

economy brick
USE jumbo brick

economy, fuel
USE fuel economy

écorché figures
USE écorchés

écorchés
VC.42 (R)
HN April 1991 descriptor moved
ALT écorché
SN Drawings, prints, or statues of flayed human or animal figures, used in the study of musculature. (MAYER)
UF écorché figures
figures, écorché

écrans à pivot
TC.440
HN January 1993 descriptor moved
ALT écran à pivot
SN Pivoting fire screens adjusted in position by a thumbscrew on a rod.

écrans à secrétaire
TC.444
HN January 1993 descriptor moved
ALT écran à secrétaire
SN Firescreens with a shelf or slide attached, to be used for writing before the fire. (WATSON)
UF écrans à secrétaire en pente
secrétaires en pente à écran

écrans à secrétaire en pente
USE écrans à secrétaire

ecru
USE grayish yellow
light grayish yellowish brown
pale yellow

Ecuadorian
FL.736 (L,B)
HN April 1990 descriptor added

écuelles
TQ.360
ALT écuelle
SN Shallow, flat-bottomed bowls with vertical sides, having two lateral handles that are level with the rim, and usually a cover, and sometimes a conforming stand.
RT brandy bowls
porringers

écus
VK.79
ALT écu
SN Use for any of various French gold or silver coins issued from the 13th through the 18th century, bearing the figure of a shield. (RHDEL2)
UF écus d'or

écus d'or
USE écus

Eden
FL.766

edge (contour)
USE contour

edge (outline)
USE outline

edge planes
TH.1502 (N)
HN March 1993 lead-in term changed, was **pianomaker's edge planes**
March 1993 lead-in term changed, was **edge planes, pianomaker's**
March 1993 lead-in term changed, was **planes, pianomaker's edge**
ALT edge plane
SN Four- to 6-inch planes with the front edge open so that the iron can cut at the very nose of the plane; used for trimming in hard to reach places. (SALAM)
UF chisel planes
edge planes, pianomakers'
pianomakers' edge planes
planes, chisel
planes, edge
planes, pianomakers' edge

edge planes, pianomakers'
USE edge planes

edge pulls, door
USE door edge pulls

edge reversal
USE Sabattier effect
solarization

edge rolls
PJ.2694
ALT edge roll
SN Firmly stuffed rolls attached to the edges of upholstered seats to make the edges more durable.
UF rolls, edge

edge rolls (moldings)
USE roll moldings

edged arms
USE edged weapons

<edged weapon components>
PJ.3133
RT blades

edged weapons
TK.4 (H)
ALT edged weapon
SN Weapons featuring a sharp edge or point for cutting, thrusting, clubbing, slashing, or various combinations thereof.
UF arms, edged
edged arms
weapons, edged
RT arrows
darts

edgers
TH.1133
ALT edger
SN Finishing tools used on the edges of fresh concrete to provide a rounded corner. (STEIN)

edges
PJ.758
ALT edge
SN Use for the narrow parts of thin, flat

objects. In books, the three outer extremities of the gatherings.
RT deckle edges
<edges: gathered matter components>

edges, cut
USE cut edges

edges, deckle
USE deckle edges

edges, deckled
USE deckle edges

edges, feathered
USE deckle edges

edges, fore
USE fore edges

edges, front
USE fore edges

<edges: gathered matter components>
PJ.3378
RT edges

edges, sight
USE sight edges

edges, straight
USE straightedges

edges, uncut
USE uncut edges

edges, unploughed
USE uncut edges

edges, untrimmed
USE uncut edges

<edging and surfacing patterns>
DG.125

edicts
USE decrees

edicule frames
USE tabernacle frames

edicules
USE aediculae

editing
KG.137   (L)
HN January 1991 scope note added
SN Collecting, preparing, and arranging materials for publication or public presentation, especially written materials, film, or tape. (RHDEL2)

edition binding
KT.771
HN January 1993 descriptor added
SN The binding of identical books in quantity, using high-speed automatic equipment, usually for a publisher or distributor and usually case binding in hard covers.
UF binding, edition

editions
PC.7
HN March 1993 descriptor moved
March 1991 scope note changed

ALT edition
SN Groups of multiples of one work issued together, such as of a book, print, photograph, or cast sculpture.

editions, abridged
USE abridgements

editions, first
USE first editions

editions, limited
USE limited editions

editions, trade
USE trade books

editorial cartoons
VC.36   (L)
HN April 1991 descriptor moved
ALT editorial cartoon
SN Use for cartoons that express editorial opinions, usually by appearing on the editorial pages of a newspaper or periodical.
UF cartoons, editorial

editorial writers
HG.480
HN December 1992 alternate terms added
ALT editorial writer
editorial writer's
editorial writers'
SN Persons who write comments on topics of reader interest to stimulate or mold public opinion, in accordance with viewpoints and policies of publication. (DOT)
UF writers, editorial

editorials
VW.384   (L)
HN November 1992 descriptor moved
March 1992 scope note changed
ALT editorial
SN Includes articles in publications expressing the opinions of their editors or publishers and statements on radio or television expressing the opinions of a station or network. (AHD)

editors
HG.377   (L)
HN December 1992 alternate terms added
ALT editor
editor's
editors'
SN Persons who revise, correct, or arrange the contents or style of literary, artistic, or musical work of others for publication or presentation. (W)

Edo (African)
FL.248   (L)

Edo (Japanese period)
FL.2060   (A,L)
UF Tokugawa

Edo-e
FL.2160

Edo, Early
USE Early Edo

Edo, Late
USE Late Edo

Edo, Middle
USE Middle Edo

<Edo-speaking cultures>
FL.246

educating
KG.257
HN April 1991 descriptor added
ALT educated
SN Use for the specific activities involved in deliberately conveying knowledge, skills, or social values to others. For the discipline that concerns the entire process of imparting such knowledge or values, use **education**. (ERIC12)
RT education

education
KD.250   (L,B,R)
HN May 1991 scope note added
April 1991 related term added
February 1991 alternate term added
ALT educational
SN Use for the discipline that concerns the entire process of imparting knowledge, attitudes, skills, or socially valued qualities of character or behavior. For the specific activities involved in deliberately conveying knowledge, skills, or social values to others, use **educating**. (ERIC12)
RT educating

education, architectural
USE architectural education

education, art
USE art education

education buildings, physical
USE physical education buildings

<education by grade level>
KD.251

<education by subdiscipline>
KD.259

<education by subject>
KD.261
HN October 1990 guide term added

education, continuing
USE continuing education

education, early childhood
USE early childhood education

education, elementary
USE elementary education

education, higher
USE higher education

education, lifelong
USE   continuing education

education, nursery school
USE   early childhood education
preschool education

education, pre-school
SEE   preschool education

education, preschool
USE   preschool education

education, primary
USE   primary education

education, secondary
USE   secondary education

education, secondary school
USE   secondary education

education, special
USE   special education

educational associations
   HN.74   (L)
HN   April 1991 descriptor moved
April 1991 descriptor changed, was
educational societies
April 1991 alternate term changed,
was educational society
April 1991 lead-in term changed,
was societies, educational
ALT   educational association
UF   associations, educational

educational buildings
USE   schools

educational complexes
   RG.52   (L)
ALT   educational complex
SN   Groupings of educational buildings
and other facilities; if possible, use a
more specific term.
UF   complexes, educational
complexes, school
educational facilities
facilities, educational
school complexes

<educational events>
   KM.69

educational facilities
USE   educational complexes

<educational functions>
   KG.256

educational media centers
USE   audiovisual centers

educational parks
   RG.54   (A,L)
ALT   educational park
SN   Complexes of schools, usually ranging from kindergarten through high
school or two-year college, that draw
students from a metropolitan area
and are intended to minimize the
effects of segregation. (ERIC9)
UF   parks, educational

educational toys
   TV.194   (L)
ALT   educational toy
SN   Use for toys with an educational or
teaching component.
UF   teaching toys
toys, educational
toys, teaching
RT   alphabet blocks
dissected maps

educators
   HG.490   (L,R)
HN   December 1992 alternate terms
added
ALT   educator
educator's
educators'

Edwardian
   FL.3411   (A,L,B,R)

Edwards Plateau
   FL.934

eel-grass
SEE   eelgrass

eel-spears
SEE   eelspears

eel spears
USE   eelspears

eelgrass
   MT.2625
HN   March 1992 descriptor moved
UK   eel-grass
SN   A submerged marine plant with
very long narrow leaves that is
found in abundance along the
North Atlantic coast. (W)
UF   grass wrack
wrack, grass

eelspears
   TK.60   (N)
ALT   eelspear
UK   eel-spears
UKA   eel-spear
SN   Forked or barbed spears for catch-
ing eels as they lie in the mud.
UF   eel spears
spears, eel

effect, moiré
USE   moiré effect

effect, Sabattier
USE   Sabattier effect

efficiency apartments
USE   studio apartments

efficiency, thermal
USE   thermal efficiency

effigies
   VC.517   (L,N,B,R)
ALT   effigy
SN   Use for sculptured representations
of the deceased on a tomb.

Effigy Mound
   FL.831

effigy mounds
   RK.839
ALT   effigy mound
SN   Use for large earthworks formed in
the likeness of birds and animals.
UF   mounds, effigy

efflorescence
   DE.19   (L,B)

Efik
   FL.241   (L)

Egba
   FL.272   (L)

egg
   MT.2517   (L,R)
HN   March 1992 scope note added
February 1992 descriptor moved
SN   Roundish reproductive bodies produced by the female of certain animals such as birds and most reptiles,
consisting of an ovum and its envelope of albumen, jelly, membranes,
egg case, or shell. (W)

egg and anchor moldings
USE   egg and dart moldings

egg and arrow moldings
USE   egg and dart moldings

egg and dart moldings
   PJ.2085
HN   April 1993 descriptor moved
ALT   egg and dart molding
SN   Moldings enriched with egg-shaped
ornaments alternating with dartlike
ornaments.
UF   egg and anchor moldings
egg and arrow moldings
egg and tongue moldings
moldings, egg and anchor
moldings, egg and arrow
moldings, egg and dart
moldings, egg and tongue

<egg and egg components>
   MT.2516
HN   January 1992 guide term added

egg-and-oil tempera
USE   egg-oil tempera

egg and tongue moldings
USE   egg and dart moldings

egg baskets
   TQ.580   (N)
ALT   egg basket
SN   Deep, open baskets of varying form
intended primarily for gathering or
transporting eggs; used especially
with reference to those with rib-
type construction.
UF   baskets, hip
baskets, jug
hip baskets
jug baskets
orioles

egg boilers
USE   egg coddlers

egg chairs
TC.495
HN January 1993 descriptor moved
ALT egg chair
UF chairs, egg
chairs, egg easy
easy chairs, egg
egg easy chairs

egg coddlers
TH.67   (N)
HN April 1993 descriptor added
ALT egg coddler
SN Vessels for cooking or coddling eggs. (HNSIL)
UF boilers, egg
coddlers
coddlers, egg
cookers, egg
egg boilers
egg cookers
RT egg poachers

<egg components>
MT.2518
HN February 1992 guide term added

egg cookers
USE egg coddlers

egg crate louvers
PJ.2311   (B)
HN March 1993 descriptor moved
July 1990 descriptor added
ALT egg crate louver
UF louvers, egg crate

egg easy chairs
USE egg chairs

egg graders
USE egg scales

egg grading scales
USE egg scales

egg holders
USE egg stands

egg-oil paint
USE egg-oil tempera

egg-oil tempera
MT.1954
HN August 1992 descriptor moved
July 1990 descriptor added
SN Tempera made using the whole egg, with oils or resins added, having qualities of both egg tempera and oil paint. (GOTTS)
UF egg-and-oil tempera
egg-oil paint
egg/oil emulsion
emulsion, egg/oil
paint, egg-oil
tempera, egg-and-oil
tempera, egg-oil

egg poachers
TQ.310
ALT egg poacher
SN Containers with a tight-fitting lid, and often an insert with separate wells, used to poach eggs. Also, vari-

ous contrivances used to poach eggs, often consisting of a stand, with a long vertical handle and a number of smaller containers, meant to be placed in a pan or skillet of water.
UF poachers, egg
RT egg coddlers

egg scales
TN.299   (N)
ALT egg scale
SN Small scales used for measuring the weight and therefore the market size of eggs, usually one by one. (HEARTH)
UF egg graders
egg grading scales
graders, egg
grading scales, egg
scales, egg
scales, egg grading

egg separators
TH.182   (N)
HN April 1993 descriptor added
ALT egg separator
SN Devices for separating the yolk from the white of the egg. (LANTZ)
UF separators, egg

egg-shaped
DC.67
HN October 1992 descriptor moved

egg-shell
SEE eggshell (animal material)

egg shell
USE eggshell (animal material)

egg shell white
USE shell white

egg slicers
TH.116
HN April 1993 descriptor added
ALT egg slicer
SN Devices with a series of cutting wires held in a frame, used for slicing hard-boiled eggs.
UF slicers, egg

egg stands
TQ.553
ALT egg stand
SN Receptacles for holding eggs while boiling or when serving them at the table. Those used for both cooking and serving are often made of twisted wire, while those used just for serving are generally earthenware or sometimes silver plate.
UF egg holders
holders, egg
stands, egg
RT breakfast services
eggcups

egg tempera
MT.1955
HN January 1993 scope note changed
August 1992 descriptor moved

SN Tempera paint using egg as its vehicle, traditionally the yolk only, in other cases, the whole egg. (GETTEN)
UF tempera, egg

egg whips
USE whisks

egg white
MT.2519
HN February 1992 descriptor added
SN The white of an egg, as distinct from the yolk; used, among other things, as a pigment binder, and in varnishes and size. For the same substance, but in the context of photographic materials, prefer **albumen**.
UF white, egg

egg yolk
MT.2521
HN March 1992 lead-in term added
March 1992 related term added
February 1992 descriptor moved
SN Yellow spheroidal mass of stored food that forms the inner portion of the egg of a bird or reptile and is surrounded by the egg white. (W)
UF yolk
yolk, egg
RT tempera

egg/oil emulsion
USE egg-oil tempera

eggbeaters
TH.136   (L,N)
HN April 1993 descriptor added
ALT eggbeater
SN Rotary beaters operated by hand for aerating eggs or liquids such as cream. (W)
UF beaters, egg
beaters, rotary
beaters, rotary egg
rotary beaters
rotary egg beaters

eggcups
TQ.494   (H,L,N)
ALT eggcup
UF coquetières
RT breakfast services
egg stands

eggplant, dark
USE blackish purple

eggshell (animal material)
MT.2522   (L)
HN February 1992 descriptor added
UK egg-shell
SN The hard exterior covering of eggs. (W)
UF egg shell
shell, egg

eggshell (pale yellow)
USE pale yellow

eggshell (pottery style)
FL.2755
HN April 1993 descriptor added

eggshell (yellowish white)
USE yellowish white

eggshell ware
HN April 1993 descriptor split, use egg-shell (pottery style) + ware

églomisé
USE verre églomisé

Egnatian
USE Gnathian

egobolis
TT.349
ALT egoboli
SN Braced musical bows of Uganda having a half-calabash resonator; the resonator is placed against the player's chest and the string is struck with a blade of grass or thin stick bent in the form of a V. (NGDMI)
UF omugobolis

egrets
USE aigrettes

Egun
USE Gun

Egyptian
FL.2859 (A,L,B,R)

Egyptian blue
MT.2101
HN April 1993 lead-in term changed, was Copper frit
April 1992 descriptor moved
January 1992 lead-in terms added
UF Ägyptisch Blau
Ägyptischblau
Alexandria blue
bleu d'alexandrie
bleu de Pouzzoles
bleu d'Egypte
bleu egiziano
bleu Egyptian
bleu fritté
blue, Alexandria
blue, Egyptian
blue frit
blue, Italian
blue, Pompeian
blue, Pozzuoli
blue, Venetian
blue, Vestorian
coeruleum
copper frit
Frittenblau
Italian blue
Pompeian blue
Pozzuoli blue
Venetian blue
Vestorian blue

Egyptian breccia marble
MT.698
HN April 1992 descriptor moved

SN A coarse breccia marble containing fragments of pophyry, basalt, quartz, and granite in a greenish or purplish ground. (RS)
UF breccia marble, Egyptian
marble, Egyptian breccia

Egyptian brown
USE mummy

Egyptian crosses
USE ankhs

Egyptian Empire
USE New Kingdom

Egyptian gorges
USE cavetto cornices

<Egyptian Paleolithic periods>
FL.2861

Egyptian paper
USE papyrus

<Egyptian periods>
FL.2860

<Egyptian pottery styles>
FL.2925

Egyptian Revival
FL.3358 (A,L,B,R)
UF Egyptian Taste
Neo-Egyptian
Revival, Egyptian

<Egyptian styles>
FL.2924

<Egyptian, Syrian and Iraqi Islamic styles and periods>
FL.3543
HN April 1993 guide term added

Egyptian Taste
USE Egyptian Revival

Egyptologists
HG.462 (L)
HN January 1993 descriptor added
ALT Egyptologist
Egyptologist's
Egyptologists'
SN Those trained or working in Egyptology.

eiderdowns
TC.204
ALT eiderdown
SN Comforters filled with the down of the eider duck.

EIF system
USE exterior insulation and finish system

EIFS
USE exterior insulation and finish system

eight lobed star Usak carpets
USE star Ushaks

eight-part vaults
USE octopartite vaults

eighteen-carat gold
MT.424
HN March 1993 descriptor moved
SN Gold which has 18 parts of gold to six parts of alloying metal. (OCDA)
UF 18-carat gold
gold, eighteen-carat

Eighteenth Dynasty
FL.2904
UF 18th Dynasty
Dynasty, Eighteenth

Eighth Dynasty
FL.2887
UF 8th Dynasty
Dynasty, Eighth

eikons
USE icons

Eile
FL.622

eilitons
USE antimensia

Einfühling
USE empathy

Ejagham
FL.237 (L)
UF Ekoi

ejectors, candle
USE pushups

ejectors, stub
USE pushups

Eket
FL.242

ekistics
KD.265 (B)
SN Scientific study of human settlements. (RHDEL2)

Ekiti
FL.273

ekklesiasteria
RK.1136 (A)
ALT ekklesiasterion
SN Use for buildings housing the meeting places of the ekklesia or sovereign assembly of an ancient Greek city.

Ekoi
USE Ejagham

ekorros
USE koras

ekphrasis
BM.20 (L,R)
SN Description of a work of art, real or imaginary, undertaken as a rhetorical exercise. (THDAT)

Ektachrome (TM)
KT.558
SN A subtractive color reversal process using a film with an integral tripack, each layer containing dyes appro-

priate to the color sensitivity of the layer. The image is formed by the chromogenic process.

El Arbolillo
FL.995

El-Omari
FL.2868

El Tajin
USE Tajin

Elamite
FL.3099 (L)

Elamite, Ancient
USE Old Elamite

Elamite, Early
USE Old Elamite

Elamite, Middle
USE Middle Elamite

Elamite, Old
USE Old Elamite

elastic buckling
KT.247
HN January 1993 descriptor moved
UF buckling, elastic

elastic chairs
TC.496
HN January 1993 descriptor moved
ALT elastic chair
SN Term for the earliest type of bent-wood chairs; patented by Samuel Gragg in 1808. (FAIRB)
UF chairs, elastic

elastic knives
TH.1160
HN December 1992 descriptor moved
ALT elastic knife
SN Plasterers' tools made of highly flexible carbon steel; used in trimming plaster. (PUTNAM)
UF knives, elastic

elastic limit
DC.178
HN October 1992 descriptor moved
SN The greatest unit stress that a material is capable of withstanding without permanent deformation. (MH)
UF limit, elastic

elastic modulus
USE modulus of elasticity

elasticity
DC.179 (L)
HN October 1992 descriptor moved
February 1992 scope note added
ALT elastic
SN The capability of a strained body to recover its size and shape after deformation in any way. (W)

elasticity, coefficient
USE modulus of elasticity

elasticity, modulus of
USE modulus of elasticity

elastomer
MT.1028 (L)
HN April 1993 lead-in term added
April 1993 descriptor changed, was elastomers
January 1993 descriptor moved
SN Polymeric material that will return to approximately its original length after stretching. (MH12)
UF artificial rubber
elastomeric material
material, elastomeric
rubber, artificial
rubber, synthetic
synthetic rubber

<elastomer by composition or origin>
MT.1029
HN January 1993 guide term moved

<elastomer by form>
MT.1045
HN January 1993 guide term moved

elastomer, epichlorohydrin
USE epichlorohydrin elastomer

elastomer, ethylene-propylene
USE ethylene-propylene elastomer

elastomer, fluorocarbon
USE fluorocarbon elastomer

elastomer, fluorosilicone
USE fluorosilicone elastomer

elastomer, isobutylene-isoprene
USE butyl rubber

elastomer, nitrile
USE nitrile elastomer

elastomer, polybutadiene
USE polybutadiene elastomer

elastomer, polyethylene
USE polyethylene elastomer

elastomer, polysulfide
USE polysulfide elastomer

elastomer, silicone
USE silicone elastomer

elastomer, sytrene-butadiene
USE styrene-butadiene rubber

elastomer, urethane
USE urethane elastomer

elastomeric material
USE elastomer

elbow chairs
TC.454
HN May 1993 lead-in term deleted, was French chairs (elbow chairs)
May 1993 lead-in term deleted, was chairs, French (elbow chairs)
January 1993 descriptor moved
ALT elbow chair
SN Term applied to armchairs, particu-

larly those with open arms and padded rests. (BEARD)
UF chairs, elbow
chairs, open-arm
open-arm chairs

elbow chairs, French
USE French elbow chairs

elbow cops
USE cowters

elbow gauntlets
TE.326
ALT elbow gauntlet
SN Gauntlets with a long cuff encircling the forearm up to the elbow where the edge often was cut at an angle to form a point. They were characteristic of foot soldiers' armor in the 16th century, and common for light cavalry from the 15th to the 17th century when they were worn on the left or bridle arm only.
UF bridle gauntlets
gauntlets, bridle
gauntlets, elbow
gauntlets, long
long gauntlets

elbow melodeons
USE lap organs

elbow organs
USE lap organs

elbow pads
USE arm pads

elbow pipes
USE uilleann pipes

elbow seams
PJ.697
HN April 1993 descriptor moved
ALT elbow seam
UF seams, elbow

elbows
USE arms
consoles
crossettes

Elda 1005 upholstered chairs
TC.497
HN January 1993 descriptor moved
ALT Elda 1005 upholstered chair
UF chairs, Elda 1005 upholstered

elder, box
USE box elder

Elder Cottage Housing Opportunity units
USE ECHO houses

elder cottages
USE ECHO houses

elderly
HG.49 (A,L,B)
HN November 1992 alternate term added
January 1991 descriptor moved
February 1990 lead-in terms added

February 1990 descriptor changed,
was **aged**
January 1990 scope note added
ALT elderly's
SN Use for those in the later stage of
life, commonly considered as 65
years of age and older.
UF aged
aging persons
citizens, senior
elderly persons
old people
older adults
older persons
senior citizens

elderly, housing for the
USE housing for the elderly

elderly persons
USE elderly

elders
HG.419 (L)
HN February 1993 descriptor moved
December 1992 alternate terms
added
ALT elder
elder's
elders'
SN Certain church officers or leaders.
(W)

election ballots
USE ballots

election districts
RG.261 (L)
ALT election district
SN Districts created for the administration of elections. (W)
UF constituencies
districts, election
districts, voting
precincts, voting
voting districts
voting precincts
wards

election returns
VW.523
HN November 1992 descriptor moved
ALT election return
SN Certified reports by election officers
on the outcome vote in an election.
(AHD)
UF returns, election

election tickets
USE ballots

elections
KM.165 (L)
HN May 1991 alternate term added
November 1990 descriptor moved
ALT election

electorates
HN.42 (H,L)
HN January 1993 descriptor added
ALT electorate
SN Administrative bodies subject to an

elector, especially within the Holy
Roman Empire.

electors, registers of
USE voters' lists

electors' rolls
USE voters' lists

electric arc welding
USE arc welding

electric blankets
TC.11 (L)
ALT electric blanket
SN Bed coverings with an inner wiring
system and thermostatic control,
which provide constant warmth.
(IWINGT)
UF blankets, electric

electric cables
PJ.773 (L)
HN March 1993 descriptor moved
November 1992 scope note changed
November 1992 related term added
February 1991 scope note added
ALT electric cable
SN Use both for electric conductors
comprising a number of twisted or
braided wire strands and for groups
of electric conductors bound to-
gether and insulated from one an-
other.
UF cables, electric
RT cable laying

electric circuit-breakers
USE circuit breakers

electric circuits
USE circuits

electric closets
HN January 1992 descriptor deleted

electric conductor
MT.2308 (L)
HN April 1993 lead-in terms added
April 1993 descriptor changed, was
electric conductors
April 1993 lead-in term changed,
was **conductors, electric**
UF conductor, electric
electrically-conducting material
material, electrically-conducting

electric conduits
PJ.775 (L,B)
HN March 1993 descriptor moved
February 1991 scope note added
ALT electric conduit
SN Use for tubes especially constructed
for the purpose of enclosing electri-
cal conductors. (STEIN)
UF conduits (electric)
conduits, electric

electric discharge lamps
PJ.2952 (L)
ALT electric discharge lamp
SN Lamps in which light, or radiant en-
ergy near the visible spectrum, is
produced by the passage of an elec-

tric current through a vapor or a
gas. (IESREF)
UF discharge lamps
discharge lamps, electric
discharge tubes
gas-discharge lamps
gaseous discharge lamps
lamps, discharge
lamps, electric discharge
lamps, gas-discharge
lamps, vapor
tubes, discharge
vapor lamps (electric discharge
lamps)

electric drills
TH.601 (L,N)
ALT electric drill
SN Portable, hand-held, motor-driven
tools used to turn a bit for boring
holes in a material and powered either by direct or alternating current. (MEANS)
UF drills, electric
drills, electric-portable
electric-portable drills
portable drills, electric

electric elevators
PC.133
HN March 1993 descriptor moved
ALT electric elevator
UF elevators, electric

electric engineering
USE electrical engineering

electric engravers
TH.842 (L)
HN February 1993 descriptor added
ALT electric engraver
UF electric engraving tools
electrical engravers
electronic engraving machines
engravers, electric
engravers, electrical
engraving machines, electronic
engraving tools, electric
machines, electronic engraving
tools, electric engraving

electric engraving tools
USE electric engravers

electric eye cameras
TH.753 (L)
ALT electric eye camera
SN Automatic exposure meter cameras
which directly control the lens aperture, in response to light falling on
the photo cell. (FOCAL)
UF automatic cameras
cameras, automatic
cameras, electric eye

electric fences
RM.235 (L)
HN April 1993 descriptor moved
ALT electric fence
SN Wire fences designed to give a shock
upon touching. (W)
UF fences, electric

electric files
USE belt sanders

electric fixtures
TC.1412   (A)
ALT electric fixture
UF electric light fixtures
fixtures, electric

electric frying pans
TQ.305
ALT electric frying pan
SN Frying pans heated electrically.
UF frying pans, electric

electric furnaces
PJ.797   (L)
HN March 1993 descriptor moved
February 1991 scope note added
ALT electric furnace
SN Furnaces in which the high-temperature heat required is produced by electricity; used especially for forging alloys and refractory materials. (W)
UF furnaces, electric

electric generating plants, tidal energy
USE tidal power plants

electric generators
USE generators

electric guitars
TT.429   (L)
ALT electric guitar
SN Electroacoustic stringed instruments more or less in the form of guitars, occurring in two types. One has a hollow body which functions somewhat like a resonator; the other has a solid body serving solely as a mounting block for the bridge and electronic apparatus, and to bear the strings. In both types the sound is electronically amplified and its tone modified by electronic controls.
UF guitars, electric

electric handsaws
USE electric-portable saws

electric heating
USE resistance heating

electric hinges
PJ.386
HN April 1993 descriptor moved
ALT electric hinge
SN Hinges designed to pass electric wires from the frame to the door for use in an electrically controlled lock. (MEANS)
UF electrically wired hinges
hinges, electric
hinges, electrically wired

electric insulation
SEE electrical insulation

electric lamps (lighting device components)
PJ.2950   (L,N,B,R)

ALT electric lamp (lighting device component)
UF electric lights
lamps, electric
lights, electric

electric lamps (lighting devices)
TC.1378   (L,N,R)
ALT electric lamp (lighting device)
UF electric lights
lamps, electric

electric light
USE electric lighting

electric light fixtures
USE electric fixtures

electric lighting
PC.218   (A,H,L,B,R)
HN March 1993 descriptor moved
April 1991 lead-in terms added
UF electric light
light, electric
lighting, electric

electric lights
USE electric lamps (lighting device components)
electric lamps (lighting devices)

electric lines
USE power lines

electric locomotives
TX.240   (L,N)
ALT electric locomotive
SN Use for locomotives whose motive power source is electricity generated on board or obtained via overhead wires or a third rail.
UF locomotives, electric

electric locomotives, diesel
USE diesel-electric locomotives

electric locomotives, gas-turbine
USE gas-turbine locomotives

electric metal-cutting
KT.1118   (L)
UF metal-cutting, electric

electric meters
TN.220   (L)
ALT electric meter
SN Devices that measure electricity by totalizing electrical quantities with time, such as watthour meters.
UF meters, electric

electric organs
USE electronic organs

electric plants, tidal
USE tidal power plants

electric plants, water-power
USE hydroelectric power plants

electric-portable drills
USE electric drills

electric-portable saws
TH.1574   (N)

ALT electric-portable saw
UF circular saws, portable
electric handsaws
handsaws, electric
portable circular saws
saws, electric-portable
saws, portable circular
saws, skill
skill saws

electric potential
USE voltage

electric power plants
USE power plants

electric power production
BM.363   (L)
HN March 1993 scope note added
November 1992 descriptor moved
SN The large-scale production of electricity for industrial, residential, or rural use, generally in stationary plants designed for that purpose.
UF power production, electric
production, electric power

electric power stations
USE power plants

electric power supply
USE power supply

electric power transmission lines
USE power lines

electric raceways
USE raceways

electric resistance heating
USE resistance heating

electric resistance welding
USE resistance welding

electric stairways
USE escalators

electric substations
RK.640   (A,L,B)
ALT electric substation
UF stations, transformer
substations
substations, electric
transformer stations

electric switches
PJ.776   (L)
HN March 1993 descriptor moved
ALT electric switch
UF switches
switches, electric

electric switchgear
USE switchboards

electric tape
USE friction tape

electric toasters
TH.80   (L)
HN April 1993 descriptor added
ALT electric toaster
SN Culinary appliances with electrically

heated elements for browning bread and similar food.
UF toasters, electric

electric transformers
USE transformers

electric utilities
HN.122   (L)
ALT electric utility
SN Use for the public service organizations that provide electricity.
UF electricity supply industry
     industry, electricity supply
     utilities, electric

electric vehicles
TX.229   (L)
ALT electric vehicle
SN Road vehicles propelled by electric motors, drawing their current either from storage batteries or from overhead cables.
UF vehicles, electric
RT trolleybuses

electric welders
USE arc welding machines

electric welding
KT.1088   (L)
SN Any of a number of methods of welding that use electricity as a source of power.
UF welding, electric

electric wiring
PJ.777   (A,L,B)
HN March 1993 descriptor moved
     February 1991 scope note added
SN Use for the aggregate of wires in electrical systems. (RHDEL2)
UF electric wiring systems
     systems, electric wiring
     systems, wiring
     wiring, electric
     wiring systems

electric wiring systems
USE electric wiring

electrical arc welding
USE arc welding

<electrical attributes and properties>
DC.21
HN October 1992 guide term added

electrical conductivity
DC.26   (L)
HN October 1992 descriptor moved
     June 1992 lead-in term added
UF conductivity, electrical
     electroconductivity

electrical drawings
VC.232
HN April 1992 descriptor moved
ALT electrical drawing
SN Use for drawings of electrical systems or parts thereof. For scaled floor plans specifically, use electrical plans.
UF drawings, electrical

electrical engineering
KD.120   (L)
UF electric engineering
     engineering, electric
     engineering, electrical

electrical engineers
HG.866   (L,B)
HN December 1992 alternate terms added
ALT electrical engineer
     electrical engineer's
     electrical engineers'
UF engineers, electrical

electrical engravers
USE electric engravers

electrical installations
USE electrical systems

electrical insulation
MT.1806   (L)
HN August 1992 lead-in term added
     June 1991 descriptor moved
UK electric insulation
UF insulation, electric
     insulation, electrical

electrical plans
VC.135
HN April 1992 descriptor moved
ALT electrical plan
SN Use for scaled floor plans showing electrical layout; may include an adjacent small drawing of an elevation, or a riser diagram. For other drawings of electrical systems, use electrical drawings.
UF plans, electrical

electrical power stations
USE power plants

electrical power systems
USE electrical systems

electrical pressure transducers
USE pressure transducers

electrical properties
DC.24   (L)
HN October 1992 descriptor moved
UF properties, electrical

electrical resistivity profiling
USE resistivity surveying

electrical resistivity surveying
USE resistivity surveying

electrical safety
BM.371
HN December 1992 descriptor moved
UF safety, electrical

electrical supply lines
USE power lines

electrical supply stations
HN January 1992 descriptor deleted

<electrical system components>
PJ.770
HN March 1993 guide term moved

electrical systems
PC.137   (A,B)
HN March 1993 descriptor moved
ALT electrical system
UF electrical installations
     electrical power systems
     installations, electrical
     power systems, electrical
     systems, electrical

<electrical systems and electrical system components>
HN March 1993 guide term deleted

electrically-conducting material
USE electric conductor

electrically wired hinges
USE electric hinges

electricians
HG.824   (L)
HN December 1992 alternate terms added
ALT electrician
     electrician's
     electricians'

electricity
BM.775   (L,R)
HN April 1993 descriptor moved
     February 1992 scope note added
SN Physical phenomenon involving electric charges and their effects when at rest and in motion. (MHDSTT)

<electricity measuring devices>
TN.218

<electricity-related concepts>
BM.794
HN November 1992 guide term added

electricity supply, emergency
USE emergency power supply

electricity supply industry
USE electric utilities

electroacoustic instruments
TT.428
ALT electroacoustic instrument
SN Musical instruments which produce barely audible sounds by acoustic methods and incorporate built-in microphones or pickups which amplify the vibrations.
UF instruments, electroacoustic

electrochemical corrosion
KT.254   (L)
HN January 1993 descriptor moved
SN Corrosion that occurs when current flows between cathodic and anodic areas on metallic surfaces. (STEIN)
UF corrosion, electrochemical
     corrosion, electrolytic
     corrosion, galvanic
     electrolytic corrosion
     galvanic corrosion

electrochemical cutting
KT.1119　　　　　　　　　　　(L)
UF　cutting, electrochemical

electroconductivity
USE　electrical conductivity

electroforming
KT.318　　　　　　　　　　　(L)
HN　December 1992 descriptor added
ALT　electroformed
SN　The technique of making an exact facsimile of a model, sometimes a wax model but often an actual article of which reproductions are sought, by depositing a thin layer of a metal, such as copper or silver, by means of an electric current.
UF　electrotyping (forming)

electrogalvanizing
KT.1107　　　　　　　　　　(L)
ALT　electrogalvanized
SN　Galvanizing by a process in which the zinc is deposited by an electroplating method. (DAC)
UF　coating, zinc
　　plating, zinc
　　zinc coating
　　zinc plating

electroless plating
KT.1111　　　　　　　　　　(L)
SN　Deposition of a metallic coating by a controlled chemical reduction that is catalyzed by the metal or alloy being deposited. (STEIN)
UF　plating, electroless

electroliers
TC.1258
ALT　electrolier

electrolysis
KT.836　　　　　　　　　　(L,B)
HN　January 1993 descriptor added
SN　The passage of an electric current through an electrolyte with subsequent migration of positively and negatively charged ions to the negative and positive electrodes. In conservation used for cleaning off surface deposits. (RHDEL2)
UF　electrolytic processes
　　electrolytic treatment
　　treatment, electrolytic

electrolytic corrosion
USE　electrochemical corrosion

electrolytic process (copying)
KT.376
HN　March 1993 descriptor added
SN　Process for producing paper copies of microform originals, depending on electrolytic image formation on a special paper having metallic layers.
UF　electrolytic reproduction process
　　Filmac (TM)

electrolytic processes
USE　electrolysis

electrolytic reproduction process
USE　electrolytic process (copying)

electrolytic treatment
USE　electrolysis

electromagnetic energy
USE　electromagnetic radiation

electromagnetic fields
USE　electromagnetism

<electromagnetic properties>
DC.28
HN　October 1992 guide term added

electromagnetic radiation
BM.777　　　　　　　　　　(L)
HN　November 1992 descriptor moved
　　November 1992 lead-in terms added
　　November 1992 descriptor changed, was **radiation**
　　September 1992 scope note added
SN　The emission of energy or energy emitted in the form of electromagnetic waves.
UF　electromagnetic energy
　　electromagnetic spectra
　　electromagnetic waves
　　energy, electromagnetic
　　radiation (electromagnetic)
　　radiation, electromagnetic
　　spectra, electromagnetic
　　waves, electromagnetic

electromagnetic spectra
USE　electromagnetic radiation

electromagnetic waves
USE　electromagnetic radiation

electromagnetics
USE　electromagnetism

electromagnetism
BM.754　　　　　　　　　　(L)
HN　November 1992 descriptor moved
ALT　electromagnetic
SN　The phenomena associated with electric and magnetic fields and their interactions with each other and with electric charges and currents. (RHDEL2)
UF　electromagnetic fields
　　electromagnetics

electromechanical instruments
TT.430
ALT　electromechanical instrument
SN　Musical instruments that produce sound by means of rotating tonewheels which themselves produce no acoustic sound but create a regular fluctuation in an electrical circuit which can be converted into an audio signal.
UF　instruments, electromechanical

electrometers
TN.221　　　　　　　　　　(L,N)
ALT　electrometer
SN　Instruments calibrated to measure

very low voltages without drawing appreciable current.

electron beam welding
KT.1097　　　　　　　　　　(L)
UF　welding, electron beam

electron diffraction
BM.719　　　　　　　　　　(L)
HN　October 1992 descriptor added
SN　The phenomenon whereby electron waves scattered by the regularly spaced atoms of a substance produce diffraction patterns characteristic of that substance. (RHDEL2)
UF　diffraction, electron

electron microscopy
KT.205　　　　　　　　　　(L)
HN　November 1992 descriptor added
SN　The use of or investigation with an electron microscope.
UF　microscopy, electron

electron microscopy, scanning
USE　scanning electron microscopy

electron paramagnetic resonance
USE　electron spin resonance

electron spin resonance
BM.761　　　　　　　　　　(L)
HN　November 1992 descriptor added
SN　The flipping back and forth between two spin directions of electrons in a magnetic field when electromagnetic radiation of the proper frequency is applied. (RHDEL2)
UF　electron paramagnetic resonance
　　ESR
　　paramagnetic resonance, electron
　　resonance, electron paramagnetic
　　resonance, electron spin
　　spin resonance
　　spin resonance, electron

electronic clocks
TN.191　　　　　　　　　　(L)
ALT　electronic clock
SN　Use for clocks driven by tiny permanent-magnet synchronous motors and electronic circuitry.
UF　clocks, electronic

electronic clocks, digital
USE　digital clocks

electronic data processing
USE　data processing

electronic data processing departments
USE　computer centers

electronic digital imaging
USE　digital imaging

electronic engraving machines
USE　electric engravers

electronic flashes
TH.787
HN　November 1992 descriptor added
ALT　electronic flash
SN　Flash lamps consisting of a gas-filled

tube activated by a discharge of electric current.
UF electronic flashtubes
      flashes, electronic
      flashes, speed
      flashtubes
      flashtubes, electronic
      speed flashes
      tubes, flash

electronic flashtubes
USE electronic flashes

electronic glue guns
      TH.606
ALT electronic glue gun
SN Instantaneous curing glue guns for synthetic thermoset adhesives. (PUTNAM)
UF glue guns, electronic
      guns, electronic glue

electronic image databases
USE image databases

electronic images
      VC.238   (L)
ALT electronic image
SN Images recorded and stored in computer and video systems.
UF images, electronic
      pictures
RT electronic imaging
      image databases

electronic imaging
      KT.359
HN February 1993 descriptor added
SN The recording, storage, and manipulation of images in computer and video systems. (MUSNEW)
UF computer imaging
      electronic photography
      imaging
      imaging, computer
      imaging, electronic
      photography, electronic
RT electronic images

electronic instruments
      TT.432
ALT electronic instrument
SN Musical instruments that incorporate electronic circuitry as an integral part of the sound-generating system.
UF instruments, electronic

electronic mail
      VW.368   (L)
HN November 1992 descriptor moved
SN Messages from one individual to another sent via telecommunications links between computers or terminals. (RHDEL2)
UF e-mail
      mail, electronic

electronic organs
      TT.433   (L,N)
ALT electronic organ
SN Electronic keyboard instruments designed to imitate the tone of con-

ventional pipe organs, and, like pipe organs, are able to sustain the tone indefinitely, play chords, and decrease or increase sustained tone.
UF electric organs
      electrophonic organs
      organs, electric
      organs, electronic
      organs, electrophonic
      organs, pipeless
      pipeless organs
RT keyboard instruments

electronic photography
USE electronic imaging

electronic photometers
USE photoelectric photometers

electronic publishing
      KG.153   (L)
SN Publishing text or images in electronic machine-readable formats such as online databases, magnetic tapes, or floppy disks.
UF online publishing
      publishing, electronic
      publishing, online

electronic records
USE machine-readable + records

electronic security systems
      PC.235   (A,L)
HN March 1993 descriptor moved
      August 1990 descriptor added
      August 1990 lead-in terms added
ALT electronic security system
SN Designates security systems dependent on electronic devices, such as card readers.
UF security systems, electronic
      systems, electronic security

electronics laboratories
      RK.1107   (A,L,B)
ALT electronics laboratory
UF laboratories, electronics

electronophones
USE electrophones

electrophones
      TT.427
ALT electrophone
SN Musical instruments that produce vibrations which must be passed through electrical circuits ending in loudspeakers before they are heard as sound. (NGDMI)
UF electronophones
      electrophonic instruments
      instruments, electrophonic

electrophonic instruments
USE electrophones

electrophonic organs
USE electronic organs

electrophotocopies
USE xerographic copies

electrophotographic processes
USE electrophotography

electrophotography
      KT.525   (L)
SN Creation of images by alteration to the electrical properties of the sensitive material as a result of the action of light. (LANG)
UF electrophotographic processes

electrophotometers
USE photoelectric photometers

electroplate
HN March 1993 descriptor deleted

electroplaters
      HG.726
HN February 1993 descriptor moved
      February 1993 lead-in term deleted, was **platers**
      December 1992 alternate terms added
ALT electroplater
      electroplater's
      electroplaters'
SN Persons who engage in electroplating.

electroplating
      KT.1112   (L)
ALT electroplated
SN Applying a protective or decorative coating of one metal to another by means of an electrolytic bath. (W)

electropolishing
      KT.299   (L)
HN January 1993 descriptor moved
      March 1991 alternate term added
ALT electropolished
SN Producing a smooth bright surface on a metal object by immersion as an anode in an electrolytic bath. (W)

electros
USE electrotypes

electrostatic copies
HN March 1993 descriptor deleted, made lead-in to **xerographic copies**

electrostatic copies
USE xerographic copies

electrostatic copying
USE xerography

electrostatic plotters
      TH.572
HN January 1993 descriptor moved
ALT electrostatic plotter
SN Plotters in which paper passes under an array of fine metal teeth that deposit electrostatic charges which then attract toner.
UF plotters, electrostatic

electrostatic printing
HN March 1993 descriptor deleted, made lead-in to **xerography**

electrostatic printing
USE xerography

electrostatic processes
USE xerography

electrotype (process)
USE electrotyping

electrotype plates
USE electrotypes

electrotypes
TH.865
HN January 1993 descriptor added
ALT electrotype
SN Metal printing plates made by using a mold of another printing surface, such as a wood engraving or set type, and electroplating with copper.
UF electros
electrotype plates
plates, electrotype
RT electrotyping

electrotyping
KT.642 (L)
HN February 1993 descriptor added
ALT electrotyped
SN The process of making printing plates by using a mold of another printing surface, such as a wood engraving or set type, and electroplating with copper.
UF electrotype (process)
electrotypy
RT electrotypes

electrotyping (forming)
USE electroforming

electrotypy
USE electrotyping

electrum
MT.419 (L)
HN March 1993 descriptor moved

elegies
VW.292 (L)
HN November 1992 descriptor moved
ALT elegy
SN Mournful, melancholy, or plaintive poems, especially funeral songs or laments for the dead. (RHDEL2)

elem
PJ.2681
UF skirts (rug components)

Elema
FL.3780 (L)

<elemental forces measuring devices>
TN.217

Elementarist
FL.3440
ALT Elementarism

elementary education
KD.254 (L)
SN Branch of education covering kin-
dergarten or grade 1 through grades 6, 7, or 8. (ERIC9)
UF education, elementary

elementary schools
RK.797 (A,L,B)
HN September 1990 scope note added
ALT elementary school
SN Use for schools generally extending from grade 1 through grades 6 or 8 and teaching the rudiments of learning; may house a kindergarten.
UF grade schools
grammar schools
primary schools
schools, elementary
schools, grade
schools, grammar
schools, primary

elements, architectural
USE architectural elements

elemi
MT.1260
HN April 1992 descriptor moved
SN Fragrant oleoresin obtained from tropical trees and used chiefly in varnish, lacquer, and printing ink. (WCOL9)

elemi, Manila
USE Manila elemi

elemi, Manilla
SEE Manila elemi

elephant enclosures
USE elephant houses

elephant houses
RK.370 (A)
ALT elephant house
UF elephant enclosures
elephant pavilions
elephant stockades
enclosures, elephant
houses, elephant
houses, pachyderm
pachyderm houses
pavilions, elephant
stockades, elephant

elephant pavilions
USE elephant houses

elephant stockades
USE elephant houses

elephant's feet
USE güls

elephants' feet
USE güls

Eleusinian marble
MT.715
HN April 1992 descriptor moved
SN A fine, black marble from Attica, prized in ancient Greece, especially for friezes and interior decoration. (MAYER)
UF marble, Eleusinian

elevated
DC.323
HN October 1992 descriptor moved

elevated freeways
USE elevated roads

elevated highways
USE elevated roads

elevated railroads
PC.193 (A,L,B)
HN March 1993 descriptor moved
ALT elevated railroad
UK overhead railways
UKA overhead railway
SN Rail transit systems of any form that run above surface traffic, primarily for local transit in urban or interurban areas.
UF elevated railway systems
elevated railways
els
overhead railroads
railroads, elevated
railroads, overhead
railways, elevated
railways, overhead

elevated railway systems
USE elevated railroads

elevated railways
USE elevated railroads

elevated roads
RM.169 (A,L,B)
HN April 1993 descriptor moved
ALT elevated road
UF elevated freeways
elevated highways
freeways, elevated
highways, elevated
roads, elevated

elevated walkways
USE skywalks

elevating
USE lifting (transporting)

elevation drawings
USE elevations (drawings)

elevation oblique drawings
VC.96
HN April 1992 descriptor moved
ALT elevation oblique drawing
SN Use for drawings in oblique projection in which the vertical plane is parallel to the plane of projection (drawing surface).
UF drawings, elevation oblique
drawings, facade oblique
facade oblique drawings
oblique drawings, elevation
oblique drawings, facade

elevation perspectives
USE one-point perspectives

elevation-sections
USE sectional elevations

elevations (building divisions)
    PJ.949   (B)
HN March 1993 descriptor moved
ALT elevation (building division)
SN Use for any of the sides or faces of a building or large interior space, however irregular, emphasizing their appearance; as distinct from **facades**, which usually constitute only those external faces which are substantially‚in one plane, and appear to have been designed with special regard to their conspicuousness or association with an entrance.

elevations (drawings)
    VC.104   (A,B)
HN April 1992 descriptor moved
     May 1991 descriptor changed, was **elevations**
     May 1991 alternate term changed, was **elevation**
ALT elevation (drawing)
SN Drawings showing the vertical elements of a building, either exterior or interior, as a direct projection to a vertical plane. (DAC)
UF drawings, elevation
     elevation drawings
     orthographs

elevations, exterior
USE exterior elevations

elevations, garden
USE garden elevations

elevations, half
USE half elevations

elevations, interior
USE interior elevations

elevations, laid-out
USE laid-out elevations

elevations, partial
USE partial elevations

elevations, perspective
USE exterior perspectives

elevations, sectional
USE sectional elevations

elevations, street
USE street elevations

elevator doors
HN March 1991 descriptor split, use **elevator** (ALT of **elevators**) + **doors**

elevators
    PC.122   (A,L,N,B,R)
HN March 1993 descriptor moved
     February 1991 scope note added
ALT elevator
SN Cars, cages, or platforms and associated machinery for the vertical conveying of goods or people to and from different levels. (W)

elevators, automatic
USE automatic elevators

<elevators by form>
    PC.123
HN March 1993 guide term moved

<elevators by function>
    PC.126
HN March 1993 guide term moved

<elevators by mode of operation>
    PC.131
HN March 1993 guide term moved

elevators, country
USE grain elevators

elevators, double-deck
USE double-deck elevators

elevators, electric
USE electric elevators

elevators, freight
USE freight elevators

elevators, grain
USE grain elevators

elevators, hydraulic
USE hydraulic elevators

elevators, hydroelectric
USE hydraulic elevators

elevators, inclined
USE inclined elevators

elevators, observation
USE observation elevators

elevators, observation car
USE observation elevators

elevators, passenger
USE passenger elevators

elevators, paternoster
USE manlifts

elevators, plunger
USE hydraulic elevators

elevators, service
USE service elevators

elevators, sidewalk
USE sidewalk elevators

elevators, slant
USE inclined elevators

elevators, traction
USE traction elevators

Eleventh Dynasty
    FL.2893
UF 11th Dynasty
     Dynasty, Eleventh

Elfenbeinschwarz
USE ivory black

Elisavetpol
USE Genje

Elisavetpols
USE Genje + rugs

elite directories
USE social registers

elitism
    BM.290   (R)
HN January 1991 alternate term added
ALT elitist
SN Belief in and advocacy of leadership or rule by an elite. (W)

Elizabethan
    FL.3283   (L,B,R)

Elizabethan Revival
    FL.3413
UF Revival, Elizabethan

ellipses
    BM.662   (H,L,B)
HN January 1991 alternate term added
ALT ellipse
     elliptical

ellipsographs
    TH.668   (N,R)
ALT ellipsograph
SN Instruments used for drawing ellipses. (W)

elliptical arches
    PJ.1585
HN March 1993 descriptor moved
ALT elliptical arch
SN Arches having the form of a semiellipse. (DAC)
UF arches, elliptical
     arches, semielliptical
     semielliptical arches

ells
    PJ.1372
HN March 1993 descriptor moved
ALT ell
SN Extensions that are at right angles to the length of buildings.

elm
    MT.2731   (L)
HN March 1992 descriptor moved

elm, American
USE American elm

elm, American white
USE American elm

elm, Chinese
USE Chinese elm

elm, English
USE English elm

elm, hickory
USE rock elm

elm, rock
USE rock elm

elm, slippery
USE slippery elm

elm, white
USE American elm

elm, wych
USE wych elm

Elmali Gördes
USE Gördes + rugs

els
USE elevated railroads

Elsner green
MT.2165
HN April 1992 descriptor moved
SN Composite pigment made with Bremen blue and a fustic lake; not used for permanent painting. (MAYER)
UF green, Elsner

elvan
MT.663
HN April 1992 descriptor moved
SN Name applied in Cornwall, England, to the local quartz-porphyry. (PEB)

émail en ronde bosse
USE en ronde bosse

emakimono
VC.261   (L)
SN Japanese handscrolls.
UF makimono

emancipating
USE emancipation

emancipation
KG.228   (L)
HN April 1993 lead-in terms added
November 1990 descriptor added
ALT emancipated
UF emancipating
manumission
manumitting

emballages
USE empaquetages

embankments
RK.1294   (L)
ALT embankment
SN Use for long ridges of earth, rocks, or gravel primarily constructed to carry a roadway; if built to retain water, use levees or dikes.

embarcaderos
USE landings (marine structures)

embassy buildings
RK.928   (A,H,L,B,R)
HN March 1993 related terms added
ALT embassy building
SN Use for the official headquarters of foreign ministers called ambassadors appointed to transact international business with a foreign government; when such headquarters are for ministers appointed primarily to oversee and protect the home country's economic interests in a host country, use consulates. For the official residences of foreign ministers in general, use legations.
UF buildings, embassy
chancelleries
chanceries

RT consulates
legations

embattlements
USE battlements

emblem books
VW.38   (L,R)
HN November 1992 descriptor moved
ALT emblem book
UF books, emblem

emblem poems
USE pattern poetry

emblems (allegorical pictures)
VC.39   (L,R)
HN April 1991 descriptor moved
May 1990 scope note changed
ALT emblem (allegorical picture)
SN Allegorical pictures, often inscribed with mottoes, common especially in the 16th and 17th centuries. Distinct from emblems (symbols), which are simpler symbolic objects or representations of an object.

emblems (symbols)
VC.68   (A,L,B,R)
HN April 1993 scope note changed
September 1992 descriptor moved
April 1991 descriptor changed, was emblems
April 1991 alternate term changed, was emblem
ALT emblem (symbol)
SN Objects, or representations of objects, symbolizing and suggesting other objects or ideas, especially by clear natural aptness or association, such as a balance as an emblem of justice. For allegorical pictures with mottoes, use emblems (allegorical pictures).

embossed inkless prints
USE embossed prints

embossed prints
VC.451
ALT embossed print
SN Prints in which the image is formed largely by areas forced into relief by the hollows of the printing plate or blocks, usually without ink.
UF blind embossed prints
embossed inkless prints
embossed prints, blind
embossed prints, inkless
inkless intaglio prints
intaglio prints, inkless
prints, blind embossed
prints, embossed
prints, inkless embossed
prints, seal
seal prints

embossed prints, blind
USE embossed prints

embossed prints, inkless
USE embossed prints

<embossed wall coverings>
TC.372
SN Wall coverings of various materials, including paper, which are characterized by embossed patterns.

embossing
KT.979   (L,R)
HN January 1993 descriptor moved
August 1991 scope note changed
ALT embossed
SN Producing raised letters or designs on a surface.

embossing, blind
USE blind embossing

embossing, imitation
USE thermography

embossing, uninked
USE blind embossing

embrasures (battlement components)
PJ.2488
HN March 1993 descriptor moved
ALT embrasure (battlement component)
SN The open spaces between two merlons or solid portions of battlements or castellated parapets. (RS)
UF crenelets
crenels

embrasures (openings)
PJ.2201
HN March 1993 descriptor moved
ALT embrasure (opening)
SN Openings in a wall with sides flaring outward, as for a door or window. (PUTNAM)

embrittlement
KT.237   (L)
HN January 1993 descriptor moved
SN Process of becoming brittle; includes the loss of flexibilty or elasticity.

embroiderers
HG.747
HN December 1992 alternate terms added
ALT embroiderer
embroiderer's
embroiderers'

embroidering
KT.1222   (L,R)
HN March 1993 scope note changed
March 1993 descriptor changed, was embroidery
March 1993 lead-in term added
March 1993 descriptor moved
ALT embroidered
SN The process of stitching decorative designs into cloth, leather, or paper by hand or machine. For the weft patterning technique of weaving raised patterns on a woven textile, use brocading.
UF embroidery

embroidery
USE embroidering

embroidery, crewel
USE crewelwork

embroidery, Persian
USE broderie perse

embroidery, white work
USE whitework

embuia
USE imbuia

embuya
USE imbuia

emeerates
USE emirates

emerald
MT.519 (L,R)
HN April 1992 descriptor moved
February 1992 scope note added
February 1992 related term added
SN A brilliant green variety of beryl,
highly prized as a gemstone. (AGI)
RT gemstone

emerald (color)
USE brilliant green
brilliant yellowish green
deep yellowish green
light green
strong yellowish green
vivid green
vivid yellowish green

emerald green
MT.2153
HN April 1992 descriptor moved
January 1992 lead-in terms added
UF English green
green, emerald
green, English
green, imperial
green, Mittis
green, Paris
green, Schweinfurt
green, Veronese
green, Vienna
imperial green
Mittis green
Paris green
Schweinfurt green
Schweinfurter Grün
Schweinfurtgrün
verde di Schweinfurt
Veronese green
véronèse vert
vert anglais
vert émeraude
vert Paul Véronèse
Vienna green

emerald green (color)
USE brilliant green
brilliant yellowish green
moderate bluish green
moderate green
moderate yellowish green
strong bluish green
strong green
strong yellowish green
very light yellowish green

emerald green, bright
USE brilliant bluish green
brilliant green
strong bluish green
strong green

emerald green, dark
USE deep green
moderate bluish green

emerald green, deep
USE moderate green

emerald green, light
USE brilliant bluish green
brilliant green
light bluish green
light green
very light bluish green

emerald green, pale
USE very light green

emerald green, vivid
USE strong bluish green

emerald oxide of chromium
USE viridian

Emeraude
USE viridian

emeraude green
USE viridian

emeraude, vert
USE viridian

emergency coinage
USE emergency currency

emergency currency
VK.137 (L)
SN Money issued under abnormal financial conditions, such as wartime
or economic panic.
UF coinage, emergency
currency, emergency
emergency coinage
emergency money
money, emergency
money, necessity
necessity money

emergency electric power supply
USE emergency power supply

emergency electricity supply
USE emergency power supply

emergency exits
PJ.2294 (A)
HN March 1993 descriptor moved
February 1991 scope note added
ALT emergency exit
SN Doors, hatches, or other devices
leading to the outside, usually kept
closed and locked, and used chiefly
for emergencies when conventional
exits fail or become inaccessible.
(MEANS)
UF exits, emergency
exits, fire
fire exits

emergency housing
RG.63 (A,L,B)
HN February 1991 related term added
UF disaster housing
housing, disaster
housing, emergency
RT crisis shelters

emergency lighting
PC.209 (A,L,B)
HN March 1993 descriptor moved
April 1991 scope note added
SN Building lighting systems that sup-
ply illumination essential to the
safety of life and property in the
event of failure of normal supply.
(IESREF)
UF lighting, emergency

emergency lights
TC.1440 (L,B)
ALT emergency light
SN Any lights designated for use during
a power outage or other emergency;
often required by municipal regulations in public buildings.

emergency medical centers
RK.743 (A)
ALT emergency medical center
UF centers, emergency medical
emergency units
medical centers, emergency
units, emergency

emergency money
USE emergency currency

emergency power supply
PC.138 (L)
HN March 1993 descriptor moved
November 1991 scope note added
November 1991 lead-in term deleted, was **power systems, standby**
February 1991 lead-in terms added
February 1991 lead-in term deleted,
was **standby power systems**
SN Use for electrical systems temporarily produced or supplied by standby
power generators when normal electric power supply fails or is interrupted.
UF electricity supply, emergency
emergency electric power supply
emergency electricity supply
power supply, emergency
power supply, emergency electric

emergency rooms
PJ.1235 (L)
HN March 1993 descriptor moved
ALT emergency room
SN Hospital areas equipped and staffed
for the prompt treatment of acute
illness, trauma, or other medical
emergencies. (RHDEL2)
UF rooms, emergency

emergency services
HN.133
ALT emergency service
UF services, emergency

emergency units
USE emergency medical centers

emergency vehicles
TX.212 (L)
ALT emergency vehicle
SN Use for specialized road vehicles designed with apparatus for emergency situations.
UF vehicles, emergency

<emergency vessels>
TX.448

emery
MT.536 (L)
HN April 1992 descriptor moved
February 1992 scope note changed
SN A gray-to-black impure variety of corundum which contains magnetite and hematite and is used as an abrasive. The stone is crushed and graded and used to make emery paper, emery cloth, and emery wheels. (AGI)

emery cloth
TH.1074
SN Finely abrasive cloth manufactured by sprinkling powdered emery or aluminum oxide onto a thin cloth coated with glue and used either wet or dry for polishing metallic surfaces. (MEANS)
UF cloth, emery

emigrants
HG.1006 (H,L)
HN January 1993 alternate terms added
May 1991 descriptor added
ALT emigrant
emigrant's
emigrants'
SN People who depart from their native or usual country or region to live elsewhere. For those who come into a country or region from another to settle there, use **immigrants.**
RT emigration
immigrants

emigrating
USE emigration

emigration
KG.198 (L,R)
HN May 1991 lead-in term added
May 1991 related term added
April 1991 descriptor moved
January 1991 alternate term added
ALT emigrated
SN Departure from a place of abode, natural home, or country for life or residence elsewhere. (W)
UF emigrating
RT emigrants

eminent domain
BM.909 (L,B)
HN February 1993 descriptor moved
UF domain, eminent
expropriation

emirates
HN.43
HN January 1993 descriptor added
ALT emirate
SN Administrative bodies in the Islamic Middle East subject to an emir, or, as in the United Arab Emirates, a sheikh.
UF emecrates

emotion
BM.996 (L,R)
HN February 1993 descriptor moved
UF feelings

empaquetages
VC.559 (L)
ALT empaquetage
SN 20th-century works of art which involve wrapping, tying, or concealing an object; often used in the context of Christo's work.
UF emballages
objects, wrapped
packaged objects (sculpture)
wrapped objects
wrappings
RT wrapping

empathy
BM.398 (L)
HN January 1991 alternate term added
April 1990 lead-in term added
ALT empathetic
SN The capacity for participating in, or a vicarious experiencing of, another's feelings, volitions, or ideas. (W)
UF Einfühling

emperors
HG.191 (L,R)
HN January 1993 descriptor moved
December 1992 alternate terms added
ALT emperor
emperor's
emperors'
SN Sovereigns or supreme monarchs of an empire. (W)

Empire
FL.3450 (A,B,R)
UF First Empire

Empire burners
USE governor burners

empires
HN.34
ALT empire

employee housing
USE industrial housing

employees' buildings
RK.577 (A,L)
ALT employees' building
UF buildings, employees'
buildings, personnel
employees' facilities
employees' service buildings

facilities, employees'
personnel buildings

employees' facilities
USE employees' buildings

employees, government
USE government employees

employees' handbooks
USE employees' manuals

employees' manuals
VW.472 (L)
HN November 1992 descriptor moved
ALT employee's manual
UF employees' handbooks
handbooks, employees'
manuals, employees'
manuals, staff
staff manuals

employees, professional
USE professionals

employees, public
USE government employees

employees' service buildings
USE employees' buildings

employing
KG.217
HN April 1993 related terms added
SN Use for the ongoing activity of providing individuals with and paying them for work. For the action of engaging the services of a person or persons for wages or other payment, use **hiring.** For the concept of the degree or extent of the provision or availability of paid work to the population, use **employment.**
RT employment
hiring

employment
BM.876 (L,B)
HN April 1993 related terms added
February 1993 descriptor moved
SN Use for the degree or extent to which paid work is provided or available to the population. For the ongoing activity of providing individuals with and paying them for work, use **employing.** For the action of engaging the services of a person or persons for wages or other payment, use **hiring.**
RT employing
hiring

employment agencies
RK.194 (H,L,B)
ALT employment agency
UF agencies, employment
employment exchanges
employment offices
exchanges, employment
exchanges, labor
labor exchanges
offices, employment

employment exchanges
USE   employment agencies

employment offices
USE   employment agencies

empresses
　　　HG.192　　　　　　　　　　　　(L)
HN   January 1993 descriptor moved
　　　December 1992 alternate terms
　　　added
ALT   empress
　　　empresses'
　　　empress's

emulsified asphalt
　　　MT.1009　　　　　　　　　　　(L)
HN   April 1992 descriptor moved
SN   An asphalt emulsion in water solu-
　　　tion; uses include surfacing floors,
　　　painting pipes, and waterproofing
　　　concrete walls. (MH)
UF   asphalt, emulsified
　　　asphalt emulsion mixtures

emulsifier
　　　MT.1692
HN   April 1993 descriptor changed, was
　　　　emulsifiers
　　　April 1993 lead-in term changed,
　　　　was **emulsifying agents**
SN   Substance that promotes the forma-
　　　tion and stabilization of an emul-
　　　sion. (WCOL9)
UF   agent, emulsifying
　　　emulsifying agent

emulsifying agent
USE   emulsifier

emulsion
　　　MT.1377　　　　　　　　　　　(L)
HN   April 1993 lead-in term changed,
　　　　was **image-bearing colloids**
　　　April 1992 lead-in terms added
　　　March 1992 descriptor moved
SN   The suspension of droplets of one
　　　liquid in another liquid in which the
　　　first liquid is not soluble. Also, an
　　　intimate mixture of a solid or semi-
　　　solid substance with a liquid, some-
　　　times with the aid of an emulsifier.
　　　In photography, the mixture of
　　　binder and final image material.
UF   colloid, image-bearing
　　　emulsion layer
　　　image-bearing colloid
　　　layer, emulsion

emulsion, egg/oil
USE   egg-oil tempera

emulsion ground
　　　MT.2478
SN   A ground made by combining or
　　　emulsifying gesso and oil. (MAYER)
UF   ground, emulsion

emulsion layer
USE   emulsion

emulsion, oil-in-water
USE   oil-in-water emulsion

emulsion paint
　　　MT.1950　　　　　　　　　　(L,B)
HN   August 1992 descriptor moved
SN   Paint having water usually as the
　　　volatile phase with the various non-
　　　volatile substances (as a linseed-oil
　　　varnish) in ₋mulsion as the binder.
　　　(W)
UF   paint, emulsion

emulsion, stripping
USE   stripping film

en camaieu
USE   monochrome

en face
USE   frontal

en ronde bosse
　　　KT.100
HN   March 1993 descriptor moved
　　　April 1990 lead-in term changed,
　　　was **email en bosse ronde**
SN   Enamel decoration characterized by
　　　an opaque coating of enamel. (DDA)
UF   émail en ronde bosse

en-tout-cases
　　　TE.427
ALT   en-tout-cas
SN   Combination umbrella and parasol
　　　for all weather, generally brightly
　　　colored but untrimmed. (CASFUP)
RT   umbrellas

enamel
　　　MT.1847　　　　　　　　　(L,B,R)
HN   April 1993 scope note changed
SN   A usually opaque, vitreous coating,
　　　composed chiefly of quartz, feld-
　　　spar, clay, soda, and borax, applied
　　　by fusion to surfaces especially of
　　　metal, ceramic, or glass; has a glossy
　　　appearance upon hardening.

enamel, baked
USE   baked enamel

enamel, dental
USE   dental enamel

enamel paint
　　　MT.1934　　　　　　　　　　(H,L)
HN   July 1990 lead-in term added
SN   Use for paint made from oil, resin,
　　　varnish, or a combination of these,
　　　mixed with finely ground pigment;
　　　usually giving a glossy finish, but
　　　sometimes giving a semigloss or flat
　　　finish.
UF   paint, enamel
　　　Ripolin

enamel, porcelain
USE   porcelain enamel

enamel process
USE   ceramic process

enamel, vitreous
USE   porcelain enamel

enamel white
USE   barium sulfate

enamelers
　　　HG.690　　　　　　　　　　　(H)
HN   December 1992 alternate terms
　　　added
ALT   enameler
　　　enameler's
　　　enamelers'
UK   enamellers
UKA   enameller
SN   Persons who engage in enameling.

enameling
　　　KT.93　　　　　　　　　　　(L)
HN   March 1993 descriptor moved
ALT   enameled
UK   enamelling
UKA   enamelled
SN   The process of applying a vitreous
　　　glaze to metal or pottery objects and
　　　then fusing it to a smooth, hard sur-
　　　face in a kiln or furnace. (QCKAIE)

enameling, copper
USE   copper enameling

enameling, filigree
USE   filigree enameling

enamellers
SEE   enamelers

enamelling
SEE   enameling

enamelling, copper
SEE   copper enameling

enamelling, filigree
SEE   filigree enameling

enamels
　　　VC.240　　　　　　　　　　　(L)
SN   Use collectively for work in enamel
　　　that includes figures or scenes or
　　　that is set into metalwork; for over-
　　　all decorative work in enamel, pre-
　　　fer **enameling**.

enanga
USE   ennangas

enangas
　　　TT.371
ALT   enanga
SN   Zitherlike chordophones of north-
　　　ern and western Uganda, having a
　　　shallow rectangular trough-shaped
　　　resonator bearing a single string
　　　laced up and down from end to end
　　　through holes or over notches.
　　　(NGDMI)
UF   engagas

enarmes
　　　PJ.3027
ALT   enarme
SN   Handles, usually of leather though
　　　very rarely of wood, riveted to the
　　　back of a shield and used to hold it.
　　　Commonly each shield has two, a
　　　fixed loop held with the hand, and

an adjustable strap buckled around the arm. (TARA)
UF braces (shield handles)

Encabellado
FL.1596

encapsulating
USE encapsulation

encapsulation
KT.882
HN November 1992 descriptor added
ALT encapsulated
SN Surrounding, enclosing, or protecting something as if in a capsule; for example, in paper conservation, the sealing of an item between two sheets of polyester film.
UF encapsulating

encarnacione
KT.450
HN June 1990 descriptor added
SN Technique used in Spanish painting which involves working the surface of a painted or carved figure to imitate flesh.
UF encarnado

encarnado
USE encarnacione

encaustic
USE encaustic painting

encaustic color
USE encaustic paint

encaustic colour
SEE encaustic paint

encaustic decoration
KT.1162
SN Use for the technique of decorating clay in which the body material is inlaid with the clay of another color. For the technique of wax wall or panel painting, use **encaustic painting**.
UF decoration, encaustic

encaustic paint
MT.1935
HN July 1990 descriptor added
UK encaustic colour
UF color, encaustic
colour, encaustic
encaustic color
paint, encaustic
paint, wax
wax paint

encaustic painting
KT.441   (L,R)
HN July 1990 scope note changed
SN Use for the technique of painting with pigments dispersed in molten wax. For the technique of decorating clay, use **encaustic decoration**.
UF cerography (wax painting)
encaustic
painting, encaustic

painting, wax
wax painting

encaustic paintings
VC.274
ALT encaustic painting
SN Creative works in the medium of encaustic paint.
UF paintings, encaustic

enceintes
PJ.2480
HN March 1993 descriptor moved
February 1991 scope note changed
ALT enceinte
SN Use for the primary line of walled fortification around forts, castles, or towns.

enclosed basin stands
TC.1073
HN January 1993 descriptor moved
ALT enclosed basin stand
UF basin stands, enclosed
inclosed basin stands
stands, enclosed basin
stands, inclosed basin

enclosed basin stands, corner
USE corner enclosed basin stands

enclosed gardens
USE walled gardens

enclosed pier tables
TC.1184
HN January 1993 descriptor moved
ALT enclosed pier table
UF pier tables, enclosed
tables, enclosed pier

<enclosing structural elements>
PJ.1730
HN March 1993 guide term moved

enclosure walls
USE curtain walls (nonbearing walls)

enclosures, choir
USE choir screens

enclosures, elephant
USE elephant houses

enclosures, toilet
USE toilet compartments

encoignures
TC.918
HN May 1993 related term added
January 1993 descriptor moved
ALT encoignure
SN Small triangular cupboards made to fit into a corner; usually made in pairs, often to match a commode.
UF armoires à encoignure
armoires d'encoignure
coins (cupboards)
corners (encoignures)
RT commodes (chests of drawers)

encolpia
USE enkolpia

Encrusted Style
USE First Style

encumbrances
BM.910   (L)
HN February 1993 descriptor moved
January 1991 alternate term added
ALT encumbrance
SN Any right or interest in land which diminishes the value of the fee but does not prevent the conveyance of the fee by the owner. Encumbrances such as taxes, mortgages, and judgements are known as liens; restrictions, reservations and easements are encumbrances but are not liens. (PUTNAM)
UF incumbrances

encyclicals
VW.354   (L)
HN November 1992 descriptor moved
ALT encyclical
SN Letters intended for wide or general circulation. (RHDEL2)

encyclicals, papal
USE papal encyclicals

encyclopaedists
SEE encyclopedists

encyclopedias
VW.849   (L,B,R)
HN November 1992 descriptor moved
ALT encyclopedia
UF cyclopedias

encyclopedists
HG.373   (L)
HN December 1992 alternate terms added
ALT encyclopedist
encyclopedist's
encyclopedists'
UK encyclopaedists
UKA encyclopaedist
SN Persons who compile or assist in the compilation of an encyclopedia. (W)

end
DC.312
HN April 1993 related term added
January 1993 scope note changed
October 1992 descriptor moved
SN Use to describe something situated at or near an extremity of a long, thin object. To refer to those extremities themselves, use **ends (portions)** from the Components hierarchy.
RT ends (portions)

end-blown flutes
USE vertical flutes

<end-blown trumpets>
TT.96
SN Collocates descriptors for tubular trumpets in which the mouthhole faces the axis. (GSJ)
RT dung-dkar

end boards
PJ.2785
HN March 1993 descriptor moved
ALT end board
UF boards, end

end-cut brick
MT.145
HN April 1992 descriptor moved
SN Brick having the end surfaces wire-cut. (W)
UF brick, end-cut

end-grain blocks
TH.859
HN February 1993 descriptor added
ALT end-grain block
SN Wood blocks cut at a right angle to the grain and used for wood engraving.
UF blocks, end-grain
RT wood engraving

end joints
USE butt joints

end lap joints
PJ.729
HN April 1993 descriptor moved
ALT end lap joint
SN Angle joints involving two members, each having been cut to half its thickness and lapped over the other in such a manner as to result in a change of direction. (MEANS)
UF joints, end lap

end leaves
USE endleaves

end matter
USE back matter

end papers
USE endpapers

end sheets
USE endleaves

end-supported beams
USE simple beams

end tables
TC.1088
HN January 1993 descriptor moved
ALT end table
SN Any small table used in relation to a couch or chair. (ARON)
UF tables, end

end users
HG.964
HN January 1993 alternate terms added
ALT end user
end user's
end users'
SN Use specifically for clients or patrons of a library, information center, or information retrieval service. For persons who themselves use products or services of the information industry to provide information services to clients or patrons, prefer **users.**
UF users, end

endangered places
RG.223   (A,B)
ALT endangered place
SN Use for usually historic open spaces, buildings, or other structures that are threatened with development or demolition.
UF endangered sites
imperiled places
imperiled sites
places, endangered
places, imperiled
sites, endangered
sites, imperiled

endangered sites
USE endangered places

endbands
USE headbands (binding components)

enderon
USE corium

endings, line
USE line fillings

endleaves
PJ.3366   (L)
ALT endleaf
SN Units of usually two leaves, the flyleaf and the pastedown, placed in the front and back of a book between the covers and the text block.
UF end leaves
end sheets
endsheets
leaves, end
sheets, end

endless saws
USE band saws

endpapers
PJ.3367   (H,L)
ALT endpaper
SN Endleaves made of paper.
UF end papers
lining papers (endpapers)
papers, end
papers, lining

endpapers, paste-down
USE pastedowns

ends (portions)
PJ.759
HN April 1993 related terms added
ALT end (portion)
SN Use for the extremities of long, thin objects. For the adjective describing the location of something at or near the end of something, use **end** from the Attributes and Properties hierarchy.
RT end
<*ends: furniture components*>

ends (warp)
PJ.3073

ALT end (warp)
SN Use for individual warp strands.
UF ends, warp
threads, warp
warp ends
warp threads

ends, astragal
USE astragal ends

<*ends: furniture components*>
PJ.2786
HN April 1993 related term added
March 1993 guide term moved
RT ends (portions)

ends, gable
USE gable ends

ends, hollow
USE hollow ends

ends, ovolo
USE astragal ends

ends, warp
USE ends (warp)

endsheets
USE endleaves

endurability
USE durability

endurableness
USE durability

endurance
USE durability

endytis
TC.348
ALT endyti
SN Altar cloths used in the Orthodox Eastern Church.

Eneolithic
FL.23
UF Aeneolithic

energy
BM.774   (A,L,B,R)
HN November 1992 descriptor moved
February 1992 scope note added
SN Generally, the capacity to do work; precisely, any quantity with dimensions that can be represented as mass times length squared divided by time squared. (NASATH)

energy, ambient
USE solar power

<*energy and related concepts*>
BM.773
HN November 1992 guide term moved

energy, atomic
USE nuclear power

energy conservation
BM.350   (A,L,B,R)
HN November 1992 descriptor moved
UF conservation, energy

energy consumption
BM.351 (L)
HN November 1992 descriptor moved
UF consumption, energy

energy conversion plants, ocean thermal
USE ocean thermal energy conversion plants

energy efficient buildings
RK.1313 (A,L,B)
ALT energy efficient building
UF buildings, energy efficient
buildings, low-energy
low-energy buildings

energy, electromagnetic
USE electromagnetic radiation

<energy-related concepts>
BM.793

energy resources
BM.354 (L)
HN November 1992 descriptor moved
UF energy sources
power resources
resources, energy
resources, power
sources, energy

energy sources
USE energy resources

enfilade
BM.63

enforcement
USE enforcing

enforcing
KG.213 (L)
HN April 1993 lead-in term added
SN Ensuring compliance with laws or regulations. (RLG7)
UF enforcement
policing

enforcing, law
USE law enforcing

engagas
USE enangas

engaged
DC.324
HN October 1992 descriptor moved
SN Partly embedded in or bonded to a supporting structure. (W)

engaged columns
PJ.1475
HN March 1993 descriptor moved
June 1991 lead-in terms added
ALT engaged column
SN Columns partially built into a surface, not freestanding. (HAS)
UF applied columns
attached columns
columns, applied
columns, attached
columns, engaged

engaged frames
TC.425

ALT engaged frame
SN Use for frames which have a structural, as well as decorative, function, in that they physically support the panels they surround and may serve to connect from two to dozens of panels in a larger structure. (BRESTA)
UF frames, engaged

Engelmann spruce
MT.2995 (L)
HN March 1992 descriptor moved
UF spruce, Engelmann

engine houses
USE fire stations
powerhouses
roundhouses

engine houses, circular
USE roundhouses

engine turning
KT.1128
HN December 1992 descriptor added
ALT engine-turned
SN The technique of engraving and decorating metal with an overall pattern of continuous, encircling, and contiguous narrow grooves, usually of a wavy character. (HNSIL)
UF guillochage
turning, engine

engineering
KD.109 (A,L,B,R)
HN April 1993 related term added
SN Science by which the properties of matter and the sources of energy in nature are made useful to humanity in structures, machines, and products. (W)
RT engineers

engineering, aeronautical
USE aeronautical engineering

engineering, aerospace
USE aerospace engineering

engineering brick
MT.102
HN April 1992 descriptor moved
UF brick, engineering

engineering, ceramic
USE ceramic engineering

engineering, chemical
USE chemical engineering

engineering, civil
USE civil engineering

<engineering concepts>
BM.595
HN November 1992 guide term added

engineering drawings
USE technical drawings

engineering, electric
USE electrical engineering

engineering, electrical
USE electrical engineering

engineering, environmental
USE environmental engineering

engineering, human
USE human factors

engineering, human factors
USE human factors

engineering, hydraulic
USE hydraulic engineering

engineering, industrial
USE industrial engineering

engineering, management
USE industrial engineering

engineering maps
VW.80 (L)
HN November 1992 descriptor moved
ALT engineering map
SN Maps, usually maintained in the public works or engineering departments of a city, showing information such as street and rail rights of way, location of bridges, and grade separations; used for planning and executing engineering work in a locality. (ULANDU)
UF maps, engineering

engineering, marine
USE marine engineering

engineering, mechanical
USE mechanical engineering

engineering, military
USE military engineering

engineering, naval
USE marine engineering

engineering physics
HN April 1993 descriptor deleted, made lead-in to **applied physics**

engineering physics
USE applied physics

engineering, plant
USE plant engineering

engineering, plastics
USE polymer science

engineering, sanitary
USE sanitary engineering

engineering schools
HN May 1991 descriptor split, use **engineering** + **schools**

engineering, structural
USE structural engineering

engineering, systems
USE systems engineering

engineering tolerances
USE tolerances

engineering, traffic
USE traffic engineering

engineering, transport
USE transportation engineering

engineering, transportation
USE transportation engineering

engineering, value
USE cost benefit analysis

engineers
     HG.854   (A,L,B,R)
HN April 1993 related term added
     December 1992 alternate terms added
ALT engineer
     engineer's
     engineers'
SN Persons trained in a branch of engineering. In some jurisdictions the designation is legally restricted in technical use to persons who have completed a prescribed course of study and complied with requirements concerning registration or licensing. (W)
RT engineering

engineers, aeronautical
USE aeronautical engineers

engineers, aerospace
USE aerospace engineers

engineers, biomedical
USE biomedical engineers

engineers' chains
     TN.38   (N)
ALT engineer's chain
SN Surveyors' measuring devices consisting of 1-inch-long steel links joined in a chain 100 feet long; succeeded surveyors' chains, but now obsolete.
UF chains, engineers'

engineers, chemical
USE chemical engineers

engineers, civil
USE civil engineers

engineers, electrical
USE electrical engineers

engineers, hydraulic
USE hydraulic engineers

engineers, industrial
USE industrial engineers

engineers, marine
USE marine engineers

engineers, mechanical
USE mechanical engineers

engineers, military
USE military engineers

engineers, municipal
USE municipal engineers

engineers, naval
USE marine engineers

engineers, nuclear
USE nuclear engineers

engineers, product
USE product engineers

engineers, safety
USE safety engineers

engineers, sanitary
USE sanitary engineers

engineers' scales
     TN.64
ALT engineer's scale
SN Flat beveled or triangular straightedges, usually of wood or plastic, graduated in multiples of ten parts per inch allowing drawings to be drawn or measured to scale in decimal values.
UF scales, engineers'

engineers, structural
USE structural engineers

engineers, traffic
USE traffic engineers

engineers, transportation
USE transportation engineers

engineers, water-supply
USE water-supply engineers

engines
     TH.932   (L,N)
ALT engine

engines (locomotives)
USE locomotives

engines, animal-powered
USE animal-powered engines

engines, dividing
USE dividing engines

engines, fire
USE fire engines

engines, gas-turbine
USE gas turbines

engines, steam
USE steam engines
     steam locomotives

engines, switch
USE switching locomotives

engines, winding
USE windlasses

English
     FL.3129   (H,L,B)

English barns
     RK.47
ALT English barn
SN Rectangular, gable-roofed barns divided on the interior into three roughly equal bays, the center of

which is a passageway entered from the center of the long sides. (WB&S)
UF 3-bay barns
     barns, 3-bay
     barns, Connecticut
     barns, English
     barns, New England
     barns, three-bay
     barns, Yankee
     Connecticut barns
     New England barns
     three-bay barns
     Yankee barns

English bond
     MT.1816
HN October 1992 descriptor moved
SN Bond composed of alternate courses of all headers and all stretchers, with the headers centered on the stretchers and on the joints between stretchers. (PCMC)
UF bond, English

English bows
USE longbows

English britannia metal
     MT.457
HN March 1993 descriptor moved
UF britannia metal, English
     metal, English britannia

English cherry
     MT.2878
HN March 1992 descriptor moved
UF cherry, English

English china
USE bone china

English, Early
USE Early English

English elm
     MT.2734
HN March 1992 descriptor moved
UF elm, English
     Ulmus procera

English flutes
USE recorders

English Gothic, Early
USE Early English

English gowns
USE sacks

English green
USE emerald green

English guitars
     TT.304   (L)
ALT English guitar
SN Type of cittern very popular in England from about 1750 to 1810, having a flat or slightly convex back and six courses of metal strings, the bottom two being single-strung and the upper four double. (NGDMI)
UF cetras
     citras
     guitars, English

English horns
    TT.165   (L,N)
ALT English horn
SN The tenor of the modern orchestral
    oboe, having a pear-shaped bell
    with a small opening and its double
    reed carried in a short metal crook.
    (NGDMI)
UF cors anglais
    horns, English
    oboes, tenor
    tenor oboes

English I-houses
USE I-houses

English locks
    PJ.3184
ALT English lock
SN A type of snaphance incorporating
    the flintlock's combined steel and
    pan cover but with a laterally, not
    vertically, operating sear working on
    the cock through an opening in the
    lock plate.
UF English snaphances
    locks, English
    snaphances, English

English oak
    MT.2829   (L)
HN March 1992 descriptor moved
UF British oak
    oak, British
    oak, English
    Quercus pedunculata
    Quercus robur

English ocher
USE moderate orange yellow

English, Old
USE Old English

English pennies
USE pennies

English pewter
    MT.461
HN March 1993 descriptor moved
SN Pewter of the 16th century con-
    taining 91% tin and 9% antimony.
    (MH)
UF pewter, English

English pink
USE Dutch pink

English poplar
USE black poplar

English pots
USE Zischäggen

English snaphances
USE English locks

English soft paste porcelain
USE bone china

English vermilion
    MT.2184
HN April 1992 descriptor moved
UF vermilion, English

English vermilion (color)
USE strong red

English walnut
    MT.2914   (L)
HN March 1992 descriptor moved
UF common Persian walnut
    European walnut
    Juglans regia
    Persian walnut, common
    walnut, common Persian
    walnut, English
    walnut, European

English white
USE whiting

engobe
    MT.2003   (L)
SN A variety of slip used for decorating
    pottery; contains color oxides as well
    as clay, feldspar, and silica. (MAYER)

engravers (incisers)
    HG.662   (L,B)
HN February 1993 descriptor added
ALT engraver (inciser)
    engraver's (inciser)
    engravers' (incisers)
SN Use for those skilled or practiced in
    incising marks on the surface of a
    hard material, such as glass or
    metal, with a sharp tool, when the
    designs or images created are for
    their own sake and not to be printed
    from. For those who practice the
    printing process of engraving, use
    engravers (printmakers).
RT engravers (printmakers)
    engraving (incising)

engravers (printmakers)
    HG.307   (H,L,B,R)
ALT engraver (printmaker)
    engraver's (printmaker)
    engravers' (printmakers)
SN Use for those who practice the
    printing process of engraving. For
    those who incise marks on the sur-
    face of a hard material, not to be
    printed from, use **engravers (in-
    cisers)**.
RT engravers (incisers)
    engraving (printing process)

engravers, block
USE wood engravers

engravers, electric
USE electric engravers

engravers, electrical
USE electric engravers

engravers' marks
HN March 1993 descriptor split, use **en-
    gravers' (printmakers)** (ALT of **en-
    gravers (printmakers)** + **marks
    (symbols)**

engravers, stipple
USE stipple engravers

engravers, wood
USE wood engravers

engravers, wood-cut
USE wood engravers

engraving (incising)
    KT.947   (L,B,R)
HN February 1993 related terms added
    October 1991 scope note changed
    October 1990 descriptor moved
    October 1990 descriptor changed,
    was **engraving (surface decor-
    ating)**
ALT engraved
SN Creating marks on the surface of a
    hard material, such as metal or
    glass, by incising with a sharp tool,
    when the designs or images created
    are for their own sake and not to be
    printed from. For printing processes
    that involve this technique plus inta-
    glio printing from the surface, use
    engraving (printing process).
RT engravers (incisers)
    engraving (printing process)

engraving (printing process)
    KT.672   (L,B,R)
HN April 1993 alternate term deleted
    February 1993 related terms added
    October 1991 descriptor moved
    October 1991 scope note changed
    October 1991 descriptor changed,
    was **engraving (printmaking)**
    May 1991 lead-in term added
SN Use for the intaglio process in which
    the design is incised into the print-
    ing plate. Distinct from **wood en-
    graving**, which is a process for relief
    printing. Historically, has sometimes
    been used to refer to printmaking
    processes in general, usually those
    employing printing plates; use the
    appropriate specific term. For the
    single step of incising the design,
    use **engraving (incising)**.
UF chalcography
RT engravers (printmakers)
    engraving (incising)

engraving, chalk
USE crayon manner

engraving, copper
USE copper engraving

engraving, copperplate
USE copper engraving

engraving, crayon
USE crayon manner

engraving, diamond-point
USE diamond-point engraving

engraving, line
USE line engraving

engraving machines, electronic
USE electric engravers

engraving, mezzotint
USE mezzotint

engraving on glass, reverse
USE verre églomisé

engraving operators
USE photoengravers

engraving, steel
USE steel engraving

engraving, stipple
USE stipple engraving

engraving tools, electric
USE electric engravers

engraving, wax
USE cerography

engraving, white line
USE white line engraving

engraving, wood
USE wood engraving

engravings
 VC.462 (A,N,R)
ALT engraving
 SN Use specifically for prints obtained from an engraved printing surface. Historically, has sometimes been used loosely to refer to all prints.

engravings, color wood
USE color wood engravings

engravings, copper
USE copper engravings

engravings, crayon
USE crayon manner prints

engravings, line
USE line engravings

engravings, mezzotint
USE mezzotints

engravings, pastel
USE crayon manner prints

engravings, process line
USE line photoengravings

engravings, reproductive
USE reproductive prints

engravings, rock
USE rock engravings

engravings, steel
USE steel engravings

engravings, stipple
USE stipple engravings

engravings, white line
USE white line engravings

engravings, wood
USE wood engravings

engsi
USE engsis

engsis
 TC.64
 SN A type of rug that served as a door at the entrance to a Turkoman tent. (DENNY)
 UF engsi
     ensis
 RT <coverings and hangings for openings>

enhancement, computer
USE computer enhancement

enhancement, image
USE computer enhancement

enkolpia
 TE.464 (H)
ALT enkolpion
 SN Pectoral medallions, suspended from the neck, bearing a sacred picture; worn by bishops of the Orthodox Eastern Church.
 UF encolpia
 RT liturgical objects

enlargement
USE enlarging

enlargements
 PE.19
 HN January 1993 descriptor moved
     March 1991 scope note added
     March 1991 lead-in term deleted, was **enlarged photographs**
ALT enlargement
 SN Copies of images or objects on a larger scale.
 UF blowups
     macrophotographs (enlargements)

enlargements, crayon
USE crayon enlargements

enlargements, frame
USE frame enlargements

enlargers
 TH.794 (N)
ALT enlarger
 SN Apparatuses for producing prints by projecting a negative or transparency onto sensitive paper; often allowing for the production of prints both larger and smaller than the original. (LANG)
 UF enlargers, print
     print enlargers

enlargers, print
USE enlargers

enlarging
 KT.602 (L)
ALT enlarged
 SN Use for the darkroom procedure in which a photographic image is magnified by being projected through an optical system; generally used for making prints from small negatives.
 UF enlargement
     macrophotography (enlarging)

printing, projection
projection printing

Enlightenment
 BM.423 (L,R)
 SN A philosophical movement of the late 18th century characterized by an untrammeled but frequently uncritical use of reason, a lively questioning of authority and traditional doctrines, a tendency toward individualism, and an emphasis on the idea of universal human progress. (W)

enlisting
USE recruiting

ennangas
 TT.227
 HN May 1993 lead-in term changed, was **enanga (arched harps)**
ALT ennanga
 SN Arched harps of the Ganda people of Uganda, with circular or oval body and eight strings. (MARCUS)
 UF enanga

enneastyle
 DC.149
 HN October 1992 descriptor moved

enology
USE wine making

ensembles (costume)
 PC.48 (L,N)
ALT ensemble (costume)
 SN Complete costume, including garments and accessories, worn for a harmonious effect. Also, two or more garments or accessories designed to complement one another.

ensembles (musical groups)
 HG.26 (L)
 HN December 1991 descriptor added
ALT ensemble (musical group)
 SN Groups of players of musical instruments and/or singers, ranging from two people to entire orchestras.
 UF groups, musical
     musical groups
 RT instrumentalists
     music
     musicians
     singers

ensis
USE engsis

enstatite
 MT.541 (L)
 HN April 1992 descriptor moved
     February 1992 related term added
 SN A mineral of the pyroxene group consisting of magnesium silicate varying in color from grayish white to olive green and brown. (W)
 RT gemstone

ensuring
USE insuring

entaalas
TT.525
ALT entaala
SN Log xylophones of the Gwere of Uganda, with six slabs supplemented by a drum, placed on two banana stems and separated by sticks; the drum is played as though it were another slab. (MARCUS)
UF mirulis

<entablature components>
PJ.1674
HN April 1993 related term added
March 1993 guide term moved
RT <structural element components>

entablature frames
USE cassetta frames

entablatures
PJ.1672 (A,N,R)
HN March 1993 descriptor moved
June 1991 scope note changed
ALT entablature
SN Use for the elaborated superstructures carried by the columns in classical architecture, horizontally divided into architrave, frieze, and cornice. Use also for similar features in other contexts, such as along the upper portions of walls.

<entablatures and entablature components>
PJ.1671
HN March 1993 guide term moved

entablatures, friezeless
USE architrave cornices

Entartete Kunst
FL.3482 (R)
UF Degenerate art

entasis
BM.78 (B)
SN The gently swelling convex curvature along the line of taper of columns, made to prevent the illusion of concavity in straight or regularly tapered columns. (A-Z)

enterprises
USE business enterprises

enterprises, business
USE business enterprises

enterprises, commercial
USE business enterprises

entertainers
USE performing artists

entertaining
KG.307 (L)
SN Diverting or amusing someone; causing someone's time to pass agreeably. (W)
UF entertainment

entertainment
USE entertaining

<entertainment and recreation spaces>
PJ.1062
HN March 1993 guide term moved

entertainment buildings
RK.975 (A,B)
HN March 1993 related term added
September 1990 scope note added
ALT entertainment building
SN Distinguished from **recreation buildings** by more narrowly designating buildings with devices or equipment for amusement or diversion and not active sports, nor for which membership is required.
UF buildings, entertainment
entertainment facilities
facilities, entertainment
RT recreation buildings

<entertainment events>
KM.75

entertainment facilities
USE entertainment buildings

entomologists
HG.528 (L)
HN February 1993 descriptor moved
December 1992 alternate terms added
ALT entomologist
entomologist's
entomologists'

entrance halls
PJ.1076 (A,L,B,R)
HN March 1993 descriptor moved
ALT entrance hall
SN Use for passages or rooms just inside the entrance of a building, but sometimes with a vestibule between it and the outdoors. Prefer **lobbies** for such spaces in public buildings.
UF entries
entryways
foyers
halls, entrance

entrance handles
PJ.336
HN April 1993 descriptor moved
ALT entrance handle
UF handles, entrance

entrance lodges
USE gatehouses

<entrance spaces>
PJ.1074
HN March 1993 guide term moved

entrances
PJ.2291 (A,B)
HN March 1993 descriptor moved
March 1991 scope note added
ALT entrance
SN Use for points or places of entering. (RHDEL2)
UF entries

entrefenêtres
TC.399

ALT entrefenêtre
SN Relatively narrow tapestries designed for the space between two windows or doors.

entrepreneurs
HG.634 (L,R)
HN December 1992 alternate terms added
ALT entrepreneur
entrepreneur's
entrepreneurs'
SN Persons who organize, own, manage, and assume the risks of a business. (W)

entresols
USE mezzanines

entretoises
USE stretchers (furniture components)

entries
USE entrance halls
entrances

entropy
BM.826 (L)
HN November 1992 descriptor moved
January 1991 alternate term added
ALT entropic
SN Includes both the quantity that is a measure of the amount of energy in a system not available for doing work, and the ultimate state in the degradation of matter and energy in the universe.

entry lamps
USE hall lamps

entryways
USE entrance halls

enumerative bibliographies
USE systematic enumerative bibliographies

enumerative bibliographies, systematic
USE systematic enumerative bibliographies

envelope chemises
USE teddies

envelope tables
USE handkerchief tables

envelopes
TQ.602 (H,L,N)
ALT envelope

envelopes, building
USE building envelopes

envelopes, bulk
USE building envelopes

envelopes, matzah
USE matzah covers

environment
BM.318 (L,B,R)
HN November 1992 scope note changed

July 1991 related terms added
April 1990 scope note added
SN Use for the aggregate of physical things, conditions, and influences surrounding and affecting an organism, object, or structure. For the branch of biology dealing with the relations and interactions between organisms and their habitat, use **ecology**. For the concept of the external world, including the forces at work in it and the nonhuman life inhabiting it, perceived by human beings as separate and independent from themselves, their activities and civilization, use **Nature**.
RT ecology
Nature

environment and behavior
USE environmental psychology

environment art
USE environmental art
environments (sculpture)

environment-behavior studies
USE environmental psychology

environment, underwater
USE aquatic environments

environmental art
VC.241　　　　　　　　　　　　(R)
HN March 1993 lead-in terms added
June 1991 scope note changed
June 1991 lead-in terms added
April 1991 descriptor moved
SN Use for 20th-century works of art, usually outdoors and on a grand scale, that surround or involve the participation of the viewer and that especially exploit or incorporate aspects of their sites. For such works that specifically manipulate the land itself, use **earthworks (sculpture)**. For indoor installations that create surroundings that can be entered by the viewer, use **environments (sculpture)**. For sculpture that is designed to be placed outdoors but is not especially site-specific, use **outdoor sculpture**.
UF ambiente
art, environmental
art, land
environment art
environmental sculpture
land art
sculpture, environmental
site sculpture

environmental artists
HG.277
HN February 1993 descriptor moved
November 1992 alternate terms added
ALT environmental artist
environmental artist's
environmental artists'
UF artists, environmental

<environmental concepts>
BM.311
HN April 1990 guide term changed, was **<environmental sciences concepts>**

environmental control
KG.162　　　　　　　　　　　　(L)
HN November 1992 descriptor added
SN Measures taken to create desirable conditions and limit specific undesirable factors within a given, often a closed, environment.
UF control, environmental
environmental management
management, environmental

environmental engineering
KD.114　　　　　　　　　　　　(L,B)
SN Professional application of scientific principles and technical practices to the management and optimum use of air, water, and land resources; also, the provision of facilities and the control of conditions for living, working, and recreation. (PG)
UF engineering, environmental
environmental management
management, environmental

environmental impact
BM.325
HN March 1993 scope note added
SN Change in one or more of various socioeconomic and biophysical characteristics of a given environment as a result of site development or new government regulation.
UF environmental risk
impact, environmental
risk, environmental

environmental impact reports
USE environmental impact statements

environmental impact statements
VW.933　　　　　　　　　　　　(A,L)
HN November 1992 descriptor moved
ALT environmental impact statement
SN Documents required by state and federal law that contain an analysis and report of the effects of major projects or programs on the quality of human, plant, or animal habitats.
UF environmental impact reports
impact statements, environmental
reports, environmental impact
statements, environmental impact

environmental laboratories
RK.1108　　　　　　　　　　　　(A,L)
ALT environmental laboratory
UF laboratories, environmental

environmental law
KD.298　　　　　　　　　　　　(A,L)
UF law, environmental

environmental management
USE environmental control
environmental engineering
environmental policy

environmental policy
BM.967　　　　　　　　　　　　(A,L)
HN February 1993 descriptor moved
November 1992 lead-in term deleted, was **environmental control**
April 1990 lead-in term deleted, was **state and environment**
UF environmental management
management, environmental
policy, environmental

environmental pollution
USE pollution

environmental protection
KG.176　　　　　　　　　　　　(A,L,R)
HN December 1992 descriptor moved
UF protection, environmental

environmental psychology
KD.227　　　　　　　　　　　　(A,L)
HN April 1990 descriptor added
SN Field of study concerned with the mutually interactive relationship between the built environment and human behavior.
UF architectural psychology
B-ES
behavior, environment and
behavior-environment studies
ecological psychology
environment and behavior
environment-behavior studies
M-ES
man-environment systems
people-environment studies
psychology, architectural
psychology, ecological
psychology, environmental
studies, behavior-environment
studies, environment-behavior
studies, people-environment
systems, man-environment

environmental radioactivity
USE radioactive (ALT of radioactivity) + pollution

environmental risk
USE environmental impact

environmental sciences
KD.127
SN Interdisciplinary area of education and research for effective resource use, resource conservation, and environmental protection. (PG)
UF sciences, environmental

environmental sculpture
USE environmental art
environments (sculpture)

environments (sculpture)
VC.505　　　　　　　　　　　　(R)
ALT environment (sculpture)
SN Use for 20th-century sculptural works that create surroundings that the viewer can enter; most often indoor installations. For outdoor works that especially exploit or incorporate aspects of their sites and that may surround the viewer, use

environmental art. For sculptural works that are composed of figures and objects arranged into a picturelike scene that the viewer does not enter, use **tableaux**.
UF environment art
environmental sculpture
sculpture, environmental

environments, aquatic
USE aquatic environments

environments, coastal
USE coastal environments

environments, marine
USE marine environments

environments, underground
USE underground environments

environments, underwater
USE aquatic environments

environments, urban
USE urban environments

envois
VC.223
HN March 1993 alternate term added
April 1992 descriptor moved
ALT envoi
SN Use for drawings required to be sent yearly from Rome to the Académie des Beaux-Arts in Paris by winners of the Prix de Rome.
UF envois de Rome

envois (correspondence art)
USE mail art

envois de Rome
USE envois

envy
BM.1000   (L,R)
HN February 1993 descriptor moved
UF jealousy

enzyme
MT.1047   (L)
HN March 1992 descriptor added
SN One of a group of complex organic substances formed in the living cells of plants and animals; it is a necessary catalyst for the chemical reactions of biological processes. (CCDICT)
UF biocatalyst
ferment
ferment, soluble
soluble ferment

eolian landforms
USE aeolian landforms

Eolithic period
USE Paleolithic

Eotile
FL.295

epaulets
TE.647   (N)

ALT epaulet
UK epaulettes
UKA epaulette
SN Ornamental trimmings mounted on the shoulder, of a type chiefly worn by military officers.
RT uniforms

epaulettes
SEE epaulets

épaulles de mouton
USE Poldermittons

épées
TK.73   (N)
ALT épée
SN Dueling or fencing swords, heavier than foils or sabers, having a cup hilt and a deeply grooved three-sided blade with a sharply pointed end and no cutting edge; those used in fencing are blunted with a button.
RT fencing swords
foils (swords)
<sports and athletic equipment>
thrusting swords

épées de chasse
USE hunting swords

epergnes
TQ.549   (N)
ALT epergne
SN A type of composite centerpiece, often tiered and quite elaborate, consisting of a metal frame with dishes, vases, or candleholders of silver, glass, or porcelain intended to hold fruits, flowers, candies or the like, and used for service or decoration.
RT dinner services

ephemera
PE.10   (L,N)
HN December 1992 descriptor moved
January 1992 scope note changed
SN Everyday items manufactured for a specific, limited use, and usually intended to be discarded thereafter, especially printed matter on paper.
UF ephemera, printed
printed ephemera

ephemera, printed
USE ephemera

ephemerides
VW.850   (L)
HN June 1992 descriptor added
ALT ephemeris
SN Use for works giving the computed positions of celestial bodies each day or other regular interval; used by navigators and astronomers. (RBGENR)

Ephyraean
FL.2745
HN April 1993 descriptor added

Ephyraean ware
HN April 1993 descriptor split, use **Ephyraean + ware**

Epi-gravettian
FL.2567

epichlorohydrin elastomer
MT.1031   (L)
HN January 1993 descriptor moved
UF elastomer, epichlorohydrin

epidote
MT.542   (L)
HN April 1992 descriptor moved
February 1992 related term added
SN A yellowish green mineral consisting of a silicate of calcium, aluminum, and iron and occurring massive or in grains, columns, and monoclinic crystal. (W)
RT gemstone

epigrams
VW.269   (H,L)
HN June 1992 descriptor added
ALT epigram
SN Use for short satiric poems or any similar pointed sayings. (RBGENR)
UF ana
sayings

epigraphers
HG.463   (L)
HN April 1993 related term added
December 1992 alternate terms added
ALT epigrapher
epigrapher's
epigraphers'
RT epigraphy

epigraphs
VW.159
HN November 1992 descriptor moved
ALT epigraph
SN Inscriptions on statues, buildings, or other structures. (AHD)

epigraphy
KD.282   (H,L)
HN April 1993 related terms added
SN Study and interpretation of ancient inscriptions, including writings, pictures, and random scratchings, incised on stone, clay, metal, or other hard surfaces. For the study of ancient modes of writing more generally, use **paleography**.
RT epigraphers
paleography

epimerization dating
USE amino acid dating

epinaoi
USE opisthodomoi

épinettes des Vosges
TT.372   (L)
ALT épinette des Vosges
SN Zitherlike chordophones of France having a long, slightly tapered shal-

low soundbox with one heart-shaped and one roseate sound hole and five strings, two of which are melody and three are drones. The melody strings are stopped in unison by a small stick held in the left hand over fixed frets fitted to the long left side of the soundbox as the right hand strums all five strings.
UF bûches
RT drone strings
    melody strings

Epipaleolithic
    FL.12

épis
    PJ.2360
HN March 1993 descriptor moved
    August 1991 scope note changed
ALT épi
SN Use for adornments found on the terminating points of roof ridges.

episcenia
    PJ.2566
HN March 1993 descriptor moved
    February 1991 descriptor changed, was **episcaenia**
ALT episcenium
SN The upper stories of the scene buildings in ancient Greek or Roman theaters. (HAS)
UF episkenia

Episcopal
    BM.474   (L,B)
HN May 1993 related term added
SN Use with reference to the Episcopal Church in America; with reference to the Church of England, use **Anglican.**
UF Anglican (Episcopal)
    Episcopalian
    Protestant Episcopal
RT Anglican

episcopal palaces
USE bishops' (ALT of bishops (prelates)) + palaces

episcopal staffs
USE crosiers

Episcopalian
USE Episcopal

episkenia
USE episcenia

epistemology
    KD.75   (L,R)
HN February 1991 alternate term added
ALT epistemological
UF knowledge, theory of
    theory of knowledge

epistle-books
USE epistolaries

epistolaries
    VW.895   (L)
HN November 1992 descriptor moved

    March 1992 scope note added
    March 1992 lead-in term added
ALT epistolary
SN Books containing the epistles to be read at the mass; by the 13th century generally folded into the missal.
UF epistle-books

epistyles
USE architraves

epitaphioi
    TC.172
ALT epitaphion
SN Large veils decorated with the body of the crucified Christ which are used in Good Friday services in the Orthodox Eastern Church.

epitaphs
    VW.160   (L,R)
HN November 1992 descriptor moved
ALT epitaph
SN Inscriptions on sepulchral monuments in the memory of those buried in the tomb or grave. (AHD)

epitomes
USE abridgements

epoxy
USE epoxy resin

epoxy, basic liquid
USE basic liquid epoxy

epoxy, multifunctional
USE multifunctional epoxy

epoxy resin
    MT.1207   (A,L,B)
HN January 1993 descriptor moved
    March 1992 lead-in term changed, was **epoxy resin**
    January 1992 descriptor changed, was **epoxy**
    December 1991 scope note changed
SN Type of synthetic resin used to produce adhesive that sets by chemical reaction, rather than through loss of solvent and coalescence.
UF epoxy
    resin, epoxy

epoxy, silicone
USE silicone epoxy

EPR
USE ethylene-propylene elastomer

EPR rubber
USE ethylene-propylene elastomer

épreuves d'artiste
USE artists' proofs

éprouvettes
USE powder testers

épures
USE full-scale drawings

equal-arm scales
USE balances

equal-armed balances
USE balances

equation clocks
    TN.185
ALT equation clock
SN Use for timepieces that indicate the difference between mean solar time and apparent time (usually based on Greenwich mean time).
UF clocks, equation

equations
    BM.651   (L)
HN January 1991 alternate term added
ALT equation
SN Statements that each of two expressions is equal to the other. (MHDSTT)

equatorial dials
USE equatorial sundials

equatorial sundials
    TN.201
ALT equatorial sundial
SN Sundials, of several varieties, whose dial plate is tilted so as to lie parallel to the earth's equator and whose gnomon is perpendicular to the plate at its center, pointing to the north celestial pole; the layout of the hour lines is not dependent on latitude.
UF dials, equatorial
    equatorial dials
    equinoctial sundials
    sundials, equatorial
    sundials, equinoctial

<equestrian armors>
    PC.42
RT spurs (accessories worn)

equestrian clubs
USE riding clubs

equestrian monuments
USE equestrian statues

equestrian statues
    VC.572   (L,R)
ALT equestrian statue
SN Sculptural groups consisting of a horse and rider.
UF equestrian monuments
    monuments, equestrian
    statues, equestrian

equestrians
    HG.919   (L,R)
HN February 1993 related term added
    December 1992 alternate terms added
    April 1992 lead-in terms added
    December 1990 descriptor added
ALT equestrian
    equestrian's
    equestrians'
SN People who ride horses. (RHDEL2)

UF horseback riders
　 horsemen
　 horsewomen
　 riders, horseback
RT jockeys

equilateral arches
　 PJ.1591
HN March 1993 descriptor moved
ALT equilateral arch
SN Use for pointed arches in which a
　 line from the springing point to the
　 pointed center equals the span be-
　 tween the springing points.
UF arches, equilateral
　 arches, equilateral pointed
　 equilateral pointed arches
　 pointed arches, equilateral

equilateral pointed arches
USE equilateral arches

equilibrium
　 BM.597　　　　　　　　　　(L)
HN November 1992 descriptor moved
SN A state of balance between opposing
　 forces that is either static or dy-
　 namic. (WCOL9)

equilibrium (composition)
USE balance

equinoctical sundials
USE equatorial sundials

equipment
　 TH.1　　　　　　　　　　(L,B)

equipment, acoustic
USE acoustic equipment

equipment, arc-welding
USE arc welding machines

equipment, astronomical
USE astronomical instruments

equipment, building
USE construction equipment

<equipment by context>
　 TH.13
HN February 1993 guide term added

<equipment by general type>
　 TH.2

<equipment by material processed>
　 TH.1116

<equipment by mode of operation>
　 TH.7

<equipment by process>
　 TH.416

<equipment by profession or discipline>
　 TH.1100

equipment, compacting
USE compacting equipment

equipment, construction
USE construction equipment

equipment, drafting
USE drafting equipment

equipment, earthmoving
USE earthmoving equipment

equipment, excavating
USE excavating equipment

equipment, firefighting
USE firefighting equipment

<equipment for business or finance>
　 TH.1101
HN November 1992 guide term added

<equipment for costume>
　 TH.346
HN January 1993 guide term added

*<equipment for engineering and building
trades>*
　 TH.1103
HN January 1993 guide term added

<equipment for music>
　 TH.1105
HN January 1993 guide term added
RT musical instruments

*<equipment for natural resource
extraction>*
HN May 1993 guide term deleted

<equipment for personal use>
　 TH.361
HN February 1993 guide term added
RT *<containers for personal use>*

<equipment for personal use: eyewear>
　 TH.364
HN January 1993 guide term added

*<equipment for personal use: grooming,
hygiene and health care>*
　 TH.371
HN January 1993 guide term added

<equipment for personal use: smoking>
　 TH.402
HN January 1993 guide term added

<equipment for science and technology>
　 TH.1107

equipment, hydraulic
USE hydraulic equipment

equipment, measuring
USE measuring devices

equipment, milling
USE milling machines

equipment, photographic
USE photographic equipment

equipment, play
USE playground equipment

equipment, playground
USE playground equipment

equipment, plumbing
USE plumbing fixtures

equipment, power producing
USE power producing equipment

equipment, sandblasting
USE sandblasting equipment

<equipment spaces>
　 PJ.1081
HN March 1993 guide term moved

equipment, stage
USE stage machinery

equipment, surveying
USE surveying instruments

equity
　 BM.878　　　　　　　　　　(L)
HN February 1993 descriptor moved
SN An interest, commonly expressed in
　 money, which an owner has in
　 property over and above all liens
　 against the property. (PUTNAM)

era
USE period

erasers
　 TH.669　　　　　　　　　　(N)
ALT eraser
SN Devices, such as pieces of rubber or
　 cloth, for removing marks made
　 with pen, pencil, chalk, or the like.
　 (RHDEL2)

erasing
　 KT.951
ALT erased
UF erasure

erasing shields
　 TH.670
ALT erasing shield
SN Thin shields used when erasing to
　 avoid erasing the surrounding
　 work. (PUTNAM)
UF shields, erasing

erasure
USE erasing

erection drawings
　 VC.199
HN April 1992 descriptor moved
ALT erection drawing
SN Shop drawings depicting compo-
　 nents and relative positions, for pro-
　 cess of erection of a structure.
　 (DAC)
UF drawings, erection

erectors
　 HG.825
HN December 1992 alternate terms
　 added
ALT erector
　 erector's
　 erectors'
SN Persons who work on a structure,
　 such as a steel building or bridge, by
　 assembling fabricated parts. (W)

Eretrian
　 FL.2709

ergastula
RK.681
ALT ergastulum
SN Use for ancient Roman domestic places of confinement for criminal offenders, usually slaves.

ergonomics
USE human factors

Erh-li-kang
USE Erligang

Erh-li-t'ou
USE Erlitou

erhu
TT.270
SN Chinese spike fiddles having two strings, a long neck of hardwood with two tuning pegs at the upper end, and a tubular, hexagonal, or octagonal resonator covered at one end with snakeskin. They are played with a horsehair bow which passes between the two strings, causing them to sound simultaneously.

Eridu
FL.3046   (L)
UF Ubaid 1

Erie
FL.1305   (L)

Erimi
USE red-on-white

Erimi ware
USE red-on-white + ware

eriometers
TN.84   (L,N)
ALT eriometer
SN Devices for measuring the diameter of minute particles or fibers based on a measurement of the diffraction pattern produced by them in monochromatic light. (W)

Erlangen blue
USE Prussian blue

Erligang
FL.1927
HN June 1990 lead-in term added
UF Erh-li-kang

Erlitou
FL.1924
UF Erh-li-t'ou
Lo-yang

eroding
USE erosion

erosion
KT.261   (L)
HN January 1993 descriptor moved
February 1991 scope note changed
ALT eroded
SN Process whereby materials are worn away and removed by natural causes including weathering, solution, corrosion, or transportation. (W)
UF eroding

erosion, alveolar
USE alveolar weathering

erosion, honeycomb
USE alveolar weathering

erosion protection works
RK.523   (A)
UF water flow control works
works, erosion protection
works, water flow control

erotica
BM.161   (L,R)
ALT erotic
SN Depiction or description of sexual love. For depiction or description of sexual activity in an exploitative, abusive, or violent context, use pornography.

Ersari
FL.1896
HN April 1993 descriptor moved
April 1993 lead-in terms added
UF Afghan (Ersari)
Arsari
Beshir
Beshire
Bukhara (Ersari)

Ersari carpets
USE Ersari + rugs

Ersari Turkoman rugs
USE Ersari + rugs

Ertebølle
FL.2568

Esa
USE Ishan

Esan
USE Ishan

escalator wells
PJ.1026
HN March 1993 descriptor moved
ALT escalator well
UF wells, escalator
wellways

escalators
PC.113   (A,L,B)
HN March 1993 descriptor moved
ALT escalator
SN Use for continuously operating, power-driven, moving stairways.
UF electric stairways
moving staircases
staircases, moving
stairways, electric

escape wheels
PJ.2652
ALT escape wheel
SN Final wheels in the going trains of timepieces which interact directly with the escapement. (IDOFC)
UF scape wheels
wheels, escape
wheels, scape

escapements
PJ.2653   (L)
ALT escapement
SN Mechanisms in clocks and watches that measure beats and control the speed of the going trains thus controling the indication of the passage of time.

escapements, anchor
USE anchor escapements

escapements, crown wheel
USE verge escapements

escapements, deadbeat
USE deadbeat escapements

escapements, Graham
USE deadbeat escapements

escapements, gravity
USE gravity escapements

escapements, lever
USE lever escapements

escapements, recoil
USE anchor escapements

escapements, verge
USE verge escapements

escapes, fire
USE fire escapes

escarpments
RD.204   (L)
HN March 1993 descriptor changed, was escarpments (landform components)
March 1993 alternate term changed, was escarpment (landform component)
ALT escarpment
UF scarps (landform components)

escarpments (fortification elements)
USE scarps

escarps
USE scarps

eschatology
KD.94   (L,R)

esclavages
TE.460
ALT esclavage
SN Necklaces composed of several rows of gold chains, beads, or jewels falling in festoons over the bosom; named for its resemblance to slave fetters. (EMAEA)

esconsons
USE reveals

escort ships
USE escort vessels

escort vessels
    TX.418
ALT escort vessel
SN Use for warships assigned to protect single ships or convoys of transports or merchant vessels during wartime.
UF escort ships
    escorts
    ships, escort
    vessels, escort

escorts
USE escort vessels

escritoires
    TC.979
HN January 1993 descriptor moved
ALT escritoire
SN Writing desks, especially of the small portable type, made since the 16th century and consisting of a nest of drawers enclosed in a box with a sloping front that is hinged along the bottom edge and may be let down to provide a writing platform. Term also applied to small, elegant desks patterned after the 18th-century French form.
UF scritoires

escritoires (desks and bookcases)
USE desks and bookcases

escritoires (secretaries)
USE secretaries (furniture)

escritorios
USE vargueños

escrows
    VW.652   (L)
HN November 1992 descriptor moved
ALT escrow
SN Any items, such as deeds, bonds, or monies, held in trust by a third party to be turned over to the grantee upon fulfillment of a condition. (WCOL9)

escudos
    VK.80
ALT escudo
SN Spanish gold coins issued beginning in the early 16th century; later, these and similar Portuguese coins; and, more recently, various coins of Spanish- and Portuguese- speaking countries.

escutcheon pins
    PJ.220
HN April 1993 descriptor moved
ALT escutcheon pin
SN Small nails, usually brass and often ornamental, used to fix an escutcheon. (MEANS)
UF pins, escutcheon

escutcheon plates
USE escutcheons (hardware)

escutcheon plates, combined
USE combined escutcheon plates

escutcheons (coats of arms)
    VW.399   (H,L)
HN November 1992 descriptor moved
ALT escutcheon (coat of arms)
UF shields (heraldry)

escutcheons (hardware)
    PJ.438   (L,N)
HN April 1993 descriptor moved
ALT escutcheon (hardware)
SN The protective plates that surround keyholes. For inserts or inlay surrounding keyholes, use **keyhole surrounds.**
UF escutcheon plates
    key plates
    lock plates (hardware)
    plates, escutcheon
    plates, key
    plates, lock
    scutcheons

escutcheons (keyhole surrounds)
USE keyhole surrounds

escutcheons, cup
USE cup escutcheons

escutcheons, drop
USE drop escutcheons

escutcheons, thread
USE thread escutcheons

Eshira
USE Shira

Eshure
    FL.97

Esie
    FL.98

eskers
    RD.152   (L)
ALT esker
SN Relatively long, narrow, winding ridges of mixed sand and gravel, deposited probably by streams of meltwater flowing through crevasses and tunnels in stagnant ice sheets. (WAYTA)

Eskimo
    FL.805   (A,L,R)
SN Use with reference to the native Arctic culture, prior to European contact. For names of specific native peoples of the present, use descriptors such as **Chugach, Inuit,** or **Katladlit.**

Eskimo, Baffinland
USE Baffin Island Inuit

Eskimo, Canadian
USE Inuit

Eskimo, Caribou
USE Caribou Inuit

Eskimo, Copper
USE Copper Inuit

Eskimo, Greenlandic
USE Katladlit

Eskimo, Labrador
USE Labrador Inuit

Eskimo, Mackenzie
USE Western Arctic Inuit

Eskimo, North Alaskan
USE Inupiaq

Eskimo, Saint Lawrence Island
USE Saint Lawrence Island Eskimo

esmalte
USE smalt

Esmeralda
    FL.1677

esonarthexes
    PJ.1270
HN March 1993 descriptor moved
ALT esonarthex
SN Inner narthexes where there is also an outer narthex (the exonarthex).

espadrilles
    TE.734   (N)
ALT espadrille
SN Rope-soled shoes originally with canvas or cotton upper, sometimes laced across the vamp and round the ankle; also, similar shoes made of other materials.
UF alpargatas

espagnolette bolts
    PJ.527
HN April 1993 descriptor moved
ALT espagnolette bolt
UF bolts, espagnolette

espagnolettes
    DG.34   (R)
ALT espagnolette
SN Motifs of female masks having a ruff around the head and under the chin, popular in 18th-century French decorative arts, especially Régence. (LDDO)

esparto
    MT.1388   (L)
HN February 1992 descriptor moved
SN The fiber of either of two Spanish and Algerian grasses (Stipa tenacissima and Lygeum spartum) used especially to make cordage, shoes, and paper. (WCOL9)
UF alfa

Esperanza
    FL.1033

esplanades
USE promenades

espontoons
USE spontoons

esquisses
    VC.583

HN April 1991 descriptor moved
ALT esquisse
SN Sketches representing an early step in the development of a pictorial composition or the design of a building, but more developed than a preliminary sketch. Used especially in the context of the École des Beaux-Arts.

ESR
USE electron spin resonance

esrajs
TT.235
ALT esraj
SN Fiddles of Bengal made in one piece, with a pear-shaped resonator waisted at the front and covered with goatskin, a long fretted neck covered by a convex wood fingerboard, and four main strings and fifteen sympathetic strings, all of metal, stretched along a bar of wood fixed along the right side of the neck.
UF esrars
RT sympathetic strings

esrars
USE esrajs

essayists
HG.361
HN December 1992 alternate terms added
ALT essayist
essayist's
essayists'
SN Writers of essays. (W)

essays
VW.270 (L)
HN November 1992 descriptor moved
ALT essay
SN Short literary compositions on single subjects, often presenting the personal view of the author. (AHD)
UF literary sketches
sketches, literary

essence
USE essential oil

essence pots
USE cassolettes

essence vases
USE cassolettes

essential oil
MT.1076 (L)
HN April 1992 descriptor moved
SN Aromatic oil found in uncombined form in various parts of plants and employed for flavoring, perfume, disenfectant, and medicine. (MH)
UF essence
oil, essential

estancias
USE haciendas

estate administration records
VW.758 (L)
HN November 1992 descriptor moved
ALT estate administration record
UF records, estate administration

estate agents
USE real estate agents

estate cars
SEE station wagons

estate inventories
VW.759 (L)
HN November 1992 descriptor moved
October 1992 related term added
ALT estate inventory
SN Lists, catalogs, accounts, or schedules, made by an estate executor or administrator of the tangible and intangible property of the estate, describing the items or classes of property so as to be identifiable and usually placing a value on each. (GAHLM)
UF household inventories
inventories, estate
inventories, household
inventories of decedents' estates
inventories, probate
probate inventories
RT inventories

estate papers
USE estate records

estate records
VW.721
HN November 1992 descriptor moved
ALT estate record
SN Use broadly for any documents concerning the real or personal property of a person or group of persons.
UF estate papers
papers, estate
records, estate

estate wagons
SEE station wagons

estates
BM.922 (H,L)
HN March 1993 descriptor changed, was **estates (law)**
March 1993 alternate term changed, was **estate (law)**
February 1993 descriptor moved
January 1991 alternate term added
ALT estate
SN Aggregate of property or liabilities of all kinds that a person leaves for his or her disposal at death. (W)

estates (country houses)
USE country houses

estates, industrial
USE industrial parks

ester
MT.2450 (L)

HN April 1993 descriptor changed, was **esters**
SN Any of a class of often fragrant compounds formed by the reaction between an acid and an alcohol usually with the elimination of water. (WCOL9)

ester gum
MT.1277
HN April 1992 descriptor moved
UF ester, rosin
gum, ester
rosin ester

ester, rosin
USE ester gum

esthetics
USE aesthetics

estilo desornamentado
USE Herreran

estimates
VW.569 (L,B)
HN March 1993 lead-in term added
November 1992 descriptor moved
ALT estimate
SN Rough or approximate calculations of cost or value, such as statements of price for which certain work will be done by one who is willing to undertake it. (GAHLM)
UF cost estimates
estimates, cost

estimates, cost
USE estimates

estimating
KG.95 (B)
HN January 1991 scope note added
SN Giving an approximate or tentative judgment regarding the value or quality of something.

estipites
PJ.1989
HN March 1993 descriptor moved
February 1991 descriptor moved
February 1991 scope note changed
ALT estipite
SN Use for pilasters with complex ornament and low-relief sculpture that taper from top to base, as commonly encountered in Spanish post-Renaissance architecture.

estocs
TK.83 (N)
ALT estoc
SN Heavy swords of the 15th and 16th centuries, having a long rigid blade of square or triangular section, and originally a simple cross hilt with a relatively long grip, used primarily for thrusting. In the late 16th century the hilt acquired a more developed guard.
UF estoques
tucks
RT thrusting swords

estofado
KT.451
HN June 1990 descriptor added
SN Technique used in Spanish painting which involves working a painted surface to create a pattern; used to embellish the robes of carved and painted figures.

estoques
USE estocs

estrays
USE animal shelters

Estridentismo
FL.1785   (R)
ALT Stridentism
UF Stridenist

estuaries
RD.125   (L)
ALT estuary
SN Water passages where tides meet the currents of streams. (W)

étagères
TC.1016   (N)
HN January 1993 descriptor moved
ALT étagère
SN Open-tiered shelves for displaying small objects; often with a mirrored back and sometimes having drawers or a cabinet below.
UF parlor cabinets
   whatnots

etch
MT.2312
HN July 1990 descriptor added
SN A solution of gum arabic and acid used in desensitizing lithographic plates and stones. (TYLER)
UF etch, gum
   etch, lithographic
   gum arabic etch
   gum etch
   lithographic etch

etch, deep
USE deep etching

etch, gum
USE etch

etch, lithographic
USE etch

etch, open
USE open biting

Etchaottine
USE Slave

etched daguerreotype prints
VC.409
HN April 1992 descriptor moved
ALT etched daguerreotype print
SN Photomechanical prints of the mid-19th century made by an etched daguerreotype process.
UF daguerreotype prints, etched
   daguerreotype prints, etched

etched daguerreotypes
prints, etched daguerreotype

etched daguerreotype process
KT.658
HN April 1993 descriptor moved
SN Use for various photomechanical processes that use a daguerreotype to make the printing plate.

etched daguerreotypes
USE etched daguerreotype prints

Etchemin
USE Malecite

etchers
HG.310   (L,B,R)
HN April 1993 scope note changed
   April 1993 related term added
   February 1993 descriptor moved
   December 1992 alternate terms added
ALT etcher
   etcher's
   etchers'
SN Artists who etch by hand metal plates used in printing.
RT etching (printing process)

etchers' needles
USE etching needles

etching (biting)
USE biting

etching (corroding)
KT.952
HN October 1991 scope note changed
   October 1990 descriptor moved
   October 1990 descriptor changed, was **etching (surface decoration)**
ALT etched
SN Creating marks on the surface of a hard material such as metal or glass, by the controlled corrosive action of acid. Use **etching (printing process)** for the series of steps that includes printing from a bitten plate.

etching (printing process)
KT.680   (L,B,R)
HN April 1993 alternate term deleted
   April 1993 related term added
   October 1991 descriptor moved
   October 1991 scope note changed
   October 1991 descriptor changed, was **etching (printmaking)**
SN Use for the intaglio process in which the design is worked into an acid-resistant substance coating the metal printing plate; the plate is exposed to acid, which etches the plate where the metal is exposed. For the single step of exposing the plate to acid, use **biting**.
RT etchers

etching, acid
USE frosting

etching blankets
USE blankets (printing press components)

etching, deep
USE deep etching

etching, fire
USE pyrography

etching ground
MT.2486
HN July 1990 descriptor added
SN An acid-resistant substance applied to a surface to stop out areas that are not to be etched.
UF ground (etching)

etching, lift-ground
USE lift-ground

etching needles
TH.843   (N)
HN February 1993 descriptor added
ALT etching needle
SN Blunt, rounded steel points used to lay open the ground when making an image on an etching plate. (PRTT)
UF etchers' needles
   needles, etchers'
   needles, etching

etching presses
USE rolling presses

etching, relief
USE relief etching

etching, soft-ground
USE soft-ground etching

etching, sugar-lift
USE sugar-lift

etching, zinc
USE anastatic printing

etchings
VC.470
ALT etching
SN Prints made from an etched printing plate.
UF etchings, hard-ground
   hard-ground etchings

etchings, hard-ground
USE etchings

etchings, relief
USE relief etchings

etchings, reverse
USE relief etchings

etchings, soft-ground
USE soft-ground etchings

eternity rings
TE.474
ALT eternity ring
SN Rings in the form of a circular band set with a continuous row of gemstones, usually diamonds, of the same size and cut. (HNDOJ)

UF alliance rings
      rings, alliance
      rings, eternity

ethanoic acid
  USE acetic acid

ether, cellulose
  USE cellulose ether

ether, ethylene glycol monoethyl
  USE ethylene glycol monoethyl ether

ethics (concept)
  BM.410   (L,B,R)
  HN January 1991 alternate term added
       January 1991 descriptor changed,
         was **ethics**
  ALT ethical
  SN System of moral principles or rules
       of conduct. (RHDEL2)

ethics (philosophy)
  KD.76   (L,B,R)
  HN September 1991 related term added
  SN Use for the branch of philosophy
       dealing with values relating to hu-
       man conduct, with respect to the
       rightness and wrongness of certain
       actions, and to the goodness and
       badness of the motives and ends of
       such actions.
  UF moral philosophy
       philosophy, moral
  RT behavioral sciences

ethics, professional
  USE professional ethics

ethics, religious
  USE religious ethics

ethics, social
  USE social ethics

<Ethiopian styles>
  FL.636

ethnic art
  BM.187   (L,R)
  UF art, ethnic

ethnic group studies
  USE ethnic studies

ethnic groups
  HG.3
  HN October 1991 lead-in term added
       September 1991 related terms
         added
       June 1991 scope note changed
       April 1991 descriptor moved
  ALT ethnic group
  SN Subgroups within a larger cultural
       or social order that are distin-
       guished from the majority and each
       other by their national, religious,
       linguistic, cultural, or sometimes ra-
       cial background. For groups that
       are the objects of prejudice or dis-
       crimination from the majority, use
       minorities. (ERIC12)
  UF groups, ethnic

RT ethnic studies
     minorities

ethnic museums
  USE enthnological (ALT of ethnology) +
       museums

ethnic studies
  KD.266   (L)
  HN September 1991 descriptor added
  SN Use for the study of the history and
       culture of ethnic groups within a
       larger cultural or social order. For
       the scientific, historic, or compara-
       tive study of the origins, characteris-
       tics, and functions of human cul-
       tures and societies, use **ethnology**.
  UF ethnic group studies
       studies, ethnic
       studies, ethnic group
  RT ethnic groups
       ethnology

ethno-archaeology
  SEE ethnoarchaeology

ethnoarchaeology
  KD.206   (L)
  UK ethno-archaeology
  SN Study of contemporary societies
       from a materialistic perspective, fo-
       cusing on variability rather than
       typical and categorical behavior,
       with the purpose of interpreting the
       past of those societies.

ethnocentrism
  BM.291   (L)
  HN January 1991 alternate term added
  ALT ethnocentric
  SN Tendency toward viewing alien cul-
       tures with disfavor; also the re-
       sulting sense of inherent superior-
       ity. (W)

ethnographers
  HG.442
  HN January 1993 descriptor added
  ALT ethnographer
       ethnographer's
       ethnographers'
  SN Those trained or working in the
       field of ethnography.
  RT ethnography

ethnographic materials
  USE ethnographic objects

ethnographic objects
  PE.95
  HN December 1992 descriptor added
  ALT ethnographic object
  SN Use for articles originating in any
       culture still living or known through
       relatively recent history when those
       articles are the concern of ethno-
       graphic or ethnological study. For
       articles from earlier periods found
       in contexts of archaeological re-
       search, prefer **archaeological ob-
       jects**.
  UF anthropological materials
       ethnographic materials

ethnological objects
     materials, anthropological
     materials, ethnographic
     objects, ethnographic
     objects, ethnological

ethnographic photography
  HN April 1993 descriptor split, use **eth-
       nographic** (ALT of **ethnography**)
       + **photography**

ethnography
  KD.212   (L,R)
  HN May 1993 alternate term added
       February 1993 related term added
       September 1991 descriptor moved
  ALT ethnographic
  SN Direct observation and descriptive
       study of the culture and way of life
       of particular societies. (TSIT)
  RT ethnographers

ethnography museums
  USE ethnological (ALT of ethnology) +
       museums

ethnological museums
  HN March 1993 descriptor split, use
       ethnological (ALT of **ethnology**)
       + **museums**

ethnological objects
  USE ethnographic objects

ethnologists
  HG.443   (L)
  HN April 1993 related term added
       December 1992 alternate terms
         added
  ALT ethnologist
       ethnologist's
       ethnologists'
  RT ethnology

ethnology
  KD.213   (A,L,B,R)
  HN April 1993 related term added
       November 1991 related terms
         added
       September 1991 scope note
         changed
       September 1991 descriptor moved
       February 1991 alternate term added
  ALT ethnological
  SN Use for the scientific, historic, or
       comparative study of the origins,
       characteristics, and functions of hu-
       man cultures and societies. For the
       study of the history and culture of
       ethnic groups within a larger cul-
       tural or social order, use **ethnic
       studies**.
  RT ethnic studies
       ethnologists
       ethnomusicology

ethnology museums
  USE ethnological (ALT of ethnology) +
       museums

ethnomusicologists
  HG.345   (L)
  HN April 1993 related term added

December 1992 alternate terms
added
ALT   ethnomusicologist
ethnomusicologist's
ethnomusicologists'
SN   Persons who study music in a socio-cultural context, especially that outside the European tradition. (WCOL9)
RT   ethnomusicology

ethnomusicology
KD.38   (L)
HN   April 1993 related term added
April 1993 scope note changed
December 1991 scope note added
November 1991 related term added
SN   Branch of musicology focusing on the study of music in its cultural context.
RT   ethnology
ethnomusicologists

ethnopsychology
KD.223   (L)
HN   September 1991 descriptor moved
UF   anthropology, psychological
cross-cultural psychology
psychological anthropology
psychology, cross-cultural

ethyl acetate
MT.2453
UF   acetate, ethyl

ethyl alcohol
MT.2445   (L)
HN   April 1993 lead-in term changed, was **Cologne spirits**
UF   alcohol, ethyl
alcohol, grain
Cologne spirit
grain alcohol
spirit, Cologne

ethyl cellulose
MT.1169
HN   January 1993 descriptor moved
SN   A colorless, odorless ester of cellulose resulting from the reaction of ethyl chloride and cellulose; forms a durable alkali-resistant coating. (MH)
UF   cellulose, ethyl
EC

ethyl silicate
MT.232
HN   January 1993 descriptor added
SN   Colorless liquid used, for example, as a source of colloidal silica in heat-resistant and acid-resistant coatings, as a protective coating for industrial buildings and castings, as a consolidant for stone, and as a bonding agent.
UF   orthosilicate, tetraethyl
silane
silicate, ethyl
tetraethyl orthosilicate

ethylene glycol monoethyl ether
MT.2423

HN   May 1990 lead-in term changed, was **cellosolve**
UF   Cellosolve (TM)
ether, ethylene glycol monoethyl

ethylene-propylene elastomer
MT.1032   (L)
HN   January 1993 descriptor moved
UF   elastomer, ethylene-propylene
EPR
EPR rubber
ethylene-propylene rubber
rubber, EPR
rubber, ethylene-propylene

ethylene-propylene rubber
USE   ethylene-propylene elastomer

etiquette
BM.266   (L,R)
SN   The forms required by good breeding or prescribed by authority to be observed in social or official life. (W)

Etowah
FL.906
UF   Etowah-Lamar

Etowah-Lamar
USE   Etowah

Etruscan
FL.2813   (A,L,B,R)

Etruscan, Early
USE   Early Etruscan

Etruscan, Late
USE   Late Etruscan

<Etruscan pottery styles>
FL.2833

Etruscan Style
FL.3359

Etrusco-Greek
USE   Greco-Etruscan

Etrusco-Italic
FL.2818

Etrusco-Roman
FL.2819

Etsako
FL.249   (L)
UF   Kukuruku

études
USE   studies (visual works)

etuis
TQ.196   (N)
ALT   etui
SN   Small cases, usually ornamental, meant to contain personal articles, such as bodkins and toothpicks. Formerly, also cases for surgical instruments.
UF   cases, pocket
pocket cases
RT   cases (containers)
housewives (containers)

etwies
TT.566
ALT   etwie
SN   Friction drums of the Akan people of western Guinea.

etymological dictionaries
VW.820   (L)
HN   November 1992 descriptor moved
ALT   etymological dictionary
UF   dictionaries, etymological

etymology
KD.60   (A,L)
HN   February 1991 alternate term added
ALT   etymological
SN   Study of the history of a particular word or element of a word, or of historical linguistic change. (RHDEL1)

Euboean
FL.2710

eucalyptus
MT.2738   (L)
HN   March 1992 descriptor moved

Eucalyptus globulus
USE   blue gum

Eucalyptus paniculata
USE   gray ironbark

Eucalyptus pilulares
USE   blackbutt

Eucalyptus regnans
USE   mountain ash

eucharistic windows
USE   squints

euchre
KQ.26   (L)

euchrome
USE   burnt umber

eulogies
VW.390   (L)
HN   November 1992 descriptor moved
ALT   eulogy
SN   Laudatory speeches or written tributes. (AHD)

eunuch flutes
USE   onion flutes

euphoniums
TT.90   (L,N)
ALT   euphonium
SN   Valved brass instruments, essentially tenor tubas, with a wide conical bore, cup-shaped mouthpiece, and built in helicon, tuba, or trumpet form, invented by Sommer of Weimar about 1843. (NGDMI)

European
FL.3123   (L,B)

European ash
MT.2688

HN March 1992 descriptor moved
UF ash, common
    ash, European
    common ash
    Fraxinus excelsior

European beech
    MT.2694   (L)
HN March 1992 descriptor moved
UF beech, common
    beech, European
    common beech
    Fagus sylvatica

European birch
    MT.2704   (L)
HN March 1992 descriptor moved
UF Betula pubescens
    birch, European
    maple, Russian
    Russian maple

European black poplar
USE black poplar

European bows
USE self bows

European box
USE boxwood

European boxwood
USE boxwood

<European Bronze Age periods>
    FL.2597

<European Bronze Age styles>
    FL.2604

<European Bronze Age styles and periods>
    FL.2596

European chestnut
    MT.2721   (L)
HN March 1992 descriptor moved
UF Castanea sativa
    Castanea vesca
    chestnut, European
    chestnut, Italian
    chestnut, Spanish
    chestnut, sweet
    Italian chestnut
    Spanish chestnut
    sweet chestnut

European green alder
    MT.2684   (L)
HN March 1992 descriptor moved
UF alder, European green
    Alnus viridis

European hackberry
    MT.2756
HN March 1992 descriptor moved
UF Celtis australis
    hackberry, European

European hop hornbeam
    MT.2772
HN March 1992 descriptor moved
UF hop hornbeam, European
    hornbeam, European hop
    Ostrya carpinofolia

European hornbeam
    MT.2769   (L)
HN March 1992 descriptor moved
UF Carpinus betulus
    common hornbeam
    hornbeam, common
    hornbeam, European
    ironwood (European hornbeam)

<European Iron Age periods>
    FL.2607

<European Iron Age styles>
    FL.2610

<European Iron Age styles and periods>
    FL.2606

European lacquer
USE lacquer

European larch
    MT.2953   (L)
HN March 1992 descriptor moved
UF larch, European
    Larix decidua
    Larix europaea

<European Lower Paleolithic styles and periods>
    FL.2538

<European Mesolithic styles and periods>
    FL.2563

<European Middle Paleolithic styles and periods>
    FL.2544

<European Neolithic pottery styles>
    FL.2590

<European Neolithic styles and periods>
    FL.2574

<European paper money>
    VK.155

<European regions>
    FL.3124

European spruce
USE common spruce

<European styles and periods>
    FL.3154

European turkey oak
    MT.2830   (L)
HN March 1992 descriptor moved
UF oak, European turkey
    Quercus catesbaei
    Quercus cerris
    Quercus laevis
    turkey oak, European

<European Upper Paleolithic styles and periods>
    FL.2548

European walnut
USE English walnut

eurythmy
USE concinnity

eutectic melting point
USE eutectic point

eutectic point
    DC.369   (L)
HN October 1992 descriptor added
SN The temperature at which a eutectic alloy or mixture melts or solidifies.
UF eutectic melting point

eutectic solder
USE fine solder

evaluating
    KG.22   (A,L)
HN April 1993 lead-in term added
SN Determining qualitative or quantitative worth or significance. (RLG7)
UF evaluation

evaluation
USE evaluating

evaluation, building
USE post-occupancy evaluation

evaluation, nondestructive
USE nondestructive testing

evaluation, post-occupancy
USE post-occupancy evaluation

evaluators
USE appraisers

evangeliaries
    VW.896   (H,L)
HN November 1992 descriptor moved
    March 1992 scope note added
    March 1992 lead-in terms added
ALT evangeliary
SN Books containing the four Gospels, or readings from the Gospels arranged for the liturgical year; by the 13th century generally folded into the missal.
UF evangeliars
    evangelistaries
    gospel lectionaries
    lectionaries, gospel

evangeliars
USE evangeliaries

evangelistaries
USE evangeliaries

evangelists
    HG.425   (L,R)
HN February 1993 descriptor moved
    December 1992 alternate terms added
ALT evangelist
    evangelist's
    evangelists'
SN Occasional preachers having no fixed pastoral charge. (W)
UF revivalists

evaporating
USE evaporation

evaporation
    KT.837   (L)

HN November 1992 descriptor added
ALT evaporated
SN The process by which any substance is converted from a liquid state into a vapor or gaseous state. (W)
UF evaporating

evaporation gauges
USE atmometers

evaporimeters
USE atmometers

even balance scales
USE balances

evening bags
　　TE.411
ALT evening bag
SN Smaller version of any bag in fashion, usually beaded, sequinned, or embroidered, or of some glamorous fabric such as kid, silver, bronze, or gold.
UF bags, evening
　　evening handbags
　　handbags, evening
RT evening dress

evening clothes
USE evening dress

evening dress
　　BM.270　　　　　　　(H,N)
HN August 1992 descriptor added
SN Formal or semiformal attire for evening wear.
UF clothes, evening
　　dress, evening
　　evening clothes
RT evening bags
　　evening dresses

evening dresses
　　TE.29
ALT evening dress
SN Dresses intended for formal or semiformal evening occasions.
UF dresses, evening
RT evening dress

evening handbags
USE evening bags

event art
USE happenings

events
　　KM.1
HN May 1991 alternate term added
　　January 1991 scope note added
ALT event
SN Occurrences taking place during a particular interval of time.

evergreens
　　RD.244　　　　　　　(L)
ALT evergreen

evicting
　　KG.284　　　　　　　(L)
HN April 1993 lead-in term added

SN Legally removing a person or persons from the premises.
UF eviction

eviction
USE evicting

eviction control
USE rent control

evolute scrolls
USE wave scrolls

evolute spirals
USE wave scrolls

evolution
　　BM.557　　　　　　　(L,R)
SN Use for the gradual development of living organisms over successive generations, from lower to higher forms, especially as articulated in Darwinian theory or in alternatives to or modifications of Darwinian theory.

evolutionary housing
USE incremental housing

Ewe
　　FL.301　　　　　　　(L)

<Ewe cultures>
　　FL.298

ewers
　　TQ.73　　　　　　　(H,N,R)
ALT ewer
SN Tall, wide-mouthed vessels, generally having a pouring lip, and that have a deep bowl on a stemmed base and a single vertical handle. The bowl is usually cylindrical, baluster-shaped, or helmet-shaped.
RT basins
　　pitchers

ex libris
USE bookplates

ex-votos
USE votive images
　　votive offerings

examination
USE examining

examination study guides
　　VW.453　　　　　　　(L)
HN November 1992 descriptor moved
ALT examination study guide
UF guides, examination study
　　study guides, examination

examinations
　　VW.391　　　　　　　(L)
HN November 1992 descriptor moved
ALT examination
SN Written questions or exercises testing knowledge, aptitude, or skills. (AHD)
UF tests

examining
　　KG.24

HN October 1992 descriptor added
SN Scrutinizing a situation or object, usually in order to determine its nature or current condition. (W)
UF examination

excavating
USE excavation

excavating equipment
　　TH.445　　　　　　　(L)
SN Equipment used in the removal of earth.
UF equipment, excavating
　　excavating machinery
　　machinery, excavating

excavating machinery
USE excavating equipment

excavation
　　KT.955　　　　　　　(L,B)
ALT excavated
UF digging
　　excavating

excavations
　　RK.1292　　　　　　(A,L,B,R)
ALT excavation
UF digs

excavators, trench
USE trenching machines

excelsior
　　MT.3009　　　　　　(L)
HN March 1992 descriptor moved
　　July 1990 lead-in terms added
SN Continuous, curly, fine wood shavings employed as a packing material for breakable articles. (MH)
UF cellulose fiber
　　cellulose fiber, wood
　　fiber, cellulose
　　fiber, wood
　　wood cellulose fiber
　　wood fiber
　　wood wool
　　wool, wood

exceptional people
　　HG.34　　　　　　　(L)
HN February 1993 lead-in terms added
　　February 1993 descriptor changed, was **exceptional persons**
　　February 1993 alternate term deleted, was **exceptional person**
　　February 1993 descriptor moved
　　January 1993 alternate term added
ALT exceptional people's
SN Persons atypical due to disabilities or giftedness. (ERIC9)
UF exceptional persons
　　people, exceptional
　　persons, exceptional
RT special education

exceptional persons
USE exceptional people

excerpts
　　VW.247

HN November 1992 descriptor moved
ALT excerpt
SN Passages reproduced verbatim from a printed work or a manuscript. (GAHLM)
UF selections

exchange, bills of
USE bills of exchange

<exchange media groupings>
PC.79

exchange pieces
USE pieces of exchange

exchange, pieces of
USE pieces of exchange

exchangers, heat
USE heat exchangers

exchanges
RK.136 (B)
ALT exchange
UF bourses
lonjas

exchanges, commodity
USE commodity exchanges

exchanges, employment
USE employment agencies

exchanges, labor
USE employment agencies

exchanges, military post
USE post exchanges

exchanges, post
USE post exchanges

exchanges, produce
USE commodity exchanges

exchanges, stock
USE stock exchanges

exchanges, telephone
USE telephone exchanges

excise marks
VW.421
HN November 1992 descriptor moved
ALT excise mark
UF marks, excise

excommunications
KM.171 (L)
HN May 1991 alternate term added
ALT excommunication

excrement
MT.2524
HN February 1992 descriptor added
SN Waste matter discharged from the body. (W)
UF excreta

excreta
USE excrement

<excretions and secretions>
MT.2523
HN May 1993 guide term added

excursion boats
TX.400 (L,N)
ALT excursion boat
SN Use for passenger vessels operated for excursions.
UF boats, excursion
excursion vessels
vessels, excursion

excursion vessels
USE excursion boats

excursuses
VW.249
HN November 1992 descriptor moved
ALT excursus
SN Appendixes or digressions that contain further exposition on some point or topic from other works. (W)

executing
KG.291 (L)
HN April 1993 lead-in term added
February 1991 alternate term added
ALT executed
SN Taking human life under judicial order. (RLG7)
UF execution (judicial function)

execution
BM.34
HN February 1991 alternate term added
ALT executed
SN Use for the actual activity of making something or carrying out a plan.

execution (judicial function)
USE executing

executioners
HG.166
HN December 1992 descriptor added
ALT executioner
executioner's
executioners'
SN Officials who inflict capital punishment in pursuance of a legal warrant. (RHDEL2)

executions
KM.160 (L,R)
HN May 1991 alternate term added
ALT execution

executive orders
VW.727 (L)
HN November 1992 descriptor moved
ALT executive order
SN Orders or regulations issued by the President, or some administrative authority under his direction, for the purpose of interpreting, implementing, or giving administrative effect to a provision of the Constitution or of some law or treaty. May also include similar state documents issued by governors or upper-level management in business. (BLACKS)
UF orders, executive

executive records
VW.724

HN November 1992 descriptor moved
ALT executive record
UF records, executive

<executive records by function>
VW.725
HN November 1992 guide term moved

<executive records by provenance>
VW.744
HN November 1992 guide term moved

executives
HG.139 (L)
HN January 1993 scope note changed
December 1992 alternate terms added
ALT executive
executive's
executives'
SN Persons who hold a high position of administrative or managerial responsibility in a private business.

exedrae (interior spaces)
PJ.1216 (A)
HN March 1993 descriptor moved
May 1991 descriptor changed, was **exedrae**
May 1991 alternate term changed, was **exedra**
ALT exedra (interior space)
SN Use for niches, recesses, or other sheltered spaces, often semicircular and lined with seats; primarily in Roman architecture.
UF exhedrae

exedrae (site elements)
RM.232
HN April 1993 descriptor moved
ALT exedra (site element)
SN Use for semicircular outdoor seats, usually of stone or concrete.

exegesis
BM.245 (R)
SN Exposition or explanation, especially critical interpretation of a portion of Scripture or other text. (W)

exercises
PE.72
HN October 1992 scope note changed
November 1990 descriptor moved
ALT exercise
SN Things made, usually writings or visual works, chiefly in order to practice or display a specific technical point or aspect, especially by students.

exercising chairs
USE chamber horses

exercising machines, horse
USE chamber horses

exergues
DG.106
HN March 1993 descriptor added
ALT exergue
SN Use for the spaces on coins, tokens,

or medals below the central design, often set off from it by a horizontal line and often containing the date; usually occurring on the reverse.

exhaust ventilation
PC.165
HN March 1993 descriptor moved
SN Ventilation that allows fresh air to enter a space through available or controlled openings and employs mechanical means such as fans to remove foul air from the same space. (MEANS)
UF ventilation, exhaust

exhedrae
USE exedrae (interior spaces)

exhibit cases
TC.998
HN January 1993 descriptor moved
ALT exhibit case
UF cases, exhibit

exhibit designers
HG.323
HN February 1993 alternate terms added
February 1993 lead-in term changed, was **exhibit designers**
February 1993 descriptor changed, was **exhibition designers**
February 1993 descriptor moved
ALT exhibit designers
exhibit designer's
exhibit designers'
UF designers, exhibit
designers, exhibition
exhibition designers
exhibition preparators
preparators, exhibition

exhibit scripts
VW.794
HN November 1992 descriptor moved
ALT exhibit script
UF exhibition texts
scripts, exhibit
texts, exhibition

exhibiting
KG.139
HN April 1993 lead-in term added
May 1991 related term added
ALT exhibited
SN Showing or presenting to public view. (W)
UF displaying
exhibition
RT alternative spaces

exhibition
USE exhibiting

exhibition booths
PJ.1204   (A,L)
HN March 1993 descriptor moved
ALT exhibition booth
UF booths, exhibition

exhibition buildings
RK.366   (A,L,B,R)

ALT exhibition building
UF buildings, exhibition
buildings, exposition
buildings, fair
exhibition facilities
exhibition halls
exposition buildings
facilities, exhibition
fair buildings
halls, exhibition

exhibition catalogs
VW.26   (L)
HN November 1992 descriptor moved
ALT exhibition catalog
UF catalogs, exhibition

exhibition designers
USE exhibit designers

exhibition facilities
USE exhibition buildings

exhibition grounds
USE fairgrounds

exhibition halls
USE exhibition buildings

exhibition preparators
USE exhibit designers

exhibition records
VW.793
HN November 1992 descriptor moved
ALT exhibition record
UF records, exhibition

exhibition reviews
HN April 1993 descriptor split, use **exhibition** (ALT of **exhibitions**) + **reviews**

exhibition texts
USE exhibit scripts

exhibitions
KM.87   (A,L,B,R)
HN May 1991 alternate term added
ALT exhibition
SN Organized displays, especially of works of art or objects of manufacture. (W)
UF expositions
shows

exhibitions, garden
USE garden shows

exhibitions, traveling
USE traveling exhibitions

exhibitions, travelling
SEE traveling exhibitions

existentialism
BM.424   (L,R)
HN January 1991 alternate term added
ALT existentialist

existing light photography
USE available light photography

exit devices, panic
USE panicproof locks

exit lights
TC.1441
ALT exit light
SN Emergency lights above exit doors.
UF lights, exit

exits
PJ.2293   (A,B)
HN March 1993 descriptor moved
ALT exit
SN Openings used solely to leave a building, room, or other enclosed area.

exits, emergency
USE emergency exits

exits, fire
USE emergency exits

exodus, rural
USE rural-urban migration

exonarthexes
PJ.1271   (H)
HN March 1993 descriptor moved
ALT exonarthex
SN The outer narthexes where there is also an inner narthex (the esonarthex).

exorcists
HG.920
HN January 1993 descriptor added
ALT exorcist
exorcist's
exorcists'
SN Those who perform exorcisms.

exotic typefaces
USE ornate (typeface group)

exoticism
BM.292   (A,L,R)
SN Interest in or adoption of the exotic. (W)

expandable dining tables
USE extension dining tables

expandable structures
USE air-supported structures

expanded dugouts
TX.504
ALT expanded dugout
UK expanded logboats
UKA expanded logboat
SN Use for dugouts broadened by softening, usually with heat, and spreading the sides.
UF dugouts, expanded
logboats, expanded

expanded glass
USE cellular + glass

expanded logboats
SEE expanded dugouts

expanded metal
MT.500   (L)
HN April 1992 descriptor moved
June 1990 scope note added
SN Sheet metal that has been slit and

expanded to form a mesh, which is used for reinforced-concrete work or plaster wall construction. (MH)
UF metal, expanded

expanded metal lath, flat
USE diamond mesh lath

expanded plastic
USE plastic foam

expanded typefaces
PJ.3495
ALT expanded typeface
SN Typefaces whose characters are especially broad in proportion to their height.
UF extended typefaces
typefaces, expanded
typefaces, extended

expanded views
USE exploded drawings

expanding bullets
TK.264   (N)
ALT expanding bullet
SN Soft-nosed bullets designed to expand their original diameter when they contact any solid resistance.
UF bullets, expanding

expanding cement
MT.43   (L)
HN April 1992 descriptor moved
SN Cement which when mixed with water forms a paste that tends to increase in volume after setting to a significantly greater degree than portland cement paste does; used to compensate for volume decrease due to shrinkage or to induce tensile stress in reinforcement. (DAC)
UF cement, expanding
cement, expansive
cement, sulfoaluminate
expansive cement
sulfoaluminate cement

expanding concrete
USE expansive concrete

expanding tables, capstan
USE capstan tables

expanding vaults
PJ.1880
HN March 1993 descriptor moved
ALT expanding vault
SN Vaults that are larger at one end than at the other. (RS)
UF conical vaults
vaults, conical
vaults, expanding

expansion
KT.241
HN February 1993 lead-in term deleted, was **heat expansion**
February 1993 lead-in term deleted, was **expansion, heat**
February 1993 lead-in term deleted, was **thermal expansion**

February 1993 lead-in term deleted, was **expansion, thermal**
November 1992 descriptor moved
ALT expanded
SN The increase in length or volume of a material, or a body, caused by temperature, moisture, or other environmental condition. (DAC)

expansion bits
PJ.2581
HN March 1993 descriptor moved
ALT expansion bit
SN Drilling bits whose blade can be adjusted to bore holes of different diameters. (MEANS)
UF bits, expansion

expansion bolts
PJ.45
HN April 1993 descriptor moved
ALT expansion bolt
SN Anchoring or fastening devices used in masonry, which expand within a predrilled hole as a bolt is tightened. (MEANS)
UF bolts, expansion

expansion bolts, star
USE star expansion bolts

expansion joints
PJ.649   (L,B)
HN April 1993 descriptor moved
ALT expansion joint
SN Joints that allow for expansion of two adjacent parts of a structure.
UF joints, expansion

expansion, thermal
USE thermal expansion

expansive cement
USE expanding cement

expansive concrete
MT.223   (A,L)
HN April 1992 descriptor moved
UF concrete, expanding
concrete, expansive
expanding concrete

expatriates
HG.1007
HN April 1993 related term added
January 1993 alternate terms added
May 1991 related term added
ALT expatriate
expatriate's
expatriates'
SN Use for persons who have withdrawn voluntarily from their native country, especially those who have renounced allegiance to it. For persons who have fled their native country or country of residence to escape danger or persecution, use **refugees**.
RT expatriation
refugees

expatriation
KG.199   (L,R)

HN May 1991 related term added
January 1991 scope note added
November 1990 descriptor moved
January 1990 alternate term added
ALT expatriated
SN Withdrawing voluntarily from one's native country, especially if renouncing allegiance to it or to its government. (W)
RT expatriates

expeditions
KM.113   (R)
HN May 1991 alternate term added
ALT expedition

experiment stations
RK.1109   (L)
HN March 1993 related term added
ALT experiment station
SN Use for buildings or outdoor facilities where research and experiments are carried out in a specific field, such as agriculture or mining, where practical applications are tested, and from where the results are disseminated. Distinct from **research stations** which are primarily for the observation of natural phenomena.
UF stations, experiment
RT research stations

experimental aircraft
USE research aircraft

experimental buildings
RK.1314
ALT experimental building
UF buildings, experimental

experimental plants
USE pilot plants

experimentation
USE experimenting

experimenting
KG.25   (L)
HN April 1993 lead-in term added
SN Testing an hypothesis or model systematically under controlled conditions to discover its qualities, behavior, or effects.
UF experimentation

expertizing
KG.23   (L,R)
SN Giving an expert or professional opinion, usually after careful study or examination.

experts
HG.882   (L)
HN January 1993 alternate terms added
ALT expert
expert's
experts'
SN People with the special skill or knowledge representing mastery of a particular subject. (WCOL9)

explicits
VW.250
HN June 1992 descriptor added
ALT explicit
SN Use for the closing phrases of a manuscript or early printed book, or a section of same, indicating its completion and sometimes giving details of its production, such as the place and date of copying or the author's name. For similar closing statements in later printed books, use **colophons**.

exploded drawings
VC.87
HN April 1992 descriptor moved
ALT exploded drawing
SN Use for drawings that show the components of a structure or object disassembled and spaced apart, but remaining in their proper relation with respect to their assembled positions.
UF drawings, exploded
expanded views
exploded views
views, expanded
views, exploded

exploded views
USE exploded drawings

explorers
HG.921 (L,R)
HN December 1992 alternate terms added
ALT explorer
explorer's
explorers'

<exploring and investigating techniques>
KT.280

explosive
MT.2314 (L,R)
HN April 1993 descriptor changed, was **explosives**
January 1993 descriptor moved
January 1992 related term added
RT <explosive weapons>

explosive actuated guns
USE stud guns

<explosive and incendiary materials>
MT.2313
HN January 1993 guide term added

<explosive weapons>
TK.101
RT explosive
fuzes

export, Chinese
USE Chinese export

exporters
HG.635
HN December 1992 alternate terms added
ALT exporter

exporter's
exporters'

exporting
KG.245 (R)
HN January 1991 scope note added
SN Carrying or sending articles of trade or commerce out of a country. (BLACKS)

exposed hinges
PJ.418
HN April 1993 descriptor moved
ALT exposed hinge
UF hinges, exposed

exposed joints
PJ.681
HN April 1993 descriptor moved
ALT exposed joint
UF joints, exposed

exposing
USE exposure

exposition buildings
USE exhibition buildings

expositions
USE exhibitions

expositions, industrial
USE industrial expositions

exposure
KT.603 (L)
HN January 1993 descriptor moved
April 1991 descriptor added
SN The act of presenting a photosensitive surface to radiant energy, especially light; also, the total amount of radiant energy received. (RHDEL2)
UF exposing

exposure meters
TN.333 (N)
ALT exposure meter
SN Light meters that convert measured data into readings that allow photographers to adjust lens apertures and shutter speeds on cameras.
UF exposure meters, photographic
light meters (exposure meters)
light meters, photographic
meters, exposure
meters, light
meters, photographic exposure
meters, photographic light
photographic exposure meters
photographic light meters
RT <camera accessories>

exposure meters, photographic
USE exposure meters

express cars
TX.273 (N)
ALT express car
SN Use for specially constructed railroad passenger train cars designed for carrying express shipments; often with facilities for handling baggage or mail. (RRDICT)
UF cars, express

express highways
USE expressways

express roads
USE expressways

expression
BM.35

Expressionist
FL.3345 (A,L,B,R)
ALT Expressionism

Expressionist, Abstract
USE Abstract Expressionist

Expressionist, New
USE Neo-Expressionist

expressways
RM.129 (L,B)
HN April 1993 descriptor moved
ALT expressway
SN Use for divided multilane highways with a minimum of traffic signals where grades are separated at important intersections, although there may be some grade crossings; can be freeways or turnpikes.
UF express highways
express roads
highways, express
roads, express
skyways
speedways

expropriation
USE eminent domain

exquisite corpses
USE cadavres exquis

extendable lamps
USE extension lamps

extended care facilities
RK.714 (L)
ALT extended care facility
UF care facilities, extended
care facilities, long-term
facilities, extended care
facilities, long-term care
long-term care facilities

extended dugouts
TX.505
ALT extended dugout
UK extended logboats
UKA extended logboat
SN Use for dugouts with sides and ends raised by the addition of planks and sometimes frames.
UF dugouts, extended
logboats, extended

extended logboats
SEE extended dugouts

extended typefaces
USE expanded typefaces

extender
MT.2327
HN April 1993 descriptor changed, was **extenders**

extender white pigment
USE   transparent white pigment

extending tables
USE   extension dining tables

extension bolts
USE   extension flush bolts

extension dining tables
TC.1133
HN   January 1993 descriptor moved
ALT   extension dining table
SN   Dining tables with extending frames whose tops can be lengthened by inserting loose leaves.
UF   dining-room tables
dining tables, expandable
dining tables, extension
dining tables, imperial
expandable dining tables
extending tables
extension tables
imperial dining tables
tables, dining-room
tables, expandable dining
tables, extension dining
tables, imperial dining

extension fire screens
TC.436
HN   January 1993 descriptor moved
ALT   extension fire screen
UF   fire screens, extension
screens, extension fire

extension flush bolts
PJ.460
HN   April 1993 descriptor moved
ALT   extension flush bolt
SN   Flush bolts whose heads connect to the operating mechanism via a rod which is inserted through a hole bored in the door. (MEANS)
UF   bolts, extension
bolts, extension flush
extension bolts
flush bolts, extension

extension keys
USE   adjustable keys

extension ladders
TH.1042
ALT   extension ladder
SN   Ladders comprising more than one section, each of which slides within the other and locks on the other, thus allowing lengthening. (MEANS)
UF   ladders, extension

extension lamps
TC.1348
HN   May 1993 descriptor moved
ALT   extension lamp
SN   Hanging lamps that have a mechanism such as a chain and pulley by which they may be raised or lowered.
UF   extendable lamps
lamps, extendable
lamps, extension

extension rules
TN.48
ALT   extension rule
SN   Use for rules having graduated sliding attachments that are extendable for taking linear measurements and inside dimensions between objects.
UF   extension sticks
rules, extension
sticks, extension

extension sticks
USE   extension rules

extension tables
USE   extension dining tables

extensions
USE   additions
wings (building divisions)

extensometers
TN.32   (L,N)
ALT   extensometer
SN   Instruments designed to measure minute changes in distance between two reference points due to contraction, expansion, or deformation.

exterior
DC.325   (B)
HN   October 1992 descriptor moved
SN   Connected with or situated at the outside or outer part of something. (W)
UF   outside

<exterior covered spaces>
PJ.1186
HN   March 1993 guide term moved

exterior elevations
VC.105
HN   April 1992 descriptor moved
ALT   exterior elevation
UF   elevations, exterior
external elevations

exterior insulation and finish system
MT.1787   (A)
HN   April 1993 lead-in term added
April 1993 lead-in term changed, was **EIF systems**
April 1993 descriptor changed, was **exterior insulation and finish systems**
July 1990 descriptor added
SN   Lightweight and economical cladding system for buildings composed of insulation and wet applied finish. (AIAENC)
UF   EIF system
EIFS
exterior insulation finish system
finish system, exterior insulation and
insulation and finish system, exterior
system, exterior insulation and finish

exterior insulation finish system
USE   exterior insulation and finish system

exterior lighting
PC.211   (A,L)
HN   March 1993 descriptor moved
April 1991 scope note added
SN   Lighting systems supplying light outdoors for safety, pleasure, or information, as for playing fields, highways, or advertising.
UF   lighting, exterior
lighting, outdoor
outdoor lighting

exterior perspectives
VC.161
HN   April 1992 descriptor moved
ALT   exterior perspective
UF   elevations, perspective
perspective elevations
perspectives, exterior

exterior profiles (ships)
USE   outboard profiles

<exterior roof components>
PJ.1798
HN   March 1993 guide term moved

exterior valances
USE   outer valances

exterior views
VC.25
HN   April 1991 descriptor moved
ALT   exterior view
SN   Use for photographs or other representations of the exterior of a building or other structure.
UF   external views
views, exterior

exterior walls
PJ.1925   (A,L,B)
HN   March 1993 descriptor moved
ALT   exterior wall
SN   Walls which are part of the building envelope, thereby having one face exposed to the weather or to earth. (DAC)
UF   external walls
periphery walls
walls, exterior
walls, external
walls, periphery

<external combustion engine-powered watercraft>
TX.532

external elevations
USE   exterior elevations

external views
USE   exterior views

external walls
USE   exterior walls

extinguisher caps
USE   extinguishers

extinguishers
PJ.2935   (N)
ALT   extinguisher
SN   Cone-shaped devices used to extin-

guish flames. For scissorlike devices with a boxlike receptacle attached to one blade, use **candle snuffers**. For scissorlike devices with flat disc-shaped ends used for pinching out a candle flame, use **douters**.
UF candle extinguishers
dousing cones
extinguisher caps
extinguishers, candle
quench-horns
wickhats

extinguishers, candle
USE extinguishers

extinguishers, fire
USE fire extinguishers

extra-rapid-hardening cement
USE high-early-strength cement

Extra Terramaricolan
USE Apennine

<extracting complexes>
RG.99

extractors
USE juicers

extractors, juice
USE juicers

extractors, staple
USE staple pullers

extractors, tea
USE tea infusers

extraditing
KG.285   (L)
HN April 1993 lead-in term added
SN Turning over a criminal suspect to another state or province in the country, the national government, or a foreign country. (RLG7)
UF extradition

extradition
USE extraditing

extradosed arches
PJ.1609
HN March 1993 descriptor moved
ALT extradosed arch
SN Use for arches with a clearly marked extrados more or less parallel to the intrados.
UF arches, extradosed

extradoses
PJ.2013
HN March 1993 descriptor moved
February 1991 alternate term changed, was **extradose**
ALT extrados
SN The outer surfaces of vaults or arches.

extraordinary ray
USE birefringence

extraterrestrial bases
RK.1299   (L)

HN March 1993 related terms added
ALT extraterrestrial base
SN Use only for manned installations established on natural extraterrestrial bodies for specific functions. For larger communities established in space or on natural extraterrestrial bodies, use **space colonies**. For manned artificial satellites set to revolve in a fixed orbit and serving as a base for specific functions, use **space stations**.
UF bases, extraterrestrial
bases, space
space bases
RT space colonies
space stations

extraterrestrial structures
RK.1298   (B)
ALT extraterrestrial structure
UF structures, extraterrestrial

extreme unction
KM.45   (L,R)
SN Formal religious act consisting of anointment with oil and the recitation of prayer, administered by a priest to a person in imminent danger of dying. (RHDEL2)
UF unction, extreme

extruded plastic
MT.1146
HN January 1993 descriptor moved
UF plastic, extruded

extruders
TH.980
HN December 1992 descriptor added
ALT extruder
SN Devices that shape materials by forcing them through a specially designed opening.

extruding
USE extrusion

extrusion
KT.319   (L)
ALT extruded
SN The process of shaping a heated or unheated material, such as plastic or metal, by forcing or pressing it through a dye or other shaping device.
UF extruding

extrusion blown plastic
MT.1147
HN January 1993 descriptor moved
UF plastic, extrusion blown

extrusive rock
USE volcanic rock

exultet rolls
VW.890   (H,L)
HN June 1992 descriptor added
ALT exultet roll
SN Rolls containing texts for the celebration of Easter, including the Exultet hymn, and having illustrations,

placed upside down in relation to the text; when the roll was draped over the lectern, the images appeared right side up to the congregation. (CALK)
UF rolls, exultet

exurbs
RD.62
ALT exurb
SN Small, usually prosperous, communities situated beyond the suburbs of a city. (RHDEL2)

Eyak
FL.1355   (L)

eye baths
USE eyecups

eye bolts
USE eyebolts

eye-catchers
RK.1274
ALT eye-catcher
SN Use for decorative features often seen in silhouette and generally placed on a distant eminence as part of an overall landscape design.

eye cups
TQ.469
ALT eye cup
SN Black-figure kylikes characterized by eyelike decorations; generally of the 6th century BCE.

eye-droppers
SEE eyedroppers

eye hospitals
RK.731   (A,L,B)
ALT eye hospital
UF hospitals, eye
hospitals, opthalmic
ophthalmic hospitals

eye-level views
VC.26
HN April 1991 descriptor moved
ALT eye-level view
UF street-level views
views, eye-level
views, street-level

eye snips, pineapple
USE pineapple snips

eye tongs
USE hammer tongs

eyebolts
PJ.47   (N)
HN April 1993 descriptor moved
April 1993 lead-in term added
April 1993 descriptor changed, was **eye bolts**
April 1993 lead-in term changed, was **eyebolts**
April 1993 alternate term changed, was **eye bolt**
ALT eyebolt
SN Anchoring devices comprising a

threaded shank with a lopped head designed to accept a hook, cable, or rope. (MEANS)
UF bolts, eye
    eye bolts

eyebrow dormers
    PJ.1816
HN March 1993 descriptor moved
    February 1991 scope note changed
    February 1991 lead-in terms added
ALT eyebrow dormer
SN Low dormers in a roof over which the roof is carried in a continuous curve. (PUTNAM)
UF dormers, eyebrow
    dormers, swept
    eyebrow windows
    swept dormers
    windows, eyebrow

eyebrow windows
USE eyebrow dormers

eyecups
    TQ.176   (N)
ALT eyecup
SN Small oval cups that have a rim curved to fit the orbit of the eye. Used to bathe the eye or for applying liquid remedies. (W)
UF eye baths

eyedroppers
    TH.384   (N)
HN January 1993 descriptor added
ALT eyedropper
UK eye-droppers
SN Devices for applying eye drops.

eyeglass cases
    TQ.197   (N)
ALT eyeglass case
SN Small cases of varying form and material intended primarily for holding eyeglasses. May be quite decorative and sometimes suspended from a chain so they can be worn on the person.
UF cases, eyeglass
RT cases (containers)

eyeglasses
    TH.366   (H,L,N)
HN January 1993 descriptor added
SN Devices to compensate for defective vision or to protect the eyes from light, dust, and the like, consisting usually of two lenses set in a frame that includes a nosepiece for resting on the bridge of the nose and which may also have two sidepieces extending over or around the ears.
UF glasses, eye
RT lorgnettes
    opticians

eyelet-holes
USE eyelets

eyelets
    PJ.17   (L)
ALT eyelet

SN Small holes, usually round and finished along the edge, as in cloth or leather for the passage of a lace or cord or as in embroidery for ornamental effect.
UF eyelet-holes
    holes, lace
    lace holes

eyelets (grommets)
USE grommets

eyelets (windows)
USE loopholes

eyesight
USE sight

Ezine carpets
USE Çanakkale + rugs

Ezine rugs
USE Çanakkale + rugs

Ezines
USE Çanakkale + rugs

fables
    VW.271   (L,R)
HN November 1992 descriptor moved
    June 1992 scope note added
    January 1991 alternate term added
ALT fable
SN Fictitious narratives usually with animals or inanimate objects as protagonists, intended to convey a hidden meaning regarding human conduct. (OCCL)

fabric
USE cloth
    materials

fabric, cover
USE top covers (upholstery components)

fabric, filling pile
USE weft pile weave

fabric, final
USE top covers (upholstery components)

fabric, finish
USE top covers (upholstery components)

fabric, luster
USE luster (textile)

fabric reinforcement, wire
USE welded wire fabric

fabric, rubberized
USE rubberized cloth

fabric, textile
USE textile

fabric, warp pile
USE warp pile weave

fabric, weft pile
USE weft pile weave

fabric, welded wire
USE welded wire fabric

fabricated chalk
    TH.661
HN February 1992 descriptor moved
UF chalk, fabricated

fabricated photographs
USE staged photographs

<fabrication attributes>
    DC.30
HN October 1992 guide term added
RT flat-woven

<fabrication attributes: watercraft>
    DC.33
HN February 1993 guide term added

fabulists
    HG.362
HN December 1992 alternate terms added
ALT fabulist
    fabulist's
    fabulists'
SN Writers of fables, especially those that carry a moral lesson. (W)

fac
USE factotum initials

fac initials
USE factotum initials

<facade components>
    PJ.1931
HN March 1993 guide term moved

facade oblique drawings
USE elevation oblique drawings

facade pavilions
USE pavilions (building divisions)

facades
    PJ.1927   (A,L,B,R)
HN March 1993 descriptor moved
ALT facade
SN Use for those exterior faces of a building which are substantially in one plane and seem to have been designed with special regard to their conspicuousness or association with entrance. Distinct from **elevations (building divisions)**, which may constitute any side or face of a building or large interior space.
UF fronts (facades)

<facades and facade components>
    PJ.1926
HN March 1993 guide term moved

facades, flying
USE false fronts

facades, screen
USE screen facades

face brick
    MT.104   (L)
HN April 1992 descriptor moved

UF brick, face
  brick, facing
  facing brick

face hammers
  TH.1355 (N)
HN December 1992 descriptor moved
ALT face hammer
SN Heavy hammers having flat faces, with one blunt end and one cutting end; used for rough dressing of blocks of quarried stone. (PUTNAM)
UF hammers, face

face joints
  PJ.682
HN April 1993 descriptor moved
ALT face joint
SN Visible joints on the surface of a masonry wall. (MEANS)
UF joints, face

face strings
  PJ.2426
HN March 1993 descriptor moved
  February 1991 lead-in terms added
ALT face string
SN Outer strings on stairs, usually of better material or finish than the carriage pieces which they cover; may be part of the actual construction or applied to the face of the supporting member. (DAC)
UF finish stair strings
  finish strings
  outer strings
  stair strings, finish
  stringboards
  strings, face
  strings, finish
  strings, finish stair
  strings, outer

faced walls
  PJ.1907
HN March 1993 descriptor moved
ALT faced wall
SN Combination walls in which the masonry facing and the backing are so bonded as to exert a common reaction under load. (PUTNAM)
UF walls, faced

faces
  PJ.566
HN March 1993 descriptor moved
  March 1993 descriptor changed, was faces (lock components)
  March 1993 alternate term changed, was face (lock component)
ALT face
SN Parts of mortise locks that show at the edge of a door through which a latch bolt or dead bolt projects. (DITTRI)

faces (typefaces)
USE typefaces

faces, quilt
USE quilt tops

faces, type
USE typefaces

Facet Cubist
USE Analytical Cubist

faceting
  KT.320
HN January 1993 descriptor added
ALT faceted
SN Shaping something, as a gem, glass, or ceramics, so that it has facets, that is, a series of relatively small flat surfaces.

facilities, administrative
USE administration buildings

facilities, agricultural
USE agricultural buildings

facilities, assembly
USE assembly halls

facilities, athletic
USE sports complexes

facilities, business
USE commercial buildings

facilities, cogeneration
USE cogeneration plants

facilities, commercial
USE commercial buildings

facilities, communications
USE communications buildings

facilities, conference
USE convention centers

facilities, congress
USE convention centers

facilities, correctional
USE correctional institutions

facilities, desalination
USE desalination plants

facilities, detention
USE detention centers

facilities, domestic
USE dwellings

facilities, educational
USE educational complexes

facilities, employees'
USE employees' buildings

facilities, entertainment
USE entertainment buildings

facilities, exhibition
USE exhibition buildings

facilities, extended care
USE extended care facilities

facilities, health
USE health facilities

facilities, horticultural
USE horticultural (ALT of horticulture) + buildings

facilities, industrial
USE industrial buildings

facilities, long-term care
USE extended care facilities

facilities management
USE facility management

facilities, medical
USE health facilities

facilities, mental health
USE mental health facilities

facilities, mental retardation
USE mental health facilities

facilities, mercantile
USE mercantile buildings

facilities, military
USE military buildings

facilities, pedestrian
USE pedestrian facilities

facilities, recreation
USE recreation areas
  recreation buildings

facilities, religious
USE religious buildings

facilities, research
USE research buildings

facilities, residential
USE dwellings

facilities, resource recovery
USE resource recovery facilities

facilities, school
USE schools

facilities, sports
USE sports buildings
  sports complexes

facilities, storage
USE storage facilities

facilities, teaching
USE schools

facilities, terminal care
USE terminal care facilities

facilities, transportation
USE transportation buildings

facilities, vocational education
USE vocational schools

facilities, welfare
USE welfare buildings

facility management
  KG.218 (A,L)
HN February 1991 descriptor moved
SN Use for the practice of coordinating the physical workplace with the workflow of an organization.
UF facilities management
  FM
  management, facility

facing
KT.118
HN January 1993 descriptor moved
ALT faced

facing brick
USE face brick

facing tile
USE wall tile

facings
PJ.3042 (L)
ALT facing
SN Linings applied to the edge of a garment for ornament or strengthening. (RHDEL2)

facings, altar
USE altar frontals

facsimile process
USE facsimile transmission

facsimile telegraphy
USE facsimile transmission

facsimile transmission
KT.366 (L)
HN March 1993 descriptor added
SN Process of copying written or printed documents by radio or telephone transmission for exact reproduction elsewhere. (RHDEL2)
UF facsimile process
facsimile telegraphy
fax
telegraphy, facsimile
transmission, facsimile

facsimiles
PE.24 (L,R)
HN January 1993 descriptor moved
May 1990 scope note changed
ALT facsimile
SN Use for precise reproductions, usually in the same dimensions as the original, especially of books, documents, prints, and drawings. Today often reproduced photographically; in the past, reproduced by engraving or other printmaking process.

facsimiles (correspondence artifacts)
USE faxes

factitious negatives
USE clichés-verre

factor, reflection
USE reflectance

factories
RK.582 (A,L,N,B,R)
ALT factory
UF buildings, factory
factory buildings
industrial plants
mills (factories)
plants (factories)
plants, industrial
works (factories)

<*factories by function*>
RK.583

<*factories by power source*>
RK.632

factories, food
USE food processing plants

factories, gunpowder
USE powder mills

factories, leather
USE tanneries

factories, sugar
USE sugar refineries

factories, textile
USE textile mills

factories, wine
USE wineries

factors, human
USE human factors

factors, shape
USE shape factors

factory buildings
USE factories

factory lamps
TC.1272
ALT factory lamp
SN Use with reference to a type of ancient pottery lamp first made in northern Italy and later copied in Germany, France, and Britain.
UF firmalampen
lamps, factory

factory lights
TC.1364 (L,B)
ALT factory light
UF lights, factory

factory lumber
MT.3034
HN March 1992 descriptor moved
UF lumber, factory
lumber, shop
shop lumber

factory marks
VW.422
HN November 1992 descriptor moved
ALT factory mark
UF marks, factory

factory outlets
USE outlet stores

factory ships
TX.382 (L)
ALT factory ship
SN Whaling vessels specifically designed for processing whales as they are caught; usually accompanying whale catchers.
UF factory ships, whale
ships, factory
ships, whale factory
whale factory ships

factory ships, whale
USE factory ships

factory sites
USE industrial sites

factory towns
USE industrial towns

factory villages
RD.54
ALT factory village
SN Designates industrial settlements purposely built by factory owners to attract workers to isolated or otherwise undesirable locations with a minimum of services.
UF villages, factory

factotum initials
PJ.3401
ALT factotum initial
SN Typographical ornaments having a hole in the center in which an initial letter is printed; common in early printed books.
UF fac
fac initials
factotums
initials, factotum

factotums
USE factotum initials

faculty clubhouses
USE faculty clubs

faculty clubs
RK.1137
ALT faculty club
UF clubhouses, faculty
clubs, faculty
faculty clubhouses

faculty housing
RG.84
HN April 1990 descriptor added
UF housing, faculty

faculty papers
VW.804
HN March 1993 alternate term deleted, was **faculty paper**
November 1992 descriptor moved
UF papers, faculty

fading
KT.229
HN January 1993 descriptor moved
August 1992 scope note added
March 1990 alternate term changed, was **fade**
ALT faded
SN A gradual loss of color or intensity.

Fagus
USE beech

Fagus crenata
USE Siebold's beech

Fagus englerana
USE Chinese beech

Fagus grandifolia
USE American beech

Fagus japonica
USE Japanese beech

Fagus orientalis
USE Oriental beech

Fagus sylvatica
USE European beech

faience
PE.108 (A,L,B)
HN January 1993 descriptor moved

faience fine
PE.109
HN December 1992 descriptor added
SN French name for earthenware covered with transparent lead glaze in imitation of English creamware.

faience tile
MT.188 (L)
HN April 1992 descriptor moved
UF tile, faience

failures, bridge
USE bridge failures

failures, building
USE building failures

failures, structural
USE structural failures

fair buildings
USE exhibition buildings

fair linen cloths
TC.349
ALT fair linen cloth
SN Long linen altar cloths, as wide as the altar top and hanging over the sides, upon which the eucharist is celebrated.
UF cloths, fair linen
linens, fair

fairgrounds
RM.99 (A,B)
HN April 1993 descriptor moved
ALT fairground
UF exhibition grounds

fairings
PE.73 (L,N)
HN December 1992 descriptor added
ALT fairing
SN Small German 19th to early 20th century porcelain ornaments, either of figures or in the form of a small box, usually depicting indelicate subjects and mass-produced for sale at fairs, bazaars, seaside stalls, and the like. (DDA2)

fairs
KM.88 (L,R)
HN May 1991 alternate term added
ALT fair

fairs, trade
USE trade shows

fairs, world's
USE world's fairs

fairy lamps
TC.1333 (L,N)
ALT fairy lamp
SN Night lamps having a base and shade of glass, burning a short, thick candle with a self-snuffing rush wick.
UF lamps, fairy

fairy stories
USE fairy tales

fairy tales
VW.272 (L,R)
HN November 1992 descriptor moved
February 1992 scope note added
February 1992 lead-in terms added
November 1990 descriptor added
ALT fairy tale
SN Narratives set in the distant past recounting events impossible in the real world, often magical and with fairies, but with humans as heroes and heroines. (OCCL)
UF fairy stories
stories, fairy
tales, fairy

faith
BM.522 (L,R)
SN Act or state of wholeheartedly and steadfastly believing in the existence, power and benevolence of a supreme being. (W)

Faiyum Neolithic
USE Fayum A

Faiyum portraits
USE mummy portraits

fakes
USE forgeries

Falasha
FL.638 (L)

falbalas
USE furbelows

falchions
TK.74 (N)
ALT falchion
SN Swords with a heavy, single-edged cutting blade, either straight or slightly convex, broadening out into a pronounced convex curve toward the tip, used in Europe roughly from the 13th to the 15th century.
RT cutting swords

falchions (tracery components)
USE mouchettes

falconets
TK.147 (N)
ALT falconet
SN Light cannons in use from the early 16th to the early 18th century, similar to falcons but comparatively smaller throughout their mutual development, firing a ball of from 1 to 3 pounds.
UF fawconets

falcons
TK.148 (N)
ALT falcon
SN Light cannons in use from the late 15th to the early 18th century, firing a ball of from 1 to 6 pounds.
UF fawcons

WITHDRAWN
No longer the property of the
Boston Public Library.
Sale of this material benefits the Library